METHODS
of
EDUCATIONAL
and
SOCIAL SCIENCE
RESEARCH

METHODS
of
EDUCATIONAL
and
SOCIAL SCIENCE
RESEARCH
AN INTEGRATED APPROACH

DAVID R. KRATHWOHL
Syracuse University

Longman

Methods of Educational and Social Science Research

Copyright © 1993 by Longman
All rights reserved.
No part of this publication may be reproduced,
stored in a retrieval system, or transmitted
in any form or by any means, electronic, mechanical,
photocopying, recording, or otherwise,
without the prior permission of the publisher.

Longman, 10 Bank Street, White Plains, N.Y. 10606

Associated companies:
Longman Group Ltd., London
Longman Cheshire Pty., Melbourne
Longman Paul Pty., Auckland
Copp Clark Pitman, Toronto

Acquisitions editor: Kenneth P. Clinton
Sponsoring editor: Naomi Silverman
Development editor: Virginia L. Blanford
Production editor: Halley Gatenby
Text design: Jill F. Wood
Cover design: Kevin C. Kall
Text art: Burmar Technical Corp.
Production supervisor: Anne P. Armeny

Library of Congress Cataloging-in-Publication Data
Krathwohl, David R.
    Methods of educational and social science research: an integrated
approach/by David R. Krathwohl.
        p.   cm.
    Includes bibliographical references and index.
    ISBN 0–8013–0255–2: — ISBN 0–8013–1039–3 (teacher's
manual)
    1. Social sciences—Research—Methodology.   2. Social sciences—
Statistical methods.   I. Title.
H62.K6793   1991
300'72—dc20   91–22541
                                                 CIP

6 7 8 9 10-MA-99 98 97

To
Charles G. and Minnie S. Krathwohl
William C., Marie Reimold, and Sarah Reading Krathwohl
Becca & Sarah Krathwohl
and Elizabeth, Jamie, & Keith Cleghorn.
Spanning five generations,
and having so greatly enriched my life.

Contents

Preface   ix

SECTION 1   The Nature of Research   1

1. Introduction   3
2. Analysis of Two Illustrative Research Studies   9
3. The Variety of Research Methods   26
4. From Findings to Knowledge   38
5. The Research Chain of Reasoning   57

SECTION 2   The Skills of Research   69

6. Finding Research Problems   71
7. Finding Links to Past Research: The Literature Review   96
8. Sampling and Representation   121
9. Conceptual Analysis   145
10. The Numeric Description of Data: Descriptive Statistics   157
11. Measurement, Testing, and Observation   191

SECTION 3   Causal Inference and the Criteria of Research   235

12. Complexities of Causal Inference   237
13. The Criteria of Research: Internal and External Validity   268
14. Other Criteria of Research   293

SECTION 4   The Methods of Research   309

15. Qualitative Research Methods   311
16. Survey Research: Questionnaires and Interviews   360
17. The Nature and Logic of Inferential Statistics   400
18. Experimental Methods and Experimental Design   440
19. The Historical Method and After-the-Fact Natural Experiments   501
20. Evaluation Studies   524
21. Longitudinal Studies, Single-Subject Designs, and Meta-analyses   554
22. Other Statistics for Inference and Multivariate Relationships   578

SECTION 5   The Larger Context of Research   613

23. Syntheses of Methods, Trade-offs, and Optimization   615
24. Alternative Conceptions of a Social Science: Implications for Method   625
25. Ethics and Legal Constraints   658
26. The Macrosystem of Educational and Social Science Research   677

Appendix: Trade-off Possibilities: The Positive
    and Negative Effects of Choices   691
Answers to Application Problems   699
Glossary   729
References   745
Name Index   771
Subject Index   776

Preface

Though combined under one heading, there are really two prefaces: student's, and instructor's. Each will find the other's of interest, but, whichever you are, you will probably benefit most from first reading the one addressed to you.

TO THE STUDENT

Intellectual mastery is rewarding. It is particularly so when the learner recognizes the cumulative power of learning, that learning one thing permits him [or her] to go on to something that before was out of reach.

J. Burner, *Toward a Theory of Instruction*

An important ingredient is a sense of excitement about the discovery of regularities of previously unrecognized relations and similarities between ideas, with a resulting sense of self-confidence in one's abilities.

J. Bruner, *The Process of Education*

What This Book Should Do for You

When learning begins with an intuitive base, it comes easily, and the exercises in chapter 2 will show you that you already have such a base to build on. Then what can this book do? It can provide a useful framework that will help organize your prior knowledge and facilitate new learning. Further, since organized material is more easily remembered, it will lower the threshold for these concepts to come to mind and be readily available.

More specifically, besides showing that you already have some knowledge of social science research on which to build, section one of this book will describe several important basic concepts:

- A continuum of research methods (chapter 3)
- How findings from a research study become accepted as knowledge (chapter 4)
- The chain of reasoning, a very useful, universal model for planning, analyzing, implementing, and critiquing research (chapter 5)

Section two will provide the knowledge and skills you will need to understand and conduct research, by addressing questions such as these:

- What are good research problems, and how do I find them? (chapter 6)
- How do I find and use past research in the development and limiting of my problem? (chapter 7)
- What are the basic principles of sampling that allow generalization from a study's sample to a population? (chapter 8)
- How do I define a concept or construct that I can't see or feel? (chapter 9)
- How do I describe in numbers as well as words? (chapter 10)
- How do I translate a concept or a construct into good instrumentation? Indeed, what characteristics mark good measures? (chapter 11)

Section three builds on the first two sections, conveying some of the complexities of inferring causation and developing the criteria by which research is judged. Here we will do three things:

- Discuss what we mean by cause and effect and upon what evidence we infer causation (chapter 12)
- Use the chain of reasoning as a base in developing criteria for how tightly the study links cause to effect—linking power, or internal validity (LP)—and how generalizable are the findings—generalizing power, or external validity (GP) (chapter 13)
- Place these criteria in a larger framework that shows both the researcher's goals as well as the constraints on research studies (chapter 14)

All this grows out of an understanding of how findings become knowledge in the first section and the various characteristics of good research noted in the second.

Section four describes particular research methods in some detail. It will accomplish the following:

- Provide an understanding of the essential characteristics of three basic research methods: qualitative methods (chapter 15), sample surveys (chapter 16), and experimentation (chapter 18)
- Explain the logic used in inferential statistics (chapter 17)[1]
- Show how the basic research methods are used in history (chapter 19) and evaluation and the additional unique aspects of these areas of research (chapter 20)
- Briefly describe the methods of longitudinal and single-subject studies (chapter 21)
- Describe meta-analysis, a method for synthesizing the findings of comparable studies to give an overall result (chapter 21)
- Describe some multivariate and other statistics not described earlier (chapter 22)

---

1. Though focused on research skills like those considered in section two, chapters 17 and 22 were moved to section four to spread out the conceptual load.

Section five stands back for a broader look. It will provide a perspective on the research system as a whole, including such questions as these:

- What about using more than one method in a study? (chapter 23)
- Why is it that in designing research, there is always a problem of "having one's cake and eating it too"? This involves study of the trade-offs in all methods; they result in the optimization of research conditions instead of ideal ones (chapter 23 and Appendix)
- Is there a single conception of what a social and behavioral science should be? (chapter 24)
- If not, how can we provide a description of the different positions and their implications? For method? For high-quality research? For how research is used and disseminated? For what research can and cannot do? For the kind of science we should build? (chapter 24)
- What are the implications of these different orientations? For research teams? For doctoral committees? For research programs? (chapter 24)
- What ethical problems surround research? (chapter 25)
- How well does the research system work? Now that we understand how findings become knowledge, does the system do what it is supposed to? What are its strengths and weaknesses? (chapter 26)

Because "a picture is worth a thousand words," you will find a greater than average number of graphics in this book. On the next page is one depicting the book's organization. The number after each topic gives the chapter in which it is covered. Arrows indicate conceptual links—which material leads more or less directly to what else so the latter can build on that material.

For example, the material in the chapters on sampling, conceptual analysis, and descriptive statistics all contribute ideas that are used in the chapter on measurement. Similarly, all of the topics in the column headed "Nature of Research and Knowledge" contribute to the section in which the research methods are described. These linkages will become apparent as the material is encountered. You may find it helpful to add your own arrows to the diagram as you discover additional linkages, labeling your new ones as well as those already there to indicate the nature of the relationship.

As you can see from the above-cited linkages plus the others shown in the diagram, from the provision of a basic model of the way research is reported, and from the development of criteria of research growing out of the way findings become knowledge, there has been a real effort to integrate and interrelate the material presented. Since material integrated into a network is easier to learn (offering "pegs on which to hang" new material) and easier to recall ("threads" in the network lead to other parts of it), an integrated approach makes good pedagogical as well as logical sense.

Assistance for Self-instruction

No doubt, having gotten this far in your education, you have some knowledge about how you learn best. But few of us work at improving how we do it. This

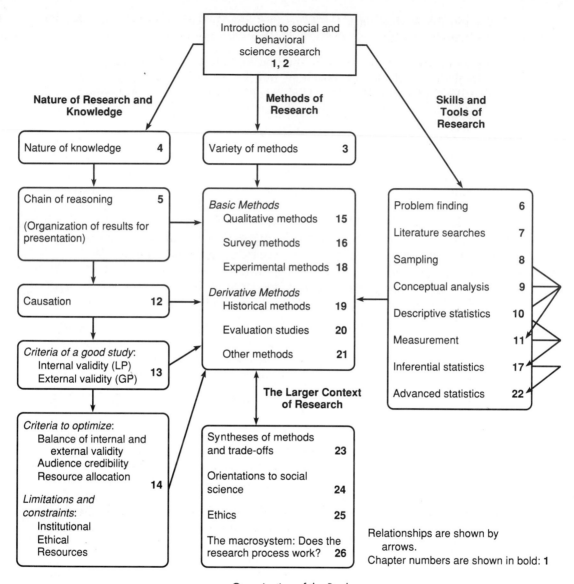

Organization of the Book

is an appeal for you to do that. A number of aids have been built into the text to help you, but it is up to you to use them most productively. Learn to employ your cognitive processes effectively.

Hall and Esposito (1985) note two examples of this. The teacher told Nancy to stop counting on her fingers when doing arithmetic problems. A friend, Susan, spent five minutes with her, and Nancy never did it again. "What did Susan do? She simply told Nancy to imagine her fingers in her head . . . [and] that eventually she would no longer need to imagine" (p. 38). In another instance, Susan was heard reading aloud to herself.

> Before rushing out for professional help, however, we decided to ask her why she was doing it. She replied that she had learned through experience that reading school assignments out loud (never books she read for fun) forced her mind to attend to what she was reading. When reading school assignments silently, her mind sometimes forgot what she was reading. (p. 39)

As Hall and Esposito note, students do attend to their cognitive processes, and more should do so. Perhaps reading the material aloud to yourself may help if you find some of the material difficult. I recently came across an instance where students read material they intended to master into a tape recorder. They then played it back while they were driving, doing household chores, or otherwise occupied physically but not mentally. Maybe that would work for you.

Bereiter (1990), studying how students succeed in learning complex material, suggests that when embarking on the study of an unfamiliar area, these students say to themselves something like this:

. . . the sheer quantity of knowledge to be acquired is larger than [I am] aware of

. . . the knowledge has a structure that is more complex than [I currently envision it]

. . . [I anticipate] trouble judging the importance of [material] so had better err on the side of overestimating importance

. . . familiar words may have special meanings . . .

. . . [I] must watch for complicating factors

. . . what makes the [material] interesting and important cannot be fully appreciated until [I] have acquired more knowledge of it (p. 617)

In my experience, as I watch students succeed in research courses, these all ring true. And with regard to the last thought, toward the end of the semester, students often tell me that it has all come together for them and makes great sense. So the above may be attitudes you want to adopt.

We know that you learn better if you can fit what you are learning into some scheme that organizes the material into proper places. Therefore, early on, in chapter 4, a point of view about how science works is presented. This leads to a framework that is begun in chapter 5 and added to in chapters 13 and 14. Where relevant, at the start of a chapter you will find a diagram that indicates where the chapter fits in that framework. The framework is referred to wherever appropriate throughout the book.

Every chapter has several features to help you learn:

■ An *overview* tells you what to anticipate in the chapter and therefore what is important. That again provides a scaffolding around which mentally to organize the material in the chapter as well as to help you set your own priorities.

- A *chapter table of contents* shows the organization of the chapter in greater detail. By examining it, you can anticipate where the material is going and the length of sections and thus process it more efficiently.

- An *introductory section* further sets the context for what is to come.

- *Summary boxes* appear after major points or sections. Processing the material as you read is especially important. To facilitate this, try to summarize the material you have read periodically in writing and compare your summary with the boxes placed throughout the text that do the same thing. Your summary may be better than the one provided, but where there are significant differences, read the material again to sort out those differences.

- A *chapter summary* supplements the summary boxes. Whereas the boxes are more complete and detailed, the chapter summary highlights the important material. Check it to see what, if anything, you missed. Many chapter summaries end with a one-paragraph bridge to the following chapter.

- An *additional reading* section follows each chapter summary. It provides suggestions if you want to read more about a topic or perhaps straighten out a point or a concept.

- A list of *important terms* follows the additional reading. When you complete a chapter, examine the list of key terms to see if you can tell what each is about and why it is significant. If you miss some, look them up in the glossary at the end of this book, which will also give you a page reference for further review. Note, however, that terms appear only in the list for the chapter in which they first appear. There will always be terms important to a chapter but not in that chapter's list because they were introduced earlier, even though they are given major treatment in the later chapter. Each important term is printed in **bold** type when it is introduced in the text.

- *Application problems* appear at the end of each chapter. Try them and then check your answers against those given at the end of the book. Again, your answer may be better than the one that is given, but be sure you understand why Richard Kenny (who came up with the majority of the problems for the book) and I gave the answer we did. (If you'd like to tell us about your alternative answer and why it is better, we'd love to hear about it. There is a reply card in the back of the book. Add it to your comments.)

- *Application exercises* begin in chapter 6, and their purpose is described on page 95. You are asked to choose a problem and then to develop it further with each successive chapter, applying the content of the chapter. This helps you learn the material, but it can also result in completing the course with the first draft of a proposal that can be developed into a dissertation. Many students in my courses have done this; it has helped change ABDs (candidates with "all but dissertation" status) into doctorates.

- Use the *glossary* to refresh your understanding of terms or to look up new ones. In addition to the glossary definition, which is often phrased differently than that in the text, there is a reference to the page where the term is discussed. Consult it for further clarification; the term is boldfaced there so you can find it quickly.

- For ease of reference, the end papers inside the front cover reprint the *chain of reasoning* of chapter 5 and its relation to internal validity (LP) and external validity (GP) described in chapter 13 as well as the *complete model* as developed in chapter 14.

Special features in the chapters on research methods highlight important aspects for researchers and for research consumers:

- *Tips* appear in the three chapters on basic research methods: qualitative, survey, and experimental. They provide researchers with pointers on participant observation, interviewing, constructing questionnaires, and designing experiments. Since advice makes for a stronger study, these suggestions add to the characteristics summarized for consumers in the hallmarks section (on occasion, tips and hallmarks are combined).
- *Hallmarks of methods.* How do you know when a research method has been used well? Or on what aspects to concentrate when you use it? All the chapters describing research methods have sections presenting the hallmarks of quality in method so that you'll recognize good work when you see it. Like the guild hallmarks of the Middle Ages, they help ensure the excellence of the product. Hallmarks for the statistical chapters are left for courses in that subject.

So a great variety of aids help you learn. Pay attention to how you master material best; talk to your friends about it. Maybe like Susan, they have some tips that will be helpful. Then practice them on this material!

Much of the book is written in an informal style. Some of you may find it inappropriate, perhaps even condescending. It is intended, as a student, Jim Ellsworth, put it, to "avoid the traditional 'droning lecture on paper' style exhibited by all too many authors" and to treat the reader "as a colleague, which is both appropriate and important for an upper-level text."

Original plans called for an appendix devoted to the dissertation proposal and dissertation process; it proved not feasible. It would have summarized my book *How to Prepare a Research Proposal* (Krathwohl, 1988); its first sections are directly applicable to the dissertation proposal, and its last two chapters give insights and suggestions regarding the dissertation process.

TO THE INSTRUCTOR

If I were faced with this book, my first reaction would be, "It's too much! I can't possibly cover all of it." My second would be, "So much of the material is new, material that is not in the typical research course—material I've not previously encountered in research courses!" Those reactions are valid. So why write a text that is going to generate such reactions? For five very important reasons.

First, we have long lacked an integrating framework in research. This book presents an important one that improves our understanding of the research process; students find it useful once mastered. It grows out of an understanding of how findings make the transition to knowledge. The point of view taken in this book is that knowledge building is a social process involving individuals making knowing judgments about knowledge claims. These judgments coalesce into a consensus around the proper interpretation of data, which, if the consensus remains unbroken from researcher to consumer, results in the findings' being accepted as knowledge (chapter 4, "From Findings to Knowledge"). The presentation of knowledge claims as a chain of reasoning (chapter 5, "The Research Chain of Reasoning") facilitates our judging them. The chain also serves as a base for making explicit the criteria for judgment that were previously only dimly sensed (internal and external validity in chapter 13, other criteria in chapter 14).[2] Students should have learned about the knowledge-building process in high school or the early undergraduate years, but for many this discussion will be new. It will give them a healthy skepticism needed in this world of specialists; it is not too late to learn this material now.

This framework also helps inform both the choice of material to include and its importance. It serves as a basis for many internal connections that integrate the material. For example, explanation credibility, a criterion of internal validity (LP), was a factor in the approach taken to chapter 9 on conceptual analysis and chapter 12 on causation. Similarly, another criterion of internal validity (LP), translation fidelity, gives particular emphases to chapter 8 on sampling and representation as it feeds into chapter 10 on numerical representation, which in turn leads to chapter 11, the translation of constructs into measurement. These are but a few of the many integrating internal connections that become obvious as the book unfolds.

Second, the material that is covered here but not typically included in research courses is important. Here are some examples:

- Conceptual analysis is a basic philosophical skill that can, among other things, facilitate problem and measurement development.
- The principles that govern sampling are pervasive throughout the research process and are also important in our daily lives.
- Chapters on the literature search usually concentrate on specific materials any good librarian could help students find instead of on knowledge of the types of indexes and their advantages and weaknesses, which is necessary for successful reference use.
- Although the terms *cause* and *effect* are used blithely, their complexities are not typically realized.

---

2. Originally, these chapters followed chapter 5 since they helped students understand the place of the various research skills described in chapters 6–11. Because I found that many students were not ready for them yet, I moved them to a later section as chapters 13 and 14. Some instructors may prefer to use them in their original sequence.

- Low correlations that are actually the result of contingent, alternative, or contributing conditions are rarely recognized as such.
- The many possible trade-offs that could be used to improve a study as the result of various design changes go unrecognized.
- Many social scientists do not understand that some of their colleagues may have differing ideas about what a social science is and therefore often talk past one another.
- Does science work? This book can't answer that question, but it should start students thinking about it.

A recent survey of graduate training in statistics, research methods, and measurement in psychology programs (Aiken et al., 1990) revealed not only the lack of training in these fields but also the slowness with which new topics have been incorporated into curricula. A comparison of their list of new topics with those included in this book indicated that most had been covered at some level.

Third, most research texts hew to a positivist point of view, stressing experimentation and ignoring or minimizing qualitative research, or, alternatively, address only qualitative research. It is clear that we have entered an era where more than the positivist paradigm is considered defensible. In this book I seek to legitimize a variety of routes to inquiry, including qualitative. Further, I hope to restore more of a balance between exploration and validation. And whereas most books either ignore or downplay differences, I seek to make visible the variety of points of view about what methods are appropriate and what kind of a social science is desirable.[3] As students recognize these differences and see them in the faculty around them, students can make more intelligent choices. Which leads to the next point.

Fourth, students need a broad understanding of methods—their logic, their strengths and weaknesses, and their complementarity. "Methodological purity," in the sense that a field espouses only one way of doing research, is on the wane. Most fields have imported the methods of others. Research at the margins of fields has stimulated the borrowing of methods. Some individuals identified with quantitative methods have become advocates of qualitative; certainly, there is increased interest in qualitative methods. To keep up with the literature of almost any field, we must have some understanding of a wide variety of methods. Such familiarity also has the potential for legitimizing choice of most appropriate method or methods regardless of disciplinary loyalty, enhancing the richness with which future researchers pursue their problems, and building greater understanding and respect for other's research.

Fifth, students don't stop learning after they leave the classroom; in fact,

---

3. Apropos of these points, Hoshmand and Polkinghorne (1992), published an interesting discussion of the problem of articulating scientific training with that of clinical practice. They call for greater attention to more than the positivist point of view and argue for greater emphasis on exploration, attending to the practitioner-researcher as a source of knowledge, and for research on reflection-in-action as suggested by Schon (1983).

the texts they have learned from feel comfortable and are familiar to them, even though they may not have covered all of the material in class. They return to them when they need to review material they think they learned but don't now remember; they consult them for the new topics not covered. Thus every really good text has both an instructional function (especially self-instructional once the student is out of class) and a reference function. If it is a good text, the student will keep it to consult later. My intent is that they will treasure this text.

The Design of This Book

The design of this book has been influenced by research in learning, problem solving, and cognitive psychology. Medical problem solving (Elstein, Shulman, and Sprafka, 1978, 1990; Swanson and Stillman, 1990) has been especially helpful. Following are some of the principles, with a brief description of how they affected the book's design.

It is unnecessary to teach general problem-solving skills; students are already using the same hypothetico-deductive process that experts use. Research in medical problem solving found that new medical students and experienced clinicians alike use the hypothetico-deductive process to diagnose problems (Swanson and Stillman, 1990). Drawing a parallel inference, by the time students get to graduate school, they know how to solve problems, so that need not be the focus of attention. Therefore, the exercise in chapter 2 shows students that they already know how to critique studies; it is other things that require learning and practice.

The difference lies in specific knowledge of the field, especially in how experts "chunk" subject matter. Since we can keep only a limited number of things in our mind simultaneously, on the average about seven, chunking is especially important to comprehend a field in perspective. Experts organize fields differently from novices. Pieces are organized into patterns, models, and frameworks that hold them in place and ease the memory task.

This text transmits the essential knowledge needed to understand research, chunking it wherever possible in terms of basic principles or characteristics that provide a framework on which to "hang" the details. Sometimes it concentrates on the basics instead of the details, especially where the details are too diverse or can be more easily picked up later; concentrating on indexing practices more than on specific references is an example.

In other instances, details are covered as well as principles. Chapter 8, on sampling, is an example. It describes the basic principles of sampling and then adds details showing that the different sampling methods are extensions of those principles. The initial statistics material (chapters 10 and 17) does not cover the many specific descriptive and inferential statistics but deals with the logic of description in numbers and the logic of inference. The latter helps students understand the logic of all inferential models. This is built on with descriptions of some advanced statistics in chapter 22. Throughout the book, there is an attempt to chunk material into basics, where possible, to get the novice closer to the expert's understanding of the material.

Problem solvers who have a model that organizes their search do better than those who don't. We can't and shouldn't give students a formula for doing research; that is a creative act people do differently. But we can give them a model of how the research process works and tell them what good research looks like. If they know that, they can creatively find their way there. Therefore, the essentials that must be covered in the product—the chain of reasoning (chapter 5), the criteria by which it will be judged (chapters 13 and 14), and an understanding of the process by which it gets there (chapter 4) are covered. In the chapters on research methods, hallmarks of good research and errors to avoid are listed.

Understanding where learning material is going and how it is organized aids comprehension. Advance organizers and summaries aid retention. Each chapter begins with an overview, a table of contents, and an introduction. Material is summarized periodically in boxes. As appropriate, chapter summaries, summary tables, lists of hallmarks of method, and lists of key terms help emphasize important material.

Deep processing of the material is essential to learning and especially to retention. The student preface stresses this point, and chapter application problems help make it possible. Much must be left to the instructor: class discussion is essential, as are additional application problems (see the *Instructor's Manual* for examples and suggestions). Integrative assignments such as the proposal development process, which begins with the application exercise at the end of chapter 6, can be of considerable help and are highly recommended. Students can complete these assignments in a log that they keep through the course and hand in from time to time for guidance. Conducting small qualitative, survey, and experimental studies makes these methods real. In addition, quizzes and examinations, especially the take-home type, facilitate it.

Using This Book in Instruction

This is largely, though not entirely, a front-end-loaded text. What do I mean by that? Consider two contrasting ways of teaching: one is to develop material logically, starting part by part and then assembling all the parts into the whole. Alternatively, we can start with a less than complete understanding of a whole and successively feed in parts as needed to provide a deeper and more complete understanding of it. In the latter instance, it is often difficult to maintain forward momentum yet retain some sense of the whole. One has to stop so often to go off on byways to cover some related topic. It also is more time-consuming since there is usually an element of discovery learning in it. Though this results in very good learning, it takes more time than can be afforded to every topic.

By contrast, a front-end-loaded text such as this one tries to have the best of both worlds. It begins with an overall view so that the students know the goal and then proceeds in a systematic way economically to teach the parts that will enable them to get there. Instructors of research courses are always pressured for time—there is so much to cover. In our one-semester course, due to time pressure, selected chapters are taken sequentially. In the two-semester course, where there is more time, the first section is followed by the methods chapters of section four, and the research skills and criteria of sections three and five are worked in. The book may be used either way.

The map of the conceptual plan of the chapters in the portion of the preface directed to the student shows the structure of the book and may help you decide which chapters to select for a course.

The Statistics Chapters. A word about the three statistics chapters: statistics material is always a special problem in research courses. The intent of these chapters is to provide an understanding of the nature and logic of statistics—what they can do for you—instead of a mastery of statistics ready for use. Statistics courses are likely to concentrate on formulas and computation—the trees instead of the forest. These chapters are the reverse, with verbal and graphic descriptions and a minimum of formulas and computation. They provide a panorama from which students can select for detailed study. Students with statistics backgrounds find that this approach gives their statistics courses new meaning. Those encountering this approach first may find statistics courses taken later easier to understand and more meaningful.

Courses with a statistics prerequisite can use the first chapter (chapter 10, on descriptive statistics) as a review. The second (chapter 17, on inferential statistics) may or may not be familiar, but students are unlikely to have approached it in this manner. Much of the third (chapter 22, on other statistics for inference and multivariate relationships) will either be new or likely summarized differently from their first contact with it.

Chapters That Need Special Consideration in Sequencing. Chapters 12, 13, and 14, on causation and the criteria of research, are placed after the research skills section to avoid too heavy a conceptual load for beginning students at the outset. For advanced students, they may be studied earlier. Chapter 12 lays the groundwork for chapters 13 and 14, but most of it can be put later in sequence, if desired, since only the middle of the chapter is relevant to them.

Similarly, chapter 24, on orientations to research, may well be considered early. It gives meaning to the continuum of possible research methods, especially if students can associate particular faculty with the positions described. It may help students trying to decide their own orientations and provides another way of considering interests, strengths, and weaknesses. Further, it breaks down the artificial distance between qualitative and quantitative. It could come after studying chapters 13 and 14, for instance.

For some students, chapter 17 in section four may be more appropriate as another of the skills to be studied in section two after the chapters on descriptive statistics and measurement.

Ethics is not formally taken up until chapter 25 but would be very appropriate to bring in at any time. Capitalize on the interest generated by an ethical problem encountered in a study or when such a discussion arises spontaneously in discussion of an application problem.

In addition, there are whole blocks of the text that can be taken in different sequence, as indicated next.

Choices. The book provides a panorama of choices. How you choose among the material and integrate it is a creative act that is yours to enjoy! You may even find that it gives a new zest to teaching to try different ones from time to time. Certainly, whatever you choose will be of value; in that sense, you can't miss! One obvious choice is to go through the book sequentially, picking chapters you find of particular interest and value and omitting others. That will probably be the most common pattern. To stimulate your thinking, however, here are other possibilities (although only complete chapters are listed, obviously, selection of material within a chapter is both expected and necessary for most classes; not all the material in a given chapter may be deemed necessary or, if too difficult, desirable):

Two-semester course—chapter sequence options:

- Begin with chapters 1, introduction, 2, two research studies, and 3, variety of methods; then, 6, finding problems, and 7, literature search (so students can get started on their own research proposals); 4, findings to knowledge; 5, research chain of reasoning; 15, qualitative methods; 12, causation; and 13 and 14, criteria of research (tying them back to qualitative method); 8, sampling (as preparation for 16); 16, sample surveys; 9, conceptual analysis, 10, descriptive statistics, and 11, measurement (as preparation for 18); 18, experimentation; selections to fit the time remaining from 19–26, being sure to include meta-analysis in 21; 23, combining methods and trade-offs; 24, orientations; and 25, ethics.
- Begin with 1, introduction, and 2, two research studies; then, 15, qualitative methods—methods that everyone can understand and feel comfortable with; 4, findings to knowledge; 5, research chain of reasoning; and 13 and 14, criteria of research (tying them back to qualitative method). Do all or selected parts of section two, on research skills (6, problem finding; 7, literature search; 8, sampling; 9, conceptual analysis; 10, description statistics; 11, measurement); 12, causation; 16, survey research; 17, statistical inference; 18, experimentation; selections to fit the time remaining from 19–26, being sure to include meta-analysis in 21; 23, combining methods and trade-offs; 24, orientations; and 25, ethics.

One-semester course—chapter selection options:

- 1, introduction; 2, two research studies; 3, variety of methods; 4, findings to knowledge; 5, research chain of reasoning; 7, literature search; 8, sampling; 10, descriptive statistics; 11, measurement; 12, causation; 13, internal and external validity; 14, other criteria; 18, experimentation; 21, meta-analysis; 23, combining methods and trade-offs; 25, ethics; and 26, macrosystem.
- 2, two research studies; 3, variety of methods; 4, findings to knowledge; 5, research chain of reasoning; 7, literature search; 8, sampling; 9, conceptual analysis; 11, measurement; 13, internal and external validity; 14, other criteria; 15, qualitative method; 16, sample surveys; 18, experimentation; 21, meta-analysis; and 25, ethics.
- 2, two research studies; 3, variety of methods; 15, qualitative method; 16, sample surveys; 18, experimentation; then as much as is deemed critical of

section two (6, problem finding; 7, literature search; 8, sampling; 9, conceptual analysis; 10, descriptive statistics; 11, measurement) and section three (12, causation, and 13 and 14, criteria of research); 25, ethics; and selections to fit the time remaining from 23, combining methods and trade-offs; 24, orientations; and 26, macrosystem.

There is no such thing as a standard research course and probably shouldn't be. What is important is that you, the instructor, make it fascinating so that students come to understand the excitement of research, that they integrate whatever material you choose to cover. Whatever you include, do so in such a way that they can view it in perspective—take the larger view, not just learn terminology and details. Then, since they continue to learn after they leave your class, they can learn from others and from their reading. Indeed, if each of you, in addition to certain basic chapters, chooses different things to emphasize, we will have researchers with different competencies—the spread of competencies necessary to attack the multifaceted problems of the social and behavioral sciences. So it is good that each of you will take from the book what you deem important. This book provides a wide smorgasbord from which to choose. In addition, obtain the *Instructor's Manual*, which has suggestions on teaching, provides some exercises, and thanks to Richard Kenny, provides sample test items. I hope it will be helpful and, perhaps, stimulating.

It is an exciting time to be teaching research methods; so many insights are developing, and even though we have greater perspective on what we are doing and why we do it, we do not yet have a consensus on many issues. Positivism is proclaimed dead but is clung to by many; talk of multiple realities confuses and leaves an uncomfortable feeling in those seeking solidity. Qualitative researchers are seeking ways of working that will satisfy critics at the same time that they maintain flexibility and freedom. You are facing the problem I faced in writing this text, that of deciding what is solidly enough agreed on to include and what is still in transition—of taking your students to the cutting edge, yet marking for them the boundary within which there is consensus.

Good choosing!

ACKNOWLEDGMENTS

Alex Haley, author of *Roots*, says, "Whenever you see a turtle on top of a fence post, you know he had a lot of help getting there." I am, for sure, like that turtle! Through a long period of development, I had much help along the way. A special acknowledgment must go to everyone responsible for establishing and administering the Center for the Advanced Study in the Behavioral Sciences, in Palo Alto, California. It is a perfect place to read, think, hold stimulating conversations with able scholars, and write—no phones in the studies! Thanks to the support of the Spencer Foundation and a sabbatical from Syracuse University, I spent a year there as a fellow, during which time much of the conceptual foundation of this book was laid. Lee Cronbach was especially supportive during this period in supplying advance copies of Cronbach (1982) as well as material from his files. Additional stimulation came from conversations with the other fellows and persons in the San Francisco Bay Area such as Michael Scriven. The result was Krathwohl (1985), upon which this book is built.

The book's instructional features resulted from consultation with Jim Cox, now of the Rochester Institute of Technology, who suggested the original layout. Richard Kenny took up that task when Jim moved on. He continues in this role, assisting me with the *Instructor's Manual*. Rick deserves special recognition, however, for the end-of-chapter problems and their answers, which are almost all his; the dialogue they develop about points made in the chapter adds greatly to the instructional thrust of the book.

Various anonymous reviewers have made many helpful suggestions and contributed significantly. They know who they are, and I am most grateful to them. Persons who helped with various parts of the manuscript who I am aware of and can acknowledge are David Erickson, UCLA; Carl Huberty, University of Georgia; Tom Knapp, University of Rochester; Emily Robertson, Syracuse University; Bruce Rogers, University of North Iowa; Gilbert Sax, University of Washington; and Eileen Schroeder, SUNY at Cortland. If errors remain, and I hope not, don't blame them, blame me. Donald Campbell, when he was Schweitzer Professor at Syracuse, was a wonderful and inspiring resource, very generous with his offprints. I am grateful to my colleague Vincent Tinto, with whom I have developed the course on which this text is based; he has been helpful, encouraging, and most patient as the book went through numerous versions and rewrites.

I thank my ophthalmologist, Dr. John A. Hoepner, whose care and conscientious monitoring controls an early case of glaucoma and saved my sight.

Students at the University of Arizona, Stanford University, and Syracuse University have been very helpful in supplying comments and suggestions. I am indebted to Larry Aleamoni at Arizona, John Krumboltz and Martin Ford at Stanford, and Martyn Berger of Twente University in the Netherlands for their willingness to use the text in draft and to supply comments. Many students wrote comments anonymously and cannot be individually credited, but among those I can credit who were especially helpful are Robin Brenner, Margaret Dobies, Amelia El Hindi, Jim Ellsworth, Tom Moats, and Judy Welter.

In addition to Richard Kenny, Afnan Darwazeh did an especially good job of checking the form and substance of the references, and Ruth Federman and I-Chen Tai helped solve some special reference problems.

Although much of this book was created on a word processor, it nevertheless involved much clerical work, and I appreciate the so-very-much-more-than-clerical assistance of Linda Froio Pitzono, who read the manuscript for form, and Carol Johns, whose patience through innumerable revisions has been a wonder. Rephah Berg very ably copyedited important parts of the manuscript on short notice, as did Gray Weaver a small section.

Finally, I have had superb assistance from Longman, whose education editor, Naomi Silverman, provided wise counsel, continuous moral support and encouragement, and tangible aid when needed. Associate managing editor Halley Gatenby has been most careful to assure accuracy, extremely helpful, and very easy to work with.

A REQUEST

As you can see, a text of this kind is not the product of one person. I've had lots of help! But it still can be improved in many ways. To do so, I need to know how you, both students and instructors, react to this material. I'd love to hear from you. You'll find a feedback card bound into the back of the book to encourage you to make comments. Let me hear from you. I'll be checking my mailbox.

The Nature of Research

- Chapter 1 introduces you to the nature of social and behavioral research and what it seeks to accomplish.
- Chapter 2 helps you recognize that you have a good knowledge base to build on.
- Chapter 3 shows the wide variety of methods that are employed in the social and behavioral sciences.
- Chapter 4 examines how the findings of a research study become knowledge.
- Chapter 5 describes a valuable general model of a study—the chain of reasoning—that we shall use throughout the book.

CHAPTER
1

Introduction

We are a scientific civilisation; that means a civilisation in which knowledge
and its integrity are crucial. Science is only a Latin word for knowledge.
Jacob Bronowski, The Ascent of Man

OVERVIEW

Although concerned people have been doing research for centuries using the
relatively dull edge of experience to cut to the heart of social problems, it is
only in this century that the keener blade of sophisticated research methods
has laid bare some fundamental explanations of individual and group
behavior. Creative efforts to describe and explain social phenomena and then
to validate those explanations have led to the development of a social science
with broad scope and a variety of methods.

CHAPTER CONTENTS

Social and Behavioral Science: Important but Historically Young   3
The Roles and Outcomes of Research   5
    Exploration and Description   5
    Explanation   6
    Validation   6
The Different Roles in Perspective   7
Summary   8

SOCIAL AND BEHAVIORAL SCIENCE: IMPORTANT BUT HISTORICALLY YOUNG

"Mom, why is Grandpa so suspicious of everyone these days? He seems
always to feel that folks are trying to hide something from him, that they are
out to get him. I'm sure not! And that stuff about not wanting him around,

where did he get that idea? He used to be so easygoing! I don't understand what's going on!''

"I wish I knew, son, but I don't. I've noticed the change, too, and it has me worried.''

Zimbardo and his associates (1981) thought they understood what was going on in cases like this. They did an experiment to test their hunch, a hypothesis that individuals who are gradually growing deaf don't realize it. Deafness changes their perception of the world, which they interpret as increasingly hostile. Testing that hypothesis was an attempt to validate the experimenters' explanation of this phenomenon, a common goal in research. We will look further at this particular study in the next chapter. This is but one example of a problem on which social and behavioral science can shed light.

Such problems have been speculated about since time began. How do you and I learn? Why do we act differently in a group than when we are alone? Why do we choose different ways to organize our governments, economies, and social groups? These are fascinating questions to which many answers have been suggested. The natural sciences have been scientifically studied for several centuries, but only in the twentieth century did we begin to investigate social and behavioral questions using systematic methods, standardized tests, carefully constructed questionnaires, sophisticated instruments, and large masses of data. Our progress has become increasingly rapid in the past few decades as we have gained experience, yet many people feel it is still much too slow, especially considering the importance and the severity of the social problems that it might ameliorate. One hope is that with improved methods and well-trained researchers, progress will accelerate. This book is intended as a step in that direction.

As might be expected of a relatively new area, social and behavioral science research methods are still evolving. You should learn enough from this book to be able to read such research with understanding and a critical eye. In many instances, you will be able to conduct that research, though you may need advanced instruction in some of the methods.

Because of their recent evolution, these methods are still close to the layperson's perspective. It does not require a lifetime of work to understand their basis. They are the result of the straightforward application of logical reasoning and will fit easily into your typical pattern of behavior once you have mastered the jargon—research, like all other fields, has its own terminology.

Just the words *statistical methods*, however, elicit fear in people uncomfortable with mathematical equations and calculations. Yet we can develop a conceptual understanding of a statistic's purpose and when best to use it, just like any other research method. Correct usage of statistics in specific situations, however, may still be daunting. Luckily, nowadays this is usually done by computer programs, so learning statistical computation is not necessary to understanding and interpreting the statistics themselves. Of course, there will always be complex statistical procedures such as canonical correlation or ridge regression that you may have to stretch a bit to comprehend. But you can usually understand enough about them to judge when to use them and when to get specialized help.

Your common sense will be a sound guide for most of what you will learn from this book.[1] A personal demonstration of that in the next chapter should allay any concerns you may have about your ability to master this material.

> The systematic study of societal and individual problems with scientific methods is a development of the twentieth century. Social science methods are of relatively recent origin, are still evolving, and are logically straight-forward. Therefore, they can be conceptually understood without having to master a wide range of complex technicalities.

THE ROLES AND OUTCOMES OF RESEARCH

Of what does research actually consist? Three of its main roles are creative description, creative explanation, and creative validation. Notice that the word *creative* is used with each of these outcomes. We often teach research as though the steps were pedestrian and routine, like a paint-by-numbers picture. Not true! All good research involves some element of creativity.

Exploration and Description

Exploration—poking around where others haven't, trying something to see what happens, bringing fresh eyes to old situations—discovers new situations and relationships to understand. It precedes **description**, which captures those findings so that we can fit them with explanations and then test or validate those explanations.

Describing often illuminates parts of our world that we might otherwise never encounter. In studying primitive tribes and third-world countries, anthropologists make real for us cultures different from our own. Sociologists often study groups that are not part of the cultural mainstream. For example, Becker (1963) devoted a book, *Outsiders*, to handicapped individuals, underground musicians, and other socially atypical individuals; Whyte's (1955) *Street Corner Society* described a group of men for whom the street corner was the focus of their community; Festinger, Riecken, and Schacter (1956) wrote of a cult that believed the end of the world would come during the period studied; and Rist (1977) and Smith and Geoffrey (1968) examined the dynamics of classrooms.

What is creative description? It incorporates creativity first in perceiving important aspects of a situation missed by others and second in organizing and

---

1. The exception is stipulative definitions—special definitions of common terms that have a particular meaning when used in the research context. For instance, the problem of "mortality" in experimentation doesn't mean that the subjects died; it means that they dropped out of the study.

presenting that perception so richly and vividly that it comes alive in the theater of the mind. Such description can make the obscure understandable and very real.

Inventiveness in description also occurs when a researcher labels important phenomena. Going beyond the creativity required to recognize a phenomenon in the first place, researchers must define it appropriately and recognizably and name it in an immediately meaningful way. Kounin (1970) did this when he noted that an important aspect of classroom control was maintaining the pace of classroom activity rather than getting bogged down in details. He called this "momentum," an apt term that borrows from its connotation in physics to convey an aspect of good teaching. Binet (1912), developing what he called an "intelligence test," introduced this important and much disputed attribute into psychology. Defining an attribute and then inventing a way to recognize it through measurement or observation is a particularly effective way of adding to our store of useful terms and concepts.

Explanation

Explanation logically follows from a good description. Explanation may take the form of creatively recognizing a relationship between and among variables, as when Dollard and Doob (1939) recognized that frustration leads to aggression (for example, in the unsocialized child who wants a toy and, failing to take it from a playmate, strikes out at him).

Explanations help us understand situations well enough to predict what will happen in them. One of the most important roles of social science is prediction; by understanding relations, we know what to expect and can take steps to change projected outcomes more to our liking. Consider aptitude testing. By noting the relationships between success and certain aptitudes, we learn which skills to encourage in children. Such prediction plays important roles in education, in social work, in economics—indeed, in nearly every professional vocation.

In explaining how something works or why a particular phenomenon occurs, we describe the relationships among its parts. Sometimes explanation is incorporated into the original description. More often, explanation follows as a result of insights gained from contrasting the phenomenon at different points in time or in different circumstances. Thus Kounin, Friesen, and Norton (1966), examining videotapes of a large number of classrooms, noted that emotionally disturbed children disrupted the classes of some teachers but not others. The teachers must be somehow responsible. The researchers studied the circumstances that preceded disruptions and contrasted them with similar situations in which no outbreaks took place. From this, they developed ideas about how teachers maintained classroom control; momentum, noted earlier, was one.

Validation

Having described a situation, we try to understand and explain what is going on. Finally, we test the explanation to be sure that it works. Hence checking, or

validation, of the explanation is the third important role and outcome of research. It determines whether predictions based on the explanation will prove accurate. Validating research uncovers incorrect explanations, oversights, one-time occurrences, limitations or restrictions, and other flaws. The validation of relationships is a major role of research for scientists who expect behavioral and social science research to be like that of the physical and biological sciences. Zimbardo's (1981) study of progressive deafness and paranoia mentioned at the outset of this chapter is one of thousands of examples of this type of research (a very creative one at that). Studies designed as experiments are usually concerned with the validation of relationships.

THE DIFFERENT ROLES IN PERSPECTIVE

The apparently simple look of these roles conceals an abundance of decisions, some routine, some complex, many that can be made creatively. Zimbardo's (1981) research is an apt illustration of creativity in validation. His use of hypnosis to study paranoia solved a very tricky ethical problem: he could hardly let elderly individuals grow deaf and not tell them, just to see if they came to view the world as a hostile place. This was typical of the many creative decisions made in any research study. Certainly the way the problem is framed in the Zimbardo study is imaginative, but so are a number of other aspects. Since we will be examining this study in more detail in chapter 2, you can see for yourself. Be alert to the wide variety of decisions researchers face and their often ingenious ways of handling them.

Although we have described these roles as if they were sequential, exploration and description leading to explanation and to validation, things aren't always that neat in real life. Often the test of an explanation fails confirmation because it rested on faulty or inadequate description, as when a person with a terrible hangover, finding a common apparently causal element in scotch and water, bourbon and water, and vodka and water, swears he'll never touch a drop of water again. An attempt to validate the causal agent by drinking water would fail and require new exploration and description. Sometimes descriptions are biased by an entirely false conception. For example, early social policy studies were based on a description of poor people as fundamentally too lazy to want to shed their poverty role. Later research showed that the early description was wrong: most poor people are eager to improve their lot, are working at doing so, and stay on welfare only for brief periods.

Not all social scientists view all three fundamental roles of research as equally important or deserving of equal emphasis. Some anthropologists, historians, and sociologists do studies that only describe; most combine description with explanation. Some psychologists, economists, and sociologists emphasize explanation and validation. For nearly all of them, however, understanding or explanation is a critical outcome.

> Three critical roles and results of research are exploration and description of social and behavioral phenomena, explanation of how and why they occur, and their validation. All have an important element of creativity about them in good research. Of the three, explaining is universally emphasized by all disciplines; the emphasis on exploration and description and on validation varies.

SUMMARY

The systematic study of societal and individual problems is relatively new as a science, and the research methods are still evolving. Three important roles of research are exploring and describing, explaining, and validating or confirming those explanations. Each involves creativity in conceptualization and implementation. Of course, not every research method is equally useful for each role. Indeed, we use a variety of methods, each of which has particular strengths. However, we have been considering the methods of the social and behavioral sciences in the abstract, and they must be made to come alive with real examples. The next chapter presents two contrasting examples of research. As noted, such studies are not so complex that you won't be able to analyze them and recognize some of their strengths and weaknesses. A demonstration of that follows.

ADDITIONAL READING

Hoaglin, Light, McPeek, Mosteller, and
   Stota (1982), especially chapter 1.

IMPORTANT TERMS

Description   Exploration
Explanation   Validation

CHAPTER
2

Analysis of Two Illustrative Research Studies

OVERVIEW

This chapter reprints the text of two research studies, illustrating different ways of approaching research. As you read them, you will sense their strengths and weaknesses and realize that certain problems may be more amenable to one approach than another.

This chapter also provides an opportunity to try your skill at analyzing studies and show how much you already know about social and behavioral science research. Though you may miss certain aspects the first time through, you will be surprised at how many you recognize when they are pointed out. Obviously, one function of this book is to make this kind of knowledge come to mind more readily.

CHAPTER CONTENTS

Analysis of Two Illustrative Studies   9
A Quantitative Experimental Study   10
    Analysis   14
A Qualitative Research Study   16
    Analysis   23
Summary   24

ANALYSIS OF TWO ILLUSTRATIVE STUDIES

In chapter 1, we noted different roles of research; these lead to studies with diverse characteristics. Showing how different these studies look and demonstrating your ability to critique such studies, even before training, are the intentions of this chapter. We will examine two articles:

First Study

- Uses quantitative methods—measures and statistics to describe phenomena
- Is a tightly designed experiment in which events are controlled by the researcher

- Employs deductive logic to predict the results from the proposed explanation
- Validates an explanation and demonstrates a relationship

Second Study

- Uses qualitative methods—verbal descriptions to portray phenomena
- Consists of unstructured interviews in which subjects expressing their own thoughts explore the topic with the researcher
- Employs inductive logic to find an explanation
- Develops an explanation for a perceived relationship

These are two contrasting but equally important methods of doing research.

A QUANTITATIVE EXPERIMENTAL STUDY

We noted in chapter 1 that the research methods of the social and behavioral sciences use straightforward logic. Untrained readers show amazing skill in critiquing important aspects of a study. Training will make you sensitive to even more aspects and, more important, will give you a framework enabling you to hold the important points in your memory. Read the following study critically, making note of its strengths and weaknesses.[1]

Induced Hearing Deficit Generates Experimental Paranoia

Philip G. Zimbardo
Susan M. Andersen
Stanford University

Loren G. Kabat
*State University of New York,
Stony Brook*

Abstract. The development of paranoid reactions was investigated in normal people experiencing a temporary loss of hearing. In a social setting, subjects made partially deaf by hypnotic suggestion, but kept unaware of the source of their deafness, became more paranoid as indicated on a variety of assessment measures. The results support a hypothesized cognitive-social mechanism for the clinically observed relationship between paranoia and deafness in the elderly.

1. "Induced Hearing Deficit Generates Experimental Paranoia" by Philip G. Zimbardo et al., 1981, *Science, 212,* pp. 1529–1531. Copyright © 1981 by the American Association for the Advancement of Science. Reprinted by permission. Paragraph numbers added.

1. Clinical observation has uncovered a relationship between deafness and psychopathology (1–3). In particular, when deafness occurs later in life and the hearing loss is relatively gradual, paranoid reactions are often observed (4–14). Delusions of persecution and other paranoid symptoms, first noted by Kraepelin (6) in 1915, seem especially prevalent among the hard-of-hearing elderly (7–9). Audiometric assessment of hospitalized, elderly patients (with age and other selection factors controlled statistically) has revealed a significantly greater degree of deafness among those diagnosed as paranoid than among those with affective disorders (10–12).

2. Maher (15) suggested that one process by which deafness may lead to paranoid reactions involves an initial lack of awareness of the hearing defect by the person, as well as by interacting others. Paranoid thinking then emerges as a cognitive attempt to explain the perceptual anomaly (16) of not being able to hear what people in one's presence are apparently saying. Judging them to be whispering, one may ask, "about what?" or "why me?" Denial by others that they are whispering may be interpreted by the hard-of-hearing person as a lie since it is so clearly discrepant with observed evidence. Frustration and anger over such injustices may gradually result in a more profound expression of hostility.

3. Observers, without access to the perceptual data base of the person experiencing the hearing disorder, judge these responses to be bizarre instances of thought pathology. As a consequence, others may exclude the hard-of-hearing person, whose suspiciousness and delusions about their alleged plots become upsetting (17). Over time, social relationships deteriorate, and the individual experiences both isolation and loss of the corrective social feedback essential for modifying false beliefs (18, 19). Within a self-validating, autistic system, delusions of persecution go unchecked (20). As such, they eventually become resistant to contrary information from any external source (21). In this analysis, paranoia is sometimes an end product of an initially rational search to explain a perceptual discontinuity, in this case, being deaf without knowing it.

4. We now report an experimental investigation of the development of paranoid reactions in normal subjects with a temporary, functional loss of hearing. Across a variety of assessment measures, including standard personality tests, self-reports, and judgments of their behavior by others in the situation, these subjects became significantly more paranoid than did subjects in two control conditions. The effect was transient and limited to the test environment [by the specificity of the instructions, by extensive post-experimental interviews (debriefing procedures), and by the healthy "premorbid" status of each participant]. Nevertheless, qualitative observations and objective data offer support for the role of deafness-without-awareness as a causal factor in triggering paranoid reactions. Although the subjects were young and had normal hearing, these results have obvious bearing on a possible cognitive-social mechanism by which deafness may eventuate in paranoia among the middle-aged and elderly.

5. Participants were 18 college males selected from large introductory classes. In the selection process, each student (i) demonstrated that he was highly hypnotizable according to the Harvard Group Scale of Hypnotic Susceptibility (22) and the Stanford Scale of Hypnotic Susceptibility, form C (23); (ii) evidenced posthypnotic amnesia; (iii) passed a test of hypnotically induced partial deafness; (iv) scored within the normal range on measures of psychopathology; and (v) attended at least one of two hypnosis training sessions before the experiment.

6. Six participants were randomly assigned to the experimental treatment in which partial deafness, without awareness of its source, was hypnotically induced. The remaining participants were randomly assigned to one of two control groups. In one of these groups, partial deafness with awareness of its source was induced to demonstrate the importance of the knowledge that one's difficulty in understanding others is caused by deafness. In the other control group, a posthypnotic suggestion unrelated to deafness was experienced (a compulsion to scratch an itchy ear) along with amnesia for it, to establish whether merely carrying out a posthypnotic suggestion with amnesia might be sufficient to yield the predicted results. Taken together, these two groups provide controls for experimental demand characteristics, subject selection traits (hypnotic susceptibility), and the rational basis for the experienced sensory anomaly (24).

7. During group training sessions, each subject was instructed in self-hypnosis and completed consent and medical history forms, a number of Minnesota Multiphasic Personality Inventory (MMPI) scales (25), and our clinically derived paranoia scale (26). In the experimental session, subjects were hypnotized, after which they listened through earphones to deep relaxation music and then heard taped instructions for one of the three treatments. The use of coded tapes randomly selected in advance by one of the researchers (L.K.) made it possible for the hypnotist (P.Z.), experimenter, (S.A.), observers, and confederates to be ignorant of the treatment assignment of the subjects. All subjects were given the suggestion to begin experiencing the changed state when they saw the posthypnotic cue ("FOCUS") projected on a viewing screen in the laboratory. In order to make the task socially realistic and to conceal the purpose of the experiment, each subject was led to believe he was participating, along with two others (who were confederates), in a study of the effects of hypnotic training procedures on creative problem solving. Because of the hearing defect that subjects were to experience, all instructions and tasks were projected automatically by timed slides, the first of which was the posthypnotic cue. While working on a preliminary anagram task, the two confederates engaged in a well-rehearsed, standard conversation designed to establish their commonality, to offer test probes for the subject's deafness, and to provide verbal content that might be misperceived as antagonistic. They recalled a party they had both attended, laughed at an incident mentioned, made a funny face, and eventually decided to work together, finally asking the subject if he also wanted to work with them.

8. The instructions had previously suggested that group effort on such tasks is usually superior to solitary responding. The subject's behavior was videotaped, observed directly by two judges from behind a one-way mirror, and scored independently by the confederates immediately after the session. After this conversation, the three participants were asked to develop stories about pairs of people in ambiguous relationships [Thematic Apperception Test (TAT)]. On the first task, they had the option of working together or of working alone. Thus, an interdependence among confederates and the subject was created [important in the natural etiology of paranoia (17, 19, 21)], which centered around developing a common creative solution. On the second TAT task, participants had to work alone.

9. After these tasks were completed, each confederate was instructed by the slides to go to a different laboratory room while the subject stayed in the room to complete evaluation forms, including the MMPI and others. Extensive debriefing followed (27), and to remove any tension or confusion, each subject was rehypnotized by the experimenter and told to recall all the events experienced during the session. Subjects were reevaluated in a 1-month follow-up.

10. Major results are summarized in Table 1, which presents group means and one-tailed t-test values derived from a single a priori planned comparison that contrasted the experimental group with the two control groups taken together (28). This analysis followed standard analysis of variance tests. As predicted, the experience of being partially deaf, without being aware of its source, created significant changes in cognitive, emotional, and behavioral functioning. Compared with the control groups, subjects in the deafness-without-awareness treatment became more paranoid, as shown on an MMPI paranoia scale of Horn (25, p. 283) and on our clinically derived paranoia scale (26). Experimental subjects also had significantly elevated scores on the MMPI grandiosity scale of Watson and Klett (25, p. 287)—one aspect of paranoid thinking. Experimental subjects perceived themselves as more irritated, agitated, hostile, and unfriendly than control subjects did and were perceived as such by confederates ignorant of the treatment. When invited to work with confederates on the TAT task, only one of six experimental subjects elected to do so; in contrast, 9 of 12 control subjects preferred to affiliate ($z = 4.32$, $P < .001$).

11. The TAT stories generated by the subjects were assessed in two ways. Subjects' own ratings of the creativity of their stories indicated that experimental subjects judged their stories to be significantly less creative than did subjects in either of the control groups. Second, the stories were scored (reliably by two judges) for the extent to which subjects evaluated TAT characters. An evaluative-judgmental outlook toward other people is a hallmark of paranoia. The experimental subjects used significantly more evaluative language, both positive and negative (for example, right–wrong, good–bad) ($t = 2.86$, $P < .01$) than controls did. In addition, they differed significantly ($z = 5.00$, $P < .001$) from the controls in their greater use of positive evaluative language. Experimental subjects reported feeling

TABLE 1. Mean Scores on Dependent Measures Distinguishing Experimental from Control Subjects

	Treatment				
		Control			
Dependent measures	Deafness without awareness (N = 6)	Deafness with awareness (N = 6)	Posthypnotic suggestion (N = 6)	t (15)	P
Paranoia measures*					
MMPI–Paranoia	1.50	.33	−.17	1.838	<.05
MMPI–Grandiosity	1.33	−.83	−1.00	1.922	<.05
Paranoia clinical interview form	.30	−.09	−.28	3.667	<.005
TAT					
Affective evaluation	83.35	16.65	33.50	2.858	<.01
Self-assessed creativity	42.83	68.33	73.33	3.436	<.005
Self-rated feelings					
Creative	34.17	55.83	65.83	2.493	<.05
Confused	73.33	39.17	35.00	2.521	<.05
Relaxed	43.33	81.67	78.33	2.855	<.01
Agitated	73.33	14.17	15.33	6.586	<.001
Irritated	70.00	25.00	7.00	6.000	<.001
Friendly	26.67	53.33	56.67	2.195	<.05
Hostile	38.33	13.33	13.33	2.047	<.05
Judges' ratings					
Confused	40.83	27.08	17.67	1.470	<.10
Relaxed	34.17	54.59	65.42	2.839	<.01
Agitated	51.25	24.59	13.75	3.107	<.005
Irritated	45.84	18.92	11.25	3.299	<.005
Friendly	23.34	48.34	65.00	3.385	<.005
Hostile	18.75	5.00	1.67	2.220	<.05

*These measures were taken before and after the experimental session; reported means represent difference scores (after minus before).

no more suspicious than did control subjects. These last two findings weaken the possible criticism that the results were based simply on anger induced by the experimental manipulation.

12. Both groups experiencing a hearing deficit reported, as expected, that their hearing was not keen, but reported no other sensory difficulties. Those who were partially deaf without being aware of the source of the deafness did experience greater confusion, which is likely to have motivated an active search for an appropriate explanation. Over time, however, if their delusional systems were allowed to become more coherent and systematized, the paranoid reaction would be less likely to involve confusion. Ultimately, there is so much confidence in the proposed paranoid explanatory system that alternative scenarios are rejected.

13. Despite the artificiality of our laboratory procedure, functionally analogous predicaments occur in everyday life. People's hearing does deteriorate without their realizing it. Indeed, the onset of deafness among the elderly is sometimes actively denied because recognizing a hearing deficit may be tantamount to acknowledging a greater defect—old age. Perhaps self-deception about one's hearing deficit may even be sufficient, in some circumstances, to yield a similar response, namely, a search for a more personally acceptable alternative that finds fault in others rather than in oneself. When there is no social or cultural support for the chosen explanation and the actor is relatively powerless, others may judge him or her to be irrational and suffering from a mental disorder. Although our subjects were young and had normal hearing, these

findings have obvious bearing on a possible cognitive-social mechanism by which deafness may lead to paranoia among the middle-aged and elderly.

REFERENCES AND NOTES

1. B. Pritzker, *Schweiz. Med. Wochenschr.* **7**, 165 (1938).
2. F. Houston and A. B. Royse, *J. Ment. Sci.* **100**, 990 (1954).
3. M. Vernon, *J. Speech Hear. Res.* **12**, 541 (1969).
4. K. Z. Altshuler, *Am. J. Psychiatry* **127**, 11 and 1521 (1971).
5. Personal communication from J. D. Rainer (14 July 1980), who has studied the psychiatric effects of deafness for the past 25 years at the New York State Psychiatric Institute.
6. E. Kraepelin, *Psychiatrie* **8**, 1441 (1915).
7. D. W. K. Kay, *Br. J. Hosp. Med.* **8**, 369 (1972).
8. F. Post, *Persistent Persecutory States of the Elderly* (Pergamon, London, 1966).
9. H. A. McClelland, M. Roth, H. Neubauer, R. F. Garside, *Excerpta Med. Int. Congr. Ser.* **4**, 2955 (1968).
10. A. F. Cooper, R. F. Garside, D. W. K. Kay, *Br. J. Psychiatry* **129**, 532 (1976).
11. A. F. Cooper, A. R. Curry, D. W. K. Kay, R. F. Garside, M. Roth, *Lancet* **1974-II**, 7885 (1974).
12. A. F. Cooper and R. Porter, *J. Psychosom. Res.* **20**, 107 (1976).
13. A. F. Cooper, *Br. J. Psychiatry* **129**, 216 (1976).
14. D. W. K. Kay, A. F. Cooper, R. F. Garside, M. Roth, *ibid.* **129**, 207 (1976).
15. B. Maher, in *Thought and Feeling*, H. London and R. E. Nisbett, Eds. (Aldine, Chicago, 1974), pp. 85–103.
16. G. Reed, *The Psychology of Anomalous Experience* (Houghton Mifflin, Boston, 1974).
17. E. M. Lemert, *Sociometry* **25**, 2 (1962).
18. L. Festinger, *Hum. Relat.* **7**, 117 (1954).
19. N. A. Cameron, in *Comprehensive Textbook of Psychiatry*, A. M. Freedman and H. I. Kaplan, Eds. (Williams & Wilkins, Baltimore, 1967), pp. 665–675.
20. A. Beck, in *Thought and Feeling*. H. London and R. E. Nisbett, Eds. (Aldine, Chicago, 1974), pp. 127–140.
21. W. W. Meisner, *The Paranoid Process* (Jason Aronson, New York, 1978).
22. R. E. Shor and E. C. Orne, *Harvard Group Scale of Hypnotic Susceptibility, Form A* (Consulting Psychologists Press. Palo Alto, Calif., 1962).
23. A. M. Weitzenhoffer and E. R. Hilgard, *Stanford Hypnotic Susceptibility Scale, Form C* (Consulting Psychologists Press, Palo Alto, Calif., 1962).
24. A fuller presentation of procedures is available by request.
25. W. G. Dahlstrom, G. S. Welsh, L. F. Dahlstrom, *An MMPI Handbook*, vol. 2. *Research Applications* (Univ. of Minnesota Press, Minneapolis, 1975).
26. We derived this scale specifically for this study: it consisted of 15 self-declarative statements responded to on 7-point rating scales. The scale was drawn from a clinical study of paranoia (*14*).
27. L. Ross, M. R. Lepper, M. Hubbard, *J. Pers. Soc. Psychol.* **35**, 817 (1977).
28. W. L. Hays, *Statistics for Psychologists* (Holt, Rinehart & Winston. New York, 1965), p. 465.
29. This report is dedicated to Neal E. Miller as part of a commemoration by his former students of his inspired science teaching. We wish to acknowledge the expert and reliable research assistance of Harry Coin, Dave Willer, Bob Sick, James Glanzer, Jill Fonaas, Laurie Plautz, Lisa Carrol, and Sarah Garlan. We thank Joan Linsenmeier and David Rosenhan for critical editing of the manuscript.

Analysis

What did you think of this study? Did you find in it things that concerned you? Were there things in it that you felt especially good about? I have discussed this study with serveral classes, and students listed these strengths and weaknesses:

Strengths

- There is an excellent explanation of the relationship of deafness to paranoia, both shown to be conditions of aging.
- Three different measures of paranoia were used just in case one might be considered suspect by a reader.
- Hypnosis was cleverly employed to substitute available subjects for ones who could not ethically be used—the researchers just couldn't let elderly subjects go deaf and not tell them!
- There was an excellent use of groups to eliminate possible alternative explanations. One eliminated posthypnotic suggestion as the cause since the group with the itchy ear did not show paranoia. The group that knew it was partly deaf showed that the phenomenon occurred only without knowledge of deafness. These two groups were like the experimental group in every way except for not having unrecognized deafness. They are called control groups and permit the researcher to eliminate alternative explanations; that is, they control for those explanations.
- Random assignment of the subjects to the groups meant that, on the average, the groups were comparable in the relevant characteristics that might otherwise bias the experiment. For example, if one group was more anxious than the other, it might have performed differently. Even though anxiety was not measured and equated over the groups, random assignment will, on average, have that effect.
- None of the individuals who had contact with the subjects or who were responsible for making observations of the development of paranoia—hypnotist, researcher, observers, and confederates—knew to which treatment any given subject had been assigned. They couldn't have made the results come out "right" even if they had wanted to. In research terms, the observers were kept blind to the treatment.
- Subjects were extensively debriefed after the study to make sure that there were no negative consequences of their participation. They were followed up a month later to provide further reassurance that there were no lingering problems.
- The first instructions were tape recordings, so subjects were treated identically before being given different treatments. Later, instructions for different treatments, given by automatically projected timed slides, served the same purpose without calling attention to the diminished hearing of two of the three groups.
- The confederates engaged in a well-rehearsed standard conversation so that all subjects were exposed to the same possibilities of misperceiving antagonistic parts of the "script."

Weaknesses

- Six persons in each group is a very small sample size.
- Only the subjects who were most susceptible to hypnosis were chosen.

- The subjects were not drawn from the population to which the results were to be generalized, the elderly; they were all male and were college students.
- The length of time the hypnotized condition existed was not given.
- Reliability and validity data were not given for the researchers' own "clinically derived" paranoia scale, so we cannot be certain that it is a valid instrument. By contrast, data on published instruments are publicly available. (They did give a reference, however, from which it was drawn.)
- Subjects knew it was an experimental setting and it was also an unusual one. They may have reacted accordingly.
- The researchers had to deceive the subjects.
- Hypnosis, an unusual procedure more associated with show business than with science, was used without explanation or defense.
- There was no assurance that the paranoia created under the experimental conditions was the same as that affecting the elderly.
- Confederates had the opportunity to learn which subjects were partly deaf since their conversation included probes for the partial deafness to ensure that it was maintained.

How did your lists compare? You might not have identified all the strengths and weaknesses. Remember that my lists are a compilation of the common responses across several classes. But no doubt when you recognized an item not on your list, you said to yourself, "Oh, I should have put that down, too!" So this is in fact a sophisticated behavioral science experiment in which many readers, without previous training in research methods, can either identify strengths and weakness or recognize them when pointed out. Further, although these weaknesses and strengths were found in an experiment, most are relevant to other research methods as well. This suggests that there is a solid base on which this book can build. Not surprisingly, Einhorn and Hogarth (1986) point out that individuals use systematic rules for assessing cause in both science and everyday life. Such rules will be further explored in chapters 12, 13, and 14 and the setting in which they operate in chapter 4.

A QUALITATIVE RESEARCH STUDY

Having examined an experimental study, let us now look at qualitative methodology, another way of working that is particularly useful in finding explanations. Christa Hoffmann-Riem studied how families who adopt a child construct the "sense of a common bond" that is perceived to exist in biologically related families. The report has been abridged for reproduction here, but nothing essential to understanding the study has been omitted.[2]

---

2. From "Adoptive Parenting and the Norm of Family Emotionality" by Christa Hoffmann-Riem, 1986, *Qualitative Sociology*, 9, pp. 162–177. Reprinted and abridged by permission. (The complete original list of references is reprinted for the purposes of chapter 7.)

Adoptive Parenting and the Norm of Family Emotionality

Christa Hoffmann-Riem
University of Hamburg

Abstract: This paper is concerned with the construction of "the sense of a common bond" in adoptive families.[1] First, I clarify how adoptive families construct this sense in relation to biological families. Second, by examining features of adoptive family life. I suggest a new way of understanding non-adoptive families. Presuppositions about "normal" family relationships dominate the start of adoptive family life. As seen from the actors' perspective, "emotional normalization" is a crucial indicator of successful adoptive family life. I outline how involuntarily childless couples try to accomplish normality when applying for a child, and how achieving the assumed normality of non-adoptive families continues after adoption.

METHODOLOGICAL ASSUMPTIONS AND THE TECHNIQUE OF THE NARRATIVE INTERVIEW

The fundamental processes which underlie the symbolic structuring of kinship and parenthood are usually invisible. Examining a special case (i.e., adoptive families) may help render these processes accessible if an appropriate method is used. Unfortunately, the sociological literature on adoption reflects the prevailing methodological orientation of the discipline, the pre-structuring of data collection by a set of hypotheses and their operationalization in a standard interview. The researcher who works with pre-structured categories will find only that which he or she has previously considered. An exception to this general trend is the work of David Kirk (1964) which draws on his own experiences as an adoptive father.

My study starts with the methodological assumption that basic structures of family life can be disclosed only if informants are given the opportunity to present their experiences in a manner I call "autonomous." Studies based on biographical documents like letters, e.g., Sorosky, Barron & Pannor (1979) or the detailed case study of an adoptive family (Huth, 1983) are the closest to my work. . . .

My research method, the "narrative interview," was drawn from the work of Fritz Schuetze (1977, see also Labov and Waletzky, 1967 and Kallmeyer and Schuetze, 1977), who recommends a strict division of the interview into two parts. The first or main part consists of the story told by the narrator without interruptions by the researcher; the second part consists of questions carefully put by the researcher in response to information already presented by the interviewee. . . .

My introductory question was formulated in the hopes of uncovering the whole history of the adoption, beginning with the decision to make an application for a child and ending with the development of their family life. After a number of introductory remarks emphasizing that the adoptive parents should tell their story the way they wanted, they were asked: "Can you still remember what it was like when you applied for a child?" I did not select a specific beginning, e.g., involuntary childlessness, for a chain of adoption events. Rather, the couples began to recapitulate the beginning of their adoption story as they saw it (e.g., childlessness) or started with the process of application and then came to recognize that something was missing. This prompted them to return to that "missing link" in the chain (childlessness) in order to enable me to have a proper understanding of their story. I interviewed couples and generally, the adoptive parents gave a combined account as a couple rather than two separate accounts. On the average, telling the story took about two hours. All interviews were recorded on tape and transcribed verbatim.

I appreciate Shulamit Reinharz' careful editing, and thank her for helping me share some of my research findings with an American audience. Address correspondence to: Institut für Soziologie, Universität Hamburg, Sedanstrasse 19, 2000 Hamburg 13, West Germany.

SAMPLING

The selection of informants was guided by the idea that ability to communicate should have priority over the representativeness of the subjects. Representative sampling would have been possible only if I had been able to use the data of the adoption agency in Hamburg. I rejected this idea since it would have associated me with the agency and possibly revived negative experiences (e.g., dependency, control) or positive associations (e.g., getting a child). Fifteen couples who participated in regular discussion group meetings of adoptive parents were selected. Most members of these discussion groups were middle class, similar to most applicants for adoption. The procedures to define class membership and a comparison of class membership between the sample and a universe of applicants for one year are presented in detail elsewhere (Hoffmann-Riem [1984], pp. 17–19, 42–45, 314, 328). I had taken part in the meetings of one group for several months to get some insight into the social world of adoptive parents. I presented my research design to the members of another discussion group and asked them to support the project.[2] I legitimized my research by referring to the fact that I needed to know more about the practical purposes, application process and the image of adoptive families. Almost all of the members were interested in participating as a means of informing the public (and the adoption agency) about adoptive family life. . . .

DATA INTERPRETATION

. . . My concern was not with the idiosyncracies of a single case but with the commonalities of all the cases. To begin, I outlined the rough chronology of events reflected in the story: (1) the couple's motivation for adoption, (2) the process of applying for a child, (3) the development of the parent-child relationship. Since each of these categories contained a wealth of information, I further differentiated within them. First I sought the shared properties of all the cases. Then I used specific data from each of the interviews to illustrate variety. For example, to analyze the "motivation process" I first showed how the desire for a child is based on conceptions of the "normal" adult role. Then I examined more closely the alternatives to being a parent en-

visioned by childless couples, how the desire for a child is integrated into male and female role definitions, and how the prospective child is instrumentalized for the adult role.

I started by comparing cases that differed widely from one another ("strategy of maximizing differences") in order to develop polar types. Then my analysis of the narratives in terms of their similarities allowed the range between the poles to be filled in.

My data interpretation is confined strictly to a reconstruction of what the research subjects themselves presented as their experiences. . . . I attempt to reflect the actor's perspective throughout the paper even if it is not explicitly stated in each sentence.

THE DESIRE FOR A CHILD

On the basis of very detailed adoption stories, I came to recognize that the majority of data can be subsumed under the concept of "constructing normality." [This idea had not been on my mind when I started the research.] . . . Before elaborating the adoptive parents' work to establish a "normal" parent-child relationship, I shall briefly outline the starting point of adoption—the desire for a child—as a chain of normalization processes.

The Federal Republic of Germany has the world's largest birth rate. Viewed against this background, narrative interviews with adoptive parents reveal that children are still very important in biographical planning for some West German adults. All the adoption stories begin with "We wanted a child." Considering the consequences of this desire, it is particularly worthy of note that no explanation is given. Seen from the narrator's perspective, no further clarification of the remark was necessary.

The motivational story preceding the decision to adopt is divided into sequences: a shift from what the couples defined as the "normal" starting point of marriage, to deviation and then, finally, to an attempt to reconstruct normality. Among these couples marriage was entered into with the aim of establishing a family. But like other couples, realization of the desire for a child was postponed until the household had been set up. As long as they practiced birth control, the couple experienced itself as being in harmony with the institutionalized pattern of the family life cycle. The unquestioned (or only slightly questioned) confidence in their joint reproductive ability made married life appear congruent with their own biographical planning for children. This enormous confidence paved the way for a crisis among these families and presumably the ten to fifteen per cent of married couples who unwillingly remain childless in West Germany.

Planning the transition from the phase of household establishment to the realization of a family is the step that progressively leads the couple away from feeling "normal." Biographical denormalization begins with the couple's first suspicions. When a certain level of fear is reached, medical help is sought so that the plan of family establishment, once regarded as something they could achieve on their own, might be pursued. Many of the narratives express the suffering the couples endured during the medical procedures. They turned to the medical option in order to rescue their original biographical plans, yet it was that very system that forced them to recognize the impossibility or improbability of its realization. A sequence of short, temporally connected sentences provides an idea of the extent to which the narrators feel rushed as they go from doctor to doctor in an effort to prevent the threat of childlessness.

ADOPTIVE MOTHER: We thought that we would like to have children.

ADOPTIVE FATHER: And since that did not work although we were trying hard—my wife was under medical treatment and I went to see a doctor—, and since it was extremely improbable that we would get children of our own, we started to think of adoption. . . . But first we have been in the university clinics for a long treatment, and a very, very good and sensible doctor was in charge of us, and we submitted to a *lot* of treatment to get an own child and be it convulsively [*sic*]. You know, then they increase the doses of hormones you get from one treatment to the next, and finally we came to the point that if there would be a pregnancy the probability was one to ten for twins and one to hundred for triplets, and that was already a critical limit. . . . And my wife had to go to the clinic every day to be checked if there weren't any negative side-effects. And then we always had to get there at a special date dependent on the cycle, for example Sunday night at 10 or Sunday morning at 9.

ADOPTIVE MOTHER: Yes, whenever ovulation was expected.

ADOPTIVE FATHER: And the doctor rushed to the clinic to wait for the right moment. Believe me, I could write a *book* about all those events in the hospital.

ADOPTIVE MOTHER: We were cared for very well, but finally we said to ourselves: Oh God, what are we doing here, why all this trouble?

Their "desperate" utilization of all the technological reproductive means available to them suggests that the definition of the family as a group of genealogically related persons is still firmly in place. It takes the couple a long time to accept the idea that being a "flesh and blood" relation is not the only way of constituting a family. Narrative interviews with adoptive parents reveal a great deal about the significance of kinship, i.e., the desire for establishing genealogical families who belong together. It takes the experience of missing parental autonomy and the suffering it causes to illustrate the way the biological family is an essential part of the normal biographical planning of many adults.

When medical procedures no longer justify the couples' hopes for a birth, the pattern of normality is redefined. The interviews reflect the couples' shift from being rushed to and fro to a new initiative of action: "And then we thought: let's adopt a child."

ADOPTING A CHILD: FROM STRANGENESS TO FAMILIARITY

Adoption does not coincide with the actors' concept of a "normal" family. Therefore, once the adoption has been carried out the normality of parental role fulfillment has yet to be reached. One means for constructing "normal" parent-child relationships is through an emotional bond. The parents define this as something that has to be worked at. While waiting for a child the applicants experience a high degree of insecurity concerning their prospective roles as parents. Experiences as prospective adoptive parents are framed by suppositions concerning the "normal" case. For example, the anxious question: "Will I be able to love a child that is not my own?" crops up in several interviews. The question illustrates how prospective parents worry about the quality of their future family life. Since the principle of biological filiation is violated, the parents fear that a quality constitutive of family life—the emotional bond—may also be adversely affected. The fact that prospective adoptive parents are so concerned about the affective bond shows how deeply the emotional parent-child relationship is accepted. When the principle of filiation is in effect, the emotional bond appears almost automatic. However, if the principle of filiation is not in effect, then the question arises as to whether the two main aspects of the "normal" family—filiation and love—are interdependent. Prospective adoptive parents hope that the constitution of a family as an emotional relationship can be accomplished even though the family has been "artificially" constructed. They hope that biological filiation is of only minor significance for the quality of their family relationship even though most had originally accepted the principle of filiation as a norm for their own biographical planning.

When the status passage from applicant to parent is achieved, the emotional quality of the parent-child relationship becomes a point of overwhelming significance. This was reflected in every narrative interview. The conditions of developing an emotional relationship differ substantially: in some cases only a few moments or hours were needed for the couple to feel attracted to a baby; but in the case of an older child, it may take years to overcome the sense of unfamiliarity. The beginning of family life may be full of happiness or irritation. Even allowing for these differences, every narrative interview arrives at some kind of statement of relationship: "And then an intensive relationship (quickly/slowly) developed between myself and the child."

For adoptive parents this process signifies the attainment of a goal. It means conformity with a central norm of family life. However, the structure of the parents' narrative shows that this statement is not the final presentation of the relational quality. It is followed by another key statement which reveals how adoptive parents organize their experiences in relation to the "normal" case. In the majority of narrative interviews, the following sentiment is expressed: "It is as if it were our own child."

Since without any interviewer guidance the majority of adoptive parents recapitulate events using this endpoint, we can assume that it refers to highly relevant experiences of family life. I am suggesting that the "achieved relationship" brings adoptive parents in line with the "normal" case. Only by evaluating their own experiences in the "primary framework" of the biological family[3] can adoptive parents ensure that the new quality of their relationship is communicated without misunderstanding. "It is like one's own child"—that is how adoptive parents indicate to themselves and others that the normality of family life has been accomplished.

Almost every narrative reflects the point at which the adoptive parents no longer need to typify their boy or girl as an *adopted* child. Whereas for a short or a long period they may have observed an emotional distance between themselves and the child because of its adoption status, ultimately they experience an emotional identification. This is a turning point in symbolic interaction with the child—the turning point from adoptive child to child. One could call this turning point the moment of emotional normalization. Emotional normalization means overcoming the strangeness of a child that is my child to be. The case of adoption presents an interesting coincidence of "The Stranger" and "The Homecomer" (Schuetz, 1972). The problem of every stranger who has to approach a new social world is accentuated in the case of adoption because the adoption stranger is expected to become a familiar person. The stranger as the homecomer who has not been at home before—that is the frame in which the interview data could be analyzed. In the following section I will describe how the chances of overcoming strangeness differ enormously, depending on the age of the child. The baby is the homecomer with minor strangeness, whereas the older child is the stranger with minor homecoming properties. Consequently, quite different trajectories of emotional normalization shall be outlined here.

Emotional Normalization When Taking In a Baby

"I've grown so fond of the child so quickly" was commonly expressed during the twenty-one interviews done with parents who adopted a child younger than seven months. Their emotional bond with the child developed unburdened by the difficulties of its long "pre-history." Attachment evolved as a matter of course, as if the process had unfolded "automatically."

ADOPTIVE MOTHER: . . . he was simply so tiny and so . . . and so in need of help that you automatically direct your affection towards the child. and that happens . . . immediately. . . .[4]

Since the development of an emotional relationship is seen as occurring automatically, the narrative recapitulation of events does not usually involve long reflections on how the result was brought about. The new quality of the parent-child relationship is regarded as normal and the parents no longer analyze it from a reflexive distance ("I don't think about it any more"). Some see the declining preoccupation with one's own special status of family as evidence of unquestionably belonging together. In the words of Alfred Schuetz and Thomas Luckmann (1979), one could call this the development of a new "natural attitude."

The baby's physical dependence in itself produces an enormous density of parental interaction. Their involvement leads to a situation in which the child, at an extremely dependent life stage, quietly turns into the little being who seems familiar to them. His/her physical growth and first efforts to communicate reveal traces of their parental influence. A number of recent studies in developmental psychology have attempted to outline in detail the process of the emerging parent-child relationship. These investigations discovered a surprisingly wide-ranging repertoire of interactive behavior which a baby of only a few weeks can initiate and sustain (Stern, 1980; Schaffer, 1980). Smiling, movements of eyes, hands and feet, the turning of its head, and finally, the first prevocal sounds—these media of expression are the active bonding part of the child to which the parents react "automatically." They are what Stern (1980, p. 24) calls "infant-elicited behavior." In parental care the child unfolds its communicative abilities and radiates the charm of a small partner.

Adoptive parents of very young babies quickly come to believe that the principle of biological filiation is almost irrelevant for an emotional relationship. Here is an example:

ADOPTIVE FATHER: What is it that really builds up the relationship? I'm not sure if it is really built up because the child has been /eh/ borne for nine months. Isn't it rather built up because /eh/ when it is still very small you have to feed it six times a day and to put on its nappies and to care for it and . . . you have to play with it

and you observe its reactions to . . . to you own /eh/ remarks and aura . . . I think that /eh/ this is much more important than bearing the child for nine months during pregnancy. . . .

According to the narrative interviews, pregnancy and birth can be renounced as binding experiences if adoptive parents are able to utilize the plasticity of the child in its most formative developmental phase,[5] and if they can superimpose social familiarity on biological strangeness. The turning point from adoptive child to child is then reached. This emotional normalization is reflected in almost every interview concerning a very young adopted child.

ADOPTIVE FATHER: . . . We take it for granted that we feel this way,
ADOPTIVE MOTHER: Yes, it's your own child, and that's it
ADOPTIVE FATHER: you adapt yourself to it; it's your own child.
ADOPTIVE MOTHER: It is your *own* child, and that's it, it is . . . /eh/ now and again you also forget that it is adopted, it's incredible how much you forget.

. . .

The narratives concerning late adoptions make it clear that the trajectory of emotional normalization includes a process of self-communication, especially on the part of the adoptive mother. It may take months or years before so-called motherly emotions for the child are directly recognized as such, since attention initially focuses on coming to terms with other immediate problems. The narrative interviews relating to a late start in family life illustrate that emotionality is often not discovered in the ongoing interaction process but is grasped retrospectively. To give an example: one adoptive mother infers from the sadness she feels when her daughter has to stay in hospital that the emotional bond must be more developed than she had assumed. The fact that her daughter shows a deeper attachment to her than she had expected reinforces the new feeling of belonging together. Another adoptive mother observes with relief that she now defends the child more against people outside of the family or that she has more sympathy for her child when it is ill or has been injured than she had in the beginning. It may take months or years before an adoptive mother is able to appreciate that she had "caught up with" the attitudes of biological parents.

CONCLUSION

The constitution of the adoptive family has been discussed in terms of the emotional work invested in parent-child relationships. The turning point from adoptive child to child is a source of relief and happiness, a sign of family authenticity. It is also a point of danger. Adoptive parents can indulge themselves in the feeling of normality to such an extent that they neglect to handle the structural difference characteristic of their family on a cognitive level. They may act as if they were the biological family, and reject the idea that they are not.[6]

Adoptive family life is family life with double parenthood. Emotional normalization is only a partial solution to the problems arising from the structural peculiarities of the adoptive family. Structuring the "awareness context" (Glaser & Strauss, 1965) towards the child and towards relatives, friends, and strangers is the work that remains after the emotional bond has been established.

Emotional normalization has been described as a process worked at by adoptive parents to minimize the difference between their own type of family and "normal" families. The process of overcoming strangeness in the adoptive family affords some insight into the conditions needed for the constitution of any family. The difficulties in constructing family reality without the principle of filiation, and without a common history of early socialization suggest that the conditions of the "healthy" personality as outlined by Erikson must be understood in terms of specific types of families. The child has to experience certain interactive relationships and the parents must initiate and sustain them in order to establish familiarity. The greater the number of developmental phases that the child has gone through before the common history of the adoptive family, the more divergent are the systems of relevance of adoptive parents and child. Hence emotional normalization may not be established for a long time or at all.

This research may be useful for adoptive parents, applicant couples, and agencies who deal with adoptive family life. It should alert agencies to the different burdens they put on parents when placing a baby or a five-year-old child. Beyond the field of adoption, the findings might have some relevance for the growing number of step-parent–child relationships where familiarity also has to be accomplished. Finally, the concept of emotional normalization might contribute to an understanding not only of parent-child relationships but other types of family interactions as well.

NOTES

1. A detailed analysis is presented in Hoffmann-Riem, Das adoptierte Kind—Familienleben mit doppelter Elternschaft (*The Adopted Child: Family Life with Double Parenthood*), Munich: Fink, 1984.
2. Twenty-three adoptive parents had adopted one child, four of them had also one biological child, two others had two or three biological children. Seven other adoptive parents had adopted two children, two of them also had one or two biological children. Among the eight cases with a combination of adoptive and biological children, there were only two where the adoptive child came first. For further information concerning the exact age see Hoffmann-Riem (1984), p. 327.
3. To use an analytical term of Goffman's (1974), the biological family is taken as a "primary framework" for determining the quality of relationship in the adoptive family.
4. All interview material is translated from German by the author.
5. One extreme statement about this dependency is Alfred Portmann's characterization of the dependence of the infant's first year as the prolongation of the fetal period ("extrauterines Fruhjahr"): A. Portmann, Die Biologie und das neue Bild vom Menschen, Bern, 1942, p. 21.
6. David Kirk conceptualized the adoptive family's alternatives as "rejection-of-difference" and "acknowledgment-of-difference" in his influential study *Shared Fate* (1964).

REFERENCES

Arbeitsgruppe Bielefelder Soziologen (eds.) 1973 Alltagswissen, Interaktion und gesellschaftliche Wirklichkeit, Vol. 2. Rowohlt.

Douglas, Mary 1970 Natural Symbols: Explorations in Cosmology, London.

Glaser, Barney G., and Strauss, Anselm 1967 The Discovery of Grounded Theory, Chicago: Aldine.

Goffman, Erving 1974 Frame Analysis, New York.

Goffman, Erving 1959 The Presentation of Self in Everyday Life, Garden City: Doubleday.

Hoffmann-Riem, Christa 1980 ''Die Sozialforschung einer interpretativen Soziologie—der Datengewinn. Kölner Zeitschrift für Soziologie und Sozialpsychologie, 22:339–372.

Hoffmann-Riem, Christa 1984 Das adoptierte Kind—Familienleben mit doppelter Elternschaft, Munich: Fink.

Huth, Wolfgang 1983 Adoption und Familiendynamik, Frankfurt/Main: Fachbuchhändlung für Psychologie.

Kallmeyer, Werner, and Schuetze, Fritz 1977 ''Zur Konstitution von Kommunikationsschemat der Sachverhaltsdarstellung.'' In: Dirk Wegner (ed.), Gesprächsanalysen, Hamburg.

Kirk, David 1964 Shared Fate, New York: Free Press.

Labov, William, and Waletzky, Joshua 1967 ''Narrative Analysis: Oral Versions of Personal Experience.'' In: J. Helm (ed.), Essays on the Verbal and Visual Arts. Proceedings of the Annual Spring Meeting, Seattle. University of Washington Press.

Portmann, Alfred 1942 Die Biologie und das neue Bild vom Menschen, Bern.

Schaffer, Rudolph 1980 Mothering, Cambridge, Mass.: Harvard University Press.

Schuetz, Alfred 1972–3 Collected Papers, Vols. I and II, The Hague: Nijhoff.

Schuetz, Alfred, and Luckmann, Thomas 1979 Strukturen der Lebenswelt, Vol. 1, Frankfurt/Main: Suhrkamp.

Schuetze, Fritz 1977 ''Die Tecknik des narrativen Interviews in Interaktionsfeldstudien.'' Arbeitsberichte und Forschungsmaterialien der Fakultät für Soziologie der Universität Bielefeld, 1: 1–62.

Sorosky, Arthur D., Baran, Annette, and Pannor, Reuben 1979 The Adoption Triangle, Garden City: Doubleday.

Stern, Daniel 1980 The First Relationship: Infant and Mother. Cambridge, Mass.: Harvard University Press.

Tyrell, Hartmann 1978 ''Die Familie als 'Urinstitution': Neuerliche spekulative Überlegungen zu einer alten Frage.'' Kölner Zeitschrift für Soziologie und Sozialpsychologie, 30: 611–651.

Tyrell, Hartmann 1979 ''Familie und gesellschaftliche Differenzierung.'' In: Helge Pross (ed.), Familie—wohin? Reinbeck: Rowohlt.

Analysis

Let us notice several things about this study that differ from the first one:

- Once the subjects had been chosen and the interview's starting point had been carefully considered, most of the creative work followed data collection—sorting the interview statements into meaningful categories and trying to make sense of them. By contrast, the creative work of an experiment goes into its careful design. Most of the work that comes after data collection follows as a result of the design. (This assumes that the study turns out as expected. If it doesn't, there is a lot of creativity in analysis, just as in qualitative studies.)

- The explanation described in the article is not what the researcher expected when she began the study. Instead of validating a previously considered notion, she was open to what the data told her—as any investigator should be, regardless of method.[3] She found a different explanation, as often occurs

---

3. Experimentalists are sometimes accused of being blind to any explanation other than the one they are seeking to validate. If this is so, they aren't very good researchers—or experimentalists!

in qualitative research. In quantitative research, the proposition being validated is usually a derivation or an extension of a prior history of investigation. A different explanation is not expected.

- Note that the explanation advanced is that "perceived" by the subjects. Essential to this point of view is the belief that people react to the world as they perceive it, influenced by past experiences, emotions, attitudes, interests, and so on. This, then, is the heart of the method for many qualitative researchers: finding the relationship between what individuals *think* is happening to them (their world as they perceive it) and what is *actually* happening. This view is the perception of detached observers trying to understand *their view in the context of their situation.* Observers looking from a detached point of view might perceive the situation differently from people involved in it, but the latter's perception of their situation is their reality. If the parents in the study perceive that it is essential to have a "normal" family, it doesn't make any difference if we protest that this is all in their minds. We might perceive that they can have any kind of family they wish, but their perception is a real influence on them and their behavior.

- There are no measures; all description is in words. We have no measure of the extent to which these parents see it as important to achieve a "normal" family relationship. Nor is there any indication of how well they succeeded, simply the statement, "It is like one's own child..." The amount of "normality" is described in words. This results in a longer report; in fact, many qualitative studies are of book length.

Clearly, there are distinct differences in methods, each with its own strengths and weaknesses. Finding the strengths and weaknesses in the qualitative study is left as an exercise. See the application problem at the end of this chapter.

SUMMARY

Critiquing the two studies just examined shows that individuals have a basic sense of what constitutes good research and that what is needed is to sharpen those skills and to make the conerns salient. But these articles use only two of the methods of research. Though they represent rather basic positions on a research continuum of possible methods, it will be helpful to see the full continuum. We will do that in the next chapter.

So far, however, we have assumed that you know how findings from a study become knowledge. Actually, this is a topic on which few of us who are not philosophers have done much thinking. It has important implications for understanding how researchers construct studies and use certain research methods, discussed in chapter 4.

In chapter 5, we will examine the research chain of reasoning. It is a framework that will help you to design and implement your own studies as well as enhance your analysis and critiques of others' studies.

================= APPLICATION PROBLEM =================

As you did for the Zimbardo study, critique the Hoffmann-Riem research and note its strengths and weaknesses. *Compare your critique with the answers beginning on page 699.*

CHAPTER
3

The Variety
of Research Methods

OVERVIEW

The two studies in chapter 2 give some substance to the nature of research but are clearly contrasting ways of going about it. This chapter examines those differences and shows how they help define a continuum of methods from quantitative to qualitative. Survey research, it points out, occupies a place between them. The chapter then describes other methods, noting how they relate to the roles of description, explanation, and validation.

CHAPTER CONTENTS

Introduction   26
A Continuum of Research Methods   29
    Qualitative Research   29
    Quantitative Research   30
    Survey Research   30
Other Research Methods   31
    Historical Research   31
    Evaluation Studies   32
    Meta-analysis   32

Longitudinal Studies   32
Single-Subject Studies   32
Model Building   33
Action Research   33
Classification Schemes and
    Theory Building   33
Comparison of Roles of Various
    Research Methods   34
Summary   35

INTRODUCTION

The contrast between the two studies in chapter 2 makes clear that there are considerable differences in the way researchers approach problems and the methods they apply. Zimbardo and his associates (1981) decided to conduct an experiment. An important characteristic of an experiment is that the researcher controls the application of whatever is hypothesized to cause an effect. That application is called a **treatment**. (In research, a treatment is any potential cause controlled by an investigator.) The investigator controls who receives the treatment, under what circumstances, and when. If there are different levels of treatment, who gets what, when, where, and under what circumstances are similarly specified. In Zimbardo's study, the experimental treatment made the subjects temporarily deaf by telling them, while hypnotized, that when they woke up, they would not be able to hear well enough to understand the conversation around them. An alternative treatment resulted in an itchy ear.

Researchers also use the term **independent variable** to refer to something they believe may be a cause. It is a broad term. Beside including treatments, it encompasses potential causes such as social status or class, variables not under the control of the investigator. If an independent variable is a cause, it follows that a **dependent variable** is an effect. For example, the effect paranoia is dependent for its appearance on the presence of the independent variable. So in the Zimbardo study, paranoia is the dependent variable, and partial deafness and social interaction are the two independent variables, which together cause the paranoia.

One of the major reasons that we use different research methods is that each method has strengths and weaknesses. To a great extent, the weaknesses of one are strengths of another. A common weakness of experiments is illustrated by Zimbardo's highly artificial situation, and it is not altogether certain that its results would apply in a more natural setting. This is of continual concern to experimenters, especially those who work in highly contrived circumstances. But such circumstances provide much control over what occurs in an experiment—in this instance, the degree of deafness, when it occurred, to whom, with what social interaction, and so on. Such control has real advantages; if the paranoia does occur, the experimenters are more easily able to eliminate alternative causes other than the treatment. Zimbardo is known for his clever experiments. In his extensive and creative use of experimentation, he is typical of the large number of researchers who become extremely skillful in a single research method or a small range of similar ones.

The degree of control attainable in a laboratory experiment is hard to come by in a natural situation, where control over the variables is ordinarily minimal or nonexistent. Yet experiments can be conducted in more natural situations. For instance, the federal government wanted to know what would happen if unemployed individuals were guaranteed an annual income. Would they use that opportunity to get an education, try out a more promising field of employment, or just lie around and enjoy life? Several such experiments were mounted with an unexpected result—greater breakup of families! Further, the data from one of the sites became only marginally useful when a state legislature unexpectedly modified its welfare payment policies and thereby changed the value of the income guarantee. Such are the many hazards in doing experiments in natural surroundings. We can learn important things from both laboratory and natural environment experiments. Each has particular advantages.

Some researchers feel that any experiment is artificial; they prefer to study individual and group behavior under completely natural conditions. Sometimes this is to see what they can make of it, whether they can understand what is happening. More often it is to see how individuals perceive the world around them, how they construct what they believe to be reality. Sometimes researchers conduct their study covertly so that the subjects do not realize they are being observed. For example, an investigator enlisted in the army (Sullivan, Queen, and Patrick, 1958) to see from the inside how it made fighting men out of recruits. The resulting study told how recruits came to understand the army's methods and to perceive changes in themselves. It is difficult to maintain cover and to continue to report objectively under such conditions. In this instance, the researcher reported his observations to a chaplain, who both recorded them and helped the researcher to maintain an "outsider's" perspective.

More often than engaging in covert observation, however, researchers simply become part of the situation, either as an observer who is recognized as such or as a participant observer. In the latter case, the individual is known to be observing but assumes some role in the situation that allows participation, thereby reducing his or her obtrusiveness. Whyte (1955), in his famous study of "street corner society" in Boston, took up residence in the community.

Though based on interviews instead of participant observation, Hoffmann-Riem's study in chapter 2 was conducted in that style or tradition. She wanted to learn how the process looked to adoptive parents. Note the difference between the starting point of Zimbardo's experiment—beginning with a hypothesis and seeking to verify it—and studies such as this. The concern is, as Hoffmann-Riem puts it, that the researcher who works with hypotheses "will find only that which he or she has previously considered." Researchers with this point of view prefer to listen to, or observe, natural behavior and then to construct their understanding of it. Hoffmann-Riem, in interviewing adopting parents, found that most of the behavior could be understood as "constructing normality," working to establish "normal" parent–child relationships. This proved a useful framework in which to understand the extent of "belonging together emotionally." But the notion of "constructing normality" emerged from her data as she listened to parents talking about their experiences. It was not an explanation she had thought of when she entered the study. This methodological orientation is typical of many participant observers and researchers doing case studies of individuals or particular groups.

So researchers differ in goals as well as methods. Some seek mainly description, as Whyte (1955) did when he told what life was like for a group of lower-class men in Boston. Some seek quite precise description, as when sample surveys estimate voter preferences to predict elections. Description frequently leads to explanation, as in Hoffmann-Riem's description of "normalization," implying that it is a way for these families to be part of "mainstream" society. Seeking explanations or causes is heavily emphasized in social science research. Reasonable fit of an explanation to the evidence in a single study is usually not totally convincing; we usually want more evidence, confirmation, and validation. Validation is illustrated in Zimbardo's research, the development of evidence to support the explanation of why paranoia may be prevalent in the elderly. Note, however, that evidence does not always support; it may lead to modification or even negation of a particular explanation.

A variety of research methods exist, from ones that maintain extensive control of the research situation to ones that use completely natural situations. Each has certain advantages and disadvantages.

Researchers' points of view also differ. Some researchers prefer to enter situations with a rather concrete idea about how to explain what is happening and test their explanation. Others enter a situation to explore and see what emerges.

A CONTINUUM OF RESEARCH METHODS

Perhaps you can sense now there are at least two different approaches to research. One works with hunches or hypotheses and validates them; the other involves situations and lets the explanations emerge. As a pedagogic device, we can show the differences in these two approaches and their methods on a continuum, like that shown in Figure 3.1.

Qualitative Research

At the left of this continuum, we have **qualitative research**, which provides descriptions of a case, a group, a situation, or an event, in what is often called a case study. The description is in words, picturing not only what happened but also *qualifying* the description with adjectives and adverbs to portray it more clearly. Qualitative researchers typically begin their observations with a target of interest but are open to whatever emerges of significance, changing

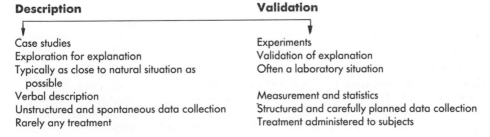

Description	Validation
Case studies	Experiments
Exploration for explanation	Validation of explanation
Typically as close to natural situation as possible	Often a laboratory situation
Verbal description	Measurement and statistics
Unstructured and spontaneous data collection	Structured and carefully planned data collection
Rarely any treatment	Treatment administered to subjects

FIGURE 3.1   The qualitative–quantitative continuum.

their data collection accordingly. They work in natural situations and seek explanations that provide the best understanding of what was observed.

Quantitative Research

By contrast, the approach on the right is referred to as **quantitative research** since the data are numbers representing quantities of whatever was measured. Because the measures must usually be constructed before the study begins, such studies typically validate one or more hypotheses that specify the variables of interest and the relationship between them.

Sometimes, like the researcher searching for cancer cures who tries all kinds of substances to see if they work, some behavioral science researchers try a variety of test items with only a vague notion that they may work and pull out those that do to construct an instrument. Even without an explanation of why they work, merely being able to show that they do is enough to produce useful research. Thus there is no explanation for why persons interested in mathematics like music, but interest inventories such as the Strong-Campbell Interest Inventory (Strong, Campbell, and Hansen, 1981) use that relationship as part of their mathematician scale because that is predictive of an interest in mathematics.

Some methods span the continuum and can, depending on the particular configuration, be considered either qualitative or quantitative. Survey research is such a method, for instance, and it introduces a middle column into our continuum (se Figure 3.2).

Survey Research

Survey research is at a true swing point in the continuum. It can be either quantitative, as when one of the big polling organizations does preelection questionnaire studies of a policial campaign, or qualitative, like Hoffmann-Riem's study. It usually attempts to provide an understanding of the group of people surveyed. Respondents to the survey are typically a carefully chosen

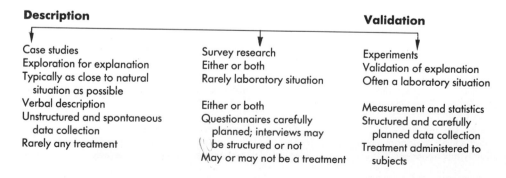

Description		Validation
Case studies	Survey research	Experiments
Exploration for explanation	Either or both	Validation of explanation
Typically as close to natural situation as possible	Rarely laboratory situation	Often a laboratory situation
Verbal description	Either or both	Measurement and statistics
Unstructured and spontaneous data collection	Questionnaires carefully planned; interviews may	Structured and carefully planned data collection
Rarely any treatment	be structured or not	Treatment administered to subjects
	May or may not be a treatment	

FIGURE 3.2   Survey research added to the qualitative–quantitative continuum of Figure 3.1.

sample, representative of some population. Thus survey researchers usually provide some careful rationale for the persons selected for study.

It should be clear, however, that though we have set up a continuum of methods for illustrative purposes, and though we will study these three methods in some detail, research is a creative act that cannot and should not be fixed into firm categories. For example, Hoffmann-Riem's study is about halfway between survey research and qualitative research. She is clearly trying to represent the views of adoptive parents, a group of people to whom she expects her data to generalize. But instead of trying to ensure that her sample in some way represents adoptive parents, she has used a sample that was convenient (for which she apologizes somewhat). Her data-collection methods were qualitative—having located homes with adopted children, she let the parents tell her what the experience was like and then tried to find a common way of understanding these comments across parents. She believes, of course, that her subjects are typical, but we have to take that on faith. A survey researcher would have used sampling methods that would provide an under-girding for such faith.

So researchers creatively combine the elements of methods in any way that makes the best sense for the study that they want to do. Their only limits are their own imagination and the necessity of presenting their findings convincingly.

- Simply to facilitate understanding, we can place methods of research on a continuum from qualitative to quantitative orientations.
- Qualitative orientations are characterized by describing in words, by exploring to find what is significant in the situation, by trying to understand and explain it, by beginning without structure but structuring the study as it proceeds, and by working in a natural situation.
- Quantitative methods are characterized by describing in numbers, by using measures, by validating hypotheses, by preplanning and structuring, and often by being carried out in a laboratory setting.

OTHER RESEARCH METHODS

Other kinds of research besides survey research make use of the full continuum of methods; certain are particularly useful in specific roles. Let us look at some examples.

Historical Research

Like survey research, historical research, the topic of chapter 19, uses the panorama of methods. Since the data of history are whatever has been left behind as records, choice of method must often defer to the kind of evidence the historian can uncover. Also, there is the problem of authenticity. The German newspaper that paid large sums for what it believed was Hitler's diary was not alone in being taken in by evidence that is not what it appears to be. Important skills of historians' methods include ways of authenticating the evidence on which their study depends.

Evaluation Studies

Evaluation studies determine the effectiveness or worth of some kind of treatment or how well units, persons, or programs are working. They may compare programs or evaluate one against some standard (for example, a 95 percent graduation rate). The federal government has been a heavy supporter of evaluation studies as it experimented with programs designed to break the cycle of poverty and to decrease unemployment. Schools are also frequent consumers of evaluation studies as they try new curricula to evaluate their effectiveness in comparison with the ones they are intended to replace.

Meta-analysis

As originally developed, meta-analysis is a way of combining statistical results from a number of quantitative studies into a single finding. But because even studies of the same phenomenon tend to be done under different circumstances, with different measures of effect, and involve different variables that modulate those consequences, meta-analysis has become a method of investigation in its own right. By grouping studies involving particular circumstances or variables, researchers can uncover those under which a relationship holds, how it changes under other conditions, and/or how it is affected by other variables.

Longitudinal Studies

Nearly every new parent in America turns to the work of Gesell, Ilg, Learned, and Ames (1943) to determine whether his or her child is developing normally. Longitudinal studies use the panorama of techniques to gather data over time and determine the pattern of changes. Gesell and colleagues followed newborn babies, noting changes in growth and determining what stages represented a normal pattern. In that respect, they were like survey researchers, describing the characteristics of "normal" newborns and their growth patterns.

Single-Subject Studies

A variation on longitudinal studies, single-subject studies usually follow one person, instead of a group, over time. But such studies are designed as experiments to provide convincing results. For example, a child who demonstrates aberrant behavior when a food dye is added to his or her food returns to normal when it is removed and then again acts up when the dye is reintroduced. In other instances, the study may qualitatively chronicle the treatment of a particular condition, like many clinical case studies.

Model Building

Economists are perhaps the best-known model builders. They describe the relationships among such things as the supply of money, the growth of government debt, the level of interest rates, and the expansion of the economy. Using data describing past events, they predict what should have occurred at some point in time. They then see whether their model provides an accurate description of what did occur. Modeling is increasingly being used in other social science fields. For example, Figure 22.3 (p. 589) shows a model development by Davis (1985) to predict not only adult earnings as a function of parental status, which is presumed to affect earnings directly, but also educational attainment. Educational attainment in turn affects earnings directly and indirectly by opening opportunities in occupations with prestige and thereby earnings. The researcher tests the model by inserting data into the model in these relationships and determining how well earnings are predicted by the model.

Action Research

Not really a method, action research or participatory research refers to the process of using any of the other methods. Concerned that findings are often not used unless they are trusted and "made real," action researchers involve in the research the people who would use the results, asking them to help plan the study, collect the data, and interpret them. Such involvement results in an "ownership" of the findings that is difficult to achieve when the study is experienced vicariously. Thus many researchers, particularly in professions such as education, social work, and library science, see this as a useful approach to carrying out research.

Classification Schemes and Theory Building

These studies are like model building, except their value is usually tested not by prediction but by their usefulness in organizing and describing phenomena and events. They are usually based on careful observation and consideration. The biological taxonomy of plants and animals provides a most useful way of classifying new living things and showing their relation to previously known ones. Similarly, a classification of educational objectives has provided a set of useful handles for describing educational goals and relating them to one another (Bloom, 1956; Krathwohl, Bloom, and Masia, 1964). But these classification schemes rarely have any empirical base of data when they are advanced. They are usually speculations that include a few well-chosen examples that show the scheme's usefulness.

Similarly, theories, like models, describe the way in which variables are related in certain situations. Because they often integrate previously disparate facts and findings they are especially treasured. They are also sometimes advanced on the basis of speculation, which follows acute observation and study. Piaget (1952), for instance, having observed a number of children, set forth a scheme describing their cognitive development. Skinner (1957), after much experimentation and observation, set forth a theory about how people learn verbal behavior. Further, he used only empirically verifiable descriptions that could be sensed directly rather than having to be inferred.[1] Both theories markedly exceeded the data available when they were set forth. But both proved useful as they were subjected to experiment for validation and as the practical implications were teased out for application to school learning. In Piaget's case, it has pointed to the most appropriate time for students to develop certain skills. In Skinner's case, it led to the development of programmed teaching materials, especially as they have been adapted to computer-based instruction.

COMPARISON OF ROLES OF VARIOUS RESEARCH METHODS

Though it markedly oversimplifies the realities of their use, Figure 3.3 indicates the common or typical relative emphases on the descriptive, explanatory, and validation role of each method by the darkness of the rectangle. The methods are arranged very roughly on our continuum from qualitative to quantitative. Notice the continuum runs vertically instead of horizontally in this diagram. In general, the heaviest shades at the qualitative end are for description (which often accompanies exploration and discovery) and at the experimental end are for the validation role. But as the chart indicates, all methods can be used in any of the roles, though the emphasis in their use tends to be as indicated. The mastery of certain basic methods provides researchers with skills for attacking a wide variety of problems. Hence in this book, we will provide considerably more detail on qualitative (chapter 15), survey (chapter 16), and experimental (chapter 18) methods and their variations. Surveys are excellent examples combining the best of both quantitative and qualitative methods. In somewhat less detail, we will examine historical (chapter 19) and evaluation (chapter 20) studies. In still less detail, but enough to understand their strengths and weaknesses, we will examine longitudinal studies, single-subject studies, and the integration of studies called meta-analysis (chapter 21).

---

1. This matter will be taken up in chapter 11, but I think you can sense that there is a difference between saying that a child is intelligent, which is a characteristic you cannot determine through the five senses, and saying that a child is good at finding figures that are hidden in the details of a picture, which can be directly observed.

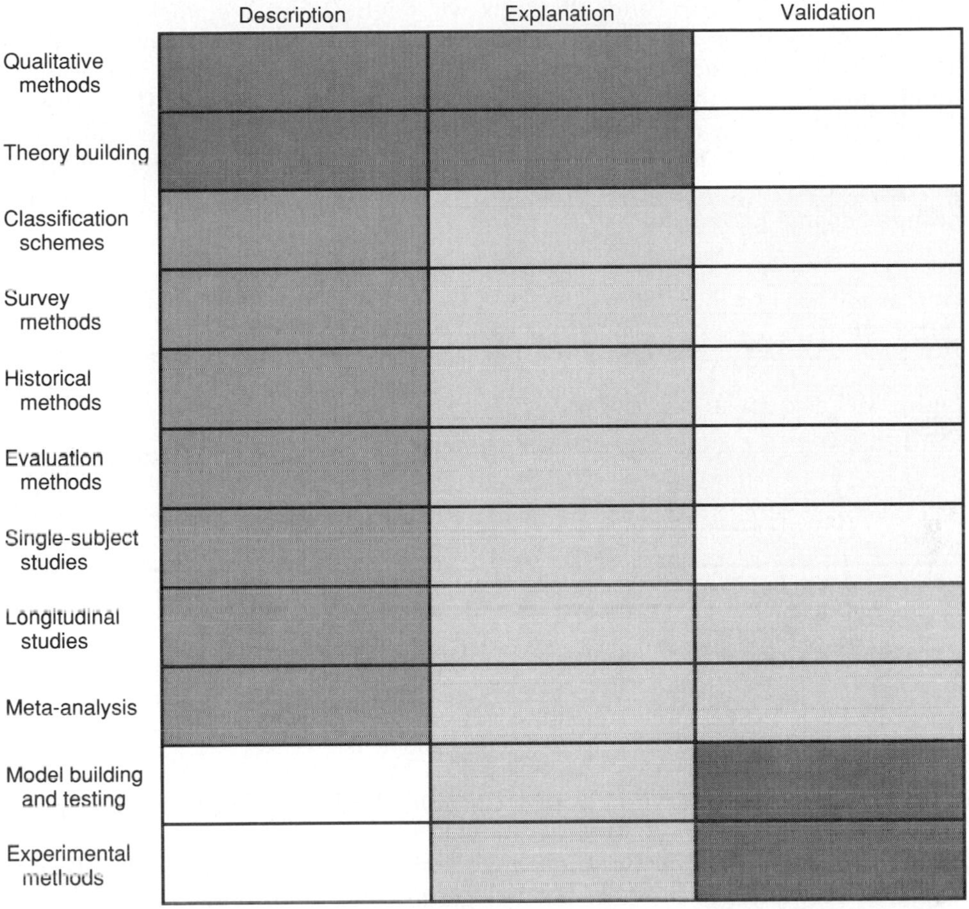

	Description	Explanation	Validation
Qualitative methods			
Theory building			
Classification schemes			
Survey methods			
Historical methods			
Evaluation methods			
Single-subject studies			
Longitudinal studies			
Meta-analysis			
Model building and testing			
Experimental methods			

FIGURE 3.3 Special emphases of various methods; the darker the rectangle, the greater the emphasis of the method on that role.

SUMMARY

A variety of methods exist to be used by the behavioral scientist researcher. For pedagogical purposes, these can be viewed on a continuum from qualitative to quantitative methods, sample surveys falling about halfway between the two. Qualitative methods collect verbal descriptions as their data; quantitative methods describe in numbers using measures and scales. Many research methods besides surveys, such as historical methods, evaluation methods, and longitudinal methods, borrow from both ends of the continuum to achieve success—some more from one end, some more from the other.

We have so far proceeded as though everyone knew how findings made the trip from the researcher's report to the encyclopedia. Few of us have thought about that trip, and although we might think we know what is involved, many of us will be surprised, perhaps even uncomfortably so. We tend to think of science as an almost mechanical process when it is really a human process and therefore fallible (though it works pretty well). And all science works this way; only the evidence is different in the physical and biological sciences. In the next chapter, because it is essential to understanding the criteria by which research is judged, we examine that trip and learn how findings become knowledge.

ADDITIONAL READING

Hoaglin, Light, McPeek, Mosteller, and
   Stota (1982).

IMPORTANT TERMS

Dependent variable
Independent variable
Qualitative research

Quantitative research
Treatment

APPLICATION PROBLEMS

1. A group of researchers conducted a study to investigate the relationship between the age of viewers of an instructional film and the gender of the narrator. Subjects in the second and fifth grades were randomly assigned to one of two groups. One watched a film narrated by an adult female, and the other group viewed the same film narrated by an adult male. The children's visual attention to the film was measured. The researchers also tested recall of the story ideas using a multiple-choice test. The results indicated that the gender of the narrator influenced the recall of the second graders but not that of the fifth graders. Also, fifth graders paid greater visual attention than the younger children. Identify the treatment and the independent and dependent variables.

2. A researcher compared low-achieving grade 6 students who left their classroom one hour per day for remedial tutoring in reading to a comparable group that received only regular classroom instruction. She wanted to ascertain whether or not the special program indeed made a difference. She found that the group that was tutored daily made significantly greater gains on a standardized test of reading skills than the other group. Identify the treatment and the independent and dependent variables.

3. Lewis Terman of Stanford University directed a classic investigation into the nature and development of gifted children. It was carried out over a 35-year period and consisted of a set of five published studies. In four of the studies, an initial group of approximately 1,400 children from elementary to high school age were identified as "gifted" and compared to a control group of 800 "nonselected" (randomly selected) students. A great deal of data was collected for these individuals, including IQ test scores, achievement test scores, interest questionnaires, reading records, a home information form filled out by the parents, an information form filled out by each individual's teachers, and medical data. These groups were reassessed after periods of 6, 25, and 35 years. A separate study was conducted of the early years (childhood to early adulthood) of 301 men and women "of great historical eminence." A variety of materials was gathered, including primary sources such as letters, essays, poems, and diaries written by these people and secondary sources such as biographies. From these data, psychologists estimated intelligence quotients. What research methods were used in this study? Where on the qualitative–quantitative continuum do they lie?

4. Two doctoral students at Syracuse University, one of whom was a librarian, were interested in the usefulness of the instruction provided as a part of a reference work kept on computer disks in the library of a local community college (reference works in such form are referred to as databases.) They wished to know if the "on-line" instructions were sufficient to allow users to search the database satisfactorily or whether users would require further help or instruction. They decided to collect data using several techniques. These included a questionnaire that would be filled out by users immediately after using the database, a rating of the printouts of their searches by an expert in on-line searching, semi-structured interviews with staff librarians concerning their perceptions of student use of the database, and logs kept by the librarians of student questions during the same period. Would their research study be considered quantitative or qualitative research?

Compare your answers with those on pages 700–701.

From Findings to Knowledge

Science is a very human form of knowledge. . . . Every judgment in science stands on the edge of error and is personal. Science is a tribute to what we can know although we are fallible.

Jacob Bronowski, The Ascent of Man

I am tempted to say that we do not look for truth, but for knowledge. But I dislike this . . . for two reasons. First of all, we do look for truth, however we define it; it is what we *find* that is knowledge. And second, what we fail to find is not truth but certainty.

Jacob Bronowski, The Identity of Man

OVERVIEW[1]

"What needs to be understood is how, scientifically, we come to know what we know" (Piel, 1986). This chapter describes the process by which the findings of an investigation become knowledge. The process starts with a knowing decision by the investigator and continues through a process of examination by peers and editors to the building of a consensus around the generalization and the proper interpretation of the research data that support it. This process is contrasted with other sources of knowledge. The norms of science that function as guides and standards for the process are described.

Understanding the process by which findings become knowledge is important for the following reasons:

- It indicates why publication is critical to the development of science.
- It helps explain the relationship of science to other methods of knowing.
- The importance of the researcher's audience becomes apparent.
- Answering that audience's questions so they make a positive judgment.
- It serves as the basis for the research criteria we will develop in later chapters.

---

1. This chapter is adapted from Krathwohl (1988), ch. 11.

CHAPTER CONTENTS

An Illustration of the Journey from
   Findings to Knowledge   39
Important Characteristics of the
   Journey   41
Knowing Judgments in Everyday Life   44
Different Sources of Knowledge   47
   Personal Observation and
      Experience   47
   Intuition   48
   Belief and Tradition   48
   Authority   48
   Science   50

The Norms of Knowledge Production   51
Universal Standards for Knowledge
   Claims (Merton's Universalism)
   51
Common Ownership of Information
   (Merton's Communism)   52
Integrity in Gathering and Interpreting Data
   (Merton's Disinterestedness)
   52
Organized Skepticism   53
Summary   54

AN ILLUSTRATION OF THE JOURNEY FROM FINDINGS TO KNOWLEDGE

We tend to think of the researcher's job as a lonely one, involved in a problem to the point where a solution is found and published and then moving on to the next problem. In truth, science is really a very social process, and each bit of knowledge involves many persons as it makes its way from being merely findings from data to becoming knowledge accepted by society.

Jacob Kounin's research (1970), mentioned in chapter 1, is our example of how research findings become knowledge. Kounin examined classroom practices to determine what teacher actions make a difference. If you've been in a classroom with an emotionally disturbed child, you know the havoc that such a child can produce; the learning process of the whole class can come to a standstill. Kounin put boxes on tripods in classrooms and left them there so that teacher and class became accustomed to them. Sometimes they contained a television camera, but only he knew when that was the case. In this way he gathered natural classroom reactions.

He noticed that children diagnosed as emotionally disturbed acted up in certain teachers' classrooms but not in others'. Why? By videotaping teachers' classrooms where they often acted up as well as those where they did not, Kounin, Friesen, and Norton (1966) and later Kounin and Obradovic (1968) found several differences. Two of these differences they named "momentum" and "smoothers." "Momentum" referred to keeping up the pace of instruction so that teaching was free from slowdowns—dwelling too long on a subject, nagging, overlaborious directions or comments. "Smoothers" referred to teachers who changed activities smoothly, as from art to mathematics. Their behavior was characterized by pausing, looking around, and sensing the group's readiness for change. By contrast, some teachers made changes whenever they felt the need, regardless of class readiness. Others would not follow through, creating confusion; they would give a transition direction and walk

away to become immersed in something else. In examining classroom recitation sessions, Kounin found a significant relationship between deviancy and
both slowdowns and nonsmoothing teacher behaviors.

How did this finding become knowledge? Many steps can be traced in the
publication records; others we must fill in.

1. First, are the three researchers, Jacob Kounin and his assistants, Wallace
   Friesen and Evangeline Norton. Each had to make a personal judgment
   that the most appropriate interpretation of the evidence showed consistent
   differences between classrooms of children emotionally disturbed to a
   comparable degree. Where momentum was maintained and transitions
   were made smoothly, there was less behavior deviancy. Their personal
   judgments we call **knowing judgments**. Such judgments will be made by
   individuals all through the rest of the journey, judgments on whether they
   accept the interpretation of the evidence as the appropriate one.
2. It took a **consensus** of knowing judgments among Kounin, Friesen, and
   Norton for them to agree on the nature of their research report. Knowing is
   a personal judgment; for a finding to be accepted as knowledge requires a
   consensus of such judgments. Furthermore, such a consensus must exist at
   each judgment point on the path from initial investigator to research
   consumer. These findings were beginning the journey down the road to
   becoming knowledge.
3. Different things happen at the next stage, depending on the researcher's
   situation. If there are immediate colleagues working in the same or a
   closely related field, most researchers will share the report with them. If
   there are no close colleagues at their own institution, some send copies to
   friends at other institutions. At this or a later stage, some send copies to
   the "**invisible college**" in their field, a designation adopted by Garvey,
   Lin, and Nelson (1970) during their study of communication in
   psychology. It describes an informal (usually unorganized)
   interinstitutional group of colleagues who have a common research
   interest. Their mutual admiration for what the others have done, their
   despair at others' "stupidity," and their hope to become the first to say
   something important in an area drive a variety of informal means of
   communication.[2]

   Because the publication process is so slow, each invisible college
   member forms a mailing list of colleagues who might be interested in his or
   her research or who may have been helpful in the past. Each routinely
   sends preprints of his or her research reports to this group, keeping them

---

2. This book owes much to Lee Cronbach's membership in an invisible college concerned with
how knowledge develops. Lee very generously shared his files with me, putting me in contact
with the mainstream and saving me hours of searching. As important as prepublication copies
of articles was the correspondence. It indicated an openness about certain conceptions that
could be only dimly discerned in publications, very encouraging signs for work contrary to
established dogma. Computer bulletin boards established by interest groups are making these
invisible colleges more visible and accessible and may largely replace them.

more up-to-date than journal readers. Persons who are cited in an important way in an article are also sent copies so that they can see how their research has been built on. Sharing data and interpretation in these ways provides feedback that can either confirm or modify notions about the proper interpretation of any set of data. The questions that invisible college members ask are likely to be among the most penetrating to be faced, since having worked in the same field, they can anticipate potential weaknesses. We assume that Kounin and his associates mailed copies of the report to interested colleagues.

4. Given positive responses, the authors probably decided to present their findings at an appropriate professional association meeting. They submitted an abstract of their report to the committee of the American Educational Research Association (AERA) charged with selecting papers on classroom research for the annual convention. The abstract was sent to each member of the committee, who independently judged whether to schedule a presentation of the report. The committee members pooled their judgments and agreed to schedule the paper. Again, there was a consensus of knowing judgments that the proposed interpretation of the data seemed appropriate and contained potentially significant findings.

5. If, as we presume, the study was presented at the next AERA convention, there would have been a discussion period following the presentation in which findings and procedures could be questioned. Informal discussions in the halls after the session would raise further questions. Again, these were colleagues knowledgeable in the field, polite but tough critics. Their questions cued the researchers to points in the report that were of concern to their audience. Since Kounin and his researchers believed they could answer these questions satisfactorily, they maintained that their interpretation was appropriate and took steps in future reports to ensure that these questions were answered.

6. They submitted the paper, revised on the basis of the questions raised at the AERA convention, to the *Journal of Educational Psychology* for publication. The authors' names and any other identifying information were stripped from the manuscript by Ray Kuhlen, the editor (a good one). He sent it to one of the journal's consulting editors and to a couple of other researchers active in the field whom he selected as competent and interested. These experts made knowing judgments that the findings held up under scrutiny, were interpreted appropriately, and constituted significant additions to the field. They recommended that the article be published, probably with some minor modifications to clarify procedure and interpretation. Note that because the reviewers were kept blind to the authors' names, the presentation had to stand on its own, unsupported by the reputation of the researchers or their institution.

   Kuhlen considered the readers' comments and his own reaction to the article very carefully. He had the authors make the few modifications needed and then scheduled it for publication. The consensus had continued to form.

7. The paper was published in 1966 under the title "Managing Emotionally

Disturbed Children in Regular Classrooms" in volume 57 of the *Journal of Educational Psychology*. The editor thought the article sufficiently important to make it the opening article of the issue.

8. The first seven steps were also involved in a replication of the earlier study by Kounin and another assistant. Replication involves doing the study again; this time, they used 50 schools instead of 30 and videotaped full days' classroom activities rather than half days. The findings proved robust and were replicated; terminology and coding of activities were further clarified. The study was published in volume 2 of the *Journal of Special Education* as "Managing Emotionally Disturbed Children in Regular Classrooms: A Replication and Extension," by Jacob S. Kounin and Sylvia Obradovic (1968).

9. John Glavin and Herbert Quay were asked to write an article summarizing research on behavior disorders for the February 1969 issue of the *Review of Educational Research*. They read the Kounin studies and decided that those findings and their interpretations were sound enough that they should include them in their review. Their article was accepted and published.

10. The findings were now in a secondary source, removed from the initial evidence and dependent for acceptance on the reader's trust of the reviewers' judgments. In addition, by 1970, a dozen other authors had cited these articles in papers. The fact that the original findings had held up under replication was an important factor in their acceptance. Their confirmation by an investigator other than the original researcher, however, would have given even stronger confirmation. But there is in social science research neither the tradition nor the funding for replication that there appears to be in the natural science fields. Unfortunately, even Kounin's own replication of his earlier study is not all that common.

11. In 1970, Kounin published a book that summarized the research to date: *Discipline and Group Management in Classrooms*. It began to take the place of the journal articles in citations by other researchers.

12. Robert Travers, a careful and meticulous worker, was charged with the responsibility of editing the second edition of the *Handbook of Research on Teaching* (1973). He asked Frank Hewett and Phillip Blake (1973), fine researchers who knew the literature and were good judges of it, to write a chapter on teaching the emotionally disturbed. They included a section on classroom management and found the Glavin and Quay references to Kounin's work. They believed it of sufficient importance to read the original studies. They included the first study in their chapter, and for that matter, so did other chapter authors. In all, there were 20 references to this body of work. The new edition of the *Handbook* was published by Macmillan in 1973. The first edition had established it as an authoritative source; this second edition benefited from that reputation and rapidly became one, too.

13. Thomas Good and Jere Brophy (1990; originally published 1977), leaders in the teaching research field, decided to write an educational psychology text. It was destined to become one of the most popular texts in the field. They had long known Kounin's work, since some of their own was based on it. They used the *Handbook* as a reference, and the many citations to

Kounin's work strengthened their own impressions of its soundness and importance. They included his findings in their text, which was published as *Educational Psychology: A Realistic Approach*. Now thousands of students were exposed to the findings as knowledge.

14. Harold Mitzel was carefully chosen as editor for the massive task of preparing the fifth edition of the *Encyclopedia of Educational Research*. On the advice of his board of editors, he asked Kevin Ryan to do an article on teacher characteristics. Ryan asked Debra Phillips to help, and they judged the Kounin work worthy of inclusion. The four-volume encyclopedia was published by the Free Press in 1982.

15. From here on, other writers of texts, encyclopedia articles, advice to teachers and parents, and articles to appear in *The Instructor* and similar journals aimed at teachers, women's magazines, and *Reader's Digest* will all treat the findings as accepted knowledge. A consensus of knowing judgments extends all the way back to the first presentation of the study's results, which have now made the transition from findings to knowledge.

Contrast that story with the stereotype of the lone scientist in his laboratory, antiseptically creating facts that are immediately accepted by a waiting public eager to be told the way the world really is. The truer picture is of a highly social process, developed, controlled, and maintained by people.

IMPORTANT CHARACTERISTICS OF THE JOURNEY

The journey from the initial findings of a research study to the acceptance of those findings is a long one. (Note the lapse of 7 years from initial publication to inclusion in the *Handbook of Research on Teaching* and another 9 years to the *Encyclopedia of Educational Research*.) The experts closest to the research and those with the greatest competency to judge it make the initial decisions as to whether findings merit a claim as new knowledge. Probably nobody is in a better position to make this judgment than those who have done research in the area and who therefore know the problems to look for— likely alternative explanations, weaknesses in methodology, and so on. Their judgment is critical to the start of the journey, in that they must determine whether the results were positive enough and the overall excellence of the study was great enough to merit reporting. (This assumes that a negative result would not be published, an assumption that is probably true. This is not entirely foolish; editors know that there are myriad ways of getting negative results but relatively few ways of getting positive ones. Therefore, they are likely to publish only negative studies that definitively close off certain otherwise attractive directions that would waste other researchers' resources.)

The experts make a data-based judgment about the proper interpretation of the findings, which they then compare with the interpretation of these data by the original researchers.

From them until they reaches the lay audience, the judgments pass to

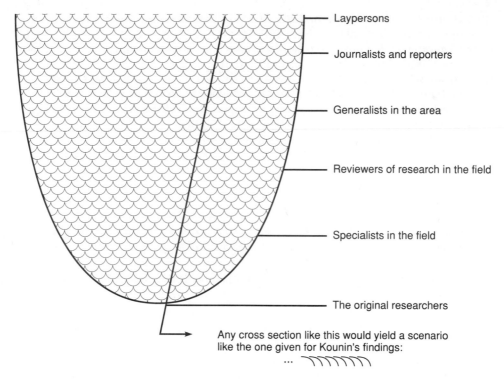

Laypersons

Journalists and reporters

Generalists in the area

Reviewers of research in the field

Specialists in the field

The original researchers

Any cross section like this would yield a scenario
like the one given for Kounin's findings:

FIGURE 4.1   The fish scale analogy of the transition of findings into knowledge.

persons removed increasingly further from the knowledge and skills involved
in the immediate focus of the research. Campbell (1988) has observed that the
knowledge and skills of each individual regarding the phenomenon of concern
overlap those of the previous person like the scales of a fish. Figure 4.1
illustrates this using the **fish scale analogy** to show the stages in the process
that we noted in the Kounin scenario.

We have traced only one path in the process, like the angled line in
Figure 4.1. Unquestionably, other people were judging and using the Kounin
results during the time frame we covered. They built on one another's work
just as Kounin and his colleagues did. These other researchers are portrayed in
Figure 4.1 by all the other "fish scales" not intersected by the angled line. No
single research study is sufficient to result in knowledge. It requires a body of
research to result in knowledge—in our example, that of Kounin and the many
who built on his work. The consensus across all these efforts results in research
making the transition into knowledge.

Each individual making a knowledge claim, or encountering such a claim,
must make a personal judgment to accept the claim as knowledge; that is, each
must make a knowing judgment. Note that the initial knowing judgments are
based on the most appropriate interpretation of the data and are made by the
people with the best basis for forming that judgment. As the claim is passed to
persons further removed from those initial judgments, except as an occasional

person goes to the source documents, the acceptance of the claim as knowledge is based on trust in the expertise of all below them in the fish scale network. It is as knowing judgments agree that a consensus is formed and the claim is accepted as knowledge.

Sometimes a field moves so fast, or the communication patterns in a field are so slow, that it is difficult for a consensus to form around findings at the periphery of knowledge. This is particularly true in the medical and biological fields, where changes are rapid. Because researchers themselves are not quite sure what parts of the knowledge base are solid, they may give different advice or make conflicting comments. This results in a loss of credibility and raises concern among practitioners and laypersons who would like to benefit from this knowledge. A technique of the National Institutes of Health (DeAngelis, 1988) is intended to speed up the process. Its "consensus conference" consists of a summarizing panel that evaluates the evidence and defines what is solid enough for practitioners to use as distinct from what is still experimental. In addition, journals such as the *New England Journal of Medicine* have made an effort to establish an "informal consensus view" in some fields. All this increases common recognition that science works by consensus.

Each individual making a knowledge claim or encountering such a claim must make a knowing judgment regarding the appropriate interpretation of the evidence. As a consensus of such knowing judgments forms, findings become accepted as knowledge.

KNOWING JUDGMENTS IN EVERYDAY LIFE

Clearly, some results do not garner a consensus. Consider, for example, the controversy over whether there is a real crisis in the use of fluorocarbons as refrigerants and in the burning of fossil fuels. Findings in these areas are rapidly being accepted as knowledge by many people. But there are still scientists who are uncertain whether these activities will result in a "greenhouse effect" or other climatic changes or whether self-adjusting mechanisms are operating, making our concern unjustified. Until there is a consensus among the experts (acceptance as knowledge), it is unlikely that the crisis will be accepted so widely that all nations will agree to appropriate action.

Laypersons, indeed all of us, are leery about accepting research findings as knowledge when experts disagree and cannot form a consensus.

Besides pointing to the fact that laypersons require agreement among the experts in order to accept something as knowledge, there are probably different thresholds for acceptance. Let us examine another way of considering this phenomenon.

Cronbach's (1982) formulation of the development of knowledge views it as one of **uncertainty reduction**. When our uncertainty about the proper interpretation of the data is high, we are unwilling to admit the research claim to the category "knowledge." When the evidence or the testimony of authorities reduces our uncertainty sufficiently, below some threshold, we accept it as knowledge.

Conceiving of knowing as resulting from uncertainty reduction—or its mirror image, the certainty with which knowledge is held—has the advantage of being able to reflect different levels of uncertainty. There is probably a threshold level of uncertainty below which something is accepted as knowledge; this threshold varies with its personal importance and relevance to our lives. For example, we may very easily accept as true a claim that a certain individual has gone over Niagara Falls in a barrel since it means relatively little to us. But a claim that a new chemical will facilitate weight loss without causing any bodily harm now or in the distant future may have a much higher threshold before the claim is accepted.

Further, we make knowing judgments differently in different areas of our lives. We allow different sources of knowledge to push us over the threshold— we accept engineering specifications for the sizes of lumber for building a house, for instance. But we may reject advice to us as parents not to use physical punishment. The latter is an instance of behavioral science knowledge and points up the fact that despite the assurances of "experts," much of it is tested against our own experiences to see whether it "rings true." Although much of the content of the natural sciences is so complex that we have no basis for knowing when or when not to trust the experts, this is much less true of sizable parts of the social and behavioral sciences. They deal with everyday life events. This presents a special problem to social science researchers. Findings that are counterintuitive are difficult to accept unless the explanation supporting them is very strong. That makes it all the more important for social science researchers to understand the process by which findings become knowledge, so that they will design research that facilitates the process of consensus building.

- Each new bit of evidence contributes to our evaluation of the certainty with which a finding or an assertion is accepted as knowledge.
- The threshold for when a finding or assertion crosses the border into the realm of knowledge varies, partly in accord with its personal importance to us.
- Social and behavioral science findings and assertions are tested against personal experience before being permitted to cross the threshold. This is not required of most natural science findings and assertions.

DIFFERENT SOURCES OF KNOWLEDGE

Science is only one source of trusted knowledge. Knowledge comes from a variety of sources, and we are constantly making knowing judgments about everything around us and in all of our interactions. We have to judge whether a source will be trusted, whether that source be our eyes; our own past experience; some source of traditional wisdom like the Bible; or a person we respect as an authority because of training and status (for example, clergy), specialized expertise (nuclear engineer, petroleum geologist, philosopher), or professional license (doctor, dentist, lawyer, teacher, clinical psychologist, social worker).

It is worth examining other sources of knowledge and their characteristics to understand science as different from them. Cohen and Nagel (1934) proposed a useful categorization—personal observation and experience, intuition, belief and tradition, authority, and science—a framework we shall develop further.

Personal Observation and Experience

Personal observation and experience is the source we trust the most. If you personally experience the maintenance of classroom order that results, as Kounin suggests, from making a smooth instead of an abrupt transition, you are likely to be convinced that this is solid knowledge. Indeed, personal observation and experience is a particularly important source of knowledge. It is the raw stuff of science, for the personal experience of scientists is both the basis for claims to knowledge discovery and for ideas and hunches that lead to new knowledge.

A characteristic of personal experience is the need for us all, infant and adult alike, to find an order, or pattern, to our existence. Where there are no patterns, we impose them. Judson (1980) notes, "Beat of the traffic, pulse of the phone, the long cycles of the angle of the sun in the sky. Patterns, rhythms, we live by patterns" (p. 28). One of the most important things that researchers do is to find order and patterns in nature, to see the relationships among things. And as Judson further notes, "Patterns set up expectations. . . . To perceive a pattern means that we have already formed an idea of what's next" (p. 28). Guessing "what's next"—predicting—is one of the most important outcomes of knowing, for if we can predict, we have the chance to change the outcomes for the better—to improve ourselves, to help others solve their problems, to have a better society—exciting possibilities.

Experiencing how things move and change is the basic experience of childhood. A child is delighted by new discoveries; a scientist experiences the same pleasure with a discovery that leads to a knowledge claim. Re-creating that pleasurable sensation can be a powerful motivator—it is the fun of doing research!

Intuition

Intuition encompasses propositions so obviously true as to be self-evident; merely stating them is enough for their acceptance. Frequently, we infer such propositions from the world around us. It was accepted for centuries that the sun revolves around the earth since this appears to be self-evident. So, too, the earth was believed to be flat since that is how it appears. Clearly, not all such propositions are true. Hence accepting such propositions involves making a knowing judgment. It is threatening when any such proposition turns out to be false because then we have no basis for knowing whether others may be equally untrue. How do we distinguish which ones to trust? There is no easy way, so we tend to wind up not doubting and not opening Pandora's box.

Belief and Tradition

This category includes all those things that "have always been true." The wisdom of the Bible, Koran, and Talmud and the advice of a culture passed from generation to generation are examples. Traditional knowledge, especially of the religious kind, tends to be set forth by authorities who help interpret it. Knowing relies on a personal judgment of whether to accept the tradition and sometimes the authority that comes with it.

Authority

Authorities are, without question, the major source of our knowledge. Why? For one thing, we can personally experience only a small part of our world. For another, few propositions are self-evidently true. An **authority** is anyone we accept as being more knowledgeable than ourselves. Most professional persons earn their livings by being accepted as authorities in some subject area. Authorities are generally accepted as experts *only* in their area of expertise, though this distinction is not always made. Heroes and persons of prominence often assert their opinions in public policy matters in which they have no special expertise. For most persons and most decisions, the knowing judgment becomes acceptance of a particular source as an authority.

Authorities are not all alike; they form a continuum. At one end are the arbitrary or **dogmatic authorities**, who assert that something is true by reason of their position or ability to enforce its truth. In the middle are authorities who are believable by virtue of their position, experience, and training. At the other end are **reasoning authorities** who, though they have a believable case and might also rest on the laurels of position, nevertheless indicate the basis for their judgment and present the case for all to judge.

Dogmatic authority is found in some traditions and religions, especially where, if there was a rationale for a given truth, it has long since disappeared. There is little doubt that moon cycles were once the best gauge for determining the earliest planting time to avoid frosts or to predict the cycles of fish travel.

Surprisingly, we can still find published advice for planting and fishing based on this lore. For many years, the Soviet Union enforced Lysenkoism with dogmatic authority. This was the theory that a plant or an animal could genetically pass onto its progeny characteristics acquired during its lifetime.

Dogmatic authority generally regards challenges as threatening; if challenge is permitted in one instance, where will it stop? And of course, should such an authority be successfully challenged, the halo of authority vanishes.

In the middle of the continuum we have the authority who, by reason of education, experience, and especially past success, is accepted. The past record is particularly important with respect to a current knowing judgment since it is one of the major bases for having been given the mantle of authority. Most licensed professionals are in this realm. Often they do not explain their decisions, nor do we often ask them to do so.

At the other end of the continuum is the reasoning authority. The characteristics of the reasoning authority are much like those of the scientist and help make science the source of much accepted knowledge. Unlike most authorities, however, every scientist's opinions are to be considered as seriously as any other's. Thus when judging manuscripts, some editors routinely remove the authors' names so that reputation will not influence acceptance. Science does not always operate on this basis, however; we can surely think of many instances where the accepted opinions of senior scientists were wrong and impeded progress. The case for the sun revolving around the earth was perpetuated by scientific authorities long after contrary evidence challenged it.

A distinguishing characteristic of reasoning authorities is the logical force of their arguments. Consider Kounin's assertion that the teacher's smoothing behavior aids in controlling emotionally disturbed children. It is more easily accepted when we understand that the teacher's behavior continuously directs the child's attention to external stimuli and away from the internal turmoil that would result in acting up.

Another characteristic is integrity: openness about what is not known, willingness to reveal weaknesses in the case, and a balanced presentation of the positive and negative sides of the case. This makes it less probable that something important and relevant is being hidden.

Challenges to the arguments of reasoning authorities do not harm the authorities' expert status; in fact, such challenges are expected and welcomed. Only through challenge can the soundness of a case be tested. Further, we can agree with such an authority in one instance where, in our judgment, the case holds up, yet disagree in another instance without rejecting the authority as a potential source of knowledge.

Of course, if repeatedly found in error, there would seem to be some uncorrected problem in procedure or thinking. But unless the individual's integrity is challenged, as in faking data or being caught deliberately with-holding knowledge that would affect its interpretation, any findings, no matter how unusual, will be seriously considered. The reasoning authority, the scientist, is the source of much of the knowledge that we have come to trust.

Science

The conception of knowledge as reducing uncertainty has the advantage of allowing many levels between the extremes of "rejected" and "accepted" as knowledge. Not everything that crosses the threshold into the knowledge category is held with the same certainty. We may reluctantly accept fluoridation of our water but buy bottled drinking water just to be on the safe side. So sometimes we accept something as knowledge but retain some uncertainty.

That is the way of science. All scientific knowledge, even the most basic, is held with a tinge of uncertainty, just enough that should more valid knowledge come to light, it could quite properly be replaced. Some knowledge, especially if replicated and reconfirmed, is held with considerable certainty—enough that we act on it as though it were unquestionably true.

Successful replication of research is essential in the natural sciences and clearly is an important kind of evidence. Replication involves repeating a study, preferably by someone other than the original researcher and possibly somewhat differently. If we obtain the same results, they are considered confirmed or validated. *Replication, especially using different methods in new situations, is the ultimate validation.* Exact replication in the social and behavioral sciences is rare. But in one common kind of replication, each successive researcher builds on the previous work. Should findings fail to be positive, either the previous work was in some way invalid or the current researcher extended it incorrectly. If the researcher can find no fault in the extension study, a replication of the earlier work may be required.

As we noted in the Kounin example, a finding must undergo the scrutiny of a host of **gatekeepers** (convention committees, editors, book authors, etc.) to make the transition to knowledge. The researcher's interpretation of the evidence is repeatedly examined to make sure that it meets each gatekeeper's standards. This process of continual challenge, when combined with the tentativeness with which we hold all scientific knowledge, is relatively unique among the sources of knowledge. It means that knowledge that is superseded can be changed as a natural part of the process without the scientific community losing its status as an important source of knowledge.

Scientists understand this, but the nature and length of the process are often not grasped by the public and by policymakers, who want concrete, correct answers and want them now! They become impatient or do not recognize science as a social process in which a network of individuals assume responsible roles to make knowing judgments that coalesce into a consensus.

- Knowledge comes to us from many sources: personal experience, intuition, tradition, authorities, and science. Of these, only science and the reasoning authority routinely seek and survive testing and challenge. The others all have trouble handling the challenges that result from unusual findings and assertions.
- In the natural process of science, knowledge is routinely challenged and

> changed as it is superseded. Changes affect science's status as an
> important source of knowledge less than they do other sources.
> ■ Replication, especially using other research methods and situations, is
> the ultimate way of validating a proposition.

THE NORMS OF KNOWLEDGE PRODUCTION

Science is a social system in which individuals assume important responsibilities in various roles:

■ Researchers design studies, carry them out, and interpret the results with
the greatest integrity.
■ Journal, handbook, and encyclopedia editors; consulting editors; reviewers;
and similarly trusted gatekeepers of means of dissemination ensure that
studies selected for publication meet appropriate standards and that pertinent criticism of already published studies is disseminated, so that an
unwarranted consensus does not develop.
■ Writers of reviews of research, textbooks, encyclopedias, and handbook
entries carefully consider the results of those studies and disseminate the
deserving findings.

Each of these roles is governed by an informal but well-understood system of
rules and norms. Some of these rules and norms are obvious, but making them
explicit helps elucidate the system, how it is maintained, and how its work is
facilitated.

Merton (1968) described the following as the norms of science: universal
standards for everyone's knowledge claims, common ownership of information, integrity in gathering and interpreting data, and organized skepticism
of all knowledge claims (note that these apply to the natural sciences as well as
the social sciences). Let us examine each norm in more detail.

Universal Standards for Knowledge Claims (Merton's Universalism)

As a neophyte researcher, you would not want your research to be judged by
harsher standards than those of a respected colleague in your field. As a
member of a minority, you would expect your work to be judged by a standard
identical to that applied to everyone else. As a researcher at East Snowshoe
State, you should not expect different standards to apply than had you been
employed by Cambridge University. The quality of the work itself, rather than
its author, sponsoring institution, or financial supporter, should be the focus of
a judgment based on **universal standards**—standards that are the same for all.

Further, each field establishes norms for what is acceptable research. Over time, these norms are raised as more is learned and the general level of methodological sophistication of the field rises. But at any point in time, the standards that gatekeepers apply should be the same for everyone.

Common Ownership of Information (Merton's Communism)

That information is owned by all and is to be shared freely—that is, **common ownership of information**—is a norm subscribed to and maintained in academic and not-for-profit research settings. As might be expected, it is not always observed in the commercial sector since industrial research is often pursued for proprietary advantage. Similarly, military research that is classified is beyond the reach of this norm. But this is the norm for all the rest, which is the great bulk of science. Most major universities have rules forbidding sponsorship of research that cannot be freely published.

This means that publication is not only a right of the researcher but also an obligation. Researchers who dabble in research simply to satisfy their own curiosity and then do not publicly share their findings not only remove themselves from the social system of science but are guilty of using for private amazement resources that are expected to be used for the public good. The universities' "publish or perish" rule for faculty expected to do research is simply an enforcement of this norm. (The point of contention here is whether we should expect all faculty to be researchers; should some be mainly instructors?)

This norm also means that the data of a study should be shared on request, once the original researchers have used the data for their purposes. The efforts of others who might want to analyze the data differently, for instance, should be facilitated in every way possible. The reasonableness of the norm is self-evident: it enables others to make sure that no errors were made in processing the data and that the most suitable methods were used to extract their appropriate interpretation.

Integrity in Gathering and Interpreting Data (Merton's Disinterestedness)

Gove[3] (1976) defines *disinterested* as "not influenced by regard to personal advantage." We all take for granted that the researcher will gather and interpret data without regard to personal predilections of what they should show. This **disinterestedness** is one of the norms to which we are presumably most sensitive when it is violated. Thus advertisers use purportedly disinterested laboratories to provide the basis for claims like "Powder-Milk Biscuits give 4

---

3. I'll bet you didn't know that Gove was the editor of *Webster's International Dictionary*. You may have wondered why I cite Gove as an authority; now you know. I had to add this footnote just in case you failed to look up the reference to make sure his authority was legitimate. This is an example of authority as a source of knowledge.

out of 10 shy persons the will to do what needs to be done!"[4] We bank on the integrity of researchers, knowing that persons with that quality will be as critical of their own behavior as would outside observers.

The pressures of success occasionally cause individual investigators to violate this norm. Indeed, no doubt many of us did so when a physics laboratory course required replication of famous experiments with a certain precision. Not realizing that these assignments are intended only to teach laboratory techniques, students often feel it necessary to generate fictitious data to meet the precision criteria. Such exercises end up teaching the wrong behavior when pressure is present for results. Though questionable pedagogically if the wrong emphasis is stressed, no great harm can be done. But it can be serious indeed if practiced on unsuspecting colleagues who expect integrity.

Broad's chapter in the *The Dark Side of Science* (1983) detailed violations both in historical times and more recently. These are instances where we know fraud occurred. How many uncaught cases are out there nobody knows. We hope and believe they are few. The peer review process is in place wherever we seek to communicate a knowledge claim, and studies that build on the findings of others are deterrents to fraud. The potential in active research areas for successful fraud seems small. Yet any at all makes us uncomfortable; the whole system is tarnished and loses credibility when even just one member violates this norm.

More difficult to handle is the behavior of researchers who believe that their past research approach is the proper one and, finding it challenged, fight strongly to defend their life's work. The history of science is rife with instances where a senior member has delayed the advance of a field by rejecting the new approaches of junior members. Such human conflicts are sometimes taken as personal challenges instead of part of the academic give-and-take. Any of the participants may lose perspective on what is ultimately at stake. Time favors the side that leads to further progress. But the interim can be difficult for the participants and for people on the sidelines whose careers are affected as well.

Organized Skepticism

We have already described this norm in our detailing of the passage of Kounin's findings into knowledge. The editors, readers, and other gatekeepers embody organized skepticism at work. Merton called attention to this aspect of the process as one of the most necessary, and you can see by now that it is a basic norm that makes science unique as a source of knowledge. **Organized skepticism** means that it is the responsibility of the community of scientists to be skeptical of each new knowledge claim, to test it, to try to think of reasons the claim might be false, to think of alternative explanations as plausible as the one advanced. This challenge to new knowledge is sought in science, instead of avoided as in other methods.

But organized skepticism cannot operate without the acceptance and

---

4. With apologies to Garrison Keillor.

observance of the other norms: the findings and the process by which data were obtained must be freely available—common ownership of information. Researchers must know that their work will be fairly and appropriately judged if they are to expose it to challenge—universal standards. The data presented must have been gathered and interpreted with integrity if we are to take the data and the report at face value. Given these conditions, organized skepticism can do its job of keeping an inappropriate and unwarranted consensus from forming and preventing invalid knowledge claims from reaching people who might otherwise unwittingly try to use them. The esteem in which scientific knowledge is held is testimony to the conscientiousness with which scientists voluntarily play their proper roles and make the system work.

Each new version of how science works is tested against the historical record. It is clear from this record that science is by no means a perfect system. We have already indicated instances in which scientists who should have been open to contrary evidence, but were not, dominated the thought of their day. There is no way of ensuring that science of a given day will tread the proper path. Yet over time, we make progress, and wrongs are righted. It is this self-correcting characteristic of science that is reassuring.

If we observe all the norms, the process will uncover errors. But any process is facilitated by an understanding of how and why it works; science is no exception. Much of the normative structure appears in one way or another in the codes of ethics of professional organizations so that we can pass these norms to new generations with an understanding of their vital roles. It is hoped that the perspective you have gained from this material will enable you to play your role more effectively, whatever it may turn out to be.

The norms of science include at least those described by Merton:

- The quality of research should be judged by universal standards regardless of the experience, race, sex, or other characteristics of the researcher.
- Scientific information is not proprietary but is owned by all in common and freely shared; publication is not only a right but an obligation of a researcher.
- The researcher displays disinterestedness—integrity in gathering and interpreting data without regard for personal advantage.
- It is the responsibility of the community of scientists to be skeptical of each new knowledge claim, to test it, to try to think of reasons the claim may be false, and to think of alternative explanations as being as plausible as the one advanced.

SUMMARY

In research, we continually make knowing judgments as to whether a knowledge claim is an appropriate interpretation of the evidence. As others agree with these judgments, a consensus forms and findings become knowledge. A network of individuals extends from those closest to the research to the lay public, with decreasing levels of expertise in judging the evidence directly; the individuals at each level, as appropriate, either judge the evidence or determine whether to accept the judgment of others closer to the research in the network. Individuals are leery of accepting research findings on which experts cannot form a consensus.

We can also consider each new piece of evidence as increasing or decreasing our uncertainty about a knowledge claim. The threshold for when a finding or assertion becomes knowledge varies, partly in relation to its personal importance to us. Though it is not possible to test many natural science assertions, social and behavioral knowledge claims are typically checked against our own personal experience.

There are a variety of knowledge sources: personal observations and experience, intuition, belief and tradition, authority (dogmatic and reasoning), and science. Science and reasoning authority invite challenges to knowledge assertions to ensure their validity. By contrast, other sources have difficulty in handling challenge and typically avoid it, for once begun, there is no way of knowing where it will stop.

The development of knowledge reveals science as a social system of individuals in roles of important responsibility governed by well-understood rules and norms. Merton (1968) has suggested that at least four norms are essential: (1) that the same standards be used in judging knowledge claims for all individuals regardless of status, personal characteristics, institutional affiliations, or other considerations; (2) that information be understood as owned by all and freely shared; (3) that there be absolute integrity in gathering and interpreting data; and (4) that it is the responsibility of the community of scientists to be skeptical of all new claims, to test them, to try to think of reasons why they may be false, and to seek alternative explanations as plausible as the ones advanced.

Looking ahead, it seems reasonable that a society with norms and standards may have found a format for reporting research that facilitates their application. We explore that in the next chapter.

──────────────── ADDITIONAL READING ════════════════

Campbell (1988)   Merton (1968)
Cronbach (1982)

──────────────── IMPORTANT TERMS ════════════════

Authority   Consensus
Common ownership of information   Disinterestedness

Dogmatic authority
Fish scale analogy
Gatekeepers
Invisible college
Knowing judgment

Organized skepticism
Reasoning authority
Uncertainty reduction
Universal standards

═══════ APPLICATION PROBLEMS ═══════

1. A Senate committee, concerned about safeguarding public funds spent on research grants, is questioning the methods of science used by the grant recipients. The committee is convinced that the process is rife with cronyism and that researchers are not adequately critical of one another's work. The senators wonder if public money is being wasted on findings of questionable quality. How would you reply?

2. You have been studying the use of color in illustrations included in school readers to facilitate children's comprehension of text. Having established children's preference for color pictures to either black-and-white illustrations or none at all, you had hypothesized that their inclusion would motivate students to attend more readily to the text and hence would increase comprehension. To your surprise, your results indicated that neither color nor black-and-white illustrations had any significant positive effect, and indeed, there was some evidence that color actually impeded understanding. What should you do with these findings? Should you submit them for publication?

3. As editor of a prominent journal in the field of information studies, you receive a paper from a psychologist who has been studying the psychological barriers that students develop to the use of computer-based information systems. The particular study had focused on the on-line catalog system at the investigator's university. Should you consider publishing this study even though the researcher is not in your field?

4. You are a junior researcher in the department of reading and are being considered for tenure this year. A senior member of your department is well known for his advocacy of the phonics approach for teaching young children to read. He is adamantly opposed to a contending theory, the whole language approach, which is the fad at other universities. You do a comparative study that produces significant findings that lend credence to the latter and undermines his position. What should you do with your findings?

Compare your answers with those on pages 701–702.

5

The Research Chain
of Reasoning

OVERVIEW

This chapter describes evidence and the way it is organized in the presentation of a knowledge claim. It thus builds on chapters 3 and 4, where it was suggested that if many individuals are making knowing judgments about studies, science must have developed procedures that make the judging process easier. This is indeed true. An integrating framework or model for the presentation of knowledge claims is described here, and important implications for designing and critiquing research studies are shown to flow from it.

CHAPTER CONTENTS

Introduction   57
The Research Chain of Reasoning   58
    The Zimbardo Article as an Example of the Research Chain of
      Reasoning   59
    Another Example: Use of the Chain of Reasoning in Study Design   62
    Four Useful Characteristics of the Chain Analogy   63
Summary   66

INTRODUCTION

Several federal reviewers are chatting about journal articles that were final reports of projects they had funded:

"I had a hard time with that last one. She started right off describing her data, and it was only later that I learned how and where she had gathered it. In the end, she had answered all my questions, but I guess I have a set of customary expectations about how a report of research should be written. I'm surprised this journal permitted such a deviation."

"Move over—I have the same expectation; there are a lot of us in that 'rut.' I must say, though, yours was an exception; the last one I reviewed was a dream—everything was there, and in good logical order."

"The report is the one thing for which we don't provide a standard federal form. I guess it is so that the researchers are free to write their report in any way that makes sense to them. Sometimes I wish we did enforce a particular sequence or outline, especially for reports that are not in journal article form. It would make them easier and faster to read and critique."

"Whoa! Come on, now, you don't really believe that, do you? There is more than enough brueaucratic regulation around here! Give them some freedom!"

"OK, I'll grant you that we don't want to stifle creativity. But most journals create expectations in their readers and authors that certain parts of the research will be reported in a particular order. I think we should too. It makes good logical sense to build one's case that way."

"Yes, and if there are headings, one knows just where to look for certain items."

"Sure, but even without headings, the organization of the write-up provides an orderly sequence so that readers can follow the argument and find what they need."

This conversation simply reinforces the fact that research is a social process; the researcher is communicating with an audience to present the study properly and convey how carefully it was done. Similarly, the reader or reviewer is trying to follow it: raising and answering questions as the report is read, judging whether it does indeed support the knowledge claim that is being asserted, and making knowing judgments. It is not surprising, therefore, that a fairly standard form or sequence of presentation has evolved. The standard has been informal and accepted by authors rather than being required by journals, though some journals rarely seem to depart from it. Depending on the journal's past record, it may be expected by reviewers. It is exemplified by the Zimbardo article reprinted in chapter 2; though it saved space by eliminating the headings used by many journals, it is organized in the typical sequence.

THE RESEARCH CHAIN OF REASONING

Articles that present a research-based knowledge claim for a generalization are typically presented as logical arguments. The parts of each article correspond to what might be thought of. as a prototypical or model **chain of reasoning**. That chain of reasoning applies to any research article, however. Even if information is not presented in the usual order, all the parts of the chain are required to supply adequate information to make the case. A representation of the chain of reasoning appears in Figure 5.1.

Research reports presenting evidence in support of a generalization do so

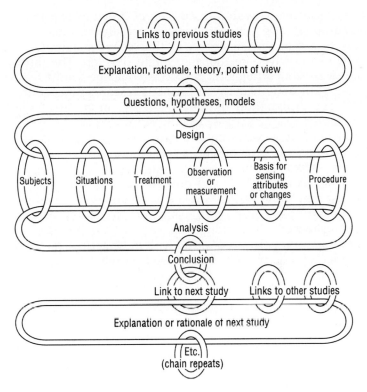

FIGURE 5.1   A prototypical chain of reasoning.

as a chain of reasoning. The chain of reasoning serves as a general model of this logical argument. To make the research chain of reasoning more than an abstract conceptualization, let us see how it applies to the Zimbardo experiment.[1]

The Zimbardo Article as an Example of the Research Chain of Reasoning

Explanation, Rationale, Theory, Point of View.   Turn back to the Zimbardo article on page 10. How does it begin? The first three paragraphs describe the rationale underlying the relationship the study is intended to demonstrate.

---

1. Does the chain of reasoning also apply to qualitative research studies using an inductive method to gather and analyze data, such as the Hoffman-Riem study of chapter 2? Yes, but only if the study presents one or more generalizations. Then, either it is presented as a chain of reasoning, as the Hoffman-Riem study is, or the links of the chain are all there but not necessarily in the same order. For example, sometimes the details of procedure and design are put in a methodological appendix. The purpose of many qualitative studies, however, is mainly description; for example, a historical account of the development of Piaget's notion of conservation, or a case study of a person, group, or culture. This type of study need not follow the chain pattern.

The article begins with a discussion of previous research showing, in the first paragraph, that psychopathology, especially paranoia, has been observed clinically to accompany deafness. In the second paragraph, a mechanism is suggested as to why a relationship might develop. The third paragraph indicates how a psychopathological response could be reinforced and maintained. All paragraphs draw heavily on previous research and writing.

The **explanation, rationale, theory, or point of view** underlying a hypothesized relationship is usually laid out at the beginning of the article as is done here. It is very important since it is the basis for understanding and interpreting the rest of the presentation. An explanation indicates how the relationship works. A rationale indicates the basis for thinking that it works this way. A theory indicates how this relationship fits into a larger scheme of things, how these variables relate to others. A point of view indicates how this researcher views this relationship and compares or contrasts this with the views of others. In building this section of the study, we draw on previous relevant work, selectively citing it to indicate that our idea is not a "bolt from the blue" but is in fact solidly based on what has gone before. In Figure 5.1, this is represented by the combination of the small links at the top of the figure labeled "Links to previous studies." The large link to which they are fastened represents the explanation, rationale, theory, or point of view based on them.

Questions, Hypotheses, Models. Next comes the "**Questions, hypotheses, models**" link. In the Zimbardo case, the hypothesis is at the end of the third paragraph: "In this analysis, paranoia. . . ." It is a hypothesis because we know enough to go beyond merely stating a question that tells us where to look. We know what we shall look for, the development of paranoia. We don't know how much paranoia or exactly how it is linked to a certain amount of deafness, so we can't make a precise prediction. That constitutes the next higher level of prior information, when we know even more about the phenomenon. When we can link all, or great many, of the variables in the situation and make a still more precise prediction, then we have a model. In Zimbardo's case, there is enough previous research to suggest that there is a relationship, but not enough to make a precise prediction or build a model. So at this link in the chain of reasoning, we have a question, hypotheses, or a model, depending on how much previous research gives us a basis for knowing what will happen.

Adapting the Format to Our Purposes. The fourth paragraph is a summary of the rest of the article. It is evidence that the chain of reasoning is a format to be followed in presenting the case, but not slavishly and rigidly. Each author adapts the format to the requirements of the readers. In this case, this article appeared in a journal that is devoted primarily to biological and physical science reports. Non-social scientists might be interested enough to read a few paragraphs but are not likely to read the whole article. Thus placing the summary early, right after the rationale and hypothesis, is savvy writing. It serves here as a motivator to read the rest of the article and provides an advance organizer for what will be found. For the hurried reader who is merely skimming the journal, this is a convenient stopping place that provides the essential information. This fourth paragraph is not part of the usual structure but illustrates an adaptation of the usual form to the needs of this particular audience.

Research Design.   After stating the expected relationship, the article begins describing how the study was carried out. Carrying out the study means translating the various facets of the presumed relationship into aspects that dramatize it, so to speak. A playwright, having described a plot as "Susie falls in love with John," must then write a script that translates that into a scene where individuals move to certain places at certain times, say certain things that convey love, and so on. In the same way, the researcher must translate in this study such terms as *paranoia*, *deafness*, and *perceptual discontinuity*. But that is not all that has to be translated.

We think of there being six aspects to look for when we examine the translation of the hypothesis link into a study. Together they constitute the **design** of the study and are represented in Figure 5.1 by the six rings interlinked with "Design." These rings correspond to the "five *W*'s and an *H*" that all journalists learn to include in a story: who, when, where, what, why, and how.[2] For research we want to know (1) *Who* was involved in the study and (2) *Where?* (3) *Why* did an effect occur (what was the cause), and (4) *What* effect occurred? (5) *How* do we know an effect occurred? And, finally, (6) *When*, or in what sequence, did the various parts of the study take place? Paragraphs 5–9 of the Zimbardo article translate the hypothesis into the design and structure of the study, the middle links in Figure 5.1.

Let us examine the choices Zimbardo and his associates made in these six facets of the study. The whole of the fifth paragraph is devoted to the who—**subjects**. The where is implied rather than specified, and it is clearly a laboratory, presumably at the author's institution—**situation**.

The cause or **treatment** (the why of the study) is described in the sixth paragraph, where part of the how by which the effect was sensed—the **basis for sensing attributes or changes**—is also described. In this instance, random assignment into three different treatment groups gives us a basis for sensing changes in the groups relative to one another that lets us sense the effect. It

---

2. This journalist's ditty, borrowed from Rudyard Kipling, may be a useful mnemonic for the six facets of design:

> I keep six honest serving men
> They taught me all I knew:
> Their names are What and Why and When
> And How and Where and Who.

For research application, this can be translated as follows:

Who	Subjects (*Who* are they?)
Where	Situation (*Where* did it take place?)
Why (the cause)	Treatment (This is *why* something would be expected to occur.)
What (the effect)	Observation or measurement (These tell *what* occurred.)
How	Basis for sensing attributes or changes (This tells us *how* we know an effect occurred.)
When	Procedure (*When* what subjects received what treatment, observations, or measures, where they received it, and when and where the effect is to occur.)

also, as we shall see, rules out alternative explanations. In the Hoffmann-Riem study reprinted in chapter 2, as in most qualitative studies, instead of sensing change, comparing the different interviews would have provided the basis for sensing an attribute that is common across a group or situation—in this instance, a desire for normality across people who adopt children.

The **observations and measures** are described in paragraphs 7 and 8. Note that Zimbardo used multiple measures of paranoia so that even if we have questions about one, it is hard to argue that all three might be wrong.

The seventh paragraph also has an extensive description of the **procedure**, as does the ninth paragraph. Thus we can see that all the important information regarding the design and structure of the study is presented in this midsection of the article. Here the concepts used in the explanation that were pulled together into a hypothesis are translated into actions. These are the basis for gathering the data for analysis.

Data Analysis and Conclusion.   The data of the study are presented in the tenth and eleventh paragraphs and the accompanying table. This is represented in Figure 5.1 in the link labeled "Analysis." The data show that the hypothesized relationship is demonstrated across all the measures and observations. This in turn leads to the conclusion, the last link in the chain of reasoning for this particular study. This is done in the last paragraph of the article, paragraph 13. There the authors note that despite the artificiality of the laboratory procedure, the rationale is sound and the findings have a bearing on the problems of the elderly.

The Next Study.   The last links shown in Figure 5.1 actually belong to the next study that builds on this one. That study is connected to this one by one of those "Links to previous studies" rings like those at the top of the figure. It would use the data from this one to undergird some further explanation of this or a related phenomenon.

In summary, the chain of reasoning begins with links to the results of previous studies that are used to build forward to an explanation, rationale, or point of view. Depending on how much previous knowledge is found, we draw from it a question, hypothesis, or model. This is in turn translated into a design, which consists of choices of subjects, situations, treatment (or independent variable), observations or measures, basis for sensing attributes or changes, and procedure. The design guides us in the collection of data, which permits us to demonstrate a relationship by means of data analysis. The demonstration of the relationship and conclusion may in turn be picked up by a new study.

Another Example: Use of the Chain of Reasoning in Study Design

A published study makes the choices in the chain of reasoning seem easy and obvious, like looking through binoculars focused on a particular phenomenon. But have you turned the binoculars around and looked through the other end? Then you see far more than the phenomenon of interest, which is embedded in

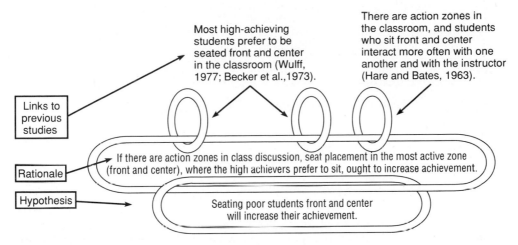

FIGURE 5.2   The first links in the chain of reasoning of a classroom seating placement study. (Adapted from Krathwohl, 1985)

a whole distracting context. So it is in developing a study. Consider the example shown in Figure 5.2. The literature suggests that there are naturally occurring zones of activity in the classroom that are normally occupied by high achievers. The rationale for the study that grows out of this literature is that perhaps this phenomenon could be turned into a treatment for students who are achieving poorly by seating them where high achievers normally sit.

Figure 5.3 shows, in the next links of the chain, a sampling of the alternatives that the researcher faces in translating this simple hypothesis into a design. Though merely touching on the possibilities, the figure gives an idea of

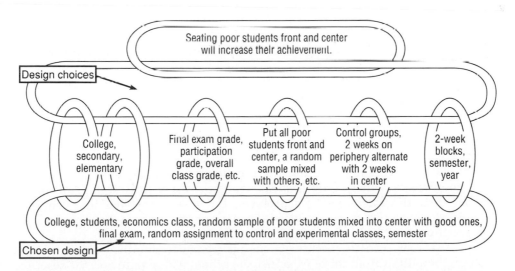

FIGURE 5.3   Design choices and the chosen design in the classroom seating placement study.

the decisions involved in choosing a design, the basis for which we will be examining in the chapters ahead. The chosen design in the figure suggests a set of reasonable alternatives that might have been combined into a study.

Four Useful Characteristics of the Chain Analogy

If the chain of reasoning were made of metal, it would have certain physical properties that, by analogy, are useful in understanding the use of the chain of reasoning in research. Four useful characteristics can be found in this analogy (Krathwohl, 1985). Let us examine them.

A Chain Is Only as Strong as Its Weakest Link.   Just as a metal chain breaks at the weakest link, so does an argument for a knowledge claim. As much as any part of the argument for a knowledge claim can be faulted, the whole chain is weakened, and experts are less likely to accept the claim. If the fault is serious enough, the chain fails, and the claim is rejected. For example, if we were convinced that the paranoia of the elderly is different from that of college males, then the "choice of subjects" link is weakened, and, depending on how serious we consider this problem, the whole argument is either weakened or fails to be convincing.

All Links in the Chain Should Be Equally Strong.   A second characteristic of a metal chain, a corollary of the first, is that all links in the chain should be built to about the same strength. This is typical of a metal chain; we do not find a set of strong links interrupted by a small, thin link. Yet that sometimes happens in a study's chain of reasoning without our realizing it or its seriousness. It makes little sense to have one link in the chain thick enough to anchor a building in a hurricane and others as thin as a decorative gold chain. Thus there would have been little point in allocating considerable resources to the instrument link as Zimbardo did—three measures of paranoia were used—if the hypnotic technique had been developed only to the point where deafness was irregularly and unpredictably maintained. Better that some resources for measures were devoted to improving the hypnotic technique. Resources should be allocated so that all the links are equally strong.

In whose judgment should the links be of equal strength? Our audience makes the final judgment; we are building a chain intended to achieve a consensus about the interpretation of the findings. We must satisfy our own personal standards first, but the interpretation of the data being advanced will be accepted by others only if their standards are met as well. Anticipating what their thresholds are is a problem, but it is a problem that cannot be avoided. Knowing these standards is part of the socialization process that maintains science.

The real problem occurs when our personal priorities about what to strengthen differ from those we anticipate others will require and the resources are not sufficient to satisfy both. Resources are always limited; trade-offs are required, and satisfying all parties is not possible. Zimbardo obviously thought a laboratory study preferable to a field study in a retirement home. He traded the positives of reality and generality and the negatives of trying to control the situation in a retirement home and the accompanying ethical problems for an alternative set of positives—good control in the laboratory and fewer ethical problems—and negatives—artificiality and problems in generalizing the results. We try as best we can to find the choice that optimizes satisfaction for all.

There are many trade-offs hidden in the research process. This is the first we have encountered, but there will be others; look for them. Because researchers differ about trade-off solutions, we often have to consider more than one "right" way to do a study, an unanticipated characteristic of science. It makes many people uncomfortable; indeed, some will argue that there is always only one best way to do a study—a position you will find is difficult to support. But such arguments are also a part of the social process, one that seems to work itself out as efforts are made to replicate or build on studies and create consensus about a particular generalization.

Each Link in the Chain Is Determined by the Link Before It. The information must be presented logically linked together. Each link is dependent on the preceding one. The explanation or rationale is built on previous research. The question, hypothesis, or model grows out of that explanation or rationale. As indicated, the extent of knowledge about the problem determines whether a question, hypothesis, or model is formulated. So the second link is dependent on the first.

The next link, the design of the study, is a translation of the preceding link into the operations that constitute the study. What can be shown in the next link, "Analysis," is dependent on the design choices. This in turn leads to the conclusion, which is clearly dependent on how the analysis of the data turned out.

By the way each step advances the argument for the knowledge claim, it sets boundaries for the next; each step is shaped by the argument to that point. Thus being aware of the desired breadth for the later links, we need to build in sufficient breadth in the earlier ones. If Zimbardo wishes to generalize his conclusions to the elderly and the use of college students is seen as narrowing the range of his conclusions, then a different choice of subjects is required in the earlier links.

Where Links Share the Load, One of Them May Be Made Stronger to Compensate for Weakness in Another. The last characteristic of the chain is not quite as obvious. Though it rarely occurs with metal chains, it is important. Where several horizontal links across the chain's breadth connect the links above and below them, each of the horizontal links shares the load. Therefore, a weak link may be tolerated if another of the horizontal links is made stronger. In the research chain of reasoning, this situation occurs at the design level. At that level, all six facets of design together link the design as a whole to the demonstration of the relationship.

Zimbardo used this principle in his study; hypnosis is a weak treatment in the sense that it will not work with some individuals. For them, the post-hypnotic suggestion might not have been very effective. He strengthened the "subjects" link by choosing subjects who were especially susceptible to hypnosis, thereby making the treatment strong.

The chain analogy is useful because it makes four points clear:

1. An argument is only as strong as its weakest link.
2. Links at all levels of the chain should be equally strong (at the design level, it is the combined strength of the six links that equals the strength at the other links). There is no point in lavishing care on one part of the argument if another part is left weak.
3. The character of links as each level advances the arugment is determined by prior levels.
4. Since all six links at the design level "help carry the load," weak links may often be balanced by strengthening other links at that level.

SUMMARY

All studies setting forth a generalization as true are expected to supply certain information that allows readers to judge the study and make a knowing judgment whether to accept the interpretation of the evidence being advanced. Most, though not all, studies follow a standard sequence in presenting the findings of their research. If they do not follow the sequence, they nevertheless include the same data.

The case for a generalization is presented (or could be arranged) in a sequence that forms a chain of reasoning. A universal or prototypical model of such a chain of reasoning may be constructed containing the essential elements of the chain. Such a model begins with an explanation, rationale, theory, or point of view that is linked to or grows out of prior research studies and writing. The generalization being advanced flows from this explanation, rationale, theory, or point of view.

The stronger the previous evidence, the more detailed in its development, the more comprehensive in its breadth, the stronger the explanation, rationale, theory, or point of view, and, therefore, the stronger the next link that flows from it. With the strongest prior knowledge, we can pose a model that links many variables. With less prior knowledge, we may still be able to make a reasonably precise prediction of how large an affect will occur, as well as where and how it will happen. With still less, we may have a hypothesis that describes the direction things may take and how they are related. And with the least prior knowledge, a question focuses our attention on certain aspects of the phenomenon of particular interest that presumably have potential for guiding further research.

The question, hypothesis, or model is translated into the design of the study. This results in making choices of who (subjects), where (situation), why (treatment), what (observations or measures), how (basis for sensing attributes or changes), and when (procedure). These choices determine how to gather data that demonstrate whatever relationship is being studied. That data are analyzed and a conclusion is drawn to represent the most appropriate interpretation of the data.

The chain-of-reasoning model is analogous to a metal chain and has some of the same properties:

1. It is only as strong as its weakest link.
2. All links should be of the same strength except when they share the load.
3. The nature of each prior link in the chain constrains the nature of successive links.
4. Where links share the load, as they do between "design" and "analysis," one or more of those links may be made stronger to compensate for weakness in one or more of the others.

Looking ahead, although the chain of reasoning begins to tell us what evidence to include in a good study and to suggest the criteria to apply to the various links, if we examined the nature of the links and what would make for strong ones, we could tease out the criteria. You may wish to do that for yourself as you go through section two of the book. It should be becoming clear that the process by which the findings of a study become accepted as knowledge has implications for the audiences it must satisfy. Further, the chain of reasoning suggests the criteria for judging the evidence we supply to that audience. These criteria will be summarized in chapters 13 and 14 of the book's third section.

ADDITIONAL READING

Krathwohl (1985)

IMPORTANT TERMS

Chain of reasoning
Explanation, rationale, theory, point of view
Question, hypothesis, model
Research design and its six facets:
   1. Subjects
   2. Situation

3. Treatment (or independent variable)
4. Observations or measures
5. Basis for sensing attributes or changes
6. Procedure

========= APPLICATION PROBLEMS =========

The following summarizes a 1987 study by Dr. David Jonassen of the University of Colorado in which he set out to verify "pattern notes" as a method to assess an individual's cognitive structure. Jonassen began his article with a brief discussion of instructional design theory. He noted that such theory had traditionally been based on experience with programmed learning and behavioral task analysis but was slowly giving way to cognitive theory. That theory assumes that knowing is a process of individually constructing our cognitive structures, or schemata, based on experience. The purpose of instruction, then, is to build the best of these structures in the learner. Instructional design theory provides techniques to determine the learner's schemata and to organize content to fit them. The problem was to find a feasible procedure for mapping cognitive structure.

Jonassen proceeded to describe the available methods, dismissing most for reasons ranging from being limited to being too difficult. His solution was "pattern notes," a form of spatial word association task first developed as a technique for taking notes during a lecture. The student placed the topic of the lecture in the middle of the page and then added related concepts around it. Lines were drawn between concepts to indicate relationships. This simple technique, he noted, depicted the relationships between concepts associated with each other and *should*, he reasoned, represent cognitive structure.

The purpose of the study was to verify this hypothesis. To do so, Jonassen proposed to compare a learner's pattern notes to a free word association task on the same topic. The free word association technique was, in his assessment, the most valid and reliable of the available methods for assessing the learner's cognitive structure. However, it requires the use of sophisticated statistical analysis. Relationships were measured by counting the number of common links between concepts—whether the lines from one concept to another in the pattern note corresponded to the response when one or the other concept was the stimulus in free word association.

Jonassen used both measures to assess the cognitive structures for Newtonian mechanics of 24 high school students, all of whom were members of an advanced elective physics course and presumed to be motivated and capable. The study was carried out on three separate days over a period of a week. The students were first administered the word association task. The order of concepts presented in each test was random for each student. The next week, they were taught how to construct pattern notes and finally were asked to construct one note for each of the concepts presented during the first test. Analysis of the data showed a significant relationship between the two measures, indicating that we could use pattern notes to assess cognitive structure as it is represented by free word association. In his concluding section, Jonassen then provided a number of suggestions for the use of pattern notes in instructional design.

1. Explain whether or not this summary of Jonassen's work follows the research chain of reasoning.
2. What do you consider to be the weak links in his argument?
3. For any weak links, indicate if Jonassen compensated by making other links stronger.

Compare your answers with those on pages 702–703.

The Skills of Research

This section is concerned with skills that are widely applicable to methods in form or in concept. For example, although sampling is most obviously used in sample surveys, it is fundamental to the concept of generalization, a matter of concern to nearly all researchers. In section one's examination of how findings become knowledge, we noted that findings intended to support generalizations are usually presented as a chain of reasoning.[1] In this section, we supply skills to strengthen various parts of that chain, beginning near the top, with problem formulation, and proceeding down it.

- Chapter 6 discusses the criteria of a good problem and provides suggestions regarding the process of finding and conceptualizing a problem. Research on creativity enhancement is introduced.
- Chapter 7 explains the relationship of a current study to previous research and thought. Building on the work of the past is necessary to avoid reinventing the wheel with each new effort. The characteristics of a good literature search and the means for doing one are described.
- Chapter 8 describes the principles of sampling and their application to various parts of the chain of reasoning. Representativeness is basic to generalization, and generalization is fundamental to the conceptualization of principles. Sampling is shown to be pervasive throughout the chain.
- Chapter 9 focuses on conceptual analysis. Because so much of social and behavioral science research deals with concepts or constructs (putting names on things that we cannot directly sense—intelligence, anxiety, fear, etc.), it is important to know how we define a concept and test that definition.

---

1. Some qualitative studies include all parts of the chain, but not necessarily in the same sequence. In some instances, aspects of the design are included in a methodological appendix.

- Chapter 10 deals with the numeric description of data. We routinely descibe our world in verbal terms, but the notions involved in describing those phenomena in numbers need to be learned as well.
- Chapter 11 explores measurement, testing, and observation. Some things can be counted (number of words produced in a minute) or measured (time between responses) and described by numbers. Others things, such as concepts and constructs, must have the definitions of chapter 9 translated into the observable behaviors that constitute a testing, measurement, or observation scheme. This chapter examines the criteria of good measurement and the means for determining how well the criteria have been met.

In the course of learning to use tools, you will be absorbing the criteria by which studies are judged. We will formalize those in relation to the chain of reasoning in section three.

Finding Research Problems

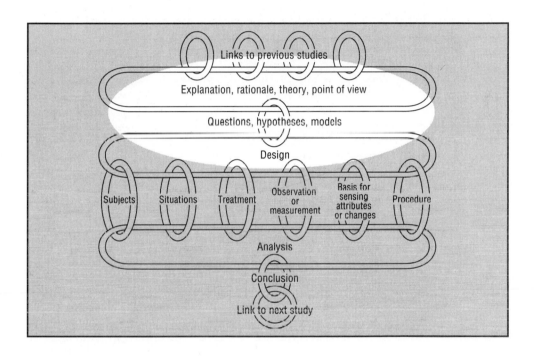

Someone once said that the difference between a scientist and an artist is the difference between discovery and creation. Another genius, some say, could have discovered Planck's constant—for it was there to be discovered—but only Beethoven could have written Beethoven's sonatas. I think that Chet Carlson's achievement was more like Beethoven's.

Sol Linowitz, former chairman of the board of Xerox Corp., commemorating the fiftieth anniversary of the invention of the xerography process by Chet Carlson (Byrne, 1988).

A question well stated is half solved!

Anonymous

OVERVIEW

Although problem selection is one of the most important of the researcher's tasks, it is often also among the most difficult. Some guidelines and suggestions are presented in this chapter.

Problem selection is usually accompanied by an explanation or a rationale, some notion of why the problem is worth working on. These contribute heavily to the first links of the chain of reasoning.

The chapter also reviews the lore surrounding creativity and discusses the criteria of a good problem.

CHAPTER CONTENTS

The Problem of the Problem 73
Problem Finding and Research
  Method 73
Success-enhancing Problem-finding
  Behaviors 75
    Fill the Mind with the Best
      Possible Relevant Material 75
    Breaking the Mind-set 76
    Enhancing Creativity 78
    Formulating the Problem
      as a Written Statement 81
    Explaining Ideas to Other People 82
    Other Useful Suggestions 83
Potential Sources of Research Problems 85
    Draw Suggestions from Other People's
      Research 85
    Keep a Log of Ideas and

Experiences 85
Use Others' Data to Answer New
  Questions 86
Use New Techniques, Instruments,
  or Models 87
Translate Significant Ideas
  from Other Languages 87
Criteria of a Good Problem 88
  Interest: A Necessary but Not
    Sufficient Condition 88
  Basis in Theory 89
  Some Impact in Its Field 90
  Originality and Creativity 90
  Feasibility 91
  Researchable Questions 93
Summary 93

THE PROBLEM OF THE PROBLEM[1]

Though the choice of problem is the most important decision each researcher makes, it is really a gamble! There is no certain way of telling at the outset whether the investment of time, energy, and resources will yield any return— with luck, a reputation can be made. But is it luck that some persons are known as good researchers? No more so than that some people can make an honest living from the stock market, generally win at cards, or beat the odds at a racetrack.

There has been little research on problem finding, but what there is suggests that some individuals are consistently better at it than others (Getzels, 1982). All of us know individuals who are particularly creative; I have known some from whom I got a good idea every time I talked with them. But Osborn and others involved with industrial training have data that suggest that creativity can be increased (Osborn, 1959; Parnes, 1967). Therefore, most of us can benefit from advice.

Clearly, some individuals improve their odds of being successful by combining knowledge of the situation with their ability to recognize an opportunity and by carrying thought into action. Indeed, studies in the past have shown that relatively few researchers account for the bulk of useful work: 10 percent of scientists account for fully 50 percent of published research, and 10 percent of published research accounts for 40 percent of the citations in books and articles (Pletz, 1965; Price, 1963). There is little reason to believe the current situation differs. So often in reading research we find that it focuses on something in a familiar situation to which we hadn't paid attention earlier. We might have noticed it, but to our regret, we did not act on it as the author had. Modifying such behaviors, as well as learning some of the behaviors that enhance problem-finding capacity, will improve research capabilities.

How can this book help with a creative process that by its very definition defies being tied to formulas or routine processes? We can describe behavior and activities characteristic of productive researchers and suggest some creativity enhancement techniques. You can then choose the behaviors that seem personally effective. Further, we can describe the criteria of good problems so that when one appears, you will recognize it. Finally, we can note the kinds of problems that are not amenable to research methods. These topics outline the plan of this chapter.

PROBLEM FINDING AND RESEARCH METHOD

Some persons prefer to find a problem, get it well defined, proceed to gather data, analyze it, and write it up. Each step follows from the next in a deductive

---

1. This is the title of an excellent chapter by Getzels (1982) on problem finding. He is one of the few people who have done research on problem finding and formulation.

sequence. Research is often visualized in this way. Although a deductive stance can be used with any research method, it is usually associated with the quantitative method. Individuals who adopt this way of working start with considerable time invested in problem finding, problem redefinition, and the literature search (the topic of the next chapter). As we have previously noted, other researchers prefer to immerse themselves in a situation of interest and let the research project emerge as they explore what is there. This is an inductive approach that is usually associated with qualitative research but can in fact be used with any method. Data collection can begin as soon as what might be called an "orienting question" is identified—one that focuses and directs our attention, although that focus can be quite broad. It may be simply a situation of interest. In the Hoffmann-Riem study presented in chapter 2, the problem began as "how parents view adoption" and ended up as "how adoptive parents normalize their lives."

Incidentally, *for most of us, research method follows problem choice.* Once we know what to study, we adapt it to a method of investigation with which we personally feel comfortable. Novice researchers often work through the details of method before they are clear on what the problem is. Working back and forth between problem and method is fine if you don't go too far with method before the problem is clear. To a certain extent, working on method helps formulate the problem, and vice versa. It is an iterative process.

The heading "Problem Finding" suggests that it is a one-time process, that a problem, once defined at the outset, does not change. Nothing could be further from the truth. In qualitative methods, problem finding is a continuous process. There is the possibility of the problem's being redefined right up through data analysis. This is also true of quantitative methods. If something new and interesting shows up in data analysis, the whole focus of the problem can shift, sometimes to a phenomenon quite different from the study's original one. But even if it doesn't shift, problem redefinition usually continues into the final stages of the study. This doesn't show in the report of the study; it is written as a deductive chain of reasoning. But such reformulation is frequently an important part of the research process. After all, only as completion of the study informs us sufficiently about the phenomenon do we understand the really important questions to ask.

- Problem finding and the redefinition of the problem and its focus are continuing processes.
- The best questions often become known only at the end of the research, when the phenomenon is better understood.
- Inductive or deductive approaches can be used with any method. The relation of problem finding to data collection and analysis is typically a function of method.
- In the typical case, a clear conception of the problem emerges earlier in quantitative methods than in qualitative methods, where it is sometimes delayed into the data-analysis stage.

SUCCESS-ENHANCING PROBLEM-FINDING BEHAVIORS

We shall describe behaviors characteristic of productive researchers. These points are drawn from autobiographies of researchers, from observation, and from the advice of people who have studied creativity.

Filling the Mind with the Best Possible Relevant Material

Filling the mind with the most relevant material from one's area of interest is one of the very best ways to find a good problem. This allows the unconscious mind to process the material. The unconscious is an amazing tool. While we are sleeping or working on other things, it organizes the material and presents us with insights that often escape us when we are too wrapped up in achieving a goal. But the unconscious must have something to process, hence the necessity for a prepared mind.

Discovery Favors the Prepared Mind. As a child, you knew your backyard, alley, or room better than anybody. You proudly showed parents or siblings things to which they had never paid attention—an interestingly shaped hole, a place where some animal lived, a spot that formed the silhouette of a person significant in your life. Such knowledge comes from long, intimate contact with the situation. Research is no different; there is no substitute for knowing the territory. Fleming's discovery of penicillin was accidental, but his prior work prepared him to recognize the breakthrough when it appeared. He noticed that his bacterial cultures seemed not to grow where there was mold on the plate and wondered why this occurred. No doubt this had happened to other investigators. Fleming, however, being curious and having worked intensely with bacterial cultures, asked why and, acting on that query, made an important discovery

Have you had the experience of learning a new word that you thought was quite rare? Once you learned it, you were surprised at how often you heard it thereafter! It must have been there before; it is a matter of the prepared mind. So dig into what is already known about a phenomenon; immerse yourself in the literature and explore each of its important facets. If that does not suggest the desired research problem, you will be sufficiently familiar with the area that when the unusual appears, you can recognize and act on it.

Read the Writings of the Seminal Minds in the Field. Productive scientists seem to read more deeply into the historical background of their problems. They read the original versions, not digests, of the best minds in the field. Often those minds will have sensed something that was not well enough understood in their time to explain clearly. In other instances, they took a problem as far as they could at the time, but now you could take it further. Reading such accounts against the background of what has happened more recently often gives a new and useful perspective and meaning. For instance, Campbell and Stanley (1963), who made important contributions to understanding social science experimentation, start with a tribute to W. A. McCall (1923), whose then 40-year-old book described many of the concepts they use in their exposition.

Behaviors that enhance problem finding include these:

■ Filling the mind with the best possible relevant material. Discovery favors a mind prepared to recognize the unusual aspects of a field.
■ Reading the writings of the seminal minds in the field, both past and present.
■ Delving into the historical background of the problem to learn which approaches have and have not proved fruitful.

Breaking the Mind-set

We have all been exposed to problems that require us to think about them differently in order to solve them. Remember the game of passing the scissors? One person passes scissors to another, saying, "I'm passing it to you crossed" or "I'm passing it to you uncrossed." Players unfamiliar with the game are puzzled; no matter how they position the scissors, they can do it correctly only by accident, if at all. They are concentrating on the scissors. Only when they realize that "crossed" or "uncrossed" refers to the position of the person's legs when the scissors are passed do they break the mind-set of concentrating on the scissors. Breaking the mind-set, viewing an area or a problem differently, is often the secret to an important piece of research. The following are often useful mindset-breaking tools.

Read Actively (Anticipate the Author; Don't Just Follow Passively).   Active reading is one of the most important skills to develop. *Anticipate* where the material is going; *project* the argument that is being fashioned instead of passively following it. We process what we read more thoroughly if we underline or make marginal comments. This reduces reading speed and allows time to think ahead to where the argument is going. As we foresee what is coming, we will often find that the author zigs where we zagged. If our logic is correct to that point, why the zig? Here is a question worth pondering; a zag might have been a more profitable course to follow. We have to retrace our steps carefully to be sure, but many new leads are discovered by active reading.

Along these same lines, actively search for inconsistencies in the argument. Look for gaps where existing ideas do not adequately account for the phenomena. This may call for revision of existing explanations or even for new ones. For example, Merton (1959) notes that regularities in cultural behavior are typically thought to result from prescriptions by cultural norms. Yet, he notes, "Men have higher suicide rates than women, for example, even when the cultural norms do not invite males to put an end to themselves" (p. xxiii). Apparently, there are regularities that result from something besides cultural norms, and the concept of cultural norms must be reworked to specify what kind of behavior lies beyond them.

Talk to Specialists in the Field.   Experts who have worked in a field for a long time have built up their own conceptions from their experiences. Although researchers who have compared the problem solving of experts and novices note little difference in strategies, they find a difference in the repertory of experiences organized in long-term memory. Chase and Simon's (1973) study of chess players illustrates this nicely. Grandmasters and masters were asked to reconstruct the positions of 22 chess pieces after viewing them for five seconds. When the positions were taken from actual games, experts could place 81 percent of them without error, whereas novices could correctly position only 33 percent. But when pieces were arranged at random, experts were no better than novices, placing only three to five pieces correctly. Experts apparently identified games in terms of patterns they had learned or experienced instead of memorizing the position of individual pieces. But note the specificity of their knowledge; their capabilities would not apply to another subject matter. Research in this field suggests that these long-term memory patterns are subject-matter-specific, so choose an expert in your field.

If you ask specialists to tell you about a problem or area, they may, to communicate easily with you, fall back on textbook formulations. Instead, try your ideas on them so that they can see your problem through your framework. They may be able to react to it intuitively in terms of their experience—especially in reconceptualizing the problem and in making connections to other areas of work that may not be readily apparent. Experts are also useful sources of pertinent things to read (despite the advances in computer searches, *the human mind is still the best retrieval device*—see the comment regarding invisible colleges on p. 114 for ways to tap it).

Assess the experts' reactions carefully, however. Some persons discourage creative ideas that weren't original with them. And some, for whatever reason, often lack of time, may not grasp your problem and react superficially. With these caveats in mind, you will find that experts can be extremely valuable and save you much time, especially by helping you avoid false and unproductive leads.

Challenge Assumptions.   When reading past research, examine the assumptions on which the arguments are based. Are they reasonable? Could we make less restrictive ones? What would be the result? If we change the assumptions, does this lead to different consequences? Consider the problem of the mentally handicapped. If we assume that they learn essentially as does everyone else, but more slowly, then given sufficient time and motivation, they could achieve normally. The consequences of this view are to give the individuals more time, to isolate them in classes where the competition is less intense, and to motivate them to achieve. A different assumption is that the conceptual structures into which they fit what they learn are not the complex ones that others can use. This assumption leads to the search for simplified conceptual structures they can learn that will result in learning approximating that of more normal children. Examining the assumptions about why slow learners are handicapped results in quite different consequences for remediation, each of which can be tested for validity. (See the application problems at the end of this chapter for other examples.)

Look for New Ways to Tease the Problem Apart. Psychologist Daniel Kahneman suggests a trick for questions about behavior that he claims derives from Lewinian psychology. Instead of asking, "Why does a person behave this way?" he asks, "Why doesn't he behave otherwise?" Instead of asking why a person is hostile in a particular setting, he asks, "Why isn't he more hostile?" "Why isn't he less hostile?" The kinds of answers made available by this reformulation are radically different from those derived from "Why is he hostile?" It may be much easier to remove the factors driving him to greater hostility and uncovered by the question "Why isn't he less hostile?" than to suppress the hostile behavior by manipulating forces that push him to be less hostile than he was. Sometimes it also helps to switch the focus of attention consciously from the result to the process of getting there.

Another way of teasing the problem apart is to look for concepts that have not been effective in differentiating important aspects of a phenomenon. Merton (1959) notes that concepts used to describe a phenomenon have often taken us as far as they will stretch. We need new concepts and new differentiations to take us further. For example, at one time, psychology talked about self-concept as though it were a single entity; one felt positively or negatively about oneself. Later, we came to realize there are different self-concepts and that we can talk about a self-concept of ability (one's capability in solving academic problems) and even self-concepts in different subject matters. Thus the term *self-concept* has come to be highly differentiated, and there are now several books available dealing with these different meanings (e.g., Wylie, 1979).

Breaking our initial view of a problem, our mind-set, is often critical to problem finding. The likelihood of breaking a mind-set is greater if we follow these suggestions:

- Read actively, anticipating where the author is heading.
- Analyze the approach the author is using and synthesize it with that of others' and our own prior knowledge.
- Challenge the assumptions that undergird a particular approach to a problem.
- For concepts that do not adequately differentiate their important aspects, look for new ways to ask the question that better target the area of interest.

Enhancing Creativity

Suggestions for the enhancement of creativity nearly always include breaking the mind-set, but they also include harnessing the unconscious, organizing material into suggestive patterns, and reducing the censorship of ideas.

Harness the Unconscious. There comes a point when we have read enough to have a flavor of what has been done, but new approaches have not suggested themselves. Here it is well to recognize that our minds do not always do their best work when we are consciously pushing at a problem. William Safire gives the first rule of holes: "When you are in a hole, stop digging!" Then let the unconscious mind take over. Read Raudsepp's (1977) recitation of the testimony of the greats on this score:

> Dostoevsky found that he could dream up his immortal, moving stories and characters while doodling. Brahms found that ideas came effortlessly only when he approached a state of deep daydreaming. And César Frank is said to have walked around with a dreamlike gaze while composing, seemingly unaware of his surrounding. . . .
>
> John Dewey stated, "I do not think it can be denied that an element of reverie, of approach to a state of dream, enters in the creation of a work of art. . . . Indeed, it is safe to say that creative conceptions . . . come only to persons who are relaxed to the point of reverie. . . ."
>
> Thomas Alva Edison also knew the value of "half-waking states." Whenever confronted with what seemed an insurmountable hitch defying all efforts, he would stretch out on his workshop couch and let fantasies flood his mind. (pp. 27–28)

Poincaré (1913) concluded that the unconscious mind collates and sorts random possibilities among pertinent variables at a rate that defies the efforts of the conscious mind.

We must all find our own best means of commanding the muse, but the unconscious is an important resource too rarely emphasized. Some people are helped by daydreaming, a reverie in which the mind floats over the problem, rejecting no possibilities. Some adopt a kind of half-awake, half-asleep posture. Still others get their best ideas at night and keep paper and pencil at hand to record ideas immediately, lest they be unable to retrieve their thoughts upon becoming fully awake. Whatever your means, use the unconscious; it is one of the most powerful tools of creativity available.

Organize Material into Suggestive Patterns. There are many ways of doing this, using the themes suggested earlier of filling the mind; letting the unconscious work on it and then analyzing and synthesizing the products; and repeating this cycle until a satisfactory solution is found. One set of steps outlined by Zwicky (1969) extend what Allen (1962) called morphological analysis:

1. Without evaluation, transfer all the material about the problem onto cards (3-by-5-inch cards cut in half are a good size)—ideas for solving the problem, achievements desired, names of persons involved, books that might be consulted, and so on.
2. Disregarding order, lay the cards out in blocks three cards wide and four cards deep. Read the cards rapidly four or five times; this transfers the ideas into your subconscious mind. For the next half hour or so, leave the cards and occupy your mind as completely as possible with other matters.
3. Study the cards and categorize them into friendly or congenial groups. Five hundred cards might reduce to 20 or 30 such groups. Place a title

card in a distinguishing color on each group; we'll call each group a "component."

4. Treat each component as you did steps 2 and 3, reducing to four to seven groups by creating more inclusive categories with titles we'll call "parameters." (Was it chance that Zwicky chose seven as the maximum? Or did he sense intuitively what memory research later showed?—in general, the mind can only handle about seven things at a time.)

5. Reduce the number of components in each parameter to seven or fewer. Prioritizing of parameters or components may be necessary to reduce the possibilities to a manageable number.

6. List each parameter, followed by its components, on a separate strip of paper, and move the strips alongside one another to suggest different combinations from which solutions may emerge.

Having such a model to follow may have value in that all the possible options are covered. Elstein, Shulman, and Sprafka (1978, 1990) have shown that in medical problem solving, having a model, or heuristic, to follow increases effectiveness.

Reduce the Censorship of Ideas. What is typically called "brainstorming" involves admitting possibilities for examination that would normally be rejected by typical problem-solving processes. Popularized by Osborn (1959), it consists of assembling a group of people to attack the problem with four basic rules of interaction: criticism is ruled out, freewheeling is welcomed, quantity is wanted, and combination and improvement of previous suggestions are sought. At one time a fad, this technique is still useful. It may lead to time-consuming consideration of impossible suggestions yet may free individuals to consider desirable ones that would otherwise have been discarded. It is sometimes particularly useful to think of analogies, such as "How is this phenomenon like an animal?" Once the bulk of the ideas has emerged, they are sifted to select the best ones for further development. Sometimes these, in turn, become the focus of brainstorming sessions and the process is repeated.

Creativity is an essential ingredient of good problem finding. Creativity may be enhanced by employing these three tactics:

1. Harnessing the unconscious, one of the most powerful of all the creativity tools.
2. Organizing the material into patterns that are suggestive of relationships.
3. Using "brainstorming" or a similar technique under which the censorship of ideas is reduced: permit no criticism, seek the largest number of ideas, encourage the combination and enhancement of ideas, and evaluate for quality only at the end of the activity.

Formulating the Problem as a Written Statement

Trying to set down our thoughts involves both clarifying and organizing. As Merton (1959) puts it, try formulating questions that register our "dimly felt sense of ignorance" (p. xxvi). Writing enforces a discipline that helps articulate half-formed ideas. Something happens between the formation of an idea and its appearance on paper, a latency that somehow results in the clarification and untangling of our thinking. Writing helps bring unconscious processing to light as articulated synthesized statements—just what we are seeking! When we are reading widely, we cram the ideas into our memory, often without checking them against what is already there; even contradictory material may exist side by side. Writing makes us confront these internal inconsistencies and put together relationships.

Sometimes continued work at a problem pays off. Witness Albert Schweitzer in a new translation of his autobiography:

> For months I lived in a continual state of mental agitation. Without the least success, I concentrated—even during my daily work at the hospital—on the real nature of affirmation of life and of ethics and on the question of what they have in common. . . . I saw the concept that I wanted to attain before me, but I could not . . . formulate it. While in this mental condition I had to undertake a long journey on the river. . . . Slowly we crept upstream. . . . Lost in thought I sat on the deck of the barge, struggling. . . . *I covered sheet after sheet with disconnected sentences merely to keep myself concentrated on the problem.* . . . Late on the third day, . . . there flashed upon my mind, unforeseen and unsought, the phrase, "reverence for life." The iron door yielded. The path in the thicket became visible. (Schweitzer, 1990, p. 155; italics added)

What struck me about this passage was the italicized sentence. It is so typical of good writers that even when blocked, they persist with provisional tries, seeking to formulate what they are after. Schweitzer "covered sheet after sheet with disconnected sentences" until he succeeded. The problem doesn't always yield, but the effort is worth making.

Slowing the writing process may help with difficult formulation. I can type when I know what I want to write, but I must write with a pen when I'm struggling, and as a last resort, a fountain pen seems to work better than a ballpoint. Note that each method takes progressively longer to form the words on paper. I can hold longer internal discussions with myself about what comes next, do a memory search for the right concept or word, and still get it down without unduly interrupting the flow of thought. This is important. Poor writers are often so taken up with grammar, spelling, or even forming words that their thinking may be interrupted to the point where they have difficulty remembering where their sentence was going.

In the preface we noted that internal processing is the name of the game, processing that results in "chunking" material into meaningful collections. The networking of these chunks makes connections that bring to mind new material. Further, the "chunks" of experts are larger and more complex than those of novices. Artists seem to have learned this process intuitively since they often spend large amounts of time practicing and rehearsing their material before producing a masterpiece. Sinclair Lewis developed notebooks that described his characters and their complete setting before he wrote a novel—their personalities, what they wore, even maps of the community and floor plans of the buildings. Did he refer to the notebooks when writing? I don't know, but I suspect that advance rehearsal chunked this material so effectively that he had little need to. Similarly, before Andrew Wyeth did his Helga pictures, sketch after sketch was discarded on the floor, some of which he even proceeded to walk on. They were chunks transferred to his mind for use in later drawings. Darwin carefully indexed the books he read and organized the material into portfolios that he consulted at the beginning of each new project (Steiner, 1984).

So everyone uses chunks in problem solving, and the best writers and thinkers find that it takes work and time to build those chunks and their relational network. Maybe that is one of the differences between the greats and the not-so-greats: the willingness to do the work that is involved in building and relating the chunks that go into a masterwork.

Explaining Ideas to Other People

Similar to writing is trying to explain our ideas to someone else, ideally an uninformed but intelligent observer. It is said that the best way to learn something is to teach it. In trying to communicate clearly with someone who is unfamiliar with your area of expertise, an idea must be formulated with a clarity that makes no assumptions and avoids jargon. In starting at the beginning to explain a concept, you may recognize aspects that you take so much for granted that they escaped your focus. Examination of those assumptions may provide new insights and lead to ways of reconfiguring the question or problem. But talking isn't enough; you must get everything down in writing while it is still fresh and you are still enthusiastic about the idea! You'll write much better sooner than later; indeed, later you may have difficulty in recapturing the idea.

Problem perspective is enhanced if we see material from a different angle or in a different context. This an intelligent observer can do better than we can for ourselves. When we are close to a problem and emotionally involved in it, we miss things that are obvious to a naive observer. An observer can maintain psychological distance from the problem. Scheerer (1963), for example, assigned subjects randomly as observers and workers. The workers were to solve a problem that required use of a missing piece of string. A string that they could use was present in the form of a hanger for a wall calendar. Only half of the workers—but all of the observers—broke the mind-set of the string as hanger and solved the problem.

Talking with others also may restore a sense of excitement and sometimes competition. Determining the structure of DNA was a race between Watson's Cambridge laboratory and others, among them Linus Pauling's at the University of California. A sense of competition was heightened through a visit of Pauling's son to discuss their parallel progress (Watson, 1968).

Making provisional tries at formulating a problem in spoken or, especially, written form is a very useful behavior in problem formulation, for four reasons:

1. It makes available the articulated and synthesized relationships formed by the unconscious.
2. It facilitates the "chunking" of material and the networking of those chunks. Building the chunks of an expert takes time and effort but is probably one of the major contributors to excellent work.
3. It provides material to which an observer can react from a different perspective and without one's own emotional biases and pre-conceptions.
4. Interaction with others not only may provide new insights but may also restore a sense of excitement.

Other Useful Suggestions

Learn Your Most Productive Working Conditions. Become aware of the conditions that make you productive. For instance, there is probably an optimal level of motivation. At a higher level, you may be unable to stay focused long enough to allow patterns to be perceived. Administrators, in particular, are inclined to think that if a little motivation is good, more must be better; this is not necessarily so.

Where and when you work can be important. Find a place without too many distractions. Many productive writers set aside a regular time for writing, staying at it during that period with provisional tries, whether they are blocked or not.

Patterns of writing are particularly likely to be unique to each person. Outlining used to be considered a *sine qua non* by many English teachers. Neil Simon, the famous playwright, was advised to try it:

> "I ... tried to make it go that way. It wouldn't! I did it 20 times! That is not the way to write a play.... Because that is not the way life is. You don't know what the end is going to be so you don't twist and push it. It just carries you along, somehow, predetermined by your character." (Rosner and Abt, 1970, p. 363)

Clearly, outlining was not for him, nor may it be for others, but there is some pattern that is better for each of us, and we must find it.

Don't Close the Problem Definition Too Quickly. Getzels and Csikszentmihalyi (1976) found the most creative solutions among artists who kept the problem open longer. They suggest that solutions must be discovered by interaction with the elements that constitute it—mucking around in the problem. Superficial solutions are also likelier to be rejected if closure is delayed.

When Having Trouble Focusing, Move to Basic Questions.   Research problems frequently grow out of the common interests or annoyances of daily work. But this often forces the researcher to look for solutions where too little is known about the phenomenon. For example, in trying to get a focus on the problem of how to induce teachers to engage in in-service training, a researcher chooses teacher centers. But what to study about such centers? He could wander over many different aspects of them with no more guidance than that. In such instances, it helps to ask more basic questions: Why do teachers seek training in the first place? What purposes does it serve besides improved teaching? Does it enhance social functions, pay improvement, chances for leadership? These begin to approach in-service training from a coherent viewpoint about the purposes it serves; we can then begin to think more reasonably about designing teacher centers around those purposes. Every problem is part of a causal chain as described in the first few pages of chapter 12. Sometimes it helps to work backward in the causal chain to earlier stages.

Trim Away Your Entry to a Problem as Soon as It No Longer Fits.   When the development of a human fetus is traced, there is always considerable surprise that it seems to go through all the developmental stages of a previous evolution, for example, developing useless gills, which then atrophy and become something else. As problem statements develop, their introductory statement tends to grow, retaining the problem's developmental history, recapitulating useless aspects that no longer contribute to the current problem. It is useful to us in that it retraces our thinking and gets us into the problem. But sometimes it is simply excess baggage. Other people can usually see this more easily than we can. It also is more apparent after the passage of time. The sooner this excess material is trimmed away, the stronger and more clearly we can develop the problem.

Some individuals find themselves rewriting the introduction to their problem every time they leave the work for a period of time. Not only is this likely to result in an introduction that needs to be trimmed, but it tends to be unproductive labor. Write where you are ready to write rather than writing linearly. You'll have to work to fit the pieces together, but you are less likely to be blocked. Rather than leaving the work at a point where a section is complete, stop at a point that cries out for completion and you know what you plan to do next. It will be easier to pick up at that point.

Suggestions for enhancing problem finding include these:

- Learn the conditions under which you are most productive.
- Keep the problem definition open and fluid until you are satisfied with the way it has been shaped.

- Move back to basic questions about a phenomenon if you are having trouble focusing.
- Trim away old entry statements to the problem so that the current one can be developed clearly and forcefully.

POTENTIAL SOURCES OF RESEARCH PROBLEMS

Draw Suggestions from Other People's Research

A review of the literature in an area of interest is the most common way to search for a problem. In reading the literature, examine the suggestions for further research in articles, at the end of dissertations, in critiques of other people's research, and especially in research reviews. Research reviews may provide only the most obvious questions, but their authors are in an especially good position to give an overall perspective. Good questions are likelier to be encountered than full-blown research suggestions. Remember, the more you know about an area, the more questions you have about it and the better you can differentiate central from tangential ones.

There is another side to these suggestions that you must keep in mind, however. Researchers may reserve their best and most practical suggestions for themselves and include in their "next steps" section only "pie in the sky" ones that they don't see a way to handle. There may be hidden problems in the suggestions that are apparent to them because of the the work just done. They will discuss such difficulties if you contact them personally but may not have gone into those aspects in their writing. A parallel to the "Peter principle" (Peter, 1969) applies to researchers: they often carry a line of investigation as far as it is profitable.[2] By contacting a researcher who has dropped an area, you may learn that it was dropped because of the attraction of new research. But the information may also save you from rediscovering a difficulty at first hand.

Keep a Log of Ideas and Experiences

Immersion in a situation of interest is one of the best ways to learn where there is research potential. Consider a pilot observational study in a role that permits you to learn. Enlist as a teacher's aide, "shadow" a social worker or administrator, work as a custodian or maintenance worker—try any of a variety of roles that allow access, preferably as unobtrusively as possible. This

---

2. The Peter principle states that persons are promoted to positions calling for higher levels of skill until they reach a level for which they are not competent. In a similar manner, researchers often work on a problem until their skills of attacking it will carry them no further.

stage can be both exciting and frustrating—exciting because of all that is new and interesting, frustrating because there are so many leads to follow. Simultaneously reading about the situation will bring new meaning to what you are reading and new understanding to what you are observing; reading and observation each inform the other. Student teachers grow tremendously in their observation of classrooms from observing who interacts with whom, how individuals play games with one another, how some individuals manifest insecurity in their overt action and others mask it. But simply observing is not enough: you must process, think, compare and contrast observations. That means keeping a log.

Keeping a log of your work and ideas is a tradition honored more in the natural than the social sciences. Past researchers made a fetish of keeping a research notebook. Thomas Edison kept copious notes on all that went on in the laboratory because they kept ideas from getting lost. Research managers usually keep notebooks to catch the ideas that flash into their minds. Often the difference between the person who is credited with an idea and one who ends up saying, "I thought of that long ago!" is that the former captured the idea and acted on it. Further, keeping a log has all the advantages discussed in the section on formulating the problem as a written statement.

Use Others' Data to Answer New Questions

Data banks are rife with records waiting to be built into significant research studies. Computerization makes access easy once the codes that facilitate labeling and interpreting the data are obtained. Data from longitudinal studies, large-scale surveys, and major social experiments are frequently available to researchers. Directories of databases (such as Williams, Lannom, and Robins, 1985) display the wide array of available opportunities.

Coleman's widely quoted studies of public and private schools (Coleman, Hoffer, and Kilgore, 1982) grew out of routine data collection by the U.S. Department of Education and exemplify the kinds of studies that can be extracted from these files. Considering the tremendous sums invested in gathering these data, the possibility of using them has obvious attractions. There are many approaches: using new or more appropriate methods to reanalyze the data, tracking a subgroup over time, partitioning the data to determine how deeply certain trends reach, or combining subgroups or even data from different studies to see whether a trend emerges.

A few words of warning are in order, however. First, most old research hands would suggest that having a question and then searching for useful data is more likely to result in a significant study than the other way around. Otherwise, you may too quickly compromise problem quality to fit available data. Second, anyone who has gathered field data quickly learns the variety of conditions that can compromise data quality and introduce anomalies. If possible, talk to the original investigators or examine any available records that bear on data quality.

Use New Techniques, Instruments, or Models

New techniques of analysis open up new avenues of investigation and permit reanalysis of significant data. When Carl Rogers began recording counseling interviews and categorizing the data, he noticed a pattern in the negative affect that had not been apparent earlier (Rogers, 1951). Over successive counseling sessions negative self-references initially rose but then declined with problem resolution. This began a significant era in counseling-methods research made possible by the advent of magnetic recording. It allowed interview statements to be carefully categorized and coded. Bales (1950) devised interaction analysis, a method for recording and analyzing the interaction of individuals in groups. It led not only to considerable fruitful research on how groups work but also to spinoff instruments for use in analyzing classroom behavior. Both groups and classrooms had previously been researched only with relatively crude judgmental scales. New instruments permit problems to be examined that were not previously reachable. Indeed, one indication of progress in a field is the accessibility of its phenomena by measures. (The University of Chicago's social science research building has Lord Kelvin's motto carved over the door: "When you cannot measure your knowledge is meager and unsatisfactory.")

Metaphors, analogies, and models are particularly helpful in examining problems. Education has typically been looked on as a necessary function for maintaining a culture and an informed electorate. When it began to be looked at as an investment, using economic terms and models, a new perspective was gained that was especially useful to third-world countries seeking to catch up to the rest quickly. Van den Haag (1956) used the idea as his dissertation and showed the very interesting consequences if all higher education were viewed as an investment and individuals were required to pay the full cost of instruction (he concluded that all fields except the humanities should pay their way). Homeostasis is another example that, used as a model for stable systems, has spread through nearly every field and is the basis for the technology of systems theory.

Translate Significant Ideas from Other Languages

Although the United States and other English-speaking countries have been leaders in data-based social science, there is a long tradition of thoughtful examination of such problems in other countries. It has resulted in some of our most important conceptualizations—Durkheim's and Freud's, for example. Finding such material and bringing it into mainstream English-language literature is important. This requires sufficient knowledge of a foreign language that you can both recognize significant ideas in that language and translate them accurately enough so as to be useful to others. Piaget's work with children was available to those who had mastered French years before his work became popular in English-speaking countries. Such lags still exist. The introduction of such ideas in understandable form is a real service and can lead to significant advances in a field.

Potential sources of problems to research include these:

- Suggestions made by others as they finish a study or review an area of research
- Problems growing out of our logs of activities in exploring an area
- Databases resulting from routine collection or past research studies
- The application of a new technique, instrument, or model to old approaches or their use to open up new ones
- Ideas in other languages and from other cultures with general applicability

---

CRITERIA OF A GOOD PROBLEM

The process of problem finding is similar to the actions of a camera buff with a new zoom lens. She goes to an area that interests her and starts with a distance wide-angle shot, surveying the landscape. As she sees something of interest, she zooms in to explore it and see if there is anything there. If there isn't, she zooms out again, exploring other facets. In time, she'll scramble to a new vantage point, looking at the scene from a new angle, again zooming in and out in a search of the nooks and crannies of the landscape. This sets her off, scrambling over rocks and hillocks for better and new views. But when is the picture just right? When does she stop the search and start composing the picture? That is the function of discussing the criteria of a good problem, so that you'll recognize one when you see it. A good problem is (1) of interest, (2) embedded in theory, (3) likely to have impact, (4) original in some aspect, and (5) feasible—within your conceptual, resource, ethical, and institutional limits. Add to these Teplin's tongue-in-cheek suggestions (Youngstrom, 1990, p. 7):

- The Goldilocks test: Is the research question so broad it's untenable, so narrow it's dull—or is it just right?
- The five-year test: A five-year-old should be able to understand the purpose of the project.
- The blood test: People besides your blood relatives should want to read the research results.

Interest: A Necessary but Not Sufficient Condition

For most researchers, interest is the prime qualification, for it provides the motivation to work on the problem. As one doctoral student put it: "It's your baby, so it better be one you can love when you are up with it at night!" (Grant, 1986). Professors' files are full of projects that failed this test and the many doctoral ABD (all but dissertation) candidates are further testimony to its importance. Clearly, it is one necessary condition; the other is feasibility. But beside these two, a problem should have as many of the following characteristics as possible.

Basis in Theory

The impact of isolated studies is trivial. But a study can contribute to explanations and significant ideas. It can provide the base of data for understanding them, for contradicting and correcting, modifying, extending, or in other ways interacting with them. Then a study's impact is multiplied. As it affects the network of previous findings, it becomes embedded with those ideas and shares in their implications and effects. Problems that either build new rationale and theory or affect previous work are less likely to get lost and more likely to have impact.

The power of Skinner to sway people to behaviorism lay not in his individual studies of learning, though these were important in building the base. Rather it lay in the rationale he built around these findings, which had important implications for explaining much of human activity; he even used the theory to suggest how language develops (Skinner, 1957).

Similarly, Piaget, whose formal experimentation must be considered minimal and whose large-scale research is nonexistent, proposed a set of stages of development that had implications for teaching children. It was the power of his theory, his explanation of phenomena, that resulted in his impact. Think of others who have had an impact on social science, and almost without exception, it is the power of their ideas that is the dominating factor. Empirical research not related to that body of thinking tends to be isolated from it and to have less impact.

Perhaps you are asking what is meant by theory. Simply put, we mean an explanation of behavior that makes good logical sense and either is consistent with the research and explanations that preceded it or convincingly negates or modifies them. Discussion of what constitutes a good theory could fill the rest of this book. Many social scientists agree that we don't have the kind of grand and precise theories that natural scientists are seen as having; some would argue that we don't have anything worthy of the name. Be that as it may, nearly all would agree that ideas that unify a variety of findings and assimilate them into a cohesive and interrelated body, as behaviorism does, for instance, are most useful. When we consider the myriad things that could be researched in a situation, theories help us find the significant variables. They suggest research directions and help locate points where research is needed to bolster arguments. They provide a network into which new findings can be integrated; the extent to which such findings fit the network tends to support or weaken our faith in them. Good problems are strengthened when they relate to theory.

When choosing or developing theory, be guided by what Yvonna Lincoln, in a speech at the American Educational Research Association convention, called the Coco Chanel principle: "Simple is always elegant, ultimately timeless and usually in fashion. Parsimony is prettier!" When choosing among explanations, choose the simplest that adequately covers the data.

Some Impact in Its Field

Beyond interest and feasibility, the criterion most researchers consider most important is impact. We have already considered one way in which you can have impact on your field, but there are other aspects to consider. Indeed, some persons have considerable difficulty finding a problem because they are not satisfied with what they perceive as the potential impact of the outcomes.

In the context of program evaluation, Cronbach (1982) describes impact with the term *leverage*, but his ideas are relevant to research as well. "Leverage refers to the influence that reducing a particular uncertainty has on decisions" (p. 226); this may be uncertainty about whether the relationship exists or uncertainty about its generality. After the study is completed, "leverage is directly visible in the response of the community to the evidence" (p. 226). A social worker is concerned because the content of in-service training is determined by the supervisor instead of the workers themselves. She does a study to show that the training is more effective when planned and implemented by the workers than by the supervisor. Her intent is that supervisors will be deterred and workers will be empowered in the determination of in-service training. But such an intent ignores the realities of responsibility and administrators' perceptions of their roles and is likely to have little impact—leverage —in changing the situation.

Similarly, a study intended to show increased effectiveness of instruction with smaller classes will have greater impact if the increased cost of schooling is related to the value of what is achieved. But a study that shows that a teacher can be more effective by using certain behaviors may have considerable impact if the cost and difficulty of learning those behaviors are low. Hence impact must be gauged by an accurate understanding of the dynamics of the situation in which change is intended and determination of responses to such questions as, "Why hasn't it changed?" "Would it change in the light of new evidence?" "What would it take to change it?"

Originality and Creativity

A good problem reflects some of the originality and creativity of its author. As Morris Klein says: "I think that in research you want to satisfy your own ego. You want to know you did it before the other fellow." (Rosner and Abt, 1970, p. 99). Yet the hard fact of the matter is that we all stand on each other's shoulders. The competitive spirit provides a useful drive, but it gets in the way when it blinds us to our dependence on others. Graduate students often refuse problems they did not invent in a kind of "second adolescence" in which they want to be independent and show they can do things themselves (Krathwohl, 1988). It helps if they recognize their adolescentlike behavior and gain perspective on the help being offered. Researchers can make problems their own by adding just enough of their own thinking to another's problem to get an "investment" in it.

How much originality is enough? It is impossible to say; the negative extremes are easier to specify. For example, some researchers try so hard to be original that they make their problem overly complex and overlook ways of simplifying. Others seem too ready to accept other researchers' ideas without trying to break the problem apart for themselves. None of us starts from scratch; it is important to find that middle ground and be comfortable with it.

Feasibility

A good problem is feasible if (1) it lends itself to investigation with the instruments and techniques that are either available or can be invented, (2) it is within the capability of the investigator's available or acquirable experience and skills, and (3) it can be accomplished within whatever social, ethical, and resource limits must be observed. As a criterion, feasibility is obviously critical, yet novice investigators, in their zeal, often feel that the only way to have impact is to choose a topic well beyond their capacity in terms of size, complexity, or required skills. This also is part of the "second adolescence" phenomenon—"I can do it, don't tell me I must cut it down, don't demean me in that way!" Such advice to reduce the scope of a study is in no way intended to devalue the person. Indeed, the hope is to keep the person from a position of self-devaluation. But unless the advice is viewed in perspective, it can be perceived incorrectly.

Surely for the novice investigator, the difficulty of doing a project itself is sufficient. Adding the task of developing a new instrument and showing its validity or mastering a new statistical or analytic technique and convincing the audience of its superiority markedly increases the burden. Each of these activities is big enough to be a research project in itself and is better treated as such. Until you have had sufficient experience, combining two such large projects into one should be avoided.

Project difficulty also comes in the form of complexity. To keep the problem within their grasp, researchers frequently shy away from problems perceived as too difficult or complex. The 4-minute mile was a boundary once thought to be beyond the capacity of the human body to exceed. Yet once broken by one man who believed he could do it, it has been exceeded many times. An amazing capacity of the human mind is the extent to which it can be stretched by concentration. There is the mistaken impression that the "greats" can pick up a problem of considerable complexity and work with it at any time. Yet in talking with such people, we realize that this is a myth. At the time of their contribution, they made a significant investment of time and effort and stayed with the problem almost continuously. Raising questions about it later usually requires a period for refamiliarization—sometimes more effort than they are willing to exert, and so they'll say they have moved on to other problems. Thus problems perceived as beyond our grasp may not be, if we are willing to spend the time and effort needed to master them.

Motivation is clearly critical, and it is more likely to be greater if what is required contributes to some later goal as well as the current one. Unfortunately, novices sometimes choose problems requiring skills that have little relevance to the area in which they hope to excel; for example, people-oriented individuals who try to master complicated numeric techniques, electronic equipment, or software programming with little relevance to their future occupation may find their motivation waning.

Social, Ethical, Institutional, and Resource Limitations.   All studies must be done within limits, for example:

- The research time required cannot be tolerated by a busy clinic.
- Leaving the control group without treatment may not be permitted by anxious parents.
- Prying into people's value structures, political affiliations, or sex lives may not be warranted by the value of the information gained in relation to the possible unpleasantness or perceived harm to the subjects.
- The cost to investigate the required number of subjects to do a study well may be beyond the resources of an investigator.

Prime considerations are what an institution will allow, what a community deems appropriate, and what ethical constraints the profession places on research. Codes of ethics in many professions provide guidelines to protect subjects from harm. Every federally supported research project must be approved by a human subjects protection committee that determines if there is the possibility of discomfort or harm and if so, if it is justifiable. Many institutions require approval by this committee even for projects without federal funding. (See chapter 25.) Finally, there are limits on our own time, funds, and energy, which, though somewhat flexible, have boundaries that we must find and observe. So feasibility is important in terms of not being intimidated by apparent limitations yet also acknowledging institutional realities.

Here are some questions to ask yourself about your problem:

- Is it of sufficient interest that I will continue to be motivated through to its completion?
- Is it embedded in theory so that it is part of a network of propositions and explanations?
- Will it have some impact on the field?
- Has it an element of originality and creativity about it?
- Is it feasible in terms of my acquired or acquirable knowledge and skills, as well as being within my social, ethical, institutional, and resource limitations?

Researchable Questions

Be sure your question is researchable; not all questions are. The most common nonresearchable problems are those that show what *ought* to be done—children *ought* to be able to read the classics by the sixth grade, clients *should* be permitted to find their own solutions in therapy, there *should* be a free market in education with the government paying for whatever means of achieving an education pupils and parents choose. Note the italicized words: *ought* and *should*. Nobody can show that something ought to be done. "Ought" or "ought not" involves a value judgment! Research can be helpful by showing the consequences if something were or weren't done. Then somebody else can decide whether those consequences merit saying, "Yes, it *ought* to be done!"

Research can also determine how well such propositions are supported in a given community. It can determine the consequences of a particular course of action such as letting a client or a pupil have the right of choice. It can show what will happen if one tries to have sixth graders read the classics or evaluate a program intended to enable them to do so. All such questions will unearth evidence that may help a decision maker determine an "appropriate" choice, but research cannot directly affirm or deny a value proposition.

> Research can help a decision maker to determine the implications of something that is desirable or desired, but it can never determine what *ought* to be—that is a value judgment.

SUMMARY

Choice of problem is the most important decision a researcher makes. Though some researchers are better at this than others, problem-finding skills can be learned. Discovery favors the prepared mind. Reading actively, reading widely, reading the seminal minds in the field, talking to specialists, challenging assumptions, looking for new ways to tease the problem apart and break the conventional way of looking at it—in short, filling the mind with the grist that allows the unconscious to sort matters out and organize thoughts—all are highly conducive to finding new research ideas. In addition, use techniques to enhance creativity such as those that organize material into suggestive patterns and reduce the censorship of ideas (brainstorming). Formulate the problem as a written statement and/or explain it to someone else. Learn your most productive working conditions. Don't close the problem definition too quickly, and when having trouble focusing, trace your problem back to more basic questions.

A log of your ideas, kept over the years, is often an excellent source of suggestions. Other researchers' data can sometimes be used; they don't necessarily have to be new. New techniques, instruments, and models often suggest possibilities and extensions of past research. Other languages and cultures often hold possibilities that await discovery and development.

Good problems are of enough interest to motivate you to carry them to completion, are typically embedded in theory, are likely to have some impact on the field, have an element of originality or creativity about them, and are feasible. Though feasibility in terms of personal skills often stretches further than you might initially think, the problem must be researchable within the ethical and institutional limits and the resources available. Research cannot affirm or deny a value judgment. It can only show the consequences of that position and the extent of support for or against it, which may be helpful to decision makers in determining policy.

Obviously, one of the most important sources of material to develop a "prepared mind" is the work of others. For this we need library skills, to which we turn in the next chapter.

ADDITIONAL READING

Getzels (1982)   Merton (1959)

APPLICATION PROBLEMS

1. Johnson (1978), drawing on the theories of Carl Jung, theorized that a person's psychological style is defined by how he or she makes decisions. He developed a two-dimensional decision-making scheme based on the way information is gathered (systematically or spontaneously) and on the way data are analyzed; that is, internally (the individual needs to think about it first) or externally (the individual needs to discuss it with someone). From this Johnson surmised that individuals could be classified into four personality types: spontaneous external, spontaneous internal, systematic external, and systematic internal. If you were interested in researching psychological styles, how could you use Johnson's theory to develop a research problem?

2. Assume that you are a graduate student in educational psychology interested in "intelligence." You have read widely on the topic and know that over the years, a number of theories have been advanced about its nature. These include such concepts as Thurstone's seven primary mental abilities; Spearman's g, or general intelligence factor; Guilford's structure of intellect model, and the idea of fluid versus crystallized intelligence championed by Cattell and Horn. To which of these should you look as the potential source of a research problem?

3. A master's student in nursing is interested in the care of brain-injured patients. She has focused on a disorder called unilateral neglect, which leaves a patient unaware of one side of his or her body. The student wishes to investigate the degree to which such patients could carry out ordinary activities of daily living and what the implications of this would be for their nursing care. How might she proceed?

4. A doctoral student in the field of educational technology is working with an adviser who has gained international recognition for his instructional model for selecting and sequencing content. The student has identified a set of motivational strategies to add to the model and is considering their verification in an instructional setting as a dissertation topic. However, the student wonders if this topic is sufficiently original, since she did not develop the original model. What would be your advice to her?

Compare your answers with those on pages 703–704.

SUGGESTED EXERCISE

Beginning with this chapter, it is suggested that you choose a topic or a problem that interests you and use it throughout the rest of the book to gain familiarity with the content of each chapter. This chapter and the next, on the review of the literature, might be combined to help find a topic of particular interest that you may be willing to stay with.

You might try some of the techniques described in this chapter to stimulate your creativity. You might try actively reading some of the references found for your topic, using the material in the next chapter. See whether there is a member of the invisible college in your school or college or whether you can locate one at a nearby institution. Get together with a small group and brainstorm. Have one person in the group play the role of observer to help you reflect on the process and make sure you follow the rules. Have this person summarize progress every 10 minutes or so or when there is a good breaking point, and have her point out any breeches of the rules. Try a morphological analysis. Read extensively and fill your mind with material; then concentrate on something else for a while and see what develops. Even if all this is effective, also try working at your project by yourself, filling a sheet of paper with ideas or whatever comes to mind to keep your mind engaged on the problem. Experimenting with these different approaches will help you learn what works best for you.

By applying the content of this and each succeeding chapter to your topic, you could easily end up with a proposal for a study that has been subjected to analysis from the standpoint of a number of skills of research and has been thought about in relation to various research methods. You'd know which skills were applicable and useful for your project. You'd have compared the potential of the various research methods for it. What could make for a stronger proposal for a research study?

Many students in the two-semester course in which this book was pioneered came out of it with proposals ready to go to their committee for final refinement. It gave them a big start on their doctoral program and helped save them from ABD status. By doing these application exercises and using the suggestions in *How to Prepare a Research Proposal* (Krathwohl, 1988), you can similarly benefit. See especially the two final chapters, which were designed specifically for doctoral students, the next-to-last giving different perspectives on the meaning of the dissertation and the last reviewing the steps involved in doing a dissertation, with suggestions and advice.

Finding Links to Past Research: The Literature Review

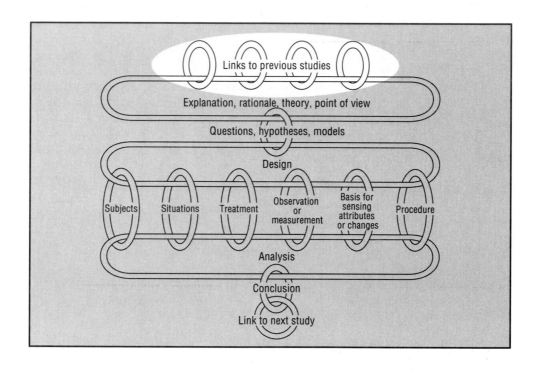

If no use is made of the labors of past ages, the world must remain always in the infancy of knowledge.

Cicero, De Oratore II

One of the diseases of this age is the multiplicity of books; they doth so overcharge the world that it is not able to digest the abundance of idle matter that is every day hatched and brought forth into the world.

Barnaby Rich, 1613 (*As quoted in Derek J. De Solla Price*, Little Science, Big Science)

Le hasard ne favorise que les esprits préparés [chance favors only the prepared mind].

Louis Pasteur

OVERVIEW

Problem formulation is facilitated by the literature review. The problem, as initially formulated, is modified by our reading, which in turn results in further considerations that are checked in the literature, and so it goes until we are satisfied. We have carried problem formulation as far as necessary, profitable, or time allows. The literature search forges the links of the chain of reasoning to past research and helps fashion the problem's rationale. Thus it contributes to building a credible explanation.

The variety of library aids is amazing. You need not learn them all. The key ones and how to use different types of indexes will be the focus of this chapter.

CHAPTER CONTENTS

The Literature Search in Relation to Research Method   97
Goals of the Literature Search   99
Beginning the Search   100
   The Starting Point   101
Understanding Indexes and the Indexing Process   104
   Cataloging Books   105
   Traditional Subject Indexes   105

Keyword Indexes   108
Citation Indexing   111
The Relationship of Starting Points to Problem Development   112
Organizing the Search   114
Computer Searches   115
Meta-analyses   118
General Suggestions   118
Summary   119

THE LITERATURE SEARCH IN RELATION TO RESEARCH METHOD

For most individuals, the literature search is the phase in which they find their research question and formulate the major direction of their study, a very early step in the research process.

We enter the literature search when we have found an area of interest and develop an "orienting question," a hunch that there is something worth pursuing—like a newspaper reporter's "sniff." That question helps to focus our attention, direct us to sources of information, and permit us to determine whether there is indeed something worth delving into.

We come out of the literature search with at least a more definitive notion about the area, its important variables, how they are interrelated, what the good questions are, and what research methods have been used. Sometimes a hypothesis will emerge. Even better, if the literature base is solid enough, we may be able to make a prediction or create an explanatory model of the interrelations of variables. At a minimum, by exploring the literature, we move a long way down the road in the development of our research focus; ideally, at that point we can fully formulate the research problem.

Recognize that research is a creative act. For every statement that most people do it one way, there are those who, for good reason, do it differently. For example, most researchers with an idea of what they want to study proceed to a literature search. Many who use qualitative or inductive methods, however, feel that to consult the literature too early will burden them with other people's perceptions. They don't want to miss what the naive eye might see; after all, we come fresh into a situation only once. They want to do the literature search after they have been exposed to the situation and begun to form their own notions about what is important, how things are related to each other, the general context, and what explanations they can advance. Then, with a very much sharpened notion of what they want to understand, they will go to the literature, ask how others have understood it, and compare that with their own understanding. Such individuals come to the literature search with quite a different background from that of persons just starting to define a problem—which is most of us.

But among qualitative methodologists there are differences about how to proceed. For instance, Wax and Wax (1980) note that reading about the situation one intends to enter "is a mark of respect to the hosts, as it demonstrates that one considers their affairs of sufficient importance to learn whatever one can about them before formal introduction. Preparation is also a mark of respect to the scholars who have studied the community in the past" (p. 6). For people who would argue that this imposes a framework that may alter the view of the situation, Wax and Wax note: "True, when one enters the field, one may be hampered by inaccurate ideas gained from prior studies, [but] the researcher will always be entering with some freight of expectations. It is better that these be grounded in past scholarship" (p. 6). So there are differences of opinion about when to study the literature with the inductive approach; researchers must decide in terms of their own style of working, their problem, and their ability to maintain openness to new perceptions.

For the rest of this chapter, we will assume that researchers are entering the literature search with only an orienting question and will discuss tools and skills that can help. This material will be equally valuable to qualitative researchers who prefer to use it at a later stage in their research. But first, let us be more specific about what the literature search is trying to achieve.

GOALS OF THE LITERATURE SEARCH

The literature search has several goals:

1. To assist in conceptualizing the problem, refining it, and, if necessary, reducing it to feasible size and scope
2. To determine the major variables of importance in the phenomenon
3. To understand the relationships among these variables
4. To find the frontier of research on the problem, how far previous researchers could solidly reach
5. To get suggestions about how to do the study, what previous mistakes to avoid, and what new methods might be effective
6. To substitute shorter, less expensive time doing the literature search for lengthier, more expensive research time rediscovering what is already known
7. To put the conceptualized problem in the context of previous research, showing how the problem relates to it yet goes beyond it

This is a long list of goals, but they indicate how crucial the literature search is to the process. Starting with a simple orienting question does not prepare us for the complexity typically encountered. Consider, for example, the seemingly simple notion of part-whole learning. When learning to swim, is it better to learn the Australian crawl as a whole or to master all the parts—arm strokes, breathing, flutter kick—and then put them together? As we enter the literature, we find that there is more than one part-whole method. For instance, we can alternate practicing a new part and integrating it into the whole, or we can start with a part and then add successive parts until the whole is achieved. The problem has taken on a new complexity. Further, the studies use these methods under different conditions of practice—massed (in a single session or in large, concentrated blocks) or distributed over time. So distribution of practice is a concomitant variable that affects learning strategy; a second complexity has been added.

Thus the literature search shows which facets of the phenomenon are important, helps redefine the problem, suggests the nature of the relationships among the variables—in this case, patterns of practice as well as learning strategy—and, if investigating all the part-whole strategies seems too much, provides the basis for cutting the problem to feasible proportions.

A function of the literature review is to find methods and designs to use as well as to avoid. You become aware of refinements to methods, especially those designed for the problem area. The literature will include instruments and measures that might be useful and may tell something about their validity. Experimental instruments for hard-to-measure characteristics usually appear first in research studies. Valuable ideas for data analysis can be gleaned from others' experiences. Studying distinctions in methods may suggest why study outcomes differ; the phenomenon may be more amenable to exploration with one method than another. But we must also determine whether the method in some way interacts with the phenomenon to potentiate it, or make it stronger. For instance, interviewing teachers about their experiences with a new curriculum might set them to solving problems they might otherwise have ignored. This would limit generality of the findings to similar instances where teachers were stimulated to consider their use of the curriculum.

The literature search shows how far previous research has come in conceptualizing and understanding the phenomena of interest, the research frontier. The frontier is a conceptual one; it is not necessarily represented by the latest studies. It may have been established by earlier work and not have been advanced much by later efforts. We hope to find the research frontier easily, but how difficult it is depends on the depth of previous work. Sometimes the number of studies is overwhelming: Glass, McGaw, and Smith (1981) found over 2,000 studies evaluating psychotherapy. Finding the frontier will also place the intended study in perspective to the work of others. Of particular value is a theory, rationale, or point of view that integrates the area.

We can look at the retrieval of knowledge on a cost-benefit basis. The literature search invests part of our time, energy, and resources in finding the research frontier; the remaining resources may then be used to advance it. Nearly every problem has been worked on by someone earlier. If the sought-after knowledge were known, would its value be greater than the cost of its retrieval? Of course, this is always an estimate, since the actual worth of the knowledge can't really be determined until it is in hand. But it is this estimate that determines how much effort to put into retrieval. The more economically we can find where previous investigators stopped, the more resources are available to "stand on their shoulders" and advance the field to a new level.

Despite the massive increase in publications over the past several decades, new retrieval methods and index types have made access easier.[1] This chapter introduces you to the tools that make retrievability possible.

BEGINNING THE SEARCH

How organized should the search be? Most people just start yanking at a corner of the problem, an aspect of it that interests them, like a loose thread on a sweater, tugging on it to unravel the garment. Often this works; problems can usually be approached from a variety of directions. Anyway, it is difficult to organize a search for something we don't know much about. So before organization there usually comes a period of broad exploration in the literature, of sleuthing, of tracking down leads, and, most important, of being flexible enough to recognize potentially profitable byways and side issues. Sometimes these turn out to be more important than what we set out to pursue. Step back

---

1. Because material is increasingly retrievable, we may find too much to digest, a relatively new phenomenon that we will have to learn to handle. It usually calls for reducing the scope of the problem. But where this is undesirable, it will call either for sampling the literature or, more likely, for judicious selection on the basis of the author's reputation and the relevance of the title.

from time to time to get a perspective on your progress; it helps maintain a balance between just following your nose—our natural inclination—and organizing the search.

Sometimes the panorama of the literature obtained from a computer search provides a perspective. Nearly all libraries have a computer search service, sometimes for a fee. To save on-line charges, librarians trained in search techniques usually do the actual searching using phone lines to enter a mainframe computer with access to the reference works. In doing the search leading up to this, bear in mind that you will have to describe your problem and the literature you seek rather precisely. Usually a preliminary search of references in print form sorts out the most relevant terms to enter into the computer. Describing your problem to the librarian has the advantage, beyond the references you will obtain, of forcing you to formulate it.

Increasingly, however, references are being placed on laser-read disks, CD-ROMs, which allow you to perform the search with a desktop computer linked to a disk reader. Many libraries have *Psychological Abstracts* (called *PsycInfo* in database form), *Sociological Abstracts* (*soclit* in database form), ERIC (Educational Resources Information Center) programs, and other reference works on disks that can be computer-searched. As libraries acquire sufficient equipment and reallocate their budgets, this will likely become the standard way to access commonly used references. Doing your own search helps you adjust your search terms selectively as you reformulate the problem more clearly. Although such searches do require that you know the structure of the database being searched, you can learn this on the CD-ROM without incurring the cost of using a mainframe search service.

Note, however, that only the more recent references are available for computer searching. Depending on when the particular reference started making computer searching available, searches involving older references must still be done from the bound volumes.

The Starting Point

Often the critical problem is knowing where to start. There are books, journals, abstracts of journal articles, indexes, bibliographies, handbooks, and encyclopedias. For long-standing problems, books, encyclopedias, and handbooks will be quite helpful. In them you can find summaries and reviews of the literature that are generally accepted as knowledge, work about which there has been a consensus.

Work that has not yet reached this level is usually included in reviews of research. Some journals are entirely devoted to such reviews, and in addition, there are annual reviews published in book form. Their chapters are organized to provide coverage of an area. A committee of relevant specialists usually puts together the annuals, allocating space to topics according to the importance and extent of recent work. Committee members are chosen who can readily identify the best experts to do the reviews. Reviewers evaluate recent work and place it in context in a way valuable to the novice.

Textbooks, journal review articles, annual review volumes, handbooks, and encyclopedias are all examples of what are termed **secondary sources**. This is in contrast to **primary sources**, which are the original research publications. Secondary sources do not report the original data; they summarize them or merely give the researchers' conclusions. In using this material, the reader is accepting expert opinion instead of judging the research personally. To locate bibliographies in a field, check the card or on-line catalog under the appropriate subject heading; then look for the subheading "Bibliography."

You will want to read the primary source, especially where you have doubts about the conclusions of a review or summary. Except for very large projects or when researchers summarize their own work in a book (as Kounin did in the example in chapter 4), research reports are found in journals. (Large projects are often published as monographs.) You will also consult journal literature to find the most up-to-date work and recently defined problems. The journal literature is accessible through a variety of indexes and abstracting services, with many specialized compilations available for nooks and crannies of subject matter (for example, *Language and Language Behavior Abstracts*, *Physical Education/Sports Index*, *College Student Personnel Abstracts*). Here is a list of selected references, including abstracting and indexing services, to give you some idea of the wide variety of resources available. The list is not intended to be a comprehensive compilation.

General and Targeted Sources of Reference Works

Aby, S. H. (1987). *Sociology: A guide to reference and information sources*. Littleton, Colo.: Libraries Unlimited.

Binger, J. L., and Jensen, L. M. (1980). *Lippincott's guide to nursing literature*. Philadelphia: Lippincott.

Conrad, J. H. (1982). *Reference sources in social work: An annotated bibliography*. Metuchen, N.J.: Scarecrow Press.

Fletcher, J. (Ed.). (1984). *Information sources in economics* (2nd ed.). Stoneham, Mass.: Butterworths.

Freed, R. K., Hess, R. K., and Ryan, J. M. (1989). *The educator's desk reference*. New York: Macmillan.

Holler, F. L. (1986). *Information sources of political science* (4th ed.). Santa Barbara, Calif.: ABC-Clio.

Reed, J., and Baxter, P. M. (1983). *Library use: A handbook for psychology*. Washington, D.C.: American Psychological Association.

Searing, S. E. (1985). *Introduction to library research in women's studies*. Boulder, Colo.: Westview Press.

Webb, W. H., Beals, B. R., and White, A. M. (1986). *Sources of information in the social sciences: A guide to the literature* (3rd ed.). Chicago: American Library Association.

Woodbury, M. (1982). *A guide to sources of educational information*. Washington, D.C.: Information Resources Press.

Woodbury, M. (1985). *Childhood information resources*. Washington, D.C.: Information Resources Press.

Annual Reviews

Annual reviews are published by Annual Reviews, Inc., 4139 El Camino Way, Palo Alto, CA 94306, in anthropology (e.g., *Annual Review of Anthropology*), psychology, and sociology as well as a number of other areas. The company also publishes reviews in some fields of medicine and in the biological and physical sciences.

Review of Research in Education is published annually by the American Educational Research Association.

Many professional associations publish yearbooks that serve the same purpose. For example, the National Society for the Study of Education publishes several yearbooks each year, each providing an examination of a particular topic.

Research Review Journals

American Sociological Review
International Library Review
International Nursing Review
Psychological Review
Reading Research Quarterly
Review of Educational Research
Social Work Review
Sociological Review

Abstracting and Indexing Services

Arts and Humanities Citation Index
Biological Abstracts
Business Periodicals Index
Business Index
Child Development Abstracts and Bibliographies
College Student Personnel Abstracts
Current Contents: Social and Behavioral Sciences
Current Index to Journals in Education (CIJE)
Dissertation Abstracts International (DAI)
Education Index
Educational Administration Abstracts
Government Reports Announcements and Index
Developmental Disabilities Abstracts
Exceptional Child Education Abstracts
Higher Education Abstracts
Index Medicus
Index to U.S. Government Periodicals
Language and Language Behavior Abstracts
Mental Retardation Abstracts
Monthly Catalog of United States Government Publications
Psychological Abstracts (PA)

Public Affairs Information Service (PAIS)
Resources in Education (RIE)
Science Citation Index (SCI)
Social Sciences Citation Index (SSCI)
Social Sciences Index
Sociological Abstracts
UNDOC: Current Index; United Nations Document Index
UNESCO List of Documents and Publications
Women's Studies Abstracts

A general source of information on reference works can be especially valuable not only in helping locate these indexes but also in pointing out the wide variety of handbooks, bibliographies, review sources, and other access points. The most general of these, and the one used by general reference librarians, is Sheehy's *Guide to Reference Books* (1986; often referred to as "Winchell" for its original author). It has sections on general reference works, the humanities, social sciences, history and area studies, and pure and applied sciences. In its subsection on bibliographies, among 14 entries, is "Bibliography Index," which is a bibliography of bibliographies arranged by subject. Sheehy's subsection on social science is divided in much the same way as the social sciences department of a typical university and contains annotations on a wide variety of reference works. Another general reference is Hillard's *Where to Find What* (1984).

There are probably targeted reference works in your area of interest. For example, Webb, Beals, and White's *Sources of Information in the Social Sciences* (1986) is a general guide to the social sciences; the quality and the datedness of its chapters vary. Two especially excellent sources are Woodbury's *Guide to Sources of Educational Information* (1982) and Reed and Baxter's *Library Use: A Handbook for Psychology* (1983). Woodbury is especially comprehensive, and since education is a broad topic, she includes information sources in nearly all the social sciences. Her abstracts of the wide variety of reference sources help readers choose the ones most appropriate for a given search. Reed and Baxter is excellent for psychology and covers the widest boundaries of that field as well. It provides detailed information on how to access such commonly used reference works as *Psychological Abstracts, Sociological Abstracts*, and the *Social Sciences Citation Index*. Freed, Hess, and Ryan's (1989) third chapter, which lists nearly 200 "Where do I go to find . . ." questions with answers, is a gem for education queries.

UNDERSTANDING INDEXES AND THE INDEXING PROCESS

Library searches are one big game of "hide and seek": the cataloger or indexer hides, and you seek! Where did the cataloger place the material that you want? Part of the problem stems from the imprecision with which we use words and the variety of different terms used for the same or similar phenomena. Another part is that the searchers don't understand how the indexer works, how the index was put together, and what it was intended to do. The former we can't remedy; the latter we can by understanding indexes and the indexing process.

Cataloging Books

Assume that you are a cataloger and that the Zimbardo article is a book to which you must assign a Library of Congress catalog number to place it on a library shelf. Since a book copy can be in only one place, you may have only one number to describe it. Where would you put it? Under "Paranoia"? "Elderly"? "Deafness"? "Hypnosis"? Probably under "Paranoia," since that is the main subject it concerns. You would turn to the Library of Congress *Subject Headings* volumes, look up *paranoia*, and assign to the book the number that accompanies the paranoia entry, RC 520.

Have you ever been in a science museum's monochromatic light room? It is a room illuminated by only a single color from the spectrum instead of white light, which contains all the colors. Usually it is a yellow light, and all clothing that doesn't contain some yellow looks a nondescript black! Folks dressed in yellow can be described beautifully, but nobody else! That is comparable to what the cataloger is trying to do, to get the right number (light color) so that the item is "described beautifully." To be so described, the illuminating light's color (the subject descriptor) must match the dominant hue (subject matter) of the item. If you are a shelf browser like me, you'll appreciate a good cataloger who lets you find the books on a topic all in one place; you need only find the Zimbardo "book" to have access to other books on paranoia. But to find books in which paranoia is not the main topic, you'll need to discover where these books might be shelved. That is where subject indexing comes in. Books may have only one place on the shelves, but they can have numerous entries in the catalog.

Traditional Subject Indexes

Instead of having only one color to shine on the item, the cataloger can use different colors to illuminate each important facet. The library catalog card or on-line entry contains subject descriptors in addition to the subject classification of the call number. These are equivalent to multiple index entries. There will be at least two such entries, one for the author and one for the title. But there will usually be other descriptive entries as well. To return to our Zimbardo example, the other terms mentioned—*elderly*, *deafness*, and *hypnosis*—might all be subject descriptors.

There are two quite different kinds of subject indexes, however. Traditional subject indexes are like those at the back of this book. Keyword indexes are a product of the computer age and, for certain purposes, have advantages over traditional subject indexing but also some concomitant disadvantages for other searches. We will examine them both, traditional indexes first.

Although the usual subject index resembles a book index, there is one important difference. The indexer for a book can use whatever terms are unique to it and adjust the entries to fit the vocabulary of the author. If an indexer of *Psychological Abstracts* were to use a particular set of terms one year and then adjust them to fit the terms used the next year, we would have a very difficult time searching across years. We would have to learn new search terms with every volume. Of course, index terms do change with time; they have to. But index terms change slowly. When a topic like "computerized instruction" comes along, we have to find under what topic indexers buried it until, convinced that it was not a "flash in the pan," they accorded it a heading of its own. Although within an index there is every attempt to maintain consistency in the way terms are used, there is little consistency from one service to another.[2] Therefore, to some extent, we must learn each reference's indexing system and the way specific terms are used within it.

Controlled Vocabulary Indexing.   To return to our color analogy, if we use a tremendous variety of color names in our efforts to describe an item precisely, we will use relatively rare terms like *mauve* and *puce*. Such names, like new technical jargon, make searches difficult for anyone not "in the know." All indexers try to maintain stability in indexing terms from year to year by having at least an in-house **controlled vocabulary**. Some publish them, which means that users have access to the thinking and decisions of indexers and can use congruent terms. For book classification, the *Subject Headings, U.S. Library of Congress* (1986) is such a set. Psychological terms in the *Dictionary of Psychological Terms* provide access to *Psychological Abstracts*. Education terms found in the *Thesaurus of ERIC Descriptors* are the list of ERIC's indexing terms for access to *Resources in Education* and *Current Index to Journals in Education*. Use *Medical Subject Headings* (MeSH) for access to *Index Medicus*. Consulting these thesauri or dictionaries to find where indexers have "hidden" terms is like getting an aerial view of a maze. It can save considerable time over entering the maze and trying to find our way on a trial-and-error basis through all its blind alleys.

The use of the analogy "getting an aerial view of a maze" is intentional. Such schemes constitute a conceptual map of the field they cover. Typically, this is a hierarchical structure that starts with a set of main headings that divide the field and then subdivides these to take account of the specialties that develop within them. We might call this conceptually based indexing because it is based on a conceptualization of the fields of knowledge and how they are interrelated. (This is truer of academically oriented services than public library–oriented ones, which simply follow the literature like the Wilson publications: *Readers' Guide to Periodical Literature, Education Index,* and *Social Science Index*, or the *Public Affairs Information Service*.)

Conceptual schemes tend to reflect the view of the field when they were developed. *Sociological Abstracts*, for instance, appends the new fields of knowledge to the end of the original scheme instead of either including them in the old one or devising a new one to organize all of them. The Library of

---

2. Look for Atkins and Ostrow's *Cross-reference Index* (1989). It indicates the terms for a topic used in different indexing and abstracting services. These may suggest additional terms to search.

Congress and the Dewey Decimal System were developed in the 1800s. We can see in them the original conceptualization of psychology as a branch of philosophy since the two are juxtaposed in those structures. Conceptually based indexing is still a major indexing approach.

Because indexers feel constrained by these controlled vocabularies, both *Psychological Abstracts* and *Sociological Abstracts* have appended descriptors to their abstracts that do not appear in their dictionaries, though in the former these appear in the computer-searchable version known as *PsycInfo*. ERIC has done the same thing with what it calls "identifiers," words that are not yet in its published scheme or are proper nouns. Such terms tend to be part of an in-house "authority list" of words that will be considered for inclusion in the next edition of the published vocabulary list.

Aids to Finding the Appropriate Index Heading. We have already cited dictionaries and thesauri as aids to finding the appropriate index heading where the index uses published controlled vocabulary. Looking at the headings will help to establish the general location of the terms you want. In addition, these publications include devices to assist you in finding the correct term; cross-reference lists are an example. The left-hand column in Figure 7.1 carries the entry "Day care services," taken from the ERIC thesaurus to show some of the **cross-references**. The right-hand column explains the entries.

Such displays not only facilitate access to the index but also help define the terms used in it. Most thesauri display the indexing terms used in different ways to enable selection of the most precise descriptors. Some, for example, use a "rotated display." Rotated-descriptor displays list all controlled vocabulary terms in the middle of a column with modifiers on either side, like the display in Figure 7.2. Unless otherwise noted, all terms are part of the controlled vocabulary and may be searched.

Although it is intended that the same terms always be used the same way, this does not always occur. The literature for tailored testing, for

Day care services	The bold type indicates that this is an index term.
UF Day care centers	UF stands for "used for" and indicates that the index term "day care services" is used in place of "day care centers," which is not an indexing term.
NT Family day care	NT stands for "narrower term" and indicates that "family day care" is a more specific index term that could be looked up as well.
BT Human services	BT stands for "broader term" and indicates that "human services" is a less specific index term that could contain relevant material.

RT Attendant trainer
   Child care
   Child rearing
   Day camp programs
   Nursery school
   Preschool children
	RT stands for "related terms," and the list indicates index terms that are related to "day care services" and so also might contain relevant material.

FIGURE 7.1 Cross-references in a sample thesaurus of ERIC descriptors display

American Indians
Nonreservation American Indians
American Literature
Spanish American Literature
American Studies
African American Studies

FIGURE 7.2   A sample rotated-descriptor display

example, appears early under "Psychometric methods" and later under "Testing." Particularly when searching terms for which there is no clear reference, if articles stop appearing or diminish markedly after a given year, a check of other relevant headings should be instituted.

Many indexes control their vocabulary but do not publish their index terms. In those instances, you must try looking up relevant headings. For such displays, indexers will follow terms that are not used in indexing with "see" references to terms that are used. This is comparable to UF ("used for") in the ERIC system. You may also encounter "see also" references, which will be either broader, narrower, or related terms.

An additional source of help is the *Cross-reference Index* (Atkins and Ostrow, 1989). This is a compilation of 42,000 subject headings used by eight major reference sources. Its tabular arrangement of headings permits you to find both the terms and the indexes in which they appear. It is particularly helpful in suggesting alternative headings. For example, it suggests that "Battered child" may be found under "Cruelty to children"; for "Educational technology," look under "Teaching aids and devices" or "Educational aids and devices." Using these sources not only helps define your body of literature and the themes in it but also helps conceptualize your problem and prepare for a computer search. For some problems, the capacity to search terms not in an index is essential; this can be done with a computer search, discussed later in this chapter.

Keyword Indexes

You might think of conceptual subject indexing as a top-down approach, one that fits the convenience of the indexer and professionals who have a conceptual map of the field. But that map may not be the one an author or a researcher has in mind. Indeed, user maps change as the emphases in a field change, especially as new topics appear and become important. Hence the second point of view is a bottom-up approach that starts with the user's orientation.

Keyword indexing takes the point of view that authors know best how terminology is being used. Under the oversight of editors who have comprehensive perspectives of their fields, authors will title their articles using new distinctions and new terms as appropriate. This avoids the inconsistencies and errors of human indexers, who are probably not as familiar with the area as the researchers. The computer age is ideally suited to this point of view because an index can be constructed from titles. The only major references employing such a scheme are the citation indexes: *Science Citation Index, Arts and Humanities Citation Index*, and *Social Sciences Citation Index* (SSCI). **Permuterm indexing** (see Figure 7.3) of all the citation indexes involves combining all the major terms of a journal title in word pairs and displaying them in every possible combination. This provides many access points for an article, 16 on average. The analysis of word pairs is also likely to suggest other terms that the searcher can use to continue the search. The Permuterm index contains references only to journal articles. (References in the citation indexes themselves include anything an article cites, including books, reviews, and movies.)

The example in Figure 7.3 shows the term *aging*. We are first referred from an alternate spelling (*ageing*) to the spelling used in SSCI, *aging*, which happens alphabetically to follow immediately; this is convenient for the example, but an alternate spelling won't always be next. Alternative terms following the term *aging* should also be considered. These are like ERIC's "related terms" and the "see also" references of most conventional indexes; indeed, they are designated with the initials *sa*, for "see also."

The first Permuterm entry is for the pair *aging, accelerated* where *aging* is the primary term and *accelerated* is the co-term; apparently the title of an article by "A. Wilkinso" contains those two words. (Computer-based indexes must often truncate names and words to fit the computer space allocated. "Wilkinso" is probably Wilkinson.) The pair will also appear in the Permuterm index with *accelerated* as the primary term and *aging* as the co-term. Some terms are not used as primary-term entries; *ahead* is such a term in the example. Such terms appear only as co-terms because they are unlikely to be consulted; we wouldn't typically look up *ahead* in an index.

The arrowhead indicates that this is the first time that this article appears under the term *aging*. Note that "Wilkinso, A" also appears under *aging, society* (we now know three words in the title). If we were interested in all the articles under *aging*, we would skip the articles without arrowheads, because these are repeats of earlier ones in the list. Having found an entry of possible interest, we consult SSCI's source index to find its complete title and location. We can probably tell from the title whether the article is relevant, but the source index also gives the references cited in the article as an additional check on relevance.

SSCI's Permuterm index is particularly useful in searching up-to-date terminology. For example, "tailored testing" is a new kind of test in which the next item given to a testee is determined by how well he or she did on the previous one. *Tailored testing* will take years to appear in controlled vocabulary indexes like *Psychological Abstracts*, if indeed it ever does, because the examinations are also called "adaptive tests." In fact, the latter is the heading *Psychological Abstracts* chose, apparently considering it the more standard terminology. However, should the article "Computerized Tailored Testing in England" be published, *tailored testing* will appear immediately in the Permuterm index. (Indeed, Wood used the terms in his title "Efficacy of Tailored Testing" as early as 1969.) This title will be referenced six times under all the possible pairs of major terms: *computerized tailored, computerized testing, computerized England, tailored testing, tailored England*, and *testing England*. Although the Permuterm

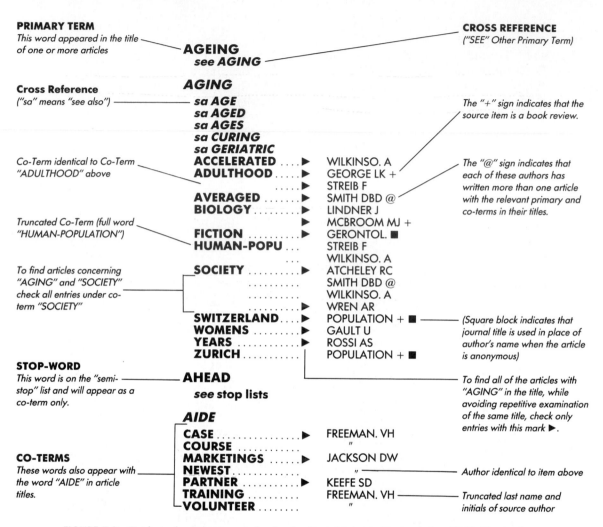

FIGURE 7.3   Guide to the Permuterm index for the *Social Science Citation Index (SSCI)*. (Copyright ©
Institute for Scientific Information. Used by permission. Permuterm is a registered trademark of the
Institute for Scientific Information, Inc.)

pair of words *tailored England* may give entirely the wrong impression to
someone interested in clothing, one of the other pairs will capture its colloquial
use in testing.

Note, however, that if you are interested in computerized testing, you
must consider the various possible variations such a subject might take. It
might be simply *computer*, as in *computer-controlled* or *computerization*. These
would be found near *computerized* and would be easy to check. But the indexer
might also use synonyms such as *automated, on-line, customized, adaptive,* or
tailored. These may show up with ''see also'' references if the indexer is
competent, but if not, you will have to think them up yourself. Use of the

Permuterm index assumes that authors will put the keywords descriptive of their study in the title, not use "cute" nondescriptive titles like "Guess What Comes Next?"

The Permuterm subject index is particularly useful in finding contemporary literature described in jargon or colloquial terms. Further, it will find articles in journals where you might not normally look because each of the citation indexes covers an extremely wide range of journals numbering into the thousands. By the same token, in looking at past indexes, you must know the vernacular of that time period to use the Permuterm index successfully.

CITATION INDEXING

Citation indexing, a product of the computer age, is by far the best way to locate works that have built on and extended a previous research report, as it will identify all published studies that cited that article. Similarly, if we know of an article that is directly on the topic of interest, it can also be used as the basis of a tightly targeted subject search finding others that cited it or its relevant references. (Note that such a search would miss uncited creative outsiders. A less tightly targeted subject search might catch them but involve considerable screening—it's a trade-off.) Whereas research reviews trace work backward, citation indexing allows us to trace it forward (and backward as well!). The *Social Sciences Citation Index*, the *Arts and Humanities Citation Index*, and the *Science Citation Index* all cover the journal literature.

These services enter all references from each published article into a computer and sort them into an alphabetical index by author referred to and title. Therefore, all the references that included a particular article in their reference lists are listed together in the citation index. Thus if we would like to follow references to an article, a book, a book review—anything that might appear in a journal article's list of references—citation indexing will let us do it.

Returning to the Zimbardo article illustration of chapter 2, all the references in the section "References and notes" at the end of the article would be put in the computer (the note comments would be discarded). Hoffmann-Riem separated notes from references at the end of her article; each item in her "References" section, from "Arbeitsgruppe Bielefelder Soziologen" to "Tyrell, H.," would be entered. These would then be sorted by author, along with all the other references picked up from the over 2,000 journals covered by SSCI. Then all the articles that used the "Arbeitsgruppe" article would be listed in the citation index, Hoffmann-Riem's among them. This gives a listing of all the authors who cited the "Arbeitsgruppe" article. That is, it lists all the authors, including Hoffmann-Riem, who used the material of the "Arbeitsgruppe" article in some way during the period the index covered. Maybe they fit it into their theory, used its findings, copied its methods; we would have to consult the articles to know.

How is this useful? Suppose we want to know who is working on tailored testing and has built on Weiss and Davison's early discussion of the subject,

Test Theory and Method (1981). We find in the SSCI citation index all journal articles in any given year that included that reference in their list. Suppose we find that in 1988, K. Johnson cited it in an article in *Educational and Psychological Measurement*. To make sure that the reference to Weiss and Davison is central to Johnson's article, we can use SSCI's source index to find the title of Johnson's article (the citation index gives only author, journal title, volume, and beginning page number). If we are still in doubt, the source index gives Johnson's complete reference list. If we have learned the literature of the area, we will be able to tell something about the article from those citations. Citation indexing uniquely permits us to trace work forward in time and, if we wish, to construct a tree of who followed up whose work and how the area grew.

More important, having found a good research study reference in our problem area, we can find out who has published work based on it and trace the development of that work to the currently published research frontier! Further, we can see the branches that stem from it, the alternative formulations and applications that differ from the original as we trace forward.

There are useful and interesting outgrowths of citation indexing. One is that we can identify the seminal and basic articles in the field by noting which are most heavily cited. We can determine the premier journals from tables prepared by the publishers of SSCI. These tables indicate how often each journal is cited, in which publications a journal is most often cited, and how long a journal's articles are typically cited (an article's average "half-life"). By seeing which journals typically cite which others, we can identify a "family" of core journals.

THE RELATIONSHIP OF STARTING POINTS
TO PROBLEM DEVELOPMENT

Table 7.1 suggests different starting points, depending on where we are in the conceptualization of a problem. Most of the content of this table has been covered, but some items in the last entry need some explanation. The Institute for Scientific Information (ISI), which prepares the citation and Permuterm indexes, produces a weekly spinoff publication, *Current Contents*. It is an excellent way to find the contents of the current journal literature in that it reproduces the tables of contents of the major journals in each field. For example, *Current Contents: Social and Behavioral Sciences* has sections for political science, sociology, psychology, education, special education, and so on. We can quickly scan the tables of contents of relevant journals in each area to find what is going on. There is also a keyword index for each issue.[3] Another ISI product, the *Index to Social Science and Humanities Proceedings*, indexes con-

---

3. Be sure to look at the front matter in each issue, which includes comments by the author of a heavily cited reference (a "citation classic"), a summary of current public comment regarding the social sciences, abstracts of new books, and an always interesting column by Eugene Garfield, founder of the company.

TABLE 7.1 Entry Points in the Literature Search

Entry Point	Purpose	Sources to Consult
A general problem area	To find the important sources of information in an area—encyclopedias, handbooks, reviews of research, etc.	■ General guides to reference books such as Sheehy's *Guide to Reference Books* (1986) ■ Reference guides specific to a field like Woodbury (1982), Brewer (1978), or Reed and Baxter (1983) ■ For computer searching, a guide such as *Directory of Online Databases* (Hall, 1986; also Gale Research Company, 1983; Lengenfelder, 1988)
A specific problem area	To learn what research has been done, what terminology is being used, where the frontier is, what keywords to pursue in journal literature	■ A library's subject index or on-line catalog for relevant bibliographies and books ■ Compilations such as handbooks (*Handbook of Experimental Psychology, Handbook of Social Psychology,* etc.) and research reviews (*Annual Review of Anthropology, Annual Review of Psychology, Annual Review of Sociology;* quarterly *Review of Educational Research;* annual *Review of Research in Education*); *Encyclopedia of Educational Research*
A specific problem	To find recent research, learn how terminology is changing, identify new fields related to the problem, explore current methodological approaches, determine the current frontier; to identify the major aspects of a topic and the prolific writers in the area	■ Appropriate indexes and abstracting services, such as *Psychological Abstracts* and *Sociological Abstracts;* ERIC and its *Current Index to Journals in Education* (CIJE) and *Resources in Education* (RIE); *Education Index; Dissertation Abstracts International;* Permuterm index of the *Social Sciences Citation Index*
A research study basic to the problem	To find out what scholars followed up on this research and what they did with it; to find the most cited authors in an area of work and the basic references to which other authors in the field refer; to trace the historical development of an area by tracing back to who was cited first in an area, who cited this work, who in turn cited that work, and so on	■ Citation index of the *Social Science Citation Index*
Latest terminology for a problem or the names of persons who are doing extensive work in an area	To locate the most recent work in an area, including ongoing work	■ For latest published work, consult *Current Contents: Social and Behavioral Science*

TABLE 7.1   *continued*

Entry Point	Purpose	Sources to Consult
		■ For ongoing research, write to the Smithsonian Science Information Exchange* or directly to researchers who have been working in the area ■ Electronic bulletin boards have been established in a number of areas to facilitate communication among researchers ■ Attend conventions and conferences for the latest papers and talk with the people doing the research; locate members of the "invisible college"

*1730 M Street NW, Room 300, Washington, DC 20036.

vention papers and proceedings on a quarterly basis. ERIC is the best source of papers given at education conventions.

The Smithsonian Science Information Exchange keeps a roster of research projects funded by the federal government and by large foundations. Its lists of ongoing research in popular areas are available for a reasonable fee. Some government agencies also have lists of their projects available. Together with attendance at conventions and meetings, these make it possible to keep abreast of ongoing research.

Why would you want to? Isn't it enough to read the journal literature? It depends on how rapidly your field is moving. In a study of communication in the social sciences, Garvey, Lin, and Nelson (1970) found that the average research project took almost $2\frac{1}{2}$ years to get published, 3 if it was sent back by the editor for corrections. That is a significant lag, and since it is an average, around half take longer. Garvey and colleagues found that because of this lag, researchers tend to establish the so-called invisible colleges mentioned in chapter 4 in the account of the Kounin article. Finding persons who are part of the invisible college is a particularly good way of keeping abreast of what is happening. This is easier still if there is an electronic bulletin board in your area, since with a computer you can tap into the board and learn the who and what of an area. Members of the invisible college will know if such a board is operating in their area. Posting a request for references targeted to your problem on such a board is a superb way to get expert help; the human mind is still the best retrieval system.

ORGANIZING THE SEARCH

There comes a point in the process where you need to stop, get some perspective on what you have done, and carry out an organized search from that point on. That point may come earlier than you anticipate, but the only way to know is to take a few minutes every so often to reflect on what you have done—consider where you are going and estimate how much more is required in order to learn the dimensions and nature of the sought-for body of literature. You will intuitively sense when the organization point comes. There is some comfortableness with what you have learned, findings begin to repeat, and your expectations that there may still be surprises in store have dimmed. At that point, just as we define the sample in a sampling problem, you "draw a string" around the sought-for body of literature and plan the future reference acquisition pattern, deciding whether, taken as a whole, the body of literature is small enough to assemble in its entirety; whether you must sample it; whether you will encompass certain parts entirely and sample the rest (the usual pattern, with the focus heavily covered and the peripheral topics sampled); or whether some other reference acquisition pattern makes sense.

If you haven't used thesauri or dictionaries before, consult them to be sure you have found the boundaries. You may want to do a computer search, if not done before. Both activities, however, are much more useful earlier than as cleanup activities.

COMPUTER SEARCHES

We have already commented on the usefulness of computer searches in certain instances such as when we are looking for a topic not well covered by printed indexes. Such searches became possible when most indexes began to be typeset by computer. This produced a magnetic record, called a database, that could be used for searching as well as typesetting. The variety of computer-accessible indexes has continued to grow. Those available are cataloged in Hall (1986), Gale Research Company (1983–), and Lengenfelder (1988). Increasingly, as noted earlier, these magnetic records are being transferred to laser-read disks so that searching with a desktop computer is possible.

A **computer search** is valuable because, in a microsecond, the computer can read the text of the abstract as well as the title and all other words in the record, such as the identifiers not in the controlled indexing vocabulary. *Thus every term in an abstract can be an indexing term.* Reviewing all the abstracts over many years would be utterly impossible for a human being but is easy for a computer.

Cooper (1985), in a study of the sources used by professional reviewers, found that their use of computer searches yielded the most references and, short of using the references from previous reviews of the area, they yielded references with the greatest centrality and significance. A computer search can be a valuable adjunct to a hand search, and this is especially true where the topic is one that is not easily located through the usual descriptors and indexing terms. That is one of several advantages of computer searches. Computer searches are especially appropriate in the following circumstances:

1. Where an aspect of an article is not prominent enough to include in the title or is unlikely to warrant an index entry but would probably appear in the

abstract. For example, we can search for methodological details (stratified samples or statistical or research methods such as analysis of variance) or instruments or measures (*Stanford Achievement Tests, Minnesota Multiphasic Personality Inventory*). This also allows the searcher to look for all forms of a word by using a truncated term like *psych+*. This would include in the search *psychology, psychiatry, psychological,* and other forms of the term. (The capability to search abstracts is a function of the search software rather than the database itself; find software that allows searching of abstracts.)

2. Where we wish to find references best identified by a combination of two or more descriptors or index terms. Again, this is a difficult task for a human being because we must match the references common to two index entries, but it is simple for a computer.

3. Where a search over a period of years must be pursued in individual volumes instead of in cumulations of years.

4. Where we wish to copy abstracts and the number is too large for machine copying.

5. Where a hand search might be constricted due to time or energy problems. It is so easy to conduct a wider search that a computer search may enlarge our horizons.

6. Where a topic is too new to have a descriptor but may be mentioned by a key phrase or term in a title or an abstract.

7. Where we seek a particular title or the work of a specific author but do not have information on the journal or date of publication. (Remember, however, that printed indexes generally extend back further in time.)

In a computer search, each word of an abstract or index entry is matched against the descriptor you have chosen; entries where there is a match are selected; and the number of such entries is indicated. You can then look at a sample of these entries to see if possible relevant ones are among them. Often looking at the indexing terms assigned to relevant entries suggests additional searches. If you have two or more descriptors, the computer searches for each one. For example, suppose you were examining the effect of inflation on education during recessions. You would look for matches to *inflation* (there are 3,605 entries), *recession* (605 entries), and *education* (20,466 entries). Since you are interested in articles that include all three, you ask for entries described by all three descriptors; this reduces the number to 121 entries. Figure 7.4 illustrates the process. If that is more entries than you wish to examine, you can use a fourth descriptor, such as articles in the past five years, to cut the number further. If you were interested only in the effect on the nonpublic sector of education, you might add "not public" to the descriptor list, and that would cut the number of education entries.

One of the problems, as can perhaps be sensed from Figure 7.4, is finding the right-sized pool of relevant items. A broad search may be very inclusive but may yield too many references to screen. A very precise specification of what you want may miss relevant items that were not quite described by the search terms. Typically, we want to search just beyond the immediate boundaries of the target area, so as to include all the relevant entries but not too many

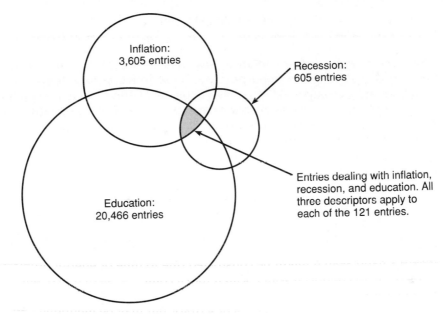

FIGURE 7.4   A sample computer search shown in graphic terms.

irrelevant ones. Finding that "just right" set of search terms is a matter partly of knowing the indexing terms of the database and partly of skill in using preliminary searches to adjust the final set of terms used in the search.

Unless references are listed together by year on the computer printout, you may not notice a change in the use of a descriptor for a certain period of time. Usually references are printed out alphabetically by author, so it is difficult to determine whether there is a break in the number found each year. Either requesting a year-by-year printout or tallying the number per year may help to determine changes in search term usage.

If you cannot use a desktop computer and must pay the full cost of a mainframe search, searching by computer can be expensive. Often you can find a library or a government-supported agency that partly or fully subsidizes such searches. It is also possible for individuals to access index and abstracting services from their own microcomputers at a reduced evening rate or to get a student rate for the Bibliographic Retrieval Service or Dialog.[4] A variety of such services are available to individuals through vendors such as CompuServe and Knowledge Index. Downloading the search in order to eliminate irrelevant entries with a word processor hastens getting the set you want.

---

4. For "BRS/After Dark," contact Bibliographic Retrieval Services, Inc., 1200 Route 7, Latham, NY 12110, or phone (800) 345-4277. Reach Dialog at 3040 Hillview Avenue, Palo Alto, CA 94304, or phone (800) DDIALOG.

META-ANALYSES

We have been considering literature searches in which the summary and analysis of the literature is done purely in descriptive verbal terms. Increasingly, these are accompanied or replaced by what have been termed meta-analyses, in which the results of studies are summarized in quantitative terms. This process will be described in chapter 21; the statistical techniques used will be covered in the intervening chapters.

GENERAL SUGGESTIONS

Perhaps the most important suggestion concerns writing the literature review. Too often the literature review aims at comprehensiveness instead of being selective of the best articles that bear on the topic. Too often previous work is merely cited instead of being related to the problem with an explanation of its contribution. Authors are prone to accept the methods of others uncritically rather than employing and demonstrating their own expertise by being appropriately critical or laudatory of aspects that deserve comment. They provide a loose collection of citations and miscellaneous facts that shows coverage but little understanding.

Aim for a coherent, integrated, critical examination of selected relevant literature! If possible, relate the problem to the network of theory and explanations already existing in the field. Show how this study fits with and "stands on the shoulders" of previous work.

In addition, keep these suggestions in mind:

1. Don't do too hurried a job. Take some time at the beginning to get the feel of the topic, and take time to organize the search when it feels right to do so.
2. Be selective in "following your nose"; do not check everything.
3. Read some primary sources, not just secondary ones, and do not depend on just one secondary source; read several.
4. Find the seminal sources, deep thinkers who really grasp the field.
5. Read in depth both forward to the cutting edge and backward in time.
6. Look for technical and design flaws to avoid.
7. Look for innovations you may use.
8. Use a thesaurus or a search term dictionary, if one is available. It forces you to think your search strategy through, avoiding trial and error. It teaches the standardized terminology of the field and sharpens your questions.
9. Notice how publications highly relevant to your topic are indexed and what descriptors are used. This gives good clues to how professional indexers would describe your problem and provides a list of terms to search.
10. Record enough data to find each reference again (5-by-7-inch cards are

good); be accurate. Better still, record the entry immediately in whatever bibliographic style you plan to use; you'll know you have all the required information.

11. When using a copying machine, be sure to label pages with the source when it is not in the heading or footer. This is especially important for preparing your set of references or for using interlibrary loans.

12. Do a search of the references in print before a computer search in order to understand how the indexers employ the terms and which are most relevant and productive.

13. Do a computer search of the journal literature, especially if your topic is not covered well by the indexing terms, if you are otherwise pressed for time, or if you want to do as complete a job as possible.

14. Remember to check sources of current information if others are likely to be currently working on your problem (SSCI's Permuterm index, *Current Contents*, Smithsonian Science Information Exchange). Check the subject indexes of the programs of recent relevant professional association meetings.

15. Actively think about, argue with, praise, and otherwise react to your reading.

16. Look for give-and-take exchanges that comment on earlier articles; such exchanges sharpen issues and often draw subtle distinctions, leading to new insights and understandings.

17. Discuss your search with the most informed expert in the field accessible to you. Nothing beats an informed mind for on-target information retrieval.

SUMMARY

Table 7.1, when combined with the general suggestions just given, provides about as good a summary of the chapter as could be written. We've noted that we may need to sample the literature; this is but one example of the ubiquitousness of the concept of sampling throughout resarch. Clearly, the principles of sampling are important, so they are discussed next, in chapter 8.

ADDITIONAL READING

Freed, Hess, and Ryan (1989)   Woodbury (1982)
Reed and Baxter (1983)

IMPORTANT TERMS

Citation indexing   Controlled vocabulary
Computer search   Cross-references

Keyword indexing

Permuterm indexing

Primary sources

Secondary sources

APPLICATION PROBLEMS

1. You are beginning an examination of how instruction in learning strategies will affect the achievement of high school students in history. You are seeking an overview of research on learning strategies and key authors in this area. Where might you start both to better define the research questions and to answer these questions?

2. A colleague has referred to articles by Wittrock and Jonassen on your topic of generative strategies in learning. How might you go about finding more on the topic and explore the work of these researchers?

3. You are studying the use of the new whole language approach in elementary basal readers. How might a computer search

make this review of the literature easier to complete?

4. Designing instruction to accommodate different learning styles has gained attention in recent years. How might you sample recent research in the field to determine where the field of learning style-based instruction has come from and is going?

5. A project to teach adults the use of computers is being developed in the local school district. You are going to be studying how effective the method of instruction to be used is with these learners. Why might you do a literature review first? Why not?

Compare your answers with those on pages 704–705.

SUGGESTED EXERCISE

Continuing the exercise begun in chapter 6, take the topic with which you began, and using Table 7.1, choose the most relevant entry point. In order to gain familiarity with the reference works at "high" and "low" entry points, perhaps choose more than one, pretending that you know more or less than you do. Consult the sources listed on pages 102–104. Be sure to include the use of such

references as a citation index, *Current Contents in the Social and Behavioral Sciences*, and at least one journal index or abstract source such as *Psychological Abstracts*, and do a computer search, if possible, on a CD-ROM. As you work, consult the general suggestions at the end of the chapter from time to time.

Sampling and Representation

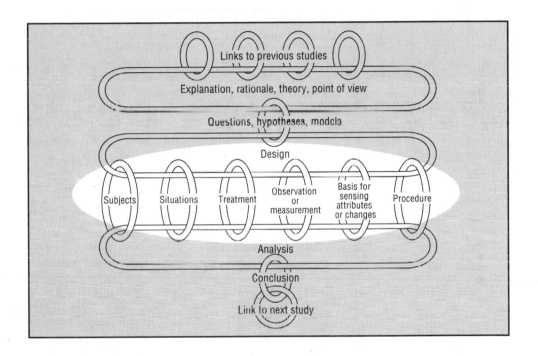

OVERVIEW

Sampling is ubiquitous throughout the chain of reasoning. Surely it is of concern in the selection of a sample of subjects. But wherever we use a subset to represent the larger whole, there is a concern with sampling. In the chain of reasoning, this is true of situation, measures, treatment, and the design of the study itself. If these choices in a study are not representative of a larger totality, the generality of the findings is limited or lacking.

This chapter describes the general principles of sampling and shows how they are used.

CHAPTER CONTENTS

Introduction   122
Principles of Sampling   123
Probability and Nonprobability
    Sampling   126
Probability Sampling Procedures   127
    Simple Random Sampling   127
    Stratified Sampling   130
    Advantages and Disadvantages
        of Simple Random and
        Stratified Sampling   132
    Systematic Sampling   133

Cluster Sampling   134
Nonprobability Sampling   136
    Judgmental and Purposive
        Sampling   137
    Quota Sampling   138
Other Sampling Procedures   139
    Snowball, or Chain Referral,
        Sampling   139
    Sequential Sampling   139
Generality and Population Definition   140
Summary   142

INTRODUCTION

The importance of any inquiry lies in its usefulness in informing us about our world. In some studies, mainly historical ones, the particular individuals involved have a unique importance in that world: a study of the U.S. Congress or the presidency, for instance. For studies of social science generalizations, the particular persons, places, instruments, and similar details are not important in themselves. They are merely marginally interesting historical facts. Indeed, most details, including the names of the subjects and the situation, are typically ignored in the usual research account. What is important is what the particular constellation of persons, places, times, and events in the study represents. What do these factors tell us about other persons, places, times, and events in our world? What is their generality to persons, places, times, and events beyond the situation in which they were researched?

Generality comes from the relationship between what is studied and the piece of the world of which it is a component and which it therefore represents. Units that are a part of a **population** of units are a **sample** of it; in sampling, we refer to the target to which we wish to generalize as the *population* or *universe*. If the population consists of reasonably similar entities, a sample of these entities will tell us about the population. Because we can interact only with small parts of our world at any given time, we are continually sampling the world around us and, on the basis of what we can see or know, making judgments about the rest, which we cannot directly sense.

> Sampling procedures are ways of selecting a small number of units from a population to enable researchers to make reliable inferences about the nature of that population.

Sampling is used in public opinion and consumer polling to make inferences about how citizens will vote on election day or how consumers will react to a new product or television program. Sampling is used in qualitative research in the selection of interviewees or persons to observe. Sampling is involved in all six facets of design choice in experimentation. Its use to find subjects and situations is obvious, but its less obvious use in measurement, for instance, is basic to measuring constructs (explored in chapter 11). So sampling is universal to the methods and is an important tool.

We intuitively use sampling principles in our everyday lives. Though without the formalities, we approximate various sampling methods, unconsciously applying the principles. From the slice we cut off, we judge whether the whole roast is done; from our neighbor's experience with a particular car, we judge whether to buy that kind; from a friend's enjoyment of his videocassette recorder, we decide it must be a "fun thing" and we purchase one too—continually making the intuitive leap from a sample to the population or universe, making judgments on the basis of incomplete information. The essential decisions are of this nature: what college to attend, whom to marry, where to live, which job to take, which house to rent or buy. We continually gather information from specific instances and generalize to new ones on the basis of their belonging to a common population of instances. In doing so, we treat information as a representative sample. So sampling is continually present in our lives. But that sampling tends to be haphazard instead of systematically applied. Unfortunately, we often find out too late that the sample chosen was not representative. As researchers well know because they use the methods, systematic application of sampling principles has the advantage of giving greater assurance of representativeness.

PRINCIPLES OF SAMPLING

As a child, you may recall reaching into a cookie jar so high on a shelf you couldn't see into it.[1] If you wanted to know the contents, you didn't

---

1. Please forgive the homely example. It seems to work, and it is how I intuitively learned sampling when I was too little to take Grandma's cookie jar off the shelf without breaking it.

necessarily take the top cookies but reached in, mixed them up, and then drew out a few cookies (random sampling of sorts, even better if the remaining cookies are mixed after each draw). We intuitively knew that we could judge from the handful we had withdrawn the freshness or staleness of the cookies we could not see or smell (the inferential leap from sample to population).

Further, we understood that the larger the sample of cookies we drew, the more certain we could be in our conclusion about the rest of the cookies (*certainty of the inference increases with sample size*).

And we also intuitively understood that if the first one was stale, as was the second, the third, and even the fourth, there was very little or no variation in freshness. Even with that small a sample, we knew we had stale cookies (*where there is very little variation among the units of the population, a small sample will do*—if the units are all identical, a sample of one tells the nature of the population!). But if the first was quite fresh, the second stale, the third in between, the fourth on the stale side, we would have a hard time judging the average freshness from a small sample. (*All things being equal, a larger sample is required to judge the nature of a highly variable population than one that is homogeneous.*)

Suppose we think the chocolate cookies are larger than the molasses ones in the jar but we aren't sure. How many cookies do we need to examine to find out? It depends. Let's say chocolate cookies vary one from another by as much as half an inch because of different baking conditions, and so do molasses cookies. In Grandma's cookie jar the typical chocolate cookie is two inches larger than the molasses, a difference easy to see even given the half-inch variability due to baking conditions. But there is another cookie jar over at Uncle Mark's house where the difference between the chocolate and molasses cookies is only half an inch. Now, the normal variation in baking conditions also causes differences of half an inch. This could mask the difference between chocolate and molasses, especially in a small sample that might consist of a bunch of big ones or small ones by accident. In a large sample, differences in baking conditions will average out over both the chocolate and molasses cookies such that the average difference in size of the two kinds will be apparent. (*A larger sample is required when a difference we are trying to sense—or estimate—is masked by the normal variation in the sample.*)

Let's stop for a moment and recapitulate what we intuitively know: We are interested in generalizing from a sample to some target we shall call a population or universe. In our example, the contents of the jar were the population about which we wished to infer freshness. As the cookie tale illustrates, sample and target need not be individuals. Although we generally think of populations as consisting of individuals, the terms *population* and *universe* can apply to anything; these words are used very broadly in research. For example, we sample not only populations of individuals but also universes of situations, of instruments, of possible treatments or variables, of possible designs and procedures; each is a realm to be sampled. In the Zimbardo study, the college student sample represented the population of persons who might develop paranoia with an unrecognized sensory deficit. The laboratory interaction was representative of social situations. The measures of paranoia were a sample of possible instruments from the universe of measures of paranoia. Each choice stood for, or represented, a target population of persons or a universe of situations or instruments and was intended to allow us to generalize to it. Although there were good reasons for the particular choices made for the study, presumably other choices would have been acceptable. Put another way, the choices made for that or any study are made from larger sets of alternatives. Presumably other choices could be made from those sets of individuals, situations, measures, and procedures with the same results. In other words, the study would replicate if it had generality.

- Required sample size is related to four factors: (1) certainty of inference desired, (2) precision of inference desired, (3) homogeneity or heterogeneity of the population on the characteristic of interest, and (4) size of the effect to be sensed in comparison with the normal sampling variation.
- A larger sample is necessary:

1. the greater the certainty required of the inferential leap from sample to population. (We want to be absolutely sure the cookies are fresh!)
2. the more precise we desire to be about the exact nature of the target population. (We want to know very accurately how fresh they are.)
3. the more the units in the sample vary from one another on a characteristic of interest—being heterogeneous rather than homogeneous. (The small sample varies in freshness, so it is hard to know just how fresh the cookies are on average.)
4. the smaller the effect to be sensed relative to the normal variation among the sampling units.

The first two principles in the box make good intuitive sense. We can do a quick pilot study with a few cases, but we intuitively know that it will only approximate the results of a larger study. Our faith in the results of the former cannot be as great as it would be in the results of the latter. If we want to know the average height of men very precisely, although we might be able to approximate it to the nearest inch with a sample of 20 or so, we can sense intuitively that a much larger sample would be required to know it to the nearest hundredth of an inch.

The third principle also seems intuitively true. When the population varies considerably with respect to a characteristic, the cases in any sample will typically vary widely on that characteristic as well. But a small sample might contain only cases at one extreme of the range on that characteristic (stale cookies), and because of the variability we wouldn't know whether the whole population was stale or whether by chance that sample of cookies contained mainly stale cookies and those in the population were mainly fresh. Only with a large sample is the chance factor minimized.

Using the fourth principle, we frequently increase the size of the sample to ensure that we will sense a positive result in a study if it occurs. We call it increasing the sensitivity, or power, of the study. The waves created in the wake of a boat are easy to see at long distances when the water has few waves but difficult to see even a short distance behind the boat in a storm. When the normal variability among units of a population is large and the effect we are looking for is small by comparison, normal variability may mask consistent differences.

Consider, again, Uncle Mark's chocolate and molasses cookies, remembering that in the population, on average, the chocolate cookies are half an inch larger. Remember too that variation in baking conditions can also create differences of half an inch. A small sample might, by chance, consist of a combination of undersized (normally larger) chocolate cookies baked under unfavorable conditions and oversized (normally smaller) molasses cookies baked under favorable conditions. Inferring the relative sizes of the cookies in the population from this small sample, we might judge them equal, no difference. Over a sample of 1,000 cookies, however, favorable and unfavorable baking conditions would average out, and as a result a sample of chocolate cookies would have quite a different average size from the sample of molasses cookies. The difference is no longer masked by the variations between samples when the samples are large and the averages therefore have little variation.

These principles govern sampling of all kinds. Indeed, it is through the use of these principles that different methods of sampling are devised. Hence we shall refresh our memory of them as we study the various sampling methods.

PROBABILITY AND NONPROBABILITY SAMPLING

Sampling methods are typically divided into probability and nonprobability techniques. **Probability sampling** enables us to make inferences about the nature of the population—for example, its average or how variable it is—with a certainty expressed by odds, like those at a racetrack. We can also set the degree of certainty that we will be right in our inferences (those odds), often at 19 times in 20, or 99 times in 100. (We'll examine that property beginning with confidence intervals in chapter 11, and go further in chapter 17).

All probability samples involve random sampling of units from the population at some stage in the sampling process. It is from this process that statisticians can construct a probability model. That model allows the construction of statistics that give us the probabilities. Recall that in the Zimbardo study there were statistics like ($t = 2.86$, $P < .01$) and ($z = 5.00$, $P < .001$). P refers to probability values that come from these "inferential statistics," as do such statements as "significant at the 5 percent level." (We will return to this topic too in chapter 17).

If probability samples involve random sampling at some stage in the sampling process, it follows that **nonprobability sampling** does not. For example, the panels used in rating television programs' audience size are not random samples but meet the profile of typical families with television receivers. They may indeed be representative of such families, but they are not probability samples, because random sampling did not enter into their choice.

If probability sampling methods allow the estimation of odds for the confidence we have in our inferences, it stands to reason that nonprobability statistics do not provide such a basis, at least not with the same certainty. That is a disadvantage, but there are trade-offs. Indeed, these trade-offs are such that most of our studies use nonprobability samples—usually convenience samples that consist of college undergraduates enrolled in a required course, making them readily available. Even professional survey research organizations often use a kind of nonprobability sample (quota sampling, described later in this chapter). Although many inferential statistics assume probability sampling, they are often computed on nonprobability samples, blurring the distinction in practice. We'll return to that problem later; for now, let us discuss probability sampling procedures.

We noted that sampling pervaded all six links at the design level of the chain of reasoning. Probability sampling, involving some form of random sampling, is more often used to select subjects or situations for study. Nonprobability methods are more often used for the selection of measures, forms of treatment, designs, procedures, and other aspects of the study design. For example, in the choice of treatment involving the teaching of outlining in English composition, we would intentionally choose a particular method of teaching it. It would be selected to be representative of the possible ways of teaching it rather than chosen by randomly sampling among the possibilities. Further, there might be other criteria such as ease of use and popularity that make nonrandom sampling appropriate.

PROBABILITY SAMPLING PROCEDURES

Simple Random Sampling

Simple **random sampling** is the basic method on which all other methods of probability sampling are built, and they all involve it at some stage in the process. It can be defined as follows:

> Simple random sampling requires that each unit of the population have an equal chance of being selected. A more precise definition is that all possible samples of a given size have an equal opportunity of being selected.

This makes it clear that the choice of any unit is independent of the choice of any other. Recall that before we drew a cookie, we mixed the cookies. That was to ensure that every unit had an equal chance at each drawing. Note that randomness is provided by the process by which we drew the sample.

How do we obtain a random sample in research? The first task is to define the population and the sampling unit. The population is that group from which the sample is to be chosen and of which the sample is to be representative. Instead of being measured directly, the nature of the population is inferred from the characteristics of this sample. Put another way, the population is the group to which you would expect the results of your study to generalize; therefore, you want your sample to reflect its nature as accurately as possible.

The list of units from which we draw the sample is called the **sampling frame**. For simple random sampling, the sampling frame and the population are the same. For a survey of teacher morale in a school district, the sampling frame might be a list of all the teachers in the district. The population would be the teachers in the district, and from the data obtained on our sample we would infer the morale of the teachers in the district. A faculty directory, a telephone book, and a club or church membership list are all examples of sampling frames. For simple random sampling, they would be the populations whose nature we would infer from the sample's characteristics and to which we would expect our results to generalize. (See Kish, 1965, for a discussion of frame problems.)

Sampling Unit.   Each case in the sampling frame is a **sampling unit**, so cases selected for the sample are chosen from among the sampling units. The sampling unit is usually also the unit used in tabulating the data. In the morale survey of a school district above, clearly the individual teachers in the district would be the sampling unit.

But the choice of unit is less clear when we make comparisons between aggregated units. For instance, when we test a new curriculum in a school, we are not interested in how Johnny did with the new and Rebecca with the old, but in how Johnny's class did with the curriculum in contrast to Rebecca's class. Is our sampling unit here the students or the classes? Ordinarily, the rule to follow is that *the sampling unit is the smallest unit receiving the treatment*. Thus in a typical curriculum, this would be the class, since all students are exposed to and interact with one another regarding the same curriculum materials. They experience the treatment together rather than independently. With a computer-based, self-guided curriculum, the individual student would be the sampling unit because each student interacts with the computer program independently of the others. Some studies examine both class and individual effects and require that attention be paid to sampling at both levels: the assignment of individuals to classes and the choice of classes.

As might be expected from the chain of reasoning, the unit used in stating the problem is usually the unit used in the hypothesis, the unit of sampling, the unit of analysis, and the unit used in stating the conclusion.

How to Choose Units.   Typically, we number the units in the sampling frame and use the numbers to choose the sample. This can involve numbering all the names on a list such as the telephone book or using the page number, column number, and location in the column as a set of numbers to designate each person. In a 20-page, two-column, 25-names-per-column directory, this would be a randomly selected five-digit number. Presumably, as is done with the military draft lottery, we could enter the numbers on slips and put the slips in a drum, then have someone who is blindfolded turn the drum to mix them and draw out the required number of slips. Partly because of the labor and partly because of the difficulty of ensuring that the slips are thoroughly mixed, we more often use a table of random numbers. The RAND Corporation (1969) has produced a book containing a table of a million random digits. Various rules for using the table provide an arbitrary starting place. Once that is located, successive groups of digits designate the units in the population chosen for the sample.

So long as it provides an equal chance for any number to be chosen from the table, any set of arbitrary rules is satisfactory. For example, using the RAND Corporation book, open the book anywhere in the random numbers section and place your finger on the page with eyes closed. Use the set of digits under your finger to designate the page on which you begin drawing the sample. Use the next appropriate pair of numbers immediately to the right to designate the row to start on that page (if there are only 20 rows, ignore all pairs above 20), and then use the next two similarly appropriate pairs of numbers to tell with which number to start in the row. If the sampling frame contains 423 units, take the numbers in any consistent direction from the starting place, three at a time, discarding any number larger than 423.

Representativeness and Bias. Why so much emphasis on randomness? To avoid bias and ensure that all the characteristics of the population relevant to whatever we are studying have an equal chance to be represented in our sample. **Bias** occurs when a sample fails to represent the population (Jaeger, 1984). There are many possible causes. You might think that stopping individuals in a shopping mall for interviews would obtain a random sample of shoppers, and with a table of random numbers, it can. But without such a guide, the interviewer may choose more men than women or may be drawn to the best-dressed people because of unconscious personal preferences. Such factors would clearly bias the sample.

A common source of bias is that the sampling frame is not complete. A most famous case is the 1931 *Literary Digest* poll. The poll had considerable success in predicting elections prior to 1931. Telephone books, their sampling frame, were used as a proxy for voter rolls. The poll predicted that the Republican presidential candidate, Herbert Hoover, would win, but the challenger, Franklin D. Roosevelt, won by a wide margin. The pollsters erred because their sampling frame excluded the many less well-to-do Democratic-voting families who did not have telephones.

A nice thing about a genuine random sample is that it will, on the average, represent all the characteristics of the units at their population level. This is especially true as larger and larger samples are taken. Characteristics of which we are not aware could affect a study if not represented according to their proportion in the population. With random sampling we are protected because, on the average, such characteristics will be close to their population representation. What does that mean in practice? Well, let us suppose that we are interested in how well a new curriculum will fare with the average youngster in a school district. A random sample will, on the average, give us a group that has not only the same average intelligence level as the students in the district but also the same motivation level and attitude toward whatever subject we are working with—all characteristics that might affect our study. In addition, it has the same average height, length of fingernails, and shoe size—characteristics that probably will not affect our study, but are on the average equalized in case they do and we couldn't anticipate it.

Sample Size: How Big Is Big Enough?   Notice that we have always hedged by saying "on the average" and "if the sample is large enough." The key is sample size. How big a sample is big enough? The answer comes in part from two decisions: how precise we want to be and how sure we want to be of our answer. It also depends on two characteristics of our data: how much variation there is in characteristics such as intelligence and motivation that we want to ensure are properly represented in our sample, and how small an effect we want to sense is in contrast to the normal variation in the sample units. As we shall see in chapter 17, there are statistical formulas that will estimate for us how large a sample is required once we decide how accurate and sure we wish to be and how variable and strong the effect is. Incidentally, that is the only way we can determine needed sample size. Conventional wisdom rules, such as "Thirty cases are enough," just won't do.

Are there other things we can do to ensure representativeness besides increase sample size? Indeed, there are; recall that a smaller sample will do the job of a larger one where the units are homogeneous. We shall use that principle in stratified sampling.

Stratified Sampling

Stratified sampling is more common than simple random sampling. Suppose that when we eat the cookies, we notice—maybe because they help retain moisture, but for whatever reason—that the number of raisins in the cookie is an approximate guide to its freshness. Suppose further that the baker was afraid he might run out of raisins and so began by using only a few, being careful to put about the same number of raisins in each cookie on the cookie sheet. Later he realized he had underestimated his stock. He grew more and more generous with each cookie sheet as the last one to be filled approached. Since the yield of each cookie sheet filled a jar, we now have a set of jars. Each jar is fairly homogeneous with respect to the number of raisins per cookie, but that number differs between each jar and the next.

Therefore, the contents of each of these homogeneous jars can be represented by fewer cookies than if the contents of each ranged over the raisin content of the entire batch of cookies. To find the freshness of the batch, a smaller random sample of cookies from each jar across the batch will give a good representation of the total batch with fewer cookies than if each jar had the full range of variation. Further, we are pretty sure that we have the full range of freshness represented because freshness is related to the number of raisins, and by sampling from all the jars we have that range covered.

This is the process of stratified random sampling: we classify the units in the sampling frame into strata on the basis of a characteristic that, if not properly represented in the sample, might bias our inferences. This reduces the variability of that characteristic in each stratum. Randomly sampling from each stratum allows us to have the same representativeness yet reduce our sample size (or, using the same size, allows us to be more exact in our estimation of the population characteristic and surer of that estimate).

Proportional Stratified Sampling. This is the most common form of stratified sampling. Consider the determination of educational achievement in a junior high school. We could take a random sample of students, but grade level is important to achievement. If sixth graders were underrepresented by chance, or seventh graders were overrepresented, our estimate for the school would be biased. To ensure proper representation of each grade in accordance with its proportion in the school as a whole, we might break the sample into strata, one for each grade. We could then randomly sample within each stratum (grade). The number taken from any stratum would be determined by the size of that stratum in relation to the school as a whole.

Because the range of achievement within each grade level would be less than that for the school as a whole, each grade is more homogeneous and can therefore be represented by fewer cases. We can take fewer from each stratum and still maintain the original precision of estimation, as from an unstratified sample. Alternatively, we can maintain the planned sample size and by stratification increase the precision of our estimates and our confidence in them.

Stratification on More than One Variable. We may stratify on more than one characteristic at a time. Thus the school sample might stratify on sex to ensure representation of both boys and girls in their correct proportions. In addition, in a racially mixed school, we might want to ensure proper representation of African-American, Hispanic, Asian, and other minority children in a three-way stratification as shown in Figure 8.1. In proportional sampling, we would randomly select some predetermined proportion that yields the proper total number of cases from each cell. For instance, there are 197 students in the set of cells in the figure. For a sample of 50, we would therefore randomly select one-quarter of the students in each cell. For example, we would randomly select 3 of the 11 sixth-grade African-American boys in the topmost left-hand cell.

Minority:	African-American			Hispanic			Asian			Other		
Grade:	6	7	8	6	7	8	6	7	8	6	7	8
Boys	11	7	7	14	13	16	2	3	1	7	8	6
Girls	13	9	8	16	11	15	2	1	1	9	9	8

FIGURE 8.1 Three-way stratification on the basis of minority, grade, and sex for an achievement study of a junior high school. (The numbers in the boxes indicate the number of students in that cell from which a random sample of pupils would be drawn.)

We gain little by using more than one characteristic unless they are independent of each other—that is, they do not overlap. For example, gender and highest level of education achieved are largely independent of each other these days. But socioeconomic status of parents and highest educational level achieved are likely to be highly related. Categorizing into strata on the basis of socioeconomic status achieves most of the advantage of stratification on educational level, meaning that additional stratification may be of little advantage. It is rare that more than a triple stratification adds much.

Intentional Oversampling.   Often while identifying individuals for classification into strata, our attention is called to small groups of special interest. These may be minority groups that might not even be present in a small sample. Yet for political or other reasons, they are of special interest. **Oversampling** permits us to study these groups separately. We would take extra cases, perhaps everyone in a cell, from those cells. But in determining the average achievement of the total sample, each cell is appropriately weighted. For example, Asians in the 25 percent sample of Figure 8.1 would be represented by three students in the sample, even if we rounded up in taking a quarter of the total of 10 Asian students. Since there is only one case in each cell, how would seventh- or eighth-grade girls or eighth-grade boys be included? If we took all 10 Asians, who make up 5 percent of the school, they would constitute 20 percent of the sample. That is overrepresentation but would characterize the subjects better. When the average achievement of the school is to be determined, however, we would weight the Asian's average at 10/197, or about 5 percent, its correct proportion in the school, for combination with the rest of the strata.

Advantages and Disadvantages of Simple Random and Stratified Sampling

Table 8.1 summarizes the advantages and disadvantages of simple random and stratified sampling. Note that even where considerable information about a population is available that would allow stratified sampling, simple random sampling does not make use of this information. Yet where such information is not available, it requires no such information to obtain, on the average, a representative sample of every characteristic of the sample.

When to Stratify.   Stratify whenever you can do so *easily*. If we randomly select within strata, we will never have a worse sample than might be obtained by simple random sampling. If the stratifying variable is *related* to the variable of interest in such a way as to increase representativeness, we will have gained. At worst, all we lose is the effort used to stratify. Note the emphasis on *easily* and *related*. Unless the stratifying variable is closely related to the variable of interest (as religion is to the abortion issue, for instance), stratifying gains little but peace of mind. Hence the concomitant emphasis on *easily*.

Peace of mind is not unimportant, however. The luck of the draw will sometimes lead to a sample that is not representative. Ten pennies are sup-

TABLE 8.1   Advantages and Disadvantages of Random and Stratified Sampling

	Description	Advantages	Disadvantages
Simple Random Sampling	Assign each population member a unique number; select members using a random number table	Requires minimum knowledge of population in advance Is free of possible classification errors Makes it easy to analyze data and compute statistics	Does not make use of knowledge of population that researcher may have Results in larger errors for same sample size than stratified sampling Requires identifying and in some studies traveling to units over whole population area
Proportional Stratified Sampling	Sort units of population into groups (strata) on basis of the characteristic(s) to be represented correctly in the sample, characteristics that might otherwise result in incorrect inferences Randomly select from each stratum cases equal in number to the ratio of that stratum's size to the population or sampling frame	Enures representativeness of whatever characteristic is used to classify units. Depending on how closely the stratifying variable is related to the variable being studied, there will be greater homogeneity in each stratum and so each can be represented with fewer cases. Thus, compared with simple random sampling, fewer cases yield equal accuracy. If size is retained, we gain greater accuracy and confidence in the estimates Facilitates analysis of strata and hence of subgroups of population; eases comparisons of subgroups	Requires accurate information on proportion of population in each stratum, or else error is increased If information for classification is not available, may make it costly to obtain and prepare lists Risks improper classification of individuals in strata due to clerical error or poor measurement

posed to come up all heads only about once in a thousand tosses, but if that one time happens to be the sample you draw, and you want a representative sample of heads and tails, you have a nonrepresentative sample. It is little consolation that your sample is an unusual one. Better to ensure representativeness through stratifying if you either have or can easily obtain the accurate information you need to do so; it is good insurance.

Systematic Sampling

Systematic sampling is one of the most commonly used and simplest sampling patterns. If we have a sampling frame of 500 names and want a sample of 50, it seems reasonable to take every tenth name instead of bothering with a random

TABLE 8.2   Advantages and Disadvantages of Systematic Sampling

Description	Advantages	Disadvantages
Using the natural order of the sampling frame, select every nth item beginning at some random point and cycling through the list; value of n is ratio of the desired size of sample to size of sampling frame	Makes sample very simple to draw If population list is ordered with a variable related to what is being studied, has the effect of stratification on that variable	May result in nonrepresentativeness if n is related to a periodic ordering in the population listing Neglecting to take stratification effect into account in the statistics will yield estimates of accuracy that are too low

number table. This often works satisfactorily if there is no periodicity in the sampling frame that is related to the characteristics we are studying. But suppose this is a list of dormitory rooms, and every tenth room is a corner room. Further, because corner rooms are preferred suites, they are assigned to elected student floor leaders. Then clearly, depending on where we start in the sampling frame, we may have either all corner rooms or no corner rooms—neither being a representative sample. If we were examining the social life of students, this could make a considerable difference. So we have to be cautious when using systematic sampling to be sure there is no periodicity to the sampling frame that is somehow related to what we are investigating.

But there is an advantage to systematic sampling if the characteristic on which the sampling frame is ordered is related to the variable being studied as a stratifying variable. In that case, systematic sampling will have the effect of stratification. Suppose the sampling frame lists individuals according to their learning ability. A systematic sample of the top group would be just like a sample taken from a top stratum, and the same is true for the middle and lowest groups. The overall sample will represent the sampling frame with respect to that characteristic just as if we had done proportionate stratified sampling. Another advantage is that in an alphabetized list of names, this approach will avoid repeat sampling from the same family.

Systematic sampling is not really simple random sampling, but it behaves like it, and cases are easier to select. Provided that we observe the cautions noted, this is an easy way to stratify. Table 8.2 summarizes the advantages and disadvantages of systematic sampling.

Cluster Sampling

We noted in Table 8.1 that if the selected units were scattered all over the city and one wished to contact them personally, random sampling would create a significant travel problem. **Cluster sampling** solves this problem. Instead of randomly selecting cases, we divide the city into units, possibly by dropping a grid over the city map so that it is divided into cells, and then randomly select cells. We may use all the cases in a cell (which may be a block or several blocks), or we may do multistage sampling, successively performing different kinds of sampling. For example, we could do cluster sampling to select clusters and then stratify within each cluster on a relevant variable. We would then randomly sample within each stratum—cluster followed by stratified and then random sampling. Cluster sampling has the advantage not only of reducing travel but also of requiring complete sampling frames only for the selected clusters. Because both travel and compilation of sampling frames can be costly, cluster sampling is widely used for studies involving interviewing.

But, you may ask, since people live in relatively homogeneous neighborhoods, how can a few cells be representative of the whole city? Unless the selected cells cover all neighborhood types, this can be a problem. Indeed, the error in estimating population values is likely to be greater with cluster than

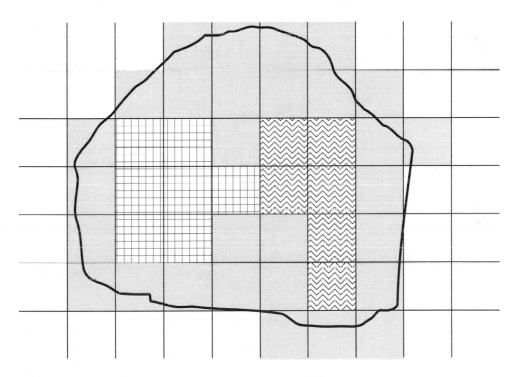

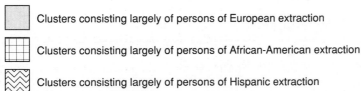

Clusters consisting largely of persons of European extraction

Clusters consisting largely of persons of African-American extraction

Clusters consisting largely of persons of Hispanic extraction

FIGURE 8.2   Design of a two-stage sample, clusters chosen within strata.

TABLE 8.3 Advantages and Disadvantages of Cluster Sampling

Description	Advantages	Disadvantages
Use as sampling unit either cells in a grid placed over a map or any other arbitrary or natural grouping; take a random sample of units and then either all individuals or a random sample of individuals in each unit	Reduces travel if clusters are used for interviews Reduces construction of sampling frames Permits studies of individual clusters and comparison of clusters Can use other persons for follow-up within a cluster if cluster was sampled, or can use other clusters	May result in larger error in estimating population values than other probability sampling methods Requires that each member of population be assigned uniquely to a cluster (for example, if clusters are families, where to assign children born out of wedlock?); otherwise may omit or duplicate cases

with random or stratified sampling for the same size sample. To ensure that neighborhood types are appropriately sampled, we sometimes use a multistage process. Clusters are stratified on a significant characteristic, and random samples of clusters are taken from within strata. Figure 8.2 shows a grid placed over a city for cluster sampling, with clusters stratified into ethnic areas. We might sample each of the three ethnic strata randomly, picking two clusters from each stratum and then randomly sampling individuals within those clusters.

Clusters need not be geographic areas. Depending on what we are studying and how we define the population, we may use classrooms, schools, or other institutions as clusters. Any already existing unit, however, is likely to be the result of factors that affect its nature. For example, all the problem cases are put in the new teacher's room or given to the new therapist. Parents seeking housing choose neighborhoods with certain school characteristics. Individuals pursuing certain kinds of jobs tend to have particular skills and values. Depending on what we are studying, the characteristics that attracted individuals to their particular cluster may cause it to be nonrepresentative, resulting in problems. The user of cluster sampling must be fully aware of its potential difficulties. Table 8.3 summarizes the advantages and disadvantages of cluster sampling.

NONPROBABILITY SAMPLING

Nonprobability sampling methods are methods that do *not* include random sampling at some stage. Because of their convenience, they are very common. Undoubtedly, the most common is the grab sample, or convenience sample: use whatever group of individuals is available. The researcher who interviews the first 100 persons entering a shopping mall at a given hour; the television or newspaper reporter who interviews the nearest shop clerks, secretaries, and police officers; the radio station that invites callers to phone in votes—these are all convenience samples.

How closely do such subjects represent community public opinion? There is no way of knowing, short of taking a probability sample. But clearly, the nature of situations, the constraints of time, and the characteristics of individuals predisposing them to act in certain ways all lead to a selective effect. For example, what kinds of individuals take the trouble to call a television station to praise it for a certain program? Or to complain? The kinds of persons entering a mall at certain times depend on whether it is in the morning, when homemakers, preschool children, and retirees are likely to predominate, or whether it is at a meal hour, when workers join in. Certain kinds of persons choose occupations that make them available to public access; others prefer to deal with things instead of people. These are all likely to be groups with characteristics that set them apart from random samples.

When any nonprobability sampling method is used, one of the first questions in the reader's mind will be the representativeness of the sample. It is the responsibility of the investigator to answer that question as best it can be answered. Usually this involves comparing the demographics of the sample on pertinent characteristics with those of the community or population to which the researcher intends the results to generalize. To allay such questions, nonprobability sampling methods often have some carefully considered base. Judgmental or purposive samples and quota samples are two such types.

> Nonprobability samples are those that do *not* involve random sampling at some stage in the process.

Judgmental and Purposive Sampling

Judgmental sampling uses the experience and wisdom of the researcher to select a sample representative of the population. The researcher selects individuals who are presumed to be typical of certain segments of the population and therefore representative of it; the composite provides the panorama of which the population is composed. This is a frequent strategy of qualitative research.

How good are judgmental samples in representing the population? In one sense, they are as good as the researcher's knowledge of the population. In another sense, the answer is a pragmatic one. If the researcher is able to predict the population characteristics from them consistently and accurately, they are useful. There may always be the instance when conditions change and the researcher doesn't change the sample appropriately. An example mentioned earlier was the *Literary Digest* poll. Only a genuine probability sample can protect against such changes. The facts that judgmental samples continue to be useful and that researchers can convince readers that their choice of individuals for a sample makes sense account for their continued use.

Many qualitative researchers go beyond judgmental sampling, however, and do **purposive sampling** for reasons other than representativeness. For example, after picking their initial sample and drawing some conclusions with that group, they test the robustness of those conclusions by seeking individuals whose actions might contradict the conclusions. That is, they deliberately choose individuals who will put their ideas to the test. Such sampling strengthens the logic of the method and, when done properly, is a stringent test of the findings.

Similarly, we may sample extreme or deviant cases to see how far a generalization extends or to see a problem in an extreme light that might give some clue about more normal situations or persons. We might sample politically important cases that if not included would cast doubt on the conclusions of our study.

Quota Sampling

Quota sampling requires prior knowledge of the characteristics related as stratifying variables to whatever we are studying. Quota sampling is a non-probability form of stratification in that we establish quotas for characteristics of individuals that we want to ensure are distributed in the sample as they are in the population. For example, knowing the sex ratio in the community, the proportion of each minority racial group, and the proportion of each religion, we could establish quotas for each of these variables to ensure that the sample taken had the required characteristics.

This often involves gathering data on a respondent's profile at the outset and proceeding with the full interview only if the respondent fits a quota not yet full. Alternatively, we can gather considerable data and discard individuals who do not fit the quotas. Still another possibility is to use all the data and simply adjust the results so as to represent each group's responses in correct proportion to its quota (provided that all quotas are adequately filled).

Unfortunately, despite the appealing logic of the methods, the individuals in any one quota are simply a convenience sample of that group. Unless properly supervised, interviewers will concentrate in areas with a large number of individuals where they can fill their quotas easily—shopping malls, entertainment areas, terminals and depots, and institutional buildings such as civic centers. Such samples will overrepresent the kinds of individuals who collect in such places and, depending on what is studied, could provide a nonrepresentative sample.

Even when interviewers are given instructions to visit certain areas so as to encounter persons who do not frequent the typical busy places, interviewers are likely to avoid less desirable locations—upper floors where there is no elevator, dilapidated buildings, hidden buildings, communities where persons are not home the first time called on, and so on. Clearly there are many potential forces that can make samples nonrepresentative.

Still, quota sampling is a favorite of pollsters who, with experience, have learned to avoid some of its problems. We shall see in chapter 16 how carefully one polling organization instructs its interviewers to select its sample.

- Whenever nonprobability samples are used, the question in the reader's mind is the representativeness of the sample.
- Judgmental, purposive, and quota sampling all involve some conception, often based on demographic data, of characteristics of the target population that could critically influence what is being studied. Judgmental and quota sampling are used by pollsters who select their samples to fit the appropriate profile of these characteristics. Qualitative researchers use purposive sampling to test their hypotheses and show generality.

OTHER SAMPLING PROCEDURES

In addition to sampling methods, there are procedures of sampling that can be useful in certain circumstances. Snowball sampling identifies a group, and sequential sampling is a procedure that can be used with any of the probability or nonprobability sampling methods.

Snowball, or Chain Referral, Sampling

Snowball sampling is a method of identifying individuals who are members of a group when that group is not otherwise visibly identified. It goes by other names: chain referral and referential sampling. Suppose we wished to learn who the influential members of the lobby group around a state legislature are. Though we might be able to identify the members of the lobbying group, we would not know which ones are influential. It could also be that there are influential lobbyists who are not visibly identified with that group. Using **snowball sampling**, we would start with an individual, such as a powerful state legislature member, and ask that person who the most influential lobbyists are and who else might know. We would then interview these as well as other individuals who would know, continuing until we came full circle and were getting names of persons already identified. This method has been used to identify members of crime groups and others engaged in covert activities. (For additional reading, see Biernacki and Waldorf, 1981.)

Sequential Sampling

Sequential sampling allows us to start with a small sample and then continue sampling until some criterion of adequacy is met. Typically, in sequential sampling, an initial sample is taken, and the data are analyzed to see if the needed statistical precision has been obtained or whether a larger sample is needed.[2] If the latter, we obtain additional cases until the desired precision is reached. Sequential sampling is increasingly used in telephone sampling polls. It may also be used with field samples where the situation is stable enough to allow us to return to the field and gather more samples like the first. The study itself must not have caused an increased awareness of the topic, which might itself lead to changes and thereby bias the results. As noted, sequential sampling can be used with any of the probability or nonprobability methods of sampling. It is of particular advantage when we know how precisely we wish to estimate the population characteristics but do not know the variability of the population.

With telephone polls, the interviewer enters the responses into a computer as the interview proceeds. The computer cumulatively computes population values as new cases accrue and stops the interviewing when the desired limit is reached. This is especially useful in quota sampling, where the interviewer obtains demographic information early in the discussion. Then the computer informs the interviewer whether this case is needed and, if not, orders an end to the interview. Where the cost of each additional case is important, this can lead to considerable efficiencies.

- Snowball sampling is used to discover the members of a group of individuals not otherwise easily identified.
- Sequential sampling involves gathering additional data in successive waves until some criterion of adequacy is met. It can save resources but assumes that the subjects do not change during the sampling process.

GENERALITY AND POPULATION DEFINITION

By now it must be clear that the generality we can attribute to a finding depends on the sample on which the study was done and what it can be presumed to represent. Therefore, the relationship between the sample and the population is crucial. Despite what generality the researcher intends, because it is always an inferential leap, it is the judgment of the experts who form the consensus about the interpretation of findings that determines the useful generality. Often this generality is less than intended. That usually results from the fact that the researcher took samples in some way that restricts it.

---

2. Statistical precision refers to estimating desired population statistics, such as the average income of the sample, with a predetermined accuracy, such as to the nearest $1,000. The procedure for doing this involves developing a confidence interval, a concept discussed in chapters 11 and 17.

Although we may have a conceptual notion about what the target population should be, it is the translation of this conceptual notion into a sampling frame that makes this concept real and is the determiner of the generality. The congruence of the sampling frame with the population we intend it to represent is what is at issue here.[3]

Suppose the faculty of a university is concerned that students do not seem to be achieving as they once did. Someone suggests the hypothesis that students are working more at jobs while trying to be students. Someone else suggests a survey to show how much outside employment graduate students engage in while working for a doctoral degree. This seems to be a straightforward question until we examine its complexities. Who is the population? Is it all students, both part-time and full-time? If only full-time students will be studied, what is the definition of a full-time student? One who takes nine hours of credit? But what about graduate assistants who take only six? Are they full-time students? If we exclude graduate assistants, we exclude the whole doctoral student enrollment of many departments. Since graduate assistants are not supposed to accept any work outside the university, to include them would clearly make the averages for outside work very low.

However we answer all these questions, the definitions of "working graduate student" and "full-time graduate student" determine who is in the sampling frame and who the population is. This is critical to what will be found, how it is interpreted, and how it bears on the original question. Clearly, the definition of the population is a critical question in designing this and many other studies.

Disjunction between the sampling frame and the target population of generalization is the most common problem. We want to generalize to all college students, but the sampling frame and sample are from one university. How representative is that sampling frame of the target population? The generality we can ascribe to the data of a study is always dependent on the study's operational definition of the population and an inferential leap from it to the target population.

Do we always have a specific target population? For applied problems, yes; the university studies described here are examples. For basic research, no. When we are seeking basic knowledge, we often deal with propositions that at least at first do not seem to be limited to specific kinds of individuals. These propositions are perceived as having generality across all individuals, so any individuals will do as a sample.

Such is the generality of the so-called Zeigarnik effect (Zeigarnik, 1927), for instance, which is presumed to apply to all individuals. It states that persons are likelier (it turns out about twice as likely) to remember interrupted tasks than tasks they have completed. It makes little difference who the sample

---

3. We shall see in chapter 13 that this is referred to as the problem of *translation fidelity*, the faithfulness with which the population in the hypothesis is translated into a list of individuals in that population, the sampling frame. We call it an operational definition because the operations of sampling form the definition of the population.

is; it could be the forever-studied students in an introductory psychology class or a group of passersby recruited off the street. The principle could be demonstrated with any group, so the nature of the sample is irrelevant.[4] Therefore, it is not always necessary to have a target population in mind when we are dealing with a proposition expected to apply universally. With a proposition not advanced as universal, defining the target population and choosing a way to sample that population become very important.

When is a proposition universal? What are our proper expectations about such propositions? When we say that a proposition is universal, we are again making an inferential leap from whatever data we have to all humankind. There is always the possibility that the generalization will not apply in another culture, at another time, and so on. Since we cannot possibly amass the evidence to show that the proposition is truly universal—we can't sample all humankind—its universality is an inferential leap of faith.

It is interesting that many social science propositions start with their universality undefined but with the clear implication that they are universal. It is only after we learn better why and how the relationship holds that we can see that it may be limited by culture, by time, or in other ways. Probably the readers and reviewers of research are likelier to limit the generality that can be inferred from a sample than the original researchers. But that is part of their natural caution in determining the proper interpretation of data. Scientists tend to be conservative, at least until a study has been replicated and an even larger consensus has developed.

- Definition of the target population in terms of sampling frame often reveals problems in specifying its exact nature. Yet this is critical to generality and to interpretation of the data.
- Generality of the results of the study to the target population depends on the appropriateness of the sampling process.

SUMMARY

Four basic principles underlie sampling: a larger sample is required (1) the greater certainty required in the inferential leap from sample to population, (2) the more precisely we desire to estimate the population, (3) the greater the variability of the population, and (4) the smaller the effect to be sensed is relative to the normal variability of the population. All probability samples

---

4. The exception might be a group that is in some way memory-impaired, and maybe even then the generalization might be demonstrable within whatever memory capacity remains.

involve random sampling at some point in the process. Random samples require that each possible sample from a population be equally likely to be drawn. Probability samples allow us to estimate the population characteristics with specified accuracy and certainty. Random, stratified, systematic, and cluster sampling are all probability sampling methods. Often they are combined in a multistage process. Their characteristics, advantages, and disadvantages are summarized in the chapter's figures.

Convenience, and grab, samples are nonprobability samples. They are popular because of their ease of use. Judgmental or purposive samples rely on the researcher's knowledge of desired characteristics of the population for an appropriate sample. Such samples are usually justified by their fit to certain demographic characteristics. Those characteristics are used as the basis for quota sampling, which selects its sample so as to include individuals in proper proportion to the population characteristics. It is in common use in survey sampling, especially telephone interviewing.

The generality that can be attributed to a study is a function of the quality of the sampling process. When well done, sampling makes the inferential leap from sample to population less tenuous. Not all studies depend on sampling for generality, only those that are intended to apply to a particular target population. Propositions that are assumed to be universal—that is, to apply to everyone—can be studied with convenience samples.

Looking ahead, we shall see that the basic principles of sampling are used in a variety of ways. In a sense, the examples we shall seek in conceptual analysis (described in chapter 9) are usually representative of a class of examples, and sampling is used in statistics and measurement as well (discussed in chapters 10 and 11).

ADDITIONAL READING

Jaeger (1984)   Kish (1965)

IMPORTANT TERMS

Bias
Cluster sampling
Generality
Judgmental sampling
Nonprobability sampling
Oversampling
Population
Probability sampling
Proportional stratified sampling
Purposive sampling

Quota sampling
Random sampling
Sample
Sampling frame
Sampling unit
Sequential sampling
Snowball (chain referral) sampling
Stratified sampling
Systematic sampling

===================== APPLICATION PROBLEMS =====================

1. A researcher wants a simple random sample of 150 students from the population of all sixth-grade pupils who attend private schools in Syracuse, New York. The total population is 900 pupils. What steps should the researcher use to get the sample?

2. Mary Wayne, doctoral student, wants to study the effect of postinstruction summaries on high school student achievement. She will use the Rochester school district, which consists of 3,000 high school students (grades 10–12). She wants an adequate sample of 300 cases by grade level (sophomores, juniors, and seniors), sex (male and female), and three different levels of reading ability (low, medium, and high). She wants to select a representative sample. (a) What type of sample should she select and why? (b) What steps should she take in selecting her sample?

3. A manager of a food company wants to test the effectiveness of a new product for marketing in California. He plans to administer a questionnaire and interview 75 persons individually. What sampling method should he use, and what criteria would influence his decision?

4. Dr. Hendrika Kuizenga of the Marley Nursing School was studying depression in first-year college students, its rate of incidence and its relation to their level of perceived stress. She wanted a sample of 200 and obtained 133 randomly selected subjects proportionally stratified by level of parents' education and by race so as to represent the entering class. To do so required sending her graduate assistants into the dormitories and personally contacting the students, a labor-intensive procedure that would run her funds low. Therefore, she asked her assistants to pick up an additional 67 cases, while in the dormitories, of any first-year female students who would cooperate with them in filling out the instruments. To answer her questions, can she combine the convenience and random samples to get the desired sample size of 200? Why or why not?

Compare your answers with those on pages 705–706.

===================== SUGGESTED EXERCISE =====================

Using the topic you have chosen to follow throughout the book, think about the generality you'd like your work to have. Then consider the kind of sample that would permit inference of that kind of generality. In addition, think about how you might apply each of the different kinds of sampling to your problem. Include both probability and nonprobability sampling procedures. You may want to reconsider your original choice after examining some of the other sampling possibilities.

Conceptual Analysis

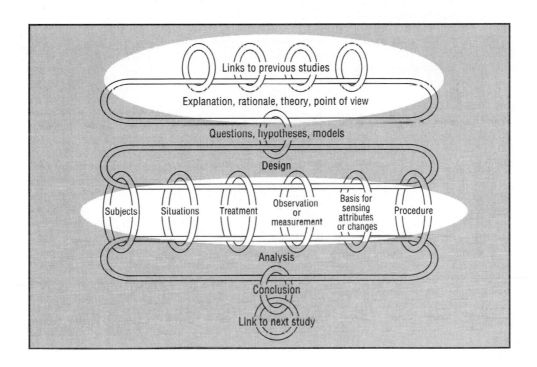

Some physical features of the world—like pencil, clock, clouds, thunder, and dog—have direct referents we can see and touch; they stand out almost begging for names. Other features—like joy, sadness, intelligence, and role—have no direct physical referent. They have to be *cut out*, as it were. These covert aspects of experience are named by the constructs of science.

After May Brodbeck

The gift of humanity is . . . that, unlike animals, we form concepts. . . . Man constantly invents ideas to express what seems to him to lie behind the appearances of nature. . . . In this sense, science is as much a play of imagination as poetry is. . . .

Man has outdistanced the other animals because he has not one but two languages: a thinking language for manipulating concepts inside his head as well as a speaking language (such as animals have) for communicating with others. A scientific discovery is searched for, a law is first guessed at . . . in the thinking language. But the exposition of science is not an account of . . . discovery . . . [;] its aim is to display the discovery definitively . . . so that everyone can then reason about it unequivocally.

Jacob Bronowski, The Identity of Man

OVERVIEW

Conceptual analysis is a process of defining constructs that is helpful both in problem formulation and in translating those constructs into measures, observations, or treatments.[1] It contributes to those links in the chain of reasoning by strengthening the credibility of the explanation and facilitating translation of the construct into the design. It is also a model for validating measures, as we shall see in chapter 11.

CHAPTER CONTENTS

Introduction   147
   Concepts and Constructs in the
     Social and Behavioral Sciences   147
   Use of Conceptual Analysis in the
     Chain of Reasoning   148
The Process of Conceptual Analysis   148
   Step 1: Find Examples of the
     Construct   149

   Step 2: Test Each of the Defining
     Conditions   152
   Step 3: Ask, "Is the Set Complete?"
     and Step 4: Ask, "If Not, What
     Must Be Added?"   152
   Some Additional Comments   153
Summary   155

---

1. I wish to thank my colleagues at Syracuse University who helped me see the value of the process of conceptual analysis. Dr. Emily Robertson has taught this unit in a research course I coordinate, and the idea for chapter 9 and its contents is directly traceable to her teaching. I am most grateful for her comments on the chapter, although, of course, problems that remain must be laid at my doorstep, not hers. I am also especially appreciative of my colleague Thomas F. Green, in whose book *The Activities of Teaching* (1971) the ideas of conceptual analysis are most helpfully and clearly developed.

INTRODUCTION

Central to comprehending a problem is understanding the exact meaning of the words that describe it—that is, learning the rules for using those terms correctly and precisely. **Conceptual analysis** helps us to understand those rules. Though called conceptual analysis, this process is particularly useful in analyzing constructs (abstract nouns that cannot be directly sensed) to find the precise way in which we use common terms in a given problem context. It is less useful with highly technical terms with agreed-on specific definitions. Conceptual analysis can facilitate organization of the literature search by illuminating the nature of a problem and its relationship to the network of concepts in which it is embedded.

Devised by philosophers, the conceptual analysis process is already used informally in science. By describing and illustrating it, this chapter calls attention to it and makes it available for use. We will encounter its parallel in construct validity in chapter 11, on measurement. As with all such techniques, how well it works depends on combining creativity with judgment.

Concepts and Constructs in the Social and Behavioral Sciences

Concepts and constructs are a prime feature of the social and behavioral sciences. The review of the literature on a problem marvelously fills our heads with such terms. Sometimes there emerges a clear image of the meaning of each. But that is the exception, because in our fields, such terms are not used with notable consistency. Let's clarify what we mean by concepts and constructs and emphasize the fact that conceptual analysis is particularly useful with constructs.

Let us consider *concept*, the broader term. Concepts are the terms that we use in our thinking language to refer to the things around us. For example, in our thinking language, the concept of clock, though perhaps learned with reference to a particular clock in our parents' bedroom, applies to any clock, whether it resembles our parents' clock or not. It can be a different color, size, or shape. As the quotation with which the chapter begins indicates, *pencil, clock, clouds, thunder, dog*, and the like are all concepts that have physical referents, that cry out for names.

Constructs are concepts, too, but whereas we have a mental image of a clock, constructs are terms that have no direct physical referent—*joy, sadness, intelligence, role*. Constructs refer to such characteristics as a person's internal state, capacities, or tendencies to act that we cannot directly sense: anxiety, spatial aptitude, racial bias. To return to the chapter's initial quotation again, they must be cut out, as it were. We must *infer* their presence from behaviors and other consequences that result from their existence. We cannot directly see, touch, smell, or hear them, only their outcomes.

Some psychologists, most notably Skinner (1957), have constructed a theory of verbal behavior development without using constructs or making such inferences. They confine their terms strictly to observable referents and their results. Although they have had some success, for most of us constructs are remarkably useful terms. Indeed, many would say they are essential; we would be lost without them. But when a construct is fuzzy, when its meaning differs markedly from person to person or instance to instance, when we use the same term in different ways, then it can be a source of difficulty and misunderstanding. A conceptual analysis of constructs removes the "fuzz" and clarifies how the term is being used. This permits clearer communication of our research and eases translation of the constructs from our thinking language into consequences that can be directly sensed in situations, actions, and results. This is necessary if we are to use constructs in our empirical research.

Use of Conceptual Analysis in the Chain of Reasoning

Clarification of terms is useful at a variety of places in the chain of reasoning. Clearly, it can be useful in the literature survey and the development of the rationale and explanation by distinguishing various ways in which the same term is being used. Besides being useful in the top links of the chain, conceptual analysis may help define the essential characteristics of a treatment, situation, population, or concept to be measured and observed, therefore having the potential to help clarify the design.

Sometimes clarification of terms can markedly facilitate the development of a field. For example, an early reading of the literature would have found the term *anxiety*, a construct that refers to uncomfortable feelings of apprehension. A conceptual analysis of the ways in which *anxiety* was used in the literature before a distinction was developed in instrumentation would have shown that the term was being used in two senses. In one, it referred to the syndrome caused by stressful situations, what was later called *state anxiety*. In the other, it referred to a more or less chronic feeling or mood, later referred to as *trait anxiety*. Although these two meanings were later distinguished in instrumentation, a conceptual analysis might have untangled them and led to earlier instrument construction.

THE PROCESS OF CONCEPTUAL ANALYSIS

Though only rarely do we engage in such formal pursuit of the meanings of terms, informally we do many of the same things, and the process is not complex. Basically, conceptual analysis involves a series of steps to help us generate ideas about the defining characteristics of a construct. These conditions are the necessary and sufficient conditions under which the term applies. **Necessary conditions** are those that must be present for the term to apply. **Sufficient conditions** are those that when present are sufficient to distinguish examples from nonexamples. Having found a set of sufficient conditions, we then test each characteristic to determine whether it really is *necessary* for the term to apply. Next we check whether we have found all the defining characteristics, that is, whether the set is *sufficient* to distinguish examples completely from nonexamples of the construct. If not, we seek the missing characteristics. Ideally, we find all the sufficient characteristics for the term. We hope that they constitute all the necessary (defining) characteristics as well. Let us look at the steps in more detail.

Step 1: Find Examples of the Construct

The first step is to examine many examples of the way we use the term describing the construct in question and make some guesses or hypotheses about its defining characteristics. These are the characteristics without which the term would not be applicable. Consider the term *desk*. A desk should have a surface on which to write, draw, or type; this is a defining characteristic; we cannot envision a desk without such a surface. But must we be able to sit down and place our legs under it? Is this a defining characteristic? No, it is not; though now rare, stand-up desks were once very popular and still are with some individuals.

Consider what it means for a person to be "creative."[2] We are concerned with creativity as a goal in school, in research, in business, in a wide variety of situations. We all have an idea in our head about what it means to be creative, and we could undoubtedly distinguish individuals whom we consider creative from those we consider not so. But creativity is not something we directly see, touch, or smell; it is a construct. To determine the defining characteristics of creativity, we must consider a number of cases of it. Thinking of certain categories of cases helps us find the central "territory" of a construct and its boundaries. Here are some examples of categories:

- **Model cases** are perfectly clear and unquestioned examples of the construct; they define the central territory; they contain the defining characteristics.
- **Contrary cases** are clearly outside that territory and help determine the boundaries. They lack one or more, if not all, of the essential defining characteristics.
- **Borderline cases** help determine the boundaries more exactly by finding those cases where it is difficult to determine whether they are examples of the construct or not.
- **Related cases** are a bit further out. They are almost, but not quite, the same as the term being analyzed. They also help establish the boundary.
- **Invented cases** give the imagination free play to see what cases might belong even though they aren't real. They attempt to make obvious "the simple regularities and conditions of our world that remain unnoticed because they are so taken for granted" (Green, 1971, p. 211).[3]

---

2. I am indebted to Emily Robertson for significant parts of this example.
3. Notice that sampling is involved. We are drawing from a population of examples of the concept for the conceptual analysis. How to sample them? We could argue that in the absence of a sampling frame or an enumeration of all the population's examples, we are using a convenience sample—those cases that come to mind. But we do better than that because we seek certain

These do not exhaust the possible categories of examples (nor will they all necessarily be useful in any given instance), but they make the point that numerous and varied examples must be explored.

An Example. What would constitute a model case of creativity? Green (1971) suggests starting with the construct's "most literal and ordinary usage,"

> the most plain and unquestioned use of the term or construct. . . .[4] One way to identify a model . . . example is to describe the conditions that you would be most likely to point to or show someone if you wanted to teach him the meaning of a certain term or the use of a certain concept. (pp. 207–208)

For *creativity*, would it not be that a person creates a work of art different from any already done by that person or any other person? What would seem to be the defining characteristics of this model case? They appear to be that the work is new in the sense that it is different from what anyone has done before. So far, so good; let us turn to contrary cases.

As Green (1971) notes:

> The study of model cases should yield some initial formulation of the necessary, if not sufficient, conditions that must be satisfied if any example is to be a genuine case of the concept. . . . The purpose in developing contrary cases is precisely to test those initial suspicions. (p. 208)

Can we think of contrary cases where the work is different from what the individual or anyone else has done before? Suppose that the work of art were to be carved out of a piece of foamglass measuring 5 by 8 by 5 inches, a problem that had been used repeatedly with previous art classes. If one student's sculpture were unique in this class but duplicated the work of many individuals in previous classes, would it still be creative? We can assume that had this been a very large class, this student's version would have appeared as a quite common solution to the foamglass problem and hence would not have been considered creative. So we learn that the uniqueness of the creation must be judged by a standard that goes beyond a comparison with other work of the moment.

What about borderline cases? Suppose the work of art resembles, but is not quite the same as, previous work by this student—it is a variation on the

---

kinds of cases. We might consider these strata, but they are still closer to quota sampling because we typically seek at least one in each category of model cases, borderlines cases, and invented cases. Contrary and related cases are sampled from nearby but different populations. How many cases need be sampled? The more varied the population, the more are needed; the more homogeneous it is, the fewer will be needed to make inferences—the same principles as before!

4. If seeking the way a construct is used in a particular problem context, start with its use in that context if it differs from common usage.

same theme. If the student's original work was unique and this is a variation on that theme, is this also to be considered original? Or must each new creation be entirely different from the previous ones to be creative? And what do we mean by different? How different is different when it is used to help define creativity? Clearly, we must make a judgment here, though difficult: one that determines whether something is creative—a judgment with which others may not agree. We have come to one borderline of the term *creativity* where things switch from being creative to not being so, depending on the judgment of how different the new piece must be.

What about related cases? Are there related terms that throw light on the nature of creativity? What about *imaginative*? Is a person who is creative also imaginative, and vice versa? When we refer to someone as imaginative, we think of that person as demonstrating repeated and varied instances of imagination, not just one. Come to think of it, that is true of saying that a person is creative: one instance won't do; creativity is shown by repeated acts. More than that, it is demonstrated in different circumstances and with respect to a variety of situations. The related case helps reveal another defining characteristic of *creativity*: that it is demonstrated in repeated acts, so much so that we could say that the individual's behavior is characterized by them. Further, the acts are repeated in more than one field of endeavor.

But are all imaginative acts creative? Sometimes we imagine things that have never existed. Where those are unique, they are creative, and both terms apply. But we can also imagine situations that have occurred before. If we are simply reliving them, we would probably not call them creative. The determination again falls in terms of the uniqueness of the experience—this doesn't add to our understanding.

What about the term *inventive*? Inventions are by definition unique instances of creativity. Are all inventions instances of creativity? Some inventions are simply modifications of something someone else thought of before. Is that the result of creativity? Probably, but here we come to the same problem we encountered in the borderline case: how much difference is required? Another blind alley; let's move on.

Finally, we come to invented cases. Sometimes it helps to release all the normal restraints and play with a construct. What would the world be like if suddenly all the highly creative people were wiped out by a special virus to which their creativity made them susceptible? What would happen? Behaviors that had been learned would continue. Individuals could learn those behaviors from others. But once those were learned by all survivors, no new behaviors would occur. Hence creative acts go beyond what one has specifically already learned.

So we have three defining characteristics of a creative person: (1) the person engages in acts unique in terms of both his or her own and others' experiences (the standard for uniqueness is a matter of judgment), (2) such acts occur with sufficient frequency and variety that we can say that they characterize the person's behavior, and (3) they go beyond what the individual has learned earlier.

Before going further, let's look back at what we have done, using Figure 9.1 to show it schematically. In the figure, the construct to be defined is

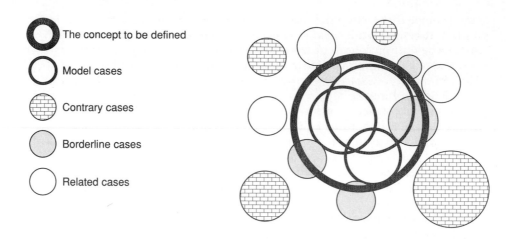

○ The concept to be defined

○ Model cases

▦ Contrary cases

● Borderline cases

○ Related cases

FIGURE 9.1   A diagram of some of the initial steps in the conceptual analysis process.

enclosed in the heaviest line, the thick black ring. Model examples fall inside that ring and illuminate its characteristics. Contrary cases help define the territory outside the ring; chosen so that they are related to the construct, they help us cut away territory that might otherwise be considered in the ring. Borderline cases help locate the position of the ring itself more precisely. Related cases are just outside the ring; like borderline cases, they help define the periphery. Since it is impossible to predict the location of imaginary cases, which could be anywhere, we have not included them in the figure.

Step 2: Test Each of the Defining Conditions

The second step is to test each of the defining characteristics to see whether it really is a necessary condition for the term to apply. To do this, we ask whether we can think of a real, honest-to-goodness instance of creativity, real or imaginary, that is not characterized by each of these characteristics. As we consider each characteristic, if the answer is no, we can't think of any instance without that characteristic, then it is defining. If, conversely, we can think of such an exception, then, of course, it is not. In our example, I could not think of such an instance.

Step 3: Ask, "Is the Set Complete?" and Step 4: Ask, "If Not, What Must Be Added?"

The third step is to ask whether the set of characteristics we have developed is complete—whether it is sufficient to delineate the instances in which the term would and would not apply. Are there situations that have all these charac-teristics to which the term would not apply? If the answer is yes, it leads to the fourth and final step of finding additional missing defining characteristics and then returning to the third to test the set once again for completeness.

So, in our example, we must ask, "Are there persons who regularly and frequently have a variety of unique thoughts that we would not describe as creative? Well, yes, individuals with delusions and hallucinations have unique thoughts, often thoughts of a kind other people would be terrified to have. They do so regularly and with respect to a variety of situations and content. Sometimes they put these down on paper as "art." Many of us have seen exhibitions of the often grotesque and erratic creations of institutionalized people. Indeed, their art is often used to help diagnose and understand their condition. Young children often form crude pieces that we say are creative but if done by an adult would be considered more bizarre than creative.

Ah, you are saying, who is to judge this as bizarre? Aren't there "modern" art pieces that some would say are bizarre and others the work of a creative genius? What about the work of van Gogh, who cut off a hunk of his ear? Obviously we have come, as the British like to say, to "a sticky wicket." For most of us, creativity must be exercised within the "rules of the game." To be considered creative, art must somehow be pleasing or at least affect our sensibilities in a way that we are willing and even eager to entertain. Haiku provides a clear example of "rules of the game." Haiku is a Japanese verse form consisting of three lines of five, seven, and five syllables, respectively. The poet must be creative within this format. Although the "rules" for art may differ among art forms, schools of art, and individuals, for most of us there is some art that exceeds our personal boundary and is judged bizarre.

So creativity has another characteristic, one we missed: it is exercised within certain boundaries or rules. But note that because some persons would argue that bizarre actions could be creative, we are making a **stipulative definition** of creativity. That is, we indicate we are going to use the term in a specific way, one that requires that creative acts result in something pleasing or at least something we willingly entertain. This is not a definition that everyone would accept, especially advocates of certain kinds of modern art.

Finally, we repeat step 3 to see whether we can think of any situation where a person socialized to what is and is not offensive regularly has unique thoughts that we would not call creative. If we can think of none, we are through. If we can think of instances, we must repeat the fourth step and again return to the third, and so on, until no new instances occur.

Some Additional Comments

Clearly, although we have illustrated all the steps in the process, not all have been helpful. Ideally, we end up having the necessary and sufficient characteristics for the term to apply. If our sampling in step 3 turns up no examples but there really are some, we have missed one or more additional defining characteristics. No doubt each reader of this material would have chosen different examples or found different ways of describing the defining characteristics. The process is unquestionably part art. But it is nonetheless highly useful. Research shows that having a model to follow facilitates problem solving (Elstein, Shulman, and Sprafka, 1978). The steps of conceptual analysis provide one such useful model.

Is the analysis of creativity helpful? It certainly tells us what characteristics to build into a measure of creativity. Such a measure should present a situation to which the individual can respond uniquely if it is natural to so do. The situation will have to be given to many individuals to learn which are the common responses and which are rare. It should include problems that sample each testee's behavior over a variety of situations and times, since one instance of creativity is not enough to characterize a person. Although a standard of common responses is established, the answers will have to be rated by someone with reasoned judgment, as it may be difficult to determine what represents a response "different" from a common one. The standard should consist of unusual situations to which the individual will not be able to apply directly, without modification, what has previously been learned. And we will need to set some "rules of the game" within which responses must be framed (for example, the response must be communicated in 25 words or less, and the first and last words must rhyme). So the analysis tells us something about how to develop situations that help us recognize creativity and suggests what we might do to measure it. We return to this topic in the discussion of construct validity in chapter 11.

Although it may seem as though we are simply playing with words, the process of conceptual analysis is analogous at a conceptual level to hypothesis testing with actual data. But instead of gathering data, we are doing studies mentally to see whether we can think of examples or situations that fit or do not fit the particular check on the term being considered (Is this a model case? A borderline case?) (D. P. Ericson, personal communication, 1990). Is this a poor substitute for data? No; in thinking through a term's meaning, it can bring past research to bear, highlight relationships to other bodies of literature, and save considerable time by rediscovering relationships through data.

Note too that conceptual analysis can map out and illuminate the conceptual framework in which the term is embedded (D. P. Ericson, personal communication, 1990). Thus our earlier analysis of creativity related it to inventions, imagination, and previously learned behavior. Clearly, we could go further and relate it to such areas as intelligence, social conformity, and spatial visualization. Each would provide additional insight into what we mean by creativity, the conditions under which we might expect it to appear, and where conditions are likely to limit its appearing. The further we carry the analysis, the more clearly we reveal the conceptual and theoretical structure that surrounds the term.

Notice that we have discussed conceptual analysis as a skill for furthering a research project. But the product, the definition of when and how a term is to be used, is sometimes a research product in and of itself. For a good example, see Green's (1971) analysis of the act of teaching. This excellent analysis is much quoted in the teaching literature.

Should we do a conceptual analysis alone or in concert with others? Going the lone road, we must keep the audience firmly in mind, as well as our problem. Remember, the set of conditions resulting from the analysis must be communicated to and accepted by the audience we intend to reach. The results of a conceptual analysis employed in a research study undergo the same scrutiny in the journey from findings to knowledge as the rest of the study. Failure of a consensus to form about the proper meaning of terms or the peculiar stipulations and conditions on a term may reduce the value and usefulness of the study. Doing the analysis with others probably reduces this risk.

A way of pooling data from others has been developed by Trochim (1986, 1989a, 1989b), using a process related to conceptual analysis he calls concept mapping. It involves sophisticated statistics, cluster analysis, and multi-dimensional scaling to develop a map describing an idea, the concepts within it, and their interrelationships. The group supplying the data may compare its map with an ideal or with maps prepared by other groups with contrasting orientations as a basis for research, planning, or evaluation.

SUMMARY

Conceptual analysis is a process for making our constructs explicit so that we can communicate them to others and use them in doing research. This process helps us to understand the construct clearly and see its relation to other terms and may lead to new and useful distinctions. The process consists of the following steps.

1. Examine many examples of the way the construct in question is used, and make some guesses or hypotheses about its defining characteristics. The following are particularly useful types of examples:
   - Model cases—examples that are the "most plain and unquestioned use of the term or construct" (Green, 1971, p. 207)—mark the heart of the construct's territory.
   - Contrary cases, which lack one or more of the defining characteristics, help define what is excluded.
   - Borderline cases, which could be either in or out of the territory, help determine how far the territory of the construct extends and where it ends.
   - Related cases, involving a term that is almost but not quite the same as the one being considered, also help set the boundaries of the territory.
   - Invented cases, which allow free play of our imagination about the construct, point up otherwise unnoticed regularities of our world.
2. Test each of the defining characteristics to determine whether we can imagine a situation where the term would apply although the characteristic is missing. If we can't find such cases, we consider it a defining (necessary) characteristic.
3. Check to see whether there are missing defining characteristics by asking whether there are situations that have all of these characteristics, yet the term would not apply. If there are none, we have what seems to be the sufficient conditions for discriminating when the term would and would not apply.
4. Find any missing characteristics; then repeat step 3 until all have been found.

Having examined some tools for handling verbal material, we next turn, in chapter 10, to tools for numeric data.

ADDITIONAL READING

Green (1971)   Wilson (1971)

IMPORTANT TERMS

Borderline cases   Model cases
Conceptual analysis   Necessary conditions
Construct   Related cases
Contrary cases   Stipulative definitions
Invented cases   Sufficient conditions

APPLICATION PROBLEM

Carry out conceptual analyses of the terms *curiosity* and *aptitude*; then compare each to the answer provided. Your analyses may, of course, differ from those given, but they should follow the same steps. *Compare your answers with those on pages 706–707.*

APPLICATION EXERCISE

Select a key term in your problem, and subject it to conceptual analysis. Choose another term from your problem that would lend itself to measurement, and do a conceptual analysis on it as well. Save the latter for further consideration in chapter 11. Does the analysis of these terms contribute to a clearer understanding of your problem? If analysis would be helpful, go on to analyze terms describing the target population to which you hope to generalize, characteristics of your situation, other potential measures, and aspects of your treatment or independent variable or variables.

CHAPTER 10

The Numeric Description of Data: Descriptive Statistics

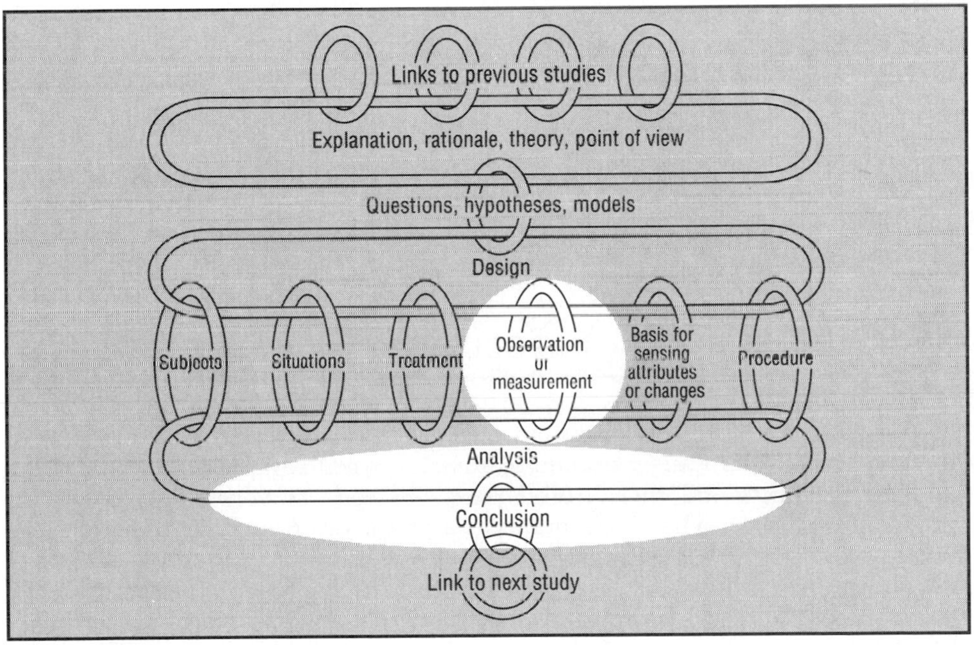
Links to previous studies
Explanation, rationale, theory, point of view
Questions, hypotheses, models
Design
Subjects
Situations
Treatment
Observation
or
measurement
Basis for
sensing
attributes
or changes
Procedure
Analysis
Conclusion
Link to next study

> For in relation to economics, to politics and to all the arts, no single branch of educational science possesses so great an influence as the study of numbers.
>
> *Plato*

OVERVIEW

Describing behavior with numbers or measures, as Zimbardo's study did in chapter 2, produces many figures. Indeed, the original data contained too many to readily comprehend unless summarized in descriptive statistics (as done there), a chart, or a graph. This chapter shows how data can be portrayed in different graphic forms and describes common descriptive statistics such as mean, median, mode, measures of variation, simple correlation, and more complex forms of correlation.

Descriptive statistics are important to the lower links of the chain of reasoning; they facilitate analyzing and summarizing data.

CHAPTER CONTENTS

Introduction   158
Picturing Groups of Numbers
    (Data Sets)   161
Descriptive Statistics   166
    Measures of Central Tendency   166

Measures of Dispersion
    and Variability   170
    Measuring Relationships   176
Comments and Caveats   185
Summary   187

INTRODUCTION

In describing a particular situation, we abstract the important parts: in a picture, we sketch in the important features; in words, we select and name the important objects and their critical parts. Indeed, Travers (1961) used this propensity to select what is important as a predictor of teaching ability. To see what was important to teachers, he asked them to draw a classroom. Did they include pupils? Where did they put the teacher? It proved a useful test; the more successful teachers included pupils and, rather than placing the teacher behind the desk, drew her in the classroom working with children. Similarly, in describing phenomena in words rather than pictures, we select what is important to us, what "hits us in the eye." Doing so is second nature to us.

We do this with numbers as well as words because we are continuously surrounded by numbers describing important characteristics of our world: the gross national product, the population of a community, the temperature of the oven, the Scholastic Aptitude Test (SAT) score of a college freshman. Nouns name these objects and their characteristics: product, population, heat, verbal learning ability. Each of these characteristics was selected from a range of possible nouns to fit the phenomenon we wish to convey. To further convey it, when describing in words, adjectives modify those nouns: enormous gross national product, small population, hot oven, bright college freshman. When describing numerically, numbers serve as adjectives.

We must decide what it is we wish to convey: a measure of some particular ability, an economic or geographic fact, or, in the case of statistics, some characteristic of a set of data. Thus as adjectives we have numbers added to nouns: $4 billion gross national product, a population of 267 persons, a 12-inch table lamp, a freshman with an SAT score of 800; we speak of a batting average of .325 or an average income of $20,000. As used in the social sciences, numbers specify some condition in a category (such as how many) or a point on some scale.

Numbers in the social sciences modify their nouns by giving a count of units (267 persons), by indicating a rank (the twelfth smallest town in the state), or by placing the characteristics on some scale (12 inches, SAT score of 800, mean of 500). They refer to only a single dimension or characteristic at a time, just as an adjective does—32 inches tall, a mean of $20,000. Numbers have the considerable advantage that we can differentiate a lot more precisely with numbers than with words. For example, students with SAT scores of 800 and 750 are both very bright, but their scores differentiate them. Even using a less-than-perfect measuring instrument, with a scale running over a large range we can differentiate many more levels of learning ability than we have adjectives to describe.

All the advanced fields of science use numbers to describe phenomena. In fact, using numbers has come to be such a hallmark of science that there are people for whom the whole purpose of social science is to describe things in numbers. It is true that where we can use numbers, they have proved effective and efficient at describing phenomena. But some experts reject this position, feeling that many characteristics have not yet been measured adequately. At the current level of development of the social sciences, there is room for both points of view, and both have merit.

> As used in the social and behavioral sciences, numbers specify a condition in a category or on some scale. Fields of science that have been able to make advances in prediction or control have used numbers to describe their phenomena.

We noted three operations for numbers: naming and counting, ranking, and placing on a scale. These correspond to different levels of measurement, each containing more information than the previous and requiring a greater degree of precision.[1] Thus if we can only put people in categories (Caucasian,

---

1. This discussion of nominal, ordinal, interval, and ratio measures perpetuates a legacy of S. S. Stevens (1946, 1951), which some statisticians would argue is best left forgotten. Certainly Stevens scale types are incomplete, as Duncan (1984) ably notes. Further, I have included

African American, Hispanic, Asian, Native American), all we can do is name them and count them. These uses are designated as the **nominal level** of measurement because persons or things in the same category are named with common characteristics. The UPC bar code on merchandise that is read at the cash register by a laser scanner is a nominal use of numbers; it names the product. We can also use numbers to modify that name by telling how many of a thing there are, that is, by counting them.

If we can differentiate among the individuals within a group, we can move up to the next level of measurement: ranking, or the **ordinal level** of measurement. We can rank several teachers in terms of their apparent skill but perhaps wouldn't want to say that the differences in skill between the first and second and between the second and third are equal. So we are not placing them on an equal-unit scale, but we do know that one is more skillful than another—ordinal measurement. The Mohs hardness scale is an example of a very useful ordinal scale. It is formed by determining which mineral will scratch the other when the two are rubbed together; diamonds, scratching everything else, rate the hardest. We have no way of expressing diamond's hardness other than this ranking.

Finally, at the next levels of measurement, we can place numbers on scales, actually two kinds of scales: one with an arbitrary zero point like the Fahrenheit temperature scale—an **interval scale**—and one with a real zero point like the scale of inches—a **ratio scale**. The advantage of the latter is that we can say that a distance of 12 inches is twice as long as one of 6 inches. But we cannot say that a day on which the temperature reaches 80 degrees is twice as warm as one on which it reaches 40 degrees. Similarly, a student with an SAT score of 400 does not have half the verbal learning ability of the student with the top score of 800. Most of our psychological and educational measures are of the arbitrary-zero type. These are called interval scales because the units from one score point to the next (400 to 401, 401 to 402) are presumed equal, but the zero point is arbitrary.

Just where ordinal measures quit and interval scale statistics become permissible has been much discussed.[2] A response scale such as "never," "sometimes," "frequently," and "always" is clearly ordinal. We often assign the values 1, 2, 3, 4 to these responses and compute means. That is, we treat them as though the attribute were being measured on an interval scale. We have no evidence that the distance from "never" to "sometimes" equals that from "sometimes" to "frequently." But the data yield useful generalizations

---

counting (which Stevens ignored) in the nominal category. It deserves a place, for when combined with good theory, counting can be as important as measurement and is certainly less controversial. So why have these measurement levels been included? Because the *interpretation* of statistics is determined by the level of data they came from. We can calculate arithmetic averages on ordinal data, but a comparison of such averages is meaningless unless we assume that the data come from scales or measures where it is reasonable to assume that scale units are approximately equal.

2. For an excellent discussion, see Knapp (1990).

when interpreted that way, so the assumption must not be totally in error. It works, so we use it.

Where the zero point is not arbitrary, we call the scale a ratio scale because we can legitimately interpret ratios such as twice as much or half as much. Time and most physical measures have this property. It makes good sense to do something in half the time or for one person to be half as tall as another. What does a zero SAT score mean? There is no such thing.

Some statistics are designed to deal with categorical data or nominal measurement, some with ranked data, and most with interval or ratio scale measurement where it is assumed we have a scale that measures in equal units.

Four uses of numbers are:

1. Nominal: numbers are used to name the members of a category and/or indicate the number in the category.
2. Ordinal: numbers are assigned to ordered data to indicate size relative to some characteristic (size, hardness, ability, etc.). No assumption is made that the differences between the numbers are equal.
3. Interval: successive numbers on a scale mark off equal units, but the scale's zero point is arbitrarily chosen.
4. Ratio: not only do numbers mark off equal units, but the zero indicates an absence of whatever the scale measures.

PICTURING GROUPS OF NUMBERS (DATA SETS)

We can describe data graphically or numerically. Suppose that we have data on the gross national product of a variety of countries, the populations of the communities of a state, the heights of a shipment of table lamps, the SATs of a freshman class. How would we describe each of these data sets? A common way is to use a graph or a chart. Another way is to use descriptive statistics, which describe one characteristic of the numbers at a time. Although the rest of this chapter is devoted to the latter, do not assume that descriptive statistics are that much more important—it just takes more words to explain them. Graphical representation has been underused, perhaps because of the extra printing costs. But the use of charts and graphs should in fact be increasing, because they help us visualize data holistically and easily and let us instantly grasp what is significant about the data. Some common graphical representations are shown in Figure 10.1, which presents nine different ways of graphically describing exactly the same data, the scores of 18 persons on a test of aggression (hence the boxing figures in chart G). Each data point is individ-

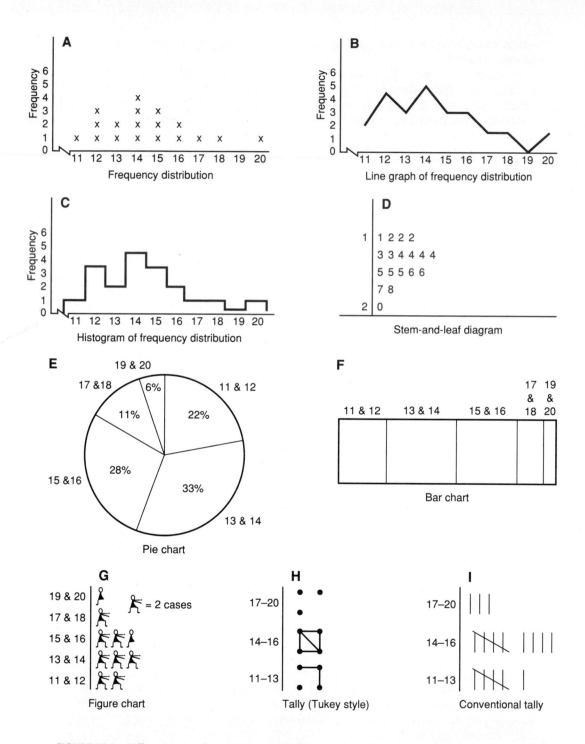

FIGURE 10.1 Different ways of portraying exactly the same data, the scores of 18 persons on a test of aggression.

ually represented in chart A, a **frequency distribution**. Frequency distributions are strongly recommended as a way of understanding how scores are distributed. In one picture a frequency distribution conveys the spread of scores, the location of the middle scores, whether the scores cluster around one or more points, whether the distribution is symmetrical, and many other things. As Cohen (1990) puts it, without them you won't know that "there are no cases between scores of 72 and 90, or that this score of 24 is somewhere in left field, or that there is a pileup of scores of 9. These . . . become immediately evident with simple graphic representation" (p. 1305).

The charts and graphs in Figure 10.1 only scratch the surface; their forms are as numerous as human ingenuity. For example, the quality of life in various states could be portrayed on a map of the United States by superimposing a face on each state. The features of the face would each represent a quality-of-life characteristic (for example, eyebrows = crime; mouth = education, etc.) and could be given a positive or negative look to reflect that aspect. A high crime rate might be given arched eyebrows; lots of educational opportunity could be indicated by a smiling mouth, little by a frowning mouth; and so on. We could convey an overall impression yet allow examination of a specific characteristic.

Some charts make interpretation intuitively obvious. Some, including the histogram (C), the bar chart (F), and the figure chart (G), permit reconstruction of the data more easily than others. The line graph (B) connects the tops of the distribution in chart A. The **stem-and-leaf diagram** (D), invented by Tukey (1977; see also Emerson and Hoaglin, 1983), is easy to construct by hand for small data sets. It shows the values of the numbers in the "leaves" at the same time it portrays the shape of the score distribution. In this diagram, the tens digit appears to the left of the "trunk," the unit digits to the right. Thus the top number is 11, with a 1 in the tens column and a 1 in the units column. Elevens and 12s would be tallied in this row or "branch," 13s and 14s in the next, 15s and 16s in the next, and so on. Thus in the second branch there are two 13s and four 14s, represented by the two 3s and four 4s, respectively. The tens digit is not repeated since it has not changed. The stem-and-leaf diagram yields a frequency diagram at the same time that all the data are present for inspection.

The pie chart (E) makes it easy to compare one circle segment with another. Unless we insert percentage figures, as here, it is harder to reconstruct the data because it is harder to estimate the area of circle segments. Area comparisons are easier in the bar chart (F), but percentages are an added help. Percentages can also be added to the columns of the histogram (C).

The tallies in H are another Tukey invention designed to minimize errors in conventional tallies, provided that the dots are made heavily. Sometimes in constructing such tallies (I is an example), we can miscount and have either too few (three) or too many (five) before making the cross mark. Arranging the tallies in a square is less subject to that error. The first four tallies are the dots for the corners, the next four become the lines connecting the corners, and the next two become the diagonals, for a total tally of 10. The tally for the scores 14–16 in chart H is for nine cases; the other diagonal would constitute the tenth case.

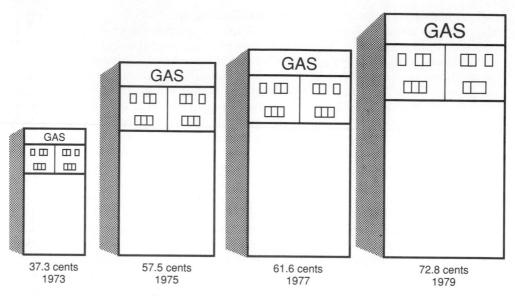

FIGURE 10.2   Misrepresentation in a picture chart of the average price of a gallon of gasoline for odd-numbered years, 1973–1979. (After a graph in *Time*, April 9, 1979, p. 57)

The icons in chart G portray the data accurately. But such picture charts are often misleading because the artist scales the characteristic of interest in only one dimension but draws it in two or three. A three-dimensional presentation is shown in Figure 10.2, where the gasoline pumps are actually scaled according to price only in the height dimension. As Tufte (1983) points out, it is the *area* of the pumps that should be scaled. The actual increase in price from 1973 to 1979 is 195 percent, which is the change in height. But because the width is also scaled up, the accompanying increase in area is actually 383 percent. Because the pumps are shown in three dimensions, if we compare the suggested volume, the apparent increase in price is 760 percent![3]

We typically choose a graphic form that facilitates the intended interpretation of the data. Charts E and F, for instance, facilitate comparisons among segments and are frequently used to display how big a portion of the federal budget is spent servicing the national debt or how small a portion of a nonprofit organization's expenses goes toward raising funds. The others can be used to emphasize outlines, flatness, peakedness, pileups at either end, where the bulk of cases lie, and so on.

Figure 10.3 shows an adapted version of a whimsical portrayal devised by the statistician W. J. Louden. It shows the bell-shaped form of a very common frequency distribution, the normal curve. His is an ingenious combination of chart and type.

---

3. Tufte (1983) is recommended reading for anyone interested in presenting data graphically and artistically. The book not only gives good advice but also is full of interesting examples.

THE
NORMAL
LAW OF ERROR
STANDS OUT IN THE
EXPERIENCE OF MANKIND
AS ONE OF THE BROADEST
GENERALIZATIONS OF NATURAL
PHILOSOPHY ◆ IT SERVES AS THE
GUIDING INSTRUMENT IN RESEARCHES
IN THE PHYSICAL AND SOCIAL SCIENCES AND
IN MEDICINE AGRICULTURE AND ENGINEERING ◆
IT IS AN INDISPENSABLE TOOL FOR THE ANALYSIS AND THE
INTERPRETATION OF THE BASIC DATA OBTAINED BY OBSERVATION AND EXPERIMENT

FIGURE 10.3   Print formed into the shape to be conveyed, in this instance, the normal probability distribution, or normal curve. (Tufte, 1983, p. 143)

Graphics have much to recommend them, especially when, as is usual, they display all the data. Always examine the frequency distributions for your data. Although we can infer certain characteristics from descriptive statistics, the frequency distribution will corroborate the accuracy of our inferences as well as our computations. We can spot computational errors if a statistic looks unreasonable in its graphical representation. Other interesting characteristics of the data may also be seen, such as flatness or peakedness, number of peaks, lack of balance around the middle and in which direction, and so on.

- Charts and graphs have the advantage of showing the data while high-lighting certain aspects of them. Unlike a descriptive statistic, such as an average, they can show more than one aspect at a time. Some, such as the frequency distribution, histogram, and stem-and-leaf diagram, show all the individual data points while displaying their distribution shape.
- Proper formulation of charts and graphs is essential to avoid misconceptions where two- or three-dimensional shapes portray one-dimensional data.
- Principles to follow in the use of graphics have been ably described by Tufte (1983): "Graphical excellence is that which gives the viewer the greatest number of ideas in the shortest time with the least ink in the smallest space" (p. 51). He also makes the following suggestions:

  The representation of numbers, as physically measured on the surface of the graphic itself, should be directly proportional to the numerical quantities represented.
  Clear, detailed, and thorough labeling should be used to defeat graphical distortion and ambiguity. Write out explanations of the data on the graphic itself. Label important events in the data. . . .
  The number of information-carrying (variable) dimensions depicted should not exceed the number of dimensions in the data. (p. 77)

DESCRIPTIVE STATISTICS

A descriptive statistic enables us to summarize some single attribute of a set of numbers. Adjectives that describe tallness, width, and other dimensions help us to visualize an object. So descriptive statistics describe different aspects of a set of data and help us gain an understanding of it. The most commonly used descriptive statistics are those describing the "central tendency" of data. They tell us something about the middle point around which most elements of a data set are found. Three descriptive statistics, the mode, the median, and the mean, are in everyday use.

Measures of Central Tendency

The **mode** is simply the score, measure, or category that occurs the most often. Categorical (nominal-level measurement) data have a mode; it is the category with the most persons or things in it. In census data displaying the number of Caucasians, African Americans, Asian Americans, and other groups, the modal category is the largest. In the case of the frequency distribution of Figure 10.1, chart A, 14 is the mode, the score with the highest frequency.

The **median** is the point below which half the scores lie. In a sample with an odd number of observations, it is the middle observation or score: in the sequence 10, 14, 15, 17, 20, the median is 15. With an even number, it is the score halfway between the two middle ones: in the sequence 10, 14, 16, 17, the median would be 15. If the middle score lies within a set of equal numbers, such as the 14s in the sequence 13, 13, 14, 14, 14, 14, 15, 16, 16, it is more complicated. In the distributions in Figure 10.1, chart A, the median score is 14.25. Why the fractional quantity? Because if more than one case has the median score, we must divide the median score appropriately.[4] A score of 14 technically scores from 13.5 to 14.4999+, and three of the 14s are below the middle score. Therefore, 0.75 is added to 13.5, making the median 14.25. No median can be formed for nominal data because they have no order, but we can find one for ordinal or higher-level data.

By far the most commonly used indicator of central tendency is the **mean**, or arithmetic average. This is simply the sum of the observations divided by

---

4. Finding the median is a little more complicated than counting to find the middle case if we have more than one score in the interval, as in this instance, or if we have grouped data. Charts E, F, and G of Figure 10.1 display grouped data; the frequencies for more than one score are combined. Charts H and I combine them three or four at a time. In these instances, each two or more successive score intervals are combined into one or more. It is common where the score range is large to group data in intervals of 5 or 10. To find the median in these instances, follow

the number of observations. It assumes the data are at least at the interval level of measurement. If the scores are displayed as a frequency distribution (Figure 10.1, charts A–D), it is the point on the baseline around which the distribution would balance if it were cut out of cardboard and put on a knife edge. The mean of the frequency distribution in Figure 10.1 is 14.5.

Like a teeter-totter or **seesaw** on a child's playground, cases that are out on the extremes have quite an effect on the mean. Picture two children in balance on the seesaw but sitting in toward the center. Now move one child to the far end of the board. The fulcrum has to be moved toward the distant child to restore the balance. So an extreme score pulls the mean significantly toward it.

Imbalance in a frequency distribution is referred to as **skewness**; if the distribution is asymmetrical with a long tail on one side, the mean is pulled toward the long tail. A long tail toward the larger values is called a positive skew; one toward the smaller, a negative skew. A skewed distribution can be detected by the order of mean, median, and mode. When the mean is largest, the median next, and the mode smallest, as in frequency distribution B of Figure 10.4, the skew is positive (a long tail toward the right); when the size order of these measures is the opposite, the skew is negative (C). When they are all very close, the distribution is likely to be symmetrical (A).[5]

A negatively skewed distribution may result when we have a test with a "ceiling" effect: it is too easy for the better students, nearly all of whom get very high scores, yet it discriminates well (provides a spread of scores) among the poorer students. Similarly, a test that is too difficult for the poor students will not discriminate among them and will therefore have a "floor" effect. All the students usually at the low end of the distribution will be bunched up at the very poor scores, but the test will spread out the better students. In Figure 10.4, there would be a "cliff" at the left end of B for a floor effect and at the right end of C for a ceiling effect.

With a skewed distribution, we are more likely to use the median or the mode rather than the mean to represent the central tendency of the data. But which measure of central tendency we use depends on the distribution and what we intend to convey. For example, the average salary paid by many

---

these steps (the parenthetical material after each step applies it to the data of Figure 10.1): (a) Find the middle case, $N/2$ (18/2 = 9); (b) Find the interval within which the middle case lies (14); (c) Determine how many cases are needed out of the interval to add up to $N/2$ cases (3 counting from the bottom); (d) Divide the number needed by the number in the interval (3/4 = 0.75); (3) Multiply this fraction by the size of the interval (in our case, the interval is 1, since each score is tallied and scores are not grouped); (f) Add this to the lower limit of the interval (our interval 14 runs from 13.5 to 14.4999; the distance between intervals is split. A 10-point interval of 10 to 19 would be considered to run from 9.5 to 19.4999. In our case, the lower limit of 14 is 13.5, so we add the 0.75 to it to obtain 14.25, the median).

5. Note that we say likely to be symmetrical but not certain. Large clump of scores close to the mean on one side could be offset by small clusters on the other side distanced further from the mean. This would be an asymmetrical distribution even though the mean, median, and mode were all lined up in the middle.

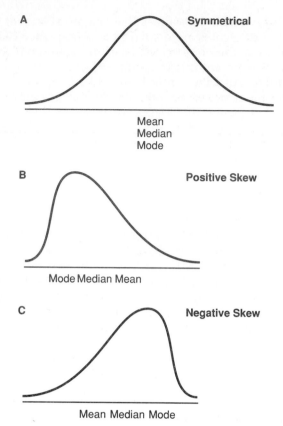

FIGURE 10.4   Symmetrical and skewed distributions and their effect on measures of central tendency.

large corporations would be better represented by the median or the mode if we wished to show what a typical salaried person was paid. Such a distribution is usually skewed, and the mean is moved higher by the salaries of the top executives.

Not all distributions are bell-shaped.[6] Those that deal with social conformity, for instance, are likely to be J-shaped. In Figure 10.5, graph A shows such a distribution for the number of parking tickets acquired by individuals in a year. Most had none, one, or two, and the drop-off is very severe from there. Some curves have more than one peak and are multimodal. An example is the bimodal graph B in Figure 10.5, which is a frequency distribution of SAT scores

---

6. True, but many are, and even Plato noticed this. In *Phaedo*, Plato remarks to Socrates, ''There are not many very good or very bad people, but the great majority are something between the two. . . . Have you never realized that extreme instances are few and rare, while intermediate ones are many and plentiful?'' (Duncan, 1984).

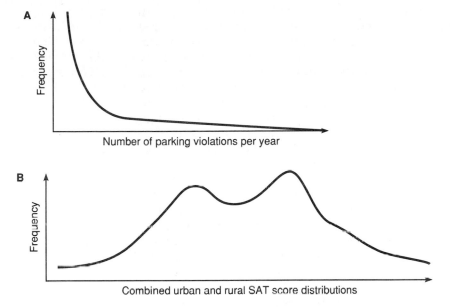

FIGURE 10.5 Frequency distributions for a social conformity variable and a bimodal variable.

for a high school with a combined rural and suburban attendance area. The suburban feeder elementary school's score distribution is represented by the higher peak, that for the rural feeder school by the lower one. When the students are merged in the high school, the combined distribution still shows these two peaks.

- Three statistics describe the central tendency of a data set:
    1. The mode is the most numerous category, measure, or score.
    2. The median is the point below which half the scores or measures lie.
    3. The mean is the arithmetic average, the sum of the scores divided by their number, the balance point of the score distribution.
- In a symmetrical frequency distribution, the mean, median, and mode are nearly equal (unless the distribution is bimodal or multimodal).
- In a negatively skewed distribution (tail to left), the mean is smallest, the median is in between, and the mode is largest.
- In a positively skewed distribution, their order is reversed.
- Negative skewness may result from a "ceiling" effect (test is too easy for high-scoring students).
- Positive skewness may result from a "floor" effect (test is too hard for low-scoring students).

We began this chapter with a discussion of four different levels of measurement: nominal, ordinal, interval, and ratio. Each level contains more information about the phenomena being described than the previous. Nominal measures simply lump people into groups. Ordinal measures provide the information to rank these groups. Interval scales add information regarding the distance between ranks but use an arbitrary zero point. Ratio scales additionally tell how far an instance is from true zero.

Statistics require a certain level of information in order to be correctly interpreted, therefore some statistics are appropriate only for certain levels of measurement. The mode, median, and mean are good examples of this. We cannot order nominal measures, so we have no median and, of course, no mean. But we can tell which category contains the largest number, so we can determine the modal category. It is obvious that where we have ordinal measures, we can determine the middle case, so we can find a median. If there are ties in rank, there is a modal rank (without ties, all ranks have one case, so there is no peak). Unless we can assume approximately equal intervals between items in the order, the interpretation of a mean ranges from difficult to impossible. (As noted earlier, we often do make that assumption; in essence we assume interval data.) Finally, with interval and ratio measures, we can find all three—mean, median, and mode.

It is a general rule that a statistic can be used with data higher than it was designed to deal with but not lower (we can find a mode for interval data but not a mean for nominal data). In using a statistic designed for lower-level data on higher-level data, we discard the additional information contained in the higher scale. Thus the mode alone includes no information from cases other than those in the modal category. The median finds the middle case, but the clustering or spread of cases on both sides of it does not affect it; such information enters only into the determination of the mean. We tend to think of statistics dealing with the lower levels of measurement as cruder measures. But especially in combination with those at higher levels, we find their insensitivity to certain characteristics helpful. For example, the insensitivity of the median and especially the mode to skewness permits us to sense the skew and its direction.

Measures of Dispersion and Variability

Range.   The second most common aspect of a distribution summarized by a descriptive statistic is its dispersion: how far apart the highest and lowest observations are and how scores are bunched around the center. The simpler of these is the **range**. It is the distance from the highest to the lowest observations. The range for the frequency distribution in Figure 10.1 (A) is 20 − 11 = 9. Because the range is totally dependent on the two extreme scores, it is independent of the way the scores are distributed between them. Therefore, for small samples, it is likely to vary considerably from sample to sample, as endpoints are likely to differ.

Semi-interquartile Range. To take account of the middle scores but include the notion of how far they are spread, we can choose some arbitrary points toward the middle of the distribution and see how far they are apart. The most common such statistic is called the **semi-interquartile range**. A **quartile**, like the median, designates a point below which a given proportion of the scores fall; for quartiles this is one-quarter of them. The first quartile, or Q_1, designates the point below which 25 percent of the observations fall; Q_2, the 50 percent point (so the median is also the second quartile); and Q_3, 75 percent.[7] The semi-interquartile range is half (semi-) the distance between Q_1 and Q_3 (the interquartile range). The quartiles are found just as we found the median, except that we divide the number of cases by 4 instead of 2. In Figure 10.1 (A), because there are 18 cases, the first quartile is halfway between the fourth and fifth cases, 12 and 13. This is 12.5. The third quartile is in an interval with two cases, so we use a procedure similar to that used to find the median, except that for the third quartile we are finding the point below which three-fourths of the cases fall.[8] It turns out to be 15.75. The semi-interquartile range is half the distance between Q_1 and Q_3 ($15.75 - 12.5 = 3.25$; $3.25 \div 2 = 1.625$).

Since we are finding the distance between points, just ranking will not do; interval or ratio scale measures are assumed. The semi-interquartile range is used primarily when only descriptive statistics are used in a study. It has no use in inferential statistics, unlike the standard deviation. Because inferential statistics are common, the standard deviation is the most frequently used measure of dispersion.

Standard Deviation and Variance. The standard deviation and the variance measure how the observations are spread around the mean. The **standard deviation** is the positive square root of the **variance**. To obtain it, we find the distance of each observation from the mean, square that distance, find the mean of those squares, and take the positive square root of that mean. Engineers call it the "root mean square deviation," which states the computational operations in reverse order.

The formula for the standard deviation (SD) of a set of scores is

$$SD = \sqrt{\frac{\Sigma(X - M)^2}{N}}$$

where Σ indicates summation, X stands for each score, M for the mean, and N for the total number of scores. The mean is subtracted from each score; these differences are summed; the sum is divided by the number of scores. The

---

7. In Figure 10.7 (page 174), on the percentile scale the 25th percentile is Q_1, the 50th percentile is Q_2, or the median, and the 75th percentile is Q_3.
8. We need three-fourths of the 18 cases, or 13.5 cases counting from the bottom. This falls in the interval 16, in which there are two cases. There are 13 cases through the score of 15, so we need only half a case from the next two, or 0.5/2, which is 0.25. We add this to the lower boundary of the interval for scores of 16, which is 15.5, to find Q_3, which is 15.75.

positive square root of that quotient is the standard deviation. The standard deviation is the square root of the variance; the variance = SD^2. When a set of scores is a sample from some population and it is the population that is of interest rather than the sample, in order to estimate the population standard deviation, use $N - 1$ rather than N in the denominator. This is necessary in order to correct for a bias in estimation, which is of greater concern with small samples (the effect of subtracting 1 from a large N is negligible).

The standard deviation indicates how broadly the scores in a distribution are spread one from another, the deviation of each score from the mean contributing its bit. Hence a class that is heterogeneous in ability will have a large standard deviation on the ability measure, whereas one that has been grouped by ability to reduce the differences among students will have a much smaller one.

The standard deviation is affected by extreme values even more strongly than the mean (on which it is based). The distance from the mean is squared, and the squares of numbers rise much faster than the numbers themselves, so the more extreme the case, the more leverage it will have. For example, consider 5, 6, 7, and 8, which are but one unit apart. Their squares (25, 36, 49, 64), however, are respectively 11, 13, and 15 units apart, and the distance between numbers one interval apart continues to increase as the numbers get larger. That means that as cases fall farther from the mean, their effect on the standard deviation is disproportionately larger than the effect of cases close to the mean. Because the standard deviation is the average of the squared deviations, it is even more sensitive than the mean to extreme cases.

Figure 10.6 shows the two measures of dispersion on a normal frequency

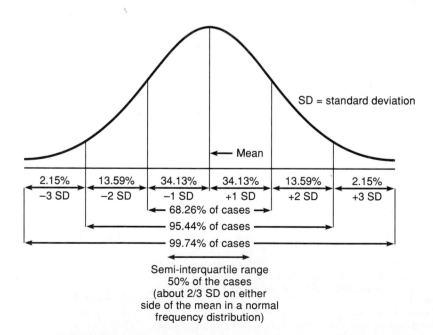

FIGURE 10.6   Two measures of dispersion shown for a normal frequency distribution (normal curve).

distribution. The **normal frequency distribution** is one of several ideal models of data. It corresponds closely enough to the score distributions of many behavioral measures to be quite useful. Note that the semi-interquartile range, by definition, includes the middle half of the cases. The standard deviation usually includes about the middle two-thirds of the cases. Therefore, the middle band including ±1SD on each side of the mean is broader than the semi-interquartile range. The range is not shown, because the highest score for a normal distribution is infinity and the lowest is minus infinity.

Three measures of dispersion are especially useful:

1. The range is the distance from the lowest to the highest score.
2. The semi-interquartile range is half the distance from the point below which a quarter of the observations lie (Q_1, first quartile) to the point below which three-fourths of them lie (Q_3, third quartile).
3. The standard deviation is the root mean square of the deviations from the mean. The square of the standard deviation is the variance. The standard deviation is the dispersion measure most used; it is strongly affected by cases far from the mean.

Standard and Derived Scores.   The standard deviation can help us to develop a kind of constant scale across different measures. A raw score typically conveys very little information because we have no meaningful zero point for our tests. Some tests are easy and others difficult; some are extremely long and some very short. But knowing the mean and the standard deviation, especially if the score distribution is roughly a symmetrical bell-shaped curve, allows us to know whether a particular raw score would be high, low, or in the middle. We met the bell-shaped curve earlier as the normal curve in Louden's clever chart-graph (Figure 10.3). Numerous test score distributions resemble it, as do many physiological functions such as height and reaction time.

Examine Figure 10.6, which is an approximation of a normal curve. The curve is really a frequency distribution just like chart B in Figure 10.1. In chart B, a line joins the tops of the columns representing the number of observations at each score value. Similarly, the normal curve joins the tops of an infinite number of columns running from the highest to the lowest score. When we mark off successive standard deviation distances on the baseline, starting at the mean, we find that one standard deviation falls just at the point where the curve changes from convex to concave. The precentages between the lines in Figure 10.6 that mark off each standard deviation indicate what proportion of the observations falls in that area. Adding the figures for the two regions adjacent to the mean gives 68.26 percent, so slightly more than two-thirds of the cases lie between ±1 standard deviation. Between ±2 standard deviations lie 95 percent of the observations (the middle four sections add to 95.44 percent), and between ±3 standard deviations lie all but 3 cases in 1,000 (99.74 percent).

A variety of score scales are based on the standard deviation. One of these, called **standard scores** (or *z*-scores), replaces the raw score with its distance from the mean in standard deviation units. For example, a raw score of 75 in a distribution with a mean of 100 and a standard deviation of 25, which is one standard deviation below the mean, would have a standard score of −1.00. Standard scores are not much used because the negative figures for all scores below the mean are somewhat difficult to handle and carry a negative connotation. Therefore, score scales are usually translated to a scale where all scores are positive. A constant such as 50, 100, or 500 is added to all scores so that the mean becomes 50, 100, or 500 instead of zero.

Figure 10.7 shows a variety of score scales that set some arbitrary serviceable number like 50 or 100 or 500 as the mean and similarly set the standard deviation conveniently (to 10 or 100) and then translate the scores to that scale. These scores are called **derived scores** (or scaled scores).

Many intelligence test results are reported as deviation IQ scores with a mean set at 100 and the standard deviation at 16. From our knowledge of the normal distribution, we can then interpret an intelligence test score of 148 as very high, for it is three standard deviations from the mean. Since only 3 cases in 1,000 exceed ±3 standard deviations, and that includes the observations in

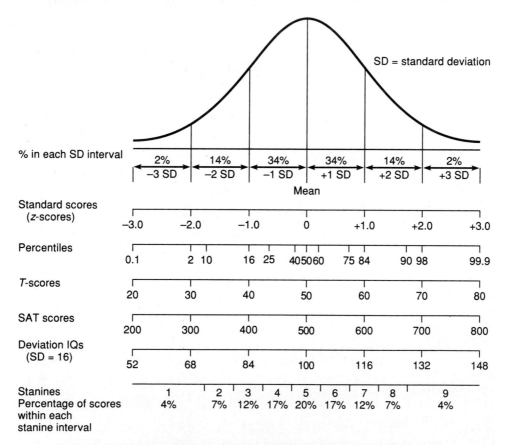

FIGURE 10.7 A variety of score scales shown in relation to the normal curve.

both tails, only 1 or 2 in 1,000 might be expected in the upper tail alone. Similarly, a score of 84 would be one standard deviation below the mean. With half of the cases above the mean and about 34 percent between the mean and one standard deviation below it, we know that $34 + 50 = 84$ percent of the cases will be above the score of 84 and only 16 percent below it.

The percentage below a given score is called the **percentile** score. Figure 10.7 shows where some percentile values fall in terms of standard deviations. Knowing the proportion of cases at points along the normal distribution, we can easily translate raw, standard, and derived scores into percentiles. Many tests have tables showing the translation.

A number of standardized tests use *T*-scores. These have a mean of 50 and a standard deviation of 10. In some, but not all, cases (you must consult the test manual, as the term *T-scores* is sometimes used loosely), the score scale is stretched and shrunk where necessary to make the proportion of cases between any two standard score points fit the proportion we would find in a normal distribution. Although the figures may not be exactly those of a normal distribution, the process results in a distribution that more closely fits normality so that inferences such as two-thirds of the cases falling between 40 and 60 are realized with little or no error. Whether this is true of the ±1 standard deviation portion of nonnormalized score scales depends on the shape of the sample's distribution.

The scores of the SAT of the College Entrance Examination Board were given a mean of 500 and a standard deviation of 100 the first year the test was administered. Test administrations in succeeding years continue to use the first year as a standard. The actual mean and standard deviation for any given year may, therefore, differ a bit from that first year. The discrepancy is small enough, however, that scores continue to be interpreted in terms of the original score scale.

Some tests use **stanine scores**. The name is a contraction of "standard nine." Each stanine is half a standard deviation wide; the middle score of 5 straddles the mean. Since so few cases normally fall in the end categories, these are open-ended, extending to the highest and lowest scores possible on the test. Like some *T*-scores, stanines are forced into a normal curve shape so the percentages found in each stanine are always the same for each test for which they are used. Stanines are intended to cut the typical score scale into nine convenient categories of equal raw score size. Considering the lack of precision of most tests, this cruder categorization of scores may be considered a more appropriate reporting of scores than using two- or three-digit derived scores, where comparison of relatively small score differences (e.g., 704 with 720 in a scale with a possible range of 600 points, like the SAT, for example) invites spurious interpretations. Depending on the relationship of raw scores to scaled scores, 720 could represent only one more question correct (one raw score point) than 714.

Using a standard half-deviation step to define each stanine, however, results in different percentages being included in each interval (4 percent in the lowest, 7 percent in the second lowest, etc.). This can be somewhat awkward unless you become familiar enough with the scores to remember them. The percentages in each stanine are shown on the last line of Figure 10.7.

- Using the standard deviation as the unit of measure and the mean as a base point, standard scores replace the raw score mean with zero and adjust the raw score standard deviation to 1.
- Using this new scale, or "ruler," all scores can be translated to show where they would fall on a standard or derived score scale.
- A variety of derived or scaled scores have been developed to translate raw scores into measures with more convenient values for the mean and standard deviation than standard scores, thus facilitating their use and interpretation.
- Such scores typically use the pattern of distribution of frequencies in the normal curve as a basis for interpretation.
- Percentile scores indicate the percentage of scores falling below a given raw score.

Measuring Relationships

So far we have dealt with the description of a single variable, but more often we have at least two variables and wish to know the relationship between them. Suppose we have grade point averages for a group of students both in high school and in their freshman year of college. We would have a pair of scores for each individual, and each pair could be plotted as a point on a graph. Such a graph is shown in Figure 10.8, where we can see that in general, individuals who did well in high school also did well in college, because the two variables vary together—they co-vary or are correlated. Such a plot is called by several names: **scatterplot**, scatter diagram, scattergram. The oval line surrounding the points is added to show the area within which the pairs of scores fall. Not a part of the computation of a correlation, the oval line will be used in other figures to represent the scatter diagram.

Pearson Product-Moment Correlation. Just as we learn to interpret the standard deviation, so also we learn the meanings of different sizes of the **Pearson product-moment correlation**. Correlations, usually represented by the symbol r, indicate the extent of relationship by a number between zero and +1.00 or −1.00. Either extreme indicates a perfect relationship. If we know one of the scores of a pair, we can exactly predict the other score; the scores track each other exactly. A correlation of less than one, either positive or negative, indicates that the relationship is less than perfect; each member of a pair of scores tracks the other less than perfectly. The lower the correlation, the more poorly one tracks the other, until with a zero correlation there is no regular relationship between the locations of the two scores. Coat or sweater size bears a close to perfect positive relationship to the distance around one's chest. High school academic achievement bears a zero relationship to shoe size or social security number, a negative but less than perfect relationship to the amount of conflict in the family or hours of television watching, and a positive but less than perfect relationship to level of education of one's parents or to one's achievement in elementary school.

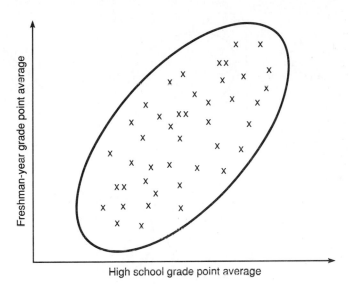

FIGURE 10.8   Correlation of high school and college grade point averages.

A characteristic of the correlation coefficient is that the extent of relationship is indicated more accurately by the square of the coefficient than by the coefficient itself. Thus the amount of relationship displayed by a correlation of .40 is more accurately represented by .16, which is considerably lower. Further, an increase of .05 in a relationship from .90 to .95 can be interpreted as a change from .81 to .90 [that is, $(.90)^2$ to $(.95)^2$], a change of .09. This is the same as the change from a correlation of .10 to .32 [$(.10)^2 = .01$ to $(.32)^2 = .10$], a difference of .22 in coefficient terms. Thus at the low end, large changes are needed to achieve the same amount of increase in relationship that a small change attains at the top end of the correlation coefficient.

The square of the correlation indicates the proportion of the variance that is accounted for by the relationship. For example, with a correlation of 1.00, 100 percent of the variance of the variables is common or accounted for by the relationship. With a correlation of .80, the proportion of variance that is common is .64, or 64 percent.

Anyone using correlations is well advised to create a scatterplot of the observations after computing it. Figure 10.9 shows scatterplots for correlations of various sizes. Correlations are often portrayed by encircling the majority of the points with an oval. As the oval narrows, it becomes a straight line for a perfect correlation, as in scatterplots C ($r = +1.00$) and D ($r = +1.00$). When the correlation decreases, the oval gets fatter until, at the zero point, it becomes a circle, as in plot E ($r = .00$). Plots A ($r = .80$ to .90) and C are positive correlations. Plots B ($r = -.20$ to $-.30$) and D are negative. An exact size was not given for each scatterplot in Figure 10.9 because the correlation depends on the distribution of the scores as well as the shape of the envelope, so these are approximations.

The importance of examining the scatterplot of a correlation is under-

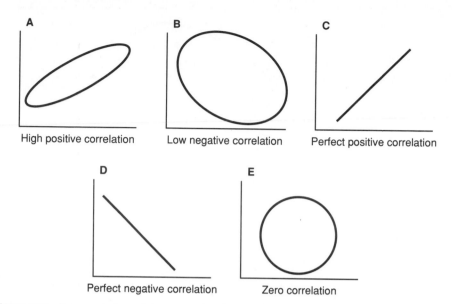

FIGURE 10.9   Representations of the scatterplots for correlations of various sizes.

scored by data from Anscombe's quartet (Anscombe, 1973, as given in Tufte, 1983, pp. 13–14). These are four sets of data, each of which produces exactly the same correlation of .82; they all even have the same means for both variables. But this set of scores for 11 cases produces the scatterplots shown in Figure 10.10. Note how different they are: A is a typical correlation scatterplot; B is a curvilinear plot; C is an almost perfect positive correlation except for one point. In D, all the y scores are the same, but one. Were we to try to infer the nature of the relationship between the variables from just the number .82, the size of the correlation alone, we would be badly mistaken. Yes, the figures were adjusted to make a point, but they make it—examining the scatterplots as well as the statistics is very important! Computerized software makes it easy to get scatterplots, but they often are not presented automatically. Ask for them.

The formula for the Pearson product-moment correlation is very simple in standard score form; it is the average of the products of the standard scores (z-scores) where we multiply the pair of z-scores for each individual (one from the x variable and one from the y variable), sum those products, and divide by the number of scores $(\Sigma z_x z_y)/N$. Since we rarely have scores in standard score form, a more common formula using raw scores (x and y) is

$$r_{xy} = \frac{N\Sigma xy - (\Sigma x)(\Sigma y)}{\sqrt{(N\Sigma x^2 - (\Sigma x)^2)(N\Sigma y^2 - (\Sigma y)^2)}}$$

EFFECT OF OUTLIERS ON THE CORRELATION.   The size of a correlation may be affected by a variety of things. Most common is the effect of one or more extreme scores. Called outliers, these are observations that lie outside the ellipse encompassing most of them. In scatterplot C in Figure 10.10, the observation at

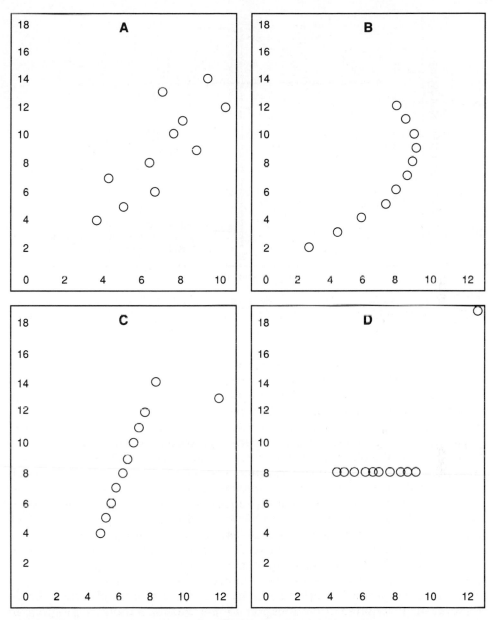

FIGURE 10.10 Scatterplots of four quite different sets of scores for 11 subjects, each set having the same mean for both variables and the scatterplots for all four sets yielding correlations of .82. (After Anscombe, 1973, as found in Tufte, 1983)

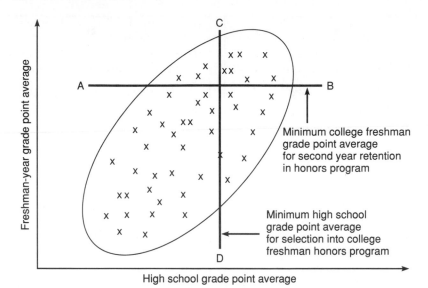

FIGURE 10.11 Selection of students for a college honors program on the basis of their high school grade point average and retention in the program on the basis of their freshman year grade point average.

the far right, which is off the line formed by the others, considerably lowers what would otherwise be a perfect correlation. In the opposite fashion, in scatterplot D, there is no relationship between most of the y-axis scores, which are all 8, and the x-axis scores, which vary over most of the score range, but the outlier in the upper right-hand corner changes the correlation to .82.[9] As these examples indicate, the extreme effect of outliers on correlations makes interpretation difficult. Often correlations are shown both with and without the outliers so that readers can see the effect and together with the interpretation and explanation judge whether the outliers should be disallowed as aberrant cases.

EFFECT OF RESTRICTION OF RANGE ON THE CORRELATION. **Restriction in range** of observations may markedly affect the correlation. This is very apparent if we look at Figure 10.11, which reproduces the data of Figure 10.8 but superimposes on them lines such as would be drawn to indicate a selection process.

Suppose the vertical line CD indicates the minimum high school grade point average required for admission to the freshman honors program in college. The horizontal line AB indicates the minimum college grade point average required at the end of the first semester for retention in that program. Students retained in the program are the cases in the sector between C and B in

---

9. Without the outlier, there is no variability. Consider, without variability, the standard deviation in the denominator of the equation would be zero. Recall your algebra? Dividing by zero was to be avoided because it gave no meaningful result. So there can be no meaningful correlation coefficient without variability.

the upper right-hand corner. Those to the left of the *CD* line never got into the program, but three of them in the sector between *A* and *C* would have made the retention grade point average if they had. Many were selected into the program but did not make the cut for retention, those in the sector between *B* and *D*.

A frequent error in studies seeking to determine the effectiveness of a screening instrument is to examine data only from subjects who survived the screening because they are the ones available. In this instance these would be the cases in the honors program, those to the right of the line *CD*. There is little relation between high school and freshman year grade point averages in this sector. Even worse, sometimes the data used are from subjects who remain after a second screening—those retained in the second year, in the *CB* sector. Finding the size of the correlation after selection has taken place markedly lowers the measure's apparent effectiveness because of the restriction in range. The cases that would have made the correlation larger, the rest of the sectors, were lost because of selection either in high school or in college.

EFFECT OF EXTENDED RANGE ON THE CORRELATION. It stands to reason that if restriction in range lowers the correlation, extending it increases the correlation. Where the range over which the instrument is to be used is less than that for which a correlation is reported, the correlation for that smaller range is likely to be lower. Suppose we are considering using a reading test as a measure of how well the student is likely to achieve. Figure 10.12 shows the relationship of a reading test to achievement for each of grades 3 through 6. Note that the correlation *in any one* of these grades is not very high. The ellipse is quite fat, almost the circle that we obtain for a very low or zero correlation. But the children do learn as they progress from grade to grade, which stretches the overall range of scores. When the grades are combined into a single scatterplot, therefore, the total range increases markedly. Although the correlation was

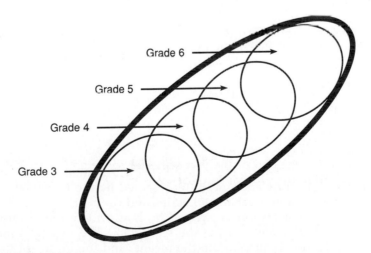

FIGURE 10.12   Effect of extended range on correlation.

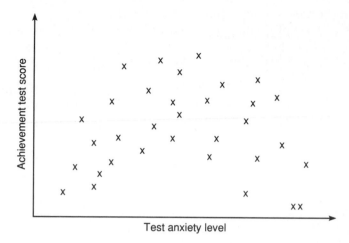

FIGURE 10.13 Curvilinear relationship between level of test anxiety and an achievement test score.

moderate to low in each of the grades taken individually, it is quite high (the heavily outlined ellipse) over the three grades. If we wished to use the reading test to examine children's likely progress in their own grade, the more modest correlation is the one we would heed.

EFFECT OF NONLINEARITY ON THE CORRELATION. From the fact that a perfect correlation is a straight line, it should be apparent that the Pearson product-moment correlation assumes that the relationship we are examining can be charted as a **linear relationship** (also called a straight-line relationship). As one variable changes, the other also changes in a proportionate amount. Relationships are not always linear, however. For example, if a student has very little anxiety about a test, he may not exert himself to do as well as he can and therefore may receive a low score. But if his anxiety is too high, he may be so nervous and unsure of himself that he is unable to exhibit his true potential and will also receive a low score. Only when moderately anxious or aroused does he attain his maximum score.

Figure 10.13 shows a scatterplot for a class, some members of which have too much anxiety about the test, some too little, and some just enough to be motivated but not too much to interfere with problem-solving behavior. Relationships such as that between test anxiety and achievement would clearly yield an inverted U-shaped or curvilinear scatterplot. Such a relationship would be markedly underestimated by the Pearson product-moment correlation.

However, the correlation ratio (represented by the Greek letter eta, η) is designed to handle **nonlinear relationships** and can be used to estimate them. Consider that the correlation is affected by how widely the observations are spread in the columns and rows of the scatterplot. The variances measure the deviations of the observations from the means, and the means of the columns will follow a pattern reflecting the relationship. Assume each anxiety score forms a column. Suppose we computed the variance in achievement for each anxiety score. Given a relationship between anxiety and achievement, the average variance of achievement *within* these columns will be much smaller than the variance of achievement for the whole group. The ratio of these two variances is the correlation ratio, η.

There are two correlation ratios for any scatterplot, one based on the variability within the rows and one based on the variability within the columns. The Pearson product-moment correlation is based on similar reasoning but examines the variation in columns and rows around straight lines that are a best fit to the column *and* row means. When these lines are a poor fit, as in a curvilinear relationship, the statistics fail to reflect the extent of relationship accurately. (For more information on the correlation ratio, see Guilford and Fruchter, 1978, pp. 296–304, or any good statistics book.)

- The Pearson product-moment correlation shows the extent of a linear relationship between two variables on a scale from zero to −1.00 or +1.00.
- Zero indicates no linear relationship.
- A negative correlation indicates that the variables vary inversely: low scores on one variable are associated with high scores on the other, and vice versa.
- A positive correlation shows that they vary together.
- The extent of relationship is portrayed more accurately by the square of the coefficient.
- Size of the correlation is affected by outliers, nonlinearity, and inappropriate range (restriction in range or too broad a range to draw appropriate conclusions).

Correlation and Causation. We often wish to use a correlation to infer that there is a causal relationship, but we must be careful. Often the relationship is caused by a third variable or by a combination of other variables. The statistician Helen Walker used to point out to her classes that if we compared the footsteps left in sand by elderly ladies with those left by younger ones, we might conclude that women tended to walk with their toes pointing outward as they grew older. Actually, there is no causal relationship between growing older and turning one's toes outward; these women simply grew up in a past age when it was considered a sign of femininity to walk that way. More cancer occurs in heavy than light smokers; therefore, there is a correlation. But is smoking the cause, or is the cause something else common to those who smoke and get cancer? Because the link is often earlier in the causal chain, we must be careful in inferring causation from a correlation.

Nonetheless, there are many instances when a correlation does permit us to predict and often, therefore, to take advantage of situations. Universities and personnel directors, looking for the most capable persons, select

TABLE 10.1 Correlations for Special Situations

Correlation	Assumptions	Attributes	Limitations
Spearman's rank correlation (Guilford and Fruchter, 1978, p. 294)	Two ranked variables (e.g., rank in class achievement against rank in social activities), equal intervals between ranks, linearity	A product-moment correlation for ranks; easy to compute for small data sets	Often slightly smaller than the Pearson when raw scores are changed into ranked data
Biserial correlation* (Guilford and Fruchter, 1978, p. 304)	A linear relationship between an interval or ratio scale variable and one that has been arbitrarily dichotomized (e.g., liberal–conservative); latter would be considered normally distributed if measured continuously	Estimates the product-moment correlation for this special situation	Cases between dichotomized parts must not be missing; oddly shaped distributions may yield $r > 1.00$; always larger than point biserial
Point biserial* (Guilford and Fruchter, 1978, p. 308)	A genuinely dichotomous variable (male–female, living–dead; not a continuous variable arbitrarily split), assumes an interval or ratio scale variable, linearity	Connot be interpreted on the product-moment scale but is an index of the relationship	Never quite reaches 1.00 but is at its maximum when the split in the dichotomous variable is 50:50

(continued)

individuals on the basis of the correlation between previous and future work. An extensive body of literature describes predictors of various kinds: to enhance learning conditions, to increase the effectiveness of teaching, to predict the stock market, to forecast college success from that in high school, and so on. We use high school grade point average (GPA), for instance, to predict freshman GPA in college. The higher the correlation, the more accurate the prediction. But unless the correlation is perfect, the predicted score (college GPA) is always less extreme—that is, closer to its mean, than the score from which it was predicted (high school GPA). This is commonly described thus: "Predicted scores regress toward their mean"—the smaller the correlation, the greater the regression toward the mean. Regression toward the mean reaches the mean itself with a zero correlation. With a zero correlation, the best prediction we can make from any score (such as high school GPA) is the mean of the other variable (mean college GPA).

The prediction of one variable from another is discussed in statistics books under the topic of **regression**. Regression, however, is a more

Correlation	Assumptions	Attributes	Limitations
Tetrachoric correlation (Guilford and Fruchter, 1978, p. 311)	Two normally distributed arbitrarily dichotomized variables (achievers– nonachievers vs. tall–short), linearity	Approximates Pearson if assumptions are observed; shortcuts typically used to estimate it	Should not be used with extreme splits (e.g., 90–10); when one cell is empty, it equals 1.00 even if other cells indicate relationship is considerably less
Contingency coefficient (Hays, 1973, p. 743)	Two categorical variables (male– female, living– dead)	Goes between zero and 1.00 with no direction to relationship; equals Pearson when the number of categories increases indefinitely; is always positive	Has a maximum value of less than 1.00 for small number of categories (e.g., .87 for 4 × 4, .97 for 15 × 15); Cramer's phi prime overcomes this
Intraclass correlation (Guilford and Fruchter, 1978, p. 270)	Two or more sets of interval or better data sets	Excellent for use in judging similarity of raters of a common situation or the reliability of repeated measures of individuals; can show members of a category or class are more alike than nonmembers (e.g., twins vs. siblings)	Theoretically, minimum is −1.00 but actually is dependent on number of cases in a class; sensitive to differences in mean and variances of groups being related, and as these differences increase, intraclass correlation decreases

*An example appears in chapter 16, pages 389–390.

complicated topic than we have room to treat here; see Guilford and Fruchter (1978) or Hays (1981).

Other Correlations for Special Conditions. A variety of correlation statistics have been devised for special situations. Some of these have the same properties as the Pearson product-moment correlation, coefficient, and many do not. Table 10.1 lists a number of these, indicating where you can read more about them, the assumptions they make about the data (special situations they fit), their special characteristics, and their limitations.

COMMENTS AND CAVEATS

The statistics of this chapter most often appear in research intended to demonstrate the validity of some hypothesis, structure, or model. But they can also be used in an exploratory mode. Indeed, they have long been used this way to look for unexpected relationships, but that activity isn't usually mentioned in the journal reports. Scatterplots are universally used in this way; we can tell a lot from scatterplots, and researchers love the exhilaration of finding something unexpected in them. Such findings can result in restructuring the direction of a whole study.

Having once experienced that "high," experienced researchers use descriptive statistics for the titillating exploration of data, almost like an addict, looking for the curiosity that may be just around the corner in the next data set. Novice researchers should try exploration; it is the major fun of research. Anyone interested in reading more about exploratory statistics should read Tukey (1977) or Leinhardt and Leinhardt (1980).

In part, exploration has been discouraged by the notion that all research is deductive, that it is cheating to look at the data to see what they show, then develop a hypothesis, and then show that the data confirm it. Right! This is like knowing the outcome of the race before placing bets! Hypotheses developed this way may be the result of happenstance in the data and have no generality. But they may very well have generality, particularly if we can find a rationale for why the data should look as they do and, better yet, show they hold in a new sample.

So always explore your data separately from checking the hypotheses you had when you started. See whether you find any interesting relationships, especially ones that provide new insights or have a reasonable explanation. Include them in your research report separately from the original hypotheses, indicating how they were discovered and your proposed explanation. If you can, check them out in another sample of data to see whether they hold up there; that markedly strengthens the case for the new hypotheses. If not, leave that to do later or for someone else to follow up. Such exploration is very important; it often leads in unexpected new directions. Exploration is important; it is a major route to new findings.

The matter of checking results with a second sample brings up a topic that is very important in statistics: the representativeness and robustness of statistics. Representativeness refers to how well the statistic represents the data. When we were discussing central tendency measures, we noted that the median, for instance, was typically a better representation of a skewed distribution than the mean. Similarly, the range is dependent on the two extreme values (lowest and highest) of any particular sample. Because the range can be changed markedly if a sample happens to contain a very atypical value, we are more likely to use a statistic like the standard deviation or the interquartile range that better represents the data. Statistics that are derived from the bulk of the data and are less affected by extreme values are likely to be robust. When choosing a statistic, choose one that will represent the data appropriately.

This raises the topic of outliers, data points outside the main body of the data set; they have undue weight in many statistics (mean, standard deviation, correlation, etc.). Should we discard outliers? Or do they tell us something special about the topic? Each situation must be judged on its own. Often talking to persons having the extreme scores will turn up the reason. Sometimes, on an achievement test, the outlier case can be accounted for by illness, a death in the family, or English as a second language. Such a case might be discarded. Alternatively, a high-scoring outlier on an art test may be looking at color plates from a different perspective due to color blindness. That would raise interesting questions about what is really being measured, the effects of different kinds of color blindness, and so on. Whatever you decide to do about outliers (keep them or discard them), note in the study report not only the decision and its rationale but also all you know about the outlier cases and their projected effects on the results.

An old saying goes, "Figures don't lie, but liars figure!" This clearly indicates that the use of statistics to mislead is an important problem. Huff (1954) is a still excellent survey of these problems. If we hope to attain a consensus around the interpretation of data, not only must we use the most appropriate statistics, but we must also anticipate problems readers may have in interpreting the research report. For instance, if our sample came from a laboratory school, our readers will suspect the students are all well above average and the range is much smaller than that of most public schools. Assuming the research is intended to apply beyond the laboratory school, we should indicate the effect curtailment in range had on the data, what might be expected under more typical conditions, and how all this affects the interpretation and generality of the results.

Anticipation of the concerns of the reader is a general strategy that will be encountered repeatedly in this material. But it is especially important in statistics and study design, since these are the most likely sources of plausible alternative interpretations of the data.

SUMMARY

The problem of describing a set of data is like that of describing a situation in words where we select the features that are important to convey, name them, and then modify them to portray the situation more accurately. With a data set, we select the feature that is important (such as the measure of central tendency) and then modify it with numbers that convey more exactly the location or amount of that feature.

Graphs and charts convey more than one feature of a data set. Statistics convey single features such as central tendency, dispersion or variation, and relationship. Statistics that convey central tendency are the mean, median, and mode; those that convey variation are the range, semi-interquartile range, and standard deviation. The mean and standard deviation are the most commonly used descriptive statistics and form the basis for standard scores. In combination with the normal frequency distribution, they can be used to translate raw scores into a variety of convenient and more easily interpreted score scales. Standard and derived scores translate the many different raw score scales into a common measure so that scores on different tests can be compared.

The Pearson product-moment correlation is most often used to convey the strength of relationships. Relationships are portrayed by means of a scatterplot, the shape of which indicates the general nature of the correlation. The Pearson assumes that the relationship is best described or approximated by a straight line. Regression permits the prediction of one variable from the other; the accuracy of prediction increases as the correlation increases.

A variety of special correlation statistics have been developed for special situations, including ones with single and multiple predictors. A criterion, whether in categorical or continuous variable form, can be predicted from continuous variables, singly or in combination.

Looking ahead, many of this chapter's statistics are used in determining quality of measurement, so we will meet them again in the next chapter, on measurement, testing, and observation. In chapter 12, we will come back to how different causal patterns relate to correlation. Chapter 17, on inference, inferring from a sample the nature of the population's value, will build on this chapter's statistics.

ADDITIONAL READING

Guilford and Fruchter (1978)
Jaeger (1983)
Moses (1986)

On exploratory data analysis, Leinhardt and Leinhardt (1980); Tukey (1977).

IMPORTANT TERMS

Derived scores
Frequency distribution
Interval scales
Linear relationship
Mean
Median
Mode
Nominal level of measurement
Nonlinear relationship
Normal frequency distribution
Ordinal level of measurement
Pearson product-moment correlation
Percentile

Quartile
Range
Ratio scales
Regression
Restriction in range
Scatterplot
Semi-interquartile range
Skewness
Standard deviation
Standard scores
Stanine score
Stem-and-leaf diagram
Variance

======================= APPLICATION PROBLEMS =======================

1. A Department of Guidance and Counseling faculty member wished to determine how the graduates of its master's program rated the instructional effectiveness of each course. She conducted a study in which graduate students were asked to rate each course on a Likert scale of 1 to 5 (in which 1 = superior and 5 = inferior). She then calculated the mean rating for each course. The department course in statistics was given a mean rating of 1.56; the courses in psychological foundations and sociological foundations had mean ratings of 3.05 and 3.21, respectively. Suppose she had concluded, on the basis of the mean ratings, that the master's graduates considered the instruction in the latter two courses twice as effective as that in statistics. Would she be correct in her assumption?

2. The following is a frequency distribution of the second-quarter house sales at a large real estate firm in Gotham City:

Price Range	Houses Sold
$225,000–$249,999	3
$200,000–$224,999	5
$175,000–$199,999	10
$150,000–$174,999	25
$125,000–$149,999	35
$100,000–$124,999	55
$75,000–$99,999	40
$50,000–$74,999	5
Total	178

(a) Calculate the median price of houses sold that quarter.
(b) If total sales were $23 million, what was the mean house price?
(c) Which is the better representation of central tendency of this distribution, the median or the mean?

3. A newly hired chemistry professor at Beltline University was put in charge of the first-year undergraduate chemistry course, which had an enrollment of over 200 students. He decided to teach the class in sections. Students would be assessed by a midterm and a final examination, each worth 50 percent of their grade. He wanted a way of making it possible for students to compare their standing on successive examinations even though the difficulty of the examinations varied. What would you advise him to do? How would he go about doing that?

4. Drawing on Bandura's (1978) self-efficacy theory of motivation, Salomon (1981) suggested that the relationship between attitude toward media and learning can be conceptualized as an inverted U. He proposed that students invest effort on the basis of two factors: the perceived difficulty of the task and the students' assessment of their skills in relation to the task requirements. Thus students who perceive a medium such as television as easy will invest little effort in television instruction. The more difficult students perceive the medium to be, the more their effort increases until they begin to consider it too difficult. At that point, effort begins to decrease. Dr. Gladys Southwind conducted an experiment to test this relationship, examining subjects' ratings of the difficulty of various media and their effort on a learning task as shown by time on a task using the medium. A Pearson product-moment correlation coefficient determined that the strength of the relationship was only .35. Dr. Southwind concluded that there was not a strong relationship. Would you agree or disagree with her? Why?

Compare your answers with those on page 708.

════ APPLICATION EXERCISE ════

Consider the data that you are likely to collect for the study you plan. How are they best summarized? Graphically? If so, what kinds of symbols or graphs would best convey what you want understood? Would statistics like means and standard deviations be helpful? How might they be presented as well? Would correlations display the strength of relationships among your variables?

Some students lay out "dummy tables" so that they can anticipate what they plan to do in the line of data analysis and can then fill in the tables when they get the data. This avoids surprises. But it also leads them to believe that they can anticipate all they are going to find, when half the fun of research is playing with the data to explore what is there. Don't make that mistake—plan to explore as well.

CHAPTER
11

Measurement, Testing, and Observation

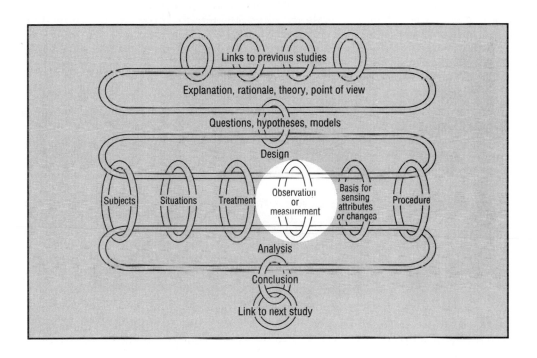

It is the faith of all science that an unlimited number of phenomena can be comprehended in terms of a limited number of concepts or ideal constructs. The constructs are . . . man-made inventions . . . not a part of nature. It is only a way of comprehending nature.

Louis L. Thurstone, Vectors of the Mind

There is no descriptive language that does not consist of general words, that is, of concepts. The gift of humanity is precisely that, unlike animals, we form concepts.

Jacob Bronowski, The Identity of Man

OVERVIEW

In chapter 10, we noted that numbers are adjectives indicating how many or how much. In this chapter, we look at the nouns the adjectives modify, the items or observations that are counted or measured. The problems of measurement are few when the scale is physical—length (how far an individual moved) or time (latency or duration of response), for example. The measurement of concepts and constructs that cannot be directly sensed is more problematic.

How do we know, if we cannot sense them, that we are measuring those constructs? What evidence can we find that an instrument is, in measurement terminology, valid? There is considerable evidence, it turns out, but we must learn what evidence to use when. Consistency is also a problem. Test items may be perceived differently a second time; the testee may be less motivated or more tired. Evidence of consistency of measurement, of reliability, is important. This chapter examines the characteristics of good measurement, in tests and on observation scales.

Constructing good measures is time-consuming and costly. Where can already developed measures be found? What problems may be encountered in choosing measures and observation scales? We will also explore these questions in this chapter.

CHAPTER CONTENTS

Introduction   193
    Measurement Builds on the
       Tools Previously Studied   194
    Measures as Operational
       Definitions   195
    Advantages of Measurement
       and Observation Records   196
Evidence of Test Validity   197
    Construct Validity: Evidence
       of Valid Measurement
       of a Construct   199
    Criterion-related Validity:
       Evidence of Valid
       Prediction   201

    Content Validity: Evidence
       of Valid Measurement of
       Achievement   202
    Face Validity: Evidence of
       Apparent Validity   203
    The Specificity of Validity   204
Test Reliability   206
    Internal Consistency Reliability
       207
    Stability Reliability   210
    Equivalence Reliability   210
    Estimates of Relationships
       under Conditions of
       Perfect Reliability   211

Generalizability Theory   212
Test Objectivity   213
The Standard Error of Measurement   215
Test Improvement through Item
　Analysis   220
　　Empirical Keying   221
Measurement Trade-offs   222

Special Measurement Problems   224
　Setting Cut Scores   224
　Special Testing Methods   225
Sources of Test Information   226
Strengths and Weaknesses of Various
　Data-gathering Methods   227
Summary   230

INTRODUCTION

Measures of constructs record ("freeze in time") a sample of behavior (for example, the ability to visualize the rotation of figures in space) for later evaluation. Observation scales provide a means for recording perceptions of a sample of behavior (who talks, who listens), judgments of persons' behavior (actively following) and internal state (happy), and characterizations of the environment (everyone free to contribute). When properly summarized and interpreted, these evaluations, judgments, and perceptions convey information about variables of interest (spatial ability, classroom climate). They provide a symbolic representation of the behavior or its perception and allow inferences about the state of constructs affecting it.

We tend to think of units and measures, especially physical ones, as obvious or "given." Indeed, some dimensions of phenomena stand out, whereas others are difficult to discern even when we are clear about them conceptually—and often we are not, which makes perception harder. But it is worth noting that dimensions and measures, even of physical characteristics, are social constructions. As Duncan (1984) observes, what we now think of as the result of multiplying width by length (area)

> was measured by cultivators in southeast [sic] Asia by the number of baskets of rice seed required to sow a field. . . . The Chinese even defined a standard vessel for measuring grain and wine in terms of the musical pitch produced when it was struck, so that a pitch pipe, its length measured by millet grains, was . . . [the] measure of capacity. (p. 15)

So cultures choose aspects from phenomena, name dimensions, and select ways to describe them—in our culture usually in units and numbers. Measurement, then, is also part of a theme begun in the early chapters that shows knowledge as the result of a social process.

- Measures pick out of our world concepts of interest to us and operationalize them in ways determined by our culture.
- Measures record information for later use and provide a representation of one of more dimensions. Measures of constructs symbolize their state.

Measurement Builds on the Tools Previously Studied

Measurement builds on other previously covered aspects of the research process: sampling, descriptive statistics, and conceptual analysis.

Sampling. Measures represent phenomena. Where have we discussed representation? In sampling! Measures and observation scales sample these sorts of things:

- The content of a course to find how well a student has learned on the assumption that the questions represent the material in the course (content or domain sampling)
- A student's behavior with respect to that content on the assumption that the sample represents that student's typical behavior with that content (behavior sampling)
- A candidate's ability to solve typical problems involved in a position he or she is seeking on the assumption that today's demonstrated ability is representative of all the tomorrows on the job (time sampling)
- The interaction of a group, coding every 2 minutes the focus of the group and the nature of the interaction, the assumption being that this record of the group's behavior is representative of a complete record such as a video-tape or other recording (time and behavior sampling)
- A pool of questions regarding ways of handling various interpersonal situations on the assumption that certain answers represent an individual's assertiveness, a construct (domain sampling)

All sampling principles apply to measurement. Other things being equal, a larger sample is required in the following circumstances:

- The more heterogeneous the target area or skill being sampled (for example, multiplication of single-digit numbers versus American history)
- The more precise we wish to be about the target (for example, our confidence that an individual's true score will be within 2 rather than 5 points of the observed score is expressed by odds of 1 to 20)
- The more certain we wish to be that the sample represents the target (for example, the confidence that an individual's true score will be within 2 points of the observed score is expressed by odds of 1 to 1,000 rather than odds of 1 to 20)

We also will see a kind of stratified sampling and sequential sampling used in measurement.

Descriptive Statistics. Obviously, to summarize the measurements of any group calls for descriptive statistics: mean, standard deviation, percentile. In addition, we will find correlations used as measures of reliability and validity.

Conceptual Analysis. Through conceptual analysis we found the conditions that enabled us to define a construct. These same conditions allow us to measure it as well. Further, as we shall see, there is a process for determining the construct validity of a measure that directly parallels conceptual analysis.

- Measuring means basically taking a sample of behavior at a sample time (which is a sample of possible times) on a sample of items taken from a domain that is a sample of a larger universe. The principles of sampling studied earlier apply to measurement, and some measures build on sampling techniques.
- Just as descriptive statistics frequently describe the characteristics of samples, so they describe the scores obtained by measures.
- The methods of conceptual analysis are useful in measurement.

Measures as Operational Definitions

We refer to the measure of a construct as its **operational definition** because the operations performed in measuring the construct determine what our data represent. The answers to the problems on an intelligence test become what we mean by "intelligence"; the responses to a series of questions on destitute people receiving government financial assistance become what we mean by "attitude toward welfare programs."

The operational definition of a construct may take three forms.

1. We may specify the operations that bring the construct about.
2. We may specify situations and circumstances that may evoke the construct.
3. We may specify descriptions of behaviors that are regular concomitants of the construct and so may be used as indicators of it.

The first form of definition is often used to bring about conditions that we are interested in studying in an experimental situation. For instance, if we are interested in the effect of the constructs "hunger" and "thirst" on the ability to concentrate, the operations that bring them about are deprivation of food and water, respectively.

The second form describes most of our measures; test items are the situations developed to evoke the behavior, and the testing situation is the circumstance in which those situations are presented. For example, we set a problem in a test situation intended to elicit the correct behavior: "Predict the increase in temperature of hydrogen gas when the pressure on a 20°C 10-gram sample is doubled from 15 ppi." The student has an opportunity to give the correct response if Boyle's law is known.

The third is reflected in observation rating scales: record on an interaction observation rating scale instances of assertiveness defined as interrupting another person, not giving others a chance to talk, or pounding the table when talking (other specific behaviors would be listed, perhaps as a checklist with space for tallies of occurrences). All three are useful ways of defining constructs.

> The operations followed in measuring a construct are its operational definition. Operational definitions may specify the operations that bring it about, the situation that evokes it, or the behaviors that are regular concomitants of it and can therefore be used as indicators of it.

Advantages of Measurement and Observation Records

Measures of a construct extend our senses, gathering more data than we could otherwise comfortably digest and summarizing them in a single number or a profile of numbers. These allow us to differentiate individuals, groups, or classes as having more or less of the construct. As an alternative, consider observing or interviewing individuals to obtain the same information, simultaneously judging it, and then verbally summarizing it in ways that differentiate hundreds of individuals. This makes apparent the efficiency of tests like the Scholastic Aptitude Test (SAT), which, with all its faults, still gathers a great deal of information in a single day's time simultaneously from tens of thousands of potential college students and puts it in usable form.

Measurement often corrects faulty impressions. A student who has done poorly in high school may obtain high scores on the SAT; the individual is not stupid, as we might infer from the grades, but perhaps bored or otherwise not motivated. We may have an impression that dissatisfaction is widespread in a group, only to find with a survey instrument that the problem is confined to a very vocal few.

Observation scales are used to make records of targeted persons (for instance, the group leader), kinds of interaction (praise or reinforcing statements), and who interacts with whom and how. One advantage of such scales is that categorizing and coding occur simultaneously with observation. The record is less voluminous than a video or an audiotape. Further, where a recording must be summarized by categorizing and coding, the tallies of an observation scale are immediately ready for analysis and interpretation. But these constitute only a partial record, colored by the viewpoints of the scale and observer. A video or an audiotape is useful when interaction is so rapid that it is impossible to keep track of all that is going on. Somewhat as the instant replay is used in telecasting professional sports, we can replay the action at slow speed to trace the effects of actions too ephemeral to follow in real time. Further, as often as it is fruitful, we can recategorize and analyze the record from fresh angles as new insights are found and can check our perceptions by having others view it as well.

It is no wonder that fields involving heavy interpersonal interaction, such as psychotherapy, organizational analysis, group leadership, and teaching, made greater strides when it became possible to record these interactions permanently. Knowledge growth seems to follow the ability to record, analyze, and measure the phenomena of a field.

- Measures allow us to differentiate individuals more precisely and accurately than we could with words.
- They permit the collection of enormous amounts of information efficiently and quickly.
- Observation scales abstract from behavior the characteristics of interest. They can be used either in the field or with film or magnetic records of field experiences. The latter allow more detailed analysis than is possible when observations are made as the action is taking place.
- There is some evidence that a field of research develops only as rapidly as the precision of its measures allows.

EVIDENCE OF TEST VALIDITY

Test **validity** refers to "whether the test measures what we want to measure, all of what we want to measure and nothing but what we want to measure" (Thorndike et al., 1991, p. 122). Note that it is referred to as *test validity* to differentiate it from other sorts, such as internal and external validity, which are discussed in chapter 13. Test validity is of concern when the test is intended to measure a variable that is a construct, something that exists in our heads but cannot be directly sensed—educational achievement, ability, attitude, and the like. The validity of measures is self-evident when we can sense the characteristic directly, as when we use a tape measure to find the size of a painting. But we may be concerned with reliability, the consistency of measurement, if it is a cloth tape measure that stretches! As we have learned, we can provide a definition of a construct in verbal terms, through a dictionary definition or conceptual analysis, that helps make explicit what we mean. Validity concerns finding evidence that, in a given context, bears on the correspondence of the interpretation of a set of scores to the verbal or pictorial definition of the construct in our heads. This means that tests may be more valid for certain uses than others and not valid at all for some. Validity is a function of a measure's *use* rather than a constant property of the measure itself. "Validity is an integrated evaluative judgment of the degree to which empirical evidence and theoretical rationales support the adequacy and appropriateness of inferences and actions based on test scores or other modes of assessment" (Messick, 1989, p. 13).

Unfortunately, measures often cover only part of what is commonly meant by a term. For example, when talking casually about "intelligent" individuals, we are likely to include social as well as academic intelligence. The latter is an aspect almost totally outside the typical test's operational definition. Further, when using the term *intelligence*, we are rarely specific about the different facets we mean to include: memory, logical reasoning, spatial visualization, social behavior, and so on. This can lead to fuzzy communication and in some instances to inappropriate action if we interpret scores on an "intelligence" test and act on them under the assumption that individuals have social and spatial skills when the construct was measured only in part. So it is not surprising that operational definitions often do not entirely correspond to the picture of the construct that we have in mind. Often that picture would be clarified by a precise dictionary definition, but especially helpful is a conceptual analysis (chapter 9). With such a definition, it is much easier to know whether the evidence of validity fits the intended construct.

Test validity involves the accumulation of evidence relating the construct and its properties to its operational definition. Different evidence can be gathered, depending on the kind of measure and the purpose for which it is to be used.

- To show that the instrument is a measure of a construct, we gather *construct-related evidence*. It demonstrates that the measure acts as we would expect if it represented the construct.
- In selecting individuals for graduate school, a sales job, or a research training program, we select persons we predict will be successful as judged by a **criterion**: grade point average, total sales, number of patents—some measure generally acepted as valid. Then we seek evidence of *criterion-related validity*.
- To measure achievement in a particular subject matter, mastery of a particular domain, or proficiency in certain job skills, we seek *content-related evidence*.
- Simply looking at the test, we judge whether it looks like a valid measure; this is *face validity*, an important characteristic when the test is used for policy decisions.

The first three are the kinds of validity evidence specified by the standards agreed on by specialists in the field (American Educational Research Association et al., 1985). The fourth, though not recognized as a "scientific" kind of evidence, is nonetheless often used by laypersons to judge the acceptability of decisions made on the basis of measurement evidence.

Past conceptualizations and test standards have discussed construct validity, criterion-related validity (which is further divided into *predictive validity* and *concurrent validity*), and content validity as different *kinds* of validity. To emphasize the unitary nature of validity where each of these contributes evidence as appropriate, the 1985 version of the test standards relabels all these as *sources of evidence*. Provided that we understand that all provide evidence in support of judgments about the validity of inferences and actions based on the measures, there seems little harm in retaining the conventional labels in our discussion. These are the terms you are likely to encounter in the field, at least during the lifetime of this edition of the book.

Test validity is of concern when measuring constructs. Validity is a judgment of the support given by empirical evidence and theoretical rationales for the adequacy and appropriateness of inferences and actions based on the measures. We use as many kinds of evidence as are relevant for the judgment.

Construct Validity: Evidence of Valid Measurement of a Construct

Construct validity is typically deemed the most important kind of validity; it involves gathering a variety of kinds of evidence to show that the measure behaves as we would expect if it represented the concept. Some experts (including Cronbach, 1984, and Messick, 1989) argue that construct validity includes all the other kinds of evidence. Since construct validity evidence shows that the test behaves as we would expect it to, and since that includes predicting in certain situations (criterion-related validity evidence) and covering certain subject matter (content validity evidence), you can see how this claim can be made. It makes little practical difference whether or not we agree with this; the important point is to have the appropriate evidence to show congruence between what we wish to measure and what we are actually measuring. For instructional purposes, we shall review the various kinds of evidence so that it is clear what kinds exist and hence what might be appropriate for which purposes.

Evidence of construct validity bears more than passing similarity to the evidence of models or cases gathered in a conceptual analysis:

- Model cases: the test in question correlates highly with other "on target" measures of the construct.
- Contrary cases: the test has low or zero correlations with measures that ought not to relate to it.
- Borderline and related cases: the test has intermediate correlations with measures that are almost but not quite the same.

An important step in conceptual analysis is to find a model example. In construct validity, it is finding other accepted measures of the concept, preferably the best available. If the test in question correlates highly with them, this is evidence of construct validity. Suppose we had a new measure of children's intelligence; we would expect it to show a high correlation with scores on the Wechsler Intelligence Scale for Children or the Stanford-Binet Intelligence Test, both widely accepted measures of intelligence. Sometimes the best measure is difficult to obtain: an accepted measure of sales ability, for instance, might require new personnel to spend several months of experience on the job before the supervisor could rate them. But those ratings would indicate how well the new test measured sales ability.[1]

In conceptual analysis, we show the boundaries of a concept by finding examples that are not instances of the target construct as well as ones that are related or borderline cases. In construct validity, the former are tests that should not correlate with the concept of interest or should be correlated less highly with it than with some other test. For example, given a new test of creativity, we could develop a set of propositions about how individuals who

---

1. If you are already familiar with validity evidence, you will recognize this as criterion-related evidence. This may seem confusing, but it is why some experts claim that construct validity encompasses the other types of evidence.

are creative would behave in certain artistic situations. These propositions would predict where we would find contrary, related, and borderline cases.

We might expect that creative people should be flexible, but not all flexible people are creative. Therefore, flexibility is a contingent (necessary but not sufficient) condition for artistic creativity.[2] This means that there might be people with both high and low creativity in their art who are flexible, but no inflexible people should be creative (contrary, or negative, case). We might inspect a scatterplot of the creativity measure against a flexibility measure to see whether there are people with high flexibility scores and low creativity scores but no persons with high creativity scores combined with low flexibility scores.

Similarly, daydreaming might be correlated with creativity, but again, it should show a low correlation, in that daydreaming might facilitate creativity, but is not a necessary condition for it (related, or borderline, case); it is a contributing condition.[3] So just as in conceptual analysis, we look for other parts of the network of measures that might be related to the construct and see whether they prove to be related as we would expect.

Factor analysis is often used to show construct validity when we hypothesize what abilities underlie performance on a test.[4] Factor analysis is a method for analyzing a table of intercorrelations, usually between test items or test scores but sometimes between person profiles or test results at different times. It indicates the underlying factors that account for the correlations. The names of the factors must be deduced from the data. If the test has construct validity, the names of the factors will be found to correspond to what the test was intended to measure. For instance, suppose we have a new measure of verbal creativity. We might predict that verbal fluency and flexibility would be two of the factors underlying such a test. A factor analysis of the intercorrelations of a battery of test scores that included measures of verbal fluency and flexibility as well as the new test scores would show whether such factors as verbal fluency and flexibility did indeed show up and how the previous and new tests related to them—evidence of construct validity.

Because establishing construct validity involves showing that the test behaves as we would expect a valid measure of the construct to behave, the kinds of evidence collected for it can involve all the other forms of validity. This can be confusing unless we realize that the others are limited evidence for validity and that construct validity provides the most inclusive evidence.

Messick (1989), in a very interesting and comprehensive discussion of validity, argues that the unitary nature of validity includes not only all the aspects of construct validity but also the value implications of test interpretation and the social consequences of test use. As he notes:

> A social consequence of testing, such as adverse impact against females in the use of a quantitative test, either stems from a source of test invalidity or

---

2. Remember this example for reference in the next chapter.
3. Remember this too; you'll encounter it also in the next chapter.
4. See pp. 585–588; Table 22.2 and accompanying text explain the use of factor analysis in construct validity.

reflects a valid property of the construct assessed, or both. In the former case, this adverse consequence bears on the meaning of the test scores and, in the latter case, on the meaning of the construct. In both cases, therefore, construct validity binds social consequences of testing to the evidential basis of test interpretation and use. (p. 21)

It is important to note that this reinforces and then goes beyond the notion of construct validity as being the preeminent and all-encompassing form of validity. But equally important, this is another in an increasing number of instances in the behavioral sciences where the interlocking nature of the relation of values and science is being explored. Researchers in qualitative research have been much interested in this relationship. They will perceive this social awareness as a healthy corrective among quantitative researchers to what they believed was a "head in the sand" approach. Some would argue that such concerns are more appropriate to a textbook on the application of knowledge than one like this concerned with its discovery and validation. But if we take an instrumentalist view of knowledge, that the main goal of knowledge is its use, such concerns are appropriate and demand the kind of further exploration taking place.

Criterion-related Validity: Evidence of Valid Prediction

We have already noted an example of criterion-related evidence in our salesperson example. Since there are two kinds of **criterion-related validity**—concurrent and predictive—it is worth discussing this example further. These terms describe when the criterion measure was obtained. If obtained at the same time as the test scores, it is evidence of **concurrent validity**; if obtained later than the test scores, it is **predictive validity**.

Returning to the salesperson example, suppose we wait several months after a new crew of salespeople have been hired so as to accumulate enough evidence to know their relative sales accomplishments. Then we give the predicting test and correlate test scores with total sales for each salesperson. This is concurrent validity. But while we were waiting for sufficient sales data to accumulate before giving the test, the unsuccessful ones dropped out or were fired. Thus the test must discriminate not between the unsuccessful and the successful salespeople but among the successful sales personnel, a much more difficult job. This results in a correlation with restricted range similar to the one in chapter 10 when we were predicting success in college (see Figure 10.11). The test might have been better able to predict who would leave and who would stay, but we will never be sure.

We would have had predictive validity had we correlated scores taken when the new crew was hired with accumulated sales at a later date. What is the relationship of concurrent validity to predictive validity? If there is no selective dropout over the course of the data collection, predictive validity is likely to be lower than concurrent validity because predictive validity involves correlation with a characteristic at a distant point in time. But if, as in our example, there is selective dropout of the weaker candidates, we have two counteracting forces: (1) the instability of the trait being predicted over the time of prediction lowers the correlation, and (2) the release from restriction in range when the dropout cases are included in the predictive validity correlation would typically increase the correlation. Whichever of these two is the stronger will determine whether predictive validity is higher or lower than concurrent validity. Since we are usually dealing with a reliable measure, the effect of the larger range resulting from including dropouts is usually the stronger. We usually consider concurrent validity to be a lower-boundary estimate of predictive validity.

Content Validity: Evidence of Valid Measurement of Achievement

Evidence of **content validity** (also called curricular validity) is important for tests that are used to measure academic achievement or competency. Examples are minimal competency examinations required for high school graduation or for obtaining a teaching certificate. *Domain validity* is more general, as a domain can be a content or a curriculum area, such as assembling a rifle or using a software program like Microsoft's Word on a computer. Such tests are shown to be valid if they adequately represent the content of an area, curriculum, or domain. In some instances, a job analysis provides specifications of the skills and content with which a test can be compared for content-related evidence, just as a curriculum does for a course in school. The initial discussion of validity indicated it was a judgment supported by empirical evidence and *theoretical rationales*; content-related evidence provides these rationales.

Evidence of content validity is basically a representation problem and therefore involves sampling. We show how well the various parts of the test represent the content by comparing the test with a "table of specifications," such as Table 11.1, for an examination dealing with test validity, reliability, and objectivity.[5] The table is constructed from behavioral objectives or goals of instruction. Such objectives state the combinations of behavior and content that the students are expected to be able to show upon completion of instruction. The content is arrayed down the left side of the table, and the behaviors are arrayed across the top. A number in a cell designates that cell as one of the combinations of content and behaviors that the student should be able to display upon completion of the course.

The table is a version of stratified sampling where, to be sure that all parts of the domain are adequately represented, we stratify on two variables, content and behavior. The whole table represents the domain to be sampled. Each cell is a subdomain within which a pool of items of varying levels of difficulty is sampled. Because some behaviors and certain content may be more important

---

5. In evaluating programs rather than individuals, each student might be given a sample of only a few items from the table so that testing time for an individual is minimized but coverage of the whole table is maximized. This process, called matrix sampling, is used by the National Assessment of Educational Progress.

TABLE 11.1 Specifications for a Test of Test Validity, Reliability, and Objectivity

Subject Matter \ Skills	Knows major terms and concepts	Can use terms correctly and intelligently	Can apply the concepts to a situation	Can construct a table of specifications	Can evaluate the usage of concepts in a study	Row weight in %
Validity	9	9	18	10	18	64
Construct	(4)	(4)	(8)		(8)	
Predictive	(2)	(2)	(4)		(4)	
Content	(2)	(2)	(4)	(10)	(4)	
Face	(1)	(1)	(2)		(2)	
Reliability	5	5	10		10	30
Internal consistency	(2)	(2)	(4)		(4)	
Stability	(1)	(1)	(2)		(2)	
Equivalence	(1)	(1)	(2)		(2)	
Stability & equivalence	(1)	(1)	(2)		(2)	
Objectivity	1	1	2		2	6
Column weight in %	15	15	30	10	30	100

than others, we can weight the columns and rows to indicate the proportion of the total test items that should come from each. These are shown as percentages in the bottom row and the far-right column. Each cell entry is the product of the percentages for the row and column defining that cell, and this number shows the percentage of the total test items that is to come from the cell. Where the domain's main emphasis is on particular cells, it may make more sense to assign weights to cell entries directly rather than use row and column weightings. The numbers in parentheses show how many items are devoted to a subtopic; they add to the total at the head of their section of the column. By comparing the test's actual sampling of items with those shown as ideal by the table of specifications, we can determine the content validity.

We tend to think of content validity as applying to a particular test in relation to a particular course. But of course, achievement tests tend to be built to apply to curricular areas and are then validated for particular courses. Crocker, Llabre, and Miller (1988) provide designs for using raters to determine the content validity of a test in relation to a curricular area so that the generalization of the content validity over different curricula can be demonstrated. They give as an example data from an international assessment of mathematics achievement.

Face Validity: Evidence of Apparent Validity

Face validity means that the measure looks as though it would be valid. Compared with the other kinds of evidence, this may seem inane, as it is simply the impression of validity. Yet because people who are not knowledgeable about measurement judge a test by its looks rather than its data, face validity can be crucial for tests used for public policy purposes. For a long time, studies have shown that a multiple-choice test involving English usage correlates with ability to write almost as well as very carefully scored written compositions (Breland, 1987). Nevertheless, the College Entrance Examination Board still uses actual composition samples instead of a multiple-choice test, which would be less expensive, less time-consuming, and quicker and easier to score. Why? The face validity of the multiple-choice test is so poor that the test's clients refuse to accept the evidence that it will do as well as an actual writing sample. Similarly, although the National Teacher Examination (now called the NTE Examination) never claimed to measure anything other than the content of the teacher preparation curriculum, it was repeatedly criticized for its poor face validity because it contained no actual sample of teaching. For tests used in making critical decisions, face validity is important, but it is not a kind of validity that is recognized in the test standards (American Educational Research Association [AERA] et al., 1974).

The Specificity of Validity

We have seen that various kinds of evidence are used to establish that a particular test is valid. Further, evidence of validity is always gathered in a particular context, and one of our concerns is the generality of that context. A test that is useful for selecting individuals for entrance to East Snowshoe State College may not be selective enough for a prestigious institution. We ask whether specificity in a situation makes it unique and limits the generality of the results from it. Is there specificity in a job or task that similarly limits generality (Schmidt and Hunter, 1981)? Because important decisions are often based on tests and because validity evidence can vary widely from instance to instance, courts have held that validity is specific rather than general.[6] Further, texts and the 1974 version of standards for psychological tests (AERA et al., 1974) have specified that validity coefficients are specific to the situations in which they were obtained.

This point of view has been contested, however, by those examining the evidence, and as Messick (1989) and Hunter and Schmidt (1990) show, a good case can be built for validity generalization if we can establish the relationship of the instance of proposed use to the accumulated evidence. Further, we must look at the social consequences as well, where important trade-offs are sometimes hidden. These can be positive as well as negative and can change with time. Use of the NTE was originally hailed as a breakthrough when African-American teachers with a high enough score could attain the same pay scale as Caucasians in certain states. Later, when pay was no longer differentiated by race, many viewed the NTE as discriminating against the minorities it originally helped.

Table 11.2 summarizes information regarding the kinds of validity, purpose, questions posed, and how evidence is obtained.

---

6. *Griggs* v. *Duke Power Co.*, 401 U.S. 424 (1971).

TABLE 11.2   Summary of the Kinds of Evidence of Validity

Kind of Evidence of Validity	Purpose	Question Posed	How Obtained
Construct validity (an inclusive form of validity; operates similarly to the first step in conceptual analysis)	To show that the test is a valid measure of the construct	Does the test behave as would be expected of a valid test of the construct?	Determine how the test would behave if valid and demonstrate that it so behaves (it should correlate with other measures of the construct, not correlate with measures not related to the construct, show an internal structure as predicted from the construct, predict success for high scorers in situations where the construct so contributes, etc.)
Criterion-related validity: Predictive validity	To demonstrate how the test would work when used to predict success and failure (criterion-related validity is gathered from a particular sample of persons, places, and times, and generalization from that instance should be done with care)	Does the test predict the success and failure of entrants?	Correlate test scores obtained at or prior to entrance to a program with a criterion measure of success obtained at end of program
Concurrent validity	To estimate predictive validity	Does the test predict success and failure of survivors?	Correlate test scores obtained at the same time as the criterion measure of success is obtained (misses subjects who had failed prior to that point; usually underestimates predictive validity)
Content validity	To show how well the test covers the domain of a subject it is designed to test	Does the test sample the content and behaviors of its domain with adequate coverage and proper emphasis?	Compare the test items with a table of specifications that describes the intersections of the content covered and the behaviors taught and indicates the relative emphasis for each intersection
Face validity	To show that the test meets our expectations of a valid test; especially important for a test used for public policy purposes with laypersons untutored in measurement	Does the test look like a valid measure?	Examine the test

TEST RELIABILITY

Reliability refers to the consistency of a test in measuring whatever it measures. The problem is that a test may be consistent even if it measures the wrong thing—reliability without validity. A commonly used analogy is to think of the test as a gun that, when valid, repeatedly hits the heart of the target and, when unreliable, spreads shots all over the target. Figure 11.1 illustrates this. The middle target is a valid test. What is important for *reliability* in this analogy is *not* that the gun hits the bull's-eye—that is, validity. Instead, it is that the gun is consistent—the shots are clustered (have high reliability—middle and right-hand targets). If the shots are clustered but not on target, the gun is at least reliable (consistent). If we can aim it properly, we will have validity as well. But a gun that is not consistent (has low reliability) will be all over the target even when properly aimed (has low validity, since it gives inconsistent scores—the left-hand target).

So reliability is a necessary condition for validity, but it is not a sufficient condition, not a guarantee that the test is valid. We examined validity first because if there is evidence of adequate validity, we don't need to worry about reliability.

Reliability is the consistency with which persons evidencing the same amount of whatever the test measures are assigned the same score under different testing conditions. Because various factors may prevent this, there are different measures of reliability:

- The test may consist of items from different, unrelated domains (spatial visualization and creativity) so that a middle score may represent excellence in only one (spatial visualization) or another (creativity) or middling levels in more than one. We don't know how to interpret the score—the test score lacks **internal consistency reliability**.
- Different samples of items assign a different score to the same level of competency or ability. Form A of a test yields different scores than form B—the scores from the different test forms lack **equivalence reliability**.

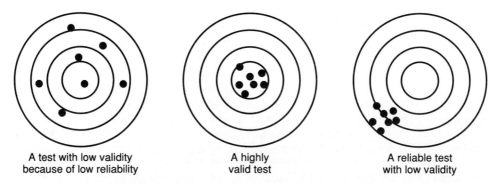

| A test with low validity because of low reliability | A highly valid test | A reliable test with low validity |

FIGURE 11.1 Reliability and validity portrayed as an analogy to firing consistent and inconsistent guns at a target.

■ The individual's responses vary over time either because perceptions of the items change or because the level of the construct changes. Today the world looks rosy and I responded accordingly; yesterday I felt depressed by the rain and darkness and it affected my answers—the test scores lack **stability reliability**.

We will examine each of these in more detail.

■ Test reliability refers to the consistency of results produced by a measure.
■ Reliability is a necessary but not sufficient condition for high validity. A valid measure is reliable, but a reliable measure may or may not be valid for the purpose intended.
■ As with validity, different evidence of reliability is used, depending on what kind of consistency is desired.

Internal Consistency Reliability

We would expect a perfectly reliable measure to be affected only by the construct of interest; all the test items should measure that construct and nothing else. Viewed in this way, the items of the test ought to be highly correlated. Individuals at the same level of the construct responding one way to a particular item ought to respond the same way to similar items. Indeed, the response patterns for individuals at the same level of ability ought to be roughly the same for all items so that all items correlate. But note that we have been talking about a test measuring one construct and all of the items correlating with one another in measuring that construct. That is what we mean by internal consistency reliability.

A test with low internal consistency may measure more than one construct, including one perhaps unrelated to the intended one. It may measure a different version of the construct we have in mind, as when a student learns material incorrectly. The responses may be affected by a pattern of random error, as when various students are distracted by external things. Often low reliability results from some combination of these factors. When this occurs, the responses to certain parts of the test may be independent of, rather than related to, those in another part of the test. A student may be correct on an item and incorrect on a similar item or do a certain part of the test flawlessly and another part poorly. When this occurs, we have difficulty knowing how to interpret the scores on the test. Unless there is consistency in responding across all items by all individuals, what does the score represent? Skill in the construct we intended to measure? Skill in an incorrect version of it? A construct that is relatively unrelated? Random error? Some blend of these? Without internal consistency, we can't tell. Score interpretability is the contribution of internal consistency reliability.

The homogeneity of a domain is not solely a function of the domain itself, especially for achievement tests and other learned responses. It is also affected by the way the domain was experienced or learned. When a student misses part of a test even though it contains relatively easy items, this may represent a portion of the course material poorly learned by the testee but well learned by others. Some subject areas tend to be more homogeneous in that a student who succeeds in one part of the domain also tends to succeed in another. Mathematics is such a subject, since people who do better at puzzling out one geometric proof or solving one equation can usually do other, similar problems. Well-learned generalizations link solutions across material and lead to high internal consistency reliability. Social studies, such as geographic and historical material, by contrast, have few such generalizations, so knowing the seventeenth century doesn't help with questions on the eighteenth or with locating modern national boundaries. For some students, visualizing the relationships of countries is easy, but remembering historical facts is hard; others may have the opposite pattern of success. The more differently individuals experience the material, the more they will diverge in terms of what is easy and what is hard, and the lower the internal consistency or homogeneity.

This makes clear the importance of internal consistency reliability. With good reliability, a high score accompanies a higher level of the construct so that we can predict individual behavior with material of which this test is a sample; with low reliability, such predictability is not possible.

Measuring Internal Consistency Reliability. There are several ways of estimating the internal consistency of a test. One is to split the test into two halves, randomly assigning the items to halves and examining the consistency of the scores between them. A perfectly reliable test would have identical scores on each half; divergence would indicate less than perfect reliability. A correlation coefficient expresses the internal consistency and therefore the reliability. Consider, however, that half the test is a smaller sample of behavior than the whole test, and we can be surer that a large sample will be more consistently representative than a small sample. The half-tests will be less consistent, and a correlation between the halves will underrepresent the reliability of the whole test. Fortunately, there is a way of estimating whole-test reliability: the Spearman-Brown prophecy formula. Using it, we can estimate the reliability for a full-length test. Such reliabilities are sometimes referred to as Spearman-Brown reliabilities.

The Spearman-Brown formula is a general one that can be used to estimate reliability for any amount of change in test length, halving it, tripling it, whatever. The formula for the corrected reliability is:

$$\frac{Kr}{1 + (K - 1)\, r}$$

where K is the ratio of items in the new test to those in the original form and r is the reliability of the original form.

Sometimes, instead of randomly splitting the test into halves, we assign the odd-numbered items to one half and the even-numbered ones to the other. Internal consistency reliability can be found this way for a test where similar items are grouped (a math section, a social studies section, etc.). This is called parallel split-half reliability. It forces a kind of stratification on the halves so that each half contains equal numbers of items from each section. Reliability on such a test will be higher than on one based on a random split.

Obviously, there are many possible random splits. Each might give a slightly different reliability estimate. An estimate of the average reliability for all random split halves is given by the **Kuder-Richardson reliability** formula 21 (for tests scored right and wrong), Cronbach's **alpha coefficient**, or Hoyt's analysis of variance estimate of reliability (either can be used with any test scoring). Kuder-Richardson formula 21 (KR21) requires only the mean, the variance, and the number of items to obtain an estimate, so it is very convenient. Because it assumes that all items are of equal difficulty, which is almost never the case, it yields a slightly lower estimate than other formulas, such as KR20, which requires additional information. The KR21 estimate may be considered a lower boundary on internal consistency reliability, since other estimates (parallel split halves, KR20, etc.) are likely to be higher.

The formula for KR21 is

$$r = \frac{k}{k - 1}\left(1 - \frac{M\,(k - M)}{k\,(\mathrm{SD}^2)}\right)$$

where k is the number of items on the test (and the maximum possible score), M is the average score on the test, and SD is the standard deviation of the test. The formula for KR20 is

$$r = \frac{k}{k - 1}\left(1 - \frac{\Sigma pq}{(\mathrm{SD}^2)}\right)$$

where p is the proportion of students passing an item and q is the proportion of students not passing it. The Σ indicates that these pq values are summed over all the items on the test. Coefficient alpha is a more generalized form of KR21 where the sum of the variances of the parts of the test replaces Σpq in the numerator of KR21. In an instance where items are scored on a 10-point scale, for example, each item would be considered a part of the test, and the variances of the items would be summed.

Time limits so short that many do not finish result in speeded tests. Such tests artificially inflate estimates of reliability, because all the items a student did not attempt will be viewed as consistently missed, and such a pattern would be more regular than if the testees had the chance to attempt them. Internal consistency and split-half coefficients are not appropriate for speeded tests.

Another way of looking at internal consistency reliability assumes that the test is a random sample of all the possible items that measure the domain from which the items came. Each individual would have a score on this universe of items. We might think of it as a universe score. The correlation between the observed test score and the universe score would be an estimate of how representative this set of items is of the universe. That is, internal consistency reliability measures the consistency with which random samples of items taken from that pool would yield consistent estimates of those scores. Obviously, we can't compute such a correlation because we do not know those universe scores, but we can estimate it from the data we have. You can perhaps sense the parallel to comparing the scores from random split halves of a test. This suggests another interpretation for Cronbach's alpha and the Kuder-Richardson formulas. They estimate the representativeness of these items of the universe or domain of which they are a sample.

Stability Reliability

Stability reliability asks, "How consistent are the scores over time?" To obtain stability reliability, we correlate two sets of scores from the same test given at two different points in time. How much time between testings? It depends on the period for which we wish to estimate stability. If we plan to compare achievement test scores taken at the beginning of a semester with those at the end, then ideally, the stability coefficient will be estimated from testings a semester apart. For an achievement test, that might raise questions whether learning some of the material could be avoided during such a long period; in practice, such periods are usually shorter. The principle is that the period should be as close to the target interval as possible, barring other influences that might affect the reliability estimate. The best trade-off between the two influences is a matter of judgment.

Equivalence Reliability

Equivalence reliability asks about the consistency of scores over two different samples of test items, such as two forms of the same test. We correlate the scores from one form of a test with those of another form of the same test. Because taking one form may facilitate the ability to do well on the second testing, we usually use a counterbalanced design. **Counterbalancing** is a general technique for eliminating the effect of the order in which individuals encounter tests, treatments, or whatever. It involves dividing the sample into as many equal groups as there are possible orderings of whatever is being administered. In this instance, there are two forms, so the group would be divided in half, one half receiving form A first and the other form B. Were there three forms and it was thought there might be an influence not only of the first on the second testing but also of the second on the third, then the sample would be divided into six, with all possible testing orders: ABC, ACB, BAC, BCA, CAB, and CBA.

What if we wish to use one form of a test at the opening of a semester and the other at the end? Then we are interested in a combination of stability and equivalence reliability. This is estimated by correlating the scores from different forms of a test administered with a suitable intervening period. Typically, that estimate will be lower than either the stability or the equivalence reliability alone, since two sources of inconsistency are involved.

Table 11.3 summarizes the information for the different kinds of reliability: the question posed, what kind of consistency is indicated, the purpose of obtaining that measure of consistency, and how it is obtained.

TABLE 11.3   Summary of the Different Kinds of Test Reliability

Kind of Reliability	Question Posed	Area of Consistency of responses	Purpose	How Estimated
Internal consistency	Are all items measuring the same thing—a single construct or dimension? Is the score interpretable?	Items of varying difficulty and content (e.g., low scorers get easy items and miss hard ones)	To determine the homogeneity of the test and the interpretability of scores	Use random split halves (split the test into random halves, correlate the scores from each half, and correct the correlation with the Spearman-Brown formula for the shortness of the half-test) or the Kuder-Richardson formula (for items scored "right" and "wrong") or Cronbach's alpha for tests with weighted responses
Equivalence	Are different forms of the test equivalent?	Different forms of a test	To determine whether the forms can be used interchangeably	Correlate the scores of form A with those of form B
Stability	Is the behavior stable over time?	Different testing times (interval should approximate that of intended use)	To determine the stability of the construct over time	Correlate the scores at one testing with those of the second testing
Stability and equivalence	Will one form of the test produce the same results as another form at a later time?	Different forms of a test given at different times	To determine the stability of the construct over time and across test forms	Correlate the scores at one testing with those on the other form at a later testing

Estimates of Relationships under Conditions of Perfect Reliability

In discussing predictive validity, we did not comment on the effect of un-reliability. But obviously, unreliability of either the predicting test or the criterion would cause the correlation to underestimate what the relationship might be if we could have had perfectly reliable tests. The **correction for attenuation** allows us to estimate the improvement in the correlation if both criterion and test were perfectly reliable. By using it, we can then tell whether the test is worth improving or whether it is measuring the wrong things. For instance, "What is the size of the relationship if the test and the sales manager ratings were perfectly reliable?" tells us whether to try to improve this test further or to take a different approach.

The formula for the correction for attenuation is

$$\frac{r_{xy}}{\sqrt{r_{xx}r_{yy}}}$$

where r_{xy} is the correlation to be corrected and r_{xx} and r_{yy} are the reliabilities of the tests involved in that correlation (see Guilford and Fruchter, 1978). Its accuracy, like that of any statistic, depends on the accuracy of the data on which it is based. For instance, lower-bound estimates of reliability from KR21, which are usually underestimates, can result in nonsense correlations of over 1.00; overestimates of reliability from using the parallel split half on a speeded test may give underestimates.

The formula can also be used to correct any correlation between two imperfectly measured variables to determine the real size of the relationship between them, given perfect measurements. This helps us to understand the extent of the relationship between constructs, devoid of measurement error. This is what we are seeking as we attempt to build theory that provides a real understanding of a phenomenon.

In using the correction for attenuation, the sources of inconsistency measured by the particular estimates of reliability used should reflect the sources of error we wish to eliminate. For instance, in the salesperson test example, because we want to predict over time, we include stability reliability. Suppose the stability reliability of the test is .80 and the stability reliability of the criterion, based on a correlation of two sales measures at different points in time, is .60. (It would also include inconsistency of the sales manager's judgment if ratings were based on characteristics besides dollar amounts of sales.) The .40 original predictability of total sales becomes .84 when corrected for the unreliability in both measures, a marked change.

> The correction for attenuation estimates the size of a correlation if both the measures involved were perfectly reliable. It is useful in determining whether a test is "on target" and merely needs to have its reliability improved and in estimating what the size of the relationship between constructs would be without measurement error.

Although we are very much concerned with reliability where individual measurements must be interpreted, we are much less concerned when group means are compared, provided that we have reasonable sample sizes. Although the differences between individual scores are unreliable, the mean of the differences is considerably less affected. For a discussion of this point, and an excellent discussion of reliability in general, see Feldt and Brennan (1989).

Generalizability Theory

Generalizability theory bridges the traditional conceptualizations of reliability and validity (Cronbach et al., 1972; Shavelson, Webb, and Rowley, 1989). It considers a test score to be a sample from a universe of possible scores and reliability to be the accuracy with which it estimates the universe value of these scores (the "true" score). It requires a partitioning of the variability of test scores (analysis of variance) to determine the variability due to the items (item homogeneity), such attributes as different samples of persons taking the test, different samples of items making up the test (such as different forms), different conditions of giving the test, and lack of consistency in scoring the test. From this analysis, the expected variance of the scores in the universe and the expected variance of the scores in the sample can be estimated, and their ratio yields a generalizability coefficient. This figure indicates how well the test embodies the variability of the universe it is intended to represent. There are very useful aspects to this approach, especially in indicating the sources of unreliability so that a cost-efficient measurement design can be constructed. Researchers have been slow to adopt it in place of the traditional distinctions between reliability and validity in general practice. Jones and Appelbaum (1990) suggest that "given the complex assumption base, both conceptual and mathematical, and the basic difficulties in the definition of a domain, a cautious approach to the use of generalizability theory still appears warranted" (p. 31).

Generalizability theory examines the sources of variability affecting a test score and is a combination of validity and reliability.

TEST OBJECTIVITY

Objectivity refers to the similarity of score or category that two or more judges would assign to a test performance or an observation. Multiple-choice tests are called objective measures because the correct answer is decided before the test is given. Any two clerks can then assign test answers to the "right" or "wrong" category with 100 percent consistency, barring clerical errors. There is no judgmental inconsistency. With essay tests, we defer judgment of responses until the test is given. Since the questions may be answered quite differently by various students, the task of judging the answers is much more difficult, and two raters are less likely to agree unless they carefully work out their scoring in advance, at least for the most common answers.

A judgment of the correct response must be made in either case. If done beforehand with a multiple-choice format, consistency of judgment of responses is ensured. But we limit the responses a testee may make. That need not be the barrier it is generally considered to be, however. There are many more forms of multiple-choice items than are typically used (Gerberich, 1956; Gulliksen, 1986; Bloom, 1956). These extend the range of skills and abilities that can be tapped by such tests. Even so, it is still not easy to measure creativity and the ability to assemble one's throughts. Alternatively, instead of using multiple-choice format, we can leave the response open and obtain constructed responses involving these skills. Then we must work hard to ensure that the scoring of those responses is done with consistency—objectivity.

Interest in objective measurement of a student's knowledge structure, a major determiner of problem solving and retention, has increased with the development of cognitive science. That would seem very difficult; it is. Nonetheless, it is instructive to see the progress that has been made in this area using computer programs to allow students to develop graphics that describe their structure or to arrange "knowledge trees" that are derivatives of it (see Lane, 1991). These methods and others, such as those in Frederiksen et al. (1990) and especially Marshall (1990), not only extend the range of measurement possibilities but also better integrate instruction and assessment of learning.

Observation scales of social interaction vary greatly in the objectivity of the inferences to be made. High-inference scales require the observer to rate dimensions or statements such as, "Group members reinforce each other's actions ____ always, ____ most of the time, ____ about half of the time, ____ occasionally, ____ almost never." Such scales require training to ensure that observers have a common framework for deciding what is "most of the time" or "occasionally."

By contrast, low-inference and, therefore, more objective scales specify the target behaviors sufficiently so that they need only be seen to be recognized. For example, a category system such as Flanders's (1970) interaction analysis for school classrooms consists of 10 clearly specified categories that can be easily learned. The observer categorizes the behavior in the classroom every 5 seconds and records a sequence of category numbers. This permits analysis of questions such as, "What happens when a child finishes talking?" Does the teacher try to clarify the child's ideas or ignore them and go off on a tangent? Many such rating scales for instruction exist. Simon and Boyer (1974) is a compilation of them.

Low-inference scales have the advantage of objectivity, but because of their highly targeted nature, they may miss the larger picture. This can be captured by high-inference measures, which provide a summary judgment on a range of group characteristics. Which to use? Another trade-off!

Another category of quite useful measures for which objectivity is a problem is projective measures. The Rorschach test, the Thematic Apperception Test (TAT), and the House-Tree-Person Test are common ones. The Rorschach inkblots are quite widely known, but what often is not realized is the skill and training required to interpret the responses. Testees are told to report what they see in black or multicolored inkblots, which look much like symmetrical clouds. The result is a set of free responses that must be clinically processed. The TAT is a set of pictures involving people in ambiguous situations into which the testee must read meaning by constructing a story about each picture. It is also clinically processed.

There have been efforts from time to time to make the scoring of these tests more objective (Beck, 1961; Klopfer, 1970; Bellak, 1986; Exner, 1986). But many clinicians feel that although something may be gained in objectivity and in comparability of one person's test with another, much clinical evidence is missed when the scoring is bound into a structured format.

A test has objectivity when different individuals judging the evidence arrive at the same conclusion. Multiple-choice tests are considered objective because two persons can score them identically except for clerical errors. Essay tests and projective tests require great effort to achieve objectivity. Tests calling for low inference tend to have objectivity; those requiring high inference, less of it.

THE STANDARD ERROR OF MEASUREMENT

It might have occured to you that the opposite of reliability or consistency of measurement is inconsistency, which suggests variability. When you hear of variability, it should suggest the standard deviation or variance. Indeed, a useful standard deviation associated with test score variability is known as the **standard error of measurement**.

Suppose we think of the test score as composed of two parts: a true score, the number assigned a testee if the test were perfectly accurate, and an error component, which represents the influence of all the factors that might cause inconsistency in measurement.[7] For any individual, the true score would not vary with retests (unless the underlying construct did, so assume here that it is stable over the measurement period). The error component would vary at random—sometimes positive, sometimes negative, usually small, rarely large. This is a description of the bell-shaped curve, the normal probability curve of chapter 10. The standard deviation of the error distribution is called the standard error of measurement and is a function of the reliability of the test scores. It is as large as the standard deviation of the test scores themselves when the reliability is zero; it is zero when the test is perfectly reliable.

A commonly used formula for the standard error of measurement is $SD \sqrt{1 - r}$ where SD is the standard deviation of the test and r is the reliability. For other formulas, see Lord (1968) or a description of item response theory (such as Weiss and Davison, 1981). Both the latter formulas produce slightly different standard errors of measurement for different score ranges and larger ones for extreme scores.

We often report standardized test scores as a score band rather than as a single score. The band is erected around the person's observed test score, using the standard error of measurement (SEM). It represents what is called a **confidence interval**, a topic developed further in chapter 17. The size of the confidence interval depends on how confident we wish to be that the interval includes the true score, where our confidence is expressed as odds, as in a wager. We derive our odds, or probabilities, from the table of the normal curve, where two-thirds of the cases lie within a band one standard deviation

---

7. This is a traditional test theory formulation; more modern test theory involves the latent variables underlying a test. The traditional formulation is simpler and serves our purposes here.

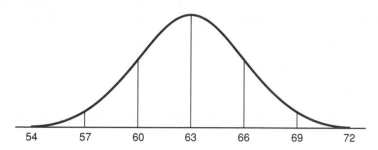

FIGURE 11.2   Distribution of observed scores for persons with a true score of 63.

wide on each side of the mean, 95 percent in a band two standard deviations wide, and 99.9 percent within three standard deviations.

Suppose we had a test with a reliability of .91, very good but not atypical. Given a test with a standard deviation of 10, the standard error of measurement would be 3. (The square root of 1.00 − .91 is .30. This is multiplied by the standard deviation of 10 to give a standard error of measurement of 3.) Figure 11.2 shows the score distribution for all persons with a true score of 63. If the tests were perfectly reliable, the scores would all pile up at exactly 63. The distribution around 63 represents the effects of error. With a SEM of 3, two-thirds of the observed scores will lie between 60 and 66, 95 percent between 57 and 69, and 99.9 percent between 54 and 72.

Suppose Rebecca obtained a score of 59 on a test with these characteristics. We don't know her true score. Graph A in Figure 11.3 shows an interval one SEM wide on each side of the observed score of 59. This is the confidence interval within which, if we set the odds at 2 to 1, the true score lies. When we set our odds of 2 to 1, we are assuming that we are willing to be wrong one time out of three, as we will be when Rebecca's true score lies beyond the limits of the two-SEM confidence interval.

A confidence interval of one SEM on each side of 59 will run from 56 to 62. Put another way, with an observed score of 59, and assuming we are accepting odds of 2 to 1, we are saying that 59 could belong to any of the seven true score distributions of 56, 57, 58, 59, 60, 61, and 62. We don't know which it is.

Graph B shows that 59 would fall within the central ±1 SEM band erected around each of these true scores. Note that these bands are around the *true* scores of 56 to 62, not the *observed* score of 59, which is shown in graph A. What this shows is that we don't know which of these true score distributions the observed score of 59 belongs to. But with a confidence expressed by the odds of 2 to 1, we believe it is one of these. The confidence interval in graph A locates this set of true score distributions for us.

Now suppose Rebecca's true score is actually 63. With an observed score of 59, at odds of 2 to 1, we would be wrong in assuming that her true score falls between 56 and 62. That is the way it is with wagers, where the odds accurately reflect reality. At odds of 2 to 1, we will be wrong one time in three, or a third of the time.

With any observed score, we will not know whether we are right or

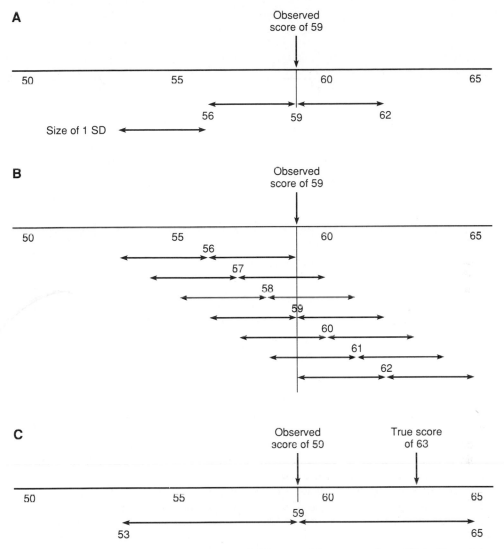

FIGURE 11.3 An observed score of 59 surrounded by a confidence interval one SEM wide and the central one-SEM-wide bands of true scores that overlap that confidence interval.

wrong, just the odds of our being so. In this instance, had we used odds of 19 to 1 reflected in a band four SEM wide, our confidence interval would have run from 53 to 65, as shown in graph C, and we would have included Rebecca's true score. But the standard deviation of the test is 10, so the confidence interval running from 53 to 65, a span of 12, is larger than the standard deviation of the test. With odds of 999 to 1, the band would be 18 score units wide, almost two standard deviations—a fairly imprecise location of Rebecca's

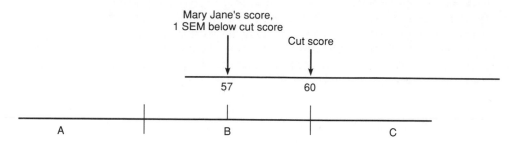

FIGURE 11.4   A score one SEM below a cut score on a certification examination and the chances of being failed in error.

score. Precision of location is traded off for certainty, and we must decide on the optimum balance between the two.

The SEM is particularly useful in determining how much faith to put in a score that categorizes an individual. Suppose any person who receives a score of 60 or below fails the nurses' licensing examination. Nelson, who falls three SEM below the cut score on a nursing certification examination, is almost certainly a failure. The confidence that his true score is above the cut line is expressed by odds of less than 1 in 1,000. However, for Mary Jane, with a score only one SEM below it, we can say with a confidence expressed by the odds of 1 in 6 that her true score is above the cut line.

Why 1 in 6 if her score is one SEM below the cut line? Look at Figure 11.4, where we have erected a confidence interval, labeled "B," one SEM on each side of the observed score. If Mary Jane were to be allowed to pass, her true score would have to lie outside this confidence interval, since all the scores inside B are at or below the cut line. So if she were to pass, her score must lie outside that interval. If the odds are 2 to 3, her score is in the interval; it follows that if they are 1 to 3 her score is outside the interval. Although outside the interval, we don't know where—whether her true score lies in the upper tail (C) or the lower (A). Since it has an equal chance of being in either, half the odds of 1 in 3, or 1 in 6, applies. So we can say with a confidence expressed by odds of 1 to 6 that with an observed score of 57, her true score is above the cut score.

Because candidates who fail a certification examination could legitimately use this argument, actual cut scores are often placed one or more SEM *below* the desired cut score. This lets some pass who should fail. Considering the personal devastation caused by an error in certification, this may be the lesser of the evils (for example, a person incorrectly held back until a high school proficiency examination is passed). Some may pass without the required skills. But that is better than holding back those who had true scores above the cut line but had failing scores on that testing because the examination is not perfectly reliable.

For an examination licensing nuclear engineers or airline pilots, whose actions place the safety of large numbers of people at stake, we may wish to err in the opposite direction. This is done by setting the cut score one or more SEM *above* the minimum level of competency. This increases the chances that everyone above the cut score really has a passing true score. Even though this may keep some candidates from being certified who might deserve to be, it may be the lesser of the evils considering the consequences if an error is made at a nuclear power plant or 35,000 feet in the air. Adjusting cut scores always involves trade-offs based on value judgments of the "greatest" good.

A refinement often not observed is worth mentioning. When we extend a confidence interval around a person's observed score to find the boundaries of the true score, we are not sure whether the true score is above the observed score or below it. Therefore, to be 95 percent confident we include it, we extend the interval in both directions around the observed score, half on each side of it. Suppose we want to know whether the true score is at least as high or as low as the desired criterion. Then the error area is all in one tail with none in the other. With the total of 100 percent to be distributed on both sides of the observed score, 50 percent would then be on one side, and the remaining 45 percent on the error side instead of 47.5 percent when it is split equally above and below. With only 45 percent, we need extend the confidence interval only 1.65 standard errors of measurement to be 95 percent confident, or only 0.44 SEM for odds of 2 to 1. Therefore, if we wish to set the cut score above or below the criterion score, the distance need only be 0.44 SEM instead of one SEM for odds of 2 to 1, or 1.65 SEM instead of 1.96 SEM for odds of 19 to 1.

Probably the best way to handle this problem is to set up a zone of indeterminacy around the criterion score. Testees who fell in this zone might have passing or failing true scores; the measurement error is such that we can't tell. The borders of the zone can be set so that scores outside the zone in either direction are, with predetermined odds, passes or failures. The width of the zone could be set wider for greater certainty, narrower for less (for example, $\frac{1}{2}$ or $1\frac{1}{2}$ SEM above and below). Most individuals would fall into the clear pass or fail area. Those whose scores fell in the zone of indeterminacy would be required to take additional tests until their combined score fell into the clear pass or fail area.

- The standard error of measurement permits us to establish a confidence interval within which we can say, with a confidence expressed by specified odds, that a person's true score will lie.
- The size of the confidence interval reflects the amount and kind of unreliability used in the computation—stability, equivalence, and so on.
- Requiring greater certainty increases the size of the confidence interval, thereby reducing precision in locating the true score.
- The standard error of measurement is often used in establishing a cut score for licensing and certifying examinations. The direction in which potential error is allowed depends on whether the individual's or society's protection is the prime consideration—a trade-off.

TEST IMPROVEMENT THROUGH ITEM ANALYSIS

Item analysis can be used to increase validity, reliability, or both. It requires analyzing how well the responses to each item predict. For validity, we determine how well they predict a criterion; for reliability, how well they predict the total score. The latter is used to increase internal consistency reliability.

A first characteristic we often look at is whether some items are too easy or too hard for most of the examinees. The percentage of test takers passing an item is called the **item difficulty index**, and the most internally consistent reliable tests generally consist of items with difficulty in the middle range. Unless the test has very high internal consistency, test items that are too easy or too hard for most students contribute less than items in the middle range. Thus we may first look for items that are too hard or too easy.

Consider item discrimination next in the process of item analysis, the extent to which each item contributes to improved predictive validity. Suppose that on a test predicting sales ability, the question "Do you like to show off at parties?" were asked. If we had a criterion measure that validly measured sales ability, such as average total value of sales per month, we could use it to correlate the responses to this question (1 for yes and 0 for no). This correlation is called the **item discrimination index**. Such a correlation would show whether sales personnel with high sales averages answered yes to this question more often than those with low sales averages. If so, the index would be a good predictor of success, and perhaps other questions modeled along these same lines might also be useful. Note that direction of correlation, positive or negative, is not of interest here. If a no answer were predictive of success, that would also usefully contribute to prediction of the criterion. But if successful and unsuccessful salespeople answered in about the same way, a close to zero correlation, this question could be dropped from the test, since it is not contributing to the prediction. In this way, items that contribute to prediction can be identified and their contribution strengthened by building parallel items. Nonfunctioning items can often be repaired. The test can also be shortened by eliminating noncontributing items, or functioning items can be substituted for nonfunctioning ones.

Often we have no criterion external to the test to check validity, so the best we can do is try to improve internal consistency reliability. For this we use the test score as the criterion. The item discrimination index becomes how well each item predicts (contributes to) the total score. Items that are measuring something different than most items on the test will have a low correlation with the total score. Therefore, they can be dropped from the test, and only those with high correlations will be retained. Removing these items may actually increase the reliability, even though it also shortens the test. It depends on which effect is stronger, removing the detracting items or decreasing test length. Patterning new items after those that remain augments reliability.

Item response theory not only examines the contribution of the correct response as a correlation but also plots the relationship of each possible response in a multiple-choice item to the criterion. This is a rapidly developing area of psychometric theory (Hambleton, 1989).

Empirical Keying

Item analysis can also be used to determine how to score a test; this is called **empirical keying**. For example, after World War II, the U.S. Army wished to select the best of its officers for retention after demobilization. A "biographical inventory blank" was devised and keyed by examining the responses of the best and poorest officers as identified by their fellow officers. It was found, for example, that the best came from small towns, were from large families, and were the firstborn. So individuals whose responses matched this profile were credited with points toward a retention score. Further, we may weight items according to their correlation with the criterion, so a respondent would get extra points for answers with the highest correlations. Should the Army have anticipated that the best officers had these characteristics and keyed them accordingly? Probably not. We can rationalize these items after the fact, but we can also build arguments against why they should be keyed this way. The relationship certainly isn't readily apparent.

Because of their weak face validity, such tests are usually subjected to repeated studies with new samples of subjects (called cross-validation) to show that the keys work and to refine them. Such tests often require a large number of representative cases to get keys that are stable from sample to sample. But tests built this way often work where tests developed by other methods fail. The Strong-Campbell Interest Inventory and the Minnesota Multiphasic Personality Inventory (used in the Zimbardo study in chapter 2), two of our most successful measures, are empirically keyed tests.

Determining what will be accepted as a criterion is often the secret but is also a matter of judgment, one around which we hope to build a consensus. Is dollar value of sales adequate as a criterion for selecting sales personnel? Since it does not include client satisfaction, client service, and other considerations, this question is a matter for discussion. As in other consensus-building instances, we must anticipate the audience's concerns.

The most common problem to watch for is criterion contamination. Suppose the supervisor made judgments of sales ability. If she had knowledge of the scores on the new test, we would have criterion contamination, because they might influence her ratings. The solution is easy: keep the rater "blind" to the scores on the test.[8] It is also important that the criterion be reliable, a topic we shall take up shortly.

---

8. The term *blind* is used to indicate that the individual is deliberately kept ignorant about certain information that might bias his or her judgments.

- Item analysis uses an item difficulty index to identify items that are too easy or too difficult and item discrimination indexes to determine how strongly each item predicts the criterion, so that the weak items can be replaced with items modeled after those that predict strongly.
- To improve validity, use the criterion to be predicted. To improve internal consistency reliability, correlate items with the total test score.
- Item analysis can also be used to determine which responses to each item predict the criterion. These responses are then keyed "correct" and sometimes weighted by how strongly they predict the criterion. This is called empirical keying.

MEASUREMENT TRADE-OFFS

Earlier in this chapter two **trade-offs** were noted:

1. Structuring a test for objectivity (as by using multiple-choice items) places a constraint on the responses but makes it difficult to construct examinations for hard-to-test complex skills and for broad topics. But the examination is easy to grade, even by a clerk. These conditions are reversed if we leave responses free from restraint (as in essay questions). We can put in the professional time beforehand in constructing the test, or afterward in grading it; it is a trade-off.
2. In setting a cut score with a fallible test, the cut can be made so that either the individual's or the public's interest is protected. But extreme protection of either one causes problems for the other—another trade-off.

The most common trade-off in measurement, however, is the breadth-versus-depth problem, that of testing broadly but shallowly versus testing narrowly but deeply. This trade-off, however, is ubiquitous throughout the research process; we encounter it in areas such as these:

- Problem finding (for example, given finite time and resources, we can tackle a problem broadly but shallowly or narrowly and deeply)
- Sampling (a given sample size may be spread across an entire population thinly, or the sample may be concentrated where the variability is the greatest)
- Measurement (using a fixed amount of testing time for a broad survey of academic achievement versus a diagnostic reading test)
- Treatment (using a variety of forms of the same treatment without having developed great skill with any one versus using one form and developing great skill in its application)

Cronbach has called this the "bandwidth fidelity problem" after its electronic analog. It refers to the problems posed by the finite capacity of a wire like a telephone cable in sending a signal—a telephone conversation, for instance. In a given time, we can either send much information with little redundancy or send less information with more redundancy. In the former case, we put through lots of information but with less certainty that it is without error (many telephone calls with little redundancy to check accuracy). Alternatively, we resend the same message. In the latter case, because we can check one transmission of the same message against another, we are more certain of the accuracy of the information—but have less of it.

Similarly, given a set amount of testing time, we may test very broadly across a subject but have little information about weaknesses and strengths. In certain areas of the subject, only a few test items, possibly only one, will sample a subarea—too small a behavior sample for reliable diagnostic scoring. Alternatively, we may reduce the coverage of subject matter and sample each subarea with many items—good information on strengths and weaknesses. Given limited testing funds and time, this is a trade-off about which decisions must always be made (for example, whether to use a reading test that is part of the broad survey of an achievement battery or a reading diagnostic examination).

Another trade-off is between the use of established tests that may not quite fit what we wish to measure and newer, possibly experimental, but not yet accepted tests that are more on target. Here we have in mind the problem of attaining credibility with our audience. The problem is compounded by limited publication space. We must choose between devoting space to evidence of the validity of the new test sufficient to allay concerns about it (space taken from describing other aspects of the study) and using an established test that is not quite on target but both understood and accepted by the audience. The latter can remove a significant hurdle to gaining a consensus around the interpretation of the data. But sometimes it can lead to less dramatic results, which must be bolstered by explanation, since they are not stark enough to speak for themselves.

Still another trade-off is between direct evidence gathering and unobtrusive measurement. The former may cause subjects to react to being observed in such a way that they mask or suppress the target behavior we wish to study. Unobtrusive measurement will lead to less reaction to being studied but may only obliquely, and possibly inaccurately, get at what we want. When people know they are being observed and evaluated, their behavior is likely to be different from normal: sometimes they try harder, sometimes they freeze or go to pieces. Use of a variety of unobtrusive methods has been suggested, including library records to measure reading behavior (but this misses magazine and newspaper reading) and one-way mirrors for observation (but this requires a good sound system to be effective) (Webb et al., 1981).

Yet another trade-off is between **norm-referenced tests** and **criterion-referenced tests**. Norm-referenced tests spread students across the range of scores and show where an individual's score stands with reference to the norm group. An achievement test's grade norms indicate how far a student is working above or below others in the same grade. Criterion-referenced tests do not attempt to spread testees among the possible scores but determine whether an individual has achieved a given criterion level with respect to particular content or skills and abilities. High school proficiency tests that students must pass before graduating are typically criterion-referenced tests: they consist of test items that the individuals should have mastered if they have achieved the desired level. Setting an appropriate passing score can be a serious problem, and procedures have been established to facilitate this process (to be disscussed shortly). Criterion-referenced tests are used for mastery learning programs to show whether a student understands a unit of subject matter and are also used for some licensing and certification tests.

In an experimental context, what is important is that whichever test we use, norm- or criterion-referenced, it should discriminate among the testees so that an effect can be sensed. A criterion-referenced test on which all or nearly all testees meet the criterion could have the same effect as a ceiling on the test. Potential differences between different treatment groups might not be adequately displayed, and the differential effect of an experimental variable might therefore not be sensed.

The conventional measures of reliability depend on having the spread of scores found on normed tests. By contrast, mastery tests are often built so that most students obtain a nearly perfect score. Therefore, there is little variability, and the conventional reliability estimates are not appropriate. Various alternative measures have been proposed (see Berk, 1986b, and Subkoviak, 1988).

Trade-offs are prevalent throughout research, and there are many of them in measurement:

- The bandwidth fidelity problem is that, given a certain amount of testing time, we trade measuring somethng broadly but minimally in each aspect for measuring fewer aspects extensively.
- Direct measures of behavior can be so obvious that they change the actions of the persons observed; the alternative, unobtrusive measures, by contrast, may be less than perfectly related to the actions to be measured.
- Norm-referenced tests spread the scores along a scale so we can determine how well individuals did relative to a norm group.
- Criterion-referenced tests determine whether a certain content has been mastered.

SPECIAL MEASUREMENT PROBLEMS

Setting Cut Scores

The example of a cut score for Mary Jane's nurses' licensing examination used in the discussion of the standard error of measurement suggested some of the complexities of using cut scores. The most difficult problem is determining where to put them. Because we are most comfortable when we have a combined judgment across experts rather than that of a single person, there is considerable literature on methods of getting and combining judgments for selection, certification, or passing an examination. Some involve asking each judge to mark all items a person who is just certifiable should be able to answer correctly. Others involve rating each item as essential, marginal, or unnecessary. Berk (1986a), Jaeger (1989), and Nedelsky (1954) are informative on this subject. Millman (1989) considers the problem of setting cut scores where multiple attempts are permitted.

Special Testing Methods

Computers have made it possible to construct branched tests, tests that allow individuals to answer the items best suited to their level of performance. Such tests can be shorter than conventional tests, because items too hard or too easy for an individual are largely eliminated. Individualized tests, such as the Stanford-Binet Intelligence Test and the Wechsler Intelligence Scale for Children, have long embodied such a principle in their vocabulary and other subtests. These tests start testees at a level just below where they would be expected to get every item correct and stop testing when they can no longer get items correct.

Tailored tests, also called adaptive tests, start everyone in the middle and then branch to easier or harder items, depending on whether the preceding item was answered incorrectly or correctly. Such tests make maximum use of testing time, because the items are so chosen as to place the individual on the scale accurately with a minimum number of items. They require high internal consistency reliability to achieve the same accuracy of classification in less testing time. A legal problem remains for their use in professional competency examinations, however—how to prove that individuals are taking comparable tests when they respond to different items. In structure, these tests are analogous to the sequential sampling plans described in chapter 8.

Computers have also made approaches to interval measurement practical. Item response theory and the Rasch models are methods of equating items on a scale that is presumably invariant with respect to population. A given test item may be easy for a college population, whereas the same item might be very difficult for someone in elementary school. Item response theory attempts to solve this problem by placing the item at the same place on a scale of item difficulty regardless of whether the data came from college or kindergarten students.[9] Tests scaled this way probably come as close as psychological measurement gets to having truly equal intervals between units on the scale for test items and may eventually help solve the legal problem noted in the preceding paragraph. They require a large number of cases for a stable scale.

Thurstone methods of psychological scaling were some of the earliest attempts at achieving equal-interval scales; the same methods have been

---

9. For additional reading on test theory, see Weiss and Davison, 1981, and Linn, 1989.

enhanced and new methods developed for scaling in more than one dimension. They are in frequent use in consumer testing, where we wish to determine individuals' preferences for one product or food over another or to rank or scale them (for more see Carroll and Arabie, 1980; Coombs, Dawes, and Tversky, 1981; Young, 1985; Geischeider, 1988).

Item scaling has contributed to another use of computers, **item banking**. Instructors and test constructors have dreamed of having pools of test items precisely classified with respect to behaviors and subject matter. Such item "banks" could be drawn on by an instructor to fit a distinctive curriculum, to fit a class, or to examine a particular individual. Various attempts have been made to construct such banks for limited subject matter and grades. Item response theory seems like the perfect answer, but the models require a homogeneous domain involving only one underlying construct, as well as a large number of subjects to achieve stable scales. Both requirements are currently being examined to determine whether strict adherence is necessary for practical use.

> Adaptive or tailored testing uses fewer test items and thereby reduces testing time when applied to measures tapping homogeneous domains. By using a computer or some other device, the testee's record on items previously passed and failed is used to determine the most appropriate next item in order to extract maximum information.

SOURCES OF TEST INFORMATION

Because test construction is such an expensive and lengthy process, retrieval systems have been developed to help find already constructed tests. This enables researchers to devote energies to improving those measures (if that is necessary) rather than starting from scratch. The longest-running series, now in its tenth volume, is *The Mental Measurements Yearbooks*, begun in 1938 by Oscar Krisen Buros and now taken over by the Buros Institute at the University of Nebraska in Lincoln. The yearbooks are noncumulative and were issued periodically. Currently they appear every other year, with supplements between issues. They provide reviews of the standardized tests that have been published since the last issue. The yearbooks are available on-line and can be computer-searched.

Very useful compendiums of sources of information have been issued by the ERIC Center on Tests and Measurements, which is currently being administered by the American Institutes of Research in Washington, D.C. Backer (1977) is an extensive annotated listing of the variety of sources of tests such as Goldman's directories of experimental tests (1974, 1978, 1982, 1985) and Chun, Cobb, and French's (1975) guide to 3,000 original sources and their applications. Fabiano and O'Brien (1987) is an updated but not as comprehensive version. Sweetland and Keyser (1987) is a listing of measurement instruments for a variety of purposes. Woodbury (1982) also has a very useful section on sources of test information. Educational Testing Service (ETS) makes available a file of unpublished research instruments called *Tests in Microfiche* and maintains, for on-site access, an extensive collection of tests and other measurement devices. It also has a file of reference tests that can be used in a factor analysis to assist in identifying factors. ETS's collection of published tests (1986, 1988, 1989, 1991) has also been cataloged.

STRENGTHS AND WEAKNESSES OF VARIOUS DATA-GATHERING METHODS

Metfessel and Michael's (1967) useful self-explanatory table, adapted as Table 11.4, summarizes the strengths and weaknesses of a variety of data-gathering devices.

TABLE 11.4 Strengths and Weaknesses of a Variety of Measurement Approaches

Approach	Strengths	Weaknesses
Data Collected by a Mechanical Device (e.g., audiotape, videotape, galvanic skin response)	■ Stays on the job, avoids human fatigue and clerical errors; has infinite patience. ■ May capture content missed by written records such as voice inflection and nonverbal communication (e.g., posture). ■ Provides a sufficiently complete record that it can often be reprocessed from a new point of view as new analytic techniques are devised or new insights are gained by further research. Often what one started out to study isn't the most interesting part of the data.	■ Can be costly to gather and may require special equipment. ■ Equipment does not make judgments and produces an extensive record that must be processed. ■ Equipment failures can be a problem, especially when failures result in missing vital parts of the data. ■ Operator error, haste, or insufficient training results in improperly collected data. ■ Period of acclimation may be necessary until targets forget the presence and purpose of the equipment (if not concealed). ■ Audiotape omits the visual, which could be important. Even videotape catches the action only from one viewpoint. ■ Visuals of group may have wrong camera angle for some individuals. Good sound record is often hard to get.
Data Collected by an Independent Observer	■ Can be used in natural as well as experimental settings. ■ Most direct measure of behavior.	■ Observer's presence changes the situation, sometimes creating an artificial one.

(continued)

TABLE 11.4 *continued*

Approach	Strengths	Weaknesses
	■ Experienced, trained, or perceptive observers can pick up subtle occurrences of interactions sometimes not available by other techniques, even may be lost on videotape if the camera is not at the right angle or the lighting is poor. ■ Analysis is often simultaneous with collection of the data.	■ There is a less complete record than with videotape. ■ Sampling may be inadequate to catch important action. ■ Ambiguities in recording and lack of objectivity in recording by different observers may lead to false interpretations or may cause an inference to be missed.
Written Accounts	■ Can use the critical incident technique, eliminating much "chaff." Critical incidents are those that respondents consider critical to triggering the target behavior of the study. Interpretation is kept separate from actual reporting so far as possible.	■ Hard to be complete. ■ Hard to avoid writing interpretations as factual data (e.g., "Mary kicked John because she was angry with him").
Observation Forms (e.g., observation schedules)	■ Easy to complete; save time. ■ Can be objectively scored. ■ Standardize the observations. ■ Have built-in point of view regarding what is important to observe.	■ Not as flexible as written accounts—may lump unlike acts together. ■ Criteria for ratings are often unspecified. ■ May overlook meaningful behavior that is not reflected in the instrument.
Data Produced by the Subject	■ Data can be collected inexpensively that would be very costly to gather by lengthy observation necessary to learn a person's attitudes, interests, values, and so on. ■ Data can be collected that is nearly inaccessible by other means (private thoughts, feelings, sensitive topics).	■ Accuracy depends on subject's self-perception, which may or may not accurately reflect how others would "objectively" describe subject. ■ Method requires conditions conducive to honest responses, nonthreatening situations. May require anonymous responses. ■ Recall of past events is modified by individual's perceptions of those events rather than accurate memory (this could be a strength if the researcher is interested in perceptions).
Diaries	■ Comprehensive, may give private thoughts and commentaries on activities.	■ Can be difficult to analyze; very different from person to person.
Checklists, Rating Scales, and Questionnaires	■ Quick and economical to administer. ■ Easy to score and summarize.	■ If data are collected by mail, may have low percentage of returns; nonrespondents may differ from respondents; other than intended respondents may have completed forms or helped.

Approach	Strengths	Weaknesses
		■ No assurance that respondents correctly understood questions or directions. ■ Subject to response sets such as the acquiescence set (a tendency to respond "true" to true–false or "yes" to yes–no queries) and to the halo effect (the tendency to respond to rating scales in terms of a general image of the person rather than rating the specific characteristic requested).
Interviews	■ Allow depth of response. ■ Can ensure that individuals understand the questions and follow directions. ■ Flexible and adaptable to individuals. ■ Nonverbal responses that reveal feelings are available for interpretation by the interviewer.	■ Very costly in time, personnel, and travel. ■ Require skilled and trained personnel. ■ Often difficult to analyze and summarize. ■ Interviewer may influence responses, especially if respondent seeks to please. ■ Certain responses may be inhibited or encouraged by demeanor or appearance of interviewer (e.g., white middle-class interviewer of black lower class interviewee). ■ Confidentiality of response less certain for interviewee than anonymous response to a questionnaire.
Sociometry (respondents indicate choices in group of best friend, lab partner, and so on; responses are usually diagrammed using arrows to indicate who chose whom as well as mutual choices)	■ Measures a unique aspect of social interaction. ■ Easy to score. ■ Can lead to clinical insights.	■ Criteria used in making choices may vary from individual to individual. ■ Can lead to complex and difficult-to-interpret diagrams. ■ Applicable mainly to small groups.
Projective Techniques	■ Lead to clinical insights. ■ Individual reveals self without realizing it; ■ No right answers, so responses are largely uncensored. ■ Nonthreatening.	■ Different clinicians may analyze the same responses differently. ■ Reliability and validity of measures are uncertain. ■ Possible ethical questions in getting individual to reveal self, if not properly used.
Tests	■ Practical—take the place of extensive observation. ■ Most reliable measures we have at present. ■ Can record products and processes of thought.	■ Because of availability and ease of use, may be used where other data-gathering techniques are more appropriate.
Tests with Constructed Responses	■ Essay tests allow students to synthesize their knowledge about a topic.	■ Difficult to cover a topic intensively with essay tests in a short time.

(continued)

TABLE 11.4   *continued*

Approach	Strengths	Weaknesses
	■ Short answer, and completion tests can be quite objective.	■ Essay tests difficult to score, and students often interpret them in the way they wish rather than in the manner intended, leaving graders uncertain whether this was intentional and should be graded down or whether credit should be given for whatever twist of the topic they used. ■ Short-answer and completion tests lend themselves to testing trivia.
Supplied-Answer, Multiple-Choice, Matching, and Ranking Tests	■ Great objectivity in scoring. ■ Ease of scoring. ■ Usually high reliability. ■ Can be item-analyzed to improve validity and reliability. ■ Wide coverage of subject matter easily achieved. ■ Diagnostic tests can be constructed. ■ Great variety of available standardized tests.	■ Problem of validity is always present. ■ Standardized tests sometimes used where specially constructed tests would be more appropriate. ■ Tests of complex problem solving are difficult to construct, so tests tend to concentrate on knowledge, facts, and details. ■ Apparent precision may result in greater faith in scores than justified.

SOURCE   Adapted from N. S. Metfessel and W. B. Michael, "A Paradigm Involving Multiple Criterion Measures for the Evaluation of the Effectiveness of School Programs," *Educational and Psychological Measurement,* 1961, *27,* 937–943.

SUMMARY

Measurement is an important characteristic of a field, for as measurement improves, the distinctions that can be made among phenomena increase and the ability to describe what is occurring improves. Measurement is basically a sampling problem: we are sampling an individual's behavior at a single time or a sample of times with respect to a sample of content or of situations.

Validity is the most important characteristic of measures, and construct validity is the most important of the validity types. Basically, we show construct validity by predicting how a measure should behave were it valid and then proceeding to show that it does so. Content validity shows that a test is a representative sample of a content domain. Empirical validity shows that a test predicts a criterion measure of success, either when the criterion measure is gathered long enough after testing to determine how well the individual succeeded on a job or in school (predictive validity) or when both test and success measures are gathered at the same time (concurrent validity). Face validity means that the test appears intuitively valid. This can be important when a test being used for important decision making must undergo scrutiny by laypersons.

Reliability is a necessary but not sufficient condition for validity. Reliability indicates whether the sample chosen is sufficiently representative that there is consistency across different samples at the item level (internal consistency reliability), at the test level (equivalence reliability), and over test samples obtained at different times (stability reliability). With the correction for attenuation, the correlation between two less than perfectly reliable tests can be estimated as if they were perfectly reliable. The standard error of measurement is useful for indicating how far the true score may possibly lie from an observed score, given the unreliability of the test.

Various means of setting cut scores for certification and licensing have been devised. Such tests are often of the domain- or criterion-referenced type, where the intent is not to spread individuals across the scores but to determine whether testees can display the intended behaviors with the specified content (Berk, 1986a). Since mastery tests result in a large proportion of high or perfect scores, reliability measures for such tests are different from those for conventional ones.

Item analysis is a test development process for improving the reliability or validity of a test. Responses to an item are correlated with some criterion. If we are seeking to improve the internal consistency reliability of the test, the total score is used. If we are improving the test's validity, a criterion that is an acceptably valid measure is used. Items that do not correlate with the criterion are either discarded to shorten the test or changed to improve the correlation.

ADDITIONAL READING

Anastasi (1982)
Cronbach (1984)

Hopkins, Stanley, and Hopkins (1990)
Linn (1989, especially Messick's chapter)

IMPORTANT TERMS

Alpha coefficient
Concurrent validity
Confidence interval
Construct validity
Content validity
Correction for attenuation
Counterbalancing
Criterion
Criterion-referenced tests
Criterion-related validity
Empirical keying
Equivalence reliability
Face validity
Factor analysis
Internal consistency reliability

Item analysis
Item banking
Item difficulty index
Item discrimination index
Kuder-Richardson reliability
Norm-referenced tests
Objectivity
Operational definition
Predictive validity
Reliability
Stability reliability
Standard error of measurement
Tailored (adaptive) tests
Trade-offs
Validity

=== APPLICATION PROBLEMS ===

1. Refer to the description of Jonassen's study in the application problems for chapter 5 (page 68). The purpose of the study was to "validate" the use of pattern notes as a measure of cognitive structure. With what type of validity was Jonassen concerned and why?

2. The dean of Watertown University was concerned about the number of freshmen who were failing. She decided to try a prestigious testing firm's new University Entrance Competency Test (UECT) and carefully examined the data on the test's validity. (a) What kind of validity should she look for? (b) How might she improve the test's validity?

3. Dr. Keith devised a typology that assigns an individual to one of four personality styles: spontaneous external, spontaneous internal, systematic external, and systematic internal. Coscarelli and Stonewater (1979) proposed that consultants use this model to help understand client decision-making behavior and thus to allow themselves to respond to the client in a supportive manner. In what sort of test validity would these researchers be interested if they were to develop a scale to measure these constructs?

4. Elizabeth Cleghorn has developed a computer-based course for teaching introductory calculus that should result in increased achievement. To verify this hypothesis, she compared a randomly selected group of 30 first-year college students with a "control" group who were taught by the "regular" (lecture) method. Each group was given a calculus achievement test at the beginning of the semester and a parallel form at the end. With what kinds of test validity and reliability would this investigator be concerned?

5. University Hospital requires its new nursing staff to pass an exam before being allowed to give medications to patients. Dr. Roberts, the hospital administrator, wondered about its validity and reliability. A study showed it had a standard deviation of 12, a Kuder-Richardson reliability of .82, and hence a standard error of measurement (SEM) of 5. If a nurse must score 80 or better to meet the hospital's standard, what score should be considered passing?

6. Recall the investigator who thought that there might be a relationship between a teacher's effectiveness and the teacher's enthusiasm. She had to measure both effectiveness and enthusiasm. To measure the latter, she decided to use two techniques: ratings by independent observers and a diary kept by the subjects. The observers were trained and filled out a 5-point rating scale for a series of indicators of enthusiasm such as facial expression, body movements, and varied vocal delivery. The diary was open-ended. Assess the strengths and weaknesses of each measure.

Compare your answers with those on pages 709–710.

=== APPLICATION EXERICSE ===

Can you find measures for the study you are thinking about? If you are dealing with variables that are standard, look up possible measures in Buros's current *Mental Measurements Yearbook*. Given the kind of study you plan, what kinds of validity and reliability will you look for? Do the tests that are candidates for your study appear to have useful levels of validity for your purposes? What about reliability? Woodbury's chapter on measures lists other sources of measurement information and ideas, including experimental measures. As you can tell from this chapter, creating your own measures is likely to be difficult and time-consuming—a study in and of itself. Try to find measures in experimental form that you can build on if nothing seems to fit exactly.

SECTION THREE

Causal Inference and the Criteria of Research

Most research is a quest for relationships—what causes relate to what effects, how they are related, and how general these relationships are. Although not all relationships are viewed in causal terms, the concept of causation is a very useful one, so much so that we take it for granted. Yet cause and effect as concepts are more complex than usually considered, and determining what evidence is sufficient for inferring causation has been a philosophical problem for centuries. Still, we do infer causation, and as shown in chapter 4, through the development of a consensus, findings do become accepted as knowledge that we act upon with confidence. If this is true, then there must be common criteria around which the consensus can coalesce—indeed, some have been touched on in previous chapters. Further, in chapter 5 it was noted that a common logic, the chain of reasoning, forms a basis for the presentation of findings supporting a generalization. The chapters in section three explore these topics further, beginning with causation and then placing the chain of reasoning in its larger context and relating the criteria to it.

- Chapter 12 examines objections to the terms *cause* and *effect*, their common uses and interpretations, and alternative interpretations. Its middle section, "Evidence for Inferring Causation," lays the groundwork for the next chapters.
- Chapter 13 is the first of two chapters on the criteria of research. It is concerned with the criteria by which a study can be judged to link variables in a relationship, its "linking power." Since this power is similar to what is commonly known as internal validity, it is designated internal validity (LP). Similarly, the criterion involved in judging the capacity of a study to support generalization beyond the instances in which the data was gathered is its external validity (GP), where GP stands in parallel fashion for its "generalizing power."

- Chapter 14 examines additional criteria and some constraints. These criteria are never completely satisfied, but we try to optimize them for each study: the extent to which we build credibility with the audience, the balance of internal and external validity, and the allocation of resources. How well we can optimize these is constrained by the limits of our resources, institutional restrictions, and ethics.

Looking at these chapters from the perspective of science as a social process, as described in chapter 4, it is apparent that the criteria and optimizing conditions follow logically from an analysis of the kinds of judgments that occur in the development of a consensus. This section's explication of that logic and those criteria develops a model that will prove useful over and over again in conceptualizing, implementing, and evaluating research studies.

Complexities of Causal Inference

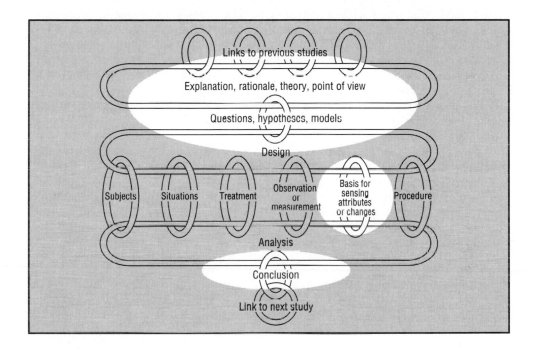

> Rags make paper, paper makes money, money makes banks, banks
> make loans, loans make poverty, poverty makes rags.
>
> *Anonymous*

> For want of a nail the shoe was lost, for want of a shoe the horse was
> lost, for want of a horse the rider was lost. . . . For want of a nail, the
> battle was lost!
>
> *George Herbert (1593–1633)*

OVERVIEW

Causation is what is explained in a rationale, proposed in a hypothesis or model, and examined in the conclusion. The "basis for sensing attributes or changes" link in the chain of reasoning provides the basis for inferring causation.

We refer to cause-and-effect relationships very casually in everyday life—for example, "The fire was caused by smoking in bed." Such simple usage hides at least three sets of complexities: (1) different understandings of what is meant by the term *cause*, (2) different perceptions of the nature of the world and their implications for the social sciences, and (3) the variety of complex as well as simple causal patterns to consider.

This chapter will sensitize you to these different understandings. It examines causal patterns other than the common ones. In particular, it examines the evidence we use to infer that a causal relationship exists (we will build on this to develop criteria in the next chapter). Finally, this chapter discusses combinations of necessary and sufficient conditions, the characteristics that permit them to be recognized, and the predictability (or lack of it) they permit.

CHAPTER CONTENTS

Introduction   239

Complexities in the Concept
of Cause   240

Which Is the Cause in
the Causal Chain?   240

Causes as Inferences   241

Validated Causal Propositions
Escape Disconfirmation   242

Complexities in Our Conception of the
World and Social Science   243

Complexities in Patterns of Causation:
Illustrative Simple Patterns   244

Complexities in Patterns of Causation:
Illustrative Multiple-Cause
Patterns   245

Evidence for Inferring Causation   246

Patterning Situations to Facilitate
Drawing an Inference of Causation:
The "Basis for Sensing Attributes or
Changes" Link   246

Evidence of Causation   250

Complexities in the Nature of
Relationships   253

Conditions Arising from the Presence
or Absence of Necessary and
Sufficient Conditions   253

An Alternative Set of Conditions:
Sufficient but Not Necessary   254

A Contingent Condition: Necessary
but Not Sufficient   257

The INUS Condition: Neither
  Necessary nor Sufficient but
  Contributing   259
Discriminating Alternative,
  Contingent, and Contributing
  Conditions in Scatterplots   260
Classification Schemes as Weak
  Explanations   261

A Key Link: The Basis for Sensing
  Attributes or Changes   262
Can Causation Ever Be Inferred?   263
Summary   264
Appendix: An Example of Difficulty in
  Identifying the Nature of a Causal
  Relationship   266

INTRODUCTION[1]

SCHOOLWORK UNDERMINED BY TV, CALIFORNIA SURVEY SHOWS

Always read the small print under the headline, my teachers used to say, and
of course, they were right. The headline, "Schoolwork Undermined by TV . . ."
ascribes a causal relationship to television viewing and poor schoolwork.

> The more a student watches television, the worse he does in school. . . . No
> conclusions were drawn as to why television watching seems to go hand in
> hand with lower reading, writing and math test scores.
> *Report on Educational Research*, November 26, 1980

As the additional material quoted from the report shows, its author was careful
to walk the fine line between association and causation. Lower achievement is
associated with more TV viewing. Instead of claiming a causal relationship, the
author uses "weasel words" —it "goes hand in hand." Perhaps the relationship can be explained by the fact that poorer students prefer exciting TV
watching to difficult and often unrewarding schoolwork. This is but one
example of the care with which the concept of causation must be used—and,
in the headline, of the way it is often abused.

Some people consider the conceptual difficulties of using the term *cause*
so serious that they believe such use should be abandoned. For instance,
Bertrand Russell wrote: "Causality . . . is a relic of a bygone age, surviving, like
the monarchy, only because it is erroneously supposed to do no harm" (1953,
p. 387). But it is so pervasive in everyday speech and among academicians that
its abandonment seems unlikely. Köbben argues, "The notion of 'cause' is
indispensable"; banning it "impoverishes our intellectual tool kit" (1973, p. 89).
Causes have been called the "cement of the universe" (Mackie, 1974).

Philosophers have devoted years to analyzing the concept of cause and
still have problems with it. This chapter cannot do justice to that volume of
literature. It will alert you to some of the common complexities and suggest
some directions to explore; you can follow up as needed.

---

1. I am most grateful to my colleague, Dr. Emily Robertson, for her very helpful comments on
this chapter.

COMPLEXITIES IN THE CONCEPT OF CAUSE

There are many complexities in the concept of cause; let us note a few. For one, whenever we use the term *cause*, we are emphasizing a part of a causal history. Consider that the car stops with the gas gauge at zero. Did it stop because it ran out of gas? That seems to be the immediate cause. But perhaps the real cause was the driver's lack of attention to the gas gauge or the fact that the driver never learned regular habits of maintenance and the necessity of providing time for them. Perhaps, even more basically, it was that his parents always took care of the maintenance tasks and so never taught him to be responsible. Each is a step back toward a more "fundamental" problem, and each is part of the causal chain. *Use of the term* cause *always means selecting the part of a causal chain that is the most salient for a particular inquiry.*

Which Is the Cause in the Causal Chain?

We usually have little trouble inferring what part of the **causal chain** is being chosen: the part that is most immediate in time, most important, most remediable, most fundamental, the part without which the event would not have occurred (the necessary condition). As Lewis (1983) notes, one cause may be salient in a particular context, another in a different context. By selectively choosing from a causal history, he argues, we "explain" an action. That is, explaining an occurrence means giving some information about its causal history. Thus we can describe the causal chain for a particular situation—as the chapter's opening quote traces the chain from the missing horseshoe nail to the lost battle. We can describe a link in a chain that generalizes across situations. That is what we do when we set forth a hypothesis or theory—for example, "frustration causes aggression." When the explanation is a hypothesis or part of a theory, we are arguing that the phenomena covered by that hypothesis or theory have a common link in their causal chains—where we see frustration, aggression follows.

Sometimes cause is defined as the link that completes the causal chain—the lack of gas in our earlier example. Consider another example: a football player flops into an antique chair; it comes apart, depositing him abruptly and painfully on the floor. He is perceived as the "cause" of the chair's demise. But in reality, he is but the last link in a years-long causal chain as the glue changed to powder, the sockets dried out and became loose, innumerable individuals of varying weights used the chair, and so on. The last link in the causal chain is usually the most immediate and obvious link.

In our modern world, we are often so accustomed to things operating correctly that should an effect cease—the lights go out, an engine stops running—the search for the cause gets considerable attention. Such cases often result from the absence of a necessary condition for the effect to occur. For example, several continuing conditions permit a car's engine to function: oxygen in the air; steady carburetion as the air is mixed with gas; negative pressure as the piston recedes, pulling in the mixture; and so on. The lack of any one of them—air, gas, negative pressure—removes a necessary condition. That breaks the cycle and causes the motor to stop. We then pronounce the cause "a clogged filter," "running out of gas," or "a leaky gasket."

Solving problems is sometimes easier from the perspective of a causal chain, as it can reveal places where intervention will affect subsequent events. For example, the threat of acquired immune deficiency syndrome (AIDS) may be combated at an early link in the chain through education for sexual abstinence. At a later link, we could promote the use of condoms or make sterile needles available free to drug users who might otherwise share them. At a still later link, we could seek a drug that will attack the virus. Of these, we might consider the earliest the least expensive, the most likely to succeed, and the most socially acceptable. Studying the causal chain suggests where to break the cause-and-effect relationship.

Causes as Inferences

A continuing puzzle for philosophers has been to determine whether the term *cause* is needed and, if it is, what conditions permit its use. David Hume (1902 [1748]) for instance, advanced three commonsense criteria: (1) cause and effect occur close together in time, (2) the cause always appears before the effect, and (3) the cause is present whenever the effect is observed. However, we can think of exceptions to the first condition: the relation of smoking to cancer or emphysema. The effect of smoking is delayed rather than contiguous. As for the second condition, when a racquet hits a tennis ball, what precedes what? This condition may be improved by changing it to "the effect did not begin before the cause began" but that does not solve all the problems.

Some people have argued that we should find the **necessary and sufficient conditions** for a phenomenon. Sufficient conditions are all those conditions in the presence of which the effect will occur. But without trying all the possible causes, we would never know whether we had missed a sufficient condition—there may still be one we hadn't tried. Causal relationships are always inferred, never proved.[2]

Causation is an inference for still another reason, a prime one: we never directly sense a causal connection. A billiard ball hits another and bounces away; we do not directly "see" the causal connection. The compression of the billiard ball material seems a reasonable explanation. But maybe it is really that oxygen atoms on the surface repel the balls. We must infer the most reasonable explanation from the circumstances; the attribution of causation is always an inference.

---

2. This may remind you of the discussion of the inference of generality in chapter 8, where it was noted that there may always be boundaries to the generality that we have not found. We will meet inference again in chapter 17.

Validated Causal Propositions
Escape Disconfirmation

Popper (1959) points out that even though causal propositions and theories cannot be proved, they can be tested. Indeed, he argues that our major responsibility is to try to falsify such relationships by posing hypotheses about them and trying to prove them false—finding instances in which, though expected to do so, they do not hold. Recall the Zeigarnik effect of chapter 9, where individuals remember interrupted tasks better than those they are allowed to complete. Suppose we found that this effect did not hold with some individuals. We would have to determine whether these individuals had some characteristic that distinguished them from the rest of the population. If they did, we would have found a boundary on the generality of the proposition. If we could find nothing distinctive about them, however, we would have to question the validity of the original proposition. Alternatively, there may be conditions under which it holds and ones where it does not. But if we can't find these, since we can't predict when it will apply and when it won't, we may have to reject it as a useful proposition.

Suppose the evidence is consistent with an explanation, even when tested in circumstances where we have deliberately tried to find an instance where it wouldn't work–as Popper would put it, "even when one has tried to falsify it." Then, as he notes, the explanation has "escaped **disconfirmation**." Theories and propositions are never proved; they merely escape disconfirmation. Of course, once they have escaped disconfirmation enough times, we consider them part of that structure we call "knowledge."

As noted in chapter 4, Cronbach (1982) views this process of escaping disconfirmation as one of "reducing uncertainty." Eventually the uncertainty is low enough that a research finding crosses the threshold for admittance into the realm of knowledge. Note that having escaped disconfirmation is consistent with the notion that we hold all scientific propositions as tentatively true and subject to disconfirmation—an important aspect of the uniquely self-correcting nature of science.

- Any explanation selects some part of the causal chain to highlight.
- The term *cause* is often used to designate the last link, or a necessary one, that completes the chain.
- Defined as the necessary and sufficient conditions for an effect to appear, causation is always an inference. Like all inferences, it can never be proved; there is always the possibility of a nonconforming case, as yet undiscovered.
- Propositions and hypotheses escape disconfirmation with each successful test. Each escape reduces uncertainty as findings move toward accepted knowledge.

COMPLEXITIES IN OUR CONCEPTION
OF THE WORLD AND SOCIAL SCIENCE

The notion of universal causation, that every event has a cause, implies a very mechanistic conception of the world. Popper (1972) thought of it as a **clocklike world**. It assumes precise mechanical determinism such as we find in the workings of an old clock with numerous gears. Turning one gear inevitably generates a response elsewhere. The physical sciences are often perceived this way. Contrast this with a **cloudlike world**, a reference to the normative behavior exhibited by a cloud of gnats in summer or a flock of birds flying south for the winter. A bird or a gnat strays only a certain distance from the center of the flock or swarm, returning when it becomes an outlier. In such a world, predictions are probabilistic rather than exact. With the loose coupling of events that the cloudlike model assumes, we would expect to find unusual results of both a positive and a negative nature from time to time. Clearly, it is much more difficult to find causal relations in a cloudlike world. But that model fits all social and behavioral phenomena more closely than the clocklike one.

Similarly, experts have argued that unlike the world of physical science, where the materials are inert and are acted on, the world of social science is one of complex interaction and so may never be predictable (Cronbach, 1975). Some such individuals do not expect ever to find a science of rules and laws and propositions like the physical sciences.[3] But, notes Phillips (1987), there are interactions in the physical sciences as well:

> Pressure and volume interact to affect the behavior of a gas—but temperature in turn is another interacting factor, and so is the initial mass of the gas and its purity. Furthermore, depending upon the precise chemical nature of the gas (another interacting factor), some surprising events may occur at specific temperatures and pressures—some gases will condense into liquids while others sublimate directly into solids.
>
> The difference between the social and physical domains is merely that the types of factors that interact are different, although, of course, the "merely" is not entirely without significance. . . . Humans are role-playing and rule-following creatures, while presumably gases neither consciously set out to follow Boyle's Law nor debate which role is appropriate for them. . . .
>
> Processes in the natural world in essence are arenas where a host of forces interact, and scientists cannot make accurate predictions because of the ensuing complexities. But this does not mean that theories are either unattainable, or useless when they are found. Popper uses the example of a storm shaking a tree and causing an apple to fall and bruise on the ground; Gage uses an autumn leaf wafting to the ground. In both cases, there are gravitational effects, air resistance, wind currents, biochemical actions in the

---

3. We will consider this matter in greater detail in chapter 24. There are real differences in the kind of "science" different researchers seek to build. If you wish to pursue this topic further, skip to that material.

plants that determined when the apple and leaf would fall, and so on. The situation in social science research undoubtedly is of similar complexity. (pp. 55–56)[4]

A very complex interactive world probably calls for equally complex explanations of its phenomena.

Complexities in Patterns of Causation: Illustrative Simple Patterns

There are a variety of patterns of causation besides the simple "A causes B" that first springs to mind.[5] Knowing a range of such patterns makes it likelier that we can find a good match to data. Where A and B occur together, it may well be that A causes B. This is the pattern we typically expect to find:

$$A \longrightarrow B$$

For example, we may think that spastic children's slurred speech and awkward movements (A) cause them to be dependent on other people (B).

But as Becker (1963) has argued, it is possible that the dependency (B) results because adults expect such individuals to be dependent on them. The child, getting desirable attention for obliging, displays dependent behavior. So Becker turns around the causal direction that most of us would have inferred. He suggests

$$A \longleftarrow B$$

A perhaps more realistic explanation might be that the child's awkwardness creates expectations and reactions in the adults, resulting in learned helplessness. That evokes even greater efforts by the adults, which reinforce the expressions of helplessness in the child, and so on. Here we are taking the perspective of a causal chain:

- What we perceive as effects may often properly be interpreted as causes or as part of a causal chain. Put another way, any effect is likely also to be a cause of some future event.
- Problem solving is often facilitated by considering, not just the endpoint, but significant portions of the causal chain.

---

4. Reprinted with permission from D. C. Philips, *Philosophy, Science, and Social Inquiry*. Copyright © 1987, Pergamon Press PLC.
5. This section is a modification of Krathwohl (1985), pp. 214–221; the term *cause* is used loosely in this discussion.

Complexities in Patterns of Causation: Illustrative Multiple-Cause Patterns

Although many of our studies deal with single-cause patterns, multiple-cause patterns are clearly more realistic. A single-cause analysis may be adequate to describe powerful variables such as intellectual ability or conditions that totally dominate a situation, such as overwhelming anger. But most variables act only in concert with others, and their effects are noticeably modulated by this interaction. This results in more complex patterns:

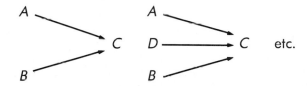

For example, visual acuity may be the result of the amount of available light and the strength of a person's uncorrected vision, an application of the first pattern:

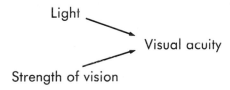

Or, like the second pattern, it may be the result of those factors plus the size of the letters to be discriminated, as on an eye test chart:

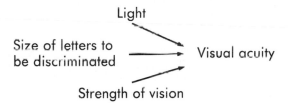

But there are still other complexities; these variables have different weights in different ranges. Thus when the light is very low, light may be the dominant factor in visual acuity, despite the strength of the person's vision. This reduces to a simple-cause pattern:

Light ⟶ Visual acuity

Some causation patterns involve a moderating variable. For example, hostile individuals often are anxious. Although they repress their hostility, this may not be totally effective, and hostility may break through. Anxiety springs from that concern. In this instance, the not-totally-trusted repression is a moderating variable:

Hostility   ⟶   Repression   ⟶   Anxiety

In still another pattern, two causal variables may be affected by a third. Inflation causes the Federal Reserve Board to raise interest rates as well as causes increases in car prices. Both of these factors depress car sales.

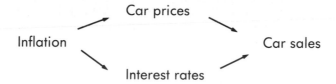

As you can see, more complex patterns result in the inclusion of additional portions of the causal clain. With that insight, you realize that we have been discussing simple examples—causal chains can be infinitely complex. This reinforces the fact that a variety of possibilities should be considered when we infer causation.

> Effects often have more than one cause, and this results in complex causal patterns. Such causal patterns may involve large portions of the causal chain.

EVIDENCE FOR INFERRING CAUSATION

Now that we have examined the complexities of defining cause and the various patterns of cause and have noted that causation can never be proved but only inferred and held as tentatively true, subject to further evidence, on what basis can causation be inferred? We can answer this question at two levels: (1) by describing the patterns in situations that facilitate drawing the inference of causation (the "basis for sensing attributes or changes" link in the chain of reasoning) and (2) by describing the evidence that most strongly permits the inference of causation in these situations.

Patterning Situations to Facilitate Drawing an Inference of Causation: The "Basis for Sensing Attributes or Changes" Link

An important link in the design section of the chain of reasoning is the "basis for sensing attributes or changes" link. This is the patterning of the situation, if we are able to manipulate it, so that we can infer the relationship of the events—we sense a change as a result of the manipulation. If we cannot manipulate the situation, then the link is the logic that we use to select events to observe to make the inference—we sense the attribute or attributes responsible. In 1843, John Stuart Mill elaborated on Sir Francis Bacon's recommendations for discovering causes in a series of what he called "canons," since he believed they were fundamental rules for proving causation. We now realize that they are not methods of proof and that they specify impossible conditions. Nevertheless, they describe the logic underlying the situations from which we infer causation; we approximate their conditions as best we can. He called his patterns of reasoning the methods of agreement, of differences, of concomitant variation, and of residuals.

The Method of Agreement.   Mill (1868) formulated the method of **agreement** thus: "If two or more instances of the phenomenon under investigation have only one circumstance in common, the circumstance in which alone all the instances agree, is the cause (or effect) of the given phenomenon" (p. 428). It is extremely rare, of course, for phenomena, especially social phenomena, to have only one aspect in common and everything else different. Yet this is a commonly used logic for finding potential causes. Where an effect occurs, we look among the commonalities to find the most plausible possibility—the attribute or activity that seems to be responsible. To return to the Kounin example of chapter 4, Kounin noted that a common characteristic of the classrooms where disturbed children were not acting out was that the teachers made smooth transitions from one activity to another. Although this was not proof, it was suggestive of a causal relationship between such transitions and the absence of acting out.

The method of agreement is often used with observation and descriptive case studies, where apparent causes in one situation are investigated in other instances to see whether they hold there as well. It is the logic that underlies qualitative methods, the subject of chapter 15. It is exemplified in the Hoffmann-Riem study of chapter 3, where in studying families with adopted children, the researcher found the common attribute across different families with different adopting circumstances to be that of seeking "normalization."

How far back do we look for a commonality? Particularly if we have reason to believe that the effect was delayed, the potential commonalities increase. Here reasonable explanation and theory help reduce the possibilities, eliminating implausible ones. All the teachers making smooth transitions might happen to have come from Peoria, Illinois. But there is no reasonable explanation that would allow us to make a connection between the teachers' growing up in Peoria and student behavior.

The Negative Form of the Method of Agreement.   Nothing can be the cause of a phenomenon that is not a common circumstance in all instances of the phenomenon. This method is most useful in eliminating potential causes. Thus if we draw up a list of potential causes, the negative method of agreement helps us definitively eliminate ones that were not present in situations where the effect occurred. Suppose we noticed that all teachers whose children acted out wore exciting red dresses. Exploration of enough cases would turn up a differently dressed teacher whose students also acted out and thereby eliminate dress color as a factor. Note that this assumes that a causal factor is necessary to the effect. As we shall see later in this chapter, there are such things as contributing causes or conditions. They are not necessary, so they may or may not be present in any given instance, and this method will not work with them.

Unfortunately, both cause and effect are usually not simply present or absent but are present in degree or kind. It is sometimes difficult to define what we mean by the "presence" of a particular cause. Mill says nothing that helps us define presence, but clearly he intends it to mean that the cause is present at greater than the threshold amount needed to result in an effect. For example, if red dresses were presumed the cause, how saturated a red does it have to be? How much of the dress must be red? Once again, there are complexities here that are not immediately apparent.

The Method of Differences.   The method of **differences** combines the method of agreement with its negative form and is the logic used in experiments. We shall give this logic much greater scrutiny in chapter 18. According to Mill (1868):

> If an instance in which the phenomenon under investigation occurs and an instance in which it does not occur, have every circumstance in common save one, that one occurring in the former; the circumstance in which alone the instances differ, is the effect, or the cause, or an indispensable part of the cause, of the phenomenon. (p. 429)

In practice, this calls for two groups as alike as possible. One, the control group, is not exposed to the experimental variable; the other, the experimental group, is exposed. If the effect shows only in the experimental group, we infer causation. As much as the groups are identical, rival hypotheses arising from differences between them that would explain the effect are eliminated. In contrast to the method of agreement, the method of differences is more often accepted as tightly associating cause and effect.

Experimentation, whereby the experimenter controls the treatment, giving it at will, is probably the most strongly accepted evidence of causation. Some people argue that it is the only acceptable evidence, but if that were true, our knowledge would be severely limited. For instance, the whole field of astronomy is built on nonexperimental knowledge.

Like the method of agreement, the method of differences requires an impossible condition—namely, that two situations be identical. No two individuals are identical; for that matter, no individual is identical from moment to moment. Attaining sufficient functional equivalence for the logic to be effective is one of the most important aspects of experimental design.

Unlike the method of agreement, which can be used to produce new hypotheses, the method of differences is useful only in eliminating possible causes. It helps narrow the field of inquiry. "Postmortem" examinations of failed experiments often suggest new explanations and hypotheses. But such after-the-fact rationalizing must be shown to hold in a new situation before it is accepted as evidence for inferring causation.

The Method of Concomitant Variation. Where it is not possible to manipulate situations experimentally, the method of **concomitant variation** may be helpful. Unlike the methods of agreement and of differences, which focus primarily on the presence or absence of cause and effect, this method asks whether cause and effect vary together in some regular way: "Whatever phenomenon varies in any manner whenever another phenomenon varies in some particular manner, it is either a cause or [an] effect of the phenomenon, or is connected with it through some fact of causation" (Mill, 1868, p. 441).

The weasel words "or is connected with it through some fact of causation" rob this method of its effectiveness. We noted in the study of correlation in chapter 10 that two things may vary together because of a common link in their causal chain. A colleague of mine, Si Halperin, is fond of pointing out to his classes that reading ability during the elementary school grades is related to weight—heavier children read better than the lighter ones. It is true that sixth graders both weigh more and read better than first graders. But would over-feeding children improve their reading capacity? Of course not! Both changes normally occur over time, and that is why they vary together.

Like the methods discussed earlier, the method of concomitant variation can be used to rule out causes, as few things that do not vary with the effect satisfy the conditions for inferring causation. A possible exception is a cause that operates in an all-or-nothing manner; a so-called step condition does not vary with the cause throughout its range. With a step function, when the cause reaches a certain level, it triggers a reaction. A smoke detector is triggered as smoke reaches a threshold but does not get louder as the smoke increases further.

The Method of Residuals. More often used in natural science research, the method of **residuals** is rare in behavioral science research. Mill (1868) states: "Subduct from any phenomenon such part as is known by previous induction to be the effect of certain antecedents and the residue of the phenomenon is the effect of the remaining antecedents" (p. 437). This method asks us to account for as much of the situation as we can, on the basis of prior work, and the cause is to be found in the residue not accounted for. This method is regularly used in trouble-shooting. A mechanic working on a stalled car may test the spark to determine whether the high-voltage electrical system is working. If it is, then one of the other systems—carburetor, fuel pump, timing, and so on—is the culprit. These are checked in order of their likelihood of contributing to the symptoms.

Clearly, the method of residuals works best in a bounded system of limited scope that has been well explored so that alternative causes can be eliminated. Problems in the behavioral sciences tend to have fuzzy boundaries and broad scope, and there is less firm knowledge about constituent parts that would permit their elimination.

Comment on the Methods. We have noted that research depends on building a logical chain of reasoning; all argumentation rests on a logical base. Mill has described the underlying logic that we use, despite its difficulties. We patch up the fact that the control and experimental groups are not alike by finding and eliminating explanations caused by differences. In qualitative methods, we deliberately look for new instances that display a common aspect but in other ways are as different from one another as possible to test the proposition we think we see emerging (see chapter 15).

Mill's methods assume a single cause; they are not as successful in cases of multiple causation. This is perhaps especially obvious with the method of residuals, as many car owners have discovered the hard way. A single weak spark plug might not cause engine failure, and neither might a bad fuel mixture. Yet together they may do so. Each might be passed over as adequate by a mechanic looking for a single cause.

Although we have discussed Mill's methods individually, clearly they may be used in combination. Thus the method of concomitant variation can be combined with the method of differences to show not only that the effect appears only in the experimental group but also that its strength is related to the strength of the cause. For example, suppose we place food dye in increasing concentration in a series of batches of processed food. We could show that the presence of the food dye above a certain level causes hyperactivity in children that does not occur when the dye is below that level or not in the food—the method of differences. By simultaneously varying at random the concentration of the dye administered and showing that the degree of hyperactivity corresponds to the level of concentration above the critical level—the method of concomitant variation—we have very strong evidence of a causal relation.

- The chain of reasoning requires a logical argument including a "basis for sensing attributes or changes."
- The logic of the "basis for sensing attributes or changes" link was described by John Stuart Mill and is still used today in inferring causation in these methods:

  1. The method of agreement (used in case studies and in historical studies)
  2. The method of difference (used in experimental studies)
  3. The method of concomitant variation (used in predictive studies and in studies examining data gathered after an event has occurred—after-the-fact natural experiments)
  4. The method of residuals

- We approximate Mill's impossible conditions as closely as possible, add such conditions as we can to strengthen the logic, and often combine the methods to support our inference.

Evidence of Causation

In chapter 13 you will meet a concept called internal validity (LP) where LP stands for "linking power"—the capacity of the study to link cause to effect. *The conditions that contribute to internal validity (LP) are those that provide evidence of causation.* They consist of conceptual evidence (evidence based on reasoning) and empirical evidence (evidence based on data). We are accustomed to examining data-based evidence for causation, so it is included in this chapter. The more detailed examination of the overall framework of internal validity (LP) and its other parts is left to the next chapter.

One of the judgments in determining the internal validity or linking power of a study is whether the evidence provides a clearly *demonstrated result.* Further, if there was a hypothesis or prediction, one must determine whether the evidence is consistent with expectations. What evidence contributes to a strongly demonstrated result? Data showing these four attributes:

- Authenticity of evidence
- Precedence of cause
- Presence of effect
- Congruence of explanation and evidence

Let us examine each of these more closely.

Authenticity of Evidence. Authenticity is important in any study but is of particular concern in historical studies. It asks the question, "Is the evidence what it purports to be?" If we claim that the moldering notebook in our library is Napoleon's diary, we must have convincing evidence that it is. We assume that scores on a test were the result achieved by a certain individual. Can we be sure that someone else did not take the test in that person's stead or help that person with it? If the test was a take-home, this is not assured. So **authenticity of evidence** is a legitimate concern we must be prepared to answer if the evidence is to be accepted as authentic.

Precedence of Cause. This evidence answers the question, "Did the cause precede or occur at the same time as the effect?" Mill argued that cause is temporally antecedent to, or concomitant with, effect, never the reverse. If a person is nervous and smokes cigarettes, does the smoking cause the nervousness? We would have to establish that smoking started before or at the same time as the nervousness appeared for smoking to be the possible cause. **Precedence of cause** is obvious in experiments. It is much more difficult to establish definitively in natural situations or in retrospective survey evidence. Often we don't know until later what causal factor we should have been attending to, so we may or may not have included evidence of its precedence in the records.

Presence of Effect. With an experimental treatment, we are sure there was an intended cause. But there is still the question, "Was there an effect?" We need no statistical test to know that penicillin is effective, that there was the **presence of an effect**. Unfortunately, most behavioral science effects are not so obvious. Even an effect in the proper direction may be a chance deviation caused by sampling or other error. We use inferential statistics to minimize the likelihood that a chance deviation is mistaken for a real effect. This assumes, however, that the correct statistics were used, were properly interpreted, and were sensitive enough to show a significant treatment result if one occurred. Cook and Campbell (1979) refer to these latter characteristics as statistical conclusion validity. In devising a study, we select the design that eliminates the most serious contenders as alternative explanations, leaving the intended explanation as the sole remaining choice for the effect.

Congruence of Explanation and Evidence.   We have noted that astronomy is not an experimental science, yet we consider it a strong one. Why? Mainly for two reasons: it has good explanations, and the explanations are shown to allow valid predictions; there is **congruence of explanation and evidence**. The first reason we shall deal with in the next chapter. The second we consider here. It is what we refer to when we ask, "Was there confirmation that evidence of the effect was congruent with the explanation?" The desired characteristics of evidence are as follows:

- *An impressive predictive feat*. Evidence is convincing when a strongly credible explanation predicts a result and that result occurs. The more detail we can supply about the prediction, the more impressive the prediction: when the effect will appear, how it will do so, in what strength in relation to that of the effect, and so on. These are all things that astronomers do in telling us where to look, when, and for what magnitude of heavenly body. It convinces us that they know what they are talking about. There are few instances in the behavioral sciences where we can make such precise predictions, but we can aspire to do so; the principle is sound.
- *A strong effect*. The larger the effect, the less likely it is to be a chance effect and the easier it is to track it to the cause. Producing the effect in the face of countervailing circumstances adds to the impression of strength. A successful treatment to reverse the decline in achievement of inner-city children through the elementary grades would be impressive not just because the children achieved but also because it reversed a countervailing tendency.
- *A demonstration that the effect follows the pattern of a manipulated cause*. This is probably the most compelling evidence of all. The more complex the causal pattern, the stronger the evidence for association. In a study of the effect of food dye on emotionally disturbed behavior, would we not be convinced that a strong causal link exists if we can show that the behavior appears when the food coloring is administered? That it disappears when the coloring is not present? That such behavior is proportional to the amount of food coloring administered? That the pattern of such behavior can be shown to follow even a random pattern of amount of coloring present that was devised by an independent observer? Such evidence can be produced by experimental time-series designs.[6]

---

6. Discussed in chapters 18 and 21.

The empirical support for inferring causation includes evidence of the following:

- That the evidence was authentic—it was what it purported to be
- That the cause preceded the effect (precedence of cause)
- That an effect did occur and, if statistics were used to sense it, that they were used correctly and were appropriately sensitive
- That there was congruence between the explanation and the evidence of the effect. The evidence is weightier if there was a detailed and accurate prediction, a strong effect, or, notably, an effect that parallels a randomly varied cause.

COMPLEXITIES IN THE NATURE OF RELATIONSHIPS

Not all relationships are as simple as the correlations studied in the chapter on descriptive statistics (chapter 10). With correlation, increases in one variable are accompanied by proportional changes in another. We have already noted step relationships where a certain level of one variable is required before another is triggered (the smoke alarm example). In this section, we will find that step functions are an example of contingent conditions, and we will explore other complexities often overlooked in the routine application of correlational statistics.

Conditions Arising from the Presence or Absence of Necessary and Sufficient Conditions

As noted earlier, one possible definition of cause is "the necessary and sufficient set of conditions for the effect to appear." Suppose we look at the combinations of presence or absence of necessary and sufficient conditions as shown in Figure 12.1.[7]

We have already commented on the impossibility of finding "the necessary and sufficient set of conditions"—the one and only cause. Not only may there be more than one set of conditions sufficient to produce the effect (**alternative conditions**) but, having found one set, we will never know whether there is another unless we test all possible situations—an inconceivable option. This is not usually a problem, however. We are often satisfied to find even one way of predicting and controlling a situation.

Contingent conditions (necessary but not sufficient) and contributing conditions (neither necessary nor sufficient) pervade the behavioral and social

---

7. I am reasonably certain that this diagram, which I used in my 1985 book, is not original with me, but efforts to locate the origin have so far failed. I would appreciate hearing from any reader recognizing the source. Kelley (1973) employs similar four-way schemata in exploring how individuals attribute causality to events, and Einhorn and Hogarth's (1986) is closer, involving alternative conditions and a cell in which the effect occurs probabilistically.

Is the cause sufficient
to produce the effect?

	Yes	No
Is the cause necessary to produce the effect? Yes	The one and only cause	A contingent condition
No	An alternative condition	A contributing condition

FIGURE 12.1   The intersections of presence and absence of necessary and sufficient conditions.

sciences. We are so used to looking for the typical correlation pattern that their presence is often not recognized. If they are noted, they are usually recognized from their distinctive scatterplots. A scatterplot, you will recall from chapter 10, results from plotting the pairs of scores for a correlation. Scatterplots for alternative, contingent, and sometimes contributing conditions may show particular patterns.

An Alternative Set of Conditions: Sufficient but Not Necessary

Alternative conditions are conditions under which the effect appears every time this set of conditions appears, although the effect may also appear when that set of conditions is not present. For example, a child's sense of low self-esteem may result from failing in competition with her peers or from being continually criticized for not doing still better despite achieving very well. They are alternative conditions leading to the same effect. (Is the low self-esteem that results from these two causes really the same? Might a finer analysis show them to be different? Whether true in this instance or not, always consider this possibility when you think you have alternative sets of conditions.)

Consider another example: a biological condition is assumed to cause certain effects (symptoms) of brain pathology. Fisher and Gonda (1955) and Fisher, Gonda, and Little (1955) noted that when a test of brain pathology, the Rorschach, yielded a certain high score indicative of the disease, the agreement with criteria was very good (94 percent). This was verified by a variety of standard neurologic procedures, including electroencephalograph tests and lumbar punctures. A particular kind of thinking that was elicited by Rorschach cards seemed to be caused by brain pathology, so high accuracy was found in predicting pathology from positive Rorschach test findings. But low scores did not indicate the absence of disease—some individuals with low scores also had brain pathology. Here is a condition (a special type of thinking as indicated by high Rorschach scores) that when present always indicates the presence of some other condition (brain pathology). The presence of an alternative condition virtually guarantees the presence of the condition of interest, but absence gives no guarantee of its absence.

Fisher (1959) noted that the scatterplot of a predictor with the criterion condition yielded what he called a "twisted pear."[8] It is perhaps better described as a triangular scatterplot. Fisher's diagram is portrayed in considerably adapted form in Figure 12.2. He labeled the quadrants in the way predictive tests are usually described: positives are scores above some criterion level (the horizontal dashed line) that defines subjects deemed to have the criterion condition—in this instance, brain pathology. Those below it are negatives. The vertical dashed line is the cut score on the test, which divides those who are presumed on the basis of the test score to have the condition (right side) from those without it (left side). Those above the criterion level who have the condition but are to the left of the cut score on the screening examination (upper left quadrant) are false negatives. They don't look as if they have it on the screening examination, but they do. Those below the criterion level who do not have the condition but are to the right of the cut score on the screening examination are false positives. They appear to have the condition on the screening examination but do not.

The errors in classification by the screening test are the cases labeled false positives and false negatives. In the diagram, there are few people whom the test identifies as having the pathology who do not (false positives). The size of this group can be a function of several things: measurement error, where the cut score is placed, and where we draw the dividing line for presence of the criterion condition. The group might be large if the test had low reliability because negatives could get high scores owing to measurement error. It could be reduced to zero if we moved the cut score for predicting the presence of the condition to the right. But this would increase the number of false negatives— a trade-off. If the criterion condition is artificially dichotomous—and many are—lowering the dividing line would also decrease false positives (for instance, if the criterion is a medical diagnosis—definitely has brain pathology, probably has it, probably does not have it, definitely does not have it—the four levels of rating provide opportunity for a lower dividing point than the dichotomous definitive determination of autopsy or invasive procedures).

The other classification errors are false negatives. In these instances, the subjects do not show the particular kind of thinking indicated by the Rorschach but have brain pathology. Such individuals would be missed by any screening procedure using only the Rorschach, even with a lower cut score. Apparently,

---

8. Unfortunately, in an otherwise excellent article, Fisher (1959) did not always distinguish in his examples between alternative and contingent conditions; both yield "twisted pear" scatterplots. He noted that overweight is sufficient to cause life insurance companies to require a higher premium, although lack of obesity may or may not accompany an early death. The presence of obesity is predictive of shortened life span, so obesity is a sufficient but not necessary alternative condition. He also indicated that IQ has a "twisted pear" scatterplot in relation to scholastic and vocational achievement. A person with a high IQ may or may not achieve, but a person with a low IQ rarely will. This is the absence of intellectual ability, a necessary but not sufficient (i.e., contingent condition) for scholastic and vocational success.

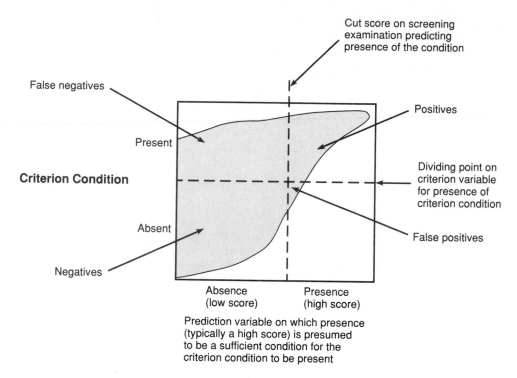

FIGURE 12.2   Scatterplot of an alternative sufficient but not necessary condition. (Adapted from Fisher, 1959, p. 152)

they are missing the symptom that shows up on the Rorschach. Like other diseases, brain pathology may show up slightly differently in some individuals than in others. Alternatively, brain pathology might grow out of several base conditions, just as some cancers seem to be the result of a virus, others the result of exposure to toxic substances, and still others the result of heredity. Brain pathology might result from a particular alternative but sufficient condition.

A caveat before we venture further. As noted earlier, although we never know when we have the "necessary and sufficient" conditions for a phenomenon, we are always satisfied to find an alternative that works. So every condition regularly accompanying an effect could be considered an alternative condition. But not all alternative conditions will show the triangular scatterplot. Only if other alternative conditions are at work in the data will the triangular scatterplot appear. Then other conditions will create the phenomenon of interest, which will appear as false negatives filling that corner of the scatterplot.

Note that in alternative conditions, it is the presence of some condition that is indicative of the presence of another condition (an "effect"), but the absence of the alternative condition is not indicative of the absence of the effect. In the case of a contingent condition—a necessary but not sufficient condition—its absence is indicative of the absence of a phenomenon, but its presence is not indicative of the phenomenon's presence.

A Contingent Condition: Necessary but Not Sufficient

A **contingent condition** is one that is always present when the effect appears. It may also appear when the effect is not present, since it is not enough by itself to cause the effect. For example, the ability to discriminate the letters of the alphabet is necessary to reading but not sufficient for reading. Without the ability to discriminate the letters, reading cannot occur, but we can discriminate letters and still not read. The skills of subtracting and multiplying are necessary to doing long division but will not produce it. We cannot do long division, however, without subtraction and multiplication. Wherever there is a hierarchy of knowledge or skills such that complex knowledge or behaviors require the prior learning of simpler ones (entry-level knowledge, skills, or abilities), contingent conditions exist.

The triangular plot for contingent conditions is oriented differently from that of alternative conditions because it is the absence of one characteristic that is predictive of absence of a second. Presence of the first yields no prediction of the second. Figure 12.3 shows that the image of Figure 12.2 is inverted.

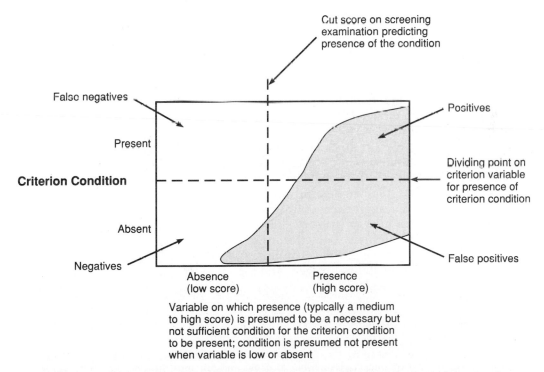

FIGURE 12.3 The contingent (necessary but not sufficient) condition and the triangular scatterplot ("twisted pear").

Figure 12.4 is an example of a contingent relationship found in the literature (Richards, 1976). It is a plot of fluency scores ("Utility Test"), interpreted as a measure of flexibility, against uniqueness scores ("Instances"), which are considered a measure of creativity. It suggests that flexibility is a necessary but not sufficient condition for creativity—subjects with low flexibility are not creative, but those with high flexibility may or may not be creative; we cannot tell. In line with the dichotomous nature of the definition of a contingent condition, each axis has been arbitrarily divided to indicate "presence" and "absence." Note that in the upper left quadrant of the scatterplot there are few cases; in the "absence" of flexibility, defined as a score of 23 or below, there are few cases with creativity, defined as 7 or above.[9] In the "presence" of flexibility, scores above 23, there may or may not be creativity. There are more cases with high scores, but there are also many low ones. Being flexible doesn't guarantee creativity. Because it is apparently a contingent relationship, we are safer predicting that with low flexibility, there will low creativity than that with high flexibility, there will be high creativity.

Contingent relationships are demonstrated by showing that below some level of a condition, the effect hardly ever appears, but as the threshold level is approached, it may. Above that level, there is often little or no relationship between the level of the cause and that of the effect. For example, consider intelligence and teaching. Instructors need some minimum mental ability to be good teachers. Up to that minimum, there are increasing numbers of competent teachers. Above that level, however, so many other factors determine teaching ability that there is little or no relation between mental ability and the teacher's competence. Some extremely intelligent persons have the wrong personality to be teachers, and some with minimal mental ability may be motivated, patient, fair, responsive, warm, friendly, and effective teachers.

Meehl (1977) suggests that in some contingent cases, the cause may have threshold or step-function characteristics: the effect appears only as the cause reaches a certain threshold level needed for the effect to occur. After that, increases may or may not occur. Once a smoke alarm is triggered, an increasing amount of smoke does not result in an increase in loudness. Another step function is the minimum level of oxygen necessary for a fire; only as that is reached can combustible materials be set afire. But levels of oxygen above the minimum increase the temperature of the fire. In parallel fashion, a child engages in physical aggression only when frustrated beyond a certain level. Additional frustration may increase the level of aggression. With these latter examples, there is an increase in effect once triggered, so both patterns exist.

An effect may have multiple contingent conditions. This is obvious for a fire: a combustible substance, oxygen, and high temperatures are all contingent conditions. This suggests a frequently appearing causation pattern, the INUS condition.

---

9. Note that for the contingent relationship to show, the test must include the proper score ranges. In this case, if the test had a ceiling effect above 6—no scores of 7 or higher—we would have had little reason to suggest a contingent relationship.

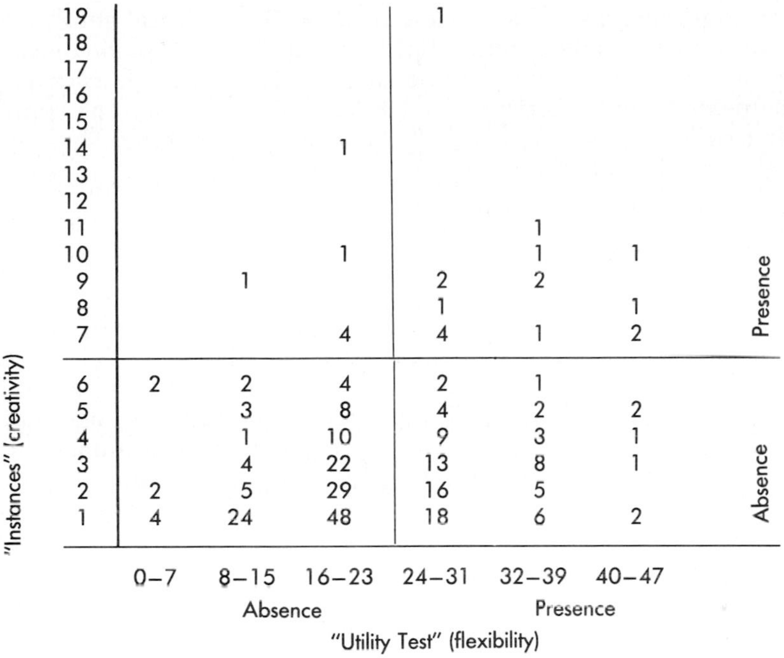

"Instances" (creativity)	0–7	8–15	16–23	24–31	32–39	40–47	
19				1			
18							
17							
16							
15							
14			1				
13							
12							
11					1		Presence
10			1		1	1	
9		1		2	2		
8				1		1	
7			4	4	1	2	
6	2	2	4	2	1		
5		3	8	4	2	2	
4		1	10	9	3	1	
3		4	22	13	8	1	Absence
2	2	5	29	16	5		
1	4	24	48	18	6	2	
	0–7	8–15	16–23	24–31	32–39	40–47	
	Absence			Presence			

"Utility Test" (flexibility)

FIGURE 12.4   Illustration of a contingent relationship in a frequency scatterplot of scores on the "Utility Test" measuring flexibility and "instances" measuring creativity. Numbers in scatterplot indicate the frequency of that pair of scores (e.g., four persons with an "Instances" score of 1 had "Utility Test" scores between 0 and 7). (Adapted from Richards, 1976, p. 162)

The INUS Condition: Neither Necessary nor Sufficient but Contributing

In a very interesting article calling attention to a variety of unusual causal patterns, Meehl (1977) discussed the INUS situation—a group of **contributing conditions** first described by Mackie (1965). The **INUS condition** explains effects resulting from a particular constellation of circumstances. Such explanations are common in qualitative research and historical studies. The name comes from the perplexing combination of the individually *Insufficient* but *Necessary* factors in a set of conditions jointly *Unnecessary* but *Sufficient* to bring about the effect. This is Mackie's way of describing the cause of an event as a set of factors each contributing to the effect but insufficient by itself to bring it about. Each is necessary in this constellation of conditions that, as a whole, is sufficient to bring about the effect. The whole constellation is unnecessary because other constellations of conditions might also bring about the same effect.

Meehl uses the example of a particular factory fire that occurs because of a short in the fuse box, no sprinkler, flammable material near the box, dry wood in the ceiling above, and a stairway to carry the fire to the rest of the building. No one of these is sufficient—the electrical short, the flammable material, the dry wood, the stairway. None of these particular items are necessary—lightning could have substituted for the electrical short, a leaking gas line for the flammable material. But the entire complex of circumstances is necessary in this constellation—the nearness of the flammable material to the short, the nearness of the stairway to the flammable material. The entire set of circumstances is sufficient to "cause" the effect. But another set could also cause a fire, so the set of circumstances is unnecessary in a "necessary and sufficient" sense.

Such explanations are a common feature of historical works and case studies. Tuchman (1962), for example, described the conditions of World War I that led to the defeat of Germany, a particular configuration of circumstances in which the German generals persisted in their preconceptions of the situation even in the face of contrary evidence. This is a set of conditions, no one of which is sufficient to bring about the particular course of the war or is necessary, since other events might have served as well. But taken together, they brought about defeat. Although such situations are unique in many aspects, we tend to look for commonalities with parallel situations to apply what was learned in them. As we shall note in chapter 24, in another reference to the Tuchman example, some individuals consider this kind of explanation of situations the essence of the social sciences.

Others, realizing that there may be alternative sets of INUS conditions producing the same effect, look for commonalities across such sets to uncover possible contributing or contingent conditions for producing the phenomenon. For example, we can look for other historical instances of rigid adherence to faulty preconceptions like Tuchman's example to determine common characteristics. This kind of analysis has been used to advantage by the effective-schools movement, which studied successful inner-city schools to reveal common elements (Stedman, 1987, Brookover, 1987).

Ericson and Ellett (1987 and their earlier papers) introduce the idea of an INUP cause, substituting *probable* for *sufficient*. They argue that this is a much more useful way of looking at complex events about which we wish to generalize but about which firm predictions are difficult or even impossible. Probably many, if not most, phenomena of interest in the social sciences are of this nature.

Discriminating Alternative, Contingent, and Contributing Conditions in Scatterplots

Many behavioral measures are bipolar, and the direction of the score is arbitrary. Thus the score of a scale for the continuum *happy–sad* may indicate the presence or absence of either happiness or sadness. Determining which is the significant condition and whether it is a contingent or an alternative condition is a matter of logic, trial, and validation rather than simply looking at the scatterplot and the direction of the scores. For an example, see the appendix to this chapter. But whereas determining whether a condition is contingent, contributing, or alternative is of research interest, it is important to realize that the relationship between variables in a triangular scatterplot is poorly represented by a Pearson product-moment correlation. Yet for lack of anything better, nearly all studies of the value of prior learning for later achievement, or those validating a hierarchical structure, have used such correlations. If you find a low correlation and have ruled out problems such as nonlinearity and floor and ceiling effects as the cause, consider the possibility of there being alternative, contingent, or contributing relationships, especially in the presence of a triangular scatterplot. Unfortunately, there does not seem to be a way of representing such relationships well statistically.[10] If you use a correlation, also display the scatterplot and describe your explanation of the relationship as contingent, contributing, or alternative together with the supporting logic.

- With an alternative condition, the presence of a condition predicts the presence of a related one. But its absence does not indicate the absence of the related condition.
- With a contingent condition, its absence predicts the absence of a related one. But its presence does not indicate the presence of the related condition.
- Conditions neither necessary nor sufficient but associated with an effect are contributing conditions or causes. They may simply show a weak correlation or a triangular scatterplot.
- The INUS causal condition is the explanation of an effect by a particular configuration of circumstances in which no one of the circumstances is itself sufficient to cause the effect, yet all of them are necessary. Together they are sufficient to create the effect, but others could substitute for any one of them in another situation. Each may be thought of as a contributing condition.
- Contingent and alternative relationships often appear as triangular scatterplots, and so sometimes do contributing conditions. In such cases, the strength of the relationship between variables is not well represented by the Pearson product-moment correlation.

Classification Schemes as Weak Explanations

The use of **classification schemes** to explain phenomena involves categorizing new phenomena into a set of previously observed groups that have some already recognized pattern, regularity, or similarity. Classifying a phenomenon

---

10. Some form of the intraclass correlation might be useful, but so far the solution has proved elusive.

with similar others tells us something about it and what we can expect, even if we do not know the causal basis. Predictions can be made and confirmed on the basis of such explanations. For example, when a newly found animal or plant is placed in a biological taxonomy, we know more about it from the characteristics of its family. A variety of such schemes have proved useful in the social sciences, some called taxonomies, some not. Jung's personality types (Jung, 1971) and the *Taxonomy of Educational Objectives* (Bloom, 1956; Krathwohl, Bloom, and Masia, 1964) are examples of such schemes.

Kaplan (1964, 1965) calls such schemes noncausal explanations and includes in this category such temporal laws as patterns of children's growth. He notes they are "weakly" explanatory in that scientists can agree on the usefulness of a taxonomic scheme even if they cannot formulate the causal laws that undergird it. He suggests, however, that the merits of such a scheme probably "depend on how clearly and nearly it can be related to causal principles" (p. 148).

Kaplan (1964, 1965) also notes that purposive statements, "explanations that attribute a causal character to behavior that is intentional" (p. 148), serve the same kind of function. Gathering of nectar by bees is purposive behavior, but we do not think of it as such because it is instinctive rather than motivated. Motivation is what drives conscious choice, as when a student does homework instead of watching television. Where choice is involved, purposive explanations, which admittedly are fictional constructs, may be useful. Eventually we will want either to replace a purposive explanation with evidence that motives are not just fictional constructs but really exist or else find another explanation.

> Associating a phenomenon with like ones in a classification scheme permits us to infer that it will have other characteristics similar to those in the classification, a kind of explanation.

A KEY LINK: THE BASIS FOR SENSING ATTRIBUTES OR CHANGES

The link in the chain of reasoning designated the "basis for sensing attributes or changes" is a key link in inferring causation. It describes the basis, usually some variation of Mill's methods, for the inference in a study. Since the inference is usually based on a comparison of persons either with themselves or with others, there are only so many possibilities. It is therefore possible to lay these out in a decision tree such as that shown in Figure 12.5. As it shows, we can compare an individual's present behavior with past or future behavior. Alternatively, this can be compared with that of other people in natural situations or ones designed for the study. The tree may be helpful in examining the research methods covered in section four of this book, because each will typically use certain alternatives in the tree more than others.

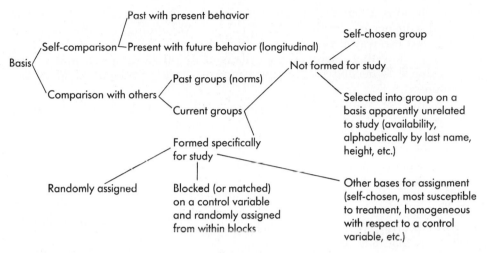

FIGURE 12.5 A decision tree of possible alternatives for the "basis for sensing attributes or changes" link in the chain of reasoning.

Further, it may suggest alternatives that ought to be considered in a particular study that were missed.

CAN CAUSATION EVER BE INFERRED?

This chapter has taken a very cautious view of inferring causality, partly as an antidote to the common assumption that studies routinely show causation and partly also to acquaint you with the complexities of this inference. Lest you come away with the impression that such an inference is almost never appropriate, some perspective is in order. Knowledge is the building of a consensus around the interpretation of data; this chapter has reviewed the kind of data that would strongly contribute to the building of such a consensus. The reality of the natural situations described with qualitative methods, combined with strong logic and a well-grounded explanation, can create a broad and useful consensus regarding the proper interpretation of the data. For nearly everyone, experimentation can provide strong evidence. This is especially true when we are able to vary the experimental variable in such a way that a concomitant effect follows its pattern. The evidence is further strengthened when we can eliminate alternative explanations—for instance, by having the experimental variable randomly varied or varied at the request of an independent observer. (Generalizing from that situation is another inference that depends on the representativeness of the key features of the study.)

Meta-analysis, a way of combining studies quantitatively that is described in chapter 21, is proving to be a strong method of providing evidence for causal propositions. Replication of a study provides the ultimate validation of it, and the combining of studies that are in some ways replications of one another to draw conclusions about the variables involved provides strong evidence that can build consensus. Further, meta-analysis, depending on the available evidence and the way it is done, can often describe the nature of the causal relationship, how that relationship is changed by other variables, and where more evidence is needed to provide a more complete understanding of the phenomenon.

Still another method of interest, also explored in chapter 21, is causal modeling. If we can construct a model showing how variables are related in a situation, causal modeling describes the fit of the model to the evidence. It shows whether these relationships are borne out by the data. Where they are, the evidence can be quite convincing that the model is an accurate representation.

So we can and do construct strong evidence for causal relationships, and our methods of doing so are continually improving. The caveats of this chapter are worth bearing in mind as we do so, however, along with the possible complexities that may be encountered.

SUMMARY

This chapter has focused on some of the complexities in the concept of causation. For example, any statement of causation emphasizes a part of a causal chain that leads to the effect. Knowing this helps to draw attention to the rest of the causal chain, which may be more amenable to study or control. Defining *cause* as the set of necessary and sufficient conditions to bring about an effect, while recognizing the impossibility of this task, helps us to understand why causation is always an inference. This suggests why it is often difficult to agree on whether something is a cause and when sufficient evidence has been amassed.

Use of the term *causation* tends to imply that the world has a mechanical, clocklike nature, a view that some social scientists do not accept. Some prefer a cloudlike conception that yields predictions only in terms of probabilities or odds. Added to all these complexities are the many possible causal patterns. If the simple "*A* causes *B*" does not fit the evidence, a variety of other patterns of causation may be considered.

Examination of the possible combinations of "necessary" and "sufficient" suggests that these combinations appear often in social science phenomena. The distinctive scatterplots of "necessary but not sufficient" (contingent) conditions and "sufficient but not necessary" (alternative) conditions help us recognize when these kinds of relationships should be considered. Their triangular or "twisted pear" scatterplot is not well suited to summarization by a correlation coefficient. Contributing conditions (neither necessary nor sufficient) also are found, usually as a low correlation or a triangular scatterplot. The INUS condition designates situations where the components are individually insufficient but necessary, and jointly unnecessary but sufficient, to create a particular effect.

Having considered causation, we will examine how the evidence for causation is assembled in the chain of reasoning and the criteria that are applied to determine where there is a cause-and-effect relationship and whether it generalizes beyond the instance in which it was demonstrated.

ADDITIONAL READING

Many useful treatments of causation go beyond this discussion. Examples are Ellsworth (1977) in psychology, Köbben (1973) in anthropology, and Hage and Meeker (1988) in sociology. Chapter 1 of Cook and Campbell (1979) is a clear and readable summarization of the progression of the philosophical positions. Guba and Lincoln (1982) similarly summarize them and argue for abandonment of causation for "plausible explanations," a construct especially congruent with qualitative positions. See also the early sections of Messick (1989).

IMPORTANT TERMS

Alternative conditions
Authenticity of evidence
Causal chain
Classification schemes
Clocklike world
Cloudlike world
Congruence of explanation and evidence
Contingent conditions
Contributing conditions
Disconfirmation

INUS condition
Method of agreement
Method of differences
Method of concomitant variation
Method of residuals
Necessary conditions
Precedence of cause
Presence of an effect
Sufficient conditions

APPLICATION PROBLEMS

1. Considering the definition of causation given in this chapter, how would you comment on the age-old question, "Which came first, the chicken or the egg"?

2. Assume you are an elementary school teacher conducting an interview with the parents of a student who has consistently demonstrated low achievement. They claim that the "real" reason for their child's performance is that he is "lazy." How would you answer them?

3. Bernard Weiner's attribution theory (1972, 1980a, 1980b) identifies several "causes" to which individuals "attribute" (use to explain) success or failure, including ability, effort, task difficulty, luck, mood, illness, and help from others. Each of these causes, Weiner asserts, shows the presence or absence of three properties: (1) stability (consistency of the attribution over time, as with luck versus ability), (2) controllability (degree to which the cause is under the person's control, such as mood versus illness), and (3) locus of control (whether the cause has an origin internal or external to the person, as in effort versus task difficulty). These are all factors in an individual's understanding of an outcome. Future behavior, then, is determined by a person's perception of these causes. Are these factors truly causes, or are some of them effects? How does this theory fit the definition of causation outlined in this chapter?

4. Consider the problem of drug abuse. Illustrate contingent, contributing, and alternative causes in explaining how such abuse occurs.

5. Examine Figure 22.5, the model of natural food purchasing on page 592, but don't read the material about it yet. This is a causal model of the role of values and attitudes in purchasing from a natural food store. Values

are posited to be of three kinds: (1) internal, having to do with self-fulfillment and self-respect; (2) external, having to do with a sense of belonging and security; and (3) interpersonal values, such as having fun and having warm relationships. These are posited to lead to attitudes that influence action. The solid lines indicate the hypothesized relationships; the dashed lines are other relationships expected to be less strong. The numbers on the lines indicate the strength of the relationships and confirm that the model is supported by the data. This illustrates how the social sciences are beginning to test causal chains. Can you think of any way in which the direction of causation might be reversed? The answer is in the text accompanying the figure.

Compare your answers to problems 1–4 with those on pages 710–711.

<hr>

APPLICATION EXERCISE

Where does your problem fall in the causal chain? What part of the chain have you chosen? The most important part? Most recent? Most easily explored? What pattern of causation do you expect to find? Might others apply? Are any contingent or con-

tributing conditions involved? Could yours be considered an INUS situation? In what way? After considering the various causation possibilities, have you changed your mind about what to expect?

<hr>

APPENDIX: AN EXAMPLE OF DIFFICULTY IN IDENTIFYING THE NATURE OF A CAUSAL RELATIONSHIP

As noted in the chapter, when a triangular scatterplot appears, it is often difficult to determine what is at work and how the relationship is best characterized. Here is an example.

Consider the left-hand scatterplot[11] in Figure 12.6, from Suciati (1990), in which students at the Indonesian Open University were asked to indicate on a four-point scale their reactions to instructional material they did not understand, 1 meaning they rarely persisted and 4 meaning they always did. The lack of cases in the upper left corner of the plot suggests that this is a triangular scatterplot. Is it that persistence is a necessary

<hr>

11. This representation of a scatterplot shows the number of individuals having each combination of scores rather than showing a dot for each pair of scores.

Scatterplot of Achievement with Persistence

Achievement score	Persists			
	Rarely 1	2	3	Always 4
70–74				1
65–69			1	
60–64			1	3
55–59			7	6
50–54		2	21	14
45–49	4	6	21	18
40–44		6	31	20
35–39		6	21	10
30–34	2	6	6	3
25–29		1	1	2
Total	6	27	110	77

Scatterplot of Achievement with Self-testing

Achievement score	Does self-tests			
	Rarely 1	2	3	Always 4
70–74				1
65–69			1	
60–64				4
55–59		1	5	7
50–54		2	11	24
45–49		4	16	29
40–44		4	21	32
35–39	1	6	11	19
30–34	1	1	8	7
25–29		1	1	2
Total	2	19	74	125

Note: Figures indicate the number of individuals with that particular combination of scores.

FIGURE 12.6 Contingent and contributing conditions related to achievement. (Adapted from Suciati, 1990)

but not sufficient condition to achieve, or is it the absence of persistence—let's call it the presence of distractibility (an alternative cause)—that is the variable involved? Is persistence a contributing variable, insufficient in itself but potent when combined with other variables? It is difficult to tell, although because of the logic and without further evidence, I suspect a contingent relationship.

Consider next the right-hand scatterplot of Figure 12.6, which has an almost identical pattern. From the same study, it shows responses to a question asking whether students used the self-tests included with the instructional material. Since it is possible to achieve without doing these self-tests, this seems more clearly a contributing condition.

Typically, we would have expected a simple linear relationship between taking the tests and achieving, and there does appear to be such a trend in the data. But the empty upper left corner and the concentration of cases at the lower right suggest that the matter may be more complex. Being aware of such additional relationships—contingent, contributing, and alternative—we may find them in situations where we hadn't anticipated them.

In neither of the instances shown in Figure 12.6 would the correlation coefficient portray the complexity of the relationships accurately. With one fat end and one narrow one, the triangular scatterplot differs significantly from the oval typical of a correlation's—a very good reason for *always* looking at the scatterplot.

The Criteria of Research: Internal and External Validity

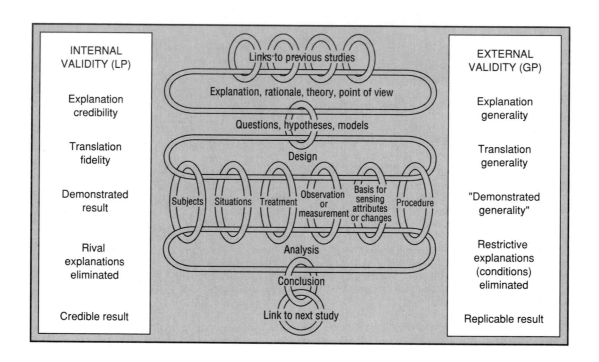

INTERNAL VALIDITY (LP)

Explanation credibility

Translation fidelity

Demonstrated result

Rival explanations eliminated

Credible result

Links to previous studies

Explanation, rationale, theory, point of view

Questions, hypotheses, models

Design

Subjects · Situations · Treatment · Observation or measurement · Basis for sensing attributes or changes · Procedure

Analysis

Conclusion

Link to next study

EXTERNAL VALIDITY (GP)

Explanation generality

Translation generality

"Demonstrated generality"

Restrictive explanations (conditions) eliminated

Replicable result

OVERVIEW

As we saw in chapter 4, audiences make knowing judgments about the proper interpretation of data; hence, findings are presented as a logical chain of reasoning. Clearly, there must be criteria that the audience applies to make those judgments. What are they?

One set of criteria determines whether a relationship exists. This is defined as the **internal validity (LP)** of a study, where LP stands for linking power. Linking power is the power of a study to link the variables in a relationship.

A second set of criteria concerns how widely the relationship applies—its generality. This will be defined as the **external validity (GP)** of a study, where GP stands for the power of the study to show generality of the findings. They are the main criteria reviewers have in mind when critiquing a study. Additional criteria, some relevant to critiquing a study and some to constructing it, are the topic of chapter 14.

CHAPTER CONTENTS

Introduction   269
Internal Validity (LP)   271
    Initial Conceptual Evidence:
        Explanation Credibility   273
    More Conceptual Evidence: Translation
        Fidelity   273
    Initial Empirical Evidence:
        Demonstrated Result   278
    More Empirical Evidence: Rival
        Explanations Eliminated   279
    Credible Result   280
    Relationship of Internal Validity (LP) to
        the Chain of Reasoning   280
    Internal Validity (LP) and External
        Validity (GP) as Reduction in
        Uncertainty   281
External Validity (GP)   281
    Dependence of External Validity (GP)
        on Internal Validity (LP)   282

Initial Conceptual Evidence:
    Explanation Generality   283
More Conceptual Evidence: Translation
    Generality   284
Initial Empirical Evidence:
    "Demonstrated Generality"   287
More Empirical Evidence: Restrictive
    Explanations (Conditions)
    Eliminated   288
Replicable Result   289
External Validity (GP) as Reduction
    in Uncertainty   289
Summary   290
Appendix: The Relation of Internal
    Validity and External Validity to
    Internal Validity (LP) and External
    Validity (GP)   292

INTRODUCTION

The norm of universal standards described in chapter 4 presupposes that common standards exist. This norm indicated that the same standards should be applied to all knowledge claims, regardless of the experience of the researcher, the reputation of the institution, and other considerations. But disciplines ask different questions and therefore emphasize different research methods. Psychology emphasizes the experimental method. Participant observation is associated with sociology. Survey techniques grew out of social psychology and are used by some political scientists. Further, to some extent, the emphasis given to particular standards varies with the method.[1] Hence it may at first appear as though common standards could not exist.

Regardless of method, however, wherever we are interested in developing generalizations, we seek to build consensus around the evidence supporting those generalizations. Therefore, there is a set of basic expectations that applies to all methods regarding the evidence to be provided and the judgments to be made of it. These are described in this chapter.

Several times now, you may have noticed that we have limited our discussion to studies involving generalizations. What is a generalization? Basically, it is a statement of a relationship between two or more variables that has generality. That means that it applies to persons, places, times, measures, and research procedures other than those involved in the original study. The two parts in the definition suggest that two separate concerns of any research are (1) whether a relationship exists in the particular constellation of circumstances studied and (2) whether that relationship has any generality.

Campbell and Stanley (1963) used the terms **internal validity** and **external validity**, respectively, to describe these conditions. Their choice of the term *validity* was both appropriate and unfortunate. It was appropriate because of the dictionary meaning of the term *validity*: "capable of being justified" or "effective, as in an argument" (Gove, 1976). This is quite consistent with the notion that the researcher is seeking to build a consensus about the proper interpretation of the data, a kind of argument.

It was unfortunate, however, because there are other contexts where the term *validity* is also appropriately used. In measurement and evaluation, for example, validity refers to a test, to quote another section of the dictionary definition, as "capable of being justified" or "effective." Again, this is a proper use of the term *validity*, since a valid test is one that is "effective." The test is an index of whatever was intended to be measured or "capable of being justified" in such use. But whereas internal and external validity refer to basic characteristics of an entire study, test validity refers only to that part of the chain of reasoning involving measurement or observation.

Unfortunately, particularly among students just becoming familiar with the technical language of research, the multiple but different uses of *validity* can be quite confusing. To keep them distinct, we need to include a modifier such as *internal*, *external*, or *test*. We will further modify the terms *internal* and *external validity* as we examine what goes into the judgments of which they consist.

---

1. However, the standards applied to a particular method are typically agreed on by the people using it within a discipline or a profession and often across such boundaries.

- The term *validity* refers to different characteristics in different research contexts.
- Internal validity refers to whether the evidence of a study supports the existence of a relationship between or among its variables.
- External validity refers to whether that relationship generalizes beyond the characteristics of the study in which it was found.
- External and internal validity are characteristics of an entire chain of reasoning supporting a generalization.
- Test validity refers to whether a test measures what was intended to be measured.
- Test validity is a characteristic of the link in the chain of reasoning for measurement and observation.

INTERNAL VALIDITY (LP)

Another view of internal validity is as the power of a study to support an inference that certain variables in it are *linked* in a relationship. Zimbardo designed the study cited in chapter 2 to have strong linking power. It has the power to develop a consensus around the authors' interpretation of the data that paranoia is linked to not being aware of gradually developing deafness. Were such power not already named "internal validity," we might refer to it as the *linking power* of a study, the power to link variables in a relationship. But because it is already named, we modify it to internal validity (LP), where LP stands for linking power. This serves as a mnemonic to help us remember the meaning of internal validity. It also distinguishes it from internal validity without the LP, which might be considered the Campbell and Stanley meaning of the term (see the appendix to this chapter).

Because we are interested in linking the concepts, not just their operational definitions, internal validity is composed of both conceptual and empirical evidence. Altogether there are five judgments in internal validity (LP). The first two of these, *explanation credibility* and *translation fidelity*, constitute the conceptual evidence linking the variables of a study. The next two, *demonstrated result* and *alternative explanations eliminated*, constitute the empirical evidence linking the variables. Finally, there is the judgment of whether there is a *credible result*. This last considers consistency with previous research and judgments of the strength of both the conceptual and empirical evidence. Together, the five judgments lead to an overall determination of the linking power, or internal validity (LP), of a study.

What do we mean by conceptual evidence? Conceptual evidence for internal validity is what links the empirical evidence to the concepts. It is as important as the empirical evidence. It involves clarifying the constructs used to describe a relationship; embedding them in an explanation, theory, or rationale; and translating them into operational definitions. These are typically the first judgments made about a study and tend to color our view of the empirical evidence if they are not favorable. Without linking the operational definitions to the constructs, we would have to describe our generalizations as sets of operations. That would be very awkward. The conceptual evidence also helps us discriminate a chance result that has no explanation from one that makes sense because it has conceptual support.

> A study with internal validity (LP) has the power to build a consensus about the proper interpretation of the data as linking the variables in a relationship. It involves judgments of conceptual evidence, empirical evidence, and a credible result.

Let us examine the five judgments that make up internal validity (LP) in some detail. Two constitute the conceptual evidence:

1. **Explanation credibility** is a judgment of the credibility of the rationale of a study: the discussion and definition of the constructs involved in the study, and the explanation of their interrelationships expressed as a question, hypothesis, prediction, or model.
2. **Translation fidelity** is a judgment of how faithfully the question, hypothesis, prediction, or model has been translated into choices at the design level of the chain of reasoning: subjects; situations; treatment, or independent variable; observation or measurement; basis for sensing attributes or changes; and procedure.

Two judgments make up the empirical evidence:

3. **Demonstrated result** is a judgment of whether some result occurred and whether it was the one expected.
4. **Rival explanations eliminated** is a judgment of whether there are plausible rival explanations that explain the data equally well and whether these can be ruled out or rendered implausible.

This is summed up and viewed in perspective in the final judgment:

5. **Credible result** is a judgment that sums the previous evidence, both conceptual and empirical; examines the external evidence to see whether this study is consistent with earlier studies; and leads to a final judgment of how strongly we can conclude that this evidence links the variables in a relationship.

We earlier found the Zimbardo study useful in adding flesh to the bones of an abstract discussion. Let us use it again to give meaning to the judgments involved in internal validity. You may wish to review the study in chapter 2 and the comments regarding the study (pages 15–16) before reading the following material.

Initial Conceptual Evidence: Explanation Credibility

What was the first thing that struck you about the Zimbardo study? Probably it was the rationale for proposing that paranoia might be related to the chain of events that begins when elderly persons do not realize that their hearing is gradually disappearing. They no longer understand what is occurring in a previously comfortable social context. They become angry and confused and perceive the environment as hostile. The explanation is well presented so that it makes the study interesting and the results plausible. The hypothesis sets the stage for the rest of the study: "paranoia is sometimes an end product of an initially rational search to explain a perceptual discontinuity, in this case, being deaf without knowing it."

This first judgment of whether the study has explanation credibility is critical. If the explanation is plausible, we are willing to pursue the rest of the study to see whether the proposed relationship is borne out by the data. If it is not, we may only reluctantly pursue it. Einhorn and Hogarth (1986) note that if we do not perceive a reasonable causal link, we may still refuse to attribute causality in spite of the evidence. Certainly, we will read it exceedingly critically, since a very high standard of evidence will be needed to be persuasive. Note that one of the strengths of the Zimbardo study was its explanation credibility; it is often the first item students put on the "strengths" list.

Einhorn and Hogarth (1986) explain that the inference of causation, which is what is involved here, is dependent on the contextual field, and the study's explanation, rationale, point of view, or theory delineates this field. They note that Mackie (1965, 1974) pointed out that this field focuses us on the part of the causal chain involved in the phenomenon, delineating it as the "figure" from its background. It also points to one important field, the background, within which alternative explanations of the event should be sought.

Explanation credibility is a judgment of the plausibility of the explanation or rationale for the study as it builds on previous investigations and thought.

More Conceptual Evidence: Translation Fidelity

What is the next thing that attracts your attention as you read the article? After ending the explanation with the statement of the expected relationship, the hypothesis, the article begins an extensive description of how the study was carried out. This requires translating the various aspects of the hypothesized relationship into the choices that form the design of the study, the "5 W's and an H" of chapter 5:

Who	Subjects (*Who* are they?)
Where	Situation (*Where* did it take place?)
Why (the cause)	Treatment (This is *why* something would be expected to occur.)
What (the effect)	Observation or measurement (These tell *what* occurred.)
How	Basis for sensing attributes or changes (This tells us *how* we know an effect occurred.)
When	Procedure (*When* what subjects received what treatment, observations, or measures, where they received it, and when and where the effect is to occur.)

The hypothesis already translates "perceptual discontinuity" as "in this case, being deaf without knowing it." But such terms as *paranoia* and *deafness* have to be translated. They have to be operationalized, used in this study in ways faithful to their meaning in the hypothesis. This faithful translation is aptly termed translation fidelity. What does translation fidelity mean in the Zimbardo article? To see, we shall examine each of the six links of the design.

Subjects.　Subjects are the who, the individuals chosen to be studied. For purposes of external validity (GP), they should be as much as possible like the target population to whom the results should generalize. Where this is not possible, the characteristics of the substitutes should have the essential characteristics of the target population. But for internal validity (LP) purposes, subjects can be anyone to whom the question, hypothesis, prediction, or model applies.

You probably felt that the use of college students in place of elderly in Zimbardo's study was a weakness of the study, that the translation fidelity was not good. The study's rationale leads us to believe that the subjects should be from among the elderly because they seem to be the target population. Although the origin of the study was a problem of the elderly, the hypothesis is more general, stating that paranoia results from a rational search to explain a perceptual discontinuity.[2] It says nothing about the kinds of individuals who experience the perceptual discontinuity of being deaf without knowing it. They could be young or old; the rationale applies to anyone who is experiencing a perceptual discontinuity of any kind. In this particular experiment, it is growing deaf without realizing it and then being exposed to social situations that can no longer be correctly interpreted because of the deficit.

A good reason for not using the elderly is that the experimenters could not ethically test subjects' hearing, not tell them they were growing deaf, and, if the hypothesis is correct, let them misinterpret their social world. So although at first we may question the use of college students as subjects, they

---

2. For example, the proposition might apply to persons with Alzheimer's disease who cannot remember from moment to moment even that they have a memory problem. Often someone will refer to something that occurred earlier that the affected individuals don't believe occurred. Since they still trust their own senses more than they trust other people, they come to distrust others and view the world as hostile.

may be an appropriate choice after all. Surely for internal validity (LP) purposes, college students are a group to whom the hypothesis is appropriate. A necessary condition in terms of choice of subjects for internal validity (LP) is that they be an example of subjects to whom the hypothesis would apply. For external validity (GP), which we shall consider in more detail later, students, though not the apparent target population, are certainly among those to whom the proposition should generalize.

Situation. Situation is the where, the location of the study. Like subjects, for external validity (GP) purposes, the situation in the study should be as much as possible like the target situation to which we hope to generalize. Where use of the real situation is not feasible, the substitute should be like it in all essential respects. But for internal validity (LP) purposes, again like subjects, any situation to which the question, hypothesis, prediction, or model would apply is appropriate.

For generalizing to the elderly, as with subjects, you may have decided that the substitution of the laboratory situation for a social situation involving elderly persons was a weakness of the Zimbardo study. But consider whether features of the normal social situation omitted in the laboratory are essential to the relationship expressed in the hypothesis. All that is important is that the situation be one where the phenomenon could be displayed. What is needed is a situation where there could be social interplay allowing individuals to discover that they couldn't understand the conversation. If you agree, then the laboratory was an appropriate situation. Further, by bringing the study into the laboratory, the social situation could be controlled so that it was almost identical for each of the subjects. We shall soon see the importance of this.

Treatment. Treatment is the why, the cause in the presumed relationship. In this case, the treatment is a sequence of three events: (1) hypnosis of the subjects, (2) three alternative posthypnotic suggestions, and (3) the social situation, which called the subjects' attention to the sensory anomaly and resulted in efforts to explain it. Each phase has to be defined operationally. Although we are told that the subjects were trained in self-hypnosis and heard "deep-relaxing" music, we are never told exactly how the hypnosis was accomplished. Zimbardo expects us to trust him that this was done well and properly.

The posthypnotic suggestions were operationally defined by tape recordings randomly assigned to the subjects. The social interaction leading to the discovery of the sensory anomaly was operationally defined as two confederates role-playing a "well-rehearsed standard conversation." Note the efforts to standardize all contact with the subjects, using slides and rehearsed conversation so that each experiences, as nearly as possible, the same situation and treatment. We will refer to that later in discussing "alternative explanations eliminated."

Because unrecognized partial deafness is essential to the study and the experimenters couldn't intentionally make people really partially deaf, the use of hypnosis to create this condition temporarily is a clever solution—provided that we accept hypnosis as a tool capable of creating the condition.

Note that the treatment in this case was administered in a laboratory-type situation. But treatments are sometimes given under natural conditions, as when studying the effects of intentionally varied housing designs (for example, effect on security and privacy of having or not having all apartments entered through a single door) or naturally occurring conditions (for example, these configurations in existing housing).

The complexities of representing a treatment are considered in chapter 18. Suffice it to note here that the treatment used in the study should faithfully represent at least one appropriate version of the treatment.

Observations and Measures.   Observations and measures are the what, the measures of the effect showing that when the cause is present, the effect appears. The effect, paranoia, must be defined operationally. This was done by using both established and new tests, as well as observations. The established measure was the Minnesota Multiphasic Personality Inventory (MMPI), a commonly used clinical tool. The new instrument, a clinically derived paranoia scale, had been devised for an earlier study. Two unseen judges served as observers and rated the social interaction of all three groups for paranoid behavior. Note that three different types of measures of paranoia were used, possibly to assure the audience that paranoia really did occur. Readers can take their choice of whichever measure they trust most; all showed the effect. Surely, one of the three indicators should be acceptable as a measure of paranoia to those among whom Zimbardo hopes to form a concensus. Clearly included in translation fidelity is the judgment that the measures or observations are appropriately reliable and valid.

There is another reason for using multiple measures, however, and that is that when these different measures all indicate the same result, we are additionally sure of the result. A surveyor establishes a particular location not by one measurement but by triangulation, using two or more sightings from different angles. Known as the **multimeasure, multimethod procedure**, such triangulation ensures that the result is not dependent on the peculiar characteristics of a single measure or of a measurement method. In the Zimbardo case, with multimeasures we find each of three different, imperfect measures indicating the same effect—triangulation support for the fact that the effect did occur. Multimethods should give us similar results from the self-report method used by the MMPI and the experimenters' own paranoia scale, as well as the observation scale method used by the observers.

In making a judgment regarding translation fidelity of measures or observations (or of the treatment, if it is subject to monitoring), we look for empirical evidence on which we can base the judgment, and we also make a conceptual judgment about the fit of the measures to what is intended (we might also do a conceptual analysis, as described in chapter 9). If tests are used, we expect evidence of test validity and/or reliability; if observation scales, evidence of objectivity and interrater reliability (both as discussed in chapter 11).

Basis for Sensing Attributes or Changes.   The how is the basis for sensing the particular characteristics of interest or the changes that resulted from treatment—the effect. A useful way to show that a relationship exists is to show that the effect is present when the cause is also present and absent when the cause is absent. We could compare subjects with themselves under the two conditions or compare comparable groups. This study used the comparable groups condition, assigning subjects to three treatment groups at random so that they would be comparable. Two of the groups were alike in that both involved partial deafness, but they differed in knowledge of the deafness. The aware group would expect and understand the sensory deficit. The researchers used a third group with a different posthypnotic suggestion (itchy ear) to eliminate a rival explanation, posthypnotic suggestion with amnesia.

Procedure. The when, the description of the study's steps, shows the operations involved in procedure. This includes who received what treatment, when and how subjects received it, who was observed and measured, and when, where, and how this was done. Note that besides ensuring comparable experiences for individuals among the three groups, the procedure was designed such that the investigator, accomplice, and observers were not privy to the subjects' treatment assignment. Subjects' assignments were given by tape recordings delivered through headphones. Judges were blind to what to expect from a subject.

The basis for sensing attributes or changes and procedure are critical facets of design where causation is to be inferred, because they provide important cues to causation: precedence of cause before effect, contiguity of cause with effect, indicators of change from some base state to a new one as the presumed result of one or more intervening causative agents, and if the state of the cause changes, a congruent pattern of change in the effect (see pages 251 and 252). Where the effect is delayed rather than contiguous, a strong, plausible explanation is required for the delay. Einhorn and Hogarth (1986) note that we typically expect both contiguity of cause and effect and congruity of the effect to the cause. By congruity we mean, for instance, that a large cause would be expected to produce a large effect and a small cause a small one. Where there are both contiguity and congruence, causation is often inferred with few conceptual links. Where either contiguity or congruence is lacking, and especially when both are, a strong conceptual "bridge" is required for the inference to be made. But when such explanations are provided and the effect appears as expected, this is potent evidence of causality (see page 252). As a prime example, to infer causality of pregnancy from intercourse where both contiguity and congruence are lacking requires either a strong conceptual bridge or very convincing evidence.

If you will review the list of strengths and weaknesses on pages 15–16, you will notice that many of them are concerned with translation fidelity. Without an accurate translation of the hypothesis, question, prediction, or model into the actual steps in a study, we are doing a different study from the one intended. If the gap in translation is serious enough, the evidence provided may be totally irrelevant. Translation fidelity is a second critical judgment in the sequence.

> Translation fidelity is the faithfulness of the design choices to the meaning of the question, hypothesis, prediction, or model as defined by the study's explanation or rationale. The design choices operationalize the concepts and constructs in the explanation or rationale.

Initial Empirical Evidence: Demonstrated Result

The basis for making this judgment was laid in chapter 12, where we discussed the evidence for inferring causation. Four conditions were noted: (1) the evidence was authentic, (2) the cause preceded or was concomitant with the effect, (3) an effect did indeed occur, and (4) the effect was congruent with the explanation. These four conditions make up a demonstrated result. Each of them was discussed in chapter 12, so we need only make a few additional comments here and examine the Zimbardo study for compliance.

Much of the responsibility for authenticity of evidence rests with the researcher. Typically, the reader trusts the researcher. As noted in chapter 26, such trust is occasionally misplaced, but most researchers do not consider this a problem. There is certainly no reason to mistrust Zimbardo and his associates; he is an established researcher, and the article appeared in a journal with good peer review and high standards.

Precedence of cause, as noted earlier, is easy to determine in an experiment such as Zimbardo's. We know when the treatment was administered and that it preceded the effect. This is sometimes much more difficult to determine in qualitative research.

The next condition is that an effect was found. With social and behavioral phenomena, it is often difficult to distinguish the large normal variation in the behavior of the untreated group from the comparatively small increment due to the treatment. In a quantitative study, we use inferential statistics, as Zimbardo did, to help make this distinction. Included in this condition is the consideration that all statistics in the study were properly used and interpreted. Without explaining the two columns on the right of Table 1 on page 13, the differences in the mean (average) scores of the groups in the first three columns of the table are apparent. So for the moment, we can accept the researchers' interpretation of these statistics as showing that the paranoia of the treated group exceeded that of the other groups on all the measures.

Was the effect congruent with the explanation or rationale and its translation into a hypothesis, prediction, or model? Clearly in Zimbardo's case it was. All four conditions were met, and we have a demonstrated result. Note, however, that in qualitative studies where the generalization arises from the data, not much evidence for congruence comes from the instance that suggested the relationship, although obviously that counts. Were it the only instance, it could have been a chance event. The evidence that is more convincing and eliminates chance as an explanation comes from the fact that there are other instances in the data (preferably numerous ones) where the relationship also holds.

> A demonstrated result appears when the evidence is authentic, there was precedence (or concomitance) of cause, and an effect occurred as was expected in terms of the relationship described by the hypothesis, prediction, or model.

More Empirical Evidence: Rival Explanations Eliminated

So far so good: the paranoia appeared when and where expected. But is there any other reasonable explanation for its appearance? Only when all reasonable alterative or rival explanations have been eliminated from consideration can we feel comfortable in interpreting the data as demonstrating the relationship. There are nearly always a variety of possible alternative explanations, some very close to the mark, some far-fetched. It is the responsibility of the researcher to anticipate any rival explanations that the audience might consider reasonable and to build the design of the study to render them implausible. A common way is to be sure that the alternative possible causative factors are present both when the treatment is present and when it is not. If the effect occurs only when the treatment is present, regardless of the presence or absence of the other factor, then the alternative factor is not the cause. In this instance, it means making the treatment and nontreatment groups comparable with respect to all the rival possible explanations. In the Zimbardo study, the researchers did this in several ways.

There are two nontreatment groups: one of them partially deaf, the other with an itchy ear. The intent is to rule out posthypnotic suggestion as a cause of paranoia. If it had been the cause, then the itchy ear group would have had as high an incidence of paranoia as the deafness groups. It didn't.

Random assignment of the subjects to the groups plus random assignment of the groups to treatment prevents the researchers from ensuring that the group most favorable to the hypothesis receives the treatment. Further, after the tapes for the treatment instructions were played in their headphones, the groups were exposed to exactly the same procedure. The posthypnotic suggestion and all succeeding directions were given by slides so that the two partially deaf groups would not be disadvantaged. The confederates conducted a "well-rehearsed standard conversation" for all the groups. This makes unlikely the possibility that the social interaction situation for the groups might have varied and therefore have been the cause of the difference in paranoia. Finally—and this is a critical feature—no one having contact with the subjects knew to which of the three groups a given subject belonged. In research terms, the judges were kept blind—they couldn't have favored the experimental group even if they had tried.

Clearly, the researchers tried to anticipate many of the possible rival explanations and eliminated them in their design of the study. Note that the design of the study is the prime protection against these rivals. If we are to satisfy this criterion, they must be anticipated and the study so designed that they are eliminated.

> For the projected explanation or rationale to be accepted, all reasonable alternative or rival explanations of the data must be eliminated. "Rival explanations eliminated" is the judgment of whether this has been accomplished.

Credible Result

Credible result is the final judgment that sums the previous evidence, both conceptual and empirical. It also includes an examination of the external evidence to see whether this study is consistent with earlier studies. (This assumes, of course, that they don't all have the same flaws or, should that occur, that the researcher is capable enough to spot them.) It results in a final judgment of how strongly we can infer that the study would create a consensus that the proper interpretation of the evidence links the variables in a relationship.

In the Zimbardo study, the four earlier judgments are all positive: the conceptual evidence of explanation credibility and translation fidelity and the empirical evidence of demonstrated result and rival explanations eliminated. The evidence is consistent with the literature, and there is no directly comparable study. We conclude that the study has strong internal validity (LP).

> Credible result is a judgment summing up the four earlier judgments and asking, in terms of external prior evidence, whether we can believe the result. It is a judgment of the extent to which the uncertainty regarding the existence of the relationship has been removed.

Relationship of Internal Validity (LP) to the Chain of Reasoning

The five successive judgments of internal validity (LP) draw their evidence from the successive links of the chain of reasoning. Showing them in relation to the chain is instructive and provides an easy way to remember them. This is done in Figure 13.1.

> Each of the judgments in internal validity (LP) can be placed alongside a certain part of the chain of reasoning where we find evidence for that judgment.

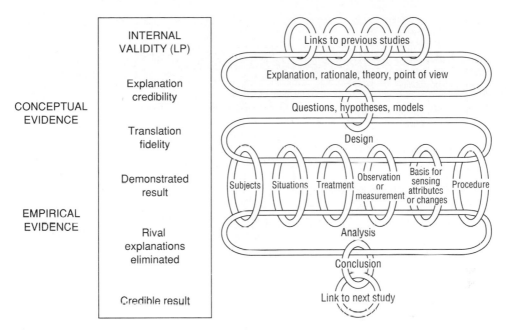

FIGURE 13.1   The judgment of internal validity (LP) superimposed on the chain of reasoning.

Internal Validity (LP) and External Validity (GP) as Reduction in Uncertainty

Just as knowledge is better viewed as a reduction in uncertainty (instead of an all-or-none, true-or-false matter), so is internal validity (LP). In this instance, we are reducing our uncertainty that the relationship exists in the circumstances in which it was investigated. The better the study meets the criteria of internal validity, the greater the reduction in uncertainty.

In a similar vein, external validity (GP) is also a reduction in uncertainty, but in this instance a reduction in the uncertainty that the relationship generalizes beyond the circumstances in which it was studied.

EXTERNAL VALIDITY (GP)

A parallel series of five sequential judgments determines external validity (GP). Each is similar in name and content to those made for internal validity (LP). They are designated external validity (GP) to indicate the power of the study to support inferences of generality of the findings, where GP stands for generalizing power.

Again, we have both conceptual and empirical evidence of generality and a wrap-up judgment. The conceptual evidence consists of two judgments: the first is a judgment of the generality claimed in the explanation, or **explanation**

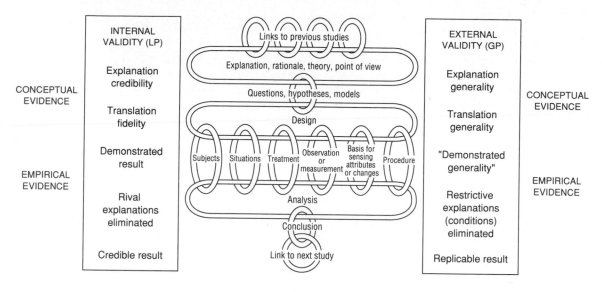

FIGURE 13.2   The judgments of external validity (GP) added to Figure 13.1.

generality; the second is the extent to which the generality claimed is operationalized in the choices made in the design of the study, or **translation generality**. The empirical evidence consists of the two judgments **"demonstrated generality"** (the quotation marks are intentional and explained in the detailed discussion that follows) and **restrictive explanations (conditions) eliminated**. Finally, a judgment is made whether there is a **replicable result**,[3] and the evidence is summed up to gauge the strength of the study's external validity (GP).

It may help if we place these criteria opposite their parallels in internal validity (LP) on the chain of reasoning. This is done in Figure 13.2.

Dependence of External Validity (GP) on Internal Validity (LP)

Some of the judgments of external validity (GP) depend on those made for internal validity (LP). For example, if the explanation makes little sense and for internal validity is therefore judged to lack explanation credibility, it doesn't matter whether it has explanation generality in external validity.[4] Similarly, if

---

3. This criterion was suggested by Cronbach (1982).
4. Even though we can't conceptually explain why they do so, a few relationships have wide "demonstrated generality" (for example, the Strong-Campbell Interest Inventory's ability to predict vocational success). They can be shown to work in a broad range of situations. In such cases, a lack of explanation credibility is a drawback to external validity (GP) only to the extent that we do not accept the pragmatist point of view (see page 634).

the translation into the operations of the study are unsatisfactory, again, it makes little sense to be concerned with translation generality. If there is no effect and no demonstrated result, there can be no "demonstrated generality." Some of the alternative explanations that were not eliminated may restrict the generality of the findings and therefore be involved in the judgment of whether restrictive explanations were eliminated. Finally, of course, if we do not have a credible result, we can hardly expect it to replicate, so replicable result is affected.

- External validity (GP) is the power of a study to create a consensus around the generality that can be ascribed to a relationship.
- It consists of conceptual and empirical evidence followed by a summary judgment, much like internal validity (LP).
- Its five judgments are parallel in name and character to those of internal validity (LP).
- Many of the judgments of external validity are dependent on judgments made with respect to internal validity.

Let us return to the Zimbardo article to see how these terms apply.

Initial Conceptual Evidence: Explanation Generality

Explanation generality makes a judgment regarding the generality stated or implied in the explanation or rationale of the study. The generality is not explicitly stated in the Zimbardo study, but by implication, we can sense that the hypothesis is intended, at least, to apply to all elderly people. As we noted earlier in this chapter, although the explanation is stated in terms of the elderly, the hypothesis is stated so broadly as to apply to anyone experiencing a "perceptual discontinuity" or "sensory anomaly." Certainly, this broader interpretation is necessary to make sense of data gathered on college students.

As in this case, the generality claimed by research studies may not be explicitly stated; it is implied or must be inferred. After all, explanations can be stated more simply and clearly if they are not cluttered with all the qualifications required to detail the boundaries within which they hold. Many explanations start out without any qualifications—as universals. Then, as a body of research develops, they are successively circumscribed as limiting conditions are found.

Regardless of whether clearly stated or merely implied, explanation generality is a judgment of whether that generality claimed is reasonable. Just as with explanation credibility in internal validity (LP) we judge the credibility of the explanation, so in explanation generality we judge the credibility of the claimed or implied generality. If the claim is reasonable, we can comfortably proceed to translation generality to see whether that extent of generality was observed in the operational translation of the study. If we reject or doubt the extent of generality claimed, we are likely to be extremely critical of the study and will be convinced only by very strong empirical evidence.

> Explanation generality is a judgment of the plausibility of the generality that is claimed or implied for the relationship.

More Conceptual Evidence: Translation Generality

Both translation fidelity in internal validity (LP) and translation generality are concerned with accuracy of translation into operational terms. The former is concerned with the accuracy of translation of question, hypothesis, or model into choices at the design level, the latter with whether the breadth of generality claimed or implied is represented in those choices. Are the choices representative of the targets to which the researcher wishes the study to generalize—the individuals, situations, times, treatment versions, alternative instruments, alternative research procedures, and so on?

Usually, the question, hypothesis, or model that stems from an explanation is only one of many that could have been explored and represents only one instance rather than the breadth of expected generality. As a test of the proposition that "frustration leads to aggression," we might study individuals in crowded elevators, but that would not validate the extent of generality. To do so would require additional evidence from a variety of kinds of individuals, situations, and so on. Clearly, whatever design choices are made should be from within the population of situations to which we hope to generalize. In addition, they ought to be representative of such situations. Let us look at the design choices in more detail.

Subjects and Situations.   Kruglanski and Kroy (1976) make the point that when a particular group is the target of generalization, a representative sample is the only appropriate set of subjects. Consider studies of how well the Scholastic Aptitude Test predicts college success. A study of students from a particular high school would not be sufficient; a cross-section of the variety of high schools represented in a typical freshman class would be needed. Cook and Campbell (1979) note that using a sample of convenience (usually college undergraduates in a required course) may save time and energy, but there is a trade-off. It is very difficult to generalize to a larger universe of which the sample might be representative.

The same advice applies to situations. Bracht and Glass (1968) use the term *ecological validity* to describe whether the choice of situation is representative of the other situations to which we intend generalization.

By contrast, in instances where a proposition is universally applicable, the characteristics of the subject and the situation make little difference. We can use anyone and any situation. The sole exception is where subject or situational characteristics might be biased in support of the proposition. Goldstein and Arms (1971), for example, hypothesized that watching aggressive athletic contests increases hostility and aggressiveness. They tested their hypothesis with spectators at a football contest. Suppose there were reason to believe that their proposition might be more applicable to sports-minded individuals than the population at large. Then, as designed, the study is a weaker demonstration of generality than, for example, one using a sample of shoppers at a mall.

In the Zimbardo study, the hypothesis seems intended to be universal—that is, intended to apply to all people who are unaware of their sensory deficit. Therefore, college students are as good as any other subjects unless something about them is particularly favorable (or unfavorable) to the hypothesis. About the only thing that might potentially affect this judgment is the fact that the subjects were chosen because they were particularly susceptible to hypnosis. But although they are a special group in this respect, it is hard to see how this has any bearing on their developing paranoia in the instance in which they did.

Treatment. In some instances, the treatment is carefully standardized. For example, in the Zimbardo study, directions were administered mechanically or electronically with tape recordings and slides. Standardization was also achieved in the social interaction by carefully training and rehearsing the confederates. Such standardization is typical where the goal is knowledge itself instead of its application in a typical field situation. It is very important for internal validity (LP) because it eliminates the alternative explanation that the differences in treatment application were in some way involved in producing the effect. Standardization that requires unusual situations or equipment may restrict the generality to similar situations or equipment, however.

Where we are interested in the useful application of a treatment, there is likely to be variability in treatment application among persons using it, in the way it is applied, in the equipment used, in the situation in which it is applied, in the circumstances immediately preceding application, and so on. For example, in studying various ways of increasing classroom learning, different teachers might apply the method in their own ways. Representativeness with respect to treatment involves including that variability in the definition of the treatment. One aspect of that definition of treatment is how the treatment will be mastered by the people who apply it. If it is to have useful generality, it should be mastered in the same manner as in normal practice. For example, if the new classroom procedure is to be mastered from a teacher's guide, learning from the guide alone is an essential aspect of the treatment. If, by contrast, teachers would typically be given extra help and explanation, either by a supervisor or by in-service training classes, then either or both should be part of the treatment.

A second aspect of treatment definition is determining how much variability to allow in the way the treatment is administered. On the one hand, we must decide how much variation can be tolerated while still maintaining the integrity of the treatment. On the other hand, some variability in the administration of a treatment is almost inevitable. The problem is to determine the in-between range that maintains effectiveness within the likely variability of application in practice. For this, we must decide the treatment's essential characteristics—those without which it would lose its effectiveness. That in-between range should be represented in the treatment.

For example, Rowe (1974) notes that as the amount of time that a teacher waits for a student's response increases, the nature of the classroom dialogue changes markedly toward more considered responses, more student-to-student discussion, higher-level thinking, and so on. How much should the time be increased? Can a teacher wait so long that the discussion drags? Clearly, there appears to be some optimum range of wait time. Defining this range and then monitoring teachers to ensure that this range was maintained would be part of treatment fidelity for internal validity (LP), and seeing that there was variety of wait times within this range appropriate to what wait times teachers typically would use would be part of translation generality in external validity (GP).

Observations and Measures.   How representative are the chosen measures or observation instruments of all possible valid measures and instruments? Could we substitute others for them without changing the results, or is there something unique about them? For example, is the measure affected by the way it is administered—paper and pencil, interview, observation? Might we get substantively different results if the information were gathered in a different way? In the Zimbardo study, the key factor to be measured was the development of paranoia. The researchers used three measures of paranoia. Fortunately, all of them showed the effect. If they had not, the researchers would have been faced with the difficult problem of deciding and justifying which measure of paranoia had the greatest construct validity and seeking a reason for the disparate results.

Time.   We seldom consider time as a factor in generality, but Cronbach (1975) points out that some generalizations decay, especially as the culture changes. Child-rearing patterns effective in one decade may not generalize to a later one. This can be a serious problem for the behavioral sciences, which are often seen as progressing by assembling findings over time into larger generalities. Cronbach notes:

> The trouble . . . is that we cannot store up generalizations . . . for ultimate assembly into a network. It is as if we needed a gross of dry cells to power an engine and could only make one a month. The energy would leak out of the first cells before we have half a battery completed. So it is with the potency of our generalization. (p. 123)

We are left with the uncomfortable feeling that our generalizations are becoming less valid even as we are discovering them—which may indeed be the case. Where a social or cultural aspect is undergoing rapid change (for example, the role of women in the past half-century), knowledge about it may not generalize to a future time. So it is important that the instance in which the study is carried out should anticipate the characteristics of the future time to which it is expected to generalize.

Basis for Sensing Attributes or Changes and Procedure.   These two final aspects of design need also to be representative of the kinds of designs and procedures that would allow generalization. For example, the Zimbardo study used a straightforward design contrasting experimental and control groups. Except for the fact that the subjects were hypnotized, there was nothing about the way the treatment, measures, and observations were carried out that would prevent generalizing the results. The use of hypnosis, however, is a condition of the experiment that is in no way implied by the hypothesis and might limit generality. Suppose we considered hypnosis only a parlor trick or believed that easily hypnotized people are different from others. Then the results would be atypical of the universal population to which the study is intended to generalize. We look for such unusual aspects of procedure and basis for sensing attributes or changes in determining translation generality.

Translation generality is a judgment of the extent to which the generality claimed or implied in the study is represented in the operational choices of its design.

Initial Empirical Evidence: "Demonstrated Generality"

The *determination of generality is always an inference*. It is a leap of faith to generalize from any given instance to others like it and assume that the same relationship will appear there as well. Indeed, it is impossible to demonstrate generality in all the instances to which the relationship is intended to apply. There is always the next one that has not yet been tested. Instead, we judge the demonstration in a sample of instances to which it should generalize and from those make an inferential leap. That leap is clearly much safer if the instances in which the relationship was demonstrated are representative of the target to which the leap is to be made. That is the importance of translation generality. We should make sure that those instances are included in the choices made in operationalizing the study.

"Demonstrated generality" asks whether the generalization held up in the instances where it should have and did not where it should not have. In the Zimbardo study, paranoia was highest in the group that was partially deaf but did not know it and, on most measures, considerably higher than in the other groups. This is, of course, just as the explanation called for.

Why is *"demonstrated generality"* in quotation marks? To call attention to the logical impossibility of demonstrating generality in all the instances where it is intended to apply. The quotation marks reinforce the point that it is an inference, not a certainty.

- "Demonstrated generality" is a judgment of the extent to which the relationship appeared in all the instances of the study in which it would be expected to do so and did not where it shouldn't.

- There is always an inferential leap from the particular instances in which the relationship is demonstrated to those to which it is intended to generalize.
- "Demonstrated generality" is in quotation marks because generality can never be completely demonstrated. There is always some untested instance in which, presumably, it might not hold.

More Empirical Evidence: Restrictive Explanations (Conditions) Eliminated

Where the conditions under which the generality is demonstrated fail to be representative of the targets to which generality is to be extended, these conditions may restrict that generality. Evidence of generality requires that these restrictive explanations (conditions) be eliminated.[5] For example, suppose that teachers were given extra assistance in interpreting the manual describing how the treatment should be administered in a learning study. Generality could then reasonably be extended only to similar situations where that kind of assistance was available. We couldn't be sure that the manual alone would be effective in conveying the essentials of the treatment from the data of that particular study.

Such restrictions are more common than might be thought. If the study was done with volunteers, their extra motivation may be necessary to make the treatment effective. If done in circumstances where the subjects knew they were part of an experiment, the desire to please the researcher or to show up well may have been an important factor. If a test was given before the treatment so that pre- and posttest scores could be compared, perhaps the pretest cued the students to what was important in the treatment. They might then have done better on the posttest than they would have otherwise. Certainty of the effectiveness of the treatment would be compromised for situations where the subjects were not volunteers, it was not perceived as an experimental situation, or there was no pretest. The most appropriate generalization of data is to situations similar to those in which they were gathered.

So this judgment looks backward to the way in which generality was translated into the study and also looks forward to the intended generality of the conclusion. It places such restrictions on the latter as are necessary in view of the special conditions under which the data were gathered.

> Restrictive explanations (conditions) that were part of the study but would not be part of the target of generalization must have been eliminated for the inferential leap to the target to be confidently made.

---

5. Dr. Jason Millman pointed out that the alternative explanations of internal validity (LP) become restrictive conditions in external validity (GP). To keep the names parallel, they are called *restrictive explanations (conditions).* They are conditions that provide explanations for restricting the generality.

Replicable Result

The heart of external validity (GP) is replicability: Would the results be reproducible in the target instances to which we intend to generalize—the subjects, situations, treatment forms or formats, measures, study designs, times, and procedures? Do we have a replicable result? Of course, we can never be sure unless we examine each of those instances, and that is an impossibility. So the final judgment of external validity (GP) is a thought experiment about the reproducibility of the results under this variety of conditions. We can use comparable studies to facilitate this judgment, if they exist.

Would the Zimbardo study replicate with elderly rather than college student subjects, with subjects less susceptible to hypnosis, in a different laboratory, in a field situation rather than laboratory, with different measures of paranoia, with observations of individuals suspected of growing deaf in a home for the elderly? These are the kinds of questions this last judgment requires. If you can see no reason that the study would not replicate in those circumstances and the four prior judgments are positive, then the external validity (GP) is strong.

Of course, this, the fifth decision of the sequence, is dependent on the preceding four: (1) the explanation must specify or imply a reasonable generality, (2) this generality must be represented in the choices for the study design, (3) the result must appear with the generality expected in those choices, and (4) the result must appear without restrictive explanations (conditions).

Replicable result is a summary judgment of the foregoing judgments and of the extent to which the results of the study could be replicated in the target to which it is being generalized.

External Validity (GP) as Reduction in Uncertainty

We noted earlier that external validity (GP) is best looked at as a reduction in the uncertainty that the hypothesized relationship will generalize beyond the instances in which it was studied. But how do we generalize to new subjects and situations? As noted earlier, external validity (GP) is usually dependent on internal validity (LP). Beyond evidence of internal validity (LP), certainty of generality depends on the strength of the study's external validity (GP) evidence. But that must be moderated by a judgment of the similarity of the constellation of characteristics in the new target to those involved in the study being generalized from. This is obviously difficult, but it is a judgment that we make continually. For example, we generalize from the evidence of the success of certain preschool programs in improving the learning of disadvantaged children and argue, therefore, that such programs should be universally available.

SUMMARY

Internal validity (LP) and external validity (GP) are two major criteria by which studies are judged. They are distinguished from internal validity and external validity as defined by Campbell and Stanley (1963) and Cook and Campbell (1979) in that they are more inclusive, encompassing conceptual as well as empirical evidence. Internal validity (LP) is the power of a study to create a consensus that the appropriate interpretation of the evidence is that the variables are linked in a relationship—that is its linking power (LP). External validity (GP) is the power to create a consensus that the appropriate interpretation of the evidence is that the relationship has generality beyond the circumstances in which it was studied—generalizing power (GP).

Each of these validities consists of five parallel judgments. Internal validity (LP) consists of two kinds of conceptual evidence, explanation credibility and translation fidelity; two kinds of empirical evidence, demonstrated result and alternative explanations eliminated; and a final summary judgment, credible result. External validity (GP) consists of a parallel set of judgments: two kinds of conceptual evidence, explanation generality and translation generality; two kinds of empirical evidence, "demonstrated generality" and restrictive explanations (conditions) eliminated; and a final summary judgment, replicable result.

Looking ahead, it is already apparent that still other characteristics affect how we build a consensus and that other criteria apply to links in the chain of reasoning. In the next chapter, we examine these other characteristics.

ADDITIONAL READING

Bracht and Glass (1968)
Brinberg and McGrath (1985)
Campbell and Stanley (1963)
Cook and Campbell (1979)

Cronbach (1982)
Krathwohl (1985)
Kruglanski and Kroy (1976)

IMPORTANT TERMS

Credible result
Demonstrated result
"Demonstrated generality"
Explanation credibility
Explanation generality
External validity
External validity (GP)
Internal validity

Internal validity (LP)
Multi-measure, multi-method procedure
Replicable result
Restrictive explanations (conditions)
  eliminated
Rival explanations eliminated
Translation fidelity
Translation generality

APPLICATION PROBLEMS

1. You are an educational researcher who is interested in the effect of cognitive styles on learning. It is your conviction that independent of ability, some individuals tend to be impulsive in their approach to learning activities while others are more reflective. You set up an experimental study to determine whether these styles exist. What conceptual evidence could you provide to show the validity of your idea?

2. You are a psychologist with a deep interest in the age-old practice of astrology. You feel that there may be some validity to the belief that astrological sign determines aspects of personality. Consequently, you decide to try to show that people who are born under the sign of Taurus tend to be more stubborn than others. What conceptual evidence could you provide for the relationship?

3. The English faculty at Local University wanted to offer its introductory writing course, using distance-delivery methods, to adults who could not come to campus. In collaboration with the computer applications department, the English department produced a computer-based writing course

that could be offered off campus without the need for an instructor. Field tests were conducted with first-year on-campus students, to whom the writing course was also normally offered. Those following the computer-based course showed significant improvements in writing scores as compared with those taking the equivalent course taught by an instructor. Proceeding from these results, the department decided to offer the course off campus in computer-based form. Was this the correct decision?

4. Criminologists conducted a five-year study of a boot camp–style correctional program for young offenders (age 20 or younger) at minimum-security institutions. Participation in the program was voluntary. "Graduates" of the program exhibited an extremely low incidence of recidivism (repeat offenses). The researchers were extremely enthusiastic about the results of their study and thought the program would work as well if applied to any offender of any age throughout the country. Was this enthusiasm warranted?

Compare your answers with those on pages 711–712.

APPLICATION EXERCISE

Consider the internal validity of your problem; do you have a strong explanation or rationale so that it has explanation credibility? The translation of the study into operational terms is yet to come, but when you did conceptual analyses, what problems, if any, did you sense there might be with translation fidelity? Demonstrated result will have to await the gathering of data, but you can think about alternative explanations that might be as plausible as your intended explanation. You'll be able to do this better after studying the research methods of section four, but what do you

anticipate now might be reasonable alternatives? Have you checked the other research evidence regarding your problem? Do you expect yours to be consistent with it? If not, are you attempting to refute prior work?

Consider external validity as well. What generality do you intend for your study? Are you examining a universal proposition, or is it bounded in some way in its applicability? What are those limits? Will the translation of your concepts plumb the boundaries of the generality you intend the study to have? Can your design choices be changed such that the generality is increased? What restrictive conditions do you see in your study as now planned that might limit generality? Would you expect your study to replicate with different design choices? If not, would better design choices allow it to?

APPENDIX: THE RELATION OF INTERNAL VALIDITY AND EXTERNAL VALIDITY TO INTERNAL VALIDITY (LP) AND EXTERNAL VALIDITY (GP)

Because you will run into the terms *internal validity* and *external validity* without *(LP)* and *(GP)* in the literature, it is important that you know something about them. Terms standardize easily when the distinctions involved "cleave nature at the joints"—that is, when they seem natural and come easily. Standardization can take longer with special definitions that do not. Unfortunately, the original special definitions of internal and external validity did not (Campbell and Stanley, 1963). As a result, these constructs continue to be defined differently in different textbooks (Krathwohl, 1985).

Internal validity was originally defined as the capacity to infer a relationship between a particular study's operational definitions of cause and effect. This definition did not take into account the conceptual evidence, the explanation and rationale. Neither did it include the last judgments of internal validity (LP) and external validity (GP): consideration of the external evidence as in credible result and consideration of replicability as in replicable result. These are important parts of internal validity (LP) and external validity (GP) and strongly influence how a study is viewed. Further, the relationship between the constructs used in the explanation and the operational definitions they represent, treated as translation fidelity in internal validity (LP), Campbell and Stanley included in external validity. But if we think of internal validity as showing a relationship among variables as conceptualized, which is what we are usually interested in, this seems to belong in internal validity. That seemingly more natural definition is the one used in internal validity (LP) and external validity (GP). The distinction between external validity (GP) and external validity is not as great as between internal validity (LP) and internal validity, since both of the former relate to generality over people, places, and things. The notions of replicable result and explanation generality, however, add elements.

Campbell and Stanley's original definitions were later split into four validities: internal validity, statistical conclusion validity, external validity, and construct validity (Cook and Campbell, 1979), and more recently, the concept of local molar validity was advanced (Campbell, 1986). For still other formulations, see Brinberg and McGrath (1985) and especially Cronbach (1982).

- The terms *internal validity* and *external validity* are used differently in different texts and are still evolving.
- Internal validity (LP) links the concepts, not just their operational definitions, as does Campbell and Stanley's (1963) original definition. There are corresponding changes in external validity (GP).
- Both internal validity (LP) and external validity (GP) include additional evidence in the judgments: explanation and rationale and the summary judgments of credible result and replicable result.

Other Criteria of Research

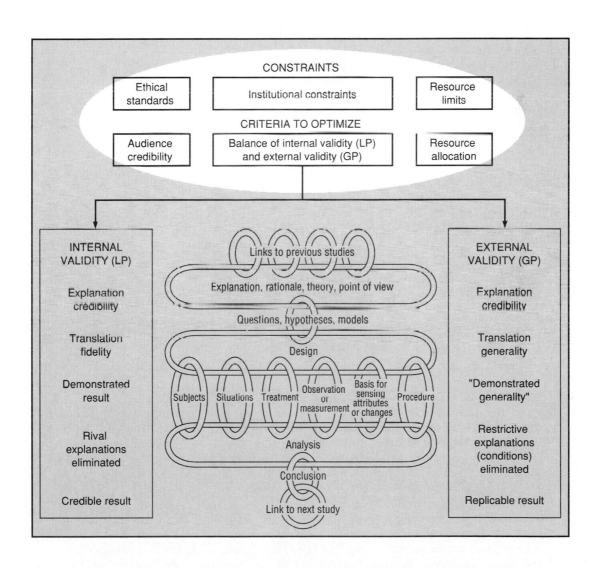

OVERVIEW

Every study must optimize three aspects: (1) the building of audience credibility, (2) the balancing of emphasis on internal validity (LP) and external validity (GP), and (3) resource allocation. These are optimized because to some extent, they are part of a zero-sum game of resources. That is, resources spent on one part of the study cannot be spent on another. Further, strengthening internal validity (LP) is usually bought at a cost to external validity (GP), and vice versa. Since optimizing these aspects for one audience will not necessarily do so for another, researchers must keep their audience in mind.

These characteristics must be optimized within the limits imposed on every study: (1) what can be ethically done, (2) what an institution will permit to be done in the name of research when its primary goal is service to clients, and (3) resource limits. Although the available resources can sometimes be increased, they are always limited—usually too much so. The relationship of these decisions to the chain of reasoning is demonstrated.

CHAPTER CONTENTS

Introduction   294
Criteria to Be Optimized   296
   Why Optimization?   296
   Audience Credibility   296
   Building Audience Credibility   298
   The Relative Weighting of Internal
     Validity (LP) and
     External Validity (GP)   300

Resource Allocation   302
Limits and Constraints   304
   Institutional Constraints   304
   Resource Limits   305
Summary   306

INTRODUCTION

Internal validity (LP) and external validity (GP) may be the criteria by which most research studies are judged, but other important criteria affect study design and effectiveness. One is the credibility readers attach to a study—the "audience credibility" of a study. Researchers must elicit credence not only from reviewers, but also from the whole audience of relevant readers and reviewers. Another is whether internal validity (LP) or external validity (GP) has the greater emphasis. The third, resource allocation, is a special concern of researchers as the study is implemented. The research report tells only the results of resource allocation, not the process that is at the heart of it. Differences in researchers' allocations of resources, especially personal time, energy, and attention, often explain how they arrive at different strategies for the same problem. Resource allocation is an important determiner of the

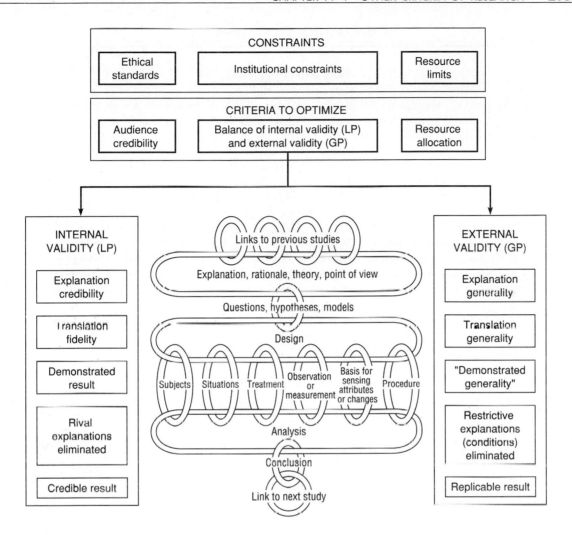

FIGURE 14.1   The complete framework of criteria and constraints.

problem formulation and design alternatives chosen at different stages in a study's development. Yet readers are typically unaware of the alternatives. Although the process of design development is infrequently discussed in print, many alternatives may have been considered and discarded or pursued only in part.

Finally, there are the constraints within which researchers must work, constraints imposed by ethics, institutions, and resources.

Figure 14.1 adds all these aspects to the model we have been discussing and shows the complete framework of criteria and constraints.

CRITERIA TO BE OPTIMIZED

Why Optimization?

In chapter 13, we discussed internal validity (LP) and external validity (GP) as though, if the proper choices were made, each could be raised to an entirely satisfactory level. Given a tractable problem, we could build a rationale that could be credible, get a satisfactory translation of the hypothesis with protection against both rival and restricting explanations, and so on. But attaining great strength in both simultaneously is another matter, since improvements in internal validity (LP) are usually bought at the expense of external validity (GP). Greater control gained by complex designs or taking the study into the laboratory typically results in decreased generality or external validity (GP). Further resources expended in pursuit of increased internal validity (LP) are lost so far as strengthening external validity (GP) is concerned, and vice versa. Since resources are always finite, and usually less than we would ideally like, we must find the proper balance of internal validity (LP) to external validity (GP) for our purposes.

Consider the problem of building audience credibility. Credibility with whom? Who are all the relevant audiences? Can we simultaneously build credibility with all of them? Pretty difficult! We must chose one or a few and find the optimal choices for them.

Resource allocation is equally complex. We have already noted that the myriad choices involved in building a design means that researchers may differ as to the ideal method. In fact, within a given method, there may be alternative "best" choices leading to different resource allocations. What is the ideal design? Even if we construct what we consider a very good design, someone might construct a better one from his or her point of view. All we can do is optimize the design for our purposes and intended audiences. With this introduction to the idea of optimization, let us understand it in more depth as we look at each criterion.

Audience Credibility

Audience credibility is a judgment on the part of the audience of the credibility it is willing to grant the researcher for having made good judgments in carrying out the study, especially for aspects not described in the report. Building a consensus around our interpretation of the evidence requires gaining credibility with the audience. Cronbach (1982) ingeniously phrased the problem this way: "Validity depends . . . on the way a conclusion is stated and communicated. Validity is subjective rather than objective: the plausibility of the conclusion is what counts. And plausibility, to twist a cliché, lies in the ear of the beholder" (p. 108).

To build that consensus, we must consider the expectations of the audience at each study stage: designing, implementing, and communicating the results. The audience may consist of gatekeepers: committee members who select presentations for professional association programs, people who review proposals for funding, journal editors. It may also include fellow researchers, researchers in related areas, and practitioners interested in applying the results.

Ignoring concerns about audience credibility may prevent a good study from being adequately disseminated if the gatekeepers reject it. Even if they accept it, lack of concern for building credibility with the ultimate consumers of the research may delay or prevent consensus development. In basic research, if such a consensus is not formed immediately, that may be remedied later. In applied research, audiences that do not understand or accept the research will not apply it, and the purpose of the study will be negated.

Relation to Integrity.   The first essential audience with whom credibility must be built is oneself. Maintaining one's integrity as a scientist and a scholar is a first priority. Do you recall Merton's norm of disinterestedness (see page 52)? This does not refer to a lack of motivation. It means that insofar as they are able, researchers prevent their personal expectations, hopes, and aspirations from influencing how they gather, analyze, and interpret their data.

Usually, the integrity conveyed when a study is presented is a reflection of one's own. (True, it is possible for individuals to succeed in playing the role of a person of integrity when that is not the case, but few researchers appear to be accomplished liars.) Integrity may require paying attention to such things as building a chain of reasoning only as strong as the data permit and not using hucksterism or propaganda techniques to build an apparently stronger one. Scientists are chided for showmanship, and such work tends to be suspect. Once an audience discovers something it thinks it should have been told, audience credibility disappears. The audience may be wrong in its perception, but that makes no difference. The line between a solid and appropriate presentation that takes full advantage of the strengths of the study without concealing its weaknesses and one that exploits its strengths and underplays its weaknesses may be a fine one. But it is a boundary that *must be found and observed*. Erring on the conservative side may delay proper recognition of a knowledge claim, but it is generally considered the lesser of the evils.

Is there a role that the researcher can adopt? The researcher's task is more akin to that of a judge writing a decision than to that of a lawyer trying to make a case. Having come to a decision, the judge prepares a document that, while recognizing the cons, presents the strongest possible argument for the pros, explaining how and why the conclusion was reached. Similarly, the researcher, having made a knowing judgment about the proper interpretation of the data, prepares the case. It is reported in such a way that we can carefully examine the argument, and it does not depend for its appeal on the eloquence of the writer (Cronbach and Suppes, 1969). In preparing that decision, both judge and researcher must consider the expectations of the audience and what concerns its members are likely to have.

The foregoing should make it clear that building credibility with the audience has nothing to do with hiding a study's weaknesses, misconstruing the data, or overgeneralizing. Protection of the progress of science is reason enough for such a stance. But from a personal standpoint, such errors reflect on one's professional competence as well.

Credibility with the audience is important to acceptance of a study's findings. It involves presenting the findings in ways that:

- provide the kinds of evidence expected by the audience,
- answer the audience's questions and allay its concerns,
- appropriately reflect the study's strengths and weaknesses, and
- convey one's integrity as a researcher.

Building Audience Credibility

How do we build audience credibility? By learning the particular expectations and concerns of our main audiences. Critiques of past studies are helpful in showing concerns that are especially salient. Journals that publish letters critiquing past articles are particularly helpful. Examples are *American Psychologist*, occasionally the *Educational Researcher*, and, although the number of social science articles is very small, *Science*. Occasionally, journals accept critiques as articles themselves, sometimes giving the original author a chance for rebuttal. An even better place to learn is at professional association conventions, where question sessions follow study presentations.

In addition to the principle of conducting oneself according to the highest code of professional conduct, it is possible to develop a few generalizations.

Build on Knowledge That the Audience Has Already Accepted. Building the study on knowledge that is already accepted by the audience is important. If the starting point of your study is questioned, you may be building on a weak foundation. Remember the use of hypnosis in the Zimbardo study? For many physical science readers of *Science*, the journal in which it was published, hypnosis is a stage trick, not based on solid accepted knowledge. Such readers will reject the study as soon as they encounter it in the report. Zimbardo and his associates assumed that the behavioral science readers of *Science* whom they were seeking to reach would not find its use objectionable. So they did not even comment on it.

Policy studies are sometimes designed to show the generality of a finding, studies with strong external validity (GP). That is fine where you are less concerned with the mechanism itself than that it worked. But in basic research, where you are trying to understand what is going on, you should make sure that the earlier work on which you are building had strong internal validity (LP) or that the lack of it has been taken into account.

Avoid the Weaknesses of Previous Similar Studies. The audience likeliest to criticize your work knowledgeably consists of the real and self-perceived experts in your area of research. Audience credibility is enhanced if you are knowledgeable about those experts' past and current work. Such knowledge will enable you to convey that your study builds on past literature and avoids its errors. Indeed, recognizing when use of a technique is controversial is important, particularly when it has been discussed in the literature. You may make some original mistakes, but to repeat the mistakes of others indicates an inability to learn from experience that is damaging to your professional credibility. Should you need to repeat problems previously encountered, explain why this was necessary to avoid inappropriate conclusions by the audience about your competence.

Use Accepted Techniques.   Other things being equal, use accepted methods, measures, definitions, terminology, and knowledge—accepted forms increase credibility (unless, of course, the contribution of the study lies in such areas as new methodology and measures). The audience's greater familiarity with conventional methods facilitates communication. It results in readers who are more comfortable, feel capable of judging the study, and have more confidence in that judgment.

Using standard methods permits the audience readily to find the hallmarks of excellence it has come to associate with particular approaches. In a questionnaire study, for instance, audience members will check to see that a special effort was made to obtain responses from a sample of nonrespondents. Showing that the latter's responses did not differ substantially from those given by people who responded to the initial request demonstrates that the data represent respondents and nonrespondents alike.

Similarly, results of accepted instruments are more readily interpreted. Given the results of a September mathematics achievement testing, an audience of experienced professionals will expect a score drop due to a summer away from school. These experts will look for that effect to be taken into account; if it is, they will have more confidence in the researcher. To reach lay or practitioner audiences, use common terminology with few technical terms. Using instruments with face validity may be particularly important.

Justify Any Use of the Nonstandard.   Whenever researchers depart from the accepted, they carry the burden of proof. Pioneering a new method, coining new terms, developing a new instrument, all require making it "self-evident" to the audience that this was appropriate. Usually, this demonstration requires a comparison with the standard choice to demonstrate the advantages of the new version.

In some instances, we must first teach the hallmarks of excellence for a new research technique and then show that these appear in the study in question. Instruction in methods and terminology may be especially necessary for an untutored or lay audience; otherwise, niceties of method may seem unnecessary complexities.

Sometimes an accepted instrument is not quite "on target" for a construct; a less well known one measures it more precisely. We trade ready acceptance of the standard measure for a better measure but must exert the extra effort to educate the audience to its merits. Another of the many trade-off decisions in research, this is part of the optimizing process.

Credibility with our audience is enhanced in several ways:

- By building on knowledge that the audience has already accepted
- By demonstrating familiarity with the relevent literature
- By avoiding the weaknesses of previous similar studies
- By using accepted research techniques, measures, definitions, and terminology
- By justifying the use of any nonstandard aspects and educating the audience to the superiority of our choices

---

The Relative Weighting of Internal Validity (LP) and External Validity (GP)

Ideally, studies have enough internal validity (LP) to create a consensus that a relationship exists and enough external validity (GP) to show appropriate generality; preferably, we optimize both. Actions taken to strengthen internal validity (LP), however, tend to weaken external validity (GP); they work against each other. So for each study, researchers must decide how to achieve a **balance of internal validity (LP) and external validity (GP)**.

For example, to strengthen internal validity (LP), we tend to narrow the scope of the question studied. This permits the phenomenon to be easily observed under controlled conditions, possibly even laboratory conditions. This artificiality shrinks external validity (GP). Bronfenbrenner (1977) described the efforts to strengthen the internal validity (LP) of developmental psychology as resulting in "the science of strange behavior of children in strange situations with strange adults for the briefest possible time" (p. 513).

Internal validity (LP) is usually stressed in the early studies of a relationship to make sure that it does indeed exist. Once the relationship has been comfortably established, there is interest in how broadly it applies. As information on a subject increases, the balancing point between these two will typically shift emphasis from internal validity (LP) to external validity (GP).

Policy studies may be done for a variety of purposes; one is to determine whether a given program or policy works. These studies are not so much concerned with what is causally related to what—internal validity (LP)—as with external validity (GP). Take, for example, the Head Start studies, which were concerned with whether it was appropriate to fund preschool programs for underprivileged children throughout the United States. The studies covered programs involving every possible range of activity to see whether they were effective with children from different cultural backgrounds, in different regions of the country, with different school milieus, and so on. Although the initial studies did not show the expected gains in achievement, for a variety of other reasons including gains in nutrition and socialization, Congress funded Head

Start anyway. Later studies, with greater internal validity (LP), showed that the expected gains did occur with Head Start (Royce, Lazar, and Darlington, 1983) and similar programs (Schweinhart and Weikart, 1985). [To the extent that we can show linkage over a wide range of persons, situations, and/or times—external validity (GP)—we become more confident about inferring internal validity (LP) in any given instance. But considering Head Start's variety of programs, there may have been different causes in different localities.] Typically, an early finding that a type of treatment was robust over situations (that is, had generality) would be followed with tight internal validity studies to determine what resulted in the effect.

Limited resources restrict the persons and places we can study, which means that external validity (GP) is often constrained. By contrast, basic research studies seeking new relationships can use any subjects, situations, or other options in which the relationship either is present or can be created. So balancing in the direction of internal validity (LP) typically results in a less expensive study.

Credibility with each new audience may require repeating previous studies in circumstances relevant to that audience. The generality of each new technique in educational technology (language laboratories, programmed instruction, educational television) has had to be demonstrated anew in each context. For example, language laboratories were tried with each of the foreign languages; programmed instruction and educational television, with each different subject matter. This is not unlike the role of the county agricultural extension agent who must demonstrate the effectiveness of a new seed corn in each county to convince farmers of the generality of its effectiveness.

The relative importance of internal validity (LP) and external validity (GP) varies with the disposition of persons and with the nature of the decision. All individuals must arrive at a knowing judgment that the interpretation of the evidence indicates that the relationship both exists and is adequate to generalize to their personal circumstances. The disposition of some individuals is to be innovators, risk takers. They are eager to take the findings of studies that emphasize internal validity (LP) and try them out before much external validity (GP) evidence is available. Others, more conservative, require stronger external validity (GP) studies before accepting a finding as likely to be useful to them.

Similarly, the nature of the decision influences which validity is emphasized. Suppose the decision requires a good bit of investment of resources (time, effort, money), and there is a relatively small return for that investment. In that case, more and stronger external validity (GP) evidence will be required than if little investment is required and the potential payoff is large. Thus each problem varies in the requirements for internal validity (LP) and external validity (GP) in terms of (1) whether it is a basic or applied study, (2) whether it requires a large investment, (3) whether the payoff is large or small, and (4) whether the audience consists of risk takers or conservatives. This may seem like a lot to bear in mind in developing and reporting a study. But successful researchers manage to balance internal validity (LP) and external validity (GP) so as to meet their own requirements as well as those of their particular audiences.

> Strengthening internal validity (LP) usually diminishes external validity (GP). Each study must find the proper balance of the two for its purposes. Basic research usually emphasizes internal validity (LP); certain applied research and policy studies may emphasize external validity (GP).

Resource Allocation

When you read a study, you see only the final choices that were made in problem choice, formulation, design, analysis, and interpretation of findings. **Resource allocation** is concerned with the invisible set of alternative choices that might have been made, many of which were undoubtedly considered and discarded before the final ones were chosen. Resource allocation determines where to invest researcher (and staff) time, energy, and other resources. How much time should be devoted to problem conceptualization? Study design? Data gathering? Analysis and interpretation? What will be required to procure research space, equipment, measuring instruments, and so on? Resource allocation is also involved in the balancing of internal validity (LP) and external validity (GP); which is more heavily weighted is determined by where resources are invested.

We noted another instance of resource allocation in discussing the chain analogy. From "a chain is only as strong as its weakest link," we drew the conclusion that all the links should be of approximately the same strength (page 64). It makes no sense to concentrate on only one link when another might allow the argument to come crashing down. Allocation of resources to bring the links to equal strength is a prime criterion of good resource allocation. As examples, let us examine how resource allocation decisions affect the links.

Question Choice and Formulation. Question choice and formulation are intertwined, but the former usually precedes the latter. Given a particular problem choice, if a satisfactory formulation for investigation cannot be found, the original problem is usually discarded and a new one sought or some new aspect tried. Clearly, some questions lend themselves to investigation more than others. The Zimbardo problem, on the face of it, appears very difficult to study; we can't let aged people grow gradually deaf and do nothing about it. Only by reformulating it to use hypnosis on college students in a laboratory did Zimbardo make it become tractable. The problem for researchers is to decide whether to pour more resources of time and energy into question reformulation or to stop. Is this formulation satisfactory enough to try it in this form? Sometimes that answer is obvious, as, once found, was Zimbardo's reformulation.

In other instances, troublesome aspects become apparent only during our work with a particular formulation. For example, we would expect that the more we spend in educating students, the better the education should be. But as soon as we unravel per-pupil expenditure figures, it becomes clear that there are many problems. There are differences in salary schedules, determinants of salary increments, costs of space and its maintenance, and so on. The problem is very difficult to formulate in terms of per-pupil expenditures as usually reported.

Most problems can be conceptualized in different ways, and there is considerable testimonial evidence on the importance of problem formulation to problem solution. Getzels (1982) quotes Albert Einstein:

> The formulation of a problem is often more essential than its solution, which may be merely a matter of mathematical or experimental skill. To raise new questions, new possibilities, to regard old questions from a new angle, requires creative imagination and marks real advance in science. (Einstein and Infeld, 1938, p. 92)

Getzels notes that this is extended by Wertheimer (1945): "Often in great discoveries the most important thing is that a certain question is found. Envisaging, putting the productive question, is often a more important, . . . a greater achievement than the solution of a set of questions" (p. 123).

A researcher faced with the problem of choosing and formulating a problem must also decide at what point to stop allocating resources to this process and proceed with the study. Frequently, we are not at all sure that we have stopped at the right place. It is quite possible that further work would have resulted in a more important problem or a better-formulated one. That is why this criterion is optimized instead of completely fulfilled—we reformulate until some inner criterion of optimality is satisfied, and then proceed, never knowing what we might have missed.

Other Links in the Chain of Reasoning.　In similar fashion, the researcher considers each link in the chain. How is the study best designed? What method or combination of methods should be used? What sample of subjects? Situations? What treatment or independent variable? The questions are legion; we allocate resources in accordance with the difficulty of finding a satisfactory choice. An appropriate measure may not be available, so we have to allocate resources for the construction of a new measure. The initial design does not rule out certain important alternative explanations, so we develop a new design. Designs are often reformulated several times before a satisfactory one is found.

We have already described in section two research skills that can be employed to strengthen some aspect of a study. Because each consumes resources that cannot then be used elsewhere, the researcher faces a plethora of choices. Concealed in the report is the fact that alternatives have been chosen and rationally integrated. Remember how long a trip seems the first time? Successive times seem much shorter. Readers of a study see it in the latter way, not as it looked to the researcher the first time through.

Resource allocation is the hidden decision making that determines the relative strength of the various parts of a study. Though confined within resource limits, what is available may be allocated in many ways. The researcher's task is to optimize the allocation to fit the problem, goal, and audience.

LIMITS AND CONSTRAINTS

Our final set of considerations is the limits and constraints: (1) what can be done ethically, (2) what an institution will allow, and (3) the limits on the resources available for the study. We shall devote chapter 25 to the question of ethics and discuss additional aspects of it in chapter 26. It suffices to note here that professional societies have developed codes of ethics. These can limit the kinds of problems open to study. Institutional human subject protection committees (and similar committees for animals) approve research projects at their institutions. They see that **ethical standards** are observed by their researchers and determine whether the potential worth of knowledge gained justifies whatever discomfort or suffering may be incurred.

Institutional Constraints

Researchers who do studies in institutional settings find research a secondary consideration to whatever activity achieves the service goals for which the institution was established. Such **institutional constraints** limit what the institution will allow researchers to do, especially if a study interferes with an institutional schedule or interrupts essential activities. Only a limited amount of time can be taken from classroom teaching or asked of a patient receiving therapy.

Limits are rarely fixed; exceptions must be negotiated by the researcher. Because most institutions try to maintain business as usual come what may, institutions that allow their schedules to be disrupted by research are unusual. Such disruptions bear testimony to some combination of the negotiating skill of the investigator, the perceived value of the research, or the atypicality of an institution. The last, of course, weakens the generality of the findings where nature of the institution is an important factor.

Access is especially difficult when controversial topics are probed or a study may reflect unfavorably on the institution. Administrators often grant access for the study of what they perceive as a desirable development only to find it reported unfavorably. Rist (1977), for example, observed the integration of black children bused to previously all-white schools in Portland, Oregon—a program of which the administration was quite proud. He pointed out, however, that integration meant assimilation to the point that black children's culture was devalued. The school administration was offended.

Similar incidents make administrators reluctant to approve researcher requests that appear more interested in revealing unfortunate conditions than in protecting the institution. Each additional highly critical report probably raises barriers to similar studies as its controversy spreads. Sometimes a no-win situation develops, and the researcher must decide who shall be harmed instead of avoiding harm altogether. Taylor (1977), for example, found institutional attendants drinking beer to the point where it interfered with their duties to the patients. Yet he did not report this, rationalizing that the impact of the study on the institutionalization problem as a whole was more important than remedying this instance of impropriety.

Whether and how to "blow the whistle" on such social problems is also an ethical dilemma for the researcher. He or she unquestionably feels that society should know about such conditions. Yet such revelations may undermine support for the institution and deny what help is now given to people who need it. In addition, the professional careers of persons who cooperated may be damaged. Although some people might argue that if they created the conditions, they deserve to suffer the consequences, that in no way enhances the researcher's image. Researchers come to be perceived by the authorities as meddlers unsympathetic to administrative complexities and lacking real understanding of the problem. Such situations interfere with the study of social problems needing correction, and institutions may consequently make them inaccessible to study.

> Institutional constraints typically prevent researchers from engaging in activities that may interfere with their ongoing routine or may reflect unfavorably on the institution, its performance, or its personnel. Such constraints have serious implications for what social problems can be investigated.

Resource Limits

Resources are rarely sufficient to do everything we hope to do. We think of the main resources as our time and energy as investigators. Graduate students writing dissertations tend to think of these as relatively unlimited—they simply put in whatever it takes. But of course these resources are limited in a practical sense. Time expended on a study must be evaluated in terms of its alternative uses, what economists call its marginal utility or opportunity cost (for example, working to earn money instead of spending that time on more dissertation development). Hence the real costs are rarely included in a researcher's decision making. Keeping a study in the perspective of alternative important activities and alternative research projects allows us to assign reasonable limits to it.

Resource limits are often fixed by the available staff, equipment, instruments, and the like, as well as by money—the size of a grant or a budget. But given positive results, new resources can sometimes be found, so limits may not be as fixed as we tend to regard them. Nonetheless, expanding such limits takes time and energy and is usually far from certain. So deciding to seek additional funds is itself part of the resource allocation process. Note also that seeking funding may subject you to the requirements of a sponsor. This can bring many changes in such areas as the focus of the study, the relative importance of various audiences, and the time schedule for completion. All these factors must be viewed in terms of the study's importance in the larger picture of your career, the needs of your discipline or profession, and your responsibility to society.

With some experience, we come to see that the same study can be built in a variety of sizes. This suggests that a resource limit may not be a bad thing, because many studies can be made to fit within it. But different study goals—large and impressive studies for Congress and lay audiences, smaller studies done to very high standards for professional audiences—suggest that there are guidelines for resource size. Optimum size for a study is determined by such variables as the need for sufficient sensitivity to show the relationship, size for representativeness and generality, and impressiveness for uncertainty reduction. This also suggests that there may be a minimum level below which the study may not have the intended effect—a study too small to reduce the uncertainty of a nonprofessional audience or too small to sense an effect, even if it should occur (more on the latter point in chapter 17).

Resource limits clearly determine the constraints within which resource allocation can take place. Since the latter is one of the essential tasks of a researcher, resource limits can be a determining factor of research quality.

- Resource limits set the boundaries on resource allocation.
- Given that studies can usually be built to different sizes, resource limits often constrain the resources devoted to a given problem to its importance in the larger scheme of knowledge development.
- There is probably both an optimum and a minimum size for a study based on the expectations of the audience, the size required to sense the expected effect, and the generality intended.

SUMMARY

Whereas it is apparent that internal validity (LP) and external validity (GP) are important characteristics of a research study, other characteristics also shape it. One, audience credibility, is strengthened by reporting the study in such a way that we anticipate the concerns of our main audiences and assuage them, providing evidence of our integrity as researchers, building trust in the way the research was conducted by using standard procedures, explaining the merits of nonstandard ones, and supplying an understanding of why we made what may appear to be dubious or controversial choices of design or procedure.

A second is the balance of internal validity (LP) and external validity (GP) such that the evidence sufficiently supports the existence of the relationship and appropriately indicates its intended generality.

A third characteristic, resource allocation, is apparent in the complex process of research in which it is practiced. Only the final product of the process appears in the research report. It permits both the intended balance of internal validity (LP) and external validity (GP) to be achieved and links in the chain of reasoning to be equally strengthened.

There are many ways in which each of the three criteria may be satisfied. Fulfilling one may be at the expense of another. Further, there may be differences among researchers concerning the optimum level on each to be achieved. Therefore, these criteria are optimized for each study rather than fully satisfied.

This optimization must be achieved within (1) the ethical limits prescribed by each discipline for the protection of both humans and animals, (2) the constraints of each institution that protect their operations in the face of research requirements, and (3) the resource limits on the researcher's personal time and energy as well as on the resources available from the institution, research grant, or contract.

We have now covered a number of the needed research skills and the criteria for judging research; it is time to examine the methods themselves, to which we turn in section four.

ADDITIONAL READING

Krathwohl (1985)

IMPORTANT TERMS

Audience credibility
Balance of internal validity (LP) and external
   validity (GP)
Ethical standards

Institutional constraints
Resource allocation
Resource limits

APPLICATION PROBLEMS

1. Reread the summary of Jonassen's study of pattern notes (chapter 5, application problem 1). His purpose was to verify this technique as a simple, practical means of assessing a learner's cognitive structure. What has he done to build audience credibility?

2. You are a researcher who is interested in the acquisition of second languages. You want to test a newly developed technique for teaching correct pronunciation in French to high school students and compare it with the program in current use. Both approaches are based on the use of listening tapes.

You are considering whether or not to bring groups of students to the university's language lab, where you can randomly assign them to one or the other approach. You have the support of local school officials and can bring in several classes. Considering internal validity (LP) and external validity (GP), what would be the advantages and disadvantages of doing so?

3. Reread the description of the study on impulsiveness–reflectiveness by Kagen and associates in the answer to problem 1 in chapter 13 (page 711). Note that the concept was developed during research on analytic versus global reasoning. From the information available, what choices did these investigators appear to make in terms of resource allocation?

4. Psychologist Sarah Ellenova compared student-generated questions about a text passage with adjunct questions inserted by the author. She sought to carry out her study in several elementary schools in the local school system. She was granted permission to investigate only one group, the grade 6 class at the "University Elementary School," a laboratory school run jointly by the university and the school board. It was, she was told, the only school properly set up to allow such research without unnecessarily disrupting school routines. How could these institutional constraints affect her study?

Compare your answers with those on pages 712–713.

=================== APPLICATION EXERCISE ===================

What constraints do you think you might encounter with your problem? Do you anticipate ethical problems? If so, you may want to jump ahead to chapter 25. Will institutions be reluctant to let you in to gather data? What might you do to mitigate such difficulties? Entry to do research is often a problem; we'll consider that further in the next chapter. Do you anticipate insufficient resources of some kind? If you may need additional monetary resources, see section four, "Finding Funding," in Krathwohl (1988), which examines sources of both public and private funding. What balance of internal validity (LP) and external validity (GP) do you anticipate? Is yours closer to basic research or applied? Do you anticipate any particular problems with audience credibility at this point in your problem's development? You may want to think about this issue again after you have chosen a research method. As for resource allocation, as your plans for your study firm up, consider doing a work plan such as is described in Krathwohl (1988) beginning on page 73.

The Methods of Research

This section's initial chapters describe the basic methods of educational and social science research: qualitative methods (chapter 15), sample surveys (chapter 16), and experiments (chapter 18). Included is a chapter on the nature and logic of inferential statistics (chapter 17), which are used in experimentation, sometimes in sample surveys and in other methods. Together with the research skills section, they constitute the basic material needed to understand and conduct studies.

They are followed by chapters that describe methods that use these basic techniques with past data (historiography and after-the-fact natural experiments, chapter 19), toward specific ends (evaluation, chapter 20), and under special conditions (longitudinal and single-subject studies, chapter 21). Also included is a discussion of meta-analysis, a method of combining the results of studies (also in chapter 21), and a chapter on some advanced statistics (chapter 22).

Chapters 15, 16, and 18–20 include a section on the hallmarks of skilled application of the method as well as one on tips on using it.

CHAPTER
15

Qualitative Research Methods

Unfortunately, events do not come with labels on them: "Look at me, I'm recurrent"; or "Ignore me, I won't happen again." Indeed, they do not even come labelled: "I am an event." Such labels must be imposed . . . by an observer. Until they have been, a scientist has nothing to work with.

George A. Miller, Spontaneous Apprentices

If one wishes to understand the term *holy water*, one should not study the properties of the water, but rather the assumptions and beliefs of the people who use it. That is, holy water derives its meaning from those who attribute a special essence to it.

Thomas S. Szasz, Ceremonial Chemistry

OVERVIEW[1]

Qualitative research methods permit the description of phenomena and events in an attempt to understand and explain them. Such descriptions may be used to seek principles and explanations that generalize. Qualitative methods are inductive: they let the problem emerge from the data or remain open to interpretations of the problem different from those held initially. The data are accounts of careful observations, including detailed descriptions of context and nearly verbatim records of conversation. They may also include analyses of documents and records.

As Biklen and Bogdan (1986) note, by contrast, some qualitative researchers gather their data from what might be called a **qualitative point of view** (also referred to as a phenomenological point of view). Biklen and Bogdan call this "thinking naturalistically." Such researchers try to understand how individuals perceive the meaning of the world around them. They argue that through our experiences, we construct a view of the world that determines how we act. Qualitative methods are used to explore a particular point of view in explaining human behavior. These result in context-dependent and sometimes multiple explanations. Although all researchers often do and probably

---

1. I am very grateful to Sari Biklen, Bob Bogdan, and Steven Taylor, who taught me much of this chapter's content.

should use qualitative methods, not all will gather their data from a qualitative point of view.

As data gathering proceeds, voluminous notes accumulate rapidly; these must be reduced to manageable form by coding. Coding categorizes data into underlying concepts and dimensions and facilitates systematic retrieval. In some instances, coding simply highlights what is there. In others, categories result from researcher insights that link aspects not necessarily perceived as related by the subjects of the study. Interpretation is separate from description, written in the form of memos that are ultimately integrated into a cohesive explanation of the data. Explanations induced from the observations are said to result in grounded theory—that is, theory grounded in the data.

Qualitative work is usually written up as a case study. Increasingly, multiple sites are used, and case studies are combined into larger reports. The internal validity (LP) and external validity (GP) of qualitative work is often carried by the conceptual evidence, especially when the empirical evidence is derived from a small sample whose representativeness is unknown. Multisite studies, or replications, provide evidence of external validity (GP) by showing generality across them. Because of the rich and vivid examples, audience credibility of qualitative research tends to be high. Unanticipated ethical problems are encountered by all qualitative researchers, who must make decisions on the spot without the opportunity to consult professional colleagues regarding what is appropriate.

CHAPTER CONTENTS

Introduction   313
    Ways of Gathering Qualitative
      Data   314
Observation   315
    Covert Participant Observation   316
    Concealed Observation or Recording
      from a Hidden or Unobtrusive
      Viewpoint   317
    Unconcealed Participant
      Observation   317
    Nonparticipant Observation   318
Participant Observation   319
    Gaining Entry   319
    Securing Acceptance   320
The Qualitative Point of View   321
Fieldwork   324
    Analytic Induction, the Constant
      Comparison Method, and
      Purposive Sampling   324
    Informants   326
    Data Validity and Triangulation   328
    Fieldnotes and Memos   329

    Ethics   334
Data Reduction: Coding, Analysis,
    and Synthesis   335
    Coding   336
    Conclusion Drawing and
      Verification   340
    Threats to the Validity of Data:
      Alternative Explanations   342
The Report   347
Internal Validity (LP), External
    Validity (GP), and Other Criteria Applied
    to Qualitative Research   348
Aids for Qualitative Researchers
    and Consumers   351
    Tips on Participant Observation   351
    When to Use Qualitative
      Methods   352
    Hallmarks of Qualitative
      Research   353
Summary and Detailed Comparison
    of Qualitative and
    Quantitative Methods   354

INTRODUCTION

We begin the section on research techniques with qualitative methods for a couple of reasons. For one, they build on the well-practiced verbal descriptive skills we have all used for years. Their methods are an elaboration of the techniques for selecting and categorizing information that we have used in writing term papers and reports since the start of high school. We come to them with both extensive experience and also some skill.

For another, familiarity with qualitative procedures is useful regardless of the method researchers may choose for specialization. They keep us close to the persons in the situation and their actions. Indeed, qualitative researchers view individuals as collaborators or teachers from whom to learn rather than as subjects to be held at arm's length and studied.

Inductive in orientation during data gathering and analysis, qualitative researchers nevertheless observe the norms of science. Like all research reports, qualitative studies that propose generalizations use a deductive format in the final report, showing the relationship between explanations and their supporting findings.[2]

In chapter 11, the trade-off between multiple-choice and essay questions was described as choosing to do the analysis up front and develop multiple-choice questions or instead collect data and do the scoring and analysis later. Multiple-choice questions are more difficult and time-consuming to construct, but the data are easier to score and analyze. Quantitative studies, like multiple-choice tests, are largely planned prior to data collection. The pattern of analysis, like multiple-choice scoring, follows from the prior work. Qualitative research is like an essay examination. The much less structured collection of data similarly results in a large and time-consuming analysis stage. Further, if the multiple-choice item developer starts with a misconception of how students will approach a problem, a poor item results. Similarly, a qualitative researcher will be misled by a misconception of the problem at hand. But the qualitative researcher lets the problem emerge during the data gathering and so is less likely to misconceive of it. Either way, however, precious research time is involved: either in quantitative study planning and design or in qualitative data gathering and analysis—there is no "free lunch."

Qualitative methods require skillful interpretation of the data. Like historians, qualitative researchers are judged by how insightfully they analyze their data, how well they present their interpretations, and how carefully and tightly they relate them to their data. Indeed, turn to page 505 and read the first two paragraphs on interpretive history, for these paragraphs apply equally well to qualitative research.

---

2. Some qualitative researchers may object to the characterization of qualitative research as inductive on the grounds that it is too narrow. In their defense, it is important to note that qualitative data can be used to validate a proposition in a deductive study just like quantitative data. But most qualitative studies are inductive, so inductive logic seems useful as a distinctive characteristic in contrast to other methods of research.

There is unnecessary tension between supporters of quantitative and qualitative methods. Qualitative researchers are sometimes defensive because their methods are said to possess less resemblance to those of the natural sciences. This stance is heightened by some quantitative researchers' view of qualitative work as "unscientific." Researchers need all the help they can get, and qualitative methods have an important and useful place among the research methods. All methods have strengths and weaknesses; our task is to learn when and where to capitalize on strengths and avoid weaknesses.

> Qualitative methods use familiar techniques for handling verbal material that makes situations "come alive"; they keep the investigator close to the data and markedly facilitate understanding of the phenomenon being studied. They can be usefully combined with all other research methods.

Ways of Gathering Qualitative Data

Some form of observation is a prime method of the qualitative approach. Because of its importance, it will constitute the major method discussed in this chapter. Interviewing, usually informal but sometimes structured, is also an important skill. Survey research uses the interview extensively, so we will cover that in the next chapter. Diaries and other personal, as well as official, records and artifacts are frequently used by qualitative researchers to gain insights. The analysis of such documents is a matter of much interest to historians, so we shall consider their use in chapter 19, on historical methods.

Like quantitative data, qualitative data may be gathered from situations as diverse as human imagination permits. Suppose we were studying communication between hospital staff and parents in a neonatal ward where extremely premature infants hover between life and death. Once we had identified a problem of communication between staff and parents, besides conducting the observation and informal interviews used by Bogdan, Brown, and Foster (1982), we might gather other kinds of data. We might interview small groups of staff and parents about the problem of communicating the right amount of hope and pessimism to parents. The group setting gives them the chance to discuss and react to one another's ideas, possibly expressing thoughts and reactions we as researchers might not have anticipated. We might show pictures taken of parent-staff conferences in the ward and ask other parents and staff to describe what was going on. It helps if the pictures are somewhat ambiguous because that allows the respondents to bring their own typical and most salient interpretations to the scene.

We might put phrases descriptive of what was going on in the ward on 3-by-5-inch cards and ask both parents and staff to sort the cards into piles, then ask them to describe the piles and explain why each card was placed there. Like the pictures, this allows the respondents to project whatever organizing schemes are most salient in their minds, schemes that may or may not be readily apparent from their actions.

We might videotape parent-staff conferences and then replay the tape to each of the participants individually. During the replay, we ask them to stop at points they think are significant, tell what they were thinking at the time, and indicate why those points were significant. In addition, we might stop the tape at points we think are significant and ask questions. Note that these are all ways of eliciting how individuals perceive situations and what organizing frameworks come readily to mind to make sense of them. Responses could be recorded either on tape or in handwritten notes kept as close to verbatim as possible. If a categorizing and coding scheme has been devised, the responses can be tallied directly into the scheme.

So there are a variety of ways of generating qualitative data. Many of the ones mentioned are similar to methods used by psychologists. Qualitative methods come more out of the sociological and anthropological traditions, where interviewing and observation are central. So let us turn to a prime source of qualitative data, observation, and examine it in some detail, leaving interviewing to the next chapter.

Qualitative data may be gathered in as many ways as the researcher's creativity permits. Although the most widely used source is observation, analysis of records and documents is also common. In addition to observation in a sociological tradition, methods of eliciting responses from individuals using interviewing or a stimulated response technique, as psychologists do, may be useful.

OBSERVATION

Our perspective in observation is like a flashlight: it lights up only where it is directed. That is to be expected. Indeed, observers are judged by whether they are sensitive enough to capture the critical aspects of what is occurring, how well they can make sense of it, and how well the explanations they induce from it fit. A central problem of observation is that individuals who are conscious of being under scrutiny are likely to behave differently, usually in the direction of what they perceive to be more socially approved or in accord with the observers' expectations. But that is not always the case, as with resentful experimental school pupils tired of being observed. Indeed, sometimes it is hard to predict how individuals will react to observation; we just know they usually do. Covert observation, where the individual is not aware of being observed, is a difficult way of solving the problem. A more common solution is to use participation by the observer to reduce obtrusiveness. We can construct a continuum of observation techniques from least to most obtrusive as shown in Figure 15.1.

Covert participant observer	Concealed recording equipment or concealed observer	Visible recording equipment made unobtrusive	Participant observation, recording done out of sight of observed	Participant observation, recording done in sight of observed	Non-participant observer

FIGURE 15.1   Observation methods placed on a continuum of obtrusiveness.

Covert Participant Observation

Covert participant observation is the most difficult of all the observation roles. There is a constant tension between the mental vigilance needed to stay in character and the effort to relax so that the role seems natural. Yet too much naturalness runs the risk that observers will "go native" and lose their professional identity. It is physically exhausting. Sullivan, Queen, and Patrick's (1958) covert observer of basic military training lost 35 pounds, presumably from role tension. Weekend meetings with the research team helped maintain his professional perspective as well as visits with a chaplain who was privy to his real identity.

There are other problems as well. Reconstruction of events over a long time period between debriefings can be a problem. An alternative, a miniature recording device, produces voluminous records that are expensive and often difficult to transcribe (two persons talking at once, disturbing noise, voices too far from the microphone, etc.). They also miss nonverbal cues. If a group is small and the behavior of the participants is neither routine nor prescribed, the observer's role may affect what the group does. To maintain a natural role in a small group, the covert observer may feel called on to initiate action, which may lead to different group outcomes than were the observer not present.

Covert participation also limits the kinds of inquires that can be made to those consistent with the observer's role. There may be questions that are too personal, too nosy, or too naive, although these questions might be asked by a researcher whose role is known and accepted (Orenstein and Phillips, 1978).

The relationships that can be developed and maintained are also limited. A teacher would not be expected to spend much time with the superintendent or central office personnel. Certain records may be inaccessible as well. And then, of course, there is a problem if the ruse is discovered. Negotiated entry for noncovert observers to institutions they end up criticizing is already difficult. It is not made easier by researchers who ask no permission and are discovered.

Cultural background, age, sex, race, appearance, manner of speaking, physical build, family situation, and other relatively unchangeable characteristics may preclude not just covert but any kind of participant observation in certain groups. Senior male professors find participation roles in any kind of youth situation difficult. The restrictions a role may place on the characteristics of an individual may well be impossible for many professionals to meet. Even under favorable circumstances, training may be necessary. The observer of military training referred to earlier was coached for nine months before assuming the part of a working-class enlisted man. Even then, he was nearly rejected by the recruiting sergeant "because by all appearances he was a juvenile delinquent" (Sullivan, Queen, and Patrick, 1958).

On the positive side, however, participants gain access to data to which no one else could be privy. Behavior is uninhibited by the presence of an outsider. How else could a researcher record how a mental, penal, or other institution looks to an inmate, how the army feels to a recruit, or how certain religious, fraternal, and political groups view their world? Further, an informant can be a main-line actor rather than the marginal and often atypical person a researcher might otherwise have to rely on (more on informants later). Despite these advantages, the difficulties involved in covert research and the dilemmas when the role involves illegal or unethical behavior result in its use being relatively rare.

Concealed Observation or Recording from a Hidden or Unobtrusive Viewpoint

Observation behind two-way mirrors or from some hidden and unobtrusive location is quite feasible in institutional settings, especially where it is possible to move into such a situation without suspicion. Experimental schools associated with universities frequently have such arrangements. As a matter of courtesy, teachers are usually informed when they are "on stage," and students are sophisticated enough to know the purpose of the mirrors as well. Requesting permission of the administration further reduces the possibility of covert recording without the subjects' being aware of it. Quite properly, few administrators will approve such an arrangement. The value of the mirrors is that the observed become accustomed to observation because neither observer nor equipment is visible to remind them. Behavior usually returns to what appears to be normal. The video record is likely to be clearer and more understandable than the soundtrack. The noise filter of the human ear and its ability to follow one conversation when several are occurring have yet to be duplicated by electronic equipment.

Alternatively, unobtrusive placement of the equipment (the third position on the continuum) is less expensive and probably as effective. Kounin (1970), for instance, placed in classrooms boxes that would conceal cameras; left in place, they came to be regarded as part of the furniture. When a record was to be made, equipment was installed in the box when the room was empty. Of course, the location is fixed, and only with expensive equipment are tracking, closeups, and perspective views possible.

Unconcealed Participant Observation

Unconcealed **participant observation** is the observer role preferred by most observers. They are open about the fact of observation, but acting as a participant at some level reduces the obtrusiveness. At the same time, it instructs the researcher in what it is like to be in the situation. This role allows access to the important places and people while still "in character." With a high level of participation (the fourth position on the continuum), making notes may have to be done on the side, but at a lower level (the fifth position) it is often done overtly. Because of the favored status of overt participant observation, it will be explored in more detail shortly.

Nonparticipant Observation

The most obtrusive of the roles, nonparticipant observation, nevertheless provides freedom to concentrate entirely on observation and to become very sensitive to the significance of what is occurring. Experienced participant observers often find that they must either adopt this role to continue in the situations they studied when they were younger or change the focus of their research to situations where they can still successfully pass as participants. Just as it is difficult for an observer to play an unnatural role, so too is it difficult for the observed to maintain "on stage" behavior over a long period of time. So even to the nonparticipant role, over time there is usually considerable accommodation on the part of the observed toward more natural behavior.

Some people might argue that without participation we are unable to appreciate fully the affective reactions of participants, but there is little evidence that this is the case. Good observers train themselves to be as empathic as they possibly can. They cultivate a combination of empathy and detachment, the former so they can understand, the latter so they can record and place in perspective what they are observing. Everett Hughes (1971) has noted that a person who is of the culture but feels not wholly a part of it often makes a good observer.

Awareness of observation changes the behavior of the people observed. Efforts to avoid this effect result in a continuum of observation methods:

- Covert observation (spying) gains access to unique situations but is difficult to carry off and involves ethical complications.
- Concealed observation is usually known to those observed, but they grow accustomed to it more rapidly in the absence of a constant visual reminder.
- Participant observation makes the observer less obtrusive because he or she becomes a member of the group.
- Nonparticipant observation requires a longer period for accommodation by those being observed to return to "natural behavior" (if they ever do entirely). But it allows the observer to concentrate on the observation process.

PARTICIPANT OBSERVATION

Participant observers are faced with the tasks of gaining entry, securing accept- ance, sampling to select informants, checking their perceptions and hunches, and building an explanation. Through it all, they must develop fieldnotes and memos that are the basis for coding and analysis and for eliminating alternative explanations.

Gaining Entry

Whether the observation is an institution, a community, or a group, field workers nearly always try to find a way of **gaining entry** that conveys that they can be trusted. Often they seek the help of a friend or colleague who either is a part of the setting or is trusted by a member of it. But negotiating entry, particularly to institutions, is often complex.

Bosk (1979) studied surgeons' errors. He started with a surgeon he had met at a party who, as supervisor of residents, was a **gatekeeper**. Although the surgeon expressed enthusiasm, he feared that his sponsorship would be a "kiss of death." He felt that Bosk needed to talk to the residents directly and be seen as his own person. "I learned . . . there was no instant access for the field- worker." Being sent to the chief resident, Bosk was not sure whether he was being given assistance or the runaround. The chief resident also approved but needed to check with his supervisors; Bosk's department provided a letter of introduction. "Gaining my initial entrée was a multistage diplomatic problem," Bosk explained. "Each action was a test, and access was the result of continual testing and retesting. Entrée was not something negotiated once and then over and done with . . . but a continuous process" (p. 194).

Bosk's experience is not uncommon, nor is his paranoia about possibly being given the runaround. The people asked may not like granting access but hate to be seen as "bad guys" who appear to be "against research and prog ress." They may refer the request to others in the hope that someone will find a legitimate objection that can be used to provide an excuse. Organizations that perceive of themselves as doing a good job and might gain favorable publicity from a report are much more willing to grant access than their opposite numbers. Sometimes it is possible to enter an area of an organization that is more secure and use the trust established there to gain entry to less accessible parts. That is often a good strategy because researchers often do not know precisely all that they will want to observe.

Often administrators ask for a quid pro quo for the privilege. They want a report on some subordinates or an evaluation of "how we are doing." Often they want some control over the project or the report: to see fieldnotes, to view the draft and make suggestions, to rule certain aspects of their operation off limits, or perhaps even to approve the report's release. Clearly, administra- tive approval is critical, and this can be a very difficult situation for the researcher because most such requests, if they do not violate academic freedom, abrogate the necessary confidentiality of informants. Clearly, the fewer restrictive conditions for entry, the better. Some people argue that such conditions can be renegotiated once the observer is at work and initial fear has been replaced by trust. Although this often happens and is certainly to be taken advantage of when possible, never promise things on the assumption that renegotiation is likely. It may be better to use another site.

- Gaining entry to institutions requires the approval of administrators who may impose conditions on the process or want a quid pro quo. This can be a serious problem.
- Negotiated entry is a continuous process that must be repeated at each level in the organization.

Securing Acceptance

To quote Bosk again, "Access—being allowed in the scene—is one thing, but approval and trust of field subjects is quite another. Just like access, cooperation . . . is earned again and again when the field-worker shows that he or she is trustworthy" (p. 194). In part, the participant role serves to demonstrate approval of what the observed are doing by helping them. Their **acceptance** in return is anticipated. Sometimes this means doing menial tasks, as when Bosk was asked to open bandage packages or retrieve charts. Sometimes the researcher is involved as a professional, as when Rist (1977) was asked to comment on classroom situations when he was observing the integration of black children bused out of inner-city schools. Acceptance may be enhanced when the observer uses personal skills to assist the observed. For example, Liebow (1967), studying a street corner society, used his knowledge of criminal proceedings to assist one of the group who had been summoned to appear as a witness in a murder trial. Whyte (1955), in a much earlier and still famous study of a similar society, employed his knowledge of the political process to organize a rally of 300 people that got hot water turned on in public showers.

The observer as participant has a difficult role. The observer must maintain close rapport with all from whom information is sought while maintaining sufficient psychological distance not to be identified with one adversarial group or another. Wax (1971) very appropriately calls this "instrumental membership" and notes that host and researcher jointly construct a suitable role. Sometimes it helps simply to explain that a researcher is not supposed to take sides. Perhaps the observed will understand, even though they will believe that, as Orenstein and Phillips (1978) put it, "'deep down' he or she is on our 'side.'"

Acceptance does not necessarily mean acting like the rest of the group. Whyte (1955) tried using some of the obscenities he heard all around him.

Conversation stopped, and one of the members said, "Bill, you're not supposed to talk like that. That doesn't sound like you" (p. 304). The goal is to become a member of the group enough to be accepted but to remain an outsider sufficiently to retain perspective on the situation and not be constrained to do all the things the group normally expects of its members.

Administrative approval of entry does not guarantee acceptance; indeed, it may delay it. Acceptance, like entry, is a continuous process and must be negotiated anew at each level and with each new informant.

THE QUALITATIVE POINT OF VIEW

Qualitative methods may or may not assume a qualitative point of view (QPV), which we shall keep distinct. QPV strongly affects what data are gathered and how they are interpreted. Although a few qualitative researchers would argue that QPV and method are inseparable, most would agree that we may use qualitative methods without adopting a qualitative point of view. Indeed, many would argue that even if a researcher rejects the qualitative point of view, *all* quantitative researchers should use qualitative *methods* at some point to understand better what their research is "really" about. This is excellent advice, and following it can turn up very useful evidence.

How does the qualitative point of view differ from qualitative method? An analogy, if not pushed too far, may be helpful. In chapter 12, we noted Popper (1972) suggested that the world might be perceived as "clocklike" or "cloudlike." A clocklike world, like the workings of an old spring-wound clock, would run with a mechanical determinism. The laws that govern behavior in such a world can be exact, and prediction is precise. This may be an appropriate model for physics. But it is too mechanistic for most social scientists, especially for those who believe in self-determination—"I am the master of my fate, the captain of my soul."

Most social scientists prefer the more loosely coupled model of the world—the cloudlike world, like the normative behavior of a cloud of gnats. Predictions will more or less hold (since most gnats are in the center of the swarm) but there can be no precise prediction. Discovering rules and laws increases the likelihood of accurately predicting loosely coupled events. Most researchers with a quantitative orientation are trying to find those rules and laws to increase the accuracy of predictions about the behavior of the swarm—normative statements. There are also some who believe that when social science is sufficiently advanced, it will result in clocklike prediction. Note that we are describing fundamental beliefs of researchers here, their orientation to what social science is all about and what kind of social science we can construct. (We will return to this in chapter 24.)

To carry the analogy a step further, those who take some form of qualitative point of view do not take the stance of the outside observer who is watching the clocklike gears or the cloudlike swarm. Rather, if we may anthropomorphize the gnats, those with a QPV try to perceive the situation like the individual gnats, trying to understand how the swarm looks to them. How do they interpret the actions of other gnats? How do they understand the behavior of always returning to the swarm whenever they find themselves outliers? One is studying the meaning-making process, asking. "How do these individuals construct the meaning of their world?" This knowledge is a social construction of behavior, a joint product of the culture and the meanings assigned by the individual.[3] So the QPV differs in terms of what is deemed important to observe and how the researcher tries to understand it.

Another difference is that knowledge is local in the sense that it applies to the gnats in this swarm. Gnats in other swarms may understand their situations differently. It is also context-dependent; how gnats interpret what is appropriate to do under certain conditions of heat and humidity may not apply to other situations.

As indicated in the analogy, QPV researchers seek to learn how people understand their world and their surroundings. But within the qualitative tradition, researchers differ with respect to the aspects of the world they emphasize in their data collection and analysis. Some distinguish these emphases with names like ethnography, symbolic interactionism, ethnomethodology, and phenomenology. These finer distinctions are not necessary for our discussion because they deal more with the "what" than the "how" of method. They simply indicate that the researcher is using qualitative methods to gather and examine data from a particular emphasis or orientation. To help understand what this means, let us examine two of these emphases.

Social scientists with an anthropological orientation typically call their work ethnography. They emphasize the role of culture in influencing behavior, study the meaning of shared patterns for behavior, and trace how culture evolves. Physical aspects of the surroundings and the behavior of others are interpreted through cultural standards.

> Researchers in this tradition say that an ethnography succeeds if it teaches readers how to behave appropriately in the cultural setting, whether it is among families in a black community (Stack, 1974), in the school principal's office (Wolcott, 1973), or in the kindergarten class (Florio, 1978). (Bogdan and Bicklen, 1982, p. 35)

Some with a sociological bent, although not denying the role of culture, tend to emphasize symbolic interaction. People are seen as acting according to

---

3. So also is quantitative interpretation a social construction. Recall that volume, which to us signifies a cubic measure, as noted in chapter 11, was at one time measured by pitch of the vessel when struck. So what characteristics of a phenomenon are attended to and how they are measured are social constructions. But such measures are so much a part of our culture that we often consider them "natural," as though that were the only way to view them.

the meaning of things and persons to them; their reality is socially constructed. From this viewpoint, it is necessary to see the world through the eyes of the actor to reach a full understanding of the purpose of that person's acts. As Bogdan and Biklen (1982) note:

> People act not according to what the school is supposed to be . . . but according to how they see it. For some, high school is primarily a place to meet friends; . . . for most, it is a place to get grades and amass credits so they can graduate. . . . The definitions they have determine their actions, although the rules and the credit system may set certain limits and impose certain costs, and thus affect their behavior. (p. 34)

We might add (as Bogdan and Biklen do) that the students' actions are also a result of how they see themselves: if they see themselves as individuals who succeed or fail in such settings, this will strongly influence their behavior as well.

Phenomenologists argue that it is an individual's perceptions that count. It does not make any difference whether you and I see a supervisor as hostile. As quantitative researchers, applying a low-inference rating scale to her overt supervisory behavior, we might find little or no evidence of hostility. But if subordinates see the supervisor's behavior as hostile, it will affect the way that they react to that person's supervision. To understand that reaction, we must understand the world as the subordinates see it; without that, the supervisor's actions might mystify us.

Although anyone can use qualitative methods, not all who do so will adopt some form of QPV. Further, those who do adopt a QPV and use data to learn how individuals construe their culture or perceive the world will not typically use tests or measures to learn this, at least not at first. Any such instrument would have been built with certain assumptions about what is important and what questions to ask. Indeed, many persons with a QPV would argue that measurement does more than simply predict, possibly incorrectly, the "ballpark" within which the individuals' perceptions will lie so that they can be measured. Stake (1978), for instance, notes that in contrast to observing, "measurement glasses do more than scale the view." They transform what is measured into a bearer of properties, into something in an array of characteristics; they objectify it. As he puts it, "Measurement is not just holding a ruler to what we see, but seeing something to hold a ruler to." So with a QPV, we might well never use a measure, but if we did, we would certainly first plumb what a person's perceptions are. Only then might we be able to select a measure that matched these perceptions as a way of gathering additional data.

Further, the kind of social science that views such knowledge as local and context-bound and encourages multiple meanings of situations without encompassing the explanation of those meanings in a single generalization is quite different from that sought by most quantitative social scientists. Social scientists in general may not embrace the natural sciences model, but neither are most willing to move as far from it as the fully committed QPVers believe is appropriate.

> Qualitative point of view involves understanding how the world looks to the people studied and how they act on that information. It therefore allows multiple interpretations of situations, depending on how the various actors perceive it. This characteristic is puzzling to people who seek single explanations of phenomena, the typical goal of the natural sciences.

FIELDWORK

Most formulations start at the same place, a first phase of trying to find what is significant in a situation. In that initial stage, the researcher is like a sponge, soaking up all that is around and listening intently. Interviewing is open-ended, and sometimes just observing is best. Whyte (1955) notes that we must "learn when to question and when not to question as well as what questions to ask" (p. 303). For example, conversation stopped when Whyte remarked to a gambler who was telling the group about his operations, "I suppose the cops were all paid off?" His friend, Doc, commented the next day that he should go easy on all the who, what, why, and when stuff or people would clam up on him. If he'd just hang around long enough, he'd learn the answers without asking. Whyte declares: "I found this was true. As I sat and listened, I learned the answers to questions that I would not even have had the sense to ask" (p. 303).

We consult documents (transcripts and minutes of meetings, court proceedings, diaries, letters, questionnaire responses, census statistics, etc.). We look for artifacts (pieces of art, choices of furniture, items on desks or tables, available equipment). In short, we seek any evidence that will be helpful in extending and deepening our understanding.

Analytic Induction, the Constant Comparison Method, and Purposive Sampling

In the next stages, the target emerges and helps us focus the following observations and inquiries. We are able to select a purposive sample that includes individuals, documents, situations, events, processes, times, and other aspects that can further develop our target area of information. Strauss (1987) and others use the term *theoretical sample* to indicate that the choice of the next subjects and situations is determined "on analytic grounds" for the purposes of developing and extending theory. Since this is covered by the term *purposive sampling* in general usage as well as in chapter 8, that term is used here.

Analytic induction calls for finding commonalities in the data leading first to a description and then to an explanation of the regularity. We also check the proposed explanation against already collected data to see how well it fits.

Where it does not, as in making over an ill-fitting dress or suit, we move back and forth between checking and modifying until the proposed explanation accounts for the data. If we are stumped by cases that don't fit, we go back to these or similar cases for information that permits appropriate adjustment to fit them as well. In this manner, we gradually develop an understanding of the phenomenon and a theory or explanation of how it works that is grounded in our observations. The analysis process may be deferred until we leave the field as a result of having become **saturated**, meaning that new observations cease to add much to previous observations.[4]

By contrast, the **constant comparison method** involves the researcher in analysis from the very start along with observation. Each item in the notes is coded in terms of the dimension or concept of which it is an indicator. New indicators of each concept are sought until the same kind of instances is found repeatedly and the concept is said to be saturated. Concepts are linked with other concepts in a theory or explanation of the phenomena. This explanation is constantly compared with new data from the field, in which we try to find negative instances, borderline instances, key examples—all the kinds of examples noted in chapter 9 on conceptual analysis, for we are engaging in the same process. It is a funnellike process as the range of new informants and situations is increasingly focused on ones that will add to and test previous formulations. Once core concepts and explanations are well developed ("densified") with detail and example, the funnel is reversed to broaden sample choice, trying to find negative cases that show the limits of the explanation and the generality of the theory. This may lead to the choice of new sites of study and a comparison of findings at the new sites with those of the old cross-site comparison.

Note the role of emerging explanation or theory in controlling the direction of the study and therefore directing purposive sampling in the constant comparative method. Cases are chosen to "flesh out" description, densify theory conceptualization, and test and extend the formulations.

For example, Gouldner (1954) studied a factory and found that workers never talked back to supervisors, did what they were told, had a schedule, and left repairs to maintenance workers even though that meant interrupting production. He considered these to be evidence of the construct "bureaucratization." (Note that whereas the quantitative researcher might build a scale consisting of indicators to measure bureaucratization that would be administered to workers, Gouldner inferred it from the many indicators of the concept across the cases observed.) At a contrasting work site, a mine, he focused his attention on the same indicators and found that workers stood up to their supervisors, made repairs themselves, rotated jobs, and had no factorylike schedules. In fact, the track-laying gang, for example, would be given only general instructions about where to work, and the supervisor would ask them how long

---

4. Be careful about declaring that saturation has been reached, for as Patton (1980) comments: "The moment you cease observing, pack your bags, and leave the field, you will get a remarkably clear insight about that one critical activity you should have observed . . . but didn't" (p. 195).

it might take. He considered these behaviors to be indicators of a lack of "bureaucratization," concluding that it was greater in the factory than in the mine (Gouldner, 1954, in Orenstein and Phillips, 1978, p. 361). With both positive and negative examples helping to define the construct, he could go on to focus on its effects.

The process just described is an example of the efforts to increase the credibility of qualitative methods through descriptive procedures that improve and discipline the process without restricting it to a set formula. Glaser and Strauss (1967) described guidelines for analytic induction intended to develop "grounded theory" and had considerable impact. They have been joined by others, including Bogdan and Biklen (1982), Guba and Lincoln (1987), Levine (1985), Miles and Huberman (1984), Strauss (1987), and Strauss and Corbin (1990).

- Most formulations begin with the observer as a sponge, listening intently and observing open-endedly.
- With the constant comparison method, as the target emerges, so do explanatory hunches that guide the further selection of cases and observations.
- Purposive sampling instead of random sampling is used to extend and densify our understanding, to test our explanation, to find the limits of its generality, and to ensure the validity of our information.
- Hunches are tested on new cases, modified as needed to fit, further tested, further detailed and related to other hunches, further modified and retested, and so on until reaching saturation. At that point, further efforts add little or nothing.
- Practitioners continue to provide discipline to qualitative methods without restricting them to a formula; Glaser and Strauss's grounded theory is an important landmark in this work.

Informants

As noted earlier, people being studied differ from subjects in experimentation in that they are treated as individuals to learn from—an egalitarian perspective. Qualitative methodologists see this as more than a difference in designation; it involves an attitudinal change on the part of the researcher as well. It has implications for how we interact with the people observed and how we treat the data obtained from them.

Bouchard (1976) makes an additional distinction between respondents and informants. The former are random or systematic samples and may be considered replicable. **Informants** are selected for their sensitivity, knowledge, and insights into their situation, their willingness to talk about it, and their ability to help gain access to new situations. Especially sensitive are persons who have less stake in the system (and so may be less defensive about it) and those who view it from a different standpoint than more central players. Examples are persons who come from another culture, social class, or community and who can contrast it with their previous experience. As newcomers, they are especially likely to note things that others might take for granted. Individuals with a new role or status are similarly sensitive; they have left one role but are not yet comfortable in the other. All such people are likely to view their new situation in terms of their old role, a potential bias but one that can often be allowed for if we are aware of it.

Other informant types may similarly have hidden agendas: rebels or malcontents welcome the opportunity to "get things off their chest." These people and former insiders who lost power are usually eager to share their views of current insiders, most likely in a negative manner. Some persons who are flattered by the attention are likely to say whatever the observer wants to hear in order to maintain that attention. Some persons are so much a part of the scene that they are too well entrenched to worry about repercussions from communicating with outsiders. They may be harder to tap, however, since they have the least to gain from doing so—unless they magnify their own roles in past actions, a problem to be sensitive to.

The most desirable informant is the "natural" (Bouchard, 1976); he or she has a perspective on the situation and is able to communicate it. Whyte's (1955) "Doc" is the prototype of such individuals. Doc had a perspective not only on his situation but also on the role that Whyte should play in the community, steered Whyte to situations, and introduced him to persons helpful in the study. Every researcher should be so lucky! Some researchers have used informants as their eyes and ears in situations where they were unable to be present because they had to be elsewhere or would be too obvious or unwelcome. Dalton (1959, 1967) even had informants introduce certain topics into a situation so that reactions could be observed. His combination of experimental and qualitative methods illustrates that it is up to the ingenuity of the investigator to use methods in ways appropriate to the target situation.

The main caveat is that the observer must always be concerned with the questions "Why is this person willing to talk to me? What point of view is she using?" Only with satisfactory answers can we determine the extent of bias that must be taken into account as the information is used.

- Informants help the observer understand the views of the people being observed, introduce new individuals and situations, and may teach the observer how to behave unobtrusively.
- Such cooperation is not without its price, and observers must ask themselves, "Why is this person talking to me and being so helpful?"
- Informants are often marginal persons who have less stake in the status quo or are not constrained by it. They may therefore be atypical, and their information must be appropriately discounted (taken with a grain of salt).

Data Validity and Triangulation

Purposive sampling is also directed toward verification of the validity of the data through **triangulation**. The term is borrowed from surveying. A property boundary can be established by simply measuring in the right direction from an established point, but it is more accurately found using two established points as the baseline of a triangle to establish a third. Denzin (1978) outlined three useful types of triangulation: (1) data triangulation, using multiple sources of data across time, space, and persons; (2) investigator triangulation, using multiple investigators; and (3) method triangulation, using multiple methods.

Data triangulation is the most common of the three and involves the use of two or more sources to establish factual accuracy. For example, we confirm an informant's recall of a meeting by checking the secretary's minutes. Denzin (1978) argues for triangulating data across samples of time, space, and person—all three. His point is well taken. For example, a finding that a school board's meeting procedures appear to discourage minority parents from presenting their concerns should be checked not only at more than one meeting but also with more than one set of parents and perhaps with regard to more than one issue. This is similar to sampling to establish the borderline of generality of a finding—external validity (GP)—or of a construct (conceptual analysis).

Data triangulation can involve a variety of comparisons. We can compare observations with past records for invariability. Answers to different questions involving the same concept should be consistent. Letting informants know we will be talking to others may make them more careful. Verbal responses can be checked against actual behavior, solitary behavior against that constrained by the presence of others. Nonverbal behavior is often a giveaway that contradicts verbal behavior—a teacher says she is concerned about the welfare of lower-class students but does other things while answering their questions or gives them less time to respond. Volunteered responses can be compared with answers to questions on the assumption that the latter may have an element of "polite agreement." Triangulation may be particularly important where we seek the covert meaning of a situation that differs from the expressed meaning.

Investigator triangulation refers to obtaining similar perceptions from different investigators of the same phenomenon. Thus we might compare the reports of two observers of a teacher's lesson for similarities.

Method triangulation uses different methods to assess the same aspect of a phenomenon. For example, we might compare observations with interviews or with questionnaire responses or compare observations of achievement in that classroom with measures of achievement (this is similar to the multi-measure, multimethod procedure, page 276).

Although triangulation is intended to provide support for a finding, as Mathison (1988) suggests, the result is often inconsistency or contradiction. The search for an explanation of the inconsistency frequently leads to new insights. In tracking teachers' activities with a new curriculum, Mathison noted that teachers reported including mathematical activities in unplanned times of the day, but a triangulation corroboration found only 14 instances in 200 classroom observations. The discrepancy turned up the fact that there was almost no unplanned time.

Taylor and Bogdan (1984) suggest that we discount the value of the information in terms not only of consistency over sources but also of such questions as these: Was it volunteered or solicited? (Just asking a question may make salient a point usually ignored.) Who was present? (People often reveal things when authority figures are not present.) Was it established through direct observation or hearsay? Finally, when reading others' research, ask who paid for it.

Perhaps the best advice is this:

> Triangulation is a state of mind. If you *self-consciously* set out to collect and double-check findings, using multiple sources and modes of evidence, the verification process will largely be built into the data-gathering process, and little more need be done than to report on one's procedures. (Miles and Huberman, 1984, p. 235)

- Triangulation is the process of using more than one source to confirm information: confirming data from different sources, confirming observations from different observers, and confirming information from different data collection methods.
- Where disconfirming information is found, seeking reasons for the contradiction frequently points to directions for extending or modifying explanations instead of discarding them.

Fieldnotes and Memos

Fieldnotes are the observers' records of what has been observed—descriptions of the individuals, the setting, and what happened, recapitulating the conversation and other interaction as completely as possible. Geertz's (1973) term *thick description* aptly captures their character. Fieldnotes should especially try to capture the language used as it shows how people define one another. Taylor (1977, pp. 117–138), for example, studied a mental institution and found that the attendants categorized patients in terms of their dominant interaction with them as "trouble-makers," "soilers," "vegetables," "runaways," "headbangers," and so on. Notes are recorded as factually as possible; because all description selects aspects to emphasize, however, they preserve what the observer believed was important.

This leads to a second aspect of the fieldnotes, the observers' reflections on the processes of selecting what was important to capture; their behavior in the situation (comfort, obtrusiveness, apparent impact on others, treatment by others); ideas or hypotheses explaining what was occurring; problems in observing, recording, or coding; suggestions for next steps and from whence they were derived; and so on. It is customary to keep these separate from the fieldnotes so that opinion is isolated from fact. Such comments are labeled *O.C.*

for "observer comment" and indented or boxed or written on new pages as personal **memos**. They assist in understanding our processes.

Typically, fieldnotes consist of a chronological account of a venture. They may include relevant incidents from outside the formal observation process as well—comments elicited at a party, reflections on an interview from an informant encountered later, and so on. They may include diagrams of the situation showing the relative positions of the participants, furniture, and the like. They typically reflect on such things as a description of the room, the dress of the participants, and the room furnishings so as to convey the context adequately. Figure 15.2 gives an example of fieldnotes (the inset material labeled "O.C." is observer comments). Only about one-fifth of the full set of fieldnotes is reproduced. An excellent example, the notes include an accidental contact at a party long after the observation that led to an insightful observer comment.

FIGURE 15.2   An example of fieldnotes. (From R. C. Bogdan and S. K. Biklen, *Qualitative Research for Education*, pp. 75–76. Copyright © 1982 Allyn and Bacon.)

March 24, 1980
Joe McCloud
11:00 a.m. to 12:30 p.m.
Westwood High
6th Set of Notes

The Fourth Period
Class in Marge's Room

I arrived at Westwood High at five minutes to eleven, the time Marge told me her fourth period started. I was dressed as usual: sport shirt, chino pants, and a Woolrich parka. The fourth period is the only time during the day when all the students who are in the "neurologically impaired/learning disability" program, better known as "Marge's program," come together. During the other periods, certain students in the program, two or three or four at most, come to her room for help with the work they are getting in other regular high school classes.

It was a warm fortyish, promise of a spring day. There was a police patrol wagon, the kind that has benches in the back that are used for large busts, parked in the back of the big parking lot that is in front of the school. No one was sitting in it and I never heard its reason for being there. In the circular drive in front of the school was parked a United States Army car. It had insignias on the side and was a khaki color. As I walked from my car, a balding fortyish man in an Army uniform came out of the building and went to the car and sat down. Four boys and a girl also walked out of the school. All were white. They had on old dungarees and colored stenciled t-shirts with spring jackets over them. One of the boys, the tallest of the four, called out, "oink, oink, oink." This was done as he sighted the police vehicle in the back.

O.C.:   This was strange to me in that I didn't think that the kids were into "the police as pigs." Somehow I associated that with another time, the early 1970's. I'm going to have to come to grips with the assumptions I have about high school due to my own experience. Sometimes I feel like Westwood is entirely different from my high school and yet this police car incident reminded me of mine.

Classes were changing when I walked down the halls. As usual there was the boy with girl standing here and there by the lockers. There were three couples that I saw. There was the occasional shout. There were no teachers outside the doors.

O.C.:   The halls generally seem to be relatively unsupervised during class changes.

Two black girls I remember walking down the hall together. They were tall and thin and had their hair elaborately braided with beads all through them. I stopped by the office to tell Mr. Talbot's (the principal) secretary that I was in the building. She gave me a warm smile.

O.C.:   I feel quite comfortable in the school now. Somehow I feel like I belong. As I walk down the halls some teachers say hello. I have been going out of my way to say hello to kids that I pass. Twice I've been in a stare-down with kids passing in the hall. Saying, "How ya' doin'?" seems to disalarm them.

I walked into Marge's class and she was standing in the front of the room with more people than I had ever seen in the room save for her homeroom which is right after second period. She looked like she was talking to the class or was just about to start. She was dressed as she had been on my other visits—clean, neat, well-dressed but casual. Today she had on a striped blazer, a white blouse and dark slacks. She looked up at me, smiled and said: "Oh, I have a lot more people here now than the last time."

O.C.:   This was in reference to my other visits during other periods where there are only a few students. She seems self-conscious about having such a small group of students to be responsible for. Perhaps she compares herself with the regular teachers who have classes of thirty or so.

There were two women in their late twenties sitting in the room. There was only one chair left. Marge said to me something like: "We have two visitors from the central office today. One is a vocational counselor and the other is a physical therapist," but I don't remember if those were the words. I felt embarrassed coming in late. I sat down in the only chair available next to one of the women from the central office. They had on skirts and carried their pocketbooks, much more dressed up than the teachers I've seen. They sat there and observed.

Below is the seating arrangement of the class today:

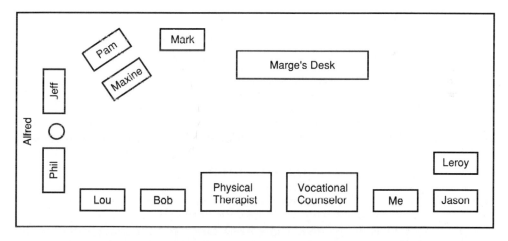

Alfred (Mr. Armstrong, the teacher's aide) walked around but when he stood in one place, it was over by Phil and Jeff. Marge walked about near her desk during her talk which started by saying to the class: "Now remember, tomorrow is a fieldtrip to the Rollway Company. We all meet in the usual place, by the bus, in front of the main entrance at 8:30. Mrs. Sharp wanted me to tell you that the tour of Rollway is not specifically for you. It's not like the trip to G.M. They took you to places where you were likely to be able to get jobs. Here, it's just a general tour that everybody goes on. Many of the jobs that you will see are not for you. Some are just for people with engineering degrees. You'd better wear comfortable shoes because you may be walking for two or three hours." Maxine and Mark said: "Ooh," in protest to the walking.

(continued)

She paused and said in a demanding voice: "OK, any questions? You are all going to be there. (Pause) I want you to take a blank card and write down some questions so you have things to ask at the plant." She began passing out cards and at this point Jason, who was sitting next to me made a tutting sound of disgust, and said: "We got to do this?" Marge said: "I know this is too easy for you, Jason." This was said in a sarcastic way but not like a strong put down.

O.C.:   It was like sarcasm between two people who know each other well. Marge has known many of these kids for a few years. I have to explore the implications of that for her relations with them.

FIGURE 15.2 *continued*

Note the wealth of detail (thick description!) in this fragment from the notes. Not knowing ahead of time what will be significant, the observer records what he was wearing as well as the attire of the important others being observed. Persons entering and leaving the school help establish the atmosphere, as do the notes about who was in the halls doing what and the observer's interaction with the students there. The use of a map of the classroom shows the relationships of students, teacher, teacher's aide, and observers. Further, note that every attempt was made to record the conversation verbatim. There is even a note that a quotation may not be exact because the observer was embarrassed about coming in late (in the full paragraph just above the class diagram).

Note also the many observer comments marked "O.C." They include introspections by the observer about his feelings, explanations of the teacher's comments, evaluative observations (unsupervised halls), and questions to check up on later—material set off from the factual observations themselves yet important to understanding those observations.

What about video or audio recordings in place of notes? Certainly these capture conversation and give-and-take more faithfully than fieldnotes. They can be useful if the observer can't be present or wishes to make an unobtrusive record with hidden equipment. Their transcription can be very expensive as well as difficult, and of course, if only the audio portion is recorded, we lose the nonverbal aspects, which can be crucial to understanding covert meanings. Extensive recording results in an overwhelming volume of detail, yet we still have the job of making notes to extract the important information.

A problem Miles and Huberman (1984) note is that we become so fascinated with the flood of particulars that we "forget to *think*, to make deeper and more general sense of what is happening, to begin to explain it in a conceptually coherent way" (p. 69). Thinking is carrying on a conversation with oneself, and memos are records of those conversations. Strauss (1987) argues that memoing should take precedence over coding or data recording so that the idea will not be lost. To illustrate different types, he reproduces 16 pages of memos from a project on the impact of medical technology on hospitals and usefully comments on their intent and actual effect (pp. 111–127). He suggests that if we do not have time to memo on the spot, we at least make a note to write the memo, then set aside time for memoing as well as coding and analysis. Figure 15.3 is an example of a memo from a study of educational innovations in Miles and Huberman (1984). The researchers note that this

Memo: Career patterns 2/22/80

In a general sense, people are riding the innovations in a state of transition; they are on their way *from* somewhere *to* somewhere *via* the project...

Where could people be going? They could be going

—*up:* from a classroom to a supervisory or administrative role or to a higher administration slot. Innovations are a lot faster than waiting for someone *else* to move on or going back for a *degree*. They get you visibility and good positioning. If it gets institutionalized, you get institutionalized with it in a new role. Also, they're less brutal than getting promotions by doing in the person above you and more convenient than having to move away to move up.

—*away:* from teaching by easing into a part-time or more flexible job. These projects tend to be marginal, loosely administered (although Tindale [one of the schools] is contrary), transition-easing. They also can allow for permutations, as in the up-and-away pattern Cary may be following at Plummet.

—*in:* the remedial programs are less choosy about formal credentials. They provide access to civil services like education to people with weird backgrounds. Aides can get positioned to become certified teachers; people from business or the arts can come into a marginal or experimental universe and ease gradually into a more formal role incumbency.

At "my" sites, the innovation services the purposes of two teachers moving into supervisory roles ("helping teachers"). One has now become Title I coordinator. The administrator at this site (Masepa) is now well positioned for promotion, since he has won (ECRI [the experimental program] has been mandated). At Banestown, the aide moves "in"; the head lab teacher does what the teacher at Masepa did with Title I: She gets the other half of her job in the same sector, thereby becoming "specialized" and ready to move "up" as *her* patron, the reading supervisor, moves "up" herself into a higher administrative post. The other lab teacher moves (back) "in" from non-teaching with a part-time post.

All this is very tentative, but it might focus us on this dimension, which is being independently flagged by 2–3 of us.

It is especially worth keeping track, as we dictate and code, of where these people have come from and where they are, or think they are, on their way to. I suggest we ask each informant:

—a little more directly, *why* he/she is doing this, in terms of roles and role changes.

—what he/she expects to be doing in 2–3 years

—if he/she has a sense of being in a transitional period.

FIGURE 15.3 An integrating memo that guided data collection. (From M. B. Miles and A. M. Huberman, *Qualitative Data Analysis: A Book of New Methods*, p. 70. Copyright © 1984 by Sage Publications Inc. Reprinted by permission of Sage Publications Inc.)

memo pulls data from many sites and reformulates them around the issue of career patterns. It occurred partway through the data collection, so it affected subsequent collection and suggested specific means of doing so.

■ Fieldnotes are the observer's record of observations. They can be made while in the field if this can be done unobtrusively and without changing the behavior of the people observed. Otherwise, they should be completed as soon as possible after leaving the field.

> - Fieldnotes should include as much verbatim conversation as possible, as well as notes regarding context.
> - Comments, inferences, and judgments should be kept separate from observations as observer comments or memos.
> - Memos are used to record hunches and the gradual development of an explanation or theory.

Ethics

Because the participant observer faces more problems in the field with less support than most researchers, it is important to discuss the issue here in addition to the discussion of ethics in general in chapter 25. Participant observers must make decisions about ethical questions on the spot without the help of subject protection committees or advisers. In some instances, illegal acts may be witnessed and should be reported. The problem is whether the outsider's own sense of justice should be substituted for whatever is the norm in the situation being observed. Bosk (1979), for instance, confronted the question of his responsibility to a patient and her relatives when he had witnessed a nursing or medical error. He decided that he would let the system handle these cases and that his disclosure of that system would be more effective than "tilting at windmills in one or two select cases" (p. 200). This is a fairly common ethical choice: to ignore the transgressions of individuals we are personally involved with in favor of making public those of the institution and its administration. The latter are perceived as the real culprits in need of reform. This is not to imply that this is an improper decision, but if made, the socially easier choice coincides with achieving the desired effect.

Maintaining confidences is especially difficult for the researcher who reveals witnessing illegal acts, since immunity from subpoena is not extended to scientists. Humphreys (1975), for instance, caused quite a stir when he reported that to study homosexual activity in public places, he had acted as lookout in public toilets and had learned the names of participating individuals by tracing their license numbers. When Humphreys learned that these data could be subpoenaed, he destroyed them.

All participant observers encounter the problem of ambiguity in inter-personal relationships.

> Once the field researcher becomes involved in the diaIy life of the community . . . he develops personal friendships. . . . These friendships are usually quite important to everyone concerned, but they are tinged with doubt over authenticity. On both sides there is often doubt as to motives, and the ·limitations of the study versus the intimacy of friendship. At times this ambiguity can become quite disturbing. . . . There are no easy solutions . . . and this ambiguity . . . must be dealt with on a day to day basis as friendships develop. If the field worker is careful to keep confidences, . . . attempts to be as dependable as humanly possible, and eventually discusses this problem with people for whom it is a matter of concern, the ambiguity of personal and professional roles will be eased. . . . Field researchers

often get so involved in observing and recording . . . that they forget to be human themselves. They forget to share their own feelings and personal histories. . . . On the other hand, this sharing makes it difficult to maintain objectivity and should for that reason be continually written about in field notes. (Fitzsimmons et al., 1973, p. A-15)

Along these same lines, P. Cusick (personal communication, July 28, 1980) writes:

In every study I've done, I've . . . found people . . . with whom I could relate on a personal level . . . and [used them] to help with understanding how people really behave in the organization. All that is fine and according to the book. . . . The problem is that when one joins a small, normative unit he agrees to abide by an ethical agreement . . . and he has to internalize those ethical constraints. [The result is] . . . when writing the study I was constrained by all the . . . internalized constraints that I took from those small affective groups. . . . I never felt it quite so strongly before, but prior studies had been of adolescents, not adults like myself. One doesn't tell tales on or even take a dispassionate view of his friends. . . . The argot of "informants" . . . etc. is one that denies an affective relation. . . . All that research talk is just a little too glib and quick. It's a paradox of course; affective involvement is essential to the study's success, but involvement places a whole set of (from a researcher's perspective) irrational constraints on the process.

- Ethical problems are inevitable in qualitative research, and many ethical decisions must be made on the spot without the support of committee discussion or ethicists.
- The betrayal of the bond of intimate friendship formed with the informants when the report is made public is always a problem.
- Serious ethical problems arise when observations include acts that are either legally or morally reportable to authorities. To report them at the least interrupts and more probably terminates the study. Not doing so can have serious consequences both for persons being abused and for the tacitly consenting observer and must be rationalized.
- Researchers and their data are not immune from subpoena. Therefore, data that might harmfully identify individuals should probably either not be collected or be quickly destroyed.

DATA REDUCTION: CODING, ANALYSIS, AND SYNTHESIS

Fieldnotes pile up rapidly and become massive as observation proceeds. Lila Sussman's fieldnotes for one day of observation at an elementary school amounted to 34 typewritten pages (Orenstein and Phillips, 1978, p. 327). Some studies run to many file drawers of notes. Clearly, data reduction is important, and Miles and Huberman (1984), who suggest a general overall pattern for analysis, indicate that a "contact summary report" is a good way to start. This one-page summary is completed after each major contact, reviewing such questions as "What were the main issues or themes?" "What, in summary, was the information obtained (or still needed) on your target questions?" "What else was salient, interesting, illuminating, or important?" "What are the next or remaining questions for this contact?" This not only summarizes a group of fieldnotes but also helps organize the next steps. In this mode, analysis is concomitant with data gathering.

Coding

Coding and book indexing have certain parallels. Did you ever turn to the index of a book to learn what it is about? The topics with many entries are clearly central to at least certain parts of the book. The "see" and "see also" references tell something about the interrelations of topics. The topics with several levels of subentries suggest the hierarchical structure—which topics subsume which others—and therefore are central to the organization of the book. A good index does more than simply make the material accessible; it communicates the author's organization of it. The indexer has analyzed the author's text to determine importance and relations of topics and inductively created an index that reflects that material. In addition, an indexer familiar with the field will relate the author's material to the commonly accepted concepts and structure of the field where a reader might expect to find them.

Now consider the problem of "indexing" (that is, coding) fieldnotes. Whereas a book has some structure, which the author imposed on the material to help readers understand it, fieldnotes are just running observations or interviews interspersed with comments. Their only organization is chronological. **Coding** makes all these different kinds of notes accessible, like indexing, but more than that, it helps us learn what is significant as we see aspects that repeat themselves—index items with many entries. As we examine these characteristics, relationships among them suggest themselves—the complex and "see" items in the index. These relationships may be organized into a theory to fit these particular data or may fit existing theory in the field so that some kind of organizational structure accounts for these characteristics and their interrelationships—the hierarchical complex entries of an index. So there are clearly helpful parallels to good indexing, keeping in mind that good coding does more than provide access to the data: it organizes them, providing lenses through which they can be viewed in a relational structure. Book indexers have most of this done by the author; coders of fieldnotes must inductively develop the organization out of the items they index.[5]

---

5. Throughout this chapter, it is assumed that the orientation of the qualitative researcher is inductive, but given an existing structure, as in an evaluation of a program to train the jobless, which suggests the topics that ought to be found in coding and their relationships, we can use this structure to analyze fieldnotes to validate the program. The good qualitative researcher, however, will also look for things outside this structure, since often these are as important to the study as the expected product. See "Goal-free Evaluation" on page 530.

So besides the summarizing and the memoing discussed earlier, both of which are steps in analysis, the most basic process is coding. In coding, we assign a descriptive word or phrase to each unit of notes. It is usually abbreviated for ease of use (numbers are shorter but removed from the concept involved). Where do these codes come from? What we code depends on what we consider relevant and important. Miles and Huberman (1984), for instance, note that codes may be descriptive, merely labeling the salient aspect of the text. Consider this text:

> Before class started, it was obvious that Johnson had decided to videotape the segment on statistics and place it in the Instruction Material Center so students could review it at their convenience. But it was equally obvious that he had never handled a video camera before and, even after class started, he was still fiddling with the equipment, apparently attempting to get it to work.

In a study concerned with instructional technology, this might be coded "vid" for videotape or "cl vid" for in-class videotape or, because there was not sufficient training, "NT/c/vid."

Often such descriptive coding is a first step to "see what is there." It helps to make a coding list and to examine it to see where there are apparent redundancies and categories that can be combined. It will suggest categories that ought to be hierarchically related so that there are different levels of coding. But *examine the material itself before making these changes*, since closer examination may reveal distinctions not conveyed by the code titles, leading to their revision. The coding list may suggest relationships that can be examined in terms of the material so coded to see what is really going on.

Growing out of this initial coding, or if the original intent of the project were clear, this same material might also be coded at an interpretive level in which we infer the intent of use of the technology: *rev* (content review), *sk* (skill learning), *sk p* (skill practice), and so on. At a still deeper level of analysis, usually arrived at later, we might code patterns of activities, themes, causal links, and other more complex aspects that relate to the theory we are building. A repeated pattern might be the instructor who decides abruptly with no training or forethought to introduce technology into the instruction, so this motif might be assigned a code (imp instr—impulsive instructor).

Many qualitative researchers, including Strauss (1987), argue for the approach of reading the fieldnotes and inductively picking out the important aspects as provisional codes that can be revised later as necessary. Certainly, our initial ideas about what is significant will bear heavily on what we look for. How to start?

- Sometimes it helps to observe or read accounts of contrasting groups so as to become sensitized to what is different about them.
- Alternatively, cut a copy of fieldnotes into segments, each containing an important aspect. Sorting them into piles of similar material forces us to decide what important aspects differentiate them and also indicates the frequency with which such characteristics occur.

- Still another approach is reading notes for common phrases as well as surprising, counterintuitive, and unexpected material. Searching for their causes is often revealing.
- Seek working hypotheses about things that follow one another regularly. These will yield classifications and principles that permit us to sort the data and observe the consistency or inconsistency of that regularity, testing with provisional trials until we are satisfied with the explanation that emerges.

Strauss (1987) suggests, as a way of getting started, coding "conditions," "interaction among actors," "strategies and tactics," and "consequences" (pp. 28–29). To find conditions, look for words like *because, since, as,* and *on account of.* To find consequences, look for *as a result of, because of,* and similar expressions. Categories will evolve as research proceeds, meaning that field-notes will have to be recoded along the way. But this approach does result in well-grounded codes, tightly knit into the theory being developed. Look for phrases or terms used repeatedly by the persons studied, then ask questions about those items and their significance to get at the kinds of codes to use. (See also Strauss and Corbin, 1990.)

Strauss (1987) suggests moving to dimensions (abstractions, concepts, constructs, generalizations) as quickly as possible, each of which will suggest comparative cases to be examined for these dimensions as well. For examples, see Strauss (1987) and Turner (1981).

By way of providing more structure, especially for beginners, Miles and Huberman (1984, p. 57) suggest Lofland's (1971) generic scheme code:

> Acts: action in a situation that is temporarily brief, consuming only a few seconds, minutes, or hours.
>
> Activities: action in a setting of more major duration—days, weeks, months—constituting significant elements of people's involvement.
>
> Meanings: the verbal productions of participants that define and direct action.
>
> Participation: people's holistic involvement in, or adaptation to, a situation or setting under study.
>
> Relationships: interrelationships among several persons considered simultaneously.
>
> Settings: the entire setting under study conceived as the unit of analysis.

Bogdan and Biklen (1982, pp. 157–162) provide a different scheme:

> Setting/context codes: general description of the setting that allows us to place the study in a larger context—for example, descriptions of elementary schools.
>
> Definition of the situation codes: how subjects understand, define, or perceive their setting or relevant study topics—for example, feminist perspectives.
>
> Perspectives held by subjects: ways of thinking shared by subjects toward the setting or some aspect of it; try to capture shared understandings—for example, "be honest but not cruel," a common recognition of what is best in informing parents in a medical setting.

Subjects' ways of thinking about people and objects: understandings of each other, of outsiders, and objects that make up their world—for example, teachers differentiate students as "immature" or "ready for school."

Process codes: sequences of events, transition from one status to another, changes over time—for example, turning points, benchmarks, stages, phases, careers.

Activity codes: regularly occurring kinds of behavior—for example, showing films, morning exercises.

Event codes: particular happenings that occur infrequently or once—for example, a strike, a pageant.

Strategy codes: ways people accomplish things, tactics, methods, techniques, ploys—for example, how students get out of hall duty.

Relationship and social structure codes: cliques, friendships, romances, coalitions, enemies, and other regular behavior not defined on the organizational chart.

Methods: problems, joys, dilemmas of the research process; usually consists of observer comments.

Tesch (1990) suggests four directions for qualitative research: (1) to study the characteristics of language, (2) to discover regularities of action, (3) to determine meaning through understanding of text or action, and (4) to discover patterns through reflection. These call for a continuum of kinds of analysis, ranging from very structured analysis of word patterns for the first to holistic treatments for the last. Tesch describes 26 types of qualitative analysis.

Without word processing, codes are usually placed in the margin of the typescript of fieldnotes, and some segments may have more than one code. The mechanical problem is to get together all the material dealing with a single code or related codes. This can be done by cutting up copies of the typescript and putting the slips into folders or by placing them on cards that can be sorted into piles.

More often, researchers now use a computer with a special program designed for qualitative analysis. One of the most sophisticated, Qualog (Shelly and Sibert, 1986; Sibert and Shelly, 1985, 1987), is a mainframe program and is especially useful for theory building. For a personal computer, programs like The Ethnograph (Seidel, Kjolseth, and Seymour, 1988) for MS-DOS machines and HyperQual (Padilla, 1990) for the Macintosh are available. Tesch (1990) has a valuable discussion of the process of analysis on computers and examines current desktop computer programs. The big task is typing the material into the computer. Although scanners that can shortcut this step for already existing documents are available, they are not yet completely reliable or widely used. Computers have the considerable advantage that they can quickly compile a list of the most frequently used words in the notes, which can be scanned for suggestions of coding categories. Search commands can be used to find text indicative of a particular code anywhere in the fieldnotes. Codes or "tags" are easily assigned to sections of the text. All the material for a code can be printed out for scrutiny, recoded, moved, and otherwise manipulated. Codes can be linked and networked, and some programs have the capacity to permit construction of graphics depicting the code structure. Because it is difficult to skim material on a computer screen, repeated printing, reading and skimming, recoding, and reprinting are required.

Coding and writing memos go hand in hand because the memos capture the inferences and abstractions that lie behind the coding and begin to unite the categories into a theoretical structure. The material in the various codes provides the operational definitions of the concepts or constructs captured by the codes and bears the same relationship that measures bear to the constructs they represent. Rename codes as you refine your constructs to ensure that titles are consistent with the examples they are intended to encompass.

Processes you have already learned—conceptual analysis from chapter 9 and construct validity from chapter 11—are useful in developing and revising codes. Drawing model, borderline, related, and contrary examples from field-notes to provide a conceptual analysis of a code can be very helpful in elucidating what is at its core and what are its boundaries. These data, in turn, demonstrate the construct validity of that particular code title. But whereas in measurement the construct remains constant and the researcher seeks measures that fit for construct validity, with code development the examples in the data must be matched and the code and its definition changed to fit. The process results in congruence of construct and operationally obtained data (construct validity), but what is changed to fit differs from quantitative (the operational definition is changed or discarded if it doesn't match the construct) to qualitative (the definition of the construct is discarded or changed if it doesn't fit the data).

Conclusion Drawing and Verification

How to proceed to find interrelationships seems to vary with the individual. Bosk (1979) kept a running analysis separate from his fieldnotes. Gans (1962) abstracted generalizations from his field diary onto more than 200 cards, which he sorted and classified. These were digested into notes listing the major generalizations. He then reread the diary and wrote the report. Strauss (1987) suggests finding families of categories and core categories that represent the higher-level abstractions making up the theoretical network. Note that these all involve writing down ideas. Putting ideas on paper, as noted in chapter 6, does more than provide a record; it helps us organize our thoughts.

Miles and Huberman (1984) find that matrices and diagrams that display the interrelationships among variables, persons, and so on are of considerable help in organizing the data, finding relationships, and eliminating hypotheses. Table 15.1 is excerpted from an example of a matrix used to summarize the results of a school improvement program across sites. Sites were arranged from top to bottom as having high, medium, or low impact. Program objectives, the direct positive and negative results, and the indirect and side effects for each site are indicated. Sources of data were indicated by *U* for user, *A* for administrator, *C* for counselor, *P* for parent, *E* for evaluator, and *S* for student. Underlined letters indicate a mention by at least two persons. An *x* indicates the presence of a dissenting or conflicting opinion.

Such matrices enable us to see many things. Do administrators always

TABLE 15.1   Matrix Summarizing the Effects of a School Improvement Program across Different Schools

| Site | Objectives | Direct Effects | | Indirect and Side Effects | |
		Positive	Negative	Positive	Negative
Masepa (externally developed innovation)	Improvement in full range of language arts skills More on-task behavior Improved discipline	Improved skills: vocabulary U, A, P; spelling U, A; phonetics Ux; punctuation U; reading comprehension Ux, E; reading decoding U; grammar U; written expression U Low achievers more productive Ux	Retention levels not good U Too little diversity U Student fatigue U	Concentration, study skills Fewer discipline problems U, A More attentive to errors U Better academic self-concept U More enjoyment, enthusiasm U, A	Some lagging, failing mastery tests U Boredom U
Carson (locally developed innovation)	Increased achievement Clearer career interests Friendliness Improved self-concept as a learner More internal locus of control	Career knowledge U, A, C		Achievement composite (use of resources) E Better classroom attitude U Attitude to school E, U Self-concept as a learner (high school) E Friendliness E Self-understanding U	Little effect on achievement U
Burton (externally developed innovation)	Knowledge and practical skills re political/ government/ legal processes (voter education, state government, individual rights)	Concept learning by being in different roles U Experienced active learning approach A	No effects discernible U		

SOURCE   Adapted from M. B. Miles and A. M. Huberman, *Qualitative Data Analysis*, p. 162. Copyright © 1984 Sage Publications Inc.

show up only on the positive comment side? Apparently. Are locally developed innovations more successful? Not according to these data. They make clear where we have data and where they are missing. Like Mendeleev's periodic table of the chemical elements, they permit prediction and search for missing entries, sometimes with useful and surprising results.

Matrices and memos are useful for another reason: they provide an "audit trail" that others can follow to reconstruct how an analysis developed, to check the translation fidelity of constructs, and to determine the logical validity of conclusions. Those who seek greater rigor in qualitative methods increasingly suggest that leaving a clear audit trail is important for several reasons. Besides letting others check our thinking, leaving a trail makes the process more explicit and thus provides perspective on how appropriately analysis is proceeding. Further, it does so without in any way restricting the options available to us.

- Observation and interviewing result in massive amounts of data, well beyond human memory capacity to retain and integrate as a whole.
- Coding, an inductive reasoning process, involves extracting similarities in behavior and/or perceptions from the data and abstracting the important concepts and dimensions for easier access and retrieval.
- Codes are the concepts eventually used in the explanation, and the coded data are the operational definitions of the concepts.
- Coding and memoing go hand in hand; memos capture the inferences underlying the codes.
- Various generic coding systems have been suggested to assist novices.
- The mechanical aspects of handling the data can be substantial but are increasingly being taken over by specialized computer programs.
- Providing an "audit trail" is important not only for others but also to provide perspective on the process for ourselves en route.

Threats to the Validity of Data: Alternative Explanations

Campbell and Stanley (1963) coined the phrase "threats to validity" for alternative explanations of data that might explain a finding as well as or better than the explanation intended by the researcher. In some cases, the researcher may not be aware of alternatives; in others, he or she may be aware but did not, or could not, protect against them. All research is besieged by such alternatives, some general ones that we can name in advance, others that plague certain research methods, and still others that are unique to a particular study. Even one uneliminated alternative that is apparent to the audience may be sufficient to destroy a consensus, however. So these are serious matters.

Some of the common alternatives were named by Campbell and Stanley (1963) and Cook and Campbell (1979). Although they were established in a treatise dealing with quantitative methods, some have applicability to qualitative methods as well.[6] Although their names are, in one sense, descriptive—mortality, instrument decay, selection—they sometimes bring the wrong picture to mind. **Mortality** refers not to the death of subjects but to individuals dropping out of a group, making it no longer representative. As we shall see, mortality is a particularly serious problem in survey research where we start with a representative sample but selectively lose subjects who do not return the questionnaire. The ones who do return the questionnaire are probably comfortable dealing with the topic, whereas those who are uncomfortable with it do not return it—the mortality factor. So an alternative explanation for conclusions based on returned questionnaires is that they are not representative of the population, only of people comfortable with the topic.

Does mortality apply to qualitative research? It often does. Our original intent is to represent the situation as it is viewed by all participants. But we often wind up with what Sieber (1973) calls an "elite bias," an overweighting of the elite of the system in the selection of informants and in the evaluation of statements. Sieber notes there are many reasons for "gravitating to the elite." Because the elite are the "gatekeepers" who grant access, the observer feels gratitude toward them and is careful to keep on good terms with them. They are likely to be more articulate and give the impression of being better informed about the group. Sieber discovered his bias when he tried to predict the results of a survey he had given teachers. "It became obvious when observing these comparisons that I had unwittingly adopted the elites' version of reality. For example, I overestimated the extent to which teachers felt that the administration accepted criticism" (p. 1353).

Instrument decay is due to a change in the measuring instrument over the course of the study. It refers, for instance, to rules made up in the course of using an observation checklist where, on encountering a situation not provided for by rules for checklist use, the researcher makes up an arbitrary one on the spot. Others using the instrument may make up other rules or, forgetting the decision, make up a different rule for the next instance. Inconsistency in using the instrument may be a reasonable alternative explanation rather than some characteristic of the group, as originally intended.

In qualitative research, the observer is the instrument. We have to wonder how the observer changes in the perception of the observed over the period of the study and how that affects the observations. Observers often will write about this in memos, but it is still a problem. Wax (1971), having studied the Japanese Americans interned during World War II, found that it "made it impossible that I ever again approach or talk to them in the way that I had . . . three or four months before" (p. 31). Clearly, the observer must be alert to such changes and take them into account.

The most serious change of this type is "going native," losing perspective

---

6. Most research texts place these under the discussion of experimental methods. We shall begin them here and note them elsewhere as they are relevant, covering the set of them again when we discuss experimentation. It is important that the applicability of alternative explanations and threats to validity be recognized beyond quantitative work.

on the group observed and becoming entirely one of them. Lang and Lang (1960) report that, during a study of a Billy Graham crusade in 1957, an observer left her observational task and "somewhere in the course of the sermon she decided to step forward. . . . The next thing she knew was that she had risen and was hurrying to the main floor to declare herself [a believer]" (p. 424).

A variation of this is the tendency to overlook or ignore the negative aspects of a group the researcher has come to identify with. Thus Orenstein and Phillips (1978) criticize Liebow's (1967) "compelling description of street corner men" because he "presents no description of their involvement in crime or drugs or violence; he describes few instances of cruelty or times when they actually were impulsive or improvident, as we all are sometimes" (p. 350).

Sadler (1981), in an article discussing the mind's cognitive limitations as they affect qualitative data gathering, notes that there is a long history of efforts to identify the sources of distortion that cause the mind to make errors of judgment and inference. He notes that these have been the subject of considerable research, and certain cognitive limitations have come to be recognized. He lists a number of "information processing limitations," many of which will be familiar to qualitative researchers but all of which should be of concern to them.[7] Knowing these limitations is the first step toward disciplining their effect.

- *Data overload*. Research suggests that most individuals are able to keep only about seven things in mind at one time. The mind can beat this limit by "chunking" things as we routinely do—we don't see four legs and a top; we see a table. But when many aspects of a situation must be considered at once, observers may be fooling themselves in thinking that they are using more of the information than they really are.
- *First impressions*. Everyone knows that first impressions are important, and research simply confirms this. Research on first impressions with regard to physical stimuli where individuals must estimate size indicates that they are affected by the first stimulus received. First impressions tend to be enduring, perhaps because new information constitutes a progressively smaller proportion of the information base: we receive a first piece of information; a second piece equal to the first doubles our knowledge base; but the next similar addition increases the base only 33 percent, the next one 25 percent, the next one 20 percent, and so on.
- *Availability of information.* A researcher who finds it difficult to find concrete supporting examples or suitable analogies for a certain understanding of events is less likely to include it in the report than one for whom such examples come easily to mind.
- *Positive and negative instances*. Evidence that supports tentative hypotheses is much more likely to be noticed than evidence that negates them. Research

---

7. Sadler (1981) cites research studies that support each of these points.

shows that people tend to ignore information that conflicts with already held hypotheses; "even intelligent individuals adhered to their own hypotheses with remarkable tenacity when they could produce confirming evidence for them" (p. 28).

- *Correlation and co-occurrences.* Co-occurrences are often seen as evidence of correlation when they may be chance occurrences. In our study of inference (chapter 17), we shall see that the presence of a reasonable explanation helps delineate chance occurrences from causal ones.

- *Internal consistency, redundancy, and novelty of information.* Two equally credible sets of data about a particular phenomena might differ, one being more extreme than the other (for example, one observer watching a teacher discipline a student describes it in routine terms; the other reports it quite graphically as an aberration in the teacher's behavior). So long as the report is believable, there is a tendency to discount the less extreme data, although redundancy of information reduces that tendency. Balancing positive and negative information does not typically cancel out, leaving no information; the more extreme tends to win.

- *Base rate proportion.* This is the frequency with which a behavior occurs. There is great difficulty judging base rates from small samples. But insensitivity to base rate data and a tendency to form impressions on clinical or observational data seem to be common problems in intuitive data processing. This may account for the novelty problem just noted. Further, as statisticians know but often themselves underestimate, there is much greater variability among small than large samples. This factor is rarely taken into account. Individuals tend to base their judgment of the generality of the findings on the representativeness of the sample or the proportion of the population it constitutes instead of the size of the sample itself.

- *Uneven reliability of information.* People tend to treat data from an unreliable source almost the same way as data from reliable sources. In one study, subjects arrived at a conclusion, and then each source was shown to be less credible than originally thought. As each source was discredited, the revisions of the original hypothesis became smaller. Even when all sources had been discredited, a residual of commitment to the hypothesis still remained.

- *Revision of a tentative hypothesis, evaluation, or diagnosis.* New information tends to be either overweighted or underweighted. With a single-stage inference, there is considerable evidence of underadjustment, as noted in the preceding example. But there is likely to be overadjustment with second-stage inferences. For example, clinical psychologists, once having formed a prediction of the future success of students in training, are then given evidence from their second most preferred clinical instrument. They seem for some reason to overadjust to accommodate it. Apparently, they carry over only the most salient data to the second-stage inference. Similarly, qualitative researchers, given new data later to which they feel they must accommodate, may overadjust to the new data. (By the way, they don't always want to accommodate; this applies only if they do.)

- *Confidence in judgment.* As noted, "once an assessment is made, people have been shown to have an almost unshakable confidence in the correctness of their decisions, even in the face of considerable, relevant, contrary evidence" (p. 30). This is where training to remain open to new evidence is very important for the qualitative researcher.

Note that even though these limitations were suggested in the context of qualitative research, many could apply just as well to the quantitative researcher: data overload (especially with computer-generated reports that give reams of data), positive and negative instances, base rate proportion, uneven reliability of information, and revision of a tentative hypothesis.

The last item, as well as others on the list, suggest that there are likely temperamental characteristics that contribute to good qualitative research. Impulsiveness, for example, might cause individuals to jump to generalizations too early. A tendency toward holistic approaches in contrast to "missing the forest for the trees" seems a necessity to induction. Flexibility, openness, and willingness to entertain the new are important, though not to the point that the new automatically displaces the old. This last item may be one of the most critical since the order of events is beyond the researcher's control and initial events form the base on which the rest is built.

Clearly, there are many sources of problems. Qualitative or quantitative researchers who wish to build audience credibility in order to secure a consensus around the findings will do well to attend to these concerns. They will also attempt to allay them in the research report, insofar as that can legitimately be done. Displays of data such as Miles and Huberman's matrices are useful in such efforts.

- The elimination of alternative explanations is a concern of all methods, including qualitative methods.
- Certain common alternative explanations, or "threats to validity," as they have been called, are applicable to qualitative methods. Examples are mortality and instrument decay.
- Besides the common alternative explanations, there are others, often unique to the individual study, which it is the responsibility of the researcher to ferret out.
- A variety of information processing limitations affect researchers. These can constitute special problems for qualitative researchers because they are free to pick and choose among the data; many can equally bedevil quantitative researchers.
- The anticipation of alternatives that will be of concern to our audience is essential if a consensus is to be formed around the proper interpretation of the data.

THE REPORT

Qualitative research is often written up as a **case study**. The case study has its origins in the medical and legal professions where, vividly and precisely conveying the characteristics of a single individual, situation, or problem, it was used to illuminate a generic problem. It has been generalized, particularly in research on policy to describe and often to evaluate an event, an institution, a process, or a program.

Case studies are bounded by a particular program, institution, time period, or set of events. Within those boundaries, whatever is the focus of attention is described in perspective to the context surrounding it. Case studies are ideal for illustrating the complexity of causation and frequently are good examples of the peculiar concatenation of circumstances described as the INUS explanation (chapter 12). The case study is often a step in a larger study where cases are combined in support of an overall explanation or theory that arises out of cross-site analysis.

In many instances, the temporal nature of the material results in a time line type of narration that organizes the case study. Many others, however, must find their organization in the explanation and description. For the latter in particular, Strauss (1987) argues for clearly specifying all the theoretical elements and their connections and then adding such illustrative material as is needed to convey reality, enhance comprehension, and build trust. Clearly, the inclusion of "real" illustrative material is one of the strengths of this kind of presentation. Strauss, however, warns not to overload because the material is "colorful and interesting—at least to the author"; "data should function . . . in the service of . . . theory" (p. 220).

What should we expect to find in a report?

1. A presentation of the facts—thick description.
2. The development of a rationale, explanation, or theory.
3. A complete meshing of facts and theory. Choice of facts must demonstrate intelligence and internal consistency. Honesty should shine through the description of how well facts support theory.
4. A talented selection of stories and quotations that illustrate the rationale, explanation, or theory, making the extent of the match clear. Good stories interweave chance and regularity in keeping with the theme that this is a unique concatenation of forces. Both the chance and regular elements are made clear.
5. The likely questions of the intended audience are answered with respect to both content and method, and where concerns are not allayed, reasons are given.

Having the report read by gatekeepers and the subjects of the study is a very useful check on both the data and their interpretation. Whyte (1955), for instance, went over the various parts of the report in detail with his informant, "Doc": "His criticisms were invaluable in my revision" (p. 341). This has its dangers, of course. Grant (1979), in a study of competency-based education, found a case study of one university so objectionable to its administrators that he had to delete it from the final draft. But most researchers feel they have benefited considerably from this process. Yin (1984) notes that one evaluator found the reviews by five schoool districts of their case studies "so insightful and helpful, the investigators not only modified their original material but also printed the responses as part of their book" (p. 138).

A criticism of qualitative research has been that the evidence from a single instance, even one described as completely as in most case studies, may still be the result of a unique set of circumstances rather than one that generalizes. Therefore, increasingly, qualitative researchers are using multiple sites and multiple case studies to increase the generality of their findings. As Miles and Huberman (1984) point out, "If each site produces 200–300 pages of field notes and ancillary material, we are rapidly awash in waves of data" (p. 151). These data must be managed well or they will be poorly analyzed. Extending the methods of single-site analysis to those of cross-site analysis, these researchers note the necessity of standardizing the codes, reporting formats, and organizing data displays for each site. They then suggest a number of tools for managing and comparing the data across sites using matrix-type displays such as Table 15.1, where the data desired make up the vertical divisions and each row is a site. (See also Ragin, 1987.)

- Most qualitative data are written up as case studies, which are ideal for describing complex causal systems "in living color."
- Inclusion of many illustrations from the data is a characteristic of these reports that makes them highly readable. Empathy permits readers to "try on" the explanation to test its validity and estimate its generality.
- Having informants and persons who gave permission for entry read drafts often helps ensure accuracy and may lead to new insights or to densifying the original material.
- Where informants strongly object to aspects the researcher equally strongly believes should not be changed or dropped, a possible solution is to report the objections.

INTERNAL VALIDITY (LP), EXTERNAL VALIDITY (GP), AND OTHER CRITERIA APPLIED TO QUALITATIVE RESEARCH

To show relationships (that is, attain internal validity [LP]), Mill's method of agreement is the main design used with qualitative methods. We look for a commonality across situations in which the same phenomenon appears but where other circumstances are different. Occasionally, when contrasting situations are used, the method of difference is applied—one situation where the phenomenon appears and one where it doesn't but everything else is the same. Because the conditions for the methods of similarity and difference are rarely adequately fulfilled, the strength of the internal validity (LP) comes primarily from the conceptual evidence presented (explanation credibility—acceptability of the explanation; translation fidelity—the groundedness of the theory in data).

The development of grounded theory, which closely relates the explanation to detailed evidence of instances where a given relation occurs, can provide strong evidence of a demonstrated result. Although other observers or interviewers might have turned up other evidence, certainly the evidence is authentic. Indeed, the detail in qualitative research reporting that is reminiscent of our own experiences makes its authenticity apparent. Qualitative research has a ring of reality about it that quantitative research often lacks. But the case for a general causal relationship can be weakened by several factors.

Precedence of cause, as noted in chapter 12, may be difficult to establish. Often we do not know until after we have left the field and the data are being analyzed just what relationships will be established. So we didn't know what was significant to observe, ask, or seek. Whereas the mere presence of both cause and effect will certainly be established by the data, precedence of cause may not have been attended to. It is to be hoped, however, that, if a causal relationship is inferred, there are enough instances in which the data on precedence can be inferred that we are confident that this condition has been satisfied.

As noted, in qualitative research, presence of effect and congruence with the explanation, the last two conditions of demonstrated result, are part of the evidence gathered in the development of grounded theory. Theory is linked strongly to convincing instances where the relationship held. As noted in chapter 13, however, there needs to be evidence that the relationship held in instances beyond those in which it was discovered; that provides the most convincing evidence. If the relationship is discovered after leaving the field, there may or may not be additional instances.

We have already discussed the problem of eliminating alternative explanations. Since we have no control over what occurs in the field, elimination may be difficult and may depend on our "discounting" certain instances—postulating what would have occurred had not some contaminating alternative influence been at work.

The strength of the judgments of explanation credibility, translation fidelity (nearly always strong in qualitative research, as the terms are well grounded in examples) and demonstrated result, and the congruence of the study to prior research all substantially contribute to the credibility of the result and the strength of internal validity (LP).

External validity (GP) also depends heavily on conceptual evidence. With the exception of studies that do cross-site sampling, the local nature of the data and limited, purposive sampling may provide little empirical evidence for external validity (GP). But the rich and detailed illustrations allow readers to "try the examples on for size" to see whether they fit their experience. They facilitate transfer to situations beyond those studies. Some studies attain considerable transfer. Margaret Mead (1928), in one of the first widely read qualitative studies, *Coming of Age in Samoa*, found in her Samoan data insights with implications for raising children in America. These had substantial impact. Although not all researchers are as explicit about the implications, all researchers expect their work to provide useful insights for other situations. Generality always involves an inferential leap—a leap of faith. Although that leap is not usually supported by empirical qualitative evidence, it is clear that many useful conceptualizations have been found with qualitative research. Often they have later been validated with quantitative or additional qualitative studies.

As noted earlier, multisite studies, particularly where the additional sites are used to confirm and validate generalizations derived from a prior site, may develop considerable external validity (GP). This is especially true if the additional sites are chosen randomly from an appropriate sampling frame. Further, the targeted approach to validation of a generality, in contrast to the inductive method used for finding generalities, markedly simplifies data gathering and analysis and makes such cross-site studies more feasible.

Lastly, the audience credibility of qualitative work tends to be very high. The dense data that make the rationale and explanations come alive are much more effective than mere numbers in conveying the characteristics of situations and people and their interrelationships. Some persons in the quantitative tradition may raise questions about the quality of data, sources of bias, and problems of causal inference, but their number is far fewer than those who find the studies acceptable and useful. Accounts of many such studies (including a number of doctoral dissertations) have been issued in paperback and widely distributed, a claim that can be made about few quantitative studies.

- Qualitative studies build strong internal validity (LP) largely through conceptual evidence, although the empirical evidence of repeated instances in which the explanation applies also contributes. In most instances, however, the empirical evidence is confined to relatively few cases, and we know little about the representativeness of those cases because they were chosen by purposive sampling. Certain alternative explanations are problems for qualitative research.
- External validity (GP) is almost entirely the result of the conceptual evidence and involves a conceptual leap to other situations. Although this is true of all research, the limited and selective nature of qualitative evidence makes the leap more speculative. Nevertheless, the qualitative researcher who attempts to explain the many by a very careful and detailed explanation of a few often succeeds brilliantly.
- Multisite studies aimed at validating generalizations found in previous studies, especially where the sites are randomly chosen from a sampling frame, can have strong external validity (GP).
- The generous examples through which the explanation is usually presented facilitate readers' testing generalizations against their own experience and lead to high audience credibility.

AIDS FOR QUALITATIVE RESEARCHERS AND CONSUMERS

Tips on Participant Observation

1. Write up the notes as soon as possible; you will remember more than expected. Writing notes may require triple or quadruple the time spent observing; allow for it. Dictation is faster than writing but requires a certain amount of skill. Dictated notes will likely be more copious and more organized.
2. When something significant happens, change something inconspicuous until you have recorded it. Sari Biklen suggests moving a ring to the other hand or turning your wristwatch around to help you remember to record it.
3. Focus on the opening and closing of conversation; you can fill in the rest later. Include contextual factors.
4. Get down keywords and phrases, outline what went on, and then go back and fill in. Develop a set of abbreviations appropriate to the study.
5. Draw a diagram not only to give the picture but also to trace your own movements.
6. Rehearse every 10 to 15 minutes what you have seen; this refreshes the memory. Play back scenes in your mind; try to visualize what your write-up of the scene would look like.
7. Keep track of your hunches; write them in the notes with O.C. before them to designate them as observer comments. Enclose them in parentheses to set them off from the narrative flow.
8. Separate inferences and interpretation from observations with observer comments and memos.
9. Ask, "Why is this person telling me this?" Be sensitive to others' and your own effect on the situation.
10. Ask not only why someone is doing something but also why the person is not doing something else!
11. Remember that actions and expressed attitudes may differ, as may verbal and nonverbal reactions. What someone does not say may be significant, too.
12. Don't get so intent on recording data that you forget to be human; share feelings and personal experiences. But also try to keep track of the effect of that sharing on the behavior being observed and your own feelings toward the situation.
13. Underline or highlight notes for ease of scanning and sorting later.
14. Look for themes. Frequently, people's language gives clues. Look for repeating events, routines, and concepts.
15. Develop typologies and classification schemes of how people categorize other people and things.
16. Have professionals in your field unfamiliar with what you are studying read the notes and point out what they see as themes, commonalities, and points of significance.

17. Consult the literature of others who have studied the same phenomenon and see what themes and explanations their work suggests. Include relevant fiction.

18. Give priority to memoing over everything else. Sort your memos from time to time, and link them conceptually.

19. There is a fine balance between sticking to a particular line of thinking and abandoning it to the lure of a seemingly more promising one. You don't want to get stuck in unproductive tracks, yet you need to follow them far enough to sense their potential. Strauss (1987) advises that you trust yourself, "your subliminal thought processes as well as your memory," and the process of sorting to bring back your older ideas "when the time is ripe. They all integrate better that way" (p. 211).

20. Remember, there is no one right way to handle your data; there are lots of "roads to Rome." Pick one that makes sense to you and is comfortable.

21. Once you have determined your core coding categories, those central to the support of your explanation, relate other categories to them. Examine what is left to see whether the core needs modifying or whether there is something significant that has been missed. After this process, discard categories totally or relatively unrelated.

22. Strauss (1987, p. 213) notes that writing the report is an excellent integrating mechanism and suggests beginning it even before integration is complete. Test each section for completeness, and see whether it hangs together. This process can result in the need to recode old data or gather new. Beginning early reduces the extent of such work.

When to Use Qualitative Methods

The use of qualitative methods is indicated in the following circumstances:

- Research is lacking in an area and must emphasize discovery rather than validation or confirmation.
- Research progress in an area has plateaued; you are seeking a new perspective for a fresh start or something that was overlooked in previous work.
- You or your audience has a methodological orientation toward qualitative methods.
- You need a well-grounded explanation of a phenomenon.
- You believe that the perceptions of the participants differ from those of outside observers in such a way as to explain their behavior.
- There are no valid and trusted measures of the phenomenon of interest.
- You want to explore a phenomenon in depth to learn about it—thick description and many nuances and details.
- You seek a holistic picture of a phenomenon.
- Measuring would be overly obtrusive or impossible.
- The focus of study is on a process and its internal dynamics more than on a product.

- You believe that side effects or unexpected consequences may be important.
- You need examples to put "meat" on statistical "bones."
- You are interested in individual outcomes rather than the normative outcomes of a process.
- You want to understand the process of local causality in depth.

Hallmarks of Qualitative Research

Here is a baker's dozen of aspects to look for in qualitative research. They seem worth making salient. Some are especially relevant to qualitative research. But some could apply equally well to any method. Though stated here with respect to this method, the points marked with an asterisk, perhaps worded differently, apply to the other methods you will be studying. Stating them here saves repeating them for each method.

These are, of course, in addition to the criteria included as part of the model either explicitly (for example, the study is consistent with previous findings in the area or, if not, there are convincing explanations for the discrepancies) or implicitly (the study includes the information needed to allow the reader to make necessary judgments about it).

*1. The author has special competence in qualitative methods as evidenced by previous work in the area, by the methodological appendix (comparable to the procedure section of a quantitative study), and/or by the details given about methods in the body of the report. Methodological detail is especially important, lacking a prior reputation for competence.

*2. There is no reason to believe that the author has special biases that would distort his or her view of the phenomenon.

*3. The study was not sponsored in such a way as to create expectations regarding the outcome of the study.

*4. Observations appear to have been made in such a way that the behavior observed was not changed by the process of observation. If it was, allowances were made and/or the changes documented.

5. From the excerpts given in the report, recording of observations appears to reflect accurately what was observed.

6. Observations appear to reflect the way those studied understand or view the phenomenon.

*7. The research examines the phenomenon in context rather than concentrating on a part to the exclusion of aspects that might give a different perspective.

8. It appropriately illustrates the complexity of the phenomenon with rich detail.

9. It appropriately takes into account the influences of personalities, politics, and time on the phenomenon.

10. It includes copious appropriate quotations and examples so that the verisimilitude between the generalizations made about what was found and observations can be judged. Abstractions are tied down with illustrations. Reduced data summaries are displayed where appropriate.

*11. The time required to complete the study was not so long that the phenomenon under investigation might have changed in such a way as to raise questions about the generality of the results.

*12. Genuine efforts to find alternative explanations for relationships that are advanced as generalizable are presented.

*13. The generality of the findings was tested in other appropriate circumstances.

SUMMARY AND DETAILED COMPARISON OF QUALITATIVE AND QUANTITATIVE METHODS

The differentiation between qualitative and quantitative methods can be overdone in the sense of making it appear that these are opposites when in fact they are complementary. Indeed, all good quantitative researchers gather qualitative data in their studies so as better to understand what they are studying, and qualitative researchers often use counts and tabulations to reduce their data to meaningful proportions. Yet there are differences that need to be understood. At the risk of making too much of the differentiation, let us summarize them in detailed tabular fashion. Table 15.2 uses the chain of reasoning and the criteria of chapters 13 and 14 as an organizing framework. The table serves not only as a summary of this chapter but also as an organizer for chapters 16 and 18, which are progressively oriented more toward the quantitative.

TABLE 15.2 Differences between Quantitative and Qualitative Methods, Examined in Terms of Links in the Chain of Reasoning, the Criteria of Internal Validity (LP) and External Validity (GP), and the Other Criteria of a Good Study

	Chain of Reasoning	
	Qualitative Method	Quantitative Method
Problem Selection	Target situation or individuals are selected, and significance of situation emerges as it is studied. "Our first job was to find out what our second job was going to be" (Miller, 1978). In multisite validation studies, the problem may be set by the prior discovery of a generalization to be validated*	Problem is developed before data are gathered; data may change perception of problem and may result in gathering of additional data.
Links to Previous Studies	Varies. Some investigators prefer cursory or no prior study of literature to avoid preconceptions. Others argue that since we always have preconceptions, they should be the most informed ones possible.	Careful development of linkage to literature prior to start of study. Search for studies to build forward from and examination of prior designs and analysis to avoid pitfalls common to prior work.
Questions, Hypotheses, or Models	Emerge as the target situation or individuals are studied; are checked and revised as study progresses.	Like problem selection, usually set at the beginning of data collection but may be modified by data. Research consumer must be informed if latter is done.

* Although qualitative methods can clearly be used in this role, in the rest of this table it is assumed that the qualitative researcher is not in a validating mode—determining the validity and generality of a generalization. Though increasing, such studies are still relatively rare, and more often confirmation and validation are by quantitative methods if appropriate measures can be found.

	Chain of Reasoning	
	Qualitative Method	Quantitative Method
Sample of Subjects	Nonprobability, purposive sampling: individuals chosen to illuminate emerging understandings and/or to check hypotheses. As study develops, nature of those sought is subject to continual change. Generality less an initial goal in determining next sample than who or what can facilitate understanding and/or check an emerging explanation. May later use purposive samples to check generality, choosing individuals to whom generalization might not apply to find boundaries.	Determined prior to data colection, though occasionally added to as need arises. Subjects often chosen with a view to generality. May use probability sampling methods.
Situations	A natural field situation selected at time subjects are chosen. May change as new subjects are sought or new hypotheses are to be tested. Entry problems are continuous as new sites are chosen. Administrators' willingness as well as that of the individuals therein must be won in each new situation to continue the study. (Entry less of a problem with participant or covert observations.)	Can range from a laboratory to a natural situation. If the latter, once permission is granted to use the site, entry may be a one-time problem.
Treatment or Independent Variables	No treatment or, if there is one, it is usually a naturally occurring phenomenon outside the control of the investigator. Examines the effects of independent variables.	Usually a cause-and-effect relationship is being studied, with the treatment or independent variable as cause.
Observation or Measurement	Usually unstructured running accounts of the target activities, persons, or documents with new aspects recorded as researcher learns what is significant to attend to. Efforts made to maintain a holistic point of view while giving sufficient attention to details that may turn out later to be important. Values, including those of the researcher, are expected to enter the study. To the extent possible, the researcher writes memos regarding where values, attitudes, and potential bias entered and how they affected data, as a way of helping to track their influence.	Measures or structured observations; emphasis on validity, reliability, and objectivity of instruments. Effort made to avoid having the values or predilections of the researcher affect the outcome of the study.
Basis for Sensing Attributes or Changes	Usually there is no treatment; rather, we are looking for common characteristics across a group of individuals (in Hoffman-Riem's case, she found a desire for a normal family across the families who had adopted children) or common changes in response to some occurrence (for example, increase in religiosity in the face of a threat of war). There can be control cases not exposed to	Usually a carefully chosen basis such as a control group or an established baseline behavior, and change is sensed as a result of the treatment.

(continued)

TABLE 15.2 *continued*

	Chain of Reasoning	
	Qualitative Method	Quantitative Method
	the variable of interest, but usually each person and setting serves as its own baseline for noting changes in the individual and situation over time. Another way of saying this is that individuals' prior behavior serves as the control for contrast with later behavior.	
Procedure	In field or participant observation, scheduling of events is outside the control of the investigator, who must go where and when something of relevance occurs. The main control is the amount of time available for observations. With interviews, considerably more control of schedule is possible.	Scheduling of administration of measures and observation, including treatment (if there is one), is controlled by the researcher. Good control of schedule.
Data Analysis	Context is extremely important, and the problem is one of determining what is the "figure" and what is the "ground." Analysis is often done as the data are collected to elucidate what is occurring and to help guide the next steps. In some instances, it is done later—but then one may miss data essential to test a hypothesis that arises after one leaves the field. Data reduction occurs by categorizing the data in themes or meanings. Few statistics except possibly counts or percentages of categories in cross-tabulations or frequency distributions.	Done after data are collected. Usually statistical to reduce mass of numbers to meaningful summary. Concentrates more on the hypothesis, typically, than on the context. Emphasizes the "figure" instead of the "ground." Should include analysis of qualitative data concomitantly gathered to understand what occurred, particularly if there are aberrations.
Conclusions and Write-up	Regularities found in data are reported; usually they are woven into an explanation of situation, perhaps into testable theory grounded in observations—grounded theory. Emphasis is on giving the reader a feel for the data through extensive examples. Description of process of doing study often a minor part of report but should not be; sometimes added as a methodological appendix.	Conclusions deduced from data, and together with the rationale, procedure, and discussion, form the report. Considerable detail on research design to show how alternative explanations were controlled and eliminated.

	Criteria	
Applicability of Criteria	Criteria of the chain of reasoning are applicable only to studies that present relationships and claim some generality for those relationships. Many studies aim to describe a complex social situation so that the reader can understand it as the participants do. They present it holistically so that dissecting it into individual relationships among variables or even viewing it as a	Most studies result in relationships and generalizable findings, so the criteria applied to the chain of reasoning are generally applicable.

356

	Criteria	
	Qualitative Method	Quantitative Method
	model is not appropriate. Studies that produce explanations resulting in grounded theory are subject to the criteria.	
Internal Validity (LP)	Lack of controls makes tightness of argument more difficult; typically less emphasis on elimination of alternative explanations than on determining the plausibility and applicability of whatever explanations are induced from the data. Extent to which alternative explanations are pursued depends on the investigator and their obviousness as threats to the explanation being advanced.	A stength of quantitative method because controls permit careful elimination of alternative explanations. Researcher is frequently judged by how well study is designed for this purpose.
External Validity (GP)	Generality lies in the perceived applicability of the user's explanation to other situations. Development of grounded theory provides explanations of considerable generality. Multisite case studies can add considerably to generality with a random sample of sites.	Generality must be built into the design choices. Emphasis is often more on internal validity, especially if it is a laboratory study. Survey studies are usually built for generality. Multisite studies can show considerable generality.
Audience Credibility	Depends on the credibility of the explanation and the verisimilitude to the reader's sense of reality of the examples used to put "flesh" on the explanation's "bare bones." Well-chosen examples, empathically described, bring audience credibility. Data displays can help immensely.	Depends heavily on the credibility of the explanation, the perceived validity of the instruments, the sizes of the effects, and the extent that expectations created by the explanation are fulfilled by the data.
Resource Allocation	Difficult to anticipate exact nature and/or length of data collection; therefore, hard to control costs. Since the trained investigator is the observation "instrument," as well as the analyzer of the data, this research is very expensive in terms of professional time. It is especially hard for inexperienced researchers to anticipate total cost.	Ability to plan study in advance allows resource allocation decisions to be deliberate and deliberated. Use of instruments allows data often to be collected by individuals trained in their use but with less than professional qualifications, markedly reducing personnel costs.
Limits and Constraints	Difficulty in planning study in advance may mean that the original expectations of institutional administrators when entry was granted may be violated; they may feel betrayed. Ethical dilemmas arise in the field wherever unacceptable conduct that the researcher would be expected to report is observed.	Ability to plan study in advance means that cost, ethical problems, and institutional constraints are typically anticipated. Ethical questions are cleared through a human subject protection committee before study begins.

Only participant observation was covered in this chapter; the other major source of qualitative data, interviewing, is examined in the next chapter. The principles described there are completely applicable to interviewing in the context of participant observation. Survey research bridges qualitative and quantitative methods.

ADDITIONAL READING[8]

The following books have methodological appendixes that illustrate the process of participant observation. Any will give a feel for the process; choose one in a topic of interest:

Medical situations: Becker (1961); Bosk (1979)
Academic situations: Becker, Geer, and Hughes (1968)
Special populations: Bluebond-Langer (1980); Humphreys (1975); Schneider and Conrad (1985)
Social communities: Liebow (1967); Lynd and

Lynd (1929; old, but appendix discusses use of multiple sources of data: observation, documents, interviews, statistics, questionnaires); Whyte (1955)

Other useful books are Bogdan and Biklen (1992); Glaser and Strauss (1967); Goetz and Le Comte (1984); Johnson (1975); Miles and Huberman (1984); Strauss (1987); Strauss and Corbin (1990); Taylor and Bogdan (1984).

IMPORTANT TERMS

Acceptance
Analytic induction
Case study
Coding
Constant comparison method
Covert participant observation
Fieldnotes
Gaining entry
Gatekeeper

Informants
Instrument decay
Memos
Mortality
Participant observation
Qualitative point of view
Saturated
Triangulation

APPLICATION PROBLEMS

1. You are interested in determining what, if any, barriers exist to children's use of microcomputers in their schooling. You decide to conduct participant observation of children at a local elementary school where staff members are just beginning a computer education program for their students. A colleague who is committed to the quantitative tradition of research questions your use of qualitative methodology. He claims that you will not be able to demonstrate the validity of the data that you collect and that your conclusions would merely be opinion. How would you answer him?

---

8. My thanks to Dr. Steven Taylor for most of these suggestions.

Your answer will depend on whether you advocate the qualitative point of view or you believe that quantitative and qualitative methods can be usefully and successfully mixed.

2. You wish to study preschool children (aged 3–4 years) at a local nursery school. In order to understand how they interpret their experience, you decide to observe them over the period of the school year. How will you go about your observation? On the continuum of obtrusiveness, which method would provide you with the most informative data?

3. You hope to conduct a study at an inner-city high school located in a lower socioeconomic district. You are aware that the community and the school have well-documented problems with juvenile crime and truancy. You want to engage in participant observation at the school in order to investigate how the youths who attend it view their schooling experience. How would you go about establishing your study? What problems would you encounter, and how would you overcome them?

4. Assume that you have gained entry to the school in problem 3 and have succeeded in conducting observations for several months. Many students have taken you into their confidence and have begun to accept you as one of them. You then observe one of these students engaged in selling cocaine to other students. What do you do?

5. Your study of children's use of computers has led you to some interesting conclusions. From your observations in two classes, one of third graders and one of sixth graders, it appears that elementary-aged children view computers as something alive or, at least, as entities with psychological characteristics. This has brought you to reflect on the question of animism. You wonder whether their apparent attitude is peculiar to these classes or this school or whether these conclusions are generalizable to other children of this age group. How would you go about extending the study using qualitative methods?

6. You live in Columbus, Ohio, a city with a large Greek immigrant population. As a researcher in the field of nursing, you are interested in the topic of folk health in immigrant populations. In particular, you wish to study the Greek folk-healing tradition, which practices *matiasma*, the beliefs surrounding the prevention, diagnosis, and treatment of the "evil eye." You wonder about the extent of this practice and how to take it into account as a nurse working with these people. Why might you incorporate both quantitative and qualitative research methodology into such a study?

Compare your answers with those on pages 713–715.

=================== APPLICATION EXERCISE ===================

How might you pursue your problem with qualitative methods? Is concealment important? If so, what method would you use? What problems of access do you expect, if any? How would you record what occurred? Would you use one of the qualitative points of view? Which? What would it add to your study? Are there persons who you think might serve as particularly useful inform-

ants? Where would you look for them? What problems, if any, might you expect with coding and analysis? Does one of the coding suggestions in the chapter seem to fit your problem better than another? Would you anticipate a single or multisite study? How might qualitative methods uniquely fit your problem?

Survey Research:
Questionnaires and Interviews

The validity of survey data depends on persuading a scientifically selected group of people to provide accurate and detailed information about themselves, their opinions and expectations, their sense of well-being, their activities, their family finances and educational background—all to a complete stranger.

Charles F. Cannell

[A census-taker's tally mark] is only in part a function of . . . the questions. It is also a function of the social interaction of the interview, of the interviewer's appearance, of the respondent's fear of similar strangers, such as bill collectors. . . . [A] questionnaire response may . . . be a function of . . . vocabulary comprehension, or individual and social class differences in the use of . . . adjectives, or . . . respondent expectations.

Donald T. Campbell, Definitional versus Multiple Operationism

OVERVIEW

Informants chosen in qualitative research presumably have a perspective on their situation and can be helpful to the researcher. They may or may not accurately reflect their group. Survey methods consider all members of the group as informants. The researcher contacts a carefully selected sample of them directly and infers the status of the entire group with respect to some characteristic—attitude, opinion, value, morale, socioeconomic status, and so on. Surveys are a halfway house on the qualitative–quantitative continuum. They may be qualitative, as when interviews or open-ended questionnaires are used, or quantitative, as when closed-end or multiple-choice questions are used. Considerably more information about a target population can be collected from a representative sample than when the same resources are spread over the thin layer of information we could afford to collect from the entire population, as in a census. This same trade-off is faced by researchers in adjusting the size of their sample and the cost of gathering information from it to stay within available resources.

Survey research has several distinguishing characteristics: the care with which the sample is chosen so that an inference can be made to the target population; the care with which the data are collected, whether by questionnaire or interview; and the integration of data collection and analysis in an interactive system with computer-assisted telephone interviewing (CATI). Largely a U.S. development, sample surveys have been the subject of much careful research to refine the methods. There is extensive literature on sample selection, interviewing techniques, and the construction of instruments, especially questionnaires.

We will explore this topic by examining the purposes of surveys and the selection of the sample. These topics are common to interviews and questionnaires. Then we will examine the nature of interviews, the different types, and the effect of the interviewer. Next we move on to the questionnaire, tracing the steps in its construction; much of this material applies to the formulation of interview questions as well. We then discuss the problem of nonrespondents, response sets, and inquiring about sensitive topics. Finally, methods of data collection are compared on a number of characteristics.

CHAPTER CONTENTS

Introduction 361
Survey Purposes and Planning 362
  Sampling 363
Interviews 367
  Special Value of Interviews 369
  Styles of Interviews 370
  Interviewer Characteristics Affecting Responses 372
  Computer-assisted Telephone Interviewing 373
  Tips on Interviewing and Hallmarks of an Interview 375
Questionnaires 376
  What to Ask 378
  How to Ask It 378
  Tips on Question Construction and Hallmarks of Questionnaires 379
  Ordering the Questions 381

Hallmarks of a Letter of Transmittal 382
Questionnaire Format 384
Improving Questions, Questionnaires, and Letters of Transmittal 385
The Nonrespondent 386
Coding and Analysis of Interview and Questionnaire Responses 388
  Analysis of Data 388
Special Problems of Interviews and Questionnaires 390
  Querying Sensitive Topics 390
  Response Sets 392
Additional Hallmarks of Survey Research 392
Summary 393

INTRODUCTION

Survey research, or **sample surveys**, as it is sometimes called, exposes a group of people representative of a target group, to which the researcher expects to generalize, to common situations or stimuli and records their reactions. The researcher is usually interested in their common responses to the questions, the variability in responses, and the interrelationships of certain responses, especially those involving demographic information or measures of social or psychological variables with positions on issues. The record may be a self-report, an audio or videotape recording, the account of an interviewer, or some combination of these. The inquiries may include questions of knowledge or fact (demographics, descriptions of past behavior under particular circumstances, participation in past events, or awareness of products or events); predictions of behavior (voting in future elections; possible need for training or anticipated occupation; expressions of opinion, interest, or valuing); problems to react to or statements to agree or disagree with (how much aid to give the homeless; all homeless people are mentally disturbed); and demonstrations of capability (problems to solve). Nearly every sphere of human behavior is subject to exploration with these methods, including topics we don't talk about to our best friends.

Surveys have practical importance for our daily lives in guiding many commercial actions. Preelection polls influence the actions of others when the results are released. Surveys determine what television programs you watch and therefore what is scheduled, what strategy your representative will use during the election campaign and how it will be changed as the campaign progresses, what foods will be placed on the grocer's shelves and how they will be packaged, which professors students believe are good teachers and which are less so, what side effects an over-the-counter drug seems to have had, which potential jurors lawyers should select on the basis of profiles of persons who will be sympathetic to their cause, and so on. Further, by disseminating the results of such surveys, political candidates often seek to persuade their competitors to step aside. Voters peg the front runners, and potential financial supporters run to get on the bandwagon while there is still time. Highly sophisticated interviewing or instrumentation is often involved. Let's look at the technique more closely.

SURVEY PURPOSES AND PLANNING

Qualitative methods allow researchers to enter a situation with a vague idea of what is significant; survey techniques are typically more targeted. They range from only slightly more targeted (you interview a school superintendent to learn the responsibilities of that job) to highly targeted (you ask how often during each day the superintendent meets with parents). The former survey may explore the superintendent's responsibilities to see where time is spent and what values are implicit in those choices. The latter may be intended to gather facts or validate hypotheses about the relationships among a set of variables (for example, that female school superintendents attend more closely to parental needs and requests than male superintendents). Sample surveys may determine the incidence of a characteristic in a target group (such as extent of child abuse) and its distribution (frequency of child abuse among different racial groups and socioeconomic classes), including its relationship to other variables (child abuse and self-concept).

Because they are targeted, surveys typically require more planning than qualitative studies. This is especially true of questionnaire studies. They also involve more out-of-pocket expenses. Plans must include the sample, the instrument, and the method of gathering data, plus at least preliminary plans for analysis. To build an internally consistent study in which each stage follows from the first, the initial purpose of the study must be clarified. This involves determining what to study, our intent in studying it, and appropriate resource limits.

Many surveys are sponsored by organizations that need information to plan their future (for example, a needs survey), to determine the source of some current problem (perceived cause of poor morale or low production), to evaluate past activities, or to determine the competency of certain units or supervisory personnel. As Davis (1964) points out, clients are interested in the specific so that they might take correct actions. Study directors, however, are often more interested in the general nature of the world, learning why things happen and contributing to sociological and psychological knowledge. As Davis puts it:

> Social research is typically conducted by (1) a study director . . . more interested in wresting an academic article from the [data] . . . , (2) a sponsor who stokes the fires with money and hopes . . . [that] the evasive, fast talking young man will complete within his lifetime a report bearing vaguely on the topic, and (3) a research organization, beset with financial woes and woefully aware of the fact that the study director (who gets no profits when the study makes money and pays no refund when he runs into the red) is capable of spending the organization into the poorhouse without shedding a tear. (p. 216)

Though a humorous overstatement, this does highlight the conditions under which many studies are done and suggests why many studies are a combination of the general and the specific, resulting in a more complex investigation than would otherwise be called for.

Sampling

One of the distinguishing characteristics of survey research is the care with which the sample of respondents is selected. The goal of a sample survey is to be able to generalize to the target group of which the sample is representative. Good survey research permits making that inferential leap with confidence. Accurate representation of the target population is a necessary but not sufficient condition for good survey research. Many of the sampling designs discussed in chapter 8, especially cluster and quota samples, have been an outgrowth of survey methodology.

Sampling Plans. As noted in chapter 8, the first step in choosing a sample is determining precisely who is included in the population of interest. If we are interested in whether university graduate students' outside work diverts them from studying, we must be clear what is meant by "university graduate students." Are these all full-time students, and if so, what is the definition of "full-time"? Is it enrolling for 12 credit hours per semester? If graduate assistants take only 9, are they considered full-time students? The definition of the population is critical to the sampling problem.

The stereotypical sample for a survey is a random sample of the population. Actually, of course, the sample is taken from the sampling frame, which is presumably an enumeration of the population or the part of it that we are sampling. As noted in chapter 8, where the frame is incomplete (for instance, a telephone book that omits individuals too poor to have a phone), this will be reflected in the sample. Random sampling is often used with questionnaires, although systematic sampling (say, taking every tenth name) is more common where only a sample of a mailing list need be used. Since stratified sampling costs little more if the information on the stratifying variable is available, random samples are often stratified. Stratified sampling requires fore-knowledge of the classification of each sampling unit so that units may be assigned to a stratum.

With quota sampling, we assign each individual to a stratum on the basis of data gathered in the questionnaire or interview. If no more cases are needed in that stratum, we can terminate the interview or, more commonly, use all cases and adjust the results according to the stratum's weight in the target population. For example, 40 percent of the data gathered might have come from blacks, but if they make up only 10 percent of the target population, their weight will be reduced to 10 percent of the total when final results are being determined.

If interviews are to be conducted, cluster sampling markedly reduces travel in contrast to random sampling. Geographic locations, called clusters, are the units sampled. A combination of sampling methods may be used, and this is especially true when cluster sampling is employed. For instance, an interview study of the availability of health services for children might combine stratification and cluster sampling in the first stage. A grid imposed on a map of the city would divide it into neighborhoods or clusters. These might be stratified according to both the average assessed value of housing and racial composition. Then a stratified sample of clusters (neighborhoods) would be taken so as to represent both variables. Within each cluster, blocks might be selected at random, and every third housing unit in the selected blocks would be visited. Lastly, systematic sampling might be used in these housing units, so that all minority families encountered would be interviewed but only every fourth Caucasian family. This would overrepresent the minority groups, but they are a subpopulation of special interest, and it would permit a more fine-grained analysis of their data. When overall population values are sought, each group's weight can be reduced to its proper proportion when combined with the rest of the data.

Sampling to Observe Changes over Time.   Most sample surveys are what we call **cross-sectional studies**. They study a cross section of the target population at one point in time, comparing, for instance, older respondents in the sample with younger ones to make inferences about changes with aging. Such inferences are subject to important alternative interpretations, however, because individuals are affected by the events and milieu around them as they were growing up and aging. Since these vary considerably from one decade to the next, contrasts between age groups are sometimes better traced to those events (war, economic depression, flu epidemic) than to aging.

Equally important is the effect of selection over time. The older group of the cross section may differ considerably from its initial composition. A cross-sectional study of college satisfaction comparing freshmen with seniors would miss all the students who dropped out. Cross-sectional studies of effects related to the passing of time, therefore, need to be viewed with some caution.

Longitudinal studies solve the problems involved in making timebound inferences from cross-sectional samples but incur other problems. There are several kinds of longitudinal studies, depending on the particular sampling process. **Trend studies** follow a trend in a particular population. If we are interested in following the change in attitude toward involving college students in making educational policy, we might sample students at three-year intervals. Not only will we be taking new samples, but the population itself will be changing over this time.

Cohort studies keep the population constant but take new samples from it. The cohort group is the sampling frame. For example, our sampling frame might be the class of 1996, which we follow as it goes through college, taking new samples of that class to determine its attitude toward being involved in policymaking.

A **panel sample** is a cohort study in which the sample is retained throughout the study and queried two or more times. It gives a stable basis for comparison provided the panel stays relatively intact during the study. When the likelihood of member loss is great, panels are made larger than needed at the outset to compensate. Alternatively, we can try to find satisfactory replacements. Because "movers" and "stayers" tend to differ on certain characteristics, if these are related to what we are studying, exact replacement may prove difficult. Because of the problem of retaining an intact group over time, panel studies tend to be shorter in duration than other longitudinal models.

The retesting or reobservation that occurs with panels, however, may have effects of its own. Having been given the instrument or interview once, individuals have time to consider their answers for the next data collection. Further, knowing that they are members of the panel may create expectations. For example, Terman's study of talent identified a panel of child geniuses. The identification itself probably created expectations that may have been self-fulfilling and changed the nature of the results (Terman et al., 1926; Cox, 1926; Burks, Jensen, and Terman, 1930; Terman and Oden, 1947, 1959).

A panel study enables us to see the changes taking place in individuals over time. Further, since the same individuals are remeasured, it is sensitive to smaller changes than comparably sized random samples would be. In a trend study, change may result either because such individuals have in general changed over the period of time or because of a change in the nature of the individuals leaving and coming into the population sampled—we don't know which. Panel studies have the advantage of noting specifically who is changing. We can then track back to the events, the characteristics of the individuals,

TABLE 16.1   Advantages and Disadvantages of Survey Designs for Studying Changes over Time

	Description	Advantages	Disadvantages
Cross-sectional Design	Data collected at one point in time from groups different in age and experience.	Considerable savings in time and money.	Researchers cannot be sure that the results are the same as would be obtained from longitudinal data.
Longitudinal Designs	Trend study Data collected at two or more points in time from different samples of the population.	No need to keep track of a group over time. No problem with dropouts.	Changes may be due to differences in persons sampled rather than changes in population. Persons entering and leaving the population may be the cause of changes.
	Cohort study Identified group of individuals sampled twice or more over time.	Traces changes in identified group. Events affecting group are known and can be linked to changes.	Changes may result from dropouts rather than changes in population. Researchers must keep track of all participants. Dropouts may be hard to replace.
	Panel study Selected group of individuals measured two or more times.	More sensitive to changes than random samples of same size. Reasons for dropouts are known, so changes in group can be adjusted accordingly.	Panel is difficult to keep intact over long periods of time. Researchers must keep track of all participants. Dropouts are hard to replace. Repeated testing or observation may create self-fulfilling expectations and/or change the nature of measured or observed behavior.

and the situations that might have contributed to the change. So there are advantages and disadvantages to each kind of sample. Table 16.1 summarizes some of these.

Sample Size.   The most common question asked with respect to samples is, "How big a sample must I have?" We will provide a definitive answer to this question in chapter 17 when we examine inferential statistics. For now, there are four points to bear in mind:

1. The principles of sampling discussed in chapter 8 apply: heterogeneity in the population plus the need for precise estimates and/or for certainty that our estimate is correct requires a larger sample.
2. Unless the population is small and the sample is a substantial part of it (10 percent or more), population size is not an important variable.[1]

3. To estimate the required sample size, estimates of the heterogeneity of the population must be obtained, usually from previous studies of this population or from a pilot study, if it is large enough to provide an estimate.
4. Additional cases increase the accuracy of the estimate considerably for small samples, but more than proportionally larger increases in sample size are required for comparable reductions in error in large samples. A useful rule is that halving the error requires a quadrupling of cases. For instance, given a question whose population response is 50 percent yes and 50 percent no, where 100 cases will give a 10 percent error, an additional 300 cases (total 400) cuts it to a 5 percent error. But an additional 1,200 cases (1,600 total) would be required to cut it in half again!

- All but unstructured surveys require advance planning to determine how data will be collected, pilot the questions for the interview or questionnaire, and determine the sample.
- Samples chosen to track changes over time may be used in a cross-sectional study or one of the longitudinal ones: trend study, cohort study, or panel study.
- Trend studies collect data from different samples of a population over time.
- Cohort studies collect data from different samples of an identified group of individuals over time.
- Panel studies collect data from a selected group of individuals over time.
- Sample size can be determined by statistical means but requires estimates of the heterogeneity of the population and decisions regarding the desired precision and certainty of results.

INTERVIEWS

Surveys typically gather their data through interviews, questionnaires, or a combination of both. Let us begin by examining interviews. As noted earlier,

---

1. For example, to determine the burning time of five freight cars of coal, I need the average chunk size. I can obtain an estimate from a sample of the cars, adjusting the size of the sample to however many accurate decimal places I need in the result, how sure I wish to be, and how variable the chunks are in size. Such an estimate, however, would be equally applicable to 50 similar carloads, 1,000, or a train reaching to the moon. The size of the population does not matter if the cars are all just as they came from the mine's coal crusher—the variability of chunk size is uniform throughout, and the chunks are "well mixed." But people tend to congregate with others like themselves, so many human samples are "lumpy." If we know the variables around which these lumps occur and can get data on these variables, we can use stratification to ensure that the "lumps" are represented appropriately.

Unstructured, exploratory, only area of interest chosen, interviewer "follows her nose" in formulating and ordering questions.	Partially structured, area chosen and questions formulated but order is up to interviewer and interviewer may add questions or modify them as deemed appropriate. Questions are open-ended, and responses are recorded nearly verbatim, possibly taped.	Semistructured, questions and order of presentation determined, questions are open-ended, interviewer records the essence of each response.	Structured questions are determined and responses are coded by the interviewer as they are given.	Totally structured; questions, order, and coding are predetermined, and the respondent is presented with alternatives for each question so that the phrasing of responses is structured. Questions are self-coding in that each choice is preassigned a code.

FIGURE 16.1   Continuum of interviews with increasing amounts of structure.

the amount of structure provided in the data-gathering process may vary. We can construct a continuum of interviews ordered by the amount of structure to show the implications of increased structure (Figure 16.1). This continuum is intended to show only some of the possible options. In comparison with commercial, governmental, and policy surveys, this chapter perhaps over-emphasizes open-ended interviewing and qualitative data collection. This is because of their value in exploratory research, in piloting questionnaires, and in understanding closed-end questionnaire responses. However, data for commercial, governmental, and policy surveys are typically gathered through questionnaires filled out during interviews or self-administered and returned by mail.

Contrasting the extremes of the continuum—the **unstructured interview** and the **structured interview**—as in Table 16.2 shows the differences in purposes and the implications of structure (entries for the unstructured interview should remind you of the material in chapter 15). Interviews structured between the extremes typically also fall between them in the various characteristics described. An exception is the unstructured exploratory interview. With it, we may be simply exploring and not much interested in generality yet. With interviews of almost any other type, generality is important, and we are concerned with ensuring representativeness of the sample.

It is clear there are many trade-offs to be decided on. Among the most important is the use of professional time: how much for the interviews, how much for analysis of the records after the data have been gathered, and what the balance between the two should be. Another is question type: whether to use open-ended questions and devote professional time to compiling and analyzing the data or to use professional time to set up closed-end questions that anticipate the meaningful responses. The latter risks missing the unexpected but is much more economical with a large sample and is by far the more common practice.

Like other measures, questionnaires and interviews may be designed to get at intangible constructs, with all the problems that entails. Just as with measures, regardless of what is intended, the questions asked become the operational definition of the construct. There are the same problems of show-

TABLE 16.2 Comparison of the Extremes in Interview Structure

Unstructured Interview	Structured Interview
■ Requires a researcher-interviewer who can direct the interview in directions that may be rewarding.	■ Interviewer may be a clerk with good social skills who can comfortably follow a script while recording answers on designated forms.
■ Profitability of such interviews depends directly on the skill in interviewing, the "nose for paydirt," and the keen recognition of insights such a person shows.	■ Compilation of the data is easy and, if computer-assisted telephone interviewing (CATI) is used, may be done as the interview is conducted.
■ Data recovered may be extensive or sparse, depending on the records kept. The interviewer may simply be looking to find what is profitable and depending on his professional skill to catch it.	■ Analysis to find and validate insights requires a professional's attention. With a structured interview, it can be preplanned so that it can be carried out by a technician to a considerable extent. A good professional, however, will want to examine the data for unexpected findings, which are often the most exciting parts of the research. This latter aspect of the analysis is the same regardless of how the data are collected.
■ Compilation of data in extensive records requires extensive and lengthy analysis.	
■ Analysis of the data requires professional expertise, especially when we are looking for unexpected findings.	
■ Nature of the sample may not be predetermined but may untold as each interview suggests where leads may appear next. Unless we are exploring the characteristics of some particular group, emphasis is not on generality but on covering the widest possible types of individuals that may suggest leads.	■ Nature of the sample will be carefully considered because the emphasis is on generality for some target population of which the sample is intended to be representative.

ing the validity of the operational definitions as with measures: the same tools and reliability and validity indexes apply. More often than with measures, perhaps, the validity of the questions seems to be apparent, so face validity is substituted for more sophisticated analyses. But as we shall see, the interpretation of questions is not always as straightforward as it appears.

Special Value of Interviews

Interviews are particularly useful in the following pursuits:

- Probing and searching
- Making sure the respondent correctly understands what is asked
- Following up incomplete or nonresponsive answers
- Getting responses from individuals who might not respond to or might not understand a questionnaire
- Identifying the aspects of situations that seem to be leading to effects
- Finding explanations for discrepancies between observed and expected effects

- Finding explanations for deviations from prevailing effects by individuals or subgroups
- Providing clues to the processes and mechanisms called into play by the situation

The last four items on this list come from Merton, Fiske, and Kendall (1956), who suggest that we seek the personal meanings of the common experience to determine what about it was significant to the respondent. They note, for example, where literature was used to stimulate voting in an experiment, an interviewer could find what aspects of the literature were significant factors, whether these factors were effective, with what groups they appeared to be effective, and what underlying mechanisms were driving voting behavior.

Styles of Interviews

There is extensive literature on the techniques of interviewing, some of which borrow from counseling and clinical techniques. Organizations that commercially engage in surveys have their own manuals for training their interviewers. That of the Survey Research Center (1976) does an excellent job of explaining how it conducts its surveys. Various approaches to interviewing have been proposed, each with its own advantages. We shall cover these few here: nondirective, focused, and multiple-interviewer and multiple-respondent interviews.

Nondirective Approach. The **nondirective approach** is important for any interviewer to master. Basically, it requires that the interviewer rephrase and reflect to the respondent the central significance and especially underlying feelings of what the respondent seems to be saying. For instance, in a survey of voting literature, the initial question might be, "What do you think of the literature you received on voting?" Respondent: "I don't like people bringing literature to my home that implies I am not a good citizen if I don't vote; I pay my taxes like anyone else." Interviewer: "You felt unhappy; they were 'putting you down.'" Note that the interviewer finds the underlying feeling of unhappiness the significant thing to reflect instead of the more superficial self-justification of paying taxes. In this style, the interviewer is attentive, and the restatement implicitly conveys the personal worth of the respondent. The restatement suggests acceptance of the respondent, whose answer was important enough to rephrase.

Nondirective responses build rapport with the respondent. They are particularly valuable in getting the respondent to talk about and elaborate on the answer. The response has an unfinished quality that calls for further elaboration but conveys the direction of what is significant to the respondent. If the restatement is incorrect or inadequate, the respondent can correct it: "I felt really mad!" On the average, structured questions result in more talk by the interviewer than the respondent; the nondirective approach reverses this ratio.

Focused Interview. Merton, Fiske, and Kendall's (1956) **focused interview** is a combination of the exploratory and the structured. It allows the respondent to set the initial course of the interview and increasingly focuses on the researcher's agenda as the interview progresses. The interview begins with broad questions and nondirective responses such as those just described, then moves to semistructured questions and finally to structured ones. The last section tests the researcher's ideas about what was significant and its effects. For example, in the voting literature study: "What did you think of the cartoons?" "Did the cartoon on the back page that showed neighbors poking fun at the protesting nonvoter make you want to prevent that from happening to you?" Early interview material provides focus for the structured parts so that the questions are continually evolving. Insights from early questions are validated by later ones.

Multiple Interviewers and Multiple Respondents (Tandem Interviewing, Group Interviews, and Focus Groups). Anyone who has done interviewing knows that there are times when help would have been extremely welcome. For example, an interviewer who becomes exasperated may need to repair rapport and regain composure. It also helps to have someone record responses while an interviewer concentrates on the interaction. **Tandem interviewing** is one answer. Kincaid and Bright (1957) used a male-female team to interview business elite. The team approach increased the accuracy of questioning because help was available for rephrasing. Leading questions, which suggested the answer, were caught. Ambiguous replies were identified and pressed to resolution—it is more difficult to "pull the wool over the eyes" of two people. Rapport was greater because the respondents had at least one interviewer's full attention at all times. Use of a team simplified recording and coding.

There can be multiple respondents as well as interviewers, thereby constituting a group interview or **focus group**. Multiple respondents permit discrimination of unique responses from those that are mainstream by merely asking for agreement by a show of hands. Such groups help get ideas for a questionnaire, determine meanings of a situation to various individuals, find the needed range of alternatives for closed-end questions, find what is significant about an issue or a political stand, or determine how people feel about an issue or a product. They are used commercially to gauge the effect of television commercials, to find the desired characteristics of a projected product, to get reactions to new products, and so on.

Focus groups are most successful with a relatively small (7–10 persons), relatively homogeneous group. Too much diversity causes some persons to withdraw. Circular seating facilitates spontaneous responses and interchange. Details and experiences of one individual may stimulate others. People have time to collect their thoughts before speaking, so the responses are often more considered than in an individual interview but may also be more carefully censored. At the same time, when one person speaks out on a sensitive issue, it releases the inhibitions of others who might not do so in a one-to-one situation.

Disadvantages include the difficulty of scheduling such a group and getting the right mix of people. Educational homogeneity seems to be an important feature. There may be a selection effect in who can or is willing to attend and speak. Strong chairing may be required to prevent certain individuals from monopolizing the discussion or so restructuring it as to focus on interesting but largely irrelevant material. (See Krueger, 1988, for more on focus groups.)

- Interviews can range from highly structured to unstructured.
- Highly structured ones are used for measuring the responses of a population, can be used with less skilled personnel, and are easier to analyze than less structured interviews, and the nature of the sample is generally carefully specified.
- Unstructured interviews are useful for exploring issues; they must be conducted by skilled personnel and analyzed by professionals; and the nature of the sample may be determined as responses suggest new leads.
- Focused interviews combine exploration and structure, starting broadly and then narrowing.
- Multiple interviewers may facilitate both the conducting of the interview and the recording of the responses.
- Multiple respondents (focus groups) have been found valuable in exploring issues and testing audience response to communications.

Interviewer Characteristics Affecting Responses

The effect on the interview of such characteristics as the race, status, sex, and religion of the interviewer has been studied. The conventional wisdom suggests that it is best to match the race of the interviewer to that of the respondent. A number of studies have shown significantly different responses under matched and mismatched conditions. But for unknown reasons, as Orenstein and Phillips (1978) point out, some questions produce different results for white and black interviewers but others do not (p. 233). They note, for example, that Schuman and Converse (1971) used both black and white interviewers to question blacks two weeks after the assassination of Martin Luther King, Jr. While discovering differences, they also found no differences where some might be expected. For example, the race of the interviewer made no difference on questions such as whether the assassination would likely drive blacks and whites further apart or whether interviewees had ever taken part in nonviolent civil rights protests.

Status and race are often confounded because whites are often perceived as high in status when interviewing low-socioeconomic-status African Americans. But considering status alone, the results are still mixed. Some investigators have concluded that biasing effects are greatest both when the status of the interviewer and the respondent are very different and when they are very much alike. Lack of rapport is a problem when they are different. But when they are alike and rapport is high, it is possible that the interview "takes on the quality of a social visit . . . as both of the participants become overly concerned about maintaining the pleasant atmosphere." Good reporting suffers (Orenstein and Phillips, 1978, p. 234).

Religion may seem to be a covert interviewer characteristic, but it has also been found to bias responses even when no apparent identification of the religion of the interviewer is given. Cosper (1972), for example, found that the reported consumption of alcoholic beverages related to the stereotype of drinking in the interviewer's religion. Protestant fundamentalists found few reports of heavy drinking, Catholics and liberal Protestants more. Hyman (1954), querying about Jewish influence in the business world, found more negative responses addressed to non-Jewish interviewers. These results seem to follow expectations with regard to the values espoused by the interviewer's religion. Perhaps an interviewer's values are conveyed more consistently than differences in race or status, or more subtly so that they work subliminally and so are harder for the interviewer to control.

Studies also show response differences with respect to same-sex and different-sex interviewers, but with the rapidly changing attitudes toward women, past data may not be a good guide to present research.

All of this suggests that if we suspect that there might be differences due to interviewer characteristics and respondent match, a pilot study with the particular instrument and population in question may well be worth the trouble.

> Interviewer-respondent interaction effects appear to be quite subtle but can influence survey results. Where suspected, pilot studies are in order to determine the nature and seriousness of such effects.

Computer-assisted Telephone Interviewing

Computer-assisted telephone interviewing (CATI) uses a computer to guide the caller through the interview questions, which appear successively on the screen. It is usually combined with random-digit dialing to automate as many aspects of the survey as possible. Once the area codes and local telephone number prefixes to be included in the survey have been selected, using some system like that of Waksberg (1978) to target residences rather than businesses, random-digit dialing generates and dials the last four digits of the number. Using the computer, the interviewer keeps track of whether the number responds or not and if not, files it for callback at a later time. The computer can be programmed to call back at another time of day and, by analyzing the information being accumulated, can determine the most appropriate time of day to reach individuals in that community. Although random-digit dialing reaches even unlisted numbers, unless steps are taken it also reaches a large number of businesses, which are typically excluded from sampling plans. Once a potential respondent is reached, the interviewer's script is displayed on the computer screen, and the interviewer is led through the interview by the computer.

Usually the interview begins with a series of questions that determine whether the person who answered the phone is part of the target sample or whether to ask for a person who is. Responses are entered into the computer by the interviewer as they are given. The computer can be programmed to tell whether to terminate the interview because this person's demographics do not fit quotas needed to fill the sampling plan. It can insert the respondent's name or other demographic information into appropriate points in the script to personalize the interview. It can remember previous answers and point out inconsistencies so that the interviewer can probe for reasons. The computer can tell the interviewer that a clerical error has been made if coding does not fit any of the acceptable codes for a given item. An important time and error saver is the computer's capacity to branch the interview to relevant questions, skipping whole blocks judged inappropriate on the basis of previous responses. Close control of the interviewing process (and useful research) is possible because all the interviewers are typically in the same location and the supervisor can easily monitor and correct them.

Telephone interviews tend to elicit shorter responses than face-to-face encounters, but total length does not seem to be shorter. With shorter responses and no transportation time between interviews, the number of interviews per worker-hour is much higher with CATI than with face-to-face interviews. Of course, with CATI, nonverbal cues that add meaning are lost, and maintaining rapport may require more interviewer responsiveness. But the impersonal aspect also permits a kind of anonymity that allows sensitive issues to be handled with less embarrassment.

In sum, CATI has many of the advantages of face-to-face interviewing; it is the method of choice when results must be obtained in a short time. Programs into which questions can be inserted are available for desktop computers, relatively inexpensive and increasingly flexible. Completely automated surveys have also been developed with precoded lead-ins and questions. Respondents answer by pressing telephone buttons: "Press, 1, 2, 3, 4, and up to 5 to indicate how strongly you agree with this statement." The computer responds to such responses as if an interviewer had keyed them in, but the respondent has actually done so. This does away with the trained interviewer, one of the most costly parts of the process. But it introduces selective factors in terms of who is willing to respond to prerecorded queries that could markedly affect the results. For interviewers, light pens can eliminate the need for keyboard skills to enter data. As software becomes more sophisticated and the cost of equipment decreases, CATI surveys will become ever more prevalent. Whether that will result in more resistant attitudes on the part of potential interviewees remains to be seen. There is some dispute about that at the present time (Anderson, 1986). Some experts argue that if the topic is of interest, individuals enjoy the opportunity to express their opinions. This puts a premium on sample selection procedures. For more information on CATI, see Frey (1989) and Groves (1990).

Computer-assisted telephone interviewing has many of the advantages of face-to-face interviews, can achieve results quickly, eliminates travel, tends to elicit shorter responses, can have the advantage of anonymity for sensitive issues, can use the computer to generate the sample and make automatic callbacks, can use less skilled personnel if the computer leads the interviewer through the questions, and can automatically check the consistency of answers. Its main disadvantage is that it cannot pick up on nonverbal cues.

Tips on Interviewing and Hallmarks of an Interview[2]

1. Identify yourself and set the respondent at ease.
2. Don't ask, "May I come in?" Simply assume that the interview will take place: "I would like to come in and talk with you about . . ."
3. Answer questions about the survey as if the person were interested and friendly. Reply in a nonspecific way: "We are interested in how people feel about . . ." does not bias the interview.
4. Have copies of clippings that show the value of past studies as an example of the worth of the interview.
5. The respondent's reaction often mirrors the interviewer. If you are uncertain and uneasy, the respondent will pick this up. A pleasant, positive, well-informed approach is reflected by the respondent's readiness.
6. Collect the data uniformly. Ask questions exactly as they are worded. If there is an interview schedule, follow the order specified. Read slowly and repeat questions that are misunderstood.
7. If you want longer and detailed responses, reinforce those kinds of answers—say, "Yes," "OK," or "I see," or nod. Using similar reinforcers for nonresponsive answers gives the wrong signal; save them for responsive answers. Study of typical interviewer feedback showed that 28 percent of interviewers gave feedback for an adequate answer, 24 percent for an inadequate answer, 18 percent for "I don't know," and 55 percent for refusal to answer (Lansing, Withey, and Wolfe, 1971). The 55 percent may consist largely of probes. But if we consider any interviewer response as positive reinforcement, which the study shows it nearly always is, this pattern is hardly likely to lead to the most responsive interview.

    To teach and motivate the respondent further, use feedback expressions like these: "Thanks, this is the sort of information we're looking for in this research." "It's important to us to get this information." "These details are helpful." "It's useful to get your ideas (your opinion)

---

2. Portions of this discussion are based on *Interviewer's Manual*, rev. ed. (Ann Arbor, Mich.: Survey Research Center, Institute for Social Research, 1976).

on this." "I see; that's useful information." "Let me get that down."
(Cannell, 1985b)

8. Master the **probe**: repeat the question, give an expectant pause (an
   expectant look or nod of the head), possibly repeat the reply. Say:
   "Anything else?" "How do you mean?" "Could you tell me more about
   it?" "I'm not sure I know what you mean by that (bewildered look)."
   "Could you tell me a little bit more?" (Don't overuse these, or the
   respondent will think you can't recognize a valid answer.)
9. When probing recall, use probes that give memory cues of items likely to
   be forgotten. For example, if probing hospitalization, say, "Well, people
   quite frequently forget; it is more difficult to remember just an overnight
   hospitalization, for instance. Was there any chance you had something like
   this?" (Cannell, 1985a).
10. Sit in a comfortable spot where you can record the responses verbatim,
    using abbreviations to get them down. Record abbreviations, probes, and
    interviewer comment in parentheses. Write on the form as the respondent
    talks. A sample interview form appears in Figure 16.2.

Much more could be discussed about interviewing, but many of the
concerns regarding question framing apply equally well to questionnaire construction; we will cover them there. A good self-instructional workbook for
both telephone and personal interviews is Guenzel, Berckmans, and Cannell
(1983).

Finally, here is a summary series of questions to ask yourself that apply
equally to interview and questionnaire data (adapted from Jaeger, 1984). Starting with the sample and questions, they track through to the interpretation:

Was the sample representative of the target population?

Was it large enough?

Did the questions have construct validity?

Did the respondents understand the questions?

Did the respondents interpret the questions as intended? Were they willing to
respond?

Did they have the knowledge or information needed to respond?

Were they honest in their responses?

Were their responses recorded accurately?

Were they transcribed and aggregated accurately?

Were they interpreted accurately?

QUESTIONNAIRES

A questionnaire gathers large amounts of data from many subjects very
inexpensively. If the topic is of interest to the respondents and there are few
questions, we may use open-ended queries, just as in an interview. But we get
less depth and richness because people will say more than they will write, and

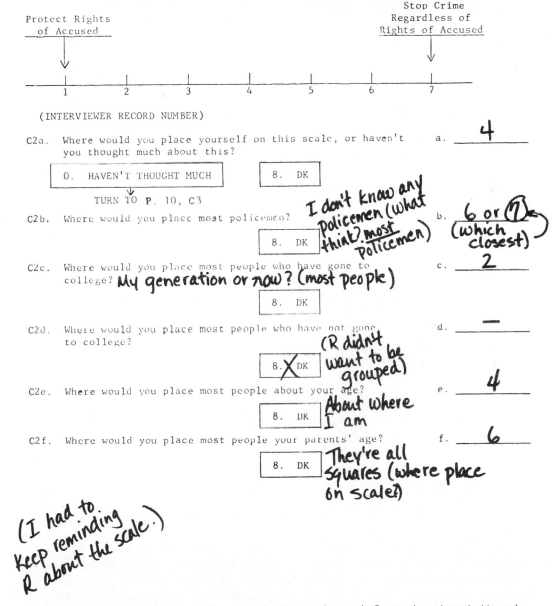

(CARD C2, ORANGE) Some people are primarily concerned with doing everything possible to protect the legal rights of those accused of committing crimes. Others feel that it is more important to stop criminal activity even at the risk of reducing the rights of the accused.

Throw them all in jail! (RQ- What # on scale shows how feel ?)

Protect Rights
of Accused

Stop Crime
Regardless of
Rights of Accused

| 1 | 2 | 3 | 4 | 5 | 6 | 7 |

(INTERVIEWER RECORD NUMBER)

C2a. Where would you place yourself on this scale, or haven't you thought much about this?   a. ___4___

    0. HAVEN'T THOUGHT MUCH   8. DK

    TURN TO P. 10, C3

C2b. Where would you place most policemen?   8. DK   b. 6 or ⑦ (which closest)

I don't know any policemen (what think? most policemen)

C2c. Where would you place most people who have gone to college? *My generation or now? (most people)*   8. DK   c. ___2___

C2d. Where would you place most people who have not gone to college?   8. ☒ DK   d. ___—___

(R didn't want to be grouped)

C2e. Where would you place most people about your age?   8. DK   e. ___4___

About where I am

C2f. Where would you place most people your parents' age?   8. DK   f. ___6___

They're all squares (where place on scale?)

(I had to keep reminding R about the scale.)

FIGURE 16.2 A completed questionnaire page. (Survey Research Center, *Interviewer's Manual*, Revised Edition, Copyright © 1976 by the Institute for Social Research, The University of Michigan, Ann Arbor, MI. Reprinted with permission.)

377

the latency involved in writing means that the responses are more closely censored. But mail questionnaires may get past doormen and secretaries who keep interviewers at bay. Further, it is easier to ensure that the responses will be confidential if the questionnaire is returned anonymously.

The considerations in questionnaire construction are what to ask, how to ask it, how to order the questions, how to format the questionnaire, and how to improve it. Nonrespondents are a serious problem. These topics form the basis of our discussion.

What to Ask

Although some questionnaires are probes to see what is there, most are targeted to obtain some specific information or to relate certain variables. Therefore, the questionnaire needs to be carefully planned. Lay out a "blueprint" of what information is needed. Some persons work backward from what the report should contain to the needed questions. This minimizes the tendency to feel, "I'd better get that now, in case I can't later." This can result in overly long questionnaires and items that never get analyzed. Yield to the impulse to add questions that allow explanations of responses, but add them where it is important. Zemke and Walonick (1980) pass along Berdie and Anderson's "litmus test" for questionnaire planning:

> Can you state the purpose of your proposed study in 25 words or less?
>
> > What do you want to know?
> > Why do you want to know it?
> >
> > What will happen as a result of answering the research question? . . .
> > [Both positive and negative consequences]
>
> Question: When you have described the goal of the study, ask yourself: "Is this study *really* worth doing?" (p. 89)

How to Ask It

As with the translation of a concept or construct into examples, which we discussed in chapter 9 on conceptual analysis, the questions become the definitions of the concepts about which we are inquiring. Careful wording is essential to portray accurately what is to be asked, to avoid biasing or leading questions, and to ensure that the response is to the full question without confusion over which part was answered or what else caused the response.

The variety of question types is limited only by the imagination. Common types, besides the open-ended, include short answers, checklists, rankings, responding on a verbal scale ("very difficult, somewhat difficult, not difficult"; "very poor, poor, good, very good"), responding on a graphical scale ("Check on the bar to show how clearly this instruction is written: very clearly _____|____|____|____|____|____|____|____|_____ not clearly at all), and a variety of other multiple-choice forms ("Use the following key to judge the following expressions of opinion: a. expresses my feelings well; b. close though not quite on target; c. not very close but somewhat; d. not close at all"). Measurement books with sample test items may suggest forms, and Payne (1951, in some respects outdated but still one of the best books on the subject), Converse and Presser (1986), Sudman and Bradburn (1982), among others, give excellent advice and suggest item formats.

Private attitudes that control our behavior are often different from those publicly expressed. Therefore, attitude scales that try to measure them directly by asking persons how closely they agree with certain positions may fail. Hence indirect measures are often used (see Webb et al., 1981). **Projective techniques** are one form of indirect measure. Three commonly used projective approaches are association, fantasy and ambiguous stimuli, and categorizing (Oppenheim, 1966).

In word association measures, we ask for the first thing that comes into the respondent's mind in response to a stimulus. The stimulus may be a word, a picture, or a graphic. This technique tends to work better in an interview because the respondent does not have time to think and censor responses. But even with a questionnaire, if there is a large number of items, responses tend to become less guarded and more revealing of underlying attitudes.

When fantasy and ambiguous stimulus measures are used, persons might be asked to produce a story ("Tell me a story about an African American person") or to discuss a stimulus (a picture of an African American child and a Caucasian child playing—"What are they saying to each other?"). The responses are revealing of the person's "building blocks" of experience and attitudes. Using ambiguous stimuli such as cloud or inkblot pictures ("Tell me what you see in these pictures") requires that the respondent assign meaning and reveal personal outlook.

Categorizing and labeling reveal how individuals see the world and thus their attitudes. Asking them to cluster photographs of faces "in whatever way you think they belong together" and then "Please explain the groupings" may tell how respondents categorize people and what characteristics of individuals are dominant in their minds. These reveal underlying thinking and suggest attitude structure. (We will return to this topic shortly.)

Tips on Question Construction and Hallmarks of Questionnaires

1. Use phrasing and language that will be understood and will appeal to all segments of the intended population. Since education and experience may vary widely, this may be very difficult because what is simple and clear for one person may seem condescending to another. Be sure to pretest with varied groups. Be careful of colloquial terms and jargon (*winnow* may be known to farmers but not city dwellers). Slang goes out of date quickly and may vary in interpretation from place to place.
2. Be sure respondents interpret the question as intended; pretesting is essential for this. ("What kind of headache remedy do you use?" may refer to the brand or to the type of medicine—pills, liquids, or lying down in a dark room for an hour.)
3. Keep both the questionnaire and individual items short and simple. Simple, short questions are better than long, complex ones for maintaining interest and imparting a feeling of movement. They are also more likely to be understood.

4. Avoid double-barreled questions. **Double-barreled questions** pose two issues at once, obscuring which is being responded to ("Have Russia's improved housing and industrialization raised the standard of living?" What if the respondent believes that housing has but industrialization hasn't?). Some such questions are very subtle, as this example from Sudman and Bradburn (1982, p. 135) shows: "The U.S. Supreme Court has ruled that a woman may go to a doctor to end pregnancy at any time during the first three months of pregnancy. Do you favor or oppose this ruling?" The issues of abortion at any time and abortion only during the first three months are intertwined. To which will the person respond?

5. Equally subtle is the one-and-a-half-barrel question, where the second issue is introduced in the alternatives, for example:

> The United States is now negotiating a strategic arms agreement with the Soviet Union in what is known as SALT II. Which one of the following statements is closest to your opinion on these negotiations? (1) I strongly support SALT II. (2) SALT II is somewhat disappointing, but on balance, I have to support it. (3) I would like to see more protection for the United States before I would be ready to support SALT II. (4) I strongly oppose the SALT II arms agreement with the Soviets. (5) I don't know enough about SALT II to have an opinion yet. (Sudman and Bradburn, 1982, p. 136)

The third response introduced adequacy of defense as a new issue and swayed responses negatively, whereas other surveys reported stronger support for the treaty.

6. Avoid biasing the response by the question. This is an obvious point, but often both sides of the issue are not included in the lead. Payne (1951) notes that when questioned on whether companies could arrange things to avoid layoffs, 63 percent of respondents said they could and 22 percent said they could not. But adding the other side of the question—"or do you think layoffs are unavoidable?"—dropped the 63 percent to 43 percent and almost doubled the 22 percent to 43 percent. Choice of words may also result in bias. Anglos react differently to "wetbacks" and "Mexican-Americans." Asking about "big business" gets a different response than just "business." Every modifier can make a difference!

7. **Framing of questions** is important. Slovic, Fischhoff, and Lichtenstein (1982) found mandatory seat belts favored by only 54 percent of respondents when the question expressed the likelihood of being injured as once in 100,000 trips. However, when the risk was stated in terms of a lifetime of driving and a rise in the chance of injury to 1 in 3, fully 78 percent favored mandatory seat belts. Tversky and Kahneman (1981) give a number of examples showing how "seemingly inconsequential changes in the formulation of choice problems caused significant shifts of preference" (p. 457). They reinforce the importance of trying out all formulations on small groups ahead of time to be sure they communicate as intended.

8. Allow respondents to protect their egos while responding. Otherwise, they may make up answers to avoid embarrassment. For instance, lead with a question undercutting the expectation of a response. Instead of asking, "What books does your child read?" first inquire, "Are you able to keep track of your child's reading?" Rephrase questions such as "Did you

graduate from college?" to "What is the highest grade in school you completed?"

9. Assuage the guilt of responding negatively by first asking for the positive: "What do you like about General Bullmoose?" "What do you dislike about him?"

10. Impersonal leads often get responses when direct questions cannot: "Do persons like yourself generally believe . . . ?" "Are you like them?"

11. Avoid negative questions if possible: "We should not admit tiny island nations to the United Nations." Respondents may miss the *not*. If the affective tone would be lost by positive phrasing, emphasize the *not* with underlining or italics.

12. With multiple-choice questions, be sure the list of alternatives is complete or an "other than the above" alternative is provided. Trying out the questions in an open-ended form with a small sample of the target group helps determine the range of likely responses and whether a "none of the above" or "other, please specify" is necessary. Supplying the respondent with an incomplete list reflects negatively on questionnaire preparation, and that is likely to be reflected in the care taken with responses.

13. The context in which a question is asked can make a big difference. A series of questions about conservation of energy preceded a question in which reasons were asked for buying a new car. Not surprisingly, fuel economy came out first. For a more accurate answer, the question should have been asked before the questions on conservation of energy.

Comparison of the answers obtained with results from an earlier poll is often helpful in determining whether the new results are trustworthy. Such analyses help us spot possible effects of context and wording that would not otherwise be noticeable. Such effects are so pervasive and so important that some pollsters argue that one question in one poll should never be trusted for very important issues. We need independent confirmation and validation of the initial results. Many data archives contain the results of past polls. Sources of data on past efforts have been compiled by the Gale Research Company since 1983. In addition, such repositories contain a wealth of question ideas that may be useful in helping develop your own instrument.

Ordering the Questions

The **order of questions** is important. The opening of the questionnaire sets the tone for the respondents regarding both motivation and purpose. Grabbing their attention and pulling them into the questions is good practice, and titles often help. Erdos (1970) suggests questionnaire titles that appeal to the ego ("A Survey of Industry Leaders"), emphasize the topic and its relevance ("Taking Inventory of Your Personal Health"), underline its importance ("A Nationwide Survey of . . ."), or emphasize the respondent-researcher tie ("For Alumni Only—A Confidential Survey").

The first few items are important in setting the tone of the questionnaire, reducing defensiveness, and allaying anxiety. Begin by asking easy-to-answer questions that personally involve the respondent: "What do you like about the location of your home?" Questions that arouse the interest or curiosity of the respondent are a good beginning, even if they are not later tabulated. Early questions also set the frame of reference for later ones. Early questions about auto safety may provide a set such that questions about auto improvement may later be confined to safety aspects unless the set is specifically broken.

Cluster similar questions so that the respondent isn't forced to change "mental set" with every question. Order them logically for flow and movement as the topic is covered. Consider such orderings as specific to general, past to present, or familiar to unfamiliar.

Leave demographic questions and other potentially sensitive questions to the end unless they are used to screen respondents to determine whether they need be questioned at all. It is well to explain why the demographics are important: "To determine how people of different backgrounds respond to this questionnaire, we'd like a few facts about you." If sensitive questions are left to the end, there is usually enough investment in the questionnaire to answer them rather than discard previous work.

Save respondent time and reading with "Skip to question X" where intervening questions are irrelevant. Arrows leading from various responses or other clever devices can help ensure that directions are followed.

The **funnel-sequenced questionnaire** parallels the focused interview in design; it starts broadly and then narrows to the topic of specific interest. As with the focus interview, the intent is to prevent the early responses from biasing those that come later. Broad questions obtain the respondent's general frame of reference. Sometimes when asking about a new topic about which an informed opinion is desired, we may invert the funnel and cover the aspects of the questions in detail. Then, at the end, we ask, "Now, taking all these things into consideration . . ."

Check the effect of order with a preliminary trial by using different orderings that seem to have merit. Often ordering affects the nature, length, and spontaneity of responses.

Hallmarks of a Letter of Transmittal[3]

Erdos (1970) provides an excellent list of characteristics and provides an example (Figure 16.3) with the characteristics identified.

1. Personalize the communication.
2. Ask a favor.
3. Indicate the importance of the research project and its purpose.
4. Indicate the importance of the recipient.
5. Stress the importance of replies in general.
6. Note the importance of replies even from readers who consider themselves not qualified to respond.
7. Indicate how the recipient may benefit from the research.
8. Note that completing the questionnaire will take only a short time.

---

3. Adapted from Erdos (1970), p. 102.

9. Point out that it can be answered easily.
10. Include a stamped envelope.
11. Describe how the recipient was selected.
12. Indicate that answers are anonymous and confidential.
13. Offer a report of the results.

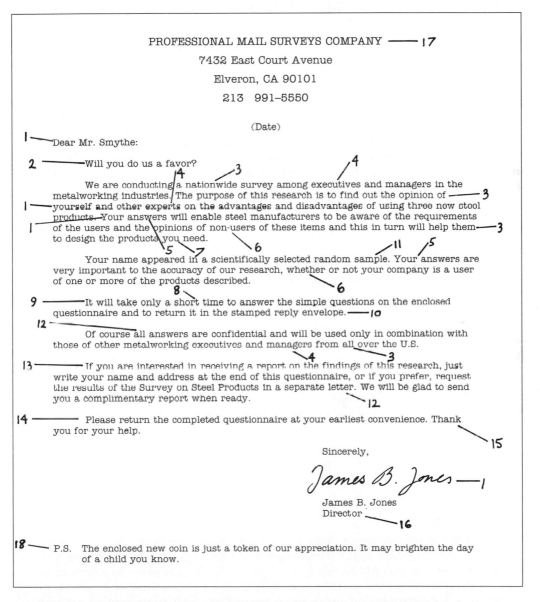

PROFESSIONAL MAIL SURVEYS COMPANY ——— 17

7432 East Court Avenue

Elveron, CA 90101

213 991-5550

(Date)

Dear Mr. Smythe:

Will you do us a favor?

We are conducting a nationwide survey among executives and managers in the metalworking industries. The purpose of this research is to find out the opinion of yourself and other experts on the advantages and disadvantages of using three new stool products. Your answers will enable steel manufacturers to be aware of the requirements of the users and the opinions of non-users of these items and this in turn will help them to design the products you need.

Your name appeared in a scientifically selected random sample. Your answers are very important to the accuracy of our research, whether or not your company is a user of one or more of the products described.

It will take only a short time to answer the simple questions on the enclosed questionnaire and to return it in the stamped reply envelope.

Of course all answers are confidential and will be used only in combination with those of other metalworking executives and managers from all over the U.S.

If you are interested in receiving a report on the findings of this research, just write your name and address at the end of this questionnaire, or if you prefer, request the results of the Survey on Steel Products in a separate letter. We will be glad to send you a complimentary report when ready.

Please return the completed questionnaire at your earliest convenience. Thank you for your help.

Sincerely,

James B. Jones

James B. Jones
Director

P.S. The enclosed new coin is just a token of our appreciation. It may brighten the day of a child you know.

FIGURE 16.3 Sample letter of transmittal. The numbers identify the characteristics listed in the text. (From P. L. Erdos, *Professional Mail Surveys*, p. 103, Copyright © 1970 by McGraw-Hill, Inc. Reprinted by permission of Robert E. Krieger Publishing Co.)

14. Include a note of urgency in the request for a response.
15. Express the sender's appreciation for the response.
16. Indicate the sender's importance to the respondent. Special populations respond to appeals from their own organizations.
17. Make the letter look professional.
18. If an incentive is included, describe it and indicate its purpose.
19. Avoid anything in the letter that might bias responses.
20. Keep it brief.

Motivating the respondent is central to getting a reply with good data. The **letter of transmittal**, which, together with a return envelope, accompanies the questionnaire, is a major means of motivation. Respondents will answer many, many items and even open-end questions if they are inspired to do so. Note the number of items above concerned with conveying the importance of the project, the respondent, and the reply—they make up almost half the list! Be sure that comments about the importance of the respondent sound sincere; obvious flattery may backfire. Limited sample size emphasizes the importance of replies ("You are one of few individuals who have moved into this area in the past 12 months; therefore . . ."). Ask for replies even from those not qualified, to keep track of them ("Send your return even if you are not a homeowner; otherwise, we'll never know").

Computer-personalized letters are so common these days that they may have lost some of their appeal, but probably not all of it. If the topic is sensitive and confidentiality is important, it is probably better to make the letter impersonal and routine. If a report is offered, be sure to supply a separate request form. A stamped envelope produces a higher response rate than a business reply envelope.

Questionnaire Format

Returns are highest on mail questionnaires that are short and easy to respond to. They should run two to four pages, not be crowded, and feature plenty of white space. Avoid giving the questionnaire a jazzy look—recipients may confuse it with junk mail. A personal rather than commercial look makes it clear that their response is important to you. Make the first page especially appealing and easy to read.

Don't number consecutively if there are many questions. Number within sections and use sectioning with interesting headings ("About You and Your Department") to provide a feeling of progress. Break lists every five lines or so. Put responses in a uniform place, usually at the right, so that the question is visible as subjects respond (unless you are dealing with a left-handed sample). A clean typeface and print make a favorable impression; print both sides, so that the questionnaire appears shorter. Use good but lightweight paper. The way the questions are arranged on the page can show the respondent the flow through the questionnaire, not only saving considerable time but also giving a feeling of progress.

IMPROVING QUESTIONS, QUESTIONNAIRES, AND LETTERS OF TRANSMITTAL

All interview schedules and all questionnaires and letters of transmittal ought always to be subjected to **pilot testing** before being used. Submit them to subjects as much like those you intend to query as you can find. Then review with these people, question by question, what they reacted to, what they meant by their answer, and why they answered as they did. This will confirm that the right meaning of each question is being conveyed and that responses can be interpreted for what they were intended to mean. It will help ensure that respondents understood the letter of transmittal and will give some indication of its motivating qualities. The time and effort involved in pilot testing will be more than repaid by the elimination of confusing wording, ambiguous questions for which the results would be uninterpretable, and frustration among both respondents and interviewers.

We never want to interrupt an interview to ask about particular responses, yet memory is selective, and underreporting of what actually occurred increases as time elapses. So querying an individual about responses to an interview after a long session may not be fruitful. **Stimulated recall** is a way of helping individuals relive their previous experiences, and the follow-up can be scheduled at a later time. For example, Bloom (1954) studied the thought processes of students in a discussion class. He replayed an audiotape, stopping it at important points and querying students about what had gone on in their minds. Kagan, Krathwohl, and Miller (1963) and Kagan, Krathwohl, and Farquhar (1965) used a similar process to study therapy and instruction with the more complete stimulation of videotapes. They also allowed the students or clients to hold the control and stop the tape at points they thought significant. In addition, the researcher could ask for it to be stopped at points not deemed significant by the other person. This provided additional insights. Given the stimulation of video or audio replays, subjects are able to report both events and inner feelings with a verisimilitude that suggests they are reliving those moments. The quality and depth of the pilot study data can be markedly enhanced by using a stimulated-recall process to probe responses to an interview or a questionnaire. Indeed, when the individual's thought processes are more relevant than the final response, it may be profitable to use this process to supplement the interviews.

For a questionnaire and a letter of transmittal, an alternative to stimulated recall is to have individuals think aloud as they go through the material. This may slow reading, but most individuals can process the letter and questionnaire at close to normal speed while giving their reactions. Again, we may not want to interrupt the flow to query them, but either an audio or a video recording can provide a record that can be played back and stopped at significant points by subject or investigator and the responses probed. Think-aloud procedures also allow us to judge the face validity of the material. This can be important in motivating adequate responses.

Where the questionnaire is intended to measure a construct, the procedures of item analysis discussed in chapter 11 will be applicable here as well, including estimates of test reliability and validity. We may also be able to shorten the questionnaire as nonfunctional items are discovered.

THE NONRESPONDENT

Nonresponse is a serious problem for questionnaires, and though rarer with interviews in person or by phone, refusals can still be a source of bias if nonrespondents differ from respondents in ways that would affect their answers. This is another example of the problem of mortality mentioned in chapter 15. Note that there are two potential sources of mortality: loss of individuals from a cohort or panel sample and lack of response from those still available.

What is a good return, and when should we be concerned about the problem? The answer lies in the representativeness of the people reached with respect to the topic of concern in comparison to the population to which we wish to generalize. If those reached are truly representative, a low response rate is acceptable.

The problem is that **nonrespondents** tend to differ from respondents in certain characteristics. Respondents are essentially volunteers. Rosenthal and Rosnow's (1975) review of the literature shows that volunteers tend to be better educated, have higher social status, be more intelligent, have a greater need for social approval, and be more sociable than nonrespondents. With somewhat less confidence, we can expect them to be more arousal-seeking, more unconventional (especially in studies of sexual behavior), more likely to be female, and less authoritarian. Likelihood of volunteering is greatest among Jews, less among Protestants, and still less among Roman Catholics. Rosenthal and Rosnow list other characteristics that we can expect with some confidence and still others with minimum confidence.

Is it important that respondents are likely to differ from nonrespondents? It depends entirely on whether the differences are related to what we are studying. In interviews, inability to reach a person after repeated callbacks may suggest a different lifestyle from the others. Whether this is serious depends on whether that lifestyle is related to what we are studying. A questionnaire study of welfare mothers would yield highly spurious results if only the better-educated and more intelligent volunteered to reply. By contrast, a questionnaire on the prevalence of cancer in the family, which seems to strike persons irrespective of the characteristics just described, might be unaffected.

The best defense against the nonrespondent problem is to do a good job of motivating respondents in the first place. Dillman, Gallegos, and Frey (1978) found that using the person's name in telephone surveys to increase rapport had little impact. Both they and Traugott, Groves, and Lepkowski (1987) found that an advance letter had a significant effect. As already noted, the letter of transmittal is important in that regard for a questionnaire. The presence of an incentive such as a coin may improve returns but probably does little to enhance quality of response. The best motivator is the internal one of wanting to do it rather than the external one of being bribed.

The "foot in the door" technique involves obtaining some type of prior commitment from a potential respondent before conducting the actual survey (Hansen and Robinson, 1980; Snyder and Cunningham, 1975). It may take the form of a postcard to be answered and returned, indicating a willingness to complete the questionnaire. Telephone solicitation of a willingness to respond to a callback at a convenient time can help with telephone interviews (Groves and Magilavy, 1981).

Follow-ups do increase returns, successive ones being less effective. A well-written postcard on first follow-up may do as much as a more expensive complete package, but replacement questionnaires on second follow-up are also often effective. Experiments have been done with certified and overnight mail; though effective, they increase expenses substantially. Be sure to allow a sufficient period for follow-ups in the time schedule; the bulk of questionnaires are returned by about two weeks following receipt.

With questionnaire studies, we often assume that nonrespondents are merely very late respondents. Tabulating responses by the three- to five-day period in which they were returned or comparing those received before and after the follow-up enables us to see whether the response pattern changes from early to late returns. If not, perhaps nonrespondents do not differ from respondents. If a pattern appears, it may be possible to extrapolate it to the nonrespondents to determine how extreme their responses might be in contrast to returns.

Especially where follow-ups are not sufficiently effective and where the nature of the nonrespondent seems important, phone follow-ups are often used to complete essential questions. Remember, however, that the respondents at this point are clearly identified and that their responses are both verbal and spontaneous. These differences need to be taken into account in comparisons with questionnaire replies. Again, depending on what is being studied, being identified and not having time to think over one's response may make little difference. However, with some topics, especially sensitive ones, it certainly may.

- Questionnaires provide structured responses and must be carefully developed, *pilot-tested*, and revised (sometimes repeating the latter steps) to obtain valid data.
- Proper framing and ordering of questions are important for obtaining valid data.

- Poor response rate is the biggest single problem for mailed question-naires. This is of concern when the answers of nonrespondents might have differed from those of respondents.
- The letter of transmittal can be important in setting the frame for responding and in obtaining a high response rate, thereby warranting careful development and pilot testing.
- A number of means of increasing response rate for mailed question-naires have been researched. Prior commitment seems to work, as may some kind of reward, but the best motivation is intrinsic interest in having one's response count toward the results.
- Follow-ups do increase returns, but each wave brings decreasing results, and responses may trend toward those of nonrespondents if respondents' and nonrespondents' answers differ.

CODING AND ANALYSIS OF INTERVIEW AND QUESTIONNAIRE RESPONSES

Precoding responses is useful for interview forms, but on questionnaires it often adds to the clutter. Once coding clerks are familiar with the form, precoding notations aren't as important, so it may be better to do without them. Keeping responses on the same edge of the paper speeds tabulation. Consider machine-readable response modes if the equipment is available to you. It saves keying the responses into a computer, with its attendant errors. You should edit the forms, however, to ensure both that the clerk will read them correctly and that the respondent has followed directions. Here are some tips:

1. Separate codes for items can always be merged later, but when, for instance, all the "Other, please specify" responses are given the same code, they cannot be distinguished later without recoding. Make at the beginning all the distinctions in coding that you may want later.
2. Make codes exhaustive of the response range but mutually exclusive so that a given response will always carry the same code.
3. Be consistent (for example, use 1 for yes and 0 for no consistently).
4. If missing data may be a significant factor, distinguish the different causes: doesn't know, skipped question, refused to respond, indecipherable, inappropriate response, and so on.
5. Where multiple responses are allowed, the most common patterns can often usefully be assigned single codes.
6. Check consistency of coding across coders and over time. Determine the desired coding of certain sheets and slip them in the batch at random intervals to provide a coding audit.
7. Provide each coder with a coding manual, and keep all manuals up-to-date as resolutions of coding problems are agreed on.

Analysis of Data

Because the main purpose of many surveys is to describe (who will win an election, levels of support for a tax increase), simple percentages often suffice to indicate the proportion of respondents giving each response. In other instances, measures of central tendency are used (most often mean or median, sometimes mode). Measures of dispersion, typically the standard deviation, indicate how broadly people differ in their responses. These were described in chapter 10.

If we wish to relate variables (for instance, to determine the influence of education on voting behavior), **cross-tabulation** tables are constructed, much like correlation scatterplots. The variables are categorical, however, and do not have a higher and lower direction. Thus a table like Table 16.3 is called a cross-tabulation or **cross-break**. Together with percentages, such tables are often themselves enough to convey relationships. For example, in this instance, it can be seen that although the Democrats have a larger total registration, their education level is more blue-collar than the Republicans'.

If we wished to summarize the relationship with a correlational statistic, we could assign arbitrary numbers to the categories and compute a correlation. For instance, we could assign 0 to the Democratic column and 1 to the Republican column; similarly, 0 to elementary-level education, 1 to high school, 2 to college, and 3 to beyond college.[4] This would provide a pair of numbers for each case from which a Pearson product-moment correlation could be computed. The correlation between educational level and political party, computed this way, is .23.

Alternatively, we could use an appropriate choice from the special correlation methods described in Table 10.1, page 184 (such as the point-biserial in this instance, which would produce the same result, .23, as just obtained). Another possibility is to reduce the data to a two-by-two cross-break by casting everyone into two categories, high school education and below or some college

---

4. If there are three or more categories, the variable must be ordered in some way for this method to work. If we included independents in the problem, for example, we could assign independents a value of 2 and Republicans a value of 3 if it were reasonable to assume that independents were in between on a scale from liberal Democrats to conservative Republicans.

TABLE 16.3 Cross-tabulation of Political Party Registration and Level of Education

Level of Education	Number of Cases (N = 423)		Percentage of Cases		Percentage by Education Level within Party	
	Democrats	Republicans	Democrats	Republicans	Democrats	Republicans
Elementary	68	21	16	5	27	12
High school	123	80	29	19	49	46
College	42	47	10	11	17	27
Beyond college	17	25	4	6	7	15
Total	250	173	59	41	100	100

TABLE 16.4   The Data of Table 16.3 Reduced to a Fourfold Table

Level of Education	Number of Cases (N = 423)		Percentage of Cases	
	Democrats	Republicans	Democrats	Republicans
High school or less	191	101	45	24
Some college or beyond	59	72	14	17

and above. This discards some of the information regarding level of education attained and assumes that high school and elementary level are pretty much the same for our purposes, as are college level and beyond. It combines the top two rows into one and, similarly, the bottom two rows, as shown in Table 16.4. The tetrachoric coefficient (also in Table 10.1) can be used to estimate the relationship of two arbitrarily categorized variables such as these. It indicates the extent of relationship as .32. Notice that depending on the assumptions made, we use different statistics to compute the size of the relationship, and somewhat different estimates result.

Chapter 17, dealing with inferential statistics, takes analysis a step further. It provides tools to distinguish data indicative of a real relationship from those more likely resulting from chance and error.

- Coding must be done carefully to maintain data validity.
- Training coders, using code books that are kept up-to-date as questions are resolved, and sampling coded questionnaires for coding accuracy and consistency all provide quality control.
- Development and analysis of cross-break tables provide information on the variation of responses with various demographic and other independent variables that may throw considerable light on the respondents' underlying value structure and thinking processes.

SPECIAL PROBLEMS OF INTERVIEWS AND QUESTIONNAIRES

Querying Sensitive Topics

Getting honest responses to questions regarding sensitive topics is a special problem. If the respondents trust the researcher's claim that the responses are truly anonymous and not identified by a secret code, the questionnaire has an advantage over the interview. This is one of those situations where the sins of shady researchers come back to haunt the innocent. Whenever a scientist is caught secretly coding presumably anonymous questionnaires, it reflects on all of us and what we do. A promise of anonymity should always be honored, even though that means that a targeted follow-up is impossible and a follow-up mailing must be sent to the whole sample.

Where individuals are likely not to trust the researcher, various forms of the randomized response technique originated by Warner (1965) can solve some of the problems (Himmelfarb and Edgell, 1980; Schuman and Kalton, 1985). Instead of being confronted with a single sensitive question, the respondent is confronted with two or more questions, one or more of which is not at all sensitive. A random device determines which the respondent is to answer. Assuming that the respondent understands the process, it removes most of the embarrassment surrounding the questioning, for instance:

> "Please flip a coin, but do not show it to me. If the coin came up heads, *when I ask you to*, please answer this question: 'Have you ever used marijuana, cocaine, or heroin or some form thereof?' If the coin came up tails, please answer this one: 'Is your birthday in December?' Now tell me your answer, please."

With a random coin flip, half the sample will answer each question. Since birthdays are spread about equally across the year, about 1/12, or 8.33 percent, will answer yes to the second question and 91.67 percent will answer no. Since they constitute half the cases, subtracting half the 8.33 percent, or 4.17 percent, from the yeses and, similarly, 91.67/2, or 45.83 percent, from the nos will yield the percentages of yeses and nos for the other half of the group. Doubling those percentages will yield an estimate of the percentages had all persons been asked the sensitive question, yet no one will know who answered which question.

Miller (1984) suggests dividing a sample randomly in half and providing two lists of behaviors. One list contains only innocuous behaviors; the other includes the sensitive behavior as well. Subjects are asked to report only the number of activities engaged in on the list. The difference between the two lists provides an estimate of the frequency of the sensitive behavior. This method appears simpler; there is nothing to be explained to the respondent, and it also seems less intrusive.

Neither of these two techniques allows the sensitive question response to be linked to any other item such as demographic information. If such linkage is needed, having the researcher's guarantee of anonymity accepted seems to be the preferred method.

Another problem has been to link the data gathered anonymously across different instruments administered simultaneously or over a period of time. The CDRGP (for "context-determined, rule-generated pseudonym") technique provides a common rule for everyone to follow in generating pseudonyms that can be placed on records (Carifio and Baron, 1977). Since the same rule is repeated at each administration, respondent error in recalling a pseudonym is eliminated. The respondent might be asked to write in successive blanks "the first letter of the month you were born in," "the first letter of the name of your street," "the first letter of your mother's first name," "the first letter of your father's first name,'' and so on. The confidentiality of certain data is protected by law in schools. Therefore, information required for breaking the code could not be obtained by the researcher without the consent of the people involved. Questions for generating pseudonyms can be based on such information.

Response Sets

Interviews and questionnaires must confront the problem that answers are often affected by **response sets** such as social desirability, acquiescence, and ''naysaying.'' These are stances that predispose individuals to respond in certain ways. For the person who wants to be thought of positively, social desirability set falsifies answers in the direction the respondent deems socially desirable. Other similar response tendency examples are a desire to gain social approval from the interviewer, to preserve one's own self-image, or to avoid feelings of discomfort (Phillips, 1971). For instance, a check of responses against records revealed that when asked whether they had contributed to the Community Chest, 44 percent of respondents gave false answers. Women were found to be more accurate than men in their reports (Cahalan, 1968). Many findings indicate that responses to questions that require admitting to socially undesirable tendencies should be viewed with suspicion. Perhaps different wording that elicits these tendencies differentially might be tried to find how much, which groups of individuals, and which wordings are affected.

Among yeasayers and naysayers, the tendency to acquiesce is considerably more common and hence the greater threat. It affects rating scales (more positive response), agree–disagree, true–false, and yes–no response modes. One way of avoiding the more prevalent acquiescence set, though it will reinforce the naysayers' set, is to make the desired response negative. Another, if it doesn't reduce the sample size unduly, is to include both negative and positive wordings and eliminate the responses of people who contradict themselves. Dropping these individuals may affect the generality of the study, however, since people who always acquiesce or are always negative probably respond differently from others in a variety of areas.

- Methods have been developed for maintaining respondent anonymity while querying sensitive topics and for anonymously linking data from several instruments.
- Researchers need to be alert to response sets, particularly the tendency to acquiesce or hew to socially desirable responses; these can create serious data validity problems

ADDITIONAL HALLMARKS OF SURVEY RESEARCH

Hallmarks of interviews, questionnaires, and letters of transmittal have already been noted. The following are some other important aspects.

1. The intent of the survey is delineated clearly.
2. The definition of the target population is consistent with the study's intent, and inferences to the target are made consistent with the quality of the sampling process.
3. The sampling technique is clearly specified, and the likelihood of systematic bias is described and, if possible, negated by demographic data from the sample. Attention to the need for stratification to ensure representativeness on key variables is displayed. A probability sample is used, if possible and appropriate.
4. Questions or questionnaires are pilot-tested to determine whether they elicit the intended response. As appropriate, "think aloud" procedures are used by respondents as they reply to make sure that their interpretation corresponds to the one intended. Revisions are also pilot-tested, as needed, to ensure that adequate corrections are made.
5. Interviewers are selected on appropriate bases (persons of a certain background to interview similar persons where this might be a factor). Data gatherers are adequately trained so that their technique does not constitute an unintended contaminating variable.
6. If sensitive data are gathered, assurances of anonymity and procedures for guaranteeing it are implemented. Protection of privacy is ensured, and individuals or institutions cannot be identified from the data without their consent.
7. An appropriate data gathering method is employed: structured, partially structured, or unstructured interviews in person or over the telephone, questionnaires administered in person or by mail, or the like.
8. Procedures ensure that the target sample was reached, including follow-up of nonrespondents. Comparison of late with early respondents or a similar practice gives clues about any nonrespondent bias.
9. Comparisons involve a large enough sample to reveal differences of a size of interest (this will be explained further in our discussion of statistical tests in chapter 17).

SUMMARY

Some important characteristics of the panorama of methods are reviewed in Table 16.5, on page 394. We turn in the chapter after next to the last of the three basic research methods, experimentation, the most structured and controlled of the three.

TABLE 16.5 Comparison of Data Collection Methods on Critical Characteristics

	Individual Interview	Group Interview	Telephone Interview	Mailed Questionnaire
Uses	Establishing rapport Ensuring that questions are correctly understood Probing answers, especially ambiguous ones Reducing "don't know" or "no opinion" responses Getting a high response rate Getting spontaneous responses Providing flexibility—interviewer can follow whatever leads seem significant	Minimizing information distortion (presence of others constrains respondents for fear of contradiction) Emboldening some to talk on sensitive issues when others do so	Contacting a geographically dispersed sample quickly Exploring sensitive topics (impersonality of the telephone emboldens respondents to speak more freely) Eliminating travel costs	Contacting large samples at very little cost Obtaining highly structured responses Obtaining considered rather than spontaneous responses
Sample	Cost usually restricts sample geographically and numerically Researcher often determines who will be chosen in field; this can bias sample if sampling plan is not carefully followed Nature of sample can be controlled in more respects than with any other method	Reduces cost considerably over individual interviews, and some believe data obtained are as good or better Not all invitees will attend and participate, so some selectivity is likely Not all ages, sexes, classes, and so on are available at same time Right mix of people is necessary to get good response	Sample can be wide and broad; no geographic restrictions exist as phone costs vary little Unlisted numbers can be reached by random number generation, but so are many businesses, usually not wanted in the sample Some members of the lower class are phoneless	Sample can be wide and broad; no geographic restrictions exist Actual sample depends on representativeness of returns Certain segments of the population are more easily reached by this method, but some segments (illiterates, disorganized people) will not respond Who in household actually answers questionnaire cannot be controlled A good sampling frame is not available for many target populations of interest (e.g., working mothers)

	Individual Interview	Group Interview	Telephone Interview	Mailed Questionnaire
Length	Very long interviews of a day or more have been held successfully	Same as individual interview, except it is harder to keep a group together for long	Interviews are generally shorter than face-to-face	Responses are comparatively short if open-end questions are used Number of structured questions is limited unless high motivation is developed
Nonresponse	Generally low, few people refuse; callbacks are expensive, however	Not all who are invited will attend group sessions; some selectivity is usually evident	Higher refusal rate than interview but it is still low Has higher response rate than interviews in urban areas where respondents are reluctant to allow strangers into their homes Callbacks are inexpensive	Return rate can be a serious problem; selective nature of dropouts may jeopardize representativeness and generality Follow-ups, initial motivation of respondent to take interest in study, and sometimes incentives can reduce dropout rate
Anonymity	Respondent is known, but good interviewer can be reassuring to most respondents	Some anonymity exists when only a group response is called for (e.g., All those who agree say "yes")	Respondent is known unless respondent appreciates anonymity of random number generation; skill of interviewer can often reassure adequately Lack of face-to-face contact eases respondent anxiety about sensitive issues	Response can be genuinely anonymous with beneficial results for sensitive issues if respondent trusts researcher's assurances that questionnaires are not secretly coded
Interviewer Bias or Coding Errors	Can be a problem, but reduced through good training Carelessness or cheating by interviewers requires regular supervisor checks Coding of open-end questions requires carefully trained workers	Same as individual interview but comparatively fewer instances to monitor	Supervisor can monitor calls for bias and for compliance with instructions; computer can be programmed to check for apparent inconsistency of responses. Interviewer can then probe for cause or correct response	No interviewer bias; responses are in own words for open-end questions, but coding requires carefully trained workers Structured questions can be read and coded by combination of document scanner and computer

(continued)

TABLE 16.5 *continued*

	Individual Interview	Group Interview	Telephone Interview	Mailed Questionnaire
Visuals	Usable	Usable	Not usable	Usable
Sensitive Issues	Reassurance by interviewer is important Method of asking questions and characteristics of interviewer may affect results; requires training and monitoring Random response methods reduce problems Ability to observe race, socioeconomic status, dress, and other nonverbal clues may affect interviewer's willingness to ask certain sensitive questions or alter their phrasing	As some respondents open up, others are encouraged to do so Method of asking questions and characteristics of interviewer may affect results; requires training and monitoring Random response methods applicable	Anonymity of phone encourages responses that might be inhibited in face-to-face interviews	Anonymity encourages fuller responses than face-to-face interviews might
Speed	Slow	Relatively fast	Fastest	Slowest of all if high rate of return is needed
Probing?	Yes, for clarification of ambiguity and to determine underlying rationale for responses	Yes; further, generality of responses can be elicited by asking how many agree	Yes, but somewhat limited if rapport is to be maintained	No, unless follow-up by phone or letter, but that requires that respondent be identified Omissions can be common but difficult to interpret; could be probed with interview
Spontaneous Reactions, Unguardedness?	Yes	Yes, for those who answer first, but others can think about response	Yes	No, person can mull over and change answer

	Individual Interview	Group Interview	Telephone Interview	Mailed Questionnaire
Adaptation of Language to Level of Respondent?	Yes	Yes	Yes, if interviewer catches on soon enough	No, must be preset; may be too simple and basic for some, not easy enough for others. Difficulty leads to nonresponse
Inclusion of Working Target Group Members?	Only if interviews are done evenings and weekends, which increases their cost	Same as individual interview	Same as individual interview	Yes
Cost	Most expensive and labor intensive	Depending on size of groups, can be least costly of interviews on per-person basis	Less than individual interview, unless extensive computer equipment is included in the cost, in which case cost per interview depends on extent of use	Least costly of methods, although extensive follow-up of nonreturns may add considerably to cost

SOURCE   Adapted from *Research Methods in Economics and Business* by R. Ferber and P. J. Verdoorn, 1962, New York: Macmillan.

ADDITIONAL READING

Cannell (1985a, 1985b)
Frey (1989)
Groves (1990)

Guenzel, Berckmans, and Cannell (1983)
Sudman and Bradburn (1982)
Survey Research Center (1976)

IMPORTANT TERMS

Cohort studies
Computer-assisted telephone interviewing
   (CATI)
Cross-break
Cross-sectional studies

Cross-tabulation
Double-barreled questions
Focus group
Focused interview
Framing of questions

Funnel-sequenced questionnaire	Projective techniques
Letter of transmittal	Response sets
Longitudinal studies	Sample surveys
Nondirective approach	Stimulated recall
Nonrespondent	Structured interview
Order of questions	Tandem interviewing
Panel sample	Trend studies
Pilot testing	Unstructured interview
Probes	

========= APPLICATION PROBLEMS =========

1. A committee was set up by the student services department of Upstate University to determine how well their services were contributing to the academic life of the university. It was the perception of the committee members that there was a lack of awareness among faculty of the department's contributions. The committee decided to conduct a survey to determine what information faculty had about the department's program, how this information was received and put to use, and the level of current faculty involvement. How might the committee carry out this survey?

2. Ruth Anne Blanchard, dean of a privately run community college, located in a city of 500,000, wished to gather information to help plan the courses the college would offer over the next five years. She decided to survey a sample of the city's residents to determine their perceived needs in order to develop projections. How should she proceed?

3. Kristin Phillips, a member of a large national professional association, wished to know whether fellow members shared her views on the need for a local chapter and the activities and services it might offer. She mailed all other members a questionnaire soliciting their opinions. Assuming that she constructed an appealing, well-designed instrument and accompanying letter of transmittal, what further problems should she be alert to, and what should she do about them?

4. David Apple is a researcher who is interested in establishing what barriers, if any, exist to children's use of micro-computers at the elementary school level. He has received permission to carry out his study at selected elementary schools and has decided to supplement his participant observation by interviewing a sample of students from all grade levels (kindergarten to grade 6). What style of interview might he use?

5. The family life and sex education team at a large urban school offers a program on human sexuality beginning at grade 7 and continuing until the end of grade 12. The team members wish to determine whether the approach they use, and the information it imparts, is having an effect on the sexual behavior of the students. How might they do so using a questionnaire?

Compare your answers with those on pages 715–717.

===================== APPLICATION EXERCISE =====================

Consider how your problem might be explored with a sample survey. Does it have aspects that might differ over time and be of interest? What kind of design might you use to study them? Cross-sectional? Longitudinal? Which longitudinal design? Why would interviewing gather useful data? What interview approach would you take? Nondirective? Structured? Funnel?

Could you use a questionnaire approach? Who would be in your sample, and how would you choose these people? How would you learn what questions to ask? What kinds of questions might you use? Why? How might you pretest your questionnaire and, if a mail questionnaire, the letter of transmittal? What motivational appeal would you use?

The Nature and Logic
of Inferential Statistics

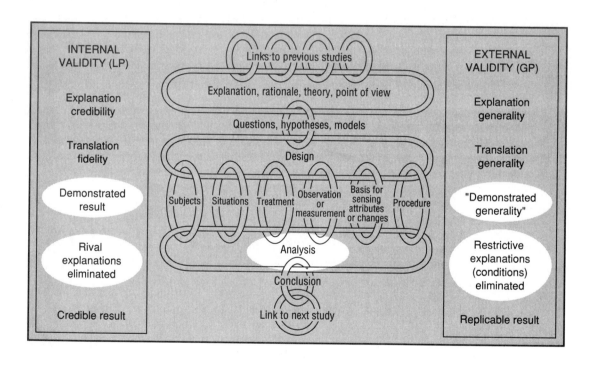

Mathematics does not develop the scientist's powers but puts its powers at his disposal; [with] its creation, something of the genius of the mathematician himself is made available to every schoolboy.
Abraham Kaplan, The Conduct of Inquiry

Like many things, statistics, though opaque in bulk, is transparent in thin slices.

Anonymous

OVERVIEW

When studying sample surveys, we encountered methods that use numbers for description. These methods may be used to reveal what is happening (discovery), but more often they are used to show that a prediction is true—to test a hypothesis. Inferential statistics help make the judgment that the data correspond appropriately to the prediction.

We typically study a sample portrayed by descriptive statistics. But ultimately, it is not the sample that is of interest. Instead, it is the applicability of the hypothesis to other samples like that one—its generality to the population of which the sample is representative. Inferential statistics provide a basis for making that generalization. Properly applied, they permit us to estimate the characteristics of the population from which the sample came. That is of interest if we must make a decision that applies to that population (a whole school district from a sample of one or a few classes) or if we wish to compare that population with some value (the district's achievement with national norms).

Inferential statistics contribute to internal validity (LP) by helping us estimate the size of any effect and giving evidence that it was unlikely that the effect was due to chance factors—key judgments in determining the internal validity of a study. So inferential statistics contribute to the third and fourth judgments of internal validity (LP): to the third in certifying that a "demonstrated result" of a certain size occurred and to the fourth in the elimination of sampling and error variation as alternative explanations of the data.

This chapter concentrates on the logic of the processes of estimation and hypothesis testing. Because the logic is the same regardless of the inferential statistic used (*t* test, analysis of variance, chi square, etc.), once we understand the logic, it is easier for us to understand how a given statistic works and when and how it is appropriate to use it. In the course of exploring this logic, the chapter explains the concepts of power (sensitivity), Type I and Type II error, and the difference between statistical and practical significance.[1]

---

1. Chapter 22 deals with statistics beyond those described in chapter 10 and here. For example, it describes statistics that apply the logic to differences between frequencies (chi square), among several means (analysis of variance), and among several means with control of a contaminating variable (analysis of covariance).

CHAPTER CONTENTS

Prologue 402
Introduction 404
Estimation 406
  Estimation in the Context of
    Measurement and in General 406
  Estimation: Another Explanation
    and Example 410
Hypothesis Testing 413
  Does the Sample Belong to This
    Particular Population? 413
  Application of the Logic to a
    Test of Differences between Two
    Observed Means 421
The t Test for Differences between
  Means 423
  An Example 425
Sensitivity, Precision, and Statistical
  Power 426

Errors of Inference 426
Ways to Increase Statistical
  Power 428
Studies Designed to Accept
  the Null Hypothesis 431
Decision Making and Knowledge
  Building 432
The Meaning of Statistical
  Significance 433
  Statistical and Practical
    Significance 433
  Proving a Proposition
    versus Its Escaping
    Disconfirmation 434
Violating Assumptions of Statistical
  Tests 435
Summary 436

PROLOGUE

Inferential statistics seem to be made up of complex operations foreign to any but the initiated. Yet even though we don't think in statistical terms, we are continually making inferences in our daily lives. Indeed, a large chunk of the work force earns its living because it is good at making inferences! Consider this example.

When you drive someone else's auto or a rental car, one of the first things you do is learn the normal noise and vibration the car makes. This is especially true of older models with lots of rattles and squeaks. These are perfectly normal or typical for a car of that age. Only when you have learned what is typical can you detect subtle but atypical noises such as a brake pad dragging or a wheel bearing starting to break up.[2] Suppose you think you hear an atypical noise in front somewhere. You take the car to a garage.

Garage managers make a good living determining what is atypical and why. How do they learn this? Probably they have listened to lots of cars. Even with normal cars there is variability. A few are very quiet, most are somewhat noisy, and a few are very noisy even though they are OK. It is that bell-shaped curve we keep encountering. So they know what typical variation is. This manager takes the car for a test ride—but only a five-minute ride; other

---

2. A flat tire is easy to sense—the effect is so great that you can recognize it immediately without knowing the normal background noise. Just so, we don't need inferential statistics to know that penicillin is effective. But when the effect is small, that is where inferential statistics come in handy.

customers are waiting. That is a small sample to use for a decision, but that is the way the world works; we usually have less information to make decisions than we wish. From this small sample, the manager must judge the kind and range of noise that might typically occur over a longer drive. That is what we call estimation, inferring from a sample what the population value is, the typical noise of the car over a long normal drive.

The next inference is whether that noise belongs to the population of noises made by "healthy" cars or to a population made by cars with defective wheel bearings. Defective wheel bearings are a serious problem. If let go too long, they become more expensive to repair, and it is possible that on a highway, they could get hot enough to seize up, freeze the wheel, and cause an accident. The service manager must decide whether the sound is atypical enough that something may be wrong. He can only tell for sure by pulling off the wheel. That deprives the owner of the use of the car and costs something for the labor. Figure 17.1 illustrates the dilemma.

These are the risks we run in making inferences. We can determine what is to be judged atypical at whatever level we wish. That will determine our **Type I error**—saying the bearing is failing when it is OK. If it is cheap to pull a wheel, we might not mind making such errors because it would avoid a possible accident and a **Type II error**—saying the car was OK when the bearing was failing. But if the level of what is judged atypical is set too conservatively so that many noises are said to be atypical when they are really typical, we are going to anger many customers who are unhappy paying for our mistake in pulling the wheel when nothing is wrong.

We can decrease Type II errors, all other things being equal, by increasing Type I errors, being conservative in saying there is a problem when there may not be. Alternatively, we can increase the accuracy of our diagnostic judgments by taking a longer test drive (bigger sample on which to base the judgment), using a stethoscope or an electronic amplifier to increase the loudness, and locating the sound or otherwise increasing our sensitivity to the atypical.

We have used the example of the automobile, but the problem faced

	Car is OK; noise is typical.	Car is not OK; noise is atypical; bearing is starting to break up, could cause accident if not corrected!
Manager says car is OK; noise is typical.	Manager is correct; customer has no further problems and has increased trust in manager's judgment.	Type II error in judgment (beta error). Customer has accident on road and says, "I *beta* never go there for service again!"
Manager says car is not OK; leave it for check and repair	Type I error in judgment (alpha error). Customer says, "If you're wrong, do I *alpha* pay da bill?"	Manager is correct; repair is made; potential accident is averted; customer builds trust in manager's judgment.

FIGURE 17.1   Type I and Type II errors of inference (puns are intended as mnemonics).

by the mechanic is also faced by the surgeon deciding whether surgery is warranted (every human being is built a little differently), the physician prescribing a drug (each of us metabolizes a chemical at a different rate), the teacher diagnosing a student's reading ability, the librarian trying to decide how open the shelves can be without unacceptable rates of book loss, the social worker trying to decide how much aid can be given a family without coming to depend on and expect it, the economist trying to determine the interest rate that will just stimulate the economy and not cause inflation.

The consequences of a Type II error may not be an accident as in the car example. If we are trying to determine the efficacy of a drug, it may merely mean that we judge the drug ineffective when it is efficacious and so miss the use of a valuable drug. If we are trying to find the proper interest rate, we may move to a lower one when the original one was already stimulating the economy, and the still lower rate may trigger inflation. Each situation has its own set of consequences. It also has its own possibilities for increasing the sensitivity of the study to make a better diagnosis.

So much for the general logic as applied to everyday life. At least you can see that the logic of inference is not foreign to you. Further, you have already encountered much of the logic as it applies to numbers in the topic of measurement, as we shall see in our discussion of estimation.

INTRODUCTION

We have already learned that words can be used in confirming an explanation or a hypothesis in chapter 15, on qualitative methods; and in chapter 16, on survey methods, the interview dealt largely with the use of words to build such cases. Chapter 10, on descriptive statistics, however, showed how numbers could be used in place of words to describe, and that is the way the results of questionnaires are usually reported in survey research—as percentages. Experimentation, one of the most common research methods, is most often associated with confirmation of hypotheses, and nearly all experimentation is reported in terms of numbers—the results of measures. So it is important to learn more about number use.

A typical poll result is reported as follows:

> Seventy percent of those queried said yes when asked whether they thought next year would be better for them financially than this one has been. Twelve hundred people were questioned, and the margin of error is three percentage points.

The phrase "margin of error" deals with **inferential statistics**. The intent of the poll is to estimate the response to the question in the population that the sample represents. The response of the sample is used to estimate population values. Without any other information, and given a 70 percent yes response in this instance, our best guess is that the percentage of the U.S. population is the same as, or close to, the percentage that so responded in the sample. But how close? That is the margin of error. It indicates that an interval of three percentage points on either side of the observed value of 70, or the range 67 to 73, contains the population value with a confidence expressed by odds of 2 to 1. (The media often say, "the chances are 2 to 1 that the real vote proportion is between 67 and 73 percent." The odds actually reflect our confidence in where the population value lies with respect to this observed value—a subtle distinction but one to keep in mind.) The odds of 2 to 1, like odds in horse racing or betting, express our confidence that the statement is true ("I'll give you two dollars for your one that my horse, Beccaboo, will win!"). Although such polls are rarely explained that way, that is what estimation in inferential statistics is about. And the techniques of estimation are used in hypothesis testing.

These statistics are called inferential because they permit us to infer the characteristics of a population from those of a representative sample. However similar the characteristics of the sample are to those of the population, they are probably not identical to them. So having set acceptable odds for possibly being wrong, we can describe on the basis of a sample the range or interval within which statistics descriptive of characteristics of the total population will fall.

Inferential statistics, because they estimate the population value from the sample, can tell us whether a difference between means, for example, is likely to result from chance error or is a "real" difference.[3] They do this by asking whether, if we examine the typical range of differences between the means of samples taken from the same population, it includes or excludes the observed difference—is it typical or atypical? If it is in the range of typical values, it is likely due to chance; but if it is atypical, something probably influenced it besides chance, so it is a "real" difference.

In a nutshell, here is what inferential statistics will do for us:

Estimation

- Using data from a random sample, we can describe an interval within which, at a decided-on level of confidence, the value of a population characteristic will be found (for example, the band within which falls the true percentage of people responding yes to the poll's question).
- Estimation allows us to set the odds of how confident we want to be that the band or interval contains the population value (by convention, these are typically odds of 2 to 1, 19 to 1, 99 to 1, or even 999 to 1. They can, however, be set at whatever odds we wish). The size of the band will increase as we insist on being surer (go from odds of 2 to 1 toward odds of 999 to 1).
- The same applies to descriptive statistics for which statisticians can mathematically determine the nature of the distribution formed under conditions

---

3. I put *real* in quotation marks because although the difference between means is very likely the result of something in addition to chance, it may or may not be the result of whatever the study hypothesized was the cause. We accept that explanation only after we have eliminated every other reasonable alternative argument. Moses (1986) suggests that if chance is rejected as the sole cause, the hypothesized cause should be accepted with the qualification "maybe so" (p. 123).

of random sampling or chance. These include all statistics in common use, such as percentages in a poll, a correlation between two variables, and the mean or standard deviation of a sample.

Hypothesis Testing

- Hypothesis testing tells whether a given statistic is likely the result of sampling and chance error (say, a difference between two means, one from a treated group, the other from a nontreated group).
- It allows us to set the probability of error in calling a result a nonchance difference when it really is a chance difference.
- With that set probability of being wrong, it eliminates one alternative explanation of the data—namely, that chance factors should be seriously considered as an alternative cause of the effect.
- Given that probability of error, it allows us to design a study with sufficient sensitivity to sense a nonchance effect of a given size with specified odds, should one appear. Usually this will involve determining appropriate sample size, but it may also result from other adjustments in the design.

ESTIMATION

Estimation in the Context of Measurement and in General

We encountered **estimation** in a different context when we discussed the standard error of measurement in chapter 11. We used that standard error to estimate the range within which, at given odds, the true score lay. With a shift in the terminology, that same logic applies to the context of estimation of population values in general. Numbers descriptive of the characteristics of a population are called **parameters**. Those descriptive of a sample are sample statistics or just statistics.[4] Estimation is concerned with parameters.

We can make the parallel clear by noting the similarities between the estimation of a true score and of a population mean. The value we wish to estimate in both contexts is the mean of a distribution of means computed from samples. In general estimation, the population mean is the mean of the average values from repeated random samples of the same size taken from a population. Similarly, in the measurement context, the true score is the mean of the distribution of scores—scores in percentage terms are also means.[5] Further, since the scores are all from the same test, they are same-sized samples of behavior, and they can be considered random samples of the subject's behavior taken at different times. The situations are comparable, but the terminology is different.

The distribution of the average values from repeated random samples of

---

4. Note the alliteration: *sample statistics* and *population parameters*.
5. Say a subject gets 30 items correct on a test with 60 items. A percentage score of 50 is a mean score—the sum of scores for each correct item (one point each) divided by the number of items.

the same size drawn from a population is the **sampling distribution of the mean**. The standard deviation of that sampling distribution is the **standard error of the mean**. It indicates the variability of the mean due to sampling and other chance influences. In the measurement context, it is called the standard error of measurement and indicates the variability of the observed scores due to sampling variability plus all the other characteristics that cause measurement error (inattention, lack of motivation, etc.). (The standard error of the mean is also increased by measurement error.) With a shift of terminology, we can now apply what was learned in measurement to the context of general estimation.

With the standard error of measurement, we constructed a confidence interval within which we could say, at a specified level of confidence, the true score lay. Refer to Figure 11.3 on page 217. In part A, a confidence interval ±1 standard error wide was constructed around the observed score of 59. Recall that the middle portion of the normal curve between ±1 standard deviation includes about two-thirds of the frequency distribution (68.26 percent, to be exact); ±1.96 SD, 95 percent of it; ±2.58 SD, 99 percent; and ±3 SD, 99.9 percent. The sampling distribution for the mean is also a normal probability distribution. (Statisticians know this as a result of the central limit theorem, which states that as the sample size increases, the frequency distribution of sample means from a common population will increasingly resemble the normal curve, whether or not the population itself is distributed normally.) Therefore, the percentages for measurement confidence intervals apply in the general estimation context as well. Thus for any observed mean of a random sample from a population, we can say with 68 percent confidence that the population mean lies within ±1 standard error of the parameter value, with 95 percent confidence that it lies within ±1.96 SE, and with 99.9 percent confidence that it lies within ±3 SE. Those figures represent our confidence that the population's mean score will be in those zones. Let us review in more detail the logic for these statements.

With an observed score of 59, the true score could be anywhere in the interval from 56 to 62 because, as part B of the figure shows, true scores of 56, 57, 58, 59, 60, 61, and 62 would all have confidence intervals that would contain 59. Constructing the confidence interval around the observed score includes all these possibilities. The only difference between the measurement context and general estimation is that test scores are generally confined to whole numbers, so there are only the seven possibilities noted. Most parameters, however, can take any value, whole or fractional.

- Numbers descriptive of a population are called parameters; those descriptive of a sample are sample statistics or just statistics.
- Suppose we calculate a descriptive statistic on repeated random samples from a population. The frequency distribution of those values is called the sampling distribution of that statistic (a mean), and the standard deviation of that distribution, a parameter, is also its standard error.
- The standard error can be used to describe a confidence interval.

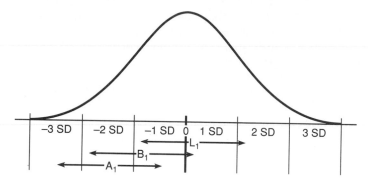

FIGURE 17.2   The ±1 standard error confidence intervals for likely (L), borderline (B), and atypical (A) values in a distribution of means of random samples from a common population.

Confidence Intervals.   The intervals described in the foregoing discussion are called confidence intervals, and they represent the range of values that includes the population value with a given confidence expressed by a percentage (for example, a 95 percent confidence interval) or odds (19 to 1). The ends of such intervals are the **confidence limits**. (for example, the 95 percent confidence limit).

The **confidence level** is the probability (for instance, 68 percent) that we will be right in saying that the confidence interval contains the population value—in this case, 68 percent of such intervals will contain the population value. The downside of this, however, is that 32 percent (100 minus 68) of them will not.

In Figure 17.2, three means are shown, chosen from the infinite number in the sampling distribution: a likely one, L_1; a borderline one, B_1; and an atypical one, A_1. Their values were chosen simply for purposes of illustration; what is considered "borderline" or "atypical" changes with the confidence level set.

When we extend a ±1 SE confidence interval around the likely mean, L_1, the band includes the population mean, the thick line running down from the middle of the distribution. The borderline value, B_1, is almost as extreme as we can get and still be within the ±1 SE zone. Yet the ±1 SE confidence interval around it includes the population mean. Using ±1 SE confidence intervals, 68 percent of those intervals constructed around the means of all possible random samples will contain the population mean. These are represented by the likely (L_1) and borderline (B_1) examples. The atypical example (A_1) represents the intervals that do not.

When we extend such a confidence interval around the atypical value, A_1, *it does not include the population's mean.* Using a ±1 SE confidence interval, about a third of the means of random samples will be atypical and not include the population value.[6] So we will be wrong one-third of the time in saying that the population mean is contained within that interval.

How often we are likely to be wrong is under our control. It depends on the confidence level we set. Frequently, we use a wider interval to lower the

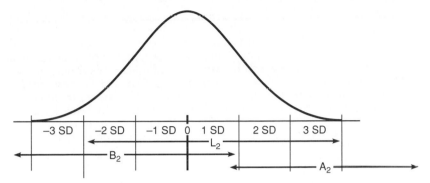

FIGURE 17.3   The ±2 standard error confidence intervals for likely (L), borderline (B), and atypical (A) values in a distribution of means of random samples from a common population.

error rate. Figure 17.3 shows the same information for a ±1.96 SE, or 95 percent, confidence interval. Again we have likely (L_2) and borderline (B_2) means that include the population value and an atypical one (A_2) that does not. But now the chances of a random sample mean being one of those that are atypical drop to only 5 percent (100 minus 95), so we will be wrong only one time in 20.

If we wish to be still more sure, we can extend our interval even more widely and use a ±3 standard error zone. But when we do that, the confidence interval becomes very broad, and we are locating the population's mean very imprecisely unless the standard error is quite small. So given data from a particular random sample, we can trade off precision of location of the population value for certainty. Other things being held constant, the more certain we wish to be, the less precise we are in locating the population mean. (Note how wide the confidence interval gets as we ask for greater certainty. A_1 is considered an atypical value with a ±1 standard error confidence interval. But a ±2 SE confidence interval would include A_1, which would no longer be atypical.)

Recall that one way of reducing the size of the standard error of measurement is to increase the reliability of the test. One of the main ways of doing this is to take a larger sample of behavior—that is, increasing the length of the test. Similarly, increasing the size of the sample reduces the standard error of the mean by reducing the variability of the sampling distribution. We can easily sense intuitively that the amount of currency men carry in their wallets when averaged over samples of 10,000 will have little variability but will be highly variable in samples of 5. Since the size of the confidence interval depends on the size of the standard error, one way of making our confidence intervals smaller, and our estimations more precise, is to increase the size of the sample. This technique is used often.

---

6. The population mean is zero in standard score terms. Not falling within the confidence interval is characteristic of a mean called "atypical." We will use that fact when we come to hypothesis testing.

- A confidence interval is a region around a sample statistic (such as a mean) that contains the population value (e.g., population mean) with a certain confidence that can be expressed in odds or as a percentage.
- The width of the confidence interval is determined by how confident we wish to be that it contains the parameter. The wider we make it, the surer we can be that it contains the parameter, but since it could be anywhere in the interval, the interval gives the parameter's possible location only within a broader range, and hence we lose precision of estimation.
- A confidence expressed by odds of 2 to 1 accompanies a 68 percent confidence interval, which is ±1 standard error wide; odds of 19 to 1 accompany a 95 percent confidence interval, which is ±1.96 SE wide; and odds of 99 to 1 accompany a 99 percent confidence interval, which is ±2.58 SE wide.
- The size of the confidence interval can be reduced, other things being equal, by increasing sample size.

Estimation: Another Explanation and Example

To review the estimation process one last time, let us use an example. As dormitory director, you are switching from an all-meals-in-the-dormitory policy to meals in any campus restaurant. You need to know how many meals on the average to budget in the dormitory. You interview 100 randomly selected students to find out how many meals per week they will take in the dormitory and come up with an average of 14.6 with a standard deviation of 2.4. How useful is that information? Not very, unless you can relate it in some way to the meal-taking habits of the rest of the dormitory population; it is that population value we want. Without further information, we'd have to say that the mean of the sample, 14.6, is our best estimate of the population mean. That is called point estimation.

But each random sample is different from the next, and this sample might have more classes close to or far from the dormitory and so its meal taking might not be exactly average. In any event, we can't be sure that its mean is the same as the population mean, even though most random sample means will be close to the population mean. If there is much variability from student to student—that is, if the variability of the population is large—samples may differ from one another by a great deal.

Since the variability of the sample means reflects the variability of the population and each sample's variability is also related to the population's, it would seem that there ought to be a way to get from the sample's variability to the variability of the sampling distribution of means. Fortunately, statisticians have found a way. The standard deviation of the distribution of means is estimated by dividing the standard deviation of the sample by the square root of the sample size minus 1.[7] In our dormitory meals example, this means dividing 2.4 by the square root of the sample size of 100 less 1, which is 9.95, yielding a standard error of 0.24.

If the standard error of the mean is 0.24 and our sample mean is 14.6, the population mean of meals taken in the dorm per person per week, at odds of 2 to 1, lies between 14.36 and 14.84. If we wish to be more certain and construct at 95 percent confidence interval, the confidence limits become 14.13 and 15.07. When multiplied by the thousands of students in the dormitories, this difference between the upper and lower confidence limits of almost a full meal per week is quite a gap. Were I this dormitory director, I'd probably go out and get additional data in order to refine the estimates. A larger sample will reduce the size of the standard error. The standard deviation of individual samples won't change much with increases in sample size, but I'll be dividing by a larger number in the denominator—the square root of the sample size less 1. As the sample size increases, the size of the fraction will decrease. Ignoring the "minus 1," note that because the square root of the sample size is used, to halve the standard error, I must increase the size of the sample by a factor of 4 (reducing it by a factor of 2 requires a sample size $2^2 = 4$ times greater). To reduce it to a quarter of my original sample's size, I must increase my sample size 16-fold.

If the students have gone home for the summer and these are all the data I can get, which confidence level do I use? That depends on many factors, such as how much of a problem an error in estimation estimation causes, how quickly it can be corrected, and how tolerant my supervisors are of error. All we can do is make a choice of confidence level based on all the factors involved in the decision, including how sure we or our supervisors wish to be.

Confidence Levels.   In our examples, we could have used any level of confidence we wished. But we have repeatedly used only confidence levels of 68, 95, 99, and 99.9 percent. Why? These are the levels that are conventionally used. Pollsters tend to report their results with ± 1 SE or 68 percent confidence. If they translate for the layperson at all, they usually express this as 2 to 1 odds. In most published work in the social and behavioral sciences, 95 percent and 99 percent levels are the most common. They represent judgments of the risk the researcher (or the audience) is willing to accept of being in error in the search for knowledge; if one study is in error, that is likely to be found out when the study is replicated or built on.

The purpose for which the data are to be used is the most important factor in determining the confidence level. For situations where we are seeking new information and an error would be remedied when a study is replicated, odds of being wrong, on the average, only 5 times in 100 seem quite accept-

---

7. In a statistics text, the "minus 1" would be explained as the loss of one degree of freedom. More on the concept of degrees of freedom can be found in chapter 22.

TABLE 17.1   Selected Entries from the Normal Probability Distribution

Distance from the Mean of the Distribution	Percentage of the Sampling Distribution in Both Tails	Percentage of the Sampling Distribution in One Tail
0.00	100.0	50.0
0.44	66.0	33.0
0.50	62.0	31.0
1.00	32.0	16.0
1.65	10.0	5.0
1.96	5.0	2.5
2.00	4.6	2.3
2.58	2.0	1.0
3.00	0.3	0.1

able. But we will never know in any given instance whether any particular study is one of the 95 or the 5, and that can sometimes be critical. Consequently, if a great deal is at stake in a particular decision, as in a life-or-death matter, we may wish to be wrong only once in 10,000 or 100,000 instances and extend the size of the confidence interval accordingly. We will return to this topic later.

Where do we find levels other than those already noted? From tables that statisticians provide us that show what proportion of the cases lie in the tails of a probability distribution. Table 17.1 presents a small sample of selected entries from a table of the normal probability distribution to give you an idea of what it looks like and how the percentages change as we go farther from the center of the distribution. Most of the statistics that social scientists now commonly use have been found to be distributed as one of five theoretical sampling distributions. Tables of probabilities such as Table 17.1 (but showing the values for smaller intervals than shown there) are available for each of them. This table of the normal probability distribution is one of the five (the others are the binomial, t, F, and chi-square distributions).

- The confidence level expresses our confidence that the population mean (parameter) falls within the confidence interval. Commonly used levels are 68, 95, and 99 percent, although these are mainly conventions.
- The confidence level needs to be set in relation to the kind of decision that flows from the data.
- A multiple of the estimated standard error, determined by the confidence level chosen, marks off the boundaries of the confidence interval around the sample value.

HYPOTHESIS TESTING

The logic of estimation can be extended to **hypothesis testing**. In estimation, we are seeking a *range* of values that probably contains the population value. Therefore, we focus on the values *inside* the confidence interval. In hypothesis testing, by contrast, we are looking at differences. These might be differences between the mean of a sample and some population value, and our question is whether our sample differs from the population value ("Are our students like a normally hearing group?"). Our usual expectations are that they are not (they are partially deaf or have extra-sensitive hearing), that they lie outside the "normal," the "typical," the "expected," the "likely." Our focus, then, is on the *atypical* values, those values that fall *outside* the confidence interval.

As another example, we often have two means (for example, one mean from a sample of subjects who have been hypnotized and told they would be hard of hearing and not realize it, and one from a similarly treated group who were told they would realize they had a hearing deficit). We examine the difference between them in relation to a sampling distribution of differences between means. Our question is whether the difference is *atypical*, larger than would be expected as a result of sampling variation and the random error built into a study. The logic involved in these two examples is slightly different, so we will examine them separately.

Does the Sample Belong to This Particular Population?

The Logic of Hypothesis Testing.   The logic builds on estimation but adds some steps. Suppose I am concerned that adolescents who are repeatedly exposed to loud music from headphones, cars, dances, and concerts are ruining their hearing. I test a randomly selected sample of 26 teenagers attending a recent concert who say they regularly listen to loud music. I find that on the Syracuse Hearing Tests, their mean score is only 69, whereas normally hearing samples have a mean of 80. I am about to go public with my results when one of my colleagues says that he is not at all sure that these students are hearing-deficient. This sample could be no different from the normally hearing population except for random sampling variation and the error built into the study, such as the error of measurement of the Syracuse Hearing Tests.

Our question is whether the difference between the sample mean of 69 and the mean of a normally hearing population of 80 can be reasonably accounted for by sampling and chance variation. Inferential statistics permit us to determine whether this explanation is reasonable or unreasonable. Figure 17.4 may be helpful in illustrating the logic.

The upper left bell curve of Figure 17.4 shows a population of adolescents who are regularly exposed to loud music. The mean of this population on the hearing test is unknown and so is indicated with a question mark. We are trying to establish whether the mean, whatever it is, differs from that of a normally hearing group. This problem is set in step 1. From what population

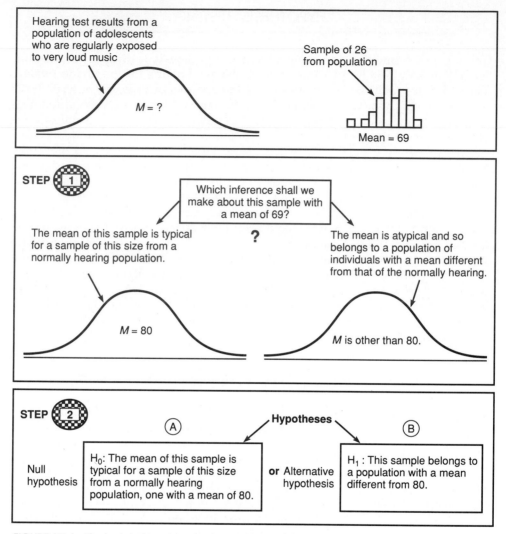

FIGURE 17.4   The logic in hypothesis testing: statement of the problem.

was our sample taken? Is it a mean from a population with a mean on the hearing test of 80—that is, a mean such as we might typically expect to obtain with a sample of this size taken from a normally hearing population? We define "typically expect" as the range within which most (e.g., 95%, 99%) means of random samples will fall. Or is it atypical and therefore more likely from a population with a mean different from 80? Notice that it is the population value about which we make inferences.

Step 2 in the figure translates the hypotheses of our problem into proper logical form for this statistical test. This involves establishing two hypotheses: the null hypothesis (A) and an alternative hypothesis (B). The **null hypothesis** is that when we take into account the sampling and random error of the study,

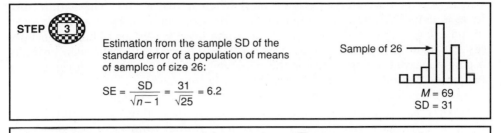

STEP 3

Estimation from the sample SD of the standard error of a population of means of samples of size 26:

$$SE = \frac{SD}{\sqrt{n-1}} = \frac{31}{\sqrt{25}} = 6.2$$

Sample of 26 →

$M = 69$
$SD = 31$

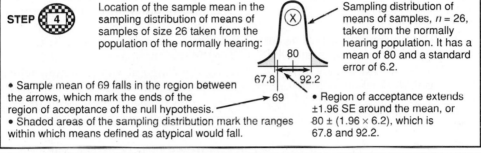

STEP 4

Location of the sample mean in the sampling distribution of means of samples of size 26 taken from the population of the normally hearing:

Sampling distribution of means of samples, $n = 26$, taken from the normally hearing population. It has a mean of 80 and a standard error of 6.2.

• Sample mean of 69 falls in the region between the arrows, which mark the ends of the region of acceptance of the null hypothesis.
• Shaded areas of the sampling distribution mark the ranges within which means defined as atypical would fall.

• Region of acceptance extends ±1.96 SE around the mean, or 80 ± (1.96 × 6.2), which is 67.8 and 92.2.

STEP 5

• Since 69 falls within the region of acceptance, it is a typical value, one likely to have been a random sample from a population with a mean of 80.
• Thus we have failed to reject the null hypothesis, H_0.
• We cannot, therefore, accept the alternative hypothesis that it is from a sample from a population with a mean different from 80.
• In making such judgments we will be right 95% of the time but will be wrong 5% of the time, if H_0 is true.

FIGURE 17.5   The logic of hypothesis testing: the solution.

the sample value is typical for a sample of this size from a normally hearing population. Put another way, it is suggesting that in reality there is no (*null*) difference between the mean of the sampling distribution from which this sample came and that of a normally hearing population. Put still another way, the strategy is to *nullify*, or reject, this hypothesis (Cohen, 1990).

The alternative hypothesis, which must be considered if the first hypothesis proves false, is that the sample came from a population with a mean different from 80. The question then becomes whether or not the null hypothesis can be rejected.

In Figure 17.5, we find a way to choose between the two inferences. Step 3 shows the calculation of the standard error of the mean, which for this example is 6.2. At step 4 in the figure, we have extended an interval around the mean of 80, just as we did in discussing estimation earlier, but here it is a region within which the null hypothesis is to be accepted—a region of acceptance. As before, we adjust its size to the error we are willing to tolerate. In hypothesis testing, we concentrate on whether the value is atypical, falls in the shaded tails—regions of rejection of the null hypothesis. So we are concerned with **significance levels**. The significance level is the complement (for example, $1 - .95 = .05$) of the confidence level and indicates the risk we are willing to run in saying that the value is atypical when it really isn't. The significance level is usually designated either by "p" for probability or by the Greek letter alpha (α): $\alpha = .05$ would be read, "The **alpha level** is .05" or "The significance level is .05." In statistical tables, this is often indicated with asterisks, typically a single asterisk being used for the .05 level and two for the .01 level. In our examples, we have used the 5 percent significance level.

We are trying to determine whether 69 falls in the range of values within which we would typically expect to find the population mean. If it does, there is no reason to say that the sample mean of 69 comes from a population with a mean different from 80. Although it is numerically different from 80, it differs by an amount that can be easily accounted for by sampling and measurement error. The null hypothesis is assumed to be true. Therefore, in step 4, the line between the arrows under distribution X is the region of acceptance of the null hypothesis around the mean of 80, showing the range of values within which the population value will be found in 95 percent of samples of 26, and it includes 69. This interval extends across the center of the distribution from 67.8 to 92.2, enclosing all but the most extreme 2.5 percent of the means in either tail, the shaded parts at opposite ends of the distribution. Sample means falling inside this are typical so the null hypothesis would be accepted as true. Means falling in the shaded areas are considered atypical, and not from a normally hearing population with a mean of 80. The shaded areas are regions for rejection of the null hypothesis as false.

The mean of 69 does not fall in the shaded regions; it falls inside the region of acceptance and so is typical—the data support H_0. "Accepting" the null hypothesis, however, does not mean we assume that the mean is really 80.[8] Rather, this indicates that within the sensitivity of this study, we simply *cannot reject* the null hypothesis. If we cannot reject the null hypothesis, we cannot accept the alternative hypothesis, H_1, and that is what counts. It is a matter of **statistical significance**: there is no statistically significant difference between this mean and the mean of 80 that cannot be accounted for by random sampling variation and chance error. We are assuming that this study is sensitive enough to show as statistically significant a difference in hearing that would be a practical hearing deficit.[9] We would have been in error had we concluded earlier that this group was hearing-impaired because its mean hearing was lower than that of the normal group.

- A difference between an observed and an expected value that falls within a region of acceptance is considered to be typical: the difference could be accounted for by sampling and chance error.

8. If it isn't 80, what is it? Using the technique of estimation covered earlier in this chapter, we could construct a confidence interval (with whatever confidence level we desire) around the sample mean to show the range within which the true mean would likely fall.
9. We'll consider statistical and practical significance, as well as studies designed to accept the null hypothesis, later in this chapter.

■ A difference that falls outside that region is considered atypical, more extreme than would be accounted for by sampling and chance error. It is considered a statistically significant difference.

One-tailed and Two-tailed Tests of Statistical Significance. Notice that in our example, we defined atypical values as being in both extremes of the distribution. Our alternative to the null hypothesis in step 2 was that the sample belonged to a population with a mean not equal to ($\neq$) 80. We were saying that a mean that was atypical in either direction was of interest. But defining the upper tail as atypical is tantamount to saying that our expectations include the possibility that the hearing of this group might be more acute than normal as a result of being exposed to loud sounds (that is, the mean of the sample is statistically significantly higher than that of the normally hearing group). This seems highly unlikely. If there is any effect, we are expecting hearing to be diminished. Therefore, our search for atypical values should be confined to the lower extreme. The alternative to the null hypothesis then becomes that the mean from which our sample came is less than ($<$) 80.

We made what is called a **two-tailed test** for statistical significance where the alternative is nondirectional ($\neq$ 80). This is quite appropriate when we do not know what to expect, whether hearing might be made more sensitive or diminished. Such might be the case if the causative factor were extensive training in pitch discrimination of very loud sounds. The training might increase sensitivity to pitch differences, but the loudness might diminish hearing entirely, and we wouldn't know whether one took precedence or whether they canceled each other out. But in our example, where loudness is suggested as causing deafness, we know in which tail to look, the lower one (the alternative $<$ 80), and a **one-tailed test** is more appropriate.

Figure 17.6 indicates in bold type the changes that must be made in Figure 17.4 to accommodate a one-tailed test of the hypothesis. Notice that the definition of the population with nonnormal hearing has changed to be not merely different from normal but lower than normal ($<$ 80). This has also changed the alternative hypothesis, B, which will be accepted if the null hypothesis is rejected.

Figure 17.7 shows in bold type the changes that must be made in Figure 17.5 to accommodate a directional hypothesis and its accompanying one-tailed test. Note that the shaded area is all in the lower tail of distribution X in step 4 of Figure 17.7 rather than split between the two tails as in Figure 17.5. Where it was split between both tails, only 2.5 percent was in the lower tail, and we had to extend the confidence limit to -1.96 SE before a mean was defined as atypical. But with 5 percent in the one tail, we need only go out as far as -1.65 SE. (Where does the 1.65 come from? See Table 17.1.) Since $68 + (1.65 \times 6.2) = 69.8$ with a one-tailed test, 69 just barely falls below the limit and so would be atypical. With a two-tailed test, you will recall, it was not. Thus with a one-tailed test, we *reject* the null hypothesis that the sample belongs to the population with a mean of 80 and *accept* the alternative hypothesis that it belongs to

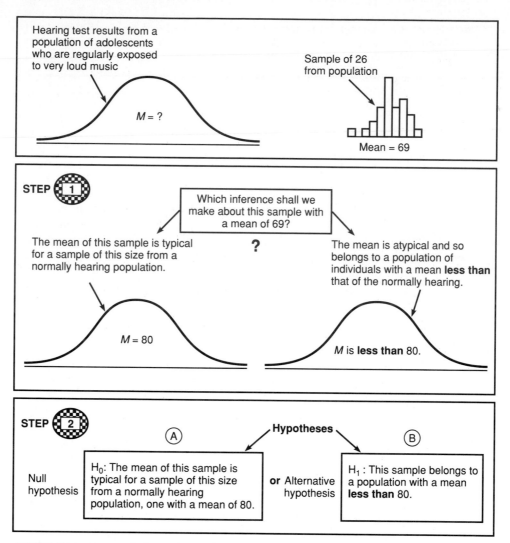

FIGURE 17.6   A one-tailed test; changes to Figure 17.4 are shown in boldface.

one with a mean lower than 80. Compared with the normally hearing population, this group, on the average, hears less well.

Notice that with the one-tailed test, we have increased the sensitivity of the study. That is, a smaller difference has become statistically significant. If the logic of the study permits us to make a sound directional prediction so that differences in only one direction are of interest, using a one-tailed test is one of the easiest ways of increasing sensitivity. It requires no changes in design, nor does it incur the cost of gathering additional data or increasing the size of the sample (the latter is the most common way of increasing sensitivity). As we

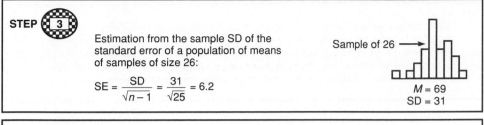

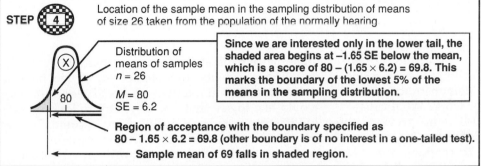

FIGURE 17.7   A one-tailed test; changes to Figure 17.5 are shown in boldface.

shall shortly see, there are other ways of increasing the sensitivity (sensitivity is also called the precision or power of a statistical test).

Directional hypotheses and therefore one-tailed tests are appropriate whenever we are studying a treatment with an expected effect, and a finding of the opposite effect (for example, a presumed sleeping pill causes agitation rather than sleep) would be ignored and would not result in new information. In improving reading scores, keeping students from dropping out, or reducing an individual's anxiety, we are interested in positive treatment effects. Negative effects are not expected or, if they occur, are presumed to be the result of chance or some factor other than the treatment. In these instances, we extend the region of acceptance only in the direction of interest. Of course, should we find the opposite of what is expected, we will not have a significant difference but will have the basis for another study to see why it happened and whether it is an artifact of the way the study was done. If it can be replicated and is a real effect, then clearly our theory or our understanding of what is going on is in error and must be remedied.

One-tailed tests of statistical significance increase the sensitivity of a statistical test and can be used whenever we have a directional hypothesis, one that tells us in which direction to look for results that will be statistically significant so far as the study is concerned. A result in the opposite direction would be considered an aberration rather than a reliable result.

Returning to our example, since 69 is a smaller mean than would likely be found as a result of sampling variability and chance error, we have a "demonstrated effect," the third judgment in internal validity. There is a cause at work. What cause? We would like to say that it is exposure to loud music. If (1) the previous three judgments in internal validity are assumed to be positive, (2) we can find no other reasonable alternative explanation (rival explanations have been eliminated, the fourth judgment of internal validity), and (3) there is no reason to assume that we do not have a credible result (the fifth judgment), then the study has internal validity, and we would say that the loss in hearing is due to the teenagers' being exposed to loud sounds.

Summary of the Logic

In abstract form, the logic of inference to determine whether an observed value belongs to a particular population goes like this:

1. We translate the study's hypothesis into two statistical hypotheses: the one we test, the null hypothesis, H_0, and the alternative, H_1, which we hope to be able to accept if H_0 is rejected.

   - H_0: The observed value is typical of means for a sample of this size from the sampling distribution of means created by random sampling and chance error.
   - H_1: The observed value is *atypical*, *not* one that belongs to the population sampling distribution created by the operation of sampling and chance or random error. It belongs to a population with a mean that differs from the mean of the chance distribution.

2. We set a significance level that expresses the risk we are willing to run of being wrong in this particular instance. Whether the observed value is atypical depends on whether it falls outside the region of acceptance of the null hypothesis constructed around the expected value.

   - If it does, we have failed to reject H_0 and cannot accept H_1.
   - If it does not, we reject H_0 and accept H_1 with a "maybe so."

Application of the Logic to a Test of Differences between Two Observed Means

Suppose we find in our survey research that one candidate has polled 45 percent among blacks and 40 percent among whites. Is there a real difference in her appeal, or is this just a chance difference? Or suppose we believe that studying from the general to the specific is more conducive to learning than working from the specific to the general. For instance, learning the logic of inferential statistics should result in superior achievement to studying specific inferential statistics and then learning the general logic. A pool of 40 volunteer students is randomly assigned: 20 to the general-to-specific treatment and 20 to the specific-to-general. A test of inferential statistics is given to both groups. The general-to-specific group's mean on the test was 46.5, and that of the specific-to-general was 38.0.

Do these means come from populations with the same mean, so that the difference results from sampling variation and test unreliability? Or are they from populations with different means? This is one of the most common questions asked of inferential statistics. We have an experimental group that received some treatment, such as the general-to-specific treatment, and a control group that received either a neutral treament or, as in this case, a less favorable alternative treatment. We want to know whether the difference between them is statistically significant—that is, reliably different from zero.

Here we appear to have two means to deal with, whereas before we dealt with only one, and an expected value. What to do now? The answer is reduce the problem to the same formulation. Instead of dealing with the two means, deal with the difference between them and test it against the sampling distribution of differences between means, finding an interval for that sampling distribution that defines the typical. Same logic as before, different application.

Assume that these two means are from sampling distributions with the same mean and the same standard error. We have one observed difference between two random samples from these distributions. But we could presumably take many more sample means and, subtracting the first from the second, construct a distribution composed of *differences between means*. On the average, the two means would be about equal; only occasionally would a large positive or negative difference occur. Therefore, the mean of this distribution would be zero, and it would have the shape of a normal distribution as the number of differences grew larger. This is the sampling distribution of the differences between means.

The variability in differences between means will be a function of the variability in each of the sampling distributions from which the means came. Therefore, the standard errors of both distributions are used in estimating the standard error of the sampling distribution of the differences between means. The logic is similar to what we examined before, but here we are dealing with the question whether the difference between the two groups belongs to a sampling distribution of differences between means with a mean of zero or to one with a mean greater than zero. Figure 17.8 shows the logic in the same kind of diagram as was used for previous examples. The top box states our

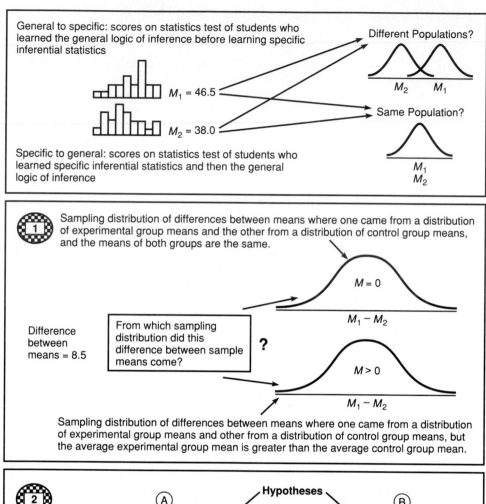

General to specific: scores on statistics test of students who learned the general logic of inference before learning specific inferential statistics

$M_1 = 46.5$

$M_2 = 38.0$

Specific to general: scores on statistics test of students who learned specific inferential statistics and then the general logic of inference

Different Populations?

M_2 M_1

Same Population?

M_1
M_2

1 Sampling distribution of differences between means where one came from a distribution of experimental group means and the other from a distribution of control group means, and the means of both groups are the same.

$M = 0$

$M_1 - M_2$

Difference between means = 8.5

From which sampling distribution did this difference between sample means come?

?

$M > 0$

$M_1 - M_2$

Sampling distribution of differences between means where one came from a distribution of experimental group means and other from a distribution of control group means, but the average experimental group mean is greater than the average control group mean.

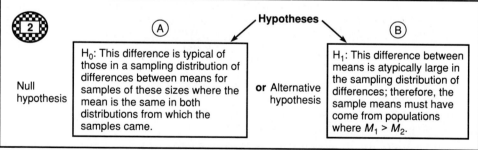

2

Hypotheses

(A)

(B)

Null hypothesis

H_0: This difference is typical of those in a sampling distribution of differences between means for samples of these sizes where the mean is the same in both distributions from which the samples came.

or Alternative hypothesis

H_1: This difference between means is atypically large in the sampling distribution of differences; therefore, the sample means must have come from populations where $M_1 > M_2$.

FIGURE 17.8 The logic of inference applied to a difference between two sample means with a one-tailed test of significance.

study question, and step 1 translates the problem into an examination of the difference between means.

The standard error of the differences between means is the square root of the sum of the squared standard errors of the individual distributions, here designated e for experimental and c for control: $\sqrt{(SE_e^2 + SE_c^2)}$, or

$$SE_{M_{e-c}} = \sqrt{\left(\frac{SD_e}{\sqrt{n_e - 1}}\right)^2 + \left(\frac{SD_c}{\sqrt{n_c - 1}}\right)^2}$$

This formula holds for independent means. Where the means come from samples where individuals are matched or paired, the product $(2r_{ec})$ (SE_e) (SE_c) is subtracted from the amount under the square root sign (r_{ec} is the correlation between the scores for the paired subjects).

We build a region of acceptance around the expected value with a width determined by the error we are willing to tolerate. Note that in this instance, we use a one-tailed test, since our hypothesis is directional. The general-to-specific treatment, M_1, is expected to be superior. Therefore, all the atypical values will be in which tail? The right one, since the difference, $M_1 - M_2$, is expected to be positive. We then determine whether the difference falls in the region of acceptance or the atypical area, the region of rejection. If it falls in the area where values are typical, we cannot reject the null hypothesis and so cannot accept the alternative. There is no statistically significant difference between studying from the general to the specific and from the specific to the general. If the difference falls outside the region of acceptance, in the region of rejection, we reject the null hypothesis and say "maybe so" to the alternative, that in this instance it pays to learn the general logic first.

- Hypothesis testing of a difference between two observed values involves a null hypothesis: the difference between the two means is typical of differences in a sampling distribution of differences between means from samples of these sizes, where the mean is the same in both populations from which the samples came. A simpler way of saying this is that the mean of the sampling distribution of differences is zero.
- The nondirectional alternative hypothesis is that the difference between means belongs to a population of differences with a mean other than zero. With a directional hypothesis, the alternative states whether the difference is greater or less than zero.
- Dealing with the difference between means rather than the two means individually allows us to reduce the problem to the logic used previously.

THE *t* TEST FOR DIFFERENCES BETWEEN MEANS

Most studies examine a difference between two means with the *t* test, especially in relatively simple designs involving either a comparison of two experimental treatments or a comparison of a control with an experimental group.

The t test and analysis of variance are probably the two most commonly used inferential statistics in the behavioral sciences. The t test uses the same logic as we have just examined but adds a couple of refinements. Instead of using the normal probability distribution to find our probability, we use a sampling distribution called the t distribution. Although this distribution becomes normally distributed with large samples, the table for it differs from the table of the normal distribution for small samples. Whereas the 5 percent level of the normal distribution requires 1.96 SE for statistical significance, the t test requires the higher value of 2.5 SE at 6 cases and even 1.98 SE at 100 cases. To use the table, we look up a number called degrees of freedom, usually abbreviated *df*. For most t tests of differences between means, this number is simply 2 less than the sum of the sample sizes. (More will be said about degrees of freedom in our discussion of chi-square in chapter 22.)

The second difference is that the usually used formula assumes a common variance for the populations from which the samples came and pools the samples' variability for a better estimate of the population value. The formula also gives greater weight to samples of larger size:

$$SE_{M_1 - M_2} = \sqrt{\frac{(n_1 - 1)SD_1^2 + (n_2 - 1)SD_2^2}{n_1 + n_2 - 2} \cdot \frac{n_1 + n_2}{n_1 n_2}}$$

Then:

$$t = \frac{M_1 - M_2}{SE_{M_1 - M_2}}$$

The t test also assumes that the groups are independent samples of a population. This is not the case where individuals are matched and then assigned to groups. As noted before, where matching occurs, a special formula should be used. If it is not, a Type II error may be made and possible statistical significance not sensed (see May, Masson, and Hunter, 1990, pp. 272–276, or Moses, 1986, pp. 189–192).

A rank test comparable to the t test and useful for small samples is the Mann-Whitney U test. It involves assigning ranks to the scores where the scores for the two groups are combined into a single distribution. The ranks belonging to each group are next sorted out and summed. If the experimental treatment is effective, the sum of its ranks should be higher than that of the control group's. Using the simple formula

$$U = n_L n_S + \frac{n_L(n_L + 1)}{2} - T_L$$

we consult the table of the U distribution to determine whether the product of the formula is significant. In the formula, n_L is the size of the sample with the larger sum of ranks, and n_S that of the smaller, and T_L is the larger sum of ranks. (For more, see Shavelson, 1981, or Hays, 1973.) The Mann-Whitney can be used in place of the t test where the populations are suspected of deviating significantly from normal or the variances are unequal. However, if

TABLE 17.2   Relationship of High and Low Test Anxiety to Various Study Patterns

Variable	High Test Anxiety		Low Test Anxiety		
	M	SD	M	SD	t
Study habits	37.2	14.8	53.4	14.2	5.42*
Total study hours	21.7	12.7	14.1	7.0	−3.11*
Cramming	4.5	1.4	4.7	1.4	0.57
Missing classes	10.5	7.7	10.7	11.1	0.08
Late exams	0.6	1.1	0.3	0.6	−1.52

*$p < .002$.
SOURCE   R. E. Culler and C. J. Holahan, "Test Anxiety and Academic Performance," *Journal of Educational Psychology*, vol. 72, p. 18. Copyright © 1980 The American Psychological Association. Used by permission.

the variances are nearly equal fairly large departures from normality can be tolerated and the *t* test used (Hays, 1981).

An Example

Culler and Holahan (1980) used the *t* test to examine the differences in study-related behaviors between two groups of college freshmen, one with low test anxiety (*n* = 31) as measured by Sarason, Pederson, and Nyman's Test Anxiety Scale, and the other with high test anxiety (*n* = 65). This is one of a large number of studies examining this problem among students. Test anxiety is "thought to produce task-irrelevant responses (concern for passing, thoughts of leaving, etc.) in the testing situation that interfere with the task-relevant responses necessary for good test performance" (p. 16). An alternative explanation is that the well-documented poorer grade performance of those with high test anxiety is "at least partially a function of differential study-related behaviors between high and low test-anxious individuals" (p. 16). Both groups of students completed the Study Habits scale of the Brown-Holtzman Survey of Study Habits and Attitudes and responded to a questionnaire. The results are summarized in Table 17.2.[10]

The data were consistent with the hypothesis that the study habits of the high test-anxious group were statistically significantly poorer than those of students with low test anxiety, using a two-tailed test. The two-tailed *t* test was significant at the 0.2 percent level. Also statistically significant were the total study hours, but the difference was in the opposite direction—a good reason for using a two-tailed test! The authors were surprised by this finding and suggest that perhaps high test-anxious students attempt to compensate for their lower study competence by studying longer. The other comparisons, degree of cramming for tests, number of classes missed, and number of exams missed and made up at a later date, were all statistically nonsignificant.

10. The asterisked figures in the table are statistically significant at the 0.2 percent level, considerably beyond the conventional levels of 1 and 5 percent. Giving additional levels of significance allows the reader to determine how to interpret the data. It also facilitates meta-analysis (chapter 21).

A *t* test allows us to test the difference between two means for statistical significance and is a commonly used statistical test for such purposes. It substitutes the *t* table for the normal probability distribution for more accurate probabilities and uses a formula that provides a more exact estimate of the standard error.

SENSITIVITY, PRECISION, AND STATISTICAL POWER

Sensitivity, precision, and statistical power are all names for the same thing, the ability of a statistical test to sense a difference of a size of interest to us. Studies should be designed with appropriate sensitivity if they are to be successful. Either too powerful or too weak a study wastes money, time, and energy. If it is not sensitive enough, it risks missing the result sought, sometimes an important one. Since most ways of increasing sensitivity require resources, an overly sensitive study uses resources that could have been put into further studies. (An exception is a study that must be large enough to be convincing to laypersons or others relatively unsophisticated in research methods.)

Errors of Inference

As already noted, when we set a confidence or significance level, we are accepting a certain level of error. With one type of error, we reject the null hypothesis, claiming that we have a real difference when in actuality the difference is not real but is due to sampling and chance variation—saying the treatment was effective when it wasn't. This kind of error has been labeled a Type I or **alpha error** (α). Type I error is always under our direct control as a result of setting significance levels, say, at 5 percent. On the average, when H_0 is true, with a 5 percent significance level, 5 times in 100 we will be wrong when we say that there is a real difference.

This is especially important when we are serious about validating a finding—that is, banking on that finding as representing the true facts, not being an atypical result. We don't want results showing that a treatment is making a difference only to find that we got them by chance. For important decisions, like building a dormitory, adding costly computer terminals, or adopting an expensive way of teaching reading, we ought to rely on accumulated evidence rather than on a single study. But if we are depending on a single study, we reduce Type I error by using a confidence level of 99 or 99.9 or even 99.99 percent. But if that is the case, why not always use such stringent confidence levels? Because for a given set of data, decreasing Type I error causes Type II error to increase. Type II error or **beta error** (β), is the opposite of Type I. It occurs when we miss a real difference and call it chance error; we accept the null hypothesis when we should have rejected it.

Decision based on sample data

	Do not reject null hypoth.	Reject null hypoth.
H_0 is true	Correct decision $1 - \alpha^*$	Type I error α^*
H_0 is false	Type II error β^*	Correct decision $1 - \beta^*$

True state of affairs

*These are the probabilities of that event occurring.

FIGURE 17.9   Type I and Type II errors and the null hypothesis.

If we pay special attention to Type I error when validating a finding, when do we especially attend to Type II error? When exploring! If we are sorting out cancer cures, we don't want to miss one by saying that an improvement was no greater than might have occurred by chance when the treatment really was effective. The effect was too small to be sensed, so it was lumped with chance errors and called "no difference." In exploring, we want a study that is sensitive enough to cull out any effect of possible interest as one that is statistically significant. Figure 17.9 may help you remember these two types of errors.[11]

Figure 17.9 also indicates the probability of occurrence of each of the events. Thus we define the Type I error as α (say, 5 percent), and that makes the probability of a correct decision when H_0 is true $1 - \alpha = 95$ percent. Unless we do some figuring ahead of time and estimate such things as the size of the standard error, we don't usually know β, the Type II error, but we know that $1 - \beta$ is the probability of a correct decision where the null hypothesis should be rejected. Indeed, because we want correct decisions, $1 - \beta$ indicates their likelihood and therefore the sensitivity of a statistic in a given instance. Hence we define $1 - \beta$ as the **power of a statistical test**, its sensitivity or precision.

- Type I, or alpha, errors occur when we decide that an observed value is atypical and not the result of sampling and chance error when it really was. Type I errors are particularly serious when we are attempting to validate a hypothesis where an important decision is involved.

---

11. Does this look familiar? It should! It is the same as Figure 17.1, in bare-bones form. Incidentally, in that figure, correct decisions build trust in a service manager's judgment and incorrect ones lead to distrust. Similarly, correct decisions lead to trust of science by laypersons and incorrect ones to distrust. In contrast to laypersons, scientists who understand how the errors occur continue to trust science.

> ■ Type II, or beta, errors occur when we decide that an observed value is not atypical and therefore not statistically significant when in fact it resulted from a real effect. Type II error is of concern when the resources are used up but the study was not built with enough sensitivity to have a positive result. They can be serious in research screening possibilities when a beneficial effect may not only be missed in that instance but possibly be excluded from further research.

The Size of Type II Error. Whereas the conventions for Type I error are typically set at 1 and 5 percent, they are not well established for Type II error. Of course, as we have noted, whether validation or screening is involved will determine whether Type I or Type II is to be emphasized. If a major screening decision is not involved and the study is but a small step in the search for knowledge, a Type II error of 10 or even 20 percent may be acceptable. Note that a large Type II error seems to be better tolerated than a large Type I, reflecting the conservative attitude of most scientists, who would rather miss a possibility than make a knowledge claim that might be wrong. In some respects, that is quite understandable, because making a false knowledge claim that cannot later be replicated is publicly embarrassing. Missing a finding is regrettable, but since few negative result studies are published, it is a private matter, and nobody else is the wiser.

Ways to Increase Statistical Power

How can a researcher increase the statistical power of a test? We have already noted one way, being able to establish a directional hypothesis, so that it becomes appropriate to do a one-tailed test. There are others.

Statistical Power and Sample Size. One of the things we all want to know when we see a poll that indicates that a candidate is winning is, "On how many cases is it based?" A poll based on 50 cases is not considered nearly as reliable as one based on 500 or 5,000 cases. Intuitively, this makes good sense because the larger sample is more likely to be representative of the population (unless there is a sampling bias, as in selecting all the cases from only one social class). But there is a statistical reason as well: the standard error decreases with sample size, as shown in Figure 17.10.

Attend to the size of the standard errors rather than the curves; although it is clear that the curves become more peaked and narrower, it is a bit difficult to judge the standard error change from the shape. If we start with a standard deviation of 10, with samples of size 1 the standard error is still 10. Doubling sample size reduces it only to 7.07. To cut it in half, we must quadruple the sample size. Similarly, to cut that in half, we must go to 16 cases. Reductions occur as a function of the square of the change in sample size; to cut the standard error by a third, we must have 9 times the cases; by a fifth, 25 times the cases; and so on. Note that with each halving in the chart, the drop in the

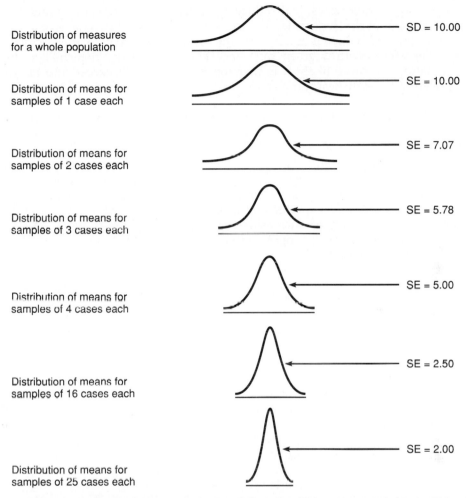

Distribution of measures for a whole population — SD = 10.00

Distribution of means for samples of 1 case each — SE = 10.00

Distribution of means for samples of 2 cases each — SE = 7.07

Distribution of means for samples of 3 cases each — SE = 5.78

Distribution of means for samples of 4 cases each — SE = 5.00

Distribution of means for samples of 16 cases each — SE = 2.50

Distribution of means for samples of 25 cases each — SE = 2.00

FIGURE 17.10 Reduction in the standard error of the mean with increases in sample size. (From J. P. Guilford and B. Fruchter, "Fundamental Statistics in Psychology and Education," Copyright 1978 by McGraw-Hill, Inc. Reprinted with permission of McGraw-Hill, Inc.)

size of the standard error is smaller and the number of cases needed to bring it about is larger.

We can see the effect of sample size more directly if we look at a simplified version of the *t* test of a difference between two means as shown in the following formula:

$$t = \frac{\text{The difference between two sample means}}{\sqrt{\dfrac{\text{A value that is a function of the variances of the samples}}{\text{A value that is a function of the sizes of the samples}}}}$$

By increasing sample sizes, we reduce the value of the fraction under the square root sign in the denominator of the formula. This reduces the size of the denominator, and when it is smaller, the value of the whole fraction gets larger. Therefore, with a given difference between means, the smaller the denominator, the more likely it is that the value of t will exceed the tabled value needed for statistical significance.

Other Ways to Increase the Power of a Statistical Test.   From the formula given, it is clear that the larger the value of the fraction, the more likely it will exceed the value required for statistical significance. We can make the fraction larger by increasing the numerator or by decreasing the denominator. We can increase the numerator by increasing the size of the difference between the means. This can be done by increasing the strength of the treatment, choosing for both control and experimental groups individuals who are especially susceptible to the treatment, increasing the motivation of the subjects, administering the treatment over a longer period of time so that the cumulative effect is greater, and similar efforts.

Another way of decreasing the denominator is to reduce the variability of the samples: choosing very homogeneous samples, eliminating all extraneous distractions by moving the study into the laboratory, masking distracting noises, and similar efforts. There are also statistics intended to control variables, such as analysis of covariance and partial correlation (see chapter 22).

Further, we can also decrease the size of the denominator by using highly reliable tests. Suppose that in trying to find the average height of women, we fail to give our data gatherers instructions on how to measure height. Some mashed down subjects' hair; some didn't. Some asked subjects to step out of their shoes; some didn't. Clearly, this inconsistency would increase the variability of the measures, and hence the standard error would be larger. To make clear that this is a matter of reliability, consider this comparable to having two forms of a test of the same ability. Thus increasing the reliability of the measures is still another common way of decreasing the size of the denominator and hence the standard error.

We have already noted that a directional hypothesis with its one-tailed test increases the statistical power, but we can also change the level of significance. Moving the significance level from 1 percent in the direction of 5 percent increases the power and sensitivity of the statistical test.

Finally, some statistical tests are more powerful than others under certain conditions. In general, tests based on interval or ratio scale data are more sensitive than those based on ranked (ordinal) or categorical (nominal) data simply because moving from interval to ranked or categorical scales discards information. However, there are special conditions, such as in sampling from nonnormal distributions, when, for example, the Wilcoxon signed-ranks test (May, Masson, and Hunter, 1990, pp. 491–494) using ranked data is more powerful than the t test (Blair and Higgins, 1980, 1985). Exploring these is beyond the scope of this book.

With these many ways of changing sensitivity, it should be clear that researchers can and should do a "statistical power analysis" during the design of a study if at all possible. For example, with the t test, such an analysis involves estimating values for all the variables in the formula except the sample sizes. This includes the t value for the level of significance we desire with the one- or two-tailed test we plan to use. If sample sizes are assumed to be equal, we have a formula with one unknown that can be solved for the proper sample size. A study designed to that size or a bit larger for good measure will show an effect of the size expected as statistically significant if it appears; the study will have designed at an appropriate sensitivity level.

Cohen (1988) gives a detailed description of how to do a power analysis for a variety of statistics. Both Cohen (1988) and Lipsey (1990) include information to allow estimation of the size of sample required and discuss the variables involved. This enables researchers to select a sample size that will provide a sufficiently powerful test to suit their purposes. This is the one and only answer to our earlier question of how large a sample is big enough.

- The power of a statistical test $(1 - \beta)$ is its ability to avoid Type II error.
- Increasing the statistical power of the test makes a statistically significant result more likely if a nonchance effect is present.
- We can increase statistical power (precision, sensitivity) by increasing the size of the effect (a stronger treatment), reducing variability (moving from field into laboratory or using more reliable tests), or reducing the standard error (increasing sample size).
- A power analysis shows the sample size needed for adequate sensitivity.

STUDIES DESIGNED TO ACCEPT THE NULL HYPOTHESIS

There are instances where we wish to show whether two statistics or distributions are the same rather than different. For instance, we are concerned that a strong alternative explanation of some results is that the sample is not representative of a population. We usually test various characteristics of the two to show that the difference between the sample and population values is not statistically significant. For example, we test the difference between the mean age of the sample and that of the population and find it not statistically significant. Does that mean that the difference is not a statistically significant difference? At the study's level of statistical sensitivity, yes; as a practical matter, it depends on whether the study's level of sensitivity is sufficient to recognize a practical difference.

We do not accept the null hypothesis in the sense of insisting the difference is really zero. Rather, we fail to reject it, meaning that it could be zero or something close to it. How close? It depends on the sensitivity of our statistical test. At the level of sensitivity of the particular statistical test used, the difference might not reach statistical significance, and so the difference could be zero. But a more sensitive test might show a statistically significant difference. This is what we did in the example of the adolescents who might have had impaired hearing from listening to loud music when we changed from a two-tailed to a one-tailed test.

How sensitive a test must we use? Here is where judgment must enter and cannot be escaped. We must decide what size difference between the sample and the population is big enough to represent an unacceptable difference. Then, with a statistical power analysis, we can determine whether an existing study is sensitive enough to detect such a difference or design one that is. Only then can we say that the particular sample does not differ significantly from the population of which it is representative. Failure to follow this logic is a common error.[12]

DECISION MAKING AND KNOWLEDGE BUILDING

The logic so far described in this chapter assumes that we are testing the truth of the null hypothesis to determine whether the alternative hypothesis (the one we are gathering data about) escapes disconfirmation. This is not unreasonable; that is usually the situation we are in at the time we do the study. In some instances, a decision is riding on this study and its data. The study stands as representative of the replications we might do. The fact that any value just missed being significant (or just barely made it, as in the hearing impairment example) is not taken into account in this logic. It is either in or out of the critical region (the shaded part of distribution in the earlier figures).

But there is a larger perspective: we do not make up our mind about a relationship on the basis of this one study. Rather this is but one in a set of interrelated studies examining the variables. Then the fact of a borderline result *is* significant. Perhaps it would go the other way in another study or would become significant with a more sensitive study. Returning to our example, suppose we argued that the group was not really hard of hearing, as an adolescent who loves loud music and doesn't want to give it up might contend. The earlier study is an aberration in a set of studies that ought to go in the other direction, producing findings of normal hearing among loud-music fans (we could argue that the ear protects itself from damage by not responding to sounds that are too loud). Given such a rationale and a conviction that the data are in error, we would want to conduct further studies.

One answer, of course, is to replicate with studies sufficiently sensitive to catch whatever represents a hearing deficit. This would determine whether the earlier result was a chance event or is replicable. If it is still borderline, perhaps the hearing deficit is just below our study's sensitivity. Repeated results of this kind are due to more than chance and deserve to be interpreted as such rather than dichotomously as significant or nonsignificant.

Indeed, it is common journal practice not just to indicate whether a result

---

12. Cohen (1990, p. 1309), however, notes that in most instances, a power analysis will show that an impractically large sample size is required, so showing similarity with considerable precision may be difficult.

is or is not statistically significant but also to tell how rare it is.[13] So we find odd probabilities like 6 percent, 10 percent, .003 percent, or even .00004 percent instead of the traditional 5 percent or 1 percent. This allows readers to make up their own minds about the data and facilitates recognizing borderline results. But it can lead to misconceptions as well, since the sensitivity of studies varies so greatly. It is difficult to compare intuitively or synthesize the result of one study based on 10 cases that is barely significant at the 5 percent level with another of 100 cases that yields a probability of 1 in 10,000. There is, however, a way of statistically combining them; see the section on meta-analysis in chapter 21. Combining the results of several borderline non-significant studies can so increase the sensitivity that we have a significant result and are also more certain of the appropriate interpretation of the outcome.

THE MEANING OF STATISTICAL SIGNIFICANCE

Statistical and Practical Significance

If it is possible to design a study so as to increase its sensitivity, it becomes apparent that any real difference, no matter how small, could be made statistically significant. If we take statistical significance as the criterion of a successful study, then this is mainly a matter of increasing statistical sensitivity—for instance, increasing sample size—until we find something statistically significant. But it must be apparent that at some point, it ceases to matter; the difference is so small that we don't care about it. We have not reached the limits of statistical significance, but we have reached the limits of **practical significance**.

Practical significance is different from statistical significance. Consider an experimental group receiving a $10,000-per-pupil reading treatment to get only a one-point gain in achievement. That difference might be statistically significant and, from the point of view of a researcher, might lead to something of interest in further research. But from the school's standpoint, so much expenditure per pupil for so little gain completely lacks practical significance. So practical significance differs from statistical significance in that it is a func-

---

13. Mathematical statisticians distinguish two points of view regarding inference: Fisher's and Neyman and Pearson's. Fisher's concentrates on rejecting the null hypothesis and uses pre-determined levels of significance (often 5 percent) and confidence intervals. Decisions are presumably based on a body of studies, and the goal is understanding. Giving the alternative hypothesis equal importance with the null, Neyman and Pearson are concerned with Type II errors as well as Type I. Their goal is decision making between the null and the alternative hypothesis. This may not seem like much of a distinction, and as May, Masson, and Hunter (1989) note, in practice, the two views often merge—studies follow the logic of a 5 percent significance level but then report whatever level is achieved. Indeed, this chapter is Fisherian in the discussion of the logic of inference, and Neyman-Pearsonian in this part that talks about power analyses. For more, see May, Masson, and Hunter (1990, chap. 7).

tion of the purpose for which the study results are to be used. What is practically significant is decided by a judgment of the value or use of the results in a particular context; for example, the school might be willing to add $300 to per-pupil costs for a 10-point gain.

> It is possible to increase the sensitivity of a study to the point where if there is any effect at all, no matter how infinitesimal, it can be made statistically significant. But whether it is practically significant is another matter entirely, a judgment based on entirely different criteria.

Proving a Proposition versus Its Escaping Disconfirmation

Suppose a study shows an effect in the expected direction and of a size that is statistically significant. Does that mean that we have proved the proposition? Don't we wish it! In the first place, you will recall that in section one of this book we noted that all knowledge is held as tentatively true until new knowledge modifies or replaces it. But beyond that, we have noted that statistical inference is such that we are never sure that a given finding is not the result of chance variation and error. All positive results can do is increase the odds of saying that the results are real; that is, they increase our confidence in our assertion. So in any given instance, we can merely say that a proposition escaped disconfirmation.

Popper (1959) and others have argued that the job of the researcher is to subject each proposition to tests of disconfirmation, to try actively to disconfirm it! With each instance in which it escapes disconfirmation, we become more confident about the proposition. Unfortunately, we are not as prone in the social and behavioral sciences to try actively to disconfirm previous findings as we are to try to confirm them in new circumstances. If we design a sufficiently sensitive study and the result does not appear or a different result appears, we consider that the original result has been disconfirmed and must go "back to the drawing board" to find out what was wrong. Alternatively, given that there is consensus that the data do support the proposition in a new application, we may feel increasingly confident about its validity. Eventually, we are confident enough about it that it crosses the threshold of what we are willing to accept as knowledge, still tentatively held but firm enough to act on.

> Statistical significance of a result does not prove that the hypothesis is true but rather that it is an instance in which the hypothesis has escaped disconfirmation. It contributes to our confidence that the proposition is valid. With sufficient confidence, a proposition becomes accepted as knowledge, which, though tentatively held as true, is considered firm enough to act on.

VIOLATING ASSUMPTIONS OF STATISTICAL TESTS

All statistical tests begin with certain assumptions that, together with the laws of probability, enable statisticians to develop the tables we use to determine statistical significance. Commonly used examples are the normal distribution, the t table, chi-square, and F, all of which are based on the laws of probability. Statistical tests that are used with interval or ratio scale data typically assume random sampling. Many further assume that the sampling is from normally distributed populations and, where two or more samples are involved, that they have variances that differ from one another no more than would be "typical." These, called parametric statistical tests, are the focus of most statistics texts and computer programs and are the most widely used and understood.

Nonparametric statistics are based on ranked or categorical data. They ask whether the patterning of the data is typically random or atypically regular. When data from an experimental and a control group are ordered by size, if nothing is at work, we would expect a random alternation between experimental group and control as we proceed from the highest to the lowest score. But if most of the experimental group's scores are grouped at the beginning and those of the control group at the end, then the ordering is atypical and something is at work. As with parametric tests, what appears to be atypical may not be. A randomly created pattern may appear too regular to be "typically" random. Ten pennies do come up all heads about once in 1,000 times, on the average. So the same kinds of logic apply, and the same errors persist. But such statistics do not depend on random sampling or the characteristics of populations, like parametric tests. The chi-square test, described in chapter 22, is such a statistic. Other such commonly used tests are the sign test, the rank test, the run test, the Mann-Whitney U test (May, Masson, and Hunter, 1990, pp. 481–490) for nonmatched samples, and the Wilcoxon signed-ranks test for matched samples.

Although parametric statistics are the norm, few studies use random samples. What is the justification for violating this assumption? May, Masson, and Hunter (1990) state that in most situations, parametric statistics approximate the nonparametric results, so parametrics result in meaningful and useful interpretations without random sampling. They also suggest that non-parametric statistics are really more appropriate for most behavioral science studies. Clearly, however, where we are concerned with building a consensus around the interpretation of data and developing credibility with the audience, using unfamiliar nonparametric statistics is an uphill battle. The prevalence of parametric statistics in teaching, textbooks, computer programs, and publications is overwhelming. In situations where parametric assumptions are seriously violated, nonparametric statistics are clearly more appropriate. But as long as useful interpretations result, the dominance of parametric statistics will continue.

One assumption of tests of differences between means (t tests, analyses of variance) is not always understood: although the means may be affected by a treatment, the variability of the distribution is not. The treatment is expected to add a constant to (or subtract a constant from) all scores but not affect them enough differentially so as to increase the variance. The sample's variability is the basis for estimating the standard error used to determine statistical significance. Therefore, this can be a problem if a treatment is expected to affect subjects differentially.

We say that a statistic is **robust** if we can interpret it meaningfully even when an assumption on which it is based has been violated. Many parametric statistics have proved surprisingly robust in the face of sampling from skewed rather than normal distributions or when having unequal variances. In a situation where assumptions have been violated, it may be desirable to use a nonparametric test or to look for studies of the behavior of the statistic under conditions where the assumptions were intentionally broken.

- Assumptions allow statisticians to use probability theory to develop the tables we use to determine statistical significance.
- Parametric statistics such as those discussed in this chapter (as well as the *t* test of difference between means and the *F* test used in the analysis of variance) assume random sampling. Sometimes they also assume sampling of normally distributed populations with equal variances unaffected by treatment.
- Nonparametric statistics using the same logic of inference do not assume random sampling. They assume that random ordering is at work and examine rankings and categorizations for regularity that is atypical and nonrandom.
- Even without random sampling, parametric statistics lead to useful results. This may be because they approximate nonparametric statistics, which do not assume random sampling.
- Tests of differences between means assume that the mean is affected by treatment but variability is not.
- A robust statistical test is one that permits accurate interpretation of the data even when an assumption on which the test is based has been violated. Parametric tests are fairly robust in the face of minor violations.

SUMMARY

Comprehending the logic of inference allows us to understand many inferential statistics because the logic is repeated in them. For estimation with interval or ratio data, it involves finding ways of determining what would be typical values for a statistic due to random sampling variability and the chance error built into the measures used in the study. Using these, we can extend a confidence interval within which the parameter value for the population from which the sample statistic came can be found with a predetermined probability. We can test a sample value to see whether it would be typical in a hypothesized distribution (such as normal hearing).

We define "typical" knowing that there will always be some cases that are normally outside that range. In those instances, we will be wrong in our inference that the population value lies in the chosen range. The range is expressed as a confidence interval, and what is typical is described by a percentage that indicates our confidence in its containing the population value in any given instance. These confidence levels are usually 95 percent (odds of 19 to 1) or 99 percent (99 to 1), and their accompanying errors, known as Type I (alpha) errors, are .05 and .01, respectively.

With hypothesis testing, our logic assumes that a given sample statistic, such as a difference between means, is typical of differences from samples of those sizes when they come from populations with the same mean (the null hypothesis). The alternative hypothesis is that they come from populations with different means, or in the case of directional hypotheses, from populations in which a particular population mean is larger than the other. We then compare the study results with the typical range to determine whether the observed difference between means falls in that range. Values lying outside the typical range are considered likely to have been influenced by something other than sampling and error variability (the alternative hypothesis) and permit rejection of the null hypothesis and acceptance of the alternative. If we fail to reject the null hypothesis, we cannot accept the alternative hypothesis.

Sometimes we will fail to consider a value atypical when it should have been. In that instance, we make a Type II (beta) error. The sensitivity of a study is determined by the extent to which such errors are avoided $(1 - \beta)$. Studies should be designed to appropriate levels of sensitivity by conducting a statistical power analysis in the planning stages. Sensitivity can be made greater by increasing the size of the sample, increasing treatment effect, or decreasing the variability of the measures (as by increasing their reliability).

Now that we have an understanding of the logic of inference, in the next chapter we examine experimentation, a method that makes considerable use of inferential statistics.

ADDITIONAL READING

Cohen (1990)
Guilford and Fruchter (1978)
Hays (1981)
Jaeger (1983)

May, Masson, and Hunter (1990)
Moses (1986)
Tukey (1977)

IMPORTANT TERMS

Alpha error
Alpha level
Beta error
Confidence level
Confidence limits

Estimation
Hypothesis testing
Inferential statistics
Nonparametric statistics
Null hypothesis

One-tailed test

Parameters

Power of a statistical test

Practical significance

Robust

Sampling distribution of the mean

Significance level

Standard error of the mean

Statistical significance

Two-tailed test

Type I error

Type II error

═══════════════════════APPLICATION PROBLEMS═══════════════════════

1. A group of researchers were interested in comparing the performance of learners working independently on a computer-assisted instruction program to that of learners working on the computers cooperatively in pairs. They were able to conduct the experiment with 60 eighth-grade students (31 male and 29 female) drawn from several health education classes and randomly assigned to either the individual learning group or the cooperative learning group. The students were given a parallel series of 16 lessons on the topic of sex education. Despite the sensitivity of the subject matter, the investigators predicted that the cooperative method would yield superior performances on a written posttest. How would the logic of inference apply here?

2. A medical researcher was interested in the long-term effects of marijuana on users. She tested the reaction time of a sample of 49 long-term users on an automobile braking time test and compared the results with the adult population average for her city (previously computed in a series of studies conducted by the local traffic safety board for use in licensing tests). The sample had a mean reaction time of 0.98 second, while the population average was 0.90. The standard error for the sample was calculated to be 0.043 second with the confidence interval for 95 percent ranging from 0.896 to 1.064 seconds using a two-tailed test and 0.909 second for a one-tailed test looking in the lower tail. Given these results, should the researcher accept or reject the null hypothesis that there is no difference be-

tween this sample's mean and that of the adult population?

3. A cognitive psychologist hypothesized that students who generated their own questions to a passage of text would demonstrate higher comprehension rates than those who were presented with adjunct questions. She decided to replicate her study with high school students. Her results were very close to showing a statistically significant difference between the two approaches in favor of the generative question hypothesis. When she examined her data, she noticed that the comprehension score for one particular student, who was part of the generative strategy group, was considerably lower than the average scores for that group. She also realized that if she were to discard his score, she would have a statistically significant result. What is her dilemma as concerns Type I and Type II error? Is it possible for her to demonstrate statistical significance using her current data without discarding the score?

4. Comment on this statement: "As we change from validation to a discovery orientation, we typically change the level of significance from 10 percent toward .1 percent."

5. Comment on this statement: "If the null hypothesis is rejected, we can say that the observed result proves that the proposition we are testing is true."

6. Teresa Wright is the superintendent of a suburban school system. Her director of research tells her that the new curriculum is statistically significantly superior to the old curriculum. What questions should she ask the director?

7. Dr. Gerrard Goetz is up for tenure. He wants to be sure that his article shows a significant result so that he can get it published. He is comparing the effectiveness of advance organizers on the learning of scientific laws with traditionally written end-of-chapter summaries. Is there anything he can do to ensure that his study will be publishable?

8. Sally Stoltz has to use a convenience sample of teachers in New York state for a questionnaire. But she would like to show that her group of teachers is like those of the state. She has 25 returns. She runs a statistical test on their ages, years of experience, and grade level and finds that the means of all three are not statistically different at the 5 percent level from those published by the state education department. She concludes that her sample can be generalized to the teachers of the state. Is she justified? Why or why not?

Compare your answers with those on pages 717–718.

APPLICATION EXERCISE

Consider how your study might be set up with an experimental and a control group (which you'll learn more about in the next chapter). How might the logic of inference apply? What would be the null hypothesis? The alternative hypothesis? Would a one- or two-tailed test of significance be more appropriate? What would be an appropriate significance level? Why? Are you concerned with statistical or practical significance?

Experimental Methods and Experimental Design

Despite the creative use of experimental design features from the seventeenth century onward, it was not until the past century or so that experimental design notions became systematized. Much more recently, as biological research moved from the laboratory to the open field, the modern theory of experimental control through randomized assignment to treatment emerged. . . . The advantages of experimental control for inferring causation have to be weighed against the disadvantages that arise because we do not always want to learn about causation in controlled settings.

Thomas D. Cook and Donald T. Campbell, "Quasi-Experimentation"

OVERVIEW

Many social scientists consider that the strongest chains of reasoning can be built with experimental design. For them, experimentation is the most effective of all methods for creating a consensus regarding the existence of cause-and-effect relationships. This effectiveness derives from several characteristics: good experimental control, the elimination or neutralizing of alternative explanations of the phenomenon, and the manipulation of the treatment in appropriate patterns that are reflected in the effect.

Study of experimental design has led to the perception of a number of common rival and alternative explanations besides those of chance and sampling variation described in chapter 17. Some weaken internal validity (LP); others restrict external validity (GP). Because they plague not only experimental studies but also other methods, these rival explanations have implications for all methods concerned with causality.

Experimentalists have developed a variety of designs to take advantage of the control features of experiments to provide the strongest internal validity (LP) and the least restrictive external validity (GP), yet fit the often peculiar conditions of particular studies. We will examine some of these designs and, in the process, learn something about the general methods of constructing them.

CHAPTER CONTENTS

Part I: Basic Principles of
  Experiments· 441
Introduction 441
  Strong Internal Validity (LP), Weak
    External Validity (GP)? 444
  The Art of Experimental Design 445
  Design as a Translation of the
    Hypothesis 446
  Manipulating Treatment to Link
    Cause Convincingly to Effect 447
Controlling for Unwanted Explanations
  or Conditions 449
  General Methods of Control 449
  Independent Variable Designs
    and Their Control of
    Unwanted Explanations 452
Common Control Problems 454
  Threats to Internal Validity (LP),
    Common Rival Hypotheses, and
    Alternative Explanations 454
  Threats to External Validity (GP),
    Common Restrictive Conditions,
    and Explanations 465
A Summary of Protection Offered by Six
  Simple Designs 471

A Summary of Common Control
  Problems and Their
  Elimination 471
  Unique Rival Explanations 476
Part II: Complex Designs, Treatment
  Problems, and Hallmarks of
  Experimentation 478
Other Designs for Single-Variable
  Studies 479
  The Nonequivalent Control
    Group Design 479
  Time-Series Designs 480
  Counterbalanced Designs 483
  A "Patched-up" Design 483
Factorial Designs 484
Experimental Treatment Problems 487
  Conceptually Defining the
    Treatment 487
  Ensuring Treatment Fidelity 488
  Problems with the Basis for
    Sensing Changes 491
Hallmarks of Experimental Design
  and Tips on Constructing
  Experimental Designs 495
Summary 497

PART I:
BASIC PRINCIPLES OF EXPERIMENTS

Experimentation is covered in two parts, divided somewhat arbitrarily, since there is no good stopping place. But it helps to have material in smaller chunks so there is a sense of movement and accomplishment. This part deals with the basics of experimentation: manipulation of treatment, some simple designs, common alternative explanations that must be protected against, and how even the simple designs provide this protection.

INTRODUCTION

Experimentation is the most structured of the three mainstream research methods. Most texts make it sound as though the extensive preplanning that goes into good experimentation were straightforward, and research reports make it look as though everything done were for the record. Actually, despite the structure of experimentation, or perhaps because of it, a great deal of time goes into pilot studies and provisional tries, fooling around to see what works, before final data collection. The length of this chapter and all it encompasses will help you understand why this is true.

The strong chain of reasoning in experiments links cause to effect. Their methods are borrowed directly from the natural sciences. Most social scientists who use them, like their natural science counterparts, see themselves as seeking the laws of nature, the rules and principles that guide individual and group behavior.

Experimentation uses the method of differences described in chapter 12. You'll recall that this required that two or more situations be exactly alike except for one thing, and that is the treatment or whatever independent variable we are studying. Although it is true that no two groups can be exactly alike—even the same group is different at a later time—the problem is to make **functionally equivalent groups**. By that we mean that they function as if they were exactly equivalent for the purposes of this study, because anything relevant to the study is made equivalent. Making the groups functionally equivalent is the purpose of control procedures that are the hallmark of experimentation. Consider the six facets of design in the chain of reasoning:

1. *Subjects*. In qualitative research, the people studied are in their natural groups. Although this may be true also in an experiment, experimentalists like to be able to assign individuals to groups and, if possible, to do so randomly.[1] Random assignment will, on the average, make the groups equivalent with regard to all characteristics, even length of toenails and size of belly button, characteristics about which we usually care not at all.

2. *Situation*. In qualitative research, the situation is determined by the field location of the individuals or group studied. This may be true of a field experiment as well. But to eliminate undesired alternative explanations of the effect, researchers often prefer doing the study in a laboratory or in some other situation less vulnerable to random events beyond their influence than most field situations.

3. *Treatment (independent variables)*. In qualitative research, the actions and reactions observed occur naturally as a result of the situation and the individuals in it. There are "natural experiments" where the researcher waits in readiness to assess the effects of a naturally occurring event. But more often, a planned cause, the treatment, is administered according to the procedure specified in the design.

---

1. Note, too, that the term *subjects* is an experimentalist term. Qualitative researchers point out that they see the persons studied as "informants" who help them understand a situation rather than as individuals to be studied, treated, and possibly manipulated. But this can be true of experimenters, as Mitroff and Kilmann (1976) showed in engaging the "subject" in an exploration of how the problem should be defined and investigated. Kruglanski (1976), too, used the postexperimental interview to draw on subjects' self-knowledge to determine how the experimental situation was interpreted and to make suggestions. Perhaps the attitude of the researcher, more than the method, is the critical variable. Most methods can be used in varying ways to fit the orientation of the user.

4. *Observations and measures.* The qualitative researcher's stock in trade is observations unfettered by instrumentation. Although experimentalists may use observations if no suitable instrument or measure is available, they prefer measures.
5. *Basis for sensing attributes or changes.* In qualitative research, changes in individuals or groups are observed over time to note the difference in various characteristics of interest. Comparison of individuals with themselves at different points in time is also the basis of some experiments. More often in experimentation, treated groups are compared with control groups (or other differently treated groups).
6. *Procedure.* With qualitative method, the order of investigator actions is determined largely by the individuals or group being studied. Even plans to interview certain individuals are not as extensive as those of experimentation. In the latter, who will get what treatment, when, and how, as well as who will be observed and measured when, where, and with what, are all generally preplanned.

So it is clear that most experimentation is at the highly structured end of the method structure continuum, much of qualitative research at the other (see Figure 3.2). Many aspects of an experimental study are under the direct control of the researcher, who plans what will occur ahead of time.

Control of the administration of the treatment provides evidence that strongly links cause with effect. The application of the treatment with a resultant visible effect is very convincing of the possibility of a causal link between them. This is enhanced when we can produce the effect on demand, particularly when production is controlled by a table of random numbers or an unbelieving observer! If the effect depends on the presence of the cause and disappears when the cause is removed, the evidence is even more strongly convincing, since it can be turned on and off at will (for example, introducing food coloring into a child's food if the coloring is suspected of producing emotionally disturbed behavior). So of all the methods we have available, experimentation is probably the one that most strongly links cause and effect.

Control is present in still another feature only hinted at earlier, although it is one of the strongest features of experimentation: the control of alternative explanations. A major function of experimental design is elimination of the variety of plausible alternative explanations to which every study is subject, regardless of the research method used. Although other methods may also work at cleaning up alternative explanations, the special capability of experimentation to do this for a wide range of alternatives is unique.

- Experimentation provides one of the strongest chains of reasoning for linking cause to effect.
- Manipulating the treatment to show that the effect follows it strongly links causes to effect.
- We can carefully plan in advance the choices for each of the six links in

> the design chain: subject, situation, treatment, observations or measures, basis for sensing attributes or changes, and procedure.
> - Careful choice of design provides control for rival explanations and restrictive conditions.

Strong Internal Validity (LP), Weak External Validity (GP)?

Experimentation clearly can build very strong internal validity (LP) (the capacity to link cause to effect). But what about external validity (GP), generality—typically considered the Achilles' heel of experimentation? This impression is reinforced by the large number of experiments using laboratory or artificial situations far from reality. Their practical applications are often difficult to discern. Given the continuous pressure for research resources, some researchers feel such studies are hard to justify. However, a variety of experts have risen to the defense of abstruse experiments (including Henshel, 1980a, 1980b; and Berkowitz and Donnerstein, 1982). They point out that the purpose of such studies is not immediate generalization but understanding of the phenomenon as it exists in the laboratory. As that understanding builds over time, eventually there may be applicability to a practical situation.[2]

Henshel (1980b) argues that learning the interrelationships of variables in an artificial situation may enable us to see how the real situation can be made to resemble the artificial one. We learn about phenomena "that are capable of existing," permitting "the creation of entirely new social structures and institutions heretofore unknown" (p. 194).[3] In support of this conjecture, he quotes Robert Lynd, an eminent sociologist, as declaring our task is to discover both "what kinds of order actually do exist . . . and what functionally more useful kinds of order can be created" (Lynd, 1939, pp. 125–126).

But experimentation is not confined to artificial settings. Recently, large-scale social experimentation has taken place in real settings. One of the largest of these, the Income Maintenance Experiment (guaranteed annual income), was even replicated in different cities. The results were very useful in deciding that such a policy was not a good idea. This was not, however, because individuals would be encouraged to laziness by the guaranteed income, the expected problem in the study, but because of an unexpected side effect, that of family breakup (Rossi and Lyall, 1976).

Ellsworth (1977) goes further in arguing for experiments in natural settings. She makes the point that the typical experimental treatment suffers from

---

2. Mosteller (1981), analyzing studies of basic research, found a long lead time (often 20 to 30 years) between publication of results and their incorporation into major developments. A substantial portion of research contributing to a given development had no relation to the application at the time the research was done. For example, he indicates this figure was 41 percent in the case of advances in cardiopulmonary medicine and surgery occurring between 1945 and 1975.

3. Among the examples Henshel cites is the propeller-driven aircraft, which does not exist in nature; indeed, humans lost their lives trying to imitate the birds.

"weakness and brevity" (p. 607). She notes that experimentally lowered self-esteem may "have nothing to do with a lifetime of low self-esteem." The anger induced in a laboratory may be "qualitatively distinct from rage" (p. 607). She notes, however, that the experimenter may "take advantage of one of nature's powerful or long-term treatments" by choosing individuals who are already subject to such treatments and then studying them in a laboratory setting. As an example, she cites Rubin (1970), who, realizing that he could not create romantic love, brought couples already in love into the laboratory. Or we can treat individuals in the laboratory and then see what happens to them in the "real world." For example, Janis (1975) turned a social psychology laboratory into a community weight reduction clinic. So there are interesting combinations.

There is also such a thing as the "natural experiment" wherein we study the effect of a "treatment" applied by nature. We have sought to learn how societies cope with disaster this way. For example, the early studies of Baker and Chapman (1962) have been followed by numerous examinations of the social reactions to earthquakes, volcano eruptions, floods, fires, transportation accidents, and other catastrophes. These have led to new summaries and understandings (Raphael, 1986; Kreps, 1989) and a collection of such research in the archives of the Disaster Research Center at the University of Delaware.

Part of the art of experimental design is choosing situations for a study that achieve the balance in internal validity (LP) and external validity (GP) that is appropriate for the researcher's goals.

- Experimentation has its greatest control potential in the laboratory study, where strong internal validity (LP) is gained at the expense of external validity (GP).
- Natural experiments, which wait for a treatment to occur spontaneously, or experiments in which a treatment is applied under field conditions, gain greater external validity (GP) at the expense of internal validity (LP).
- The researcher's task is to achieve a balance of the two types of validity appropriate to the goal of the study.
- Basic research that aims at understanding phenomena or inventing conditions that do not yet exist but might is often seen as a first step toward application.

The Art of Experimental Design

From the foregoing it is clear that experiments are intentional acts that call for careful advance planning. Creating the appropriate experimental design, which is the heart of that planning, requires proper choices for all six facets of design: subjects, situation, treatment, observation or measurement, basis for sensing attributes or changes, and procedure. Appropriate choices can create convincing demonstrations linking cause to effect, eliminate undesired alternative explanations of a phenomenon, and prevent undue restriction of generality.

The researcher's task is to use the available time, personnel, money, equipment, measures, etc., to translate the hypothesis into a design within the constraints of those resources he or she can tap, institutional limitations, and ethical boundaries. In addition, they must maximize audience credibility in the chain of reasoning being developed. If inferential statistics are being used, the design must have sufficient statistical power to sense the effect. The sample of subjects must be large enough to be convincing to the audience. The choices of persons, situations, measures, and treatments must be representative enough to support the desired generality.

Clearly, this requires a balancing of many things and, hence, in some respects, experimental design is an art: there are so many choices that could be made differently. What one person weighs as a serious alternative explanation, another might take more lightly and so prefer a different design. Where one emphasizes the practical implications of whether a treatment will be broadly effective and so is interested in external validity (GP), another is more interested in how the treatment works and what aspects of treatment cause what effects and so tips the balance toward internal validity (LP). Choice of design is made easier by the fact that many frequently used designs have been analyzed for strengths and weaknesses.

- Design is part science and part art—so many choices can be combined in so many ways to protect against the alternative explanations deemed most threatening.
- Researchers may differ in design choices to provide protection, the alternative explanations viewed as most potentially damaging, and the chosen balance between internal validity (LP) and external validity (GP).

Design as a Translation of the Hypothesis

By now it will not be news that the *design is an operational definition of the hypothesis*. In experimentation, however, we soon learn that certain terms in the hypothesis are associated with or require certain design features. For example, the terms on the left of the following list are typically linked to the features on the right.

Terms	Associated Features
Trend	At least two observations or measures
Retention versus immediate recall	Multiple posttests
Curvilinear trend	At least three observations or measures
Change in trend	At least two measures before change and at least one after it, preferably two or more

Terms	Associated Features
Gain measures	Either pretests and posttests or a control group
Relationship	Measure of two or more variables on the same group
Cumulative effect	Multiple treatments with testing after each treatment or after selected treatments
Different levels of treatment intensity	Multiple experimental groups
Weak treatment	Large sample, increased length of treatment, stratification or blocking to reduce random "noise" and make study more sensitive, use of subjects sensitive to the treatment, a directional hypothesis, one-tailed test of significance, 5 or 10 percent level of significance rather than 1 percent

The list could be extended, but the point is clear that we can determine some of the features of our design from the way the hypothesis is stated. Note that the terms on this list are not peculiar to experimental research; establishing of trends, for instance, may also be a part of survey or qualitative research.

- Design is basically an operational definition of the hypothesis; indeed, certain terms that appear in hypotheses have their design counterparts.

Manipulating Treatment to Link Cause Convincingly to Effect

One of the essential tasks of the design is to manipulate the treatment so as to give a clear illustration of the relationship of cause to effect.[4] This is done in several ways:

1. Use a theory or a rationale to predict the appearance of the effect. Do so in as much detail as possible, indicating when it will appear, how strongly, how long it will last, and so on. Show the agreement of prediction and results.
2. Make the difference between untreated and treated as big as feasible.
3. Show that the effect follows the cause.
4. Vary the treatment, and show that the effect has the same pattern.

---

4. This discussion builds on material in chapter 12, especially that presented under "Evidence for Inferring Causation" (page 246).

Astronomy is not an experimental science. Yet an astronomer can tell you that if you will look at a certain point in the sky at a certain time with a telescope of a certain strength, you will see Halley's comet. If that turns out to be right, you are convinced that the astronomer knows a great deal about the comet. In similar fashion, suppose that we theorize that having skipped a developmental task in choosing a vocation, even individuals who were initially pleased with it will become discontent with their vocation after a period of about 10 years. We find individuals who are about 10 years into their chosen occupation and compare the satisfaction of those who can recall having completed that developmental task with those who do not recall having done so. If the data are confirmatory, that is strong evidence. The more detailed our predictions can be made, the more compelling the evidence for the expected relationship when the prediction is validated. Using a theory or a rationale to predict the effect in as detailed a fashion as possible is an important way of strengthening the evidence.

The second alternative, showing a large effect, is not uncommon in the natural sciences but is rarer in the social sciences.[5] Dramatic results from trials of a medical drug or procedure are front-page news. But such strong effects are almost unknown in the social sciences. Yet, as chapter 17 indicates in describing how to increase the sensitivity of an inferential statistic, there are many aspects of a study that can be changed to increase the size of an effect.

A condition of cause-and-effect relationships is that, timewise, the effect follows the cause. Experiments have a big advantage in that the treatment is administered so appearance of effect only after the administration of treatment can be easily observed.

The link of cause to effect is most convincingly demonstrated by showing congruence in the pattern of cause and effect. There are a variety of ways in which the pattern of cause may be changed. We can change the frequency, the strength, and the duration of application. The changes can be made in large enough steps to produce measurable results. They can be made in equal steps (a single unit of strength, twice as strong, three times, etc.) or in accelerating fashion (twice as strong, 4 times as strong, 16 times, 256 times, etc.). Administration can be clustered between intervals, and the pattern of clustering and length of intervals can be changed. A random pattern of administration can be used. Any of these patterns, when accompanied by a similar pattern in the effect, will very convincingly link cause to effect.

You can easily see how such patterns would apply to drug testing with on-and-off patterns as the drug is given or withdrawn. But teaching and other treatments with residual effects do not lend themselves quite as well to this method, since the "off" period may show no loss. In forgetting, there may be only a slight loss, often not measurable during the short period of the study. To pattern the "on" treatment, we may use two or more treatment strength levels—more practice problems or increased contact time—levels different enough from each other to be reflected in the strength of the effect. Large changes in the strength of treatment will not always be reflected in the effect,

---

5. However, see the Rosenthal reference on p. 568. Do we ask for too much?

however, because there are sometimes learning "plateaus" that do not correspond to either strength of treatment or extent of practice.

CONTROLLING FOR UNWANTED EXPLANATIONS OR CONDITIONS

General Methods of Control

There are three main methods of obtaining protection from the effect of an unwanted variable: (1) remove it, (2) measure and adjust for it, and (3) spread its effect across all the groups being compared so that they are equally affected. Of these, removing it is the most desirable. Measuring and adjusting is the next but is difficult to do. Spreading the effect equally across the comparison groups is the least desirable because it adds to the variance already present. This reduces the power of the statistical test, making it less sensitive to a small effect. Yet this method is the one most commonly employed. What we can't eliminate or measure and adjust for, we make sure is present in the control and other groups being compared.

Removing and Excluding. Use of the laboratory, or some specially designated area where we have control over what goes on, is the most common method of removing and excluding unwanted variation. But that is not always possible, so other techniques that have the effect of removal are also used. **Camouflage**, for instance, was used by Kounin (1970), who placed a box on a pedestal in classrooms. Students and teachers never knew whether the box was empty or held a camera and soon came to ignore the box. Similarly, the participant observer, by participating, seeks to lose the stigma of an outsider and take on the role of group member.

Masking of one variable with another is sometimes effective. In "landscaped" offices, which use 5-foot partitions instead of walls, "white noise" is introduced to mask sounds coming over the partitions. Thurstone (1947) used darkness to mask the movement of a penlight, which, after being moved in a designated pattern, was placed in a holder. Subjects were to trace the movement of the light on paper. This study of autokinesis found that subjects mapped movement long after the pen was in the holder. Darkness masked the holder, so subjects could not tell when the penlight was placed there.

Promising deferred treatment of the control group after the experimental group sometimes allays compensatory action. For example, when parents demand that their children also receive the experimental treatment, administrators promise that the control group will be treated next or build a waiting list that is used as a control.

Restricting the range of the variable to be controlled will also eliminate that variable as a factor in the effect. Using a very bright group or a group in which IQs vary little will eliminate the variability so that differences in intelligence would not be a factor in the effect.

Measurement and Adjustment. Partial correlation and analysis of covariance are the two methods most commonly used for reducing the effect of unwanted variables (these are discussed in chapter 22). But just as in trimming the fat from a piece of meat, it is difficult not to trim too much or too little. Therefore, these methods have problems making the proper adjustment. We can build the unwanted variation into the study as an independent variable. This allows us to determine its effect. A third method employs factorial designs, which are described later in this chapter.

But the Achilles' heel of all these methods is measurement of and adjustment for the unwanted variable. Where this is easy and accurate, the methods work well (as in controlling for length of practice time). But how do we use analysis of covariance to measure and adjust for the private schoolchild's perception of his parents' expectations for success? Coleman, Hoffer, and Kilgore (1982) tried to correct for the socioeconomic bias of private schools with analysis of covariance. The controversy surrounding that study indicates the difficulty of building a consensus around the interpretation of data when these methods are used (Goldberger and Cain, 1982).

Spreading the Effect to All Comparison Groups. Making sure that the groups compared are alike in all respects except that of the treatment is basically the goal when we spread the effect of rival explanations to all the groups. Thus if giving a pretest is likely to boost the posttest scores, be sure that the control group is also pretested. If the recipients of the experimental treatment feel special because the treatment was given obtrusively, then give the control group a placebo treatment devoid of the treatment's "active ingredient" and make them feel special, too. The different ways in which individuals react to the pretest and to obtrusive treatment will add to the variance of the study. That will increase the minimum effect size that will be needed for a statistically significant effect, but that is part of the trade-off for the control of these variables.

How can we be sure that groups are exactly alike except for the treatment variable? Certainly, they can't be exactly alike; individuals change from moment to moment. But they must be enough alike with respect to the vital variables that, were they not alike, would constitute strong alternative explanations of the effect. If an experimental group starts out at a higher level of achievement than the control group and it ends higher, we don't know which produced the effect, the treatment or prior achievement.

Random assignment of individuals to groups is the statistician's preferred way of ensuring that groups are comparable from the outset. Indeed, where it is not known which of two treatments is more effective, it can be argued that random assignment is the fairest way of allocating them. Where there is a surplus of applicants for a presumed more effective treatment, random assignment is the democratic way of distributing the favor. Most important of all, on the average, random assignment makes groups comparable in all of the variables we think might present problems *and also in all other things we had not expected.* Randomization buys so much for so little!

Campbell and Stanley (1963) thought random assignment so important a contributor to internal validity that they devised the term "true experimental designs" to describe those where random assignment was used and named other designs "quasi-experimental." This distinction has the unfortunate consequence of sounding as though so-called true experimental designs protect against all rival hypotheses. Of course they do not. For example, where random assignment is evident to the subjects, it may actually increase the feeling of being special noted earlier by indicating that the individuals are participating in an experimental situation.

As a method of control, random assignment tends to be intuitively resisted by researchers. In the first place, it can be obtrusive. There are so few instances where people are normally assigned to situations by the luck of the draw. To counter this perception, Boruch, McSweeney, and Soderstrom (1978) produced a bibliography of some 300 field tests using random assignment in delicate as well as uncontroversial areas. Similarly, Boruch and Wothke (1985, appendix 1) list 10 such studies in employment training programs. Further, the latter show how random assignment can be used to study important policy matters. It describes eight social experiments that used random assignment in problems as different as those involving welfare versus work incentive programs, arrest and nonarrest in domestic assault cases, treatment of depression, use of mediation in judicial litigation, and hospital versus community treatment of the chronically mentally ill. They make a strong case for seriously considering random assignment even in situations where we might think it normally impossible. Further, random assignment, having once been found defensible in an area, is more easily used in new studies.[6]

Researchers often object to apportioning a key variable among groups by random assignment alone. Although it equates all variables over groups "on the average," it is cold comfort to a researcher that it failed to equate them in the current study. No one wants to invest time and energy in a situation when, just by the luck of the draw, a bad break occurred. As with stratification, where random sampling within the strata provides the random element, so random assignment within blocks (strata) provides the random element. Adding blocking, stratifying, or matching ensures that the blocked or matched variable will be equated between or among the groups so that we can have the best of both worlds.

- Random assignment protects not only from unwanted variables that have been identified but also from those that have not even been thought of.
- So-called true experimental designs are those in which the groups are equated by random assignment. Despite the connotation of the name, these designs are not immune from all rival hypotheses.
- Random assignment of individuals to groups from within blocks (strata) is a preferred way of equating the characteristics of individuals within groups.

---

6. Appendix 2 in Boruch and Wothke (1985) lists six objections to random assignment with counterarguments, and the book's final chapter describes strategies for increasing the chances of making randomization feasible through advance planning.

> ■ Ensuring equality across groups by blocking and then randomly assign-
> ing provides the protection of stratification as well as that of randomness.

Independent Variable Designs and Their Control of Unwanted Explanations

To provide a basis for understanding how designs protect against rival explanations, let us look at a set of six designs. Each successive design can be used to study the effect of a single treatment with a bit of an advantage over the previous one.[7] This will illustrate how designs evolve and some desirable design characteristics.

Here is a simple case. Mrs. Kimball, a first-grade teacher in the inner city, is concerned about her children's progress. She has heard that the Bereiter-Engleman curriculum, which is based heavily on Skinnerian techniques, has been highly successful. She gives it a four-month trial and then tests the children on the Stanford Achievement Test. In comparison with the test's norms, it appears that her group's score, though still below what should be expected, is better than it might have been.

How would we describe her design? A fairly standard notation for such depiction was developed by Campbell and Stanley (1963) using X to indicate a treatment and O to indicate an observation or a measurement. Events are sequenced in time from left to right, and each group occupies a separate line. To describe the teacher's experiment, we need only one line because there was but one group; it appears thus:

Design 1: Case study   X O

This indicates that the Bereiter-Engleman curriculum was applied (X) and then the students were measured with the Stanford Achievement Test (O for observed). This is the case study design.

You can sense that this is not the strongest design. Although the teacher believes that the students are ahead of where they might be, the basis on which change is sensed is a comparison with the test's norms. If the students in this year's class are different from those on whom the test was normed, the norms may not be applicable. But if the teacher had known where the students started, she wouldn't have had to depend on the norms to show change. Actually, they might have started as high as they ended; we can't tell from the case study design. So a stronger design in this respect would have tested them both before and after the treatment:

Design 2: One-group pretest-posttest design   O X O

Such a design will at least show the change: the students are being used as their own control group—compared with themselves at an earlier point in time. This is the **one-group pretest-posttest design**.

---

7. This does not illustrate the full variety of designs, which is almost limitless; more complex ones are discussed later in this chapter.

The mention of a control group suggests that the teacher might have used one in her study, but the control group must be just like the experimental group. How to get one? She might use another teacher's class, a preformed group that might be comparable to hers. A preformed group is one formed for purposes other than the experiment. Since such groups are not formed by random assignment, we do not know their comparability to one another, and this is indicated by a line between the rows in design 3.

There the C indicates that this is a control treatment, just as the X indicates the administration of the treatment with the "active ingredient." Recall that the groups are to be "functionally equivalent." This may mean that there is no special treatment, as in this case, where Mrs. Kimball's usual free-play kindergarten curriculum might be contrasted with Mrs. Johnson's very structured curriculum. The "traditional" kindergarten curriculum is, nevertheless, a treatment, so we designate it as the control treatment with the C.

Suppose we were studying the effect on an experimental group of over-active children receiving caffeine and the control group received nothing. It may be that the *expectation* of some effect, as when a pill is administered, is really the "active ingredient"—this is known as the **placebo effect.**[8] A placebo treatment would create that expectancy but would not contain caffeine. It might contain sugar or other neutral substances. The C, therefore, symbolizes a control or placebo treatment in this **nonequivalent control group design**:

Design 3: Nonequivalent control group design
$$\frac{O\ X\ O}{O\ C\ O}$$

A way of ensuring that, on the average, the groups will be comparable is to set them up specifically for this study. Randomly assign the individuals from a pool of subjects to either the control or the treatment group by a flip of a coin. Once half of the total has been assigned to one group, the rest go in the other. If, at the beginning of the year, all the kindergarten children were assigned by the flip of a coin to either Mrs. Kimball's or Mrs. Johnson's class, we would expect them, on the average, to be equivalent. Then, again by the flip of a coin or a random device, the Bereiter-Engleman treatment is assigned to one of the two teachers to administer. Random assignment of subjects and treatment to groups is designated by an R in a square. The pretest tells us whether randomization worked and the groups are really comparable. This is the **pretest-posttest control group design**:

Design 4: Pretest-posttest control group design
$$\boxed{R}\ \ \begin{array}{c} O\ X\ O \\ O\ C\ O \end{array}$$

If we trust randomization to make them really comparable, perhaps there is no need for the initial testing, and we could simply compare them at the posttest. This is the **posttest-only control group design**:

---

8. In medical research, an unmedicated pill given to the control subjects in place of the experimental medicine is called a placebo.

Design 5: Posttest-only control group design $\boxed{R}$ X O
                                              C O

But perhaps we are not sure enough that randomization has really worked; we'd like a check to make sure. Let's combine the last two into a single design, known as the **Solomon four-group design**:

Design 6: Solomon four-group design $\boxed{R}$
O X O
O C O
X O
C O

In design 6, subjects from a pool are assigned to one of four groups: two experimental (one pretested and one not) and two control (one pretested and one not). Such a design has the combined advantages of designs 4 and 5, as we shall see. But it requires more subjects, and four rather than two groups must be treated.

Each of the six designs successively provides added protection from an alternative explanation of the effect—a rival hypothesis to the one being tested. But each such design typically provides protection from more than the single problem noted, yet has weaknesses we have not yet considered. Let us proceed to in-depth coverage of some of the common alternative explanations—rival hypotheses from which we seek protection. These six designs will be sufficient to allow us to illustrate how experimental design eliminates many of them or, in some cases, fails to do so.

COMMON CONTROL PROBLEMS

Threats to Internal Validity (LP), Common Rival Hypotheses, and Alternative Explanations

Part of the empirical evidence supporting internal validity (LP) is the elimination of alternative explanations or rival hypotheses. This is the fourth of five judgments of internal validity (LP). Campbell and Stanley (1963) described these as **threats to validity**, since they are threats to internal or external validity. The three terms in the heading of this discussion refer to eliminating the same thing—sufficiently plausible alternative explanations of the effect in question. If one of them is present we can't be sure that the intended explanation is the true cause. If they are not eliminated, our audience is as likely to consider one or more of them equally plausible causes, and a consensus will not form around our intended explanation. Design is used to ensure that the intended cause is linked as tightly as possible to the intended effects.

Sometimes the term **confounding** is employed because alternative explanations are variables that occur at the same time as the independent variable or treatment. In Mrs. Kimball's study, because the effect of the pretest no doubt lingered into at least the beginning of the Bereiter-Engleman curriculum, the variables are said to be confounded (students encountering certain material in the curriculum covered by the pretest pay extra attention to it, expecting to be retested). That is, the effects each variable had are inextricably entangled (confounded) with each other to the point that they cannot be separated; we cannot tell the effects of the curriculum from those of the pretest.

Confounding occurs when two variables are present at the same time in a situation so that we cannot tell which might have been the cause of whatever effect occurred (or whether both contributed).

Campbell and Stanley (1963) and later Cook and Campbell (1979) named and called attention to a variety of common alternative explanations. It should be emphasized that these are by no means all the alternative explanations we need be concerned about; many studies have unique alternatives. The work of these researchers has, however, contributed to a very useful list. We shall examine their explanations plus other alternatives in relation to some of the designs we have just reviewed. *Beware not to take their names literally;* I have used the names Campbell, Stanley, and Cook gave them, but the meanings are often different or broader than the names imply. *Maturation*, for instance, includes changes in the individual between testings due to growth, as the name implies. But it also refers to any change over time, such as growing more tired, less motivated, or more test-wise.

Sampling Error and Chance Error. Consider, first, the case study design, where Mrs. Kimball applied a treatment to the children in her class and then measured their achievement. She says that the average score, "though still below what should be expected, is better than it might have been." That is damning her effect with faint praise, but we have to wonder whether there really was an effect. After all, merely taking different samples of subjects and measurement error would cause the mean to bounce around, sometimes higher and sometimes lower. This could have been an upward bounce without any treatment effect, just chance variation—a reasonable alternative explanation. Inferential statistics help us determine the odds that this is nothing but chance sampling error. So by using inferential statistics, sampling and chance variation is the first alternative explanation eliminated. We determine whether there is a statistically significant difference between the achievement level on the norms and that found by testing. If there is, sampling and chance error is discarded as an alternative explanation, and we must consider others.

Note, however, that for a correct decision to be made regarding chance error as an alternative explanation, we must have designed the study with appropriate statistical power to sense an effect of interest, should one occur. Boruch and Gomez (1977) point out that a treatment shown to be effective in a typical controlled setting may require increased sensitivity to show equal effectiveness in the field. They use as their example the evaluation of a program designed to increase student achievement by half a standard deviation with a sample of 40 and a significance level of .01 (Type I error) under controlled conditions. The study has sufficient statistical power (1—Type II error) that it will show a statistically significant difference 9 times out of 10 if an effect of the expected size (half a standard deviation gain) occurs. But things change when the evaluation is moved to the field:

> A standardized achievement test chosen for convenience . . . for instance, may only be 75% relevant to program content. And because of natural random variation in the quality of measurement, the test's reliability [could dip as low as] . . . .80. Further, it will usually be the case that the treatment delivered in the laboratory will not be the treatment delivered in the field. Simple indifference among field staff may reduce the treatment's fidelity to 75% of its design value, and natural random variation in staff delivery and in student receipt will reduce the uniformity of treatment as well. It is easy to show under all these conditions, the power drops to . . . [3 chances in 10]. (p. 412)

They further point out that the effect of these degradations is multiplicative rather than additive. So we need to bear these considerations in mind in substituting laboratory for field values in estimating appropriate statistical power in a field experiment.

- Sampling and chance error is an alternative explanation made improbable by inferential statistics.
- Estimation of statistical power based on laboratory conditions may underestimate requirements for adequate power under field conditions.

Testing. You'll recall that Mrs. Kimball improved her design by adding a pretest as well as a posttest. If they show a significant difference, then there was a gain over the period of the study. Suppose such a gain appears; now what?

Maybe the students did better the second time they took the test because they were more comfortable with it, knew what to expect, had thought about the questions in the meantime, and were more ready for them. Crane and Heim (1950) showed students gained 3 to 5 IQ points just as a result of retaking the test without any instruction on items initially missed. In personality testing, retesting is likely to result in an increase in apparent "adjustment" (Windle, 1954). Certainly increased awareness of socially approved answers might develop between testings, once subjects were sensitized to the topic and had a chance to think and converse about it.

The effect of the pretest on the posttest is called **testing**. So a reasonable alternative explanation for the effect with a one-group pretest-posttest design (design 2) is perhaps that testing created the effect, rather than the Bereiter-Engleman treatment.

How do we eliminate the effect of testing? Use a control group; consider the nonequivalent control group or the pretest-posttest control group design (designs 3 and 4). The control group would be tested twice so that it would exhibit the effect of the pretest on the posttest. Thus we compare two post-tests, both influenced by the effect of testing. Another way is to eliminate the pretest, as in the posttest-only control group design (5). The Solomon four-group design has the advantages of both designs 4 and 5.

> Testing, as a rival hypothesis, occurs whenever two or more testings occur with the same or closely related instruments, since the experience of having been tested earlier may affect later tests.

Regression.   Wherever we retest a group that was split off as a high or low section of a parent group, we should suspect the alternative explanation of **regression**. It is one of the most subtle rival hypotheses. Suppose that Mrs. Kimball had used the Stanford Achievement Test as a pretest to select the lowest quarter of the students for treatment with the new curriculum. This is group A, the group to the left of the cut score in Figure 18.1. When she retested them, even if her treatment were totally ineffective, she would have observed an improvement in scores due to the effect of regression! You may be able to recall studies where just this kind of claim occurred: a remedial group was retested and the treatment was proclaimed a success. Alternatively, a top-notch group, group B in Figure 18.1, was selected for accelerated instruction. On retest, students in this group would be found to have gained little, per-haps even to have lost. The treatment would be deemed ineffective, perhaps incorrectly, also because of the effect of regression.

Regression causes the mean of the split-off section to "regress," or move toward the mean of the parent group, on retest. As shown in Figure 18.2 for group A, it moves higher in low or remedial groups, showing an apparent

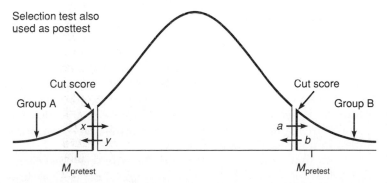

FIGURE 18.1   Groups subject to the regression effect as a result of having been separated from a parent group by means of a selection test later used to measure treatment effect.

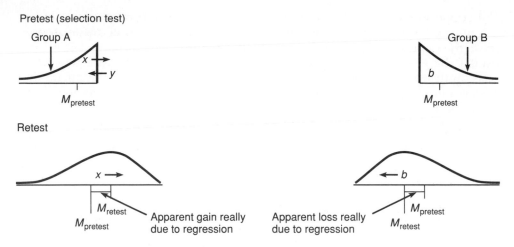

FIGURE 18.2   Regression effect in the selected groups at retest.

gain. If there is a treatment effect, it looks better than it should because it is added to the regression effect. In accelerated or enrichment groups, group B in the same figure, regression moves the mean lower, showing an apparent loss. Since the regression and treatment effects typically work in opposite directions for high-achieving groups, a treatment looks worse than it otherwise would. Assuming that the treatment is designed to raise scores, with a high group, the *apparent* treatment effect will be less than the *actual* effect. In fact, if regression exceeds the treatment effect, students will appear worse off than at pretest.

This kind of regression results from a less than perfect correlation between any two tests for any reason. In pretest-posttest designs, that reason is the unreliability of the test. When retesting with the same test, we have the influence of stability reliability (described in chapter 11). Retesting with an alternative form involves both the inconsistency due to instability and any lack of equivalence between forms. The greater the unreliability, the greater the regression effect.

How does unreliability cause regression? If a test is not perfectly reliable, an individual's score will vary from testing to testing. Say an individual has what we might think of as her true score. Suppose that we could hypnotize the testee and give the test an infinite number of times, giving the posthypnotic suggestion each time that she is to forget she ever took it before. With multiple retests, we would get a normal distribution of scores, and its mean would represent her true score. At any testing, her score may be any one from the distribution of scores around the true score—this is the result of un-reliability. Like the spread of shots from an unreliable gun, sometimes her score will be too high, other times too low.

It is the fact that a different score from the true score distribution appears each time a person is tested that results in regression. Here is how: consider just the cases labeled x and y adjacent to the cut score for group A in Figure 18.1. The positions of the letters x and y indicate their scores on the pretest.

But suppose that X's true score is above the cutoff; he is in the remedial group because of error. On retest, his score is likely to be closer to his true score and be higher. Y's situation is just the opposite. With a true score below the cut score, on retest, her score is likely to become closer to her true score and therefore to be lower. The movement of scores from pretest to retest is indicated by the arrows. If the groups were not split apart, on retest these scores around the cut score would merely change places within the distribution, leaving the overall shape unchanged. But when the big middle segment of the parent distribution is removed, y is no longer part of the remedial group, so only the effect of x appears in the retest.

This is shown in Figure 18.2, where the distributions of scores for the tails alone are shown at retest. Concentrate on the lower tail. When the tail is isolated from the middle, and X's score is likely to be closer to its true score on retest, it goes above the cut score, and a tail now extends to the right, in place of an abrupt absence of cases above the cut score. There are no scores above the cut score moving down to maintain the balance; those were removed when the tail was isolated from the midsection. The result is that the mean of group A moves higher on retest.

If we concentrate instead on the upper tail, the exact reverse process occurs. Persons with true scores lower than the cut score (they don't belong in the enrichment group) are trapped in the upper tail (like score b). When that group is removed for an enrichment treatment and retested to find its effect, with no treatment effect and only regression operating, their scores naturally move down. There are no scores to counterbalance, so again the scores tail off, this time downward, and the mean of the isolated segment moves lower. Thus a supposedly "enriching" treatment may appear to show no gain (if the treatment and regression effects are equal), a small gain (if treatment is slightly larger), or even a loss (if the regression effect is stronger than the treatment effect or there is no treatment effect).

Equivalent control groups, also chosen from the bottom or the top of the parent distribution in a manner identical to that used for the remedial or enrichment group, would be equally affected by regression on retest. Therefore, any design with such a control group protects against regression. If individuals are assigned at random to experimental and control groups so that the groups are, on the average, equivalent, the difference between the control and experimental posttest means gives a measure of the treatment effect without any regression effect. An alternative way of controlling for regression is to retest the selected group before treatment and use the average of the test and retest scores as a basis for sensing change. This provides a larger sample of the subjects' behavior; it is thus more reliable, and scores that were too high will generally come down and those that were too low will come up on retest.

Another kind of regression, which acts the same way as that just discussed, results from instigating a remedial treatment when an effect is at the peak of its display and would move toward the mean without any intervention. In a critique of a study of the effectiveness of a program for delinquents that compared their arrest records before and after treatment, McCleary and colleagues (1979) noted that the 365 delinquents had been selected from a pool of eligible delinquents because of their comparatively higher arrest rates. "Second, in each case the time of intervention has been selected also, apparently, as a reaction to a particularly high rate of arrest" (p. 633). Another way of putting this is that the arrest rate for these delinquents was at a peak in comparison with the pool in general as well as their own personal record of arrests. From this example, it is clear this is a special difficulty in assessing the effectiveness of remedial programs. Remediation is not likely to begin until the problem has become so serious that various ameliorating mechanisms in society are already coming into play. This makes it difficult to interpret evaluation studies of the effect of an intervention where there is no control group and no preintervention measure of trend to indicate whether the problem was already on the decline.

- Regression is a rival explanation wherever an extreme group is selected for treatment (remediation, enrichment, or special treatment) using a pretest-posttest design with no control group.
- Regression may also be found where a remedial treatment is employed at the height of a problem that would subside in time without treatment.
- A control group will also be affected by regression. A comparison of control and experimental means controls for this problem.

Local History.   It is quite possible that Mrs. Kimball's Stanford Achievement Test scores are higher because many of her students were watching *Sesame Street*, a television program that that month happened to be giving practice on the kinds of problems the test emphasized. Alternative events that could have caused the target effect are called **local history** or just history.

If we have a comparable control group, is there any reason to believe that those children will not also watch *Sesame Street* and so also gain on the posttest? No, they probably would, so a comparable control group protects against local history.

Local history is a threat to validity whenever events occur before the posttest that might also cause the effect. A control group that would also be subject to those events is an effective control for this problem.

Mortality.   It is possible that the poorest students in Mrs. Kimball's class had the poorest attendance records. If they were absent when the test was given, that would have raised the average considerably. Their dropping out from the measure of the effect is called mortality, not because the subjects are dead, but because of the selective loss of cases that could affect the test average.

Survey studies are particularly vulnerable to the rival explanation of mortality when there is a low return rate for a questionnaire or when interviews are not completed because the persons were never home when the interviewer called.

As before, a comparable control group would presumably have the same rate of absenteeism as the experimental group, so it would provide a measure of the effects of mortality. Therefore, for internal validity (LP) purposes, comparison of experimental and control groups will permit linking treatment with effect excluding any differential impact of mortality because it is presumed that the two groups are affected equally. However, to the extent that mortality creates a sample that differs in relevant characteristics from the target group to which we hope to generalize, external validity (GP) may be diminished.

Mortality is a rival explanation wherever individuals leave an experimental group prior to completion of the study. The danger is that the composition of the group is changed by the loss, and the measure of effect may differ because of this change. A control group with loss of individuals comparable to those in the treated group in both proportion and nature protects against this problem for internal but not external validity.

Maturation. **Maturation** includes "all those biological and psychological processes which systematically vary with the passage of time independent of specific external events" (Campbell and Stanley, 1963, pp. 177–178). Thus between observations, students might have grown older, more tired, more bored, capable of more mature reasoning, more serious about getting an education, as well as biologically and socially more advanced. In Mrs. Kimball's study, with the passage of only four months, biological growth would show too small an effect to be noticeable. Such processes as growing tired or bored, quite likely to be a factor in a study lasting only a single session, are unlikely to have persisted for over a month. So maturation seems an unlikely alternative in our particular example. But in a longitudinal study lasting several years or a two-hour study in which young children were expected to sit quietly, we can sense that maturation might well be an issue.

Once again, a control group would presumably be affected by maturation in the same way as the experimental group is affected and so would protect against it.

Maturation is a rival hypothesis whenever there is growth or change in the individuals that would affect the measured effect. The term applies not only to natural growth patterns but also to changes such as growing bored, tired, or hungry and other characteristics that might change with the passage of time. A control group provides protection.

Instrument Decay. As described in chapter 15, instrument decay refers to changes in the measuring process between instances of observation or measurement in ways that might account for the observed effect. It can happen in many ways, especially if the instrument is relatively unstructured or a high-inference measure. In qualitative research, the researcher is the instrument and very likely accommodates to unpleasant or shocking events, is less attuned to notice the unusual as the setting becomes familiar, has different expectations as anticipations become more realistic, and so on. In grading essay examinations, expectations are highest (or lowest) for the first papers read, becoming more realistic for later ones. Similarly, we can generally expect an observer to grow more sympathetic with the subjects being observed over a period of time as understanding grows about why they behave as they do.

Instrument decay is rare with multiple-choice tests and is similarly less likely with an observation device that is tightly structured so that the coding of observed behaviors is clear and unambiguous. But even with the latter, observers may become more skilled in using it, make up different rules for handling new situations, or gradually change the rules to make observation easier or more pleasant. Two or more observers may use the instrument quite differently. Interviewers may become more comfortable with an interview schedule or more skilled in eliciting responses. In all these instances, the nature of observations or measures may change with time, and those changes could account for an effect.

Another type of instrument decay involves a change in the scale used between pretest and posttest due to ceiling or floor effects. The scale may be adequate to spread the group across the scale at the pretest, but because of learning during the intervening period, it may be too easy on posttest, and scores pile up at the top. Because scores can't go beyond a perfect score, the mean is lower than it would be if there were additional difficult items that would differentiate among individuals in the top group and spread those scores. This is called the ceiling effect. When the test is too hard at pretest but does a good job at posttest, the opposite happens. The pretest mean will be higher than if the pileup of scores at the bottom could have spread out to still lower scores—a floor effect. Both effects can be spotted by noting the skewness of the frequency distributions as the scores pile up against the floor or the ceiling. This can be avoided only by using measuring instruments that can differentiate across the entire range of behaviors we expect to encounter.

A control group can protect against instrument decay only if the measurment or observation is done in comparable ways and at comparable times in the two groups. If we were to run the experimental group and follow it with measuring or observing a control group (or vice versa), instrument decay could account for differences between measures of the groups.

Use of structured low-inference instruments or training of observers with high-inference measures will reduce or eliminate instrument decay. Repeated use of training videotapes to ensure continued calibration of observers throughout the study is important. So also is the sharing of experiences where new problems are encountered so that agreed-on procedures are used by all.

> ■ Instrument decay refers to changes in the way an instrument is used to measure the effect during the study, as in reinterpreting the meaning of categories of an observation instrument or moderating the strictness of grading on an essay test. Decay may occur from different usage over time or from differences in usage between observers.
>
> ■ Ceiling and floor effects occur when tests are, respectively, too easy or too hard.

Selection.   **Selection** occurs when subjects are present in a group as the result of a selective factor that causes the same effect as the treatment. Especially where it is unrecognized, it can lead to wrong conclusions. For example, if we were to judge from the bottles that wash up on the beach, we would conclude that all bottles discarded in the ocean have their caps on. Of course, we know that those bottles are the survivors; the others sank. Similarly, some of the groups we study—seniors in high school, college students, and graduate students—are survivors.

When a selective factor differentiates persons assembled into groups, we start with nonequivalent groups. A common example is where we ask for volunteers who are willing to use a treatment; they constitute the experimental group. The nonvolunteers become the control group. From Rosenthal and Rosnow's (1975) review of the literature, we know that in contrast to non-volunteers, volunteers have many positive characteristics: they are more intelligent, better educated, higher in social status, and more sociable. In general, they are higher in need for social approval and more likely to be female (except for physically demanding or stressful situations, where males are more likely to volunteer), to be interested in arousal-seeking situations, and to be somewhat unconventional. They tend to be less authoritarian and are more likely Jewish than Protestant and more likely Protestant than Catholic. This listing includes only the findings that Rosenthal and Rosnow believed were supported by enough research to merit considerable confidence. They list other differences, with less convincing evidence, that could be important under particular circumstances.

It is no wonder that studies with volunteer experimental and non-volunteer control groups are suspect. The range of characteristics likely to differentiate such groups is so broad as to affect all but a few studies. Where getting volunteers is the only way to do the study, their use in both experimental and control groups improves internal validity (LP). But it reduces external validity (GP) by placing a restrictive condition on the generality of the findings to nonvolunteers.

Random assignment of subjects to experimental and control groups is the most common antidote to the selection effect. If the groups are small, some form of stratification ("blocking," as it is called in experimental design) is practiced. For example, to ensure that groups are comparable in socioeconomic status, we sort the individuals in the sample into high, middle, and low socioeconomic strata or blocks. Then individuals in the high-socioeconomic-class block are randomly assigned to experimental and control groups, and similarly the middle and low blocks. Matching individuals on the control variable is the extreme of blocking: every pair of matched experimental and control individuals constitutes a block or stratum.

- Selection is a rival explanation when the choice of subjects has been exposed to a selective factor that causes the same effect as the treatment. It also occurs when a selective factor differentiates persons assembled into groups with respect to characteristics that may influence the measure of effect. Use of volunteers for the experimental group and nonvolunteers for the control is a common example.
- Random assignment to groups usually avoids the selection effect.

Base Rate Problems.   Where an effect is part of a larger series of events, unless the **base rate** of the series is taken into account in judging the effect, the base rate can be an alternative explanation of the findings. For example, Baron and Ransberger (1978) examined 102 major riots in the United States between 1967 and 1971 and concluded that there was a curvilinear relationship with the temperature on the day of the violence. This was in contrast to the conventional wisdom that riots are sparked by very hot weather. Carlsmith, Merrill, and Anderson (1979) noted that the original study did not take into account the base rate, the number of very hot days that would have provided conditions for riots. When they adjusted the analysis for this base rate, they found that the probability of a riot increased linearly with the temperature.

Interactions Affecting Internal Validity (LP).   **Interaction** effects occur when the treatment effect is inappropriately strengthened or weakened by a characteristic of another treatment, the study situation, or the individuals in it. For example, in **instrument decay by treatment interaction**, an observer might be so influenced by a treatment as to issue harsher or more lenient judgments. Or in a study of democratic and authoritarian-led groups, an observer may be pleased by the collaboration and teamwork in the democratic group, and hence may focus on its positive attributes. Similarly, the observer may react to the stifling ordering of the authoritarian roles by being especially sensitive to negative behavior. Clearly, this would make the democratic group look better than it should and the authoritarian group worse, resulting in a greater difference between the two groups than should have been shown. A structured instrument combined with training might be the best antidote.

Another example of interaction is selection-maturation interaction, which occurs when the maturation levels of the individuals selected into groups differ in such a way as to cause the effect. Suppose we differentially assigned individuals to groups in such a way that one group tires more easily or grows more bored or less motivated than the other. Engineers compared with social scientists in a required humanities course might differ both in the skills they brought and in their motivation, especially as the former became interested in fields they had not had a chance to explore. Such factors could well create a difference between the two groups that could be inappropriately interpreted as due solely to the treatment. As before, random assignment to control and experimental groups will control for this.

> Interaction effects can make a treatment appear more or less effective than it should. Examples are instrument decay by treatment interaction and selection-maturation interaction.

Threats to External Validity (GP), Common Restrictive Conditions, and Explanations

Just as there are alternative explanations that weaken internal validity (LP), there are restrictive conditions and explanations that pose threats to external validity (GP) and limit generality.[9] These are restrictive conditions found in the study that would not typically be found in the target situation to which we hope to generalize. A thorough examination of external validity is in Bracht and Glass (1968). They coined the terms *population validity* to describe studies that allowed generalization to the intended target population or subjects and *ecological validity* to allow generalization to the intended situations. By extension, you can see that any unusual conditions that are attendant on the choice of one of the six links of design would have restrictive effects on generality:

1. *Subjects*: An unusually intelligent sample volunteered.
2. *Situation*: Treatment and data collection were done in a laboratory.
3. *Treatment*: Experimenters administering the treatment were given expensive training for a year.
4. *Observation or measure*: The measure of creativity depended solely on written verbal responses, a limited measure of creativity.
5. *Basis for sensing attributes or changes*: There was competition between the experimental and control groups.
6. *Procedure*: A pretest sensitized the experimental group to the parts of the treatment that were essential to learn, even though a pretest would not normally accompany the treatment.

---

9. In Campbell and Stanley (1963), Bracht and Glass (1968), and Cook and Campbell (1979), these are simply called "threats to validity." The distinction is not made between alternative, or rival, hypotheses that *weaken* linking power [internal validity (LP)] and restrictive conditions or explanations that *limit* generalizing power [external validity (GP)]. The latter limit generality to situations and conditions similar to those encountered in the study.

It is clear there can be a variety of study characteristics that would restrict generality to circumstances similar to those in which the study was carried out. As internal validity (LP) has common rival explanations to which researchers need to be alert, so external validity (GP) has common restrictive conditions and explanations. Some of the more important ones will be described here; Bracht and Glass (1968) describe a few additional ones.

Obtrusiveness and Reactivity. **Reactivity** is the host of effects that result when individuals realize they are the subjects of study. This happens when the study occurs with enough **obtrusiveness** that the normal conditions existing in the situation are disrupted. Here is a sampling of the reactions to obtrusiveness:

1. "I'm special!" This is often called the **Hawthorne effect** after an experiment at the Hawthorne plant of the Western Electric Company. In that study, Roethlisberger and Dickson's (1939) improvement of the working conditions of a department resulted in increased production. But they found that even negative changes, reducing the amount of lighting, for instance, also increased production. They concluded that it was the psychological effect of giving special attention to the experimental unit that was the cause, rather than the physical changes. The Hawthorne effect could be expected to increase the treatment effect beyond what might be expected under normal conditions.[10]

2. "What does she expect from me? I'd like to please her!" **Hypothesis guessing** by subjects is common: most often subjects want the researcher to think well of them. This is especially true where there is a status difference, with the researcher perceived as a professional. A researcher who can help a subject in some way during or after the study—for example, an instructor who uses her advisees as subjects—is likely to observe very eager-to-please behavior. The subject is trying to determine what is going on and reacting in terms of that perception to facilitate the effect. Expectancies created by a study are part of what are called its demand characteristics (more on this later in the chapter).

3. "I don't want to be a guinea pig!" This appears where the treatment is perceived to be aversive or dangerous or where research sites are too frequently used—laboratory or experimental schools, for instance.

4. "I want my child to get that special treatment!" This complaint causes administrators to provide compensatory treatment to the control group, thus decreasing the apparent treatment effectiveness.

5. "I don't want my group to be disadvantaged; by the luck of the draw, it

---

10. Adair, Sharpe, and Huynh (1989) examined 86 studies that they believe are the body of studies involving the use of control groups to counteract the Hawthorne effect. Control procedures were classified as alternative activity, special attention, or awareness of being studied. Attention had the largest effect but was not statistically significant. They concluded that there is no such artifact as the Hawthorne effect as currently operationally defined. If there is, it is too small to be of significance, since 86 studies did not find it. Since it is widely considered one of the most important manifestations of reactivity I decided not to drop it from the list—yet. There is not enough evidence to know whether other reactivity manifestations might yield similar findings; be alert for such studies.

became the control group." Compensatory rivalry is a frequent response of control group teachers who see to it their subjects do just as well as "those special ones." It is sometimes called the John Henry effect, after the legendary railroad worker who pitted his skill against a steam railroad spike driver. For an example, see Zdep and Irvine (1970).

6. "That's new and interesting: I like it!" This is the novelty effect. Even though it requires extra work, a new curriculum is taught with enthusiasm the first time and maybe even the second time. But the gusto wears off, and effectiveness may decrease along with it.

7. "We can't compete with that group—it's getting all that special help! Why try? Let's quit." Demoralization and feelings of dismay may cause the comparison group to be less effective than it would otherwise be, making the treatment look better.

8. "Have you heard about the easy new way we are learning long division? **Diffusion**, whereby a treatment is communicated on the playground, may or may not be a reactivity effect, but is more likely under nonroutine conditions. It decreases the apparent treatment effect.

9. "I'm especially pleased he's studying me." In one-to-one situations, a close emotional bond may develop between subject and investigator. This is all right if the treatment is always to be administered this way, since reactivity is part of the treatment. But the findings clearly may not generalize to less intensely monitored situations.

Obviously, the best way to reduce reactivity is through **unobtrusiveness**, by making the experiment—both treatment and measures—part of the regular activities of the subjects so that there is no realization that an experiment is being carried out. In an institutional experiment, have the regular personnel carry out the treatment and measurement as part of the routine (instead of having a special treatment administrator or tester). If treatment materials are distributed as they normally are and tests are given with little fanfare, perhaps most of the effects will be mitigated (unless the materials themselves are too novel).

In some instances, the treatment can be given and observations made without the subjects' awareness. Observations can be made of subjects' behavior from behind two-way mirrors, with concealed observers, without reactivity if subjects don't know the mirrors' purpose. Since many students do, it helps if they know that the mirrors aren't always in use. This helps subjects grow accustomed to the special circumstances over time. Webb and colleagues (1981) provide a very useful treatment of unobtrusive measurement and offer suggestions.

The reactions to being observed or being part of an experiment, with the attendant special circumstances, are termed reactivity. Obtrusive study procedures increase it, and using unobtrusive methods of treatment, observation, or measurement can reduce it.

Researcher Expectancy Effects. "Did the rat find the target? He stuck his nose in the box. I'll count it." Research assistants who know what is expected are probably more likely to perceive events in the desired direction, especially if the behavior is somewhat ambiguous. For that matter, even the researcher may be unconsciously biased this way. Rosenthal (1969, 1976) and Rosenthal and Rubin (1980) call this the **researcher expectancy effect**. Researchers or their assistants may inadvertently tip the scales in favor of an experimental treatment in a variety of ways, both verbally (for example, with encouragement and clues) and nonverbally (for example, smiling for right answers or frowning for wrong ones).

Rosenthal and Rubin (1980) studies 345 instances of interpersonal expectancy effects, ranging from reaction time studies to learning and animal studies. For instance, experimenters were told they were running especially able mice; teachers were told that certain children could be expected to show remarkable gains. In actuality, mice and children were randomly chosen yet showed the expectancy effects (in humans this is called the Pygmalion effect, after George Bernard Shaw's play). Only 2 of 9 reaction time studies showed an expectancy effect, but 11 of 15 animal studies did. The unintended impact of the expectancy effect may be as large as the intended effect of many treatments.

Researcher expectancy is controlled by using **double-blind procedures**. Neither anyone involved with the treatment (persons applying treatments and recipients) nor anyone observing the effects can distinguish the control group or treatment from the experimental group or treatment. Treatments used appear identical or at least similar, but subjects are coded in such a way that some uninvolved party can tell them apart after treatment. Subjects in both groups therefore believe that they may be receiving the treatment—they are kept "blind." The control treatment is often called a placebo or placebo treatment.

Double-blind procedures *cannot* be used in certain circumstances:

1. When subjects' knowing they are being treated is part of the treatment itself
2. When it is obvious which treatment is to be favored from merely observing the treatment or being exposed to it
3. If the treatment can be readily identified from side effects
4. If withholding a more favorable treatment would have ethical consequences
5. If the use of therapeutic knowledge is sacrificed to methodological precision (the judge's sensitivity is reduced by uncertainty about what to look for); this can be demoralizing to both professionals and subjects

Depending on the obviousness of treatment and side effects, some objections can be met by using an independent individual or team who participate in the study only to assess the results. They are kept blind even though those who administer the treatment are not (Guy, Gross, and Dennis, 1967).

Even when every effort has been made to keep them so, are the people who administer the treatment or evaluate its effects really blind, or do shrewd guesses defeat efforts to control their knowledge? This is an empirical question. Asking them to identify the experimental treatment or the subjects receiving it and comparing their responses with chance may help determine the extent to which they have correctly guessed the study's intent. This alerts the researcher to a problem so that the data can be interpreted more conservatively (Kazdin, 1980).

- Researcher expectancy effects may appear when the people responsible for giving the treatment or assessing its effects can identify the experimental treatment, experimental subjects, or intended treatment effect.
- Unintended expectancy effects can be as large as or even larger than some intended experimental effects.
- Keeping observers, measurers, treatment administrators, and subjects blind to which are the experimental group and treatment and which the control (or having independent evaluators who are) may eliminate these effects.
- Whether such efforts are successful is an empirical question that can and often should be checked.

Various Treatment Interaction Effects. A treatment can interact with some of the study's conditions or other treatments in such a way as to potentiate or weaken the treatment effect. Here are some common ones to watch for.

MULTIPLE-TREATMENT INTERACTION. Where two or more treatments are administered in sequence to the same persons, the effect of one may carry over to the next to either intensify or weaken it. Such **multiple-treatment interaction** may make generalization to situations where the treatment is given by itself difficult. For instance, halfway through the school year, having tried the Bereiter-Engleman program and finding it only moderately successful, Mrs. Kimball decides to switch to the curriculum for inner-city children devised by the Southwest Educational Laboratory. She finds it very effective and begins with it the next year, only to find that it is no more effective than the Bereiter-Engleman. The learning resulting from the Bereiter-Engleman may have made the Southwest curriculum more effective than it was when used by itself. Unless validated in some other way, the findings of the first study for the Southwest curriculum are limited to situations where it follows the Bereiter-Engleman, a restrictive condition on external validity (GP).

To study this effect, divide the group into as many subgroups as there are treatments, and keeping the treatments in the same order, rotate each treatment into the first position with one of the groups. If there is no sequencing effect, then the data from the groups can be combined. If there is a sequencing effect, some indication of the treatment's effectiveness alone can be found from the sample in which it was given first.

> Multiple-treatment interaction occurs when the residual effects of one treatment influence a later one such that its apparent effect is different than if it were given by itself. Designs that rotate the treatment into first position can estimate the interaction effect.

TESTING-TREATMENT INTERACTION. Where a pretest is given, individuals may be sensitized to parts of the curriculum that are very similar to pretest problems. They may be motivated to learn these parts better than they would otherwise. In that case, the pretest will have a potentiating effect, known as **testing-treatment interaction**. As a restrictive condition on generality, we cannot assume that the treatment will be as effective without a pretest. Experimental evidence shows, however, that the effect of a pretest is not always to potentiate; Hovland, Lumsdaine, and Sheffield (1949) reported that movies were less effective changers of attitude when used with a pretest.

Testing-treatment interaction may be present in any pretest-posttest design (2, 3, and 4) but is eliminated by the posttest-only design (5). Alternatively, consider the Solomon four-group design (6), which gives an estimate of its size.

> Testing-treatment interaction occurs when the treatment effect is strengthened or weakened as a result of pretesting.

SELECTION BY TREATMENT INTERACTION. People who are attracted to or perhaps have a special need for the treatment try to get into the experimental group, especially in the case of experimental therapeutic treatments. Conversely, individuals who are repelled by the treatment try to avoid that group. In either case, the true effect of the treatment is masked: **selection by treatment interaction** overlays it.

In another scenario, we seek institutions to cooperate in the study and are turned down by all but a few because of characteristics of the treatment—it disrupts the schedule, takes too much time, is not compatible with the organization's orientation, and so on. Are the institutions that welcome the study a representative sample of institutions? Not likely; they are similar to individual volunteers in distinctiveness. The use of only volunteers to compose both treatment and control groups is the usual remedy for these problems. As pointed out earlier, this strengthens internal validity (LP) and weakens external validity (GP).

> Selection by treatment interaction may be present when the treatment affects who is selected (or is self-selected) for the experimental or control group or both.

MORTALITY BY TREATMENT INTERACTION. Returning to Mrs. Kimball, if the reason children had high absenteeism was that they disliked the Bereiter-Engleman curriculum, we have a selective factor, an interaction between the treatment and the subjects who dropped out. This is **mortality by treatment interaction**. The scores may be higher because children who disliked the curriculum dropped out and those who were motivated to study it remained. Though sometimes difficult, collecting data from all individuals initially assigned to a group provides evidence that has more generality.

> Mortality by treatment interaction occurs when individuals selectively drop out of the treated group in reaction to the treatment.

A SUMMARY OF PROTECTION OFFERED BY SIX SIMPLE DESIGNS

Table 18.1 summarizes the opportunity for protection potentially offered by the six designs with which this discussion began. It is important to recognize that this table cannot be taken too literally. Each situation must be analyzed to make sure that the design will work as intended. It is mainly useful for making comparisons by showing the protection (+) or lack of it (−) that various designs potentially confer. Question marks indicate that depending on the particular circumstances, this rival explanation may or may not be a problem. You can see in design 4 that the combination of random assignment and a control group confers a great deal of protection. And the Solomon and posttest-only designs, 5 and 6, by removing the pretest in whole or in part, go this one better since the minus is removed for testing-treatment interaction. The latter are very strong designs but do require random assignment to groups, and the Solomon requires four groups, so the instances in which they can be used may be limited.

A SUMMARY OF COMMON CONTROL PROBLEMS AND THEIR ELIMINATION

Table 18.2 is a summary of common rival explanations affecting internal validity (LP) and external validity (GP). As noted in the column "Gains and/or Losses," often these involve trade-offs. Both Appendix A and chapter 23 analyze the problem of trade-offs in detail. That material along with this table will provide a good basis for making design choices.

TABLE 18.1   Protection Potentially Offered by Six Basic Designs against Common Alternative Explanations

Design	History	Maturation	Testing	Instrumentation	Regression	Selection	Mortality	Interaction of Selection and Maturation, etc.	Interaction of Testing and Treatment	Interaction of Selection and Treatment
1. XO	−	−	−			−	−			
2. OXO	−	−	+	−	?	+	+	−	−	−
3. OXO / OCO	+	+	+	+	?	+	+	−	−	?
4. [R] OXO / OCO	+	+	+	+	+	+	+	+	−	?
5. [R] XO / CO	+	+	+	+	+	+	+	+	+	?
6. [R] OXO / OCO / XO / CO	+	+	+	+	+	+	+	+	+	?

NOTE   As demonstrated on page 481, the pluses and minuses depend on the study's circumstances and should not be taken too literally.

SOURCE   Adapted from D. T. Campbell and J. C. Stanley, *Experimental and Quasi-experimental Designs for Research*, p. 178. Copyright © 1963 Houghton Mifflin Co.

TABLE 18.2 Summary of Rival Explanations and Their Control

Problem	Method of Control	Operation	Gains and/or Losses Resulting from Method of Control or Operation (Trade-offs)
Base rate problems	Measure and adjust.	Determine whether opportunities for the phenomenon to occur were constant or varied in some way related to your hypothesis.	Measuring the base rate determines the extent to which the effect is influenced by changes in the base rate in contrast to the treatment or the independent variable.
Demand characteristics	Measure and adjust or redesign study.	Use stimulated recall, think-aloud procedures, or interviews to obtain subjects' perceptions of the study as it proceeds.	Obtaining subjects' perceptions ensures the fidelity of the original plans for study. Think-aloud procedures may change the way subjects approach what is asked. Recall may not be accurate or may be modified to please the researcher.
Instrument decay	Eliminate.	Train carefully in the use of instruments and use calibration checks during study; use double-blind conditions; hold regular conferences of observers to resolve use and interpretation problems.	Training is expensive; researcher needs a pilot to tell how much training is sufficient; determining the success of training requires checks on observer reliability.
Local history	Eliminate.	Discard affected cases, such as those interrupted by a fire drill.	Discarding cases decreases power by reducing sample size. Researcher may not know all persons exposed. Exposure may have been selective. Replicating the study to recover lost cases is expensive; data may be impossible to reproduce.
	Equalize across groups.	Be sure the control group is as likely to be exposed to the same events as the experimental group; ideally keep in close proximity.*	Proximity may result in increased chance of rivalry, other reactivity, and diffusion.

(continued)

---

*Local history is one of the most difficult problems to control because it is impossible to predict what to expect, when, or how serious it will be. Keeping close to the groups so that we will know when something untoward occurs is the main line of defense.

TABLE 18.2 *continued*

Problem	Method of Control	Operation	Gains and/or Losses Resulting from Method of Control or Operation (Trade-offs)
Maturation	Measure and adjust.	Use norms to determine growth of comparable groups or measure trend prior to treatment and extrapolate to posttreatment expectation.	Norms on comparable group may not be available. Nonlinear growth is hard to extrapolate; growth could be linear prior to treatment and nonlinear after.
	Equalize across groups.	Use random, blocked, and matched groups.	Blocking and matching decrease variability and increase the sensitivity of the study unless the variable being used to stratify is unrelated to the relationship studied (only loss then, however, is the labor of blocking).
Mortality	Eliminate.	Provide incentive for completion of study.	Incentives are likely to be obtrusive; reward becomes part of the treatment.
	Measure and adjust.	Discern the kinds of individuals who dropped out and remove equivalent individuals from the other groups.	Loss of cases reduces the statistical power and generality of the study.
	Equalize across groups.	Assign to groups randomly and make placebo treatment of the control group as similar to the experimental treatment as possible.	Mortality by treatment interaction may still occur if the "effective ingredient" is unpleasant or difficult.
Multiple-treatment interaction	Eliminate.	Use a separate group for each treatment.	Separate groups eliminate interaction but require more groups with concomitant treatment and measurement for each.
	Equalize.	Assuming interaction is equal among treatments, divide into subgroups, each receiving one of the possible orderings of treatments, and combine data.	Such studies are usually done on one or a few subjects because of the scarcity of such persons and/or the cost of treatment.
Reactivity	Eliminate.	Use low obtrusiveness conditions for treatment and measurement or observation; keep groups separate—in different buildings, locations, and so on.	Groups and situations may not be comparable; local history may cause variation in effects.

Problem	Method of Control	Operation	Gains and/or Losses Resulting from Method of Control or Operation (Trade-offs)
Regression	Reduce regression effect.	Use the most reliable measure possible; double-test individuals.	Reliable measures and double testing do not correct for the type of regression that occurs when corrective measures are instigated at the peak of a problem that would subside without remediation.
	Equalize across groups.	Use randomly assigned experimental and control groups.	Presence of control provides a measure of gain in the control group.
Researcher expectancy	Eliminate.	Use double-blind procedures—neither treatment nor test administrators nor observers know which group is experimental and which is control.	If clinical knowledge is required of the treatment administrator, observers must be blind.
Selection	Eliminate.	Use random assignment with matching and blocking on all relevant variables.	Special assignment to group procedures may result in obtrusiveness and its effects.
	Measure and adjust.	Use ANCOVA or partial correlation (see chapter 22), built in as an independent variable.	Elimination may be incomplete, depending on the validity and reliability of the measure.
Testing	Eliminate.	Use posttest only.	Posttest only eliminates testing-treatment interaction; reduces testing cost, and only one form is needed, but researchers may not be sure the groups were equivalent.
	Reduce testing effect.	Use different forms of test or different tests at pretest and posttest.	The more alike the forms are, the greater the comparability of pretest and posttest but the greater the likelihood of a residual testing effect. The latter is reduced by using different tests, but so is the comparability of pretest and posttest, another trade-off.
		Use a different group for each testing; use the Solomon four-group design.	Use of extra groups, such as the Solomon design, requires a much larger sample, and groups may not be comparable. It increases the cost of testing but controls for testing-treatment interaction.
	Equalize across groups.	Give experimental and control groups the same pattern of observation.	Same observation patterns do not control for testing-treatment interaction.

Unique Rival Explanations

The Demand Characteristics of a Study. The list of alternative and restrictive explanations described so far is by no means complete. Any study may have uncommon, and sometimes unique, alternative explanations. In many instances, these stem from what psychologists call the **demand characteristics** of the study. What the subjects perceive the study seems to demand of them may not be what the researcher intended. It was noted earlier that Kruglanski (1976) interviewed subjects after the study to try to understand how they interpreted what was being asked of them. The researcher expectancy effect and many of the obtrusiveness problems described as restrictive conditions for external validity (GP) are all part of the demand conditions. Determining the demand conditions of a study can be a very important aspect of ensuring that the findings can be interpreted as we hope.

A personal example of unanticipated demand conditions occurred in a study where students were to learn from one of two versions of a programmed text. The text consisted of questions about the material that the students were to answer; the answer was then explained. Students were randomly assigned to a text in which the questions were logically organized as the material was usually taught and one in which, although each question and its answer were kept together, the questions were randomly scrambled. Surprisingly, performance on the randomly scrambled material was found not to be significantly different from learning with questions in the proper order (Krathwohl, Gordon, and Payne, 1967). We couldn't believe that the scrambling would not have an effect until we talked with some of the students. We learned that we were not studying the effect of scrambling. We had inadvertently turned the scrambled material into a challenging puzzle. It forced the individuals into an active learning process. Instead of merely reading questions and answering passively, subjects had to rehearse the parts in order to remember them as they were fitted together. They had to analyze and organize the questions to place them in proper sequence. All this facilitated learning and yielded our unexpected answer.

It is important to look at the demand characteristics of a study and to determine the alternative explanations, as well as to avoid the common rival explanations. The explanation just given, though not on published lists of alternatives, is obvious once suggested. When such insights occur after the study has been written up, researchers are inclined to believe that they should have anticipated them during the study's design. But hindsight can be 20/20; research design never is!

Other Unique Alternative Explanations. Demand characteristics constitute one kind of unique rival explanation for studies, but besides the standard set we have just explored, there are likely to be other explanations. They are often unique to the particular study, its setting, or its procedure. Zeigarnik (1927; see also Denmark, 1984) argued that unreleased tension has an effect on memory. She proceeded to illustrate this by giving subjects a lengthy series of common tasks (such as winding thread), a randomly selected half of which were interrupted when the subject was thoroughly engaged. The others were completed without interruption. Subjects were then asked to recall all the tasks. She found that the interrupted tasks were better remembered.

It was argued, however, that the impact of being interrupted was what caused the increased memory. To answer this alternative explanation, all the tasks were interrupted with a new set of subjects, who were then allowed to complete half of them. Again, the uncompleted tasks were better remembered.

But maybe these were better remembered because they were to be completed later? So still two more studies were done with instructions that indicated either that the task would be completed later or that it would not be worked on anymore. Again, interrupted tasks were better remembered. This cascade of studies to answer new objections illustrates nicely the problem of new alternative explanations springing up that are unique to the particular study. It also illustrates the handling of them.

Should the researcher have anticipated these alternatives and designed protections into the original study? It would have been ideal if she had. But what is obvious later isn't always obvious when the study is being done. The best the researcher can do is consider the common rival explanations, try to anticipate all the unique rival explanations imaginable, and then protect against the ones that seem most serious. The better this is done, the shorter the route to building a consensus around the interpretation of the data and acceptance as a contribution to knowledge.

Sometimes, however, we miss a common alternative explanation because it occurs outside the usual context in which we have been trained to look for it. Such instances can be very difficult to discern. Mark (1990) notes an instance that escaped the careful monitoring of two individuals who are among the most significant contributors to the literature of social science experimental design. Both were members of the dissertation committee of Seaver's (1971) study of teacher expectancies, an ingenious study that examined a "natural experiment" where such expectancies had theretofore only been studied under artificially manipulated circumstances.

Seaver observed that elder siblings created expectancies in teachers for their younger brothers and sisters. He hypothesized that depending on whether the elder one had done well or poorly, the siblings would, on the average, achieve more in a like direction than if they had been assigned to a different teacher. The results confirmed the hypothesis. Considerably later, Reichardt (1985) noted that these results might have been due to the students' having been assigned to good or poor teachers. Any two siblings who had the same *good* teacher did well, but the younger sibling assigned to a different teacher had a *closer-to-average* teacher and did more poorly, a regression toward the teacher mean. Similarly, any two siblings assigned to a poor teacher did poorly, but the younger sibling assigned to a different teacher also had one closer to the average, in this instance a better one, and so did better. The usual clues to regression—extreme groups, retesting, and remediation or enrichment groups—are missing.

Mark (1990) notes still another explanation: there really were no differences in expectations, because teachers in a small school communicated with one another about their children. Thus the "different" teachers of younger siblings actually held the same expectations as the teachers who had had the elder siblings. This alternative explanation could have been examined, however, by pretesting the teachers' expectations of these children had the researcher thought of it when the study was planned. We may take comfort in the fact that the acknowledged experts missed these alternative explanations, but it is at the same time discomforting to note how subtle these effects can be, discerned only long after the study was planned and executed.

Special Internal Validity (LP) Problems in Field Experiments. As noted earlier, Boruch and Gomez (1977) suggest that the careful design of an experiment is often eroded in ways that decrease its power to sense an effect in field experiments. For example, treatment fidelity is likely to suffer as the treatment undergoes adaptation by people administering it in different situations. If standard measures are used so that the results can be trusted and easily understood, they may fit the goals of the treatment poorly or only partially. Measures of effect may be degraded once publicly identified. Boruch and Gomez also note that these effects are not additive but multiplicative, thereby more severely degrading the power of the study to sense an effect.

Once a measure is defined as the measure of success or failure in a policy decision, it is likely to be corrupted to some degree. Where achievement tests are identified in advance, teachers "teach to the test." Although the test is intended to sample a domain to be mastered, the teachers emphasize only the knowledge and skills necessary to solve specific test items. Achievement in the domain beyond what is specifically tested is therefore left untaught. Corruption can occur in a project judged in part by how few of its members drop out when the definition of *dropout* is changed to allow more absences before an individual is so classified. Alternatively, herculean efforts to retain students may result in less emphasis on more important but unmeasured goals. Bogdan (1976) noted that when special education legislation decreed that Head Start classes should include special education students, many students who had not previously been, were so classified. Examination showed that such classifications were questionable. Experiments involving policy decisions need to be alert to such problems.

PART II:
COMPLEX DESIGNS, TREATMENT PROBLEMS,
AND HALLMARKS OF EXPERIMENTATION

In part I, we noted that starting with the simplest design, the case study, we could add features to provide substantial protection from alternative explanations. Building on this foundation, this second section begins by examining common single-treatment designs. First we examine the most common, the nonequivalent control group design, and then two special-purpose designs, time-series designs for studying trends and changes over time and counterbalanced designs where the order of treatment is a concern. A so-called patched-up design demonstrates how we create unique designs by adding features to solve particular problems. Increasingly, research includes multiple treatments or control variables (or both); the very common multiple-independent-variable factorial design is described for these situations. Generic advice is presented on design construction especially for the "treatments" and "basis for sensing attributes or changes" links in the chain of reasoning. Tips for researchers and a list of hallmarks of experimentation provide a summary. Note that in addition to the designs considered here, what is often referred to as the ex post facto design, the after-the-fact natural experiment, is considered in chapter 19. It is an important additional design, usually considered with other experimental designs; I have placed it with the historical method for reasons explained there.

OTHER DESIGNS FOR SINGLE-VARIABLE STUDIES

The Nonequivalent Control Group Design

Because of its prevalence, the nonequivalent control group design (design 3 in Table 18.1) deserves our further attention. In many instances we cannot arrange groups but must take them as they come:

$$\frac{OXO}{OCO}$$

Much has been written about this design, and Cook and Campbell (1979) devote considerable space to it and its variations. A particularly common problem occurs when the experimental group begins and ends ahead of the control group. What are we to conclude? Cook and Campbell point out that under these conditions, this design is subject to the following alternative explanations:

- Local history (the experimental group was in a classroom that had just won the school's achievement award; its members were "on a roll")
- Testing (the level of the test at which the control groups scored was not as sensitive to changes as that at which the experimental group scored)
- Regression (since they started at different levels, they regressed at different rates)
- Selection-maturation interaction (with self-selection, the more able opted for the treatment, thus differentially selecting the groups in such a way that they changed at different rates)[11]
- Selection-history interaction (most members of the more academically oriented experimental group found a public broadcasting television program that dealt with the treatment topic attractive enough to put other things aside and watch it)

Bracht and Glass (1968) noted that this design is most interpretable when the experimental group is below the control at pretest and their positions are

---

11. This will occur when one group is more able than another. The more able will learn faster than the less able, so that the differences between the groups will grow over time—a case, as Cook and Campbell (1979) point out, of "the rich getting richer and the poor getting poorer."

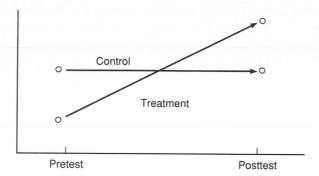

FIGURE 18.3 Outcome of the nonequivalent control group design when the treatment group overtakes the control group.

reversed at posttest, as in Figure 18.3. As Cook and Campbell (1979) point out, this pattern makes several alternative explanations unlikely. A ceiling effect might explain why an initially lower treatment group drew even with the control when it hit the ceiling, but it could not explain why it drew ahead. A regression effect is also unlikely because the initially lower-scoring group might be expected to regress upward toward the group mean and possibly come close to catching up, but there is no reason that it would be expected to overtake the higher mean.

The temptation is to find which group is lower after the pretest and assign it to the experimental treatment and hope that the experimental group overtakes the control. Cook and Campbell (1979) warn, however, that if the growth rate of the experimental group is lower than that of the control, as is possibly indicated by their lower start, the lines may not cross. We are more likely to have a finding of no statistically significant difference. This may be due to a lack of treatment effect or to the canceling out of the treatment effect by the slower growth rate; we will not be able to tell which. Cook and Campbell also discuss a number of variations of the basic design.

The nonequivalent control group design is in common use because researchers must often work with preformed groups. The design is interpretable if the experimental group begins below the control group and then overtakes it. Deliberately designing a study in this way, however, may underestimate the typical effect.

Time-Series Designs

Design 7 is a **time-series design** that can be employed with groups but is especially useful with single subjects. An individual will be observed for a period of time to establish a baseline. A treatment will be introduced, and then the posttreatment baseline will be established. Since there is no control group, the effect of local history is not controlled but with a single subject could probably be easily detected (see Table 18.3). Depending on the changes expected, maturation is controlled by repeated observations. Testing effect wears off with repeated measurements, as does regression. Testing-treatment interaction could be a problem, depending on the study. In a study of the effect of food dye on hyperactivity, the presence of a small amount of dye could be concealed by the natural color of food. There is no control for instrument decay as would be provided by a control group, so the continued calibration of instruments or observers would be important. Depending on the subject and the obtrusiveness of the procedure, there might or might not be selection by treatment interaction (a particularly susceptible person who sought out the treatment) and reactivity. You can see in the foregoing how the circumstances of the particular study can modify the pluses and minuses of Tables 18.1 and 18.3, so the warning against taking them too literally is warranted.

The multiple measurements before the treatment establish any trend, whether linear or curvilinear. This allows us to predict what the posttreatment effects should be if the treatment is not effective. Deviations from those predictions are presumably the result of the treatment if there is no other alternative explanation. This variation of the time-series design is called a regression discontinuity design and is discussed extensively in Cook and Campbell (1979).

Design 7: Time-series design   O O O X O O O

Another variation of the design (it has many useful ones) is shown in design 8, where the treatment is turned on and off (X_1 and C_0, respectively). This is essentially a replication of the treatment. It would take a very persistent local history event recurring over the whole series of treatment replications to be a problem; hence the plus in that column in Table 18.3. But it is unlikely that we could unobtrusively turn the treatment on and off repeatedly, so a minus appears for reactivity. Depending on the persistence of the effect of treatment, one may have multiple-treatment interaction since the second treatment administration may build on the residual of the first. Hence the minus for it. Still, if the periodicity of treatment follows that of a randomly applied treatment, it is a very powerful design.

Design 8: Time-series design   O X_1 O C_0 O X_1 O

Entries 7 and 8 in Table 18.3 summarize the protection potentially offered by these designs for comparison with the others. Note that design 8 is considerably stronger than design 7 but can be used only where there is no residual treatment effect.

Time-series designs provide good control for a number of common rival explanations and are especially useful in studying the behavior over several treatments, alternating treatment and control conditions.

TABLE 18.3 Protection Potentially Offered by Four Additional Designs

Design	History	Maturation	Testing	Instrumentation	Regression	Selection	Mortality	Interaction of Selection and Maturation, etc.	Interaction of Testing and Treatment	Interaction of Selection and Treatment
7. OOOXOOO	−	+	+	?	+	+	+	+	−	?
8. $Ox_1OC_0Ox_1O$	+	+	+	+	+	+	+	+	−	?
9. $X_1OX_2OX_3$ $X_2OX_3OX_1$ $X_3OX_1OX_2$	+	+	+	+	+	+	+	?	?	?
10. $\boxed{R}$ O (X) X O $\boxed{R}$ O C C O	+	+	+	+	+	+	+	−	+	+

SOURCE Adapted from D. T. Campbell and J. C. Stanley, *Experimental and Quasi-experimental Designs for Research*, p. 178. Copyright © 1963 Houghton Mifflin Co.

Counterbalanced Designs

Design 9 is of interest if we are concerned about multiple-treatment interaction. It allows each treatment an opportunity to be first and to be preceded by all the other treatments. In this way, some estimate of the persistence and interaction of one treatment with another (multiple-treatment interaction). It also permits us to enter all subjects into all treatments. Such designs have been called **counterbalanced**, crossover, switchover, and rotation designs. The particular design illustrated is called a Latin square and is often used for assignment of treatments to groups. The pattern of a Latin square can be extrapolated from the example, where each row starts one treatment lower and then cycles through the treatments in order. Each treatment appears once in each column and row.

Design 9: Counterbalanced designs

$$X_1 \ O \ X_2 \ O \ X_3 \ O$$
$$X_2 \ O \ X_3 \ O \ X_1 \ O$$
$$X_3 \ O \ X_1 \ O \ X_2 \ O$$

If we cumulate treatment effects across groups, selection effects may balance out. But interactions between selection and maturation, between testing and treatment, or between selection and treatment might be specific to a treatment or a group, so these would not be protected against. Nevertheless, this design is widely used because it economically gives an estimate of the effect of treatment, place in the rotation (first, second, etc.), and differences among groups, if any. Random assignment of groups to rows markedly strengthens the design.

Subjects with physical disabilities are always in short supply. We would like to compare several hearing aids on the same persons but are concerned about interaction effects. This design permits us to use all the identified subjects with all the hearing aids, yet to estimate whether there is any treatment interaction and if so, its extent.

Counterbalanced designs are especially useful in studying multiple-treatment interaction effects by exposing all the members of a group to all the treatments.

A "Patched-up" Design

The tenth design is intended to overcome the common field limitation of using intact groups (school classes, churches, etc.) where observation of a group is easier to arrange than its treatment. The separate-sample pretest-posttest control group design involves pairs of two separate experimental and control groups. The $\boxed{R}$ indicates that the groups are randomly assigned to experimental conditions within the first pair and last pair, so the two sets of pairs may not be equivalent. The X in parentheses stands for any treatment that is administered with an obtrusiveness comparable to that of X, the treatment of interest.

Design 10: "Patched-up" design

$$\begin{array}{l} \boxed{R} \quad O \ (X) \\ \qquad \ \ X \ O \\ \hline \boxed{R} \quad O \ C \\ \qquad \ \ C \ O \end{array}$$

Since both of the first pair receive treatments and neither of the second pair does, reactivity is controlled within each pair. The second pair controls for history, maturation, and mortality. It is possible that there is a selection difference between the two sets of pairs (for example, one pair of classes is older and less likely to grow tired than the others). Selection might interact with time (interaction of selection and maturation), so this appears as a minus in the selection column in Table 18.3. The lack of a pretest in the experimental group controls for testing and for testing-treatment interaction.

Campbell and Stanley (1979) note that this design has been called the simulated before-and-after design (Jahoda, Deutsch, and Cook, 1951). They think of it as a "patched-up" design with peculiar patterns of groups and of testing in order to provide proper control. But as they note, this approach, which creates a design to solve particular problems, should be typical of the spirit in which designs are developed.

> Many designs are "patched-up" designs that use peculiar patterns of groups and measures that fit particular situations. They can usually be so designed as to provide the kind of protection that is important for a given study.

FACTORIAL DESIGNS

So far we have considered only single-treatment designs, but increasingly the preponderance of studies include more than one independent variable. This may result from the comparison of two or more treatments or, equally often, from the inclusion of other characteristics (demographic, situational, personality, ability) as independent variables in the design. Sometimes variables are introduced for control purposes so as to eliminate the effect of a contaminating variable. In other instances, they are intervening variables that might potentiate or weaken the effect.

Suppose we are interested in whether there is greater grade inflation in undergraduate or graduate school. We suspect that part of it may be due to higher grades being given to women graduate students, whose numbers have

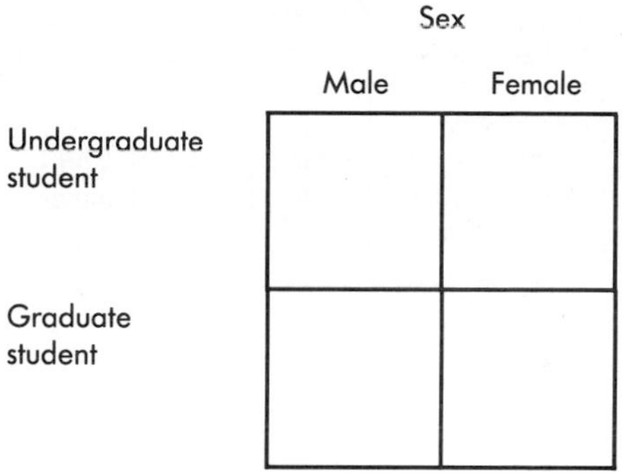

Sex

	Male	Female
Undergraduate student		
Graduate student		

FIGURE 18.4 A simple 2 × 2 factorial design.

increased markedly over recent years. Control for sex of student can be built in as a second control variable that examines grades between the levels, sex differences in grades, and the combination. A common approach, particularly among psychologists, is called a **factorial design**. It investigates all the interactions of the variables and, for our sample problem, would have four cells as shown in Figure 18.4.

A *factor* is simply another term for a variable in the treatment or any other independent variable in a study. Factorial designs permit us to examine the effect of factors taken singly and in every possible combination. Each factor is present in two or more *levels*. Sex would have two levels, male and female; a treatment applied individually by a tutor, individually by a computer, and in a group with a tutor would have three levels. Factorial designs provide a separate group for each of the possible combinations of factors and levels and are labeled by the number of categories for each factor. Our sample problem requires a 2 × 2 design since there are two factors each having two categories or levels.

Consider a study of the control of speeding on the New York State Thruway involving a 12-week trial of (1) the use of (a) marked and (b) unmarked police cars driven by (2) male police officers who (a) are uninstructed and do what they normally would (control group) or are specially instructed to (b) require an immediate court appearance, (c) issue a ticket for a later court appearance, (d) issue a ticket that can be handled by mail, or (e) give a stern warning (experimental groups). (3) It is suspected that it makes a big difference whether the stretch of highway is (a) heavily traveled by commuters or (b) unlikely to be traveled repeatedly except by truckers. To control for the commuting factor, it is built in as an independent variable; half the stretches are commuter and half noncommuter. Five-mile stretches are chosen for the study, each with comparable terrain. The criterion is the average speed during the experimental period in each highway segment.

The study calls for a 2 × 5 × 2 design because there are three factors: (1) two kinds of police cars, marked and unmarked, (2) five ways of handling a violation, and (3) two kinds of highway, commuter and noncommuter. Factorial designs call for a data collection for each combination. In this case,

Treatment of Violators

Marked car	Control		Immediate trial		Delayed trial		Mail		Warning	
	Com-muter	Non-com-muter	Com-muter	Non-com-muter	Com-muter	Non-com-muter	Com-muter	Non-com-muter	Com-muter	Non-com-muter
	Site x	Site x	Site x	Site x	Site x	Site x	Site x	Site x	Site x	Site x
Unmarked car	Site x	Site x	Site x	Site x	Site x	Site x	Site x	Site x	Site x	Site x

FIGURE 18.5   A 2 × 5 × 2 factorial design for a study of speeding.

2 × 5 × 2 = 20 sites would be needed, and the study can be diagrammed as in Figure 18.5. "Site *x*" appears in each of the cells to designate one of the 20 randomly assigned 5-mile stretches of highway. The data for each cell would consist of the average speed over a period of time (daily, length of a trooper's shift, etc.).

By analysis of variance (discussed in chapter 22), we can determine (1) whether using a marked car makes a difference, (2) whether the various treatments of violators differentially reduced the average speed, and (3) whether the speed slowed more on commuting or noncommuting stretches of highway. In addition, we can determine whether the variables interact with others to form a more potent or weaker effect in combination than alone. For example, was the mail-in ticket treatment more effective with commuter or noncommuter traffic? With marked or unmarked cars? Lastly, we can examine whether all three characteristics formed a pattern that together raised or lowered the average speed. Thus we can check the effect of each major factor by itself and in all possible combinations.

Nested designs reduce the number of groups to those combinations in which we are particularly interested and allow confounding of variables where we are not concerned. For example, suppose we placed both the severe treatments (immediate and delayed court appearances) upstate and the less severe ones in the downstate New York City area. We would have to assume that there are no differences between upstate and downstate drivers in their reaction to treatments, since these would be confounded or "nested" with the treatments and could not be separated out. To investigate these differences in a factorial design, however, would require doubling the number of 5-mile highway samples to 40!

■ Factorial designs are popular because they permit estimation of the effect of the treatment and other independent variables singly and in all possible combinations.

- Variables we wish to control are built into such designs as independent variables so that the extent of their effect can be determined.
- Where we are not interested in all the combinations of variables, nested designs reduce the demand for cases.

EXPERIMENTAL TREATMENT PROBLEMS

The experimental treatment is the cause in a cause-and-effect relationship. The general problems of observing and measuring discussed in chapter 11 are usually associated with measures of effect. But these problems, plus others, apply as well to the cause, the treatment. We will discuss four of these problems:

1. Conceptually defining the treatment
2. Operationally defining and sampling the treatment to be certain that the study is representative
3. Ensuring that the treatment was administered as intended (fidelity of treatment)
4. Establishing a basis for sensing change due to the treatment such that the characteristics that are essential to the conceptualization of the treatment are the ones that can be clearly delineated as determining the effect

Conceptually Defining the Treatment

Most hypotheses contain a number of constructs: "The more that students actively participate in the social and academic life of the university campus, the less likely they are to dropout of college." Here we must define the constructs: students, social life, academic life, university, campus, active participation, various levels of participation, dropout. As soon as you begin to sense a need for specification, think of conceptual analysis (chapter 9). Model cases provide excellent illustrations of operational definitions. The borderline examples delineate the rim of the definition, and negative examples show instances to avoid.

As is always the case, an understanding of the theory or rationale underlying the hypothesis helps in discriminating among different possible meanings. Conceptual meanings can often be derived from the original context. Our hypothesis here comes from the work of Tinto (1987), who drew a parallel with Durkheim's analysis of suicide cases. Persons too isolated from their society to benefit from its support are like college dropouts who similarly isolate themselves from the social and academic support that results from an active campus life. Therefore, we define levels of participation in social and academic life in terms of their capacity to involve and support students and prevent feelings of isolation and disconnectedness.

Cronbach's (1982) various discussions of treatment, especially his Chapter 8, are very useful additional reading.

> Conceptually defining the treatment (conceptual analysis) develops the conceptual base that relates it to the underlying theory or rationale. It also helps delineate the parts of the treatment that are the "active ingredient."

Ensuring Treatment Fidelity

Treatment fidelity ensures that the treatment administered was the treatment intended. There are three aspects: congruence of the operational definitions with the conceptual definition, representativeness of the operational definition of whatever generality is intended, and assurance that the administration of the operational definitions was followed as designed.

Operational Definitions of Treatment.   A first aspect is ensuring that the operational definitions of treatment are congruent with intentions. Just as measures of effect are translated into operational definitions, so must the treatment be translated. On rare occasions, treatments come specified in operational terms: "Full-time students who become members of university-recognized clubs are less likely to become dropouts than those who never join such organizations." The university has a definition for who is a full-time student and probably already has a mechanism for officially recognizing campus clubs. Further, since clubs have rules for determining who is a member and the registrar has a definition for what constitutes a dropout, this hypothesis comes ready to translate into a study.

Just as with measures of effect, it does not matter what was intended; the operationalization defines the treatment for the study. If the treatment is not an accurate reflection of what was intended, the evidence will be irrelevant to the intent of the study. For example, defining involvement as being a member of an official university organization is a very limited definition. There is no guarantee that the individual took part in club activities; indeed, it is possible the individual joined and then never attended another meeting. We must always judge whether the operationalization is an accurate reflection of what was intended in the context in which the concepts and constructs are used.

A common problem that arises involves judgments that must be made about noncomparable situations. Just as there may be multiple measures of a construct, so there may be many ways of giving the treatment. Thus what realistically constitutes involvement at a local junior college, where many students have jobs and therefore not much time for student life, may not be considered involvement at a small four-year residential college. So reasonable and appropriate standards of activity, the levels of involvement, and the kinds of activities may call for different operational definitions for each campus type. Operational definitions may need to be fitted to each situation.

As noted earlier, where there is a pretest, sometimes it interacts with treatment so as to potentiate it, at other times, to weaken it (testing-treatment interaction). In such instances, the operational definition of the treatment, in a very real sense, includes the pretest, especially where it has a potentiating effect.

- Treatment fidelity involves translation from the concepts in which treatment is expressed into operational terms.
- Conceptual analysis may be helpful in operationally translating constructs.
- The operational definition is the treatment, and an inaccurate representation makes the data irrelevant to the study's intent.
- A judgment must be made about the congruence of the operationalization with the intended treatment as one aspect of treatment fidelity.

Representativeness of Treatment. A second aspect of treatment fidelity concerns either studying the particular intervention used or providing generality beyond it. In the former case, we choose treatments because they are of particular interest—often those most commonly used. To provide generality, the treatment must be chosen to reflect typical examples of the construct or to reflect the relevant range of possible examples of the treatment.[12] For example, if we were studying outlining in relation to instruction in English composition, we should choose a method of instruction that includes the content and a method of its delivery that is typical of ways of teaching outlining.

Treatment is not always representative, however. For example, Mrs. Kimball's use of the Bereiter-Engleman curriculum might be simply a test of that particular curriculum. But if she considered it to be a representative example of a preschool behavior modification curriculum, we are back to seeking broader generality again.

Where faithfulness of translation of treatment into operations is to have generality, treatments selected for study may be typical examples or representative of the range.

Treatment Administration. If we are to attribute the effect to the treatment, treatment fidelity must include assurance that the treatment really was given as intended. In too many instances, the latitude exercised by the person giving the treatment may be so great that the administered treatment no longer

---

12. Readers familiar with models of analysis of variance will recognize the parallel of the first point to the fixed model, of interest in and of itself, the second to the random model, representative of the typical, and the third to the mixed model, where examples of special interest represent the range. For further explanation, see page 601.

properly represents the original design. In other instances, where more than one treatment administrator is involved, the variation may be so extreme that it significantly blurs the definition of the treatment or even constitutes an important experimental variable in its own right.

The complexity of the judgments involved in determining fidelity can be surprising. Consider these questions that might arise about a curriculum designed to teach certain mathematical concepts:

How much time must be devoted to this topic for the treatment to be authentic? Must all the content be covered? If not, how much? Must it be spread over a certain period, or can it be concentrated? If the latter, how much?

Are some topics essential, others desirable, others marginal? Must certain ones be included for the treatment to be authentic? Which ones?

May other material be included in the teaching of these concepts, or must these be the only things taught in this block?

What activities constitute teaching? Lecture? How must it be organized and delivered? Discussion? What kinds of questions should be asked? What kinds of answers should be given? Should questions be drawn from the text or from the work of the class?

How much must the students be involved in doing problems? What constitutes adequate assignment of problems? What constitutes adequate attempts at solving problems?

What level of absenteeism constitutes the threshold for noncompletion of treatment?

Obviously, we have not exhausted the list of items, and perhaps some items on the list are nonessentials. That, of course, is the point; we must decide which are the essentials, the "active ingredients," if we are to ensure treatment fidelity.

Once we have defined the "active ingredients," how do we ensure appropriate judgments about treatment implementation? Observation and measurement of treatment administration are often built into the design. Often this involves changing to low-inference observation and developing a detailed description of the behaviors involved so that a faithful administration of treatment is easily recognized—an observation checklist of the critical aspects.

Developers have sometimes tried to ensure effectiveness by structuring a curriculum to the point where it was "teacherproof" (effective with even the rawest and poorest of professionals and designed so that the teacher wouldn't meddle with it). Instead they found that teachers resisted the structure so strongly that its original potency was ruined (Leonard and Lowery, 1979). There are probably limits to the effectiveness of structuring treatments administered by humans instead of by books, machines, or computers.

In some instances, we intentionally have a low structure requiring improvisation. By observation of the treatment in use, we learn both the variety of implementation and how skilled personnel make basic structure effective. We lose the standardization that permits easier determination of the effective agent, however.

Studies of an innovative treatment still in the process of adoption will find that the extent and fidelity of adoption may vary considerably from site to site. Hall and Loucks (1977) devised the "levels of use of the innovation" scale to estimate the stage of adoption. The scale value for each site can be used as a control variable. We can compare effects of sites at the same stage of adoption in an analysis of variance design.

A treatment that is not highly structured will typically vary in the way it is applied in the field. To avoid a restriction on external validity (GP) and generality, that variation should be represented in the study. For example, suppose a curriculum will be disseminated in booklet form, but the teachers on whom its effectiveness was tested received workshop training in its use. Teachers' implementation from booklets alone may be quite different—the training workshops were part of the treatment. Another example comes from a famous study by Haney, Banks, and Zimbardo (1973), in which college students were randomly assigned to the roles of prisoners and guards, and a discussion was held with the students assigned as guards in which their proper role was defined. But just as would realistically occur in training sessions in a real prison, what the students carried away from those discussions and their resulting behavior were matters of personal interpretation. What happened in fact was that the guards became so abusive and the prisoners so submissive, the experiment had to be stopped early.

- Treatment fidelity involves administration of whatever is considered the "active ingredients" of the treatment.
- Observations of treatment administration can ensure fidelity.
- For maximum generality, conditions of treatment administration should be like those under which the treatment is intended to be used. Pretests and special training may limit generality.

Problems with the Basis for Sensing Changes

Sometimes we compare a treatment with the lack of it or with rival treatments. Often, however, we test the effectiveness of certain characteristics. Such studies call for a placebo treatment. A placebo has all the characteristics of the experimental treatment except for the "active ingredient" or cause. The need for monitoring the experimental treatment is clear, but we must also monitor any alternative treatments to ensure that the expected contrast is maintained. Sometimes the experimental treatment spreads to these groups (through diffusion, discussed as a rival hypothesis earlier in the chapter).

Suppose learning to solve five different types of mathematics problem is defined as the essence of the curriculum. Each individual student is expected to score 80 percent correct on a test. The teacher can devote as much time as she wishes, teach however she pleases, and involve the students in any way and as much or little as she desires, so long as the problem types are learned and the minimum test level is obtained. This also defines the placebo. It should devote an equal amount of time to the content, follow the same teaching style including that of involvement of the students, and in all other ways be like the teaching in the experimental section. The one difference—it should not include the five problem types as such. Although the teacher might teach the solutions to similar problems, they would be taught as solutions to specific problems rather than as types. By making the placebo a completely parallel treatment, we eliminate many potential alternative causes: length of instruction, kind of instruction, involvement of students in active learning, and so on.

The "Swahili syndrome" is often encountered in curriculum studies. We teach the experimental group Swahili and ignore the control group. Lo and behold, the experimental group knows more Swahili at the end of the study![13] When stated so starkly, the study seems ridiculous. Yet new curricula usually include some aspect not included or considerably less emphasized in the old one. It should be superior just by definition in this respect. Still we see studies comparing the two on a test that includes or perhaps even emphasizes the new material. Beware of the Swahili syndrome.

Statistics are often essential to demonstrating that an effect occurred. While it goes without saying that these must be correctly applied and interpreted, often unnoticed are the problems of the researcher in handling data, comparable to those of the qualitative researcher. The problems of cognitive limitations discussed in chapter 15, pages 344–346, are extremely relevant to the experimentalist.

- The placebo treatment should be exactly like the experimental treatment or as much like it as possible, except for the characteristics that delineate the treatment itself.
- Monitoring treatment administration, both experimental and placebo, ensures treatment fidelity as well as appropriate contrast of treatments.

The Placebo Effect. Although it has long been recognized that, medically speaking, placebos do indeed have an effect, it has only recently been found that, biologically, the effect is in many respects a genuine organismic response. Thus a group getting medical placebos has been found to develop antibodies and in other ways muster the body's defenses therapeutically. Ross and colleagues (1962) demonstrated a design for separating the effects of a drug from the placebo effect. Their design involved constructing four groups, each given orange juice:

1. Orange juice used to swallow a pill containing the drug (obtrusive administration of treatment)

---

13. I am indebted to Gavriel Solomon for this stark rendition of the problem.

2. Orange juice used to swallow a placebo pill (obtrusive administration of placebo)
3. Drug put in the orange juice, no pill (unobtrusive administration of treatment)
4. Orange juice only (unobtrusive administration of placebo)

A comparison of 2 with 4 estimates the placebo effect and of 1 with 3 indicates whether the drug is potentiated or weakened by the placebo effect. Although the design requires a vehicle such as orange juice to allow a "silent administration" of the treatment (Gottschalk, 1961), this could presumably be done with treatments involving interpersonal interaction as well.

For example, consider an experiment to determine whether it is the adaptation of the instruction to the individual or the placebo effect that makes adaptation appear effective. The latter is simply the expectancy of efficacy on the part of students who realize that the material has been adjusted to fit each of them personally. Which is the "active ingredient"? Suppose we have a new, very flexible set of course materials dealing with the United States Constitution that can be adapted to fit each individual student. Material in each unit is written several ways so as to fit different learning styles. I very conspicuously tell students about this wonderful new study approach, which should ensure that they each will raise their grade as I change the material to fit their individual needs. I make changes in the material very obtrusively, posting the unit assignments for each student on a large wall chart for all to see. In addition, I make assignments in such a way as to maximize the learning for each person in terms of that person's learning style (condition 1 of the Ross et al. design).

For condition 2, I do the same thing except that the assignments for each student are chosen from a random number table instead of being intentionally assigned. For condition 3, nothing special is said about the course material; it is just another assignment. Individual assignments are made unobtrusively as I walk around the room interacting with students as I normally would during seatwork. Condition 4 is like condition 3 except that the assignments for each student are random instead of intentional.

In summary, condition 1 is obtrusive and individual, 2 is obtrusive and random, 3 is unobtrusive and individual, and 4 is unobtrusive and random. Assuming that the random assignment of material resulted in equal learning conditions in each group, comparison of conditions 2 and 4 tells me whether obtrusively changing the course material potentiates learning; whether there is a placebo effect. Comparison of 3 with 4 shows whether intentional individual assignment results in greater learning than random assignment of those materials: whether the treatment was effective. Comparison of conditions 1 and 3 indicates whether the placebo effect potentiates the treatment effect: results in greater effectiveness of the individual adaptation of course materials.

In many social science situations, the placebo effect, the expectation of efficacy of treatment, is an intended part of treatment. Counseling and psychological therapy can be effective only if the client wants to participate in it and has some hope, however small, of benefiting from it. Thus the expectation of efficacy, the placebo effect, is often intentionally a part of treatment, in which case we aren't interested in separating out its effect.

> ■ If the treatment can be given without the subjects' being aware they are receiving it (silent treatment), the placebo effect can be determined by varying the obtrusiveness of placebo and treatment.
> ■ The placebo effect is often consciously made a part of treatment because subjects are likely, consciously or unconsciously, to render ineffective treatments of no expected benefit to them.

Possible Bases for Sensing Attributes or Changes. The options for sensing attributes or changes are displayed in the decision tree shown in Figure 18.6, which repeats Figure 12.5. Starting at the beginning of the tree, individuals can be compared with themselves over time, or with others. If with others, these may be individuals measured in the past (a previous class) or norms (as on a standardized test). Alternatively, individuals may be compared with current groups, either formed by existing processes or formed specifically for this study. Commonly, we use groups formed by a regularly occurring process such as subjects' availability in a certain time block, subjects' choice, or an institutional scheduling procedure, often computerized. The problem with such bases is that although they may appear to form groups similar to those formed by random assignment, unrecognized selection factors are often at work. This is especially true when student choice is involved, because a student's interest in a subject, a group of friends, or an easy-grading teacher may be the selective factor. Such selection forces could affect the nature of a

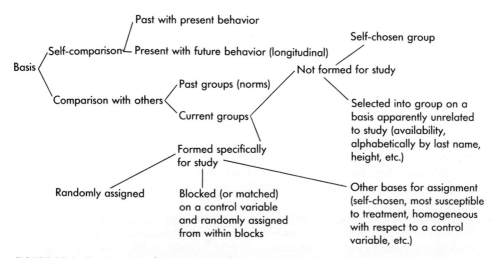

FIGURE 18.6 Decision tree showing options for sensing attributes or changes.

group so as to form a rival explanation for an effect. Thus the use of preformed groups is always open to some suspicion.

Groups formed specifically for the study, especially those involving random assignment, are to be preferred. The bottom branches of the tree show some alternatives for such groups. Straight random assignment, as noted earlier, is less preferred than blocking and random assignment. In addition, we often assign subjects in such a way as to build in the effect of a control variable. For instance, we might develop groups varying in ability from high to low so as to see the interaction of ability with treatment.

HALLMARKS OF EXPERIMENTAL DESIGN AND TIPS ON CONSTRUCTING EXPERIMENTAL DESIGNS

Too many studies involve a single treatment administrator (teacher, nurse, social worker), nonrandom assignment of treatment groups, intact groups with potential selection factors, short-term treatments, and lack of long-term follow-up. To prevent such lapses, you should be mindful of the following points regarding experimental designs. Some refer to the process of constructing designs and are unlikely to appear in the published study. These are tips. Others refer to aspects that are likely to appear in the report and so are hallmarks of good design. These are the asterisked items.

1. The best experimental designs are often developed through a series of iterations. That is, make a provisional try at a design, and whenever you see something wrong, fix it. That will make apparent either a new alternative explanation or one not previously noticed. It will require changes in the basic design again, perhaps starting over, and so it goes. Keep going until you are satisfied, but remember that nearly all designs are compromises because of the trade-offs involved. Trade-offs are discussed further in chapter 23 and the Appendix.

2. Start with a translation of the hypothesis; then add features needed to protect against such alternative explanations as are likely to be important in the eyes of your intended audience.

*3. Control undesired variables by eliminating them, if that does not unduly affect whatever external validity (GP) is required (for example, laboratory versus field). Control others by building them into the design as independent variables, if possible. For still others, spread their effect equally among the groups.

*4. Indicate in the write-up that rival explanations not protected against but of possible concern to your audience were present by conscious choice, usually a trade-off compromise, rather than ignorance. Explain the reasons.

*5. Don't freeze the design until you have done a pilot study, including gathering qualitative data (see point 17). Then do a power analysis to ensure that the study is sensitive enough to detect a result of interest.

*6. Random assignment to experimental groups and a well-constructed placebo control group buy more protection than any other design feature. Block on what seem to be important variables not otherwise controlled. You lose only your labor if the variable turns out not to be important, and you make the study more sensitive if it is. But if such procedures cannot be done unobtrusively, they will reduce external validity (GP).

*7. Use double-blind methods, if possible, to control for expectancy effects. (Follow up with point 17—the subjects may not have been as blind as you thought!)

*8. In learning studies, tests of later retention are often more sensitive to differences in treatment than immediate posttests.

*9. In studies of treatments that do not have residual effects, vary the treatment in an on-off, on-off pattern, possibly at random intervals or in randomly constructed patterns for maximally convincing results.

*10. Besides an on-off pattern, either different levels of treatment or reversal of treatment (using its opposite where feasible and ethical) can provide convincing data (for example, in a study of the effect of praise on achievement, vary the frequency of praise or even scold instead of praise). (See Cook and Campbell, 1979.)

*11. Find out how stable or variable the phenomenon of interest is in the nonexperimental state. Multiple observations will reveal a trend; at least three observations are required for a curvilinear trend. Changes in trend as a result of treatment can be handled by a design of the regression discontinuity type, where the equation describing the pretreatment trend is compared with that describing the posttreatment trend. An effective treatment will show that the trend has been displaced upward and may also angle upward more sharply. (See Cook and Campbell, 1979.)

*12. Carefully delineate the "active ingredients" in the treatment through a supporting rationale or theory. If possible, build them into the experimental treatment alone, putting all its other characteristics in the control (placebo) treatment as well.

*13. Assign a group to each separate combination of independent variables; vary them systematically from group to group for ease of analysis (factorial design).

*14. Counterbalance the order of measures or multiple treatments when the order is expected to have an effect (counterbalanced design).

*15. Use unobtrusive measures and administer treatments as unobtrusively as possible for increased external validity (GP).

*16. Remember that replication is the ultimate validation; repeating a study with the same or similar results is very strong evidence.

*17. Every experimental study should have an element of qualitative research in it. This helps you understand what is going on from the point of view of the subject, the treatment administrator, and the observer or measurer. Often interviewing the subjects after the study reveals that the treatment was perceived quite differently from what was intended (the demand characteristics of the study) and leads to new and important rival explanations. It also provides anecdotes that help vivify the phenomenon being studied and flesh out the statistics.

*18. Consider that when you subtract an unreliable score that might be too high or too low from another similarly unreliable score, the difference score is still more unreliable than the scores that made it up. Although such scores have been found useful, using random assignment with posttest-only designs where feasible avoids pretest-posttest change scores.

*19. Where the effect of repeated testing is expected to be significant, establish multiple comparable groups (possibly by splitting experimental and control groups), one for each testing.

20. Evaluate carefully all design changes made after the pilot study; let them gestate for 24 hours before acting on them.

21. Conduct data gathering in the least amount of time that is appropriate. This reduces the likelihood of local history events, the possibility of selection, mortality, and maturation effects, and personnel costs (usually the largest budgeted item). Remember that even if personnel costs are not budgeted, you still incur what economists call opportunity costs, the potential of using that time in other ways.

*22. Experimentation is designed to validate hypotheses, but afterward, *explore*! Talk to subjects and co-workers about their experiences. Explore conceptually some "what if's" and gather a bit of information about some of the more promising leads. Explore your data with scatterplots and distributions; try different cross-breaks and look for patterns. It's exciting, fun, and often fruitful! Your most precious finding may be something other than what you were looking for, so keep your horizons wide.

SUMMARY

Experimentation produces one of the strongest chains of reasoning for the validation of a hypothesis. Design is the heart of experimentation, since it allows the development of a plan to collect the data that will provide the strongest chain. The researcher's manipulation of the treatment, especially where such manipulation allows the effect to follow the pattern of the treatment, provides especially strong evidence of cause-and-effect linkage. Control is also a hallmark of a strong design. Control of the effect of unwanted variables by removing these effects makes for a more statistically powerful design than making sure the effect is present in the control as well as the experimental group. In particular, through control, we provide protection against rival hypotheses (alternative explanations, threats to validity), potential weakeners of internal validity (LP), as well as against restrictive explanations or conditions that weaken external validity (GP), reducing generality.

Although each study may have particular rival explanations or restrictive conditions that are unique, a useful set of common ones has been developed in the context of experimentation. But they may apply equally well to other research methods. Since these are problems of which most experienced audiences are now aware, researchers seeking to build a consensus should be especially wary of designs that do not provide protection against them. Where weak designs must be used, researchers should make clear that this choice was intentional and give reasons for the choice.

Experimentation runs the gamut from laboratory to so-called natural experiments where society or nature is the treatment administrator. In between are treatments applied under field conditions. The laboratory approach offers considerable control over problem variables and hence provides evidence with strong internal validity (LP). The other approaches seek greater external validity (GP), at the possible expense of internal validity (LP).

After-the-fact natural experiments are discussed in chapter 19. They are a common type of design, especially where experimentation is ethically impossible. Longitudinal studies and single-subject designs, considered in chapter 21, are elaborations on time-series designs. Design considerations are also discussed in chapter 23 and the Appendix, where the effects of different trade-offs are evaluated, especially the trade-off between internal validity (LP) and external validity (GP), a perennial problem for experimenters.

So far in section four, three basic methods—qualitative, survey, and experimental—have been presented. These methods incorporate most of the logic and considerations used in other methods, although they have their own problems to which careful attention must be given. We next move to two methods that make use of the techniques of these three: history (chapter 19) and evaluation (chapter 20). These will show how the base methods are further developed and added to and point out special considerations of which to be aware. Chapter 21 is a potpourri of other interesting methods that cannot be covered in detail.

ADDITIONAL READING

Campbell and Stanley (1963) and Cook and Campbell (1979) are excellent materials to read for the detailed analysis of a great many designs. In addition, both contain a variety of examples that make the principles come alive. Both books are quite understandable, although the material on statistical analysis in Cook and Campbell is somewhat difficult. This latter also has an excellent section on analysis of causation.

IMPORTANT TERMS

Base rate
Camouflage
Confounding
Counterbalanced designs
Demand characteristics
Diffusion
Double-blind procedures
Factorial design
Functionally equivalent groups
Hawthorne effect
Hypothesis guessing

Instrument decay by treatment interaction
Interactions
Local history
Masking
Maturation
Mortality by treatment interaction
Multiple-treatment interaction
Nested designs
Nonequivalent control group design
Obtrusiveness
One-group pretest-posttest design

Placebo effect
Posttest-only control group design
Pretest-posttest control group design
Random assignment
Reactivity
Regression
Researcher expectancy effect
Selection

Selection by treatment interaction
Solomon four-group design
Testing
Testing-treatment interaction
Threats to validity
Time-series designs
Treatment fidelity
Unobtrusiveness

═══════ APPLICATION PROBLEMS ═══════

1. You are a researcher in science education who is interested in the role of diagrams in instruction. These are usually combinations of text and arrows to indicate what phenomenon leads to what other phenomenon. Examples are the oxygen and water cycles. You wish to investigate whether using small pictures in place of text within the diagrams will facilitate comprehension of the principles and concepts taught. To do so, you have developed a grade 8 geography unit on the water cycle that incorporates the liberal use of diagrams. How would you design your study?

2. A state government curriculum team wished to demonstrate the superiority of its new approach to the junior high school level social studies program. Team members selected a sample of teachers from around the state to carry out a one-year pilot study of the new program. All the teachers were volunteers.

(a) Assume that students who were taught using the new approach scored significantly higher on a test of comprehension of key concepts than comparable students in the regular program. What alternative explanations to the claim that the new approach was better could be advanced? How could these be avoided?

(b) Assume that the control (regular curriculum) group scored significantly higher. What could explain this result?

3. A university mathematics instructor has developed and incorporated an extensive computer-assisted instructional (CAI) program into his own course on introductory calculus. Wanting to assess the effectiveness of his approach, he decided that he would randomly assign students to each section of the course and compare the mean scores on the final exam at the end of the semester (the posttest-only control group design). He hypothesized a significant difference between the means in favor of his approach. What alternative explanations represent a threat to his design? How could he avoid them?

4. Recall the study (chapter 3, problem 1) in which a group of researchers investigated the interaction between the age of viewers of an instructional film and the gender of the narrator. Subjects in the second and fifth grades were randomly assigned to one of two groups. One group watched a film narrated by an adult female, and the other group viewed the same film narrated by an adult male. During the film, the investigators measured the children's visual attention to the program. They also tested recall of the story ideas using a multiple-choice test. What research design would these investigators probably have used and why?

5. A nursing graduate student investigated the neurological problem of unilateral neglect (in which a patient is unaware of one side of the body). She decided to compare unilateral neglect patients who also suffered from another, related problem, anosognosia (the inability to recognize that anything is wrong with them), with those who did not. She believed that the patients with both unilateral neglect and anosognosia would experience more difficulties with self-care activities. Assuming that she has located a reliable measure of self-care, how would she design a study to compare the two groups?

Note that these disorders are relatively rare. Take into account, as well, that such medical conditions tend to be unstable; that is, the severity of the symptoms varies with such factors as patient fatigue and stress. In addition, such patients do tend to improve, albeit slowly.

Compare your answers with those on pages 718–720.

―――――――――――――――― APPLICATION EXERCISE ――――――――――――――――

For you to explore the possibilities of using experimentation with your problem, you will need some kind of hypothesis and treatment. If these would not normally be part of your problem, find an aspect about which enough is known that setting forth a hypothesis is reasonable. What kind of experiment does a translation of the hypothesis lead to? What terms in the hypothesis automatically translate into design features?

How would you define the treatment? Should you check to be sure that it is being administered faithfully to what is intended? How would you do that? Are you interested in the treatment per se? Or is it intended to be representative? If so, of what and what are the implications of this?

How might you administer the treatment so as to have the most convincing evidence of cause and effect? What kind of design does that suggest? Do you need an alterna-

tive or a placebo treatment? Of what would it consist? What essential characteristics of treatment must be excluded from it, and what other characteristics must be included because they go with the treatment but are not really part of it?

What alternative explanations are likely to be a threat to the internal validity (LP) of the study? How would you protect against them? Can you protect against the worst threats? If you can't, what would you do? Are there alternative designs among which you could choose? What trade-offs would be involved in selecting one design over another?

Would you be concerned with generality? If so, what restrictive conditions should you be aware of that might limit external validity (GP)? What design considerations might be involved?

CHAPTER
19

The Historical Method and After-the-Fact Natural Experiments

Sometimes historians search for a single fact as when Mosteller and Wallace . . . sought to determine whether Madison or Hamilton wrote the Federalist papers. In other instances, they try to understand the meaning of the past to the living as when the black historian John Hope Franklin tutored the Supreme Court lawyers in the 1954 case that overturned the "separate but equal" doctrine. He demonstrated convincingly ". . . in the view of the framers, the Amendment meant equality . . . and that if they were around today they wouldn't support segregation and discrimination."

J. Starr, "Above All, a Scholar"

Through an understanding of the past many historians seek to contribute to our current knowledge of the human condition. They explain if not predict. In this role they follow the same rules as do other behavioral scientists. For their finding of patterns in the past, historians are to be especially treasured. True, hindsight is on their side. But it is difficult enough to make progress when one can set one's own stage for data collection. Making sense of the leavings of a culture is a tough job!

David R. Krathwohl

OVERVIEW

This chapter consists of two sections. The first examines history and the methods it uses; the second, after-the-fact natural experiments. History consists of the discovery, selection, organization, and interpretation of evidence to describe a situation or to answer a question about past events. Free to choose and interpret their data, historians are judged by the intelligence and honesty they bring to the task. They often seek to interpret data from a new standpoint. They rely on a variety of social science research methods, though history has its own unique problems, such as the authentication of evidence.

After-the-fact natural experiments face many of the same problems. They use the posttest-only control group design in which the control group is formed after the fact from available data. The intent is to be able to draw conclusions—ideally, causative conclusions—about the relationship between variables. Most evidence of the relationships between cancer and tobacco smoke, fish oils, pesticides, and other substances comes from such studies. The problems of finding comparable controls and establishing adequate conditions for inferring causation are formidable.

CHAPTER CONTENTS

Introduction   502
    Methods of the Historian   503
    History as Selective
      Interpretation   503
Steps in a Historical Study   506
    Problem Formulation, Problem
      Modification, and Hypothesis
      Development   506
    Validating Evidence   508
    Accuracy of Account   508
    Problems of Analysis and
      Alternative Explanations   510

Inferring Causation   511
After-the-Fact Natural Experiments   514
    A Common Design Where
      Treatment Is Impossible   515
    Problems of After-the-Fact
      Designs   516
    Example of an After-the-Fact
      Natural Experiment   517
Hallmarks of Historical and
    After-the-Fact Designs   519
Summary   520

INTRODUCTION

What is a historical study? There are probably as many definitions as there are historians. I like the definition provided by Fischer (1970, p. xv): "A historian is someone (anyone) who asks an open-ended question about past events and answers it with selected facts." He notes that "questions and answers are fitted to each other by a complex pattern of mutual adjustment." Facts teach us how to formulate the questions; that leads to a different selection of facts, which in turn requires reformulation of the questions. Thus Fischer sees the logic of history as neither inductive nor deductive. Instead, it is adductive reasoning, where *adducing* means "leading out the answer . . . to specific questions so that a satisfactory explanatory fit" is attained. The result "may take many forms: a statistical generalization, or a narrative, or a causal model or a motivational model, or . . . maybe even an analogy" (p. xv).

    Historical studies serve many purposes. Sometimes they help us see a parallel between present and past events. Allison (1971) analyzed the Cuban missile crisis in which the United States and the Soviet Union stood toe to toe in a nuclear confrontation with disaster. He points out that a historian's analysis was important: "Kennedy . . . saw how miscalculation . . . could turn this path into a slippery slope. Having recently read Barbara Tuchman's *Guns of August* he mused about the miscalculations . . . within each government [that] allowed them to tumble into war" (pp. 218–219). Allison shows how

Kennedy resisted his own bureaucracy to provide time for the Soviets so as to minimize hurrying that would lead to miscalculations.

Sometimes history is used to support theoretical positions. For instance, Laslett (1980), employing Marx's theory of social change, used contrasting groups and time frames. She showed the explanatory power of the theory. She used it to anticipate the 1850–1870 change from the extended family to the smaller nuclear family structure as a result of the shift from farming for consumption for the family and local area to production patterns of farming.

In other instances, historians give us perspective so that we may better judge progress. Historical views provide still another way of studying a particular social science problem that may yield unique and useful insights.

Methods of the Historian

History displays the increasing unity of the social sciences in borrowing techniques from other fields. All of human experience being the stuff of history, it is natural that historians should search widely for techniques to facilitate their work. Most commonly used is the qualitative method's analysis of context. But also used are the statistical analyses associated with experiments and surveys; the analytic techniques of the linguist to determine the authorship of texts; carbon dating and ink chemistry to date various artifacts, especially documents; and the instincts of the detective to track down the obscure records, lost manuscripts, forgotten diaries, and other evidence of the past. Historians have to become adept at authenticating their evidence and determining how it bears on the particular problem they are studying. The good historian is a jack-of-all-trades and the master of as many of them as possible.

Many historians consider themselves "the real interdisciplinarians." Dealing mainly in words, like other fields, historians have their concerns about the "number crunchers" (cliometricians). Indeed, historians have succumbed to the siren call of numbers for the same reasons others have: "Correct or not, they speak to us with authority; they have rhetorical force" (Barzun and Graff, 1977, p. 201). Hence some historians, like William Aydelotte, have actively sought to illustrate how quantitative methods contribute to historical understanding (Aydelotte, 1971; Aydelotte, Bogue, and Fogel, 1972). Historians have also borrowed theory from other behavioral sciences. For example, psychohistorians describe their psychological insights into the reasons public figures acted as they did, as in Mazlish's (1972) study of President Nixon.

History as Selective Interpretation

The match of a strongly developed rationale with carefully selected and organized data to show their congruence is always partly an art. The skills of the writer are critical in all research methods that rely on narration to make their case; the qualitative method is a prime example. The best historians are very good writers: they think clearly and logically, and they write the way they think—words flow effortlessly through the narrative, piquing reader interest as they simultaneously drive home the points to be made. Consider Fisher's (1970) description of a local antiquarian:

> In every New England town library, there is likely to be an ancient Puritan virgin, shriveled and dried in the snows of sixty Massachusetts winters and suitably shrouded in black bombazine, who has been at work for the past twenty years on the story of her home town from 1633 to 1933 when Franklin Roosevelt was inaugurated and history came to an end. (pp. 140–141)

For some historians, just as for some qualitative researchers, description is an adequate goal. For many historians, however, there are only too many stories that could be told. For them, it is not the story that is significant but the generalizations that can be drawn from it. If they are to select facts and tell stories, they prefer to select those that provide an explanation or a rationale, clarify a principle, reveal a point of view. This gives forward-looking usefulness and perspective to their work. Out of this mold have come writers like Toynbee, Spengler, Nietzsche, Malthus, and Voltaire. Probably the great majority of historians are between these two extremes, neither solely telling a story for the story's sake nor explicating some grand theory. More likely, they are using an explanation to throw light on a corner of history not yet illuminated from that angle.

Every research method has its special demands, and clearly the ability to combine strong storytelling with an organizing rationale is critical to the historical method. Nevins (1975) tells a story of Lincoln Steffens, who on seeing a man bearing a glittering fragment of truth warned Satan "that man has hold of some truth. He could kill you if he tried. . . . 'No danger,' Satan replied. 'He will take that fragment home, chisel it, rub it, dull it until it has no power whatsoever.'" "Not so," says Nevins. "Truth, like the South African diamond, is a dull cloudy pebble when first discovered. Long labor and the nicest art have to be applied to cut it into those well polished facets that give it scintillating power" (pp. 41, 42). That is the work of the historian.

Scientific History. With a longer tradition than other social sciences, history has watched many views of its role become dominant and then fade. For example, scholars, seeing the success of the methods of the physical sciences, have suggested that history attempt to be completely objective in writing the chronicle of some event or era. Such "scientific history" attempted to re-create what "really" occurred in great detail and resulted in what has been called "dry as dust" history (Barzun and Graff, 1977). Undoubtedly, some still hold this view. Certainly, the effort to be objective in the sense of accurately interpreting the evidence is a matter of considerable pride to every historian. Still, as with any observation, historians also realize that there can never be a complete picture. Nor, if that were possible, would we want one; all the details are not important to what is usually of interest to us.

Interpretive History. Most historians would argue that all history is interpretive; the human mind continually seeks patterns in the events that pass before it. The historian interprets not only in selecting what is important but also in how important facts are juxtaposed and organized; the latter implicitly creates relations and imparts ideas. To say that "Jimmy Carter won the election over the conservative Gerald Ford" implies, in some way, that conservativeness caused the defeat. How the historian arranges that pattern is at once an important contribution and, to the extent that another person would arrange it to convey something else, a problem.

"The objection that historians select their facts to suit themselves is seen to be no objection but a helpful necessity. They are meant to think and to choose and they are judged by the intelligence and honesty with which they do both" (Barzun and Graff, 1985, p. 190). And as they indicate, historians must wrestle with the problem of making a single stream of words weave a multidimensional tapestry. It must include the various strands occurring simultaneously at different locations viewed from whatever perspective has been chosen.[1]

With this, there is the realization that all history is interpretative, the extent of interpretation varying with the author, the author's purpose, and the reader's perception of the events. This interpretiveness may be particularly apparent when the author is advancing a hypothesis and is marshaling evidence for it, especially if we suspect that facts are being selectively overemphasized or underemphasized to make a point. Some people have so criticized Toynbee's analysis of past civilizations, which contends that their fall was not just the result of external attacks but of internal defects or failures. Where the reader's view of the facts is congruent with the historian's, the extent of interpretation may be perceived as relatively minor, as in Tuchman (1962). In retelling the story of World War I, she shows how individuals set in motion events over which they lose control and then repeatedly interpret the evidence selectively to fit their predispositions.

More, perhaps, than professionals in other fields, historians restudy problems. Doing revisionary history, reinterpreting previous accounts, imposing a new explanatory framework, adding new data, and discounting old data are common activities. There is a cliché that history must be rewritten by every generation. Barzun and Graff (1985, p. 204) note that this is not so much that the earlier expositions were untrue as that the picture is never finished.

The past cannot help but be reconceived by the present, for historians' outlook and way of thinking are products of the age in which they live. Each new generation of historians reinterprets events from its own perspective. Barzun and Graff (1985) explain reinterpretation using an analogy in which events are a mountain. The climber sees only the part of the mountain passed en route. The airplane pilot flattens it out and sees it in a different perspective. The traveler from afar sees its outline. Thus early historians view the Protestant Reformation

> as mainly a theological and military event; in . . . the eighteenth century . . .
> as a reshaping of the map of Europe, a strenghtening of emergent states

---

1. As indicated in chapter 15, notice how well these two paragraphs apply to the report of any qualitative study; they are right on target!

and a furthering of intellectual freedom. In the nineteenth century [it is seen] . . . as a religious movement with profound social implications; in the twentieth . . . a social and economic revolution with religious and political side effects. (Barzun and Graff, 1977, p. 156)

The authors point out that knowing the full history requires reading successive treatments just as a researcher of an event "seeks out all its witnesses" (p. 156).

When setting forth a generalization, historians employ the same chain of reasoning we have found useful in analyzing other research methods. As before, the chain does not describe how they do their work so much as how they present the results. How the historian constructs different parts of the chain will become clearer as the chapter progresses.

- Historians seeking generalizations find, assemble, organize, and interpret evidence.
- They may adduce a rationale or an explanation from the evidence or may have developed it in advance and seek to demonstrate its validity.
- Selectively choosing and organizing the evidence, the historian seeks to show effectively, yet honestly, the correspondence between it and the proposed explanation.
- Historians are judged by the intelligence and the integrity with which they perform this task.

STEPS IN A HISTORICAL STUDY

Problem Formulation, Problem Modification, and Hypothesis Development

Just as the methodologist with a new tool seeks problems that can be attacked with it, the historian may start with a lucky find and work backward to learn what interesting questions can be asked of that evidence. Sometimes a new set of papers will be given to an institution or be made available by an archivist for study. Often, as in other fields, the initial formulation of a problem is considerably modified by later findings. Then the whole problem is recast as we learn both what evidence can be found and what questions are appropriate to ask of it. No more than in any other field do historians necessarily conduct their studies in the neat way the evidence is reported.

Historians often begin like participant observers, determining the important aspects of the person or event as they proceed, though probably having predetermined notions about where to look. For them, the design links of the chain of reasoning—persons (subjects), situations, causes (treatments) and effects (independent variable, observation or measurement), basis for sensing the attributes or changes that occurred—are only partly determined at the outset. They emerge more clearly as we repeatedly cycle back through the data deciding what is important, finding and examining it, analyzing it, deciding more precisely what is needed next, searching for and finding it, examining it, deciding still again, and so on. Thus the chain of reasoning evolves as the study is defined more clearly.

For the historian with a hypothesis dimly in mind, the first steps are like those of any other researcher—to see what others have done and to clarify concepts. The main difference lies in the references consulted; certain topics have their own access routes. For example, there are Adams's *Dictionary of American History* (1976–1978), Johnson's *Oxford Companion to American History* (1966), Langer's *Encyclopedia of World History* (1972), the *Harvard Guide to American History* (Friedel and Showman, 1974), and the American Historical Association's series ending in the 1961 *Guide to Historical Literature*.

Just as other researchers have difficulty cutting their problem to fit their time and energy, historians, too, are likely to take on too large an initial problem. Barzun and Graff (1985) define a just-right-sized problem as one where the "facts and ideas . . . presented . . . leave no questions unanswered WITHIN the presentation, even though questions could be asked OUTSIDE of it" (p. 19).[2] Comparable to the feasibility problem in other research, there is the limitation of whether there are adequate records, artifacts, or other evidence to permit the investigation planned. Such evidence was not often designed to help the historian. It consists of what someone else thought was worth collecting and saving and is nearly always incomplete. It is thin in times of intense action when historians would like a complete and accurate immediate record instead of a self-edited retroactive one. It can be fullest when there is little else to do, during a time of less interest.

Historians can't manipulate treatment, create new data, or take new measures. They are confined to the objects, artifacts, and records left to them by the past. Often they must resort to indirect evidence. A classic example of this is the problem of showing the growth of the British bureaucracy in the days before organizational charts. Records of the growth of government procurements of sealing wax very nicely documented the expansion. Failing such evidence, there is little the historical researcher can do if the records aren't there. However, a good bit of ingenuity goes into both divining evidence that might have been kept and undertaking the detective work of finding it; a good bit of luck helps, too.

Like the lawyer who distrusts hearsay evidence, historians most value firsthand accounts by participants instead of secondary reports by persons who have heard about, read about, or perhaps talked to participants. They seek the former in official records and reports, minutes of meetings, photographs, recordings, bulletins, catalogs, licenses, certificates, and other documents likely to be generated in the activities they are studying. The author's relation to the event is important. Was it an immediate or a retrospective account? If the latter, how much time elapsed between event and report? Was the event viewed directly, or is the account based on what other people saw?

Oral history has special problems (Vansina, 1965; Davis, Back, and

---

2. This is an excellent specification of problem size for any research method, not just history!

MacLean, 1977; Rosaldo, 1980). Just as in interpreting documents, oral statements must be understood as cultural products, and it must be learned when to take them literally, figuratively, or in some instances, ironically (for example, do they really mean to "kill the ump" in a baseball game?).

Validating Evidence

How can the researcher be sure that the evidence unearthed is what it purports to be? In a few instances, artifacts may be forgeries, like the Hitler diaries unveiled with much fanfare some years ago. Sometimes they are not what they appear to be—records may be drafts, an autobiography may really be a biography. Authenticity of dubious historical evidence may be hard to establish; we typically proceed by looking for consistencies in its content, its physical condition, and the context in which it was found. We may examine the dates of other material found with it, may subject ink and paper to chemical analysis and carbon or other radioactive dating techniques, examine watermarks and word usage for typicality at the time of presumed production, and look for facts and allusions appropriate for the time as well as assuring the absence of inappropriate ones. In some instances of disputed authorship, counts of unusual word usages and constructions can be made by computer, and the document can then be analyzed to determine its resemblance to the base rates of the contending authors in other documents. Mosteller and Wallace (1984) used this technique to analyze the Federalist Papers to determine whether Hamilton or Madison authored them. Their evidence strengthened the prevailing opinion favoring Madison.[3]

Accuracy of Account

A document may be genuine in that it was produced at the time and by the person presumed to have produced it but still be an inaccurate account of what is of interest. To evaluate the accomplishments of President Franklin Roosevelt, we would not take the campaign speeches of 1942 as accurate. Not only are they deficient because they are campaign speeches, but also, a war was being fought, so there might be things that could not be revealed at that time. The person, the circumstances under which the document was produced, the purposes it is to serve, and the question we are trying to answer all affect our estimate of the likelihood of an accurate account. For example, if not a record of accomplishments, Roosevelt's speeches would still document the kinds of anxiety that people in the government felt had to be allayed during those difficult times.

---

3. Authentication of artifacts has been called "external criticism," and the problem of establishing their accuracy or worth, "internal criticism." For a variety of reasons, these terms seem less used these days; they are noted here in case you come across them.

An analysis of the other work of an author or the records of a clerk may help to establish whether the individual was accurate in instances where there is certainty regarding what occurred. Internally inconsistent reporting destroys the credibility of the reporter. Obvious errors in totals or apparent inconsistencies in recording data brand a writer as untrustworthy.

The training of the author may be helpful in this regard, particularly if the training was in the phenomenon involved so that there would be some familiarity with what would be significant in the situation. The television sports commentator points out many aspects of the game a novice would otherwise miss. But knowledge is only part of the story. A professor visiting another professor's classroom may be thoroughly familiar with the subject matter. But a trained observer who has been observing classrooms might give us a report that we would prefer for its accuracy and its attention to detail regarding teaching methods. Both knowledge of the phenomenon and experience in observing and reporting it on the part of the author increase our confidence in that author's report.

The circumstances under which the report is made also affect its accuracy. We might expect that routine records would generally be kept accurately and without bias. Yet when these are the basis for punitive administrative or other action, they may not represent the facts. For example, the statistics for the New York State narcotics law should show the size of the drug problem. But because the law mandates long sentences on conviction, judges may be more reluctant to find the person guilty of that particular crime in the first place, thus biasing the conviction record. Similar pressures may make open letters of reference less reliable than those never intended to be seen by the subject.

Lastly, the purpose for which the report is made is important. A public record is one thing, a private report another. A report to a superior may be written to impress, whereas a staff report, intended for guidance in decision making, may be more objective. Propaganda and advertising contrast with report writing, though the latter, too, may have less obvious but equally distorting hidden agendas. Ascertaining purpose obviously helps us judge the author's motives.

Historians are reconciled to the fact that some truths may never be known where accounts differ. Did President Truman fire Secretary of State James F. Byrnes? Truman's memoirs say he did. Byrnes, in his autobiography, says he didn't. "Barring the presence of an unsuspected witness, . . . precision must often remain an ideal and finality a dream" (Barzun and Graff, 1970, p. 159).

The historian is responsible for not only finding but also authenticating evidence and then determining its worth and its contribution to the problem under consideration. Authenticity is a necessary but not sufficient condition that evidence will make a worthwhile contribution.

Problems of Analysis and Alternative Explanations

The relation of constructs to their operationalization is a problem for the historian just as for other researchers, but it has a special twist. Is the meaning of the construct consistent from one time period to another, or does it change in ways that might suggest alternative explanations? For example, in considering changes in family size as judged from census data, we must make sure that the meaning of "household size" was constant. For instance, did it count as a family, in addition to husband, wife, and children, adult sisters and brothers living together? (Apparently it did at one time.) Did it include boarders who ate and lived with the family? The latter, in particular, could have a significant effect on apparent household size but would also constitute a different concept of a household from any usual meaning.

Whereas we usually think of operationalization as moving from construct to evidence, the reverse process is equally important for the historian where the intended purpose of an artifact in a culture is not clear. Consider the many spoofs of how today's indoor toilets might be interpreted by historians of the future as places of religious ritual and sacrifice to unknown gods. The difficulty of inferring the meaning of things in another time and place is readily apparent.

Alternative Explanations.   Most of the alternative explanations listed in chapter 18 on experimentation apply to historical events as well. Especially prevalent is selection, since we nearly always use intact groups (no mystical figure was out there arranging randomly assigned ones so that we could do research later!). Such groups are almost always subject to some selection pressure, often related to the topic being studied. We are not even free of the problem of volunteers, since many groups are self-selected. For example, were people who immigrated to the United States those who were the most unhappy in their homeland, the most aggressive and proactive in seeking solutions to problems, the misfits and maladjusted, the uneducated? All of these are possible selection factors that might have contributed to the nature of their lives. Differential mortality is also a factor in that potential immigrants who returned disgruntled to their homeland were not a random sample of the original group. Selection was a factor in the representativeness of the army during the U.S. Civil War. Although there was a draft, it was both legal and common practice for wealthy men to hire others to take their place.

Just as selection may occur with respect to the individuals involved, it may also occur with respect to the records. Laslett (1980), for example, noted the belief that extended families were the dominant form in preindustrial societies. She wondered whether this belief was a reflection less of commonality than of the fact that wealthier families tended to live in larger and more complex households. Since such families were more likely to create diaries, letters, and other artifacts and to preserve these records, the impression may have been more a function of the selective availability of records than of reality.

Society and culture determine what is important to record. The kinds of persons who make and retain records are different from those who don't. Only certain kinds of events are typically recorded. There are, for example, plenty of probate records in precolonial Maryland but no regular methods of recording births and marriages. Exactly the reverse is true of Massachusetts; both reflect what was important in the religion and life of that time. Clearly, knowledge of the culture is essential to correct interpretation.

Many alternative explanations can be eliminated if there is a control group. Establishing such groups requires creativity and ingenuity. Briggs (1978), for example, wanted to show how children of Italian immigrants in the United States compared with their non-Italian classmates in achievement. He compared each child with an Italian surname in three Rochester public schools over the years 1910–1924 to the child nearest on the class roll with a non-Italian surname. With this group he could compare age in grade, attendance, and promotion to next grade. Children of Italian immigrants tended to be older but had better attendance and had very slightly less chance of repeating a grade. Briggs was concerned about the middle-class bias of the district as a whole, so, instead of comparing these children with district averages, he sought a comparable working-class control group. His scheme depended, of course, on the assumption that the neighborhood attendance area for a school was relatively homogeneous with respect to socioeconomic status, a not too improbable assumption in that day.

Historians face special problems of analysis, including these:

- The necessity of understanding the meaning of constructs in the culture and at the time studied
- The possibility that constructs change in meaning over time
- The difficulty of inferring the meaning of artifacts except as we understand their meaning in the culture
- The fact that society and culture determine what is important to record so that selectivity with respect to records may be an important factor to take into account
- The difficulty of establishing control or contrasting groups in past data; much ingenuity is required
- Historical studies are subject to the same alternative explanations as other studies, but selection and mortality may be especially common.

Inferring Causation

Like other behavioral scientists, historians are very much interested in causation, the internal validity (LP) of their study. Some work on a grandiose scale, like Marx, who viewed the world in terms of the social forms of production and its consequences. Others are concerned with less cosmic events, such as the cause of a particular war or battle or of the triumph of an individual over circumstances. Causation pervades history.

Nearly all the voluminous writing on the historical method has considered problems of causation. Historians have certain advantages. They can choose selectively among the wide scope of past events to prove their point. They are not caught up with and blinded by the passions of the time studied. They have the advantage of hindsight, of knowing what happened, and they can trace backward for causes. But authors agree that the historian's task is formidable, even with the clarity of hindsight. Given, among other problems, faulty and partial records and differing perspectives, people who think deeply about the problem generally believe only "highly plausible connections" can be demonstrated.

But historians want to write forcefully and present a strong case, often doing so dramatically. Many write as though the cause were clear, using words like *inevitable, unavoidable,* and *inescapable*. Carr (1962), in discussing causation, suggests that we should do without such terms: "Life will be drabber. But let us leave them to the poets and metaphysicians."[4] Barzun and Graff (1985, p. 187) propose using the term *conditions* and talk of the "probability of events." These are the exceptions. Just like all other behavioral scientists, historians make the strongest case the evidence permits for each of the internal validity (LP) judgments.

Satisfying the Conditions for Inferring Causation. The rationale or explanation plays the same role in historical studies as in other studies. We show the fit of the rationale to the data and the extent to which changes in causes resulted in changes in effect. If we argue that emigration is a function of economic conditions, the more tightly the rate of emigration follows the gyrations of the economic indicators, the stronger is the presumption of a causative relationship.

One of the most convincing conditions, the production of an effect at will, is denied the historian, who can only pick and choose to illustrate past events and cannot create them. But in one important sense there are predictive possibilities: predicting the as yet unknown or undiscovered on the basis of the known. The historian who supplies missing pieces later confirmed by new discoveries is in much the same position as the astronomer who predicts the existence of an unseen planet or moon later shown to be present. Such evidence is very convincing. Sometimes such predictions can be made from one period to another when the data from the other period have not yet been analyzed in that way. This serves exactly the same purpose as a cross-validation sample or replication does in quantitative research.

The presumption of causation is strengthened by showing repeated examples in varying circumstances—Mill's method of agreement applied to historical data. Toynbee, for example, tracing his thesis about the rise and fall of civilizations over a range of cultures, shows that his argument holds under a variety of circumstances.

Demonstrating that cause precedes effect is difficult, if not impossible. Fischer (1970), for instance, disagrees with Potter's (1954) *People of Plenty*, which argues that much of Americanism resulted from affluence. Only recently

---

4. But he is nevertheless partial to vivid writing: on the next page, he asks to be excused for not getting rid of *inevitable* in his own work (p. 126).

have people thought of themselves as affluent, says Fischer; "portraits of our ancestors have a lean and hungry look. . . . They became American and *then* became affluent" (p. 172). Which came first? Were Americanism and affluence interactive? Have we an amplifying loop? Precedence as a condition may not be possible to show, nor may it make much sense in this or other historical situations. The large number of historical phenomena that are really relatively self-contained interactive systems makes precedence useful only for analyzing isolated sections of the chain of events.

Multiple Causes. Can historians ever claim to have found the single necessary and sufficient cause of an event? It is true that there are events in history that appear to be the key to what follows? For example, Fischer (1970, p. 173) notes that enemy possession of Confederate General Robert E. Lee's General Order 191 allowed Union General George B. McClellan to anticipate where Lee would mass his troops. It may have been fatal to the loss of Antietam, a defeat that may have lost the South the possibility of European intervention and hence the Civil War.

Others, however, may build competing chains of events. Which is correct? Perhaps all are! Perhaps the possession of the Confederate order played a contingent or contributing role to the battle, which may be seen as an example of the INUS form of causation discussed in chapter 12. In Mackie's (1965) INUS form of causation, there may be multiple conditions, all of which contributed to the eventual outcome.

Like all behavioral scientists, historians abstract and simplify. But they are confronted with complex people in biographies, with institutional histories, with a range of people and institutions in important events and over periods of time. Therefore, historians are much less prone to the highly simplified single-variable descriptions of the psychologist or the more complex pictures painted by many sociologists. Patterns of multiple causation are the norm instead of the exception. With the acceptance of multiple causation, complex social phenomena can be looked at from different points of view, each making good sense.

David Tyack (1976) demonstrates this very nicely in an essay explaining the rise of compulsory schooling as driven by five different intents or causes: (1) as a means of binding students to the nation-state, (2) as a means to satisfy the ethnocentric demands of religious and ethnic groups, (3) as an outgrowth of the developing school bureaucrat, (4) as an investment in human capital, and (5) as a way of reproducing the class structure of American society, a Marxist interpretation. Each explanation is shown to fit the facts, some better at certain periods than others, but all apparently having some validity.

Not only does the Tyack example demonstrate how a single event can be open to multiple understandings, but also it indicates the creativity that historians bring to the reinterpretation of events. Often they reconstruct the past from a new angle, bringing a different insight to past explanations. In some instances, such as the Laslett (1978, 1980) example described previously, these grow out of a theory, such as the Marxist viewpoint, about how all or some part of society functions. Many scholarly pieces have been written exploring the Marxist view of history.

- Historians face the same problems of showing causality as other social scientists. Those who have thought about it seriously doubt that tight cases are possible. Yet historians, like others, continually attempt to build convincing cases for causality.
- Historians cannot vary causes and show that effects follow, but they can selectively seek instances where that has occurred naturally.
- Precedence of cause may be difficult or impossible to prove.
- With complex phenomena, explanations involving multiple causes are the most common and make the most sense. They open phenomena to multiple useful interpretations. They also result in useful reinterpretations, or revisionist history.

AFTER-THE-FACT NATURAL EXPERIMENTS

After-the-fact natural experiments have a posttest-only control group design wherein the intervention was not under the experimenter's control and the control group is formed after the fact, that is, after the variable of interest has had its effect. Researchers arrange the data to make comparisons that will allow them to draw inferences about the relationship between variables. The very clever study by Briggs (1978) of the school achievement of the children of Italian immigrants, cited earlier in this chapter, is an example of such a study.

Why treat this kind of study in a chapter on historical methods instead of one on experimentation? There are several reasons:

1. When historians use quantitative methods, the after-the-fact natural experiment is typically the kind of model they use.
2. Like history, this method is restricted to the data that are available in records or, like students of contemporary history, to the retrospective accounts of individuals.
3. After-the-fact studies share the same data problems as historical studies. For example, researchers are confined to data gathered earlier, usually before the event of interest occurred. There is the problem of authenticity of data, that is, ensuring that the data really represent what they are supposed to and do so consistently over the time period studied. (For example, are self-ratings of degree of nervousness sufficiently comparable across individuals to serve as an index? Have improving methods of detecting lung cancer inflated the number of cases?)
4. The after-the-fact approach has the same problems as history in showing causation, such as problems in determining precedence of cause, inability to manipulate treatment, and inability to assign individuals to groups randomly.

So it seems clear that although not all after-the-fact studies are historical studies in the usual sense, they share many of the same characteristics.

A Common Design Where Treatment Is Impossible

The world is such that we can't experiment with many of the phenomena that interest us most. What is the effect of low socioeconomic status on school achievement? What is the effect of low spatial visualization on creativity? Manipulating these variables as we would a treatment is impossible; we must examine them as they exist in the world and try to understand their consequences.

The evidence for many policy statements rests on arranging existing data so as to examine the effect of some variable—the effects of eating meat by studying vegetarians and fish eaters, the protective effect of certain fish oils by studying people who routinely ingest them in contrast to those who don't, the effects of exposure to Agent Orange among Vietnam veterans who were exposed to it and those who weren't, and so on. Such studies are often bolstered by animal studies or statistical modeling studies that hypothesize relationships among variables and ask, "What if . . . ?" But the most convincing evidence is that from humans, so after-the-fact natural experiments often carry a great weight in making policy. The critical problem in all such studies is that of establishing proper conditions for inferring causation. In many instances, where only the suspicion of causation can be inferred—for example, the role of cholesterol in strokes and heart disease—belief in the possibility of such a relationship is enough to establish a dietary policy.

Unfortunately, a universally satisfactory name for such analyses is lacking, so I have chosen to call them descriptively "after-the-fact natural experiments."[5] They are natural experiments in that the treatment and effect have occurred as they would in their natural states. We use available data to find individuals who possess the variable or variables of interest (smoking, lung cancer, or both). This target group forms the treatment group, and our problem, after-the-fact and by a combination of logic, wizardry, and luck, is to develop an experiment by creating a control group that is functionally equivalent to the treatment group in every necessary way. Because there are rarely "before" data on both groups, it is usually analogous to a posttest-only control group design:

$$\frac{X\ O}{C\ O}$$

To create a control group, we must either arbitrarily form such a group from an existing pool of individuals on which appropriate data are available or find an already formed group that will serve the purpose. In either case, the actual equivalence of the groups is always a nagging question.

---

5. Many authorities, like Kerlinger (1973), call them "ex post facto studies," from the Latin for "after the fact"; Kerlinger changed their name to the too inclusive term "nonexperimental studies" in the next edition (1986). Babbie (1986) refers to them as the "elaboration model." Others refer to them as "causal comparative studies." None of these names seems satisfactory, and since terminology is nonstandard anyway, it seemed wise to invent something descriptive, so I have opted for "after-the-fact natural experiments."

Problems of After-the-Fact Designs

Finding Comparable Groups.   We define the experimental group in terms of people who possess the variable of interest. This characteristic may be either the cause (treatment or independent variable in experimental design terms) or the effect (dependent variable). For example, we might start with people who possess what we presume to be the cause (smoking, high spatial visualization, a record of juvenile delinquency). Or we might define the group in terms of those with an effect (lung cancer, high achievement scores in geometry and mathematics, no high school diploma). Or we may start with individuals with both cause and effect (smokers with cancer). Such individuals, selected from the natural environment, must be taken just as they exist. Their sex, socio-economic status, age, and perceptual ability are already set—they come as a combined set of variables. This complicates the problem of forming comparable groups. It may also give us problems if we want to analyze variables separately. For instance, there may be too few upper-class dropouts to analyze because not many wealthy persons drop out. We can disproportionately sample such cases or markedly increase the sample size to include such rare cases.

We can't randomly assign individuals to groups since our target experimental group is already formed. Yet the control group must be as much like the experimental group as possible except for the characteristic(s) of interest, so we must provide a matching group on all the variables we think are relevant. But what are the relevant variables? We don't always know!

Even when we do, the fact that variables do not act independently but rather, often, in "bundles" or "constellations" gives us problems. Consider, for example, that for some characteristics, such as smokers or dropouts, there is a certain element of self-selection of lifestyle that is almost impossible to duplicate for the control group—otherwise, those people would also be smokers or dropouts. Even when we match on variables such as age and occupation, there are no doubt differences between these groups of people who chose to smoke and those who didn't. The latter, health-conscious and self-controlled enough to avoid smoking, quite possibly have attitudes and personality characteristics that carry over to more than nonsmoking behaviors and that could be related to lung cancer incidence. That makes it hard to relate lung cancer to smoking.

Consider another common problem: we are often asked to evaluate the effectiveness of a program after it has taken place—for example, the establishment of a comparison group for children who received Head Start treatment. We can't ask parents to volunteer their children for Head Start and then randomly assign them to experimental and control groups, withholding treatment from some even though there is money to treat them. Rather we take those most in need and work with them. But how do we find a comparable group? It's not easy. We could take the group of subjects just above the cutoff point. But they already had a better start, so if the Head Start group does not equal or surpass them, we won't know whether it is because they had a better start or because the program is ineffective. Match them with students in another community without a Head Start program? Are there community and background differences? Finding equivalent groups is difficult.

The chain-of-events notion considered in chapter 12 suggests that after-the-fact natural experiments may be examining late links in the causal chain. The critical link may have occurred much earlier. For example, maybe it is really nervousness that causes people to smoke and thence get lung cancer. The real difference between the groups is then the degree of nervousness, and smoking is simply a symptom of the nervousness. We often encounter suggestions like this when presenting the results of an after-the-fact study. That sets us off on a new study to compare groups that are equally nervous, assuming that we can find them, composed of smokers and nonsmokers. And when that study is presented, someone raises a new alternative explanation, which calls for still a new study. The evidence is totally convincing only when nobody can advance a new plausible explanation.

Additional Problems of After-the-Fact Natural Experiments. Like historians, researchers engaging in after-the-fact natural experiments must make do with evidence already gathered. Suppose data on occupation but not age are available for the study of lung cancer. Unless we are ingenious enough to find a way to infer missing data from other sources (for example, matching names with driver's license records), we have to leave open the fact that differences in age between the groups might be an alternative explanation for any difference in cancer rates. If the nonsmokers' group were enough younger, the cancer might not have had time to show up yet. Thus one weakness of such studies is an inability to bring variables under control where no relevant data were gathered on them.

A second weakness is an inability to manipulate the treatment. Because smoking is self-chosen, randomization is impossible. Neither can we vary the cause in a particular pattern to show that the effect displays the same pattern as the cause; if natural variation happens to do this, we are very fortunate.

A third problem is that of the establishment of precedence of cause. Suppose that we do find that lung cancer patients smoked more and are nervous. Did nervousness come before smoking, which preceded cancer, or did smoking come before nervousness? Unless prior data are available, order of precedence may be hard to determine.

All of the foregoing makes such studies particularly vulnerable to second guessing, to alternative explanations that in turn raise new plausible explanations despite a carefully crafted chain of reasoning.

Example of an After-the-Fact Natural Experiment

Carlsmith's (1964) study of the effect of early father absence on boys' scholastic aptitude is an interesting example of an after-the-fact natural experiment. It deals with the effect of nonmanipulable variables—sex of subject and father absence—and shows the combination of arranging available data with an active pursuit of missing data to study a phenomenon. As part of a larger study of sexual identity, Carlsmith studied the differential development of mathematical and verbal ability.

Females are generally superior to males in verbal ability, whereas males are usually superior to females in quantitative areas. The Math and Verbal Aptitude scores of the College Entrance Examination Board seemed to be good operational definitions of these two abilities. Carlsmith postulated that boys deprived of their father's presence in the early formative years should show a greater similarity to the feminine pattern than those whose parents were not absent. Since children born during the years of World War II were just finishing high school and attending college at the time of this study, it was a fortuitous time to study these students—the condition for this natural experiment.

Using college freshmen at Harvard as well as seniors in nearby high schools as her example, Carlsmith administered a simple questionnaire to learn if and when the father was absent. Students whose fathers were in the service overseas were selected, their SAT scores were obtained, and a Math minus Verbal score was computed. Carlsmith was able to show that if the father had left before the son was 12 months old and was gone for more than a year, the son's Verbal score is relatively superior to the math score. Math ability increases with shorter separations or if separation occurs later in life.

Having shown this, the problem now becomes one of eliminating plausible alternative explanations, that is, asking what else might also account for this relationship. Carlsmith used the discussion section of her article to consider the most serious alternative explanations. For instance, it might be that the Verbal score is potentiated instead of the Math score being depressed by the father's absence. Carlsmith called on studies of problem-solving ability to argue that what is being measured by the two scores is a conceptual approach to problem solving instead of a difference in aptitude. It is rather surprising to find this argument at the end of the article when the prior presentation of the data all argued in terms of the fact that these were differences in aptitude. This illustrates some of the difficulties of eliminating alternative explanations in after-the-fact experiments.

A second alternative explanation deals with the possibility that anxiety in the father-absent boys had more of an effect on the Math than the Verbal scores. An earlier study suggested that the Verbal scores are more resistant to the effects of stress. This is countered with a second study in which both Verbal and Math scores show the effect of stress except in individuals who were severely emotionally disturbed; these students weren't.

Carlsmith also studied small subsamples matched on such variables as age, occupation, and education of parents; number and age of siblings; and high school experience in the subject matter. She found that the relationship held, thus ruling out these variables as alternatives. Lastly, to bolster the conclusions, she cited other studies with similar findings.

Whether the reader is convinced depends on whether the arguments for alternative explanations are accepted and whether other alternatives the researcher did not consider important are advanced by the reader. The study illustrates the logic used, however, as well as the difficulties encountered.

Published reports on after-the-fact natural experiments nearly always support the presumed relationship they set out to demonstrate. Unless the after-the-fact evidence is clearly contrary to either normal expectations or those created by previous research, a study showing the lack of a relationship would probably not be published. After all, there are so many variables we could study after the fact that *wouldn't* show something. Unless there is a strong rationale (explanation credibility), negative studies can rarely compete for precious publication space.

- After-the-fact natural experiments provide a comparison of a target group of interest possessing either a cause, an effect, or both with a group so constructed as to be comparable in all important ways.
- The latter does not possess the presumed cause and so, it is hoped, does not show the effect.
- Alternatively, we may start with persons with the effect and show that they were exposed to the cause, whereas similar persons without the effect were not.
- The intent is retrospectively to show a causal relation.
- Besides the usual problems of historical studies, the difficulty of constructing comparable groups that exclude alternative explanations is especially serious.
- Such studies are often used to gather evidence for policy decisions where experimentation is impossible.

HALLMARKS OF HISTORICAL AND AFTER-THE-FACT DESIGNS

1. A reasonably complete search for sources of evidence has been conducted.
2. The sources of information are indicated.
3. Primary sources were used; where secondary sources were used, this is made clear.
4. The approach to the evidence appears evenhanded and open.
5. A credible rationale or explanation is presented. If it builds on previously available evidence, it extends, clarifies, and revises prior interpretations.
6. The evidence presented is appropriate to the constructs employed.
7. Sufficient instances of evidence are given that the reader is able to judge its adequacy.
8. Important alternative explanations have been carefully weighed and, as appropriate, rejected or presented as possibilities.
9. There is a close correspondence between the rationale and the evidence.
10. Where generality is claimed, evidence from more than one instance is cited (preferably considerably more, depending on the generality sought).
11. If the authors are venturing into a field or time period that is new to them, they teamed up with someone having the appropriate expertise.
12. The authors makes clear any biases that might have affected their judgment.

In addition to these hallmarks, an after-the-fact natural experiment has that of a comparison group that disallows any serious alternative explanation of the data. Difficult to fulfill as this may be, it is a key hallmark.

SUMMARY

The historian, in advancing a rationale or an explanation of an event (or a set of them), provides the reasoning that persuades us that the relationship being advanced does exist. The better the match of rationale to events, the more convincing the case. The art and skill of the historian is in the selection and organization of the facts and data to show congruence without distorting either data or theory. Historians range widely, looking for strong and convincing explanations to encompass a set of events. They borrow from all the behavioral sciences the propositions, viewpoints, and research methods that can be applied to retrospective data.

After-the-fact natural experiments are basically simulated experiments using past data. They involve the comparison of data previously gathered for a target group with previously gathered, retrospective, or new data from a group intentionally formed to be comparable in relevant ways. The intent is to show a relationship, ideally a causal one, between variables present in different amounts in the two groups. Such studies are used by historians to show relationships in historical times, as well as contemporaneously where experimentation is impossible. In either case, they must try to make sense of the natural distribution of characteristics and events. Many policy studies regarding the effects of drugs, lifestyles, and past educational practices are of this nature.

ADDITIONAL READING

Aydelotte, Bogue, and Fogel (1972) presents nine examples of historical studies demonstrating different quantitative approaches.

Barzun and Graff (1985) is readable and practical, with much useful detail.

Fischer (1970) is a fantastic laundry list of errors of historians, full of lively examples.

See also Gottschalk (1956); Moehleman et al. (1969); Nevins (1975).

IMPORTANT TERM

After-the-fact natural experiments

APPLICATION PROBLEMS

1. Burton (1988) traced the evolution of school discipline in the United States from the mid-nineteenth century until the present.

At the heart of her study was the analysis of 475 journal articles from 1940 to 1980 with a specific focus on elementary public schooling. This was supported by a general review of the history of school discipline and an analysis of the social, political, and economic changes in American society based on such social analysts as Galbraith, Henry, and Potter.

Burton delineated three historical periods, indicating what she thought to be the overriding societal philosophy pertaining to school discipline for each, and compared them to the modern era. From the mid- to late nineteenth century there was a search for a theory of discipline that would "provide self-disciplined citizens and workers for a rapidly growing, industrializing young nation"—a production-oriented society. During the first quarter of the twentieth century, the philosophy of John Dewey, the spirit of social cooperation, and community life dominated—interest was the key to discipline. During the mid-twentieth century, discipline was based on self-control and the recognition of each individual's "responsibilities to the group consonant with good citizenship in a democratic society." In the last half of the twentieth century, two major social changes affected both the purpose and the methods of school discipline. One was a recognition of social diversity and individual rights. The second was a shift from a producer to a consumer society—increased consumption became the cornerstone of democratic and economic security.

On the basis of this analysis, Burton argued that American educators now face unrecognized and therefore unaddressed conflicting social purposes. They are disciplining for the needs of a consumer-oriented society, the purpose of which is present gratification. This runs counter to traditional American beliefs and standards— "the production-oriented goals of thrift, sobriety, diligence, responsibility, hard work, and delayed gratification are not conducive to, [or] supportive of, a consumer society." The response of educators has been to concentrate on workable methods of immediate control in the classroom without regard to general, long-term social purpose.

How does Burton demonstrate internal validity (LP) in this study?

2. Laslett (1978) describes past and present family structure in American society, how and why it has changed, and its importance in contemporary society. She begins her study with a brief discussion of two contradictory sociological views of family. The first is that the institution is in trouble—that it is "alive but not well," a view predicting its demise and borne out by a steady increase in divorce rates and in family violence. The second view is that the family is "here to stay," contending that society depends on it for the development of personal identity and the satisfaction of personal needs.

Laslett argues the second viewpoint, stating that "changes in household composition, in the demography of kinship, and in the relationship between family and other institutions have contributed to the greater emotional significance of the family through their impact on the socialization process" and have increased its significance for personal identity and emotional gratification. The problems of divorce and violence are the negative result of the intense feelings generated by this increased intimacy.

To make her argument, Laslett attempts to trace the changes over time and compare family in the past to that in the present. Thus household composition of preindustrial society is held to have included others unrelated to the conjugal family unit, such as boarders, lodgers, and employees; today's family rarely does. Further, in the past, adolescence tended to be spent outside the family home (job hunting, apprenticeships, etc.). Today, adolescents tend to remain at home with increased identification of the self based on the particular family. Increased life span and improved means of communication have led to the modern availability of ascendant kin—grandparents, aunts, and uncles—who may elaborate the meaning of kinship.

Finally, the ideology of family living has changed from the Puritan view of family as guardian of the public good to that of the private family and the home as a personal sanctuary where a sense of personal control and intimacy can be found. This has been further accentuated by the separation of home and work and of home and schooling. These historical changes have resulted in an increased weight of meaning attached to the personal relations of the family.

What has Laslett attempted to do in this study? Is her argument convincing?

3. Genesee (1976, 1978) examined the importance of general academic ability for success in both Early Total Immersion (entry at kindergarten and instruction during the first three years totally in French) and one-year Late Immersion (entry in grade 7 and program half in English, half in French). Students were native English-speaking Canadians. Using the Lorge-Thorndike group-administered IQ test, students were classified into three groups: below average, average, and above average. Academic achievement was assessed by a battery of English language, French language, and mathematics tests and compared to students in the regular English program in the same grades.

Comparisons in the three ability levels on the English-language tests indicated no significant difference between those in the two immersion programs and those in the regular program. As expected, immersion students significantly outperformed their regular English-program counterparts on all of the French-language tests (listening comprehension, speaking, reading, and grammar). Further, although low-ability immersion students scored significantly lower on the literacy-based French-language skills (reading) than students in the other groups, they scored at the same level on tests that assessed interpersonal com-munication skills (speaking and listening). This pattern was most consistent with the Early Total Immersion students. Thus Genesee concluded that immersion students, especially those of below-average ability (thought to be most at risk), were not handicapped in their first-language development as a result of being in the program and benefited from increased competency in the second language.

Is Genesee able to demonstrate satisfactory internal validity (LP) in these studies?

4. A 1986 study by De Back and Mentkowski attempted to answer the question of whether or not nurses with baccalaureate degree preparation were more competent than those graduating from a hospital-based or two-year diploma program. They hypothesized that baccalaureate graduate nurses would have more nursing competencies than other graduates, as would nurses with more experience regardless of training. These competencies were broadly defined as a set of "generic" abilities that represent the underlying characteristics of nursing performance. The investigators described these in behavioral terms inferred from descriptions of effective and ineffective behaviors on the part of professional nurses.

To do so, they selected three midwestern health care settings with excellent reputations: an acute-care setting, a long-term care environment, and a community agency. Nursing staff members were asked to cite "outstanding" and "good" nurses; 90 percent of them returned the questionnaire. A group of 45 "outstanding" nurses and 38 "good" nurses equally weighted for education were selected for interviews. They were asked to describe three critical incidents in which they felt they were effective and three in which they were ineffective. They also completed a biographical questionnaire. There was no significant relationship between the nominations and either education or experience.

A codebook model of nine generic nursing competencies (conceptualizing, emotional stamina, ego strength, positive expectations, independence, reflective thinking, helping, influencing, and coaching) was developed from the interviews and used to evaluate 502 critical incidents gathered. A 2 × 2 analysis of variance (education × experience) yielded statistically significant results in favor of baccalaureate preparation for six of the nine competencies: independence, ego strength, coaching, helping, conceptualizing, and reflective thinking. Three statistically significant effects favoring the two-year program were also shown (influencing, conceptualizing, and helping). There were no significant interaction effects (between education and experience), but level of education was significantly correlated with setting (the community agency had almost all baccalaureate-prepared nurses) and, in the acute-care setting, with supervisory position.

De Back and Mentkowski concluded from this analysis that nurses with baccalaureate preparation exhibited more competencies than those with associate degrees or diplomas and that such education had long-term benefits. Was this an after-the-fact natural experiment? Are the researchers' conclusions warranted?

Compare your answers with those on pages 720–721.

========================= APPLICATION EXERCISE =========================

How might your problem be examined in historical perspective? What might this add to your understanding of it? How might it give a clearer picture of the causal chain of events? What, if any, might be the problem of obtaining data and records? Of authenticating them?

Could your problem be examined as an after-the-fact natural experiment? What might be the problems of constructing an adequate comparison group? What alternative explanations might such a group be open to? Is there any way of reducing their plausibility or eliminating them?

CHAPTER
20

Evaluation Studies

Evaluative investigation is an art. The design must be chosen afresh in each
new undertaking and the choices to be made are almost innumerable. Each
feature . . . offers particular advantages and entails particular sacrifices.
Lee J. Cronbach, Designing Evaluations of Educational and Social Programs

Conceptualizing an evaluation depends on understanding self-interest:
yours and theirs. Useful evaluations put theirs first.
Michael Quinn Patton, Qualitative Evaluation Methods

OVERVIEW

Evaluation differs from research not by its methods, which are borrowed from
research, but in other aspects:

- It is **decision-driven** instead of hypothesis-driven. That is, its intent is to
  facilitate making a decision about the worth of something. Like research,
  it seeks a consensus around the proper interpretation of data, but the
  consensus may be limited to two persons—the evaluator and the client.
  Alternatively, it may be broader, as when a congressional committee, a
  group of decision makers, or people affected by the outcome (**stakeholders**)
  are involved. Any way we look at it, however, evaluation generally deals
  with a more targeted group than research.
- Because it is decision-driven, the value of an evaluation lies in its usefulness
  in that process. Therefore, **utilization** is a prime criterion. An evaluation that
  is a nice piece of research but does not create the desired consensus and is
  therefore not accepted as a basis for decision making has failed its purpose.
- Because utilization requires trust in the results, the process of evaluation
  may be as important as the product.
- Policy choice is nearly always made on the basis of incomplete information. The intent of evaluations is to reduce the uncertainty, to provide
  an information-rich decision-making environment. Just as with research,
  absolute proof cannot be given, but by providing information that is plausible

even though not completely certain, evaluations provide a better basis for informed action.

- Because the audience is limited and the goal is usefulness, the way in which results are reported can and must be tailored to that audience. This may include audience involvement in the evaluation. It may mean giving audience members control over certain parts of the process of evaluation. It may mean using a form of evaluation that is consistent with the audience's idea of what a social science ought to and can be.

CHAPTER CONTENTS

Introduction 525
    Examples of Evaluation 527
    A Comparison of Research and
        Evaluation Studies 527
Alternative Evaluation Approaches 529
    Objective- and Goal-based
        Approaches 529
    Goal-free Evaluation 530
    Management-oriented
        Approaches 531
    Consumer-oriented
        Approaches 533
    Expertise-oriented Approaches 534
    Adversarial Approaches 536
    Naturalistic Approaches 536
    Participant-oriented
        Approaches 538

The Panorama of Evaluation Choices 539
    Choices Affecting the Entire
        Evaluation 540
    Choices at Different Stages
        in the Evaluation 541
The Political Nature of Evaluation 543
    The Conservative Nature of
        Evaluation 544
    Who Controls the Study? 545
    Pressures for a Favorable
        Report 545
The Evaluation Standards: Protection
    for Evaluators and Clients 546
Hallmarks of Evaluation Studies:
    Suggestions for Doing Evaluations 549
Summary 550

INTRODUCTION

Evaluation studies are concerned with improving a program or product (**formative evaluation**) or determining its value or worth (**summative evaluation**). The term *evaluation* applies so broadly, however, that it can be applied to almost anything—a person, for instance. Each such evaluation category (personnel evaluation, teaching evaluation, student achievement evaluation) would require a chapter by itself to do it justice. This chapter, therefore, is limited to the evaluation of social and educational programs and of products, such as curricula and instructional materials.

Policy research is often indistinguishable from evaluation. Policy research is the broader category, including the search for feasible alternative solutions to problems, often by simulations, as well as the determination of their comparative effectiveness. Most federal program evaluations are considered policy research since they are intended to lead to the development or modification of social legislative policy.

Evaluation as an aspect of research had been developing for years. But it blossomed in the 1970s, largely as a result of the simultaneous trend toward management by objectives and the interest of the federal government in knowing if its expensive social programs were effective. Probably no area of behavioral science methodology has received as much attention; in 1977 alone, $234 million was earmarked for program evaluation in 39 different government departments and agencies.

As with most such emphases, when the pendulum swings one way, it also swings back; evaluation is now budgeted at more modest levels. But the scrutiny of evaluation processes left a residue of new thinking and advanced our understanding. Having no methods of its own, evaluation borrowed from all the social sciences. The importance of utilization forced evaluators to confront questions of when and why knowledge was accepted as such. This made explicit for researchers questions previously largely left to philosophers. It revealed a broad collection of choices for both sponsor and evaluator of ways of doing evaluations. Contributing to these choices were contrasting schools of thought about what evaluation ought to be, some of which are still maturing.

It has been said that knowledge is power. Where some people saw knowledge resulting from evaluation as a tool for more effective management of programs, others saw it as a means of empowerment for the people affected by those programs (House, 1976, 1980; Cronbach, 1982). Where some saw it directed by a highly competent professional opinion, others saw it as a transactional endeavor in which professionals and stakeholders together sought the answers (Rippey, 1973). Where most saw it as a means to conclusions and recommendations, some saw it as a process of negotiation with and among stakeholders, the product being an agenda for further negotiation (Lincoln and Guba, 1986; Argyris, Putnam, and Smith, 1985). Some saw it as an effort to be responsive to the concerns of the stakeholders (Stake, 1991). Where some saw it as embedded in measurement and experimentation, others saw it as a place for connoisseurial judgments by an area's experts (Eisner, 1981). Widely divergent perceptions about the proper role of evaluation have developed and are still being debated.

- Evaluation studies are concerned with improving a product or a program or determining its value or worth.
- Formative evaluation is used in the development stage to guide the evolutionary process.
- Summative evaluation determines the worth of a more mature program or process. But in a sense, even this is formative since it usually leads to appropriate program modification.
- Different points of view with respect to the evaluation process emphasize product, process, stakeholder rights, administrator concerns, and client rights.

Examples of Evaluation

Examples come from the full range of social, educational, psychological, and economic problems. In the field of health, for instance, evaluation of the substitution of nurse practitioners for physicians suggested that the substitution was desirable and cost-effective. It resulted in a loss of income to the physicians, however, because of government reimbursement policies (Spitzer et al., 1974). A negative income tax means that people earning less than a certain income receive payments from the government instead of paying taxes—a minimum income is guaranteed. Evaluation of the effects of guaranteed income on health care showed the effects to be more a function of lifestyle than income (Elesh and Lefcowitz, 1977). When the 55-mile-an-hour speed limit was evaluated in cost-benefit terms, benefits were shown to outweigh the economic cost, though the policy may be a second or third best way of achieving such goals as fuel conservation (Clotfelter and Hahn, 1978). When a correctional institution program was subjected to cost analysis, a 6 percent reduction in recidivism was found but at a cost of $38,000 per inmate (Bloom and Singer, 1979). Some evaluations, such as the negative income tax study, were conducted on a scale of resources undreamed of in the behavioral sciences only a short time ago and still rare.

Many educational programs have been evaluated. Three very different such studies are the evaluation of the Perry Preschool Program, educational vouchers, and Outward Bound. The Perry Preschool Program attempted to show what could be done with preschool programs such as Head Start if carefully developed. The evaluation extended longitudinally, following the students to age 19, and included causal models of what contributed to both positive and negative long-term outcomes (Berrueta-Clement, Barnett, and Weikart, 1985). Voucher programs gave parents and children freedom to use a tuition voucher to choose any school they wished—initial discouragement was misleading, as found in later evaluations (Wortman, Reichardt, and St. Pierre, 1978). Outward Bound is designed to expose participants to the physical challenges of the wild and help them learn more self-reliance. The evaluator went through the program and gave a fascinating qualitative account as well as some quantitative data (Smith et al., 1976).

A Comparison of Research and Evaluation Studies

This chapter is concerned with program and product evaluations commissioned by an administrator, an institution, or a policy-shaping community, often pluralistic in interests (for example, a legislature, a consortium of lobbying or interest groups, a professional association). The concern is to improve a program or product or to determine whether to discontinue, continue, or expand it. Whereas research is designed to discover or validate a hypothesis, evaluations are aimed at helping someone make a decision. They are, therefore, decision-driven.

A research finding can sit on the shelf until someone deems it useful; evaluations, by contrast, are intended to be useful in decision making from the outset, so an evaluation that fails utilization in some way (not always that intended) is an evaluation that has not served its purpose.

To say that evaluations are to be utilized is another way of saying that we are building a consensus around the proper interpretation of the findings. But here the consensus is to be produced among the people intended to use the evaluation product. Primarily this will be the client, if it is a sponsored evaluation. But particularly if the client is the administrator of the program, the client is not the only stakeholder. Equally important, many people would say more so, are other stakeholders: those affected by the program—both directly, as the program's clients, and indirectly, as taxpayers or supporters who are concerned that the program achieve appropriate goals. If the client and stakeholders are to have faith in the product of the evaluation, they must have faith in the process that produced it. Therefore, the evaluation process can be, and often is, as important as the product.

Certainly, some program evaluations are research; they conform to all the criteria of research, are published in research journals, and are intended either to show the superiority of a program over others or to demonstrate that it meets certain standards. But an evaluation that is a nice piece of research but does not create a consensus about a proper interpretation of the data among appropriate groups has failed its purpose.[1]

The key assumption is that the evaluation is decision-driven; the other implications flow from it. Though the characteristics just described are crucial, they by no means reflect all of the decision-driven consequences. A number of implications require that evaluators and sponsors make choices about the initiation, development, conduct, and reporting of the evaluation.[2] These choices have been synthesized into positions about the proper role and conduct of evaluations, positions we will consider next. After that, we will examine stages in the evaluation process and the choices involved.

- Evaluation uses research methods but is decision-driven: the results are intended to be so used.
- Utilization is therefore a prime criterion of a successful evaluation.
- Having faith in the product sufficient for decision-making is another way of talking about building a consensus around the proper interpretation of the data.
- Having faith in the product means having faith in the process by which it was derived.

---

1. Note that consensus within a stakeholder group is not necessarily unanimous. An evaluator may recognize as the client only the person who sponsors the evaluation, with the result that the proper interpretation of the data may be disputed by other stakeholders. Some evaluators consider this appropriate evaluation practice; others do not. The point is that an evaluation should facilitate decision making by someone. Determining who and within what scope may be two of the evaluator's most important and difficult decisions.
2. One consequence of evaluation thought has been an exploration of what a social science ought to be. We will consider this in chapter 24.

- The process may therefore be as important as the product.
- Consensus must be built among the stakeholders, as they are defined by the sponsor and the evaluator.

ALTERNATIVE EVALUATION APPROACHES

Differences in approaches to evaluation tend to be matters of emphasis. Proposers frequently seek to remedy flaws in previous efforts. For example, some perceive that evaluation has always served management to the detriment of consumers; they seek to redress this imbalance. Others intend to provide different kinds of evaluation to fit various management purposes. Let us examine some of the major approaches.[3]

Objective- and Goal-based Approaches

One of the oldest approaches to evaluation was advanced by Ralph W. Tyler in the 1930s (Tyler and Waples, 1930; Tyler 1934). Developed in the context of education, it was intended as a means of building a curriculum and evaluating its success. A **goal-based evaluation** argues that the goals or objectives of an intervention should be stated in terms of **behavioral objectives**. If we can describe the behavior the intervention is intended to bring about, we can recognize whether the program was successful. We use these behavioral descriptions to construct educational objectives. A goal such as "the student should be able to appreciate a painting" would be broken into behavioral statements such as "On studying a painting, the student should be able to describe how the artist used perspective to achieve her goals." The latter is behavior that can be recognized; the former is covert behavior that cannot.

Further, we can use the objective to construct a situation in which, if the behavior has been learned, it can be elicited as an appropriate way of responding. Although this is typically considered a measurement-oriented approach, Tyler did not limit testing to using paper and pencil alone. He indicated that any relevant evidence should be used. Thus as evidence of appreciation of painting, we might search the library records to see if the student checked out prints from the collection of reproductions. If there are records of art gallery attendance, perhaps we might note the number of visits in the gallery's guest book.

This approach emphasizes the specification of the goals or objectives of the intervention and their operationalization in terms of observable behavior. Such specification requires most interveners to think about their program in concrete ways and in a degree of detail not previously considered. It assumes, however, that all goals can be broken into observable behaviors without losing

---

3. This discussion is patterned in large measure after Worthen and Sanders (1987), a very useful treatment of evaluation.

a wholeness or essence that may be a prime characteristic. Thus it is very difficult to specify and observe the affective thrill of a painting that may be considered the very heart of that objective.

Emphasis on measurement and therefore measurable behaviors may simplify the process, but it may also result in emphasizing only the simple behaviors that lend themselves to measurement. Further, by accepting the avowed goals of the program to guide the evaluation, we may miss the actual effects. A boring history curriculum might teach students to dislike history and to gain considerable skill in avoiding being called on. Since these results are not included in the intended goals of the course, the evaluation will not pick up such effects if it focuses only on avowed purposes.

From this comes the concern of who should specify the evaluation objectives. Should it be the sponsor, the program staff, the stakeholders affected by the intervention, some policy-shaping community? If there is agreement on the objectives by the people with an interest in the evaluation, all is well, but in a diverse, pluralistic society, that is unlikely. The sponsor may believe that the main goal of a job-training program is preparing mothers for work; however, program staff may know that, equally important, it provides otherwise unaffordable day care and some time away from children for the mothers themselves. Though these are not incompatible objectives, they could result in quite different outcomes.

Preceding industry's similar "management by objectives" emphasis by many years, the objectives-based approach has been widely used and has had considerable influence. Its most recent manifestation is in the U.S. National Assessment of Educational Progress (NAEP), which determines important common objectives for major areas of the curricula in American schools. The program assesses the achievement of a cross section of pupils with respect to these objectives, allowing comparisons over time as well as, eventually, state by state. Some critics argue that the effect of such an evaluation is not just to find out what is achieved but also to change the curriculum. Teachers will "teach to the test" so that their students show up well. If state-by-state comparisons are made, a national curriculum will in effect be established, and the freedom to choose state and local goals will be diminished.

> Goal-based evaluation takes the intended goals sought for the program, project, or product and determines how thoroughly they have been met. A key factor, or course, is who determines the goals and how. Clients and stakeholders involved in a program or project may differ on these questions.

Goal-free Evaluation

An obvious antidote to goal-based evaluation is **goal-free evaluation**, in which the evaluator examines the implementation of the intervention to determine what the real effects have been and thence to infer what goals have been achieved. These results can then be compared with the goals the program was intended to satisfy to determine the success of the intervention. Proposed by Scriven (1972), the evaluator purposely avoids becoming aware of the goals of the project, having minimal contact with the program manager and staff until the actual outcomes have been determined.

Often side effects are more important than the original goal. For example, the toy-lending library was an intervention intended to help the poor obtain certain advantages of the middle-class home. It made available a collection of toys these households would not otherwise have been able to afford. The librarian who checked out the toys was typically consulted by the mother as to what toys would be most appropriate for her child. A side effect, the education of the mother by the librarian, turned out to be the most important outcome of this project.

Clearly, goal-based and goal-free evaluation can complement each other. A goal-based evaluation could be pursued by an internal evaluator—a staff person or a hired evaluator. A goal-free evaluation could be conducted simultaneously by an external evaluator who has no contact with the project beyond being employed to conduct the evaluation.

Goal-free evaluation examines outcomes and infers the intended goals from these. Goals achieved can then be compared with goals intended.

Management-oriented Approaches

Management-oriented evaluation approaches serve administrators; their intent is to provide information that will improve the administration of the intervention. A management information system provides a continuous evaluation of an operation and may be viewed as formative evaluation. In addition, there are intermittent or cyclical evaluations, which are closer to summative evaluations. Stufflebeam's CIPP model (Stufflebeam and Shinkfield, 1985) is a frequently cited management-oriented approach. It consists of four kinds of decisions, corresponding to the initials of its name:

1. *Context* evaluations involve planning decisions such as identifying the target audience and determining the needs to be met by the intervention. As noted in our job-training example, the need perceived by outsiders is not always the one considered most important by the program's stakeholders.
2. *Input* evaluations involve determining the resources that can be used, the alternative strategies to be considered, and how best to lay a plan that will meet the needs determined through context evaluations.
3. *Process* evaluations examine how well the plan was implemented. They determine where these implementation problems are and ask how they can be solved.
4. *Product* evaluations examine what results were obtained, whether the needs were met or reduced, and what plans should be laid for the future.

Rossi and Freeman (1985) list six areas of accountability and assessment with which managers would typically be concerned. Their titles indicate what is involved more directly than the CIPP model does. The first is the sole focus of most evaluations; the others are relevant areas that should also be considered.

1. *Impact assessment.* This is the usual assessment of whether the intervention achieved its goals.
2. *Efficiency assessment.* Impact is evaluated in relation to program costs; that is, program costs are judged in relation to the benefits as well as cost-benefit assessments of alternatives.
3. *Coverage assessment.* Are all the targets served? What are their numbers and characteristics? What proportion of potential targets are served (the technical term for this is *penetration*)? What proportion drop out (what is the *mortality*)?
4. *Service delivery assessment.* How well does delivery conform to plans? Of the services anticipated, were all actually provided? . . . by appropriately qualified staff? Was quality up to expectations?
5. *Fiscal assessment.* Accountability for funds is clearly important, but in addition there may be questions about the costs per client or per service, about the marginal cost of serving additional clients, and variations in costs depending on load, program site, and other factors.
6. *Legal assessment.* Have legal and quasi-legal concerns, such as "informed consent, protection of privacy, community representation on decision-making boards, equity in provision of services, and cost sharing" (p. 95), been attended to?

Cost-benefit and cost-effectiveness analyses are frequent concerns of administrators. They are alluded to in the input concerns of the CIPP model and the efficiency and fiscal concerns of Rossi and Freeman. Although such procedures are not without controversy, there is some agreement on their major steps and parameters (Levin, 1983; Wortman, 1984; Yates, 1985). **Cost-benefit analysis** requires that the outcomes of the project be translated into monetary terms or some kind of measure of value so that their relation to costs may be determined. This is often a controversial aspect of such studies since it is very difficult to determine the monetary value of, for instance, learning. Health measures are a little easier in the sense of being able to estimate the savings in later medical attention, but the inferences are "soft." Often such analyses are run several times with different assumptions about the value of certain outcomes, and they take into account outside influences such as inflation that would affect the estimates.

Cost-effectiveness analysis allows us to compare and rank "choices among potential programs according to the magnitudes of their effects relative to their costs" (Rossi and Freeman, 1985, p. 330). Cost-effectiveness analysis requires only measures of outcomes across programs in comparable terms; the outcome measures need not be translated into monetary estimates. Hence scores on tests, number of visits, client satisfaction ratings, and so on, may be the basis for comparison among programs in terms of impact. We then find the input costs and relate them to the impact measures on a per-score, per-visit, or per-rating-unit basis. Thus we might find that, for private school speech therapy programs, for each $1,000 spent, 1.2 children take their place in a regular instead of special classroom. We could contrast this with 0.8 child in public schools.

Cost figures are often greatly affected by assumptions regarding difficult-to-estimate indirect cost figures such as the expense of physical facilities in different states of repair, or personnel costs of individuals with different levels of qualifications. Measures of impact are seldom beyond question either. For example, how comparable are judgments above when a child is ready to join the regular classroom, and are they the same in the private as well as the public school program? Such studies should not be taken as the final word in judging a program, but they may provide useful data.

- Evaluation that is intended to inform management has been a focus of considerable interest involving different models.
- Cost-benefit analyses translate benefits into monetary terms so that judgments comparing the use of resources for different goals can be compared.
- Cost-effectiveness analyses make comparisons of different treatments to attain the same goal so that the most effficient and effective may be selected.

Consumer-oriented Approaches

If there is a management-oriented evaluation approach, can a **consumer-oriented evaluation** approach be far behind? Many individuals have developed consumer-oriented criteria and checklists for use with educational materials such as curricula, textbooks, films, and other instructional devices. Here, as elsewhere, some of these efforts have been spurred by the decision-making needs of the federal government to judge whether the materials from its research and development efforts were worth the additional dissemination investment. The Joint Dissemination Review panel of the U.S. Department of Education, for example, established standards (Tallmadge, 1977) to determine approval of a new program for deployment by the National Dissemination Network.

Scriven (1974), the Educational Products Information Exchange (EPIE), and Tyler, Klein, and Associates (1976) have all produced product checklists. Tyler and Klein's list is based on a set of standards for such materials similar to those produced for tests. It is reproduced here.

Is the value of the objectives substantiated?
Is the basis on which the content of the program was selected explained?

Are students given opportunities to practice skills that are related to what they are supposed to be able to do at the end of instruction?

Is an evaluation package available?

Does the technical manual (or guide) state what the students are supposed to be able to do (or think or feel) at the end of instruction or use of the materials?

Does the technical manual (or guide) describe the students for whom they were developed? (by age, grade, race, socioeconomic level, etc.)

Is evidence available about the effectiveness and efficiency of the materials?

Is evidence available as to unanticipated outcomes?

Does the technical manual cite any field-testing that could be used to estimate the effect the materials will have on your students?

Does the technical manual or guide describe what teacher skills will be necessary?

Does the price listed represent the full cost of utilization of the materials?

Does the technical manual give instructions or cautions about special care or special facilities which may be needed?

Is evidence from recent studies on the use of materials reported?[4]

EPIE was started as a kind of consumers union for educational products. It intended to gather field reports from member institutions, then collate and redistribute this information to show how well various products were working. Although this model did not work as planned, it has produced a variety of useful evaluations of materials and equipment.[5]

> Consumer-oriented evaluation has focused on the evaluation of products and the determination of appropriate criteria for judging them.

Expertise-oriented Approaches

The **expertise-oriented evaluation** approach (Eisner 1976, 1981) is the most common and the oldest form of evaluation. It is ubiquitous: personnel promotion, salary raises, award of funding, certification or accreditation, evaluation of essay and oral examinations (including doctoral and publication peer reviews). The familiar charges of "cronyism," bias, and unequal standards applied to different people or by different judges all attest to the difficulties of this method. It depends on the wisdom, fairness, integrity, professional knowledge, and judgment of the "expert." It is most widely used where measurement is impossible because of the many "right" answers. A pilot can fly

---

4. L. L. Tyler, M. F. Klein, and Associates, *Evaluating and Choosing Curriculum and Instructional Materials.* Copyright © 1976 Educational Resource Associates. Used by permission.

5. EPIE reports are available from EPIE, 475 Riverside Drive, New York, NY 10027.

from Chicago to New York in many different ways under a variety of flight conditions. The combinations of possibilities are so numerous that measurement would be difficult, if not impossible. But evaluation by a flight observer is considered the fairest method of assessing such a performance.

What can be done to make the judgments less subject to criticism? Expert judgment evaluations that conform to the following five criteria probably provide the least opportunity for criticism of unfairness:

1. Evaluations are made in a structured way that all agree is fair. What evidence will be available, what kinds of individuals will judge it, what the criteria will be, and on what cycle the judging will be done—all are clearly stated and understood.
2. Criteria for judgment are publicly available in written form, preferably have been arrived at by the efforts of both the judges and the judged, and are as close to low-inference criteria as is appropriate, given what is to be evaluated.
3. More than one judge is involved in the evaluation. Just how many should be used is hard to say. one is too few; 15, too many.
4. A written report of the evaluation is made available in some appropriate form to the person evaluated or to some other trusted party who will provide an appropriate summary of the judgment. The person evaluated has the opportunity to respond, if desired.
5. The report of the evaluation and any response, together with minutes of any meetings, should be reviewed and approved by a group that is selected as a fair review group by both judges and judged.

The public nature of the process and the criteria go a long way toward preventing abuses. The use of more than one evaluator makes it less likely that any one judge's attitude or personality will determine the outcome. The requirement of a written report makes it less likely that the Dr. Fell phenomenon can operate.[6] The opportunity for presenting a rebuttal helps point up aspects that may have escaped notice and hence resulted in inopportune decisions. Lastly, the approval of a group that reviews the whole procedure, including any response to the evaluation, provides a safety net for catching flaws that had not previously been provided for.

> The judgment of a clinical or connoisseurial expert is often necessary if there are many ways of achieving a goal, the criteria are very complex, or comparable evaluations are not made often enough to warrant developing a low-inference procedure for any one type or style.

---

6. This phenomenon was named after a nursery rhyme: "I do not like you, Dr. Fell; the reason why I cannot tell; I only know and know quite well, I do not like you, Dr. Fell."

Adversarial Approaches

The model of a law court, continually evaluating cases presented disputatiously by opposing parties, is a ready-made analogy for **adversarial evaluation**. As a model, however, the strict procedures of the courtroom have been considerably loosened. Wolf (1975, 1979) proposed a judicial evaluation model that included a statement of charges, opposing presenters of the cases who could call witnesses (including experts), a judge or hearings officer, and a jury or panel to render a verdict. Four stages were proposed: (1) issue generation, in which the possible issues are developed for consideration; (2) issue selection, in which the issue to be argued at the hearing is selected and further developed as necessary; (3) preparation of the cases, in which the presenters seek appropriate evidence, try out their arguments on friends and supporters, and generally develop the approach they will use at the hearing; and (4) prehearing meetings, during which procedures are agreed on. As Wolf (1979) makes clear, the object is not so much to win as to provide an insightful examination that educates the audience to the complexity of the issues. The interchange among the presenters may result in insights into one another's points of view that themselves become major outcomes of the process.

The process is expensive and may be used as an alternative way of analyzing and presenting data collected under another evaluation scheme. It is an interesting way of presenting evidence and may be of special value for topics of great interest, especially since all sides get their due. One large-scale trial sponsored by the National Institute of Education (NIE) was on the topic of minimum competency testing. The trial was recorded and televised; a three-volume transcript was prepared by NIE; and Popham (1981) and Madaus (1981) presented their cases in print. There was no jury; the intent was to educate audiences to the complexity of the issues.

The complexities of procedure must not overwhelm the process, and the focus should be kept on illuminating the issues and presenting points of view. Where more than two points of view are dominant, the format may follow the model of a hearing more than that of a trial. The ability of the presenters must be comparable; otherwise, as in legal trials with star lawyers, the case may be swayed more by style than by the evidence.

Adversarial evaluations, borrowing procedures from law, are useful for educating a public or set of stakeholders regarding the complexity of the problem and the value judgments involved.

Naturalistic Approaches

As Rossi and Wright (1986) point out, there is a belief that

> social programs tend to develop their goals as they proceed; thus to saddle them with evaluations that stress *a priori* goals does an injustice to the

evolving nature of most programs. . . . Many potentially innovative social projects are funded with vague goals supposed to be achieved using unspecified procedures. An experimental approach that demands fixed procedures and unchanging goals simply does not work in the "real world" where both goals and procedures are continually being changed in an effort to find something that appears to work. (p. 60)

Researchers uncomfortable with the objectives-oriented approach typically believe that there are better ways of gathering data. Worthen and Sanders (1987) found this beautifully descriptive quotation in Huxley (1982):

> The best way to find things out is not to ask questions at all. If you fire off a question, it is like firing off a gun—bang it goes, and everything takes flight and runs for shelter. But if you sit quite still and pretend not to be looking, all the little facts will come and peek round your feet, situations will venture forth from thickets and intentions will creep out and sun themselves on a stone: and if you are very patient, you will see and understand a great deal more than a man with a gun does.

Not that observers will necessarily be that passive—especially once they think they understand the situation, they may poke and query too—but the difference in attitude was well expressed by Huxley.

This obviously suggests the qualitative research method called "naturalistic" or sometimes "responsive" in the context of evaluation. But whereas qualitative evaluators are guided solely by their personal understanding of what they perceive and are told, researchers engaged in **naturalistic evaluation** gather evidence that is responsive to the stakeholder audience. "The responsive approach is an attempt to respond to the natural ways in which people assimilate information and arrive at understanding" (Stake, 1975, p. 23). It describes the activities of a program and leaves inferences regarding the nature of goals and of success in reaching them to the audience to infer: "We need a reporting procedure for facilitating vicarious experience. We need to portray complexity. We need to convey holistic impression, the mood, even the mystery of the experience" (p. 23). The report of one example of responsive evaluation included detailed descriptions of science programs and totaled well over 1,000 pages (Stake and Easley, 1978a, 1978b). The typical report may be an informal one instead of, as in this case, a published volume, but evidence of results is likely to be presented in case studies of a small sample of persons affected. But since qualitative researchers are likely to find multiple perceptions and value patterns, the findings are likely to emphasize the pluralistic nature of the situation and to present alternative instead of single recommendations.

Clearly, results of this kind are sometimes more easily understood than scores on tests, examinations, or behavior checklists newly minted to cover the goals of a particular project. Where statistics seem to be accepted with a shrug, the portrayal of individuals in a case study can be the stuff of which headlines are made that sway legislatures to action. So presenting the evidence in a "natural" way has its advantages. And for projects still in the discovery stage or trying to find their way, the descriptive approach has its advantages.

But this qualitative approach also has its limits. For large-scale projects with clear goals and established procedures, the qualitative approach is likely to yield questionably representative and fuzzy estimates of success. In addition, to be truly representative, the amount of data gathered would be large and very expensive to collect, process, and present. It has been noted that the large-scale projects to which qualitative approaches were applied, such as Model Cities (Kaplan, 1973) and revenue sharing (Nathan, Cook, and Rawling, 1981), had only vaguely stated goals.

- Naturalistic or responsive evaluation seeks to portray the complexity of situations in a way that people naturally gather information and assimilate understanding.
- It has advantages, particularly where the project is small and where goals are not sharply defined.
- It may be less effective with programs having sharply defined goals and with large projects.

Participant-oriented Approaches

As you can see, stakeholders are involved in the qualitative approach, where large amounts of descriptive data may be presented to them for interpretation. Indeed, many advocates of qualitative evaluation favor **participant-oriented evaluation**, the involvement of stakeholders in the evaluation process well beyond mere interpretation of the evidence. If we return to the prime assumption that a successful evaluation is one that is used, then clearly one of the most effective ways of getting the evidence used is to involve the stakeholders in as much of the evaluation process as possible. Although it may make them more aware of the fallibility and inevitably incomplete nature of the evidence, it should also make them more properly cautious about drawing inferences from it.

Rippey (1973) noted that the findings and recommendations of evaluations done by an evaluator and a sponsor and then delivered to the stakeholders as a *fait accompli* were often rejected. But if the stakeholders had a role in the evaluation process, what he called "transactional evaluation," rejection was less likely, not only because they had ownership in the process and might therefore trust it more, but also because they had become educated to the problem in the process of evaluating it.

Guba and Lincoln (1987) have provoked considerable thought about the stakeholder's role in evaluation. They espouse responsive evaluation but go beyond it to what they are calling fourth-generation evaluation. Taking the point of view of the qualitative method (see chapter 15), they argue that all reality is constructed.

The concept of a single objective reality onto which inquiry can converge . . . is replaced by the concept that reality is *multiple* and *constructed* in form. . . .

> These constructions are made by persons and it is in the minds of persons
> that one find them, not "out there." (p. 76)

They argue for value pluralism and for involving all stakeholders: "Recognizing
that different stakeholders may base their judgments on very different value
patterns, [the evaluator] is concerned that no one of them be given unfair
reference" (p. 76).

The role of the evaluator, in this model, becomes that of a negotiator.

> Once the concept of value-pluralism is admitted and the criterion of fair-
> ness is invoked, it becomes plain that fair judgments can be reached only
> through negotiation, if at all. . . . The stakeholding audiences are given
> the opportunity to provide inputs *at every stage* of the evaluation. . . . The
> inclusion of these divergent views into anything resembling a viable course
> of action requires extreme political dexterity, persuasiveness, compromise,
> and let it be noted, integrity. . . . *Evaluation is a social-political process.*" (Guba
> and Lincoln, 1987, pp. 78–79)

In addition, it is clear that the evaluator is both learner and teacher. There is
a concern that this method of evaluation will be rejected by clients, administrators, and sponsors because of the power sharing that it implies.

The position is still evolving and, though not yet widely embraced, it
poses real challenges to previous approaches, causing careful thought to be
given to the points made. Even if not adopted in its entirely, it will probably cause evaluators either to consider new options or to provide shifts in
emphasis.

> The results of participant-oriented evaluations are more likely to be accepted
> and used by stakeholders since they have a hand in developing them.
> This shifts the role of the evaluator to consultant, teacher, and negotiator.
> The power sharing involved is not acceptable to all administrators.

THE PANORAMA OF EVALUATION CHOICES

The variety of positions described in the foregoing suggests many of the
choices among which evaluator, sponsor, and stakeholders must decide.
House (1990) cites a multidimensional scaling exercise by Williams (1989) of
the positions of 14 evaluation theorists. "He found the major theoretical
issue on which they were differentiated was qualitative versus quantitative
methodology" (p. 26). The second was whether studies should be used to hold
individuals accountable for the results or mainly to inform. "The third . . . was
client participation versus nonparticipation" (p. 26). In addition to these major
issues, there are others that affect an evaluation. It would be redundant to

point out all the choice points. Therefore, we shall examine selected choices, some influencing the entire evaluation, others only certain stages of it.

Choices Affecting the Entire Evaluation

Most of the choices that affect the entire evaluation are suggested in the differences among the positions we described:

1. Who should evaluate? Should it be a formative or a summative evaluation? Cronbach (1982) rightly argues that in an ultimate sense, all evaluation is formative since summative judgments have a formative effect on policy. Nonetheless, there is a sense in which the distinction is useful, not the least of which is whether to use an internal or an external evaluator. Typically, an external evaluator evokes more trust in the results of a summative evaluation. An internal evaluator might be influenced not only by friendly feelings for colleagues but also by the possibility of eliminating his or her own job.

2. Related to the formative/summative distinction is whether the intervention is perceived as new and evolving or whether it is a stable one that has reached relative maturity. This will affect the evaluation approach, as an objective-based approach is probably less appropriate to an evolving project than to a mature one.

3. Who besides the evaluator should be involved in decisions? The sponsor? Almost by necessity, sponsors are involved if they choose to be. Program staff? If it is a formative evaluation, involvement of both staff and stakeholders may be welcomed since all have a stake in improving the project. But a summative evaluation, which may mean the termination of the project, causes divergent interests to enter. When resources are taken from other programs to create a magnet school in the inner city, there are conflicting interests when that program is evaluated for continuance. The answer in any given situation is a combination of values, political reality (the art of the possible), negotiating skills of the various parties, administrative philosophy and style, the interests of the sponsor, and, sometimes, the terms of the legislation that allocated the funds. Each situation will be unique.

4. Also related is whether the evaluation is intended to be large-scale, with generality sought, or small-scale, with limited generality. This also affects the possible approaches because it is difficult to use a qualitative approach in large-scale evaluations where generality is sought.

Choices affecting the entire evaluation include these:

- Who should do the evaluation, and should it be formative or summative?
- Is the intervention evolving or stable?
- Who besides the evaluator should be involved in the decisions?
- Is generality sought?

Choices at Different Stages in the Evaluation

Problem Formulation. Programs don't always start out with clear goals. Head Start, for instance, was intended to improve the lot of culturally deprived preschool children so that once they entered school, they would not fall further and further behind. But what was its real goal? It could be conceived as many things: a supplement to a relatively uneducated mother's efforts to bring up children; to socialize children into middle-class norms who would otherwise have accepted lower-class ones; to give them better nutrition and identify children needing medical attention earlier than the usual school entry age; to provide the hidden curriculum of the middle-class home, lack of which would put children at a disadvantage; to provide mental stimulation to the psychological growth that should have been taking place but might not under cultural deprivation.

Boruch and Gomez (1977) note three problems in identifying and measuring treatment in evaluations: (1) vaguely formulated policy (for example, racial integration is operationalized as a program, such as busing, when real racial integration clearly involves much more than that, (2) imperfectly implemented programs, and (3) programs variously received or delivered at the individual level—for example, tutors "do not spend the same time with each child nor are [they] uniformly enthusiastic, energetic or perceptive with each child" (p. 427).

This doesn't end the list, but it does suggest the problems of the evaluator in trying to determine what to include in an evaluation and how to set priorities. Further, it does not begin to look at the needs of stakeholders. For example, the child care provided by Head Start was as important as the education for the many stakeholders who could not afford day care. No doubt, perceived through their eyes, there were other advantages and disadvantages. In this, as with many problems, a needs analysis of the client group might have been a place to start in defining the problem. Needs analyses are very helpful since they reveal whether the proposed solution is addressing the problems that are important to the program's clients. It is quite possible to have a fine program that leaves the most pressing needs untouched while addressing lesser ones.

Needs analysis, whereby a situation may be seen differently from various perspectives, raises the question of whose definition of the problem should be used. Should it be that of the sponsor? The sponsor may have a clear-cut set of goals, whereas the staff sees situations as much more fluid, with goals emerging from action. Should it be the staff? The staff may set goals that are less important to clients than others. Whose view should prevail?

This, like many other concerns, needs to be negotiated at the outset by the evaluator. As noted, many evaluation theorists are egalitarian in outlook and argue that all stakeholders should be involved in at least the planning of the evaluation. But as Cronbach (1982) correctly points out, this is a political act that imposes the values of the investigator on the sponsor. Employed by a sponsor who is very clear about wanting to know whether the intended goals were indeed served, evaluators may have little choice: accept the sponsor's terms, or do not do the study. When we discuss evaluation standards later in this chapter, we will return to this as one of several dilemmas the evaluator faces.

Of considerable importance at this and other stages is the investigator's role in teasing out the implications of a policy or the dimensions of a program (Cronbach, 1982). For example, an evaluation of most written policies on mainstreaming would show that it would apply equally well to keeping gifted and talented children in the mainstream as well as the handicapped. That implication may not be acceptable and call for rethinking what is meant by mainstreaming. The evaluator as educator is an important role.

- Needs analyses help to ensure that the intervention meets the needs of clients as well as those of the sponsor.
- The implications of policy sometimes go beyond those anticipated; the evaluator should tease them out if possible.

Design. Design is under the evaluator's control in policy research where a new or a proposed policy is under trial, as in the large-scale field experiments of the 1960s and 1970s. The best-noted evaluations were the negative income tax studies, which were basically experiments to determine the effects of income maintenance, especially as work disincentives. But there were also studies involving prisoner release, police patrols, medical insurance, and housing.[7] In all instances, these were "true to life" studies where the policy involved was used in a limited geographic area with random assignment to treatment and control. Thus unintended effects, such as the negative income tax's family breakup where both members of the family could qualify for support, were uncovered.

The significant thing about these and similar studies is that they demonstrated that large-scale evaluations on a randomized basis were logistically and politically feasible, but also very difficult. Further, they seemed applicable only to new programs instead of ongoing ones with established clienteles. It was hard to keep the experimental groups uncontaminated over a sufficiently long period for effects of the intervention to develop naturally. Interventions that don't change over the course of the study, like payments, seem more likely candidates than provision of services that evolve in response to conditions and clientele. But such studies gather useful data about real contexts that policymakers are likely to accept as being indicative of the results if the policy

---

7. Five negative income tax experiments were conducted in the United States (Watts and Rees, 1976; Rossi and Lyall, 1976; Moffitt, 1979; Robins et al., 1980). Other studies included transitional aid to prisoners (Rossi, Berk, and Lenihan, 1980), which provided unemployment compensation to prisoners to provide a time of transition and reduce recidivism; housing allowance (Struyk and Bendick, 1981; Bradbury and Downs, 1981; Friedman and Weinberg, 1983), which paid subsidies to poor families to permit them to purchase better housing (another study required the housing purchased to conform to certain health standards); the effects of alternative police patrols on crime rates (Kelling et al., 1974); and subsidized medical insurance on consumption of health care (Newhouse et al., 1980).

were adopted. These pioneer studies should markedly benefit later ones.

Some of the problems of evaluating treatments in field studies were noted in chapter 18. An additional problem with large-scale evaluations is the time required to mount them, carry them out, and analyze the data. The income maintenance studies took place over six years. By the end, enthusiasm for the intervention had dissipated somewhat. Concern for the persons suffering while the research drags on often prevents withholding action until research is complete. By training and instinct, researchers do not necessarily agree that partial data—which may be misleading—are better than none. Decision makers, who know that they never have all the data they need, may prefer to take their chances with what is available. Legislative, budgetary, and administrative deadlines may lead to conflict and confrontation. Timing is often all-important on the political scene; it is usually difficult, if not impossible, to make timing of the study conform to political opportunism.

Of even more concern than these problems, as Rossi and Wright (1986) point out, are the "close-to-zero effects." "When 'no significant difference' is interpreted as a program failure, the burden of proof is placed on the innovation" (Cronbach, 1982, p. 33). Part of the problem may be how programs are implemented. There is often considerable difference between the way a program is conceptualized and how it is implemented. For these reasons, some educators have tried to invent "teacherproof" curricula that essentially take the teacher out of the learning process. Though implementation is a problem, the challenge for program designers may be to develop programs that either are robust over a variety of implementation strategies or have "natural" paths to correct implementation built in. Alternatively, they may require that implementation take place, then study it to see how and why modifications took place to see whether they can be controlled (Fairweather and Tornatzky, 1977; Hamilton, 1979).

- The large government studies of the 1960s and 1970s showed that it was possible to do large-scale experiments with randomization to study social policies.
- Timing is important in reporting results, yet it is very difficult to co-ordinate political and evaluation timing.
- Since close-to-zero effects are usually considered failures, a focus on program implementation to ensure maximum effect is sometimes important. Examining how the program was modified may throw light on implementation problems.

THE POLITICAL NATURE OF EVALUATION

The political nature of evaluation manifests itself in many ways. If the prime criterion of an evaluation is utility, the evaluator is, by definition, not solely in charge. The evaluation process has become a negotiation (Krathwohl, 1980), and negotiations, like politics, seek the "art of the possible." Because evaluations favor the people in charge, they reinforce the conservative end of the political spectrum. Findings of "no significant difference" for incremental improvements, a common result, conservatively reinforce the status quo and tend to discourage the search for change. Pressures for favorable results often bring more heat than light to the evaluation process.

The Conservative Nature of Evaluation

Evaluation may be considered conservative when it reinforces the dominant scientific view of the world.[8] Looking for "standard" ways of implementing interventions, most evaluators believe there can be general conclusions about what are the best practices. "For them, standardization is a feature of rational management, not just of investigation" (Cronbach, 1982, p. 34). Other evaluators have a different view of the complexity of the world. We might call them humanists. They "believe that probabilistic generalizations are almost worthless, since much of what happens is determined by the specifics of a situation and perceptions of participants." (p. 34). They fear authorities who, trusting generalizations, will inappropriately force a program to conform. We have already alluded to different views about what the world is like and what a social science can be. Suffice it to say that these differences exist and that they tend to be accompanied by preferences for certain kinds of research methods and evidence.

Further, there is a tendency for society to move into administrative positions individuals who view scientific findings as valuable and who prefer analytic reports. Such individuals will likely view quantitative evidence more favorably than qualitative. Whereas an administrator may find a statistical report interpretable and useful, a kindergarten teacher may find a case study approach describing the impact on specific children more meaningful. Thus evaluators need to be aware of how clients and stakeholders view social science research and what they think it can contribute. If an evaluation is to be used, evaluators should either conform to these notions in research method, nature of evidence, and reporting style or be prepared to educate these individuals to accept a different point of view.

Berk and Rossi (1976) argue that evaluation is inherently conservative because it is limited to the politically feasible. The negative income tax experiment investigated only a narrow range of incentives that Congress might consider. Such options are much more limited than the range that would contribute to an understanding of the phenomenon and might be investigated in a research project. Further, such studies shed light only on the dominant view of social problems. The negative income tax arose out of concern that persons, satisfied with the dole, would withdraw from the work force. Improved health and enrichment of lives as outcomes were either neglected or downplayed.

---

8. Participant-oriented approaches do not always do so, however; it depends on the participants.

Who Controls the Study?

Control of the study by sponsor or manager is another aspect of evaluation as a conservative force. Employed by the sponsor, the evaluator serves the side where power lies: "Evaluators help political figures remain in power if they supply them with information that other participants in the political process do not possess" (Cronbach, 1982, p. 35). Although the evaluator may negotiate for the voices of powerless publics to be included, it is the funder who ultimately determines this. An evaluator thus gives evidence of personal values by the evaluation opportunities accepted.

Administrators who, threatened by an evaluation, are out of sympathy with it can make access and data gathering very difficult. They can, of course, deny access. But that is too overt. They can instead hold up scheduling interviews, require approval of all instruments by boards or committees, subtly undermine their requests to teachers or parents to cooperate by the way they are phrased or delivered, informally marshal the "insiders" to resist the "outsiders," and so on, repeatedly and indefinitely. Similarly, those being evaluated, if antagonistic to the evaluation, can delay returning questionnaires, leave items blank, change or remove code numbers, give vague responses, and limit observations to favorable times and places. The whole process is controlled by those who have a stake in the outcome. Brickell (1978) refers to the needed "instinctive ability of every born evaluator" to "bite the hand that feeds you while seeming to be licking it" (p. 95). Bogdan (1976) argues, "You can only afford to do evaluation if you can afford not to do it" (p. 65). This doesn't mean that evaluations can never be done where there are hostile staff or participants, but there are clearly serious difficulties if they don't want to be evaluated. Hence the considerable interest in making stakeholders participants in the evaluation process.

Pressures for a Favorable Report

Evaluation as a political process conjures up the vision of conflict and compromise and, indeed, the life-or-death stakes for programs undergoing evaluation can lead to that. Consider this example: Brickell (1978) was employed by the board of education to evaluate the impact of teacher aides, but it was the district superintendents who employed them. One of the superintendents warned Brickell:

> "Okay you evaluators. Let's get one thing straight . . . these paraprofessionals . . . not only . . . help kids learn but . . . link us to the community [not a criterion the evaluator was employed to consider]. We're not looking for a report . . . that will cause any trouble . . . downtown. They've got their reasons . . . we've got ours. . . . We're going to keep our para-professionals. Don't make it difficult." Alerted thus, we made our study. And we were lucky that time. We found that the presence of para-professionals did in fact improve pupil achievement. (p. 95)

Here is a second example:

> While serving as the external evaluator of a large-scale program ... our first submission ... was a formative evaluation report. ... Our report was ... returned ... and we were told that 100 pages was too much help. ... He [the sponsor] asked us to shrink the length ... cut out some of the negative material and try to write with a more balanced viewpoint. Then he could submit a copy of the report to his funding agency. We cut it in half, rethought the negative things we had said, eliminated some, and softened others. (p. 95)

Sponsors may ask to see the report before it is released; they may demand the right to edit the final version. Even a report that is not censored may be made unavailable, and this applies to the federal government as well as smaller evaluation employers. Coleman (1972) reports that since small differences were found in the resources put into black and white schools, his widely discussed *Equality of Educational Opportunity* report was perceived as damaging the case for programs aiding minorities. This finding was obscured in the summary report, though not in the larger one. The summary report was released with a press interview that suggested that the report contained nothing new. Even when Senate testimony and media coverage publicized the findings, the full report remained unavailable for a year after the small initial printing was exhausted. Availability of the report is one of the many conditions that must be agreed on at the outset of an evaluation.

It is because of situations like these that evaluation standards were developed that would spell out the appropriate conduct for both evaluator and client. We turn to these standards next.

The political nature of evaluations has implication because:

- The evaluator is not solely in charge, and if utilization is a prime criterion, negotiations to find the "art of the possible" are important—evaluations are limited to the politically feasible.
- Evaluations may reinforce the dominant scientific view of society.
- Data gathering may be made difficult or impossible by individuals unsympathetic to the evaluation.
- There may be pressures for a favorable report by individuals whose positions or careers may be jeopardized by unfavorable results.

THE EVALUATION STANDARDS: PROTECTION FOR EVALUATORS AND CLIENTS

The evaluation standards, like the test standards in chapter 11, were a joint project of the American Psychological Association, the American Educational Research Association, and the National Council on Measurement in Education.

In fact, they grew out of the test standards effort and were developed by a committee of representatives from these three organization plus those of evaluation practitioners and users. Thirty standards are grouped under the four main concerns of evaluation: utility, feasibility, propriety, and accuracy (Joint Committee on Standards for Educational Evaluation, 1981). Each standard includes an overview of intent, guidelines for application, common pitfalls, caveats (trade-offs where more than one standard applies), and an illustration of the standard's application. A functional table of contents indicates which standards apply to the major evaluation tasks. These are the 30 standards that represent the agreed characteristics of good practice:

Utility Standards[9]

1. Audiences involved in or affected by the evaluation should be identified, so that their needs can be addressed.
2. The persons conducting the evaluation should be both trustworthy and competent to perform the evaluation, so that their findings achieve maximum credibility and acceptance.
3. Information collected should be of such scope and selected in such ways as to address pertinent questions about the object of the evaluation and be responsive to the needs and interests of specified audiences.
4. The perspectives, procedures, and rationale used to interpret the findings should be carefully described, so that the bases for value judgments are clear.
5. The evaluation report should describe the object being evaluated and its context, and the purposes, procedures, and findings of the evaluation, so that the audiences will readily understand what was done, why it was done, what information was obtained, what conclusions were drawn, and what recommendations were made.
6. Evaluation findings should be disseminated to clients and other right-to-know audiences, so that they can assess and use the findings.
7. Release of reports should be timely, so that audiences can best use the reported information.

Feasibility Standards

8. Evaluations should be planned and conducted in ways that encourage follow-through by members of the audiences.
9. The evaluation procedures should be practical, so that disruption is kept to a minimum, and that needed information can be obtained.
10. The evaluation should be planned and conducted with anticipation of the different positions of various interest groups, so that their cooperation may be obtained, and so that possible attempts by any of these groups to curtail evaluation operations or to bias or misapply the results can be averted or counteracted.

---

9. From Joint Committee on Standards for Educational Evaluation, *Standards for Evaluations of Educational Programs, Projects, and Materials*, Copyright 1981 by McGraw-Hill, Inc. Reprinted with permission of McGraw-Hill, Inc.

Propriety Standards

11. Evaluations should produce information of sufficient value to justify the resources expended.
12. Obligations of the formal parties to an evaluation (what is to be done, how, by whom, when) should be agreed to in writing, so that these parties are obligated to adhere to all conditions of the agreement or formally to renegotiate it.
13. Conflict of interest, frequently unavoidable, should be dealt with openly and honestly, so that it does not compromise the evaluation processes and results.
14. Oral and written evaluation reports should be open, direct, and honest in their disclosure of pertinent findings, including the limitations of the evaluation.
15. The formal parties to an evaluation should respect and assure the public's right to know, within the limits of other related principles and statutes, such as those dealing with public safety and the right to privacy.
16. Evaluations should be designed and conducted, so that the rights and welfare of the human subjects are respected and protected.
17. Evaluators should respect human dignity and worth in their interactions with other persons associated with an evaluation.

Accuracy Standards

18. An evaluation should be complete and fair in its presentation of strengths and weaknesses of the object under investigation, so that strengths can be built upon and problem areas addressed.
19. The evaluator's allocation and expenditure of resources should reflect sound accountability procedures and otherwise be prudent and ethically responsible.
20. The object of the evaluation (program, project, material) should be sufficiently examined, so that the form(s) of the object being considered in the evaluation can be clearly identified.
21. The context in which the program, project, or material exists should be examined in enough detail, so that its likely influences on the object can be identified.
22. The purposes and procedures of the evaluation should be monitored and described in enough detail, so that they can be identified and assessed.
23. The sources of information should be described in enough detail, so that the adequacy of the information can be assessed.
24. The information-gathering instruments and procedures should be chosen or developed and then implemented in ways that will assure that the interpretation arrived at is valid for the given use.
25. The information-gathering instruments and procedures should be chosen or developed and then implemented in ways that will assure that the information obtained is sufficiently reliable for the intended use.
26. The data collected, processed, and reported in an evaluation should be reviewed and corrected, so that the results of the evaluation will not be flawed.
27. Quantitative information in an evaluation should be appropriately and systematically analyzed to ensure supportable interpretations.
28. Qualitative information in an evaluation should be appropriately and systematically analyzed to ensure supportable interpretations.

29. The conclusions reached in an evaluation should be explicitly justified, so that the audiences can assess them.
30. The evaluation procedures should provide safeguards to protect the evaluation findings and reports against distortion by the personal feelings and biases of any party to the evaluation.

Although aimed at education projects, the standards have much wider applicability. Wildemuth (1981) prepared an annotated bibliography addressing each of them. The standards are particularly useful in the development of a contract between sponsor and evaluator in suggesting some of the potential points of conflict that might evolve out of their relationship as the project progresses. The standards can also be helpful in what has been termed "meta-evaluation," the assessment of how well an evaluation study was done.

HALLMARKS OF EVALUATION STUDIES: SUGGESTIONS FOR DOING EVALUATIONS

Together with the standards just discussed, the following suggestions for doing evaluations make clear the hallmarks of a good evaluation.

1. Be sure you want to do the project. Having to work at being nice in continuous contact with protagonists, antagonists, and various stakeholders can be wearing and reduce your effectiveness. But if all evaluators were too choosy, only advocates would be available; keep a balance.
2. Try to anticipate potential problems and work through the gray areas with the sponsor regarding problem definition and scope, stakeholders' rights in the evaluation, report editing and documentation, the public's right to know, the time schedule, and fiscal details. Be sure they meet your personal and professional standards. Have a written contract.
3. Have a means of modifying the contract in case sponsor/evaluator negotiations fail; provide for flexibility and accommodation.
4. An advisory group of right-to-know audiences may be helpful in identifying potential "minefields." Depending on your philosophy and that of your sponsor, probe for additional audiences not apparent earlier, and work through their acceptance.
5. Using this group and the sponsor, decide whether a targeted or goal-free evaluation is appropriate. Goal-free evaluation may be a first stage that targeted evaluation can follow. For a targeted evaluation, use such a group to explore the variety of questions of concern (called the *divergent* phase by Cronbach, 1982). Find those important to all, those negotiated as important to enough groups to include, and those with no agreement (Cronbach's *convergent* phase). Allocate resources to the first type of questions and to the second as resources allow. Consider questions of the third type in terms of their intrinsic merit, the powerlessness of the group to get them attended to, resources available, and so on.
6. Act as an institutional resource by bringing appropriate outside research

findings to bear and organizing them into a conceptual scheme related to the decisions to be made.

7. Choose methods of investigation appropriate to the questions and to the preferences for kinds of evidence of relevant stakeholders. Remember the importance of the evaluation *process* in instilling trust. "It is . . . of fundamental importance that justice be done, but it should manifestly and undoubtedly be seen to be done" (Stewart, 1924, p. 259).
8. Educate the advisory committee and the sponsor regarding trade-offs in the study; have them help in the trade-off decisions.
9. Do not take for granted that the program was implemented as planned or conceptualized. Reasons for any discrepancy may bear on the feasibility of implementation in a wider sphere.
10. Expect political pressures to increase in the later stages; the study's potential impact is getting closer.
11. Use a format (written or oral report, graphics), style (informal, formal), and wording (technical, nontechnical) that will best communicate with your audience.
12. Pace reporting so that it is absorbed. Leak results early in small interim reports dealing with easily understood segments. Negative evidence may be accommodated more comfortably this way. The big report's summary may restore perspective, but the report itself may be mainly archived.
13. Reinforce the limits and constraints of the study to the audience.
14. Separate recommendations and advocacy from interpretation of findings; make clear the judgmental aspects and possible biases.

Bear in mind that the audiences reading a report will want to know the special competencies of the authors, who sponsored the study and why, what their responsibility was, how well these results match those of comparable studies, and, if the evaluation is controversial, where the response of opposing parties can be found (Hoaglin et al., 1982).

SUMMARY

Evaluations are typically decision-driven rather than hypothesis-driven like most research. The need to make some kind of decision initiates and guides the evaluation with the expectation that it will facilitate decision making. Consensus around the interpretation of the data is generally within a more targeted group than in research. It may be only the sponsor and the evaluator, but more often it includes other stakeholders. Utilization of an evaluation is a prime criterion of its success. If the results are to be utilized, stakeholders must trust the process that produced them. Therefore, often the process by which the evaluation was carried out is as important as the product. Formative evaluations are intended to help a program improve. Summative evaluations are used to determine whether to continue a program or which of several programs is best. Evaluations are unavoidably political acts.

There are various approaches to evaluation:

goal-based approaches—the evaluation concentrates on the intended goals of a program; a major question is whose version of intended goals is used, that of sponsor, administrator, staff, clients, etc.

goal-free approaches—the evaluator looks at what occurred and compares that with intended changes

management-oriented approaches—evaluations are designed to assist managers in the administration of projects, often concerned with efficiency and effectiveness

consumer-oriented approaches—evaluations are intended to help consumers decide what program to use, what product to buy, etc.

expertise-oriented approaches—evaluators employ experts to judge what has occurred

adversarial approaches—evaluators prepare cases to represent the two or more alternative solutions to a problem and present their cases as in a court of law

naturalistic approaches—evaluations use qualitative methods to describe what occurred and seek to be responsive to the stakeholder audience

participant-oriented approaches—the stakeholders are taught how to carry out the evaluation themselves

Each has certain advantages and disadvantages and is useful under certain circumstances. As the differences among the approaches suggest, the many decision points can lead to quite different evaluations.

Evaluations tend to be conservative. Questions of who does the evaluation, who controls the process, and who controls the report are often points of contention. Evaluation standards have been developed to guide both sponsors and evaluators.

ADDITIONAL READING

Cronbach (1982)
Eisner (1981)
House (1980, 1990)
Guba and Lincoln (1987)

Patton (1980)
Rippey (1973)
Rossi and Wright (1986)
Stake (1991)

IMPORTANT TERMS

Adversarial evaluation
Behavioral objectives
Consumer-oriented evaluation
Cost-benefit analysis

Cost-effectiveness analysis
Decision-driven
Evaluation
Expertise-oriented evaluation

Formative evaluation
Goal-based evaluation
Goal-free evaluation
Management-oriented evaluation
Naturalistic evaluation approaches

Participant-oriented evaluation
Stakeholders
Summative evaluation
Utilization

═══════════ APPLICATION PROBLEMS ═══════════

1. The success of the Children's Television Workshop (CTW), especially its best-known program, *Sesame Street*, has been attributed to CTW's unique three-stage program development model, summarized as follows:

  a. A long preproduction stage (up to one year)
    (1) Instructional designers conduct needs analysis and hammer out detailed behavioral objectives linked to the founder's definition of the educational problem to be solved.
    (2) The executive producer and designers agree on the behavioral objectives.
    (3) Educational researchers and production staff develop program philosophy and format.
  b. Pilot Show
    (1) Internal, laboratory-style research is done on comprehensibility and appeal to the viewer population and consequent modification of program segments. Small groups of preschool children are brought to the studios.
    (2) A pilot show is produced and used to estimate audience appeal and comprehensibility (as measured by interview, questionnaire, and assessment of eye movement) and to select the best program and features.
    (3) Findings are discussed through informal, supportive teamwork.
  c. Full Production: Production takes place with continuing feedback from researchers and subject content experts.

Consider the activities described in stages b

and c. Are they research or evaluation? Why?

2. Two doctoral candidates at Upstate University were asked to evaluate the Developmental Economic Educational Program (DEEP) run by a local community college. This program was primarily funded by the Joint Council for Economic Education, a private, nonprofit organization, and additional funds came from the state education department. The local DEEP center was administered by a director and four faculty advisers. It had contracts with 35 school districts, each of which had a resident DEEP coordinator. It ran in-service workshops designed to familiarize the primary and secondary teachers in the districts with the DEEP curriculum (now mandated by the state) and to aid them in developing and implementing their own individual curricula. The director wished to determine if the teachers were really using the DEEP curriculum and if so, to what extent. He wanted to know whether the workshop was successful in helping them to do so and if it met their expectations. What approach might the evaluators have taken?

3. The superintendent of curriculum of the Fayetteville school board was given the task of developing a teacher evaluation process after the state education department disbanded its inspection system and turned control over to the school boards. What approach would you advise her to take?

4. The directors of a large charity organization in Sandstone City are concerned about the program at their halfway house for teenage girls. The halfway house serves local girls who have no alternative home life and are referred by child care agencies. Most are in legal trouble. At any one time, the home might have between a half-dozen and a dozen residents. The program attempts to teach the girls life skills such as self-care, personal hygiene, home care, and shopping skills. The basis of the program is a behavior modification system in which they earn points to move up level by level and obtain increased privileges. Some of the directors are concerned about the persistent reports that the program is being used to maintain control over the residents and that the point system is merely a means of punishment. They are also alarmed at the high rate of turnover of both staff and residents. They have hired you to evaluate the program. How would you proceed?

Compare your answers with those on pages 721–722.

APPLICATION EXERCISE

Are there aspects of your problem that are like an evaluation or could be? If there are, consider who would be the stakeholders, who ought therefore to be involved in some way in the evaluation. How should they be involved? What problems might be associated with their involvement? Which kind of evaluation would be most appropriate? Which would most likely be utilized? Considering the evaluation standards and the hallmarks of an evaluation, which of them do you think might cause the greatest problems? How might you find your way around them?

CHAPTER
21

Longitudinal Studies, Single-Subject Designs, and Meta-analyses

OVERVIEW

This chapter examines three methods in common use: longitudinal studies, single-subject designs, and meta-analyses. Longitudinal designs follow individuals over time and thus are able to discern personal changes as well as those of the group. Things that cross-sectional studies miss, longitudinal studies can make salient. Keeping a panel intact, repeating measures, selection, and reactivity can cause problems.

Single-subject designs are useful for studying changes in individuals as well. They are especially good when the kinds of cases required are rare or when treatments are prolonged, expensive, hard to administer, or effective only under certain conditions. They constitute a useful exploratory technique but unless replicated lack generalizability.

Initially perceived as a method of strengthening literature reviews, meta-analysis has evolved into a research method in its own right. A meta-analysis obtains a quantitative measure reflecting the combined research results of the studies available on a given problem. We estimate the average size of the effect over these studies. As results are cumulated over different conditions, in the presence of different variables, and involving different strengths of variables, we can also ascertain what potentiates or weakens a relationship, the pattern in which that occurs, and where and how the effect is maximized.

CHAPTER CONTENTS

Introduction   555
Longitudinal Studies   555
  Difficulties of Longitudinal
    Studies   557

Hallmarks of Longitudinal
  Studies   558
Single-Subject Studies   559
  An Example   560

The Internal Validity (LP) of Single-
Subject Experimental Studies   560
External Validity (GP) Concerns   563
Hallmarks of a Single-Subject
Study   563
Meta-analysis   564
The Initial Meta-analysis Model   567
Weaknesses in Meta-analytic
Methodology   568

Meta-analysis Methods   569
Advantages and Disadvantages
of Quantitative Literature
Summaries   571
Hallmarks of Meta-analytic
Studies and Tips
for Doing Them   573
Summary   574

INTRODUCTION

This chapter could have been much longer, considering the number of techniques that could have been included. Longitudinal studies, single-subject designs, and meta-analyses are three of the most commonly encountered. Advanced statistical techniques are also used; some of these are covered in the next chapter. Among techniques not included here are these:

- *Q technique* is a data-gathering pattern in which subjects sort a set of statements into ranked categories to express their opinion on a subject. It simplifies individual comparisons. (See Stephenson, 1953, or Kerlinger, 1986, ch. 32).
- The *delphi method* obtains a group judgment on an issue or a prediction. The researcher starts by selecting experts and getting them to answer questions such as what the most appropriate topics are for a research course (Todd and Reece, 1989) or to make predictions and give reasons therefor (for example, how will word processing change in the future?). Their reactions are cumulated in anonymous form and sent back to the experts, with their previous response indicated. The experts consider their colleagues' responses and decide whether and how to modify their own. A second round is similarly cumulated and circulated for response. Usually three rounds suffice to get sufficient convergence of opinion. (See Linstone and Turoff, 1975, and Quade, 1982).

These by no means exhaust the possible topics, especially when it comes to alternative statistical treatments; they only hint at the richness of the methodology field.

LONGITUDINAL STUDIES

We tend to think of longitudinal studies in connection with following development with maturation or changes with age. But as Featherman (1981) notes, life-span orientation "is questioning the longstanding assumption that age is a reliable predictor of behavior. It calls attention to the variability across persons . . . [and] emphasizes the malleability of personality and behavior in persons of all ages" (p. 69). So longitudinal studies are better thought of as examining any kind of changes in persons, usually targeted ones, over time. They involve repeated observation, measurement, and/or self-assessment of a panel of individuals over a period of time. In this respect, they are like a panel study in a survey. A panel that is representative of some group is identified and followed over a period of time and assessed periodically. Though the data are usually quantitative, narrative qualitative evidence gathered at the same time is extremely useful in explaining the quantitative data.

A longitudinal study involves the confounded effects of three sources: (1) the normal developmental processes of the individual, including the physical effects of aging; (2) events that occur during a particular historical period (war, drafts, depression, affluence, governmental instability); and (3) the accumulated experiences of each particular cohort of individuals. Each cohort starts at a different point in time and therefore views history from its own distinct perspective.

Longitudinal studies are expensive. Costs add up rapidly: holding staff together, keeping track of the sample, collecting and analyzing mounds of data. If the same information can be gained through a cross-sectional study, comparing freshmen with graduates, new teachers with the long-employed, new residents of a community with old-timers, that is preferable; faster and less expensive, it permits a great many questions to be answered.

But the different experiences of individuals over their lifetimes make many questions impossible to answer by means of cross-sectional designs. Studying divorce on a cross-sectional basis would compare individuals raised in a period when divorce was not an acceptable outcome of a marriage, whereas those married today accept it as much more possible. Higher-education administrators, concerned about the attrition rates from freshman year to graduation, were considerably reassured by longitudinal studies that showed that a very high percentage of students finished somewhere, sometime.

Statistics aggregated over time may conceal more than they reveal. As Hoaglin and colleagues (1982) note, continuing unemployment figures of around 7 percent were thought to reflect a hard core of unemployables. A longitudinal study (Parnes, 1980) found, however, that it consisted largely of around 20 percent of the work force who are marginally employed and move back and forth between temporary employment and welfare. Only longitudinal studies can give an accurate picture in such cases.

- Longitudinal studies involve repeated observation, measurement, and/or self-assessment of a panel of individuals over a period of time.
- Longitudinal studies are likely to encounter confounding effects with the developmental processes of the individual, the events of the period studied, and the accumulated experience of each cohort.

Difficulties of Longitudinal Studies

One problem of longitudinal studies has already been noted, that of cost, particularly in relation to expected benefits. There are others.

Keeping the Panel Intact.   It has been said that 20 percent of Americans move every year. Whether that is currently true, or not, we are certainly a mobile society. Keeping a panel intact is a difficult and expensive process. Asking panel members to identify individuals who would always know where they are helps. Freedman, Thornton, and Camburn (1980) gathered this information to help locate women nine years later and found 94 percent of their original sample, one-third through using this information. Most researchers try to estimate expected attrition and begin the study with a sample large enough to compensate for losses. In some longitudinal studies, missing cases have been replaced with substitutes. But even though they are matched on major characteristics, there is always the question as to whether available replacements are a select group and thus not really representative.

Experience has shown that it is the better-educated, upper class panel members who are easiest to retain and most likely to respond to requests for information. Thus it is easy to bias the sample increasingly over time unless we correct for it.

Avoiding Floor and Ceiling Effects.   We seek instruments that are not too hard at the beginning of the study or too easy at the end (floor and ceiling effects, described in chapter 11). This is a large order if considerable change is expected. Further, achievement tests usually change content and underlying skills from level to level so that end tests may be quite different from beginning ones, posing problems of comparability.

Statistical Comparisons over Time.   Like most studies, longitudinal ones are more likely to use intact groups than randomly assigned ones. This results in the problem of finding some way of ensuring that initial differences between groups do not account for later differences—the dilemma of nonequivalent groups encountered in experimental design (chapter 18). The statistical problems of analyzing longitudinal data have been discussed extensively (see Nesselroade and Baltes, 1979). Rogosa (1987), in an excellent but technical article, examines nine statistical myths of these discussions. The preferred solution has been to use the difference between the actual posttest and a score predicted from the pretest. Rogosa argues that under most conditions, this difference is no more reliable than a difference score. Using just the pretest-posttest difference markedly simplifies analysis.

One advantage of longitudinal studies, however, is that there are multiple data points over time rather than just a pretest-posttest difference. Rogosa (1987) suggests that curve-fitting rather than adjustment techniques are the best currently available solution to this problem. It seems clear, however, that most researchers will want to consult the best statistician they can find for the latest word on this continuing controversy.

Selection Problems.   In addition to the problem of mortality (persons dropping out of the study), there is the problem that persons who volunteer for a study, especially one that continues over time, may not be typical of the population.

Reactivity Problems.   Individuals repeatedly queried with the same or similar questions may be changed by the process of responding. They may differ from people not so exposed by trying always to give the same response so as not to appear inconsistent. Having thought about a question repeatedly may solidify a response that might otherwise have changed. One way to handle this is to start with a sufficiently large panel that we will need data from only a portion of it at any one point in time. By rotating the people used in any single sample through the panel, we query each individual less often.

Further, being part of a study may cause individuals to react differently from the way they might otherwise. There is much speculation as to whether Terman's study of geniuses, which followed schoolchildren well into adulthood, created expectations by their identification, which subjects then tried to meet (Terman and Oden, 1947, 1959). There is, of course, no way of knowing. It is hard to prevent panel members from knowing the kind of a study in which they are participating, though in some instances it may be desirable.

> The difficulties of longitudinal studies include keeping the panel intact over the period of the study, floor and ceiling effects of instruments, the complexities of statistically analyzing the data, and selection, mortality, and reactivity as alternative explanations of the data.

Hallmarks of Longitudinal Studies

1. The sample was chosen so that dropouts were allowed for or replaced with comparable individuals. Selection was eliminated as an alternative explanation of the data.
2. Any measures used were valid and reliable over time; floor and ceiling effects were avoided. If observations or other qualitative data were used, some means was employed to ensure that the method of eliciting the data remained stable.
3. The effect of repeated measures was dealt with through comparable forms, by using different samples of persons, or in some other way.
4. Reactivity and expectancy problems were anticipated and dealt with by using unobtrusive measures, blind observers, or some other method.
5. Arrangements were made to collect missing data.
6. Records were kept of the changing context in which the study was carried on so that these aspects could be considered in interpreting the data.

SINGLE-SUBJECT STUDIES

Single-subject studies are time-series experimental designs with a sample size of one. They basically consist of two alternating phases: the **baseline phase**, in which measures are taken to determine the starting point (condition A), and the **treatment phase**, in which a treatment is given and the effect observed (condition B). The basic design is an **AB design**, but there are many variations: a return to baseline, an ABA design; the AB conditions repeated, an ABAB type of design; repeated additional times ABABAB . . .; the A condition given at random times; additional conditions (C, D, etc.) introduced; and so on. If the treatment is effective, the effect should copy the pattern of treatment administration in timing and strength.

Such studies are important in a variety of professional service situations, such as psychotherapy, counseling, medicine, social work, special education, and tutoring. Since the subject serves as his or her own control, no control group is required, and the problem of withholding treatment from the control group is eliminated. This design is particularly useful where the expense, length, timing, and situational requirements of the treatment prohibit large samples. It is useful when the average tends to obscure differences in treatment results across individuals, situations, or both. The design is ideal for rare cases where a large sample would be very difficult to put together. We can easily study different ways of administering the treatment, dosage rates, sequences of treatments, and timing of applications.

The plan for treatment can easily be changed to take into account new insights regarding the intervention, client, or situation with little or no loss of validity. We simply look for the effect to be replicated with the same or other individuals. With all these advantages, you might wonder why it is not more common. Indeed, when psychology first started, the single-case study was *the* method of investigation. But the hazardous inferential leap from a single case to a class of individuals means that results are held more tentatively, and additional cases are required for widely generalizable knowledge.

Replication of results and a clear congruence of the pattern of cause with effect are at the heart of these designs. Indeed, advocates have argued that merely plotting the responses should make evident whether the treatment is effective. Though the results are sometimes self-evident, in practice, statistics are often useful to ensure that the effects are not due merely to chance.

- Single-subject studies are time-series experiments with a sample size of one and alternate phases of baseline (condition A) and treatment (condition B, C, etc.) effect measures such as AB and ABC and sometimes replications (ABAB, ABACAB, etc.).
- Single-subject studies are ideal for rare cases, where expense, length, timing, and situational requirements prohibit large samples, or where differential effects may be masked by group results.
- Replication of results rather than statistical significance is the heart of these designs; the effect follows the pattern of the treatment.

An Example

Hannum, Thoresen, and Hubbard (1974) sought to improve the self-esteem of three elementary teachers who were too self-critical. In the first phase, self-monitoring was employed to establish a baseline frequency of positive and negative thoughts. In the second phase, the teachers were taught to sub-vocalize the word *stop* to reduce negative thoughts. The third phase involved finding a high-frequency behavior (looking at the wall clock) and inserting a stimulus cue (a small blue decal on its face) to remind the teacher to think a positive thought. In the follow-up phase, the cue was withdrawn, and the teachers continued to monitor their thoughts.

Figure 21.1 shows the data from this study, for teacher S1 at the top, S2 in the middle, and S3 across the bottom. The frequency of positive thoughts is indicated by the solid line; of negative thoughts, by the dotted one. The four phases—baseline, thought stopping, positive intervention (cuing), and follow-up—are divided by the vertical lines. The effect of treatment is discerned by comparing the baseline phase with the intervention phase. Each phase is usually continued until a stable and reliable measure has been taken. The behavior being monitored should change in level, rate (acceleration or de-celeration of incidents as shown by a rising or falling line, respectively), or both rate and level. In Figure 21.1, teacher S1's negative thoughts change in rate in the last two phases; there is a downward slope to the line. Teacher S2's positive thoughts change more in level over the three treatment phases than in slope; each phase wobbles about the same level but moves to a higher level with the next phase.

We do not need statistics to see that positive thoughts increase with each intervention phase and remain higher than the baseline during the follow-up for all three subjects; negative thoughts similarly decrease.

Note that S2 began the second and following phases three days later than S1—a **lagged treatment**. Similarly, S3, who missed the thought-stopping phase entirely due to an out-of-town trip, began the positive intervention phase a day after S1 did. The lagging of the beginning of the intervention for S2 and S3 behind S1 was intentional to protect against an alternative explanation, history—an event that might have caused the same effect as the intervention. Although such an event might affect a case on one particular day, its effect would be obvious by comparison with the other two. This brings us to the various designs used by such experiments to build strong internal validity (LP) and external validity (GP).

The Internal Validity (LP) of Single-Subject Experimental Studies

A strong feature of experimental design is its protection against alternative explanations to build strong internal validity (LP). We have already noted achieving such protection against one alternative, history, by lagging the time of intervention when two or more subjects are used. Another is to replicate the

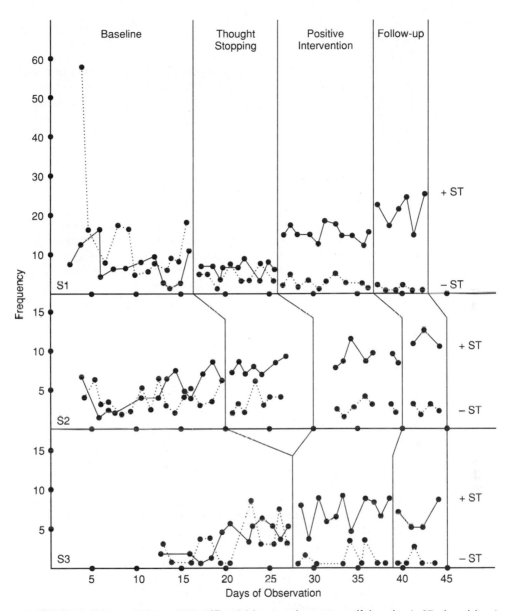

FIGURE 21.1 Positive self-thoughts (+ST, solid lines) and negative self-thoughts (−ST, dotted lines) reported by three teachers (S1, S2, S3) and plotted against days of observation. (From M. J. Mahoney and C. E. Thoresen, *Self-control: Power to the Person*, p. 149. Copyright © 1974 Wadsworth Publishing Co., Inc. Reprinted by permission of the publisher, Brooks/Cole Publishing Co., Monterey, Calif.)

initial AB phase one or more times to give an ABAB or ABABAB design. It is unlikely that a history event will be timed to occur simultaneously each time we switch into B, the intervention phase.

Note that in combination with an understanding of the intervention and how it creates its effect, we can manipulate treatment to create weak and strong effects at will. We can even do so at intervals specified by a random number table. This targeted replication provides considerable protection against a whole set of threats to internal validity: history, testing, maturation, and regression.

Maturation can also be protected against if the initial baseline period is long enough to become stable. A trend can then be noted, and postintervention behavior should break with that trend in rate, level, or both.

Most single-subject studies are susceptible to sequence effects (multiple treatment interference or carry-over effects) where a prior intervention has an effect on a later phase. Thus learning taking place in a treatment (B) phase does not disappear upon return to a baseline (A) phase. This was illustrated by White, Nielsen, and Johnson (1972), who used isolation in a special room for 1, 15, or 30 minutes to control deviant behavior. The one-minute period was quite effective when it was the first treatment used but lost its effectiveness when it followed one of the longer periods.

Just as in other studies, depending on how obtrusively the intervention is administered and the effect observed, reactivity may or may not be present. Since the teachers were monitoring their own behavior, reactivity is clearly part of the intervention in the teacher self-esteem treatment described. Nor were the follow-up studies free of it. They might have been, had manifestations of self-esteem appeared that an unobtrusive classroom observer could rate. Except where reactivity is part of a treatment, ideally the treatment should be given completely unobtrusively and the effect observed by observers blind to the timing of the intervention.

As can be noted in the behavior recorded in Figure 21.1, there is a great deal of normal variability in most of the behaviors being observed. A Type II error, finding that there is no effect when in fact there is one, can occur when the treatment effect is weaker than the normal fluctuation of the behavior being observed. That is, if the effect is buried in the normal variation, it is unlikely to be detected.

- The internal validity (LP) of single-subject designs can be strengthened by using two or more subjects and by lagging the time of intervention or administering the intervention to a single subject at random times.
- Sequence effects or multiple-treatment interference can be a problem, as can obtrusiveness or reactivity (except when the latter is part of the treatment).
- Normal variability may be large enough to mask the effect of treatment.

External Validity (GP) Concerns

The generality of findings from a single subject is usually not very great. It may be suggestive of applicability to similar individuals, but we are much more confident if several cases are run. The extent of variation from individual to individual then becomes apparent, as well as the extent to which some individuals are unusually susceptible to the intervention and others resistant to it. Replication across individuals is important for external validity (GP).

Problems with respect to sequence or multiple-treatment interference and reactivity are pretty much the same for external validity (GP) as for internal validity (LP)—as are the solutions.

Experimenter expectancy, or what has been called the demand characteristics of the experiment, may also lower generality. Thus if we run individuals through the study without the intervention phases, does the effect occur? Are there personal, environmental, or other characteristics that of themselves "demand" the response? This is a variation of reactivity, but one that should be noted, since generality to conditions other than the experimental ones may be jeopardized.

Alternative ways of giving the treatment, giving it under other conditions, and altering the situation in which the effect is to be displayed all give evidence of generality. The robustness of effects as experimental variations are replicated within and among individuals over time and situations lends still greater generality to the findings. It is possible to build a substantial case for generality by combining these kinds of intentional variations and running sufficient cases.

> As with all small-sample studies, it is difficult to infer strong external validity (GP) from single-subject studies.

Hallmarks of a Single-Subject Study

A good single-subject study will show the following characteristics:

1. It starts with a baseline condition and stays in that condition until the target behavior has been reliably and stably observed or measured (phase A).
2. It follows the baseline condition with an intervention condition and observes or measures the effect (phase B).
3. If the intervention does not have strong learning or carry-over effects, intervention and baseline conditions alternate. The more replications of the AB phases, the greater the internal validity (LP).
4. In successive intervention (B) phases, the researchers vary the timing, strength, duration, and other relevant conditions that should have an effect on the target behavior.

5. In replications over subjects, the interventions lag in time so that they are not administered simultaneously.
6. The study replicates changes in interventions over individuals.
7. Intervention and baseline patterns for each individual are adjusted to take account of new knowledge about the interaction of individual, situation, and timing, and these adjustments are replicated with other similar individuals.
8. The characteristics of intervention—its timing, the conditions under which it is given, the conditions under which the effect is observed—are varied over the persons, situations, and times to which the researcher hopes to generalize.
9. Where reactivity is not properly part of the treatment, treatment is administered and effects are observed unobtrusively and under double-blind conditions.
10. Statistics are used as an aid in judging the results where they add information or certainty.

A number of books on single-subject designs are available, among them Barlow and Hersen (1984), Kazdin (1982), and Kratochwill (1978).

META-ANALYSIS

Traditionally, literature reviews have sought to evaluate and integrate the body of research relevant to a question or a proposition. Since rarely are studies exact replications of previous ones, how can we combine these apples and oranges? Does putting them together make fruit salad? Or garbage? In the past, such a synthesis was strictly a matter of judgment. The reviewer estimated the contribution of a given study to the synthesis being constructed by weighing such characteristics as sample representativeness and size, tightness of the design, control of important moderating conditions such as socioeconomic status or time on task, and validity of instrumentation. Next the combined nature and direction of the studies had to be assessed, bearing in mind the appropriate weighting for large studies, for studies exceptionally well done, for exceptionally representative samples, or for studies with unusually valid instrumentation. Since the human mind can hold in memory a maximum of only seven to nine things at a time, the variety of characteristics to weigh and juggle quickly leads to the conclusion that this is a very difficult task.

Quantitative summaries do not completely replace the judgmental aspects of traditional summaries, but they do have certain advantages where the studies being summarized include quantitative results. Such a summary has been called a **meta-analysis**, using the Greek prefix *meta-*, a meaning of which is "after," to make an "after-analysis," an analysis of completed studies.[1] Their

---

1. In like manner, meta-evaluations are assessments of evaluations done after they are concluded.

appeal so far as inferential statistical studies are concerned derives from three main considerations:

1. A study's result may be in the hypothesized direction but not statistically significant, due to a design without quite enough power. Several of these near misses lead to the conclusion that this is more than happenstance. Yet statistical purists refuse to count a close but not significant difference as positive evidence. Combining these studies in a meta-analysis, however, yields a power greater than any one study and together usually tips the balance to statistical significance.

2. In doing judgmental reviews, the tendency is to try to figure which of the studies is the best estimate of the effect rather than to consider the study results as samples from a population of effect sizes. As Jackson (1980) notes, "Sampling theory indicates that when there is a set of studies from a given population, the findings will vary some. About one-half of the study findings will be greater than the population parameter, and about one-half will be less" (p. 447). Therefore, with a small positive true **effect size**, we might expect some negative studies. The difficulty of judgmentally weighing a set of results this way is enormous, especially when it comes to evaluating negative studies. The subjective feeling is that "any is too many." But such weighing is comfortably within the realm of statistics.

3. From a single study, it is hard to judge the effect of moderating variables such as personal attributes, characteristics of the setting or environment, and the way the study was done. The combined results of several studies can help us target the specific set of circumstances under which an intervention can be most effective. Again, such characteristics are difficult to spot in a judgmental review.

For all these reasons and more, quantitative literature reviews have increased rapidly in popularity. Meta-analyses now "appear in disciplines from marketing (to synthesize studies of advertising) to meteorology (. . . an overview of 750 cloud-seeding experiments), and from education (. . . studies of class size . . .) to epidemiology (. . . studies of the health effects of power lines)" (Mann, 1990, p. 476).

Actually, as Bangert-Drowns (1986, p. 389) indicates, such studies have been done for years: "Ghiselli (1949, 1955, 1973) for instance averaged correlation coefficients from numerous studies to estimate the validity of different tests in predicting proficiency in different occupations. Bloom (1964) aggregated correlation coefficients to summarize evidence of stability and change in behavior." In addition to combining correlation coefficients, the combining of probabilities from inferential studies emerged even earlier as a way of combining studies in agriculture and was imported into the social sciences. A simple approach was the vote count: How many studies favored treatment A? How many B? If there is no difference between them, half will favor each treatment. Through inferential statistics (the sign test, a very simple one), a chance difference favoring A or B could be distinguished from one unlikely to be a chance result. But such a finding does not tell anything about the size of the effect.

When Glass (1976) showed that studies could be combined in terms of a standard measure called effect size and coined the term *meta-analysis* for the process, quantitative literature summaries increased markedly. Kulik (1984) estimated that about 300 of them had been done by 1984. Rosenthal (1978) demonstrated an alternative method, but Glass's term has stuck as the name for all the quantitative summary methods, and his form of measuring effect size, rather than a correlation coefficient or binomial effect size display (BESD) as proposed by Rosenthal (1984), seems preferred.

Glass proposed that effects measured by different operational definitions of the same construct could be compared by putting them in what amounted to a standard-score form—a form routinely used to compare different test results. Standard scores remove the inches, units of time, and other contexts of the raw scores by dividing scores (in this instance, the score difference between two means) by an appropriate standard deviation. Scores can thus be expressed in standard deviation units.

But what should be used as the standard deviation in this instance? Since it is supposed to be uncontaminated by treatment, Glass suggested the standard deviation of the control group. The difference between experimental and control group was divided by the standard deviation of the control group. It would then represent, in standard deviation terms, the superiority of the average student in the treated group over the untreated group. We could average the effect sizes of a set of studies to obtain an overall estimate of average size of treatment effect. Thus an average effect size of 1 would indicate that the average treated person's score exceeded that of an untreated one by a full standard deviation. If it were a normal distribution, we could translate the treated person's gain into percentiles. An effect size of 1.00 would locate the average treated person at the 83d percentile of the untreated group's distribution. This puts combined results into quite understandable terms.

Meta-analysis has evolved as a research method that does more than provide a single effect size as a summary of the literature. As past data are assembled into subsets in which particular conditions can be contrasted (for example, differing levels of socioeconomic status—SES), we can find the circumstances under which a relationship is strengthened (for example, fairly high classroom activity structure, which facilitates learning for low SES students) or weakened (too high and inflexible a structure, which reduces learning for high SES students). In addition, the shape of the relationship may be plotted to determine where it is maximized or minimized. An example, the relation of class achievement to class size (Glass and Smith, 1979), is described later in this chapter.

- Meta-analysis combines the results of studies of the same relationship.
- Effect size is a kind of standard score that permits combining results. Effect size is found by dividing the difference between experimental and control group means by the standard deviation of the control group. (Correlation coefficients are also sometimes used.)
- Each study yields an estimate of the population effect size.

- The average effect size for a sample of studies may be considered an estimate of the population effect size.
- Meta-analysis gives a different perspective to a mixture of positive, negative, and not-statistically-significant results. If the effect size mean for the population is near zero and half the results fall above and half below it, negative and no effect results appear as a matterr of course. Therefore such a mixture of results indicates a weak relationship rather than one that does not exist, which is what a judgmental review would be likely to find.
- Meta-analysis has evolved as a new research method. As subsets of published data provide estimates of effect sizes under contrasting conditions, they indicate whether a phenomenon is strengthened or weakened by certain conditions and, with enough data, permit mapping the nature of that relationship.

The Initial Meta-analysis Model

Glass brought meta-analysis to the world's attention in a striking way. Ever since clinical psychology began, people have been arguing the effectiveness of "just talking about a problem." Many studies were done to convince skeptics of the effectiveness of psychotherapy, but questions remained. Indeed, some of the studies had negative results—the control groups did better than the treated groups! How could any method be effective when that occurred? And of course, there were many studies that showed no significant differences. Glass, in a presidential address to the American Educational Research Association and later in written form (Smith, Glass, and Miller, 1980), described a meta-analysis of this research. He and his colleagues selected 375 studies for intensive analysis from over 1,000 in the literature. Though the 375 contained weak as well as strong designs, all included an untreated as well as a treated group; they yielded 833 effect sizes from over 25,000 subjects.

The average effect size over all measures of improvement was .67. This means that the average client in the treated group was about two-thirds of a standard deviation better off than the average person in the untreated control—that is, better off than the person at the 75th percentile in that group. Whereas 12 percent of the effect sizes were negative, fully half of them would have been negative had there been no effect. If measures of fear or anxiety reduction were used as a criterion, the effect size was nearly 1, equivalent to the 83d percentile in the untreated group. Effect sizes on criteria of achievement or work improvement were only .31, about the 62d percentile in the untreated group; these are harder to change.

By categorizing studies in terms of their inclusion of other independent variables or in terms of certain study conditions, we can determine the dependence of results on these factors. For instance, Smith and Glass (1977) coded the studies on overall quality and found no difference in effect size between the stronger or weaker studies. (This has not always proved true in other studies.) They also examined the studies according to the kind of psychotherapy practiced and found that systematic desensitization therapy yielded the largest effect, .9, averaged over 200 effect sizes from more than 100 studies.

What is considered a strong or a weak effect seems relative to the field. Effects of 1 are considered strong in the behavioral sciences; ones of .3 or below, weak. Rosenthal (1990) notes a study of the effect of aspirin on heart attacks in physicians. The results were considered so dramatic that a randomized double-blind experiment was ended prematurely to break the good news. What was the correlation? he asks. .90? .80? .50? .20? Actually, it was .034, a correlation that would be considered too small to notice in a behavioral science study.

Weaknesses in Meta-analytic Methodology

If 833 effect sizes came from 375 studies, it is clear that most studies provided two or more measures of the effect and so were represented several times in the overall result. For example, were the Zimbardo study of chapter 2 used in a meta-analysis, it would yield three effect sizes since there were three measures of paranoia. It would thus be represented three times in any average effect size across studies. Any flaws in the Zimbardo design would therefore be represented three times in that average.

Glass argued that the studies were done independently, so the weak point of one might be the strong one of another, canceling each other. Therefore, he included weak studies. But if a study is represented several times in a meta-analysis, the average is not composed of independent estimates.

Further, in general, we would expect larger samples to yield estimates closer to the population value than small studies. Therefore, when a finding on a small sample is given equal weight in an average with the results from large samples, another question is raised (the ratio in sample sizes is sometimes 50 to 1).

There is also an apples-and-oranges problem. If we include measures of changes in attitude with changes in skills, the effect of psychotherapy is moderated by the kind of effect that is being measured. In such an instance, the variability of the effect sizes would be greater than if measures from a single domain were being averaged.

Turning the data in a published report into effect sizes requires some backward reasoning and often some assumptions when the original data are not available. For example, a *t* test reported without giving the difference between means or standard deviation could still be turned into an effect size using the statistical significance level, if given exactly (for example, 7 percent). Using the sample size, we could consult a *t* table to determine what ratio yielded that significance level; that would be the effect size. This assumes that the control group standard deviation is close to that used in the denominator of the *t* test, usually a reasonable assumption. If no exact probability is given (for example, significant at the 5 percent level), we can only estimate a minimum effect size level from the data. Glass, McGaw, and Smith (1981), Hedges and Olkin (1985), and Rosenthal (1984) provide instructions for translating most statistics into effect sizes or, alternatively, into a combined significance test, if that is preferred.

Corrections have been developed for small-sample studies (Hedges and

Olkin, 1985) and for restricted and unreliable variables (Hunter, Schmidt, and Jackson, 1982). In the former case, the correction is so small that it is rarely of potential significance, and in the latter case it must be used with care by someone who understands the statistics. Hauser-Cram (1983) has suggested a number of cautions to observe in synthesizing research studies.

Summaries based solely on published research tend to overestimate treatment effect size since the published literature is biased toward positive results (Glass, McGaw, and Smith, 1981). This is reasonable, as editors dislike using their space for studies showing no significant difference—there are so many possible ways a study can go wrong. Therefore, average effect sizes solely from published literature are usually higher than those that include unpublished studies such as dissertations or the lengthy reports of government projects. Rosenthal (1979, 1984) provides a formula for estimating the extent to which a meta-analysis is resistant to the "file drawer effect," the effect of including unpublished studies that were rejected for publication or never submitted. Effect sizes large enough to require a ridiculous number of such studies to negate the result (sometimes called a fail-safe number) are considered real, not the creation of editorial selection.

These concerns show that although meta-analysis is a relatively simple idea, it cannot be done perfunctorily—important judgments must be made. Alternative models of meta-analysis have emerged, including study effect meta-analysis and a variance-partitioning procedure. Meta-analyses of the same area, following different rules, can yield different answers. The holy grail of a single completely objective "right" answer has escaped again!

These are some of the potential problems of meta-analysis:

- It assumes that each effect estimation is independent of every other. This assumption is violated when more than one estimate from a single study is included in the combined estimate.
- Larger samples yield estimates closer to the population value than smaller ones.
- Is combining different kinds of effects (for example, achievement and attitude) meaningful?
- Using the limited data that are published to reconstruct an effect size often requires assumptions.
- If based solely on published studies, average effect sizes are likely to be overestimates. Studies not published, dissertations, and studies rejected for publication may show smaller effects.

Meta-analysis Methods

Hunter and Schmidt (1990) describe a variety of ways of doing meta-analysis, from the least sophisticated vote-counting methods to their latest version, which they call psychometric meta-analysis. Included is an excellent analysis of artifacts that may affect study results and their impact on a meta-analysis. Let us look at two methods designed to overcome problems considered serious.

Study-Effect Meta-analysis.   **Study-effect meta-analysis** (SEMA) attacked the problem of allowing more than one effect size from a single study to enter a combined analysis. SEMA thus took the study as the unit of analysis instead of all the individual findings within a study as Glass had done (Mansfield and Busse, 1977; Bangert-Drowns, 1986). In doing this, however, we throw away valuable information. For example, a study might show that a curriculum had three positive effects: achievement, attitudinal, and study skills. We must choose one of these, probably achievement, to represent the study. (If other studies also gathered attitudinal and study skills effect data, however, we could do additional meta-analyses, one on attitudinal and one on study skills effects.) In addition, SEMA calls for the researcher to exclude studies sufficiently deficient as to distort the study outcome. Further, SEMA weights the studies in the overall average in relation to sample size, thus giving more weight to the better estimates from larger samples. By limiting the studies included to those involving a particular treatment and a particular kind of outcome, the procedures' conclusions are limited to these variables; they do not paint a broad picture of a research area, such as psychotherapy, as Glass's procedures did (Hunter and Schmidt, 1990).

Variance-partitioning Meta-analysis.   Ideally, if studies were replications of one another, instead of using the study as the unit, perhaps we could pool the individual subjects into one huge study. Since the studies are not replications, we can only approximate data pooling. Further, the variability in the results may be so great that it is clear that the results are the consequence not only of the treatment variable but also of variations in method, instruments, and so on. Given a background in analysis of variance, this suggested to researchers that they could do **variance-partitioning meta-analysis** to determine the effect of the various sources of variance and subtract it to determine the effect of the independent variable of interest. Hedges (1982) and Rosenthal and Rubin (1982) worked out statistical tests for the homogeneity of effect sizes so as to determine whether they could be accounted for by a single variable. If not, then the variance needs to be partitioned into subgroups on some reasonable basis (by type of outcome measure, by treatment variation, by research study quality, etc.) until it can be shown to be homogeneous. Hunter, Schmidt, and Jackson (1982) propose a similar approach, but instead of using statistical tests for homogeneity, they estimate the sampling error. If it is no greater than 25 percent of the total variance, they assume that the variance is homogeneous and can be accounted for by a single variable.

Hunter and Schmidt (1990), in their psychometric meta-analysis, take this procedure a step further and make corrections for the unreliability of the instruments, code the studies for a variety of characteristics that might be related to the phenomena under study (such as gender of subjects), and also note any study artifacts that might systematically affect the pool of results (for example, artificial dichotomization of continuous variables or restriction in range). Study artifacts are corrected for, if possible. They correlate study-characteristic codings with effect sizes to determine whether there are relationships between outcomes and these variables, and they correct for unreliability in the measures of these characteristics. A regression of corrected effect sizes on the corrected study characteristics is presumed to give a picture of the causal relationships of the study characteristics and the effect. Clearly, many assumptions are involved in these procedures, and it is too early to know the effect of all these corrections. This method, however, is attempting to find the potential inaccuracies in the estimates provided by simple meta-analytic methods and to find ways of making allowances for them.

- Study-effect meta-analysis uses only one effect size from each study in the combined estimate and weights studies in relation to sample size.
- Variance-partitioning meta-analyses allow analysis of subgroups of studies to determine the variables that affect treatment size.

Advantages and Disadvantages of Quantitative Literature Summaries

Cooper and Rosenthal (1980) early demonstrated one of the major advantages of quantitative literature summaries. Judgmental reviewers rarely make a positive finding. They are most likely to see so many flaws or have so many reservations that they do not find a proposition strongly supported and so end up by calling for more and higher-quality research.

Cooper and Rosenthal showed that a quantitative literature summary was more likely to yield a clear-cut answer than traditional judgmental summaries. They chose seven studies that they believed supported the same hypothesis. They gave them to 41 judges, randomly assigned to meta-analytic and traditional procedures. Judges were asked to determine whether the studies upheld the proposition. More than twice as many of the traditional reviewers found "probably or definitely" no support for the proposition (73 percent) as meta-analytic reviewers (32 percent). In commenting on the study, Glass, McGaw, and Smith (1981) note:

> The entire set of studies occupied . . . fewer than 56 journal pages. One can imagine how much more pronounced would be the difference between these two approaches with bodies of literature typical of the size that are increasingly being addressed with meta-analytic techniques. (p. 17)

This very important finding indicates that meta-analytic techniques are here to stay.

Further, meta-analytic reviews help us to understand the phenomena better. For instance, Glass and Smith (1979) and Glass, McGaw, and Smith (1981) plotted class size against achievement. They found that achievement increases only very slightly from huge class sizes into the low teens and then accelerates rapidly, especially with class sizes below 10. It reaches a maximum with a class size of one—tutoring. By plotting the effect sizes against class size, a much clearer idea of the nature of the relationship was gained. Incidentally, stronger designs yielded a larger effect size when the sample studied was smaller than weaker ones did.

Light (1984) notes that research syntheses can answer several important questions. They can explain which features of a treatment are critical. For example, Raudenbusch (1984) examined 18 studies of the expectancy effect. He found only a small effect overall (.11). But by comparing the studies with a strong expectancy effect with those with a weak one, he discovered the important finding. Teachers who met their children *after* they were given information creating the expectancy showed a strong effect. Those who met the children first showed almost none. Unless this were hypothesized, it is unlikely that it would be determined from a single study. In the same way, syntheses can examine the robustness of treatment across sites and sometimes explain conflicting results.

Light and Pillemer (1984) emphasize as a critical feature of such summaries the decision of what studies to combine and how to combine them. The system used for classifying studies into homogeneous groups is important in determining both how well a meta-analysis illuminates the interrelations of independent to dependent variables and what variables are related to the effect. Providing a classification system adequate for the variables being studied is critical to the acceptability of the summary.

For example, a study of whole (W) versus part (P—P1 for part 1, P2 for part 2, etc.) learning of psychomotor skills must clearly delineate the variety of different possible styles of part learning if it is to be useful: W, P, W; (P1), (P1 + P2), (P1 + P2 + P3), and so on; P1, W, P2, W, and so on. These variations of treatment were found to be administered under conditions of massed practice (all at one learning session) or distributed practice (distributed over several sessions), or both. So a second variable was introduced, and studies had to be sorted into the different possible combinations of variations of whole versus part learning with massed versus distributed practice. Developing such a structure from an analysis of the literature is one of the most important tasks of the quantitative literature reviewer. The structure facilitates understanding the field. It shows where research has and has not been done and hence where new research is most needed. Conceptual analysis (chapter 9) to clarify the meanings the terms involved may be helpful in constructing such a framework.

In chapters 4 and 12 we noted that replication is the ultimate validation of a generalization; meta-analyses bring together the data from replications. We tend to think that results in the social and behavioral sciences are less replicable than those in the physical sciences. Hedges (1987) notes that "essentially identical methods are used to test the consistency of research results in physics and psychology" (p. 443). He compared 13 exemplary reviews from each domain and found that the results of physical experiments are not strikingly more consistent than those of social or behavioral experiments. This welcome news contradicts a stereotype about the "softness" of behavioral science results. Hedges suggests that "study of the actual cumulativeness found in physical data could inform social scientists about what to expect from replicated experiments under good conditions" (p. 443).

- Meta-analyses are more likely to yield a clear-cut answer regarding the existence of a relationship than traditional literature reviews.
- They permit the determination of the shape and nature of the relationship as affected by other variables.
- They are dependent on the framework used in classifying the studies for clarity of results.

Hallmarks of Meta-analytic Studies and Tips for Doing Them

A good meta-analytic study should meet the following guidelines:

1. Enter each study in the meta-analysis only once or, alternatively, show the effect size with and without multiple measures from the same sample.
2. Estimate the effect size from the best studies as well as the total composite.
3. Develop a reasonable framework for classifying the studies that includes the variables likely to be found together in that domain.
4. Indicate where studies are adequate for the analysis and where they are lacking in terms of that framework.
5. Make clear the criteria for inclusion of studies in the composite analysis.
6. Provide a list of the studies, their sample sizes, and the effect sizes they contribute (this may not be published but should be available on request).
7. Trace the sources of variation among studies to variables that might reasonably be considered to account for them.
8. Include unpublished studies such as dissertations and compare the composite effect sizes of published and unpublished studies.
9. Judgmentally evaluate the adequacy of the kinds of studies done (if all research in the area is weak, or if weak studies predominate, that is an important caveat).
10. Discuss any interesting results or side effects discerned in borderline studies that just missed being included in the set analyzed because of the definition of the variables.

Combining a meta-analytic study with traditional judgmental qualifications about the nature of the studies is probably the most reasonable course to follow. Slavin (1985) has also argued for "best-evidence synthesis," which is a combination of judgmental and quantitative methods. So too have Light and Pillemer (1984), who prepared an excellent analysis of the problems of both narrative reviews and quantitative reviews.

SUMMARY

Longitudinal studies involve the repeated assessment of a panel of individuals over a period of time, often years. They provide evidence of growth and change that can be only approximated by less time-consuming and less expensive cross-sectional methods. In addition to their expense, however, longitudinal studies encounter problems of floor and ceiling effects, the effects of repeated measures, statistical comparisons over time, selection and mortality, and reactivity.

Single-subject studies, as the name implies, are studies of individuals over time, usually in an experimental mode, with treatment applied and then removed in some pattern. Effects that do not result in learning or permanent changes should vary with the cause. Such studies are very powerful means of linking cause with effect, particularly because the cause is varied in a random pattern that is followed by the effect. Like longitudinal studies, floor and ceiling effects, effects of repeated measures, statistical comparisons over time, and selection and reactivity may be problems. Further, there is a problem of external validity (GP) if we intend to generalize from a single case.

Meta-analysis combines the results of studies of the same relationship to produce an overall estimate of the size of the effect. It provides a perspective on mixtures of positive, zero, and negative results, which are then seen as merely studies at the low end of a distribution of the effect of a weak treatment rather than as negating the expected relationship. Providing a framework within which the studies can be analyzed throws light on the variables that are important and their interrelationships; it is conducive to theory and model building. Meta-analysis can show the moderating effect of variables, of research methods, and of measures in addition to estimating the overall treatment effect. It is one of the most important advances in integrating findings and unifying a fragmented field of research studies.

ADDITIONAL READING

Longitudinal studies: Nesselroade and Baltes (1979)
Single-subject studies: Kratochwill (1978)
Meta-analysis: Glass, McGaw, and Smith (1981); Hedges and Olkin (1985); Hunter and Schmidt (1990); Hunter, Schmidt, and Jackson (1982).

IMPORTANT TERMS

AB design
Baseline phase
Effect size
Lagged treatment
Longitudinal studies

Meta-analysis
Single-subject studies
Study-effect meta-analysis
Treatment phase
Variance partitioning meta-analysis

============================= APPLICATION PROBLEMS =============================

1. In a 1985 article, Stanley wrote a historical note about research methodology in which he summarized the following study by Terman. In 1939–1940, the latter administered his Concept Mastery Test (vocabulary and verbal analogies) to 768 of his "gifted" subjects (see chapter 3, problem 3). Their average age was 29.5 years. He retested them with a comparable form between 1950 and 1952—approximately 12 years later. At this time, they averaged 41.5 years of age. In addition, he tested and retested 335 husbands and wives of the gifted subjects across the same time period. The years of birth of the gifted subjects ranged from 1903 to 1920. The oldest male spouse was 70 at the time of his second testing, and the oldest female spouse was 52. At each testing, he gave the Concept Mastery Test and the Stanford-Binet Intelligence Test to a random sample of college students. Each time, he was able to compare these results by age, sex, occupation, and group (gifted subject, spouse, or regular college student). The main conclusion of the study was that synonym/antonym and analogical reasoning ability, as measured by the Concept Mastery Test, increased over a bright adult's lifetime—at least through age 50. What sort of study is Stanley describing? Why did Terman design the study in such a manner?

2. The San Diego Unified School District had to comply with a 1980 court order to raise the overall achievement of students in its racially isolated schools to 50 percent of the national norm in reading, language, and mathematics as measured by the Comprehensive Tests of Basic Skills (CTBS) by 1985. Having anticipated the court order, the school district's administration and teachers developed and instituted the Achievement

Goals Program (AGP) in 1980. This plan integrated four elements found in the effective schools research: mastery learning, teacher-directed instruction, elimination of classroom distractions and interruptions, and time on task. The California Assessment Program (CAP) was also used to assess the results of the program. Districtwide testing with CTBS gave baseline data from 1975 and permitted the time-series design for reading and mathematics scores shown at the bottom of this page.

In order to judge the stability and makeup of the target population during this period, the district also gathered socioeconomic and demographic information from its Pupil Ethnic Census Reports of 1975–1985 and from the program on Aid to Families with Dependent Children and Non-English-Proficient Children. Further, the AGP was put into effect in the non–racially isolated schools beginning in 1982 with CTBS and CAP data gathered from that point. The CTBS and CAP results showed a steady rise, beginning in 1981, in mean scores for the racially isolated school students from the flat baseline score of below 30 percent of the national norm in the 1975–1980 period to 51 percent in 1985. Demographic data showed that the racial mix in these schools remained essentially the same from 1980 to 1985. There was, for instance, a small increase in the nonminority (white) population, but the numbers of minorities (including African Americans, Hispanics, and Asians) also increased proportionally. There was a 23 percent increase in minorities districtwide during this period.

Clearly, the district was able to comply with the court order. The investigators concluded, however, that the AGP was responsible for the observed gains in achievement

O   O   O   O   O   O X O X O X O X O X O
1975 1976 1977 1978 1979 1980 1981 1982 1983 1984 1985

because it provided a "critical mass" of school effectiveness factors. Are they justified in drawing this conclusion?

3. Kelly and Schoen (1988) describe a single-subject study in which they designed and instituted a social and academic change program for an 11-year-old educable mentally retarded girl with Down syndrome. They used two treatments concomitantly, a token economy and verbal praise, in order to reduce the girl's inappropriate social behavior (specifically, noncompliance to instructions) and to improve her mathematics proficiency. Compliance was defined as responding to or initiating a response to a command within five seconds; proficiency in mathematics was set as 85 percent mastery of a given concept during daily seatwork following direct instruction.

The program was carried out in the student's regular classroom and in the library four days a week for 40 minutes a day. The investigators used an ABC design in their study. They first recorded baseline data on the targeted behavior for four days during which there was no mention of the project to the subject (condition A). Next social praise was used alone for two days: the subject was thanked for her behavior and praised for doing what she was asked the first time (condition B). This intervention was followed by 11 days on which a token economy and praise were used together (condition C). The subject was praised but also given a bingo chip (collected in a paper cup) that could be traded in at the end of the period for such reinforcers as stars, stickers, erasers, pencils, and markers. The directions given were very specific, and noncompliant behavior was ignored. A sole researcher applied the program. The subject was also involved in the program by being shown a graph of her academic performance daily and being given an extra chip each day "the line goes up."

The results of the study were as follows: baseline noncompliance averaged 65 percent and increased to 86 percent during the praise-alone intervention. It dropped to an average of 35 percent (with a clear downward trend) during the combined intervention. Academic behavior during baseline was 61 percent; it dropped to 54 percent during the praise-only intervention and increased to an average of 75 percent for the combined treatment. Kelly and Schoen claimed that this was evidence that a token economy system combined with praise was an effective method to decrease noncompliance while increasing academic performance. Was this claim justified? What threats to internal validity (LP) are there for this study?

4. David Ausubel's concept of advance organizers has been heavily studied and so is a prime candidate for meta-analysis. (Advance organizers, placed at the beginning of material to be studied, convey the concepts of that material in terms that relate it to what the student already knows without using the terms in the material—for example, by analogy). In one such project, Luiten, Ames, and Ackerson (1980) did a study-effect meta-analysis because they believed that advance organizers might have small but consistent treatment effects that might not always show up as statistically significant. They found 170 published and unpublished studies, including 76 doctoral dissertations, for the period from 1960 to 1979. The authors focused on both learning and retention effects. Learning was defined as measured within 24 hours of the treatment. Retention was divided into five periods ranging from 2–6 days to over 22 days. Mean effect sizes ranged from .21 for the aggregate learning scores to .38 for the 22+ periods. Even the lowest effect size of .21 meant that with the advance organizer, the average student performed better than 58 percent of those without it. Luiten and colleagues concluded that advance organizers have a facilitating effect on retention.

They also considered the effect of advance organizers by grade level, by subject type, and by ability level. For example, for the four years of college, average learning effect size was .28 and retention was .21. For the primary grades 3–8, learning was .17 and retention was .33. They reached a number of conclusions:

(a) The studies showed a trend toward increased effect size over time, thus indicating that advance organizers provide a permanent advantage rather than a short-term "warm-up" effect.

(b) Advance organizers are effective with individuals of all ability levels and most effective with those of high ability.

(c) Advance organizers are useful at all grade levels, but grade level is an influencing variable since college-age students showed the highest effect for learning but those in the primary grades had the greatest average effect in terms of retention.

(d) Advance organizers facilitate learning and retention in a wide range of subject areas since positive average effect sizes were found for all subject groupings.

Based on the data available to you, do these conclusions seem justified?

Compare your answers with those on pages 722–723.

========================= APPLICATION EXERCISE =========================

How might your problem be examined from a longitudinal perspective? Might you use one of the cohort sampling designs described in chapter 8? What possibilities might such an approach hold that conventional ones might not? What would be the problems of maintaining your sample over time?

Would a single-subject approach be feasible with some definition of your problem? Would it lend itself to experimental mani-

pulation with, say, an AB-type design? What would be the advantages and disadvantages of this approach?

Have enough studies been done on some aspect of your study to mount a meta-analysis? How might the results from such an analysis help in the reformulation of your problem? Which form might such a meta-analysis take? SEMA? Variance partitioning? Vote count? Average effect sizes of all studies as they are?

Other Statistics for Inference and Multivariate Relationships

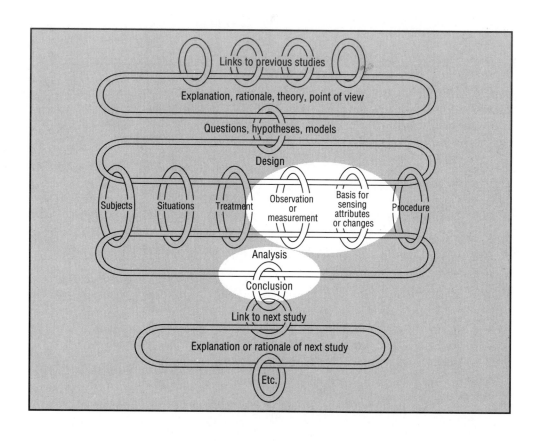

OVERVIEW

This chapter describes techniques for going beyond two-variable cause-and-effect relationships to dealing with multiple variables. The first part deals with relationships by using multiple correlation, factor analysis, canonical correlation, discriminant analysis, and structural modeling. Building on the discussion of inference, the second part describes chi-square and analysis of variance. There is also a brief discussion of controlling unwanted variation through the use of covariance and partial correlation.

CHAPTER CONTENTS

Introduction   579
Relationships among Multiple
    Variables   579
    Multiple Regression and Multiple
        Correlation   580
    Canonical Correlation   584
    Discriminant Function Analysis   585
    Factor Analysis   585
    Structural or Covariance
        Modeling   588
    An Example of the Use of Relationship
        Statistics   590
Statistics for Differences   593
    Chi-Square   593
    Testing Differences among Several
        Means: Analysis of Variance   597

Correcting for a Contaminating
    Variable: Analysis of Covariance
    and Partial Correlation   604
    Description   604
    Characteristics, Interpretation,
        Limitations, and Assumptions   606
Using the Proper Statistic and
    Understanding Data   607
    Statistical Consulting and the
        Availability of Other Statistics   607
    Computerized Statistical Programs and
        Understanding Data   608
    Selecting the Proper Statistic   608
Summary   608

INTRODUCTION

The purpose of this chapter is help you understand just enough about a number of commonly used statistics to recognize where they might be useful. For some statistics, caveats are in order. Having an idea of what statistic might be appropriate is the first step; then you can go elsewhere for the help needed to learn more about it and use it.

RELATIONSHIPS AMONG MULTIPLE VARIABLES

We have already noted that where there is a relationship, we can use regression—a close relative of correlation—to predict the dependent variable from the independent variable. To improve these predictions, we often use techniques that employ more than one independent variable. Although such techniques involve complex computation, that is now easily done by computers. Our ability to handle many variables at once takes us closer to real situations. So ease of computation plus closeness to reality means that multivariate studies are becoming the norm.

The ultimate in understanding relationships is the development of a theory that explains a causal chain of events. Such structural modeling (also called covariance and causal modeling) is appearing with ever greater frequency in the literature. It seems a likely direction of future research as we learn better how to work with multivariate analyses of situations and as our theory improves our ability to conceptualize them. The most widely used techniques deal with smaller parts of a causal chain—multiple regression, canonical correlations, and discriminant function analysis. This portion of the chapter starts with them and works up to structural modeling.

Multiple regression predicts an interval- or ratio-scaled dependent variable from two or more interval- or ratio-scaled independent variables. Ordinal-scaled variables can also be used if they can logically be treated as interval-scaled. **Multiple correlation** shows the size of this predictability. The dependent variable is typically called the **criterion** variable, or just the criterion. Sometimes we have multiple criteria and sometimes a nominal-level (categorical) criterion rather than interval-level criterion to predict. Figure 22.1 shows the match of techniques to different combinations of data and number of criterion variables, the techniques that are discussed next.

Multiple Regression and Multiple Correlation

Because many college scholarships are awarded to the students most likely to succeed, scholarship officers would like to be able to predict college grade point average (GPA). With **multiple regression**, we could improve the pre-

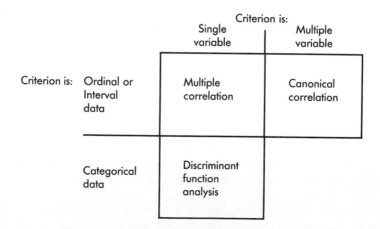

FIGURE 22.1   Relation of multivariate techniques to level of data and number of variables in criterion.

diction of college GPA by combining high school GPA with the predictive power of the Scholastic Aptitude Test, a scale to measure motivation, a measure of personality adjustment, and so on. Using this year's freshman class, we would develop a prediction equation that could be used on next year's freshmen so as to distribute the scholarship money more effectively. The result would be an equation that would multiply the scores for each of the predictors by a weight and total them to yield a predicted college GPA. When compared with the actual GPAs for this year's class, there is no set of weights that would yield lower squared differences between actual and predicted grades for this particular set of predicting variables—what is called a "least squares fit."[1]

The coefficient of multiple correlation (typically designated R) is the Pearson product-moment correlation of those predicted scores with the GPAs actually obtained. The multiple correlation can be interpreted as a product-moment correlation, and like it, the square of the correlation is a better representation of the predictability of the criterion. In fact, R^2 is called the coefficient of multiple determination. It tells us the proportion of the variance in the criterion that is associated with and predicted by that correlation. A multiple correlation of .80 thus has 64 percent of the variance accounted for, while the remaining 36 percent is not related to the predictors. Like the Pearson, the multiple correlation also assumes that the variables are linearly related and underestimates the relationship when it is curvilinear. All multiple correlations are positive, because direct and inverse relations with the predictors are reflected in the signs ascribed to the weights.

What does the order in which the variables are entered into the equation have to do with predictability? Predicting the criterion with one variable predicts the part of the criterion related to that variable. How do you pick the second variable to predict the remainder, the residual? The answer would seem to be one that is highly correlated with the criterion but not so highly correlated with the first variable that it will predict only the part of the criterion already predicted. We want to predict the residual. So the order in which the variables enter the predicting equation determines the nature of the residual and therefore which variables will be most effective in adding substantially to predictability. The various rules for finding the best prediction when the independent variables are related is a topic in itself. Suffice it to say that when maximum predictability is sought in these circumstances, the order must be attended to.

An Example. Wilson and Matheny (1983) examined the predictors of mental development for a set of 116 families participating in a study of identical and fraternal twins. They had measures of the adequacy of the home environment, mother's temperament (such as "tension, tolerance for frustration, mood and activity level"), mother's cognitive ability ("intellectual and verbal facility plus home-management skills"), mother's social affect ("ratings of the mother's

---

1. Similarly, the standard deviation is a least squares fit around the mean since the mean is the point in the distribution around which the squared differences are at a minimum.

TABLE 22.1 Predictability of Mental Test Scores at Three Ages as Variables Are Added to the Multiple Regression Equations

Predictor Variables	Entry Order Correlation	Multiple *R*	Original Correlation with Criterion Score
24-Month Scores (*N* = 207)			
Adequacy of home environment	1	.48	.48
Maternal cognitive	2	.50	.40
Maternal social affect	3	.52	.27
Father's education	4	.54	.40
3-Year Scores			
Adequacy of home environment	1	.56	.56
Maternal temperament (−)	2	.57	.03
Maternal social affect	3	.59	.36
Maternal cognitive	4	.61	.42
Maternal temperament (−)	Remove		
Father's education	5	.64	.51
Mother's education	6	.65	.49
Adequacy of home environment	Remove		
6-Year Scores			
Adequacy of home environment	1	.55	.55
Maternal cognitive	2	.59	.51
Maternal temperament (−)	3	.61	−.05
Maternal social affect	4	.62	.27
Father's education	5	.66	.55

SOURCE Adapted from R. S. Wilson and A. P. Matheny, Jr., "Mental Development: Family Environment and Genetic Influences," *Intelligence, 7*, p. 206. Copyright © 1983 Ablex Publishing Corp. Used with permission.

sociability, talkativeness and interpersonal warmth"), and father's and mother's level of education in terms of years of schooling (p. 201).

Table 22.1, adapted from their data, shows the predictability of mental test scores from combinations of the predictors at three successive ages. The researchers specified the order in which the program would enter the variables (starting with the most global, adequacy of home environment), and worked toward more specific and less central predictors: maternal cognitive, maternal temperament, maternal social affect, father's education, and mother's education. The program examined each variable in this order, indicating those that made a significant contribution to prediction. Next it recycled to examine whether the residual could now be predicted by variables that had not been statistically significant in the prior cycle. Finally, it determined whether an early predictor should be removed since the variance it predicted was covered by later predictors. The program was used with each age group to determine how the predictability changed over the years. Thus in the 3-year age group, the middle set of data, maternal temperament was the third predictor entered into the equation, but the variance that it predicted was apparently also predicted by the next variables in the equation so that after the fourth iteration, it was removed. Similarly, adequacy of home environment which was the first variable, was removed as the last step in the prediction of the 3-year-olds.

Note that correlation improves from accounting for 29 percent (.54 squared) of the variance at the 2-year (24-month) stage to about 42 percent (.65 squared) at the 3-year stage, and then it plateaus. The overall measure of home environment is the best predictor at all levels and is augmented by some mother variables and father's education (which is a good predictor by itself at the 6-year level). Father's education was a significant predictor at all ages and apparently reflected aspects not captured by the characteristics of mother and home. From these data, when the home was geared for fostering development (adequacy of home environment) and when the mother was intellectually alert, positive in mood, and free of tension and frustration, children tended to have higher IQ scores than expected.

Exploratory use of multiple regression helps differentiate the important from the unimportant variables and therefore has a special use in the initial stages of investigation of an area. As further knowledge of the area develops and we understand how the variables relate, entry of the variables into the equation in an order dictated by this theoretical conception is a kind of test of the model and is the thing to do where scientific understanding is the goal (Serlin, 1987).

Achieving Maximum Prediction.   The weights in the standard score form of the regression equation reflect the additional contribution of each variable to the prediction. In Figure 22.2, the amount of correlation between variables is reflected by the overlap in the circles. Since high school rank has the highest correlation with college academic success, it has the largest overlap and will predict segments A and B. The residual, segments C and D, remains to be predicted. Though there will be a comparatively large weight for high school rank, it is the correlation of the motivation scale with the residual that determines the contribution and therefore the weight given to the motivation scale; this is segment C. Although it also predicts B, that segment has already been predicted by high school rank. Therefore, as much as possible, the overlap among predictors should be minimized. Ideally, each new predictor should cut

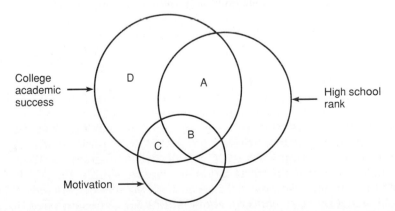

FIGURE 22.2   Prediction of college academic success from high school rank and motivation measures.

off a section of the criterion that has not yet been covered. A diverse set of variables is thus more likely to yield a prediction of a complex criterion than one where the measures are redundant; strive for the most valid measures of uncorrelated predictors.

Cross-validation of Multiple Correlations.   A limitation of multiple correlation is that the weights obtained from a study are so designed as to maximize the relationship for that particular sample. To the degree that the samples to which it will ultimately be applied differ from those used in the study, the weights will not be quite as appropriate. Prediction will be less accurate, and therefore the correlation between the actual and predicted scores—the multiple correlation—will be lower. It is as if we used the measurements from a small sample of size 12 persons to design size 12 dresses for everyone of that size. Though the product fits the *original* sample very well, it is unlikely to fit other samples quite as well. So it is with the weights; they exactly fit the sample from which they were derived, but they are unlikely to predict another sample accurately. This process of trying the weights on a completely independent sample to determine the extent of shrinkage of the multiple correlation is called cross-validation. There are formulas for estimating it.

This problem of differences between the samples on which weights are determined and those to which the weights will be applied is common to all the methods of estimating weights in prediction (including the Pearson when it is used in regression). Therefore, cross-validation should be expected in all studies where the weights are expected to generalize to a new sample.

Canonical Correlation

Canonical correlation extends linear multiple correlation's one-variable criterion to a situation where two or more variables are combined to form a criterion. For example, rather than a single measure for the criterion, grade point average, we may wish to include measures of both creativity and leadership, which as a threesome will define academic success. As with multiple correlation, the criterion is predicted by a combination of two or more predictors. Canonical correlation forms a weighted combination of the criterion variables that is the "most predictable criterion." This particular weighted combination of criterion variables is maximally predicted by a weighted combination of predictor variables.

Walberg and Ahlgren (1970) used canonical analysis to find the relationship between students' perception of classroom social environment and a set of measures of achievement and attitudes toward school. They sought the classroom environment most closely associated with positive school achievement and attitudes. As this example shows, the distinction between criterion and predictors is not really necessary since we are simply seeking to identify the most predictable relationship between the two sets of variables. The need for cross-validation and concern about shrinkage when applied to a new sample pertain to canonical correlation as to multiple correlation. An example of canonical correlation is given later in this chapter (pages 592–593).

See Thompson (1991) for a helpful discussion of the method, its uses, and an example. As Thompson notes (p. 81), it can be shown that canonical correlation analysis is a general method of which many common parametric statistics are special cases (e.g., t tests, ANOVA, and discriminant analysis). Canonical correlation analysis computations are so difficult, however, that such analyses were not feasible before computers; their interpretation remains complex.

Discriminant Function Analysis

Where the criterion is categorical, that is, where individuals belong to categories rather than being measured on a continuous scale, the extent to which individuals in one group can be discriminated from those in another can be found by a technique called **discriminant function analysis** (or just discriminant analysis). Discriminating who will drop out of college during their freshman year from who will continue would be such a problem. We might further divide the dropouts into those who left for financial reasons, illness, academic failure, and miscellaneous reasons. Discriminant analysis, using interval- or ratio-scaled measures as predictors, would show whether these four groups could be successfully discriminated one from the other by such measures as the Scholastic Aptitude Test, a health inventory, the rating on the parents' financial aid form, the dorm director's rating of involvement in extracurricular activities, and so on.

Factor Analysis

Factor analysis is not one method but a general label applied to a set of procedures intended to help determine the underlying constructs that might account for a set of interrelationships. For example, given a set of intercorrelations, can we find one or more constructs that seem to account for those intercorrelations? Given intercorrelations among spatial visualization test items, does a single factor of spatial visualization account for the intercorrelations? Given intercorrelations among the subtests of the Stanford-Binet Intelligence Test, does a single factor of intelligence account for those relations, or do we need a verbal and an abstract reasoning factor? Given intercorrelations among individuals on a personality test, how many types of persons are necessary to explain the original correlations, and what are the types? Given correlations among individuals on repeated testings of the same test as they grow older, does a single factor of maturity explain the relationships, or must we posit a factor for schooling as well? These are all possible factor analysis problems.

With canonical correlation we were finding a pattern of predictors that best predicted a pattern of relationships in a criterion. The predictor measures represented constructs deemed related in some way to the criterion measures.[2] With factor analysis, we could find the relationship between the criterion measures and a set of hypothetical constructs that could account for the relationships, the so-called basic variables underlying them. We could make measures of those constructs out of combinations of those criterion measures, taking a little bit of this and some of that, which together might indicate the nature of the basic constructs. Using these combinations as models, perhaps purer measures of these "latent" variables could then be constructed. Alternatively, if we have some measures that we think are measures of a particular construct, we could use factor analysis to see whether our notions are confirmed.

So one use of factor analysis is exploratory, to determine what constructs lie behind a set of relationships. Thurstone (1935, 1947), for example, examined large sets of ability measures looking for what he called the "primary mental abilities" using the method of "multiple factor analysis" that he developed. He found a variety of such abilities: verbal reasoning, vocabulary, abstract reasoning, spatial ability, and so on. He believed that rather than a single score representing intelligence, we could better describe an individual's abilities with a profile of scores representing different capacities. More recently, also using factor analysis, Cattell (1963) reduced intelligence to two major categories: "fluid" and "crystallized." The former is the capacity to perceive relationships without benefit of prior experience or education, and the latter is the ability to solve problems using a core of broadly applicable learned abilities.

Osgood, Suci, and Tannenbaum (1957) provide another example of the exploratory use of factor analysis. Exploring how adjectives modify meaning, they used factor analysis of adjectives to find the dimensions through which concepts might be characterized more accurately. Ultimately, they hoped that every concept could be most accurately described as a combination of these different basic factors (so much of this plus so much of that, etc.). They found three such main dimensions, each of which they described by adjective pairs. Evaluation, one dimension, was described by adjective pairs such as *good–bad*, *pleasant–unpleasant*, *beautiful–ugly*, and *clean–dirty*. Potency or strength, the second dimension, was indicated by pairs such as *large–small*, *heavy–light*, *strong–weak*, and *rugged–delicate*. Activity, the third dimension, included these adjective pairs: *active–passive*, *sharp–dull*, *fast–slow*, and *hot–cold*. From this research they produced an instrument called the semantic differential whereby any concept or stimulus (this book, for instance) could be rated on adjective pairs:

pleasant : ___ : ___ : ___ : ___ : ___ : ___ : ___ : unpleasant
heavy : ___ : ___ : ___ : ___ : ___ : ___ : ___ : light
active : ___ : ___ : ___ : ___ : ___ : ___ : ___ : passive

---

2. Recall that in canonical analysis, the distinction between predictors and criteria is not meaningful; thus with canonical analysis we might simply ask what pattern of personality variables is most closely related to what pattern of cognitive variables. The distinction is used here for convenience merely to differentiate the two sets of variables.

TABLE 22.2 Sample Questions from the Religious Problem Solving Scales Related to the Three Factors Revealed through Factor Analysis

Test Item	Factor 1	Factor 2	Factor 3
When it comes to deciding how to solve a problem, God and I work together as partners.	.85*	−.02	.01
When considering a difficult situation, God and I work together to think of possible solutions.	.80*	−.05	.04
After I've gone through a rough time, I try to make sense of it without relying on God.	−.04	.82*	.02
When deciding on a solution, I make a choice independent of God's input.	.00	.72*	.08
In carrying out solutions to my problems, I wait for God to take control and know somehow he'll work it out.	−.01	−.07	.80*
I do not think about different solutions to my problems because God provides them for me.	−.05	.06	.78*

*High factor loading (correlation between scores on that factor and answering the question positively) that indicates this question should be used to help name the factor.
SOURCE K. I. Pargament, J. Kennell, W. Hathaway, N. Gravengoed, J. Newman, and W. Jones, "Religion and the Problem-solving Process: Three Styles of Coping," *Journal for the Scientific Study of Religion, 27,* pp. 96–97. Copyright © 1988 Society for the Scientific Study of Religion, Inc. Used with permission.

Usually a 5- or 7-point scale is used and each subject checks one of the spaces that describes his or her impression. More than 50 adjective pairs were used in the original research, and Di Vesta (1984) and others have suggested other dimensions.[3] With appropriately selected dimensions, the semantic differential is often used to evaluate quality of instruction, reaction to a meeting, and the like.

Factor analysis is frequently used in a confirmatory way to supply evidence of construct validity by showing that the measure behaves as it should if it were valid. Pargament and colleagues (1988) constructed a measure of problem-solving styles related to religion. From interviews and the literature they posited three styles: self-directing, deferring, and collaborative. The self-directing person believes that problem solving is the individual's responsibility and takes an active stance. God is seen as providing the freedom and resources to direct their lives. The deferring stance "waits for solutions to emerge through the active efforts of God" (p. 92). People with a collaborative stance believe that "God is my partner" and view both God and the individual "working together to solve problems" (p. 92). Table 22.2 shows sample items related to each of the three factors that emerged when the instrument was factor-analyzed. The figures in the columns, called factor loadings, indicate the correlation of the item with the factor.

Factor analysis provides no interpretation of the factors, only data indicating which items are heavily related to a given factor. We must determine

---

3. Here is an excellent example of the value of the *Social Science Citation Index*. It is the ideal reference work to trace forward from Osgood, Suci, and Tannenbaum (1957) to see who has validated or added to the basic set of dimensions.

the meaning of the factor from the items that correlate highly with it. Thus, in Table 22.2, factor 1 correlates highly with the first and second items and very poorly with the other four items, so we name it in terms of what is measured by those first two. From their nature it is clear that factor 1 represents the collaborative stance. Similarly, we can identify factors 2 and 3 as representing, respectively, self-directing and deferring stances. Note that even though the order of the factors is different in the table from their order in the text where the three styles were described above, we have no trouble identifying factors from loadings. With these interpretations, it is clear that the factors and their loadings conform to the rationale used in developing the test and therefore provide evidence of its construct validity. Another example of factor analysis appears later in this chapter.

The initial factor analyses resulting from most statistical software packages yield uncorrelated factors (called orthogonal factors). If these factors are identifiable, fine, but that is often not the case. The factors are most clearly identified when loadings of the items that relate to a single factor are maximized and loadings on other factors are minimized. This often requires rotating the axes, a procedure too complicated to explain here but available as an option in statistical software packages. It results in factors that are intercorrelated (oblique rather than orthogonal). That is what was done in this study, where the factor intercorrelations for the complete test are: $r_{12} = -.61$, $r_{13} = .47$, and $r_{23} = -.37$. The loadings in Table 22.2 reflect the relationships with the intercorrelated (rotated) factors.

Structural or Covariance Modeling

Sociologists, economists, and more recently, psychologists are interested in causal chains and the relationships between links in those chains. **Structural modeling** is a set of statistical techniques designed to permit causal inferences in such a chain. It is also called covariance modeling and causal modeling. These techniques are often applied to nonexperimental data, which makes them particularly useful for exploring policy issues where variables cannot be manipulated. The methods allow us to assess the contribution of each factor to a dependent variable at each stage of a longitudinal process or, alternatively, the projected influence of a variety of variables on one another and thence through intermediate (intervening) variables to the dependent variable. The methods yield the equivalent of correlations that represent the contribution of each variable. Figure 22.3 shows an example adapted from Davis (1985) in which the relationships among the variables are indicated by lines A, B, C, D, and E in the diagram. Earnings is the dependent variable, which is influenced by parental status both directly and through the intervening variable of educational attainment. Educational attainment affects earnings both directly and through an intervening variable, occupational prestige. That is, education, by opening the gates to careers with occupational prestige, determines potential earning levels.

You can immediately see a parallel to multiple regression. But these techniques go beyond it by examining the relationships through the inter-

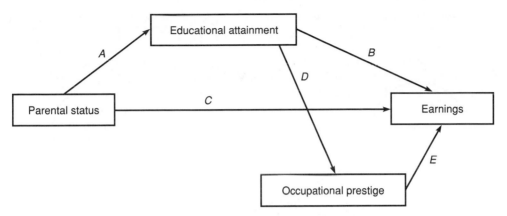

FIGURE 22.3 Example of structural modeling. (Adapted from J. A. Davis, *The Logic of Causal Order*, p. 17. Copyright © 1985 Sage Publications Inc. Used with permission.)

vening variables: parental status through educational attainment and occupational prestige to earnings. As in factor analysis, we can combine measures to form constructs in the causal structure. Figure 22.4 shows such a model adapted from Maruyama and Walberg (1982) that contains both measures (rectangles) and underlying dimensions or constructs (circles). In this instance, we use one or more measures (Maruyama and Walberg used three) that together in some combination provide an assessment of the construct. We then examine the relations of the constructs to the dependent variable.

In the model in Figure 22.4, school achievement is seen as determined in part by the constructs "ability" and "peer acceptance." The latter is affected by both "ability" and the construct "adult acceptance." Each construct is assessed by three separate measures, which are combined to provide a score for an individual.

Structural modeling, like the previously discussed techniques, assumes linear relationships. Further, in some techniques, like path analysis, devised by Sewall Wright (1921) for work in genetics, causation is assumed to flow in only one direction, down the causal chain. Feedback from peer acceptance, which modifies perceived ability, cannot be handled by such techniques. Path analysis is, however, one of the most commonly used ones. Like the other methods, structural modeling is useful for both validating and exploring. We can explore the relative contributions of factors in order to determine those that are the most influential. Validation of theoretical views of a phenomenon is done by determining their fit to data. But structural modeling has been criticized as a method for determining causation because it is essentially correlational. Further, there is always the question as to whether there is another model including more or different variables or ones with better measures that might more fully explain the data (technically referred to as misspecification of the model, or just misspecification). For critiques of structural modeling, see Baumrind (1983), Freedman (1987), and Lipsey and Pollard (1989).

A computer program known as LISREL (Jöreskog and Sörbom, 1988)

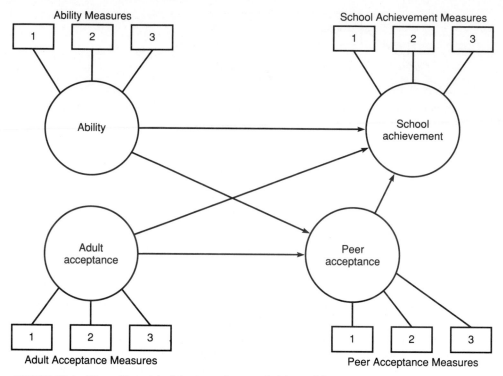

FIGURE 22.4 "Causal" model of the interrelations of ability, adult acceptance, peer acceptance, and school achievement. (Adapted from Maruyama and Walberg: "Causal Modeling" in *Encyclopedia of Educational Research*, Fifth Edition, Harold E. Mitzel, Editor in Chief. Copyright © 1982 by the American Educational Research Association. By permission of Macmillan Publishing Company, a Division of Macmillan, Inc.)

provides a much more sophisticated approach to handling causation flowing in both directions and, like factor analysis, developing hypothetical constructs and determining their relationships in the model. (See also Bollen, 1989, and Loehlin, 1987.)

An Example of the Use of Relationship Statistics

Homer and Kahle (1988) used factor analysis, discriminant analysis, canonical correlation, and structural modeling to determine whether a commonly accepted theory—that values lead to attitudes determining behavior—is valid. The study was done in the context of consumer buying at so-called natural food stores. Such stores stock foods grown without commercial pesticides or fertilizer as well as health and nutrition food supplements and educational materials.

Their model assumed two categories of values, internal and external, with natural food shoppers placing more importance on internal values that relate to control over their lives, including dietary decisions. Nonshoppers would

TABLE 22.3   Factor Analysis of Homer and Kahle's (1983) List of Values Scale

Variable	Factor Loadings		
	Factor 1	Factor 2	Factor 3
Self-fulfillment	.70*	.18	.08
Excitement	.63*	−.03	.43
Sense of accomplishment	.74*	.11	.15
Self-respect	.75*	.27	−.07
Sense of belonging	−.05	.81*	.29
Being well-respected	−.03	.76*	.40
Security	.26	.64*	.13
Fun and enjoyment	.25	.05	.84*
Warm relationships	−.03	.40	.75*
Percent of variation explained	37.2%	15.0%	12.1%

* High factor loadings for a List of Values test score used in naming the factor.
SOURCE Adapted from P. M. Homer and L. R. Kahle, "A Structural Equation Test of the Value-Attitude Behavior Hierarchy," in *Journal of Personality and Social Psychology*, Vol. 54. Copyright 1988 by the American Psychological Association. Adapted by permission.

be more externally oriented, concerned with relations with others and with security. These attitudes, in turn, would influence attitudes toward nutrition, which would influence shopping behavior.

They began with a List of Values scale that measured the nine values listed in the "Variable" column of Table 22.3. They factor-analyzed these nine scores and found that three factors accounted for 64 percent of the original variance of the measure. The relationship of each of the nine values to the three factors is shown in the factor loadings.

As noted earlier, factor analysis gives only statistical information like this. We must determine the meaning of the factor, the nature of the underlying construct, from the relationships of the factors to each variable. Homer and Kahle named their factors in terms of the asterisked variables. Factor 1 (self-fulfillment, excitement, sense of accomplishment, and self-respect) represents individual internal values. Factor 2 (sense of belonging, being well-respected, and security) represents external values. Factor 3 (fun and enjoyment in life and warm relationships with others) also represents interpersonal values, but "people who value warm relationships with others are motivated by the internal gratification received from such interactions, which renders this an internally oriented value" (p. 641). This is a typical example of how factor analysis works. The interpretation of the factors is supplied by the researcher with the expectation that a consensus with respect to that interpretation will be created among the editor, article reviewers, and readers.

Figure 22.5 displays the model they hypothesized, the causal relationships, and their path coefficients. Variables contributing to a construct are connected to it with short dashed lines, paths not part of the model have longer dashed lines, and the model is shown in solid lines. Path coefficients, the numbers on the lines, indicate the contribution of the pathway to the causal relationship.

The path coefficients that are not part of the model (−.02, −.14, and .07)

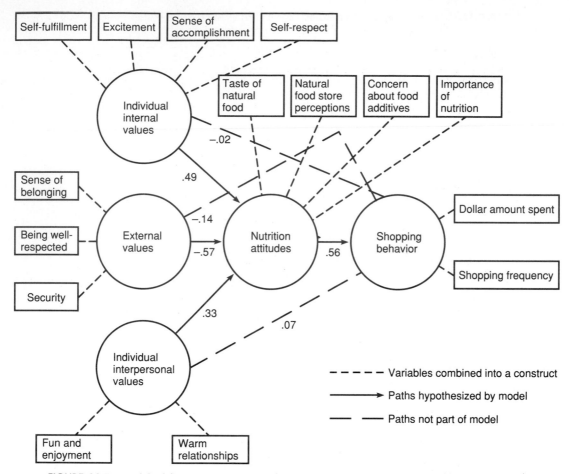

FIGURE 22.5 Model of the relationship of values to attitudes to buying behavior in a natural food store. (Adapted from P. M. Homer and L. R. Kahle, "A Structural Equation Test of the Value-Attitude Behavior Hierarchy," in *Journal of Personality and Social Psychology*, Vol. 54. Copyright 1988 by the American Psychological Association. Adapted by permission.)

are considerably lower than those on the solid lines, which are .49, −.57, .56, and .33. This is as it should be if the data fit the proposed model. The fit of the model was tested by the LISREL computer program and found to fit. The authors note that the direction of causation must be determined by theory rather than by the statistics. For example, an alternative explanation reverses the direction: people " 'caught' in natural food stores might attempt to answer in socially desirable ways that make them appear to be more internally oriented and to have more positive attitudes toward nutrition" (p. 644). In response, the authors argue that they have provided "sufficient prior research and compelling theory to justify" their model.

The authors also computed a canonical correlation between the four variables making up the nutritional-attitudes construct and the nine scores of the List of Values scale and found it to be .29. This indicates a fairly low correlation between values and attitude, lower than might be expected from the fact that the model fits. It is difficult to compare this correlation meaningfully* with the path coefficients, however, since they are affected by other interrelationships in the model. It serves mainly to indicate that though the model fits, the proportion of variance explained is still small. (A possible partial explanation for so little of the variance being accounted for is that although this model fits, another might fit as well or better.)

Various statistics exist to assist with multivariate relationships:

- Given data that are at the interval- or ratio-scale level, multiple regression will predict a dependent variable from two or more independent variables, and multiple correlation will indicate the size of the relationship between the dependent variable (often called a criterion) and the predicted scores.
- Given two or more dependent variables to be related to two or more independent variables, canonical correlation will indicate the size of the relationship between the latter and a "most predictable composite criterion."
- Given a categorical (nominal-scale) variable to relate to two or more interval- or ratio-scale variables, discriminant analysis will indicate whether some combination of the latter can classify individuals into their correct categories.
- If we have a theory that supports a causal chain, structural modeling eliminates the alternative explanation that the data can be explained by sampling and chance error and indicates the influence various paths have on the outcome.

STATISTICS FOR DIFFERENCES

Let us take a look now at two commonly used statistics that help eliminate the alternative explanation of sampling and chance error to account for differences between frequency counts (chi-square) or means (analysis of variance).

Chi-Square

Chi-square (mathematicians call it *chi squared*) is a useful statistic.

- It can test a hypothesis about whether one variable is related to (or contingent on) another when the data are in frequencies, proportions, or percentages.
- It can test whether the data fit a particular model or distribution.
- It can combine probabilities derived from independent samples into a single probability over the data set (another way of doing a meta-analysis).

Frequencies, proportions, and probabilities are often displayed in tables. Polling results, for example, may indicate the differences in responses between groups of individuals (men and women, say, or the responses among inner-city dwellers, urban non-inner-city dwellers, and suburbanites). Such tables are called contingency tables because we are often interested in whether there is a relationship between persons' responses and their gender or where they live. The pattern of entries in such tables may be due to the influence of gender, for instance, or might be accounted for by sampling and chance error. Chi-square may be used to eliminate the latter alternative explanation.

We can also use chi-square to test the fit of a model. For example, the LISREL computer program used chi-square to test the fit of the model in the Homer and Kahle (1988) modeling study just described. The likelihood that the set of path coefficients could be accounted for by sampling and chance error was less than one-tenth of 1 percent. In some instances, we may be interested in whether a frequency distribution differs from the normal distribution only by sampling and chance error. With chi-square we can compare frequencies from the two distributions and determine whether the data are too atypical and so could not be.

Chi-square can be used to combine the probabilities from a series of studies into a single significance test of the set. Although chi-square appears not to be the preferred statistic, it can be used in meta-analyses as described in chapter 21. For example, suppose four studies compared teaching swimmers the sidestroke by having them practice the parts separately—kick, arm movements, and breathing—in contrast to practicing the whole stroke at once. None of the studies showed significant results, but the means of the whole method showed shorter learning times than the part method in three of the four studies. Using chi-square, we could combine the probabilities of the four studies as though they were a single study with four replications. The test over the set, with the increased power provided by the replications, would probably reach statistical significance.[4]

The formula for chi-square (χ^2) is quite simple. It involves finding the difference between the observed frequency and the frequency that would be expected by chance, squaring it, dividing it by the expected frequency, and summing these over all the observed data:

$$\chi^2 = \sum \frac{(f_0 - f_e)^2}{f_e}$$

where f_0 is the observed frequency found in the data, f_e is the expected frequency, and Σ indicates that the fractions are to be summed.

An Example.   Culler and Holahan (1980), in a study of test anxiety and academic performance, gave a test anxiety scale to entering freshmen in a class of

---

4. Combining chi-squares requires a formula different from the one in the next paragraph; see Rosenthal, 1984, and Guilford and Fruchter, 1978.

	Actual Frequencies and Percentages				**Expected Frequencies**		
	High Test Anxiety		Low Test Anxiety		High Test Anxiety	Low Test Anxiety	
GPA	Frequency	Percent	Frequency	Percent			
Less than 2.00	19	29	2	7	14.2	6.8	21
2.00 and above	46	71	29	93	50.8	24.2	75
Totals	65	100	31	100	65	31	96

FIGURE 22.6 Contingency table showing the relationship of test anxiety to grade point average. (Adapted from R. E. Culler and C. J. Holahan, "Test Anxiety and Academic Performance: The Effects of Study Related Behaviors," in *Journal of Educational Psychology*, Vol. 72, No. 1, 1980. Copyright 1980 by the American Psychological Association. Adapted by permission.)

96 introductory psychology students. Using a 2.00 grade point average (GPA) as a cutting point (2.00 was required for graduation on a scale of 0 to 4.00), they divided students into high and low groups on the test-anxiety scale. Figure 22.6 shows the data.

In contrast to 29 percent of the high-test-anxiety group failing to meet this minimal requirement during their first semester of college work, only 7 percent of the low-anxiety group failed to do so. This would appear to be a significant deviation from a chance distribution. But is it? Chi-square will tell us.

The figures at the left give the actual data, whereas those at the right show us how the frequencies would have been distributed if chance were at work. Thus there are $19 + 2 = 21$ cases who failed to meet the 2.00 GPA. If this were a chance distribution, since the ratio of high test anxiety to low test anxiety is 65 to 31 out of 96 cases, then 65/96 of the 21 cases would be low in anxiety and 31/96 would be high in anxiety. This gives us the figures 14.2 and 6.8 in the top row of the expected frequency table. The second row is similarly derived. Now, is the deviation of the observed from the expected such that it could reasonably be accounted for by sampling variability, or is it atypical?

Chi-square uses the differences between the actual frequencies and the expected frequencies as the basis for its calculations. These differences are squared, divided by the expected frequency, and summed over all the cells:[5]

---

5. If one or more expected frequency is less than 10 for a 2×2 table, Yates's correction for continuity must be used. It moves the frequencies to the middle of the interval by subtracting 0.5 from observed frequencies greater than expected and adding 0.5 to those lower than expected. This correction has been applied to the numbers in the equation (for example, 19 becomes 18.5 because it is larger than 14.2).

$$\chi^2 = \frac{(18.5 - 14.2)^2}{14.2} + \frac{(2.5 - 6.8)^2}{6.8} + \frac{(45.5 - 50.8)^2}{50.8} + \frac{(28.5 - 24.2)^2}{24.2} = 5.34$$

We will need the number of **degrees of freedom** to find our probabilities in the chi-square table. The concept of degrees of freedom refers to the freedom of the data in successive samples to vary. Once one of the expected frequencies is found, the others can be found by subtraction. Thus given that 14.2 is found by the foregoing process for the top left cell entry, the remainder of the 21 cases in the row have to be in the top right cell, or 6.8. Similarly, the remainder of the 65 cases in the left column must be in the lower left cell, or 50.8. The rest of the 96 cases must be in the remaining empty cell. This is what is meant by a 2 × 2 table having only one degree of freedom. Given the row and column totals, once one cell entry is determined, the rest are as well. So we say that the table has only one degree of freedom.[6] All fourfold tables like this one have one degree of freedom. In general, chi-square tables have $(r - 1)(c - 1)$ degrees of freedom, where r is the number of rows and c the number of columns.

Looking in any chi-square table (such as Guilford and Fruchter, 1978, p. 515) under the 5 percent significance level and one degree of freedom, we find that anything larger than 3.84 is atypical. The chi-square of 5.34 is clearly atypical, so the differences are statistically significant. As a handy rule of thumb, since the average value of chi-square is the number of degrees of freedom, unless the result of the equation is greater than the degrees of freedom, don't bother to look it up in a table. Whether we accept the data as supporting the hypothesis that students with low GPAs have greater test anxiety than those with GPAs over 2.00 will depend on whether we can conceive of reasonable alternative explanations. Chi-square has allayed a major one, that the distribution in the table is the result of sampling and error variation.

Assumptions and Limitations.   In using chi-square, it is assumed that each observation can be correctly classified in only one cell and that the observations are independent of one another. For instance, a person can clearly be classified with respect to GPAs, and one student's GPA does not affect the GPA another

---

6. With one degree of freedom, as Moses (1986) notes, we can lay out all the possible tables, inserting successive values of 1, 2, 3, and so on in the upper left-hand cell of the frequency table. We would have as many such tables as the lowest of the marginal frequencies, in this instance, 21 of them. Moses then notes that we can find the probabilities empirically by making up a deck of cards to represent the data. Suppose we combine two decks of playing cards, selecting 21 red cards to represent students with GPAs under 2.00 and 75 black ones for those over 2.00. Shuffling them thoroughly, if we dealt 65 cards and counted the number of red cards, that would indicate the number in the upper left cell. We could continue doing this, deriving a table of how often each of the 21 possible distributions of cases would appear and from that would be able to judge the probability that any particular one would do so. Chi-square, of course, does this much more easily for us. The point of this is to illustrate the probability base underlying chi-square. There is such a base underlying each of the inferential statistics. Each could be derived empirically, as done here, though it would be very complex to do so. Chi-square for one degree of freedom makes it easier to see that base than other tests do.

individual will have. Chi-square is based on the assumption that we are sampling from a continuous normal distribution, but this assumption can be violated for large samples.

Chi-square handles only categorical (nominal) data, frequencies, or figures based on them like percentages or probabilities. The GPAs were interval data, so Culler and Holahan threw away information when they categorized students as high or low on GPA in order to use chi-square. Since it was statistically significant and illustrated the desired point, this is not of concern and is often done. However, had a *t* test been statistically significant and the chi-square not significant because of the information discarded when the data were dichotomized, an investigator who ran only the chi-square might have been led to a Type II error. Typically, except when exploring the data to see what they tell you, it is better to use statistics appropriate to your original data level than to discard information in order to use a simpler test. In this instance, it might have been more appropriate to correlate the GPA with test anxiety scores to determine the strength of the relationship. However, this example demonstrates that there are many ways in which data can be summarized and presented. It is up to the researcher to use statistics appropriately to make a point.

Chi-square can be used in the following ways:

- To determine whether the frequencies in a contingency table are arranged according to chance or whether they fit some particular model or pattern of expectations
- To determine whether the data deviate from a particular model such as a normal distribution more than would be expected by random sampling and chance error
- To combine the probabilities from several independent observations into a single probability

---

Testing Differences among Several Means: Analysis of Variance

Analysis of variance (ANOVA) is one of the most commonly used statistics in the experimental literature.[7] Edgington (1974), analyzing journals published by the American Psychological Association from 1962 to 1972, found that 71 percent of the articles involving statistical inference used ANOVA. The situation has probably not changed markedly. ANOVA lends itself well to complex experimental designs, those where more than two groups are being compared. Indeed there may be many groups exposed to different conditions. For example, we might study the effect of directive and nondirective coun-

---

7. Although widely used, in many instances the researcher would do as well or better with a multiple regression model; see Cohen (1968, 1990), and Pedhazur (1982).

seling (two treatments) under conditions where the counselors were of the same or opposite gender (two conditions) and may do so for teenagers, adults, and the elderly (three categories of subjects) and for males and females (two categories of subjects). This is a $2 \times 2 \times 3 \times 2$ design involving 24 cells and lends itself to ANOVA. ANOVA can be used when subjects are stratified into homogeneous groups to hold gender, age, ability, or background constant. In experimental design terms, stratification is called **blocking**, and a stratum (such as teenagers) is a *block*.

ANOVA allows us to partition the variance of the study to find the part that is attributable to any variable that was a part of the design. This allows us to test the statistical significance of the contribution of any variable (gender, age, treatment) to the effect and also to test the combined effect of variables (gender combined with treatment, age with treatment, etc.). In addition, by removing all the sources of variance accounted for in the study design, the residual is closer to being the result of sampling and chance error. This allows for more powerful and precise tests of statistical significance. With a complex design, we have many more data to use in population estimation, thereby making the estimates more accurate and the tests more sensitive. Finally, where there are many groups, there would be many pairs of means to examine with a *t* test. If there are 20 possible pairs, the 5 percent level for Type I errors has gone up since, on the average, one of the pairs will be statistically significant just as a result of chance alone. ANOVA keeps the Type I error at 5 percent by making a single simultaneous test of all means that tells us whether they are equivalent except for differences traceable to chance variation. If they are not, we can go in and find where statistical significance lies.

Analysis of variance proceeds by comparing two independent estimates of the population variability based on different aspects of the sample's variability. One of the estimates is from data that might be inflated by the treatment effect (or whatever effect we are interested in sensing). The other is free of it. The null hypothesis is that the two are estimating the variability of the same population and that there is no difference between them that cannot be reasonably accounted for by chance.

This is tested by dividing the population estimate of the variance embodying the treatment effect by another population estimate presumed free of it. If both were from the same population, on the average, the fraction would be 1, since the two estimates would be approximately equal. This is the null hypothesis: they are not more different from each other than would be expected by chance. The alternative hypothesis is that the variances are so different that the deviation from one will be greater than might be expected by random sampling and chance variation at whatever significance level we are using to protect from Type I error. Presumably, this is due to whatever independent variable was included in the numerator's estimate of the population variance.

An Example Designed for Explanatory Purposes. To show how analysis of variance works, a simple fictitious example may be most helpful. Suppose we are interested in how effective nondirective, psychoanalytic, and behavior modification therapy are in improving clients' social adjustment. We have a random sample of 15 people who come from the same normally distributed population, the members of which would, on the average, score 10 on a measure of social adjustment. Let us assign them in terms of the mean score randomly to three groups of five.

Group 1	Group 2	Group 3
10	10	10
10	10	10
10	10	10
10	10	10
10	10	10

But the fact that the mean of the population is 10 doesn't mean that everyone will have an observed score of 10. Were we to administer a test, some subjects might score 10, but most would not. Some would score higher, some lower—the variability in social adjustment we would get from random sampling. In addition, the unreliability of the test, the different conditions under which the subjects took it, the way they reacted to those conditions, their motivation to take the test, their ability to concentrate that day, and many other factors all contribute to the variability of test results. We can represent the totality of such variation by inserting the social adjustment scores in the table of the 15 individuals we selected in the first step. We show their scores as the mean plus or minus their deviation from it since this shows the variation. We also randomly assign treatments to the groups.

Nondirective Therapy	Psychoanalytic Therapy	Behavior Modification Therapy
$10 + 2 = 12$	$10 + 0 = 10$	$10 + 1 = 11$
$10 + 5 = 15$	$10 - 6 = 4$	$10 + 0 = 10$
$10 - 6 = 4$	$10 + 2 = 12$	$10 - 1 = 9$
$10 + 7 = 17$	$10 - 8 = 2$	$10 - 4 = 6$
$10 - 3 = 7$	$10 - 4 = 6$	$10 - 9 = 1$
$M = 11$	$M = 6.8$	$M = 7.4$

Grand mean (mean of all the data) = 8.4

The combined effect of sampling, measurement, and other errors is represented in the variability of the scores. How do we get two independent estimates of the population variability from these data? The variability in the population would contribute both to the variability within each sample of five scores and also to the variability between the means of the three separate samples. So one estimate could come from the variability of these scores around their column mean, the other from the variation of the three column means around the mean of the whole set of data. In our sample data, the estimate of the population variance based on the between-the-means data is 25.8; that from within the columns is 21. The ratio, called an F ratio, of 25.8 to

21 yields 1.23. The F value for 2 and 12 df[8] is 3.89 (see any statistics text, such as Hays, 1981). To be statistically significant, the F ratio would have to exceed this. Therefore, we cannot reject the null hypothesis that these three groups are no more different from one another than we would expect by chance error if they were drawn from the same population. That is reasonable; we have not yet added treatment effect.

Suppose now we add a treatment effect to these scores: 10 for nondirective therapy, 3 for psychoanalytic therapy, and 1 point for the behavior modification therapy. The treatment effect must conform to the assumption that it affects the mean but not the variability. That is, it adds a certain amount to each score depending on the size of the treatment effect (in the case of a negative effect, it subtracts). So although the scores in a column may go up (or down) as a whole, the treatment doesn't increase the variability of the scores about the mean. On that basis, the variation within the columns about each column's mean would give us a measure of population variability independent of treatment effect. By contrast, the column means are clearly affected by the treatment. Therefore, the variability of these means from each other would be the result of a combination of the treatment effect and chance error. So if the treatment had an effect, when we estimate the population variability from them, it ought to be larger than the other estimate.

Nondirective Therapy	Psychoanalytic Therapy	Behavior Modification Therapy
10 + 2 + 10 = 22	10 + 0 + 3 = 13	10 + 1 + 1 = 12
10 + 5 + 10 = 25	10 − 6 + 3 = 7	10 + 0 + 1 = 11
10 − 6 + 10 = 14	10 + 2 + 3 = 15	10 − 1 + 1 = 10
10 + 7 + 10 = 27	10 − 8 + 3 = 5	10 − 4 + 1 = 7
10 − 3 + 10 = 17	10 − 4 + 3 = 9	10 − 9 + 1 = 2
$M = 21$	$M = 9.8$	$M = 8.4$

Grand mean = 13.1

The estimate of population variance based on the differences among means of the columns that have been affected by treatment now is 238.48, while the within-columns variability (which has not been affected by treatment) remains at 21. Once again, we examine the F ratio of the variance estimate from between the means of the columns to that from within the columns, or $238.48/21 = 11.36$. Compared with 3.89, which we found earlier was the tabled value for 2 and 12 degrees of freedom, this is clearly atypical. The means were affected by the treatment. But that is a rather crude test. Where is there a difference among the groups?

If we had hypotheses prior to the study that nondirective counseling would do better than psychoanalytic which, in turn, would do better than behavior modification, then we can test these **planned comparisons** with t

---

8. The degrees of freedom between columns is one less than the number of columns, or 2. Within columns, it is the number of cases, less one for the mean of each column: $15 - 3 = 12$. Both degrees of freedom are needed to use the F table.

tests. If we had no hypotheses but were just looking to see what would be the result, we are making what are called **post hoc comparisons**. That is, we are making comparisons after the fact, knowing now which came out larger. Comparisons made on this basis most commonly use Scheffé's test or Tukey's HSD (honestly significant difference) test. These, as well as the t test, can be found in many statistics texts (such as Hays, 1981).

The example just given is known as a fixed-model analysis of variance. There are also random and mixed models. These terms refer to the generality to be attributed to the treatment categories chosen. The importance of knowing which model applies is twofold: it affects both the way the test of significance is done and the seriousness of violating certain assumptions on which ANOVA is based.

Generalization from the **fixed model** is only to treatments exactly like those tested. The treatment's strength and nature are directly represented—the nondirective, psychoanalytic, and behavior modification treatments, *as used in the study*, were the ones we desired to learn about.

In the **random model**, the treatments used are assumed to be a random sample of the possibilities that might have been used, and the results are intended to generalize to those possibilities. In our example, we used three specific therapies, but there are many more schools of therapy than these three, and our random sample might have included some of them. The question we are asking is whether it makes any difference which school of therapy a psychologist follows, and these three represent the variety of such schools.

Finally, there is a **mixed model** for studies where the categories involve both fixed and random characteristics. This is common in studies with different levels of treatment that represent random samples of treatment levels, but the treatment itself is fixed in that we are interested in studying it as it is used in the study, not generalizing to other forms of which it might be representative. For example, we might study nondirective counseling at different randomly selected lengths of treatment.

Much more complex designs than our fictitious example are quite common. For instance, we might be interested in adding other variables to the previous design: whether it yields the same results for men and women and for subjects of low as well as middle or high socioeconomic status. This would increase the complexity and possibly result in interactions, combinations of variables with which a given therapy is more effective. Nondirective therapy, for instance, might be more effective with upper- and middle-class girls but behavior modification more effective with lower-class boys. The nature of interactions will be made clearer when we discuss Table 22.5.

An Example from the Literature. Darley and Batson (1973) examined the reactions of seminary students to a person apparently ill and in need of help. The "ill" person, an accomplice, was stationed on a path subjects were directed to follow. Seminarians were randomly assigned to one of two conditions: given instructions to hurry to an appointment (hurry condition) or sent to speak on the parable of the Good Samaritan (message condition). The question was whether these conditions individually or together would influence the seminarians' willingness to stop and help an individual apparently in trouble. Table

TABLE 22.4   Means for Combinations of the Three Levels of Hurry Condition and Two of the Message Condition

Message	Low	Hurry Medium	High	Summary over Hurry Conditions
Helping relevant	3.8	2.0	1.0	2.3
Task relevant	1.7	1.7	0.5	1.3
Summary over message conditions	3.0	1.8	0.7	

SOURCE   Adapted from J. M. Darley and C. D. Batson, "From Jerusalem to Jericho: A Study of Situational and Dispositional Variables in Helping Behavior," in *Journal of Personality and Social Psychology*, Vol. *27.* Copyright 1973 by the American Psychological Association. Adapted by permission.

22.4 shows their results in terms of ratings of their helpfulness. Note that the means for the hurry condition alone as indicated in the summary line at the bottom of the table diverge quite widely and are in the expected directions. The means for the message condition in the summary column at the right side of the table are also in the expected order, but closer together. If we were to run *t* tests, look at all the pairs we would have to compare. Analysis of variance tells us whether it is legitimate to look for differences among pairs.

The data for ANOVA are usually presented in a standard format. Table 22.5 shows such a table for the Darley-Batson study. The horizontal entries in the table indicate the data for each of the conditions studied. These entries show the between-means variation for message (whether the seminarian was to speak on the parable or not), hurry (the variation between means under hurry and no-hurry conditions), and the interaction, the combination of hurry with message (speech but no hurry, speech and hurry, no speech but hurry, no speech and no hurry).

The label "error" is frequently used for the within variation data. This is the variation within each of the conditions, a variation presumably not affected by the treatment since the treatment was expected to elevate or depress the mean but not change the variability.

The sum of squares for each condition is difficult to interpret by itself. However, when divided by the degrees of freedom (shown in the column labeled "df"), it yields an estimate of the population variance, which is shown

TABLE 22.5   A Typical ANOVA Data Table

	Sum of Squares	df	Mean Square	F	p
Whether or not the subject was being sent to speak on the parable (message)	7.766	1	7.766	2.65	NS
How much of a hurry the subject was in (hurry)	20.844	2	10.422	3.56	<.05
Hurry by message interaction	5.237	2	2.619	0.89	NS
Error	99.633	34	2.930		

SOURCE   Adapted from J. M. Darley and C. D. Batson, "From Jerusalem to Jericho: A Study of Situational and Dispositional Variables in Helping Behavior," in *Journal of Personality and Social Psychology*, Vol. *27.* Copyright 1973 by the American Psychological Association. Adapted by permission.

in the next column, labeled mean square. Note that the estimates range from a low of 2.619 to a high of 10.422. It is the ratio of the between estimates to the within, or error, estimate which yields the F ratios shown in the next column. Those F ratios can then be compared with the tabled value for 1 and 34 degrees of freedom for hurry and for 2 and 34 df for both message and interaction. These provide the probability values shown in the right-hand column.

Only the probability for the hurry condition is statistically significant (NS means "not statistically significant"), at less than the 5 percent level. The interaction condition asks whether some combination of hurry with message (such as low hurry with thinking about the parable) is more effective than hurry or message alone. In this instance, since F is less than 1 and since only ratios larger than 1 can be statistically significant, this one is not. We might have expected such an interaction, but it apparently did not occur.

Error, the within variation, is a combination of sampling variation, measurement unreliability, and other extraneous sources of variation not explicitly built into the design—differences in depth of religious faith, for example. Randomization should have equated depth of faith among the treatments, but if it affected how individuals reacted in the situation, it might contribute to the variability in responses and hence to the variance. If we had thought this might contribute significantly to helping behavior, it could have been built into the design. We might divide the seminarians into four levels of depth of faith, giving a $4 \times 2 \times 3$ design; this would have permitted its variance to be removed. A decrease in the size of the error variance would have resulted, and this would have increased the F ratios, making them more likely to be statistically significant. Note that the data for the message condition are in the hypothesized direction but are not significant. A more powerful design might have avoided what appears now to be a possible Type II error.

Assumptions. ANOVA assumes random sampling from a normally distributed population, but studies of this assumption have shown ANOVA is quite robust to violations of normality. If violation is severe, moving the 5 percent level to the 1 percent level seems to make adequate compensation. As noted earlier, the test assumes that the variances of the groups are not affected by the treatment and vary from one another no more than would occur by chance. This assumption, called **homogeneity of variance,** used to be of concern, but studies have shown ANOVA to be robust with respect to violations, though somewhat less so than for violations of normality.

Since each group is assumed to be a separate random sample of the population, each is assumed to be independent, and treatment effect or observations of one should not affect another.

- Analysis of variance (ANOVA) allows for more precise inference by estimating and removing the variance due to factors built into the design. This allows a more accurate estimate of the error variance and a more powerful design.
- It allows the testing of the statistical significance of the effect of classi-

fying individuals according to that variable as well as the combined effect of variables.

- It avoids the inflation of the probabilities problem that would result when more than two means are compared. Since the probability of getting a statistically significant difference by chance increases as more tests run, the true Type I error level becomes inflated over the stated level.
- There are different ANOVA models, depending on whether the treatments being tested are the actual ones of interest (fixed model), they are a random sample of the treatments of interest (random model), or there is a combination of these fixed and random conditions (mixed model).

CORRECTING FOR A CONTAMINATING VARIABLE: ANALYSIS OF COVARIANCE AND PARTIAL CORRELATION

Description

Where we desire a measure of the relationship between two variables, we often find that a third variable gets in the way, and we want to be free of its effect. For example, we want to know the effect of various strengths of a new fertility treatment on ovulation rate but know that anxiety level affects it. Or, for example, we are looking at the relationship between measures of achievement and creativity but are concerned that differences in intelligence may mask the actual relationship. These are not easy corrections to make, and our ways of making them are, at best, controversial. **Analysis of covariance** (ANCOVA) can be used to increase the accuracy of our estimate of a relationship by removing the effect of an unwanted variable. It is also used to adjust for differences among groups. **Partial correlation** adjusts Pearson product-moment correlations, removing the effect of an unwanted variable.

What do we mean by removing the effect of a variable? Recall that a high correlation is an oval. If we plotted the correlation of three variables in space, that oval becomes, in three dimensions, like a blimp taking off into the air, its nose pointed up and its tail down, as shown in Figure 22.7. Suppose we want to find the correlation between the two variables, creativity and school achievement, that form the base of the three-dimensional cube that surrounds the blimp. The variable that rises vertically is intelligence. Now consider average intelligence, which will be midway up that variable, and think of taking a slice through the blimp in the horizontal plane (the middle oval of the five ovals that cut horizontally through the blimp). The arrow from that oval points to a diagram of the scatterplot between creativity and achievement for that particular level of intelligence (looking down at that cut from above). We have, in effect, held intelligence constant at that level.

We could compute the correlation between creativity and achievement at

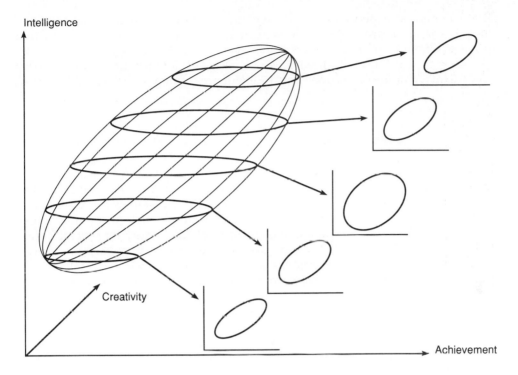

FIGURE 22.7 Model of a partial correlation adjusting the correlation between achievement and creativity for the effect of intelligence level. (Adapted from A. E. Treloar, *Elements of Statistical Reasoning*. Copyright © 1939 John Wiley and Sons, Inc. Used with permission.)

that level. But we want it over other levels as well, since we want to pool our estimates of the relationship over more than just that one slice. Figure 22.7 shows only four additional slices, but suppose we cut the blimp into an infinite number of slices, computing the correlation at each slice and averaging them. Then we would have found the correlation between creativity and school achievement at all levels without the influence of intelligence, since there is no variability in intelligence in each slice to affect that slice's correlation. Conceptually, that is the way in which these statistics remove the effect of a third variable; we say we "hold it constant" (which is what we do in taking those successive slices).

Coleman, Hoffer, and Kilgore (1982) used ANCOVA to compare the achievement of students attending public and private high schools using data from the National Center for Education Statistics. Because students attending private shcools differ from those attending public schools, having chosen to avoid public schools voluntarily (or their parents' having chosen for them), analysis of covariance was used to adjust the private school means for these differences between the two groups. Using demographic information like family income, parents' education, family composition, number of rooms in the home, parental expectations, and race, the researchers made what they believed was an appropriate adjustment in the means. But the conclusion that private schools provided superior achievement was strongly challenged by Goldberger and Cain (1982), who were concerned, among other things, about the adequacy of the correction. This problem occurs frequently with ANCOVA.

Characteristics, Interpretation, Limitations, and Assumptions

Presumably, the results of an ANCOVA or correlation study are interpreted after the adjustment, just like an ANOVA or a correlation. But removing the effect of one or more variables is both conceptually and statistically difficult, as we can see from examining the criticism of the example just given. Goldberger and Cain (1982) object to the methods of the Coleman study on several bases. One basis is a general statistical one discussed earlier by Cronbach and Furby (1970); namely, under the conditions in which ANCOVA is usually used, we cannot tell whether it overcorrects, undercorrects, or is in the middle (Cronbach et al., 1976).

But on logical grounds, also, we can sense that it would be most difficult to correct differences in achievement for the effect of the expectancies of parents who are so concerned about their children's education that they not only pay their children's tuition in private schools but at the same time shoulder the tax burden of supporting the public schools. Clearly, there is a strong commitment to achieve here that is probably passed on to the children in terms of expectancies.

Similarly, there would be conceptual problems in interpreting the results of correcting for SES with partial correlation to determine the relationship of creativity to achievement as depicted in Figure 22.7. SES is highly correlated with most measures of achievement as well as some creativity tests. So eliminating SES's effect removes something from each, depending on the measure used. Interpreting the correlation for the relation between the residual constructs, creativity and achievement, would be difficult.

These methods must be used with great care and considerable caution. Certainly, we must take note of the criticisms of the methods and indicate why we are justified in using them in any particular case. Magidson (1977) reviews alternatives to ANCOVA that have been suggested and adds one of his own.

ANCOVA and partial correlation are based on the same assumptions as the statistics they are intended to correct.

Analysis of covariance (ANCOVA) and partial correlation are statistical ways of removing the effect of a variable not wanted in a study. They must be used with considerable care.

USING THE PROPER STATISTIC
AND UNDERSTANDING DATA

Statistical Consulting and the Availability of Other Statistics

Only a few commonly used statistics have been described. You should be aware that there are a large number of statistical techniques designed to fit specific situations. For example, log-linear and logit-linear models have been developed for qualitative data as an analogue of ANOVA (see Baker, 1981). LISREL (Jöreskog and Sörbom, 1988) is a very complex and powerful computer program for uncovering the complex structure underlying a set of constructs. LISREL takes into account the fact that some constructs cannot be measured directly, so it relies on multiple efforts to estimate these unmeasurable factors. LISREL also gives reliability estimates so that we can correct relationship measures for unreliability (refer to our discussion of correction for attenuation in chapter 11).

Statistics is such a rapidly evolving field that researchers should get a conceptual grasp of the statistics they intend to use (that is what has been attempted in this chapter) so as to have a basis for intelligent conversation with a consultant as well as for making choices among the possibilities presented to them. Methods themselves often suggest research questions: What are the underlying variables? What is the nature of the causal chain? The greater the variety of data analysis techniques we know, the better the questions we can ask.

But though there are many possibilities, there is not a statistic for every situation. Indeed, statistical consultants dread the researcher who, having collected all the data, asks, "What statistic shall I use?" The time for statistical consultation is *before* the data are gathered! This is not to say that the study should be designed around a statistical model, though some studies are. *Statistics should be a tool of science, not its master.* But it is not an either/or situation. If consultation is sought in time, often simple changes will make the analysis much neater and allow the statistics to fit more exactly.

- A broad knowledge of statistical techniques suggests questions we might ask, thus possibly improving problem conceptualization—problem "homesteading."
- Statistics should be a tool of the researcher rather than the researcher distorting studies to fit a particular statistical analysis. Consulting competent professionals *before* data are gathered can often avoid problems, and minor changes often allow a particular statistical analysis to be more effective.

Computerized Statistical Programs and Understanding Data

Computerized statistical programs make available a much wider range of possibilities than existed in the past and in many instances introduce users to opportunities they would not have thought of had the options not been available on the program menu. In some instances, however, this has resulted in studies that are so immense and complex that they can be handled only through the computer, as though the researcher, like a worker in a laboratory handling radioactive material, were manipulating mechanical hands by remote control from a room outside a sealed data container. With no sense of the data, there is little basis for suspecting an absurd result, and we are at the mercy of the computer printout. Pictures are worth a thousand numbers. People are sensitive to patterns in plots, graphs, and other displays of the kind provided by these same computer programs. Request them. Make certain that the numbers are congruent with what you intuit from the data plots, and also look for other patterns not caught by your planned analyses.

It nearly always pays to play with a sample of the data using either exploratory data analysis techniques like those described in Tukey (1977) or easily computed nonparametric tests that handle ranked or categorical data. What's more, such exploration is fun! Chapters on nonparametric statistics can be found in Hays (1981); Hinkle, Wiersma, and Jurs (1979); and Guilford and Fruchter (1978). With these preliminary analyses from a small set of cases, we have an idea of what to expect. If the computer analysis differs, we are aware that a possible error has been made.

Selecting the Proper Statistic

A number of charts and decision trees can assist in selecting appropriate statistics. One of the most complete of the decision trees is that of Andrews and colleagues (1981). Nearly all are organized on the basis of matching statistics to the level of data (nominal, ordinal, interval, ratio). They are useful in suggesting statistics to consider. A less complete aid than Andrews's is given in Table 22.6. Descriptions of the statistics at the rank (ordinal) and categorical (nominal) level appear in the references for nonparametric statistics given in the paragraph above.

SUMMARY

Appropriate statistics exist for most of the situations in which you will want to use them: for dealing with single variables or multiple ones; for data that are categorical, ranked, or measured; for estimating relationships; and for determining statistically significant differences. This chapter described statistics

TABLE 22.6 Suggested Statistics for Different Conditions

Level of Data	Description of Central Tendency or Variability	Testing differences or making inferences using:			Correlation and prediction with:	
		Single variable	Two variables	More than two variables	Two variables	Three or more variables
All interval data	■ Mean ■ Standard deviation ■ Semi-inter-quartile range ■ Range	■ Confidence interval (test against a theoretical value) ■ Chi square or Kolmogorov-Smirnov (test of fit of a distribution, e.g., normality)	■ *t* test	■ Analysis of variance	■ Pearson product-moment correlation	■ Multiple correlation (one variable predicted from others) ■ Canonical correlation (two or more variables predicted from two or more variables) ■ Factor analysis (clustering of related variables; determination of underlying structure)
One variable nominal, other interval			■ *t* test	■ Analysis of variance	■ Correlation ratio ■ Biserial correlation (dichotomous variable)	■ Discriminant analysis (predicts dichotomous or polychotomous—three or more categories—criterion from multiple interval level predictors)
All ordinal data	■ Median		■ Sign test ■ Median test ■ Mann-Whitney (independent samples) ■ Wilcoxon (matched samples) ■ Run test ■ Chi square	■ Kruskal-Wallis (one-way ANOVA with ranks) ■ Friedman (two-way ANOVA with ranks)	■ Spearman rank correlation ■ Tau	■ Kendalls' coefficient of concordance (agreement among three or more variables)
All nominal	■ Mode	■ Chi square ■ Cochran's Q test (dependent variable is two-valued, e.g., pass-fail, yes-no)	■ Chi square		■ Contingency coefficient ■ Phi (for two dichotomous variables) ■ Tetrachoric (for two dichotomous variables derived from a normal distribution)	

that fit some of these categories. Let us review common ones likely to be encountered:

- Multiple regression indicates, for interval- or ratio-level data, the relationship between a dependent variable and two or more independent ones.
- Discriminant function analysis indicates whether a set of interval- or ratio-level variables can accurately categorize individuals who fall into two or more catagories (nominal level).
- Canonical correlation combines a set of interval- or ratio-level variables into a linear composite that can be maximally predicted by another set of interval- or ratio-level variables similarly combined.
- Factor analysis indicates whether a set of intercorrelations between a given number of variables can be accounted for by a set of variables less than that number.
- Structural (covariance or causal) modeling shows whether data representing the real situation fit a theoretical model proposed as explaining the causal relations among a set of variables that produce an effect.
- Chi-square indicates whether two variables are independent or are more likely to be related.
- Analysis of variance tests whether sets of means are equivalent except for chance variation or whether there is greater than chance variability among them. This avoids the inflation of probabilities—"probability pyramiding"—that can result in Type I errors when a large number of significance tests are run.
- Analysis of covariance and partial correlation are intended to correct for the effect of some variable that contaminates a result of interest.

Having concluded our discussion of methods, we take a step back in section five to see the research process in perspective. This starts in the next chapter with a discussion of the advantages of combining methods and the problems of trade-offs.

--- ADDITIONAL READING ---

Multivariate relationships: Pedhazur (1982); Thompson (1984).
Analysis of variance and covariance: Bray (1985); Edwards (1979); Hays (1981); Iverson (1987).

Structural modeling: Asher (1983); Cuttance and Ecob (1987).

--- IMPORTANT TERMS ---

Analysis of covariance
Analysis of variance
Blocking

Canonical correlation
Chi-square
Criterion

Degrees of freedom
Discriminant function analysis
Fixed model
Homogeneity of variance
Mixed model
Multiple correlation

Multiple regression
Partial correlation
Planned comparisons
Post hoc comparisons
Random model
Structural modeling

─────────────── APPLICATION PROBLEMS ───────────────

1. Dr. Dee Arkay has devised a new test of artistic aptitude that can be used to select students for the visual arts curriculum at Fayetteville State University. In addition to measuring creativity, it is presumed to measure aesthetic sensitivity and manual skill. What questions do the techniques described in our discussion of relationship statistics suggest with respect to this test, and how might the techniques be used?

2. A researcher in mathematics education has developed a computer-based course for teaching introductory calculus to university students. He hypothesizes that it will be more motivating than the regular classroom instruction and consequently will have a positive effect on student attitude toward mathematics in general. To verify this hypothesis, he randomly assigns 100 students, half to this treatment and half to receive their instruction via the regular (lecture) method. Each group is given a mathematics attitude scale once the course has been completed. What statistic should he use?

3. Two doctoral students at Syracuse University were interested in the usefulness of the instruction provided as a part of a database on a computer disk used in the library of a local community college. They wished to know if the on-line instructions were sufficient to allow users to search the database or whether they would require further help or instruction. The researchers decided to collect data using several techniques. One of their methods was a self-rating questionnaire that was filled out by users immediately after using the database.

The investigators wished to use the results from this survey to compare the frequencies of different groups of users on two self-ratings: their judgment of whether or not the on-line instructions provided sufficient information to allow them to use the system and whether or not the information obtained was viewed as satisfactory. The investigators wondered if there would be a significant difference between more experienced users, such as graduate students and faculty, and less experienced users, such as undergraduates. What statistical technique should they use to analyze these data?

4. Dalton, Hannafin, and Hooper (1989) used a 2 × 2 × 2 factorial design (see chapter 18) to compare the performance of learners working independently on a computer-assisted instruction program to that of learners working on the computers cooperatively in pairs. The researchers were interested in the effect of gender and ability (dichotomized as high or low) as well. A total of 60 eighth-grade students (31 male and 29 female), drawn from several health education classes, were randomly assigned to either the individual learning group or to the cooperative learning group. They were given a parallel series of 16 lessons on the topic of sex education. As the subject matter was sensitive, the investigators also wanted to establish whether attitude (measured by a 20-item Likert-type scale) toward the subject content, as well as the instructional technique, would have an effect. They predicted better learner performance as a result of cooperative learning, a preference for cooperative learning, and a proportionately greater gain for low-ability students using cooperative methods. They chose to analyze their data by means of a fixed-model analysis of variance. Was this an appropriate technique for this study? Why?

Compare your answers with those on pages 723–724.

━━━━━━━━━━━━━━ APPLICATION EXERCISE ━━━━━━━━━━━━━━

Sometimes the availability of new statistics suggests questions that we hadn't thought about before. Consider the different statistics discussed in this chapter in relation to your problem. Do any of them stimulate you to mull over new possibilities? For example, is enough known about your problem that you could convert your rationale or theory into a model of the interrelationships of your variables that could be tested? If not, are there other statistics that might shed light on which variables are significant in your relationships? Would factor analysis help in analyzing the structure of one or more of your variables, or in demonstrating the construct validity of a measure?

The Larger Context of Research

Having examined the tools and methods of research, each of the chapters in this section steps back to take a longer view, to place the previous material in a larger context. Much of what is examined here has been hinted at earlier: the advantages of using both quantitative and qualitative methods in the same study, the costs and advantages of increasing the power of a study to sense an effect, the different conceptions of what a social science ought to be, the ethical problems that pervade research, and whether and how social science works.

- Chapter 23 examines the advantages of combining methods for the study of a problem and the trade-offs involved in various steps one might take in upgrading the approach to a problem.
- Chapter 24 presents a typology of orientations to research that shows that not all social and behavioral scientists have the same idea of what a social science is or should be. It has important implications for collaborative research, for panels responsible for funding research, and for doctoral committees, among other things.
- Chapter 25 describes some of the ethical problems of doing research, the safeguards that the federal government has erected to protect human subjects, and the codes of conduct that professional societies have developed to guide researchers. Whereas specific ethical problems have been mentioned in discussing various methods, this pulls the problems together and puts them in perspective.
- Chapter 26 examines why social science research is needed and what is involved in ensuring that it works properly at the individual level, the peer level, and the societal level. It is a heuristic chapter intended to raise questions for further thought rather than provide answers.

C H A P T E R
23

Syntheses of Methods, Trade-offs, and Optimization

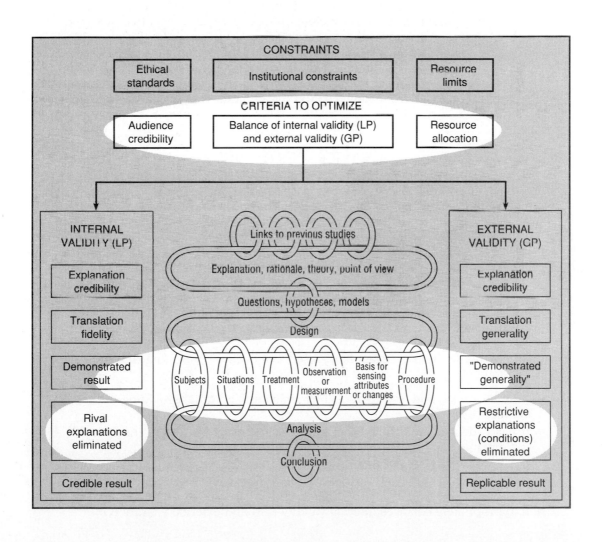

Let us . . . get on with the business of attacking our problems with the widest array of conceptual and methodological tools that we possess and they demand.

Martin Trow, "Comment on Participant Observation and Interviewing"

A study can meet two out of three criteria—good, fast, and cheap—but not all three!

Phillip L. Doughty

OVERVIEW

This chapter notes the strengths to be gained by combining complementary research methods to attack a problem optimally. It also notes that trade-offs pervade the research process; handling them well is important to a strong study. The Appendix makes concrete the positive and negative trade-off implications of a variety of common design enhancements (for example, increasing sample size). It is also a useful heuristic of enhancements to consider. Because many of the trade-offs relate to a variety of designs, the Appendix is placed at the back of the book for easy reference. Lastly, the chapter notes that replication is the ultimate validation for all methods.

CHAPTER CONTENTS

Synthesis of Methods   616
     Examples of Multimethod Use   619
Trade-offs   620
The Power of Replication   621
Summary   622

SYNTHESIS OF METHODS

Ideally, a researcher's problem lends itself to a chain of reasoning that does all of the following:

- It links cause and effect as tightly as possible, thus providing internal validity (LP).
- It has wide applicability to other people, situations, and times, thus providing external validity (GP).
- It explores sufficiently that side effects are noticed, aberrations in procedure are sensed, and the strongest possible explanation is discovered and advanced.
- It appropriately balances internal validity (LP) and external validity (GP).

- It gains acceptance by its intended audience (audience credibility).
- It allocates available resources so as to build the strongest possible chain of reasoning.
- It fits within resource, institutional, and ethical constraints.

It is not easy to achieve all this simultaneously; indeed, it may be impossible if a researcher sticks to a single method of doing research.

In a book devoted to advancing multimethod approaches, Brewer and Hunter (1989) argue: "Our individual methods may be flawed, but fortunately the flaws are not identical. A diversity of imperfection allows us to combine methods not only to gain their individual strengths but also to compensate for their particular faults and limitations" (pp. 16–17).[1] In addition, within each method there are myriad variations among which researchers may chose. Which methods are best? Which choices within a method should they make? The decisions depend on many things, but especially on the question to be answered, the audience, and personal conceptions of what is good research and of what research should achieve. We'll consider this last factor in the next chapter.

Modern architects often argue that the form a building takes should follow the function it is to serve. A building that serves its purpose well will have a beauty of its own. This is in contrast to an architect's designing a beautiful façade and having to compromise the interior design. Analogously, if we view problem as function and method as form, then form follows function in behavioral science research. The problem, the function to be served, is the all-important determiner of the method, the form the study will take. Once we have determined the problem we intend to investigate and who our audience is, the possible methods almost suggest themselves. Thus policy research for a

---

1. There once was a hen from Nantasket
   Who put all her eggs in one basket.
   The basket was deep, with colors replete,
   And filled up with eggs qualitatively sweet.

   Along came a hen from Lanerick
   Whose eggs were in baskets numeric.
   In measures exact it was clear she could revel
   With small standard error and confidence level.

   Qualities, quantities, which is the better?
   Let us decide to use them together!
   Qualities show us holistic missions;
   Quantities measure effects of conditions.

   Adapted with thanks from a 1985 presentation by Doug R. Berdie to the American Educational Research Association, *Survey Research: A Qualitative/Quantitative Synthesis.*

   Eisner (1981) notes, "The issue is not qualitative as contrasted with . . . quantitative. . . . With both we can achieve binocular vision. Looking through one eye never did provide much depth of field" (p. 9).

large and unsophisticated audience nearly always requires field studies of applied problems. Such audiences are suspicious, perhaps rightly so, of the uncertain transfer of results to real situations from laboratory conditions. These audiences like the case studies that result from a qualitative approach because they are so much easier to understand than statistics. But how solidly does the qualitative study link an intervention with its effects? And how generally applicable are the results? We can add surveys and sometimes even experimental interventions to strengthen a study by adding evidence not gained otherwise and to allay concerns about alternative explanations.

Marks and Shotland (1987) summarize three ways of combining methods to enhance an investigation. The first is *triangulation*: we approach the problem from different angles, with the anticipation that they give congruent answers free of method bias. The second, described by Reichardt and Gollob (1987), is the *bracketing model*. They argue that error may not average out in the triangulation model, and we should instead consider the results as alternative estimates. The trick, then, is to use methods that are biased in opposite directions so that the true value is bracketed. Ideally, the bias is small so that the bracket is narrow and the average is a good estimate. The third enhancement method, *complementary multiplism*, was described on the previous page (Brewer and Hunter, 1989). Different methods play complementary roles; together, they provide evidence that is markedly strengthened.

As Marks and Shotland (1987) point out, complementary multiplism may serve many purposes. We may use different methods to build greater credibility with particular audiences and enhance the interpretability of the results. We may use them to protect against different alternative explanations. And we may use them to investigate different aspects of a phenomenon, as when participant observation is used to catch social aspects, tests to assess psychological aspects, and physiological measures to find bodily concomitants. It should also be clear that the bracketing model can be used in complementary multiplism where we might use different methods to bracket the true value within the physiological measures (for example, clinical observations and laboratory tests). So there are many models to choose from in synthesizing methods to attack a problem.

Some researchers argue, however, that combining qualitative and quantitative methods in the same study is inappropriate. If we maintain a "qualitative point of view," it is hard to think of quantifying that perspective. If we maintain the mind-set of finding the "insider's view,' switching to measurement and experimentation is not very compatible. Certainly, a barrier to introducing an intervention into a qualitative field study is the point of view that there are no "subjects," only informants who are helping researchers understand the situation. We don't "treat" informants without their knowledge and consent. But since informed consent is now a requirement of most human-subject experiments, a main reason for not combining methods is that their skillful use depends on the competence and perspective of the researcher. The qualitative expert may not be so masterful in quantitative methods, and vice versa; so one or the other may be done poorly. There are undoubtedly instances where that is the case, but at most institutions, both competencies are available if a researcher is of a mind to enlist the help.

Examples of Multimethod Use

There are many examples of use of multiple methods. Smith and colleagues' (1976) combination of qualitative and quantitative methods in the evaluation of Outward Bound is a good example. Outward Bound is a voluntary program intended to increase participants' self-confidence and awareness of their dependence on others. Participants train for a wilderness experience that tests their physical, mental, and emotional capacities. Smith provided a qualitative account that not only conveys how a participant experienced it but also made the program come alive for the reader. This was accompanied by quantitative evidence of its success in achieving its goals.

Rossi and Lyall's (1976) income maintenance study combined a field experiment, survery methods, and intensive case studies. Together these provided the picture that kept from becoming policy what seemed to be a promising plan for helping low-income families escape poverty. Case studies caught the family breakup that unexpectedly resulted and also helped the researchers understand why it occurred. The researchers learned from the survey data the extent of this side effect and the good consequences of income maintenance that had been expected. Thus the combination of three research methods provided evidence of relationships plus explanations of why they occurred.

Duffy and Roehler (1990) provide still another example in their study of the effect of explicit instruction of mental processing on reading. Volunteer teachers were randomly assigned to experimental and control treatments. Both sets of teachers were taught ways to improve student engagement on academic tasks. The experimental teachers were also taught to provide instruction in mental processing. Both groups were observed seven times during the year to determine the explicitness of the instruction and to interview students to determine the extent of their awareness of their mental processing. Students were also tested on reading achievement. This nice combination of experimental and qualitative techniques provided the data needed to show the success of explicit instruction for low-reading students.

Indeed, as noted earlier, every experimental study should have, formally or informally, an element of the qualitative case study in it. Good researchers stay close to their treatment administration and data collection to learn whether things went according to plan, how subjects viewed the study, what the subjects (informants) were expecting, and how they reacted. Unanticipated events, side effects, or misperceptions can completely alter a study. The demand conditions of a study may convey quite a different perception to the subject than that planned. If a treatment is intensely disliked, students may do poorly on the measure of effect out of spite. Unless researchers are aware of such events, they will completely misinterpret the results. In a large study where data are mainly gathered by assistants, there is no substitute for the researchers' gathering some firsthand.

In many instances, only multiple methods provide the optimal combination to cover the data required to provide the powerful combination of evidence and explanation that will gain a consensus. That possibility should always be given consideration if the necessary skills to carry through the required methods competently can be obtained.

TRADE-OFFS

From the outset, this book has pointed out how difficult it is to eat your cake and have it too; we are forced to trade off one "good" to get another. We engage in trade-offs to achieve adequate sensitivity to an effect, generality without losing much linking power, the tightest possible chain of reasoning, and optimal allocation of resources. As you must realize by now, trade-offs are a critical feature of research, and the competency displayed in trade-off decisions can make or break a study. They occur at every level of the study:

- *Choice of problem*: Basic or applied research? How broadly or deeply shall it be studied?
- *Formulation of a question, hypothesis, or model*: Shall we describe? Explore? Explain? Validate? We probably don't do as good a job of exploring if we are trying to validate a hypothesis, or as good a job of validating if we are mainly exploring.
- *Choice of method or methods*: The power of the laboratory to link cause and effect is traded for the generalizing power of the field study. The detailed realistic reporting of the case study, with the possibility of well-grounded theory and explanation, is traded for the measures and numbers of experimental conditions wherein the logic and clear comparison provide compelling validation of relationships. Alternatively, one can choose the detailed responses of the sample survey wherein the combination of a clearly understood process and large amounts of data can create a sharply etched representative picture of a situation, group, or problem. Costly professional time can be devoted to qualitative observation, designing a study, building instruments, or some combination.
- *Choice of study design*: All the trade-offs involved in choices within the various facets (see the Appendix).
- *Involvement*: Should the audience or stakeholders be involved in doing the study and interpreting its data? What are the implications for the use of professional time?

A major determiner of trade-offs is whether we are conducting applied, evaluation, policy, or basic research. Each type involves contrasting trade-off choices. In a basic research study, we are describing a phenomenon and linking cause to effect. The emphasis is on understanding what is going on and how variables are linked (for example, how anxiety is linked to achievement). Strong internal validity (LP) is a key criterion. Audience credibility is almost automatic since the audience demands are typically the ones that basic researchers make of themselves to maximize the descriptive, linking, and explanatory power of the study.

As certainty that we understand a phenomenon increases, we look for practical implications and do applied studies. Internal validity (LP) is still a consideration, particularly if previous studies were done in a laboratory. But there is more concern with generality, external validity (GP), seeing whether and how the phenomenon works under real conditions. To the extent that the target audience is less sophisticated in the ways of research, we may need to use well-established instruments and familiar research methods.

Applied studies are sometimes used to determine or change policy. The studies are being done not just to find the effects but to obtain evidence that will convince particular audiences to take action based on the findings. There are usually multiple audiences: the staff of the program, its clients, other people or programs affected by it (including those it might replace), policy-makers, and legislators. Quite often these interests are antagonistic (for example, the various points of view regarding busing to provide racial integration in the schools), but the credibility of the study must be such that as many of the groups as possible—ideally, all—will accept its findings.

Each such decision involves trade-offs since taking a study in one direction typically excludes others. These are trade-offs at the macro level in terms of method. When we get to the micro level, the particular study design within a method, the trade-off possibilities become quite numerous. Each decision carries with it implications that may not always be apparent. To facilitate the process of rational design choice, the Appendix provides an accounting of what is involved in taking commonly used actions to strengthen designs. For each design enhancement, the Appendix lists both positive and negative implications. Reading through this material will suggest enhancement possibilities and facilitate weighing the trade-offs between the positive and negative implications for your particular study. As noted in the introduction to the Appendix, each study can have unique implications. Therefore, the applicability of the general direction of a design enhancement has to be carefully considered in the light of the particular circumstances of your study.

In analyzing the options of the Appendix, you will note frequent references to cost implications. These are an important factor in planning a study with or, especially, without special funding. The allocation of resources through proper choice of trade-offs to build the strongest possible chain of reasoning within a budget has always been, and will remain, a key skill of a good researcher.

THE POWER OF REPLICATION

In a chapter concerned with multimethod research, it is very important to note that for *all* methods, replication is the ultimate validation. In discussing experimentation, we noted that nothing more convincingly links two variables than to show repeatedly, and under a variety of circumstances, that a particular effect follows the administration of a cause (see pages 252 and 481). We tend to associate such evidence with experiments, but when qualitative research provides evidence of replication, it is also a convincing validation of the existence of a relationship.

When using qualitative methods, the more numerous the replications, under different circumstances, the greater the credibility; and the more varied the replications, the greater the generality. As situations and subjects are varied, alternative explanations are being ruled out—local history and instrument decay, for example. If the situations and subjects are highly varied and randomly selected, maturation and selection may be eliminated as well. There is no testing effect since there is only observation. Regression effect could be a factor, if subjects for study were selected at the top or bottom of a group; in choosing individuals for a purposive sample, we could look for subjects and settings that would help rule it out. Mortality and treatment mortality interaction could be a factor. So could reactivity, but having thought of these, we could similarly look for them in situations and, if they are present, find other situations that would help rule them out as well.

From the foregoing it is apparent that the case study, given replication under the appropriate conditions and implementation, can be a method with considerable internal validity (LP) as well as external validity (GP). As appropriate steps are taken, the evidence takes on characteristics of a meta-analysis of qualitative studies without the effect size estimate. It is less storytelling of particular instances and more describing the variety of instances and circumstances under which the phenomenon occurred.[2]

SUMMARY

The various research methods provide different kinds of evidence about phenomena. By combining methods, not only can we compensate for the flaws of one method with the strengths of another, but we can obtain different perspectives, "depth of field," and detail. Using more than one method provides complementary evidence that can reinforce our confidence in the results. It can bracket a phenomenon to reveal its dimensions. All methods involve trade-offs, however; we gain one thing but are likely to lose something else. The art of research is the balancing of trade-offs to provide the strongest study possible to achieve our goals within our resources and constraints. Replication of results with a variety of methods under a variety of circumstances is the strongest and ultimate validation of a generalization.

ADDITIONAL READING

Brewer and Hunter (1989)
Fielding and Fielding (1985)
Reichardt and Cook (1979)

Sieber (1973)
Smith (1986)

---

2. Interestingly enough, this appears to have been the method that such people as Piaget (1952) and others have used in developing and presenting their theories. The evidence gathered through their observations are, indeed, quite convincing.

=========== APPLICATION PROBLEMS ===========

1. A medical researcher wished to investigate the sensitive topic of incest in American society. Her problem was to find out what incest is and to understand the behavior of the participants. To conduct the study, she had to establish a strong rapport with a sample of affected families. Further, to identify a sufficient number of cases, the investigator had to work with an educational treatment agency. "Obtrusive" procedures such as surveys, questionnaires, and psychological tests were actively discouraged by the agency. However, the agency worked with about 500 families. What research method(s) would she have used?

2. Two nursing scholars, Johnson and Lauver (1989), were interested in the relationship between medical patients' ability to cope with stressful experiences and nursing interventions that provided them with information to prepare for each such experience.

In particular, they wished to test the predictions of two theories, emotional drive theory and self-regulation theory, which presented alternative hypotheses about how people cope. To do so, they conducted a study using patients suffering from prostate cancer who had to undergo the taxing experience of radiation therapy. The patients were randomly assigned to either a treatment group in which they listened to experimental tape-recorded messages or a control group in which they were visited by a research team member who inquired about their well-being. All patients received the usual care provided by the radiation therapy department. What trade-offs did the investigators make with this design?

3. A group of educational psychologists (Corkhill et al., 1988) were interested in whether or not advance organizers would help learners recall learned material. Normally, advance organizers are introduced ahead of the material to be learned. They are verbal or visual passages written at a more abstract or general level than the material and are intended to help learners relate the material to what they already know. Thus they aid in encoding the information. The investigators hypothesized that having learners read the advance organizer for a second time just before a recall test would aid them in retrieving the information.

The researchers conducted a series of six experiments that varied the delays between reading the material to be learned and the recall test from immediately after to two weeks later. Experiments 1–3 and 5 and 6 were conducted using the same materials with samples of university undergraduate education students. They were all laboratory studies, and all students participated for course credit. Experiment 4 was carried out with different materials and a group of grade 7 students at a university experimental school in their regular classroom. Sample sizes varied between 30, for experiment 2, and 98, for experiment 1. Experiments 3–6, those with delays of 24 hours or more between the treatment and the recall test, produced statistically significant results in favor of the investigators' hypothesis. What trade-offs did these researchers make?

4. Cunningham and Stewart (1983) were interested in testing the effectiveness of an innovative counselor training model. Thirty-two masters'-level counselor trainees from a large U.S. midwestern university participated in a 10-hour workshop consisting of three sessions spread out over the course of a week. The trainees were randomly assigned to either the treatment group or control group. Both groups received parallel training and instructional materials, with the exception of the cognitive material presented. The experimental group received discrimination training, which emphasized the integration of knowledge of responses to the client with knowledge of the counseling process, while the control group was instructed in another useful counseling skill, the formulation of behavioral objectives for difficult-to-define client problems. Both workshops were conducted concurrently.

Each trainee group was assessed on three measures of counselor effectiveness, a 25-item multiple-choice instrument, 25 free-response questions regarding audiotaped counseling situation descriptions, and a rating of a 10-minute audiotaped counseling interview. Three equivalent forms of each were used. Internal consistency reliability scores for these measures varied between .55 and .95. Each trainee was given a pretest at the first session to check equivalence between the groups and a posttest at the conclusion of third session. A follow-up testing of 22 trainees who agreed to participate was conducted after six weeks. Statistical analysis revealed significant differences between the experimental and control groups for both the initial and the follow-up studies. What trade-offs did the researchers make concerning choices involving observation and measurement?

Compare your answers with those on pages 724–725.

APPLICATION EXERCISE

Consider how you might use multiple methods to bolster the study of your problem. Are you doing basic or applied research? If the former, are there aspects of internal validity (LP) not covered by the method you were planning to use? As you considered your problem from the standpoint of different chapters in section four of this book, were there methods you considered useful? Is there a combination of these that would strengthen the case for your study? If you are doing applied research, what aspects of external validity (GP) need strengthening, and how might other methods facilitate this?

Consider the different enhancements for design described in the Appendix with respect to any tentatively chosen design you may have developed. Examine the trade-offs for those enhancements that might make your design stronger. What are the positive and negative aspects of the enhancements that might be helpful? On balance, do the positives outweigh the negatives? If not, which enhancements would you drop to strengthen the overall picture? Which additional ones might you use?

CHAPTER
24

Alternative Conceptions of a Social Science: Implications for Method

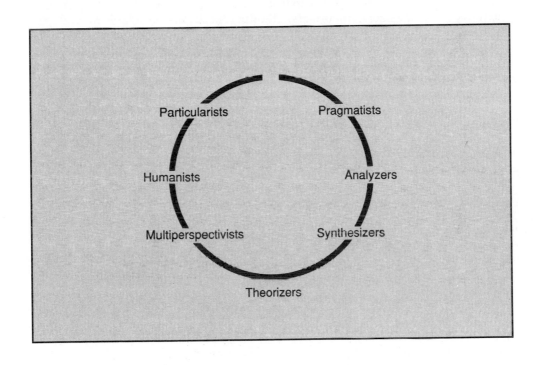

If we understand that science is not simply about the acquisition of knowledge but is a means of expressing ourselves—and of forming, transforming, and generally coping with our world—we can approach this endeavor in a new way. In so doing, we will be able to steer clear of the delusion that it is possible to know in an absolute sense of "being right" and devote our energies to the more constructive process of dealing with the implications of our different ways of knowing.

Gareth Morgan, Beyond Method

OVERVIEW

Alternative views exist among researchers of what a social science can and should be. Researchers themselves are not very conscious of this fact. These differences can, however, cause problems in communication and disagreements as to how to pursue a research problem. This chapter presents a typology of alternative orientations of researchers consisting of seven types: pragmatists, analyzers, synthesizers, theorizers, multiperspectivists, humanists, and particularists. Each has different preferred research methods as well as alternative views of what is good research. Individual researchers may hew to a single type or, quite often, take them as different roles to be assumed as appropriate to the problem.

CHAPTER CONTENTS

Introduction 626
Different Orientations to
   the Social Sciences 627
      Three Basic Strands 627
      Additional Orientations 630
Approaching a Problem from Different
   Orientations: An Example 632
The Orientations in Detail 634
      The Pragmatist 634
      The Analyzer 635
      The Synthesizer 635
      The Theorizer 636
      The Multiperspectivist 637
      The Humanist 638

The Particularist 639
Summary and Examples of
   the Orientations 640
How the Types Differ in Making
   Research Decisions 640
      Choice of Research Problem 640
      Criteria of Excellence 643
      Choice of Research Methods 644
      Strengths and Weaknesses
         of the Types 644
Perpetuation of Orientation Types 653
Team Research 654
All Types Are Valued 655
Summary 655

INTRODUCTION

Chapter 23 discussed trade-offs in terms of the many detailed decisions through which to strengthen a particular problem approach. This chapter steps back from the detail to examine what underlies approach choice. Did you think this was settled with the statement "Form follows function"? In large measure, it is true that the nature of the problem limits appropriate methods. But in that discussion we also noted that some individuals work only on problem particularly susceptible to their preferred research method; problem and approach are always synchronized. That preference is examined here.

Underlying many such preferences for method are different conceptions of what social science can and should be, conceptions I am calling **orientations to the social sciences**. From the start when we examined qualitative and quantitative studies and their differences in chapter 2, you might have sensed that these differences went deeper than words versus numbers. But researchers themselves often have not thought deeply about the underlying differences. This chapter describes a typology intended to cover major ways in which behavioral scientists view their science. It also examines how this affects their research methods. This makes differences explicit, laying them on the table for all to examine. Then, as Morgan (1983) suggests, we can "devote our energies to the more constructive process of dealing with the implications of our different ways of knowing" (p. 18).

This typology was stimulated by a set of four types based on Jungian thought described by Mitroff and Kilmann (1978). Their work considerably facilitated this derivation and is gratefully acknowledged. Two of the orientations, the particularist and the analyst, are very similar to their types.

The typology describes a continuum of orientations and methods from those closest to the natural science traditions to those nearest to the humanistic ones. Each point on the continuum characterizing a type describes a pattern of work that occurs with some frequency, a pattern in which graduate students are trained. As in any field of study, behavioral scientists are socialized by those who have gone before, learning their points of view and methods of research.

Like the nursery tale of the blind men and the elephant, each of whom characterized this strange beast by the part he was holding, so researchers' views of social science are molded by their ways of working and the content with which they work. Their knowledge claims reflect this. Some are socialized narrowly. Others are more broadly oriented, particularly in professions that cross disciplines, such as the information sciences, social work, and education. Many individuals will see the orientations as roles they assume as the characteristics of particular problems require them. Such individuals' roles usually span several orientations. Mature researchers probably bridge types more often than novices.

DIFFERENT ORIENTATIONS TO THE SOCIAL SCIENCES

Three Basic Strands

Imagine the earliest humans, huddled together in a cave around a campfire telling stories of their accomplishments. These myths conveyed the way they deal with both the everyday problems of life and, especially, its unusual catastrophes. The teller's tales suggested to others how they might do likewise.

Such wisdom helped individuals not only hunt and gather but also live in harmony. These sagas were the beginning of social science, and stories have not disappeared as a way of learning about people and their individual and communal lives.

Now imagine a much later age in the Middle East where a wise king (presumably Hammurabi) in a hot and dusty kingdom, wanting to avoid war and disputes, asked his ministers to find ways of laying down rules of conduct that would provide guides for proper living together. Thus began the rules and principles of social science that tell us how actions are related to each other and to their effects. This second step represents the wisdom of experience rationally distilled into what is presumed to be an accurate picture of the way the world works.

In due time, someone thought about testing these rules against evidence. We tend to think of this happening during the Renaissance, when the empirical began to compete with the purely rational as a basis for knowledge. But whenever it occurred, it established a third way of developing social science knowledge, the empirical work of science.

You can see these three streams of knowledge persisting to this day, though they no doubt serve different roles than previously. Where stories were the mainstream in the earliest days, they are less so now. Where social science at one time focused on theoretical treatises in what we now call philosophy and political science, we have added many additional fields where individuals speculate about the nature of economies, social and cooperative endeavor, and the mind.

Perhaps most prominent of the three in our culture is the third stream, empirical science. The social scientist who emulates aspects of physical science method has become very prominent. Indeed, the tools of measurement and statistics have pervaded all behavioral science fields. Even the historian who persists in telling and analyzing the events of the past in story form often now uses tools of quantitative investigation. And of course, such historians try their hand at theorizing and propounding principles based on past events (as did, for example, Arnold Toynbee). So the three strands by which knowledge is developed and conveyed are present today, and we use all three to learn more about our world and ourselves.

As a way of thinking of these streams, we might place them at different points on a circle, giving them names descriptive of their heritage and their roles. Let us call the first strand, which tells us stories that inform our lives, **humanists**. Such individuals follow the tradition of the humanist historians who seek out, describe, and explain those events of the past (and the present) that help us best to learn about the world. Second, there are those who encode our wisdom into rules, principles, and explanations. These we shall call **theorizers**, not so much because what they produce is worthy of being called theory but because its construction is their ultimate goal. Lastly, those following the scientific tradition of proposing hypotheses and testing them we shall call **analyzers** for their essentially deductive tradition.

These three can be placed at roughly equally distanced points around a circle to help describe their relationships (see Figure 24.1). Toward the top of the circle, we have the data- and evidence-based orientation. Toward the

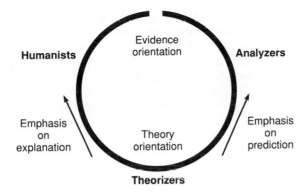

FIGURE 24.1   The relationship of humanists, analyzers, and theorizers.

bottom is that based more heavily on abstract conceptualization and rational thought alone. On the right, the emphasis is on prediction and control, which increasingly gives way to explanation as we swing clockwise around the circle. We will break the circle at the top to indicate that, though bent into the shape of a circle, it is really a continuum.

Consider now the kind of knowledge that can be gained from each of these three strands. The strand on the right depends on the simplification and reduction of the causal chain to relatively few variables, ideally to those that can be handled in an experiment. Even the most complex multivariate experiments reduce the complexity of situations so as to make clearer what leads to what. (This reductionist stance is occasionally blamed for some of the dissatisfaction with the slow growth of social science knowledge.)

Next consider the humanist side. Here, in describing situations, we include great detail and many variables. We illustrate the complexity of the situation. Why was a conflict lost? It is rarely a single factor, such as the nursery rhyme's "for want of a nail the battle was lost." More likely it was a case of INUS causation, a concatenation of particular circumstances (see chapter 12). And what truth do readers draw from the story? It is hard to predict; different individuals may see different things. Aspects likely to be salient for one may not be for another, depending on circumstances, pressures, and needs. The shadowy truths that lie beneath the surface in such tales are useful in guiding behavior, but not in the same way as principles or rules or social science "laws" (such as "frustration begets aggression").

Persons who program robots are concerned with many of the processes studied in the behavioral sciences: learning, perceiving, and problem solving—the area of artificial intelligence. At first, their approach was that of the reductionist stance of breaking everything into units so that each aspect to be perceived and each action of response was to be programmed. This is the stimulus-response orientation of behaviorism in psychology. Behaviorism is an approach that tries to make sense of behavior strictly from the outside, from the observables, without inferring anything that is going on inside the human. It had been sufficiently successful in therapy and behavioral modification that those involved in the programming of robots were very optimistic about their eventual success. It is an approach very close to that of the analyst.[1] But this approach has proved very resistant; both stimuli and response are so complex that the code for the computer became too large to write or process.

Another orientation to psychology is the cognitive approach. This approach argues that we are continually processing the world around us in terms of patterns. We interact with and process the stimuli in terms of patterns that we know and have learned. Perception is not a passive but an active process.

> Beat of the traffic, pulse of the phone, the long cycles of the sun in the sky. Patterns, rhythms. We live by patterns. . . . Patterns set up expectations. Patterns in time. To perceive a pattern means that we have already formed an idea of what's next. (Judson, 1980, p. 28)

We find that experts in a field perceive phenomena in patterns based on their experience and so are different from novices. As noted earlier, expert chess players looking at a chess board with randomly placed pieces were able to reproduce it no better than novices. But chess pieces placed as would result from a game were reproduced considerably more accurately by experts than by novices. Because they are built from experience, such patterns are, we think, context-dependent.

People concerned with programming robots now believe that the cognitive approach, which looks for patterns, will be a much more fruitful approach. But of course, the problem is determining which patterns to use for which situations. Many researchers are currently engaged in studying differences in the way experts and novices view various situations. Does the cognitive approach move us closer to the approach of the humanists? Probably, though the extent is not yet clear. Yet here, in an entirely different and contemporary context, we find elements of both the analyzer and humanist strands emerging.

Additional Orientations

The behaviorist approach, while similar to the analyzer approach in some respects, is really deserving of its own characterization. Where the behaviorist approach refuses to recognize the need for constructs and concepts, few of us can do without them. Certainly, most typical analyzers use them and find them very useful. Therefore, we shall split off a group that deals only with the operational definitions of things, with what works; we shall call them **pragmatists**.

Another group, like the analyzers, also looks for the relationships, rules,

---

1. It is in fact the pragmatist orientation, discussed later.

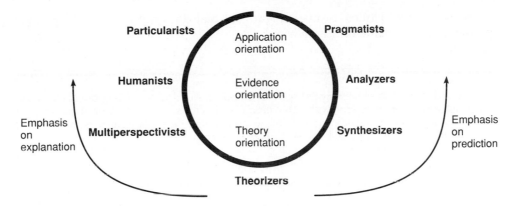

FIGURE 24.2 The complete set of seven types of social scientists, differentiated by orientation to the social sciences.

and principles that form the basis of social sciences. They are discontent with the deductive approach used by analyzers, starting with a conceptual explanation and setting up hypotheses to test. Preferring to start at the bottom, perhaps as participant observers, this group of what we shall call **synthesizers** prefers to see what emerges as significant in terms of how the people in the situation construe it. Close to the analyzers, but with characteristics like the theorizers, who also induce the important characteristics from situations, we shall place them between the analyzers and the theorists on our diagram (see Figure 24.2).

In addition, there are two other orientations that should be recognized. One is halfway between the humanists and the theorizers, the **multiperspectivists**. Like the humanist, multiperspectivists attempt to explain situations but use perspectives drawn from different disciplines or outlooks.

The final orientation is held by persons who believe that the world is so complex and each individual is so unique that a social science is impossible. You can learn from me, and I from you, and in interaction we may make sense of our world. But it is primarily in this interaction that we construe meaning. Such individuals we shall name **particularists**.

Viewing the model in its entirety, as we move from the pragmatists clockwise around to the humanists, phenomena are perceived as more complex and more context-dependent. With positions closer to the humanist end, a science composed of simple generalizations and principles, the natural sciences model, becomes increasingly difficult to attain but also less attractive. Emphasis on prediction yields to explanation going around the circle in the same direction. The pragmatist totally emphasizes prediction. Explanation is closely associated with prediction for the analyzer. Synthesizers and all to their left are content to explain; if prediction seems possible, that is an added plus. Explanation and prediction are disassociated for the humanist. Historians, for example, clearly realize this; they may be able to explain what happened in a particular battle, a series of battles, or even a war. But that does not mean that they can predict the next battle or a new war.[2]

> Some social scientists model their attempts to build a science around the natural science model with operational definitions, laws, and principles. Others seek a science more like the humanities that attempts to explain particular situations but eschew generalizations. Between these positions and around them extend a set of seven orientations to what a social science should be that helps illuminate differences in these positions.

APPROACHING A PROBLEM FROM DIFFERENT ORIENTATIONS: AN EXAMPLE

Sarah is working on an interesting doctoral dissertation. She is trying to be as objective and unbiased as possible in determining the factors contributing to the outcome of a presidential election. She has worked long, hard hours with her major professor to develop a comprehensive questionnaire to be used in predicting the election's outcome. It was initially limited to a variety of demographic and personal characteristics that could be described in concrete, observational terms. At the suggestion of a psychology professor, she added some scales intended to measure "personal security" and "fate control" (Can I control my fate, or is it mainly luck?). Her major professor is not very happy about these additions as he prefers to stay with concrete characteristics, whereas these can't be directly sensed. But he decides to let them stay in the study; he believes they won't add anything to the prediction anyway.

Before collecting her data, Sarah seeks approval of her research plan by her dissertation committee. The committee members seem to tolerate, more than be enthusiastic about, the questionnaire. Indeed, one of them reacts by suggesting that Sarah extend her plans to include mingling with the voters as they leave the polls to learn how they made their decisions. That leads another

---

2. As Scriven (1980) notes, an explanatory pattern is open-ended—it can be implemented in many ways that are impossible to predict. Scriven uses the example of coroners not being able to predict that a person 50 pounds overweight would die of a heart attack if he ran up 50 stairs. "But they can nevertheless be sure of that exertion as the cause of death after an autopsy.... The fit can be made *exact* when the events fall into place. Explanations are possible where predictions are not" (p. 18).

   Gergen (1980) makes the same point in his description of human development, calling attention to the flexibility of the developmental pattern: "From this perspective, existing patterns appear potentially evanescent, the unstable result of the peculiar juxtaposition of contemporary historical events. For any individual the life course seems fundamentally open-ended. Even with full knowledge of the individual's past experience, one can render little more than a probabilistic account of the broad contours of future development" (pp. 34–35).

committee member to suggest that she add some studies of how these voters made up their minds over the 90 days prior to the election.

Sarah thinks, "They must be crazy! Not only is that a lot of extra work, but it doesn't belong in an empirical study like mine! I'm just trying to see what predicts the results. Mingling with the voters gets into a lot of soft stuff that can't be measured! And for that matter, how could such a small sample of case studies predict anything? It takes a large number of representative cases to make a valid prediction."

Before she can voice her reaction, however, the historian member adds his suggestion: "How about reading the various analyses of the election and then doing a retrospective that merges the best of the questionnaire results, the case studies, and the analyses into a single discussion that explains the event?" Sarah despairs, "It gets even worse! How can we call it science when we pick and choose among the data and analyses to select whatever we wish? It's so confusing! Here are all these competent behavioral scientists, clearly sincere in their efforts to help me. Each seems bent on making my study the best ever, but their suggestions are so diverse! And worse yet, they seem to ask me to do things that run counter to what I've been taught about science. Why can't they live with the questionnaire study as first designed? It is a good predictive study with 'hard' data to determine what forecasts the outcome of the election."

With the perspective provided by this chapter, it is hoped that Sarah, and students like her, will better understand that, yes, each *is* bent on improving her study, but *from his or her own point of view*—and those views differ. For some quantitative methodologists, like Sarah's major professor, variables that can be directly sensed are the stuff of which science is made. If we can't directly sense something, then deal strictly with operational definitions instead of trying to guess what construct lies underneath; we so often guess wrong. By contrast, the historian member of her committee recognizes that selecting what to include in a study is a subjective decision—indeed, the quality of a historian's work is judged by how well those decisions are made (Barzun and Graff, 1977). The historian's approach seeks an explanation of the election results in a specific context and emphasizes the importance of context in understanding phenomena. His approach envisions the situation as interactive instead of proceeding from cause to effect, process to product, like Sarah's major professor's. Further, for the latter, instead of context dependence, context independence is the goal, generalizations that apply beyond the context in which they are studied. Yet both are researchers contributing to the behavioral sciences.

Working from their orientations, the committee members sought different evidence to provide the best demonstration of the determining factors of the election as they would approach the problem. Each was interpreting the criteria of a good behavioral science study in terms of what seemed to contribute to building that science as he or she understood it.

The orientation types seem most meaningful when you can personalize them, matching them to persons you know. This gives a greater sense of reality to these abstract conceptions. The fit typically will not be exact (everyone wants to adjust the scheme to fit personal predilections). But the scheme has proved useful in stimulating thought about the linkage of method to conceptions of what the behavioral sciences are and ought to be.

THE ORIENTATIONS IN DETAIL

The Pragmatist

Pragmatists seek instruments, rules, principles, equations, and models that predict with better than chance accuracy and therefore permit some measure of control. Note that it is the instruments they seek, not the constructs those instruments measure. Pragmatists wish to do without constructs and concepts that cannot be physically sensed and therefore are never directly measured. These researchers are concerned with finding *what works*, regardless of whether it can be explained or seems reasonable.

The Strong-Campbell Interest Inventory (Strong, Campbell, and Hansen, 1981) is a pragmatist product. It consists of a variety of questions to be asked of persons seeking to make a vocational choice. It compares an individual's responses to those of persons who have already chosen particular fields of work. Congruence of response suggests that the individual has the interests and values of people in the field and so might be successful there. For years, this and similar measures have been our most effective instruments, and they often work in areas of very difficult prediction. But many of the predictions lack explanation credibility. There is no particular reason why, for instance, an interest in music should be related to an interest in being a mathematician, but it turns out that it is!

Another example is the work of Skinner (1957). He avoids using concepts and constructs and sticks strictly to operational definitions. He desires to build a psychology without having to infer what is in the mind—the contents of the "black box" that can't be sensed directly. For example, a reinforcer is not defined as something that gives pleasure. That is the meaning the term has come to have with many persons, especially as it is associated with M&M candies. Skinner defines it in observable terms: whatever has the effect of increasing the probability of a given behavior the next time the same circumstances occur. Nonpragmatists may infer that it is the pleasure (a construct that can't be directly sensed) that leads to learning (another construct), which results in the increased frequency of the correct response. Pragmatists skip all in-between speculation about what goes on in the mind.

Pragmatists often use statistical prediction techniques such as multiple correlation and regression, discriminant function analysis, canonical correlation, and factor analysis. They are most often found in psychology and economics.

Pragmatists assume Popper's clocklike world, endorsing the classical norms of the natural sciences as the most valid ways of knowing. Subscribing to Merton's norms (see chapter 4), they see science as impersonal, value-free, precise, reliable, valid, causal, and exact, with clear standards for judgment. They are less concerned with explaining, with understanding, or with theory than with what works in contexts other than those in which first discovered. Such findings have context independence. (Probably no prediction is totally context-free, but the greater the context independence, the greater the generality, and that is what pragmatists seek.) We may not entirely understand why an economic model works; it involves so many variables, and their relations are so complex. The important point is that the model predicts. To pragmatists, science is more finding operations that work across contexts than finding explanations.

The Analyzer

Validating hypotheses is the analyzer's main business. Analyzers seek to confirm rules, principles, and propositions that relate variables (constructs) or events. Such confirmation may also constitute a test of theory. Analyzers prefer carefully designed studies. Experimentation is their main technique, but they may also do natural or field experiments. Although many are satisfied to confirm a single hypothesis, ideally, they integrate findings to build an explanation or a theory. Other researchers are critical of the former practice, believing that it leads to bits and pieces of literature that do not add to anything important.

Like pragmatists, analyzers subscribe to science as the prime method of knowing and support its norms. They place considerable emphasis on science as a method of reducing or eliminating the biasing effects of personal values on observation and try to be value-free. They seek propositions that are context independent, much like pragmatists. Often they give the appearance, and sometimes the reality, of cutting down a problem to fit the method instead of adjusting the method to fit the problem. They use a cause-and-effect model for studying phenomena.

Behavioral science literature, particularly in psychology but also in sociology, political science, and economics, heavily represents the work of analyzers. Indeed, whole issues of the *Journal of Experimental Psychology*, the *Journal of Educational Psychology*, and even the *Journal of Counseling Psychology* are filled with such writing. The Zimbardo, Anderson, and Kabat study of chapter 2 is an example.

The Synthesizer

Synthesizers study phenomena in their natural surroundings and are oriented to fieldwork. From observations, possibly as unobtrusive participants in the phenomenon being studied, synthesizers produce an explanation of its essential workings. They may produce theory grounded in these observations (grounded theory).

Synthesizers take an interactive view of phenomena, perceiving the world as a system with homeostatic states being maintained through the constant adjustment of variables and conditions. Where analyzers seek teacher behaviors that permit the maintenance of order and result in gaining students' attention, synthesizers see such a search for context-free behaviors as hopeless. Teacher and student behaviors are interactive and context-based. For example, when students are tired, the teacher must make an effort to attract their attention and maintain order. By contrast, when students are fresh, eager, and seeking stimuli, maintaining order is more a matter of providing a focus. In the view of synthesizers, there is no simple correlational relationship between the frequency or strength of a particular teacher's behavior and classroom control. Both teacher and pupil behaviors are continually adjusting to each other. In this instance, at least four variables are involved: student tiredness, teacher attention-attracting activity, teacher providing foci for attention, and student attending.

Synthesizers are more concerned with description and explanation than with prediction. In providing generalized explanations, as in grounded theory, they delineate the most common causative factors from relatively rare ones in a particular context. Synthesizers prefer a holistic approach to phenomena instead of piecemeal studies that are likely to cut the phenomenon to fit the requirements of method.

Synthesizers subscribe to the norms of science and to science as a way of knowing. But they are much more aware of the role of values in science because of their potential for biasing observations—the mainstay of their work.

Most sociological and anthropological case studies that seek to derive generalizations or develop theory are the work of synthesizers (for example, Blau, 1963). Such studies often help us understand groups that are not obvious in daily life—sexual minorities (Humphreys, 1975), the black underclass (Liebow, 1967), working-class families (Rubin, 1976), an Italian ghetto (Whyte, 1955). They show how these subjects perceive their situation and reveal how consistent their behavior is with how we might behave in their circumstances. Some historians are synthesizers as well, using the records of the past in the way sociologists use contemporary observations.

The Theorizer

The theorizer, like the synthesizer, works back and forth between abstractions and a phenomenon itself. The abstractions are designed to capture essential characteristics that explain the phenomenon. In a theorizer's typical method of work, an explanation is derived from a few carefully observed cases or from the integration of some past research. Perhaps a few small studies or more observations are added to check the explanation. The conceptual explanation is adjusted to fit, further checks are made, and so on. Construction of the typology of this chapter was a typical theorizer effort.

Theorizers are found in nearly every field. They produce very attractive explanations that keep analyzers busy in attempts to confirm them. Consider all the studies that have been inspired by Durkheim, Erikson, Freud, Kohlberg, Maslow, Piaget, Redfield, Riesman, and others like them who did substantial theorizer work.

Theorizers, like synthesizers, are sufficiently close to observations that the "cloudlike" character of phenomena can be a problem. But they have an uncanny ability to find common patterns across groups, aggregating at an appropriate level so that random noise cancels and pattern is apparent. Historians, like Toynbee (1948) and Spengler (1926), fit this pattern. But whether these two went beyond their data, as many theorizers do, is a matter for critics to debate. Theorizers' ideas are not always on target, and their ideas must often be modified by other researchers. But their captivating suggestions contain enough of the germ of reality that their conceptualizations are tenacious.

Numerically, in comparison with the three types already discussed, successful theorizers are rare. But those who succeed can be tremendously powerful figures who set the course for a field and strongly influence its research agenda. They would no doubt say they subscribe to the norms of science. But instead of presenting evidence with a sizable formal database, they depend more on the method of intuition (the self-evidently true nature of their theory or explanation) to build a consensus. Carefully chosen and very powerful examples make their case. Confirmation, as already noted, becomes the work of others. An example of a theorizer's writing that had considerable impact is Piaget's (1929, 1930, 1952). In it, the alternation between theoretical explanation and example is obvious and compelling.

Indicative of the fact that these orientations are often better thought of as roles instead of indelibly categorizing types is the case of Skinner. His role was as a pragmatist in *Verbal Behavior* (1957)—building a psychological theory without constructs, using only behavior that can be directly sensed and manipulated. At a later career stage, he is a theorist in "The Science of Learning and the Art of Teaching" (1968). The enthusiasm and cogent arguments of his writing sparked substantial experimentation on programmed learning and teaching machines. As it became apparent that more than small steps between right answers were required to build a program that students and teachers use willingly, the fires of enthusiasm were banked. The wide availability of microcomputers in education may rekindle the flames. But as of now, most of that literature stands as a tribute to the tremendous efforts of analyzers to validate a position set forth by a skilled theorizer.

The Multiperspectivist

Depending on their work, multiperspectivists may be more like theorizers or like humanists. They are therefore placed between these types. Like theorizers, they usually operate from observations and examples instead of a formal database. Platt (1964) attributes to T. C. Chamberlin (1897/1985), a geologist at the University of Chicago, the statement of the "method of multiple hypotheses":

> The moment one has offered an original explanation for a phenomenon which seems satisfactory, that moment affection of this intellectual child springs into existence, and as the explanation grows into a definite theory his parental affections cluster about his offspring and it grows more and more dear to him. . . . There springs up also unwittingly a pressing of the

theory to fit the facts and a pressing of the facts to make them fit the theory. . . .[3]

To avoid this grave danger, the method of multiple working hypotheses is urged. It differs from the simple working hypothesis in that it distributes the effort and the affections. . . . Each hypothesis suggests its own criteria, its own means of proof, its own method of developing the truth, and if a group of hypotheses encompass the subject on all sides, the total outcome of means and of methods is full and rich.

Chamberlin very neatly states both the multiperspectivist position and some of its advantages in contrast to other modes of work.

Multiperspectivists are still fewer than successful theorizers, although their numbers seem to be increasing and their work is widely admired. Potentially, their impact is great, but so far it has not, in general, been realized. Perhaps one reason is that we are unaccustomed to multiple explanations. Having been taught all our lives to look for "the" explanation, we are often uncomfortable with multiple correct answers. The often unintegrated, sometimes almost contradictory nature of the proposed explanations stimulates considerable thought but decreases the ease with which explanations translate into action. Consider, for example, competing Marxist and capitalist explanations of economics or the examination of the role of hospitals from complementary political, social, psychological, historical, and economic viewpoints.

Whereas theorizers aim to find explanations with generality over persons, places, and times, like Piaget's stages of growth or Skinner's learning principles, multiperspectivists usually take on more limited tasks. Their explanations are more like those of the historian.

Allison's (1971) study of the Cuban missile crisis is a very good example of multiperspectivist work, one that dramatically called attention to this approach. It examines the puzzles of the crisis from three perspectives: that of the rational-man model, that of an organizational bureaucracy with standard operating procedures, and that of governmental politics and bargaining. Each viewpoint raises different questions, provides different answers, and reaches different conclusions. The rational-man model views nuclear war as unthinkable and suggests that low-level military actions can be engaged in without fear of escalation. But both the organizational and political models suggest that "irrational stumbling into a nuclear war is quite possible and nuclear crises are inherently chancy" (p. 260).

The Humanist

Humanists believe that causation is so complex and so context-bound, each event being the result of a nearly unique pattern of causative factors, that rules and principles will not provide adequate explanations. Humanists leave research consumers to find their own real-life parallels to the patterns they

---

3. We could read this paragraph as a criticism of analyzers and synthesizers.

make evident and thus to form their view of how the world works. Through the study of enough such accounts—some of which may be personal, some group or institutional, and some even fictional—we learn to recognize patterns that help us adjust our behavior successfully to meet future events. The humanist seeks accounts that have the power to instruct and models of literary, personal, and historical accounts that do so.

Presumably, timeless literature has successfully found these models; certainly, much literature consciously attempts this goal. Prescott (1982) noted a current attempt in his eulogy to John Cheever:

> He observed and gave voice to the inarticulate agonies that lie just beneath the surface of ordinary lives. . . . In "The Bus to St. James," a man watches his daughter in dancing school; ". . . It struck him that he and the company that crowded around him . . . were bewildered and too confused in principle, too selfish or too unlucky to abide by the forms that guarantee the permanence of a society . . . [that] their fathers and mothers had [used]. . . . Instead, they put the burden of order onto their children and fill their days with specious rites and ceremonies."

In contrast to previous types, the humanist still further disassociates explanation from prediction, being content to explain a given event or historical movement as completely as possible. Humanist studies may be of contemporary phenomena, such as White's *Making of the President* (1961, 1965, 1973), as well as historical ones.

Instead of laws, rules, and principles of a physics-like behavioral science, the humanist helps us build "cognitive maps" so we can recognize parallel situations when we encounter them. For example, President John F. Kennedy is said to have read Barbara Tuchman's *Guns of August* (1962) just before the Cuban missile crisis. In it, Tuchman describes how German generals in World War I persisted in their preconceptions of situations even in the face of contrary evidence. Kennedy saw a parallel to Khrushchev's handling of the missile crisis and modified his behavior accordingly.

The line between synthesizer and humanist is determined by whether a researcher seeks a behavioral science consisting of relatively context-free generalizations, typical of the synthesizer, or those that are very much context-bound, typical of the humanist. Humanists prefer to explain a situation and let readers draw inferences for their own cognitive and affective maps and lives.

The Particularist

The useful organization of the events of the world for the particularist is a personal phenomenon, unique to each individual. The particularist assumes that we must each discover the patterns that work for us. Much of the grist for that discovery comes from personal experience and intuition, but some comes from vicarious experiences described by others. Because it is a personal pattern, criteria for what is accepted into the pattern differ and may be aesthetically as well as rationally oriented.

The researcher working from a particularist orientation learns from another person, and, in turn, that person learns from the researcher. But this information instructs the individuals involved rather than builds a science. The particularist contributes mainly indirectly to science by suggesting leads and stimulating researchers of other orientations to consider ideas.

A position very close to the particularist is that of action research as described by Zweier and Vaughan (1984), who note that it is also called "participatory," "endogenous," or "dialectical" research with slight changes in emphasis. In action research, researchers are working participants instead of passive observers. The relationship of the observer to the situation deserves study, and the situation is seen as changing during the research. In fact, the researcher often introduces social knowledge into the situation to test its effect. The knowledge acquired is context-bound, specific to the particular constellation in which it was generated rather than generalizable. The social scientist is seen, not as objective, but as learning from the people in the situation, making them part of it by helping them learn at the same time. Examples in Reason and Rowan (1981) are very similar to the particularist position. They involve voluntary desegregation programs, prison environments, and banking systems, and their main benefits accrue to the subjects participating in the research.

SUMMARY AND EXAMPLE OF THE ORIENTATIONS

Table 24.1 summarizes the characteristics of the orientations in the seven columns. Descriptive characteristics of each orientation highlight in successive rows the similarities and differences in the orientations' guiding principles, what they believe to be the nature of behavioral science knowledge, their criteria of good work, their preferred research methods, stereotypes, the role of values, and their strengths and weaknesses. The stereotypes suggested in the fifth row are intended to be helpful but, carried too far, can be misleading. They may be the least important of the information in the table. It would be better for you to find your own examples that fit the characteristics in the first four rows.

The table gives more detail than the text in describing the characteristics of each orientation and presenting all seven in a form that facilitates comparison. Read down the columns to get a renewed sense of each type and then across the rows to note differences.

HOW THE TYPES DIFFER IN MAKING RESEARCH DECISIONS

Choice of Research Problem

Researchers typically view problems through two screens: their subject matter orientation and their typology orientation. The first suggests what in the problem to focus on; the second, the approach to use in studying it. Consider

TABLE 24.1 Summary of the Seven Orientations

	Pragmatist	Analyzer	Synthesizer	Theorizer	Multiperspectivist	Humanist	Particularist
Guiding Principle	Produce an instrument, rule, principle that will usefully predict.	Test propositions and thereby confirm them.	Produce an explanation embodying the essential characteristics of a phenomenon.	Produce theory to explain phenomena	Produce explanations of phenomena from different perspectives—for example, political, economic aspects.	Find the most powerful data-based images and models that foster human understanding.	Emphasize importance and uniqueness of person or organization; help subjects know selves and achieve self-determination.
Nature of Behavioral Science Knowledge	Impersonal, that which empirically predicts.		Impersonal; the consensus of a scientific community where individuals with relevant competencies monitor the work of peers and pass their approval or disapproval to those less qualified to judge.			Largely personal, provides understanding to self and culture in terms of conceptual patterns and scenes that have value in guiding future behavior.	Personal, provides self-understanding as a unique person or group; science often less useful than older ways of knowing (art, poetry, mysticism, etc.).
Criteria of Excellence	Predictions replicate on new samples.	Solid theory or rationale produces strongest possible predictor confirmed by data. Alternative explanations eliminated. Narrows problems for control.	Production of an accurate description of phenomenon and, if possible, an explanation of its essential characteristics. Production of theory grounded on data. Holistic view.	Production of a theory or framework that explains a phenomenon. Logical, internally consistent convincing examples	Choice of approaches that contribute significantly to understanding.	Explanation that mediates well between the world and persons. Provides useful models and examples of analysis.	Personal growth of person or organization; may also be aesthetically pleasing.
Preferred Research Method	Quantitative data involving statistical prediction techniques; usual forms of correlation.	Quantitative data and as close to good experimental design as possible.	Qualitative data, verbal descriptions, case studies, enthnography, participant observations.	Very careful observation of few cases. Often cases chosen for special characteristics and sometimes placed in special circumstances.	Choice of approaches that contribute significantly to understanding.	Gathering of personal accounts that will stir minds, hearts, and souls and bring new insights.	Sharing of personal experiences and knowledge by subject and researcher. Action research.
Stereotypes (helpful in visualizing types but likely to be controversial)	Developers of instruments like the MMPI and Strong-Campbell; some personnel psychologists; many economists.	Most quantitatively oriented psychologists and sociologists; many economists.	Some sociologists and anthropologists; many historians.	Famous theorists of behavioral science, including Freud, Parsons, Piaget, Skinner.	Allison, possibly McLuhan. Well-known persons in behavioral sciences are rare. In natural sciences, Bronowski, Sagan.	Many historians; some ethnographers; many clinicians, literary critics.	Some clinicians; people reacting against the dehumanizing of persons by science.

(continued)

TABLE 24.1 *continued*

	Pragmatist	Analyzer	Synthesizer	Theorizer	Multiperspectivist	Humanist	Particularist
Role of Values	Research is nonpartisan, sees science as value-free.		Researcher tries to control possible biasing value positions but describes personal bias to allow reader to judgment of its possible effect.	Can be like either analyzer or synthesizer.	Value differences may highlight different aspects of a phenomenon and so may be sought, but their presence is made explicit.	Values are an integral part of knowledge; they help give it meaning and serve as motivators.	
Strengths	Starts new fields where little understanding exists; trial-and-error approach serendipitously produces leads that can then be studied to gain explanations; empirical keying of measuring instruments often yields most accurate predictions.	Tests and confirms propositions; experimentation is the strongest and most convincing method for demonstrating relationships.	Locates "heart" of phenomenon; theory has close correspondence to data; provides theory and propositions for analyst to confirm.	Explains important phenomena in ways that, in hindsight, fit conventional wisdom; usually very convincing, especially in use of examples.	Reflects the complexity of reality; contrasting viewpoints provide breadth and depth of view.	Emphasizes the personal, human, and historical as a repertoire from which to draw; source of ideas for scientific validation; seeks answers where laws and theorist fail.	Produces knowledge highly useful to person or organization; source of ideas for scientific validation.
Weaknesses	Requires ability to handle statistics; does not supply understanding and explanations; some items are counterintuitive, and others may be without any apparent logical basis for predicting.	Requires ability to handle statistics; narrowing of problems may reduce significance; hard to do "tight" validation and show wide generality at same time; not all important phenomena are measurable.	Requires ability to integrate masses of data and find patterns; observer biases are a potential problem; requires a separate validation step for theories and propositions.	Is typically not grounded in demonstrations of any size or representativeness; leaves validation to others; boundary conditions within which theory holds are rarely set forth, must be found.	Requires breadth of skill and training; heavy conceptual load; relative importance of contrasting points of view requires synthesis.	Contributes little to consensual knowledge; requires conceptual grasp of large amounts of material to select relevant portions to weave into integrated story.	Has little generality; each person and institution must start anew.

how an analyzer psychologist and a synthesizer sociologist might study doctor-parent interaction in an intensive care facility for newborns. The analyzer psychologist might focus on the personality characteristics and typical social response tendencies of staff and parents and hypothesize how and where these might mesh or clash. The psychologist might then set up several alternative experimental situations intended to minimize clashes and maximize meshings and see whether predictions of which situations had what effects were accurate. Where they went astray, the researcher would seek the cause, reformulate the study, and try again, iteratively learning the combination yielding the most productive interaction. The synthesizer sociologist, by contrast, might act as participant observer of the social communication of staff and parents and from the data accumulated establish the types or roles each group created in its perception of the other. The researcher might use these with examples to explain how parents and professionals interact and why. In each instance, the researchers focused on the part of the problem to which prior training sensitized them and then applied the research procedure that their training suggested would typically be most helpful.

Some researchers' work is narrowed by these two screens to a single research method and a strictly held orientation. Some have even a single-minded missionary zeal about the "rightness" and power of their approach. Other researchers work at avoiding being constrained by the screens and are eclectic in their approach. Each position has its advantages. Researchers with a single orientation have the advantage of focusing their technique, so they develop methodological excellence. But they may be limited in the problems they work on and may not have the broad perspective of researchers who range across problems widely. The latter, with less practice in any one method, may have less methodological expertise. Further, they may regard as trivial the distinctions and terminolgoy that are important to the deeply specialized researchers. Probably most researchers find themselves between these extremes, seeking at least one area of methodological excellence but ranging into problems that require other skills.

In contrast to such disciplines as psychology and sociology, methodological socialization is less strong in professional fields. Many individuals in the latter fields are eclectic in both orientation and method and flexibly adopt the role that the problem seems to require. Where acculturation to method is strong, however, or method requirements are difficult to master, as in statistics, such eclecticism is reduced.

Criteria of Excellence

The variation in what constitutes excellence is one of the most striking contrasts in Table 24.1. Reading across from pragmatist to particularist, note the differences:

- Being able to predict and control
- Well-controlled, though possibly narrow, experimental studies that are very satisfying demonstrations that a relationship exists

- Production of theory that is grounded in observations and captures the holistic characteristics of a phenomenon
- Developing a theoretical approach to a problem supported by very persuasive and compelling examples
- Application of a variety of perspectives to a single problem
- Stories that mediate well between reality and the person
- Personal growth and meaning

That is quite a spectrum!

You can already see seeds sown for communication problems and even conflict among differing orientations. Increasing the chance of conflict is the vexation of some persons over the often greater acceptance of work closer to the natural science model, which implies a lesser status for their orientation. When preferences for a particular definition of excellence are built into funding or tenure criteria, this can be an even more serious problem.

Choice of Research Methods

One method or technique of research fits each orientation better than the others and so is preferred. The matches of orientation to method in the table appear to make good intuitive sense. What the table does not make clear, however, is that when someone uses a nonpreferred method, it is usually used in a way consistent with that person's orientation.

Consider questionnaire technique, for example. A pragmatist would likely convert questionnaire responses into a single score, weighting the questions according to their predictive value. An analyzer might either convert them to a single score or examine them item by item to determine each item's relation to a proposition or theory. A synthesizer might use the questions as a basis for observations or possibly an interview. A humanist or a particularist might use the questions as a basis for mutual exploration in a discussion between researcher and subject.

We have come to think of method as a prime descriptor of behavioral scientists. But the research type or orientation, by describing how a given method is used, may be an even better way of differentiating among behavioral scientists.

Strengths and Weaknesses of the Types

Pragmatist.   Pragmatists' research is important because whatever predicts also has potential for control. Control can be used to remedy a situation, avoid a problem, or select an option with a greater payoff. These are actions with significant benefits for our daily lives. The weakness of the viewpoint is that without an explanation, merely showing that something works in a given situation may be viewed as an isolated, chance finding. It is not calculated to weld the consensus needed to be accepted as knowledge.

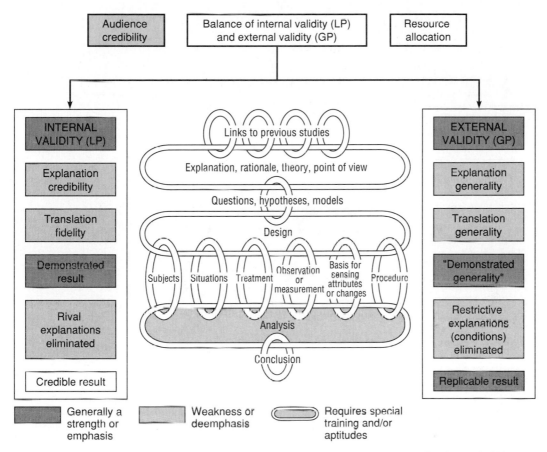

FIGURE 24.3 Strengths and weaknesses of the pragmatist orientation graphically depicted in the chain-of-reasoning model.

For example, we don't know why achievement is greater when a teacher calls on each child in turn in a small reading circle than when the teacher calls on the children randomly, but research evidence indicates that it is (Anderson, Evertson, and Brophy, 1979)—a counterintuitive finding. It seems as though children would learn more if they believed they needed to be ready all the time in case they were called on, instead of getting ready only for their own predictable turn. Left at that, as a pragmatist might do, we might consider this a nonreplicable finding.

Consider how differently you feel about this finding when it is explained that being able to anticipate what we will be called on to read allows us to prepare and rehearse ahead of time. This increases the likelihood of a triumphant reading experience, the "I can do it" motivation that underlies successful learning. No longer is the finding counterintuitive. But without an adequate explanation, we are left questioning.

In Figure 24.3, the items with dark shading represent strengths or emphases. For example, "Internal validity (LP)" is darkly shaded because

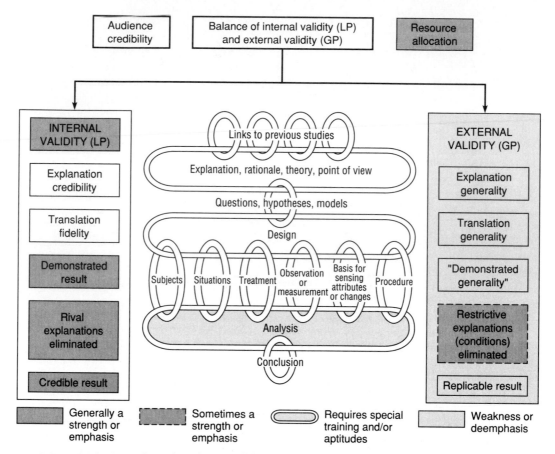

FIGURE 24.4 Strengths and weaknesses of the analyzer orientation graphically depicted in the chain-of-reasoning model.

operational definitions are strongly linked to demonstrated result, which is a strength. "External validity (GP)," "Demonstrated generality," and "Replicable result" are emphasized because findings are typically cross-validated to ensure applicability to other than the original sample.

Light shading designates characteristics previously discussed as weaknesses (such as "Audience credibility") or not emphasized. For example, "Explanation credibility," "Translation fidelity," and "Rival explanations eliminated" and their external validity (GP) counterparts do not merely lack emphasis; they are almost irrelevant since there is no attempt at explanation. The lightly shaded areas within the chain require special training and aptitude. For example, the oval "Analysis" reflects the special requirements of the pragmatist's statistical techniques, especially some of the more complex ones like ridge regression and LISREL.

Analyzer. In a culture like ours that reveres science and experimental research, analyzers are generally considered to be in the strongest position to command the consensus needed for acceptance of knowledge. This is one reason why analyzers find confirming other ideas rewarding, for in doing so, the ideas gain their most complete general acceptance. With satisfying explanations, unbiased and representative samples, confirmed predictions, and the elimination of otherwise reasonable alternative explanations, the studies provide strong confirmatory evidence, or, when negative evidence appears, they raise strong doubts. As represented graphically in Figure 24.4, their studies usually have very high internal validity (LP) and are particularly good at sensing small effects when built with adequate power (demonstrated relationship). They effectively eliminate alternative explanations (but only sometimes restrictive explanations, hence the broken outline there). Their carefully designed studies allow efficient use of resources (resource allocation).

When analyzers narrow and clean up a problem to control for other explanations, however, it can be argued that they change and delimit the problem. This is a definite weakness that limits the generality of the findings. Analyzers are more likely to dissect and work on parts of a problem instead of involve all its holistic interrelationships, for they prefer controlled situations instead of naturalistic but uncontrolled fieldwork. For both of these reasons, external validity (GP) appears as a lightly shaded region.

To be an analyzer, one must have training in experimental design, which, especially as it is linked to sophisticated statistical analyses, requires some measure of mathematical skill—not everyone's cup of tea; hence the light shading of "Analysis."

Synthesizer. Synthesizers (summarized in Figure 24.5) are oriented to holistic approaches and the discovery of key interrelationships. Whereas analyzers typically look for a consistent behavior across situations, synthesizers will carefully observe a situation to determine the roles of various behaviors in interaction. Remember the example of the teacher interacting with students to hold their attention when they are fresh as opposed to when they are tired? The methods lend themselves well to exploring phenomena and discovering new approaches.

The grounded-theory approach of synthesizers provides strong internal validity (LP), as indicated in Figure 24.5. Such theory tightly ties a convincing explanation to the evidence out of which it arose; hence the dark shading of "Explanation credibility" and "Translation fidelity." Synthesizers have not always been strong in eliminating rival explanations, but this is less true now than before this problem was recognized. Because their explanations are context-bound, external validity (GP) is shown as a lightly shaded area. Audience credibility, with explanations strongly tied to evidence, is a strength.

As indicated by the light shading on the facets of design, the gathering of data requires training in what to note, how to record it, how to handle personal biases, and other matters. Similarly, data analysis and reduction to generalizations are important hurdles for the synthesizer. Not everyone is able to integrate a mass of detail into holistic pictures and discern the patterns that identify the determiners of significant actions. Some researchers gather mountains of data and then cannot complete the task of delineating the patterns, a heartbreaking experience for all concerned.

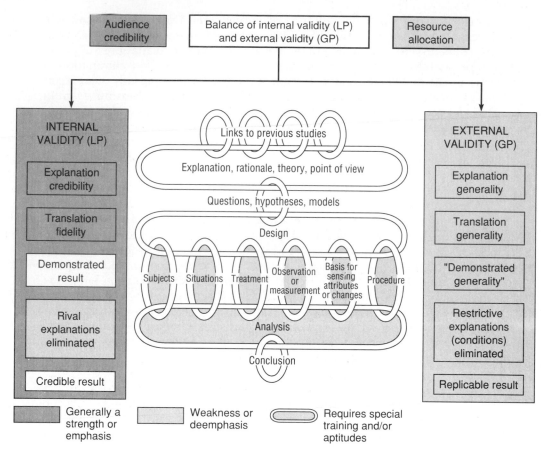

FIGURE 24.5 Strengths and weaknesses of the synthesizer orientation graphically depicted in the chain-of-reasoning model.

Resource allocation is often a problem for this approach and is therefore shaded. Working in the field, the synthesizer does not always have control over what will be done next and on what schedule. If the data are analyzed in the field, the time devoted to analysis is combined with observing, and the researcher can decide when to stop. But data saturation and analysis may not be complete when resource limits are reached. If done after leaving it, however, the amount of time required by the analysis is difficult to estimate in advance, making resource control difficult.

If the three constraints had been included in these graphics as they are in the full model in chapter 14, the area of ethical standards would be lightly shaded. Very difficult ethical problems crop up often in the field. An administrator or public official demands information about illegalities you apparently observed and did not immediately report. To whom should your allegiance go: those you observed, the public, the administrators who granted you admittance? These are knotty problems!

To the analyst, interested in objective views, potential observer bias is a

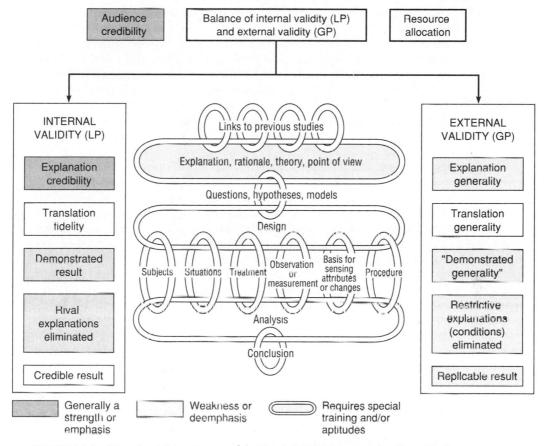

FIGURE 24.6 Strengths and weaknesses of the theorizer orientation graphically depicted in the chain-of-reasoning model.

persistent problem. To the synthesizer, the researcher's viewpoint is a valid interpretation of what was seen. What is considered a weakness depends in part on your point of view.

Theorizer. Successful theorizers have the considerable advantage of being able to propose very believable explanations. Making sweeping generalizations with important implications, theorizers can have considerable impact, the largest, in fact, of all the orientations. They find the simple, powerful, plausible explanations that seem to basically underlie phenomena. Their strengths and weakness are portrayed in Figure 24.6.

Like the synthesizer, who provides illustrations from voluminous data to flesh out generalizations, so too do theorizers. These well-illustrated and appealing generalizations have explanation credibility and garner considerable audience credibility. Therefore, these criteria in the figure are darkly shaded. But synthesizers, unless they do a multisite study to cross-validate their findings, typically realize that their findings may be context-bound. By contrast, theorizers usually make broad generality implicit in their very credible explanations and examples.

This generality may be more apparent than real, however. Indeed, one of the real concerns about theorizers is that they often oversimplify reality. They rarely delineate the boundary conditions within which a generalization holds. To do so would complicate their explanations and reduce the impact of their claims. Their sweeping statements often greatly annoy analyzers, who, as a result, challenge the claims, try to validate them, and in the process limit and modify them. Therefore, "Explanation generality" has a light shading in the diagram.

The foundations underlying the explanations of synthesizers and theorizers differ. Synthesizers base their examples on extensive data and typically have a number of instances to draw on. By contrast, theorizers usually have no formal database. From their acute observations, current and past, they carefully select persuasive examples. Indeed, we can never be entirely sure of the extent of their database or what group it represents. Because their empirical evidence is usually limited to their examples, "demonstrated result" and "rival explanations eliminated" in internal validity (LP) and the three lowest labels in external validity (GP) are lightly shaded. Because of the generally convincing nature of their arguments, "credible result" is not.

"Explanation, rationale, theory, point of view" has light shading because the skill of the theorizer is the development from observations of very plausible explanations that are widely accepted. The rarity of recognized theorizers indicates the difficulty of doing this successfully.

Multiperspectivist.   As noted earlier, multiperspectivists are like theorizers, so the graphic representing their strengths and weaknesses resembles it. Like Allison's (1971) explanation of the Cuban missile crisis, multiperspectivists explain a single event or set of circumstances; therefore, their graphic depiction (Figure 24.7) also resembles that of the humanists. Dark shading of "Explanation credibility" and "Audience credibility" is common to all three. So also is the problem of finding a plausible explanation that fits the evidence; hence the light shading of "Explanation, rationale, theory, point of view." Because plausible alternative explanations are advanced instead of eliminated—and this is one of the strengths of the orientation—that item has been changed and darkly shaded.

To provide evidence for their relationships, multiperspectivists, like Allison, gather the same extensive database for an event as a humanist historian. But ambitious efforts like Tyack's (1976) are more like theorizers' work with selective examples. Tyack showed how compulsory schooling could be explained from five points of view: as a political construction (to create citizens and legitimize the state), as an outgrowth of ethnocultural conflict (compulsory attendance laws were largely passed by Republican pietists and evangelical ministers who were leaders in the common school crusade), organizational integration (education should be taken out of politics and shifted to superintendents who employed attendance officers), investment in human capital (economists argue that education has considerable power in explaining economic development), and Marxist theory (workers won schooling for their children,

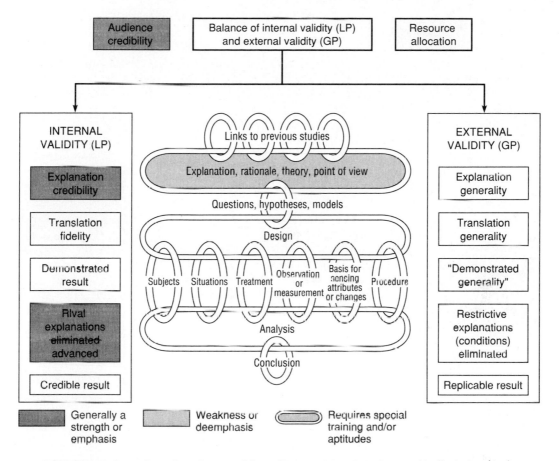

FIGURE 24.7 Strengths and weaknesses of the multiperspectivist orientation graphically depicted in the chain-of-reasoning model.

but the ruling class controlled decision making in education). Thus the extent of generality—external validity (GP)—claimed depends on the study and is therefore neither emphasized nor deemphasized in the graphic.

Humanist.   Like synthesizers and theorizers, humanists must have considerable conceptual capability. Finding patterns is often difficult and requires the ability to extract generalizations from the mass of detail in extensive descriptive data. Thus we find similarities in their graphic (Figure 24.8) to their predecessors' in the shading of "Explanation, rationale, theory, point of view" and the highlighting of "Audience credibility" and "Explanation credibility." Humanists formulate the accounts and stories that are most likely to lead to good internal cognitive maps of how the world works, a most difficult task. When successful, this kind of map considerably exceeds the explanatory and predictive power of simple propositions and sometimes of theories.

Humanists carefully develop the relation between evidence and explana-

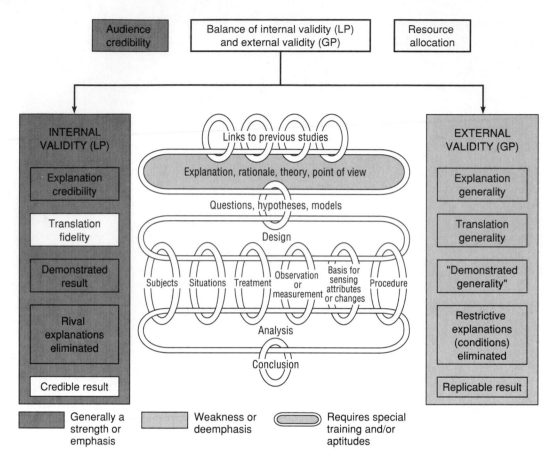

FIGURE 24.8   Strengths and weaknesses of the humanist orientation graphically depicted in the chain-of-reasoning model.

tion, hence the emphasis of "Demonstrated result" in the graphic. They are typical quite careful to ensure that their terms reflect the actual event accurately. They explore alternative explanations to make certain that none of these is a better fit than the one they are advancing and try to find evidence to eliminate them; hence, the dark shading of "Rival explanations eliminated." Together with strong explanation credibility, this gives them strong internal validity (LP), so it is darkly shaded as well. Like those of synthesizers, humanists' explanations are context-bound, so the whole of external validity (GP) is lightly shaded.

Humanist accounts draw attention to the situational aspects of behavior that so often are determining factors. But they are very difficult to describe in sufficiently general terms that they can be added as boundary conditions to generalizations. To do so would make the theories as complex as the humanists' stories, so the simplifying advantage of theory would be lost.

Particularist. Particularists reject generality claims for knowledge about people. Each person is distinctive, and laws about behavior threaten that uniqueness. But we cannot build a behavioral science without beliefs in generality of some kind. So particularists do not contribute directly to behavioral science; hence we can provide no graphic for this orientation. They are relevant to this typology, however, both because we need to understand individuals who are in social science positions who hold this orientation and because they do contribute to social science by stimulating suggestions in others for further investigation.

As the particularist knows, nothing is more useful than knowledge built intuitively out of one's own experience. It usually comes more readily to mind than what has been learned vicariously.

Particularists believe that researchers of other orientations must often accept satisfying others' criteria rather than their own. Particularists contend that they are "truer to themselves." To some extent this is true. The shadow of the natural sciences is cast over all orientations, and insofar as research does not meet its criteria and norms regardless of whether these are appropriate, some individuals will perceive the work as less than satisfactory. Particularists, as well as some humanists, perceive their peers to have been inappropriately swayed to use statistics and experimental methods by this pressure.

PERPETUATION OF ORIENTATION TYPES

The characteristics that determine a graduate student's orientation or type are partly brought by him or her to the acculturation process and are partly the result of it. The contributed part results from the match of the student's skills and values to those of the faculty or a mentor, a match that probably attracted the student to the field in the first place. As Roe's (1953a) studies show, there are differences in capabilities and interests among scientists in different fields—indeed, even between the theoretically and the experimentally oriented in a single field. Preferred methods are, in part, a function of subject matter. The psychologist's statistical and experimental design skills would be of little use to an anthropologist trying to capture the essential characteristics of a primitive culture. Where experimental methods require precise measurements and statistical manipulation, anthropological ethnomethodology uses verbal narration. It is no surprise, therefore, to find eminent anthropologists with lower mathematical scores but higher verbal scores than psychologists (Roe, 1953b, p. 28).

Since some orientations tend to be associated with certain fields of study, a person's capabilities, predilections, interests, and values are all likely to influence the selection of a field and the socialization process that results. Students without appropriate skills for a field either select themselves out to avoid failure, are counseled out by faculty members, or cannot find someone to serve as their adviser. Those remaining find that co-workers respond positively to their interests and values; a mutual attraction binds them cognitively and affectively.

These bonds are strengthened by the extensive socialization processes that accompany graduate training. Socialization takes place not only in coursework but also in apprentice roles on research projects. The many informal discussions among students and between faculty members and students are especially important in forging the affective undergirding of attitudes, values, and interests that develop and maintain the socialized role.

The socialization continues as the graduate student becomes "a member of the club" through joining a university faculty or some other work unit of like professionals. "In-service socialization" occurs through contacts with colleagues at the work level and in professional association affairs. The "right" roles are reinforced: in the promotions given for "good" work and award of tenure, in the models set by those receiving dissertation prizes and young researcher awards, by what gets published and what rejected, by the records of persons appointed to various institutional and association committees, in what receives positive attention at conventions, in the similar models of mature professionals honored with professional association prizes and awards for outstanding research, and in the records of who is elected to prestigious association officer positions.

Indeed, you might wonder why variation exists in a discipline at all were it not that competition also does. Everyone wants to succeed, and where success is defined as new knowledge, other orientations may be perceived as more successful routes, especially for certain problems. Competing graduate students and faculty members may see an advantage in diverging from a discipline's typical training; they break the pattern to exploit the potential of another orientation. Thus although traditional modes dominate, we find a variety of methodological orientations among mavericks in any field.

Of course, occasionally, socialization fails. Some such failures can be traced to the reduced control of fate many graduate students experience at the time they enter graduate school. They typically go where financial inducements are highest and only later realize the nature of the field. Many are able to live with their choice, but some are not and become resentful. Faculty members are probably more consciously aware of the prerequisites for a successful match than graduate students. But the faculty's ability to predict who will be good partners in the match is far from perfect. Further, the pool of sufficiently capable potential students is often not large enough for faculty to apply what they do know. Consequently, faculty may prefer to take a chance on a highly capable student who is switching fields and may not realize what he or she is getting into, than on a mediocre one whose previous experience indicates he or she does.

TEAM RESEARCH

Team research is increasingly prevalent because problems have different skill requirements, expertly mastering more than one orientation is difficult, and having different perspectives brought to bear on a problem (from the standpoint of subject matter as well as methodology) has significant advantages (witness chapter 23). To facilitate team formation, research corporations have developed a matrix-type organization. Individuals are employed in disciplinary departments that are responsible for recruiting the best personnel in a given field. The departments provide a disciplinary home for researchers with support from other persons who share the same point of view. Work, however, is done in interdisciplinary task forces chosen from appropriate departments as each problem dictates. This pattern combines the advantages of depth of specialization with the breadth of viewpoint that provides for exploration of the widest range of approaches. Note, however, that this interdisciplinary structure provides for continuous in-service socialization through the department.

ALL TYPES ARE VALUED

Greater understanding of the orientations should lead to increased tolerance of positions other than your own, as well as to greater appreciation of each orientation's strengths and weaknesses. The weaknesses seem to be emphasized more often than the strengths. It is worth remembering that, except for the particularist, all these orientations make valid contributions to research.[4] What is more, the behavioral sciences have benefited from this variety. No one orientation has so far demonstrated that it is the sole source of significant knowledge. We need all the orientations; each has its advantages. We should educate audiences about both the strengths and the contributions of all the orientations and the problems created by insistence on making natural science criteria the sole basis for valuing research in the behavioral sciences.

SUMMARY

Although we seldom attend to them, researchers in the social and behavioral sciences often have differing orientations toward the kind of social science they think is possible and desirable. Such views sometimes underlie differing advice about how to approach a research problem or improve a study. Individuals with different orientations tend to prefer different research methods and hold different ideas about what is good work and what role the values and guiding principles of research should play. A set of seven such orientations can be delineated: pragmatist, analyzer, synthesizer, theorizer, multiperspectivist, humanist, and pragmatist. Individuals may adopt these as different roles for different problems or may hold firmly to one of them as their position. We can analyze the chain-of-reasoning model in relation to each orientation to see the strengths and weaknesses of each. Although any one researcher may hold that a particular orientation is preeminent, all contribute to knowledge and are useful.

---

4. For an example of a similar effort to show the value of different approaches to the social sciences and their potential, see Morgan (1983).

=========== ADDITIONAL READING ===========

Krathwohl (1985)   Morgan (1983)

=========== IMPORTANT TERMS ===========

Analyzers   Particularists
Humanists   Pragmatists
Multiperspectivists   Synthesizers
Orientations to the social sciences Theorizers

=========== APPLICATION PROBLEMS ===========

1. Daniel Bertaux and Isabelle Bertaux-Wiame (1981) studied the artisanal bakeries in France. Their intention was to determine how bakers and bakery workers work and live, how they come to choose this field, and, especially, why (at the time) 90 percent of the bread in France was still produced by small bakeries. The authors described their approach as "structuralist-Marxist" and stated that their ultimate aim was to unravel the patterns of sociostructural relations underlying the daily process that produces the daily bread. Their research method was to work mostly with life stories gathered by means of interviews. They collected close to 100 life stories of bakers and bakery workers as well as published material on artisanal bakeries, available statistics (apparently few), and conversations with "key informants" (mill owners, sales agents, etc.). Bertaux-Wiame, a historian, also carried out a historical study of artisanal bakeries.

The result was a series of "central hypotheses" about why 45,000 artisanal bakeries can still be found in France, such as a ready supply of cheap, trained labor from the rural areas, the recent (twentieth-century) development of rural bakeries that produced this supply, and the desire of bakery workers to become self-employed. The report was written in the form of a narrative description of the baker's trade, how it developed historically, and its present nature. To what research orientation would these investigators belong? Why?

2. Here are two quotes from leading scholars concerning the nature of learning and instruction. What would be the research orientation of each of these authors?

(a) There is no mystery; it is all a matter of the scheduling of reinforcements. A good program of instruction guarantees a great deal of successful action. Students do not need to have a natural interest in what they are doing.

(b) The hypothesis is that human learning with understanding is a generative process. Stated more directly, all learning that involves understanding is discovery learning. We can determine the effects of instruction in terms of what the instruction causes the learner to do. Effective instruction causes the learner to generate a relationship between new information and previous experience.

3. Two psychologists, McKim and Cowen (1987), published a study of young children's school adjustment that they characterized as multiperspectivist. The main purpose of the study was to "assess the relationships among five perspectives of young school children's adjustment: teacher, peer, parent, and self-ratings and behavior observations." According to the authors, each of these five measurement perspectives "has its own substantial literature." Secondary purposes were to assess relationships between adjustment and achievement, to compare the adjustment of suburban and urban children, and to compare children referred for mental health services to children not referred. The investigators studied 462 second- and third-grade children from four urban and two suburban schools. The measures were all quantitative and consisted of a series of psychometric rating scales, standardized achievement tests, and a classroom observation protocol. The scores obtained on the 27 dependent measures were compared using Pearson product-moment correlation coefficients. Analysis of variance was used to test for difference between location and gender. Given the typologies used in this chapter, is the approach described here truly multiperspectivist? Why or why not?

4. The following passages are from various commentaries on research. What is the research orientation of each of the authors?

 (a) Teachers [should participate] in collaborative research [with each other] to become agents of their own change. . . . Not only do teachers identify practical theories that apply to their own idiosyncratic settings, but they also can formulate these practical theories as general hypotheses which have the potential for universal applicability.

 (b) He is not dependent on the categories of established theory and technique, but constructs a new theory of the unique case. His inquiry is not limited to deliberation about means which depends on a prior agreement about ends. He does not keep means and ends separate but defines them interactively as he frames a problematic situation.

 (c) Personal structural analysis was devised by Baldwin to focus on one woman through review of a long series of personal letters. The object of interest was her unique thought structure. Again, emphasis is on unique individual pattern rather than parts.

 (d) [Nurses] reflect on the experience and phenomenologically describe the calls they receive, their responses, and what they come to know from their presence in the nursing situation. It is believed that compilation and complementary syntheses of these descriptions over time will build and make explicit a science of nursing. (From *Humanistic Nurses*)

Compare your answers with those on pages 726–727.

================= APPLICATION EXERCISE =================

Consider which of the orientations comes closest to your beliefs about the desired nature of the social sciences. How might you, using other points of view about the social sciences, conceptualize your problem differently?

If you find it hard to think of your problem from different points of view, get a group of seven fellow students together and have each role-play one of the orientations. Discuss each group member's problem, examining it from the standpoint of the different orientations. How would each orientation conceptualize it differently? Research it differently? How would the end product of the research differ?

Can you pick faculty with different orientations to discuss your problem with? How would they differ in their recommendations to you? After talking with them, consider whether your expectation of their orientation was accurate. If not, why not? Do they perhaps play different roles, depending on the problem?

Ethics and Legal Constraints

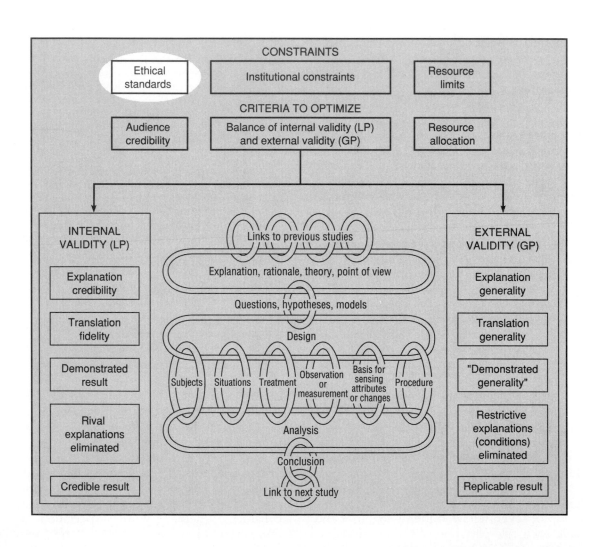

Whether you wish to become an ethicist in your particular discipline is not at issue. . . . You became one the minute you joined the profession. The only . . . issue now is whether you are going to be a good ethicist or a bad one. . . . You cannot use a human being [in a study] . . . without asking yourself, "Ought I to be doing this, in this way, to this person, at this time?" The moment the word "ought" is muttered, you have entered the realm of ethics.

T. M. Grunder, Informed Consent

OVERVIEW

Ethical standards impose one of the three constraints on research. The topic of ethics can be divided into two aspects: (1) the legal and institutional constraints on research designed to protect the people from whom data are gathered and (2) the responsibility of the individual researcher for proper conduct of the study above and beyond legalities. The former is covered by U.S. federal regulations and the procedures they establish. The government wants assurance from the researcher's institution that adequate safeguards are provided for the protection of human subjects. Its regulations must be observed in all federally funded research involving humans.[1] In addition, most institutions apply them to all research, not only that of faculty, for instance, but that of graduate students as well.

Above and beyond what the government requires, the actions of any individual affect the image of the rest of us when a problem becomes public knowledge. Although professional associations have established useful codes of conduct, what is done in the privacy of the professional office is almost impossible to police; trust and integrity are the cornerstones of the enterprise. This chapter deals with the investigator's conduct in selecting problems, adopting roles in the investigation (as in covert observation), and giving appropriate credit to others who also worked on the project. Analyzing and reporting data with integrity are taken up in the final chapter of the book, which is concerned with whether and how well science works.

CHAPTER CONTENTS

Introduction   660
Legal and Institutional Protection
    of Human Subjects   661
        Institutional Review Boards   661
        Informed Consent   663
Codes of Ethics from Professional
    Associations   666
Additional Common Ethical
    Concerns   668

Problem Choice   668
Data Confidentiality and
    Personal Privacy   670
Gaining Entry for Studies   671
Ownership of the Data   672
The Researcher's Responsibility
    to the Institutional
    Review Board   673
Summary   674

1. The regulations' reference is 45 CFR 46. Similar regulations exist for the protection of animals used in research.

INTRODUCTION

Although published professional standards in psychology were formulated as early as 1951 (American Psychological Association, 1951), extensive emphasis on the protection of human subjects arose primarily as a result of government intervention. Prior to that, many members of the professions were concerned by studies that, though they made important points, did so by deceiving the subjects. Milgram's (1963) study provoked an early outcry. A subject in a cubicle thought he was helping another subject in an adjoining cubicle to learn. The first subject did so by applying electric shocks to the second subject at the request of the investigator. When asked to do so, the first subject moved the level, presumably increasing the shocks into what was labeled as the "danger" level even after hearing a groan and then silence from the person receiving them. Individuals were informed during **debriefing** after the study that no shocks were given and that the other person was a confederate.

Milgram thought the study important, for it showed that ordinary persons could be made to do extraordinary things under certain circumstances. As Sieber and Stanley (1988) put it, blind obedience to authority is "more contextual and less characterological than most [people] have assumed" (p. 52). Milgram believed that the evidence bore on the questions involved in the Nuremberg trials of Nazi officials as war criminals when they claimed they were merely following orders. This created quite a furor, and people argued as to whether the circumstances were comparable enough to those in Nazi Germany that a parallel could be drawn.[2] This dispute was important because it also gave prominence to the issue of whether the value of the information gained might have been worth the discomfort of the subjects requested to do such awful things.

A second issue involved the protection of subjects. They had not asked to have such distasteful knowledge of themselves, nor did they realize they were going to receive it. A person could find it very disturbing to realize that he or she was capable of such behavior. Whether deception of subjects that can result in self-knowledge and stress is conscionable is at issue.

On what are such ethical judgments based? We noted early in the book that knowledge results from the development of a consensus around the appropriate interpretation of evidence. Similarly, a consensus is required for ethical decisions to be accepted. There are two differences, however: usually there is no evidence to form the basis for judgment—the consensus must be formed around what each person projects as likely to happen; and a value must be placed on the anticipated consequences to determine whether gains outweigh costs. Clearly, these conditions make it much more difficult to form a consensus. People differ in their predictions of likely consequences, on the seriousness of potential negative effects, and in their estimate of the potential

---

2. Milgram (1974) notes, incidentally, that there were no objections to his study until the results were known. This raises the interesting question of how many of the criticisms resulted because the conclusions ran counter to what people wanted to believe.

value of the knowledge sought. Adding to the difficulty of getting a consensus are persons who are absolutists when it comes to values. To them, for example, there is never any way that gains in knowledge can offset harm to subjects; deception of subjects is always unacceptable.

How to proceed? From whom can we gain a consensus that ensures meeting acceptable ethical standards? Two groups, the federal government and the professional associations, have stepped into the breach. We shall examine first the federal apparatus for the protection of human subjects and then the principles established by professional associations to guide researchers.

LEGAL AND INSTITUTIONAL PROTECTION OF HUMAN SUBJECTS

Two U.S. federal laws provide for regulation in ethical matters: the Family Educational Rights and Privacy Act[3] and the National Research Act 93-348 of 1974. The latter provides for what are known as **institutional review boards** (IRBs), which have the responsibility for ensuring that projects forwarded for funding are perceived as ethically permissible. Technically, the IRBs are responsible only for research funded by the U.S. Department of Health and Human Services (HHS), but Grunder (1983) found that 96 percent of institutions have been applying the regulations to all research whether funded by HHS or not.

Institutional Review Boards

The membership of an institutional review board is specifically prescribed in the regulations:

- It must have at least five members.
- It may not consist of all men or all women.
- It must include at least one nonscientist (examples given are lawyers, ethicists, clergypersons).
- It must include one person not affiliated with the institution or part of the immediate family of persons affiliated with it.
- Persons with a conflict of interest are to be excluded except to provide information.
- Persons with competency in special relevant areas may be invited to assist in the review but may not vote.
- If the board regularly reviews research involving a vulnerable category of subjects (such as the mentally retarded), the IRB must include one or more individuals "who are primarily concerned with the welfare of these subjects" (Sec. 46-107).

---

3. P.L. 93-380, Title V, Sec. 513 (b)(2)(i), 88 Stat. 574; 34 CFR Part 99.

Approval is by majority vote. These boards have the responsibility of approving research plans. They also have the authority to suspend or terminate approval of research that is not being conducted in accordance with the IRB's requirements or where unexpected serious harm occurs. Adequate documentation of all IRB meetings and actions is required.

In addition to a lengthy discussion of informed consent (our next topic for discussion), the criteria for IRB approval include concerns for the safety of subjects:

- Risks to subjects are to be minimized; this means that the risks of harm must be "not greater, considering probability and magnitude, than those ordinarily encountered in daily life or during the performance of routine physical or psychological examinations or tests" (Sec. 46-103).
- "Risks are reasonable in relation to anticipated benefits, if any, to subjects, and the importance of the knowledge that may reasonably result" (Sec. 46-111). Note that this makes the IRB specifically responsible for evaluating the trade-off—for deciding how much risk this knowledge is worth.
- "Selection of subjects is equitable" (Sec. 46-111); this means, for example, that friends are not put at less risk or have greater potential benefits than strangers.
- Adequate provision is made for monitoring the safety of subjects, where appropriate.

As Grunder (1986) notes, the IRB is "a work of bureaucratic genius," a reasonably satisfactory solution to a very complicated problem to which no solution will be lauded by everyone. It transfers the responsibility from the government to the institution but specifies what the institution must do to comply. It means there is no "Ethical FBI," as he puts it, to check out rumors; "no army of investigators lurking around thousands of laboratories" (p. 7). It solves the problem of where and among whom to obtain a consensus by specifying the board as the place where agreement must be found and by reducing "consensus" to a majority. It provides guidelines, leaving it to the board to interpret them and to decide when a rule is violated. The penalty for violation is the removal of eligibility for all future research monies involving human subjects for the researcher *and the institution*—a very severe penalty for a research institution!

The work of IRBs has become of such importance that it now has its own journal, *IRB: A Review of Human Subject Research.*[4] In it are discussions of such issues as IRBs' being too responsive to community pressure or too resistive, too zealous in protecting subjects, and so on. Just as the body of law is helped by precedents, no doubt IRB judgments will be refined by experience and discussion.

---

4. Published by the Hastings Center, Institute of Society, Ethics and Life Sciences, 360 Broadway, Hastings-on-Hudson, NY 10706.

- Institutional review boards bear the responsibility for determining whether projects are ethically permissible and, if there are ethical questions, for deciding whether the potential knowledge gained is worth the potential risk involved.
- Although established under federal regulations for funded projects, IRBs are used for other research conducted at most institutions regardless of funding.

Informed Consent

A key part of work with human subjects is obtaining **informed consent**. It is especially important where

- there is any possibility of risk,
- minors are involved,
- privacy may be invaded, or
- potentially distasteful self-knowledge may result from participation.

Consequently, 45 CFR 46 deals with it extensively. Like the other topics in the values arena, there is more to it than meets the eye. Who can give informed consent? Can a jailed prisoner? A psychotic? A mentally retarded person? What constitutes sufficient information? How do we know when a person really understands and so can provide "informed" acquiescence? Once again, certain safeguards have been put in place, and a number of aids have been developed. Grunder (1986) is such an aid and an excellent one. He provides a checklist on written consent forms and the procedures surrounding their use. In addition, a number of sample situations test the reader's mastery of the rules. Much of the following material is patterned after Grunder. For starters, he notes that informed consent may be obtained on a short or long form.

Short and Long Consent Forms.   The short form accompanies a verbal explanation and indicates that the individual has been given information regarding the study, understands what he or she is committing to, and has received answers to all questions. Two copies must be signed and dated by the subject and a witness, a disinterested third party who was present during the presentation of the information. The presentation should give the information needed to make an informed decision. With short or long form, a reasonable opportunity must be given the subjects to decide whether to participate. Those not signing should be dismissed courteously. Whether short or long form is used, the participant retains one of the two signed and dated copies.

The long form includes all the information that would be given verbally. It does not need to be witnessed, although Grunder notes that that is still a good idea. Under either short or long form, a witness can affirm that the assent was freely given, not coerced, nor the person deceived into signing the form.

The witness can attest that a person who refused to sign was allowed to leave with no sign of disfavor. Grunder prefers the long form because it points out the positive features of the study to the participant in writing for later reference. When the long form is used, it is read aloud to the participant to reinforce its content and to be certain that it is read in its entirety. A brief verbal summary follows the reading.

Content of the Consent Form.   What must the consent form contain? These are the minimum requirements:

- Information as to who is doing the study; its nature; its purpose; procedures; hazards, risks, and inconveniences; benefits; if therapeutic, the alternative treatments that could be chosen; duration; and the identification of any experimental procedures
- Availability of compensation and treatment if an injury should occur in cases of more than minimal risk
- The extent, if any, to which confidentiality of records identifying the subject will be maintained
- The name of the contact person to whom to address questions or report an injury
- Notification that participation is voluntary and that refusal to participate or discontinue participation will be without penalty or loss of benefits to which the person is otherwise entitled

In some instances, where appropriate, it should also reveal the following information:

- The fact that some risks are unforeseeable
- The investigator's right to ask a subject to leave the study (usually the criteria for termination are given to show that this is not arbitrary)
- The promise that subjects will continue to be informed as information develops that may bear on participation
- Additional costs to the subject resulting from participation
- The consequences of withdrawal and the procedure for orderly termination of participation
- The approximate number of subjects

The consent form must be so written that its reading level makes it understandable to the subjects. Readability formulas can be used to determine this, and Grunder (1986) includes those in his manual. Stanley, Sieber, and Melton (1987) note that such studies as have been made indicate that in general, the risk disclosure required by the consent process has had only a minimal influence on decision making with regard to medical procedures. That seems consistent with the few available studies of psychological studies as well.

Altering or Waiving the Consent Process.   The decision to alter or waive the consent process can only be made by an IRB. It can do so only if the research does not involve greater than "minimum risk," the rights or welfare of the subjects will not be adversely affected, the research could not be done otherwise, and the subjects will be debriefed. Consent documentation can be waived if the consent form links the individual to data that, if made public, could be harmful to the subject. For example, in a study of drug pushers, merely being identified as part of such a study might be considered the basis for subpoenaing the data to search for an illegal act. Humphreys (1975) makes fascinating reading on this latter problem. He studied homosexual behavior in public places—illegal then as now—identifying participants through their license plate numbers, tracking them down, and interviewing them. Realizing later that he could not protect his files from subpoena, he destroyed them. Social science researchers have immunity under the law like doctors and lawyers only under special dispensation. "Scientists engaged in research on mental health can obtain certificates of confidentiality from the Department of Health and Human Services which provide immunity from subpoenas. The Department of Justice can provide grants of confidentiality to protect data gathered in research projects involving drugs" (Nelkin, 1984, p. 52).

Obtaining Consent When the Individual Is Incapable of Giving It. Can freely given informed consent be obtained from children, prisoners, and the mentally handicapped? Each is a special case. With children, informed consent must be obtained from *one* parent or legal guardian. In addition, assent—agreement to take part in the procedures—must also be sought from the child, and the IRB must determine if the child is capable of giving assent. The definition of who is a child is found in state rather than federal statutes since the age of legal majority varies from state to state.

Prisoner consent must not involve procedures that would compare too favorably with normal prison conditions so as to serve as an enticement. Risks must be comparable to those of nonprisoner volunteers. The selection of subjects must be fair. Participation must have no effect on parole, and subjects must be so informed.

Procedures for working with the mentally handicapped and the elderly are not addressed by the regulations. Grunder (1986) strongly suggests using a professional who regularly works with the population in question and who has no ties to the project. This person can attest that consent procedures were followed, that consent or assent was obtained during a period when the subject was lucid, and that if assent is not within the realm of capability, the lack of objection may be enough if minimal risk is involved. In cases of more than minimal risk but benefit to the patient, approval from a court of competent jurisdiction should be sought. Grunder suggests reading chapter 1 of the report of the National Commission for the Protection of Human Subjects of Biomedical and Behavioral Research as a guide.

Individuals used as subjects in a study, especially if there is any potential risk, if minors are involved, if privacy may be invaded, or if potentially distasteful self-knowledge may be gained, should give their voluntary consent. Problems arise when individuals are unable to do so because of such circumstances as incapacity, lack of freedom to make decisions, or minor status.

CODES OF ETHICS FROM PROFESSIONAL ASSOCIATIONS

Most disciplinary professional associations have developed a set of ethical standards for their field. Typical of these is *Ethical Principles in the Conduct of Research with Human Participants* by the Committee on Protection of Human Participants in Research of the American Psychological Association (APA) (1982). The **code of ethics** consists of 10 principles. "Each section begins with a review of the problem or issue that gives rise to the need for a guiding Principle. Then . . . a discussion relates the Principle to various problems, research settings, and populations of research participants" (p. 25). An excerpt from the committee's statement that includes the 10 principles follows:

The decision to undertake research rests upon a considered judgment by the individual psychologist about how best to contribute to psychological science and human welfare. . . .

A. In planning a study, the investigator has the responsibility to make a careful evaluation of its ethical acceptability. To the extent the weighing of scientific and humane values suggests a compromise of any principle, the investigator incurs a correspondingly serious obligation to seek ethical advice and to observe stringent safeguards to protect the rights of human participants.

B. Considering whether a participant in a planned study will be a "subject at risk" or a "subject at minimal risk," according to recognized standards, is of primary ethical concern to the investigator.

C. The investigator always retains the responsibility for ensuring ethical practice in research. The investigator is also responsible for the ethical treatment of research participants by collaborators, assistants, students, and employees, all of whom, however, incur similar obligations.

D. Except in minimal-risk research, the investigator establishes a clear and fair agreement with research participants, prior to their participation, that clarifies the obligations and responsibilities of each. The investigator has the obligation to honor all promises and commitments included in that agreement. The investigator informs the participants of all aspects of the research that might reasonably be expected to influence willingness to participate and explains all other aspects of the research about which the participants inquire. Failure to make full disclosure prior to obtaining informed consent requires additional safeguards to protect the welfare and dignity of the research participants. Research with children or with participants who have impairments that would limit understanding and/or communication requires special safeguarding procedures.

E. Methodological requirements of a study may make use of concealment or deception necessary. Before conducting such a study, the investigator has a special responsibility to (1) determine whether the use of such techniques is justified by the study's prospective scientific, educational, or applied value; (2) determine whether alternative procedures are available that do not use concealment or deception; and (3) ensure that the participants are provided with sufficient explanation as soon as possible.

F. The investigator respects the individual's freedom to decline to participate in or withdraw from the research at any time. The obligation to protect this freedom requires careful thought and consideration when the investigator is in a position of authority or influence over the participant. Such positions of authority include, but are not limited to, situations in which research participation is required as a part of employment or in which the participant is a student, client, or employee of the investigator.

G. The investigator protects the participant from physical and mental discomfort, harm, and danger that may arise from research procedures. If risks of such consequences exist, the investigator informs the participant of that fact. Research procedures likely to cause serious or lasting harm to a participant are not used unless the failure to use these procedures might expose the individual to risk of greater harm or unless the research has great potential benefit and fully informed and voluntary consent is obtained from each participant. The participant should be informed of procedures for contacting the investigator within a reasonable time period following participation should stress, potential harm, or related questions or concerns arise.

H. After the data are collected, the investigator provides the participant with information about the nature of the study and attempts to remove any misconceptions that may have arisen. Where scientific or humane values justify delaying or withholding this information, the investigator incurs a special responsibility to monitor the research and ensure that there are no damaging consequences for the participant.

I. Where research procedures result in undesirable consequences for the individual participant, the investigator has the responsibility to detect and remove or correct the consequences, including long-term effects.

J. Information obtained about a research participant during the course of an investigation is confidential unless otherwise agreed upon in advance. When the possibility exists that others may obtain access to such information, this possibility, together with the plans for protecting confidentiality, is explained to the participant as part of the procedure for obtaining informed consent.[5]

These principles repeat and clarify many aspects already discussed.[6] The APA also publishes a set of ethical standards for psychologists in its annual directory, which cover not just research but all professional activities.[7] Most would apply to any social science.

In addition to ethical standards, associations have formulated standards for various fields of work such as standardized testing (see chapter 11) and evaluation (see chapter 20). Although in no way intended to have legal standing, these carefully crafted statements are often cited as expert opinion in

5. Copyright © 1982 The American Psychological Association. Used with permission.
6. The committee's statement makes clear that the principles should be interpreted in terms of the context provided in the complete document offered as a supplement to them.
7. To assist in the interpretation of the principles, a casebook has been developed citing actual instances considered by the APA's Ethics Committee (American Psychological Association, 1987).

legal cases. They have therefore come to have a marked influence beyond what might otherwise be expected of pronouncements set forth for voluntary compliance.

Professional associations have developed codes of ethics and standards for the guidance of both the lay public and members of their professions. Although without legal standing, they are sometimes cited in legal cases.

ADDITIONAL COMMON ETHICAL CONCERNS

Problem Choice

As indicated by the quotation at the start of this chapter, researchers are ethicists whether they want to be or not. This ethical role often includes the choice of problem, as is made clear by these two excerpts:

> Some years ago, I did research on attitudes toward cheating among college students. One could observe cheating, however, only by deceiving subjects. I could have used a technique such as returning already graded multiple-choice exams for (supposedly) self-grading and then counting answers that are changed by students during grading. Such techniques seemed to me to raise very serious questions about relations between people. . . . Was this my right as a scientist? I decided not to pursue the project in this direction.

> I have conducted a number of participant-observation studies in which subjects were unaware that they were being observed. Each time I conduct such a study, the ethical problem arises concerning the very act of disguised participant observation. My resolution of the ethical problem of invasion of privacy, disguising one's true role, and so on, essentially is based on a rudimentary cost-benefit analysis. That is, I consider at length the value of the data sought, the possible effects of publication of the findings on the subjects, and the relative degree of privacy that actually is being violated. If I have serious misgivings about any of these factors, I will not conduct the research.[8]

Clearly, not all studies raise such ethical dilemmas. But as stated earlier, it is the responsibility of the researcher to search for the ethical aspects of each problem and to make a judgment as to whether to pursue it.

---

8. Both from American Psychological Association, Ad Hoc Committee on Ethical Standards in Psychological Research, *Ethical Principles in the Conduct of Research with Human Participants*, p. 20. Copyright © 1973 The American Psychological Association. Reprinted with permission.

Deception. It can be argued that some topics cannot be studied without **deception of subjects**; it is necessary to withhold from the subjects true knowledge of the nature of the study. Studies of entrance procedures to college to determine the effect of racial and sexual identification, the effects of subliminal messages, the effects of certain drugs, and other topics may all require concealment of the true purpose of the study. The Zimbardo study of chapter 2 is such an example. Institutional review boards do approve such studies from time to time (e.g., the Zimbardo study), so why do some persons categorically reject such procedures? Baumrind (1985), summarizing the arguments from different points of view, notes that such approvals fail to take into account long-range costs that are "unknown and therefore easy for investigators and review boards to dismiss" (p. 167). For example, deception may

> offend participants or damage their self-esteem, give . . . research a bad name and work to the detriment of the research of others, lower the level of the participants' confidence in the quality of their relationships with others or provide them with a bad example on which they may model their behavior. (American Psychological Association, 1973, pp. 11–12)

It is difficult to obtain evidence regarding the absence of harm to subjects that is acceptable to opponents of deception. For instance, Milgram (1974, 1977) argues that he adequately debriefed his subjects, and in a one-year follow up, 80 percent said they were glad to have taken part and less than 1 percent of his subjects regretted it. Patten (1977), however, argues that the evidence comes from "destructively obedient" individuals; we could hardly expect them to say otherwise. Further, Baumrind (1985) notes that when queried about the study, such subjects need to deny they have allowed themselves "to be treated as objects, and . . . [therefore] most will say that they were glad to have been subjects" (p. 169). In the face of such arguments, it is difficult to gather evidence acceptable to people who oppose the practice.

Decreased trust of others is a cost to both the individual and society. Debriefed subjects have been found to be less inclined to trust experimenters to tell the truth (Fillenbaum, 1966). That same distrust rubs off on the profession since the community is less likely to be supportive of research that runs contrary to accepted values. Baumrind (1985) also sees the practice as deteriorating researchers' "ethical sensibilities and integrity" in addition to their credibility. She argues that the continued use of such practices is self-defeating because enough subjects are made suspicious that the naiveté of subjects becomes a variable itself. Page (1973) showed that the behaviors of subjects who are suspicious are generally different from those of subjects who are not.

There are clearly strong arguments against using deception, and IRBs should and no doubt do weigh carefully any proposal for its rare use. Certainly, careful debriefing by a skilled professional is one condition of its use. If it is employed, Sieber's (1983) recommendations are worth consulting, and Mills (1976), who attempted to educate his subject in the process, may provide a model.

> Certain research topics cannot be pursued without deception. Some people feel that they should be excluded from the research agenda; others decide each project on a cost-benefit basis.

Data Confidentiality and Personal Privacy

Confidentiality and privacy are often mistakenly assumed to relate to the same concern. **Confidentiality** refers to control of access to information; **privacy** to a person's interest in controlling boundaries between self and others (Sieber and Stanley, 1988). In most research, ensuring confidentiality of data is just plain good practice. As noted earlier, the researcher has no immunity from subpoena like some professionals, so researchers must gather data in such a way that anonymity is ensured from the outset.[9] Usually, the main use of identifiers is to link items of data such as test scores with other data from the same person. Various means that do not violate confidentiality can be used to link data or to gather responses to sensitive questions (see chapter 16). Data gathered with identifiers can be made anonymous by tearing off this information once it is no longer needed. Sometimes a neutral third party can receive the data, remove the identifiers, and pass the data on to the researcher. The keys for identification can be held by a neutral person in another country, where subpoenas cannot be served. As noted earlier, immunity from subpoena can be granted for particular data by the National Institutes of Health and the Department of Justice for certain kinds of projects. In short, there are enough ways of handling this situation that the problem more often stems from inadequate attention to solutions than from a lack of them.

Inadequate provision for protection can cause problems. Consider the *Chronicle of Higher Education* report (Dispatch Case, 1986) that the government of Sweden ordered all clues to the identity of participants destroyed. It thus terminated and rendered useless past sociological information on 15,000 Stockholm residents who had been part of a longitudinal study since 1966. It quotes Professor Jansson, who started the project, as writing: "It is grotesque that people under study can deprive me of material I have worked on for more than 20 years; fantastic that they think they own information on themselves" (p. 42). Critics called the comment "academic arrogance." We can criticize the project as not having adequately attended to confidentiality concerns. But it should also be noted that such concerns were not as great when the project started as they have become with the advent of computer databases.

Confidentiality of information from school records is within the jurisdiction of the U.S. Family Educational Rights and Privacy Act, also known as

---

9. Nelkin (1984) reports that "between 1966 and 1976 at least 50 scholars were served subpoenas in 18 different cases, ordering them to reveal the identities of sources and subjects of research; another 30 scientists were threatened with subpoenas" (p. 51).

the **Buckley amendment**. This act requires that before information may be gathered from school records, a waiver must be obtained from the parent or guardian or, if over 18 years of age, the student. The waiver must indicate what records will be disclosed, the purpose of the disclosure, and the persons to whom disclosure will be made. The act exempts school personnel with a legitimate educational interest, as well as organizations conducting studies for local or state agencies for the purpose of developing and validating tests, administering student aid programs, or improving instruction. Although this last category seems broad, the local institution is the final judge of what constitutes "improving instruction," and its approval must be obtained. Data so gathered must be reported so that individuals cannot be identified, and the date must be destroyed when the study is completed.

Privacy of subjects is a problem when a person reveals more than intended to a skilled investigator. The subject may reveal this information more readily if he or she suspects that it is available anyway and that concealing or lying about it may create problems. Such information may then result in public policy such as mandatory AIDS testing, quarantine, or similar actions that might not have occurred had the information been withheld (Sieber and Stanley, 1988). IRBs are alert to this problem, but clearly, ultimate responsibility for respecting privacy rests with the researcher.

- Confidentiality of data must be maintained so that individuals or institutions cannot be identified in ways that may be harmful or invite undesirable comparisons.
- Invasion of privacy is a problem when subjects reveal more than they intended in the course of a study.
- Except as special status is obtained in a funded project, social science investigators have no immunity from subpoena. Special steps must be taken from the outset of data collection to make sure that subjects are not at risk.

Gaining Entry for Studies

It goes without saying that one must obtain permission to collect data in an institution. Yet many dilemmas may arise in this process. The natural inclination is to follow the "chain of command" and seek initial approval from the top down, starting with the administrative officer, the school superintendent, the hospital administrator, the counseling center director. Yet to do so may cause problems. Teachers, for instance, may feel that the superintendent cannot commit their time and effort, that the researcher should seek their permission first, then the superintendent's. This places the researcher in a difficult position, since many superintendents don't want such contacts made in their schools without their permission. There is no simple answer; each situation must be judged in terms of the rules in effect at the time and the procedures that seem to have been followed in the past. That is not terribly helpful advice since mistakes in gaining entry can be costly not only to the researcher but to those who follow him, who also lose access. Yet there is no single, simple solution.

Equally perplexing ethical decisions are often encountered in the course of field research as noted in chapter 15. Where illegal acts, incompetence, or serious mistakes are observed (such as an incompetent surgeon who makes a serious error), should we report them? Alternatively, we can hope that in revealing the overall situation, as Bosk (1979) did, the general situation will be corrected, even though this particular surgeon may not be caught. Researchers in the field encountering such problems usually have to make their decisions on the spot without any opportunity to consult others or an IRB.

A special problem in gaining entry is the administrator who wishes to control the flow of information emanating from the study. Such a desire may seem unreasonable from a scientific point of view. But since unfavorable reports may cost the administrator's job, this is not an illogical request. The researcher may feel that an administrator who has anything to hide ought to lose the job, but that won't win entry. Once again, individuals' rights as human beings, society's needs for protection from incompetence and wrong-doing, and the scientist's freedom to explore and provide the free flow of information that is the lifeblood of science come into conflict. It is a conflict that each researcher must resolve. Many prefer not to use a site rather than submit to censorship or to deceive in order to obtain the data.

> Entry to field situations, especially where a negative report may reflect on the people giving such access, causes serious ethical dilemmas, especially when the public's right to know is also involved.

Ownership of the Data

There are at least two ethical issues with respect to ownership of the data: its availability to others for secondary analysis and who gets credit at the study's publication. Ideally, the rules are clear for each of these areas. So far as availability of the data for secondary analysis is concerned, it is becoming increasingly important for researchers to keep their data so that others may use it to check their findings. This has developed because of the awareness of frauds in science. A problem that can develop, however, is that the anonymity of the data could be compromised if individuals try to check on the way they were collected or to follow up on cases. Nelkin (1984) cites cases where federal granting agencies claimed *and were granted* access to data that researchers obtained under the promise of confidentiality. Ownership of data and maintenance of confidentiality should be agreed on at the time a grant is negotiated.

Who should get credit upon publication is covered well in principle 17 of the American Psychological Association's "Ethical Standards of Psychologists" (republished yearly in its membership directory). It is useful in deciding authorship of work on which a graduate student and a faculty member have collaborated, perhaps a dissertation initiated at the behest and with the guidance of a faculty member but carried out by the student:

> Credit is assigned to those who have contributed to a publication, in proportion to their contribution, and only to these.
>
> a. Major contributions of a professional character, made by several persons to a common project, are recognized by joint authorship. The experimenter or author who has made the principal contribution . . . is first listed.
>
> b. Minor contributions . . . [such as] clerical or similar non-professional assistance . . . are acknowledged in footnotes or . . . an introductory statement.
>
> c. Acknowledgment through specific citations is made for unpublished as well as published material that has directly influenced the research or writing.

Other associations have similar statements and mores.

- The right of outsiders to obtain data for secondary analysis may pose a dilemma for the investigator who has promised confidentiality to subjects.
- Publication credit should be given in direct proportion to contribution to the project.

The Researcher's Responsibility to the Institutional Review Board

Although it is the IRB's responsibility to make the final decision, the board depends on the researcher to present the case. This can be a dilemma for researchers, who must anticipate the negative consequences as well as the positive side of each new study. It is easy to see the IRB as the enemy to be thrust aside. But the attitude everyone must take is not much different from the impartial attitude that researchers assume, insofar as they can, in assessing data in which they have invested their time, their resources, and sometimes their reputations. As Koshland (1990) notes:[10]

> Scientists are the servants of society, not its masters, and we should remain so. . . . It is our special responsibility to spell out the disadvantages as well as the advantages of a new discovery as far as we can. What is good for science is not necessarily good for the country. . . .

---

10. From Daniel E. Koshland, Jr. "To See Ourselves as Others See Us," in *Science*, Vol. 247, beginning on p. 9, 01/01/90. Copyright 1990 by the AAAS. Reprinted with permission.

As architects of change, we have occasionally oversold the product, implying that it will bring unmixed good, not acknowledging that a scientific advance is a Pandora's box with detriments or abuses as well as benefits. By confessing that we are not omniscient we may lose some awe and admiration, but we will gain in understanding and rapport.

If you are turned down, try to understand the position of the IRB. Often simple adjustments in the research plan will take care of the matter. In other instances, there may be counterarguments that can and should be expressed. Careful listening, genuine understanding, and a real attempt to view the situation from the other side of the table are essential to keeping this decision process working as it should before a counteroffensive is launched.

Researchers must also help IRBs understand the opportunistic nature of science. Quoting Koshland (1990) again:

No one can assess at the inception of an invention all of its social implications. We could not predict that an understanding of radio waves would change the way we communicate, that understanding control of bacterial growth would lead to a population explosion, or that a simple equation, $E = mc^2$, would lead to a change in the nature of warfare. . . . [We must] explain the serendipitous nature of science, . . . display our own limitations with candor, . . . express our intentions and reservations in clear, nonspecialized terms, and . . . empathize and communicate with those whose lives . . . [may] be changed.

SUMMARY

Ethical principles to guide the work of the researcher have been established by the federal government and by professional associations. The government has entrusted the enforcement of these principles to institutional review boards (IRBs), which must be established at institutions seeking federal funds for research involving humans. In most institutions, these boards must approve all research, not just that federally supported. IRBs are responsible for holding harmless, both physically and mentally, individuals who serve as subjects for research. They also enforce quite specific rules with respect to eliciting freely given informed consent from subjects and protecting the confidentiality of data and the privacy of subjects. Federal specifications protecting the privacy of information obtained from school records must also be observed.

In addition, professional associations, through the publication of ethical standards and their explications, have sought to be helpful in many areas of research not covered by federal regulation as well as in fields such as testing, evaluation, and personnel selection.

Despite all these standards, there is deep concern over fraud in science. Do scientists live up to the standards set for them? Can their work be trusted? And this concern raises questions as to whether the whole system works. It is to those questions that the final chapter of this book is devoted.

=================== ADDITIONAL READING ===================

See Koshland (1990)
Schuler (1982) examines ethical questions
    from a historical viewpoint on both sides
    of the Atlantic. The codes of eight

European nations are presented, as well
as an examination of alternatives to
laboratory experiments for sensitive
problems.

=================== IMPORTANT TERMS ===================

Buckley amendment
Code of ethics
Confidentiality
Debriefing

Deception of subjects
Informed consent
Institutional review boards
Privacy

=================== APPLICATION PROBLEMS ===================

1. The rapid spread since the beginning of the 1980s of the virus that causes the acquired immune deficiency syndrome (AIDS) has brought about considerable medical research on the topic and, with it, a series of controversies. One surrounds research into the effectiveness of drugs, such as AZT, meant to control the disease. Medical researchers and government regulatory bodies such as the U.S. Food and Drug Administration have restricted the distribution of such medications until they have been clinically tested. Further, during such tests, some groups of AIDS patients would receive the experimental drugs while others would not. Some of the latter might even receive a placebo in order to provide a control for the experiment. AIDS patients have objected strenuously. What is the ethical dilemma here?

2. The AIDS epidemic has also led to another ethical problem. Two of the major groups identified as at risk are male homosexuals and intravenous drug abusers. Homosexuality is legal in many countries, including the United States and Canada; in others it is not. Regardless, many gays are sub-

jected to discrimination. Drug abusers are most often in contravention of the law. Research to find ways to control and eventually cure the virus must necessarily involve these groups. What is the problem?

3. An educational sociologist was interested in determining if there was a relationship between teachers' socioeconomic backgrounds and their job performance. She decided to begin with an exploratory approach using several qualitative research techniques including classroom observation, interviews, and document analysis. She met with a local school superintendent to negotiate entry to the schools and permission to interview teachers. The superintendent agreed to arrange for her to meet several school principals and, in the meantime, provided her with copies of various documents from the personnel files of teachers in the district. Is there an ethical problem here? If so, for whom?

4. A cognitive psychologist wanted to study the effect of modeling behavior on school-aged children's willingness to persist in a task. To do so, he chose a task, solving a wooden puzzle, and developed two video-tapes to provide a model. The first showed a child of comparable age as the subject solving the puzzle easily (a positive model); the second featured a child having great difficulty, becoming very frustrated, and not finishing (a negative model). Each videotape was also accompanied by one of three audio messages explaining what to do in the task and stating whether or not the child would succeed. One message was positive, one neutral, and one negative. Combining each audio message with each videotape provided six treatments. Having designed the experiment, the psychologist approached the local school authorities for permission to carry it out with local school children in grades 5 and 6. He received permission from the superintendent of schools and from the principal of the particular school. Need he have done more?

5. A team of social psychologists wished to investigate the cognitive processes underlying the concept of altruism. They decided to conduct a surreptitious field experiment in order to study the phenomenon under "natural" conditions. This was carried out in an urban subway to determine whether assistance to an "ill" passenger would be affected by the severity of the problem (blood or no blood). A "passenger" (member of the experimental team) with a cane would collapse in a subway car. In some cases, "blood" would trickle from his mouth. The responses of the "participants" (regular, unsuspecting passengers) were observed and timed. If no regular passengers came to his aid within a specified time period, a "helper," disguised, for example, as a clergyman, would assist the victim and help him off at the next station. What ethical issue was involved with this experiment?

6. Daniels (1983) used participant observation to study wealthy women involved in charity organizations. She gained acceptance into the group and, in particular, developed a close friendship with some of the women (her key informants), who were aware that she was engaged in research. This relationship involved such activities as frequent lunches together and the exchange of gifts. As the study wound down, the investigator found herself bored with the friendship and wishing to terminate it. In effect, it no longer served a research purpose. Is it ethical for a researcher to develop such a friendship in the first place?

Compare your answers with those on pages 727–728.

Compare your answers with those on pages 727–728.

===================== APPLICATION EXERCISE =====================

Consider what problems of informed consent you might have with your proposed project. Will you be collecting data from individuals from whom informed consent can be obtained, or will you need to contact parents or guardians? Is there a problem in terms of confidentiality? Will you be the only one seeing the data? Can you assure that no one else has access to it? Is there any reason you can't destroy identifying information shortly after the data is collected? Better still, can you collect data without identifying information and still get the subjects' cooperation?

Are you collecting data about which there might be a privacy question? If so, how will you handle it?

Does your institution require that both federally and nonfederally sponsored grants be approved by its institutional review board? If so, do you know the procedure? Why not get one of the board's forms now and fill it out for your project? See what potential problems it brings to mind.

If you plan to do the project with others, have you decided how you will allocate credit and authorship?

The Macrosystem of Educational and Social Science Research

Few of us realize how short the career of what we know as "science" has been. Three hundred and fifty years ago hardly any one believed in the Copernican planetary theory. . . . The circulation of the blood, the weight of air, the conduction of heat, the laws of motion were unknown; the common pump was inexplicable.

R. Reynolds and Sons, Some Problems of Philosophy *(1911)*

You may think all this nonsense, but I tell you these are great times. . . . Before many centuries more, science will be the master of man. The engines he will have invented will be beyond his strength to control. Some day science may have the existence of mankind in its power and the human race commit suicide by blowing up the world.

Henry Adams (1862)

After close to two centuries of passionate struggles, neither science nor faith has succeeded in discrediting its adversary. On the contrary, it becomes obvious that neither can develop normally without the other. And the reason is simple: The same life animates both. Neither in its impetus nor its achievements can science go to its limits without becoming tinged with mysticism and charged with faith.

Pierre Teilhard de Chardin, S.J.

OVERVIEW

This chapter examines the system we call science, starting at the individual level and working successively through the peer to the societal level. It examines some of the problems at each level, asking whether and how well it works. Lastly, having explored in chapter 24 orientations that argue for different conceptions of social science, we look here at whether, as has been presumed throughout the book, a social science is possible.

CHAPTER CONTENTS

Introduction   678
Does Science Function as Intended
   at the Individual Level?   679
      Fraud in Science   679
      Can We Trust What We See?   680
Science at the Peer Level   681
      Does Peer Review Function
         as Intended?   681
      Conditions for Productive
         Science   682

Does Science Function
   as Intended
   at the Societal Level?   683
      Dissemination Research   684
      The Contribution of
         Science to Policy   686
What Are the Limits of the Social
   and Behavioral Sciences?   687
      The Need for the Humanities   689

INTRODUCTION

This chapter takes up a variety of questions that have not been directly examined elsewhere in the book: Does the system we call science function as intended at the individual, peer, and societal level? We are dealing with a system wherein each level depends on the workings of the previous level.

Anyone expecting answers should be aware that the chapter's purpose has to be heuristic. In the first place, there are not yet satisfactory answers to most of the questions raised. Perhaps there never will be since many depend on value judgments on which researchers differ. Second, there is room here for only a cursory examination. The goal is to raise questions otherwise taken for granted and suggest topics deserving of thought. Due to this greater awareness, perhaps you will pursue new discussions of them as you encounter them in professional reading or your own research.

Questioning whether we need a social science and how well it works is very important. Support by the lay community depends on satisfactory answers. Natural sciences are supported more as a matter of faith. The lay community doesn't understand much of what the natural sciences do but sees occasional important applications. By contrast,

> the social sciences seldom get full credit . . . because the discoveries, once labeled, are quickly absorbed into conventional wisdom. This is easily demonstrated: note the number of social science concepts common to our vocabulary: human capital, gross national product, identity crisis, span of control, the unconscious, price elasticity, acculturation, political party identification, reference group. (Prewitt, 1981, p. 659)

Further, the content of social and behavioral science is the stuff of everyday life in which all of us are our own "experts." Such work is therefore judged by everyone—witness your own expertise in analyzing the research of chapter 2! This "transparency" makes it even more important that the research process for building social science knowledge should work as well as possible.

DOES SCIENCE FUNCTION AS INTENDED
AT THE INDIVIDUAL LEVEL?

There is an amazing amount of trust in the integrity of the investigator in research. We tend to think of research reports as containing enough information to judge the study, and in many respects, this is accurate. But research reports omit much of the detail that would be very important in replicating it. If you don't think that is true, consider the Zimbardo study of chapter 2. Think about all the aspects you would have to supply to replicate it—the method of hypnotism, many of the instruments, and most surprisingly of all, a timetable. How long did the actual sessions take? Thirty minutes? An hour? A day? Several days? They actually took only about half an hour to an hour, but that information was contained in a newspaper article about the study (Hunt, 1982), not in the study itself.

Fraud in Science

Largely because of contemporary problems in the biomedical field, trust in the individual investigator is being increasingly questioned. Summerlin at Sloan-Kettering painted spots on a mouse (Broad, 1983); Soman at Yale admitted falsifying work; Darsee at Harvard could not produce raw data for his research; and Spector at Cornell used the wrong tracer, a mistake a peer believed could not have been an accident (Broad and Wade, 1983). Sir Cyril Burt, knighted in 1946 for his contributions to psychology, was shown four decades later to have faked his data (Dorfman, 1978). Broad and Wade (1983) trace fraud from the days of Ptolemy and argue that it is more prevalent than supposed and that it has always been around. They also argue that the response of the scientific community to fraud has been inappropriately feeble.

It is unknown, of course, how widespread fraud in science really is. The uncovering of fraud at esteemed institutions in the 1980s caused considerable unease. So much so, in fact, that the federal government stepped in, requiring all institutions receiving federal research monies to have a procedure in place for dealing with fraud.

The unexpectedness of any fraud at all, combined with the inability to determine how frequently it occurs, undermines confidence in the whole research enterprise. Everyone is tainted with the stain. Why does it occur? Pressure to publish, to win research grants, to succeed, and to be first with the significant finding no doubt all contribute. Various studies (among them Katz, 1973, and Tuckman, 1976) have shown that publications contribute significantly in all fields of research to salary increases. Centra (1977) showed that the most important information for tenure, salary, and promotions was the number of articles in quality journals and the excellence of the research as judged by peers. Clearly, these are pressures that every academic researcher feels, and no doubt, although specific pressures differ, the situation is similar outside academia.

The rush to publish is endemic to the scientist's world. As Price (1963) points out:

> At the root of the matter is the basic difference between creative effort in the sciences and . . . the arts. If Michelangelo or Beethoven had not existed, their works would have been replaced by different contributions. If Copernicus or Fermi had never existed, essentially the same contribution would have had to come from other people. There is, in fact, only one world to discover. (p. 69)

The first person to publish is recognized as the discoverer and gets the credit.[1]

It is difficult to convey adequately the excitement of the race to discover. Unfortunately, there are few reports of research competition. One is the story of the unraveling of DNA by Watson and Crick as told by one of those Nobel Prize–winning researchers (Watson, 1968). The intensity of that race is conveyed especially effectively when Watson tells of the laboratory visit of the son of Linus Pauling, who headed a rival team. Watson and Crick's efforts to covertly assess where the two teams stood with respect to the problem solution and their elation at believing they were ahead are fascinating.

Another account is that of the marathon between Nobelists Guillemin and Schally to discover the interaction between the brain and the pituitary gland (Wade, 1978). Wade analyzes the way in which the rivalry shaped their approaches, trying to assess whether the competition helped or hindered. Certainly it interfered with cooperation between the teams, but it also " 'stimulated both men to do their very best and check each other's work. They learned from each other.' " (Wade quoting Meites, a historian of the field, p. 513). Though neither example is from the social sciences, the interpersonal relations and team experiences are likely to be similar.

Given these innate features of research, there is no easy solution to the problem of avoiding fraud. As with other ethical problems, we cannot have laboratory police chasing data. The responsibility rests with the individual researcher. Fraud may be uncovered in the long run by replications. But the damage in the short run of building new work on inaccurate information, plus the damage to the reputation of all scientists when the fraud comes to light, is too great a price. Researchers must be vigilant to the possibility of fraud. Instead of letting possible incidents pass, we must be more willing to challenge our peers to guarantee that it is not present. How much fraud is there in the social sciences? We are inclined to think very little. But we don't know for sure. And when any is uncovered, trust is destroyed, and that is very difficult to reestablish.

Can We Trust What We See?

Considerably more prevalent than fraud are the mechanisms likely to bias interpretation of data. The expectancy effect that Rosenthal and Rubin (1980) showed to be so pervasive, where in a variety of fields, results confirm the

---

1. Just as nobody remembers vice presidents of the United States, so those who come in second serve the purpose of validating the discovery but are not usually associated with the discovery. This may contribute to the lack of replication of research in the social sciences.

researchers' expectations, is an example of this problem. Researchers need to be aware, according to Hanson (1958), that "there is a lot more to seeing than meets the eyeball" (p. 7). Clearly, perception organizes what we see into learned patterns. Phillips (1987) cites research in which playing cards were flashed tachistoscopically, mixing in trick cards such as a black six of hearts. Regular cards could be routinely identified; trick cards were either misread or seen as a blur. Moreland and Zajonc (1977) flashed abstract designs on a screen at a speed below perception threshold, so fast that the designs were not perceived as seen. Later these designs were mixed with other abstract designs, and the subjects were to indicate how well they liked each design. The designs with which they were familiar as a result of prior subliminal exposure were better liked! Ferris (1981) notes:

> The eye . . . delivers not television pictures to be observed . . . but processed information, much of it . . . hypotheses. . . . And in the dialogue between the eye and the rest of the brain, what we see can become what we expect to see. A field mouse is transformed into a snake to the hiker who fears snakes. (p. 61)

How many such influences are there? How pervasive are they? How much and what effect do they have? We don't know for sure. Just as qualitative researchers look inward to become aware of how their actions and reactions affect data gathering, so must all researchers seek the effect of their perceptual problems on the data.

SCIENCE AT THE PEER LEVEL

Does Peer Review Function as Intended?

You'll recall that peers are the first level in the development of a consensus around the interpretation of data. Peers are also gatekeepers to journals and convention presentations. How well does peer review work? Is peer review a matter of buddy taking care of buddy instead of attending to the concerns of science? Do people with famous reputations get by with things that lesser-known researchers cannot?

Several studies illuminate these issues. First, are reviews really blind, or do reviewers generally know the authors? Ceci and Peters (1984) found that psychology respondents to a survey believed, on the average, that author identities were known about 72 percent of the time. Using six psychology journals from a broad range of areas, Ceci and Peters showed that only about a quarter of reviewers were able to identify the author of a sufficiently blinded manuscript, about one-third the commonly suspected rate.

Does blind review make a difference? Tobias and Zibrin (1978) used the abstracts submitted for an educational convention program to examine this question, comparing four evaluations of each proposal—two blind and two with identifying information. They found no differences between these conditions! They also examined the question of the effect of prominence of author. They found that prominent individuals received significantly more favorable evaluations than others, but they did so under both the blind and nonblind conditions. This finding serves as "a kind of validity check on the prominence of the individuals" (p. 16).[2]

Lastly, do reviewers agree on the criteria of research excellence, and do they agree in their evaluations of articles? The picture is mixed, but with significant problems. Fiske and Fogg (1990), in a careful study of 402 reviews of 153 papers submitted to 12 different psychological journals, found that "reviewers did not . . . disagree on particular points; instead, they wrote about different topics, each making points that were appropriate and accurate. As a consequence, their recommendations about editorial decisions showed hardly any agreement" (p. 591). Intraclass correlation of reviewers' ratings was .20, lower than some other studies. Gottfredson (1978), again with psychological journals, showed that psychologists associated with the decision-making processes of nine journals that covered a range of psychological literature substantially agreed on the desirability of article characteristics. But even using scales developed out of the research on desirable characteristics, agreement between judges was quite modest. Comparability of reviewers is a problem. It is understandable, however, when we consider the different trade-offs in chapter 23 and the Appendix and the comparison of apples and oranges that result when we stretch them along a single dimension of quality. It will be a difficult problem to solve.

Conditions for Productive Science

Under what conditions are researchers most productive? Every research and development center director would like to know the answer to that question. There is some research on it, but the results are far from conclusive. Knorr and colleagues (1979), in a book comparing the effectiveness of research groups in six European countries, looked at the effects of quality of leadership and group climate where the latter included dedication, cooperation, and innovativeness. They found the expected positive relationships. Stankiewicz (1979), in the same volume, examined size of research group. He hypothesized that larger groups would be more fruitful because of the greater opportunities to interact, to pursue alternative research strategies in parallel, and to attack different aspects of a complex problem. Beyond a certain point, size would prove counter-productive because of problems of communication. Examining only research groups in Sweden, he found an increase in effectiveness from three to five members and from five to seven, depending on the performance measures used, but a decline after that.

---

2. The researchers also examined the effect of prominence of reviewer, sex of author, and sex of reviewer. Neither prominence of reviewer nor sex of author interacted with the review process comparing blind and nonblind conditions. Female reviewers gave more favorable ratings to the importance of the problem than male reviewers, but that was the only difference.

In an excellent comparison of U.S. and Soviet science, Gustafson (1980) observed that the Soviets could concentrate enormous resources on crucial problems in basic research. Senior colleagues are oriented more toward theory than toward experimentation and provide planning and coordination for younger researchers. This was seen as producing at best teamwork, at worst conservatism, deference to superiors, immobility, and logrolling. The American belief in individual initiative, tolerance for risk and conflict, and lack of respect for authority were seen as producing a dynamic and competitive system with a zest for "unplanned opportunity" (p. 58). Highly productive, the American system lacks the predictability of support of the Soviet system, and there is considerable lack of coordination of what governmental support there is. Gustafson was careful to note that large, block-funded institutions in the United States experienced many of the same problems as the block-funded institutions of the Soviet Union.

Glaser and Taylor (1973) compared successful applied research projects sponsored by the National Institutes of Mental Health with their less successful ones. They found the successful projects characterized by both internal team communication and external communication with clients and administrators, especially the latter. This is consistent with research on the problem of dissemination, which we shall come to in a moment.

One of the most interesting omissions is the lack of findings that more resources make a difference. It is clear that in the physical and life sciences, expensive equipment is a necessity for certain lines of work. But this is rarely true in the social and behavioral sciences. Indeed, Weick (1984) argues for "small wins," cutting social problems into manageable pieces. "Small wins are like miniature experiments that test implicit theories about resistance and opportunity and uncover both resources and barriers that were invisible before the situation was stirred up" (p. 44). For instance, he notes that the feminist movement failed at the equal rights amendment, but they found that sex references in speech were more susceptible to change than had been thought. The opponents were "more dispersed, more stuffy, and less formidable than anticipated" (p. 44). He provides a number of arguments for "small wins" as a strategy.

Obviously, there are many unsolved problems in this area; many are probably context-dependent. Can we learn to maximize conditions for research? It is not at all clear that we can. In contrast to "hard" science, the "soft" social sciences, as must be clear from this book, are still evolving standards and goals and improving their methods. It is harder to tell that the target has been hit when it is still moving.

DOES SCIENCE FUNCTION AS INTENDED
AT THE SOCIETAL LEVEL?

The topics of social science have been the subject of thought and speculation since time began. Although such thought was often the product of extremely intelligent persons, the best-educated of their day, we would today consider them amateurs. Herodotus, for example, was not a trained historian. But these amateurs described their work in the vernacular of their day, which made it immediately available to other educated people in all fields. And since it concerned topics of interest, it was often widely read.

The social sciences as disciplines developed relatively late among the arts and sciences. For the University of Chicago to build a special building for the social sciences in the late 1930s was an important act of faith. Although psychology had its own national society and considered itself a discipline, for example, it was still merged with philosophical societies in some regions of the United States as late as World War II. Emergence of separate departments for each of the social sciences resulted in many changes: better training for new entrants and the development of more sophisticated research methods, for example.

A negative effect was that the fields moved further from the understanding of the common person as jargon grew up around each area. A useful shorthand within a field, jargon impedes communication to the general public, increases the problems of dissemination, and expands the social distance between researchers and practitioners who might benefit from their work. This leads to the charge that social scientists write mainly for other social scientists. True, but that is so for all scientists. Yet when findings are translated into the vernacular and end up sounding like platitudes, public esteem for the enterprise decreases. This denies to social scientists a trust that their work will eventually be of a value at least equivalent to that more freely given to physical scientists, but, perhaps, no more merited.

The increased distance between professional and practitioner has led to efforts to understand the field of dissemination of findings. Not only has a field of research on knowledge utilization developed, but now a publishing and consulting industry also translates the material of science for the intelligent layperson. Witness the extensive front section of the journal *Science* and publications like *Scientific American, Popular Science, In Health, Discover*, and others.

Dissemination Research

Dissemination research has been extensively sponsored by agriculture, which had the problem of getting research implemented by farmers. The agricultural extension agent translated research for the farmer. He showed how it applied in a specific situation and grew demonstration plots to show the results of new practices. This proved effective but expensive. Research showed that individuals could be divided into three classes: early adopters—individuals who were ready and eager to try new things—a middle group, and a late group. The early adopters are important sources of practices for the middle group, who tend to follow their lead with successful innovations.

Research has also shown that individuals tend to go through stages of information use in the adoption process:

1. *Awareness* sensitizes them to pay attention when they encounter a demonstration of an innovation or literature about it.

2. *Interest* encourages them to seek information about it.
3. *Evaluation* lets them estimate the chances of its success in their situation.
4. *Trial* involves making a small commitment to the innovation to determine whether it acts as anticipated.
5. *Adoption* is the result of a successful trial.

Characteristics that enable people to predict the probability of successful implementation have also been studied. A first characteristic is the relative advantage of the innovation over alternatives. So cost-effectiveness, especially when it saves time and effort, is important, as is the immediacy of the results. Consider the adoption of wait-time in teaching, which will presumably change the character of student responses to a much higher level of thinking (Rowe, 1974). It costs the embarrassment of silence following a question and may cause discomfort for the students initially. But the discussion that is likely to follow will be at a much more satisfyingly high level than is produced by a bombardment of simple questions.

A second characteristic is compatibility with the existing values, needs, standards, and practices of the adopter. The better the match, the less change is needed and the more likely the innovation will be adopted and integrated into ongoing practice. Wait-time will result in the kinds of responses the teacher values, those much closer to desired standards, and the questioning pattern is not a drastic change from previous practice.

A third aspect is complexity: the simpler, the better. It is a relatively simple matter to extend the time we wait for an answer to a question before modifying it, substituting another, calling on a student, and so on.

A fourth property is trialability—the extent to which a small commitment on the part of the adopter will permit a trial that provides sufficient evidence to determine whether to make a complete commitment to the innovation. Certainly, wait-time can easily be given a trial.

A final characteristic is observability, the degree to which the results are apparent to potential adopters. If the research on wait-time is correct, the result should be a rather immediate change in the quality and level of class discussion.

Key in all the literature on adoption of innovations is administrative support, involvement of adopters in the adoption decision, adaptation to their situations, and their trial of the innovation to obtain evidence firsthand. Administrative support is a necessary but not sufficient condition. Involvement of the adopter, however, is a sufficient condition if adoption results are sufficiently rewarding in and of themselves. So involvement is stressed in nearly all the literature.

Research on dissemination provides a basis for researchers to be more effective in getting their innovations adopted. A basic problem, however, is that the involvement of the adopter in the adoption process is costly and time-consuming. Informational materials seem to go only so far. Research is still needed that will find ways to decrease the cost of the adoption process and make it more effective.

The Contribution of Science to Policy

Probably the earliest involvement of the social sciences in U.S. policy was the 1832 grant to the Franklin Institute to study the causes of explosions in steamboat boilers. "Professor Bates . . . reported that 'sometimes there is a little carelessness in stoking the fire.' A bursting steam boiler is not just a matter of chemistry and physics; it is also a matter of operator training and human behavior" (Prewitt, 1980, p. 2). Years later, the President's Commission on the Accident at Three Mile Island "similarly concluded that it was 'people-related problems and not equipment problems' that brought the nation so close to a major tragedy" (p. 3). Repeatedly, government has recognized the importance of the human element in its attempts to regulate and plan.

A tremendous surge in the utilization of social science knowledge in policy decisions came with the use of social science evidence in the federal courts in such cases as the landmark desegregation decision, *Brown* v. *Board of Education of Topeka* (347 U.S. 483); the development of accurate survey samples that provided information regarding the public's view on important policy decisions; the increased use of planning, programming, and budgeting techniques under Robert McNamara in the Defense Department, which spread into business and industry as well as across government; and concern over the effectiveness of federal programs by Congress and federal agencies, resulting in many large-scale evaluations.

The increased involvement in policy decisions resulted in new understandings by researchers of themselves. They found that they differed from policymakers in important ways. Their time scale for studies was determined by the problem rather than politics. The problems they chose to work on were ones of interest to them and easier to study rather than selected on the basis of societal need and resistance to solution. Scientists preferred to hedge and qualify their findings rather than starkly state preferences. Further, administrators, who had been decision makers long before they were responsible for public policy, have nonscientific ways of identifying policy options besides the scientific ones. So researchers have not always found themselves and their work at center stage when they were ready. They have had their research used for purposes for which it was not intended. They have been forced to try to be useful before they were ready. They have regularly given equivocal opinions when asked for concrete choices. And in general, they have behaved in ways that, though consistent with their values, lifestyle, and milieu, did not endear them to policymakers.

Researchers have had to learn that timing is extremely important. Policy development goes through stages, and the role of research and the demands on it differ with each stage. At the earliest stage, when policymakers are trying to articulate policy interests and demands, research helps define the problem. At the second stage, which involves the deliberation, modification, and aggregation of support for various proposals, research turns desires into concrete alternatives for action. It may pilot them to determine implications if there is time. In the priority-setting and allocation-of-resource stages that follow, research helps indicate effect sizes of alternative or competing programs. Research is probably more powerful in killing proposals than in improving their chances. The Income Maintenance Experiment, for example, killed this alternative when the side effect of family breakup was discovered.

At the final stage, that of legislative oversight, summative evaluation studies indicate how well the programs are working, formative evaluation shows how they might work better, and comparative evaluations show which programs to emphasize and which to downsize or eliminate. So different kinds of research are needed at the different stages, and the timing of the research, so that the results are available when decisions must be made, is crucial. Academic researchers, with teaching, advisement, committees, and many other demands on their time, have not been very good at crash research intended to produce results on call. As a result, a large private sector has developed to meet those demands. Time demands are most severe in the early stages, when support is being aggregated for a given policy, and in later stages, when budget deadlines must be met for reauthorization of funding.

What can be most discouraging to researchers, however, is the apparent politicization as choices are made for implementation. It often appears that policymakers seek out research that fits their point of view and ignore whatever does not. But policymakers, who are used to making decisions in the absence of complete information, argue that they must take many more things into account than the usually simplified evidence provided them by research.

Clearly, inquiry is not ideally suited to policymaking as currently practiced by academic researchers. Whether the private sector will supply the research needs for policy or whether academic researchers will find it in their interests to find a way to be more responsive remains to be seen. Certainly, much more could be done to adjust information needs to the research process and vice versa.

WHAT ARE THE LIMITS OF THE SOCIAL AND BEHAVIORAL SCIENCES?

Throughout this book we have been suggesting that building stronger chains of reasoning is a goal of social science, and we have been concentrating on the methodology that would facilitate this. Pierce, a famous philosopher writing in 1868, took the chain analogy a step further: "The reasoning should not form a chain which is no stronger than its weakest link, but a cable whose fibers may be so slender, provided they are sufficiently numerous and intimately connected." Good point!

The cable analogy, with its numerous and intimate connections, clearly refers to theory that integrates knowledge—always a higher goal to be sought, as I hope this book has also made clear. But consider the fact that two psychological theories as different as cognitive psychology, which views behavior as inwardly controlled, and behavioral psychology, which focuses on its external control, can both coexist and be useful at the same time. This says something about the present state of our knowledge.

Certainly, we have a long way to go. But how far is the journey? What is the end? Boulding (1968) suggests:

> It is only by the . . . activities of the . . . social sciences that we can hope to understand the social system sufficiently well to be able to control it and to be able to move into a positive image of the future through our own volition and policy. Otherwise we are merely slaves of necessity or victims of chance. (p. 107)

Along these same lines, Asimov (1977) tells of inventing "psychohistory," the mathematical analysis of every kind of sociological trend. We could then predict, with a high degree of accuracy, the social movements of the future. He based his idea on the kinetic theory of gases in which, though trillions and trillions of molecules are moving randomly, we can predict exactly what will happen to a gas if it is heated or compressed. "All the random behavior of the individual molecules ends up by making the gas, as a whole, a completely predictable system" (p. 11).[3] No doubt this is the dream of many social scientists. Some, however, don't believe even that level of predictability can be achieved, let alone that of the individual's behavior—the prisoner seeking parole, the developmental path of a mentally retarded child.

Religious persons might ask whether, given God's purposes in the world, such a search for behavioral predictability is an evil act, whether it is more knowledge than humans should have. Berger (1961) argues that the scientist must assume that the fundamental integrity in a universe ruled by God is meant to be plumbed. It is an act of faith—an exploration that leads us to understand and appreciate ever more the intricate complexities of our being and to wonder how it all came about.

Many scientists have always assumed that if we only knew enough, the world would be completely predictable. Thus the insatiable drive of science has been to learn enough about everything so that it would be understandable. It is only very recently that scientists have begun to believe that there are phenomena that are inherently unpredictable. They can be predicted only statistically; the odds of a given condition can be stated. Although Poincaré noted this phenomenon when he tried to extend Newton's equations of gravitational attraction from two bodies to three, the implications of his work were not understood. Newton's model of a predictable, clocklike universe prevailed. But more recently, interest in what is known as chaotic systems has rediscovered the phenomenon.[4] Pool (1989) notes that Joseph Ford, a physicist who has been working in the field since 1950, was intrigued by the question, "Where does [the] randomness necessary for statistical behavior come from if the universe is at heart an orderly, deterministic place? Chaos theory may offer an answer" (p. 26).

Under some conditions, systems that behave in nonlinear fashion may be so very sensitive to small differences in the initial or starting conditions that unpredictable behavior results. For example, it is now assumed that the weather may no longer be perfectly predictable because it is impossible to

---

3. Does this remind you of Popper's gnats and a cloudlike world?
4. An excellent discussion of chaos, from which many of the illustrations in this material were drawn, is an episode of the Public Broadcasting Service program *Nova* called "The Strange New Science of Chaos."

know the starting conditions completely enough to make an entirely accurate forecast. Even the slightest change in a starting condition, such as a gust from a butterfly's wing, may result in quite different forecasts. Examples in nature of chaotic behavior are the turbulent flow of a stream, never the same twice, and the smoke from a cigarette, which floats smoothly upward and then dances wildly about.

Most chaotic systems in nature seem to be predictable under "low-stress" conditions and become unpredictable with increases in speed or pressure. A dripping faucet may show clearly predictable drips at a slow pace but when forced to a faster level may turn chaotic. Normally linked actions are no longer able to feed back properly. In the case of a dripping faucet, the surface tension snaps a drop closed when the drip is slow; the surface tension is the same on each drop. It turns to variable when the drip is so fast that the surface cannot completely snap back, and the next drip is variably and unpredictably affected by the previous one. A similar thing happens in a heart attack. Fibrillation results when the aortic pacemaker is working so rapidly that the ventricular pacemaker, which normally takes its signal from the aorta, is bombarded by stimuli and "loses its place," so to speak. In many of the physical conditions so far studied, chaotic behavior does not typically yield to complete unpredictability. Rather it seems to oscillate within certain bounds, set by what is called a "strange attractor." The nature of such strange attractors is under study.

Only recently developed, applications of chaos theory are now being sought. It is not clear whether all instances in which it appears to apply really are examples of chaotic behavior.[5] But the analogy to human behavior is so tempting as to suggest that it will find its application here as well. If it applies to behavior as to natural phenomena, certain behaviors would be predictable only when not under some kind of stress; past some breaking point, they would no longer be predictable. This certainly corresponds to the stereotype of how people react. Precise predictions would prove impossible, and we could predict behavior only within certain ranges. That would be no surprise either, yet would also be consistent with chaos theory. It will be interesting to watch chaos theory develop and to learn more about its possible applications.

The Need for the Humanities

Ultimately, the answer to how the social sciences will develop is an empirical one that will be increasingly uncovered by the work of you, the future researchers. Whatever occurs, you can be certain that science alone does not hold all the answers. Frye (1981) notes that there are three different ways in which language can be used. One is the language of science, which seeks to convey information about the world. A second is the language of transcendence, used in philosophy and religion, an "abstract, analogical language that expresses

---

5. See Pool (1989) for a discussion of how it is being applied. This article is the last of a six-part series of articles in *Science* exploring chaos theory and its applications.

what by definition is really beyond verbal expression" (p. 129). Third, there is the language of immanence, of poetry, where "natural objects can become images of human emotions" (p. 129).

It is in the languages of transcendence and immanence that the goals of science are found. As Frye (1981) puts it:

> The arts and sciences, . . . for all their obvious differences, have a common origin in social concern. . . . When we think . . . of a world to be remade, we find we need a model or imaginative vision of what we are trying to achieve. . . . The world of dream and fantasy can be a source of models . . . and models are the first product of the chaos of hunch and intuition and guesswork and free association out of which the realities of art and science are made (pp. 130–131).

We have been studying the processes of science with the intent of improving the quality of our journey through life. But it is to the humanities that we must turn to understand our goals, what "quality" means, and where the journey leads.

APPENDIX

Trade-off Possibilities:
The Positive and Negative
Effects of Choices

APPENDIX CONTENTS

Choices Involving Subjects   692
Choices Involving Situations   693
Choices Involving Treatment   694
Choices Involving Observation
    or Measurement   695

Choices Involving the Basis
    for Sensing Attributes or Changes   698
Choices Involving the Procedure   698

Much of the intent in trade-offs is to make studies adequately sensitive to an effect, to increase generality without losing much internal validity (LP), to tighten a chain of reasoning, and to consider alternatives in the allocation of resources. We shall list enhancements to design that you might choose to achieve one of these goals. Each such design change has positive and negative implications. Analyzing the consequences of a choice provides a basis for deciding what positive aspects you want badly enough to tolerate the negative aspects that accompany it.

Each design change described here is worded in a single direction of change, for example, increasing the number of persons. You can and should, however, interpret these implications in both directions; with reduction in sample size, negative consequences become positive consequences, and vice versa. For example, increasing sample size for an individualized treatment may cause problems of treatment fidelity—treatments have to be standardized and administered by many different people. The treatment fidelity attained in a small sample might be preferable to the increased statistical sensitivity achieved with a large one. So though worded in one direction, each section should be considered bidirectional and consequences considered for the most appropriate direction for a particular study.

Even though the language in which the various possible actions are described often implies experimentation, with a little thought and translation the discussion can be applied to qualitative research as well. In an experimental study, we can select individuals who are particularly susceptible to a treatment and assign them to experimental and control groups. Comparably, in a qualitative study of the effect of a curriculum, we can focus on persons with the particular characteristics we deem necessary to heighten the effect. These might be particularly able students or an enrichment group. Except for our discussions of treatment and its manipulation, the following material has rather universal applicability (and in some instances even manipulation is possible in a qualitative study).

Consideration is given to changes in each of the links at the design level in the chain of reasoning: subjects, situations, treatment, observation or measures, basis for sensing attributes or changes, and procedure. The plus sign (+) indicates a usually desirable outcome, the minus (−) an undesirable one. When the direction could go either way, both signs are shown (±). *You are cautioned to consider the particular circumstances of your study; what holds in general may not apply in your situation.*

CHOICES INVOLVING SUBJECTS

Increasing the Number of Persons (Increasing Sample Size)

+ 1. Increases the statistical sensitivity of the study to weak effects
+ 2. May make it practical to:
     - Block or stratify
     - Study subgroups
     - Establish additional experimental and/or control groups
     - Isolate main or contaminating effects
     - Study additional relationships
+ 3. Is likely to increase generality as the search for additional cases leads us to broaden the boundaries within which cases are considered suitable
− 4. May increase the treatment fidelity problem where treatment is individualized and/or personalized
− 5. May lead to a selection effect, especially if added subjects are hard to find and groups with different qualities must be used, especially volunteers
− 6. Increases costs for treatment and observation of the added cases; increases the complexity of administration of the study

Selecting Persons with Certain Characteristics

We typically select persons who meet the following criteria:

+ 1. Who ensure representativeness of a target group; for example, stratification ensures the inclusion of persons with certain characteristics (increases generality)
+ 2. Who are more susceptible to treatment (increases sensitivity)
+ 3. Who will hold constant a characteristic that would otherwise provide an alternative explanation (removes a threat to validity)
+ 4. Who are more or less skilled with respect to a factor that has an impact on the effect (increases sensitivity; for example, in a study of nonverbal communication, compare expert poker players with novices)

Be aware of several caveats with respect to selecting persons with certain characteristics: Ensuring representativeness requires knowledge of the distribution in the population of key characteristics relevant to the study as well as the nature of those characteristics for each person in the sampling frame. This increases costs unless the data are already available. Further, we run the risk of missing a key characteristic (for example, we may get representativeness on conceptual ability but not on motivation). Selection for susceptibility to treatment limits generality (for example, using the most capable students in a learning study may increase the treatment effect, but are the findings applicable to any but able students?). Use of a narrow range of average students to hold a variable constant may also lack generality outside the narrow range used.

CHOICES INVOLVING SITUATIONS

Increasing the Number of Situations

+ 1. Increases the possibility of investigating subgroups of situations and isolating various effects
+ 2. Results in greater generality
± 3. Is more likely to result in a field than a laboratory-type study, with the concomitant advantages and disadvantages
± 4 Increases the possibility of getting more subjects, with the pros and cons noted for increasing sample size
− 5. May increase the treatment fidelity problem if a number of sites must be coordinated
− 6. Increases the cost and complexity of the study, especially in terms of the overhead costs of establishing good interpersonal relations at each site, regardless of the volume of data gathered there
− 7. Is likely to increase travel costs, both out-of-pocket and in personnel time
− 8. May have to confront different institutional constraints to which the study must conform at each site
− 9. May result in lowered generality through use of sites with special characteristics (for example, reluctant or uncooperative sites may affect data collection adversely)

Selecting Situations for Greater Control

We may seek greater control over the conditions under which a study is done than we have in the field and therefore change to a partial or complete simulation or a laboratory-like situation. Moving in this direction generally has the following results:

+ 1. Greater assurance that treatment preceded effect
+ 2. Greater potential for eliminating a variety of rival hypotheses, but especially those deriving from the environment of the study (noise and distractions, communications with other subjects, etc.)
+ 3. Increased sensitivity since greater control eliminates random effects that contribute to the variability of behavior
+ 4. Reduced costs with a laboratory study than with a field study unless simulation is expensive; sometimes the equipment costs of a laboratory study are large, but these costs would typically be even larger if the same kinds of control were attempted in the field
+ 5. Elimination of the constraints of institutional and social norms except those involved in what is ethically proper

± 6. Greater fidelity of treatment since there is more control over its administration (however, fidelity may be lessened if the situation cannot be realistically simulated in the laboratory)

− 7. Greater potential for reactivity since it is very difficult to be unobtrusive about a laboratory study; therefore, all the reactive possibilities—trying to please the investigator, presenting one's best behavior, trying to guess the purpose of the study, and so on—are present

− 8. Decreased generality

CHOICES INVOLVING TREATMENT

We can change several characteristics of the treatment: its obtrusiveness, the forms in which it is given, its intensity, or a combination of these.

Decreasing Obtrusiveness

Decreasing the obtrusiveness of treatment makes the situation more natural, with the following results:

+ 1. Reduced reactivity

± 2. Conversion to a field study, with a reversal of the pros and cons noted under "Selecting Situations for Greater Control"

± 3. Increased generality but less control over treatment, especially as treatment occurs naturally (since naturally occurring variability represents the conditions of typical use, it adds generality)

− 4. Possibly greater costs (for installation of two-way mirrors or concealed cameras and sound equipment)

Increasing the Forms of Treatment

The same treatment can often be given in different forms. For example, we may change the mode in which the treatment is given from live people to videotape, audiotape, or interactive video. The reward for completing workbook exercises in a curriculum may be changed from reading adventure stories to extra recess time. We may change the form of remuneration in an income maintenance study from food stamps, which can be exchanged only for food, to cash, which buys anything.

Of course, the essential question is whether the new form is the same or a new treatment. This forces us to be clearer about the "active ingredient" in a treatment. If the active ingredient of drill and practice problems is mainly the reinforcement of learning, this suggests carefully sequenced problems of gradually increasing difficulty in which the student makes few errors. The active ingredients are the reinforcement of nearly error-free responses resulting from the correct gradation of item difficulty. It should make little difference whether administered by people or computer. But if the feedback is individualized to the person's responses or for incorrect answers, success depends on the program developer, who must correctly anticipate all the important errors and provide feedback that is effective for all persons making the same error. Whether we have a different treatment or a different form of the same treatment may be learned only by exploring differences in effects, both cognitive and affective.

Increasing the forms of treatment has the following advantages and disadvantages:

+   1. Greater generality by showing the robustness of effects as treatment format is varied
−   2. Possible problems of treatment fidelity
−   3. Increased cost and complexity of administration

Increasing the Intensity of Treatment

We can increase the intensity in many ways: increasing its strength, if that is possible (as by turning up the voltage for an electric shock), increasing the length of treatment, repeating the treatment, or switching to a form more effective for the kind of individuals involved (as in changing printed learning instructions to a spoken recording in Spanish for migrant workers), with the following results:

+   1. Greater sensitivity, since presumably the effect will be larger or more certain to occur as the treatment increases in stength
+   2. Greater generality and audience credibility if the increased length of treatment is more typical of normal practice than the brief exposures common in experiments
−   3. Greater chance of treatment-maturation interaction with prolonged treatment as well as other problems that accompany increased project length (waning institutional commitment, schedule conflicts, budget problems; see the sections on situations and procedure)
    4. Reactivity to the increased length or number of treatment sessions
−   5. Greater likelihood of treatment-mortality interaction if the sessions do not hold the subject's interest.
−   6. Increased cost for the additional treatment

CHOICES INVOLVING OBSERVATION OR MEASUREMENT

Increasing Observations

We can increase the amount of time spent in observation or the number of observations, or both. This usually has the following consequences:

+   1. Increased sensitivity because the larger sample of behavior increases the reliability of measurement and thus is more likely to pick up treatment effects (recall the Spearman-Brown formula of chapter 11)
+   2. Increased generality because the larger sample of behavior is more likely to center around typical behavior
+   3. Increased representation of a construct because multiple tests of the same construct make it more likely the essential characteristics of the construct will be covered (greater validity); if different testing techniques are used (e.g., written answers versus multiple-choice), methods effects will be minimized
+   4. Plateaued testing effect because with each repeat of a testing procedure, the subject typically learns to do a little better and gets more test-wise; but with each testing the amount of gain is reduced and soon declines to nearly zero, so there is little or no increase due to testing effect with later tests
+   5. Increased number of observations to permit the sensing of trends
      ■ If done as pretests, allays the alternative explanation that apparent gain was a continuation of an established trend.
      ■ If done as posttests, detects residual effects, usually the most

important consequences of any treatment. Retention is sometimes a more sensitive measure of treatment effect than immediate testing. For example, Krumboltz and Weisman (1962) tested the effect of having the student write in the answer to programmed instruction in contrast to choosing among suggested answers. They found achievement differences in retention but not immediate posttreatment. Reduction in the time required to relearn to a given criterion level is also a sensitive test of residual effect.

±   6. Reactivity changes
- ■ (−) The initial effect may be an increase of feeling "we are special," leading to positive feelings about the study as well as wanting to please the observer and give the "right" responses.
- ■ (+) Over time, this wears off, and the observer is no longer noticed; more typical behavior asserts itself.
- ■ (−) If testing is involved, a negative reaction may set in with prolonged testing.

−   7. Increased costs for supplies, personnel time, and possibly travel; possibly also increased administrative complexity

−   8. Increased opportunity for instrument decay because as observation is prolonged, the likelihood that there may be calibration problems among different observers increases; so does the difficulty of holding constant the standard of judgment

−   9. Conflicts with institutional or observer schedules due to the increased time required by observations

−   10. Increased testing-treatment interaction; if this effect is present to begin with, increased testing gives more opportunity for the subjects to be sensitized to the relation of testing to the treatment; they can be especially attentive to those parts during treatment

Increasing Observations to Include Preexisting Conditions

Increasing observations to include measures of preexisting conditions can be used to ensure that there was indeed change, that control and experimental groups were equivalent at the outset, and that any preexisting trend was sensed that might by itself have caused the change instead of the treatment. Observations of preexisting conditions can be done either on the same experimental and control groups from which posttreatment measures are taken or on pretest-only groups that are like the treatment groups.

Effects of Pretesting and Posttesting the Same Group
+   1. Precedence of treatment is clearly established.
+   2. The cost of establishing posttest-only groups is avoided unless a Solomon four-group-type design is used.
+   3. Assuming that the measures are reliable, we can be certain that a change took place.
+   4. If control and experimental groups are both pretested, we know whether the control group started even with or ahead of the experimental group. If the experimental group then overtakes the control group, this adds to the credibility of a study with the audience (but is a conservative measure of treatment effect).
±   5. Testing effect and testing-treatment interaction are likely but may be controlled by a Solomon four-group design, which requires additional groups.

Effects of Pretesting and Posttesting Different Groups

+   1. Testing and testing-treatment interaction effects are avoided.
−   2. More groups are needed; it may be more difficult to find suitable situations.
±   3. Comparability of groups at the beginning is not established if the groups are preestablished groups. With random assignment, comparability is ensured, on the average, and so is usually assumed (but may not be present in any given instance with small groups).

Effects of Using Solely Posttest-Only Groups

+   1. Testing and testing-treatment interaction effects are avoided.
+   2. Fewer groups are needed.
±   3. Comparability of groups at the outset is not well established unless subjects are randomly assigned. Effect on the comparability assumption depends on trust in randomization—probably safe if groups are large.
−   4. Pretreatment trend is not sensed if present.

Observations during the Treatment

Observations during the treatment can have the following effects:

+   1. Ensures fidelity of treatment
+   2. Points up changes during the course of treatment, especially important if the effect is nonlinear or is an "all or none" change (up to the point of change no visible effects occur; when the "cause" exceeds a threshold, the change takes place)
+   3. Permits speed of change and patterns of change to be determined
−   4. Presents the disadvantages of pretesting.
−   5. When used to enforce treatment fidelity, becomes a restrictive condition on generality to situations where no such enforcement occurs

Increasing the Objectivity of Observations or Measures

Changing from high-inference observations or measures (such as participant observation or open end questions or essay tests) to low-inference instruments (observation checklists, multiple-choice tests) can have these consequences:

+   1. Increases the reliability of measures by decreasing or removing observer variability
+   2. Increases the sensitivity of the study
+   3. Yields more precise measures of behavior that can distinguish small differences (between groups, times, etc.)
+   4. Provides efficient data-gathering mechanisms for large numbers of cases
±   5. Tends to focus the observations and measures on fewer behaviors (greater depth on few behaviors, less breadth)
±   6. Requires decision regarding what behaviors are worth observing
±   7. Transfers researcher time from categorizing and evaluating responses to construction and validation of the instrument (may not be worth constructing an instrument for small sample)
−   8. May miss the unexpected or side effects
−   9. May present difficulties when constructing such an instrument for affective responses

− 10. May increase obtrusiveness if nonparticipant observation using a checklist or a structured observation form is employed in the presence of the people observed

CHOICES INVOLVING THE BASIS
FOR SENSING ATTRIBUTES OR CHANGES

Choices for experiments involving the basis for sensing attributes or changes may be viewed along a continuum as follows:

| Single experimental group, compared with performance of a comparable group of test norms | Single experimental group, compared with previous measures of the group from files or records | Single experimental group, pretest compared with posttest | Experimental group compared with a control group | Experimental group compared with multiple control groups (also possibly multiple experimental groups) |

As we move along this continuum, we obtain the following:

+ 1. Through the use of control groups, greater protection against history, maturation, testing (with posttest-only groups), instrument decay, statistical regression, selection, mortality, and their interactions
+ 2. Greater sensitivity in that any consistent effect of contaminating variables can be measured and removed from the estimate of random error used as a basis for sensing changes
+ 3. Greater generality and audience credibility as multiple control and experimental groups provide replications of the study
+ 4. Greater opportunity to isolate specific effects through changing the conditions in a consistent manner from group to group
− 5. Increased cost for new groups as well as for the increased complexity
− 6. Greater difficulty in locating cooperative sites that will be able and willing to supply all the groups needed
− 7. Different social and institutional constraints to be observed in terms of schedules, local problems, and so on as number of sites used increases

CHOICES INVOLVING THE PROCEDURE

The procedure deals with the scheduling of observations and treatment. Since we have already dealt with the effects of lengthening observation and treatment schedules, we have implicitly dealt with the effects of lengthening time schedules. Several points are worth stressing, however:

− 1. In the absence of adequate controls, the longer the schedule, the greater plausibility of such problems as history, maturation, mortality, treatment-maturation interaction, selection-maturation interaction, and diffusion.
− 2. Costs increase. Personnel costs make up as much as 75 to 80 percent of many budgets; therefore, reduction in project length is the researcher's most effective cost-cutting measure.
− 3. Floor (too hard at the beginning) and ceiling (too easy at the end) effects in tests are increasingly likely.

Answers to
Application Problems

CHAPTER 2

Strengths

- The explanation makes sense; that is, the account that couples experience a progression from trying to have their own child to seeking a medical solution to adopting a child is plausible. Further, the explanation of the process of emotional normalization also has intuitive appeal—that once a child has been adopted, an emotional attachment develops like that of a biological family.

- The research was presented to the couples in a manner that would encourage cooperation, saying that the purpose was to inform the public (and adoption agencies) about adoptive life.

- The choice of couples from existing support groups aided communication. The researcher could safely assume that since these couples were accustomed to discussing their problems and experiences about adoption, they would more readily discuss them with an interviewer.

- Hoffmann-Riem recorded and transcribed the interviews. Recording could have a negative effect on an interview, but given the apparent cooperativeness of the subjects, it appears that it did not. Combined with the investigator's own observations, it provided an accurate and detailed record of each interview.

- The interviews were open-ended. In the first part, the couples were encouraged to "tell their story" without interruption. In the second part, Hoffmann-Riem used their comments to probe further. She was open to their accounts and did not attempt to lead or direct the discussion.

- The adoptive parents were interviewed as couples. This could be seen as both a strength and a weakness. Its strong point is that both members could fill in details, add to each other's comments, and so enrich the information.

- Hoffmann-Riem began the study with only a general idea of what she might discover. She was able to let the couples tell their stories and to let her conclusions develop inductively, to "emerge from the data." She was less likely to be blinded by her preconceptions and miss an important point.

- Her sample could be considered representative of adoptive parents in general as most were members of the middle class, the segment of West German society that adopted most.

Weaknesses

- The data collected consisted entirely of narrative (words). There was no way to analyze it statistically. Another investigator could, presumably, interpret it differently.

■ Since Hoffmann-Riem provides only small samples of her data, there is no way to verify her conclusions.

■ There was no control on researcher expectancy effect, that is, no guarantee that Hoffmann-Riem was not leading or directing the interviews in some way (even subconsciously, perhaps) toward predetermined conclusions.

■ The interview technique relied on self-reporting by the couples. The investigator had no real check on whether or not what they said was truly what they felt or believed. Further self-reports may limit information to whatever is comfortable or reflects favorably.

■ The couples were interviewed together. A possible weakness in this approach is that one of the couple might dominate the interview or bias the spouse's answers. Separate interviews might provide different information.

■ The sample could be viewed as unrepresentative because the couples were all members of a particular support group. Adoptive parents who participate in such groups may well have different attitudes from those who do not. Also, the support group itself could lead to changes in their views that would not otherwise have occurred.

■ Fifteen couples is a small sample on which to base generalizations to all adoptive couples, although such sample sizes are not atypical in this kind of research. Further, the researcher drew the interviewees from only two support groups rather than sampling several such groups. Self-selection of groups compatible with one's own point of view probably results in group differences.

■ Though Hoffmann-Riem did refer to prior research to justify her choice of methods, she might also have used it to help support her conclusions.

■ Accuracy of translation is often a problem where two languages are involved. Perhaps this is not an issue in this instance because of the researcher's apparently excellent command of English. Back-translation into the original language by someone not familiar with the study permits comparison with the original statements for accuracy. This method is often used to check on the accuracy of translation of a test or measuring instrument.

CHAPTER 3

1. Two separate treatments were compared in this study: the film with narration by a woman and the film with narration by a man. The independent variables were viewer age (grade level) and gender of the narrator. There were two dependent variables: a measure of visual attention and a test of recall of story ideas. Both gender of the narrator and age were employed as presumed causes.

2. The treatment was the remedial tutoring received by the experimental group; the independent variable was prior achievement level (low); the dependent, each student's level of reading skills as measured by the standardized test.

3. Terman and his confederates used a wide variety of methods to validate and to describe, although mostly they did the latter. No part of the study was truly an experiment. It took place entirely "in the field" (rather than in a laboratory or similar setup), and no treatment was applied. However, both the IQ and achievement tests could be seen as validation of the category of giftedness (that is, quantitative research) and certainly involved both measurement and statistics and structured data collection. Furthermore, the 800 nonselected individuals provided a group (a control) against which to compare the gifted group as in an experiment.

The interest questionnaires, reading records, information forms, and medical data, by contrast, were all forms of survey research. Most (like the interest questionnaire) would likely have provided numeric data, but there would have been narrative data to analyze as well. All were probably structured and hence are closer to the quantitative side of the continuum.

The study of the 301 eminent personalities was historical research. The case study method, a qualitative approach, was used, and the data were verbal. However, by assigning IQ scores based on these data, the investigators gave the method a quantitative twist.

All in all, although the methods of Terman et al. spanned the continuum, their orientation was toward quantitative data.

4. The methods chosen for the study were used entirely in a descriptive manner and were to be used at the library (the natural situation). The questionnaire and the expert ratings were forms of survey research and produced numeric data. As such, they were a form of measurement and hence quantitative. The interviews and the logs were not fully structured and provided spontaneous verbal data. These latter methods were more qualitative. Thus the methods again span the continuum; it would be hard to classify this study, since both quantitative and qualitative data make important contributions.

CHAPTER 4

1. Respond to the committee by describing the journey of findings to knowledge, explaining the thoroughness and professionalism with which research findings are examined by members of the field even before they are published. Explain that research findings are normally submitted for judgment first to colleagues at one's own institution and then to members of the "invisible college," an informal interinstitutional group of colleagues with a common interest in the particular topic. In this way, the people most likely to know the potential weaknesses of the study are given a chance to respond to the methodology used and to the interpretation given to the results. They make a "knowing judgment" of the study. Any findings that progress further in the journey would have already been subjected to substantial scrutiny.

Given positive responses to this point, findings would likely be submitted for presentation at an appropriate professional association meeting. Abstracts submitted to convention program committees normally have the names removed and are submitted "blind" to committee members. Each paper is again judged by members of the field who pool their knowing judgments. Therefore, before a paper is scheduled, a consensus has been reached that the interpretation of the data seems appropriate and that the findings are significant. At the presentation itself and informally during the convention, the findings would again be questioned.

Finally, if the researcher is satisfied that all questions have been answered appropriately, the findings would likely be submitted to a professional journal for publication. Similar to the process used by the convention program committee, the paper would be submitted to a blind review by both a consulting editor and other experts in the field. The findings are again subjected to knowing judgments. Only after these people are satisfied that the findings have been interpreted appropriately and are significant additions to the field is the paper published.

Although the findings may not yet be accepted by the field as knowledge, they have been subjected to a thorough and professional review process.

2. You should attempt to disseminate your information. Negative findings may function to close off otherwise attractive research directions that would waste other researchers' resources. By submitting your findings either for presentation at a professional meeting or for publication, you put them up for peer review and allow others in the field to judge their merit. In doing so, you are subscribing to the principle of Merton's communism, or common ownership of information. This principle implies that publication is the obligation of any researcher participating in the social system of science who uses resources intended for the public good.

3. The functioning social system of science extends beyond the perceived boundaries of a particular field. This researcher would presumably be following the same norms of knowledge production as members of your field. Merton's universalism (universal standards for knowledge claims) applies to this case. That is, you should judge the quality of the work according to what is considered acceptable research for the methods commonly used in your field. While you, as editor, must use your judgment to filter out obviously inappropriate submissions, findings from another field may provide the members of your field with enlightening and useful knowledge that might not otherwise reach them. Thus you must make an initial knowing judgment based on the nature of the study, not the identity of the investigator and, if appropriate, allow the findings to be judged on their merits by putting the study through your review process.

4. Although you are in a politically sensitive situation, you should submit your findings to the peer review process and share your information with others in the field. As in the study on color illustrations in problem 2, Merton's communism applies: ownership of the data is shared, and you have an obligation to disseminate your results. Perhaps your first step is to seek the feedback of the particular researcher concerning your interpretation of the findings. He will likely be one of your most severe critics and may help confirm or modify your analysis. You may also wish to provide copies of the study to other members of the department or friends at other institutions to garner their reactions. After seeking such informal feedback and making any appropriate modifications, you should submit your findings for presentation at a professional meeting or for publication. You should allow the community to judge the merits of the study.

CHAPTER 5

1. Jonassen did follow the chain of reasoning, but with a slight twist. He began with a rationale for the study and a statement of the problem rather than with conclusions from previous research studies. He described traditional instructional design theory first and then described how it was changing as a result of new theory, cognitive psychology. His rationale, though, was based on prior research. Once he had stated his problem—to find a feasible procedure for mapping cognitive structure—he explored the research, examining the available techniques. Only then did he offer a hypothesis—that pattern notes would provide a practical technique for mapping cognitive structure—and it, too, was based on previous research.

The next step was to translate his hypothesis into a research design. The *who*, 24 high school students in an advanced physics class, the *where*, in the high school classroom, and the *when*, over three separate school days, are clearly specified. To demonstrate *what* effect occurred, that pattern notes measure cognitive structure, Jonassen again returned to the literature to find a method to measure cognitive structure. He chose free word association, a technique that he felt was the most valid and reliable measure of cognitive structure available. A high relationship between the scores on the free word association task and on the pattern notes would demonstrate *how* he knew that the effect had occurred. Perhaps the most difficult task was to demonstrate *why* the effect happened—in this case, why pattern notes (and free word association) could be said to measure cognitive structure. This he did by means of a theoretical assumption—that the relationship between two concepts can be determined by their links in free association or in the notes. The why, then, was shown by counting the corresponding links between the concepts produced by the students in pattern notes and by free word association.

Although not indicated in our summary, both the experimental and analysis procedures were described in some detail. The relationship was demonstrated statistically and the conclusion, that pattern notes were a valid measure of cognitive structure, was based on the analysis of the data. Jonassen concluded his report by relating the pattern note technique to instructional design theory and thus provided the link on which future studies could be built.

2. Possibly the weakest link is Jonassen's assertion that cognitive structure can be represented by the number of references of one concept to another. It is a means of inferring what cannot be observed directly. We must accept his argument that this is true in order to believe that cognitive structure was actually being measured.

We may also consider his choice of sample a weak link. It was, first of all, quite small (24 students). However, a sample of 20 or more can be sufficient, under the right circumstances, to demonstrate an effect. (See power analysis in chapter 17, pp. 428–431.)

Second, the effect may have resulted from the characteristics of this one sample. The class was advanced, and the students were probably more capable than average, so maybe intelligence accounted for the relationship. Further, it was quite a uniform group; it did not have the variability of a group representative of that grade. This might not have been a weakness since it was necessary that each student have a well-developed cognitive structure in this subject to provide something to measure. The researcher's purpose was to demonstrate that pattern notes could be used to measure cognitive structure, not necessarily to show that the technique worked for all learners. The study would surely require replication with samples having different characteristics before we could accept the technique as widely useful.

Finally, we could advance an alternative explanation, that of the added motivation that results from the special attention of being part of an experiment (often called the Hawthorne effect). However, the experiment was carried out in the students' own classroom, which would probably dampen any such effect.

3. Not that you can tell from this summary. In the article, Jonassen (1987) strengthened the "observation and measurement" link for measuring cognitive structure by basing the technique solidly in theory and prior research. He indicated considerable theoretical and research support for it.

CHAPTER 6

1. Do you find these assumptions believable, or do you find yourself questioning them? One approach would be to challenge Johnson's assumptions. Examine their basis. Is there an alternate explanation that comes to mind? Are these personality types really stable aspects of an individual's personality, or are they a function of the particular situation? If they are based on exhibited behavior, is there another way of explaining that behavior?

Conversely, you may find these assumptions appealing. Note that they have a basis in established theory. You would be well advised to review Jung's theory rather than relying on Johnson's interpretation. However, you may be able to come up with a way of extending, validating, or applying these conclusions. Coscarelli and Stonewater (1979), for instance, suggested that these personality types could be useful in a model of consultation to help determine the best way to work with a client.

2. All have potential. You could apply the criteria of a good problem here. First, which of the approaches interests you, makes most sense to you, perhaps gets you excited? Does any of them suggest a question to you immediately? Second, all of them are embedded in theory, but is one developing a stronger network than the others? Does it seem to fit better into our developing knowledge base? Third, in terms of impact, which of them appears to be the most current? Exploring a problem based on a theory of prevailing interest in one's field is more likely to produce findings that have an impact than exploring one based on a theory that has been replaced or discarded. Fourth, which allows you to be creative? Do any of them lend themselves to analysis by a new technique, instrument, or model? This is one way to revive an older theory and still have impact.

3. She should begin, of course, by immersing herself in the literature of this topic. It would be worth her while to talk to anyone available to her who has experience or expertise with this disorder. Such experts may be able to answer questions about such matters as certainty of diagnosis, spontaneous recovery, and length of disorder. She should learn the best current explanation of the disorder and how well it is embedded in the network of theory that explains it and similar problems. Then she may turn to the problems of feasibility: Will patients with this disorder be available to her and, if so, in sufficient number to conduct a study? How would she evaluate how well they carry out the activities of daily living? Knowing that this is of concern in special education and with the mentally retarded, she might look for scales in those fields that could be applied here.

4. You should advise her to proceed with her question. If her adviser's model is indeed well recognized, she is in effect embedding her problem in current theory. She is more likely—particularly as a novice—to have an impact on her field in this way than to produce a more original but isolated study. Second, by adding her own touch to the model and providing an interesting and possibly useful extension to it, she has demonstrated originality.

CHAPTER 7

1. The education encyclopedias and handbooks might be the best places to start. You could determine what terminology is used for this topic, gain an overview of the field, pick out keywords and authors, and locate references to current research. The information on keywords and authors might then be used to access the journal indexes. Descriptors or keywords (or both) may be used, depending on the index. If a CD-ROM or on-line search service is available, these might be used for a more comprehensive search once the terms have been determined. These indexes can provide an overview of current research, help locate review articles, identify authors who appear frequently, and show various aspects of a topic. Once key authors and works are found, the SSCI citation index could be used to determine who has cited these authors and thus possibly contributed to furthering the directions of this research.

2. To trace the works of the authors, you could search some of the major indexes by author to locate all their works. Then you might check the citation index of SSCI to determine who has cited their works on generative strategies. This could lead you to more recent work on the topic.

It would also be useful to locate review articles that deal with learning and specifically touch on generative strategies. This would help situate the topic on a conceptual map and lead you to other sources that might contain information on the topic or be related to it.

To find still more on this topic, you would probably first check the thesauri for cross-reference terms that are broader, narrower, related to, or used for "generative learning strategies." If "generative learning strategies" or its parts are not used in the major indexes with thesauri, keyword searching would be the next step. This is possible in SSCI or in ERIC or *Psychological Abstracts* on-line or on CD-ROM. When relevant articles appear, look at the descriptors or subject headings used to index those articles for further leads to search. References in the articles themselves are usually relevant to the topic and provide additional avenues to follow.

3. Computerized searching makes it easier to search for terms that are not descriptors or subject headings, such as *whole language approach*. This is especially true for new terms or very specific topics that might be subsumed in larger concepts. It will also allow the search to combine more than one concept in a search. For example, the search in this case could look for articles that are about whole language, about basals, and about the elementary level all at the same time. This is a great timesaver.

If the whole language approach is a recent idea in the literature, this computerized search will also help identify the appropriate indexing terms. It will point out the major authors in the field and reveal the research frontier on the topic.

4. Encyclopedias, handbooks, and the card or on-line catalog will give you a start in tracing the history of the field of learning style–based instruction. Bibliographies on the topic, located through the card or on-line catalog or through *Bibliographic Index*, would also be useful. Review articles on the topic can be found in ERIC and *PsycInfo*. This is especially easy when searching these indexes on-line.

You could use the large number of journal indexing and abstracting services to locate articles and then narrow the topic to something workable. *Dissertation Abstracts International* is good for locating dissertations, *Resources in Education* in ERIC for conference proceedings or speeches.

5. A literature review before the study begins would provide background on adult learners and methods of instruction in computer use. It could point out what methodologies work and what ones don't. It could help determine the variables, relationships, and confounding factors in other such studies. In addition to showing the state of research on the topic, it could help the developers avoid reinventing the wheel.

Others might argue that such a literature review done before the study might bias the observations through preconceived notions of what should happen. If the treatment and the sample are already set, it might predispose the researcher to expect certain results based on prior research.

CHAPTER 8

1. (a) Obtain a list of the names and addresses of all private elementary school principals in the city of Syracuse from the superintendent of schools. **(b)** Contact each principal by mail and request a roster of sixth-grade pupils enrolled in that school. **(c)** Assign a number to each name. **(d)** Use a table of random numbers to draw the desired sample from that list by doing the following: **(i)** Select a starting point randomly and then follow a row, column, or diagonal and, since the population consists of 900 cases, read the numbers in sets of three. **(ii)** Skip any set of three on the random table that exceeds 900, since there are only 900 cases in the population. **(iii)** Continue taking numbers until a sample of 150 pupils has been selected.

2. (a) An adequate sample might be obtained through proportional stratified sampling, since Mary has to adjust her sample to more than one variable at a time (grade level, sex, reading ability). She should also take into consideration the proportions of variables in the target population. **(b)** The steps in the proportional stratified sampling are as follows: **(i)** Get the names, sex, and reading scores of the high school students from the superintendent of the Rochester school district. **(ii)** Classify the students into sophomores, juniors, and seniors. This yields students in three cells. **(iii)** Classify students as male or female within each grade level. The three cells are now divided into six. **(iv)** Set scores that are the dividing points for low, medium, and high reading ability according to a reading ability test. Divide students in the six cells into high, medium, and low groups according to the reading test cut scores. This yields 18 cells. The cells will not have equal numbers because the classes may be of unequal size and boys more numerous than girls, and the scores determining low, middle, and high reading ability will not necessarily divide the whole group into equal thirds, let alone those in a cell. **(v)** Since there are 3,000 students in the schools and we want a sample of

300, we can take 10 percent of each cell. We can use a table of random numbers to select a random sample from each of the 18 cells. Alternatively, since the list of names in each cell is probably unordered, taking every tenth name will likely give us a random sample (this is systematic sampling).

3. He should use cluster sampling. The state of California is so large that one researcher cannot cover every city, area, street, and block. Traveling and interviewing are expensive and time-consuming.

4. This problem nicely illustrates the difference between the inferences that can be derived from a random and a convenience sample. Where Dr. Kuizenga is concerned with the level of incidence of depression, she is concerned with a context-specific estimation, the incidence of depression in a specific population. The 67 convenience sample cases may or may not be representative of first-year college students at the institution; there is no way to know. They showed a 25 percent incidence, similar to other studies that used convenience samples. On average, however, the 133-case random sample will be representative, so incidence of depression should be estimated from it; it showed a 15 percent incidence. The difference in incidence rates, especially if it holds up with additional studies, could be a significant finding.

The relationship of depression to perceived stress is not unique to first-year women. The relationship of depression to stress, if it exists, is postulated as a universal, so there is no reason that she cannot combine the samples for purposes of examining the relationship of depression to a variety of stress variables. However, since some of the stress variables may be related to culture, she may wish that she had oversampled certain combinations of parents' level of education and race.

CHAPTER 9

Curiosity

Step 1: Find Examples. To what would you point if you wished to teach someone the meaning of this concept? What is the model case of curiosity? A curious person (meaning one demonstrating curiosity as opposed to merely being unusual) would show an eagerness to learn or know. The defining characteristics of this case would be not only that the person shows interest but also that there is some strength or apparent level of motivation behind this interest. This decision would involve a degree of judgment.

What about contrary cases? Are there cases that lack some or all of the defining characteristics? What if a person were to have been offered some form of reward or threatened with punishment or otherwise persuaded to demonstrate interest in some topic? Would this person then be curious? No, although the level of reward or punishment may affect enthusiasm, the person would not be genuinely eager to know or learn. The enthusiasm must be internally derived or intrinsic to the person.

How about borderline cases? Where are the boundaries of "curiosity"? What if the person is intensely interested in one particular subject or topic—for instance, a student interested only in art? Is that person curious? Perhaps, but it seems that a genuinely curious person should have wider interests, should be inquisitive about things generally. Deep interest in only one topic may indicate narrowness or fanaticism rather than curiosity. Like the creative person, the curious person should demonstrate such behavior on more than one occasion and in more than one area.

Consider related cases next. What terms are almost but not quite the same as *curiosity* and shed light on the concept? How about *nosy* or *prying*? Is a nosy or prying person curious as well? The terms *nosy* and *prying* imply excessive interest in a topic that is known to be private and in which outsiders have no legitimate reason for being interested. This is obviously a judgment call, but these terms do carry a negative connotation that goes beyond being merely curious to being interested for illegitimate reasons. A curious person, then, shows interest in things where there is a legitimate interest and often demonstrates interest for interest's sake.

Finally, what about invented cases? What if all someone did was to pry into things and go off into each newly encountered situation to see where it led? Nobody would get anything done. The curious person, therefore, demonstrates curiosity in a reasonable degree that does not interfere with normal activities but merely adds interest to them and enriches them. Again, this is a judgment call, but an important one.

The defining characteristics of curiosity, then, are that the person is eager to know or learn (the tendency to show interest characterizes the person's behavior), that this is a mental act, that the person's motivation is innate (interest for interest's sake), that it is engaged in legitimate pursuits, and that it is manifested in a reasonable degree in relation to other activities.

Step 2: Test Defining Conditions. Is each of the conditions in step 1 necessary for the term to apply? Can you think of someone you consider to be a curious person for whom one or more of the conditions would not apply? I could not.

Steps 3 and 4: Exhaust Possibilities. Are there persons who are eager to learn but who are not curious? Again, I could not think of any, so the analysis is considered complete. Maybe in following this analysis you thought of such persons. If so, repeat steps 3 and 4.

Aptitude

Step 1: Find Examples. What is the model case of a person exhibiting an aptitude for something? That person must first be capable of some particular task or skill, must be good at something. Further, the person must have a natural capability or inclination—a talent for that task or skill.

What about contrary cases? Does a person who has been taught a task or skill have an aptitude for it? Presumably yes, or the person should not have been capable of learning it. So having been taught about the task or skill is not an excluding characteristic. What if a person demonstrates an ability to do something once but can't repeat it despite practice and instruction? It is possible this was a chance performance. A sharpshooter who hits the bull's-eye of a target one time out of many tries cannot be considered to be demonstrating an aptitude. Thus we must take consistent performance into account.

How about borderline cases? Do we really have to be talented to be able? What degree of aptitude equates with being "apt"? What constitutes being good at something? Often comparison is made with others to place an individual somewhere on a continuum. The research literature on the topic of aptitude, for example, is rife with interpretations of high, medium, and low aptitudes. In each such study, a standard for high, medium, or low is set. A student showing high verbal aptitude, for instance, might be judged so on the basis of performance on some standardized scale.

There is also a judgment here of ease of doing or learning something. An athlete who is considered to be a natural usually outperforms others but also learns the sport more easily. The term *aptitude* implies the ability to learn a skill easily.

What of related cases? What about a person's nature or temperament? Is aptitude a function of volition or willingness? What role does motivation play here? You have probably known a person whom you judged an "underachiever," a capable student or athlete, for example, who normally wasn't motivated to perform yet occasionally demonstrated great skill or could do so on demand. Aptitude, apparently, is something beyond interest or willingness. One person can be better at a task or a skill than another as the result of instruction or practice. But presumably, if the latter had greater aptitude for it, then with the equivalent training, the latter would outperform the former.

How about invented cases? What if individuals could not improve their performance of a particular task or skill by learning, practice, and so on? What if motivation played no part in its performance either? In that case, either people would differ in their performance on the basis of aptitude, or they wouldn't differ at all. The latter seems unlikely though, given the biological differences among people. Hence there appears to be an innate quality to aptitude.

The defining characteristics of a person demonstrating a particular aptitude, then, are that the person be capable of that task or skill (the standard for capability being a matter of judgment), that this capability have some innate quality, and that the person be able to demonstrate the task or skill at the judged level with some degree of consistency (again a matter of judgment).

Step 2: Test Defining Conditions. Is each of the conditions in step 1 necessary for the term to apply? Can you think of any exceptions? Consider *overachievers*. This term implies that individuals can learn to perform at a level beyond their supposed aptitude. But can this really happen? Can people actually achieve more than what they are capable of? To me, the term *overachiever* merely indicates that an individual has worked (studied, practiced) harder than the majority of others against whose performance that person's is compared. All others of the equivalent aptitude level should be capable of the same. It is not an exception to the defining characteristics.

Steps 3 and 4: Exhaust Possibilities. Are the defining characteristics sufficient for the term to apply? Can you think of situations that have all the characteristics but to which *aptitude* does not apply? I could not, so the analysis is considered complete.

CHAPTER 10

1. No! Scales such as this have no real zero point; therefore, they are not ratio scales. We don't even know for sure that the units of measurement are equal to one another for an interval scale. The scales are at least ordinal, and we treat the data as though they were interval because we have found that we can make useful interpretations this way that correspond to real-world phenomena when we test them out. Although it is convenient to calculate mean ratings by way of comparison between groups, it is not correct to interpret them in terms of ratios.

2. (a) To get the middle case, divide the number of cases by 2; $178 \div 2 = 89$, which is in the third category ($100,000–$124,999). Counting from the bottom, 44 more cases are needed from that category, which contains 55 cases. So $44 \div 55 = 0.8$, and $0.8 \times \$24,999$ (the size of the category) $= \$19,999$. To find the median house price, add $19,999 to the lower boundary, which is $100,000. Thus the median price is $19,999 + $100,000 = $119,999.

(b) Mean sale price $= \$23,000,000 \div 178 = \$129,213$.

(c) The median would be a better representation than the mean because the frequency distribution is positively skewed; that is, the majority of house prices are in the lower part of the distribution. The mean is more sensitive to extremes and in this case is high because it is influenced by the expensive houses sold.

3. Advise him to change the raw scores to a derived score with some easy-to-remember mean and standard deviation, such as a mean of 50 and a standard deviation of 10. To do this, he would subtract the mean for a test from each raw score on that test, divide it by the raw score standard deviation, multiply that standard score by 10, and add 50. Then all the tests would have a mean of 50 and a standard deviation of 10 regardless of how easy or hard they happened to be.

4. From the description of Salomon's theory, Dr. Southwind probably should have expected a curvilinear relationship: little effort for easy media, increased effort as a medium was perceived as more difficult, and effort falling off again as the medium was seen as very difficult. Nonlinear relationships are underestimated by the Pearson product-moment correlation. Statistics like the correlation ratio (η), not covered in this chapter, would provide a more accurate estimate of the relationship. A scatterplot would be very useful in showing whether the relationship really is U-shaped.

CHAPTER 11

1. The purpose of the study was to seek evidence to confirm the technique of pattern notes as a measure of cognitive structure. Therefore, Jonassen needed to demonstrate construct validity—that is, to determine whether pattern notes were a measure of an individual's schemata, or knowledge structure, a construct.

2. **(a)** She would have been interested in criterion-related validity and, specifically, in predictive validity, a predictor of a student's first-year grade point average. Presumably she is into the academic year when she notices freshmen dropping out because of failing grades. She could ask the remaining freshmen to take the UECT and correlate its scores with end-of-year grade point average. This would be concurrent validity, which would underestimate predictive validity because students who have already dropped out are not included in the testing. To estimate predictive validity, the UECT should be given to next year's freshmen at the beginning of the academic year and correlated with their GPA at the end of the year.

(b) To improve predictive validity, she might item-analyze the test to determine which items did not predict dropouts, replacing them with new items similar to those that did predict them. To do this, she would compare the way dropouts answered each item with the way those who did not drop out answered it. Items that showed a large difference would be predictive of dropping out.

3. They would be interested in both construct validity and predictive validity. First, they would want to know whether the scale truly did measure the existence of the four personality styles theorized by Keith's model. To estimate this, they might ask individuals to nominate people who know them well. The latter persons would then be asked to rate the individuals on each of the four personality types, and these ratings would be correlated with the test scores. High correlations would be evidence of construct validity.

Second, they proposed that a consultant use his or her knowledge of the client's style in determining how to approach the relationship. If the measure did differentiate people according to psychological style, it would presumably then predict how that client would behave when making decisions. Clients would be given the test at the beginning of the relationship, and their personality type classification would be compared with their decision-making style to determine predictive validity.

4. She should check the content validity of the test against the course. The table of specifications for the examination should match the content and skills taught in the course in both coverage and emphasis. In terms of reliability, she would be concerned with a combination of stability and equivalence reliability. Since she will be measuring the effect of semester-long instruction, she will be comparing the results from two tests given several months apart. She would want to know that without instruction, students' scores would stay approximately the same over that period of time. She will also be comparing the students on two parallel forms of the test and would be concerned that the two forms consistently measure the same concepts—that is, that they are truly equivalent.

5. This depends very much on whose welfare it is deemed most important to protect. If a nurse who cannot achieve a score of 80 is a threat to the patient and might not be caught by other checks in the system, a cut score above 80 might be in order. If the other checks in the system will catch a nurse who should not have passed and, because of a nursing shortage, one is concerned about failing nurses whose true score is above the cut line, then a cut score below 80 would be appropriate. How far from 80 the cut score should be placed in either case depends on the amount of error the hospital is willing to tolerate and how efficient the other systems are for sensing testing errors. If a cut score of 85 is set, then the confidence interval within which the true score lies, with a confidence expressed by the odds of 2 to 1, extends from 80 to 90. But at the same time, at odds of 1 in 3, some persons will lie outside this interval, half of them above 90 and half below 80. Therefore, at odds of 1 to 6, a nurse's score might lie below 80. Is 1 in 6 too high or too low? That is a judgment that must be guided by the conditions surrounding the decision.

6. The data collected by the observers were a direct measure of the teachers' behavior and perhaps the most objective available to the investigator. Since a checklist was used, analysis of the data would have been straightforward. However, the presence of the observers likely had an effect on both the teachers and the students. Moreover, the observers were restricted to predetermined indicators of enthusiasm, which may or may not have been valid measures. Thus enthusiastic behavior not reflected by the checklist may have been overlooked. These observations would have been time-consuming, and possibly costly, if the investigator had to pay the observers.

The diaries were a form of data produced by the subjects themselves. Their flexible form could have provided comprehensive insight into a particular teacher's behavior, particularly into private thoughts and feelings. They were inexpensive. The major weakness of this form of measure is that it depends on self-perception and may not accurately reflect how others (in this case, the students) would have perceived the teacher's level of enthusiasm. In addition, filling out a diary requires recall of past events, albeit recent ones, which may have been modified by the teacher's memory. Finally, the diary data would have been time-consuming, and possibly difficult to analyze and summarize.

CHAPTER 12

1. Needless to say, the question does not refer to any specific chicken or any particular egg but to chickens and eggs in general. It addresses the problem of precedence of the cause before the effect and is an example of what appears to be a simple causal pattern that has been, with tongue in cheek, turned around. Did there have to be a chicken egg from which the first chicken hatched? If so, where did the egg come from? Which was the "cause" and which was the "effect"? Was the egg the cause, by hatching the first chicken (the effect), or was the first chicken the cause, laying the first chicken egg (the effect)? The saying is an example in popular terms of the fact that everything is part of a causal chain, and we use this saying in nonresearch problems to make the causal chain salient.

2. Your answer would naturally depend on the specific circumstances: the particular student, his instructional history, his environment, and so on. You would likely emphasize that patterns leading to low achievement are never simple and that there might be alternative explanations. In effect, there is a causal history to the student's behavior, and its pattern should be explored. Maybe the causes are multiple and affect each other in complex ways. What, for example, is the home situation? Have the parents encouraged or discouraged learning? What is the student's perceived or measured ability level? Has he in the past made an effort but not succeeded? Is he now achieving at his ability level? Is he learning-disabled? What is his medical condition? All are possible explanations for, or factors involved in, his behavior, some of which may be more important than others. It is likely that the cause is some constellation of these factors and not one simple answer (such as "The student is lazy"), perhaps an INUS condition.

3. The causes are probably best explained as all being part of a causal chain in a multiple-cause pattern. Some will be real and some perceived. Not all will be present in any one circumstance, but some group of them will act one on the other, or in concert, to affect an individual's understanding of a situation. Consequently, they will influence that person's choice of behavior in that situation or in similar ones in the future. Take an individual who normally does poorly on exams and believes himself to be a poor student. He may prepare well for a test and be successful. Yet instead of identifying the cause of his success as his ability or his effort (or both), he may attribute it to conditions such as luck or the exam being "easy." He might then choose to depend on luck the next time rather than believing in his ability and therefore preparing for the exam. In each case, multiple factors or causes, both real and perceived, produce a behavior.

4. The availability of drugs in the community and prior use before abuse are necessary but not sufficient (contingent) conditions for drug abuse. A prior addiction to a drug is a sufficient but not a necessary condition for drug abuse and therefore an alternative cause. Peer pressure, boredom, and poverty are neither sufficient nor necessary conditions for drug abuse but may make it more probable and may therefore be considered contributing conditions.

5. Answer is given on page 592.

CHAPTER 13

1. First, consider explanation credibility. Is your rationale plausible? In this case, it makes good sense intuitively that some people respond quickly to situations while others prefer to take their time and ponder. It is especially apparent in exam situations. Is there existing research evidence that might help explain the idea? In fact, these categories *did* grow out of research into analytic versus global reasoning. Kagen and colleagues (1964) developed a categorization test (the Conceptual Style Test) to compare the concepts. As a side product of their research, they found that children who adopted an analytic reasoning style took significantly longer to answer the test questions than those who gave relational answers. It led the researchers to wonder whether the tendency to delay responses was a stable characteristic of certain individuals. Their explanatory evidence, then, had its roots in prior research.

Second, consider translation fidelity. How well have you operationalized this explanation? What is your hypothesis here, and how have you designed your study? Kagen et al. (1964) operationalized the concept of "impulsiveness–reflectiveness" by stating it as a tendency to delay a response to a task. Because the hypothesis involved time, it was easily measurable. Furthermore, so was the individual's error rate. Kagen and associates developed another test, the Matching Figures Test, consisting of sets of very similar pictures in which the task was to pick out the ones that match exactly. Time and error scores were kept. Individuals were classified as above or below average on each score. An impulsive person would be quick (below average on time) but would make many errors, while a reflective person would be slow (above average on time) with few errors. The researchers appear to have soundly operationalized their construct. That their studies were corroborated by other researchers gives evidence of this.

2. The evidence for this concept may not be as easy to provide as for impulsiveness–reflectiveness! Again, consider explanation credibility. To some people, the relationship between signs of the zodiac and personality is intuitively obvious; witness the popularity of astrology columns in many newspapers. To others, the idea of any relationship between personality and star patterns is inherently ridiculous. To the first group, the explanation is plausible, but to the second, it will be a hard sell! You will have to provide strong empirical evidence. Is there any research evidence to support the idea?

Think about translation fidelity. How would you operationalize this concept? Members of the sign of Taurus are indicated by birth date. But you will need a convincing measure of stubbornness. If you do find or develop such a test, you may be able to sense an effect—that is, demonstrate that a relationship exists. Even so, you will have a problem eliminating rival explanations. For example, how will you show that the relationship is caused by the zodiac and not the season of the year? Personality issues are extremely complex, and so are the influences on them.

3. No, the faculty should have repeated the study with the target audience *in situ*.

There is a problem here both with translation generality and with whether all restrictive explanations (conditions) have been eliminated. The field test was not conducted with the adult population to whom the course would be offered. The faculty members cannot be certain that the significant findings would be repeated with this group. Are the learning needs of adults and undergraduates the same? For example, the undergraduate students may be more experienced or more comfortable with computers.

In addition, the conditions of the study do not appear to be the same as those under which the course would be offered. Since the field test was conducted on campus, it seems likely that assistance from instructors, both with the subject matter and with use of the computers, was available to students taking the computer-based course. Any such assistance could very well be quite significant and could account for the findings. This is a restrictive condition with strong implications for "stand-alone" (without human intervention) computer-based instruction.

4. No, again there are problems with translation generality and with whether all explanations (conditions) have been eliminated. One translation generality problem is that these inmates had volunteered for the program and therefore probably already had a willing attitude. They may well have been in the process of "going straight" anyway, and this program only served to shorten their prison terms. Furthermore, there is a restrictive condition. The program may have taken them from an environment (prison) that could otherwise have negatively affected them and therefore contributed to recidivism. If conducted in the prisons, it might not be as effective.

Further, these offenders were from a very specific population (translation generality again). They were young offenders (20 years or under) who had committed less violent crimes. The investigators have no way of knowing if the technique would work with older, more "hardened" inmates or with the more violent. The study may hold promise, but it also needs replication.

CHAPTER 14

1. First, Jonassen built his study on knowledge that the audience had already accepted. He began his article with a discussion of existing instructional design theory and pointed out what he thought was missing. He next compared the various techniques available for assessing cognitive structure and, on the basis of that information, presented his rationale for choosing to use pattern notes instead. Part of this explanation showed why he felt the existing methods were not appropriate. Thus he also attempted to avoid the weaknesses of previous similar studies.

Second, he used an existing, accepted technique, free word association, to validate pattern notes as an assessment method. It was, he noted, the most valid and reliable method available for assessing a learner's cognitive structure.

2. You want to demonstrate that the new approach is more effective than the current one—internal validity (LP)—but you would also like to show that this is true with other such groups and in other situations—external validity (GP). Conducting the study in the lab would allow you tight control of most variables and would probably help to strengthen internal validity (LP). Most important, you would be able to use such methods as the random assignment of students to either treatment and the standardization of your instructions to eliminate rival hypotheses. It is, however, an artificial situation (for these students) and not one in which the approach will normally be used. That in itself could account for a demonstrated effect.

A demonstrated relationship in a study conducted in the schools—in the natural environment—would certainly improve external validity (GP). The new approach would be shown to be superior in the situation in which it would normally be used.

Such a result would also be more difficult to obtain. Unless the schools also have language laboratories, it would be hard to standardize your treatments. Furthermore, random assignment of students to the two approaches could be unacceptable for ethical or administrative reasons. You would generally be less able to guarantee the equivalence of your samples, and it would be more difficult to eliminate rival explanations.

In this case, however, it is probably essential to know whether any advantage attributed to the proposed technique will hold up when it is used in the schools. So you may wish to emphasize external validity (GP) and conduct your study in the schools if at all possible.

3. Resource allocation reflects the hidden decisions that a researcher makes, such as what question to choose, how to formulate it, and where to invest time and energy. Perhaps the most obvious (and important) choice that Kagen et al. made was that of the question. They were originally studying these other concepts when they noticed the tendency of analytic individuals to take longer to respond to questions. It led them to wonder whether this was a stable trait and to want to investigate it.

Once they had chosen this question, its formulation was fairly easy: measure the time taken to complete questions or problems and the error rate in doing so. However, they also had to invest considerable effort in the development and validation of a new measure, their Matching Figures Test, before they could actually test for the concepts in question.

4. They could strongly affect the generalizability of any results she might obtain. Though perhaps not totally a laboratory situation, such a school probably would not represent the other schools in the district. We would expect more (and more varied) visitors than in a typical school. It would likely be staffed with exceptionally enthusiastic and capable teachers who had agreed to work in a more public atmosphere and to be equipped with extra resources and paraphernalia for research, such as two-way mirrors.

All of this could contribute to an unusual atmosphere in the school, perhaps allowing for more highly motivated students than would be found in an average school. It is probable that the school would be the site of a variety of experimental programs. Further, if such a school were located in a residential district near the university, we might also find a higher proportion of children from professional families who might be expected to be, on the average, more capable than those in a more average school.

CHAPTER 15

1. (a) *Qualitative Method:* You may need to explain to your colleague what participant observation entails and how data are collected and verified. You should point out that in choosing this method, your intent is to do a case study of the children in this particular school in order to understand their interactions with the medium in the natural setting. You should explain that the process involves collecting a considerable quantity of data (in narrative form). Checks on researcher bias are provided **(i)** by detailed fieldnotes containing as much verbatim reporting (direct quotes) as possible and **(ii)** through self-reflection in the form of observer comments and memos. These notes to yourself reflect your feelings, biases, and reactions, as well as your methodology. Point out as well that some qualitative studies include an extensive appendix reflecting methods used or else include such explanation within the body of the report. All this helps you as the researcher be aware of where data are influenced by opinion and, when included in the report, informs the reader as well.

(b) *Mixing Quantitative and Qualitative Methods:* Although some researchers who advocate the qualitative point of view likely might not accept the mixing of the two methods in the same study, most qualitative researchers see these techniques as complementary. From this viewpoint, qualitative methods provide an excellent exploratory device to allow researchers to develop a solid understanding of the circumstances in which they are interested. Qualitative methods can be extremely useful to help identify questions that will later be verified experimentally, which is your intent in this study.

(c) *The Qualitative Point of View:* Some investigators are of the opinion that to carry out qualitative research, researchers *must* adopt this point of view. If you agree with this argument, you will have to add to the statements in answer (*a*) above. For instance, you would explain that the qualitative point of view involves understanding how the circumstance looks to the people being studied and how they act on that information. From this standpoint, knowledge is a joint product of culture and the meanings assigned by the individual. Thus in your school study, you would expect a variety of behaviors, depending on the particular children involved. Your choice of participant observation as a research method will allow you to understand these behaviors from their point of view and to document them. The plausibility of your explanation would be induced from, or "emerge from," the data. The process is inductive rather than deductive. It is true that others looking at the data might come up with different interpretations. However, this methodology provides reasoned opinions based on the data.

2. (a) *Nonparticipant Observation:* Included here are both overt and covert recording and nonparticipant observation. They are the least obtrusive techniques, especially if covert (say, done from behind two-way mirrors), and therefore allow observation of "natural" actions. However, they limit action to special rooms and/or the range of equipment. They will provide behavioral and descriptive data but will not afford you the opportunity to gather any explanation from the children's point of view.

(b) *Participant Observation:* Within this category is a continuum of possible researcher behaviors. At one end, you may make it clear that you are conducting research and make it obvious by means of low interaction with your subjects. At the other extreme, you may observe covertly. You could adopt an authority role within the situation, such as being a teacher (covert observation), or try to become a part of the situation (with minimal explanation—at least to the children). Some researchers conducting such studies have gone so far as pretending to be one of the children, playing with them as if they were a child. Perhaps the most common approach within this tradition, however, is to adopt the friendship role, maintaining your status as an adult but eschewing a position of authority. By adopting this role, you would be able to minimize your influence on the situation and to develop trusting relationships in which you are able to ask the children for their own explanations.

3. Your problem is the one faced by all investigators who wish to engage in participant observation. You have the dual task of gaining entry and securing acceptance.

Gaining Entry: You need to find a way to enter that conveys the message "I am to be trusted." Your first step will probably be to secure the approval of the school administration—possibly the superintendent—or begin the process of approval with a member of the particular school board. In one such study of students at a junior high school, the researcher, Everhart (1977), was able to legitimize his presence at the school through his role as evaluator for a government agency. Even so, the school administration resisted his entry for several weeks. The administrator with whom you are dealing may also impose conditions on your study or demand some sort of quid pro quo for the privilege. You must be careful that such conditions neither violate academic freedom nor abrogate the confidentiality of your informants. In Everhart's case, the school principal set the parameters for the study by limiting it to students (that is, excluding teachers) and by insisting that the researcher's role be one of observer and not "confidant." Everhart was restricted to specific classes and limited interviewing. Fortunately, he was able to renegotiate these conditions once on site for a couple of months.

Securing Acceptance: Once you are on site, you will have to gain the approval and trust of your field subjects—in this case, the students. Simultaneously, you must remain enough of an outsider to avoid the constraints of the behaviors the group expects of its members. Everhart slowly developed the role of friend to his respondents. He did so first by developing an explanation of his presence (he was a writer there to do a story about what students did in junior high) that made sense to them and indicated that his presence was legitimate. He was then able to present himself as a friend both by spending a considerable amount of time with the students and by reducing his contact with the adults. In time, he became so well accepted by the students that he was able to become an ex officio member of certain groups in the school.

4. This is an example of an ethical dilemma to which the answer may not be as clear-cut as it first appears. It is a no-win situation that is frequently encountered in this kind of research. Reporting the people involved to the authorities may well identify you as a part of the authority structure and disrupt any special relationships that you have developed, thus terminating your study. Conversely, you may endanger yourself and your study by becoming party to a criminal act. A fairly common choice is to ignore such transgressions in favor of completing the study and letting the natural corrective forces of society come into play. You should understand, however, that unlike an attorney, you are *not* in a privileged position. You cannot protect the anonymity of your informants or subjects. Furthermore, once published, your information is public knowledge. Your notes can be subpoenaed by a court of law.

5. Your first step would be to conduct further observations in other classes in the same school and, if possible, at the same grade levels as those you have already studied. Develop your understanding and densify it with detail and example. Test your understanding with negative instances, borderline cases, and key examples. Extend your observations to other grade levels within the school. Once the concept becomes saturated (the same kinds of instances are being found repeatedly) within the school, reverse the funnel and broaden your sample choice to gather new data. First, include other similar schools (in terms of age level, socioeconomic status, exposure to computers, etc.). Then move to less similar schools until you are no longer able to discover new instances of your theory. Continue this process until you develop a solid understanding of the phenomenon—in this example, how children interpret their interactions with computers.

6. Such a study was carried out by Tripp-Reimer (1983) in Columbus with the intent of identifying the extent of such beliefs across the generations in order to help plan health care. She used the qualitative methods of semistructured interviews and participant observation in the Greek community in order to establish baseline data concerning the description of *matiasma*. The descriptions she obtained allowed her to develop categories indicating levels of belief in *matiasma* and levels of knowledge of the practice.

Tripp-Reimer also used a questionnaire to quantify the distribution of these beliefs and practices within the population. It was devised to elicit demographic and social characteristics of the population, including sex, age, and generation.

CHAPTER 16

1. The committee could use either a mailed questionnaire or some form of interview, depending on whether or not it wished to reach all the faculty or a sample thereof. The choice may depend, in part, on the urgency of getting the information. The questionnaire represents a method of reaching a majority of faculty quickly and cheaply. With the support of academic administration, a high return rate might also be expected. On the one hand, in light of the possibly sensitive nature of the information sought, the anonymity of the questionnaire might provide more open and honest responses. On the other hand, the questions will be structured and might restrict the answers given, possibly allowing important information to be missed.

The committee could also consider two forms of interview: individual or telephone. Both offer the flexibility of probing answers and ensuring that questions are answered clearly. Individual interviews offer the opportunity to establish rapport but are time-consuming and would restrict the committee to a small sample of the faculty. In this instance, since the calls are local and inexpensive, telephone interviews might permit more thorough coverage while retaining most of the advantages of both the individual interviews and the questionnaire.

2. Dean Blanchard is faced with two problems: finding the perceived educational needs and determining the size of the clientele for each educational program designed to answer a need. These call for different survey techniques. An exploratory technique such as some kind of open-end interviewing in depth with a small sample to find the unfilled perceived needs is required for the initial phase. A focus group might work well too. Once the perceived needs have been determined, a sample questionnaire or telephone survey of potential clients is required to estimate demand. The questionnaire would be cheaper and easier, but individuals might say they would sign up just to preserve their options. A telephone interview might be able to probe just how serious they are about entering a program and so might provide better data.

The focus groups might be made up of selected previous clients. They might also be in the best position to identify groups who, similar in situation to themselves, might be interested in enrolling. The sampling plan for the second phase depends on the kinds of programs proposed. If there is uncertainty about what population to tap to determine interest in the programs, a random sample might be the best bet. If questionnaire or telephone interviewing were used, geographic location of the respondents would not matter. If face-to-face interviewing were used, cluster sampling would reduce travel should the area served by the college be large.

3. After mailing the questionnaire, Phillips's major problem is one of response. She needs a good return rate, but she needs especially to know that the people who do reply represent the membership. It may be, for instance, that those who responded are the members most supportive of establishing a chapter or most interested in specific services. To overcome this problem, Phillips would have begun by writing a good letter of transmittal to motivate as many respondents as possible to answer the first questionnaire. Next, she could have attempted to increase the return rate with a mailed follow-up (a reminder postcard or a replacement questionnaire).

To determine whether the responses she is receiving represent the membership, she could see whether late-arriving responses are like early returns. If they are, even if the response rate is low, as long as the sample is representative, unless it is quite small, the responses may be extrapolated to the population. If late responses are not like early ones, it is quite possible that nonrespondents are different; a comparison of responses received in successive weeks might indicate the trend. Remembering that phone follow-ups may differ from written responses, Phillips may phone a sample of nonrespondents to approximate their written answers. Using the trends established from the comparison of early with late respondents and the answers of phone-contacted nonrespondents, she may extrapolate results for the total membership.

4. Children represent a special and often difficult group with which to conduct interviews. Further, the responses Apple might obtain from the youngest will likely be quite different from those of the older children. Given that and the fact that his purpose here is exploratory, he will want to use either an unstructured or a partially structured style. These approaches will allow him to ask open-end questions and to follow up any leads or unusual answers. Use of a nondirective technique would allow him to establish better rapport with the children and to encourage freer responses. Conducting group interviews, particularly with the younger children, might help overcome their natural shyness toward strangers.

5. Faced with the problem of querying a sensitive topic, the team will want to clear its questionnaire with all parties: representative parents, school administrators and teachers, and the school board. Obviously, an anonymous questionnaire with no secret coding should be used. The simplest method and the one needing the least information would involve dividing the group in two and giving one half a list with the behaviors of interest. The other half would receive a list that does not include them. Each list would include innocuous as well as targeted behaviors, and each questionnaire might be a combination of lists, some innocuous and some not, the other questionnaire being a mirror image. Thus the two groups would answer similar but not identical questions.

CHAPTER 17

1. It would be used in hypothesis testing. The investigators would be interested in examining the difference between the means of the two groups and, expecting a greater effect for the cooperative learning group, would choose directional testing using a one-tailed test. Thus they might adopt the null hypothesis that the difference between the means of the two groups belongs to a population of differences with a mean of zero. Any observed difference is due to chance and sampling error, and the two samples actually belong to the same population. If they were able to reject the null hypothesis, they would likely accept the alternative hypothesis that the difference between the means belongs to a population of differences with a mean greater than zero and that there was a significant difference between the instructional treatments in favor of the cooperative treatment.

2. The answer depends on which test the researcher chooses, the one-tailed or the two-tailed t test. The latter includes the population mean within the 95 percent confidence interval; the former does not. Thus the one-tailed test is more sensitive and indicates statistical significance. But is the researcher justified in using it here? It depends on whether or not we would expect the drug to slow or quicken an individual's reaction time. The choice of the one-tailed test is justified if the researcher had a directional hypothesis that marijuana slows an individual's reaction, and if it were found to speed it up, she would consider that an aberration in the study rather than a finding. (If she could find nothing wrong with the study, she might then switch her hypothesis and replicate the study.)

3. The psychologist does not want to reject the null hypothesis and claim an effect that really does not exist—that is, commit a Type I (alpha) error. However, especially given the problem of one extreme value within her sample, she also does not wish to reject the possibility of an effect that is really there despite the statistics—that is, commit a Type II (beta) error. She could strengthen the sensitivity of her study in a number of ways. First, she could, of course, discard the data for the one subject, provided that she can demonstrate a valid reason for doing so (perhaps he was ill that day, or it turned out he was from another country and had weak English skills, for example). She should, of course, report this decision. If she had analyzed the first data using a two-tailed test, she probably would have a valid argument for choosing the more sensitive, one-tailed test with the replication, which, since she is close, might well provide statistical significance. That is, she has a directional hypothesis, though recognized only after the study had been completed. If her sample were small, it might be possible to repeat the experiment with a larger group to dampen the variability due to size. Finally, if able to return to the sample, she could increase the treatment time (perhaps test the subjects with more text passages) to attempt to strengthen its effect.

4. With a discovery orientation, such as we have in screening remedial reading programs for one that works, we don't want to miss a potentially good one. We are willing to tolerate what we call false positives, findings that look significant but are Type I errors. So we change the confidence level in the opposite direction, from 0.1 percent toward 10 percent. Some of those 10 percent are going to be called statistically significant effects and turn out not to be, but that is OK because we will be less likely to miss those that do validate on replication as significant effects.

5. If that were the case, it would make research much easier! No, all we can say is that the null hypothesis escaped disconfirmation this time. We ought to be putting our propositions to the most rigorous tests we can find. Each time we test a proposition and it is validated, we say that it escaped disconfirmation. After it has escaped enough times that we are confident about using it, we eventually act as though it were a true proposition. But science is the only method of knowing wherein every proposition is held as tentatively true until disconfirmed. Thus any proposition could, in theory, at least, be disconfirmed at any time. Of course, this would markedly upset our ideas about the way the world works, but in some respects that is what Einstein did with the theory of relativity.

6. Here we run into the problem of statistical significance versus practical significance. Wright needs to know not only that the effect was statistically significant but also whether it was large enough to be practically significant. So she wants to know how big it is in terms of the gains that children normally show at that grade.

7. Dr. Goetz should conduct a pilot study to find estimates of the standard deviation of his variables, as well as an estimated difference between treatments. When he has these, he can design a study that will be sufficiently sensitive that if that size of effect recurs, it will be statistically significant.

Alternatively, he can devise a design that is as sensitive as possible. To do this, he can change the confidence level from 1 percent toward 5 percent, use a directional hypothesis and a one-tailed test of significance, increase the size of the difference between treatments by writing the advance organizers for maximum effect, comparing the two treatments over many samples of material, giving the two treatments to a bright group that might be more susceptible to the effect of advance organizers, and so on. In addition, he could increase the size of the sample of subjects or decrease the variability. The latter can be done by using more reliable tests or measures, by moving into the laboratory to decrease random noise that would decrease attention, by uniformly motivating the students but ensuring that different trials used the same directions for testing, and similar things.

8. Apparently, the difference between the means for these characteristics in Stoltz's sample and those of the population were such as to likely be due to sampling error for samples of 25. But that assumes that the sensitivity of the statistical test that she ran was powerful enough to pick up a difference that was practically significant so far as she was concerned. Sally must determine what size difference means a practically significant difference between her sample and the population. If this turns out to be within the sensitivity of her study as already designed, all is well. If not, then getting a larger sample is probably the easiest way to fix the study.

CHAPTER 18

1. You will be designing a single-variable study and have many options, depending on the availability of subjects and your control over the situation. If you are able to bring the students to a laboratory or otherwise rearrange their natural classroom groupings for the purposes of the study, you may be able to assign your subjects randomly to each treatment. It is unlikely that you could successfully assign different units (with or without the pictures within the diagrams) on a random basis within each classroom as the students would soon realize the differences and compare materials (the diffusion threat to validity). If you are able to assign subjects randomly (rearrange the classes), the best choice would be the randomized posttest-only control group design (design 5), in which the no-pictures group is the control. This would allow you to avoid any testing effect caused by a pretest.

Most likely, however, you will have to give each treatment to existing, presumably comparable classes. Besides, as your study involves the use of full units and requires some time to carry out, a counterbalanced design in which each treatment is applied.to all subjects is not feasible (unless you use more than one unit, but then you would likely be stretching the cooperation of the school authorities). Therefore, your design choice would, of necessity, be the nonequivalent control group design (design 3). Since this design includes a pretest, you may wish to assign the class with the lower mean to the treatment. This is risky because if the latter does not catch up to the other (control) class, you will not have a statistically significant result. If the experimental group does outscore the control on the posttest, however, you may have an interpretable result.

2. (a) If the treatment group did score significantly higher, we could point to several alternative explanations, including selection, since all the pilot study teachers were volunteers; the Hawthorne effect, since the students would likely have been aware of belonging to an experimental group; the novelty effect, if the approach was substantially different from standard classroom procedure; and possibly even a researcher expectancy effect, if members of the curriculum team or its supporters were involved in the measurement of the effect.

(b) A significant result in favor of the control group might have resulted from compensatory rivalry, or the John Henry effect. This is more likely if the teachers using the regular program were opposed to the introduction of the new approach. They may well have made an extra effort to demonstrate that the old approach was equally effective or even more effective.

3. We could argue for several alternative explanations: a researcher expectancy effect, a Hawthorne or novelty effect, and, if the regular section was superior, the John Henry effect (compensatory rivalry). The instructor couldn't very well keep the section leaders blind to the treatment, given its obvious inclusion in the course. One way that he could avoid the expectancy and John Henry threats is by gaining the section leaders' support and involving them in the use of the CAI program in their sections. This might reduce, though not entirely eliminate, researcher expectancy, since the section leaders would probably not have the same vested interest in the outcome. Gaining their agreement to use the program themselves would also remove the possibility of their trying to improve the standard approach to compete with the CAI.

Eliminating a Hawthorne or novelty effect might be more difficult because of the obvious and unusual nature of the treatment, communication between students, and other factors. One possibility is using a placebo (perhaps a CAI program containing topics not examined) so that all students are exposed to CAI in the course and are kept blind to the actual treatment. Lastly, the researcher could use the nonequivalent control group design (design 3) by using the CAI with all the introductory calculus students one semester and comparing results with past exam results or with those of a future group not exposed to the treatment.

4. The investigators would probably have used a $2 \times 2 \times 2$ factorial design, because they tested children of two different age groups (second and fifth grades) on two variables (recall and attending) to determine the effects of two treatments (a film with a male narrator and the same film with a female narrator). Use of analysis of variance would have allowed them to determine the effect of each factor in turn and also the various possible combinations. In actual fact, Klein et al. (1987) did report a combination effect: second graders showed a significant difference on attending in favor of the male narrator.

5. She is restricted in her choice of design for several reasons. The most obvious is that her study is actually observational and not truly experimental. That is, it is a "natural experiment" in which she intends to study the "treatment" applied by nature. In effect, the treatment is the disorder of anosognosia acting in concert with unilateral neglect. So rather than apply a treatment, she would need to locate, in sufficient numbers, two groups of neurological patients: one whose members exhibit unilateral neglect only and another whose members have that disorder and anosognosia. If she considers the disorders to be a form of treatment, she could consider one of the experimental designs, the nonequivalent control group design (design 3). She could not, of course, apply a pretest, because she cannot identify ahead of time who will develop the disorders. The randomized posttest-only control group design (design 5) would be the strongest choice, but she could not randomly assign the subjects to each group, as they have to suffer from each particular disease. In actuality, she would have to conduct a series of case studies (design 1).

Consequently, her study would be subject to a variety of threats to internal validity (LP), the most serious of which are selection, local history, and maturation. The first is important because it might be argued that the subjects who volunteered (or whose families agreed to the study) might well differ from those who did not. The second, local history, is a serious threat because the severity of these syndromes varies with such factors as patient stress and fatigue. The third, maturation, is perhaps the biggest threat, as patients do tend to get better. Since the numbers of such patients are small, she may be compelled to assess various subjects in different stages of the progress of disease.

She might be able to control for the threats of local history and maturation by using a variation on the time-series design and conducting several assessments of each of the subjects throughout their convalescence. The problem of selection, however, may be difficult to avoid, since the numbers of such patients are small, and the researcher may have to accept the patients to whom she can gain access.

CHAPTER 19

1. Remember that the basis of the historical method is interpretation, the extent of which varies with the author, the author's purpose, and the reader's own perceptions. Internal validity (LP) is demonstrated by means of a strong organizing rationale, one that effectively shows a correspondence between the explanation (the construct) and the evidence (the data). Burton developed her theme first from historical sources and then supported it with an analysis of an exhaustive series of studies (475) drawn from a 40-year period. She further strengthened her rationale by tying her themes to contemporary social analysis. Her rationale makes sense based on her selective interpretation of the evidence.

2. Laslett has tried to show causality. She has presented a thesis: that the role of the family has changed from preindustrial to modern times and that society is now dependent on it for the development of personal identity and the satisfaction of personal needs. To support her argument, she has tried to demonstrate a pattern of multiple causes all acting together to produce the current situation. To be convincing, she needed to satisfy the conditions for inferring causation. Does her rationale fit the data? Does it make sense? Although insufficient information has been presented in this summary to permit judgment, she seems to have put forward a convincing argument.

3. This researcher had the usual problem in after-the-fact natural experiments of ensuring comparable groups. These were descriptive studies designed to measure the impact of existing school programs. Consequently, Genesee could not manipulate the treatment to ensure the equivalence of the members of the experimental (immersion-program) and control (regular-program) groups on all variables except the treatment. Entry in such programs is voluntary, and the investigator would have been dependent on existing groups. Thus although he was able to match the groups on socioeconomic status and IQ test scores, he could not be certain that there were not differences between the two groups such as attitude toward schooling that could have affected his measures. Otherwise his data are convincing. Do you regard such explanations as sufficiently plausible to pose a threat?

4. It was an after-the-fact natural experiment. The investigators were unable to control the variable of interest, which was the possession of baccalaureate nursing training. They were, however, able to select a stratified random sample, which provided them with comparable groups in most respects. They could not, however, control for self-selection. This, since they are arguing for baccalaureate preparation for nurses, is an important alternative explanation. Perhaps nurses who complete the higher degree have greater ability (for example, intelligence) or are more strongly motivated. It may be that these characteristics are responsible for the difference in these competencies and would display their effect regardless of education.

Also, to agree with their conclusion, one would have to accept De Back and Mentkowski's definition of nursing competencies. Does their rationale make sense? Does it support their hypotheses? Though not presented in this summary, the investigators did indeed develop their hypotheses from a theoretical basis and from past research evidence. The operationalization of the hypotheses also appears to be sound since the codebook was developed from the descriptions by the actual subjects of effective and ineffective nursing behavior.

CHAPTER 20

1. Though there are elements of research involved here, this is formative evaluation. It is decision-driven, designed to render judgments about what to include in the programs (pedagogical decisions) and whether particular program segments appeal to and are understood by the intended audience (programming decisions). The emphasis is on in-house teamwork in which a consensus is sought at each stage of development. The purpose is to make production decisions rather than to test hypotheses about the effectiveness of programs as instructional treatments.

2. They would likely have used a management-oriented approach like that of Rossi and Freeman. The intent of this evaluation was to provide information that would improve the administration of the particular intervention, the DEEP program. Their client was the local director, who was interested in assessment of classroom impact, coverage of all the affected teachers in the districts, and the delivery of service. However, since there were many stakeholders, including the program's sponsors (the state education department and the joint council) and the clients of the program (the school districts' administrators and the teachers), whose input might have been important, a qualitative or participant-oriented approach might have been both informative and politically expedient in gathering evidence responsive to their concerns.

3. The evaluation of teaching competency, looked at from the administrators' point of view, requires current knowledge of both teaching practice and curriculum. But since utilization is a prime criterion for an evaluation and since these evaluations will clearly affect stakeholders such as the teachers evaluated, they are of concern to more than the sponsor. Further, they may well be affected by local circumstances of which teachers would be aware (teaching practice certainly being different in a large city from that in a rural setting). Therefore, some kind of evaluation that involved the stakeholders in the development of the evaluation process would be important: teachers, parents, school board, administrators, and experts in the evaluation of teaching would need to be included (though members of the stakeholder group guiding the evaluation might study the literature to become their own experts).

A common strategy is to develop a standard teacher evaluation procedure with an appeal process. A fair process should take into account the five criteria mentioned in the chapter. Thus the evaluation should be structured, making clear who will make the judgment, when, and on the basis of what criteria. These criteria should be jointly developed by the stakeholders and be made publicly available in written form. Such evaluations should be conducted by more than one person—for example, by two different school administrators or peers. A written report of the evaluation should be given to the teacher with the opportunity to respond and, if possible (or desired), have the evaluation judged by a review group seleted to be fair (again, possibly including peers).

4. Since you want to understand what is truly happening at the home, you would need to collect information that is responsive to the staff and residents as well as the directors. This is, in effect, a case study. In this situation, a naturalistic, or qualitative, approach, in which you conduct unstructured interviews or engage in participant observation, would be most informative. Entering with few preconceptions, you may get a better grasp of the differing perceptions of the people involved, understand the pluralistic nature of the situation, and come up with alternative recommendations. Perhaps only by involving the staff and the residents in every stage of the evaluation will you be able to overcome suspicions and resentment and make a viable recommendation.

CHAPTER 21

1. This study is both cross-sectional and longitudinal. At each testing, Terman was able to compare subjects and spouses of different ages (cross-sectionally). The second testing after 12 years allowed him to compare each subject against his or her previous performance on the test (longitudinally). The sets of data supplement each other. The use of both techniques allowed the investigator to circumvent two major problems of conducting this study solely as a longitudinal one. The alternative might have been to follow one age group for a long period (40 to 50 years). He would have had both the problem of keeping his panel together over an extended period of time and guaranteeing that he himself would be around.

2. This depends on whether you agree that the investigators were measuring the right things and that they have controlled for alternate explanations. Translation fidelity is strengthened by using well-known, validated tests and by collecting data using two different instruments. The investigators eliminated many potentially troublesome alternate explanations. For instance, although complete data have not been provided here on subject mortality, the investigators were presumably using very large samples with subjects of varying backgrounds and grade levels and could compensate for lost cases. They were able to use demographic information to indicate that the overall makeup of the targeted schools had not changed substantially during the study. They avoided the threat of instrument decay by using both low-inference tests and two measures of achievement. The history effect threat was countered with demographic data and the time-series design, which allowed them to demonstrate a steady improvement. A particular event would have showed up as an unusual set of results for one particular year. Finally, perhaps the greatest threat to their study was the explanation of reactivity—in this case, the teachers reacting to the court order with a superhuman effort. It is questionable whether such an effort could have been maintained over 10 years, however, and the researchers were able to demonstrate a comparable improvement in schools using the AGP and not affected by the court order. The conclusion appears to be justified.

3. The investigators clearly succeeded in improving the girl's behaviors as defined by them. Their claims for the cause of this success (concomitant praise and a token economy system) have to be tempered by several other factors. First, there were other treatments: the consistent feedback in the form of charting daily behavior, the setting of goals, the personal attention, and the student's own interest in the program. These likely contributed to the results but were not controlled during the study. Another possible factor influencing academic improvement was improved instruction in terms of the specificity of the directions given to the subject. There may as well have been a reactivity effect due to the unusual circumstances. The combined praise and token economy treatment probably had an effect, as indicated by the demonstrated change in behavior, but was likely a necessary but not sufficient condition.

Considering that behavior deteriorated during condition B, it is possible that the results of condition C might have been even more impressive had it not been preceded by condition B.

There may also have been regression toward the mean. The burst of abnormal behavior during the praise phase might have been followed by a return-to-normal phase that may have been further affected by the token economy phase.

The case would have been much stronger had the researchers used an ABCDC design where D would have been the token economy alone. If the treatments were mutually reinforcing, we would expect a deterioration of behavior over the D condition and its restoration during the second C condition.

4. Given that the authors are noting trends, their assumptions appear reasonable. Though we may disagree with the groupings they used to analyze their data, they have, on the one hand, used a straightforward classification system for dividing the studies into homogeneous groups for analysis and hence for examining the relationship between independent and dependent groups. They have also used each study only once for a particular conclusion and have included unpublished as well as published sources.

On the other hand, the investigators have not provided any criteria for inclusion of studies. It is implied, but not stated, that they used every study that they could find. Their conclusions should be interpreted with caution.

CHAPTER 22

1. (a) Does the test measure what it is purported to measure? We might factor-analyze the test items to determine whether the factor pattern that emerges corresponds to the characteristics the test was designed to measure. If it does not, we might determine whether the test should be revised to include relevant aspects that were not measured. It might also show that relevant aspects not designed to be measured were included in the test.

(b) Does the test improve prediction of success in the program? Using multiple regression, we might combine the new test with others previously used to predict success and determine whether the multiple correlation with grade point average is improved.

(c) What criteria of success does the prediction battery now measure? Using multiple measures of success, such as faculty judgments of creativity, awards in exhibitions, and peer nominations of individuals most likely to succeed, we might develop a canonical correlation between the prediction battery and the measures of success to see which aspects are predicted and which are not. This might show where to improve the battery.

(d) Does the new prediction battery discriminate potential dropouts better than the previous one? Waiting until dropout data were available, we might compare the previous prediction batteries' discriminant analysis of dropouts from stayers with the battery augmented by the new test.

2. His exeriment is a relatively simple design involving a comparison between an experimental treatment and a control group. Since he will be calculating the mean difference in attitude toward mathematics over the semester for each group, he would be justified in choosing a t test for the difference between two means.

3. Since they have recorded their data here as categorical judgments (each judged as "whether or not") rather than as scaled ratings, the appropriate choice would be a chi-square used to test the difference between frequencies. It would allow them to judge whether there was any significant difference in ratings among the different groups. The test should preferably be used with fairly large samples.

4. Yes, the ANOVA allowed them to analyze, first, whether or not the set of results, as a whole, was attributable to chance. They then followed this up with planned comparisons between means. Their choice of ANOVA was appropriate for several reasons. They needed a method for testing the differences among several means. Using *t* tests would leave them susceptible to the problem of inflation of probabilities. In this case, they compared 18 different groups, including various combined scores (for example, high ability for males, females, and combined genders), and could expect at least one significant result just by chance (1 in 20). The use of ANOVA instead allowed the investigators to avoid this problem and also to test quickly and easily for an effect distinct from sampling and other types of error. Further, since ANOVA is robust (effective even when its assumptions are violated), they had randomly selected fairly large samples and could assume a fairly normal distribution. Therefore, ANOVA was an appropriate technique for analyzing their samples.

Was fixed-effect ANOVA correct? Gender is clearly a fixed variable, in that it does not represent a random sample of measures of treatments. But the measure of ability and the way the treatments were administered were intended to be representative of ability measures and of other ways of working cooperatively on problems, so these are random variables in the ANOVA sense. Hence, the researchers have a mixed model.

They could instead have used multiple regression analysis, which would have provided them with an indication of the strength of each relationship as well as an indication of effect. However, they were apparently interested in whether or not the predicted effects occurred rather than how much of a difference there was.

CHAPTER 23

1. In this basic research study, in which the investigator is interested in understanding and describing the phenomenon of incest, strong internal validity (LP) is the key criterion. This very study was carried out by Patricia Phelan (1987) in San Francisco. She was able to mix qualitative and quantitative methodology in an innovative way to explain the phenomenon. To gain entry, she became involved as an intern counselor in the treatment program and began with an ethnographic study using participant observation. This allowed her to understand the treatment community, including clients and staff, and the treatment model used.

Once accepted, she was able to conduct intensive interviews to reveal the family dynamics involved. Since surveys and other quanititative methods were not permitted and interviews with the large number of families was not feasible, Phelan conducted structured interviews with the counselors to gather detailed descriptions of the incestuous relationships. From this she was able to carry out a numeric analysis and test for statistical significance. Combining the two types of data, numeric and narrative, provided her with a comprehensive picture of the phenomenon.

2. The investigators made trade-offs, in terms of both subjects and situation. First, they chose to study people with a very specific problem, prostate cancer. Thus the treatment was limited to mostly older men with that disease who had agreed to undergo radiation therapy. This would have helped to ensure that the sample would consist of people coping with a stressful experience who were representative of the target population. They would also presumably be susceptible to the treatment—the coping information. And finally, the group was homogeneous, both in factors such as age and sex and also with respect to various clinical variables related to their disease and medical treatment. These factors all help to strengthen the internal validity (LP).

But it would be difficult to generalize beyond such a narrow group to patients with different characteristics or coping with different problems.

Second, even though the theories could be relevant to coping with other aspects of physical illness, such as being diagnosed with a life-threatening disease or having to live with a chronic, debilitating illness, the investigators restricted this to the study of coping with a stressful medical treatment. The situation was a hospital-based treatment program (an acute-care setting). This provided a number of benefits related to greater control such as assurance that treatment preceded effect, more chance of elimination of a number of rival hypotheses (for example, other contacts providing information to help cope), and greater fidelity of the treatment since the stressful experience would also take place at this setting. But as before, it would be hard to generalize beyond this circumstance.

3. These investigators made choices concerning subjects, situation, and treatment. By conducting several studies with the same materials, they were, in effect, increasing sample size and hence the statistical sensitivity to the effect of the treatment. Since they were able to replicate their results with a different age group and in a more natural environment (the classroom), they were able to increase the generalizability of their results. With that exception, however, their subjects were a narrow sample: undergraduate university students who had volunteered to gain credits. This acted to decrease generalizability.

All but one of the studies were conducted in the laboratory. This provided the benefits, again, of greater control over treatment. Thus the researchers increased assurance that treatment preceded effect, eliminated rival hypotheses and random effects contributing to variability of behavior, and provided greater fidelity of treatment since they were able to control its administration. It also helped, presumably, to keep the costs to a minimum. In addition, except for the grade 7 group, institutional restrains were likely minimal. Even then, the children attended a university experimental school. These are typically set up to encourage research and would present fewer constraints than a regular school. Regardless, the study in the school represented a natural use of the treatment and helped increase generality.

One factor helping decrease control was the need to give delayed recall tests. Hence the subjects would not have been under laboratory control for the duration of the study. There would have been some threat of diffusion as the students would have had the chance to discuss the study. Further, the laboratory situation would have increased the potential for reactivity.

Finally, asking the subjects to read these a second time may have increased the intensity of the treatment and thereby increased the sensitivity of the statistical test. Though unusual, such rereading is not impractical.

4. The investigators used multiple measures of the construct "counselor effectiveness." This would have increased the internal validity (LP) by making it more likely that its essential characteristics were covered. Since they used different testing techniques, method effects would have been minimized. The follow-up tests increased the number of observations and allowed detection of any residual effects, in this case, the retention of the counseling skills training. However, the large number of observations increased the opportunity for instrument decay error and also for testing-treatment interaction.

Further, the use of a pretest-and-posttest design had its effects as well. It allowed the investigators to ensure the equivalence of the treatment and control groups and, since they demonstrated the reliability of their measures, to be sure that a change actually took place. Again, the negative was the likelihood of testing and testing-treatment interaction.

Finally, the use of volunteers for the follow-up probably inflated that measure of effect because 10 of the original 32—nearly a third—were not followed up. No information is given as to whether the mortality was equal among groups, but if not, that might have compounded the problem.

CHAPTER 24

1. These researchers are clearly synthesizers. Their stated intention was to "unravel the patterns of socio-structural relations" in the artisanal bakery trade, that is, to produce an explanation embodying the essential characteristics of the phenomenon. Their central hypotheses were grounded in their data. Further, though they used more than one research method (specifically, field studies and historical description), they are not multiperspectivists. In fact, they label themselves as adhering to a particular socio-logical school, the structuralist-Marxist. Rather than explain the artisanal bakery phenomenon from different perspectives, they have synthesized several into one narrative explanation.

2. (a) This quote is by B. F. Skinner as reported by Green (1984, p. 24). Skinner at different times could be characterized as a pragmatist or a theorist. In this quote, he is demonstrating his pragmatist orientation. He is indicating that a principle, the scheduling of reinforcements, works; that is, it "guarantees a great deal of successful action" and therefore predicts learning.

(b) This quote, by Wittrock (1974, p. 182), sounds like the writing of a theorist. He is advancing a theory, the generative learning hypothesis, to explain a phenomenon, learning with understanding. But it is difficult to tell from only this much evidence. He could be an analyst; he uses the term *hypothesis*. This could be an analyzer's lead-in to a study involving a specific proposition to be tested.

3. This study was not multiperspectivist as the term is used in this chapter. Multiperspectivists operate using multiple hypotheses and attempt to explain a phenomenon from competing viewpoints—for example, Marxist and capitalist expla-nations of economics. These authors are testing several complementary and related propositions: what are the relationships between different perspectives of young school children's adjustment; what is the relationship of adjustment to achievement; and how do suburban children compare to urban children and referred children to nonreferred children? The investigators attempted to answer these questions from different meas-urement perspectives, but it is questionable whether or not these could be considered as "competing." McKim and Cowen are perhaps best characterized as analyzers who attempt to test and confirm these propositions empirically.

4. (a) This quote is taken from an article on action research by Noffke and Zeichner (1987, p. 3). At first, it sounds like a particularist's point of view—"research [with each other] to become agents of their own change." But a particularist would stop with the "idiosyncratic setting" and not go on to an identification of general principles. So the researchers are somewhere on the right-hand side of our orientation continuum, using a collaborative approach; they are probably synthesizers. We would need more evidence to tell.

(b) This is a quote from Schon (1983, p. 68), *The Reflective Practitioner*. The author, describing the practicing professional (doctor, teacher, etc.) as a researcher-in-action, actually bridges several orientations. In the quote, he appears to be advocating a particularist approach in that he is emphasizing personal patterns and context-bound knowledge. However, he is also describing the reflective practitioner; that is, he is trying to explain a phenomenon and could fit either the synthesizer or the theorist mode. The quote does not provide enough information for us to decide.

(c) This quote was taken from a discussion of nursing theory (Malinski, 1986, p. 74). It is suggesting an appropriate research technique for conducting investigations based on this theory. The theory is considered humanist, and Baldwin's technique, focusing on the unique thought structure of one person, indicates a humanist orienta-tion as well. The thorough analysis of one person's individual pattern would presum-ably provide a model to further human understanding and perhaps to guide future research.

(d) Paterson and Zderad (1988, p. 3) are actually synthesizers rather than humanists as the book title implies. They are advocating here a phenomenological approach to nursing research that advances participant observation as a methodology. The intention is to gather "complementary syntheses" and, over time, to build "a science of nursing." Unlike humanists or particularists, they have adapted a physical science model that seeks context-free generalizations.

CHAPTER 25

1. The dilemma is the choice between the rights of the patients and the responsibilities of the regulatory agencies. The latter must ensure valid assessment of the drugs before their general use is allowed. Balancing this are the rights of terminally ill patients to any treatment that might offer them a chance of life. This may be a situation in which the cost to the subjects (probable death) outweighs the gain in knowledge about an effective treatment for a deadly disease, as is evidenced by the 1989 decision by the U.S. Food and Drug Administration to modify its policies and make certain of these drugs more readily available. However, the decision is not simple even concerning the cost to the patient with AIDS. A drug that has not been thoroughly tested may well be discovered to have side effects that worsen the patient's condition rather than ameliorate it. There is a cost to society as well. Properly controlled tests of these drugs may be necessary in order to allow medical researchers to build knowledge about the disease and eventually find a control or a cure. Premature distribution of a particular drug may well impede research into its effectiveness.

2. The problem is one of confidentiality. Researchers generally have no immunity from subpoena unless granted special immunity by government bodies such as the National Institutes of Health or the Department of Justice. For homosexuals and drug abusers, breaches of confidentiality could result in great social harm, including imprisonment and a criminal record, loss of employment, or loss of insurance. Furthermore, the disease of AIDS itself carries a stigma. Understandably, many members of at risk populations would be reluctant to jeopardize their privacy in order to participate in research on this problem. To gain access to these important groups, researchers have to take extraordinary steps to ensure the privacy of their subjects.

3. There is a possible invasion of privacy here with legal implications that should concern both the investigator and the superintendent. It involves the issues of gaining access to and ownership of the data and obtaining consent. It appears that the superintendent released information from confidential files without the permission of the teachers involved. Since the consent of particular teachers was not sought or obtained, the question becomes one of ownership of the data. Were the data contained in the files the sole property of the school system, in which case the superintendent may have been within his rights, or was this a case of joint ownership? Without seeking the involvement and permission of the teachers, both the superintendent and the investigator could be leaving themselves open to grievance and possibly litigation. Their best course of action would have been to obtain consent before the release of the information.

4. Yes, he should have obtained the consent of each child's parent or guardian and also of the children themselves. His institutional review board should have required him to determine if the children were willing to give assent. Furthermore, since his experiment seems likely to produce psychological discomfort in at least some of the subjects, in obtaining consent from the children, he would have the responsibility to make clear the nature of the task and, perhaps, to debrief the children afterward.

5. This controversial experiment was conducted as described by Piliavin and Piliavin (1972). It clearly involved deception and also likely invoked considerable anxiety on the part of subjects who were not given the opportunity to consent to the treatment. It was actually quickly terminated because of dramatic participant reactions and the possible danger to them as well as a result of harassment from subway police. The research was inspired by the highly publicized attack and murder of a young woman in plain daylight, observed by a number of people who did nothing to help. The research problem thus appeared to have significant social value (the gain). It was conducted surreptitiously in order to create a "natural" situation and allow "valid," interpretable results. The cost was to the subjects who had not consented, may have experienced negative effects, and certainly gained no direct benefit (other than perhaps the satisfaction of assisting a fellow citizen).

6. The question of ethics in the study by Daniels (1983) focuses on deception. There does not appear to be any serious breach of ethics. The respondents were informed that Daniels was conducting a research study and had consented to participate. The question the investigator was asking was whether or not she had deceived these women by appearing to have developed a friendship and then letting it lapse as the study wound down. Since friendships usually have a basis in some common interest and since the investigator was not otherwise involved in these charities, this may well have been the natural course of events.

Glossary

The number following each entry indicates the page in the text where the term is first discussed. You are encouraged to consult the glossary regarding the meaning of key terms when reviewing material as well as when studying. The necessarily succinct statements in the glossary may pull together the material in ways that are helpful. Use the index to find additional places in the book where the term is discussed. For a few terms, the most complete discussion may be considerably after their first mention.

AB design A time-series design in which a control phase called the baseline (A) usually precedes a treatment phase (B). 559

Acceptance The process in qualitative research by which the people being observed become sufficiently accustomed to the observer that their behavior is normal. 320

Adversarial evaluation The process whereby evaluation teams prepare cases for opposite sides of an issue and present them to judges or a jury in a quasi-judicial proceeding. 536

After-the-fact natural experiments Studies in which the data are assembled after the presumed cause and effect occurred in an attempt to demonstrate a causal relationship. Also called *ex post facto studies* and causal comparative studies. 514

Agreement (method of) If two situations of a phenomenon under investigation have only one circumstance in common, the instance in which they agree is presumed to be causally related to the phenomenon. 247

Alpha coefficient A measure of internal consistency reliability. 209

Alpha error Type I error. 426

Alpha level The percentage of instances, on the average, that a researcher will conclude that a value is atypical (there is a statistically significant difference) when in fact it is not (there is none). 416

Alternative conditions Conditions sufficient for an effect to occur, but since the effect may occur in the absence of the conditions as well, they are not necessary. 253

Alternative explanations See *rival explanations*.

Analysis of covariance A statistical technique for adjusting the means of groups for the effect of an unwanted variable. 604

Analysis of variance (ANOVA) Estimates of the population variance are made from the variability between groups (which is presumed to be affected by the intervention or independent variable of interest) and from the within-group variability (which is not so influenced). Comparison of estimates from these two sources shows whether the former is larger than the latter by a ratio (F ratio) greater than would be expected by the influence of random sampling and chance error. 597

Analytic induction Finding commonalities and regularities in qualitative data, seeking their explanation, and finding other situations in which to test the generality of that explanation. 324

Analyzers Researchers who see challenging and validating hypotheses as the main business of science. They are like the natural scientists in method and outlook. 628

Audience credibility   Judgment on the part of the audience of the credibility they are willing to grant the researcher for having made good judgments in the design and implementation of the study, especially for aspects not directly described in the report. 296

Authenticity of evidence   Reassurance that the evidence is what it purports to be—for example, that a test score represents a sample of a particular individual's behavior and not someone else's. 251

Authority   A figure who believably asserts that something is true either without explanation or rationale (*dogmatic authority*) or with it (*reasoning authority*). 48

Balance of internal validity (LP) and external validity (GP)   Balancing the study's capacity to link cause and effect with its capacity to show the generality of the relationship. Internal validity (LP), linking cause and effect, can be strengthened by tight controls and/or using a laboratory. These characteristics decrease external validity (GP), generality, which is strengthened by using natural—usually field—conditions. 300

Baseline phase   The phase of a time-series design during which the natural state of the subject is determined before the intervention is applied. 559

Base rate   The rate at which an event occurs naturally. When not taken into account, the base rate may affect study outcomes in ways that are confounded with treatment. 464

Basis for sensing attributes or changes   The basis on which we can determine whether an attribute is present or there was a change in the dependent variable as a result of the independent variable or treatment. 61

Behavioral objectives   Objectives stated in terms of the behavior to be learned or acquired with respect to specified content. 529

Beta error   Type II error. 426

Bias   In sampling, an influence that systematically prevents obtaining a representative sample. 129

Blocking   Grouping individuals with a similar level on a characteristic perceived to be related to the effect. See also *stratified sampling*. 598

Borderline cases   Cases used in conceptual analysis to help define the boundaries of the term being analyzed. 149

Buckley amendment   A federal law that protects the privacy of information held by an institution or an organization regarding an individual until it is released by the individual or his or her guardian. 671

Camouflage   A method of control whereby a characteristic that is otherwise prominent is made to become part of the background. 449

Canonical correlation   The prediction of a criterion composed of two or more dependent variables by two or more independent variables. 584

Case study   A careful, in-depth study of an individual or a situation usually using qualitative research methods; in quantitative research, an application of treatment followed by observation and measurement. 347

Causal chain   The sequence of events that results in an effect. 240

Causal modeling   See *structural modeling*. 588

Chain of reasoning   The steps in the presentation of a logical argument in support of a knowledge claim. 58

Chain referral sampling   See *snowball sampling*.

Chi-square   A statistic that helps determine whether the pattern of frequencies found in data assigned to categories is likely due to chance or is atypical. Also used to compare data with a model to determine whether the data's fit is within the typical range of sampling and chance error. Also used to combine the results of independently conducted studies to determine overall statistical significance. 593

Citation indexing   Indexing of all references during a given time period that cited a given journal article including when and where cited. 111

Classification schemes   Schemes that classify events into an organization or a structure that in some way reflects a causal or developmental relationship and thus is a weak form of causal explanation. 261

Clocklike world A conception of causation as resulting from tightly coupled events, such as the meshing of a train of gears. 243

Cloudlike world A conception of causation as resulting from loosely coupled events such as a cloud of gnats always maintaining a cloud rather than dispersing. 243

Cluster sampling Random samples of cells in a geographic grid placed over a map, or random samples of units organized on some prior basis such as schoolrooms. 134

Code of ethics A set of rules for ethical behavior; usually drawn up by a professional organization for the guidance of its members. 666

Coding Categories of recurring facts, themes, comments, and the like selected from fieldnotes for attention because they are likely to help explain a situation of interest. Once established, new fieldnotes are coded into these categories. 336

Cohort studies Studies of change over time using a constant population but taking new samples during each data-gathering period. 365

Common ownership of information A norm of science that states that information is owned by all and is to be shared freely. Researchers have an obligation to share their findings through universally available publications. Data should be shared on request once its use by the researcher is completed. Supporting data for knowledge claims should be open to examination by others. 52

Computer-assisted telephone interviewing (CATI) Random-digit dialing used to select a sample randomly from among telephone subscribers for interviews. The computer is programmed to determine whether the respondent fits the quota sample, what questions to ask, and in what order. Responses *immediately* entered directly into the computer are checked for consistency and errors. 373

Computer search Use of a computer to find specific terms in relevant sections of a computer-readable version of an abstracting or indexing source or to search the entire source for those terms—an utterly impractical task with the printed version. 115

Conceptual analysis A process for finding the characteristics that define a term. Especially useful for defining constructs and concepts. 147

Concomitant variation (method of) Phenomena that consistently vary together are presumed to be connected to one another, directly or indirectly, through a causal relationship. 249

Concurrent validity A test correlates with a criterion measure obtained at the same time as the test was administered. 201

Confidence interval An interval constructed around an observed value such as a test score or a mean within which the true value is believed to lie with a confidence expressed by certain odds. The greater the odds (e.g., from 19 to 1 to 100 to 1) and the less reliable the test, the wider the confidence interval. 215

Confidence level The odds we are willing to accept that express our confidence that the population value is contained within the confidence interval. 408

Confidence limit One end of a confidence interval. 408

Confidentiality Refers to control of access to information gathered during research or obtained for other purposes but made available for research purposes. Assurance is given that none other than persons working on the study will have access to the data without the subject's permission. Typically, identifying information is destroyed as soon as no longer needed for research purposes. 670

Confounding Reflecting the fact that two or more variables that might have caused an effect were simultaneously present, so that we do not know to which to attribute the effect. 454

Congruence of explanation and evidence Evidence that an effect occurred agrees with the explanation advanced for the cause-and-effect relationship; a condition strengthening the inference of causation. 252

Consensus The agreement of individuals making separate knowing judgments. 40

Constant comparison method   Fieldnotes are coded as the study progresses, and new instances of a dimension or a concept of interest are sought until *saturation* (which see). These concepts are linked with others to develop a theory or an explanation that is constantly compared with new data from the field. Discrepancies call for modification or additions that increase understanding. 325

Construct   A concept of which we have a mental image but that has no direct physical referents; an abstract noun. 147

Construct validity   A test behaves as the definition of the construct predicts that it should. 199

Consumer-oriented evaluation   An evaluation intended to serve the information needs of consumers; contrasts with management-oriented approaches. 533

Content validity   Comparison of the items of the test with a table of specifications or test blueprint to determine if the items representatively sample the behaviors and content of the subject matter the test is intended to cover. Also called *curricular validity*. 202

Contingent condition   A condition that is necessary for an effect to occur but not sufficient to make it appear. 257

Contrary cases   Cases that are sufficiently beyond the boundaries of a term that they help delineate its boundary; used in conceptual analysis to help establish defining characteristics of a term. 149

Contributing conditions   Conditions that make an effect more likely to occur but are neither necessary nor sufficient to cause it to appear. 259

Controlled vocabulary   The dictionary or thesaurus that lists the stable set of subject-matter terms used to describe abstracts or index entries. 106

Correction for attenuation   A formula for correcting a correlation coefficient for unreliability in the measures and estimating the size of the relationship if the reliability were perfect. 211

Correlation   See *Pearson product-moment correlation*.

Cost-benefit analysis   Determination of the costs of achieving certain benefits. 532

Cost-effectiveness analysis   Determination of the cost of achieving certain levels of effectiveness. 532

Counterbalanced designs   Studies designed such that if two or more treatments are administered in sequence, the treatments are administered in all possible sequences so as to reveal and eliminate the effect of ordering. 483

Counterbalancing   In equivalence reliability, eliminating the effect of the order in which two tests were taken by giving half the group one order and the other half the reverse order and analyzing the combined results. 210

Covariance modeling   See *structural modeling*.

Covert participant observation   An observation method whereby the observer becomes part of the situation in such a way that individuals are not aware they are being observed. 316

Credible result   A summary judgment of the conceptual and empirical evidence for internal validity (LP) together with a judgment of the consistency of the evidence with prior studies, which results in a determination of the internal validity (LP) of the study. 272

Criterion   A measure generally accepted as valid; a measure to be predicted; a standard to be attained. 198; 580

Criterion-referenced tests   Tests whose scoring is based on meeting the mastery requirements of a content area rather than placing the score in the context of a reference group like norm-referenced tests. 223

Criterion-related validity   See *concurrent validity* and *predictive validity*.

Cronbach's alpha   See *alpha coefficient*.

Cross-break   See *cross-tabulation*.

Cross-references   Alternative terms that might also be used to describe a particular word or phrase to which the reader is referred by an abstracting or indexing service. 107

Cross-sectional studies Studies of change that compare current individuals of different age or experience on the variable of interest rather than waiting for change over time. 364

Cross-tabulation Tabulation of data in terms of two or more variables. For example, respondents' choices of each of five possible answers to a question are tabulated; the tabulations for each response are then categorized by another variable, such as gender. Results would be displayed in a 2 (male, female) × 5 (the possible responses) table with the frequency of responses displayed in each cell. 389

Debriefing Informing an individual who has been deceived in an experiment of that fact and assuaging any unfortunate consequences. 660

Deception of subjects Involvement in an experiment in which subjects are told that one thing is occurring when the point of interest is really something else. 669

Decision-driven evaluation An evaluation used to help in the making of a decision, thus influencing both development and implementation. 524

Degrees of freedom The number of data entries free to vary when their total is fixed. 596

Demand characteristics Responses that subjects perceive as required by the study. 476

"Demonstrated generality" Evidence that the effect appeared in instances where it was expected within the limits of generality provided by the study and did not show where it should not have. 282

Demonstrated result Evidence that four conditions were met: (1) the evidence was accepted as authentic, (2) cause preceded or was concomitant with effect, (3) an effect occurred and was sensed—if sensed by inferential statistics, these were correctly applied and interpreted, and (4) the effect was congruent with the expectations created by the explanation, hypothesis, prediction, or model. 272

Dependent variable A variable presumed to be affected by a treatment or by an independent variable. 27

Derived score A standard score in which the mean and the standard deviation have been changed to numbers chosen for ease of interpretation or computation. Also called *scaled score*. 174

Description The perception, naming, organizing and verbally portraying of a situation to highlight its important features, to put those features in context, and to show the interrelations among them. 5

Design A translation of questions, hypotheses, or models into choices of subjects, situations, treatments, observation or measurement, basis for sensing attributes or changes, and procedure so that greater understanding or validation of the former results. 61

Differences (method of) A situation in which a phenomenon occurs and one in which it does not occur are exactly alike save for one circumstance in the former. The circumstance in which they differ is presumed to be causally related to the phenomenon. 248

Diffusion Spread of a treatment to the control group; spread of a finding to the people who can make use of it. 467

Discriminant function analysis Determination of the capacity of two or more independent variables to predict correctly the categorization of individuals scaled on a nominal variable. 585

Disconfirmation The process of trying to invalidate a proposition. Causal relations can never be proved; there may always be some as yet untested circumstance under which the relationship does not hold. With each successful test, the relation is said to have escaped disconfirmation. 242

Disinterestedness Ignoring personal advantage when interpreting data. 52

Dogmatic authorities See *authority*.

Double-barreled question   Two questions rolled into one, making it impossible to determine to which the respondent is responding. 380

Double-blind procedures   Neither the subject nor the treatment administrator knows whether the treatment being given is a placebo or the actual treatment. 468

Effect size   The average size in standard deviation units of an effect as determined by data combined from several studies. 565

Empirical keying   The answer scored is determined by the answers given by some criterion group and discriminate that group from others. 221

Equivalence reliability   Evidence that a test measures consistently across different equivalent forms. 206

Estimation   The process in statistical inference whereby a confidence interval is constructed around an observed value within which the population value is presumed to lie with a confidence expressed by odds (such as 19 to 1). 406

Ethical standards   Rules that set limits on what can be done in good faith in a study; one of three constraints on research. 304

Evaluation   Determination of the worth or value of something in order to decide whether to continue it, how to improve it, or how to adjust it to the needs of a certain clientele or management. 525

Expertise-oriented evaluation   Judgments by experts of the value or worth of something. 534

Explanation, rationale, theory, point of view   A description of the relationship among variables that portrays the sequence of events and attributes causal and moderating roles to certain variables or events in that sequence or, where this is not yet possible, as much of such description as the current state of knowledge permits. 6; 60

Explanation credibility   The plausibility of the explanation advanced for a phenomenon. 272

Explanation generality   The generality that is claimed, implied, or must be inferred from the study's problem statement. 281

Exploration   To examine phenomena that have not previously been studied in the same way; to try different things in a situation to determine what happens; to examine previously examined situations from new points of view to see whether a difference is significant. 5

Ex post facto studies   See *after-the-fact natural experiments.*

External validity   The capacity of a study to support inferences regarding the study to other persons, situations, and measures. 270

External validity (GP)   The generalizing power (GP) of a study; the power of a study to permit inferences regarding the generality of the findings. 269

Face validity   The appearance of being a valid test. 203

Factor analysis   Clustering the variables most highly correlated with each other into homogeneous groups called "factors" and making inferences of the constructs measured by the factors from the size of the variables' correlations with them. 200

Factorial design   A study design in which data on every combination of variables in the study are provided by a separate group from which their effect can be determined. 485

Fieldnotes   The observer's records of what has been observed. 329

Fish scale analogy   Knowing judgments made by each person in sequence extending from the researcher to laypersons. Each, being less expert than the previous person, looks at the evidence presented by previous judges and determines whether to accept their judgment. 44

Fixed model   A form of analysis of variance in which the treatments used are exactly those to which the researcher expects to generalize rather than being representative of them. 601

Focus group   A panel, selected to be representative of a population, interviewed on a topic of interest. Probes determine the popularity of various comments and points of view and the depth of feeling toward them. There may also be trials of material to determine how the panel's reactions could be changed. 371

Focused interview   Interview in which the respondent is allowed to set the initial course but increasingly focuses on the researcher's agenda as the interview progresses. 371

Formative evaluation   Evaluation intended to provide information that can be used during the development of a project to guide progress toward its goals. 525

Framing of questions   Stating a question in such a way that the respondent understands and reacts to the question exactly as intended. 380

Frequency distribution   A graphic portraying the frequency with which each score occurred in a set of data, the scores being arranged in order from low to high. 161

Functionally equivalent groups   Groups that function as though they were identical to each other in every way that is relevant to the experiment. 442

Funnel-sequenced questionnaire   A questionnaire that, like the focused interview, begins broadly and narrows to the target of interest. 382

Gaining entry   Obtaining permission to observe a situation from the people in authority as well as from the people to be observed. 319

Gatekeepers   Individuals who give approval to conduct a study, such as institution administrators, school boards, and department heads, who approve the presentation of a study to an audience, such as editors and convention scheduling committees. 50; 319

Generality   The ability to generalize to subjects, situations, treatments, measures, study designs, and procedures other than those used in a given study. 122

Goal-based evaluation   Use of the goals of the project as a basis for evaluation and for determining whether they have been met. 529

Goal-free evaluation   Inferring the goals of a project from observations and measures of what has occurred as a result of the project. These goals, and the success with which they have been achieved, are compared with the intended goals. 530

Hawthorne effect   The subject's perceived feeling of being special as a result of being part of an experiment and the resulting impact on the effectiveness of treatment. 466

Homogeneity of variance   Circumstance wherein the variance of groups differs by no more than would be expected as a result of random sampling and chance error. 603

Humanists   Researchers who explain a particular effect in terms of the occurrence of a certain set of events. They seek the most powerful images and models that foster human understanding. 628

Hypothesis guessing   Subjects' guessing what the researcher has in mind and reacting accordingly. 466

Hypothesis testing   The process in statistical inference whereby the likelihood that an observed value, such as a difference between means, is typical of what might be expected as a result of random sampling variation and chance error (at certain odds, such as 19 to 1, the Type I error we allow) or is atypically larger and therefore the result of some other influence. 413

Independent variable   A variable believed to be a cause. 27; 61

Inferential statistics   Statistics that allow us to estimate population values and to test hypotheses that the results of a study differ from the population value only by amounts typical of random sampling variation and chance error. 404

Informants   Persons selected for their sensitivity, knowledge, and insights into their situation, their willingness to talk about it, and their ability to provide access to new situations. 326

Informed consent   Consent freely given by an individual who has been informed of the nature of the study, understands its procedures, knows who to contact if harmed, and understands he or she may withdraw at any time without malice. 663

Institutional constraints   Constraints imposed on a research study by institutions cooperating with the study's requirements while either keeping their regular program going or interrupting it minimally. 304

Institutional review boards   Boards established by institutions receiving federal research funds that are responsible for ensuring either that individuals involved in the research will not suffer any harmful consequences or that if the possibility of some risk is involved, the benefits outweigh the risks. 661

Instrument decay   A change in the way a measure or observation schedule is used over the course of a study that might provide an explanation for a phenomenon other than the one proposed; in qualitative studies, a change over time in observational point of view or attitude toward the people observed that affects the nature of one's observations in ways one would be concerned about if aware of it. Written about in memos when suspected. 343

Instrument decay by treatment interaction   Treatment-induced change in the way an instrument, measure, or observation schedule is used over the course of a study. 464

Interaction   Potentiation or weakening of the effect of an independent variable or treatment due to the presence of another variable or condition. 464

Internal consistency reliability   Evidence that the items of a test are homogeneous, measure a single construct, and correlate highly with one another and that the score is therefore interpretable. 206

Internal validity   "The capacity of a study to link [its] operational definitions of cause and effect" (Campbell and Stanley, 1963). 270

Internal validity (LP)   The power of a study to link the variables in a relationship— linking power (LP). 269

Interval scale   A scale whose units are presumed to be equal (for example, the difference between a score of 8 and 9 is the same as that between 20 and 21). 160

INUS condition   A particular concatenation of conditions that results in an effect where the conditions taken individually are *insufficient*, *necessary*, *unnecessary*, and *sufficient*. Each cause is insufficient by itself. Each of the conditions must be present for the effect to occur, so together they are necessary. Another set of causes might also bring about the effect, so they are unnecessary. Together they bring about the effect, so they are sufficient. 259

Invented cases   Cases that release the restrictions of reality to see what kind of characteristics might belong to a term being examined in a conceptual analysis. 149

Invisible college   A group of researchers interested in the same problem who communicate regularly with one another by exchanging drafts of articles, corresponding or phoning regarding problems, or trading messages on an electronic bulletin board. 40

Item analysis   A method of improving a test by correlating the items with either the total score or a criterion measure. Reliability is improved by correlating with the total score, keeping only items that correlate highly with it and changing others to be like those kept. Validity is improved by a similar process, except that a valid measure (criterion) is used rather than a total score. 220

Item banking   The development of a comprehensive and redundant set of items testing an area of interest from which items can be drawn to make up a test. 226

Item difficulty index   An index indicating how hard a test item is; usually the percentage of students passing a test item. 220

Item discrimination index   An index indicating the correlation between the item score (say, 1 for correct, 0 for wrong) and some criterion. To improve validity, the criterion is some index of success outside the test; to improve internal consistency reliability, the total test score is used. 220

Judgmental sampling   Samples chosen nonrandomly in such a way as to be representative. 137

Keyword indexing Indexing with a controlled vocabulary descriptive of a field. An article is found by determining the intersection of two or more keywords descriptive of it. 108

Knowing judgment Each individual's judgment of the acceptability of a knowledge claim or, in the case of the original research, a judgment about the appropriate interpretation of the data. 40

Kuder-Richardson reliability A measure of internal consistency reliability. 209

Lagged treatment Treatment applied to individuals at different times to avoid the effect of certain alternative explanations such as local history. 560

Letter of transmittal The letter accompanying a questionnaire that is intended to motivate the respondent to complete and return it. 383

Linear relationship A relationship between two variables best described by a straight line; that is, as one variable increases, the other consistently either increases or decreases proportionately. Also called a *straight-line relationship*. 182

Local history An event that occurs during the course of a treatment that could have the same effect as the treatment. 460

Longitudinal studies Studies of change in a particular individual or group over time. 365

Management-oriented evaluation An evaluation intended to serve the information needs of management in contrast to serving the needs of all stakeholders in a project. 531

Masking A form of control whereby an unwanted variable's effect is mitigated by a stronger variable that blocks the unwanted one from perception by subjects. 449

Maturation Changes that occur in subjects over the course of a study that, because they could also have caused the effect, are confounded with it; includes such changes as growing tired or bored. 461

Mean The arithmetic average of a set of scores. 167

Median The middle score of a set of scores; also, the second quartile. 166

Memos Notes written by a qualitative method observer to record some insight or some aspect of a process that may be helpful in the interpretation of the data. 330

Meta-analysis Combining the statistical results of studies of the same question into a single result to enhance statistical power, to find the average size of the effect, to determine the nature of the relationship, and to find how the relationship is affected by other variables. 564

Mixed model A form of analysis of variance in which there are both random and fixed factors. 601

Mode The most frequently occurring score in a set of scores. 166

Model cases Perfectly clear and unquestioned examples of a construct; used in conceptual analysis to help define a term. 149

Mortality Changes in the composition of the sample due to individuals dropping out of the study before its completion that could also have caused the effect and are confounded with it. 343

Mortality by treatment interaction Changes in the composition of the sample due to reactions to treatment that caused some individuals to drop out of the study before its completion. (See also *mortality*.) 471

Multimeasure, multimethod procedure Multiple measurement or observation of the same phenomenon or attribute with different methods. This triangulation ensures that the researcher knows if characteristics of the measure or the method of measuring or observation are affecting the result. 276

Multiperspectivists Researchers who seek to explain phenomena from more than one point of view. 631

Multiple correlation The correlation between the criterion and the values of the dependent variable as they are predicted from two or more independent variables. 580

Multiple regression Prediction of a criterion from two or more variables. 580

Multiple-treatment interaction   The effect of earlier treatments on later ones. 469

Naturalistic evaluation   Use of the qualitative approach in evaluation to determine the goals of the project as in goal-free evaluation as well as the needs and expectations of the stakeholders in the projects. Sometimes called *responsive evaluation* because it is intended to respond to the information needs of the stakeholders. 536

Necessary condition   A condition that must be present for an effect to occur or for a term to apply. 148; 241

Nested designs   Factorial designs that reduce the number of groups to the combinations in which one is particularly interested and allow confounding of variables in the remainder. 486

Nominal level (of measurement)   The grouping of like individuals or units (such as institutions) into categories. 160

Nondirective approach   Interviewing design in which the interviewer rephrases and reflects the interviewee's responses, especially to draw out the underlying feelings and central significance of each response. 370

Nonequivalent control group design   Experimental design in which individuals are not randomly assigned to groups so there is no assurance that they are equivalent. Usually uses preformed groups such as schoolrooms. 453

Nonlinear relationship   A relationship between two variables best described by other than a straight line; as one variable increases, the other does not consistently either increase or decrease, or if it does, it does not do so proportionately (for example, a distribution best described by a U or J). 182

Nonparametric statistics   Inferential statistics that assume random assignment or random categorization as a basis for determining probabilities rather than random sampling. 435

Nonprobability sampling   Any sampling procedure that does not involve random sampling at some stage. 136

Nonrespondents   Persons who do not return questionnaires or other instruments and must be recontacted to obtain a large enough sample and to determine whether their responses differ from those whose responses have been received. 386

Normal frequency distribution   A frequency distribution with a particular shape produced by the action of probability in a chance event over an infinite number of trials. Often used as an approximation or model for test score distributions. 173

Norm-referenced tests   Tests on which performance is interpreted in the context of the performance of a group with whom it is reasonable to compare the individual (for example, achieving at the 3.4 grade level). 223

Null hypothesis   The observed value is the result of randomness and chance error; that is, there is a null (no) difference between the value and what typically results from chance error; the value derived from a sample is typical of those in its sampling distribution for samples of that size. 414

Objectivity   The similarity with which two or more judges would evaluate or record a test performance or observation. 213

Observation, measures   The means by which the effect is sensed, assurance is gained that the treatment was given as intended, and/or the nature of variables that may have a moderating impact on the effect is sensed. 62

Obtrusiveness   The change in a typical pattern of events, schedule, or situation such that it has the same effect as the treatment or independent variable and is perceived as sufficiently significant by subjects as to affect their actions (e.g., an unfamiliar adult visiting a kindergarten class). 466

One-group pretest-posttest design   Experimental design in which a group is measured, treated, and then remeasured to determine change. 452

One-tailed test   A test on which all Type I error is assumed to be in one tail of the sampling distribution; a directional hypothesis forecasts the direction of the expected change (for example, experimental group mean greater than control group mean). 417

Operational definition The definition of a construct formed by the operations of measurement. 195

Order of questions Sequence in which the respondent is asked the questions, important because prior questions can affect later responses. 381

Ordinal level (of measurement) The ranking of individuals or units (such as institutions). 160

Organized skepticism The process whereby new knowledge claims in science are routinely challenged by other researchers to determine their validity. 53

Orientation to the social sciences The point of view held by a researcher about what good social science research is and what it can accomplish. 627

Oversampling Taking more samples from a stratum than its proportional share of the sample. 132

Panel sample A panel chosen so as to be representative of a population; usually used in order to study change over time. 365

Parameter A statistic descriptive of some aspect of a population, such as the mean or the standard deviation. 406

Partial correlation A statistical procedure for holding constant the effect of a third variable on a correlation. 604

Participant observation Circumstance wherein individuals are aware that they are being observed, but the observer, by participating in the situation as normally as he or she can, is as unobtrusive as possible. 317

Participant-oriented evaluation Involvement of the stakeholders in the evaluation in a range of roles extending from advisors to the process to having them actually carry out the evaluation, the evaluator acting as teacher and consultant. 538

Particularists Persons who believe that individuals are too complex to be explained by rules and theories and that we can mainly learn from one another. 630

Pearson product-moment correlation A number between -1.00 and $+1.00$ indicative of the strength of relationship between two variables where zero indicates no relation. Positive correlations indicate that they vary directly; negative ones, inversely. At $+1$ they vary perfectly proportionally; between ±1 and zero, they vary increasingly imperfectly as zero is approached. 176

Percentile The percentage of cases in a frequency distribution that fall below that score (e.g., the median is the 50th percentile because 50% of cases have lower scores than the median). 175

Permuterm indexing Using the important words in journal article titles to form an index that displays these words in all possible pairs. 109

Pilot testing Trying out an instrument or a procedure to determine problems before the actual study is begun. 385

Placebo effect The effect that results from a treatment that is just like the actual treatment but lacks the active ingredient. 453

Planned comparisons Comparisons for statistical significance that were planned in advance of computing statistics on the data. (Compare with *post hoc comparisons*.) 600

Population The total group to whom a researcher expects to be able to generalize and which is to be represented in a sample. 122

Post hoc comparisons Statistical comparisons made after learning how the data are going to turn out rather than before the data are gathered. 601

Posttest-only control group design Experimental design in which individuals are randomly assigned to experimental and control groups, treated, and then measured to determine effect. 453

Power of a statistical test The capacity of a statistical test to avoid a Type II error; to avoid missing statistical significance when a more sensitive test would find it. 427

Practical significance A difference large enough to cause some practical consequence, in contrast to *statistical significance*, which may be so small that nobody cares about it. 433

Pragmatists Researchers who seek instruments, rules, principles, equations, and models that predict with better-than-chance accuracy and thereby permit control; explanations are not their forte. 630

Precedence of cause Evidence that a cause precedes or occurs simultaneously with an effect. 251

Predictive validity Evidence that a test correlates with a criterion obtained at an earlier time, before a selection decision or choice was made. 201

Presence of effect A necessary condition for inferring causation; the fact that an effect did indeed occur as indicated by one's measures or observations; often determined by inferential statistics. 251

Pretest-posttest control group design Experimental design in which individuals are randomly assigned to experimental and control groups, measured before treatment, treated, and remeasured. 453

Primary sources The original sources of data, facts, findings, theory; the publications of the original authors rather than quotation, summary, or paraphrase of the material by other authors. 102

Privacy Individuals' right to restrict inquiries about themselves to those areas in which they knowingly and willingly provide access. 670

Probability sampling A sampling procedure that involves random sampling at some stage. 126

Probe An interviewing technique designed to cause the respondent to amplify a response or to jog the respondent's memory. 376

Procedure The determination of who is administered what treatment as well as who is observed or measured and when and where all this is done. 62

Projective techniques Techniques used to indirectly measure; what is being measured is not apparent. For instance, individuals may merely be asked to respond to the stimulus by telling what is seen, telling a story about it, or giving the first response that comes to mind. 379

Proportional stratified sampling A method wherein the percentage of cases randomly selected from a strata is the same as the percentage that the strata represents in the population. 131

Purposive sampling Samples assembled by intentionally seeking individuals or situations likely to yield new instances and greater understanding of a dimension or concept of interest. Also used to test the generality of a coding category, finding, or principle. Employed in analytic induction. 138

Qualitative point of view The observer takes the stance of trying to learn how the people being observed see their situation, how they understand it, what it means to them. Also called the *phenomenological point of view*. 321

Qualitative research Research that describes phenomena in words instead of numbers or measures. 29

Quantitative research Research that describes phenomena in numbers and measures instead of words. 30

Quartile The point below which one-quarter of a set of scores fall (first quartile, or Q_1), half the scores fall (second quartile, median, or Q_2), or three-quarters of the scores fall (third quartile, or Q_3). 171

Questions, hypotheses, models The link in the chain of reasoning that is forged out of the rationale, theory, or point of view. It focuses the direction of the study in a quantitative study and emerges from the data in a qualitative study. Whether a question, hypothesis, or model emerges depends on the extent of the information available. 60

Quota sampling Using the frequency distribution of characteristics in the population to choose units in the sample such that those characteristics are in the same proportion in the sample as they are in the population. 138

Random assignment Assigning individuals to control and experimental groups by a random process. 450

Random model   A form of analysis of variance in which each intervention is a random sample of its possible forms. 601

Random sampling   Choosing samples by chance in such a way that every sample has an equal chance of being selected each time a sample is drawn. 127

Range   The distance from the lowest to the highest score. 170

Ratio scale   An interval scale with a true zero point that represents the complete lack of what is being measured. 160

Reactivity   Change in individuals' behavior due to their perception that they are part of an experimental study. 466

Reasoning authorities   See *authority*.

Regression   The prediction of one variable from another variable. Alternatively, scores of individuals selected as low or high on a characteristic with a less than perfectly reliable measure and placed in separate groups will move closer to the mean of their original group on retesting. Also, a phenomenon measured at a peak will appear to have improved if remeasured at more typical levels. 184; 457

Related cases   Cases that are almost but not quite the same as the term being examined in a conceptual analysis. They help distinguish the term's boundary. 149

Reliability   Evidence that a test measures consistently in some respect. 206

Replicable result   A judgment as to whether the result would be replicable with new choices of any or all of the facets of the study design or whether the results are dependent on some or all of the design choices, thus limiting generality. 282

Researcher expectancy effect   Researchers or judges, knowing what to expect, believe they perceive it. 168

Residuals (method of)   Subtract from any situation all aspects known to be the cause only of phenomena other than the one of interest, and the cause of the phenomenon of interest is in the residual. 249

Resource allocation   The allocation of resources to achieve the purposes of a study, especially to achieve the appropriate balance of internal validity (LP) to external validity (GP) and to build a strong chain of reasoning. 302

Resource limits   The limits on resources available for a study, especially limits on the researchers' time and energy, a constraint. 305

Response sets   Tendency of respondents to answer questions in certain directions (such as "yes" or "true") regardless of the actual question. 392

Responsive evaluation   See *naturalistic evaluation*.

Restrictive explanations (conditions) eliminated   Conditions of the study that restrict the generality that may be inferred from the evidence. In the interests of greater generality, it is desirable these be eliminated in the study's design. 282

Restriction in range   If the range of values on which a correlation coefficient is based is restricted in comparison with the typical situation of which it is intended to be an estimate, the estimate will be too low. 180

Rival explanations   Explanations other than the intended one proposed to explain the phenomenon or effect under study. A major purpose of experimental design is their elimination. 272; 454

Robust   Describes a statistical test that can be accurately interpreted even when the conditions of its use violate certain of its assumptions. 436

Sample   A means by which cases are taken from a population in such a way as to accurately represent the variables of interest in that population; thus a study of the smaller sample may economically be substituted for a study of the entire population. 122

Sample surveys   The gathering of questionnaire or interview data from a sample drawn so as to be representative of a population of interest. 361

Sampling distribution of the mean   The frequency distribution of a statistic formed from repeated samples from a population. 407

Sampling frame   An enumeration of all the units in the population or in a cluster from which the sample is to be drawn. 128

Sampling unit   The units that make up the population and are chosen in a sampling procedure. 128

Saturated   Describes a situation in qualitative research where so many examples of a dimension or a concept of interest have been gathered that nothing new is being learned. 325

Scatterplot   The plot of scores developed when one variable is measured on the vertical axis (usually the dependent variable) and the other on the horizontal axis. Also known as a *scatter diagram* or *scattergram*. 176

Secondary sources   Quotation, paraphrase, or summary of data, facts, findings, or theory by other than the original authors. 102

Selection   Assignment of individuals to groups in such a way that any characteristic that could have caused the effect is not equated between the groups and is therefore confounded with the treatment. 463

Selection by treatment interaction   Assignment of individuals to groups (often self-selection) because of the attractiveness or repulsiveness of the treatment in such a way that a characteristic that could have caused the effect is not equated between the groups and is therefore confounded with the treatment. 470

Semi-interquartile range   Half the distance from the first quartile to the third quartile. 171

Sequential sampling   Taking successive samples until the required precision of measurement and stability of the data across samples is attained. 139

Significance level   The frequency or probability (e.g., 1 time in 19, or 5%) with which one is willing to be wrong in saying that a value is atypical and not due to chance error (i.e., statistically significant) when it *is* the result of chance error. 415

Single-subject studies   Studies in which individuals are studied over time, usually with repeated instances of treatment and measurement of effect. 559

Situation   The situation wherein the data are collected; often determined by where the subjects are. 61

Skewness   A deviation of the frequency distribution from symmetry. Positive skewness has a long tail to the right toward the high scores; negative skewness, the opposite. 167

Snowball sampling   The identification of the members of a group by asking individuals who would be expected to know the members to identify them, continuing until no new information is being obtained. Also called *chain-referral sampling*. 139

Solomon four-group design   A combination of the pretest-posttest experimental and control group design with the posttest-only experimental and control group design. 454

Stability reliability   Evidence that a test measures consistently over time. 210

Stakeholders   Individuals who are affected by the outcome of a project and who therefore have a stake in how it is developed, implemented, and evaluated. 524

Standard deviation   A measure of the variability or spread of scores; the square root of the average of the squared deviations of the scores from the mean of the set of scores. 171

Standard error of the mean   The standard deviation of a sampling distribution. 407

Standard error of measurement   A measure of the reliability or consistency of measurement; it permits the construction of confidence intervals. 215

Standard score   A raw score divided by its standard deviation. Also known as the *z-score*. 174

Stanine score   A test score (one of a *standard nine*, from whence comes the name). Each stanine score is a half deviation wide, and nine of them cover the score range since the top and bottom scores are open-ended. 175

Statistical significance   Evidence that a value is atypical in a sampling distribution, that it would not typically result from the operation of random sampling variation and chance error and would appear with a rarity expressed by long odds such as 19 to 1 or 100 to 1. 416

Stem-and-leaf diagram Tabulation of scores in small score intevals down a vertical line. See Figure 10.1. 163

Stimulated recall Audio- or videotaping the respondent during a session and later playing back the tape, stopping it, and asking the respondent to explain his or her thoughts and feeling at that time. 385

Stipulative definition The use of a term in a particular way other than that in which it is commonly used; usually a modification of the latter. 153

Stratified sampling Dividing a population into groups (strata) on the basis of some variable such that the groups are more homogeneous on the variable of interest than in a simple random sample. Units are randomly sampled from within strata, usually proportionally to the size of a stratum in relation to the total sample. 130

Structural modeling Developing a hypothesized casual chain and its test with data. Also called *causal modeling* or *covariance modeling*. 588

Structured interview An interview in which the questions and their order are predetermined. 368

Study-effect meta-analysis (SEMA) A meta-analysis in which each study is allowed to contribute only one result to the combination determining effect size. 570

Subjects The units (usually individuals, but can be classes, groups, or institutions) that are the subject of the investigation. 61

Sufficient conditions (In relation to causation) all those conditions, in the presence of which the effect occurs, (in relation to conceptual analysis) conditions which are sufficient to distinguish all examples from nonexamples of a term. 148; 241

Summative evaluation Evaluation intended to determine the value or worth of something. 525

Synthesizers Researchers who study phenomena in their natural surroundings and seek to induce an explanation of the phenomena from the data collected. 631

Systematic sampling Choosing every *n*th unit (for example, every tenth person) from the sampling frame. 133

Tailored tests Tests that are adjusted to the appropriate level of difficulty for each subject by having each subject who passes an item branched to a more difficult item and each who fails branched to an easier one. Also called *adaptive tests*. 225

Tandem interviewing Conducting an interview as a team of two. 371

Testing Changes in the scores of individuals resulting from familiarity with a test taken two or more times; the resulting higher scores are confounded with treatment. 456

Testing-treatment interaction Changes in the scores of individuals resulting from individuals having been sensitized to aspects of treatment by a pretest subsequently paying greater attention to those aspects during treatment than they otherwise would; confounded with treatment effect. 470

Theorizers Researchers who infer theories and explanations with very convincing examples, usually with very little data since they are more oriented toward observing and thinking than toward validating hypotheses. 628

Threats to validity See *rival explanations*.

Time-series designs Experimental designs that follow subjects through time, treating and remeasuring them to determine changes. 480

Trade-off A gain in one aspect of a study at the cost of loss in another (e.g., breadth vs. depth—a good general achievement test does a poor job of diagnosing specific weakness in an area covered). 222

Translation fidelity The faithfulness with which the terms in the question, hypothesis, or model are translated into the six facets of design. 272

Translation generality A judgment of the extent to which the translation of the question, hypothesis, or model into the six design facets supports the generality claimed or implied by the problem statement. 282

Treatment   A potential cause controlled by the investigator. 27; 61

Treatment fidelity   Evidence that the treatment was administered as it was intended to be administered. 488

Treatment phase   The phase of a time-series experimental design during which the treatment is administered. 559

Trend studies   Studies of changes over time. 365

Triangulation   Determining the consistency of evidence gathered from different sources of data across time, space, and/or persons, by different investigators and/or different research methods. 328

Two-tailed test   A test in which Type I error may be found in either tail of the distribution; we do not have a directional hypothesis; we expect an effect but do not know its direction. 417

Type I error   The error of erroneously indicating that an effect is statistically significant when in fact it is the result of random sampling variation and chance error. 403

Type II error   The error of indicating that a given value is due to sampling variation and chance error when it is not. 403

Uncertainty reduction   The reduction that progressively occurs as a proposition is sufficiently validated that we can accept it as knowledge and/or act as though it were true. 46

Universal standards   Criteria governing research quality that apply to all researchers regardless of status or lack of it. 51

Unobtrusiveness   Administration of treatment or measures in such a way that they appear to be part of the situation normally expected by the subjects. 467

Unstructured interview   Interview in which the interviewers, taking their cue from previous responses, formulate and order questions on the spot to obtain the desired information. 368

Utilization   The use of evaluation or research results in an applied setting. 528

Validation   Checking an explanation or a hypothesis to determine whether predictions made from it are accurate. 7

Validity   Evidence that a test measures what it is intended to measure. 197

Variance   A measure of the variability of the scores in a frequency distribution; more specifically, the square of its standard deviation. 171

Variance-partitioning meta-analysis   A meta-analysis in which the variance of the effect is partitioned, as in analysis of variance, to determine the contribution of different variables to the effect. 570

References

Adair, J. D., Sharpe, D., and Huynh, C. (1989). Hawthorne control procedures in education experiments: A reconsideration of their use and effectiveness. *Review of Educational Research, 59*, 215–228.

Adams, J. T. (1976–1978). *Dictionary of American history* (rev. ed., 8 vols.). New York: Scribner.

Aiken, L. S., West, S. G., Sechrest, L., and Reno, R. R. (1990). Graduate training in statistics, methodology, and measurement in psychology: A survey of Ph.D. programs in North America. *American Psychologist, 45*, 721–734.

Allen, M. S. (1962). *Allen morphologizer.* Englewood Cliffs, N.J.: Prentice-Hall.

Allison, G. T. (1971). *Essence of decision: Explaining the Cuban missile crisis.* Boston: Little, Brown.

American Educational Research Association, American Psychological Association, and National Council on Measurement in Education. (1974, 1985). *Standards for educational and psychological testing.* Washington, D.C.: American Psychological Association.

American Historical Association. (1961). *Guide to historical literature.* New York: Macmillan.

American Psychological Association (1987). *Casebook on ethical principles of psychologists.* Washington, D.C.: American Psychological Association.

American Psychological Association, Ad hoc Committee on Ethical Standards in Psychological Research. (1973). *Ethical principles in the conduct of research with human participants.* Washington, D.C.: American Psychological Association.

American Psychological Association, Committee on Ethical Standards for Psychology. (1951). Ethical standards in research. *American Psychologist, 6*, 436–443.

American Psychological Association, Committee for the Protection of Human Participants in Research. (1982). *Ethical principles in the conduct of research with human participants.* Washington, D.C.: American Psychological Association.

Anastasi, A. (1982). *Psychological testing* (5th ed.). New York: Macmillan.

Anderson, J. G. (1986). *Questionnaire design and use revisited: Recent developments and issues in survey research.* Paper presented at the convention of the American Educational Research Association, San Francisco.

Anderson, L., Evertson, C., and Brophy, J. (1979). An exploratory study of effective teaching in first grade reading groups. *Elementary School Journal, 79*, 193–233.

Andrews, F. M., et al. (1981). *A guide for selecting statistical techniques for analyzing social science data* (2nd ed.). Ann Arbor: Survey Research Center, Institute for Social Research, University of Michigan.

Anscombe, F. J. (1973). Graphs in statistical analysis. *American Statistician, 27*(1), 17–21.

Argyris, C., Putnam, R., and Smith, D. M. (1985). *Action science: Concepts, methods, and skills for research and intervention.* San Francisco: Jossey-Bass.

Asher, H. B. (1983). *Causal modeling*. Beverly Hills, Calif.: Sage.

Asimov, I. (1977). The future of futurism. *American Way, 10*(4), 11–12.

Atkins, T. V., and Ostrow, R. (Eds.). (1989). *Cross-reference index: A guide to search terms*. New York: Bowker.

Aydelotte, W. O. (1971). *Quantification in history*. Reading, Mass.: Addison-Wesley.

Aydelotte, W. O., Bogue, A. G., and Fogel, R. W. (Eds.). (1972). *The dimensions of quantitative research in history*. Princeton, N.J.: Princeton University Press.

Babbie, E. R. (1986). *The practice of social research*. Belmont, Calif.: Wadsworth.

Backer, T. E. (1977). *A directory of information on tests*. (ERIC TM Report 62-1977). Princeton, N.J.: ERIC Clearinghouse on Tests, Measurement and Evaluation, Educational Testing Service.

Baker, F. B. (1981). Log-linear, logit-linear models: A didactic. *Journal of Educational Statistics, 6*(1), 75–102.

Baker, G., and Chapman, D. (Eds.). (1962). *Man and society in disaster*. New York: Basic Books.

Bales, R. F. (1950). *Interaction process analysis: A method for the study of small groups*. Cambridge, Mass.: Addison-Wesley.

Bandura, A. (1978). The self system in reciprocal determinism. *American Psychologist, 33*, 344–358.

Bangert-Drowns, R. L. (1986). Review of developments in meta-analytic method. *Psychological Bulletin, 99*, 388–399.

Barlow, D. H., and Hersen, M. (1984). *Single case experimental designs: Strategies for studying behavior*. New York: Pergamon.

Baron, R. A., and Ransberger, V. M. (1978). Ambient temperature and the occurrence of collective violence: The long hot summer revisited. *Journal of Personality and Social Psychology, 36*, 351–360.

Barzun, J., and Graff, H. F. (1970, 1977, 1985). *The modern researcher* (2nd, 3rd, 4th ed.). New York: Harcourt Brace Jovanovich.

Baumrind, D. (1983). Specious causal attributions in the social sciences: The reformulated stepping-stone theory of heroin use as exemplar. *Journal of Personality and Social Psychology, 45*, 189–198.

Baumrind, D. (1985). Research using intentional deception: Ethical issues revisited. *American Psychologist, 40*, 165–174.

Beck, S. J. (1961). *Rorschach's test* (3rd ed.). New York: Grune & Stratton.

Becker, F. D., et al. (1973). College classroom ecology. *Sociometry, 36*, 514–525.

Becker, H. S. (1961). *Boys in white*. Chicago: University of Chicago Press.

Becker, H. S. (1963). *Outsiders: Studies in the sociology of deviance*. New York: Free Press.

Becker, H. S., Geer, B., and Hughes, E. C. (1968). *Making the grade: The academic side of college life*. New York: Wiley.

Bellak, L. (1986). *The TAT, CAT, and SAT in clinical use*. Orlando, Fla.: Grune & Stratton.

Bereiter, C. (1990). Aspects of an educational learning theory. *Review of Educational Research, 60*, 603–624.

Berger, P. (1961). *The voice of solemn assemblies*. Garden City, N.Y.: Doubleday.

Berk, R. A. (1986a). A consumer's guide to setting performance standards on criterion-referenced tests. *Review of Educational Research, 56*, 137–172.

Berk, R. A. (Ed.). (1986b). *A guide to criterion-referenced test construction*. Baltimore, Md.: Johns Hopkins University Press.

Berk, R. A., and Rossi, P. H. (1976). Doing good or worse: Evaluation research politically re-examined. *Social Problems, 23*, 337–349.

Berkowitz, L., and Donnerstein, E. (1982). External validity is more than skin deep. *American Psychologist, 37*, 245–257.

Berrueta-Clement, J. R., Barnett, W. S., and Weikart, D. P. (1985). Changed lives: The effects of the Perry Preschool Program on youths through age 19. In L. H. Aiken and B. H. Kehrer (Eds.), *Evaluation studies review annual* (Vol. 10, pp. 257–279). Beverly Hills, Calif.: Sage.

Bertaux, D., and Bertaux-Wiame, I. (1981). Life stories in the baker's trade. In D. Bertaux (Ed.), *Biography and society: The life history approach in the social sciences.* Beverly Hills, Calif.: Sage.

Biernacki, P., and Waldorf, D. (1981). Snowball sampling: Problem and technique of chain referral sampling. *Sociological Method and Research,* 10(12), 141–163.

Biklen, S. K., and Bogdan, R. C. (1986). On your own with naturalistic evaluation. In D. D. Williams (Ed.), *Naturalistic evaluation.* (New Dimensions for Program Evaluation No. 30). San Francisco: Jossey-Bass.

Binet, A. (1912). *A method of measuring the development of the intelligence of young children.* Lincoln, Ill.: Courier.

Blair, R. C., and Higgins, J. J. (1980). A comparison of the power of Wilcoxon's rank-sum statistic to that of student's *t* statistic under various nonnormal distributions. *Journal of Educational Statistics,* 5, 309–335.

Blair, R. C., and Higgins, J. J. (1985). Comparison of the power of the paired samples *t* test to that of Wilcoxon's signed-rank test under various population shapes. *Psychological Bulletin,* 97, 119–128.

Blau, T. (1963). *Dynamics of a bureaucracy: A study of the interpersonal relations in two government agencies* (2nd ed.). Chicago: University of Chicago Press.

Bloom, B. S. (1954). The thought processes of students in discussion. In S. French (Ed.), *Accent on teaching: Experiments in general education.* New York: Harper.

Bloom, B. S. (Ed.). (1956). *Taxonomy of educational objectives: The cognitive domain.* New York: Longman.

Bloom, B. S. (1964). *Stability and change in human characteristics.* New York: Wiley.

Bloom, H. S., and Singer, N. M. (1979). Determining the cost-effectiveness of correctional programs: The case of Patuxent Institution. In L. Sechrest, S. G. West, M. A. Phillips, R. Redner, and W. Yeaton (Eds.), *Evaluation studies review annual* (Vol. 4). Beverly Hills, Calif.: Sage.

Bluebond-Langer, M. (1980). *The private worlds of dying children.* Princeton, N.J.: Princeton University Press.

Bogdan, R. C. (1976). Conducting evaluation research—integrity intact. *Sociological Focus,* 9, 63–72.

Bogdan, R. C., and Biklen, S. K. (1982). *Qualitative research for education: An introduction to theory and methods.* Boston: Allyn & Bacon.

Bogdan, R. C., Brown, M. A., and Foster, S. B. (1982). Be honest, but not cruel: Staff-parent conversation on a neonatal unit. *Human Organization,* 4(1), 6–16.

Bogdan, R. C., and Taylor, S. (1976). The judged, not the judges: An insider's view of mental retardation. *American Psychologist,* 31, 47–52.

Bollen, K. (1989). *Structural equations with latent variables.* New York: Wiley.

Boruch, R. F., and Gomez, H. (1977). Sensitivity, bias, and theory in impact evaluations. *Professional Psychology,* 9, 411–434.

Boruch, R. F., Mc Sweeney, A. J., and Soderstrom, E. J. (1978). Bibliography: Illustrative randomized field experiments for program planning, development, and evaluation: An illustrative bibliography. *Evaluation Quarterly,* 2, 655–695.

Boruch, R. F., and Wothke, W. (Eds.). (1985). *Randomization and field experimentation.* (New Directions for Program Evaluation No. 28). San Francisco: Jossey-Bass.

Bosk, C. L. (1979). *Forgive and remember: Managing medical failure.* Chicago: University of Chicago Press.

Bouchard, T. J., Jr. (1976). Field research methods: Interviewing, questionnaires, participant observation, systematic observation, unobtrusive measures. In M. D. Dunnette (Ed.), *Handbook of industrial and organizational psychology.* Chicago: Rand McNally.

Boulding, K. E. (1968). *Beyond economics.* Ann Arbor: University of Michigan Press.

Bracht, G. H., and Glass, G. V. (1968). The external validity of experiments. *American Educational Research Journal,* 5, 437–474.

Bradbury, K. L., and Downs, A. (Eds.). (1981). *Do housing allowances work?* Washington, D.C.: Brookings Institution.

Brand, M. (1979). Causality. In P. D. Asquith and H. E. Kyburg, Jr. (Eds.), *Current research in philosophy of science: Proceedings of the Philosophy of Science Association Critical Research Problems Conference.* East Lansing, Mich.: Edwards Brothers.

Bray, J. H. (1985). *Multivariate analysis of variance.* Beverly Hills, Calif.: Sage.

Breland, H. (1987). *Assessing writing skill.* New York: College Board Publications, College Entrance Examination Board.

Brewer, J., and Hunter, A. (1989). *Multimethod research: A synthesis of styles.* Newbury Park, Calif.: Sage.

Brewer, J. G. (1978). *The literature of geography: A guide to its organisation and use* (2nd ed.). London: Bingley.

Brickell, H. M. (1978). The influence of external political factors on the role and methodology of evaluation. In T. D. Cook, M. L. Del Rosario, K. M. Hennigan, M. M. Mark, and W. M. K. Trochim (Eds.), *Evaluation studies review annual* (Vol. 3, pp. 94–98). Beverly Hills, Calif.: Sage.

Briggs, J. W. (1978). *An Italian passage: Immigrants to three American cities, 1890–1930.* New Haven, Conn.: Yale University Press.

Brinberg, D., and McGrath, J. E. (1985). *Validity and the research process.* Beverly Hills, Calif.: Sage.

Broad, W. (1983). Frauds from 1960 to the present. In B. K. Kilbourne (Ed.), *The dark side of science: Proceedings of the annual meeting of the Pacific Division of the American Association for the Advancement of Science* (Vol. 1, Part 2). San Francisco: Jossey-Bass. (ERIC Document Reproduction Service No. ED 245 917)

Broad, W., and Wade, N. (1983). *Betrayers of the truth.* New York: Simon & Schuster.

Bronfenbrenner, U. (1977). Toward an experimental ecology of human development. *American Psychologist, 32,* 513–531.

Brookover, W. (1987). Distortion and overgeneralization are no substitutes for sound research. *Phi Delta Kappan, 69*(5), 225–227.

Burks, B. S., Jensen, D. W., and Terman, L. M. (1930). *The promise of youth: Follow-up studies of 1,000 gifted children* (Vol. 3.). Stanford, Calif.: Stanford University Press.

Burton, M. A. B. (1988). School discipline: Have we lost our sense of purpose in our search for good method? Paper presented to 1988 Convention of the American Association of Colleges for Teacher Education (ERIC Document Reproduction Service No. ED 291 686).

Byrne, G. (1988). Random samples. *Science, 242,* 198.

Cahalan, D. T. (1968). Correlates of respondent accuracy in the Denver validity survey. *Public Opinion Quarterly, 32,* 607–721.

Campbell, D. T. (1986). Relabeling internal and external validity for applied social scientists. In W. M. K. Trochim (Ed.), *Advances in quasi-experimental design and analysis.* (New Directions for Program Evaluation No. 31). San Francisco: Jossey-Bass.

Campbell, D. T. (1988). Descriptive epistimology: Psychological, sociological, and evolutionary. In E. S. Overman (Ed.), *Methodology and epistemology for social science: Selected papers Donald T. Campbell* (pp. 435–486). Chicago: University of Chicago Press.

Campbell, D. T., and Stanley, J. C. (1963). Experimental designs for research on teaching. In N. L. Gage (Ed.), *Handbook of research on teaching.* Chicago: Rand McNally.

Cannell, C. F. (1985a). Experiments in the improvement of response accuracy. In T. W. Beed and R. J. Stimson (Eds.), *Survey interviewing: Theory and techniques.* North Sydney, Australia: Allen & Unwin.

Cannell, C. F. (1985b). Overview: Response bias and interviewer variability in surveys. In T. W. Beed and R. J. Stimson (Eds.), *Survey interviewing: Theory and techniques.* North Sydney, Australia: Allen & Unwin.

Carifio, J., and Baron, R. A. (1977). Soliciting sensitive data anonymously: The CDRGP technique. *Journal of Alcohol and Drug Education, 23*(2), 47–66.

Carlsmith, L. (1964). Effect of early father absence on scholastic aptitude. *Harvard Educational Review, 34*(1), 3–21.

Carlsmith, L., Merrill, J., and Anderson, C. A. (1979). Ambient temperature and the occurrence of collective violence: A new perspective. *Journal of Personality and Social Psychology, 37*, 337–344.

Carr, E. H. (1962). *What is history?* New York: Knopf.

Carroll, J. D., and Arabie, P. (1980). Multidimensional scaling. In M. R. Rosenzweig and L. W. Porter (Eds.), *Annual Review of Psychology* (Vol. 31, pp. 607–649). Palo Alto, Calif.: Annual Reviews.

Cattell, R. B. (1963). Theory of crystallized intelligence: A critical experiment. *Journal of Educational Psychology, 54*, 1–22.

Ceci, S. J., and Peters, D. (1984). How blind is blind review? *American Psychologist, 39*, 1491–1494.

Centra, J. A. (1977). *How universities evaluate faculty performance: A survey of department heads.* (Rep. BRED-75-5bR). Princeton, N.J.: Graduate Record Examinations Board. (ERIC Document Reproduction Service No. ED 157 445)

Chamberlin, T. C. (1897/1985). The method of multiple working hypotheses. *Journal of Geology, 5*, 837. Reprinted in *Science, 148*, 754–759.

Chase, W. G., and Simon, H. A. (1973). Perception in chess. *Cognitive Psychology, 4*, 55–81.

Chun, K. T., Cobb, S., and French, J. R. P. (1975). *Measures for psychological assessment: A guide to 3,000 original sources and their applications.* Ann Arbor: Institute for Social Research, University of Michigan.

Clotfelter, C. T., and Hahn, J. C. (1978). Assessing the national 55 m.p.h. speed limit. *Policy Sciences, 9*, 281–294.

Cohen, J. (1968). Multiple regression as a general data-analytic system. *Psychological Bulletin, 70*, 426–443.

Cohen, J. (1988). *Statistical power analysis for the behavioral sciences* (2nd ed.). New York: Academic Press.

Cohen, J. (1990). Things I have learned (so far). *American Psychologist, 45*, 1304–1312.

Cohen, M. R., and Nagel, E. (1934). *An introduction to logic and scientific method.* New York: Harcourt Brace.

Coleman, J. S. (1972). *Policy research in the social sciences.* Morristown, N.J.: General Learning Press.

Coleman, J. S., Hoffer, T., and Kilgore, S. (1982). *High school achievement: Public, Catholic, and private schools compared.* New York: Basic Books.

Converse, J. M., and Presser, S. (1986). *Survey questions: Handcrafting the standardized questionnaire.* (Quantitative Applications in the Social Sciences Paper No. 63). Beverly Hills, Calif.: Sage.

Cook, T. D., and Campbell, D. T. (1979). *Quasi-experimentation: Design and analysis issues for field settings.* Chicago: Rand McNally.

Coombs, C. H., Dawes, R. M., and Tversky, A. (1981). *Mathematical psychology: An elementary introduction.* Englewood Cliffs, N.J.: Prentice-Hall.

Cooper, H. M. (1985). Literature searching strategies of integrative research reviews. *American Psychologist, 40*, 1267–1269.

Cooper, H. M., and Rosenthal, R. (1980). Statistical versus traditional procedures for summarizing research findings. *Psychological Bulletin, 87*, 442–449.

Corkhill, A. J., Bruning, R. H., Glover, J. A., and Krug, D. (1988). Advance organizers: Retrieval context hypotheses. *Journal of Educational Psychology, 80*, 304–311.

Coscarelli, W. C., and Stonewater, J. K. (1979). Understanding psychological styles in instructional development consultation. *Journal of Instructional Development, 3*(2), 16–22.

Cosper, R. (1972). Interviewer effect in a survey of drinking practices. *Sociological Quarterly, 13*, 228–236.

Cox, C. M. (1926). *The early mental traits of three hundred geniuses* (Vol. 2). Stanford, Calif.: Stanford University Press.

Crane, V. R., and Heim, A. W. (1950). The effects of repeatedly testing the same group on the same intelligence test, Part III: Further experiments and general conclusions. *Quarterly Journal of Experimental Psychology, 2*, 82–197.

Crocker, L., Llabre, M., and Miller, M. D. (1988). The generalizability of content validity ratings. *Journal of Educational Measurement, 25*, 287–299.

Cronbach, L. J. (1975). Beyond the two disciplines of scientific psychology. *American Psychologist, 30*, 116–127.

Cronbach, L. J. (1982). *Designing evaluations of educational and social programs.* San Francisco: Jossey-Bass.

Cronbach, L. J. (1984). *Essentials of psychological testing* (4th ed.). New York: Harper & Row.

Cronbach, L. J., and Furby, L. (1970). How we should measure "change"—or should we? *Psychological Bulletin, 74*, 68–80.

Cronbach, L. J., Gleser, G. C., Nanda, H., and Rajaratnam, N. (1972). *The dependability of behavioral measurements: Theory of generalizability of scores and profiles.* New York: Wiley.

Cronbach, L. J., Rogosa, D., Floden, R., and Price, G. G. (1976). *Analysis of covariance in nonrandomized experiments: Factors affecting bias.* (Occasional papers, Stanford Evaluation Consortium). Stanford, Calif.: Stanford University, Department of Education.

Cronbach, L. J., and Suppes, P. (1969). *Research for tomorrow's schools: Disciplined inquiry for education.* New York: Macmillan

Culler, R. E., and Holahan, C. J. (1980). Test anxiety and academic performance: The effects of study-related behaviors. *Journal of Educational Psychology, 72*, 16–20.

Cunningham, N. J., and Stewart, N. R. (1983). Effects of discrimination training on counselor trainee response choice. *Counselor Education and Supervision, 23*, 46–61.

Cuttance, P., and Ecob, R. (Eds.). (1987). *Structural modeling by example: Applications in educational, sociological and behavioral research.* New York: Cambridge Universtity Press.

Dalton, D. W., Hannafin, M. J., and Hooper, S. (1989). The effects of individual and cooperative computer-assisted instruction on student performance and attitudes. *Educational Technology Research and Development, 37*(2), 15–24.

Dalton, M. (1959). *Men who manage: Fusions of feelings and theory in administration.* New York: Wiley.

Dalton, M. (1967). Preconceptions and methods of men who manage. In P. E. Hammond (Ed.), *Sociologists at work: Essays on the craft of social research.* New York: Basic Books.

Daniels, A. K. (1983). Self-deception and self-discovery in fieldwork. *Qualitative Sociology, 6*, 195–214.

Darley, J. M., and Batson, C. D. (1973). From Jerusalem to Jericho: A study of situational and dispositional variables in helping behavior. *Journal of Personality and Social Psychology, 27*, 100–108.

Davis, C., Back, K., and MacLean, K. (1977). *Oral history: From tape to type.* Chicago: American Library Association.

Davis, J. A. (1964). Great books and small groups. In P. E. Hammond (Ed.), *Sociologists at work: Essays on the craft of social research.* New York: Basic Books.

Davis, J. A. (1985). *The logic of causal order.* (Quantitative Applications in the Social Sciences No. 55). Beverly Hills, Calif.: Sage.

De Angelis, T. (1988). Gerontologists lament practice-research gap. *APA Monitor, 19*(2), 9.

De Back, V., and Mentkowski, M. (1986). Does the baccalaureate make a difference? Differentiating nurse performance by education and experience. *Journal of Nursing Education, 25*, 275–285.

Denmark, F. L. (1984). Zeigarnik effect. In R. J. Corsini (Ed.), *Encyclopedia of psychology* (Vol. 3). New York: Wiley.

Denzin, N. K. (1978). *The research act: A theoretical introduction to sociological methods* (2nd ed.) New York: McGraw-Hill.

Dillman, D. A., Gallegos, J. G., and Frey, J. H. (1978). Reducing refusal rates for telephone interviews. *Public Opinion Quarterly*, 40, 66–78.

Dispatch Case. (1986, April 16). *Chronicle of Higher Education*, p. 42.

Di Vesta, F. (1984). A developmental study of the semantic structures of children. *Journal of Verbal Learning and Verbal Behavior*, 5, 249–259.

Dollard, J., and Doob, L. W. (1939). *Frustration and aggression.* New Haven, Conn.: Yale University Press.

Dorfman, D. D. (1978). The Cyril Burt question: New findings. *Science*, 201, 1177–1186.

Duffy, G., and Roehler, L. (1990). The tension between information giving and instructional explanation and teacher change. In J. Brophy (Ed.), *Advances in research on teaching, Vol. 1: Teaching for meaningful understanding and self-regulated learning.* Greenwich, Conn.: JAI Press.

Duncan, O. D. (1984). *Notes on social measurement: Historical and critical.* New York: Russell Sage Foundation.

Edgington, E. S. (1974). A new tabulation of statistical procedures used in APA journals. *American Psychologist*, 29, 25–26.

Educational Testing Service (1986). *The ETS test collection catalog, Vol. 1: Achievement tests and measurement devices.* Phoenix, Ariz.: Oryx Press.

Educational Testing Service (1988). *The ETS test collection catalog, Vol. 2: Vocational tests and measurement devices.* Phoenix, Ariz.: Oryx Press.

Educational Testing Service (1989). *The ETS test collection catalog, Vol. 3: Tests for special populations.* Phoenix, Ariz.: Oryx Press.

Educational Testing Service (1991). *The ETS test collection catalog, Vol. 4: Cognitive aptitude and intelligence tests.* Phoenix, Ariz.: Oryx Press.

Edwards, A. L. (1979). *Multiple regression and analysis of variance and covariance.* San Francisco: Freeman.

Einhorn, H. J., and Hogarth, R. M. (1986). Judging probable cause. *American Psychologist*, 99, 3–19.

Einstein, A., and Infeld, L. (1938). *The evolution of physics.* New York: Simon & Schuster.

Eisner, E. W. (1976). Educational connoisseurship and criticism: Their form and function in educational evaluation. *Journal of Aesthetic Education*, 10, 135–150.

Eisner, E. W. (1981). On the differences between scientific and artistic approaches to qualitative research. *Educational Researcher*, 10(4), 5–9.

Elesh, D., and Lefcowitz, M. J. (1977). The effects of the New Jersey–Pennsylvania negative income tax experiment on health and health care utilization. *Journal of Health and Social Behavior*, 18, 391–405.

Ellsworth, P. D. (1977). From abstract ideas to concrete instances: Some guidelines for choosing natural research settings. *American Psychologist*, 32, 604–615.

Elstein, A. S., Shulman, L. S., and Sprafka, S. A. (1978). *Medical problem solving: An analysis of clinical reasoning.* Cambridge, Mass.: Harvard University Press.

Elstein, A. S., Shulman, L. S., and Sprafka, S. A. (1990). Medical problem solving: A ten-year retrospective. *Evaluation and the Health Professions*, 13, 5–36.

Emerson, J. D., and Hoaglin, D. C. (1983). Stem-and-leaf displays. In D. C. Hoaglin, F. Mosteller, and J. W. Tukey, *Understanding robust and exploratory data analysis.* New York: Wiley.

Erdos, P. L. (1970). *Professional mail surveys.* New York: McGraw-Hill.

Ericson, D. P., and Ellett, F. S., Jr. (1987). Teacher accountability and the causal theory of teaching. *Educational Theory*, 37, 277–293.

Everhart, R. B. (1977). Between stranger and friend: Some consequences of "long term" field work in schools. *American Educational Research Journal*, 14, 1–15.

Exner, J. E. (1986). *The Rorschach: A comprehensive system* (2nd ed.). New York: Wiley.

Fabiano, E., and O'Brien, N. (1987). *Testing information sources for educators.* (TME Report 94). Princeton, N.J.: ERIC Center on Tests and Measurements, Educational Testing Service.

Fairweather, G. W., and Tornatzky, L. G. (1977). *Experimental method for social policy research.* New York: Pergamon.

Featherman, D. L. (1981). The life-span perspective in social science research. In *Five-year outlook on science and technology.* Washington, D.C.: National Science Foundation.

Feldt, L. S., and Brennan, R. L. (1989). Reliability. In R. L. Linn (Ed.), *Educational measurement* (3rd ed., pp. 105–146). New York: American Council on Education/Macmillan.

Ferris, T. (1981). The spectral messenger. *Science, 81,* 66–71.

Festinger, L., Reicken, H., and Schacter, P. (1956). *When prophecy fails.* Minneapolis: University of Minnesota Press.

Fielding, N. G., and Fielding, J. L. (1985). *Linking data.* (Qualitative Research Methods Series, Vol. 4). Beverly Hills, Calif.: Sage.

Fillenbaum, S. (1966). Prior deception and subsequent experimental performance: The "faithful" subject. *Journal of Personality and Social Psychology, 4,* 532–537.

Fischer, D. H. (1970). *Historians' fallacies: Toward a logic of historical thought.* New York: Harper & Row.

Fisher, J. (1959). The twisted pear and the prediction of behavior. *Journal of Consulting Psychology, 23,* 400–405.

Fisher, J., and Gonda, T. A. (1955). Neurologic techniques and Rorschach test in detecting brain pathology: A study of comparative validities. *Archives of Neurology and Psychiatry, 74,* 117–124.

Fisher, J., Gonda, T. A., and Little, K. B. (1955). The Rorschach and central nervous system pathology: A cross validity study. *American Journal of Psychiatry, 3,* 487–492.

Fiske, D. W., and Fogg, L. (1990). But the reviewers are making different criticisms of my paper! *American Psychologist, 45,* 591–598.

Fitzsimmons, S. J., Herriott, R. E., Kidder, S. J., Miller, P. S., and Muse, D. N. (1973). The role of the on-site researcher in Project Rural. In S. J. Fitzsimmons, R. E. Herriott, S. J. Kidder, P. S. Miller, and D. N. Muse, *Evaluation and documentation of experimental schools projects in small schools serving rural areas, phase II plan* (Vol. 2). Cambridge, Mass.: Abt Associates.

Flanders, N. A. (1970). *Analyzing teacher behavior.* Reading, Mass.: Addison-Wesley.

Florio, S. E. (1978). Learning how to go to school: An ethnography of interaction in a kindergarten first grade classroom. *Dissertation Abstracts International, 39,* 3239A. (University Microfilms No. 78–23, 676)

Frederiksen, N., Glaser, R., Lesgold, A., and Shafto, M. G. (Eds.). (1990). *Diagnostic monitoring of skill and knowledge acquisition.* Hillsdale, N.J.: Erlbaum.

Freed, M. M., Hess, R. K., and Ryan, J. M. (Eds.). (1989). *The educator's desk reference: A sourcebook of educational information and research.* New York: Macmillan.

Freedman, D. A. (1987). As others see us: A case study in path analysis. *Journal of Educational Statistics, 12,* 101–128.

Freedman, D. S., Thornton, A., and Camburn, D. (1980). Maintaining response rates in longitudinal studies. *Sociological Methods and Research, 9,* 87–98.

Frey, J. H. (1989). *Survey research by telephone* (2nd ed.). Newbury Park, Calif.: Sage.

Friedel, F., and Showman, R. K. (Eds.). (1974). *Harvard guide to American history* (Vol 2., rev. ed.). Cambridge, Mass.: Belknap Press of Harvard University.

Friedman, J., and Weinberg, D. (Eds.). (1983). *The great housing experiment.* Beverly Hills, Calif.: Sage.

Frye, N. (1981). The bridge of language. *Science, 212,* 127–132.

Gale Research Company (1983–). *Surveys, polls, censuses and forecasts directory.* Detroit, Mich.: Gale Research.

Gans, H. J. (1962). *The urban villagers: Groups and class in the life of Italian-Americans*. New York: Free Press.

Garvey, W. D., Lin, N., and Nelson, C. (1970). Communication in the physical and social sciences. *Science, 170*, 1166–1173.

Geertz, C. (1973). Thick description: Toward an interpretive theory of culture. In C. Geertz, *The interpretation of cultures: Selected essays*. New York: Basic Books.

Geischeider, G. A. (1988). Psychophysical scaling. In M. R. Rosenzweig and L. W. Porter (Eds.), *Annual review of psychology* (Vol. 39, pp. 169–200). Palo Alto, Calif.: Annual Reviews.

Genesee, F. (1976). The role of intelligence in second language learning. *Language Learning, 26*, 267–280.

Genesee, F. (1978). A longitudinal evaluation of an early immersion school program. *Canadian Journal of Education, 3*, 31–50.

Gerberich, J. R. (1956). *Specimen objective test items: A guide to achievement test construction*. New York: Longman.

Gergen, K. J. (1980). The emerging crisis in life span developmental theory. In P. B. Baltes and O. G. Brim (Eds.), *Life-span development and behavior* (Vol. 3). New York: Academic Press.

Gesell, A., Ilg, F. L., Learned, J., and Ames, L. B. (1943). *Infant and child in the culture of today: The guidance of development in the home and nursery school*. New York: Harper.

Getzels, J. W. (1982). The problem of the problem. In R. M. Hogarth (Ed.), *Question framing and response consistency*. (New Directions for Methodology of Social and Behavioral Science No. 11). San Francisco: Jossey-Bass.

Getzels, J. W., and Csikszentmihalyi, M. (1976). *The creative vision: A longitudinal study of problem findings in art*. New York: Wiley.

Ghiselli, E. E. (1949). The validity of commonly employed occupational tests. *University of California Publications in Psychology, 5*, 253–258.

Ghiselli, E. E. (1955). The measurement of occupational aptitude. *University of California Publications in Psychology, 8*, 101–216.

Ghiselli, E. E. (1973). The validity of aptitude tests in personnel selection. *Personnel Psychology, 26*, 461–477.

Glaser, B., and Strauss, A. (1967). *The discovery of grounded theory: Strategies for qualitative research*. Chicago: Aldine.

Glaser, E. M., and Taylor, S. H. (1973). Factors influencing the success of applied research. *American Psychologist, 28*, 140–149.

Glass, G. V. (1976). Primary, secondary, and meta-analysis research. *Educational Researcher, 5*(10), 3–8.

Glass, G. V., McGaw, B., and Smith, M. L. (1981). *Meta-analysis in social research*. Beverly Hills, Calif.: Sage.

Glass, G. V., and Smith, M. L. (1979). Meta-analysis of research on class size and achievement. *Educational Evaluation and Policy Analysis, 1*, 2–16.

Glavin, J., and Quay, H. (1969). Behavior disorders. *Review of Educational Research, 39*, 83–102.

Goetz, J., and Le Compte, M. (1984). *Ethnography and qualitative design in educational research*. Orlando, Fla.: Academic Press.

Goldberger, A. S., and Cain, G. G. (1982). The causal analysis of cognitive outcomes in the Coleman, Hoffer and Kilgore Report. *Sociology of Education, 55*, 103–122.

Goldman, B. A. (1974, 1978, 1982, 1985). *Directory of unpublished experimental mental measures* (Vols. 1–4). New York: Behavioral Publications.

Goldstein, J. H., and Arms, R. L. (1971). Effects of observing athletic contests. *Sociometry, 34*, 83–90.

Good, T., and Brophy, J. (1990). *Educational psychology: A realistic approach*. White Plains, N.Y.: Longman.

Gottfredson, S. D. (1978). Evaluating psychological research reports: Dimensions, reliability, and correlates of quality judgments. *American Psychologist, 33*, 920–934.

Gottschalk, L. A. (1956). *Understanding history*. New York: Knopf.

Gottschalk, L. A. (1961). The use of drugs in interrogation. In A. B. Bidermand and H. Aimmer (Eds.), *The manipulation of human behavior*. New York: Wiley.

Gouldner, A. W. (1954). *Patterns of industrial bureaucracy*. Glencoe, Ill.: Free Press.

Gove, P. P. (Ed.). (1976). *Webster's third new international dictionary of the English language* (unabridged). Springfield, Mass.: G. & C. Merriam.

Grant, G. P. (1979). *On competence: A critical analysis of competence-based reforms in higher education*. San Francisco: Jossey-Bass.

Grant, R. (1986). Advice to dissertation writers. *PS, 19*, 64–65.

Green, J. O. (1984). B. F. Skinner's technology of teaching. *Classroom Computer Learning, 4*(7), 23–29.

Green, T. F. (1971). *The activities of teaching*. New York: McGraw-Hill.

Groves, R. M. (1990). Theories and methods of telephone surveys. In W. R. Scott (Ed.), *Annual review of sociology* (Vol. 16). Palo Alto, Calif.: Annual Reviews.

Groves, R. M., and Magilavy, L. J. (1981). Increasing response rates to telephone surveys: A door in the face for foot-in-the-door? *Public Opinion Quarterly, 45*, 346–358.

Grunder, T. M. (1983). DHHS human subjects protection: The new regulations revisited. *Health Matrix, 1*(2), 37–41.

Grunder, T. M. (1986). *Informed consent: A tutorial*. Owings Mills, Md.: National Health Publishing.

Guba, E. G., and Lincoln, Y. S. (1982). *Causality vs. plausibility: Alternative stances for inquiry into human behavior*. Paper presented at the annual meeting of the American Educational Research Association, 1982.

Guba, E. G., and Lincoln, Y. S. (1987). The countenances of fourth-generation evaluation: Description, judgment, and negotiation. In D. S. Cordray and M. W. Lipsey (Eds.), *Evaluation studies review annual* (Vol. 11). Newbury Park, Calif.: Sage.

Guenzel, P. J., Berckmans, T. R., and Cannell, C. F. (1983). *General interviewing techniques: A self-instructional workbook for telephone and personal interviewer training*. Ann Arbor: Survey Research Center, Institute for Social Research, University of Michigan.

Guilford, J. P., and Fruchter, B. (1978). *Fundamental statistics in psychology and education* (6th ed.). New York: McGraw-Hill.

Gulliksen, H. (1986). Perspective on educational measurement. *Applied Psychological Measurement, 10*, 109–132.

Gustafson, T. (1980). Why doesn't Soviet science do better than it does? In L. L. Lubrano and S. G. Grossman (Eds.), *The social context of Soviet science* (pp. 31–68). Boulder, Colo.: Westview Press.

Guy, W., Gross, M., and Dennis, H. (1967). An alternative to double-blind procedure. *American Journal of Psychiatry, 123*, 1505–1512.

Hage, J., and Meeker, B. F. (1988). *Social causality*. (Contemporary Social Research Series No. 16). Boston: Unwin Hyman.

Hall, G. F., and Loucks, S. F. (1977). A developmental model for determining whether the treatment is actually implemented. *American Educational Research Journal, 14*, 263–276.

Hall, J. L. (1986). *Online bibliographic databases: A directory and sourcebook* (4th ed.). Detroit, Mich.: Gale Research.

Hall, V., and Esposito, M. (1985). *What does research on metacognition have to offer educators?* Paper presented at the conference of the Northeast Educational Research Association.

Hambleton, R. K. (1989). Principles and selected applications of item response theory. In R. L. Linn (Ed.), *Educational measurement* (3rd ed., pp. 147–200). New York: American Council on Education/Macmillan.

Hamilton, W. L. (1979). *A social experiment in program administration: The housing allowance administrative agency experiment*. Cambridge, Mass.: Abt Associates.

Haney, C., Banks, C. W., and Zimbardo, P. G. (1973). Interpersonal dynamics in a simulated prison. *International Journal of Criminology and Penology, 1*, 69–97.

Hannum, J. W., Thoresen, C. E., and Hubbard, D. R., Jr. (1974). A behavioral study of self-esteem with elementary teachers. In M. J. Mahoney and C. E. Thoresen (Eds.), *Self-control: Power to the person.* Monterey, Calif.: Brooks/Cole.

Hansen, R. A., and Robinson, L. M. (1980). Testing the effectiveness of alternative foot-in-the-door manipulations. *Journal of Marketing Research, 17*, 359–364.

Hanson, N. R. (1958). *Patterns of discovery.* Cambridge: Cambridge University Press.

Hare, P., and Bates, R. (1963). Seating position and small group interaction. *Sociometry, 26*, 480–487.

Hauser-Cram, P. (1983). Some cautions in synthesizing research studies. *Educational Evaluation and Policy Analysis, 5*, 155–162.

Hays, W. L. (1973; 1981). *Statistics for the social sciences* (2nd ed.; 3rd ed.). New York: Holt, Rinehart & Winston.

Hedges, L. V. (1982). Estimation of effect size from a series of independent experiments. *Psychological Bulletin, 92*, 490–499.

Hedges, L. V. (1987). How hard is hard science, how soft is soft science? *American Psychologist, 42*, 443–455.

Hedges, L. V., and Olkin, I. (1985). *Statistical methods for meta-analysis.* Orlando, Fla.: Academic Press.

Henshel, R. L. (1980a). The purposes of laboratory experimentation and the virtues of deliberate artificiality. *Journal of Social Psychology, 16*, 406–478.

Henshel, R. L. (1980b). Seeking inoperative laws: Toward the deliberate use of unnatural experimentation. In L. Freese (Ed.), *Theoretical methods in sociology: Seven essays.* Pittsburgh: University of Pittsburgh Press.

Hewett, F., and Blake, P. (1973). Teaching the emotionally disturbed. In R. M. W. Travers (Ed.), *Handbook of Research on Teaching.* New York: Macmillan.

Hillard, J. (1984). *Where to find what: A handbook to reference service.* Metuchen, N.J.: Scarecrow Press.

Himmelfarb, S., and Edgell, S. E. (1980). Additive constants model: A randomized response technique for eliminating evasiveness to quantitative response questions. *Psychological Bulletin, 87*, 525–530.

Hinkle, D., Wiersma, W., and Jurs, S. (1979). *Applied statistics for the behavioral sciences.* Boston: Houghton Mifflin.

Hoaglin, D. C., Light, R. J., McPeek, B., Mosteller, F., and Stota, M. A. (1982). *Data for decisions: Information strategies for policymakers.* Cambridge, Mass.: Abt Associates.

Hoffmann-Riem, C. (1986). Adoptive parenting and the norm of family emotionality. *Qualitative Sociology, 9*, 162–177.

Homer, P. M., and Kahle, L. R. (1988). A structural equation test of the value-attitude-behavior hierarchy. *Journal of Personality and Social Psychology, 54*, 638–646.

Hopkins, K. D., Stanley, J. C., and Hopkins, B. R. (1990). *Educational and psychological measurement and evaluation* (7th ed.). Englewood Cliffs, N.J.: Prentice-Hall.

Hoshmand, L. T., and Polkinghorne, D. E. (1992). Redefining the Science—Practice relationship and professional training. *American Psychologist, 47*, 55–66.

House, E. R. (1976). Justice in evaluation. In G. V. Glass (Ed.), *Evaluation studies review annual* (Vol. 1). Beverly Hills, Calif.: Sage.

House, E. R. (1980). *Evaluating with validity.* Beverly Hills, Calif.: Sage.

House, E. R. (1990). Trends in evaluation. *Educational Researcher, 19*(3), 24–27.

Hovland, C. I., Lumsdaine, A. A., and Sheffield, F. D. (1949). *Experiments on mass communication.* Princeton, N.J.: Princeton University Press.

Huff, D. (1954). *How to lie with statistics.* New York: Norton.

Hughes, E. C. (1971). *The sociological eye.* Chicago: Aldine.

Hume, D. (1902). *Enquiry concerning human understanding.* (L. A. Selby-Bigge, Ed., 2nd ed.). Oxford, England: Clarendon. (Originally published 1748)

Humphreys, L. (1975). *The tearoom trade: Impersonal sex in public places* (2nd ed.). Chicago: Aldine.

Hunt, M. (1982, September 12). Research through deception. *New York Times Magazine,* *66,* 138–144.

Hunter, J. E., and Schmidt, F. L. (1990). *Methods of meta-analysis.* Newbury Park, Calif.: Sage.

Hunter, J. E., Schmidt, F. L., and Jackson, G. B. (1982). *Meta-analysis: Cumulating research findings across studies.* Beverly Hills, Calif.: Sage.

Huxley, E. (1982). *The flame trees of Thika: Memories of an African childhood.* London: Chatto & Windus.

Hyman, H. H. (1954). *Interviewing in social research.* Chicago: University of Chicago Press.

Iverson, G. R. (1987). *Analysis of variance* (2nd ed.). Newbury Park, Calif.: Sage.

Jackson, G. B. (1980). Methods for integrative reviews. *Review of Educational Research,* *50*(3), 438–460.

Jaeger, R. M. (1983). *Statistics: A spectator sport.* Beverly Hills, Calif.: Sage.

Jaeger, R. M. (1984). *Sampling in education and the social sciences.* New York: Longman.

Jaeger, R. M. (1989). Certification of student competence. In R. L. Linn (Ed.), *Educational measurement* (3rd ed.). New York: American Council on Education/Macmillan.

Jahoda, M., Deutsch, M., and Cook, S. W. (1951). *Research methods in social relations with especial reference to prejudice.* New York: Dryden Press.

Janis, I. L. (1975). Effects of social support for stressful decision. In M. Deutsch and H. Hornstein (Eds.), *Applying social psychology: Implications for research practice and training.* Hillsdale, N.J.: Erlbaum.

Johnson, J. E., and Lauver, D. R. (1989). Alternative explanations of coping with stressful experiences associated with physical illness. *Advances in Nursing Science,* *11*(2), 39–52.

Johnson, J. M. (1975). *Doing field research.* New York: Free Press.

Johnson, R. H. (1978). Individual styles of decision-making: A theoretical model for counseling. *Personnel and Guidance Journal,* *56,* 530–536.

Johnson, T. H. (1966). *Oxford companion to American history.* New York: Oxford University Press.

Joint Committee on Standards for Educational Evaluation. (1981). *Standards for evaluations of educational programs, projects, and materials.* New York: McGraw-Hill.

Jonassen, D. H. (1987). Assessing cognitive structure: Verifying a method using pattern notes. *Journal of Research and Development in Education,* *20*(3), 1–14.

Jones, L. V., and Appelbaum, M. I. (1990). Psychometric methods. In M. R. Rosenzweig and L. W. Porter (Eds.), *Annual review of psychology* (Vol. 40, pp. 23–44). Palo Alto, Calif.: Annual Reviews.

Jöreskog, K. G., and Sörbom, D. (1988). LISREL VII: Analysis of linear structural relationships by maximum likelihood and least squares methods. In *Statistical Package for the Social Sciences.* New York: McGraw Hill.

Judd, C. M. (1987). Combining process and outcome evaluation. In M. M. Mark and R. L. Shotland (Eds.), *Multiple methods in program evaluation* (pp. 23–42). (New Directions for Program Evaluation No. 35). San Francisco: Jossey-Bass.

Judson, H. F. (1980). *The search for solutions.* New York: Holt, Rinehart & Winston.

Jung, C. G. (1971). Psychological types. In *Collected works of C. G. Jung* (2nd ed., Vol. 6). Princeton, N.J.: Princeton University Press.

Kagan, N., Krathwohl, D. R., and Farquhar, W. (1965). *IPR: Interpersonal process recall by videotape in exploratory studies of counseling and teaching-learning.* East Lansing: College of Education, Michigan State University. (ERIC Document Reproduction Service Nos. ED 003 230 and ED 017 946)

Kagan, N., Krathwohl, D. R., and Miller, R. (1963). Stimulated recall in therapy using video-tape: A case study. *Journal of Counseling Psychology,* *10,* 237–243.

Kagen, J., Rosman, B. L., Kay, D., Albert, J., and Phillips, W. (1964). Information processing in the child: Significance of analytic and reflective attitudes. *Psychological Monographs: General and Applied,* *78*(1, Whole No. 578).

Kaplan, A. (1964). *The conduct of inquiry: Methodology for behavioral science*. San Francisco: Chandler.

Kaplan, A. (1965). Noncausal explanation. In D. Learner (Ed.), *Cause and effect*. New York: Free Press.

Kaplan, M. (1973). *Urban planning in the 1960's: A design for irrelevancy*. New York: Praeger.

Katz, J. (1973). A new conception of service: Principles and strategies. In J. Katz (Ed.), *Services for students* (pp. 127–139). (New Directions for Higher Education No. 3). San Francisco: Jossey-Bass.

Kazdin, A. E. (1980). *Research design in clinical psychology*. New York: Harper & Row.

Kazdin, A. E. (1982). *Single-case research designs: Methods for clinical and applied settings*. New York: Oxford University Press.

Kelley, H. H. (1973). The processes of causal attribution. *American Psychologist, 28*, 107–128.

Kelling, G. L., Pate, T., Dieckman, D., and Brown, C. E. (1974). *The Kansas City preventive patrol experiment: A technical report*. Washington, D.C.: Police Foundation.

Kelly, M. M., and Schoen, S. F. (1988). It worked in my classroom: A social and academic behavior program. (ERIC Documentation Service No. ED 299 785)

Kerlinger, F. N. (1973, 1986). *Foundations of behavioral research* (2nd ed., 3rd ed.). New York: Holt, Rinehart & Winston.

Kincaid, H. V., and Bright, M. (1957). The tandem interview. *Public Opinion Quarterly, 21*, 304–312.

Kish, L. (1965). *Survey sampling*. New York: Wiley.

Klein, J. D., Voss, D. R., Reiser, R. A., and Gardner, G. N. (1987). The effect of age of viewer and gender of the narrator on children's visual attention and recall of story ideas. *Educational Communication and Technology Journal, 35*, 231–238.

Klopfer, B. (1970). *Developments in the Rorschach technique*. Yonkers-on-Hudson, N.Y.: World Book.

Knapp, T. R. (1990). Treating ordinal scales as interval scales: An attempt to resolve the controversy. *Nursing Research, 39*, 121–123.

Knorr, K. D., Mittermeir, R., Aichholzer, G., and Waller, G. (1979). Leadership and group performance: A positive relationship in academic research units. In F. M. Andrews (Ed.), *Scientific productivity: The effectiveness of research groups in six countries* (pp. 95–120). Cambridge: Cambridge University Press.

Köbben, A. S. F. (1973) Cause and intention. In R. Naroll and R. Cohen (Eds.), *A handbook of method in cultural anthropology*. New York: Columbia University Press.

Koshland, D. E., Jr. (1990). To see ourselves as others see us. *Science, 247*, 9.

Kounin, J. S. (1970). *Discipline and group management in classrooms*. New York: Holt, Rinehart & Winston.

Kounin, J. S., Friesen, W. V., and Norton, A. E. (1966). Managing emotionally disturbed children in regular classrooms. *Journal of Educational Psychology, 57*, 1–13.

Kounin, J. S., and Obradovic, S. (1968). Managing emotionally disturbed children in regular classrooms: A replication and extension. *Journal of Special Education, 2*, 129–135.

Krathwohl, D. R. (1980). The evaluator as negotiator. *Educational Evaluation and Policy Analysis, 2*(2), 25–34.

Krathwohl, D. R. (1985). *Social and behavioral science research: A new framework for conceptualizing, implementing, and evaluating research studies*. San Francisco: Jossey-Bass.

Krathwohl, D. R. (1988). *How to prepare a research proposal: Suggestions for funding and dissertations in the social and behavioral sciences* (3rd ed.). Syracuse, N.Y.: Syracuse University Press.

Krathwohl, D. R., Bloom, B. S., and Masia, B. (1964). *Taxonomy of educational objectives: Handbook II. The affective domain*. New York: McKay.

Krathwohl, D. R., Gordon, J., and Payne, D. (1967). The effect of sequence on programmed instruction. *American Educational Research Journal, 7,* 125–132.

Kratochwill, T. R. (Ed.). (1978). *Single subject research: Strategies for evaluating change.* New York: Academic Press.

Kreps, G. A. (Ed.). (1989). *Social structure and disaster.* Newark: University of Delaware Press.

Krueger, R. A. (1988). *Focus groups: A practical guide to applied research.* Newbury Park, Calif.: Sage.

Kruglanski, A. W. (1976). On the paradigmatic objections to experimental psychology. *American Psychologist, 31,* 655–663.

Kruglanski, A. W., and Kroy, M. (1976). Outcome validity in experimental research: A reconceptualization. *Representative Research in Social Psychology, 7,* 166–178.

Krumboltz, J. D., and Weisman, R. G. (1962). The effect of overt and covert responding to programmed instruction on immediate and delayed retention. *Journal of Educational Psychology, 53,* 89–92.

Kulik, J. A. (1984). *The uses and misuses of meta-analysis.* Paper presented at the annual meeting of the American Educational Research Association, New Orleans.

Lane, S. (1991). Implications of cognitive psychology for measurement and testing: Assessing students' knowledge structures. *Educational Measurement: Issues and Practice, 10,* 31–33, 36.

Lang, K., and Lang, G. E. (1960). Decisions for Christ: Billy Graham in New York City. In M. Stein (Ed.), *Identity and anxiety: Survival of the person in mass society.* Glencoe, Ill.: Free Press.

Langer, W. L. (Ed.). (1972). *An encyclopedia of world history: Ancient, medieval, and modern, chronologically arranged* (5th ed.). Boston: Houghton Mifflin.

Lansing, J., Withey, S., and Wolfe, A. (1971). *Working papers on survey research in poverty areas.* Ann Arbor: Survey Research Center, University of Michigan.

Laslett, B. (1978). Family membership, past and present. *Social Problems, 25,* 476–490.

Laslett, B. (1980). Beyond methodology: The place of theory in quantitative historical research. *American Sociological Review, 45,* 214–228.

Leinhardt, G., and Leinhardt, S. (1980). Exploratory data analysis: New tools for the analysis of empirical data. In D. C. Berliner (Ed.), *Review of research in education.* Washington, D.C.: American Educational Research Association.

Lengenfelder, H. (1988). *Libraries, information centers, and databases in science and technology: A world guide* (2nd ed.). New York: Sauer.

Leonard, W. H., and Lowery, L. R. (1979). Was there really an experiment? A quantitative procedure for verifying treatments in educational research. *Educational Researcher, 8*(6), 4–7.

Levin, H. M. (1983). *Cost-effectiveness: A primer.* (New Perspectives in Evaluation No. 4). Beverly Hills, Calif.: Sage.

Levine, H. G. (1985). Principles of data storage and retrieval for use in qualitative evaluations. *Educational Evaluation and Policy Analysis, 7*(2), 169–186.

Lewis, D. (1983). Causal explanation. In D. Lewis (Ed.), *Philosophical papers* (Vol. 2). Oxford: Oxford University Press.

Liebow, E. (1967). *Talley's corner: A study of Negro street corner men.* Boston: Little, Brown.

Light, R. J. (1984). Six evaluation issues that synthesis can resolve better than single studies. In W. H. Yeaton and P. M. Wortman (Eds.), *Issues in data synthesis* (pp. 57–73). (New Directions for Program Evaluation No. 24). San Francisco: Jossey-Bass.

Light, R. J., and Pillemer, D. (1984). *Summing up: The science of reviewing research.* Cambridge, Mass.: Harvard University Press.

Lincoln, Y. S., and Guba, E. G. (1986). But is it rigorous? Trustworthiness and authenticity in naturalistic evaluation. In D. D. Williams (Ed.), *Naturalistic evaluation.* (New Directions for Program Evaluation No. 30). San Francisco: Jossey-Bass.

Linn, R. L. (Ed.). (1989). *Educational measurement* (3rd ed.). New York: American Council on Education/Macmillan.

Linstone, H. A., and Turoff, M. A. (Eds.). (1975). *The Delphi method*. Reading, Mass.: Addison-Wesley.

Lipsey, M. W. (1990). *Design sensitivity: Statistical power for experimental research*. Newbury Park, Calif.: Sage.

Lipsey, M. W., and Pollard, J. A. (1989). Driving toward theory in program evaluation: More models to choose from. *Evaluation and Program Planning, 12*, 317–328.

Loehlin, J. C. (1987). *Latent variable models: An introduction to factor, path, and structural analysis*. Hillsdale, N.J.: Erlbaum.

Lofland, J. (1971). *Analyzing social settings: A guide to qualitative observation and analysis*. Belmont, Calif.: Wadsworth.

Lord, F. (1968). *Statistical theories of mental test scores*. Reading, Mass.: Addison-Wesley.

Luiten, J., Ames, W., and Ackerson, G. (1980). A meta-analysis of the effects of advance organizers on learning and retention. *American Educational Research Journal, 17*, 211–218.

Lynd, R. S. (1939). *Knowledge for what? The place of social science in American culture*. New York: Grove Press.

Lynd, R. S., and Lynd, H. M. (1929). *Middletown: A study in contemporary American culture*. New York: Harcourt Brace.

Mackie, J. L. (1965). Causes and conditions. *American Philosophical Quarterly, 4*, 245–264.

Mackie, J. L. (1974). *The cement of the universe: A study of causation*. Oxford: Clarendon Press.

Madaus, G. F. (1981). NIE clarification hearing: The negative team's case. *Phi Delta Kappan, 63*(2), 92–94.

Magidson, J. (1977). Toward a causal model approach for adjusting for preexisting differences in the nonequivalent control group situation: A general alternative to ANCOVA. *Evaluation Quarterly, 1*, 399–420.

Malinski, V. M. (1986). *Explorations on Martha Roger's science of unitary human beings*. Norwalk, Conn.: Appleton & Lang.

Mann, C. (1990). Meta-analysis in the breech. *Science, 249*, 476–480.

Mansfield, R. S., and Busse, T. V. (1977). Meta-analysis of research: A rejoinder to Glass. *Educational Researcher, 6*, 3.

Mark, M. M. (1986). Validity typologies and the logic and practice of quasi-experimentation. In W. M. K. Trochim (Ed.), *Advances in quasi-experimental design and analysis* (pp. 47–66). (New Directions for Program Evaluation No. 31). San Francisco: Jossey-Bass.

Mark, M. M. (1990). Methodological training: Dispensation from logic, blinders, or what? On using your head in evaluation. In C. Rinne (Ed.), *Proceedings of the 1990 Edward F. Kelly evaluation conference*. Albany: Evaluation Consortium, Albany School of Education, State University of New York.

Mark, M. M., and Shotland, R. L. (1987). Alternative models for the use of multiple methods. In M. M. Mark and R. L. Shotland (Eds.), *Multiple methods in program evaluation* (pp. 95–100). (New Directions for Program Evaluation No. 35). San Francisco: Jossey-Bass.

Marshall, S. P. (1990). Generating good items for diagnostic tests. In N. Frederiksen, R. Glaser, A. Lesgold, and M. G. Shafto (Eds.), *Diagnostic monitoring of skill and knowledge acquisition*. Hillsdale, N.J.: Erlbaum.

Maruyama, G. M., and Walberg, H. J. (1982). Causal modeling. In H. E. Mitzel (Ed.), *Encyclopedia of educational research* (5th ed.). New York: Free Press.

Mathison, S. (1988). Why triangulate? *Educational Researcher, 17*(2), 13–17.

May, R. B., Masson, M. E. J., and Hunter, M. A. (1990). *Application of statistics in behavioral research*. New York: Harper & Row.

Mazlish, B. (1972). *In search of Nixon: A psychological inquiry*. New York: Basic Books.

McCall, W. A. (1923). *How to experiment in education*. New York: Macmillan.

McCleary, R., Gordon, A. C., McDowall, D., Maltz, M. D. (1979). How a regression effect can make any delinquency intervention look effective. In L. Sechrest, S. G. West, M. A. Phillips, R. Redner, and W. Yeaton (Eds.), *Evaluation studies review annual* (Vol. 4, pp. 626–652). Beverly Hills, Calif.: Sage.

McKim, B. J., and Cowen, E. L. (1987). Multiperspective assessment of young children's school adjustment. *School Psychology Review, 16*, 370–381.

Mead, M. (1928). *Coming of age in Samoa: A psychological study of primitive youth for Western civilization*. New York: Morrow.

Meehl, P. E. (1977). Specific etiology and other forms of strong influence: Some quantitative meanings. *Journal of Medicine and Philosophy, 2*, 33–53.

Merton, R. K. (1959). Notes on problem-finding in sociology. In R. K. Merton, L. Broom, and L. Cotrell (Eds.), *Sociology today: Problems and prospects*. New York: Basic Books.

Merton, R. K. (1968). *Social theory and social structure*. New York: Free Press.

Merton, R. K., Fiske, M., and Kendall, P. L. (1956). *The focused interview: A manual of problems and procedures*. Glencoe, Ill.: Free Press.

Messick, S. (1989). Validity. In R. L. Linn (Ed.), *Educational measurement* (3rd ed., pp. 13–104). New York: American Council on Education/Macmillan.

Metfessel, N. S., and Michael, W. B. (1967). A paradigm involving multiple criterion measures for the evaluation of the effectiveness of school programs. *Educational and Psychological Measurement, 27*, 931–943.

Miles, M. B., and Huberman, A. M. (1984). *Qualitative data analysis: A book of new methods*. Beverly Hills, Calif.: Sage.

Milgram, S. (1963). Behavioral study of obedience. *Journal of Abnormal and Social Psychology, 67*, 371–378.

Milgram, S. (1974). *Obedience to authority: An experimental viewpoint*. New York: Harper & Row.

Milgram, S. (1977). Ethical issues in the study of obedience. In S. Milgram (Ed.), *The individual in a social world* (pp. 188–199). Reading, Mass.: Addison-Wesley.

Mill, J. S. (1868). *System of logic: Ratiocinative and inductive: Being a connected view of evidence and the methods of scientific investigation* (7th ed.). London: Longman.

Miller, G. A. (1977). *Spontaneous apprentices: Children and language*. New York: Seabury Press.

Miller, J. D. (1984). A new survey technique for studying deviant behavior. *Dissertation Abstracts International, 45*, 319A. (University Microfilms No. DA84-10-488)

Millman, J. (1989). If at first you don't succeed: Setting passing scores when more than one attempt is permitted. *Educational Researcher, 18*(6), 5–9.

Mills, J. (1976). A procedure for explaining experiments involving deception. *Personality and Social Psychology Bulletin, 2*, 3–13.

Mitroff, I. I., and Kilmann, R. H. (1976). On organizational stories: An approach to the design and analysis of organizations through myths and stories. In R. H. Kilmann, L. Pondy, and D. Slevin (Eds.), *The management of organization design*. Amsterdam: North-Holland.

Mitroff, I. I., and Kilmann, R. H. (1978). *Methodological approaches to social science: Integrating divergent concepts and theories*. San Francisco: Jossey-Bass.

Moffitt, R. A. (1979). The labor supply response in the Gary experiment. *Journal of Human Resources, 14*, 477–487.

Moehleman, A. H. (1969). *A guide to computer-assisted historical research in Amercian education*. Austin: Center for History Education, University of Texas.

Moreland, R. L., and Zajonc, R. B. (1977). Is stimulus recognition a necessary condition for the occurrence of exposure effects? *Journal of Personality and Social Psychology, 35*, 191–199.

Morgan, G. (Ed.). (1983). *Beyond method: Strategies for social research*. Beverly Hills, Calif.: Sage.

Moses, L. E. (1986). *Think and explain with statistics*. Reading, Mass.: Addison-Wesley.

Mosteller, F. (1981). Innovation and evaluation. *Science, 211,* 881–886.

Mosteller, F. K., and Wallace, D. L. (1984). *Applied Bayesian and classical inference: The case of the Federalist papers* (2nd ed.). New York: Springer-Verlag.

Nathan, R. P., Cook, R. R., and Rawling, V. L. (1981). *Public service employment: A field evaluation.* Washington, D.C.: Brookings Institution.

Nedelsky, L. (1954). Absolute grading standards for objective tests. *Educational and Psychological Measurement, 14,* 3–19.

Nelkin, D. (1984). *Science as intellectual property: Who controls research?* New York: Macmillan.

Nesselroade, J. R., and Baltes, P. B. (Eds.). (1979). *Longitudinal research in the study of behavior and development.* New York: Academic Press.

Nevins, A. (1975). *Allen Nevins on history.* New York: Scribner.

Newhouse, J. P., Rolph, J. E., Mori, B., and Murphy, M. (1980). The effects of deductibles on the demand for medical care services. *Journal of the American Statistical Association, 75,* 525–533.

Noffke, S. E., and Zeichner, K. M. (1987). *Action research and teacher thinking: The first phase of the action research project at the University of Wisconsin—Madison.* Paper presented at the annual meeting of the American Association for Educational Research, Washington, D.C. (ERIC Document Reproduction Service No. ED 295 939)

Oppenheim, A. N. (1966). *Questionnaire design and attitude measurement.* New York: Basic Books.

Orenstein, A., and Phillips, W. R. (1978). *Understanding social research: An introduction.* Boston: Allyn & Bacon.

Osborn, A. (1959). *Creative imagination: Applied imagination principles and procedures of creative thinking.* New York: Scribner.

Osgood, C., Suci G., and Tannenbaum, P. (1957). *The measurement of meaning.* Urbana: University of Illinois Press.

Padilla, R. (1990). *HyperQual, Version 3.* Desert Hot Springs, Calif.: Qualitative Research Management.

Page, M. M. (1973). On detecting demand awareness by post-experimental questionnaire. *Journal of Social Psychology, 91,* 305–323.

Pargament, K. I., Kennell, J., Hathaway, W., Gravengoed, N., Newman, J., and Jones, W. (1988). Religion and the problem solving process: Three styles of coping *Journal for the Scientific Study of Religion, 27,* 90–104.

Parnes, H. S. (1967). *Creative behavior workbook.* New York: Scribner.

Parnes, H. S. (1980). *The national longitudinal survey.* Report prepared for the U.S. Department of Labor, Manpower Administration. Washington, D.C.: U.S. Government Printing Office.

Paterson, J. G., and Zderad, L. T. (1988). *Humanistic nursing.* New York: National League for Nursing.

Patten, S. C. (1977). Milgram's shocking experiments. *Philosophy, 52,* 425–440.

Patton, M. Q. (1980). *Qualitative evaluation methods.* Beverly Hills, Calif.: Sage.

Payne, S. L. (1951). *The art of asking questions.* Princeton, N.J.: Princeton University Press.

Pedhazur, E. (1982). *Multiple regression in behavioral research: Explanation and prediction* (2nd ed.). New York: Holt, Rinehart & Winston.

Peter, L. J. (1969). *The Peter principle.* New York: Morrow.

Phelan, P. (1987). Compatibility of qualitative and quantitative methods: Studying child abuse in America. *Education and Urban Society, 29,* 35–41.

Phillips, D. C. (1987). *Philosophy, science and social inquiry.* Oxford: Pergamon.

Phillips, D. L. (1971). *Knowledge from what? Theories and methods in social research.* Chicago: Rand McNally.

Piaget, J. (1929). *The child's conception of the world.* (S. Tomlinson and A. Tomlinson, Trans.). London: Routledge & Kegan Paul.

Piaget, J. (1930). *The child's conception of physical causality*. (M. Gabian, Trans.). London: Routledge & Kegan Paul.

Piaget, J. (1952). *Origins of intelligence in children*. New York: International Universities Press.

Piel, G. (1986). The social process of science. *Science, 231*, 201.

Piliavin, J. A., and Piliavin, I. M. (1972). Effect of blood on reactions to a victim. *Journal of Personality and Social Psychology, 23*, 353–361.

Platt, J. R. (1964). Strong inference. *Science, 146*, 347–353.

Pletz, A. (1965). Psychology of the scientist: XI. Lotka's law and research visibility. *Psychological Reports, 16*, 566–568.

Poincaré, H. (1913). *The foundations of science: Sciences and hypothesis, the value of science, science and method*. New York: Science Press.

Pool, R. (1989). Chaos theory: How big an advance? *Science, 245*, 26–28.

Popham, W. J. (1981). The case for minimum competency testing. *Phi Delta Kappan, 63*(2), 89–91.

Popper, K. R. (1959). *The logic of scientific discovery*. New York: Basic Books.

Popper, K. R. (1972). Of clouds and clocks: An approach to the problem of rationality and the freedom of man. In K. R. Popper, *Objective knowledge: An evolutionary approach*. Oxford: Clarendon Press.

Potter, D. M. (1954). *People of plenty: Economic abundance and the American character*. Chicago: University of Chicago Press.

Prescott, P. S. (1982, June 28). The bard of St. Botolph's. *Newsweek*, p. 77.

Prewitt, K. (1980). Kenneth Prewitt, Frederick Mosteller, and Herbert A. Simon testify at National Science Foundation hearings. *Items, 34*, 1–7.

Prewitt, K. (1981). Usefulness of the social sciences. *Science, 211*, 659.

Price, D. J. D. (1963). *Little science, big science*. New York: Columbia University Press.

Quade, E. S. (1982). *Analysis for public policy decisions*. New York: Elsevier North-Holland.

Ragin, C. C. (1987). *The comparative method: Moving beyond qualitative and quantitative strategies*. Berkeley: University of California Press.

Rand Corporation. (1969). *A million random digits with 100,000 normal deviates*. Santa Monica, Calif.: Rand Corp.

Raphael, B. (1986). *When disaster strikes: How individuals and communities cope with catastrophe*. New York: Basic Books.

Raudenbusch, S. W. (1984). Magnitude of teacher expectancy's effects on pupil IQ as a function of credibility of expectancy induction: A synthesis of findings from 18 experiments. *Journal of Educational Psychology, 76*, 85–97.

Raudsepp, E. (1977, April). Daydream a little. *American Way, 10*, 27.

Reason, P., and Rowan, J. (Eds.). (1981). *Human inquiry: A sourcebook of new paradigm research*. New York: Wiley.

Reed, J. G., and Baxter, P. M. (1983). *Library use: A handbook for psychology*. Washington, D.C.: American Psychological Association.

Reichardt, C. S. (1985). Reinterpreting Seaver's (1973) study of teacher expectancies as a regression artifact. *Journal of Educational Psychology, 77*, 231–236.

Reichardt, C. S., and Cook, T. D. (1979). *Qualitative and quantitative methods in evaluation research*. Beverly Hills, Calif.: Sage.

Reichardt, C. S., and Gollob, H. F. (1987). Taking uncertainty into account when estimating effects. In M. M. Mark and R. L. Shotland (Eds.), *Multiple methods in program evaluation* (pp. 7–23). (New Directions for Program Evaluation No. 35). San Francisco: Jossey-Bass.

Richards, R. L. (1976). A comparison of selected Guilford and Wallach-Kogan Creative Thinking Tests in conjunction with measures of intelligence. *Journal of Creative Behavior, 10*, 151–164.

Rippey, R. M. (Ed.). (1973). *Studies in transactional evaluation*. Berkeley, Calif.: McCutcheon.

Rist, R. (1977). *The invisible children: School instruction in American society*. Cambridge, Mass.: Harvard University Press.

Robins, P. K., Spiegelman, R. G., Weiner, S., and Bell, J. G. (Eds.). (1980). *A guaranteed annual income: Evidence from a social experiment*. New York: Academic Press.

Roe, A. (1953a). *The making of a scientist*. New York: Dodd, Mead.

Roe, A. (1953b). A psychological study of eminent psychologists and anthropologists and a comparison with biological and physical scientists. *Psychological Monographs*, 2 (Whole No. 253).

Roethlisberger, F. J., and Dickson, W. J. (1939). *Management and the worker*. Cambridge, Mass.: Harvard University Press.

Rogers, C. R. (1951). *Client-centered therapy: Its current practice, implications, and theory*. Boston: Houghton Mifflin.

Rogosa, D. (1987). *Myths about longitudinal research* (87-CERAS-23). Stanford, Calif.: Center for Educational Research, Stanford University.

Rosaldo, R. (1980). Doing oral history. *Social Analysis*, 4, 89–99.

Rosenthal, R. (1969). Interpersonal expectations: Effects on experimenters' hypotheses. In R. Rosenthal and R. L. Rosnow (Eds.), *Artifact in behavioral research*. New York: Academic Press.

Rosenthal, R. (1976). *Experimenter effects in behavioral research* (Enlarged ed.). New York: Irvington.

Rosenthal, R. (1978). Combining results of independent studies. *Psychological Bulletin*, 85, 185–193.

Rosenthal, R. (1979). The "file drawer" problem and tolerance for negative results. *Psychological Bulletin*, 86, 638–641.

Rosenthal, R. (1984). *Meta-analysis procedures for social research*. Beverly Hills, Calif.: Sage.

Rosenthal, R. (1990). How are we doing in soft psychology? *American Psychologist*, 45, 775–777.

Rosenthal, R., and Rosnow, R. L. (1975). *The volunteer subject*. New York: Wiley.

Rosenthal, R., and Rubin, D. (1980). Summarizing 345 studies of interpersonal expectancy effects. In R. Rosenthal (Ed.), *Quantitative assessment of research domains*. (New Directions for Methodology of Social and Behavioral Science No. 5). San Francisco: Jossey-Bass.

Rosenthal, R., and Rubin, D. (1982). Comparing effect sizes of independent studies. *Psychological Bulletin*, 92, 500–504.

Rosner, S., and Abt, L. (1970). *The creative experience*. New York: Grossman.

Ross, S., Krugman, A., Lyerly, S. B., and Clyde, D. J. (1962). Drugs and placebos: A model design. *Psychological Reports*, 10, 383–392.

Rossi, P. H., Berk, R. A., and Lenihan, K. (1980). *Money, work, and crime: Experimental evidence*. New York: Academic Press.

Rossi, P. H., and Freeman, H. E. (1985). *Evaluation: A systematic approach* (3rd ed.). Beverly Hills, Calif.: Sage.

Rossi, P. H., and Lyall, K. (1976). *Reforming public welfare: A critique of the negative income tax experiments*. New York: Russell Sage Foundation.

Rossi, P. H., and Wright, J. D. (1986). Evaluation research: An assessment. In D. S. Cordray and M. W. Lipsey (Eds.), *Evaluation studies review annual* (Vol. 11, pp. 48–69). Beverly Hills, Calif.: Sage.

Rowe, M. B. (1974). Relation of wait-time and rewards to the development of language, logic and fate control, Part 1: Wait-time. *Journal of Research in Science Teaching*, 11, 81–94.

Royce, J. M., Lazar, I., and Darlington, R. B. (1983). Minority families, early education, and later life chance. *American Journal of Orthopsychiatry*, 53, 706–720.

Rubin, L. B. (1976). *Worlds of pain: Life in the working-class family*. New York: Basic Books.

Rubin, Z. (1970). Measurement of romantic love. *Journal of Personality and Social Psychology*, 16, 265–273.

Russell, B. (1953). On the notion of cause, with applications to the free-will problem. In

H. Feigl and M. Brodbeck (Eds.), *Readings in the philosophy of science*. New York: Appleton.

Ryan, K., and Phillips, D. (1982). Teacher characteristics. In H. Mitzel (Ed.) *Encyclopedia of Education Research* (5th ed.). New York: Free Press.

Sadler, D. R. (1981). Intuitive data processing as a potential source of bias in naturalistic evaluations. *Educational Evaluation and Policy Analysis, 3*(4), 25–31.

Salomon, G. (1981). *Communication and education, social and psychological interactions*. Beverly Hills, Calif.: Sage.

Scheerer, M. (1963). Problem solving. *Scientific American, 208*(4), 118–128.

Schmidt, F. L., and Hunter, J. E. (1981). Employment testing: Old theories and new research findings. *American Psychologist, 36*, 1128–1137.

Schneider, J. W., and Conrad, P. (1985). *Having epilepsy: The experience and control of illness*. Philadelphia: Temple University Press.

Schon, D. A. (1983). *The reflective practitioner: How professionals think in action*. New York: Basic Books.

Schuler, H. (1982). *Ethical problems in psychological research*. (M. S. Woodruff and R. A. Wicklund, Trans.). New York: Academic Press.

Schuman, H., and Converse, J. M. (1971). The effects of black and white interviewers on black responses in 1968. *Public Opinion Quarterly, 35*, 44–68.

Schuman, H., and Kalton, G. (1985). Survey methods. In G. Lindzey and E. Aronson (Eds.), *The handbook of social psychology* (3rd ed.). New York: Random House.

Schweinhart, L. J., and Weikart, D. P. (1985). Evidence that early childhood programs work. *Phi Delta Kappan, 66*, 545–551.

Schweitzer, A. (1990). *Out of my life and thought: An autobiography* (A. B. Lemke, Trans.). New York: Holt, Rinehart & Winston. (Originally published 1933.)

Scriven, M. (1972). Pros and cons about goal-free evaluation. *Evaluation Comment, 3*, 1–4. Reprinted in *Evaluation Practice, 12*, 55–62.

Scriven, M. (1974). Standards for the evaluation of educational program and products. In G. D. Borich. (Ed.), *Evaluating educating programs and products*. Englewood Cliffs, N.J.: Educational Technology Publications.

Scriven, M. (1980). Self-reference research. *Educational Researcher, 9*(6), 11–18, 30.

Seaver, W. B. (1971). Effects of naturally induced teacher expectancies on the academic performance of pupils in primary grades. *Dissertation Abstracts International, 32*, 3426–3427.

Seidel, J. V., Kjolseth, R., and Seymour, E. (1988). *The ethnograph* [computer program]. Littleton, Colo.: Qualis Research Associates.

Serlin, R. C. (1987). Hypothesis testing, theory building, and the philosophy of science. *Journal of Counseling Psychology, 34*, 365–371.

Shavelson, R. J. (1981). *Statistical reasoning for the behavioral sciences*. Boston: Allyn & Bacon.

Shavelson, R. J., Webb, N. M., and Rowley, G. L. (1989). Generalizability theory. *American Psychologist, 44*, 922–932.

Sheehy, E. P. (1986). *Guide to reference books* (10th ed.). Chicago: American Library Association.

Shelly, A. L., and Sibert, E. E. (1986). Using logic programming to facilitate qualitative data analysis. *Qualitative Sociology, 9*, 145–161.

Sibert, E. E., and Shelly, A. L. (1985, April). *Logic programming: Computer programming that complements qualitative research*. Paper presented at the annual meeting of the American Educational Research Association, Chicago.

Sibert, E. E., and Shelly, A. L. (1987). *Qualog user's manual (Vax/VMS version)*. Syracuse, N.Y.: School of Computer and Information Science, Syracuse University.

Sieber, J. E. (1983). Deception in social research, Part 3: The nature and limits of debriefing. *IRB: A Review of Human Subjects Research, 5*(3), 1–4.

Sieber, J. E., and Stanley, B. (1988). Ethical and professional dimensions of socially sensitive research. *American Psychologist, 43*, 49–55.

Sieber, S. D. (1973). The integration of fieldwork and survey methods. *American Journal of Sociology, 78,* 1335–1359.

Simon, A., and Boyer, G. E. (1974). *Mirrors for behavior.* Philadelphia: Communication Materials Center/Humanizing Learning Program, Research for Better Schools.

Skinner, B. F. (1957). *Verbal behavior.* New York: Appleton-Century-Crofts.

Skinner, B. F. (1968). The science of learning and the art of teaching. In B. F. Skinner, *The technology of teaching.* New York: Appleton-Century-Crofts. (Original version published in *Harvard Educational Review,* 1954, 24, 86–97)

Slavin, R. E. (1985). Best evidence synthesis: An alternative to meta-analytic and traditional reviews. *Educational Researcher, 15,* 5–11.

Slovic, P., Fischhoff, B., and Lichtenstein, S. (1982). Response mode, framing, and information-processing effects in risk assessment. In R. M. Hogarth (Ed.), *Question framing and response consistency.* (New Directions for Methodology of Social and Behavioral Science No. 11). San Francisco: Jossey-Bass.

Smith, L. M., and Geoffrey, W. (1968). *The complexities of an urban classroom: An analysis toward a general theory of teaching.* New York: Holt, Rinehart & Winston.

Smith, M. L. (1986). The whole is greater: Combining qualitative and quantitative approaches in evaluation studies. In D. D. Williams (Ed.), *Naturalistic evaluation.* (New Directions for Program Evaluation No. 30). San Francisco: Jossey-Bass.

Smith, M. L., Gabriel, R., Schott, J., and Padia, W. L. (1976). Evaluation effects of Outward Bound. In G. V. Glass (Ed.), *Evaluation studies review annual* (Vol. 1, pp. 400–421). Beverly Hills, Calif.: Sage.

Smith, M. L., and Glass, G. V. (1977). Meta-analysis of psychotherapy outcome studies. *American Psychologist, 32,* 752–760.

Smith, M. L., Glass, G. V., and Miller, T. I. (1980). *Benefits of psychotherapy.* Baltimore, Md.: Johns Hopkins University Press.

Snyder, M., and Cunningham, M. R. (1975). To comply or not comply: Testing the self-perception explanation of the "foot-in-the-door" phenomenon. *Journal of Personality and Social Psychology, 31,* 64–67.

Spengler, O. (1926). *The decline of the West.* New York: Knopf.

Spitzer, W. O., et al. (1974). The Burlington randomized trial of the nurse practitioner. *New England Journal of Medicine, 290,* 251–256.

Stack, C. (1974). *All our kin: Strategies for survival in a black community.* New York: Harper & Row.

Stake, R. E. (1975). To evaluate an arts program. In R. E. Stake (Ed.), *Evaluating the arts in education: A responsive approach.* Columbus, Ohio: Merrill.

Stake, R. E. (1978). Seeing and measuring. *Journal of Curriculum Studies, 10,* 265.

Stake, R. E. (1991). Excerpts from "Program evaluation, particularly responsive evaluations." *Evaluation Practice, 12,* 63–77.

Stake, R. E., and Easley, J. A., Jr. (Eds.). (1978a). *Case studies in science education, Vol. 1: The case reports.* Washington, D.C.: U.S. Government Printing Office.

Stake, R. E., and Easley, J. A., Jr. (Eds.). (1978b). *Case studies in science education, Vol. 2: Design, overview and general findings.* Washington, D.C.: U.S. Government Printing Office.

Stankiewicz, R. (1979). The size and age of Swedish academic research groups and their scientific performance. In F. M. Andrews (Ed.), *Scientific productivity: The effectiveness of research groups in six countries* (pp. 191–222). Cambridge: Cambridge University Press.

Stanley, B., Sieber, J. E., and Melton, G. B. (1987). Empirical studies of ethical issues in research: A research agenda. *American Psychologist, 42,* 735–741.

Stanley, J. C. (1985). Historical note about cross-sectional versus longitudinal studies. *Journal of Special Education, 19,* 359–361.

Stedman, L. C. (1987). It's time we changed the effective schools formula. *Phi Delta Kappan, 69,* 215–227.

Steiner, J. (1984). *Notebooks of the mind.* Albuquerque: University of New Mexico Press.

Stephenson, W. (1953). *The study of behavior*. Chicago: University of Chicago Press.

Stevens, S. S. (1946). On the theory of scales of measurement. *Science, 103*, 677–680.

Stevens, S. S. (1951). Mathematics, measurement, and psychophysics. In S. S. Stevens (Ed.), *Handbook of experimental psychology*. New York: Wiley.

Stewart, Lord. (1924). Rex vs. Sussex Justices, Nov. 9, 1923. *Kings Bench Reports, 1*, 259.

Strauss, A. (1987). *Qualitative analysis for social scientists*. Cambridge: Cambridge University Press.

Strauss, A., and Corbin, J. (1990). *The basics of qualitative research: Grounded theory procedures and techniques*. Newbury Park, Calif.: Sage.

Strong, E. K., Campbell, D. P., and Hansen, J. (1981) *Strong-Campbell Interest Inventory*. Palo Alto, Calif.: Stanford University Press/Consulting Psychologists Press.

Struyk, R. J., and Bendick, M., Jr. (1981). *Housing vouchers for the poor: Lessons from a national experiment*. Washington, D.C.: Urban Institute.

Stufflebeam, D. L., and Shinkfield, A. J. (1985). *Systematic evaluation: A self-instructional guide to theory and practice*. Boston: Kluwer Nijhoff.

Subkoviak, M. J. (1988). A practitioner's guide to computation and interpretation of reliability indices for mastery tests. *Journal of Educational Measurement, 25*, 47–56.

Suciati. (1990). *The effect of motivation on academic achievement in a distance education setting: An examination of latent variables in an Indonesian case*. Doctoral dissertation, Syracuse University.

Sudman, S., and Bradburn, N. M. (1982). *Asking questions: A practical guide to questionnaire design*. San Francisco: Jossey-Bass.

Sullivan, M. A., Queen, S. A., and Patrick, R. C., Jr. (1958). Participant observation as employed in a study of a military training program. *American Sociological Review, 23*, 660–667.

Survey Research Center, Institute for Social Research (1976). *Interviewer's manual* (Rev. ed.). Ann Arbor: Institute for Social Research, University of Michigan.

Swanson, D. B., and Stillman, P. L. (1990). Use of standardized patients for teaching and assessing clinical skills. *Evaluation and the Health Professions, 13*, 79–103.

Sweetland, R. C., and Keyser, D. J. (Eds.). (1987). *Tests: A comprehensive reference for assessments in psychology, education and business* (2nd ed.). Kansas City, Mo.: Test Corporation of America.

Tallmadge, G. K. (1977). *Ideabook: The joint dissemination review panel*. Washington, D.C.: U.S. Government Printing Office. (ERIC Document Reproduction Service No. DL 48329).

Taylor, S. (1977). The custodians: Attendants and their work at state institutions for the mentally retarded. *Dissertation Abstracts International, 39*, 1145–1146.

Taylor, S., and Bogdan, R. C. (1984). *Introduction to qualitative research methods: The search for meanings* (2nd ed.). New York: Wiley.

Terman, L. M., and Oden, M. M. (1947). *The gifted child grows up: Twenty-five years' follow-up of a superior group* (Vol. 4). Stanford, Calif.: Stanford University Press.

Terman, L. M., and Oden, M. M. (1959). *The gifted group at midlife* (Vol. 5). Stanford, Calif.: Stanford University Press.

Terman, L. M., et al. (1926). *The mental and physical traits of a thousand gifted children* (Vol. 1). Stanford, Calif.: Stanford University Press.

Tesch, R. (1990). *Qualitative research: Analysis types and software tools*. New York: Falmer.

Thompson, B. (1984). *Canonical correlation analysis: Uses and interpretation*. Beverly Hills, Calif.: Sage.

Thompson, B. (1991). A primer on the logic and use of canonical correlation analysis. *Measurement and Evaluation in Counseling and Development, 24*, 80–95.

Thorndike, R. M., Cunningham, G. K., Thorndike, R. L., and Hagen, E. P. (1991). *Measurement and evaluation in psychology and education* (5th ed.). New York: Macmillan.

Thurstone, L. L. (1935). *Vectors of the mind*. Chicago: University of Chicago Press.

Thurstone, L. L. (1947). *A development and expansion of the vectors of the mind: Multiple factor analysis*. Chicago: University of Chicago Press.

Tinto, V. (1987). *Leaving college: Rethinking the causes and cures of student attrition*. Chicago: University of Chicago Press.

Tobias, S., and Zibrin, M. (1978). Does blind reviewing make a difference? *Educational Researcher, 7,* 14–16.

Todd, R. F., and Reece, C. C. (1989). *Desirable skills and knowledge outcomes for an introductory educational research course: A Delphi study*. Memphis, Tenn.: Memphis State University. (ERIC Document Reproduction Service No. ED 305 342)

Toynbee, A. J. (1948). *A study of history*. London: Oxford University Press.

Traugott, M. W., Groves, R. M., and Lepkowski, J. M. (1987). Using dual frame designs to reduce nonresponse in telephone surveys. *Public Opinion Quarterly, 51,* 522–539.

Travers, R. M. W. (1961). *Measured needs of teachers and behavior in the classroom*. Salt Lake City: Department of Educational Psychology, University of Utah.

Treloar, A. E. (1939). *Elements of statistical reasoning*. New York: Wiley.

Tripp-Reimer, T. (1983). Retention of a folk-healing practice (matiasma) among four generations of urban Greek immigrants. *Nursing Research, 32*(2), 97–101.

Trochim, W. M. K. (1986). Conceptualization for planning and evaluation. *Evaluation and Program Planning, 9,* 289–308.

Trochim, W. M. K. (1989a). Concept mapping. *Evaluation and Program Planning, 12,* 87–110.

Trochim, W. M. K. (1989b). An introduction to concept mapping for planning and evaluation. *Evaluation and Program Planning, 12,* 1–16.

Tuchman, B. (1962). *The guns of August*. New York: Macmillan.

Tuckman, H. P. (1976). *Publication, teaching and the academic reward structure*. Lexington, Mass.: Heath.

Tufte, E. R. (1983). *The visual display of quantitative information*. Cheshire, Conn.: Graphic Press.

Tukey, J. W. (1977). *Exploratory data analysis*. Reading Mass.: Addison-Wesley.

Turner, B. A. (1981). Some practical aspects of qualitative data analysis: One way of organizing the cognitive processes associated with the generation of grounded theory. *Quality and Quantity, 15,* 225–247.

Tversky, A., and Kahneman, D. (1981). The framing of decisions and the psychology of choice. *Science, 211,* 453–458.

Tyack, D. (1976). Ways of seeing: An essay on the history of compulsory schooling. *Harvard Educational Review, 46,* 355–389.

Tyler, L. L., Klein, M. F., and Associates. (1976). *Evaluating and choosing curriculum and instructional materials*. Los Angeles: Educational Resource Associates.

Tyler, R. W. (1934). *Constructing achievement tests*. Columbus: Ohio State University.

Tyler, R. W., and Waples, D. (1930). *Research methods and teacher's problems: A manual for systematic studies of classroom procedure*. New York: Macmillan.

Van den Haag, E. (1956). *Education as an industry*. New York: Kelley.

Vansina, J. (1965). *Oral tradition: A study in historical methodology*. Chicago: Aldine.

Wade, N. (1978). Guillemin and Schally: A race spurred by rivalry. *Science, 200,* 510–513.

Waksberg, J. (1978). Sampling methods for random digit dialing. *Journal of the American Statistical Association, 73,* 40–46.

Walberg, H. J., and Ahlgren, A. (1970). Predictions of the social environment of learning. *American Educational Research Journal, 7,* 153–167.

Warner, S. L. (1965). Randomized response: A survey technique for eliminating evasive answer bias. *Journal of the American Statistical Association, 60,* 63–69.

Watson, J. D. (1968). *The double helix: A personal account of the discovery of the structure of DNA*. New York: Atheneum.

Watts, H. W., and Rees, A. (Eds.). (1976). *The New Jersey income maintenance experiment* (Vol. 2). New York: Academic Press.

Wax, M. L., and Wax, R. H. (1980). Fieldwork and the research process. *Anthropology and Education Quarterly, 11,* 29–37.

Wax, R. H. (1971). *Doing fieldwork: Warnings and advice.* Chicago: University of Chicago Press.

Webb, E. J., Campbell, D. T., Schwartz, R. D., Sechrest, L., and Grove, J. B. (1981). *Nonreactive measures in the social sciences* (2nd ed.). Boston: Houghton Mifflin.

Webb, W. H., Beals, A. R., and White, C. M. (1986). *Sources of information in the social sciences* (3rd ed.) Chicago: American Library Association.

Weick, K. E. (1984). Small wins: Redefining the scale of social problems. *American Psychologist, 39,* 40–49.

Weiner, B. (1972). *Theories of motivation from mechanism to cognition.* Chicago: Markham.

Weiner, B. (1980a). A cognitive (attribution)-emotion-action model of motivated behavior: An analysis of judgments of help-giving. *Journal of Personality and Social Psychology, 39,* 186–200.

Weiner, B. (1980b). *Human motivation.* New York: Holt, Rinehart & Winston.

Weiss, D., and Davison, M. (1981). Test theory and method. *Annual Review of Psychology, 32,* 629–658.

Wertheimer, M. (1945). *Productive thinking.* New York: Harper.

White, G. D., Nielsen, G., and Johnson, S. M. (1972). Timeout duration and the suppression of deviant behavior in children. *Journal of Applied Behavior Analysis, 5,* 111–120.

White, T. H. (1961). *The making of the president, 1960.* New York: Atheneum.

White, T. H. (1965). *The making of the president, 1964.* New York: Atheneum.

White, T. H. (1973). *The making of the president, 1972.* New York: Atheneum.

Whyte, W. F. (1955). *Street corner society: The social structure of an Italian slum* (2nd ed.). Chicago: University of Chicago Press.

Wildemuth, B. M. (1981). *A bibliography to accompany the joint committee's standards on educational evaluation.* Princeton, N.J.: ERIC Clearinghouse on Tests, Measurement, and Evaluation, Educational Testing Service. (ERIC Document Reproduction Service No. ED 222 512)

Williams, J. E. (1989). A numerical taxonomy of evaluation theory and practice (Mimeo.). Los Angeles: Graduate School of Education, University of California.

Williams, M.E., Lannom, L., and Robins, C. G. (Eds.). (1985). *Computer-readable databases: A directory and data sourcebook.* Chicago: American Library Association.

Wilson, J. (1971). *Thinking with concepts.* Cambridge: Cambridge University Press.

Wilson, R. S., and Matheny, A. P., Jr. (1983). Mental development: Family environment and genetic influences. *Intelligence, 7,* 195–215.

Windle, C. (1954). Test-retest effect on personality questionnaires. *Educational and Psychological Measurement, 14,* 617–633.

Wittrock, M. C. (1974). A generative model of mathematics learning. *Journal for Research in Mathematics Education, 5,* 181–196.

Wolcott, H. (1973). *The man in the principal's office: An ethnography.* New York: Holt, Rinehart & Winston.

Wolf, R. L. (1975). Trial by jury: A new evaluation method. *Phi Delta Kappan, 57,* 185–187.

Wolf, R. L. (1979). The use of judicial evaluation methods in the formulation of educational policy. *Evaluation and Policy Analysis, 1*(3), 19–28.

Wood, R. (1969). Efficacy of tailored testing. *Educational Research, 11,* 219–222.

Woodbury, M. (1982). *A guide to sources of educational information* (2nd ed.). Arlington, Va.: Information Resources Press.

Woodbury, M. (1985). *Childhood information resources.* Arlington, Va.: Information Resources Press.

Worthen, B. R., and Sanders, J. R. (1987). *Educational evaluation: Alternative approaches and practical guidelines.* White Plains, N.Y.: Longman.

Wortman, P. M. (1984). Cost-effectiveness: A review. In R. F. Connor, D. G. Altman, and C. Jackson (Eds.), *Evaluation studies review annual* (Vol. 9). Beverly Hills, Calif.: Sage.

Wortman, P. M., Reichardt, C. S., and St. Pierre. R. G. (1978). The ███████ education voucher demonstration. *Evaluation Quarterly, 2,* 193–214█

Wright, S. (1921). Correlation and causation. *Journal of Agricultural Rese██ Chemistry, 20,* 557–585.

Wulff, K. M. (1977). Relationship of assigned classroom seating area to ach██ variables. *Educational Research Quarterly, 2,* 56–62.

Wylie, R. C. (1979). *The self-concept* (Rev. ed.). Lincoln: University of Nebraska Pre█

Yates, B. T. (1985). Cost-effectiveness analysis and cost-benefit analysis: An int█ duction. *Behavioral Assessment, 7,* 207–234. Reprinted in D. S. Cordray and M. W█ Lipsey (Eds.). (1986). *Evaluation studies review annual* (Vol. 11, pp. 315–342). Beverly Hills, Calif.: Sage.

Yin, R. K. (1984). *Case study research: Design and methods.* Beverly Hills, Calif.: Sage.

Young, F. W. (1985). Scaling. In M. R. Rosenzweig and L. W. Porter (Eds.), *Annual review of psychology* (Vol. 35, pp. 55–81). Palo Alto, Calif.: Annual Reviews.

Youngstrom, N. (1990, September). Psychologist receives NAMI science award. *APA Monitor, 21,* 7.

Zdep, S. M., and Irvine, S. H. (1970). A reverse Hawthorne effect in educational evaluations. *Journal of School Psychology, 8*(2), 89–95.

Zeigarnik, B. (1927). Untersuchungen zur Handlungs- und Affektpsychologie, herausgegeben von K. Lewin, Teil 3: Das Behalten erledigter und unerledigter Handlungen. *Psychologisches Forschung* [Psychological Research], *9,* 1–85.

Zemke, R., and Walonick, D. (1980). The non-statistician's approach to conducting and analyzing surveys. *Training/HRD, 17,* 89–90, 93, 96–99.

Zimbardo, P. G., Anderson, S. M., and Kabat, L. G. (1981). Induced hearing deficit generates experimental paranoia. *Science, 212,* 1529–1531.

Zweier, G., and Vaughan, G. M. (1984). Three ideological orientations in school vandalism research. *Review of Educational Research, 54,* 263–292.

Zwicky, F. (1969). *Discovery, invention, and research through the morphological approach.* New York: Macmillan.

first year of the

rch and Food

vement

s.

o-

Name Index

Abt, L., 83, 90
Adair, J. D., 466n
Adams, Henry, 677
Ahlgren, A., 584
Aiken, L. S., xvii
Allen, M. S., 79
Allison, G. T., 502–503, 638, 650
Ames, L. B., 32
Andersen, Susan M., 10
Anderson, C. A., 464
Anderson, J. G., 374, 378
Anderson, L., 645
Andrews, F. M., 608
Anscombe, F. J., 178, 179
Appelbaum, M. I., 213
Arabie, P., 226
Argyris, C., 526
Arms, R. L., 285
Asimov, I., 688
Atkins, T. V., 108
Ausubel, David, 576
Aydelotte, William, 503

Babbie, E. R., 515n
Back, K., 507
Backer, T. E., 226
Bacon, Francis, 247
Baker, F. B., 607
Baker, G., 445
Baltes, P. B., 557
Bandura, A., 189
Bangert-Drowns, R. L., 565, 570
Banks, C. W., 491
Barlow, D. H., 564
Barnett, W. S., 527
Baron, R. A., 391, 464
Barron, Annette, 17
Barzun, J., 503–507, 509, 512, 633
Batson, C. D., 601, 602
Baumrind, D., 589, 669
Baxter, P. M., 104
Beals, A. R., 104
Beck, S. J., 214
Becker, H. S., 5, 244

Bellak, L., 214
Bendick, M., Jr., 542n
Berckmans, T. R., 376
Berdie, Doug R., 617n
Bereiter, C., xviii
Berger, P., 688
Berk, R. A., 224, 225, 231, 542, 544
Berkowitz, L., 444
Berrueta-Clement, J. R., 527
Bertaux, Daniel, 656
Bertaux-Wiame, Isabelle, 656
Biernacki, P., 139
Biklen, S. K., 311, 323, 326, 338
Binet, A., 6
Blair, R. C., 430
Blake, Phillip, 42
Blau, T., 636
Bloom, B. S., 33, 213, 262, 385, 565
Bloom, H. S., 527
Bogdan, R. C., 311, 314, 323, 326, 329, 338, 478, 545
Bogue, A. G., 503
Bollen, K., 590
Boruch, R. F., 451, 455–456, 478, 541
Bosk, C. L., 319, 320, 334, 340, 672
Bouchard, T. J., Jr., 326, 327
Boulding, K. E., 687–688
Bracht, G. H., 284, 465, 479–480
Bradburn, N. M., 379, 380
Bradbury, K. L., 542n
Brahms, Johannes, 79
Breland, H., 204
Brennan, R. L., 212
Brewer, J., 617
Brickell, H. M., 545–546
Briggs, J. W., 511, 514
Bright, M., 371
Brinberg, D., 292
Broad, W., 53, 679
Bronfenbrenner, U., 300

Bronowski, Jacob, 3, 38, 146, 192
Brookover, W., 260
Brophy, J., 42, 645
Brown, M. A., 314
Burks, B. S., 365
Buros, Oscar Krisen, 226
Burt, Cyril, 679
Burton, M. A. B., 520–521
Busse, T. V., 570
Byrne, G., 72
Byrnes, James F., 509

Cahalan, D. T., 392
Cain, G. G., 450, 606
Camburn, D., 557
Campbell, D. T., 30, 75–76, 252, 270, 271, 284, 292, 342, 360, 440, 450–452, 454, 455, 461, 465n, 479, 480, 484, 496, 634
Cannell, C. F., 360, 376
Carifio, J., 391
Carlsmith, L., 464, 517, 518
Carlson, Chet, 72
Carr, E. H., 512
Carroll, J. D., 226
Cattell, R. B., 586
Ceci, S. J., 681
Centra, J. A., 679
Chamberlin, T. C., 637–638
Chapman, D., 445
Chase, W. G., 77
Cheever, John, 639
Chun, K. T., 226–227
Cicero, 97
Clotfelter, C. T., 527
Cobb, S., 226–227
Cohen, J., 163, 431, 432n, 597n
Cohen, M. R., 47
Coleman, J. S., 86, 450, 546, 605
Converse, J. M., 372, 379
Cook, R. R., 538
Cook, S. W., 484

771

A. S., xviii, 80
, J. D., 163
L., 381, 383
D. P., 154, 260
M., xii
R. B., 714
C., 645
., 214

, 227
, G. W., 543
., 385
D. L., 555–556
212
97
., ..81

Culler, R. E., 425, 594–595
Cunningham, M. R., 387
Cunningham, N. J., 623
Cusick, P., 335

Dalton, D. W., 611
Dalton, M., 327
Daniels, A. K., 676, 728
Darley, J. M., 601, 602
Darlington, R. B., 301
Darwin, Charles, 82
Davidson, M., 111–112
Davis, C., 507
Davis, J. A., 33, 363, 588, 589
Davison, M., 215, 225n
Dawes, R. M., 226
De Back, V., 522, 523, 721
Denmark, F. L., 476
Dennis, H., 468
Denzin, N. K., 328
Dewey, John, 79
Dickson, W. J., 466
Dillman, D. A., 387
Dollard, J., 6
Donnerstein, E., 444
Doob, L. W., 6
Dorfman, D. D., 679
Dostoevsky, Feodor, 79
Downs, A., 542n
Duffy, G., 619
Duncan, O. D., 159n, 168n, 193

Easley, J. A., Jr., 537
Edgell, S. E., 391
Edgington, E. S., 597
Edison, Thomas Alva, 79, 86
Einhorn, H. J., 253n, 273, 277
Einstein, Albert, 303
Eisner, E. W., 526, 534, 617n
Elesh, D., 527
Ellenova, Sarah, 308
Ellett, F. S., Jr., 260
Ellsworth, P. D., 444–445

Festinger, L., 5
Fillenbaum, S., 669
Fischer, D. H., 502, 504, 512, 513
Fischhoff, B., 380
Fisher, J., 254–256
Fiske, D. W., 682
Fiske, M., 370, 371
Fitzsimmons, S. J., 335
Flanders, N. A., 214
Fogel, R. W., 503
Fogg, L., 682
Ford, Joseph, 688
Foster, S. B., 314
Frank, César, 79
Frederiksen, N., 214
Freed, M. M., 104
Freedman, D. A., 589
Freedman, D. S., 557
Freeman, H. E., 532, 721
French, J. R. P., 226–227
Freud, Sigmund, 87
Frey, J. H., 374, 387
Friedman, J., 542n
Friesen, W. V., 39, 40
Fruchter, B., 183–185, 212, 429, 594n, 596, 608
Frye, N., 689, 690
Furby, L., 606

Gallegos, J. G., 387
Gans, H. J., 340
Garvey, W. D., 40, 114
Geertz, C., 329
Geischeider, G. A., 226
Genesee, F., 522
Geoffrey, W., 5
Gerberich, J. R., 213
Gergen, K. J., 632n
Gesell, A., 32
Getzels, J. W., 73, 83–84, 303
Ghiselli, E. E., 565
Glaser, B., 22, 326
Glaser, E. M., 683
Glass, G. V., 100, 284, 465, 479–480, 566–569, 571
Glavin, John, 42

Goldberger, A. S., 450, 606
Goldman, B. A., 226
Goldstein, J. H., 284–285
Gollob, H. F., 618
Gomez, H., 455–456, 478, 541
Gonda, T. A., 254
Good, Thomas, 42
Gordon, J., 476
Gottfredson, S. D., 682
Gouldner, A. W., 325, 326
Gove, P. P., 52, 270
Graff, H. F., 503–507, 509, 512, 633
Grant, G. P., 88, 347–348
Green, J. O., 726
Green, T. F., 149, 150, 154, 155
Gross, M., 468
Groves, R. M., 374, 387
Grunder, T. M., 659, 661–665
Guba, E. G., 326, 526, 538–539
Guenzel, P. J., 376
Guilford, J. P., 183–185, 212, 429, 594n, 596, 608
Gulliksen, H., 213
Gustafson, T., 683
Guy, W., 468

Hahn, J. C., 527
Hall, G. F., 491
Hall, J. L., 115
Hall, V., xii
Halperin, Si, 249
Hambleton, R. K., 221
Hamilton, W. L., 543
Haney, C., 491
Hannafin, M. J., 611
Hannum, J. W., 560
Hansen, J., 30, 634
Hansen, R. A., 387
Hanson, N. R., 681
Hauser-Cram, P., 569
Hays, W. L., 184, 424, 601, 608
Hedges, L. V., 568–569, 570, 572–573
Heim, A. W., 456
Henshel, R. L., 444
Herbert, George, 238
Hersen, M., 564
Hess, R. K., 104
Hewett, Frank, 42
Higgins, J. J., 430
Hillard, J., 104
Himmelfarb, S., 391
Hinkle, D., 608
Hoaglin, D. C., 163, 550, 556
Hoffer, T., 86, 450, 605
Hoffmann-Riem, Christa, 16–18, 28, 31, 59n, 62, 74, 247, 700
Hogarth, R. M., 253n, 273, 277
Holahan, C. J., 425, 594–595
Homer, P. M., 590–592, 594
Hooper, S., 611

Hoover, Herbert, 129
Hoshmand, L. T., xviin
House, E. R., 526, 539
Hubbard, D. R., Jr., 560
Huberman, A. M., 326, 329, 332, 333, 336–338, 340, 341, 346, 348
Huff, D., 187
Hughes, Everett, 318
Hume, David, 241
Humphreys, L., 334, 636, 665
Hunt, M., 679
Hunter, A., 617
Hunter, J. E., 204, 569, 570
Hunter, M. A., 424, 430, 433n, 435
Huth, Wolfgang, 17
Huxley, E., 537
Huynh, C., 466n
Hyman, H. H., 373

Ilg, F., 32
Irvine, S. H., 467

Jackson, G. B., 565, 569, 570
Jaeger, R. M., 225, 376
Jahoda, M., 484
Janis, I. L., 445
Jensen, D. W., 365
Johnson, J. E., 623
Johnson, K., 112
Johnson, R. H., 94
Johnson, S. M., 562
Jonassen, D. H., 68, 307, 702, 703, 712
Jones, L. V., 213
Jöreskog, K. G., 589, 607
Judd, C. M., 618
Judson, H. F., 47, 630
Jung, Carl, 94, 262
Jurs, S., 608

Kabat, Loren G., 10
Kagan, N., 385
Kagen, J., 308, 711
Kahle, L. R., 590–592, 594
Kahneman, D., 78, 380
Kallmeyer, Werner, 17
Kalton, G., 391
Kaplan, A., 262, 538
Katz, J., 679
Kazdin, A. E., 469, 564
Kelley, H. H., 253n
Kelly, M. M., 576
Kendall, P. L., 370, 371
Kennedy, John F., 502–503, 639
Kerlinger, F. N., 515n, 555
Keyser, D. J., 227
Kilgore, S., 86, 450, 605
Kilmann, R. H., 442n, 627
Kincaid, H. V., 371
King, Martin Luther, Jr., 372

Kirk, David, 17
Kish, L., 128
Kjolseth, R., 339
Klein, J. D., 719
Klein, M. F., 533, 534n
Klein, Morris, 90
Klopfer, B., 214
Knapp, T. R., 160n
Knorr, K. D., 682
Köbben, A. J. F., 239
Koshland, D. E., Jr., 673–674
Kounin, J. S., 6, 39–43, 47, 49, 102, 247, 317, 449
Kraepelin, E., 11
Krathwohl, D. R., 33, 90, 244n, 262, 292, 308, 385, 476, 501, 543
Kratochwill, T. R., 564
Kreps, G. A., 445
Kreuger, R. A., 372
Kroy, M., 284
Kruglanski, A. W., 284, 442n, 476
Kuhlen, Ray, 41
Kulik, J. A., 566

Labov, William, 17
Lane, S., 214
Lang, G. E., 344
Lang, K., 344
Lannom, L., 86
Lansing, J., 375
Laslett, B., 503, 510, 513, 521, 522, 722
Lauver, D. R., 623
Lazar, I., 301
Learned, J., 32
Lee, Robert E., 513
Lefcowitz, M. J., 527
Leinhardt, G., 186
Leinhardt, S., 186
Lengenfelder, H., 115
Lenihan, K., 542n
Leonard, W. H., 490
Lepkowski, J. M., 387
Levin, H. M., 532
Levine, H. G., 326
Lewis, D., 240
Lewis, Sinclair, 82
Lichtenstein, S., 380
Liebow, E., 320, 344, 636
Light, R. J., 572, 573
Lin, N., 40, 114
Lincoln, Y. S., 89, 326, 526, 538–539
Linowitz, Sol, 72
Linstone, H. A., 555
Lipsey, M. W., 431, 589
Little, K. B., 254
Llabre, M., 203
Loehlin, J. C., 590
Lofland, J., 338
Lord, F., 215

Louck
Louden,
Lowery, L
Luckmann,
Lyall, K., 444
Lynd, Robert, 4

Mackie, J. L., 239, 2
MacLean, K., 507
Madaus, G. F., 536
Magilavy, L. J., 387
Maher, B., 11
Malinski, V. M., 726
Mansfield, R. S., 570
Mark, M. M., 477, 618
Marshall, S. P., 214
Maruyama, G. M., 589
Masia, B., 33, 262
Masson, M. E. J., 424, 430, 433n, 435
Matheny, A. P., Jr., 581, 582
Mathison, S., 328
May, R. B., 424, 430, 433n, 435
Mazlish, B., 503
McCall, W. A., 76
McCleary, R., 459–460
McClellan, George B., 513
McGaw, B., 100, 469, 568, 571
McGrath, J. E., 292
McKim, B. J., 656–657, 726
McNamara, Robert, 686
McSweeney, A. J., 451
Mead, Margaret, 349–350
Meehl, P. E., 258–260
Melton, G. B., 664
Mentkowski, M., 522, 523, 721
Merrill, J., 464
Merton, R. K., 51, 54, 76, 78, 81, 370, 371, 634
Messick, S., 199, 201, 204
Metfessel, N. S., 227, 230
Michael, W. B., 227, 230
Miles, M. B., 326, 329, 332, 333, 336–338, 340, 341, 346, 348
Milgram, S., 660, 669
Mill, John Stuart, 247–250
Miller, George A., 311
Miller, J. D., 391
Miller, M. D., 203
Miller, R., 385
Miller, T. E., 567
Millman, J., 225, 288n
Mills, J., 669
Mitroff, I. I., 442n, 627
Mitzel, Harold, 43
Moffitt, R. A., 542n
Moreland, R. L., 681
Morgan, G., 626, 627, 655n
Moses, L. E., 405n, 424, 596n
Mosteller, F., 444n, 508

Nagel, E., 47

S. F., 491
W. J., 164
R., 490
Thomas, 490
543n, 21
619

59, 273, 513

, R., 526

E. S., 555
erbert, 42
. A., 316, 317

C., 348
, V. M., 464
., 445
ch, S. W., 572
E., 79
L., 538
640
, 555
104
., C. S., 477, 527, 618

A., 73, 80
Osgood, C., 586, 587n
Ostrow, R., 108

Padilla, R., 339
Page, M. M., 669
Pannor, Reuben, 17
Parnes, H. S., 73, 556
Pasteur, Louis, 97
Paterson, J. G., 726
Patrick, R. C., Jr., 316, 317
Patten, S. C., 669
Patton, M. Q., 325n, 524
Pauling, Linus, 82–83
Payne, D., 476
Payne, S. L., 379, 380
Pedhazur, E., 597n
Peter, L. J., 85
Peters, D., 681
Phelan, Patricia, 724
Phillips, D. C., 243–244, 681
Phillips, D. L., 392
Phillips, Debra, 43
Phillips, W. R., 316, 320, 326, 335, 344, 372, 373
Piaget, J., 34, 87, 89, 622n, 637
Piel, G., 38
Piliavin, I. M., 727
Piliavin, J. A., 727
Pillemer, D., 572, 573
Plato, 158
Platt, J. R., 637
Poincaré, H., 79
Polkinghorne, D. E., xviin
Pollard, J. A., 589
Pool, R., 688
Popham, W. J., 536
Popper, K. R., 242, 243, 321, 434, 634
Potter, D. M., 512
Prescott, P. S., 639
Presser, S., 379
Prewitt, K., 678, 686
Price, D. J. D., 679–680

Reicken, H., 5
Reynolds, R., 677
Richards, R. L., 257, 259
Rippey, R. M., 526, 538
Rist, R., 5, 304, 320
Robertson, Emily, 149n, 239n
Robins, C. G., 86
Robins, P. K., 542n
Robinson, L. M., 387
Roe, A., 653
Roehler, L., 619
Roethlisberger, F. J., 466
Rogers, C. R., 87
Rogosa, D., 557
Roosevelt, Franklin D., 129
Rosaldo, R., 508
Rosenthal, R., 386, 468, 566, 568–571, 594n, 680–681
Rosner, S., 83, 90
Rosnow, R. L., 386
Ross, S., 492–494
Rossi, P. H., 444, 533, 536–537, 542n, 543, 544, 619, 721
Rowan, J., 640
Rowe, M. B., 286, 685
Rowley, G. L., 212
Royce, J. M., 301
Rubin, D., 468, 570, 680–681
Rubin, L. B., 636
Rubin, Z., 445
Russell, Bertrand, 239
Ryan, J. M., 104
Ryan, Kevin, 43

Sadler, D. R., 344
Safire, William, 79
Salomon, G., 189, 708
Sanders, J. R., 529n, 537
Schacter, P., 5
Schaffer, Rudolph, 21
Scheerer, M., 82
Schmidt, F. L., 204, 569, 570
Schoen, S. F., 576
Schon, D. A., xviin, 726
Schuetz, Alfred, 20, 21
Schuetze, Fritz, 17

Schuman, H., 372, 391
Schweinhart, L. J., 301
Schweitzer, Albert, 81
Scriven, M., 531, 533, 632n
Seaver, W. B., 477
Seidel, J. V., 339
Serlin, R. C., 583
Seymour, E., 339
Sharpe, D., 466n
Shavelson, R. J., 212, 424
Sheehy, E. P., 104
Shelly, A. L., 339
Shinkfield, A. J., 531
Shotland, R. L., 618
Shulman, L. S., xviii, 80
Sibert, E. E., 339
Sieber, J. E., 343, 660, 664, 669–671
Simon, H. A., 77
Simon, Neil, 83
Singer, N. M., 527
Skinner, B. F., 34, 89, 147, 634, 637, 726
Slavin, R. E., 573
Slovic, P., 380
Smith, D. M., 526
Smith, L. M., 5
Smith, M. L., 100, 527, 567–569, 571, 618–619
Snyder, M., 387
Soderstrom, E. J., 451
Solomon, Gavriel, 492n
Sörbon, D., 589, 607
Sorosky, Arthur D., 17
Southwind, Gladys, 189
Spengler, O., 637
Spitzer, W. O., 527
Sprafka, S. A., xviii, 80
St. Pierre, R. G., 527
Stake, R. E., 323, 537
Stankiewicz, R., 682
Stanley, B., 660, 664, 670, 671
Stanley, J. C., 75–76, 270, 271, 292, 342, 450–452, 454, 455, 461, 465n, 484, 575
Starr, J., 501
Stedman, L. C., 260
Steffens, Lincoln, 504
Steiner, J., 82
Stephenson, W., 555
Stern, Daniel, 21
Stevens, S. S., 159n, 160n
Stewart, Lord, 550
Stewart, N. R., 623
Stillman, P. L., xviii
Stonewater, J. K., 703
Strauss, A., 22, 324, 326, 332, 337, 338, 340, 347
Strong, E. K., 30, 634
Struyk, R. J., 542n
Stufflebeam, D. L., 531
Subkoviak, M. J., 224

Suci, G., 586, 587n
Suciati, 266
Sudman, S., 379, 380
Sullivan, M. A., 316, 317
Suppes, P., 297
Sussman, Lila, 335
Swanson, D. B., xviii
Sweetland, R. C., 227

Tallmadge, G. K., 533
Tannenbaum, P., 586, 587n
Taylor, S., 305, 311n, 329, 683
Teilhard de Chardin, Pierre S. J.,
    677
Terman, L. M., 365, 575, 701, 722
Tesch, R., 339
Thompson, B., 585
Thoresen, C. E., 560
Thorndike, R. M., 197
Thornton, A., 557
Thurstone, L. L., 192, 586
Tinto, V., 487
Tobias, S., 681–682
Todd, R. F., 555
Tornatzky, L. G., 543
Toynbee, Arnold, 628, 637
Traugott, M. W., 387
Travers, R. M. W., 42, 158
Treloar, A. E., 605
Tripp-Reimer, T., 715
Trochim, W. M. K., 155
Truman, Harry, 509
Tuchman, Barbara, 260, 505, 639
Tuckman, H. P., 679
Tufte, E. R., 164–165, 178, 179
Tukey, J. W., 163, 186, 608
Turner, B. A., 338

Turoff, M. A., 555
Tversky, A., 226, 380
Tyack, David, 513
Tyler, L. L., 533, 534n
Tyler, R. W., 529

Van den Haag, E., 87
Vansina, J., 507
Vaughan, G. M., 640
Verdoorn, P. J., 397

Wade, N., 679, 680
Waksberg, J., 373
Walberg, H. J., 584, 589
Waldorf, D., 139
Waletzky, Joshua, 17
Walker, Helen, 183
Wallace, D. L., 508
Walonick, D., 378
Waples, D., 529
Warner, S. L., 391
Watson, J. D., 82, 83, 680
Wax, M. L., 98
Wax, R. H., 98, 320, 343
Webb, E. J., 223, 379, 467
Webb, N. M., 212
Webb, W. H., 104
Weick, K. E., 683
Weikart, D. P., 301, 527
Weinberg, D., 542n
Weiner, Bernard, 265
Weiss, D., 111–112, 215, 225n
Wertheimer, M., 303
White, C. M., 104
White, G. D., 562
White, T. H., 639
Whyte, W. F., 5, 28, 320–321, 324,

Wiersm[...]
Wildemu[...]
Williams, J[...]
Williams, M[...]
Wilson, R. S., [...]
Windle, C., 456
Withey, S., 375
Wittrock, M. C., 726
Wolf, R. L., 536
Wolfe, A., 375
Woodbury, M., 104, 227
Worthen, B. R., 529n, 537
Wortman, P. M., 527, 532
Wothke, W., 451
Wright, J. D., 536–537, 543
Wright, Sewall, 589
Wyeth, Andrew, 82

Yates, B. T., 532
Yin, R. K., 348
Young, F. W., 226
Youngstrom, N., 88

Zajonc, R. B., 681
Zdep, S. M., 467
Zderad, L. D., 726
Zeichner, K. M., 726
Zeigarnik, B., 141, 476
Zemke, R., 378
Zibrin, M., 681–682
Zimbardo, P. G., 4, 7, 10,
    271–278, 283–289, 491
Zweier, G., 640
Zwicky, F., 79

ect Index

NAME INDEX

775

327, 347, 636
W., 608
B. M., 549
E., 539
86
581, 582

...g services lists, 103–104
Acceptance, securing in qualitative
    research, 320–321
Achievement
    of public and private high
        school students, 605–606
    structural model of, 589, 590
    study of class size and, 571–572
Achievement Goals Program
    (AGP), 575
Achievement tests, content
    validity of, 202–203
Acquired immune deficiency
    syndrome (AIDS), 671, 675
Action research, 33, 640
Adaptive tests. *See* Tailored tests
Adjectives, factor analysis of,
    586–587
Adoptive parenting study, 17–24,
    28, 30, 31, 247
Adversarial evaluation, 536–538
After-the-fact natural experiments
    example of, 517–519
    explanation of, 514–516
    hallmarks of, 519
    problems of, 516–517
Agreement, method of, 247–248
Alpha coefficient, 209, 210
Alpha error, 403, 416, 426, 427,
    717
Alternative conditions, 254–257,
    260–261
Alternative explanations
    control problems and, 454–465,
        476–478
    historical studies and, 510–511
    qualitative method and, 342–346
Alternative police patrols study,
    542n
American Educational Research
    Association (AERA), 41, 546
American Institutes of Research,
    226
American Psychological

Association, 546, 597
    code of ethics of, 666–667
Analogies used in problem
    finding, 87
Analysis of covariance (ANCOVA),
    450, 604–606
Analysis of variance (ANOVA)
    assumptions of, 603
    examples of use of, 598–603
    explanation of, 597–598, 603–604
    use of, 424
Analytic induction, 324–325
Analyzer orientation
    explanation of, 628–629, 635,
        641–642
    strengths and weaknesses of,
        646–647
Annual reviews, 101–103
Anscombe's quartet, 178
Arbitrary-zero type measures, 160
Artificial intelligence, 629–630
Arts and Humanities Citation Index,
    109, 111
Association, as projective
    technique, 379
Assumptions
    challenges for, 77–78
    of statistical tests, 435–436
Attribution theory, 265
Audience credibility, 294, 647
    discussion of, 296–297
    integrity and, 297–298
    methods of enhancing, 298–300
    of qualitative work, 350
    trade-offs and, 620
Audiotape use, 385
Authenticity of evidence, 251
    in historical method, 508
Authority
    explanation of, 48–49
    obedience to, 660

Balance of internal validity (LP)
    and external validity (GP),

300–301
Bandwidth fidelity problem,
    222–224
Bar charts, 163
Baseline phase, 559
Base rate, 464, 473
Base-rate proportion, 345, 346
Basis for sensing attributes or
    changes
    explanation of, 61–62
    as facet of design in chain of
        reasoning, 443
    as link in inferring causation,
        246–247, 250, 262
    decision tree for, 263, 494
    problems with, 491–495
    trade-off possibilities and, 698
    translation fidelity and, 276–277
    translation generality and,
        286–287
Behavioral objectives, 202–203, 529
Behaviorism, 629–630
Beliefs as knowledge source, 48
Bereiter-Engleman curriculum
    study, 452–456, 469, 489
Beta error, 426, 428
Bias
    explanation of, 129
    interviewer characteristics and,
        372–373
    in questionnaires, 380
    sources of, 129
Bibliographic Retrieval Services,
    117
Bibliographies, 102, 104
Biserial correlation, 184, 389–390
Blind review, 41, 681–682, 701
"Blind" judging, 15, 221, 277, 279,
    468, 496, 558
Blocking
    stratification as, 598
    use of, 451, 452
Borderline cases in conceptual
    analysis, 149–152

Bracketing model, 618
Brainstorming, 80
Brown v. *Board of Education of Topeka*, 686
Buckley amendment (Family Educational Rights and Privacy Act), 661, 670–671
Bureaucratization, 325, 326

California Assessment Program (CAP), 575
Camouflage, 449
Canonical correlation, 584–585, 592–593
Case studies, 347–348
Categorical data, 166, 184–185, 593–597
CATI. *See* Computer-assisted telephone interviews
Causal chain, 240–242
Causal comparative method. *See* After-the-fact natural experiments
Causal modeling, 588–590
Causation
    complexities in patterns of, 244–246
    correlation and, 183–184
    evidence for inferring, 246–253
    explanation of, 238
    inferred, 263–264, 511–514
    overview of, 238, 239
Cause
    complexities in concept of, 240–242
    and conception of world and social science, 243–253
    explanation of, 240, 242
    precedence of, 251
Cause-and-effect relationship
    experimentation and, 442
    manipulation of treatment and, 447–449
CDRGP technique, 391
CD-ROMs, 101
Ceiling effects
    explanation of, 167, 169
    instrument decay and, 462, 463
Central limit theorem, 407
Chain of reasoning
    article used as example of, 59–62
    and basis for sensing attributes or changes, 61–62, 246–247, 250, 262. *See also* Basis for sensing attributes or changes
    characteristics of, 63–66
    experimentation and, 442–444
    explanation of, 58–59, 616–617
    quantitative vs. qualitative methods examined in terms

of, 354–357
    relationship of internal validity (LP) to, 280, 281
    study design and, 62–63, 65
    use of conceptual analysis in, 146, 148
Chain referral sampling, 139
Chance and sampling error, 405, 455–456, 593–595, 598
Charts
    advantages of, 165
    types of, 163–164
    use of, 161–163
Checklists, 214, 228–229
Chess players study, 77
Children's Television Workshop (CTW), 552
Chi-square
    assumptions and limitations of, 596–597
    example using, 594–597
    explanation of, 593–594, 597
    formula for, 594
Chronicle of Higher Education report, 670
CIPP model, 531, 532
Citation indexes, 109, 111–112
Classification schemes, 33–34, 261–262
Classroom discipline study, 6, 39–44
Classroom size study, 571–572
Clocklike world, 243, 321–322, 688
Close-to-zero effects, 543
Cloudlike world, 243, 321–322, 636
Clusters, 364
Cluster sampling, 134–136, 364
Coco Chanel principle, 89
Codes of ethics
    as guidelines, 92
    of professional associations, 304, 666–668
Coding
    explanation of, 336–337, 342
    of interview and questionnaire responses, 388
    schemes for, 337–340
Cognitive psychology, 630
Cohort studies
    advantages and disadvantages of, 366
    explanation of, 365
College Entrance Examination Board, 175, 204
College grade point average prediction, 580–581
Common ownership of information, 52
Comparison and control groups, 450–452
Complementary multiplism, 618

Comp...
    S...
CompuSer...
Computer-as...
    intervie...
    advantages of...
    use of, 361, 373...
Computers
    used for qualitative...
    339–340, 342
    used for searches, 101, 1...
    used in testing, 225, 226
Computer software
    qualitative analysis, 339–340
    statistical, 608
Concept mapping, 155
Concept Mastery Test, 575
Concepts
    explanation of, 147
    in social and behavioral sciences, 147–148
Conceptual analysis
    in chain of reasoning, 146, 148
    of codes, 340
    comments regarding use of, 153–155
    construct validity and, 199–200
    explanation of, 146, 147
    measurement and, 195
    process of, 148–153
Conceptual evidence
    external validity (GP) and, 283–287, 349, 350
    internal validity (LP) and, 271–278
    meaning of, 271–272
Conceptually based indexing, 106–107
Concomitant variation, method of, 249
Concurrent validity
    discussion of, 198, 201–202
    evidence of, 205
Conditions
    alternative, 254–257, 260–261
    arising from presence or absence of necessary and sufficient, 253–254
    contingent, 254, 257–261
    contributing, 254, 259–261
    INUS, 259–261
Confidence intervals
    discussion of, 408–409
    explanation of, 215, 216, 219, 407, 410
Confidence levels
    determining, 411–412
    explanation of, 412
Confidence limits, 408
Confidentiality, 670–671
Confounding, 454, 455

rehensive Tests of Basic
ills (CTBS), 575
ve, 117
sisted telephone
s (CATI)
374, 375
374
alysis,
5–117

...ive research codes,
340
discussion of, 199–201, 292
evidence of, 205
Consumer-oriented evaluation,
533–534
Content validity
discussion of, 198, 202–203
evidence of, 205
Contingency coefficient, 185
Contingent conditions, 254,
257–261
Contrary cases in conceptual
analysis, 149, 150
Contributing conditions, 254,
259–260
Controlled vocabulary, 106
Convenience sampling, 136–137
Correction for attenuation,
211–212
Correlations
canonical, 584–585
causation and, 183–184
correlation ratio, 183
effect of extended range on,
181–182
effect of nonlinearity on,
182–183
effect of outliers on, 178, 180
effect of restriction of range on,
180–181
examination of scatterplot of,
177–178
multiple. See Multiple correlation
partial, 450
Pearson product-moment. See
Pearson product-moment
correlation
for special situations, 184–185
Cost-benefit analysis, 532
Cost-effectiveness analysis,
532–533
Counterbalanced designs, 483

rbalancing, 210
nce modeling, 588–590
participant observation,
16–317. See also
bservation; Participant
bservation
y
g characteristics of,
9–153
ription, 5–6
ement of, 73, 78–80
lem, 90–91
ation, 7
r. See Audience
libility; Explanation
redibility
ible result
discussion of, 280
explanation of, 272, 280
Criterion-referenced tests, 223–224
Criterion-related validity
discussion of, 198, 201–202
evidence of, 205
Criterion variable, 198, 580
Critiques, 298
Cronbach's alpha. See Alpha
coefficient
Cross-break tables, 389, 390
Cross-reference Index (Atkins and
Ostrow), 108
Cross-references, 107
Cross-sectional studies
advantages and disadvantages
to, 366
explanation of, 364–365
Cross-tabulation tables, 389, 390
Cross-validation, 221, 512, 584
Current Contents: Social and
Behavioral Sciences (ISI), 112
Current Index to Journals in
Education (ERIC), 106
Curricular validity. See Content
validity
Curvilinear relationship, 178,
182–183, 446, 464, 481, 496,
581, 708. See also Nonlinear
relationship

Data
alternative explanations for,
342–346
categorical, 166, 184–185, 593–597
confidentiality issues regarding,
670–671
issues regarding ownership of,
672–673
overload of, 344, 345
use of others', 86
validity of, 328–329
Data analysis
chain of reasoning and, 62
of interview and questionnaire

responses, 389–390
of qualitative, 335–346
shift in focus of problem
resulting from, 74
Database directories, 86, 88
Data-gathering methods. See also
various data-gathering methods
integrity in, 52–54
for qualitative data, 314–315
strengths and weaknesses of
various, 227–230
Data interpretation, integrity in,
52–54
Data reduction
and alternative explanations,
342–346
coding used for, 336–340
need for, 158–159, 335–336
and process of conclusion
drawing and verification,
340–342
Data sets, 161–166
Data triangulation, 276, 328, 618
Deafness. See Zimbardo induced
hearing deficit study
Debriefing, 15, 660
Deception of subjects, 16,
669–670, 726–727
Decision driven
evaluation as, 528
explanation of, 524
Decision trees, 262, 263, 494
Degrees of freedom, 596
Delphi method, 555
Demand characteristics, 471
Demonstrated generality
discussion of, 287–288
explanation of, 282
Demonstrated result
discussion of, 278
explanation of, 271, 272, 279
Department of Justice, 670
Dependent variables, 27
Derived scores, 174, 176, 566
Description
explanation of, 5, 7
qualitative-quantitative
continuum and, 29, 30
Descriptive statistics
comments on use of, 185–187
to describe data sets, 161
explanation of, 166
measurement and, 194
and measures of central
tendency, 166–170
and measures of dispersion and
variability, 170–175
measuring relationships with,
176–184
overview of, 158–161
Designs. See Experimental designs
Diagrams in qualitative research, 340

Diaries, 228, 507
Dictionaries, 106, 107
Dictionary of Psychological Terms (American Psychological Association), 106
Differences, method of
  experimentation and, 442
  explanation of, 248
Diffusion, 467
Discipline and Group Management in Classroom (Kounin), 42
Disconfirmation
  causal propositions and, 242
  and proving a proposition, 434
Discriminant function analysis, 585
Disinterestedness, 52–54, 297
Dispersion measures, 170–173
Dissemination research, 684–685
Documents, 508–509
Dogmatic authority, 48–49
Domain validity, 202
Double-barreled questions, 380
Double-blind procedures, 468
Dr. Fell phenomenon, 535

Early father absence study, 517–518
Ecological validity, 284, 465
Editors, 51
Educational Products Information Exchange (EPIE), 533–534
Educational Psychology: A Realistic Approach (Good and Brophy), 43
Educational Testing Service, 227
Educational voucher evaluation, 527
Effect *See also* Cause-and-effect relationship
  presence of, 251–252
Effect size, 565–567
Elite bias, 343
Empirical evidence
  external validity (GP) and, 287–289
  internal validity (LP) and, 278–280
Empirical keying, 221, 222
Encyclopedia of Education Research (Mitzel), 43
Encyclopedias, 102
Entry gaining
  ethical standards and, 671–672
  for participant observation, 319–320
Equality of Educational Opportunity (Coleman), 546
Equivalence reliability, 206, 210–211
ERIC (Educational Resources Information Center), 101, 106–109, 226
Errors of inference (Types I and II), 426–428
Essay tests, 213, 215, 222, 313
Estimation
  confidence levels and, 411–412
  in context of measurement in general, 406–409
  example of, 410–411
  explanation of, 405–406
  of true score, 215–219
Ethical Principles in the Conduct of Research with Human Participants (American Psychological Association), 666–667
Ethical standards, 304, 659
  codes of ethics as, 92, 304, 666–668
  confidentiality and privacy issues and, 670–671
  gaining entry and, 671–672
  informed consent and, 663–666
  institutional review boards and, 661–663, 673–674
  overview of, 659
  ownership of data and, 672–673
  problem choice and, 668–670
  problems in qualitative research, 334–335
  whistle blowing and, 305
"Ethical Standards of Psychologists" (American Psychological Association), 673
Ethnography, 322
Evaluation
  choices affecting entire, 540–541
  choices at different stages in, 541–543
  examples of, 527
  explanation of, 32, 525–526
  formative, 525, 526, 540
  hallmarks of, 549–550
  overview of, 524–526
  political nature of, 543–546
  research vs., 527–528
  standards for, 546–549
  summative, 525, 526, 540
  types of choices in, 539–540
Evaluation approaches
  adversarial, 536
  consumer-oriented, 533–534
  expertise-oriented, 534–535
  goal-free, 530–531
  management-oriented, 531–533
  naturalistic, 536–538
  objective and goal-based, 529–530
  participant-oriented, 538–539
Evaluation standards, 546–549
  accuracy, 548–549
  feasibility, 547
  proprietry, 548

ut
Eviden
  authen
  congruen
    252, 25
  validation of,
Ex post facto stu
  After-the-fact
  experiments
Experience, as source o
  knowledge, 47
Experimental designs
  after-the-fact natural experiments, 514–520
  counterbalanced, 483
  factorial, 484–487
  nonequivalent control group, 453, 479–480
  "patched-up," 478, 483–484
  single-subject, 559–564
  time-series, 480–482
  tips on construction of, 495–497
  See also Experimentation
Experimental treatment problems
  with basis for sensing changes, 491–495
  and complex designs, 478, 479
  conceptually defining the treatment for, 487–488
  ensuring treatment fidelity in, 488–491
  trade-offs, 694–695
Experimentation
  art of, 445–446
  complex designs and treatment problems in, 478, 479
  control of unwanted explanations or conditions in, 449–454
  and evidence of causation, 248
  hallmarks of, 495–497
  internal validity (LP) and external validity (GP) and, 440, 444–445
  linking cause to effect, 447–449
  natural environment vs. laboratory, 27–28
  overview of, 440–442
  and protection offered by simple designs, 471, 472
  and rival explanations, 476–478
  summary of control problems and their elimination in, 471, 473–475
  threats to external validity (GP), common restrictive conditions, and explanations in, 465–471
  threats to internal validity (LP), common rival hypotheses, and alternative explanations in, 454–465

ity, 547
idity of, 251, 508
e of explanation and,
508
ies. See
atural

ic induction, the constant
mparison method, and
rposive sampling in,
4–326
lidity and triangulation
328–329
es and memos for,
–334
v of, 324
ethics in, 334–335, 665
nformants in, 326–327,

rts, 163
ee Research findings
e analogy, 44
model ANOVA, 601
oor effects
  explanation of, 167, 169
  instrument decay and, 462, 463
  in longitudinal studies, 557
Focus groups, 371–372
Focused interview, 371
Foreign language literature, 87
Formative evaluation, 525, 526,
  540
Framing of questions, 380. See also
  Questions
Franklin Institute, 686
Fraud, 53, 679–680
Frequency distributions
  skewness in, 167
  symmetrical, 161, 168, 169
  use of, 161–164
Functionally equivalent groups,
  442
Funnel-sequenced questionnaire,
  382

Gaining entry
  ethical standards and, 671–672
  for participant observation,
    319–320
Gale Research Company, 115
Gatekeepers
  elite as, 343
  in qualitative research, 319
  standards of, 50
Gender of interviewers, 373
Generality
  chain of reasoning and, 59. See
    also Chain of reasoning
  demonstrated, 282
  discussion of, 122, 140–142, 270
  explanation, 281–284
  and multi-site studies, 350
  restrictive effects on, 465–466
  translation, 282
Generalizability theory, 212–213
Goal-based evaluation, 529–530
Goal-free evaluation, 530–531
Good samaritan study, 601–603

GP. See External validity (GP)
Grab sampling, 136–137
Grade point average (GPA), 184,
  596–597
Graphs, 161, 164–166
Group interviews
  compared to individual
    interviews, telephone
    interviews, and
    questionnaires, 393–397
  use of, 371–372
Guaranteed annual income
    experiment, 27, 444, 527,
    542, 544, 619, 689
Guide to Reference Books (Sheehy),
  104
Guide to Sources of Educational
  Information (Woodbury), 104

Handbook of Research on Teaching,
  42–43
Handbooks, 101–102
Hawthorne effect, 466
Head Start studies, 300–301
Hearing deficit, 4, 7, 10–15, 60.
    See also Zimbardo induced
    hearing deficit study
High-inference scales, 214, 215
Histograms, 163
Historical method
  advantages of, 511–512
  and after-the-fact natural
    experiments, 514–519
  goals of, 504
  hallmarks of, 519
  inferring causation, 511
  interpretative, 504–506
  methods of, 31–32, 503, 506–507
  overview of, 501–503
  problems of analysis faced by,
    510–511
  scientific, 504
  steps in, 506–514
Homeostasis, 87
Homogeneity of variance, 603
House-Tree-Person Test, 214
Housing allowance study, 542n
Hoyt's analysis of variance
  estimate of reliability, 209
Humanist orientation
  explanation of, 628–629,
    638–639, 641–642
  strengths and weaknesses of,
    651–652
Humanities, 689–690
Human subjects. See also Subjects
  codes of ethics to protect, 92,
    304, 666–668
  legal and institutional protection
    of, 661–666
  protection of, 660–661
HyperQual, 339

nce and,
  252, 253
  role of, 6–8, 60
Exploration, 5, 7
External criticism, 508n
External validity, 292
External validity (GP)
  applied to qualitative research,
    312, 349–350
  and conceptual evidence, 281,
    283–287
  dependence on internal validity
    (LP), 282–283
  and empirical evidence, 287–289
  experimentation and, 440, 444,
    445
  explanation of, 269, 270,
    281–282
  as reduction in uncertainty, 289
  restrictive conditions and
    explanations that pose
    threats to, 465–478
  and single-subject studies, 563
  situations and, 275
  subjects and, 274, 275
  weighing of internal and, 294,
    295, 300–302

Face validity, 198, 203–205
Factor analysis, 200, 585–588
Factorial designs, 484–487
Family Educational Rights and
    Privacy Act (Buckley
    amendment), 661, 670–671
Feasibility of research problem,
    91–92
Fieldnotes
  coding of, 337–338
  data reduction techniques for,
    335–336. See also Data
    reduction
  examples of, 330–332
  explanation of, 329, 333–334

Hypothesis
    chain of reasoning and, 60, 65,
        66
    design as translation of, 446–447
    disconfirmation and, 242, 434
    evidence supporting, 344–345
    method of multiple, 637–638
    null, 414–415, 420
    revision of tentative, 345, 346
Hypothesis guessing, 466
Hypothesis testing
    and differences between two
        observed means, 421–423
    explanation of, 406
    logic of, 413–416
    and one-tailed and two-tailed
        tests of statistical
        significance, 417–420

Illegal acts, 334, 335
Impressions, first, 344
Income Maintenance Experiment,
    27, 444, 527, 542, 544, 619,
    687
Independent variables, 27
Indexes
    citation, 111
    controlled vocabulary in,
        106–107
    function of, 336
    keyword, 105, 108–110
    overview of, 104–105
    Permuterm®, 109
    traditional subject, 105–108
Indexing services listings, 103–104
Index Medicus, 106
Index to Social Science and
        Humanities Proceedings (ISI),
        112, 114
Inference
    causes as, 241, 242
    Fisher's and Neyman and
        Pearson's, 433n
Inferential leap, 124, 125, 140–142,
    287–288, 350, 363
Inferential statistics
    decision making and knowledge
        building and, 432–433
    and errors of inference, 426–428
    and estimation, 405–412
    explanation of, 404–405
    and hypothesis testing, 413–423
    increasing statistical power with,
        428–431
    and null hypothesis, 431–432
    overview of, 401–405
    statistical significance and,
        433–434
    statistical tests and, 435–436
    and t test for differences
        between means, 423–426

Informants
    draft reading by, 348
    perspective of, 360
    use of, 326–327, 335
Information, common ownership
    of, 52
Information, errors in using,
    344–346
Informed consent
    altering or waiving process of,
        664–665
    content of forms for, 664
    explanation of, 663, 665–666
    for individuals who are
        incapable of giving it, 665
    short and long forms for,
        663–664
Institute for Scientific Information
    (ISI), 112
Institutional constraints, 304–305
Institutional review boards (IRBs)
    eplanation of, 661–663
    privacy issues and, 671
    researcher's responsibility to,
        673–674
Instrument decay
    design control for, 475, 482
    examples of, 462
    explanation of, 343, 463, 473
    by treatment interaction, 464
Integrity
    and audience credibility,
        297–298, 506, 534, 659, 669,
        679
    as characteristic of reasoning
        authorities, 49
    and norms of science, 51–54
    of treatment, 285
Intelligence quotents (IQ), 255n
Intelligence tests, 174–175
Interaction analysis, 87, 214
Interaction of rival hypotheses
    instrument decay by treatment,
        464
    mortality by treatment, 471, 622
    multiple-treatment, 469–470, 477,
        562
    selection by history, 479
    selection by maturation, 464
    selection by treatment, 470
    testing-treatment, 470, 724
Interactions, ANOVA, 601–602
Internal consistency reliability
    discussion of, 206–208
    improvement of, 220, 222
    measurement of, 208–210
    summary of, 211
Internal validity, 292
Internal validity (LP)
    applied to qualitative research,
        312, 348–350
    and conceptual evidence, 271–278

co...
    depen...
        (GP...
    and empi...
    experimentat...
        454
    explanation of, ...
    inferential statistics...
    interactions affecting, ...
    judgments in, 271, 272...
    as reduction in uncertain...
        289
    and relationship to chain of
        reasoning, 280, 281
    of single-subject studies, 560,
        562
    trade-offs and, 620
    treatment standardization and,
        285
    weighing of external and, 294,
        295, 300–302
Interpretive history, 504–506
Interval measurement, 160, 161,
    170
Interviewers
    effects of characteristics of,
        372–373
    multiple, 371, 372
    training for, 370
Interviews
    approaches to, 370–372
    benefits of, 369–370
    coding and analysis of
        responses to, 388–390
    continuum of structure in, 368
    focused, 271
    group, 371, 393–397
    individual, 393–397
    strengths and weaknesses of,
        229
    tandem, 371
    telephone, 140, 361, 373–375,
        393–397
    tips for, 375–376
    use of, 367–369
    word association in, 379
Intraclass correlation, 185, 261n,
    682
Intuition as knowledge source, 48
INUS conditions, 259–261
Invented cases in conceptual
    analysis, 149, 151, 152
Investigator triangulation, 328
Invisible college, 40, 114
IRB: A Review of Human Subject
    Research, 662
Item analysis
    empirical keying and, 221
    explanation of, 220, 222
Item banking, 226
Item difficulty index, 220, 222

ditions that contribute to,
250–253
ence of external validity
on, 282–283
al evidence, 278–280
on and, 440, 445,

9–272
and, 401
464–465
y, 281,

ychology (Reed and
xter), 104
lationship, 182, 267, 464,
, 481, 581, 584, 589, 607
hs, 163
ower, 269, 271. *See also*
rnal validity (LP)
9–590, 592, 594, 607
est poll (1931), 129, 137
earch
ndexing used in,
12
ts in, 112–114
9–100
and indexing process
sed in, 104–111
.eta-analysis and, 118. *See also*
    Meta-analysis
organization of, 114–115
and relationship of starting
    points to problem
    development, 112–114
in relation to research method,
    97–98
steps in, 101–104
suggestions for, 118–119
use of computer for, 101,
    115–117

sampling, 137–139

Keyword indexes, 105, 108–111
Knowing judgments
    consensus of, 40–43, 45
    in everyday life, 45–46
    explanation of, 40
Knowledge
    characteristics of findings
        acceptance process, 43–45
    example of transitions of
        findings to, 39–43
    fish-scale analogy of transition
        of findings to, 44
    resulting from evaluation, 526
    sources of, 47–51
Knowledge claims
    chain of reasoning and, 63–64
    universal standards for, 51–54
Knowledge production, 51–54
Kuder-Richardson reliability
    formula 20 (KR20), 209, 210
Kuder-Richardson reliability
    formula 21 (KR21), 209, 210,
    212

Lagged treatment, 560
Latin square, 483
Laypersons, 45–46, 203–204, 426,
    684
Least squares fit, 581
Legal problems, resulting from
    witnessing illegal acts, 334,
    335
Letters of transmittal
    example of, 384
    improvements for, 385–386
    pilot testing of, 385
    use of, 383–384, 387, 388
Leverage as a criterion in problem
    choice, 90
Library Use: A Handbook for

Local history as threat to validity,
    460, 476
Local molar validity, 292
Log keeping, 85–86
Longitudinal studies
    difficulties of, 557–558
    explanation of, 32, 365, 556
    hallmarks of, 558
    overview of, 555–556
Low-inference scales, 214, 215
LP. *See* Internal validity (LP)

Management-oriented evaluation,
    531–533
"Managing Emotionally Disturbed
    Children in Regular
    Classrooms: A Replication
    and Extension" (Kounin
    and Obradovic), 42
"Managing Emotionally Disturbed
    Children in Regular
    Classrooms" (Kounin,
    Friesen, and Norton), 41–42
Mann-Whitney *U* test, 424, 435
Masking as a control stratagem,
    449
Matrices, used to find
    interrelationships, 340–342
Matrix sampling, 202n
Maturation as a threat to validity,
    461, 473–474, 476–477
Means
    difference between two
        observed, 421–423

explanation of, 167, 169
nonparametric tests of
    differences between,
    435–436
skewed distributions and, 168
t test for differences between,
    423–426, 428–430
Measurement
    advantages of, 196–197
    conceptual analysis and, 195
    descriptive statistics and, 194
    estimation in context of,
        406–409
    interval level of, 160, 161, 170
    nominal level of, 160, 161, 170
    ordinal level of, 160, 161, 170
    overview of, 193
    problems related to, 224–226
    ratio scale level of, 160, 161, 170
    reliability of, 206–212
    sampling and, 194
    standard error of, 215–219, 407
    strengths and weaknesses of
        approaches to, 227–230
    trade-off possibilities and,
        695–698
    trade-offs in, 222–224
    validity of, 197–205
Measures
    as facet of design in chain of
        reasoning, 61
    as operational definitions, 195
    translation fidelity and, 276
    translation generality and, 286
Median, 166–169
    skewed distributions and, 168
Medical Subject Headings (MeSH),
    106
Memos
    coding and, 340, 342
    example of, 333
    use of, 330, 332–334, 342
Mental development study,
    581–583
Mental Measurements Yearbooks
    (Buros Institute), 226
Mental processing and reading
    study, 619
Meta-analysis
    advantages and disadvantages
        of, 571–573
    discussion of, 564–566
    and evidence for causal
        propositions, 263–264
    explanation of, 32, 118, 566
    hallmarks of, 573
    initial model of, 567–568
    methods of, 569–571
    problems in, 568–569
    study-effect, 570
    variance-partitioning, 570–571
Meta-evaluations, 564n

Metaphors, use in problem
finding, 87
Method triangulation, 328
Mind-set, breaking of in problem
finding, 76–78
Minnesota Multiphasic Personality
Inventory (MMPI), 12, 116,
221, 276
Mirrors, two-way, 317
Mixed model ANOVA, 601
Mode
explanation of, 166, 169
skewed distributions and, 168
Model building, 33. *See also*
Structural modeling
Model cases in conceptual
analysis, 149, 150
Model Cities, 538
Models
chain of reasoning and, 60
used to examine problems, 87
Mohs hardness scale, 160
Momentum, 39, 40
Morphological analysis, 79–80
Mortality
explanation of, 343
as threat to validity, 460–461,
477
by treatment interaction, 471,
662
Multi-measure, multi-method
procedure, 276
Multiperspectivist orientation
explanation of, 637–638, 641–642
strengths and weaknesses of,
650–651
Multiple-choice questions. *See also*
Questionnaires; Questions
formulation of, 313
tips for use of, 381
Multiple-choice tests
construction of, 313
strengths and weaknesses of,
230
use of, 213, 215, 222
Multiple correlation and regression
cross-validation of, 584
example using, 581–583
explanation of, 580, 581
and maximum prediction,
583–584
Multiple-treatment interaction,
469–470, 477, 562
Multiple variables
and canonical correlation,
584–585
and discriminant function
analysis, 585
and example of use of
relationship statistics,
590–593
and factor analysis, 585–588

methods of studying, 579–580
and multiple regression and
multiple correlation, 580–584
and structural or covariance
modeling, 588–590
Multisite studies, 350

Narrative interview, 17–18
National Assessment of
Educational Progress
(NAEP), 202n, 530
National Center for Education
Statistics (NCES), 605
National Commission for the
Protection of Human
Subjects of Biomedical and
Behavioral Research, 665
National Council on Measurement
in Education, 546
National Dissemination Network,
533
National Institute of Education
(NIE), 536
National Institutes of Health
(NIH), 45, 670
National Institutes of Mental
Health (NIMH), 683
National Research Act of 1974,
661
National Teacher Examination
(NTE Examination), 204
Natural experiments, 445. *See also*
After-the-fact natural
experiments
Naturalistic evaluation, 536–538
Necessary condition, 148, 200,
206, 240–241, 253–261, 275
Needs analysis, 541, 542
Negative income tax studies. *See*
Income maintenance
experiments
Negatively skewed distributions,
167, 169
Nested designs, 486, 487
New England Journal of Medicine, 45
Nominal-level measurement, 160,
161, 166, 170
Nondirective, psychoanalytic, and
behavior modification
therapy study, 598–601
Nondirective interview approach,
370
Nonequivalent control group
design, 453, 479–480
Nonlinear relationship, 182–183.
See also Curvilinear
relationship
Nonparametric statistics, 184–185,
435
Nonparticipant observation, 318
Nonprobability sampling
explanation of, 126, 137

ju
purpos
324–
quota samp
364, 374
representativen
Nonrespondents, 3
Normal curve, 164, 1
Normal frequency distr
172–173
Norm-referenced tests, 223,
NTE Examination, 204
Null hypothesis
explanation of, 414–415, 420
studies designed to accept,
431–432
type I and II errors and, 427
Numeric description. *See*
Descriptive statistics
Nurse practitioner evaluation, 527

Obedience to authority, 660
Objectives-based evaluation,
529–530
Objectivity, 213–215, 222, 335
Observation
continuum of, least to most
obtrusive, 315–318
as facet of design in chain of
reasoning, 62, 443
in qualitative research,
concealed or hidden, 317
in qualitative research, covert
participant, 316–317
in qualitative research,
nonparticipant, 318
in qualitative research, overview
of, 315
in qualitative research,
participant, 316–321
in qualitative research,
unconcealed participant,
317–318
as source of knowledge, 47
strengths and weaknesses of,
227–228
trade-off possibilities and,
695–698
translation fidelity and, 276
translation generality and, 286
Observation scales, 195–197
Observed test score, 215–217
Observer comments (O. C.),
330–332
Observer perspective, 343–344
Obtrusiveness
decreases in, 694
as threat to validity, 466–469,
477
One-and-a-half-barrel questions,
380

mental sampling and,
7–138
e sampling and, 138,
26, 349
ling and, 138–139,
ss of, 137
6–388
utions,
224

scores, 175, 176
m® indexing, 109–111
school Program
luation, 527
bservation, 47

nants, 360
343–344
research in, 7
ple, 85
logy, 322–323
nces, comparison with
sciences re causation,
44
arts, 164
arts, 163
ot studies and pilot testing, 85,
367, 373, 379, 380, 382, 385,
387, 393, 442, 476, 495, 718
Placebo effect
discussion of, 492–494
explanation of, 453
Placebo treatment, 468, 491–492
Planned comparisons, 600–601
Point biserial correlation, 185,
389–390
Point of view
and qualitative methods, 311,
321–324
role of, 60
Policy, research contributions to,
686–687
Population
defining, 128
explanation of, 122
judgmental samples and,
137–138
in statistics, 406
target, 140–142
Population validity, 465
Positively skewed distributions,
167–169
Post hoc comparisons, 601
Posttest-only group design
and after-the-fact natural
experiments, 514, 515
explanation of, 453–454
Power of a statistical test, 427–431
Practical significance, statistical
vs., 433–434
Pragmatist orientation
explanation of, 630, 634–635,
641–642
strengths and weaknesses of,
644–646
Precedence of cause, 251, 278
Predictive validity, 198, 201–202
Presence of effect, 251–252, 278,
287
Presidential election outcome
example, 632–634
Pretest-posttest control group

design, 453, 457
Primary literature sources, 102
Privacy of personal information,
661, 670–671
Probability sampling procedures
and advantages and
disadvantages of simple
random and stratified
sampling, 132–134
cluster sampling, 134–136
explanation of, 126
simple random sampling,
127–130
stratified sampling, 130–132
systematic sampling, 133–134
Probing in survey research,
369–372, 376
Problem formulation in evaluation
studies, 541–542
Problems
behaviors that enhance problem
finding, 75–85
choice and formulation of, 303
criteria of good, 88–93
ethical concerns in choice of,
668–670
overview of, 73
potential sources for, 85–88
research method and, 73–74
as spoken statements, 82–83
trade-offs in, 222
as written statement, 81–82
Procedure
as facet of design in chain of
reasoning, 62, 443
trade-off possibilities and, 698
translation fidelity and, 277
Projective techniques
objectivity and, 214
strengths and weaknesses of,
229
types used in sample surveys,
379
Proportional stratified sampling, 131
Propositions, tests of
disconfirmation for, 242, 434
Pseudonyms, artificial to ensure
privacy in surveys, 391–392
Psychological Abstracts (PsycInfo),
101, 104, 106, 107
Psychology
behavioral approach to, 629–630,
635
cognitive approach to, 630
study of communication in, 40
PsycInfo, 107. *See also Psychological
Abstracts*
Purposive sampling
explanation of, 326
and external validity (GP), 349
in qualitative research, 324–326,
349

Outward Bound evaluation, 527,
618–619
Oversampling, intentional, 132

Panel samples, 365
Panel studies, 366
Parallel split-half reliability,
208–209
Parameters, 406
Parametric statistics, 435, 436
Paranoia, 10–15, 27, 60. *See also*
Zimbardo induced hearing
deficit study
Partial correlations, 450, 604, 606
Participant observation
concealed, 317
covert, 316–317
ethics and, 334–335
gaining entry for, 319–320
guidelines for, 351–352
securing acceptance for, 320–321
unconcealed, 317–318
Participant-oriented evaluation,
538–539
Particularist orientation
explanation of, 631, 639–640,
641–642
strengths and weaknesses of,
653
Path analysis, 589. *See also*
Structural modeling
Pearson product-moment
correlation, 389, 581. *See
also* Correlation
discussion of, 176–183
formula for, 178
relationship between alternate,
contingent, and contributing
conditions represented by,
261
Peer review, 41, 51–52, 53–54,
681–682

use of, 138, 139, 324
and verification of data validity
through trangulation, 328
Pygmalion effect, 468

Q technique, 555
Qualitative methods. *See also*
Qualitative researchers
analysis software, 339–340
analysis of study using, 23–24
compared to essay testing, 313
compared to quantitative
methods, 354–358
data reduction used in, 335–346
example of study using, 17–22
explanation of, 10, 29–31, 314
fieldwork techniques used for,
324–335
hallmarks of, 353–354
internal validity (LP) and
external validity (GP) and
other criteria applied to,
348–350
methods of gathering data for,
314–315
overview of, 311–314
participation observation used
in, 315–321
and point of view, 311, 321–324
points to be aware of in,
353–354
qualitative point of view in
(QPV), 311, 321–324
quantitative vs., 354–357
report resulting from, 347–348
tips on using, 351–352
when to use, 352–353
Qualitative researchers
information processing
limitations of, 344–346
orientation of, 336n
tempermental characteristics of,
346
tension between quantitative
and, 314
Qualog, 339
Quantitative literature summaries,
571–573. *See also*
Meta-analysis
Quantitative methods
after-the-fact natural
experiments, 514–519
analysis of study using, 14–16
example of study using, 10–14
experimentation, 440–500
explanation of, 10, 24, 30, 31
longitudinal studies, 555–559
measurement, 191–234
meta-analysis, 564–577
qualitative vs., 354–357
single-subject studies, 559–564

statistics for, 157–190, 400–439,
578–612
Quartile, 171
Questionnaires
coding and analysis of
responses to, 388–390
compared to interview method,
393–397
construction of questions in,
379–381
dealing with sensitive topics in,
390–392
double-barreled, 380
example of, 377
explanation of, 376, 378,
387–388
format for, 382–385
funnel-sequenced, 382
improvement, measures for,
385–386, 393
methods of expressing questions
of, 378–379
mortality factor in using, 343
ordering of questions on,
381–382
pilot testing of, 379, 385
planning involved in, 363
research orientations and use
of, 644
response sets and, 392
strengths and weaknesses of,
228–229
tips for, 379–381
what to ask on, 378
Questions to research
chain of reasoning and, 60
choice and formulation of,
302–303
use of researchable, 93
Quota sampling, 138–139, 364, 374

Race of interviewers, 372
RAND Corporation, 129
Random assignment
as method of control, 450–451
selection effect and, 464
Random-digit dialing, 373–374
Random digits table, 129
Randomized response technique,
391
Random model ANOVA, 601
Random sampling. *See also*
Sampling
methods for, 127–128
probability sampling and, 126,
127
simple, 127–130
stratified, 130–131, 364
systematic, 364
Range
effect of extended on

expla...
restricti...
180–...
semi-interqu...
Ranking tests, 2...
or Mann-W...
Rasch models, 225...
Rating scales
effect of tendency to a...
on, 392
strengths and weaknesses...
228 229
Rationale for hypothesis, 60
Ratio scale level of measurement,
160, 161, 170
Reactivity
longitudinal studies and, 558
as threat to validity, 466–469,
477, 694
Reading study, 619
Reasoning. *See* Chain of reasoning
Reasoning authority, 48–49
Reference sources, 102–104
Regression
and prediction, 184
as threat to validity, 457–460
See also Multiple correlation and
regression
Related cases in conceptual
analysis, 149, 151, 152
Relationships, complexities in,
253–262
Relationship statistics, 176–184,
580–593
Reliability. *See* Test reliability
Religion of interviewers, 373
Replicable result, 282, 289
Replication
explanation of, 42
in physical science, 572–573
power of, 621–622
in single-subject studies, 559
as validation, 50, 51
Representativeness
of nonprobability sampling,
137
random sampling and, 129–130
of statistics, 186
Research
chain of reasoning and design
of, 61–62
dissemination of, 684–685
evaluation studies vs., 527–528
in other languages, 87, 88
roles and outcomes of, 5–8
as social process, 38–56, 58,
677–690
team, 654–655
Researcher expectancy effect
as threat to validity
effects of, 468–469, 478

correlation, 181–182
ation of, 170, 173
n in and correlation,
81
rtile, 171
0. *See also* Tests
itney U test
cquiesce
of,

method, 249
llocation
n, 296
n of, 302–304
e of, 294
nits, 305–306
Education (ERIC), 106
te to questionnaire,
88
ts, 392
valuation, 536–538
planations eliminated,
8
range, effect on
tion, 180–181
planations
and characteristics of study
as, 476
elimination of 271, 272, 279–280,
454
and special internal validity (LP)
problems in field
experiments, 478
summary of, 476–478
unique alternative explanations
as, 476–477
Robust statistics, 436
Rorschach test, 214, 254–256
Rotated-descriptor displays, 107

Sample size
factors of required, 123–125
increases in, 692
methods for determining, 130,
366–367
statistical power and, 428–431
Sample surveys. *See* Survey
research
Sampling. *See also* Survey research
cluster, 134–136
explanation of, 123
measurement and, 194
nonprobability, 126–127, 136–139
to observe changes over time,
364–366
planning for, 363–364, 367
principles of, 123–126
probability, 126–136. *See also*
Probability sampling
purposive, 138, 324–326, 349
sequential, 139–140
simple random, 127–130,
132–133
snowball or chain referral, 139
trade-offs in, 222
used in adoptive parenting
study, 18
use of, 69, 122, 123
Sampling distribution of the
mean, 407
Sampling and chance error as
rival explanation, 455–456

*. See also various
research methods*
choice of in relation to
orientation to social
sciences, 644
comparison of roles of, 34, 35
continuum of, 29–31, 34
examples of use of multiple,
618–619
literature search in relation to,
97–98
overview of, 26–29, 270
research problem selection and,
73–74
synthesis of, 616–618
Research orientations to nature of
social sciences
analyzer, 628–629, 635, 641–642
and choice of research problem,
640, 643
criteria of excellence, 643–644
example of different, 632–634
humanist, 628–629, 638–639,
641–642
multiperspectivist, 637–638,
641–642
overview of, 627–632
particularist, 631, 639–640,
641–642
perpetuation of types of,
653–654
pragmatist, 630, 634–635,
641–642
summary and examples of,
640–642
synthesizer, 631, 635–636,
641–642
theorizer, 628–629, 636–637,
641–642
tolerance for various, 655
Research reviews as research, 8
Research studies, examples of,
10–14, 17–23

Sampling frame
bias and, 129
explanation of, 128
in simple random sampling, 128
Sampling unit
method for choosing, 128–129
in simple random sampling, 128
Saturation in qualitative research,
325
Scaled scores. *See* Derived scores
Scanners for computers, 339
Scatterplots
correlation ratios for, 183
discriminating various causal
conditions in, 260–261
examination of, 177–178
explanation of, 176, 179
triangular, 255–258, 266
Scholastic Aptitude Test (SAT),
175, 196, 284, 585
School achievement structural
model example, 589, 590
Science, 298
Science
knowledge and, 50–51
limits of social and behavioral,
687–690
norms of, 51–54
responsibilities of individuals
involved in, 51
as social process, 38–56,
677–690
working of at individual level,
679–681
working of at peer level,
681–683
working of at societal level,
683–687
Science Citation Index, 109, 111
Scientific history, 504
Score scales, 173–176
Secondary sources in literature,
102
Selection
by history interaction, 479
by maturation interaction, 464
as threat to validity, 463–464,
478
by treatment interaction, 470
Self-concept, 78
Self-esteem of elementary teachers
study, 560, 561
Semi-interquartile range, 171, 173
Seminary students study, 601–603
Sensitive issues, querying in
sample surveys, 390–392
Sequence effects, 210, 562
Sequential sampling, 139–140
Significance levels, 415–416, 420
Simple random sampling. *See also*
Random sampling
advantages and disadvantages
of, 132–133

use of, 127–130

Single-subject studies
example of, 560, 561
explanation of, 32–33, 559
external validity (GP) concerns and, 563
hallmarks of, 563–564
internal validity (LP) of, 560, 562

Situations
as facet of design in chain of reasoning, 61, 442
trade-off possibilities and, 693–694
translation fidelity and, 275
translation generality and, 284–285

Skepticism, organized, 53–54

Skewed distributions
explanation of, 167, 168
negatively, 167, 169
positively, 167–169

Smithsonian Science Information Exchange, 114

Smoothers, 39

Snowball sampling, 139, 140

Social Sciences Citation Index (SSCI), 104, 109–111, 587n

Sociological Abstracts (*Soclit*), 101, 104, 106, 107

Sociometry, 229

Solomon four-group design, 454, 457

Sources of Information in the Social Sciences (Webb, Beals, and White), 104

Spearman-Brown prophecy formula, 208

Spearman's rank correlation, 184

Stability reliability, 207, 210, 211

Stakeholders, 524, 527, 528, 529, 530, 531, 536, 538–539, 541, 544, 545, 549, 550, 551

Standard deviation (SD)
explanation of, 171–173
formula for, 171–172
score scales based on, 173–175

Standard error
of the differences between means, 423
of the mean, 407

Standard error of measurement (SEM)
discussion of, 215–218
explanation of, 215, 219, 407
formula for, 215
use of, 218–219

Standard scores, 174, 176, 178, 566

Stanford Achievement Test, 452, 457

Stanford-Binet Intelligence Test, 199, 225, 575

Stanine scores, 175

Statistical conclusion validity, 292

Statistical methods, 4–5, 157–190, 400–439, 578–612

Statistical power
analysis of, 430–432
estimation of, 456
methods to increase, 428–431

Statistical precision, 140

Statistical significance, 416
one-tailed and two-tailed tests of, 417–420
practical vs., 433–434
of result, 434

Statistical tests
power of, 427, 430–431
violation of assumptions of, 435–436

Statistics
descriptive. See Descriptive statistics
inferential. See Inferential statistics
for multivariate relationships, 593
nonparametric, 435
parametric, 435
robust, 436
statistical consulting and availability of other, 607, 609

Stem-and-leaf diagram, 163

Stimulated recall, 385

Stipulative definition, 153

Stratified sampling
advantages and disadvantages of, 132–133
explanation of, 130
on more than one variable, 131–132
proportional, 131
use of, 130–131, 364

Strong Campbell Interest Inventory, 30, 221, 282n, 634

Structural modeling, 588–590

Structured interviews, 368, 369

Study-effect meta-analysis (SEMA), 570

Subject Headings, U. S. Library of Congress, 106

Subject indexes. See also Indexes
use of traditional, 105–108

Subjects
deception of, 669–670
as facet of design in chain of reasoning, 61, 442
human. See Human subjects
as informants, 442n
trade-off possibilities and, 692–693
translation fidelity and, 274–275
translation generality and, 284–285

Subs[...]
s[...]

Sufficient[...]
206, [...]

Summative e[...]
540

Supplied-answer [...]
also Tests

Surgeons' errors study[...]

Survey research
coding and analysis of [...]
used in, 388–390
comparison of data collectio[...]
methods used in, 393–39[...]
computer-assisted telephone interviewing, 373–375
data collection techniques, summary of, 393–397
explanation of, 30–31, 34
hallmarks of, 392–393
impact on daily lives of, 362
interviews for, 367–376, 385. See also Interviews
letters of transmittal, 383–388
mortality in, 343
overview and discussion of, 360–362, 392–393
problem of nonrespondents in, 386–388
purpose and planning for, 362–364, 367
questionnaires for, 376–386. See also Questionnaires
sampling in. See Sample size; Sampling; Sampling unit
special problems occurring in, 390–392

Survey Research Center, 370

Swahili syndrome, 492

Symbolic interactionism, 322–323

Synthesizer orientation
explanation of, 631, 635–636, 641–642
strengths and weaknesses of, 647–649

Systematic sampling, 133–134, 364

Tailored tests, 225, 226

Tandem interviews, 371

Taxonomy of Educational Objectives (Bloom et al.; Krathwohl, Bloom, Masia), 33, 262

Teacher self-esteem study, 560, 561

Teaching ability study, 158

Telephone interviews, 140. See also Computer-assisted telephone interviews
advantages of computer-assisted, 374, 375
compared to individual interviews, group interviews, and mailed questionnaires, 393–397

...ized medical insurance
...tudy, 542n
...conditions, 148, 200,
...241, 253–261
...aluation, 525, 526,

...ests, 230. *See*

..., 319

...ethods

...s and weaknesses of,
...650

...and developing, 89–90
...0, 101, 118, 283, 419
...ding, 33–34
...dy, 598–601
...6, 107
...*ERIC Descriptors*, 106
...procedures, 385–386
...lidity, 454–479
...ethods of
...logical scaling,
...
...ion generality and,

...eries designs, 480–482
...de-off possibilities
choices involving the basis for
    sensing attributes or
    changes, 698
choices involving the procedure,
    698
choices involving observation or
    measurement, 695–698
choices involving situations,
    693–694
choices involving subjects,
    692–693
choices involving treatment,
    694–695
overview of, 691–692
Trade-offs
    examples of trade-off instances,
        65, 111, 127, 222–224, 284,
        300, 313, 361–362, 368, 450,
        474, 476–478, 495, 550, 662
    explanation of, 222
    use of, 620–621
Traditions, 48
Transitional aid to prisoners study,
    542n
Translation fidelity
    discussion of, 273–277
    explanation of, 271, 272, 278
Translation generality
    discussion of, 284–287
    explanation of, 282, 287
Treatment. *See also* Experimental
        treatment problems and
        treatment fidelity
    conceptually defining, 487–488
    explanation of, 27
    as facet of design in chain of
        reasoning, 61, 442
    interaction effects of, 469–471
    trade-offs in, 222, 694–695
    translation fidelity and, 275–276
    translation generality and,
        285–286
Treatment fidelity
    operational definitions of
        treatment and, 488–489

...specifications for test of,
    202–203
stability, 207, 210
stability and equivalence,
    210–211
Tests
    achievement, 202–203, 452, 457
    intelligence, 174–175
    item analysis of, 220–222
    setting cut scores in, 218–219,
        224–225
    sources of information for,
        226–227
    standards for standardized, 667
    strengths and weaknesses of,
        229–230
    tailored, 225, 226
Tests in Microfiche, 227
Test validity
    concurrent, 201–202
    construct, 199–201
    content, 198, 202–203
    criterion-related, 198, 201–202
    face, 198, 203–204
    generalizability theory and,
        212–213
    item analysis to increase, 221
    overview of, 197–198
    predictive, 201–202
    specifications for test of,
        202–203
    specificity of, 204–205
Tetrachoric correlation, 185
Textbooks in knowledge
        development process,
        101–102
Thematic Apperception Test (TAT),
    214
Theoretical sample, 324
Theorizer orientation
    explanation of, 628–629,
        636–637, 641–642

representativeness of treatment
    and, 489
treatment administration and,
    275–276, 489–491
Treatment phase, 559
Trend studies
    advantages and disadvantages
        to, 366
    explanation of, 365
Triangulation
    data validity and, 328–329
    investigator, 328
    use of, 276, 618
t test
    for differences between means,
        423–426, 429–430
    explanation of, 426
    scores of, 175
    use of, 600–601
Two-tailed test for statistical
    significance, 417
Type I error, 401, 403, 426, 427
Type II error
    consequences of, 404
    explanation of, 403, 426, 428
    occurrence of, 424
    and power of a statistical test,
        427–431
    size of, 428

Uncertainty reduction
    explanation of, 46
    external validity (GP) and, 289
    internal validity (LP) and, 281
Unconscious mind, 79
Universal standards for knowledge
    claims, 51–52, 54
Unobtrusiveness, 467
Unstructured interviews, 368, 369
Utilization of evaluation findings,
    528

Validation
    explanation of, 6–7
    qualitative-quantitative
        continuum and, 29, 30
    replication as ultimate, 50, 51
    use of, 28–29
Validity. *See also* External validity;
        Internal validity; Test
        validity
    construct, 199–201, 205, 292
    concurrent, 201–202
    content, 198, 202–203, 205
    criterion-related, 198, 201–202,
        205
    data, 328–329
    domain, 202
    ecological, 284, 465
    face, 198, 203–205
    meaning of, 270
    population, 465
    predictive, 198, 201–202

threats to, 454–479
Values study, 590–593
Variables. *See* Dependent variables;
    Independent variables;
    Multiple variables
Variance. *See also* Analysis of
    variance (ANOVA)
  explanation of, 171
  homogeneity of, 603
Variance-partitioning
    meta-analysis, 570–571
Videotape use, 385

Voucher programs, 527

Wechsler Intelligence Scale for
    Children, 199, 225
Where to Find What (Hillard), 104
Whistle blowing, 305
Whole-test reliability from
    split-half, 208
Wilcoxon signed-ranks test, 430,
    435
Word association, 379

Working conditions, productive,
    83
Written statements in problem
    finding, 81–82

Zimbardo induced hearing deficit
    study, 10, 26–28, 59–62,
    64–66, 105, 111, 124,
    271–280, 283, 285–287, 289,
    302, 568, 635, 669, 679
Z-scores. *See* Standard scores

It's Your Turn!

This is your opportunity to tell me how the book can be improved: where I wasn't clear, what could be omitted or shortened, what needs further development or should be added (heaven forbid the book should be longer!). Any and all suggestions and comments are welcomed. To get an idea of who you are and what kind of course you are commenting on, please answer the demographic questions.

When finished, cut along the dotted line, fold and place in a stamped envelope, and drop in mailbox. Thanks so much!

Feedback Card for Krathwohl,
Methods of Educational and Social Science Research

I'm studying for a _____ Bachelor's, _____ Master's, _____ Doctor's Degree in

(field) _____ . This was a ___one-, ___two-semester course

in the department of _____

at (school) _____ .

I have prior coursework in ___ statistics, ___ measurement, ___ neither statistics nor measurement.

Please circle or check the number of each chapter assigned in your course:

1 intro, **2** two studies, **3** variety methods, **4** fndings to knwldg, **5** chain reas, **6** prob find,

7 lit srch, **8** smplng, **9** cncpt anal, **10** dscrptv stat, **11** meas, **12** caus, **13** int ext val, **14** oth crit,

15 qual mthd, **16** survys, **17** infer stat, **18** exprmnts, **19** hstry, **20** eval, **21** oth mthds,

22 adv stat, **23** trade-offs, **24** orientatns, **25** ethics, **26** mcrosystm

In addition, I read or consulted these unassigned chapters: _____

I did the application exercise at chapter's end asking me to successively develop my own
problem further with each chapter for ___all, ___most, ___few, ___none of the chapters assigned
and found this (check all that apply) ___helpful, ___unhelpful, ___hard, ___easy,
(supply your own adjectives): _____

I have these suggestions, comments, and/or problems:

(suggestions, comments, and/or problems, *continued*)

Please place in envelope and return to:

Longman Publishing Group
Attn: Education Editor
10 Bank Street
White Plains, NY 10606